Culture in History

Photograph by Ralph Norman

Paul Radin

CULTURE IN HISTORY

Essays in Honor of Paul Radin

Edited by STANLEY DIAMOND

Published for BRANDEIS UNIVERSITY

by COLUMBIA UNIVERSITY PRESS

NEW YORK 1960

PUBLISHED IN GREAT BRITAIN, INDIA, AND PAKISTAN

BY THE OXFORD UNIVERSITY PRESS

LONDON, BOMBAY, AND KARACHI

LIBRARY OF CONGRESS CATALOG CARD NUMBER: 59-13776

PRINTED IN THE NETHERLANDS

Paul Radin died on Saturday, February 21, 1959, in New York city. This book, conceived in his lifetime and left exactly as conceived, is now his visible memorial.

FOREWORD

By Abram Leon Sachar

PRESIDENT, BRANDEIS UNIVERSITY

THAT THE FIRST *Festschrift* to appear over the imprint of Brandeis University should be devoted to anthropology and dedicated to Dr. Paul Radin is not only a felicitous but, I think, a significant event.

Anthropology is one of the descriptive sciences which is basic to the study of both history and psychology—the study of what men do and how men feel and think. In it lies a key to immemorial customs, to the obscure origins of morality, and to the source as well as the understanding of the arts. No subject is more pertinent to that humanism which Brandeis University believes to be the aim, the focus, and the fruit of higher education. Like all sciences, anthropology must—as a goodly number of the essays in this volume will illustrate—explore what to the layman are technical, when not arid, minutiae; it must spin a web of theories in the hope of catching now and then an elusive conclusion. Yet these patient and painstaking labors are informed with a loving concern for humanity. They are penetrated and ennobled by the conviction that mankind is the proper study of man; and if, in reading the contributions that follow, a touch of this spirit brushes us, anthropology will again fulfill its function of strengthening our allegiance to the humanistic values of life.

The distinguished scholar in honor of whose seventy-fifth birthday the present studies are offered as the tribute of appreciative colleagues and grateful disciples, exemplifies the type of thinking and interests which has governed anthropology at its best. Dr. Radin has persistently sought the individual behind the tribe, the mind behind the ritual, the hand behind the tool, and the man behind humanity. His own personal warmth and cheer are but another manifestation of that abundant sympathy, at once profound and delicate, which is requisite to the science he has enhanced. It is further evidence of his still resilient and pioneering temper that this internationally eminent anthropologist should now bring his wisdom and skills to the youngest of American universities.

What Brandeis in its youth will give this veteran would be a little presumptuous to state; but what we, not altogether unselfishly, can assuredly offer him is the fervent hope that his vigor and creativity will long remain unabated. On the other hand, what he can offer us is clear. "One who learns from the old," said a Talmudic master, "is like one who eats ripe grapes and drinks old wine." In joining the salute and congratulations accorded Dr. Radin by the academic world, I congratulate, too, the new generation of Brandeis scholars who are privileged to take the cup of learning from his hand and in turn pass it on to their successors; for in it is the wine of life.

PAUL RADIN: AN APPRECIATION

By Cora Du Bois

HARVARD UNIVERSITY

PAUL RADIN stems from two distinguished traditions: German-Russian intellectualism in Europe and Boasian anthropology in America. These two heritages converge in their dedication to things of the mind. Radin's father was a rabbi of the reform movement and a Hebrew scholar with a rare command of both living and dead languages. This linguistic gift his sons inherited. But in addition to scholarship and linguistic aptitude, the father instilled in at least two of his sons, Max and Paul, a skeptical liberalism that consistently informed both their lives.

There were three boys in the Radin family: Herman, born in Germany in 1878, became a New York physician; Max, born in 1880, also in Germany, was a distinguished jurist in the Law School of the University of California; Paul, born in 1883 at Lodz (Poland), is one of the formative influences in contemporary anthropology both in the United States and in Europe.

In 1884 the family left Europe for Elmira, New York. There the second of two sisters was born. Their mother, who came from a distinguished German family, never fully recovered from the death of these two daughters in a scarlet fever epidemic shortly after moving to New York City in 1890. The three sons were to receive the major part of their education in the New York public school system. Paul entered the College of the City of New York as a sub-freshman at the age of fourteen and, after a five-year course, graduated in 1902. The schools of that day had not yet become the *smörgasbord* of contemporary American education. The training was exacting and intended for an intellectual élite rather than for the general citizen.

After graduating from college, Paul Radin began a flirtation with zoology at Columbia. "Tiring of fish," as he says, after writing a thesis on the embryology of sharks, he found himself in his second year attracted to history, then being taught with distinction at Columbia by James Harvey Robinson.

Like so many young scholars of the day he was drawn to Europe, which he had already visited with his mother in 1892. He went in 1905 and returned in 1907. Those two years were important not only because they crystallized an affection for West European intellectual life, but also because they confirmed a penchant for anthropology. During his first year, at Munich, Radin substituted physical anthropology for the zoology of fish. And Ranke, the nephew of the famous historian and himself an anthropologist of note, reinforced in Radin the influence of James Harvey Robinson. The following year Radin transferred to the University of Berlin, where men like Von den Steinen, Ehrenreich, and Seler turned him irrevocably to anthropology. That year Radin published his first anthropological paper, "Zur Netztechnik der Sudamerikanischen Indianer" (1906), in the *Zeitschrift für Ethnologie*. Despite this early sortie into technology, Radin was to show little interest or aptitude in later years for the problems of material culture or even for the quasi-historical studies of the diffusionists. He had always manifested a fine disdain for the technological aspects of contemporary life and a profound respect for written history.

However academically formative, these two years were essentially Radin's *wanderjähre*. He walked in Germany, Switzerland, and Italy; he worked for a month in the museum at Prague; he spent three months in Florence. He was beginning, between the ages of twenty-two and twenty-four, the process of self-cultivation that exclusive concentration on studies and academic life rarely produces.

In 1907 Radin resumed his studies at Columbia with a major in anthropology and a minor in statistics, both under Franz Boas, and a second minor in history under James Harvey Robinson. Whether Radin really understood Boas's famous course on statistics that was the nemesis of many young anthropologists of the period is a moot point. But Radin insists that he could at least ask questions that convinced Boas of his grasp of the subject. Radin seems never to have forgotten the art of asking probing questions.

When he came up for his Ph.D. orals in 1910, Radin recalls that Boas quizzed him primarily and considerately on linguistics, but that James Harvey Robinson grilled him relentlessly on medieval education and the order of argument in St. Augustine's *De Civitate Dei*. Obviously anthropologists were expected to be men of wide interests and to be grounded in their own culture before being considered fit for the study of another.

Those were the days when Boas's broadly informed mind was beginning to shape the curriculum of American anthropology. It was that group of early Boas students, all of whom came to their graduate work from other disciplines, that made the United States one of the major centers of anthropology. Among Boas's early students, whom we now esteem as elder statesmen and among whom Radin ranks high, were Alfred Kroeber and Clark Wissler. They had recently graduated from Boas's hands when Radin began his graduate studies at Columbia. Edward Sapir and Robert Lowie were in their last year of graduate work during Radin's first. His age mates were Speck, Goldenweiser, Skinner, and Laura Benedict.

The year 1910, in which Radin passed his final orals, proved a fateful one. As he was preparing for his examinations, his father died and Paul found it necessary to tutor German at CCNY. In this year he also married his first wife.

With 1911 began a series of appointments that were to take him widely around North America and that deepened further his professional interests and tastes. There was a year (1911–12) in the Bureau of American Ethnology. Then another year (1912–13) on a joint fellowship from Columbia and Harvard to study Zapotec linguistics and mythology. The next four years were spent with his lifelong friend, Edward Sapir, in the Geological Survey of Canada; Radin's assignment was the Ojibwa of southeast Ontario, on which a number of reports were published.

In this busy and diversified period, the first field trips to the Winnebago, from 1908 to 1913, were crucial. Whatever other field research was to follow, the Winnebago remained Radin's primary devotion. To judge from monograph after monograph that resulted from these and subsequent visits, his diligence on the early trips must have been as monumental as his affection and respect for these people was deep and lasting. His command of their language and his respect for their unwritten literature have had few parallels in the history of ethnographic investigations. Through the Bollingen Foundation, materials from Radin's Winnebago notebooks are still appearing and, we hope, may continue to appear. Here another strand in Radin's intellectual interests was woven into the pattern of his life. Radin and the

Winnebago may not be precisely synonymous, but his name is as indelibly associated with them as Boas's is with the Kwakiutl.

The humanistic quality of Radin's mind was certainly already set by this time, but the Winnebago experience gave it depth and form. By 1920 he had published *The Autobiography of a Winnebago Indian* in the California series in anthropology. It was one of the first significant life histories of an American Indian viewed as a unique human being. Two years later Elsie Clews Parsons edited *American Indian Life* (1922). It was an early "popular" book on the American Indians to which her collaborators contributed biographies of Indians from the various tribes among which they had worked. Too often these putative biographies were nothing more than skeletons on which to hang ethnographic sketches. When Radin's *Autobiography of a Winnebago Indian* appeared as a commercial publication in 1926 under the title *Crashing Thunder,* the general reader was in a position to judge the difference between real and contrived biographies.

At this point one might have expected Radin to move toward a more searching psychological approach to anthropology. But, like Kroeber, who had flirted with psychoanalysis, Radin failed to pursue further the psychological implications of his work. Perhaps true humanism and psychology, particularly of that day, seemed strange bedfellows.

It was also during the period from 1910 to 1920 that the first of Radin's archival contributions to Winnebago ethnography and religion began to appear. "The Winnebago Tribe," for example, was published in the *Annual Report* of the Bureau of American Ethnology for 1915–16, although the actual manuscript had been completed in 1913. As one reviews Radin's publications in conjunction with his field research, one cannot but be impressed both by the promptness of his first reports and by the continuity of his interests.

During this seminal decade three productive years, from 1917 to 1920, were spent in Berkeley at Mills College and on the University of California campus. The former president of Mills College, Aurelia Reinhardt, was a warmly supportive admirer. More importantly, these three years initiated Radin's intermittent professional and personal association with Kroeber and the group of vigorous anthropologists who were drawn to Kroeber and subsequently to his colleague Robert Lowie. The Lowie and Radin families had been intimate since the youth of both men. In Robert Lowie, Paul Radin had throughout life a loyal friend with a devotion to intellectual life and an admiration for German scholarship comparable to his own.

With the end of the First World War Radin left again for Europe, from which he had been separated not only by the war but by his preoccupation with writing and field research. In 1920 he went to England and for the next five years continued his work at Cambridge, where he held a lectureship under Rivers and supplemented his income by teaching German at the Perse School. His acquaintances in that period were Bartlett and Elliott-Smith. But in these years, aside from Rivers, it was C. G. Jung in Zurich who provided intellectual grist to a man who was already much interested in comparative religion and literature. That Radin was never a Jungian goes without saying. Perhaps his very contact with Jung's cultivated but mystical mind served to reinforce Radin's skeptical rationalism and alienated him from explorations in at least the murkier depths of the unconscious. But that he found Jung and his group stimulating influences would be only natural. It was in 1927 that Radin published *Primitive Man as Philosopher,* which was essentially his declaration of faith in the universal rationality of man and a riposte to the influence of Zurich.

The United States was, however, still Radin's other home, and he returned in 1925 to do field work among the Ottawa for the University of Michigan. In 1927 a brief summer trip of four months in Europe was sandwiched into a chronically peripatetic existence. In the late 1920s Outhwaite of the Rockefeller Foundation recognized the quality of Radin's mind and provided him with a year's fellowship through President Angell of Yale and Clark Wissler of the American Museum of Natural History in New York. The following year (1927) Outhwaite was instrumental in an appointment at Fiske. This post Radin held until 1930. During his stay at Nashville he collected life histories of former slaves and accounts of Negro conversion experiences that are still unpublished. He also returned to Mexico to continue his survey of Mexican languages.

With the onset of the Depression Radin moved to Berkeley, which was to remain his official headquarters until 1949. Here Paul Radin met and married his present wife, Doris Woodward. But no personal matters deflected him from his indefatigable productivity. From 1930 to 1940 Radin worked on the analysis of one of the Penutian languages of California (Patwin), on surveys of minority groups in the San

Francisco Bay area, and in the Sutro Library—of whose rich collection of Mexican pamphlets Radin still speaks with the gleam in his eye of the incurable bibliophile with a penchant for historical source material. After all, he did prepare a catalogue of the collection that ran to a thousand pages!

It was in these years that I knew Paul Radin best, and one of my favorite memories of him is with a load of volumes from a second-hand bookstore tucked under one arm, his cane (from which he was inseparable) hung over the other, and his large reflective face surmounted by the inevitably battered gray felt hat. He knew all of our interests and, on foraging trips that must have consumed endless hours and required much perspicacity, he unearthed book after book that we coveted for our personal libraries.

It was also in this period that I learned to appreciate Radin's rare qualities as a teacher. These qualities were not manifest in the class room. They had no relation to the meticulous fulfillment of administrative tasks having to do with bluebooks and grades. Rather his gift as a teacher lay in establishing warm and interested relationships with young students of his own choosing and leading them into broad-ranging, skeptical, exploratory conversations, often until late at night. For a man who entertained a fine impatience for the drudgery of schoolteaching, he has today a singularly wide and grateful circle of students whom he chose to instruct in his own informal and often caustic fashion.

All this should account sufficiently for any man's time during the difficult years of the Depression. But it was precisely in those hard-pressed years of national upheaval that Radin not only wrote, but published, in a time when publication was a feat, *Social Anthropology* (1932), *Primitive Religion* (1937), and perhaps most important, *Method and Theory of Ethnology* (1933). The last antedated by four years Lowie's *History and Theory of Anthropology* (1937). It seems probable that the close association of these two scholars during Radin's residence in Berkeley was productive for both of them. Whatever reciprocal influences these two authors had on each other from 1930 to 1937 (and I believe their books should be read together) each in his own way summarized his theoretical position at the midpoint of his life. Radin was fifty when his *Method and Theory of Ethnology* appeared; Lowie was fifty-four when he published *History and Theory of Anthropology*. Both books were landmarks.

Intermittently from 1941 to 1944 Radin filled an academic appointment much to his taste in the informal and experimental atmosphere of Black Mountain College. But Radin is essentially an urban man and could never resign himself long to a limited and bucolic environment. The arrangements that followed proved even more to his taste. Through Mary Mellon and later the Bollingen Foundation he was freed to devote himself to his writing, to editing the work of others, and to teaching one semester a year at Kenyon College. And, of course, there was always the pull of Europe.

In 1949 he was invited to lecture at the four major Swedish universities, and in the same year he delivered the first of a series of lectures at the Eranos conferences in Ascona. In 1952 the intermittent trips abroad finally stabilized into four years of residence at Lugano in Switzerland. From this base a new series of activities developed. There were lectures at Oxford, Cambridge, and Manchester, as well as at Jung's Institute in Zurich. Working steadily on grants from the Bollingen Foundation, he wrote a series of papers on Winnebago religion which appeared with the imprint of the Ethnographical Museum at Basel. The Rhein-Verlag at Zurich published, among other works, his *Gott und Mensch in der Primitiven Welt* (1954).

When Paul Radin was invited to Brandeis in 1957, New England added another figure of stature to the roster of intellectuals in which it has always taken pride.

This bare chronology of Radin's life has been reviewed because, with characteristic unwillingness to either label or be labeled, he has rarely bothered to have himself listed in *Men of Science, Who's Who,* or even the *International Directory of Anthropologists.* But the usual dead categorizations of a man's life tell us nothing, or next to nothing, of his endless and steady productivity, his tastes, his singular consistencies in the face of apparent restlessness. Radin is a man who respects himself, as he respects others, for internal integrity. It was this very inner integrity which made him ill-adapted to routine, to egalitarian amiability and the cooperativeness that can so often be stultifying. If at times he seemed inconsiderate of his friends, it was only when they pressed him to undertake uncongenial responsibilities and routine tasks. Radin is a rational and skeptical man, even if at times he has appeared unreasonable. He is a man with his own sense of form, one that is as sophisticated intellectually as it is simple socially. He has never coveted wealth or courted approval. He is acquisitive only of books. It is entirely consistent that his erudition in comparative religion, adorned by an unparalleled private library in the field, centered on the Apollonian rather than Dionysian aspects of religion; that a loving care was expended year after year on texts, and that it was he who wrote *Primitive Man as Philosopher.*

Paul Radin's professional accomplishments, great as they are, would be diminished were they divorced from a personal appreciation of the man. He is many faceted, but he is of one piece. He has pursued his intellectual interests tenaciously and with an ever deepening curiosity. For seven decades he has been indestructibly himself.

To salute him with honor and affection on his seventy-fifth birthday is a duty we owe ourselves as his epigones.

EDITOR'S PREFACE

THE PARTICIPANTS in this celebration of Paul Radin responded with a warmth and spontaneity rare in academic life. The *Festschrift* was conceived in the summer of 1957, six months after Radin came to Brandeis University; by the spring of 1958 fifty-one papers had been received, along with scores of letters from accomplished European and American scholars. It would be superfluous to quote from these letters, whether written by Jung or Lowie or Klüver; the book itself testifies to their sentiment. It is, I think, doubtful that any other living anthropologist could have stimulated a reaction of such depth, from so many disparate quarters.

In the course of preparing the volume for publication, I have often reflected on the meaning of this response. Obviously, Radin's academic standing has long been of an international order. As early as 1923, Marcel Mauss wrote in *L'Année Sociologique:* "M.R. est un des meilleurs ethnographes de sa génération et son Autobiography of a Winnebago est, à notre avis, un des meilleurs documents, acquis avec une méthode des plus nouvelles, qui ait été publié pendant la décade où l'Année sociologique a été interrompue. Cette façon de trouver un indigène qui se raconte rend compte, mieux qu'aucune autre, de la façon dont un individu se situe dans un clan et dans une tribu."

By 1927, John Dewey, in his foreword to *Primitive Man as Philosopher,* was writing enthusiastically on the revolutionary character of Radin's work. Yet high intellectual attainment alone does not ensure a response of the dimensions we enjoyed. Nor is Radin the kind of man who desperately cultivates friendships. He is not above being disliked; it does not displease him. Yet, liked or disliked, he is usually loved, for love is what he subtly demands in return for the gift of his being, the man and his work inseparable. He has a sorcerer's charm, undimmed by age; he bewitches. In conversation, he can suddenly switch to a trickster's view of the world, obliterating cant and puncturing the ordinary pieties. And to his friends (he has no enemies, only antagonists) his character is a legend; he has, of course, the storied defects of his virtues.

Let me put it this way. When Confucius returned from his apparently apocryphal visit with Lao-tzu, "to whom etiquette meant hypocrisy and nonsense," he told his disciples: "Of birds I know that they have wings to fly with, of fish that they have fins to swim with, of wild beasts that they have feet to run with. For feet there are traps, for fins nets, for wings arrows. But who knows how dragons surmount wind and cloud into heaven? This day I have seen Laotsu and he is a dragon."

Paul Radin is such a dragon, heaven-bent, indestructible, achieving the unheard of, even the outrageous, as if it were a part of nature. At a time of low civil courage and wild careerism, amply reflected in the academy but evident everywhere in our civilization, Radin is a figure that heartens. When he came to Brandeis, he reached across the generations and lifted up undergraduates to a view of anthropology not as a career, but as a way of life. For that is what, through many trials, it has been for him. Freely, he shared his experience, and in his very presence conveyed what it meant to be one's own man. Radin's fierce individualism, his simplicity, his passion for diversity and love of culture, his downright intelligence, a rarer trait than realized among intellectuals, have kept him on the margin of the orthodox academy while enabling him to contribute mightily to the field he loves. He has never retreated into jargon, nor has he deflected his concern from the great, recurring, troubling themes in human history. Above all, he has never merely analyzed the lives of people called primitive; by some alchemy of insight he transmuted himself into their spokesman.

It is for these reasons that I believe Paul Radin has become a charismatic person, teaching us the rewards and penalties, no less than the techniques, of selfhood in an anonymous age. The words of Lao-tzu, rendered by Witter Bynner, are perfectly appropriate:

A sound man by not advancing himself
Stays the further ahead of himself,
By not confining himself to himself
Sustains himself outside himself;
By never being an end in himself
He endlessly becomes himself.

ACKNOWLEDGMENTS

FIRST OF ALL I wish to thank Stanley Moore, philosopher and long-time friend of Paul Radin, who helped shepherd this work through the press when prior field work commitments took me to Nigeria.

The generosity of the Bollingen Foundation, supplemented by grants from the Samuel Rubin Foundation, the Wenner-Gren Foundation, and Brandeis University made publication of the volume possible. They have my gratitude and that of the contributors.

Gratitude is due also to other friends and colleagues who have worked with Paul Radin through the years and who were prevented from contributing essays in his honor only by force of circumstances beyond their control. Among them are Professor Max Gluckman of the University of Manchester; Edward Winslow Gifford, professor emeritus at the University of California; Dr. Alfred Métraux of UNESCO; and Dr. Nels Nelson, former curator of the American Museum of Natural History.

Richard P. Werbner, Radin's youngest disciple, prepared the bibliography and helped in many other ways; I am grateful to him. Vergene F. Leverenz, editor at Columbia University Press, treated the manuscript as if it were her own and fiercely protected the rights of all concerned; she has our unanimous respect. To my wife, Olga, and our children, who suffered with me as I turned too slowly into a weathered editor, goes the inexpressible word of thanks.

STANLEY DIAMOND

Brandeis University
September, 1959

Note.—Joseph Campbell's contribution to this volume, "Primitive Man as Metaphysician," appears in somewhat altered form in his book *The Masks of God: Primitive Mythology* (New York, The Viking Press, 1959; London, Secker and Warburg, 1960).

CONTENTS

Part III.   Ritual, Religion, and Myth

Part IV. History, Social Theory, and Law

Part V. Language

PART I

The Primitive World View

THINKER AND INTELLECTUAL
IN PRIMITIVE SOCIETY

By Robert Redfield

AGAINST THE BACKGROUND of prevailing anthropological concentration upon cultures, groups, customs and institutions there stands out Paul Radin's long-maintained interest in *particular* individuals in primitive societies and especially in the intellectually creative productions of some of them. In two ways he has been a pioneer. Publication of "The Autobiography of a Winnebago Indian" stimulated the now widespread use of autobiographies in the study of cultures and of personalities in cultures. Both Clyde Kluckhohn[1] and Margaret Mead,[2] in discussing anthropological uses of extended documents recording first-person statements by informants, have given expression to a general recognition that it was *Crashing Thunder* which directed professional attention to the making of such documents and to their interpretation. Another door opened for us when Paul Radin found among primitive peoples certain individuals who were thinkers, persons with a vocation for things of the mind, who worked upon the ideas and images of their tradition to make them coherent and, maybe, abstract.[3] This discovery ran counter to notions at that time current as to the unreflective, custom-bound life of primitive peoples. It also contradicted those philosophers who found the origins of philosophy in the religious beliefs and rites of the unreflective many. John Dewey declared that if Dr. Radin's work was even approximately right, it required a thoroughgoing revision of prevailing ideas of the intellectual history of mankind.[4] In primitive society, Radin was saying, there are already philosophers. In commenting here on this second important contribution to anthropology I shall try to say just what type of being Radin discovered or asserted to exist, and to connect or compare this type with some others.

This human type, the thinker, is put forward as a kind of man or mind performing a kind of role or function. It is both a temperament and an

---

The late Dr. Redfield was Professor of Anthropology at the University of Chicago.

activity. Let us look first at the former aspect of this type. Radin makes no attempt to describe a total personality; he describes only certain qualities of mind. The thinkers are those who have "a marked capacity for articulating their ideas and for organizing them into coherent systems."[5] A thinker is "constrained to answer certain questions, to try to discover why there is an effect...." He does not accept the world as a mere series of events "on the same level," he requires explanations; for him "some type of coordination is imperatively demanded."[6] These qualities may be, says Radin, "basic and inherent."[7] They appear in marked degree in only a few individuals in any society.

This type contrasts with its opposite, "the man of action," whose mind does not require integration of event and meaning into systems. Presumably these types are ideal, and in actual individuals are more or less purely represented. Radin's terms may not be the most felicitous that could be found; at least it may be said that some men who lack the special qualities of mind attributed to thinkers do not always act very conspicuously, but rather plod along in routine; and further it seems that there are many very thoughtful men who do not consider fundamental and comprehensive questions at length or integrate event and meaning into coherent wholes. The Mayan villager, Eustaquio Ceme, of whom I have written,[8] was a very thoughtful man in that he considered, persistently and penetratingly, many questions—religious, moral, political. He would pause when a problem occurred to him and take it away to give it thought; later he would set out, in careful words, the opinions or conceptions or explanations to which his cogitation had brought him. But he was primarily a man of action in that he planned and executed courses of action; he was a leader of his people in a period of transition and crisis.

It might be simpler, at least in these paragraphs, to say that Radin showed us evidences of the activities of certain primitive minds in conceiving and articulating the nature of things as coherent, as coordinated by some principle or principles. This is a very special kind of thinking. Whether it corresponds to the thinking done by philosophers in civilized societies is a question. The nature of this special quality of mind is known to those who have read Isaiah Berlin's essay on Tolstoy. Berlin interprets a line of the Greek poet Archilochus to "mark one of the deepest differences which divide writers and thinkers, and, it may be, human beings in general." The one type, "the fox," consists of men who live by ideas scattered and often unrelated to one another. But the man of the other type, "the hedgehog," relates "everything to a single central vision, one system more or less coherent or articulate . . . a single, universal, organizing principle . . . ." [9] Berlin is writing about great Western literature and sees Dante as a hedgehog and Shakespeare as a fox, but, I think, he is talking about qualities of mind similar to those which Radin has found in primitive "thinkers." Radin discovered the hedgehogs in primitive society.

How do we know that any particular human being has this quality of mind? If today we had him before us for testing, it is probable that we should use ink blots to find out. Dr. Mead made Rorshach tests of her best Arapesh informant, Unabelin. Dr. Klopfer, looking at the protocols and without other acquaintance with that Arapesh, declared that he had "no intellectual positive interest in organizing the material on one card into a concept . . ." and "no capacity for abstract organization of material . . . no theoretical mind whatever." [10] Unabelin was no hedgehog. I received the impression of his alert and curious foxiness just by reading the edited transcript of his interviews with Margaret Mead. He was interested in many things, but there was nothing philosophical about his interest. It is the exceptional human individual who has the quality of mind that Radin has made us recognize in primitive society.

By their works shall we know them. Radin presents to us contrasting texts of myths from the same society and asks us to accept his judgment that one was written by a thinker and the other by what he calls a man of action. I do not know if he knew personally the tellers of the two Winnebago myths he gives us, but I am almost sure he did not know the Maori or the Dakota whose tales he also offers as the products of thinkers. He recognizes the thinkers from the coherent and abstract organization of idea and symbol in the accounts that they gave to this or that anthropologist. In the texts Radin uses I too see this difference: texts that march along like a catalogue or a mere sequence of events, and texts that have an intellectual and often esthetic integrity. If we accept this kind of proof that the thinker-qualities existed in the tellers, we are using the text—speaking now broadly—as a projective test. The tradition provides the people of that society with elements of symbol and event, with mythic content;

there is a certain flexibility or ambiguity in these elements; they may be interpreted and articulated more or less particularly, more or less coherently and integrally.

When a native informant speaks to an anthropologist at length the document that results is more or less autobiographic, more or less "auto-ethnographic" (Kroeber's word).[11] It tells about the personal experiences and thoughts of the teller, or it describes the ways of life of his people. Many of the recently published personal documents from primitive people are primarily autobiographic; the informant was told to tell about himself and found it not too difficult to do so. *The Son of Old Man Hat*,[12] *Sun Chief*,[13] Du Bois's *Alorese*,[14] and most of the short Walapai narratives published under Kroeber's editorship,[15] are autobiographies. In the autobiography given Mead by her Arapesh there is much auto-ethnography also. The recent strong interest in personality and its formation has stressed the production of autobiographies and on the whole it has been the revelation of personality rather than of a native mind working on a tradition that has interested the anthropologist.

But the relative emphasis on autobiography or auto-ethnography depends also on the interests and the temperament of the informant. I repeat a twice-published observation when I say that when Kluckhohn asked the Navaho, Mr. Moustache, to tell everything about his life, he produced no autobiography but rather "a philosophic homily."[16] This happened because Mr. Moustache was by temperament suited to be a moralist, in later life had become one, and was quite conscious of his role in transmitting the moral tradition (as Kroeber's discussion of the case well shows).[17] Autobiographies tend to expose not only personality in culture as analyzed by the anthropologist and psychologist, but also the teller's self-conception; and this self-conception in not a few cases is a statement of how the teller's career seems to *him* to fulfill statuses and roles recognized by the society. Later, when these remarks come to deal with roles, this aspect of the autobiography will become relevant. But in discovering the hedgehog-thinker it is the auto-ethnography—the account of custom, the myth, the description of the universe and its meanings, the tale that expresses reflection and perhaps questioning—that is most useful to us. Even a philosophic individual, looking back on his life, sees much that is episodic, insubordinate to principle and unified meaning. We see a unified whole not so much in our experiences as in our thoughts about the meaning of life. So the thinker is to be found in his works of the mind and accounts of the origin or nature of things, rather than in the story of what happened to him.

It would be interesting to learn whether several judges, reading a group of texts of auto-ethnographies, would come to the same conclusion as to which of them are productions of "thinkers" and which are not. Further, it would help us along in identifying the thinkers and their works if we considered several versions of the same myth as told by different informants. Have we examined the collections of variant myths that we now have with this question in mind? Beyond this possible enquiry lie important and less accessible questions. Perhaps the text cannot be used as a test of the mental qualities of the teller. Does a given myth, coherent, integrated and abstract, reflect the mental qualities of the narrator or those of preceding thinkers whose production the present narrator is reproducing, as an unpoetical person might recite a poem? I do not read Dr. Radin as necessarily asserting that the Dakota or the Maori who told the myth was himself a thinker; Radin's first purpose is to show that *some* thinkers have worked upon the tradition. Further, how much originality, how much rearranging of the elements of a tradition, is accomplished by even the best thinkers in primitive societies? Is it not possible that the most impressive of these productions, such as the Polynesian accounts of the origin and development of things, have come to the forms in which we know them by small increments of elaboration and systematization taking place in a multitude of oral reproductions over a long period of time?

Such a very impressive production, a really astonishing system of ideas in a primitive or archaic society, has come to our knowledge through the work of the late Professor Griaule and his associates among the peoples of the French Sudan. The publications[18] about the Dogon include several versions of long and complicated origin myths, a study of a secret language, a study of the meanings of 266 graphic signs, and, of immediate interest here, a long report of thirty-three interviews Griaule had with one informant. This book, *Dieu d'Eau*,[19] was produced for a general public and is without the apparatus of scientific publication; it is presumably something less than a complete account of what went on in this series of interviews. I shall here take it, however, at its face value. In these interviews Ogontêmmeli, an old blind man, once a hunter, gave Griaule in logical sequence an account of the origin and the nature of all things. One cannot read it, I think, and fail to recognize it as a work of the mind. All things—plants, animals, tools, man's social life, his rituals and the divine beings— are linked together in an intricate system of related meanings. The linkage is both genetic and static: everything has some connection with events going back to creation; and everything is bound to a system of parallel forms, of symbols—as, for example, the village is a human body; this body is also the primordial body of the first god; the house represents man's pedigree back to the gods; even pots are images of the universe. Further, this primitive Great Design is a definition and justification of human conduct; the same elaborately integrated system of symbols defines the significances of human life. In *Dieu d'Eau* this immense and complex work is reproduced by one man, virtually un- assisted by other men and of course, in the darkness of his blindness, without immediate mnemonic aid. Reading it one sees that this is not a case of memorizing a chant or other ritual form. It is not the order and form of words that matter to Ogontêmmeli; he is not reciting; he is thinking about the right relations of ideas and things, and his mind sees the outlines of a unified structure. He is thinking as hedgehogs think; his mind demands that coordination of which Radin speaks; a multiple general principle, causal, developmental and analogical, holds together a great mass of detail. Of explicit abstraction there is not much, but occasionally Ogontêmmeli speaks as if formulating, out of his own cogitations, this or that comprehensive principle. At the twentieth interview he says that in all sacrifices "first one's self is nourished, one is strengthened, then by the Word the strength is given back to the people. As each one gives to all, each receives from all. Between men there is a continuous interchange, a ceaseless movement of invisible flow . . . ." And at the seventh interview, after recognizing the complementarity of water and fire, and describing the way in which the sun's rays draw up water which then descends as rain, he in effect generalizes: "Draw up and make descend, draw up and make descend, that is the life of the world."

Here, it seems, we have the record of a primitive philosopher at work. But further examination of the document suggests some doubts or qualifications. Ogontêmmeli is reproducing a vision of the universe, and it is plain that he wants to get it right. He thinks about where a detail belongs in the vast scheme; at a few points where he is not sure he suspends his account and goes and asks someone else about it. But I do not find evidence that he struggles with difficulties and inconsistencies to resolve them by a creative effort of his own powers of intellect. In one or two places he gives two versions of a mythical episode; he just gives the two versions and offers no judgment of choice or attempt at reconciliation. From time to time Professor Griaule puts questions to him. To most of them Ogontêmmeli gives no answers, or says something that is unresponsive. It seems to me that the more explicit effort to reflect upon this material and provide connections and principles is made by Griaule in his questioning of the old Dogon. There are some small exceptions, a few places in the record where Ogontêmmeli does answer Griaule directly. Griaule asks why it was the *seventh* Nommo who became Master of the World, and the Dogon answers, "Because seven is the greatest number." When Griaule asks why seven is the greatest number, the reply comes, "Because it is the sum of three and four," three being associated with maleness and four with femaleness (from the numbering of the genitalia). But evidences of original contributions from Ogontêmmeli are few. If to think long and deeply about the nature of the world and its origins as tradition has proposed explanations to one, is to be a philosopher, Ogontêmmeli is a philosopher. He is not, if a philosopher is one who struggles with intellectual problems in abstract terms and offers solutions of some originality.

This is not to say, of course, that among the many Dogon there may not be more philosophical minds than Ogontêmmeli's. In another publication[20] Griaule suggests that these Dogon who have attained to the highest level of cosmogonic learning do not feel over them a "ceiling of knowledge"; rather, they think that they can still advance their understanding. On the other hand, such developments of thought that in fact do occur result from the play of different natures on traditional knowledge and lead only to variant conclusions resting always on the same basic principles. And elsewhere[21] he tells us that it is very difficult to introduce any significant novelty into Dogon ideas—both because they find expression in an intricate and tightly interrelated system of symbols, and because any departure from tradition would run against the opinions of a large intellectual elite and the more diffuse conceptions of the less instructed mass. The question recurs: Are there nevertheless still taking place small and unnoticed changes such as may account for the development of this vast system over much time? Or is it that with complexity and unification, such systems of thought reach a more or less stable condition so that what is recorded by Griaule is a finished edifice on which no further construction can take place?

The foregoing remarks tend to the conclusion that in primitive societies some individuals have those qualities of mind attributed by Radin to his "thinker," and that some expositions as to the origin or nature of things written down by anthropologists show the effects of such minds upon the body of knowledge in their society, and that, presumably, the more comprehensive, coherent, extensive and esoteric formulations of tradition that we have in our literature have resulted, however slowly, largely from the intellectual activities and oral reproductions of individuals with such qualities of mind. I do not think we know very much about the contributions to these structures of thought made by particular individuals.

Presumably, other things being equal, individuals with these special qualities of temperament are drawn into the restating of a tradition; for the Dogon Griaule assures us that it is those who have the required intelligence and curiosity who attempt to learn the higher levels of knowledge.[22] But we do not always find esoteric knowledge lodged in the minds of men with intellectual curiosity and ability to integrate thought. I recall that interviews (unpublished) had by Alfonso Villa Rojas with eight or nine h-menob, priestly functionaries of the Yucatec Maya, suggest that many of these men were repositories of special knowledge of prayers and rites, but were without unusual qualities of intellect. A man can enter into professional life by accident or for reasons of temperament having nothing to do with capacity to provide intellectual integration.

I turn to the professionalization, in primitive and not quite so primitive societies, of the life of the mind. The interest now shifts to the ways in which the kind of intellectual activity discussed above is carried on in statuses and roles, in institutions and perhaps offices, that are parts of the social organization or structure of the society. I should like, if possible, to limit the topic to the institutionalization of thoughtful consideration and coherent, possibly abstract, formulation of the traditional understanding of the nature of things. Specialists who memorize knowledge unknown to others, and use the knowledge in magical or religious activity, as do many priests, sorcerers and diviners, are not by that fact exemplars of the life of the mind. To know something other people do not know, and to use this knowledge in ways recognized in that society is to perform a role, possibly to occupy an office, but it is not necessarily to be a thinker, in Radin's special sense. The specialists who carry on institutionalized thinking depend upon the existence of recognized traditional learning, of a body of ideas and symbols susceptible to thoughtful consideration. As Radin has used "thinker" for someone with a kind of temperament and intellectual capacity, we might use the familiar word "intellectual" for one who performs a role in cultivating the life of the mind; he has or is expected to have employed the thinker's capacity in the cultivation of learning; in many cases he is a thinker. Intellectuals have their functions and their roles; they are seen by their fellows as doing something characteristic in society. The intellectuals of the Europe of modern times are associated with their effects on social or political movements.[23] The *literati* of traditional China, many of them scholars or creative writers, constituted a ruling class.[24] So we might ask whether there are intellectuals in primitive societies and if so, what are their functions and their roles.

The answer is probably either "not quite," or "yes, in some degree." We see something fully recognizable in civilizations—law, foreign policy, originally creative artists—and, looking back at this or that isolated nonliterate society we see in one or another of them something that represents or at least foreshadows what in civilizations has greatly developed. So with learning and intellectuals. In this or that primitive society tradition has become complex; its transmission and perhaps its elaboration is the work of specialists; there is perhaps recognition of roles to be fulfilled in performing this work; there is a separation between the learning of the professional and that of other people in the society; and perhaps in the future the creative contribution of the individual thinker may become apparent to us.

In making some order among the proto-artists and proto-intellectuals one might begin by attending to two familiar and probably very widespread tendencies in even the simplest societies: the tendency to recognize wisdom in the experience accumulated by old people; and the tendency to vest special knowledge, often esoteric, in practitioners of the ritual arts of one kind or another. Tradition must be held in minds; there may be so much of it that only parts of it can be held in any one mind, that of chanter or priest, diviner or sorcerer. Factors of personality presumably contribute to the recruitment of both the specialized memorizer and the generally thoughtful and usually elderly repository of tradition. Kroeber has shown us[25] one type of thoughtful old person (represented by Kuni, the Walapai, and Mr. Moustache, the Navaho): a personality responsible, conservative, pious, sober, disposed to accept established forms; a self-conception fulfilling a role as preserver of tradition. The recorded utterances of Mr. Moustache[26] are predominantly moral advice; he is one who tells people not so much about the nature of things as about what a man ought to do; he sees the good life as right conduct. Kroeber's suggestion that such a type, both of person and of role, may be quite widespread, is readily acceptable.

In other aspects of the cultivated tradition we see other kinds of specialists—neither moralists nor intellectuals—but rather artists and entertainers. The occasional individual who is recognized by his fellows as unusually good at telling traditional tales may have qualities of personality that we have not yet fully identified; they are surely qualities different from those conspicuous in Mr. Moustache and Kuni. This function is performed by occupiers of recognized statuses or offices in some societies where great social and practical importance is attached to a content of tradition that must be remembered and from time to time restated. One thinks of the genealogies of Polynesian peoples and of the bardic chanter who establishes the illustriousness of the lineage of his patron. This is an office, an art, and—one imagines—in cases a personality type. Skill in poetic composition and in certain styles of vocal utterance, as well as the memorizing of genealogies, composed the art of the Hawaiian *Haku-mele,* "Master of Song." [27] The bardic castes of India perform similar functions, and master similar arts of composition and voice.[28] This is a type of cultivator of tradition that has appeared more than once in human history and that continues into civilized society.[29]

Moralist and bardic chanter, types of specialists maintaining tradition and exercising upon material some degree of considered and individualized creative effort, are not, however, intellectuals. The intellectual's special activity is predominantly neither homiletic nor poetic; it consists of a disposition to conceive and present an integral view of all things. He too remembers and transmits tradition, but for him it is the comprehensive questions as to the origins and the nature of man and the universe that are to be understood and communicated. The documents that express this kind of thinking tell of how things came to be as they are or explain how it is that they are as they are. They are causal or genetic or symbolic explanations of the meaning of life. Do we have also integrated statements of moral judgment— primitive ethics? In such documents as are given us for the Navaho, the ethics is implied rather than explicated; it is reflected from assertions as to particular conduct, right or wrong, bad or good. But bodies of mythology, or explanation of things and customs, obedient to apparent unifying ideas, are common in anthropological literature.

The enquiring mind, attentive to questions of ritual, cosmology and the symbolic significance of acts and objects, is frequently shown to exist in one nonliterate group or another. It is clear that in primitive societies there occur disagreements as to details of ritual, the form of the act or its interpretation; that elements of myth or ritual may have different meanings for different people of the same group, or different meanings for the same individual at different times; that improvised explanations are sometimes made; that these matters become a subject of discussion; and that primitive people commonly recognize the superior knowledge in such matters of some members of their group as compared with others.[30] In seeking the beginnings of intellectualism more is to be asked: do we find the thinkers constituting an institutionalized group or class carrying on the perpetuation and consideration of world view in fulfillment of a role, or in occupation of an office to which recognized duties are attached?

Much could be assembled that would suggest if not display some beginnings, in one circumstance or another, of learning and the intellectual life. Some comments on one outstanding instance of organized learning among an African people—the Dogon—may suggest one direction for further enquiry and comparison.

The accounts of the Dogon that I have seen[31] show that the knowledge of these people is highly organized, systematically and in some respects theoretically arranged, formally taught to child, youth and older person, conceived as attainable progressively through increasingly abstruse degrees of understanding, and bound together by fundamental organizing ideas. It is, emphatically, knowledge about the nature of things; the justifications and directives it offers for human conduct are apparently implied rather than declared; the Dogon learns what we might feel to correspond roughly to our natural history, sociology, theology, history and metaphysics. The amount of this knowledge is enormous; it is clear that no one could grasp its every detail, although the older and the most advanced in instruction certainly comprehend the great design into which fit endless details. One sample of this learning,[32] having to do with insects (including some other small creatures not arthropods), shows the nature of the knowledge and the progressively arcane nature of learning. Children are told to collect insects; these are sorted out by the elders, who then teach the names, uses, taboos and mythology connected with each. We are told that insects, like many other classes of natural or artificial things, fall into twenty-two categories, and that the order in which the twenty-two categories of insects are taken up for instruction is not the same as the properly traditional order. This latter order is revealed to the young person only after initiation; it is among the more arcane matters having to do with insects, including the correspondences of the insect-categories with those classifying birds, quadrupeds, reptiles, plants and the twenty-two parts of the human body. Later, also, comes revelation of the conventional graphic signs—groupings of simple lines—associated with certain of these categories and their meaning. This instruction of the young with regard to insects is but a small part of all the knowledge about nature, the technical arts and their products, and the mythological beings and events, and of a series of instructions that begins with lessons given, at least ideally, by the old man who is familial head to "the male members of the family *lato sensu*," and continues through a series of instructions and initiations. Women have their own body of knowledge, in which the same design of all things appears through study of things, events and occupations characteristic of women; and specialists in crafts know more about the meanings connected with that craft than do other people.

Griaule was told of four degrees of understanding recognized by the adult Dogon, and expressed in certain graphic signs that were shown to him. The knowledge at the next higher degree is not knowledge about kinds of things different from that at the lower degree; it is deeper knowledge of the same kind of thing. As the student advances, his learning becomes more and more profound and the organizing ideas of the whole become more apparent. The fourth and most profound degree is thought of as a culmination; degrees one, two and three are respectively "in front," "on one side," and "behind," but the fourth is "clear knowledge"; it is knowledge in its ordered complexity. Truly the ways of the hedgehog are institutionalized for all Dogon!

Griaule was given the names of eighty men of one Dogon community who had reached "clear knowledge." These men constituted 5 or 6 percent of the total population of that community, or about 12 percent of the adult male population. Ogontêmmeli was not one of these advanced initiates; Griaule says that his account represents only levels two and three; of the "clear knowledge" we are given a sample in the monograph about Sirius and the calculation of the exact period (of about sixty years) between celebrations of a certain ceremony. So this society includes a recognized group of especially learned men, not moralists or artists, but men of advanced knowledge.

Are they intellectuals? One wishes one knew something of the discussions they carry on with one another—if they do—and as to how they conceive their role in society. It is a fair assumption that they well know their importance in preserving and communicating the higher learning and in regulating religious ceremony. They surely have something in common with learned Brahmins, elderly mandarins, and modern philosophers. On the other hand—although I may have missed something in these publications that I should have seen—there is lacking evidence of criticisms of tradition, of important original contributions by individuals, of notable reformulations. Knowledge is apparently conceived as substantially fixed, to be progressively revealed as one goes through life. And the thorough integration of the degrees of learning and of those who have attained to the various degrees, in one body of thought, in one society of people sharing a common life, becomes notable as one begins to think about intellectuals in the great civilizations. For in these there is a tendency for the life of the mind to be carried on at some distance from the life of ordinary people and in its own, now somewhat separate, stream of tradition. The learning of the Mayan priest-astronomer surely connected, at necessary points of thought and action, with the practices and ideas of the peasantlike people of the villages; yet the priest-astronomer thought and worked apart in the shrine center, presumably communicated with other priest-astronomers, and advanced his abstruse calculations to knowledge not easily connected with what the villager knew. The Brahmins maintained their separation through caste, and the most learned of them shared knowledge with others like himself across much of India but touched the villager's thoughts only at points, and imperfectly through people of intermediate learning. Where a society has become so large and complex as to move the intellectual away from other people, where the learned inhabit a temple, a city, or a monastery, where learning is communicated among learned people distant from one another, where perhaps writing is added to help these developments to take place and to encourage the restatement of learning in a form consultable over long periods—where these things happen the more civilized instances of institutionalized intellectualism are to be recognized. In the case of the Dogon, learning may seem to us (but apparently not to them) to be a single-stepped pyramid up which the qualified man way ascend. In the great civilizations the pyramidal form is less easily suggested; the degree of separation of the intellectuals from other people suggests parallel but interrelated structures of thought, two or more streams of tradition flowing into one another and yet cutting somewhat distinct channels. This compounding or dividing of traditional knowledge is one of the characteristics of civilized life.

What we are told about the Dogon is a presentation of a way of life as traditional ideas perpetuated and perhaps cultivated. This way of life, like others, might be conceived as a society, as characteristic relationships among kinds of people. That Griaule and his associates have not done so, but have instead made us see first the integrated body of thought that is Dogon learning, a learning that rules, that gives meaning to, institutions and activities, may in part be a consequence of the bent of interest of the investigators, but it is also brought about by the fact that with these Sudanese learning is indeed complex and is systematically conceived and studied. Social structure seems to follow from the Dogon view of the universe rather than world view to emerge from social structure. In the great civilizations of Asia this manner of thinking about ways of life is also invited. Where a tradition is thoughtfully reproduced and perhaps cultivated, and especially where the learned are markedly distinguished from the unlearned, we may think of that central entity of our consideration, culture-society, as a body of knowledge, more or less pyramidal, more or less multilineal.

NOTES

[1] Clyde Kluckhohn, "The Personal Document in Anthropological Science," in *The Use of Personal Documents in History, Anthropology and Sociology* (Bulletin No. 53, Social Science Research Council, 1945), pp. 79-175.

[2] Margaret Mead, "The Mountain Arapesh: V. The Record of Unabelin, with Rorshach Analysis," *Anthropological Papers of the American Museum of Natural History*, Vol. 41, part 3 (1949).

[3] Paul Radin, *Primitive Man as Philosopher* (New York and London: D. Appleton & Co., 1927); *The World of Primitive Man* (New York: Henry Schuman, 1953).

[4] Radin, *Primitive Man as Philosopher*, pp. xv-xvii.

[5] Radin, *The World of Primitive Man*, p. 171.

[6] *Ibid.*, p. 39.

[7] *Ibid.*, p. 37.

[8] Robert Redfield, with Alfonso Villa Rojas, *Chan Kom, a Maya Village* (Washington, D.C.: Carnegie Institution of Washington Publication No. 448, 1934); *A Village That Chose Progress* (Chicago: University of Chicago Press, 1950).

[9] Isaiah Berlin, *The Hedgehog and the Fox* (New York: Mentor Books, The New American Library, 1957), pp. 7-8.

[10] Mead, "The Mountain Arapesh," pp. 378, 383.

[11] A. L. Kroeber, "A Southwestern Personality Type," *Southwestern Journal of Anthropology*, III (1947), 109.

[12] Walter Dyk, *The Son of Old Man Hat* (New York: Harcourt, Brace and Company, 1938).

[13] Leo W. Simmons, ed., *Sun Chief* (New Haven: Yale University Press, 1942).

[14] Cora Du Bois, *The People of Alor* (Minneapolis: The University of Minnesota Press, 1942).

[15] Fred Kniffen and others, *Walapai Ethnography*, ed. by A. L. Kroeber (Memoirs of the American Anthropological Association, No. 42, 1935).

[16] Clyde Kluckhohn, "A Navaho Personal Document with a Brief Paretian Analysis," *Southwestern Journal of Anthropology*, I (1945), 273.

[17] Kroeber, "Southwestern Personality Type."

[18] I am indebted to M. Claude Tardits for helping me to some acquaintance with these publications.

[19] Marcel Griaule, *Dieu d'Eau* (Paris: Editions du Chêne, n.d.).

[20] Marcel Griaule, "Le Savoir des Dogon," *Journal de la Société des Africanistes*, Tome XXII (1952), Fascicles I and II.

[21] Marcel Griaule, "L'Enquête orale en ethnologie," *Revue Philosophique de la France et de l'Étranger*, CXLII (1952), 540.

[22] *Ibid.*, p. 33.

[23] Roberto Michels, "Intellectuals," *Encyclopaedia of the Social Sciences*, VII, 118.

[24] Max Weber, "The Chinese Literati," in *From Max Weber: Essays in Sociology*, trans. and ed. by H. H. Gerth and C. Wright Mills (New York: Oxford University Press, 1946). Following Toynbee's special use of *intelligentsia*, that word might be reserved for those who have learned enough of the ways of a society dominating their own to enable their own community to deal with the

invaders. These men may not be intellectuals at all. The anthropologist encounters intelligentsia in tribal or peasant societies undergoing acculturation.

[25] Kroeber, "Southwestern Personality Type."

[26] John Ladd, The Structure of a Moral Code (Cambridge, Mass.: Harvard University Press, 1957), pp. 335-406. Mr. Moustache was Ladd's principal informant in the course of his study of Navaho morality. See also Kluckhohn, "A Navaho Personal Document."

[27] Martha Beckwith, The Kumulipo, A Hawaiian Creation Chant (Chicago: University of Chicago Press, 1951), pp. 35-41.

[28] A. M. Shah, "The Vahivancha Barots of Gujerat." Unpublished MS.

[29] Ibid. In Gujerat there are still bardic chanters who retain in memory the substance of their verses, but their importance declines while similar castes that make use of written records—their professional secrets—have a larger place in the affairs of their society. Some of the "followers of the written tradition" also recite or compose bardic chants and tell stories.

[30] For example, Monica Wilson, Rituals of Kinship Among the Nyakussa, "Publication of the International African Institute" (London: Oxford University Press, 1957), pp. 48, 106, 240.

[31] Marcel Griaule, Dieu d'Eau; "Le Savoir des Dogon"; "L'Enquête orale en ethnologie." Marcel Griaule and Germaine Dieterlen, "La Harpe-luth des Dogon," Journal de la Société des Africanistes, XX (1950), 209-28; "Un Systeme soudanais de Sirius," ibid., 273-94; "Signes graphiques soudanais," L'Homme, cahiers d'ethnologie, de geographie, et de linguistique, 3 (1951). I have not had access to G. Dieterlen, Essai sur la religion bambara (Paris: Presses Universitaires, 1951).

[32] Griaule, "Le Savoir des Dogon."

OJIBWA ONTOLOGY, BEHAVIOR, AND WORLD VIEW

By A. Irving Hallowell

UNIVERSITY OF PENNSYLVANIA

> It is, I believe, a fact that future investigations will thoroughly confirm, that the Indian does not make the separation into personal as contrasted with impersonal, corporeal with impersonal, in our sense at all. What he seems to be interested in is the question of existence, of reality; and everything that is perceived by the sense, thought of, felt and dreamt of, exists.
>
> PAUL RADIN

Introduction

IT HAS BECOME increasingly apparent in recent years that the potential significance of the data collected by cultural anthropologists far transcends in interest the level of simple, objective, ethnographic description of the peoples they have studied. New perspectives have arisen; fresh interpretations of old data have been offered; investigation and analysis have been pointed in novel directions. The study of culture and personality, national character and the special attention now being paid to values are illustrations that come to mind. Robert Redfield's concept of world view, "that outlook upon the universe that is characteristic of a people," which emphasizes a perspective that is not equivalent to the study of religion in the conventional sense, is a further example.

"World view" [he says] differs from culture, ethos, mode of thought, and national character. It is the picture the members of a society have of the properties and characters upon their stage of action. While "national character" refers to the way these people look to the outsider looking in on them, "world view" refers to the way the world looks to that people looking out. Of all that is connoted by "culture," "world view" attends

The courtesy of the Stanford University Press is acknowledged for permission to use portions of a paper by the author which appeared in *Person Perception*, ed. by R. Tagiuri and L. Petrullo.

especially to the way a man, in a particular society, sees himself in relation to all else. It is the properties of existence as distinguished from and related to the self. It is, in short, a man's idea of the universe. It is that organization of ideas which answers to a man the questions: Where am I? Among what do I move? What are my relations to these things? . . . Self is the axis of "world view."[1]

In an essay entitled "The Self and Its Behavioral Environment," I have pointed out that self-identification and culturally constituted notions of the nature of the self are essential to the operation of all human societies and that a functional corollary is the cognitive orientation of the self to a world of objects other than self. Since the nature of these objects is likewise culturally constituted, a unified phenomenal field of thought, values, and action which is integral with the kind of world view that characterizes a society is provided for its members. The behavioral environment of the self thus becomes structured in terms of a diversified world of objects other than self, "discriminated, classified, and conceptualized with respect to attributes which are culturally constituted and symbolically mediated through language. Object orientation likewise provides the ground for an intelligible interpretation of events in the behavioral environment on the basis of traditional assumptions regarding the nature and attributes of the objects involved and implicit or explicit dogmas regarding the 'causes' of events."[2] Human beings in whatever culture are provided with cognitive orientation in a cosmos; there is "order" and "reason" rather than chaos. There are basic premises and principles implied, even if these do not happen to be consciously formulated and articulated by the people themselves. We are confronted with the philosophical implications of their thought, the nature of the world of being as they conceive it. If we pursue the problem deeply enough we soon come face to face with a relatively unexplored territory—ethno-metaphysics. Can we penetrate this realm in other cultures? What kind of evidence is at our disposal? The forms of speech as Benjamin Whorf and the neo-Humboldtians have thought?[3] The manifest content of myth? Observed behavior and attitudes? And what order of reliability can our inferences have? The problem is a complex and difficult one, but this should not preclude its exploration.

In this paper I have assembled evidence, chiefly from my own field work on a branch of the Northern Ojibwa,[4] which supports the inference that in the metaphysics of being found among these Indians, the action of persons provides the major key to their world view.

While in all cultures "persons" comprise one of the major classes of objects to which the self must become oriented, this category of being is by no means limited to *human* beings. In Western culture, as in others, "supernatural" beings are recognized as "persons," although belonging, at the same time, to an other than human category.[5] But in the social sciences and psychology, "persons" and human beings are categorically identified. This identification is inherent in the concept of "society" and "social relations." In Warren's *Dictionary of Psychology* "person" is defined as "a human organism regarded as having distinctive characteristics and social relations." The same identification is implicit in the conceptualization and investigation of social organization by anthropologists. Yet this obviously involves a radical abstraction if, from the standpoint of the people being studied, the concept of "person" is not, in fact, synonymous with human being but transcends it. The significance of the abstraction only becomes apparent when we stop to consider the perspective adopted. The study of social organization, defined as human relations of a certain kind, is perfectly intelligible as an objective approach to the study of this subject in any culture. But if, in the world view of a people, "persons" as a class include entities other than human beings, then our objective approach is not adequate for presenting an accurate description of "the way a man, in a particular society, sees himself in relation to all else." A different perspective is required for this purpose. It may be argued, in fact, that a thoroughgoing "objective" approach to the study of cultures cannot be achieved solely by projecting upon those cultures categorical abstractions derived from Western thought. For, in a broad sense, the latter are a reflection of *our* cultural subjectivity. A higher order of objectivity may be sought by adopting a perspective which includes an analysis of the outlook of the people themselves as a complementary procedure. It is in a world view perspective, too, that we can likewise obtain the best insight into how cultures function as wholes.

The significance of these differences in perspective may be illustrated in the case of the Ojibwa by the manner in which the kinship term "grandfather" is used. It is not only applied to human persons but to spiritual beings who are persons of a category other than human. In fact, when the collective plural "our grandfathers" is used, the reference is primarily to persons of this latter class. Thus if we study Ojibwa social organization in the usual manner, we take account of only one set of "grandfathers." When we study their religion we discover other "grandfathers." But if we adopt a world view perspective no dichotomization appears. In this perspective "grandfather" is a term applicable to certain "person objects," without any distinction between human persons and those of an other-than-human class. Furthermore, both sets of grandfathers can be said to be functionally as well as terminologically equivalent in certain respects. The other-than-human grandfathers are sources of power to human beings through the "blessings" they bestow, i.e., a sharing of their power which enhances the "power" of human beings. A child is always given a name by an old man, i.e., a terminological grandfather. It is a matter of indifference whether he is a blood relative or not. This name carries with it a special blessing because it has reference to a dream of the human grandfather in which he obtained power from one or more of the other-than-human grandfathers. In other words, the relation between a human child and a human grandfather is functionally patterned in the same way as the relation between human beings and grandfathers of an other-than-human class. And, just as the latter type of grandfather may impose personal taboos as a condition of a blessing, in the same way a human grandfather may impose a taboo on a "grandchild" he has named.

Another direct linguistic clue to the inclusiveness of the "person" category in Ojibwa thinking is the term *wíndígo*. Baraga defines it in his *Dictionary* as "fabulous giant that lives on human flesh; a man that eats human flesh, cannibal." From the Ojibwa standpoint all *wíndígowak* are conceptually unified as terrifying, anthropomorphic beings who, since they threaten one's very existence, must be killed. The central theme of a rich body of anecdotal material shows how this threat was met in particular instances. It ranges from cases in which it was necessary to kill the closest of kin because it was thought an individual was becoming a *wíndígo,* through accounts of heroic fights between human beings and these fabulous giant monsters, to a first-hand report of a personal encounter with one of them.[6]

The more deeply we penetrate the world view of the Ojibwa the more apparent it is that "social relations" between human beings

(*änícinábek*) and other-than-human "persons" are of cardinal significance. These relations are correlative with their more comprehensive
categorization of "persons." Recognition must be given to the culturally
constituted meaning of "social" and "social relations" if we are to
understand the nature of the Ojibwa world and the living entities in it.[7]

Linguistic Categories and Cognitive Orientation

Any discussion of "persons" in the world view of the Ojibwa must
take cognizance of the well known fact that the grammatical structure
of the language of these people, like all their Algonkian relatives,
formally expresses a distinction between "animate" and "inanimate"
nouns. These particular labels, of course, were imposed upon Algonkian languages by Europeans;[8] it appeared to outsiders that the Algonkian differentiation of objects approximated the animate-inanimate
dichotomy of Western thought. Superficially this seems to be the case.
Yet a closer examination indicates that, as in the gender categories of
other languages, the distinction in some cases appears to be arbitrary,
if not extremely puzzling, from the standpoint of common sense or in
a naturalistic frame of reference. Thus substantives for some, but not
all—trees, sun-moon (*gízis*), thunder, stones, and objects of material
culture like kettle and pipe—are classified as "animate."

If we wish to understand the cognitive orientation of the Ojibwa,
there is an ethno-linguistic problem to be considered: What is the
meaning of animate in Ojibwa thinking? Are such generic properties
of objects as responsiveness to outer stimulation—sentience, mobility,
self-movement, or even reproduction—primary characteristics attributed to all objects of the animate class irrespective of their categories as physical objects in our thinking? Is there evidence to sub-
stantiate such properties of objects independent of their formal linguistic
classification? It must not be forgotten that no Ojibwa is consciously
aware of, or can abstractly articulate the animate-inanimate category
of his language, despite the fact that this dichotomy is implicit in his
speech. Consequently, the grammatical distinction as such does not
emerge as a subject for reflective thought or bear the kind of relation
to individual thinking that would be present if there were some formulated dogma about the generic properties of these two classes of objects.

Commenting on the analogous grammatical categories of the Central
Algonkian languages with reference to linguistic and nonlinguistic

orders of meaning, Greenberg writes: "Since all persons and animals are in Class I (animate), we have at least one ethnoseme, but most of the other meanings can be defined only by a linguiseme." In Greenberg's opinion, "unless the actual behavior of Algonquian speakers shows some mode of conduct common to all these instances such that, given this information, we could predict the membership of Class I, we must resort to purely linguistic characterization."[9]

In the case of the Ojibwa, I believe that when evidence from beliefs, attitudes, conduct, and linguistic characterization are all considered together the psychological basis for their unified cognitive outlook can be appreciated, even when there is a radical departure from the framework of our thinking. In certain instances, behavioral predictions can be made. Behavior, however, is a function of a complex set of factors —including actual experience. More important than the linguistic classification of objects is the kind of vital functions attributed to them in the belief system and the conditions under which these functions are observed or tested in experience. This accounts, I think, for the fact that what we view as material, inanimate objects—such as shells and stones—are placed in an "animate" category along with "persons" which have no physical existence in our world view. The shells, for example, called *mígis* on account of the manner in which they function in the Midewiwin, could not be linguistically categorized as "inanimate." "Thunder," as we shall see, is not only reified as an "animate" entity, but has the attributes of a "person" and may be referred to as such. An "inanimate" categorization would be unthinkable from the Ojibwa point of view. When Greenberg refers to "persons" as clearly members of the animate grammatical category he is, by implication, identifying person and human being. Since in the Ojibwa universe there are many kinds of reified person-objects which are other than human but have the same ontological status, these, of course, fall into the same ethnoseme as human beings and into the "animate" linguistic class.

Since stones are grammatically animate, I once asked an old man: Are *all* the stones we see about us here alive? He reflected a long while and then replied, "No! But *some* are." This qualified answer made a lasting impression on me. And it is thoroughly consistent with other data that indicate that the Ojibwa are not animists in the sense that they dogmatically attribute living souls to inanimate objects such as stones. The hypothesis which suggests itself to me is that the allocation of stones to an animate grammatical category is part of a culturally constituted cognitive "set." It does not involve a consciously formulated theory about the nature of stones. It leaves a door open that our orientation on dogmatic grounds keeps shut tight. Whereas we should never expect a stone to manifest animate properties of any kind under any circumstances, the Ojibwa recognize, *a priori,* potentialities for animation in certain classes of objects under certain circumstances.[10] The Ojibwa do not perceive stones, in general, as animate, any more than we do. The crucial test is experience. Is there any personal testimony available? In answer to this question we can say that it is asserted by informants that stones have been seen to move, that some stones manifest other animate properties, and, as we shall see, Flint is represented as a living personage in their mythology.

The old man to whom I addressed the general question about the animate character of stones was the same informant who told me that during a Midewiwin ceremony, when his father was the leader of it, he had seen a "big round stone move." He said his father got up and walked around the path once or twice. Coming back to his place he began to sing. The stone began to move "following the trail of the old man around the tent, rolling over and over, I saw it happen several times and others saw it also."[11] The animate behavior of a stone under these circumstances was considered to be a demonstration of magic power on the part of the Midé. It was not a voluntary act initiated by the stone considered as a living entity. Associated with the Midewiwin in the past there were other types of large boulders with animate properties. My friend Chief Berens had one of these, but it no longer possessed these attributes. It had contours that suggested eyes and mouth. When Yellow Legs, Chief Berens's great-grandfather, was a leader of the Midewiwin he used to tap this stone with a new knife. It would then open its mouth, Yellow Legs would insert his fingers and take out a small leather sack with medicine in it. Mixing some of this medicine with water, he would pass the decoction around. A small sip was taken by those present.[12]

If, then, stones are not only grammatically animate, but, in particular cases, have been observed to manifest animate properties, such as movement in space and opening of a mouth, why should they not on occasion be conceived as possessing animate properties of a "higher" order? The actualization of this possibility is illustrated by the following anecdote:

A white trader, digging in his potato patch, unearthed a large stone similar to the one just referred to. He sent for John Duck, an Indian who was the leader of the *wábano*, a contemporary ceremony that is held in a structure something like that used for the Midewiwin. The trader called his attention to the stone, saying that it must belong to his pavilion. John Duck did not seem pleased at this. He bent down and spoke to the boulder in a low voice, inquiring whether it had ever been in his pavilion. According to John the stone replied in the negative.

It is obvious that John Duck spontaneously structured the situation in terms that are intelligible within the context of Ojibwa language and culture. Speaking to a stone dramatizes the depth of the categorical difference in cognitive orientation between the Ojibwa and ourselves. I regret that my field notes contain no information about the use of direct verbal address in the other cases mentioned. But it may well have taken place. In the anecdote describing John Duck's behavior, however, his use of speech as a mode of communication raises the animate status of the boulder to the level of social interaction common to human beings. Simply as a matter of observation we can say that the stone was treated *as if* it were a "person," not a "thing," without inferring that objects of this class are, for the Ojibwa, necessarily conceptualized as persons.

Further exploration might be made of the relations between Ojibwa thinking, observation, and behavior and their grammatical classification of objects but enough has been said, I hope, to indicate that not only animate properties but even "person" attributes may be projected upon objects which to us clearly belong to a physical inanimate category.

The "Persons" of Ojibwa Mythology

The Ojibwa distinguish two general types of traditional oral narratives: 1. "News or tidings" (*täbătcamowin*), i.e., anecdotes, or stories, referring to events in the lives of human beings (*ănícinábek*). In content, narratives of this class range from everyday occurrences, through more exceptional experiences, to those which verge on the legendary. (The anecdotes already referred to, although informal, may be said to belong to this general class.) 2. Myths (*ätíso'kanak*),[13] i.e., sacred stories, which are not only traditional and formalized; their narration is seasonally restricted and is somewhat ritualized. The significant thing about these stories is that the characters in them are regarded as living entities who have existed from time immemorial. While there is genesis through birth and temporary or permanent form-shifting through transformation, there is no outright creation. Whether human or animal in form or name, the major characters in the myths behave like people, though many of their activities are depicted in a spatio-temporal framework of cosmic, rather than mundane, dimensions. There is "social interaction" among them and between them and *änícinábek*.

A striking fact furnishes a direct linguistic cue to the attitude of the Ojibwa towards these personages. When they use the term *ätíso'kanak,* they are not referring to what I have called a "body of narratives." The term refers to what we would call the characters in these stories; to the Ojibwa they are living "persons" of an other-than-human class. As William Jones said many years ago, "Myths are thought of as conscious beings, with powers of thought and action."[14] A synonym for this class of persons is "our grandfathers."

The *ätíso'kanak,* or "our grandfathers," are never "talked about" casually by the Ojibwa. But when the myths are narrated on long winter nights, the occasion is a kind of invocation: "Our grandfathers" like it and often come to listen to what is being said. In ancient times one of these entities (*Wísekedjak*) is reputed to have said to the others: "We'll try to make everything to suit the *änícinábek* as long as any of them exist, so that they will never forget us and will always talk about us."

It is clear, therefore, that to the Ojibwa, their "talk" about these entities, although expressed in formal narrative, is not about fictitious characters. On the contrary, what we call myth is accepted by them as a true account of events in the past lives of living "persons."[15] It is for this reason that narratives of this class are significant for an understanding of the manner in which their phenomenal field is culturally structured and cognitively apprehended. As David Bidney has pointed out, "The concept of 'myth' is relative to one's accepted beliefs and convictions, so that what is gospel truth for the believer is sheer 'myth' and 'fiction' for the non-believer or skeptic. . . . Myths and magical tales and practices are accepted precisely because pre-scientific folk do not consider them as merely 'myths' or 'magic', since once the distinction between myth and science is consciously accepted, the acquired critical insight precludes the belief in and acceptance of magic and myth."[16] When taken at their face value, myths provide a reliable source of prime value for making inferences about Ojibwa world outlook. They offer basic data about unarticulated, unformalized, and unanalyzed concepts regarding which informants cannot be expected to generalize. From this point of view, myths are broadly analogous to the concrete material of the texts on which the linguist depends for his derivation, by analysis and abstraction, of the grammatical categories and principles of a language.

In formal definitions of myth (e.g., *Concise Oxford Dictionary* and Warren's *Dictionary of Psychology*) the subject matter of such narrative often has been said to involve not only fictitious characters but "supernatural persons." This latter appellation, if applied to the Ojibwa characters, is completely misleading, if for no other reason than the fact that the concept of "supernatural" presupposes a concept of the "natural." The latter is not present in Ojibwa thought. It is unfortunate that the natural-supernatural dichotomy has been so persistently invoked by many anthropologists in describing the outlook of peoples in cultures other than our own. Linguists learned long ago that it was impossible to write grammars of the languages of nonliterate peoples by using as a framework Indo-European speech forms. Lovejoy has pointed out that "The sacred word 'nature' is probably the most equivocal in the vocabulary of the European peoples . . ."[17] and the natural-supernatural antithesis has had its own complex history in Western thought.[18]

To the Ojibwa, for example, *gízis* (day luminary, the sun) is not a natural object in our sense at all. Not only does their conception differ; the sun is a "person" of the other-than-human class. But more important still is the absence of the notion of the ordered regularity in movement that is inherent in our scientific outlook. The Ojibwa entertain no reasonable certainty that, in accordance with natural law, the sun will "rise" day after day. In fact, *Tcakábec,* a mythical personage, once set a snare in the trail of the sun and caught it. Darkness continued until a mouse was sent by human beings to release the sun and provide daylight again. And in another story (not a myth) it is recounted how two old men at dawn vied with each other in influencing the sun's movements.

The first old man said to his companion: "It is about sunrise now and there is a clear sky. You tell the sun to rise at once." So the other old man said to the sun: "My grandfather, come up quickly." As soon as he had said this the sun came up into the sky like a shot. "Now you try something," he said to his companion. "See if you can send it down." So the other man said to the sun: "My grandfather, put your face down again." When he said this the sun went down again. "I have more power than you," he said to the other old man, "The sun never goes down once it comes up."

We may infer that, to the Ojibwa, any regularity in the movements of the sun is of the same order as the habitual activities of human beings. There are certain expectations, of course, but, on occasion, there may be temporary deviations in behavior "caused" by other persons. Above all, any concept of *impersonal* "natural" forces is totally foreign to Ojibwa thought.

Since their cognitive orientation is culturally constituted and thus given a psychological "set," we cannot assume that objects, like the sun, are perceived as natural objects in our sense. If this were so, the anecdote about the old men could not be accepted as an actual event involving a case of "social interaction" between human beings and an other-than-human person. Consequently, it would be an error to say that the Ojibwa "personify" natural objects. This would imply that, at some point, the sun was first perceived as an inanimate, material thing. There is, of course, no evidence for this. The same conclusion applies over the whole area of their cognitive orientation towards the objects of their world.

The Four Winds and Flint, for instance, are quintuplets. They were born of a mother (unnamed) who, while given human characteristics, lived in the very distant past. As will be more apparent later, this character, like others in the myths, may have anthropomorphic characteristics without being conceived as a human being. In the context she, like the others, is an *ätíso'kan*. The Winds were born first, then Flint "jumped out," tearing her to pieces. This, of course, is a direct allusion to his inanimate, stony properties. Later he was penalized for his hurried exit. He fought with *Misábos* (Great Hare) and pieces were chipped off his body and his size reduced. "Those pieces broken from your body may be of some use to human beings some day," *Misábos* said to him. "But you will not be any larger so long as the earth shall last. You'll never harm anyone again."

Against the background of this "historic" event, it would be strange indeed if flint were allocated to an inanimate grammatical category. There is a special term for each of the four winds that are differentiated, but no plural for "winds." They are all animate beings, whose "homes" define the four directions.

The conceptual reification of Flint, the Winds and the Sun as other-than-human persons exemplifies a world view in which a natural-supernatural dichotomy has no place. And the representation of these beings as characters in "true" stories reinforces their reality by means of a cultural device which at the same time depicts their vital roles in interaction with other persons as integral forces in the functioning of a unified cosmos.

Anthropomorphic Traits and Other-than-Human Persons

In action and motivations the characters in the myths are indistinguishable from human persons. In this respect, human and other-than-human persons may be set off, in life as well as in myth, from animate beings such as ordinary animals (*awésiak*, pl.) and objects belonging to the inanimate grammatical category. But, at the same time, it must be noted that "persons" of the other-than-human class do not always present a human appearance in the myths. Consequently, we may ask: What constant attributes do unify the concept of "person"? What is the essential meaningful core of the concept of person in Ojibwa thinking? It can be stated at once that anthropomorphic traits in outward appearance are not the crucial attributes.

It is true that some extremely prominent characters in the myths are given explicit human form. *Wísekedjak* and *Tcakábec* are examples. Besides this they have distinctive characteristics of their own. The former has an exceptionally long penis and the latter is very small in size, yet extremely powerful. There are no equivalent female figures. By comparison, Flint and the Winds have human attributes by implication; they were born of a "woman" as human beings are born; they speak, and so on. On the other hand, the High God of the Ojibwa, a very remote figure who does not appear in the mythology at all, but is spoken of as a "person," is not even given sexual characteristics. This is possible because there is no sex gender in Ojibwa speech.

Consequently an animate being of the person category may function in their thinking without having explicitly sexual or other anthropomorphic characteristics. Entities "seen" in dreams (*pawáganak*) are "persons"; whether they have anthropomorphic attributes or not is incidental. Other entities of the person category, whose anthropomorphic character is undefined or ambiguous, are what have been called the "masters" or "owners" of animals or plant species. Besides these, certain curing procedures and conjuring are said to have other-than-human personal entities as patrons.

If we now examine the cognitive orientation of the Ojibwa towards the Thunder Birds it will become apparent why anthropomorphism is not a constant feature of the Ojibwa concept of "person." These beings likewise demonstrate the autonomous nature of Ojibwa reification. For we find here a creative synthesis of objective "naturalistic" observation integrated with the subjectivity of dream experiences and traditional mythical narrative which, assuming the character of a living image, is neither the personification of a natural phenomenon nor an altogether animal-like or human-like being. Yet it is impossible to deny that, in the universe of the Ojibwa, Thunder Birds are "persons."

My Ojibwa friends, I discovered, were as puzzled by the white man's conception of thunder and lightning as natural phenomena as they were by the idea that the earth is round and not flat. I was pressed on more than one occasion to explain thunder and lightning, but I doubt whether my somewhat feeble efforts made much sense to them. Of one thing I am sure: My explanations left their own beliefs completely unshaken. This is not strange when we consider that, even in our naturalistic frame of reference, thunder and lightning as perceived do not exhibit the lifeless properties of inanimate objects. On the contrary, it has been said that thunder and lightning are among the natural phenomena which exhibit some of the properties of "person objects."[19] Underlying the Ojibwa view there may be a level of naïve perceptual experience that should be taken into account. But their actual construct departs from this level in a most explicit direction: Why is an avian image central in their conception of a being whose manifestations are thunder and lightning? Among the Ojibwa with whom I worked, the linguistic stem for bird is the same as that for Thunder Bird (*pinésī*; pl. *pinésīwak*). Besides this, the avian characteristics of Thunder Birds are still more explicit. Conceptually they are grouped with the hawks, of which there are several natural species in their habitat.

What is particularly interesting is that the avian nature of the Thunder Birds does not rest solely on an arbitrary image. Phenomenally, thunder does exhibit "behavioral" characteristics that are analogous to avian phenomena in this region.[20] According to meteorological observations, the average number of days with thunder begins with one in April, increases to a total of five in midsummer (July) and then declines to one in October. And if a bird calendar is consulted, the facts show that species wintering in the south begin to appear in April and disappear for the most part not later than October, being, of course, a familiar sight during the summer months. The avian character of the Thunder Birds can be rationalized to some degree with reference to natural facts and their observation.

But the evidence for the existence of Thunder Birds does not rest only on the association of the occurrence of thunder with the migration of the summer birds projected into an avian image. When I visited the Ojibwa an Indian was living who, when a boy of twelve or so, saw *pinési* with his own eyes. During a severe thunderstorm he ran out of his tent and there on the rocks lay a strange bird. He ran back to call his parents, but when they arrived the bird had disappeared. He was sure it was a Thunder Bird, but his elders were skeptical because it is almost unheard of to see *pinési* in such a fashion. But the matter was clinched and the boy's account accepted when a man who had *dreamed* of *pinési* verified the boy's description. It will be apparent later why a dream experience was decisive. It should be added at this point, however, that many Indians say they have seen the nests of the Thunder Birds; these are usually described as collections of large stones in the form of shallow bowls located in high and inaccessible parts of the country.

If we now turn to the myths, we find that one of them deals in considerable detail with Thunder Birds. Ten unmarried brothers live together. The oldest is called *Mätcíkīwis*. A mysterious housekeeper cuts wood and builds a fire for them which they find burning when they return from a long day's hunt, but she never appears in person. One day the youngest brother discovers and marries her. *Mätcíkīwis* is jealous and kills her. She would have revived if her husband had not broken a taboo she imposed. It turns out, however, that she is not actually a human being but a Thunder Bird and, thus, one of the *ätíso'kanak* and immortal. She flies away to the land above this earth inhabited by the Thunder Birds. Her husband, after many difficulties, follows her there. He finds himself brother-in-law to beings who are the "masters" of the duck hawks, sparrow hawks, and other species of this category of birds he has known on earth. He cannot relish the food eaten, since what the Thunder Birds call "beaver" are to him like the frogs and snakes on this earth (a genuinely naturalistic touch since the sparrow hawk, for example, feeds on batrachians and reptiles). He goes hunting gigantic snakes with his male Thunder Bird relatives. Snakes of this class also exist on this earth, and the Thunder Birds are their inveterate enemies. (When there is lightning and thunder this is the prey the Thunder Birds are after.) One day the great Thunder Bird says to his son-in-law, "I know you are getting lonely; you must want to see your people. I'll let you go back to earth now. You have nine brothers at home and I have nine girls left. You can take them with you as wives for your brothers. I'll be related to the people on earth now and I'll be merciful towards them. I'll not hurt any of them if I can possibly help it." So he tells his daughters to get ready. There is a big dance that night and the next morning the whole party starts off. When they come to the edge of Thunder Bird land the lad's wife said to him, "Sit on my back. Hang on tight to my neck and keep your eyes shut." Then the thunder crashes and the young man knows that they are off through the air. Having reached this earth they make their way to the brothers' camp. The Thunder Bird women, who have become transformed into human form, are enthusiastically received. There is another celebration and the nine brothers marry the nine sisters of their youngest brother's wife.

This is the end of the myth but a few comments are necessary. It is obvious that the Thunder Birds are conceived to act like human beings. They hunt and talk and dance. But the analogy can be pressed further. Their social organization and kinship terminology are precisely the same as the Ojibwa. The marriage of a series of female siblings (classificatory or otherwise) to a series of male siblings often occurs among the Ojibwa themselves. This is, in fact, considered a kind of ideal pattern. In one case that I know of six blood brothers were married to a sorority of six sisters. There is a conceptual continuity, therefore, between the social life of human beings and that of the

Thunder Birds which is independent of the avian form given to the latter. But we must infer from the myth that this avian form is not constant. Appearance cannot then be taken as a permanent and distinguishable trait of the Thunder Birds. They are capable of metamorphosis, hence, the human attributes with which they are endowed transcend a human outward form. Their conceptualization as "persons" is not associated with a permanent human form any more than it is associated with a birdlike form. And the fact that they belong to the category of *ätíso'kanak* is no barrier to their descending to earth and mating with human beings. I was told of a woman who claimed that North Wind was the father of one of her children. My informant said he did not believe this; nevertheless, he thought it would have been accepted as a possibility in the past.[21] We can only infer that in the universe of the Ojibwa the conception of "person" as a living, functioning social being is not only one which transcends the notion of person in the naturalistic sense; it likewise transcends a human appearance as a constant attribute of this category of being.

The relevance of such a concept to actual behavior may be illustrated by one simple anecdote. An informant told me that many years before he was sitting in a tent one summer afternoon during a storm, together with an old man and his wife. There was one clap of thunder after another. Suddenly the old man turned to his wife and asked, "Did you hear what was said?" "No," she replied, "I didn't catch it." My informant, an acculturated Indian, told me he did not at first know what the old man and his wife referred to. It was, of course, the thunder. The old man thought that one of the Thunder Birds had said something to him. He was reacting to this sound in the same way as he would respond to a human being, whose words he did not understand. The casualness of the remark and even the trivial character of the anecdote demonstrate the psychological depth of the "social relations" with other-than-human beings that becomes explicit in the behavior of the Ojibwa as a consequence of the cognitive "set" induced by their culture.

Metamorphosis as an Attribute of Persons

The conceptualization in myth and belief of Thunder Birds as animate beings who, while maintaining their identity, may change their outward appearance and exhibit either an avian or a human form exemplifies an attribute of "persons" which, although unarticulated abstractly, is basic in the cognitive orientation of the Ojibwa.

Metamorphosis occurs with considerable frequency in the myths where other-than-human persons change their form. *Wisekedjak,* whose primary characteristics are anthropomorphic, becomes transformed and flies with the geese in one story, assumes the form of a snake in another, and once turns himself into a stump. Men marry "animal" wives who are not "really" animals. And *Mikīnāk,* the Great Turtle, marries a human being. It is only by breaking a taboo that his wife discovers she is married to a being who is able to assume the form of a handsome young man.

The senselessness and ambiguities which may puzzle the outsider when reading these myths are resolved when it is understood that, to the Ojibwa, "persons" of this class are capable of metamorphosis by their very nature. Outward appearance is only an incidental attribute of being. And the names by which some of these entities are commonly known, even if they identify the character as an "animal," do not imply unchangeableness in form.

Stith Thompson has pointed out that the possibility of transformation is a "commonplace assumption in folk tales everywhere. Many of such motifs are frankly fictitious, but a large number represent persistent beliefs and living tradition." [22] The case of the Ojibwa is in the latter category. The world of myth is not categorically distinct from the world as experienced by human beings in everyday life. In the latter, as well as the former, no sharp lines can be drawn dividing living beings of the animate class because metamorphosis is possible. In outward manifestation neither animal nor human characteristics define categorical differences in the core of being. And, even aside from metamorphosis, we find that in everyday life interaction with nonhuman entities of the animate class are only intelligible on the assumption that they possess some of the attributes of "persons."

So far as animals are concerned, when bears were sought out in their dens in the spring they were addressed, asked to come out so that they could be killed, and an apology was offered to them. [23] The following encounter with a bear, related to me by a pagan Ojibwa named Birchstick, shows what happened in this case when an animal was treated as a person:

One spring when I was out hunting I went up a little creek where I knew suckers were spawning. Before I came to the rapids I saw fresh bear tracks. I walked along the edge of the creek and when I reached the rapids I saw a bear coming towards me, along the same trail I was following. I stepped behind a tree and when the animal was about thirty yards from me I fired. I missed and before I could reload the bear made straight for me. He seemed mad, so I never moved. I just waited there by the tree. As soon as he came close to me and rose up on his hind feet, I put the butt end of my gun against his heart and held him there. I remembered what my father used to tell me when I was a boy. He said that a bear always understands what you tell him. The bear began to bite the stock of the gun. He even put his paws upon it something like a man would do if he were going to shoot. Still holding him off as well as I could I said to the bear, "If you want to live, go away," and he let go the gun and walked off. I didn't bother the bear anymore.[24]

These instances suffice to demonstrate that, at the level of individual behavior, the interaction of the Ojibwa with certain kinds of plants and animals in everyday life is so structured culturally that individuals act as if they were dealing with "persons" who both understand what is being said to them and have volitional capacities as well. From the standpoint of perceptual experience if we only take account of autochthonous factors in Birchstick's encounter with the bear his behavior appears idiosyncratic and is not fully explained. On the other hand, if we invoke Ojibwa concepts of the nature of animate beings, his behavior becomes intelligible to us. We can understand the determining factors in his definition of the situation, and the functional relations between perception and conduct are meaningful. This Indian was not confronted with an animal with "objective" ursine properties, but rather with an animate being who had ursine attributes and *also* "person attributes." These, we may infer, were perceived as an integral whole. I am sure, however, that in narrating this episode to another Indian, he would not have referred to what his father had told him about bears. That was for my benefit!

Since bears, then, are assumed to possess "person attributes," it is not surprising to find that there is a very old, widespread, and persistent belief that sorcerers may become transformed into bears in order better to pursue their nefarious work.[25] Consequently some of the best documentation of the metamorphosis of human beings into animals comes from anecdotal material referring to cases of this sort. Even contemporary, acculturated Ojibwa have a term for this. They all know what a "bearwalk" is, and Dorson's recent collection of folk traditions, including those of the Indian populations of the Upper Peninsula of Michigan, bears the title *Bloodstoppers and Bearwalkers*. One of Dorson's informants gave him this account of what he had seen:

When I was a kid, 'bout seventeen, before they build the highway, there was just an old tote road from Bark River to Harris. There was three of us, one a couple years older, coming back from Bark River at nighttime. We saw a flash coming from behind us. The older fellow said, 'It's a bearwalk, let's get it. I'll stand on the other side of the road (it was just a wagon rut) and you stand on this side.' We stood there and waited. I saw it 'bout fifty feet away from us—close as your car is now. It looked like a bear, but every time he breathe you could see a fire gust. My chum he fall over in a faint. That brave feller on the other side, he faint. When the bear walk, all the ground wave, like when you walk on soft mud or on moss. He was goin' where he was goin'.[26]

It is clear from this example, and others that might be added, that the Indian and his companions did not perceive an ordinary bear. But in another anecdote given by Dorson, which is not told in the first person, it is said that an Indian "grabbed hold of the bear and it wasn't there—it was the old woman. She had buckskin bags all over her, tied on to her body, and she had a bearskin hide on." [27] I also have been told that the "bearwalk" is dressed up in a bearskin. All such statements, of course, imply a skeptical attitude towards metamorphosis. They are rationalizations advanced by individuals who are attempting to reconcile Ojibwa beliefs and observation with the disbelief encountered in their relations with the whites.

An old-fashioned informant of mine told me how he had once fallen sick, and, although he took various kinds of medicine these did him no good. Because of this, and for other reasons, he believed he had been bewitched by a certain man. Then he noticed that a bear kept coming to his camp almost every night after dark. This is most unusual because wild animals do not ordinarily come anywhere near a human habitation. Once the bear would have entered his wigwam if he had not been warned in a dream. His anxiety increased because he knew, of course, that sorcerers often transformed themselves into bears. So when the bear appeared one night he got up, went outdoors, and shouted to the animal that he knew what it was trying to do. He threatened retaliation in kind if the bear ever returned. The animal ran off and never came back.

In this case there are psychological parallels to Birchstick's encounter with a bear: In both cases the bear is directly addressed as a person might be, and it is only through a knowledge of the cultural background that it is possible fully to understand the behavior of the individuals involved. In the present case, however, we can definitely say that the "animal" was perceived as a human being in the form of a bear; the Indian was threatening a human person with retaliation, not an animal.

A question that I have discussed in *Culture and Experience* in connection with another "bearwalk" anecdote, also arises in this case.[28] Briefly, the Ojibwa believe that a human being consists of a vital part, or *soul*, which, under certain circumstances may become detached from the body, so that it is not necessary to assume that the body part, in all cases, literally undergoes transformation into an animal form. The body of the sorcerer may remain in his wigwam while his soul journeys elsewhere and appears to another person in the form of an animal.

This interpretation is supported by an account which an informant gave me of a visit his deceased grandchild had paid him. One day he was traveling in a canoe across a lake. He had put up an improvised mast and used a blanket for a sail. A little bird alighted on the mast. This was a most unusual thing for a bird to do. He was convinced that it was not a bird but his dead grandchild. The child, of course, had left her body behind in a grave, nevertheless she visited him in animal form.

Thus, both living and dead human beings may assume the form of animals. So far as appearance is concerned, there is no hard and fast line that can be drawn between an animal form and a human form because metamorphosis is possible. In perceptual experience what looks like a bear may sometimes *be* an animal and, on other occasions, a human being. What persists and gives continuity to being is the vital part, or soul. Dorson goes to the heart of the matter when he stresses the fact that the whole socialization process in Ojibwa culture "impresses the young with the concepts of transformation and of 'power', malign or benevolent, human or demonic. These concepts underlie the entire Indian mythology, and make sensible the otherwise childish stories of culture heroes, animal husbands, friendly thunders, and malicious serpents. The bearwalk idea fits at once into this dream world— literally a dream world, for Ojibwa go to school in dreams."[29]

We must conclude, I believe, that the capacity for metamorphosis is one of the features which links human beings with the other-than-human persons in their behavioral environment. It is one of the generic properties manifested by beings of the person class. But is it a ubiquitous capacity of all members of this class equally? I do not think so. Metamorphosis to the Ojibwa mind is an earmark of "power." Within the category of persons there is a graduation of power. Other-than-human persons occupy the top rank in the power hierarchy of animate being. Human beings do not differ from them in kind, but in power. Hence, it is taken for granted that all the *ätíso'kanak* can assume a variety of forms. In the case of human beings, while the potentiality for metamorphosis exists and may even be experienced, any outward manifestation is inextricably associated with unusual power, for good or evil. And power of this degree can only be acquired by human beings through the help of other-than-human persons. Sorcerers can transform themselves only because they have acquired a high order of power from this source.

Powerful men, in the Ojibwa sense, are also those who can make inanimate objects behave as if they were animate. The *Midé* who made a stone roll over and over has been mentioned earlier. Other examples, such as the animation of a string of wooden beads, or animal skins, could be cited.[30] Such individuals also have been observed to transform one object into another, such as charcoal into bullets and ashes into gunpowder, or a handful of goose feathers into birds or insects.[31] In these manifestations, too, they are elevated to the same level of power as that displayed by other-than-human persons. We can, in fact, find comparable episodes in the myths.

The notion of animate being itself does not presume a capacity for manifesting the highest level of power any more than it implies person-attributes in every case. Power manifestations vary within the animate class of being as does the possession of person-attributes. A human being may possess little, if any, more power than a mole. No one would have been more surprised than Birchstick if the bear he faced had suddenly become human in form. On the other hand, the spiritual "masters" of the various species of animals are inherently powerful and, quite generally, they possess the power of metamorphosis. These entities, like the *ätíso'kanak,* are among the sources from which human beings may seek to enhance their own power. My Ojibwa friends often cautioned me against judging by appearances. A poor forlorn Indian dressed in rags might have great power; a smiling, amiable woman, or a pleasant old man, might be a sorcerer.[32] You never can tell until a situation arises in which their power for good or ill becomes manifest. I have since concluded that the advice given me in a common sense fashion provides one of the major clues to a generalized attitude towards the objects of their behavioral environment—particularly people. It makes them cautious and suspicious in interpersonal relations of all kinds. The possibility of metamorphosis must be one of the determining factors in this attitude; it is a concrete manifestation of the deceptiveness of appearances. What looks like an animal, without great power, may be a transformed person with evil intent. Even in dream experiences, where a human being comes into direct contact with other-than-human persons, it is possible to be deceived. Caution is necessary in "social" relations with all classes of persons.

Dreams, Metamorphosis, and the Self

The Ojibwa are a dream-conscious people. For an understanding of their cognitive orientation it is as necessary to appreciate their attitude towards dreams as it is to understand their attitude towards the characters in the myths. For them, there is an inner connection which is as integral to their outlook as it is foreign to ours.

The basic assumption which links the *ätiso'kanak* with dreams is this: Self-related experience of the most personal and vital kind includes what is seen, heard, and felt in dreams. Although there is no lack of discrimination between the experiences of the self when awake and when dreaming, both sets of experiences are equally self-related. Dream experiences function integrally with other recalled memory images in so far as these, too, enter the field of self-awareness. When we think autobiographically we only include events that happened to us when awake; the Ojibwa include remembered events that have occurred in dreams. And, far from being of subordinate importance, such experiences are for them often of more vital importance than the events of daily waking life. Why is this so? Because it is in dreams that the individual comes into direct communication with the *ätiso'kanak,* the powerful "persons" of the other-than-human class.

In the long winter evenings, as I have said, the *ätiso'kanak* are talked about; the past events in their lives are recalled again and again by *änícinábek*. When a conjuring performance occurs, the voices of some of the same beings are heard issuing from within the conjuring lodge. Here is actual perceptual experience of the "grandfathers" during a waking state. In dreams, the same other-than-human persons are both "seen" and "heard." They address human beings as "grand-child." These "dream visitors" (i.e., *pawáganak*) interact with the dreamer much as human persons do. But, on account of the nature of these beings there are differences, too. It is in the context of this face-to-face personal interaction of the self with the "grandfathers" (i.e., synonymously *ätíso'kanak, pawáganak*) that human beings receive important revelations that are the source of assistance to them in the daily round of life, and, besides this, of "blessings" that enable them to exercise exceptional powers of various kinds.

But dream experiences are not ordinarily recounted save under special circumstances. There is a taboo against this, just as there is a taboo against myth narration except in the proper seasonal context. The consequence is that we know relatively little about the manifest content of dreams. All our data come from acculturated Ojibwa. We do know enough to say, however, that the Ojibwa recognize quite as much as we do that dream experiences are often qualitatively different from our waking experiences. This fact, moreover, is turned to positive account. Since their dream visitors are other-than-human "persons" possessing great power, it is to be expected that the experiences of the self in interaction with them will differ from those with human beings in daily life. Besides this, another assumption must be taken into account: When a human being is asleep and dreaming his *òtcatcákwin* (vital part, soul), which is the core of the self, may become detached from the body (*mīyó*). Viewed by another human being, a person's body may be easily located and observed in space. But his vital part may be somewhere else. Thus, the self has greater mobility in space and even in time while sleeping. This is another illustration of the deceptiveness of appearances. The body of a sorcerer may be within sight in a wigwam, while "he" may be bearwalking. Yet the space in which the self is mobile is continuous with the earthly and cosmic space of waking life. A dream of one of my informants documents this specifically. After having a dream in which he met some (mythical) anthropomorphic beings (*mémengwécīwak*) who live in rocky escarpments and are famous for their medicine, he told me that he had later identified precisely the rocky place he had visited and entered in his dream. Thus the behavioral environment of the self is all of a piece. This is why experiences undergone when awake or asleep can be interpreted as experiences of self. Memory images, as recalled, become integrated with a sense of self-continuity in time and space.

Metamorphosis may be *experienced* by the self in dreams. One example will suffice to illustrate this. The dreamer in this case had been paddled out to an island by his father to undergo his puberty fast. For several nights he dreamed of an anthropomorphic figure. Finally, this being said, "Grandchild, I think you are strong enough now to go with me." Then the *pawágan* began dancing and as he danced he turned into what looked like a golden eagle. (This being must be understood as the "master" of this species.) Glancing down at his own body as he sat there on a rock, the boy noticed it was covered with feathers. The "eagle" spread its wings and flew off to the south. The boy then spread his wings and followed.

Here we find the instability of outward form in both human and other-than-human persons succinctly dramatized. Individuals of both categories undergo metamorphosis. In later life the boy will recall how he first saw the "master" of the golden eagles in his anthropomorphic guise, followed by his transformation into avian form; at the same time he will recall his own metamorphosis into a bird. But this experience, considered in context, does not imply that subsequently the boy can transform himself into a golden eagle at will. He might or might not be sufficiently "blessed." The dream itself does not inform us about this.

This example, besides showing how dream experiences may reinforce the belief in metamorphosis, illustrates an additional point: the *pawáganak*, whenever "seen," are always experienced as appearing in a specific form. They have a "bodily" aspect, whether human-like, animal-like, or ambiguous. But this is not their most persistent, enduring and vital attribute any more than in the case of human beings. We must conclude that all animate beings of the person class are unified conceptually in Ojibwa thinking because they have a similar structure—an inner vital part that is enduring and an outward form which can change. Vital personal attributes such as sentience, volition, memory, speech are not dependent upon outward appearance but upon the inner vital essence of being. If this be true, human beings and other-than-human persons are alike in another way. The human self does not die; it continues its existence in another place, after the body is buried in the grave. In this way *änícinábek* are as immortal as *átíso'kanak*. This may be why we find human beings associated with the latter in the myths where it is sometimes difficult for an outsider to distinguish between them.

Thus the world of personal relations in which the Ojibwa live is a world in which vital social relations transcend those which are maintained with human beings. Their culturally constituted cognitive orientation prepares the individual for life in this world and for a life after death. The self-image that he acquires makes intelligible the nature of other selves. Speaking as an Ojibwa, one might say: all other "persons"—human or other than human—are structured the same as I am. There is a vital part which is enduring and an outward appearance that may be transformed under certain conditions. All other "persons," too, have such attributes as self-awareness and understanding. I can talk with them. Like myself, they have personal identity, autonomy, and volition. I cannot always predict exactly how they will act, although most of the time their behavior meets my expectations. In relation to myself, other "persons" vary in power. Many of them have more power than I have, but some have less. They may be friendly and help me when I need them but, at the same time, I have to be prepared for hostile acts, too. I must be cautious in my relations with other "persons" because appearances may be deceptive.

The Psychological Unity of the Ojibwa World

Although not formally abstracted and articulated philosophically, the nature of "persons" is the focal point of Ojibwa ontology and the key to the psychological unity and dynamics of their world outlook. This aspect of their metaphysics of being permeates the content of their cognitive processes: perceiving, remembering, imagining, conceiving, judging, and reasoning. Nor can the motivation of much of their conduct be thoroughly understood without taking into account the relation of their central values and goals to the awareness they have of the existence of other-than-human, as well as human, persons in their world. "Persons," in fact, are so inextricably associated with notions of causality that, in order to understand their appraisal of events and the kind of behavior demanded in situations as they define them, we are confronted over and over again with the roles of "persons" as *loci* of causality in the dynamics of their universe. For the Ojibwa make no cardinal use of any concept of impersonal forces as major determinants of events. In the context of my exposition the meaning of the term *manitu*, which has become so generally known, may be considered as a synonym for a person of the other-than-human class ("grandfather," *ätíso'kan, pawágan*). Among the Ojibwa I worked with it is now quite generally confined to the God of Christianity, when combined with an augmentative prefix (*k'tci manītu*). There is no evidence to suggest, however, that the term ever did connote an impersonal, magical, or supernatural force.[33]

In an essay on the "Religion of the North American Indians" published over forty years ago, Radin asserted "that from an examination of the data customarily relied upon as proof and from individual data obtained, there is nothing to justify the postulation of a belief in a universal force in North America. Magical power as an 'essence' existing apart and separate from a definite spirit, is, we believe, an unjustified assumption, an abstraction created by investigators."[34] This opinion, at the time, was advanced in opposition to the one expressed by those who, stimulated by the writings of R. R. Marett in particular, interpreted the term *manitu* among the Algonkians (W. Jones), *orenda* among the Iroquois (Hewitt) and *wakanda* among the Siouan peoples (Fletcher) as having reference to a belief in a magical force of some kind. But Radin pointed out that in his own field work among both the Winnebago and the Ojibwa the terms in question "always referred to definite spirits, not necessarily definite in shape. If at a vapor-bath the steam is regarded as *wakanda* or *manitu,* it is because it is a spirit transformed into steam for the time being; if an arrow is possessed of specific virtues, it is because a spirit has either transformed himself into the arrow or because he is temporarily dwelling in it; and finally, if tobacco is offered to a peculiarly-shaped object it is because either this object belongs to a spirit, or a spirit is residing in it." *Manitu,* he said, in addition to its substantive usage may have such connotations as "sacred," "strange," "remarkable" or "powerful" without "having the slightest suggestion of 'inherent power', but having the ordinary sense of these adjectives."[35]

With respect to the Ojibwa conception of causality, all my own observations suggest that a culturally constituted psychological set operates which inevitably directs the reasoning of individuals towards an explanation of events in personalistic terms. *Who* did it, *who* is responsible, is always the crucial question to be answered. Personalistic explanation of past events is found in the myths. It was *Wísekedjak* who, through the exercise of his personal power, expanded the tiny bit of mud retrieved by Muskrat from the depths of the inundating waters of the great deluge into the inhabitable island-earth of Ojibwa cosmography. Personalistic explanation is central in theories of disease causation. Illness may be due to sorcery; the victim, in turn, may be "responsible" because he has offended the sorcerer—even unwittingly. Besides this, I may be responsible for my own illness, even without the intervention of a sorcerer. I may have committed some wrongful act in the past, which is the "cause" of my sickness. My child's illness, too, may be the consequence of my past transgressions or those of my wife.[36] The personalistic theory of causation even emerges today among acculturated Ojibwa. In 1940, when a severe forest fire broke out at the mouth of the Berens River, no Indian would believe that lightning or any impersonal or accidental determinants were involved. *Somebody* must have been responsible. The German spy theory soon became popular. "Evidence" began to accumulate; strangers had been seen in the bush, and so on. The personalistic type of explanation satisfies the Ojibwa because it is rooted in a basic metaphysical assumption; its terms are ultimate and incapable of further analysis within the framework of their cognitive orientation and experience.

Since the dynamics of events in the Ojibwa universe find their most ready explanation in a personalistic theory of causation, the qualitative aspects of interpersonal relations become affectively charged with a characteristic sensitivity.[37] The psychological importance of the range and depth of this sensitive area may be overlooked if the inclusiveness of the concept of "person" and "social relations" that is inherent in their outlook is not borne in mind. The reason for this becomes apparent when we consider the pragmatic relations between behavior, values, and the role of "persons" in their world view.

The central goal of life for the Ojibwa is expressed by the term *pīmädäzīwin*, life in the fullest sense, life in the sense of longevity, health and freedom from misfortune. This goal cannot be achieved without the effective help and cooperation of *both* human and other-than-human "persons," as well as by one's own personal efforts. The help of other-than-human "grandfathers" is particularly important for men. This is why all Ojibwa boys, in aboriginal days, were motivated to undergo the so-called "puberty fast" or "dreaming" experience. This was the means by which it was possible to enter into direct "social interaction" with "persons" of the other-than-human class for the first time. It was the opportunity of a lifetime. Every special aptitude, all a man's subsequent successes and the explanation of many of his failures, hinged upon the help of the "guardian spirits" he obtained at this time, rather than upon his own native endowments or the help of his fellow *ánicinábek*. If a boy received "blessings" during his puberty fast and, as a man, could call upon the help of other-than-human persons when he needed them he was well prepared for meeting the vicissitudes of life. Among other things, he could defend himself against the hostile actions of human persons which might threaten him and thus interfere with the achievement of *pīmådäzīwin*. The grand-father of one of my informants said to him: "you will have a long and good life if you dream well." The help of human beings, however, was also vital, especially the services of those who had acquired the kind of power which permitted them to exercise effective curative functions in cases of illness. At the same time there were moral responsibilities which had to be assumed by an individual if he strove for *pīmådäzīwin*. It was as essential to maintain approved standards of personal and social conduct as it was to obtain power from the "grandfathers" because, in the nature of things, one's own conduct, as well as that of other "persons," was always a potential threat to the achievement of *pīmådäzīwin*. Thus we find that the same values are implied throughout the entire range of "social interaction" that charac-terizes the Ojibwa world; the same standards which apply to mutual obligations between human beings are likewise implied in the reciprocal relations between human and other-than-human "persons." In his relations with "the grandfathers" the individual does not expect to receive a "blessing" for nothing. It is not a free gift; on his part there are obligations to be met. There is a principle of reciprocity implied. There is a general taboo imposed upon the human being which forbids him to recount his dream experiences in full detail, except under certain circumstances. Specific taboos may likewise be imposed upon the suppliant. If these taboos are violated he will lose his power; he can no longer count on the help of his "grandfathers."

The same principle of mutual obligations applies in other spheres of life. The Ojibwa are hunters and food gatherers. Since the various species of animals on which they depend for a living are believed to be under the control of "masters" or "owners" who belong to the category of other-than-human persons, the hunter must always be careful to treat the animals he kills for food or fur in the proper manner. It may be necessary, for example, to throw their bones in the water or to perform a ritual in the case of bears. Otherwise, he will offend the "masters" and be threatened with starvation because no animals will be made available to him. Cruelty to animals is likewise an offense that will provoke the same kind of retaliation. And, according to one anecdote, a man suffered illness because he tortured a fabulous *wíndīgo* after killing him. A moral distinction is drawn between the kind of conduct demanded by the primary necessities of securing a livelihood, or defending oneself against aggression, and unnecessary acts of cruelty. The moral values implied document the consistency of the principle of mutual obligations which is inherent in all interactions with "persons" throughout the Ojibwa world.

One of the prime values of Ojibwa culture is exemplified by the great stress laid upon sharing what one has with others. A balance, a sense of proportion must be maintained in all interpersonal relations and activities. Hoarding, or any manifestation of greed, is discountenanced. The central importance of this moral value in their world outlook is illustrated by the fact that other-than-human persons share their power with human beings. This is only a particular instance of the obligations which human beings feel towards one another. A man's catch of fish or meat is distributed among his kin. Human grandfathers share the power acquired in their dreams from other-than-human persons with their classificatory grandchildren. An informant whose wife had borrowed his pipe for the morning asked to borrow one of mine while we worked together. When my friend Chief Berens once fell ill he could not explain it. Then he recalled that he had overlooked one man when he had passed around a bottle of whiskey. He believed this man was offended and had bewitched him. Since there was no objective evidence of this, it illustrates the extreme sensitivity of an individual to the principle of sharing, operating through feelings of guilt. I was once told about the puberty fast of a boy who was not satisfied with his initial "blessing." He demanded that he dream of all the leaves of all the trees in the world so that absolutely nothing would be hidden from him. This was considered greedy and, while the *pawágan* who appeared in his dream granted his desire, the boy was told that "as soon as the leaves start to fall you'll get sick and when all the leaves drop to the ground that is the end of your life." And this is what happened.[38] "Overfasting" is as greedy as hoarding. It violates a basic moral value and is subject to a punitive sanction. The unity of the Ojibwa outlook is likewise apparent here.

The entire psychological field in which they live and act is not only unified through their conception of the nature and role of "persons" in their universe, but by the sanctioned moral values which guide the relations of "persons." It is within this web of "social relations" that the individual strives for *pīmädäzīwin.*

NOTES

[1] Redfield 1952, p. 30; cf. *African Worlds.*

[2] Hallowell 1955, p. 91. For a more extended discussion of the culturally constituted behavioral environment of man see *ibid.,* pp. 86-89 and note 33. The term "self" is not used as a synonym for ego in the psychoanalytic sense. See *ibid.,* p. 80.

[3] See Basilius 1952, Carroll in Whorf, 1956, Hoijer, 1954, Feuer, 1953.

[4] Hallowell 1955, chap. 5.

[5] Bruno de Jésus-Marie 1952, p. xvii: "The studies which make up this book fall into two main groups, of which the first deals with the theological Satan. Here the analysis of exegesis, of philosophy, of theology, treat of the devil under his aspect of a personal being whose history—his fall, his desire for vengeance— can be written as such." One of the most startling characteristics of the devil ". . . is his agelessness" (p. 4). He is immune to "injury, to pain, to sickness, to death . . . . Like God, and unlike man, he has no body. There are in him, then, no parts to be dismembered, no possibilities of corruption and decay, no threat of a separation of parts that will result in death. He is incorruptible, immune to the vagaries, the pains the limitations of the flesh, immortal" (p.5). "Angels have no bodies, yet they have appeared to men in physical form, have talked with them, journeyed the roads with them fulfilling all the pleasant tasks of companionship" (p. 6).

[6] Hallowell 1934b, pp. 7-9; 1936, pp. 1308-9; 1951, pp. 182-83; 1955, pp. 256-58.

[7] Kelsen 1943, chapter 2, discusses the "social" or "personalistic interpretation of nature" which he considers the nucleus of what has been called animism.

[8] In a prefatory note to *Ojibwa Texts,* Part I, Jones says (p. xiii) that " 'Being' or 'creature' would be a general rendering of the animate while 'thing' would express the inanimate." Cf. Schoolcraft's pioneer analysis of the animate and inanimate categories in Ojibwa speech, pp. 171-72.

[9] Greenberg 1954, pp. 15-16.

¹⁰ I believe that Jenness grossly overgeneralizes when he says (p. 21): "To the Ojibwa ... all objects have life. ..." If this were true, their *inanimate* grammatical category would indeed be puzzling. Within the more sophisticated framework of modern biological thought, the Ojibwa attitude is not altogether naïve. N. W. Pirie points out (pp. 184-85) that the words "life" and "living" have been borrowed by science from lay usage and are no longer serviceable. "Life is not a thing, a philosophical entity: it is an attitude of mind towards what is being observed."

¹¹ Field notes. From this same Indian I obtained a smoothly rounded pebble, about two inches long and one and a half inches broad, which his father had given him. He told me that I had better keep it enclosed in a tin box or it might "go." Another man, Ketegas, gave me an account of the circumstances under which he obtained a stone with animate properties and of great medicinal value. This stone was egg shaped. It had some dark amorphous markings on it which he interpreted as representing his three children and himself. "You may not think this stone is alive," he said, "but it is. I can make it move." (He did not demonstrate this to me.) He went on to say that on two occasions he had loaned the stone to sick people to keep during the night. Both times he found it in his pocket in the morning. Ketegas kept it in a little leather case he had made for it.

¹² Yellow Legs had obtained information about this remarkable stone in a dream. Its precise location was revealed to him. He sent two other Indians to get it. These men, following directions, found the stone on Birch Island, located in the middle of Lake Winnipeg, some thirty miles south of the mouth of the Berens River.

¹³ Cognate forms are found in Chamberlain's compilation of Cree and Ojibwa "literary" terms.

¹⁴ Jones, *Texts,* Part II, p. 574*n*.

¹⁵ The attitude manifested is by no means peculiar to the Ojibwa. Almost half a century ago Swanton remarked that "one of the most widespread errors, and one of those most unfortunate for folk-lore and comparative mythology, is the off-hand classification of myth with fiction. ..." On the contrary, as he says, "It is safe to say that most of the myths found spread over considerable areas were regarded by the tribes among which they were collected as narratives of real occurrences."

¹⁶ Bidney 1953, p. 166.

¹⁷ Lovejoy and Boas 1935, p. 12; Lovejoy 1948, p. 69.

¹⁸ See, e.g., Collingwood 1945, also the remarks in Randall 1944, pp. 355-56. With respect to the applicability of the natural-supernatural dichotomy to primitive cultures see Van Der Leeuw 1938, pp. 544-45; Kelsen 1943, p. 44; Bidney 1953, p. 166.

¹⁹ Krech and Crutchfield 1948 write (p. 10): "clouds and storms and winds are excellent examples of objects in the psychological field that carry the perceived properties of mobility, capriciousness, causation, power of threat and reward."

²⁰ Cf. Hallowell 1934a.

²¹ Actually, this was probably a rationalization of mother-son incest. But the woman never was punished by sickness, nor did she confess. Since the violation of the incest prohibition is reputed to be followed by dire consequences, the absence of both may have operated to support the possibility of her claim when considered in the context of the Ojibwa world view.

²² Thompson 1946, p. 258.

23 Hallowell 1926.

24 Hallowell 1934a, p. 397.

25 Sorcerers may assume the form of other animals as well. Peter Jones, a converted Ojibwa, who became famous as a preacher and author says that "they can turn themselves into bears, wolves, foxes, owls, bats, and snakes.... Several of our people have informed me that they have seen and heard witches in the shape of these animals, especially the bear and the fox. They say that when a witch in the shape of a bear is being chased all at once she will run around a tree or hill, so as to be lost sight of for a time by her pursuers, and then, instead of seeing a bear they behold an old woman walking quietly along or digging up roots, and looking as innocent as a lamb" (Jones 1861, pp. 145-46).

26 Dorson 1952, p. 30.

27 Ibid., p. 29. This rationalization dates back over a century. John Tanner, an Indianized white man who was captured as a boy in the late eighteenth century and lived with the Ottawa and Ojibwa many years, refers to it. So does Peter Jones.

28 Hallowell 1955, pp. 176-77.

29 Dorson 1952, p. 31.

30 Hoffman 1891, pp. 205-6.

31 Unpublished field notes.

32 See Hallowell 1955, Chapter 15.

33 Cf. Skinner 1915, p. 261. Cooper 1933 (p. 75) writes: "The Manitu was clearly personal in the minds of my informants, and not identified with impersonal supernatural force. In fact, nowhere among the Albany River Otchipwe, among the Eastern Cree, or among the Montagnais have I been able thus far to find the word Manitu used to denote such force in connection with the Supreme Being belief, with conjuring, or with any other phase of magico-religious culture. *Manitu*, so far as I can discover, always denotes a supernatural personal being.... The word *Manitu* is, my informants say, not used to denote magical or conjuring power among the coastal Cree, nor so I was told in 1927, among the Fort Hope Otchipwe of the upper Albany River."

34 Radin 1914a, p. 350.

35 Ibid., pp. 349-50.

36 "Because a person does bad things, that is where sickness starts," is the way one of my informants phrased it. For a fuller discussion of the relations between unsanctioned sexual behavior and disease, see Hallowell 1955, pp. 294-95; 303-4. For case material, see Hallowell 1939.

37 Cf. Hallowell 1955, p. 305.

38 Radin 1927, p. 177, points out that "throughout the area inhabited by the woodland tribes of Canada and the United States, overfasting entails death." Jones, *Texts*, Part II, pp. 307-11, gives two cases of overfasting. In one of them the bones of the boy were later found by his father.

REFERENCES

African Worlds: Studies in the Cosmological Ideas and Social Values of African Peoples. 1954. Published for the International African Institute. London, Oxford University Press.

Baraga, R. R. Bishop. 1878. A Theoretical and Practical Grammar of the Otchipive Language. Montreal, Beauchemin and Valois.

Baraga, R. R. Bishop. 1880. A Dictionary of the Otchipive Language Explained in English. Montreal, Beauchemin and Valois.
Basilius, H. 1952. "Neo-Humboldtian Ethnolinguistics," *Word*, Vol. 8.
Bidney, David. 1953. Theoretical Anthropology. New York, Columbia University Press.
Bruno de Jésus-Marie, père, ed. 1952. Satan. New York, Sheed and Ward.
Chamberlain, A. F. 1906. "Cree and Ojibwa Literary Terms," *Journal of American Folklore*, 19:346-47.
Collingwood, R. G. 1945. The Idea of Nature. Oxford, Clarendon Press.
Cooper, John M. 1933. "The Northern Algonquian Supreme Being," *Primitive Man*, 6:41-112.
Dorson, Richard M. 1952. Bloodstoppers and Bearwalkers: Folk Traditions of the Upper Peninsula. Cambridge, Mass., Harvard University Press.
Feuer, Lewis S. 1953. "Sociological Aspects of the Relation between Language and Philosophy," *Philosophy of Science*, 20:85-100.
Fletcher, Alice C. 1910. "Wakonda," in *Handbook of American Indians*. Washington, D.C.: Bureau of American Ethnology, Bull. 30.
Greenberg, Joseph H. 1954. "Concerning Inferences from Linguistic to Nonlinguistic Data," in *Language in Culture*, ed. by Harry Hoijer. (Chicago University "Comparative Studies in Cultures and Civilizations.") Chicago, University of Chicago Press.
Hallowell, A. Irving. 1926. "Bear Ceremonialism in the Northern Hemisphere," *American Anthropologist*, 28:1-175.
—————— 1934a. "Some Empirical Aspects of Northern Saulteaux Religion," *American Anthropologist*, 36:389-404.
—————— 1934b. "Culture and Mental Disorder," *Journal of Abnormal and Social Psychology*, 29:1-9.
—————— 1936. "Psychic Stresses and Culture Patterns," *American Journal of Psychiatry*, 92:1291-1310.
—————— 1939. "Sin, Sex and Sickness in Saulteaux Belief," *British Journal of Medical Psychology*, 18:191-97.
—————— 1951. "Cultural Factors in the Structuralization of Perception," in John H. Rohver and Muzafer Sherif, *Social Psychology at the Crossroads*. New York, Harper.
—————— 1955. Culture and Experience. Philadelphia, University of Penna. Press.
Hewitt, J. N. B. 1902. "Orenda and a Definition of Religion," *American Anthropologist*, 4:33-46.
Hoffman, W. J. 1891. The Mide'wiwin or "Grand Medicine Society" of the Ojibwa. Washington, D.C., Bureau of American Ethnology 7th Annual Report.
Hoijer, Harry, ed. 1954. Language in Culture. Memoir 79, American Anthropological Association.
Jenness, Diamond. 1935. The Ojibwa Indians of Parry Island, their social and religious life. Ottawa, Canada Department of Mines, National Museum of Canada Bull. 78, Anthropological Series 12.
Jones, Peter. 1861. History of the Ojibway Indians. London.
Jones, William. 1905. "The Algonkin Manitu," *Journal of American Folklore*, 18:183-90.
—————— Ojibwa Texts. (Publications of the American Ethnological Society, Vol. 7, Parts I and II.) Leyden: 1917; New York: 1919.
Kelsen, Hans. 1943. Society and Nature: A Sociological Inquiry. Chicago, University of Chicago Press.

Krech, David, and Richard S. Crutchfield. 1948. Theory and Problems of Social Psychology. New York, McGraw-Hill.

Lovejoy, Arthur O. 1948. Essays in the History of Ideas. Baltimore, Johns Hopkins Press.

Lovejoy, Arthur O., and George Boas. 1935. Primitivism and Related Ideas in Antiquity. Baltimore, Johns Hopkins Press. Vol. I of A Documentary History of Primitivism and Related Ideas.

Pirie, N. W. 1937. "The Meaninglessness of the Terms 'Life' and 'Living,'" in Perspectives in Biochemistry, ed. by J. Needham and D. Green. New York, Macmillan.

Radin, Paul. 1914a. "Religion of the North American Indians," Journal of American Folklore, 27:335-73.

———— 1914b. Some Aspects of Puberty Fasting among the Ojibwa. Geological Survey of Canada, Department of Mines, Museum Bull. No. 2, Anthropological Series, No. 2, pp. 1-10.

———— 1927. Primitive Man as Philosopher. New York, D. Appleton & Co.

Randall, John Herman, Jr. 1944. "The Nature of Naturalism," in Naturalism and the Human Spirit, ed. by H. Krikorian. New York, Columbia University Press.

Redfield, Robert. 1952. "The Primitive World View," Proceedings of the American Philosophical Society, 96:30-36.

Schoolcraft, Henry R. 1834. Narrative of an Expedition through the Upper Mississippi to Itasca Lake, the Actual Source of the River . . . . New York, Harper.

Skinner, Alanson. 1915. "The Menomini Word 'Häwätûk,'" Journal of American Folklore, 28:258-61.

Swanton, John R. 1910. "Some practical aspects of the study of myths," Journal of American Folklore, 23:1-7.

Tanner, John. 1830. Narrative of the Captivity and Adventures of John Tanner, ed. by E. James.

Thompson, Stith. 1946. The Folktale. New York, Dryden Press.

Van Der Leeuw, G. 1938. Religion in Essence and Manifestation. London, Allen and Unwin.

Whorf, Benjamin Lee. 1956. Language Thought and Reality: Selected Writings of Benjamin L. Whorf, ed. with an introduction by J. B. Carroll; Foreword by Stuart Chase. New York, Wiley.

THE WORLD OF THE KERESAN
PUEBLO INDIANS

By Leslie A. White

UNIVERSITY OF MICHIGAN

WHEN CORONADO and his party entered the American Southwest in 1540 they found many Indian tribes living in towns, or pueblos, with rows of terraced houses two to four stories high. They were peaceful Indians who raised corn, beans and squash, cotton and tobacco. They had dogs and kept flocks of domesticated turkeys. They made a good grade of pottery and wove cotton fabrics on simple looms. They were the Pueblo Indians.

The land occupied by the Pueblo tribes was wild and beautiful. Great mesas of solid rock alternated with sandy plains. Deep canyons cut sharply into mesas and mountains. The lower elevations were a mile above sea level, but huge mountain ranges—the Jemez and the Sandias—raised their peaks ten and eleven thousand feet above the sea. Huge Ponderosa pines and Douglas firs grew high upon the mountain slopes; the mesas and lowlands were dotted with clumps of juniper, yucca, and cactus. Cottonwoods and willows followed the river valleys.

The pueblo country is an arid one. Streams are few and many of them are bone-dry most of the year. But during the summer months the rain may fall in torrents, quickly filling the dusty channels with swift and turbulent currents. The summers are hot, a brassy sun glares fiercely out of a deep blue sky, great white clouds are piled at random above a distant horizon. Lizards sun themselves on hot, flat rocks, or dart swiftly to cover at a sign of danger. But in winter bitter storms, bringing snow and ice, occasionally descend from the mountains, and all life is stilled for a time.

The actual holdings of the Pueblo Indians were meager indeed in comparison with the vast expanse in which they lived. They had little farms near their villages, either in valleys where irrigation was possible, or out on the barren plain or hillside. But most of the land was nature's domain, the home of deer and bear, of turkey, puma, and antelope. These great tracts were exploited for game and plant food, for minerals and dyestuffs, for boughs of fir for dance costumes, and willow twigs for prayersticks. Sacred springs were visited to fill the medicine bowls upon their altars. The hazards of the open country were faced when the pueblo peoples attended each other's ceremonies. And dangers there were, for wild nomadic tribes, the feared and hated Moshomi—the Navahos and Utes, the Comanches and Apaches—infiltrated their land, visiting them with murder and theft.

This was the world of the Pueblo Indians as the early Spaniards saw it, and indeed as the Americans saw it after the Treaty of Guadalupe-Hidalgo. The Indians themselves saw all of this, too. But they saw much more—and they still do today, even as in 1540 when Coronado broke in upon their world.

The world of the Pueblo Indians[1] was not created in the beginning; it was always there—or here. But it was somewhat different in the beginning than it is now. The Earth was square and flat; it had four corners and a middle. Below the surface of the earth there were four horizontal layers; each one was a world. The lowest world was a white one. Above that lay the red world and then the blue one. Above the blue world, and just beneath this world that we are living in today, was the yellow world.[2]

In the beginning the people were living deep down inside the earth, in the white world, with their mother, Iyatiku. Finally it was time for them to come out, to ascend to this world. Iyatiku caused a great evergreen tree, a spruce or a fir, to grow so that the people could climb up its trunk and boughs to the next world. But when the tree reached the next world above it found its way blocked by a hard layer of earth and rock. So Iyatiku had Woodpecker make a hole through the layer into the next world. The people climbed up into the red world and lived there for four years. Then it was time to climb up into the blue world. Again Iyatiku had a tree reach up to the world above, and again she had someone make a hole through the hard layer so the tree and the people could pass through.

At last the people were ready to ascend into this world. Iyatiku had Badger make a hole through the hard crust. He made so much dust in his work that there was danger that the people might be blinded, so Whirlwind Old Man went up and held the dust in his arms until Badger got through. Then Cicada was asked to line the opening so it would be smooth and safe to pass through. Iyatiku asked Badger to look out into this world and tell her what it looked like. Badger looked out. "It is very beautiful up there," he told Iyatiku, "there are rain clouds everywhere." So Iyatiku decided it was all right for the people to complete their ascent and to emerge into this world. Iyatiku had created societies of medicine men in the lower worlds and had given them their altars and ceremonies. These societies—the Flint, Fire, Giant, and Kapina medicine men—came out with the people. There were some evil spirits, too, who also came out. They were *kanadyaiya,* 'witches,' but no one knew this at that time.

They came out at a place in the north called Shipap. Everything was new and "raw." The earth was too soft for people to walk upon so Iyatiku had the mountain lion use his magic power to harden it. When it was sufficiently hard, the people came out. They stayed near the opening at Shipap for a time, but it was too sacred a place for permanent residence, so Iyatiku told them they were to migrate toward the south. She said: "I shall not go with you. I am going to return to my home in the white world, but I will be with you always in spirit. You can pray to me and I will always help you." Before she left she appointed a man to take her place. "You shall be Tiamunyi," she told him and the people. "You will be my representative among my people. You must look after them and work for their welfare." Then Iyatiku gave Tiamunyi an ear of corn. "Take this," she told him. "This corn is my heart. This is what you will live on; its milk shall be to you as milk from my breasts."

Iyatiku returned to the lower world and the people began their journey to the south. They stopped at a place and established a pueblo. They called it Kashikatchrutiya, or White House. They lived here a long time.

There were two sisters, Utctsityi and Naotsityi, living with the people. They were supernatural beings. Naotsityi felt superior to her sister and challenged her to a number of contests so that she could demonstrate her superiority. They had a number of contests, but Utctsityi always came out on top. Finally Naotsityi decided to go away, so she took her people and left. Naotsityi's people became the white people; the children of Utctsityi became the Indians.

In these early days lots of things happened. There was a girl who was out in the mountains one day picking pinyon nuts. She became impregnated by the Sun and in due course bore twin sons. She named the first born Masewi, the younger Oyoyewi. They grew rapidly and soon showed signs of great supernatural power. They were very venturesome and wanted to explore the world. Their mother, fearing for their safety, tried always to keep them at home. The boys were determined to go to the place of the sunrise to meet their father, and, ignoring their mother's protests, they set out. When they got to the Sun's house they announced that they were his sons and had come to meet him. But the Sun was unwilling to accept them as his sons and devised a number of tests to settle the question of paternity. In one of these tests he put the boys into a big oven full of glowing coals. But Masewi and Oyoyewi had some magic shells in their mouths which they spat out upon the fire and remained unharmed. Each time the boys passed the test so finally the Sun acknowledged them as his own sons. He gave them bows and arrows and throwing sticks of great potency and they returned home.

Masewi and Oyoyewi had many other adventures. They used to take trips far and wide to see what they could see. On one of these trips they met a huge woman-like creature. She was a Shkoyo. She was big and ugly and carried a basket on her back. She picked up Masewi and Oyoyewi and put them in her basket. When she got home she built a fire in her oven; she was going to roast the boys and eat them. But Masewi and Oyoyewi were too smart for her, and they killed her. On another adventure the two boys turned an entire pueblo and its houses into stone—all except one couple—for being inhospitable to strangers. Eventually it became clear to everyone that Masewi and Oyoyewi were supernatural; they were war-gods. They finally left the people and went to make their home in the Sandia mountains where they now live. But they are represented today in the Pueblos by two men, the war chiefs, who bear their names.

While the people were living at White House they came to know all about the world they were living in, and how to behave toward it. First of all there was the Earth, Naiya Ha'atse, 'Mother Earth.' It was the Earth that we live on. It was square and flat, although marked with mountains and valleys here and there. It was very large, also; one could not reach its edges in many days' journey, although one could easily see them on the distant horizons. Above the earth was Howaka, 'the Sky.' This was not merely empty space, but a real something, a structure that arched like a great dome above the earth upon which it rested.

At each corner of the Earth was a house and in that house lived a god. In the northwest corner was the House of Leaves, the home of Tsityostinako, or 'Thought Woman'; she could cause things to happen merely by thinking of them. Spider Grandmother lived in the House of Boards in the southwest corner. Turquoise House was in the southeast corner; Butterfly lived there. And in the northeast corner lived Mocking Bird Youth in Yatkana house.

The cardinal points were important. They were called "middle north," "middle east," and so on, meaning that the points were midway beween the corners of the earth. In addition to the four points on the horizons, zenith and nadir were distinguished and named. Each of the six directions had a color: the north was yellow, west blue, south red, east white, zenith brown, and nadir black. At each of the cardinal points lived a god. Shakak lived at Kawestima, the north mountain; he was the god of winter and of snow. Shruwitira, a man-like god, lived at Tspina, west mountain. A gopher-like god named Maiyochina lived at Daotyuma, or south mountain; he helped crops to grow. Shruwisigyama, a bird-like god, lived at east mountain, a fox-like god at the zenith, and a mole-like god at the nadir.

Each one of the six directions had its own animal: the puma lived in the north, the bear in the west, bobcat in the south, wolf in the east; eagle lived at the zenith, shrew at the nadir, and the badger in the middle—the middle of the whole world. Each cardinal point had also a woman, a tree, a snake, and a warrior. The women had colored faces, each one with the color appropriate to her cardinal point.

Thus, everything was well ordered in the world in which the Keresan Pueblo Indians found themselves, and neatly arranged according to the cardinal points.

There were still other gods, each with his, or their, home. In the middle east was Koaikutc, 'Sunrise Place,' located a short distance south of Yastya Kot, 'Dawn Mountain.' The Koshairi lived at Koaikutc, and just south of them the Kwiraina had their home at Shell Spring. In the northwest, but not at the corner of the earth, lived Gotsa, the patron of game animals. Whirlwind Old Man lived in the southwest near the house of Spider Grandmother. In the middle west, but not as far as the edge of the world, was Wenima, the home of the

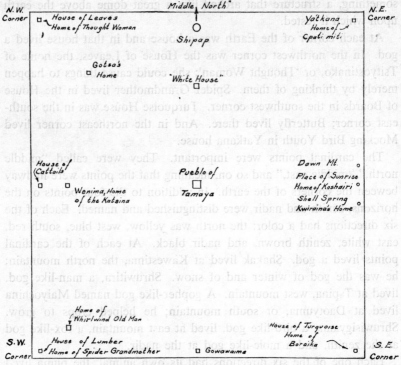

MAP OF THE MYTHOLOGICAL WORLD OF THE
PUEBLO OF SANTA ANA
From White, *The Pueblo of Santa Ana, New Mexico* (1942)

Katsina, the rain makers. Water Snake, with a horn on his head and cloud designs on his sides, lived in the earth and the Rio Grande river.

It was while the people were living at White House that the way of life which they have followed since that time was organized. They raised corn, beans, squash, cotton, and tobacco, and they hunted deer and turkey in the mountains. The medicine societies performed their ceremonies in their houses. Two *kivas* were built for other ceremonies and dances. The people learned how to make prayersticks and how to pray to all the gods and spirits with them. They prayed with corn meal, too.

When people died their bodies were buried, but their souls went back to Shipap, the place of emergence, and returned to their mother in the fourfold womb of the earth. Every year they would come back to White House to visit their relatives. But when the time came for them to return, the living people wanted to accompany them. But Iyatiku told them that they could not do this, that they would have to wait until they died and became like little children again before they could reenter the place of their birth. So every year, now, the souls of the dead come back to the pueblos of the living and visit their relatives and eat the food that has been placed for them on their graves and on the road toward the north. The living entertain their dead relatives, but do not accompany them when they leave. Some people become *katsinas* after they die.

The *katsinas* used to come to White House during the summer to dance for rain and crops. It always rained after a visit from the *katsinas,* the crops grew abundantly, and the people prospered and were happy. But one time a quarrel arose between the people and the *katsinas*. Accounts differ somewhat as to just what happened, but, in any event, the *katsinas* felt that they had been insulted and they decided not to come to the Pueblo again to dance for rain. The people were staggered by the decision; without the *katsinas'* help they would have no rain and consequently no crops; they would starve. The *katsinas* finally relented to the extent of allowing the men of the Pueblo to impersonate them by wearing masks and costume, and to put on the dances just like the *katsinas* did. "We will be there with you in spirit," they told the people.

This was the way the Keres came to have the masked dances which they perform today. They had to learn to impersonate the Koshairi and the Kwiraina, too. These were the two groups of spirits whose homes were in the east, near the Place of Sunrise. They have great power to promote fertility of crops, animals, and people. They—or rather, their impersonators—have charge of dances today. The Koshairi act as buffoons in the plaza between dances and occasionally engage in scatological rites.

After the unfortunate quarrel with the *katsinas* at White House the people fell to quarreling among themselves. Iyatiku, their mother, deep down in her home within the earth, knew all about what had happened and she was deeply distressed. One night she changed the language of the people, causing each faction to speak a different tongue. The people decided to abandon White House. So they set out, one group going in this direction; another, in that. They settled at various places.

Sometimes they would live at a site for a time and then move on to some other place. Finally they came to establish their homes permanently where they are now found. This is why we find so many pueblo ruins today, and why the Pueblo Indians speak different languages.

Thus the great mythical era of the Pueblo Indians came to an end, and the modern era began. But by the time this change took place, the Indians had their culture—their institutions, their clans, medicine societies, officers, dances, and ceremonies—well established. The Cacique, or Tiamunyi, was the head of the Pueblo. He was the representative of the mother, Iyatiku. There were two war chiefs, Masewi and Oyoyewi, who represented the war-god twins. The *katsinas* and the Koshairi and Kwiraina were impersonated by appropriately initiated and costumed men. There were a number of medicine societies—the Flint, Fire, Shikame, Giant, and Kapina societies. Some of the pueblos had a Snake society which performed a ceremony with living snakes.

Life was not too difficult for the Pueblos, but they did have problems to face and solve. The most important one was to get enough to eat; in their arid land this problem sometimes became critical. And game was not always plentiful. There were enemies, the wild Moshomi, to be opposed. Sickness and disease were always to be reckoned with; sometimes a whole pueblo would be stricken. But the Pueblos had means and aids to cope with these problems. There were the vast powers of the supernatural world to be enlisted in their behalf. With good hearts, powerful songs, prayers, paraphernalia, and ritual they could accomplish anything.

Everyone worked and prayed for rain. The Cacique prayed and fasted. The medicine societies performed their ceremonies; men impersonated *katsinas* in dances; the Buffalo dances brought snow in wintertime; and even the scalps of slain Moshomi had power to moisten the earth. Cloud, rain, and lightning symbols were everywhere, on altars, medicine bowls, and masks; the horned water snake was painted on dance kilts. Carved and feathered prayersticks were offered to all kinds of spirits, in the mountains, in the springs, and in the heavens. The whole supernatural world was constrained by prayer and song to give up its fructifying fluid so that the people might raise abundant crops and have enough to eat.

There was a special society to bring success to hunters. This was the Shaiyak society. The mountain lion was the principal god of the hunt, but other predatory animals assisted also. The medicine men of the Shaiyak society had songs, paraphernalia, ritual, and prayers to insure success. Each hunter carried a *mokaich,* a little stone figure of the mountain lion, in his pouch. When a deer was killed the first thing the hunter did was to feed the *mokaich* by dipping his head and mouth in the fresh blood. The deer were taken back to the pueblo where they were received with ceremonial display and adopted into the village; their heads and horns were adorned with fluffy feathers and placed upon the housetops next to the chimneys.

The Moshomi, especially the Navahos, were not only ruthless men who killed and plundered the Pueblos; they were possessed of supernatural powers as well, and one had to have supernatural power to overcome them. Fortunately, the Keres had their twin war-gods, Masewi and Oyoyewi, who were ever ready to help them through their human representatives the war chiefs. There was also a society of warriors called Opi. This was composed of men who had scalped an enemy and "taken his clothes," i.e., his supernatural power embodied in a charm or medicine bag. To be sure, the enemy had to be killed in order to do this, but the mere killing was not as significant as overpowering him on the supernatural plane and taking his scalp. The Opi were the first line of defense against the nomadic marauders. The Flint society, too, had powers for war and helped the Opi and common men alike to overcome their foes.

Scalps were taken back to the pueblo where they were greeted with a war dance. They were adopted into the pueblo and kept in a special chamber in one of the ceremonial houses. They were fed, given cigarettes, and bathed periodically. Once they had become residents of the pueblo they had power to bring rain.

But a man who had come into direct contact with a slain enemy became contaminated in a supernaturalistic way. The power of the enemy was upon him, and his life would be in danger until he was put through a ceremony to cleanse him and restore him to his customary life within the pueblo.

As we noted earlier, there were some Evil Ones who came up out of the lower world with the people of the pueblos. They were *kanadyaiya,* or witches. They were human beings, like the others, but they had two hearts, one good, the other bad. When they grew up they expressed their evil nature by making people sick. They would shoot objects of various kinds—broken glass, cactus thorns, dirty rags, or sharp stones—into people causing them to become ill. Sometimes they stole a person's "breath-heart," his *tsats-winoshka*.

The *kanadyaiya,* or witches, had some affinity with owls and crows which sometimes enabled one to recognize them. But for the most part they could be detected only by medicine men. Along with rain making, the curing of sickness is an important function of the medicine men organized in the Flint, Giant, Fire, and other societies. The real doctors, however, were animal gods; the Indian medicine men must obtain their power to cure from them. The animal doctors include the bear, eagle, badger, wolf, and shrew. The bear is by far the most important of these. Medicine men wear necklaces of bear claws and put the foreleg skins of bears on their arms when performing curing rituals. The spirits of the animal doctors are induced to enter the curing chamber by means of songs. There they invest their respective stone figures and lend their powers to the medicine men. Wooden slat altars, meal paintings on the floor, medicine bowls, corn ear fetiches of Iyatiku, comprise the equipment of a medicine society. Some of the doctors have a quartz crystal which gives them second sight; this enables them to locate the evil spirits that have caused the sickness. Curing consists of withdrawing the objects which have been injected into the body. This may be done with eagle wing feathers, but it is usually accomplished by sucking. If diagnosis reveals that the sick one's heart has been stolen, it must be restored if the patient is to live. When the doctors retrieve a stolen heart it turns out to be a small ball of rags in the center of which are some kernels of corn. If these are in good condition the patient will live; if they are mouldy or scorched the sick one will probably die. In either case, he is given the corn to swallow.

When the Spaniards settled in New Mexico in the seventeenth century they brought new gods and spirits to the Pueblo Indians. At first the Indians were unwilling to accept these foreigners, but after the Great Revolt of 1680 failed they found themselves obliged to submit. The Catholic gods of the Spaniards came to live in the pueblos and were eventually adopted and assimilated to the Indian way of life and belief. A Catholic church was built in each pueblo, and each village acquired a patron saint. The birth of Jesus is celebrated every year, and Easter ceremonies are observed. Important among the

Catholic spirits are saints, particularly Santiago and his horse. Santiago, San Geronimo, and a comparable spirit with an Indian name, Boshaiyanyi, are impersonated by men who "ride" little hobby horses. They may take part in the celebration for the patron saint or they may come at other times. They ride through the corrals and sprinkle the horses with holy water. Santiago has great and beneficent power for horses.

Associated with the saints and the equestrian impersonations is the *gallo,* or "rooster pull," ceremony. A rooster is buried in the sand with only his head and neck protruding. Horsemen ride by until one of them succeeds in pulling the rooster out of the sand. When one has done this he dashes away as fast as his horse can gallop, pursued by the other horsemen. When the horseman with the rooster has been overtaken a fight over the possession of the fowl ensues. Bit by bit the poor bird is torn to pieces. "Rooster blood is good for rain." The foamy lather on the horses' flanks is like the foamy waters rushing down an arroyo after a heavy rain. At the end of the ceremony the riders go around to houses of persons named for the saint of that day where they are doused with water. This, too, helps to bring rain.

But, with rather few exceptions, the Keresan Pueblo Indians have not become Christians, or Catholics. They have merely adopted some alien spirits and have taken them into the pueblos to live. Santa Ana and Santiago have become *maiyanyi,* that is, spirits like Masewi and Oyoyewi, or Spider Grandmother. In an altar painting in one of the Pueblo missions John the Baptist has become Naotsityi, the mother of non-Indians; Jesus has become Utctsityi, the mother of Indians. Prayersticks may be offered to God as they are to Iyatiku and other Indian gods.

Despite more than three centuries of contact with Christian faiths, both Catholic and Protestant, the Keresan Pueblos remain Indian. Even some of the individuals who leave their pueblos to live among white men and adopt their ways cannot always succeed by any means. I once knew well an old man who had gone to a Presbyterian mission school as a young man. He became a Christian, or so he thought. He used to say grace before meals in Christian fashion, but, curiously enough, he addressed the Deity in the Keresan language even though his English was fluent. His transfiguration was never really accomplished, as the following incident makes clear. He told me one

morning that he had dreamed that he had died and gone to heaven. "I went up to heaven," he told me, "and I stood there before God." "What was heaven like?" I asked, eager to know how an Indian would conceive of this place. "It was just like in a bank," he said, "God was sitting there at a big desk, just like in a bank." "What did God look like and how was he dressed?" I asked. "He was a white man and he was wearing a business suit." "I stood there before God," he said, "and finally God looked up at me. 'You've come,' he said. 'Yes,' I told him. 'Where is your license [credentials]?' God asked me. 'Right here,' I told him, and I handed him the Bible they gave me when I was in the Mission boarding school. God took the Bible and studied it for a while. Then he handed it back to me and said, 'No, this is not your license.' Then he pulled out a drawer in his desk and took out a prayerstick. '*This* is your license,' he said and he gave it to me."

We may be sure that when this old man left this world it was with a prayerstick in his hand—and in his heart.

Man's visions of his world are myriad and kaleidoscopic. The world that the Keres believed in and lived in is one of those visions. It was dramatic and picturesque; it was intimate and reassuring. Their vision has sustained them for centuries on end, and it will continue to do so as long as they remain Indians.

NOTES

[1] From here on, this essay is confined to the historic Keresan pueblos, namely, Acoma, Laguna, Santo Domingo, San Felipe, Santa Ana, Sia, and Cochiti.

[2] There are many versions of the origin myths. We shall try to present a fair consensus of them.

REFERENCES

Benedict, Ruth. Tales of the Cochiti Indians. Bulletin 98, Bureau of American Ethnology, Washington, 1931.

Boas, Franz. Keresan Texts. Publications of the American Ethnological Society, Vol. VIII, Parts 1 and 2, 1925, 1928.

Stevenson, Mathilda Coxe. The Sia. Eleventh Annual Report, Bureau of American Ethnology, Washington, 1894.

Stirling, Matthew W. Origin Myth of Acoma. Bulletin 135, Bureau of American Ethnology, Washington, 1942.

White, Leslie A. The Pueblo of Santa Ana, New Mexico. Memoir 60, American Anthropological Association, 1942.

NAVAHO CATEGORIES

By Clyde Kluckhohn

HARVARD UNIVERSITY

PAUL RADIN'S reputation has many bases. But I think that he is famed as much as anything for his analyses of primitive thought and for his intensive studies of the Winnebago. It seems appropriate, therefore, to offer a contribution upon some of the categories of another tribe that has been studied in depth. It is not yet possible to write a definitive account of Navaho categorization because some areas of thought remain to be investigated and because some available field materials still await analysis. Nevertheless, it may be useful at this point to bring together a provisional synthesis of some of the published and unpublished data.

An English-speaking informant once said to Wyman: "The Navahos are great categorists" (Wyman and Harris, 1941, p. 9). All field workers who have known even a little of the Navaho language have been struck by Navaho delight in sharply defined categories, by their pleasure in filing things away in neat little packages, their readiness to argue about small distinctions that would strike even a philosopher as hair-splitting. Indeed the formal structure of the language itself introduces elaborate classifications. For example, many verb stems "refer not to a characteristic type of event such as *stand* or *give* or *fall,* but to the class of object or objects conceived as participating in such an event, whether as actor or goal ... there is no simple verb *to give* but a number of parallel verb themes consisting of a certain sequence of prefixes plus a classificatory verb stem" (Hoijer, 1945, p. 13). Hoijer lists only the more frequently occurring classificatory stems that must be differentiated in a wide range of verbs: round object, long object, living being, set of objects, rigid container with contents, fabric-like object, bulky object, set of parallel objects, a mass, wool-like mass, rope-like object, mud-like mass.

It is evident that every Navaho must use a rather well developed sensitivity for categorization. Of course, the finer distinctions are the province of the various specialists, and it is they whom we shall have

primarily in mind in the course of this paper. Nevertheless one should not underestimate the extent to which a representative Navaho adult man will both categorize firmly all sorts of objects and events outside his own occupational specialty *and* systematize all of these—crudely and yet with some coherence—in a master scheme. In my opinion, Reichard (1943, p. 360) goes too far when she writes: "Thus Navajo dogma connects all things, natural and experienced, from man's skeleton to universal destiny, which encompasses even inconceivable space, in a closely interlocked unity which omits nothing, no matter how small or how stupendous...." Yet I know from experience and from reading the literature on the Navaho what she means. The more articulate and thoughtful Navahos, especially some of the ceremonialists, do exhibit a tendency in this direction.

It therefore appears inviting to examine in some detail standard Navaho categories in various spheres, trying to discover the criteria, explicit and implicit, applied in each area and seeing the extent to which some criteria tend to pervade all or many areas. It will be more convenient to use Western categories for the broad divisions, but I shall indicate the major places where this does violence to Navaho thinking. I shall begin with the supernatural world because it is here, on the whole, that Navaho thought exhibits its most distinctive elaborations and shadings. In fact, Goodwin (1945, p. 506) sees the main distinction between the ceremonialism of the Navaho and the closely related (biologically and culturally) Western Apache in the fact that "the latter people have not bothered to go in for minute classification; the Navaho have."

The Supernatural World

Detailed documentation will be found in Haile (1947a, 1947b), Kluckhohn and Wyman (1940, esp. pp. 184-90), Reichard (1950), Wyman and Kluckhohn (1938), Wyman (1957).[1] These sources do not agree completely on every point, but there is a highly satisfactory consensus on most issues. Much of such disagreement as exists is to be attributed to the same phenomenon among the Navaho themselves. There are a host of matters on which all unacculturated Navaho are unanimous. There are others where regional and generational variations are prominent. There is also contention traceable to the competitive rivalry of various "schools" of ceremonialists. In other instances it is a question of sheer ignorance. I have, for example, shown (Kluck-hohn, 1938) that a sample of 60 women (out of about 210 in this particular Navaho group) were—age group for age group—much less familiar with ceremonial categories than the men of the same band. However, the women aged fifty years and over were quite positive on the main outlines of Navaho theology.

The most fundamental category is that represented by a Navaho word which is commonly translated "holy" but which is more precisely rendered as "supernatural." For this term is applied to all individuals, things, and events that are beyond ordinary experience, charged with a special kind of power and danger. "Holy" has the wrong connotation because the word is applied also to evil people and events (e.g. witch-craft). "Supernatural" does not have its paired opposite to designate the phenomena of the mundane world. "Earth-surface People" are regularly contrasted with "Supernatural People," but there is no general category embracing everything in ordinary experience.

Within the supernatural sphere there are distinguished "behavior" (literally: "here and there [in a place] one person goes"),[2] "myth," and "beings."

Behavior. Colloquially one can render the Navaho word as "some-thing is going on" or "something is being done." Contextually, it becomes perfectly clear that the meaning is something like this: "An organized attempt is being made to influence the course of events by supernatural techniques."[3] The word is applied freely to a major ritual, a small ceremony; to witchcraft, to ritual practices employed in trading and gambling; to events directed in the supernatural world by super-naturals. It designates any *act* in the supernatural sphere, as opposed to words or "personalities."

There is a major dichotomy of behavior relating to the supernatural. English-speaking informants will frequently speak of "the good side" and "the bad side." Navaho terminology on this point is not altogether con-sistent. Navahos use a variety of words which can be roughly translated as "evil," "ugly," "bad" (cf. Kluckhohn, 1956) to refer to all ritual activi-ties that are culturally disapproved, that involve an improper and mali-cious use of supernatural techniques. The distinction is approximately that between all forms of evil magic and ceremonialism (which is defined as "good"). Actually, the use of magic in trading and gambling with aliens and, to some extent, personal enemies is condoned, but these

behaviors are close enough to witchcraft in the narrow sense that informants uniformly group them "on the bad side."

Navahos who pride themselves on their rigor will deny that there is any generic term in Navaho for "witchcraft." They grant that in loose, popular usage two words that properly designate two of the special techniques of witches are in fact used to cover the whole range of culturally prohibited behaviors which strict Navaho thinking classes only vaguely together. The categorization of these is primarily by techniques:

1. Poison Witchcraft. The Navaho term means literally "by means of it something is being done terminatively," but the technique is exclusively that of administering noxious substances.

2. Spells. The Navaho term is "evil-wishing"—i.e. witchcraft by a technique primarily verbal.

3. Pellet Witchcraft. The technique is that of magically shooting dangerous foreign objects into the victim's body. The word is literally "they cause something, emaciation" (by these injections).

4. Frenzy Witchcraft. The technique involves administration of narcotic plants, especially Datura, and is used primarily to obtain women. The stem refers to recklessness in any form.

Actually, to represent Navaho thinking fully a dotted line should be run between 3 and 4. While all four of the above will be mentioned and associated by every unacculturated Navaho, careful analysis of the data shows a less explicit subclassification. The first three are grouped together on the ground that these three kinds of "witches" (and only these three) move about at night as were-animals and participate in the Witches' Sabbath. There are also two named subvarieties of "Spells." While small differences in technique are specified for each, the basis of the subclassification seems clearly to be that one is connected with Game Way[4] (a hunting rite) and the other with Eagle Way, a Navaho chant.

The "good side" includes a very large number of ceremonies. The most sweeping and clear-cut distinction is that between "chants" and all else.[5] The Navaho word which means "chant" or "sing" refers to those ceremonials differentiated by a simple and consistent operation: those which include singing accompanied by some kind of rattle. Chants are subdivided fundamentally in two ways. The first refers merely to the duration, and one hears therefore of one-night, two-night, five-night, and nine-night chants. Or a patient may have only an "excerpt" from a chant or other ceremonial. This may be a blackening or a making of a sacrificial figurine (cf. Haile, 1947a).

The other subdivision is according to the "ritual" by which they are carried out: Holy[6] Way or Ugly[7] Way or Life Way.[8] Several chants provide for performance according to all three rituals; a much larger number for performance by Holy Way and Ugly Way only. The ritual is selected in accord with the assumed etiology of the disease of the patient being treated. If the illness is thought to be caused by angry supernaturals, Holy Way is appropriate. If the "cause" be the ghosts of fellow tribesmen or (sometimes) witches, Ugly Way is selected. The Life Way ceremonials are primarily for those suffering from injuries attributed to accidents, either recent or past. Special circumstances may call for some combination of rituals within a performance of a single chant (Haile, 1947b, p. 9). Each ritual implies certain choices of procedures, equipment, songs, and symbolism. Thus in Angry Way subritual reds are turned in, blues out; in Peaceful Way blues are toward the figure, reds out (Haile, 1947b, p. 12). Holy Way ritual makes provision (at least in the case of certain chants) for three subrituals: Weapon Way,[9] Angry Way, and Peaceful Way. Here likewise the decisive factor is the "diagnosis" of the origin of the illness.

The specific chants which may be conducted according to one or more of the rituals and subrituals are loosely associated by the Navaho into subgroups which are derived in the first instance from the particular corpus of mythology on which the chants are based and, in the second instance, from well-known techniques or features prominent in or distinctive of these connected chants. Thus, for example, in Holy Way we get:

I. Shooting-Chant subgroup

Hail Way
Water Way

Shooting Way, Male Branch
Shooting Way, Female Branch

Red Ant Way
Big Star Way

Flint Way, Male Branch
Flint Way, Female Branch[10]

II. Mountain Chant subgroup

Mountain Top Way, Male Branch
Mountain Top Way, Female Branch (Old Woman's Branch)
Mountain Top Way, Cub Branch (Her Son's [woman speaking] Branch)[11]
Mountain Top Way, Male Shooting Branch
Mountain Top Way, Female Shooting Branch[12]

Excess Way, Male Branch
Excess Way, Female Branch

Way to Remove Someone's Paralysis[13]

Moth Way

Beauty Way, Male Branch
Beauty Way, Female Branch

III. Those Which Have Impersonators of the Supernaturals

Night Way, Rock Center Branch (Darkness Beneath the Rock Branch)
Night Way, Big Tree Branch
Night Way, Water Bottom Branch[14]
Night Way, Pollen Branch
Night Way, Across the River Branch

Big God Way
Plume Way
Dog Way
Coyote Way
Raven Way

IV. Wind-Chant subgroup

Navaho Wind Way, Male Branch
Navaho Wind Way, Female Branch

Chiricahua Apache Wind Way

These four groups all represent Navaho classification with fair consistency. However, only Group III is consistently given the same Navaho designation,[15] perhaps because these chants may be given only "while the thunder sleeps." There are other small subgroups: Eagle Way and Bead Way; one subgroup containing only one chant (Hand Trembling Way); and three (probably more[16]) extinct Holy Way chants of uncertain affiliation: Earth Way, Awl Way, and Reared in Earth Way.

Some principles of Navaho classification, including a few that we shall meet more than once again, emerge from study of the above table. There is the tendency exhibited in a number of cases to specify a male and a female part. The chant names refer either (a) to a central episode in the accompanying myth (e.g., Red Ant Way) or to a particular episode taken as basic for the elaboration of a particular branch (e.g., Night Way, Across the River Branch); or (b) statement of symptom or etiology (e.g., Excess Way and Hail Way). There is also a manifestation of the tendency to syncretism which appears elsewhere in Navaho chant classification: the Mountain Top and Shooting Chants are mingled. There may also be syncretism between Navaho Wind Way and Hail Way and the Game Way complex (Wyman and Bailey, 1946, pp. 214-15).

The foregoing does not begin to exhaust the ways in which Navahos classify their ceremonials. For example, chants of Group III may be given without the masked impersonators in which case they are called "just visiting" chants (Haile, 1947c, p. 36). There are the *features* (with sandpaintings, prayersticks, jewels, and various other paraphernalia which may or may not be added). There are the public exhibitions[17] and "vaudeville acts" which can be included as "extras" with certain chants. There are the "etiological factors" specified with some chants and influencing the precise details of their conduct: Upper Regions Side or Thunderstruck Side; From Under Plants (the reference is really to snakes as the cause of illness); Striped Side.[18] If one asks a chanter what ceremonial he is conducting, his answer will vary[19] with a number of circumstances, but if he trusts you and feels that you understand the language and the ceremonial system and really want him to be precise, he is perfectly capable of coming out with something like the following: "Holy Way, Male Shooting Branch; nine nights; Angry Way and Peace Way subrituals; Thunderstruck Side: with Sun's House and Dark Circle of Branches."

Actually, there are still further specifications possible which it would take too long to explain here. To give just two instances: (1) careful ceremonialists distinguish two forms of Shooting Way, Female Branch, with one held to be of Jicarilla and the other of Navaho origin (Kluckhohn and Wyman, 1940, p. 155); (2) the order of the component ceremonies of a chant may be reversed to cure a singer who has given a chant too often—this is designated a "reverse chant" (*ibid.*, p. 107).

To turn to the "non-chants" there are (leaving aside small, essentially personal songs and rites for crops, livestock, good luck in traveling, girl's adolescence, and the like) the following groups:

> Blessing Way (in five varieties)
> Prayer Ceremonials (three main varieties)
> War Ceremonials (at least two varieties)
> Hunting Ceremonials (many varieties)
> Rites of Divination (four varieties)

Blessing Way is sung but not to the accompaniment of a rattle. Although it is short and of fixed duration (two nights), it is stated by almost all Navahos to be the very keystone of their whole ceremonial system. In addition to its existence as an independent ceremonial, each chant has "its Blessing Way part,"[20] and many minor rites such as the Girl's Adolescence Ceremony are essentially built up out of Blessing Way. Blessing Way is differentiated in function as well as in form and content; its purpose is not to cure illness but rather "for good hope" (e.g. for a pregnant woman or a person about to start on a journey). The named varieties of Blessing Way are:

> Talking God Blessing Way (Two Go for Water Blessing
>   Way; also, Night Way Blessing Way)
> Enemy Monster Blessing Way
> Chief Blessing Way
> Mountain Peak Blessing Way (Eagle Way Blessing Way)
> Game Way Blessing Way

All except one of these names and synonyms refer to mythic episodes and/or related ceremonials (syncretism again). Chief Blessing Way is designated by a main though not exclusive function of this rite—the induction of a "chief" or "headman." Most informants when they say simply "Blessing Way" in Navaho have in mind Talking God Blessing Way, though a few vigorously maintained the primacy of Chief Blessing Way.

The prayer ceremonials are mainly associated with Blessing Way, even though they have forms given in connection with chants conducted according to Ugly Way ritual. They are not sung but often include drypaintings of pollen on buckskin (rather than the "sandpaintings" made of sand, charcoal, and minerals on the floor of the hut). Alone among Navaho ceremonials they have a duration of four nights. Prayer ceremonials are intended primarily for cure of witchcraft and for protection against witches. The names of each of those still well known today have a definite witchcraft implication: Self-Protection, Bringing Up, and Bringing Out.

Just as the prayer ceremonials "fall on Blessing Way side," so most[21] of the war ceremonials are felt to have a marked affiliation with Ugly Way ritual. The myths of Ugly Way chants and war ceremonials frequently interlock (cf. Haile, 1947b, p. 6) and are, indeed, at some points almost indistinguishable. With one exception, war ceremonials have been extinct or obsolescent for some time save as preserved in fragments of rites ("excerpts," especially some of the "blackenings") and some myths. Enemy Way, the public part of which is widely known to the English-speaking population of the Southwest as "the Squaw Dance," is still very frequently performed, though only during the summer months. This is the treatment for "ghost infection" from aliens, whereas the Ugly Way chants are for illness caused or threatened by native ghosts. But Enemy Way falls out of the chant pattern in three respects: (a) not a rattle but a rattle-stick is used, and the singing is accompanied by a potdrum; (b) the ceremonial lasts *three* nights; (c) Enemy Way is not unequivocally in charge of a single individual; two, if not four, persons share the responsibility. Navaho differentiation of Enemy Way as non-chant is reflected in the fact that the patient of Enemy Way is called by a different term from that applied to the patients in all chants.

Navaho informants are agreed that the other war ceremonials (Enemy Monster Way, Monster Men Way, Two Went Back for Scalp Way, Ghosts of Every Description Way, and Where the Two Came to their Father Way) are not chants, but it is not so clear how, in other particulars, they fit into the Navaho scheme of ceremonial categories. Some excerpts were revived and rather popular during and immediately after the Second World War, but only the myth and drypaintings of the last-named have been recorded in detail (Oakes, 1943). The first two may represent rather minor versions of a basic ceremonial. Oakes's principal informant says (Oakes, 1943, p. 57) that Enemy Monster Way was another "side" of Where the Two Came to their Father that was used in enemy country on the battlefield. Two Went for Scalp Way may be merely an old synonym for the basic native-ghosts chant, Upward-Reaching Way. Ghosts of Every Description Way may be a special designation for the end of Enemy Way or for a slightly un-

orthodox combination of Upward-Reaching Way and Enemy Way (cf. Kluckhohn and Wyman, 1940, p. 190). From the Oakes monograph and from scattered fragments of other information, some resemblances to Blessing Way and to the prayer ceremonials are evident: drypaintings and prayers are prominent; prevention and protection are intended as much as (or more than) cure. On the other hand, while Oakes's informant admitted the similarity of his rite to Blessing Way, he likewise insisted that it was separate, "has nothing to do with it" (Oakes, 1943, p. 56). One painting is from Blessing Way, but "this is used because it gives a personal blessing which has nothing to do with war" (*ibid.*). In sum, the evidence indicates that these war ceremonials were regarded as being in a special category but with felt linkage to chants conducted according to Ugly Way ritual.

The game ceremonials[22] are also substantially extinct. There were two main divisions corresponding to the hunting of deer and the hunting of antelope. The known varieties of ritual deer hunting are named again partly on the basis of technique (e.g. Encircling by Fire or Tiptoe) or myth (e.g. Big Snake Way and Talking God Way).

Types of divination are distinguished by technique: hand-trembling, stargazing, listening, and *Datura* divination. In each case the practitioner goes into a kind of trance to "diagnose" the cause and history of an event (illness, loss, theft, adultery) and to make a prognostication of a favorable course of action (what ceremonial to have for an illness, where to hunt, when and how to raid or retaliate in war). It is also relevant to remark that "diagnosticians" seldom carry out other ceremonials. Divination is a specialty, and Navahos rather generally assume implicitly it is an exclusive one. In fact, some evidence (cf. Kluckhohn, 1939) indicates that strong temperamental and selective factors operate to distinguish between "diagnosticians" and other ceremonialists. All other ceremonials are learned; one becomes a diagnostician by a sudden "gift." To a lesser extent, singers of Blessing Way are likely to stick to this specialty, not becoming either chanters or "diagnosticians." They do often carry out prayer ceremonials. Presumably because of close affiliation between one technique of divination (hand trembling) and the chant of the same name, these chanters also strongly tend to restrict themselves to this single chant (cf. Kluckhohn and Wyman, 1940, p. 169).

Beings. Almost everything known to the Navaho is personalized in the supernatural context: animals, plants, mountains, winds, and rain. "They are conceived as existing 'in man form'" (Haile, 1943, p. 67). "A number of natural phenomena are taken possession of by ... 'one who lies within it' ... this inner form is a being independent of the object which it happens to occupy. To instance, the sun disc ... is quite distinct from its carrier ... 'who carries a round object here and there in daytime'" (*ibid.*, p. 68). The personalized "inner forms" of animals, plants, and inanimate natural phenomena are addressed in prayers and mentioned in myths and ceremonials. They are legion, and there does not seem to be an evident Navaho classification of them except insofar as they are often grouped in pairs, frequently as either male and female or older and younger.

As to the Navaho "gods" (as this word would usually be understood in the tradition of the West), there are many. The sun appears really in three guises: as object, as "inner form" of this object, and as a completely individualized being who is one of the major Navaho supernaturals. (The moon,[23] on the other hand, appears only under the first two aspects, and although the earth is invoked as "the earth, our mother," the earth likewise does not seem to be completely individuated[24]). The wife of the sun, Changing Woman[25] is regarded by many Navahos as the principal Navaho divinity. Another "school" assigns this place to an hermaphroditic deity (whose name means literally 'breast-grabber') who is portrayed as the creator. There are grounds for suspecting that Breast-Grabber represents a foreign, not fully assimilated element in Navaho theology, and one which has in recent times been sharply remodeled under Christian influence. In the main stream of Navaho thought, the principal divinities appear to be the Sun and Changing Woman; their children, the Hero Twins; First Man and First Woman. Note that just as the dual form is prominent in the Navaho language, the main deities appear in pairs. Changing Woman herself is often equated with a remarkably similar personage, Turquoise Woman. The Hero Twins are differentiated in accord with Navaho kinship terminology into "older brother" and "younger brother." Each of the Twins has an "alias." Monster Slayer appears as Reared in the Earth, Child of the Water as Changing Grandchild. These terms are used when Navaho lore wishes to emphasize special manifestations of their "personalities" (Reichard, 1950, p. 482). There is also another "form" of the Twins: The Stricken Twins (*ibid.*, p. 481).

Reichard (1950, chap. 5) has grouped Navaho divinities:

Persuadable deities
Undependable deities
Helpers of deity and man
Intermediaries between man and deity
Unpersuadable deities
Dangers conceived as deities
Beings between good and evil
Order of monsters, dangers, and beings-in-between

This is not a Navaho categorization, though a correct ordering of certain regularities in Navaho statements. Reichard herself (p. 53) says her classification is "intended to be suggestive rather than definitive." Navaho categories remain to be satisfactorily worked out. There are three terms in common use. The first, "Supernatural People,"[26] seems to be the generic one which can be applied to all individual divinities and personalized powers, to all "people" of the preemergence world as contrasted with Earth-surface People, even to chanters when they are saturated with supernatural power at the height of a ceremonial. Neither the Navaho nor Father Berard Haile have been able to translate the second Navaho word, so the latter proposes (1947c, p. 37) using Anglicized *ye-i*. The *ye-i* occupy a prominent place in Navaho legend, but sometimes the word or its correlate, 'Maternal Grandfather of the Supernatural Monsters,' is used to designate divinities who are not represented as monstrous animals. The third term which is literally 'Failed-to-Speak People' would appear to be a colloquial usage, deriving from the fact that the impersonators of the divinities at the public exhibitions attending some chants never talk but only hoot, holler, and sing.

Navaho deities are strikingly less fully categorized than the ceremonials, though each ceremonial tends to be associated with a particular figure. Changing Woman is, so to speak, patron of Blessing Way and the prayer ceremonials. The Sun is prominent in the Shooting Way complex. First Man and First Woman are connected with all evil magic. Breast-Grabber is first and foremost the tutelary deity of hunters. The Hero Twins, great warriors, bulk large in most ceremonials telling of war. Black Supernatural, however, conducts Enemy Way. Reviewing the evidence thus far available, one must conclude that for some reason the Navaho were not interested in an elaborate grouping here. They found it sufficient to speak of the Supernatural People and then to name each individual divinity and personalized "inner form." The other two terms do not appear to be more than colloquial variants, handy in specific contexts. Haile (1947b, pp. 6-7) regards the ye-i and the Failed-to-Speak ones as an identical subclass of the Supernatural People. They were created by First Man. The myth Haile quotes lists seven: Talking God, Calling God, Male God, Female God, Shooting God, Whipping God, and Red God. In Night Way, however, there are six each of "Male God" and "Female God" (i.e. ordinary male and female ye-i) and the following possible additional impersonators: Black God, Monster Slayer, Born for Water, Water Carrier (Gray God), Hump Back, Fringed Mouth, Red Failed-to-Speak, Destroyer, Whistling Failed-to-Speak, Shooting Failed-to-Speak (Haile, 1947b, p. 37).

Myth. Roughly speaking, alike from the point of view of the observer and of the Navaho, one distinguishes the more secular from the more sacred stories, although the same Navaho word is applied to both. "More" is a necessary qualification, because in Navaho feeling the supernatural world is involved in all. Definitely in the "sacred" category belong the legend—or rather the various legends—dealing with the emergences of the Navaho from the eleven lower worlds (a very widely distributed plot among Indians of Western North America but with variations and elaborations more or less special to each tribe or group of tribes). Likewise "sacred" are the myths that are the rationale for the various ceremonials. As a matter of fact, the emergence myth or part of it is incorporated into the justificatory legend of many ceremonials. In a somewhat intermediate class are the legends of the different clans. These often begin with part of the emergence story and then recount the wanderings and subsequent development of that clan. Most on the "secular" side are what would usually be designated as "folktales." These are the Navaho equivalent of Aesop's Fables or of Brer Rabbit. The best known to most Navahos are the Trotting Coyote Stories. There are also other quasi-obscene cycles like those of Tooth-Gum Woman. Some tales, like some chants, are reserved for the winter months (Haile, 1954, p. 39).

While themes and passages of the emergence and ceremonial myths and clan legends (and even the folktales) weave in and out of each other in a manner most bewildering to a non-Navaho, they still consti-

tute in some sense a fairly unified corpus. A knowledgeable Navaho who is recounting or talking about mythic materials will say most definitely but at a point that strikes an outsider as altogether arbitrary, "here Blessing Way begins." The origin legends of numerous ceremonials may be almost identical up to a certain point and then they "branch off." Beauty Way (cf. Wyman, 1957) and Mountain Top Way are independent continuations of the story of the war against the Pueblo Indians of Taos, a story which the Navaho seem to regard as having been begun in the myth of Monster Way and that in turn in the emergence story. The origin legend of the divinatory rites of stargazing and listening appears to take off from the buzzard episode of Enemy Way. As Wyman (1945, p. 382) says:

As more Navaho myths are recorded the more apparent it becomes that the total mythology possesses a somewhat limited number of episodes and incidents of types thereof which recur over and again in the origin legends of different chants. It is almost as in the construction of the chants themselves, where a limited number of types of ceremony are combined in different ways and with various individual minutiae ... With a store of legendary events to pick from, and evidence in the existing myths that "picking" must have occurred in the past, the temptation to create new combinations and thus new myths would seem to be present.

Discussion. Navaho beliefs and practices relating to the supernatural certainly constitute a ramified system. From the Navaho viewpoint everything is related to everything else. It has not been possible to specify in detail here all actual relationships. Most chants are connected with particular animals. Many are related to specific mountains (especially the sacred mountains of the four directions) and to other localities. Every ceremonial has a color, directional, sex, number, and sound symbolism. The intricacies remind one of the contrived systematic symbolism of Joyce's *Ulysses.*

In part, these interrelationships are made quite explicitly and consistently. "Causation" is a keynote. You begin by finding out what "caused" your illness or who stole your property or indulged in adultery with your wife; where the enemy or the game animals are at the moment. A course of action is then indicated in "logical" terms. The system with its categorizations tells you. If the diagnostician maintains that you have "Thunderstruck" sickness, then obviously you must have recourse to a practitioner of one of the Shooting Ways. The chanter.

on the basis of his information on what details divination has revealed and his knowledge of the full mechanics of etiology as set forth in the myth, will know what ritual, subritual, branch, and features of Shooting Way are indicated; what divinity or divinities must be given special attention in the symbolism of the chant.

And at points almost inseparable the keynote is "origin." Is "ghost sickness" attributable to native or foreign ghosts? Was there a failure in treatment because superficial "diagnosis" prescribed Enemy Way but, as the legends show, the story of Enemy Way begins "farther back" in Monster Way and therefore it was this latter that was required? Technique likewise receives some accentuation, often following the familiar principles of sympathetic and holophrastic magic. Mountain Lion Way is one branch of Game Way because mountain lions are notably successful as hunters of deer. Since some forms of witchcraft utilize the clothes or offal of the victim, an appropriate prayer ceremonial for someone suffering from such a technique is one which incorporates "in a good way" some part or product of the person. Technique is also a basis of naming in a descriptive sense. Thus Flint Way is popularly called Hoof Way (from the hoof rattles used); Chiricahua Wind Way is popularly designated by one of its refrains or is called Toothgum Way; Blessing Way is referred to as No Sleep from the all-night performance of the second night.

Other general principles of Navaho classification appear at a number of points. For the Navaho everything comes in twos (or in fours, the multiple of two and the number of the directions recognized by the Navaho). The pair may be male and female, older and younger, "outer" and "inner," siblings or counterparts, without reference to relative age. Many divinities appear in duplex or multiplex forms. Holy Young Man and Holy Boy appear to be the same "person," as do Changing Woman and Salt Woman. Indeed, Changing Woman also appears as White Shell Woman and as Turquoise Woman. Reichard (1950, p. 76) suggests that First Man and First Woman are the respective manifestations of Sun and Changing Woman in the worlds below and that (p. 77) First Woman is "a rudimentary archetype of Changing Woman." She likewise implies that various aspects of the Sun's personality are represented by:

Breast-Grabber (the darkness of the sun)
Black Supernatural (the darkness of the sun)

Talking God
Speechless God

She specifically proposes (p. 79) that Coyote, the "exponent of irresponsibility and lack of direction," "seems to be an uncontrolled aspect
of either the Sun himself or his child." Similarly, Changing-Bear
Maiden "is the female apotheosis of evil as Changing Woman is of
good" (*ibid.*, p. 414).

How the Navaho name (i.e. classify) a supernatural depends upon
quite standardized features of context. The elder of the Hero Twins
is called Monster Slayer when arrayed in armor, Holy Man otherwise
(*ibid.*, p. 55). Place and situation are also determinative of the various
appellations of the twins: Reared-in-the-Earth, Child-of-the-Water,
Holy Boy, Changing Grandchild. There is also a marked tendency to
project into the supernatural world the main categories of persons
found in the actual world. The supernatural beings include parental
categories (Sun and Changing Woman; First Man and First Woman;
Male Supernatural and Female Supernatural); children (First Boy and
First Girl; the Hero Twins and some of the "inner forms" of natural
phenomena—e.g. Thunder Boy and Thunder Girl); Changing Grandchild; the "maternal grandfather of the *Ye-i*," and so on. It may be
significant that the relationship between maternal uncle and maternal
nephew, so important in Navaho social organization in recent centuries,
has only a minor place in Navaho myth and ceremonialism. Breast-
Grabber, the hermaphrodite, is the supernatural representation of the
culturally recognized category of the transvestite. The most pronounced
tendency is pairing by sex: Rock Crystal Boy, Rock Crystal Girl;
Whiteshell Boy, Whiteshell Girl; Dawn Boy, Dawn Girl; White Corn
Boy, Yellow Corn Girl; Evening Light Boy, Abalone Girl; Mirage
Stone Boy, Carnelian Girl; Soft Goods Boy, Soft Goods Girl.

While categorizations of ceremonials, myths, and beings are interrelated and cross-cut in a number of explicit and consistent ways, there
remains the fact that the relative elaboration of categories in various
spheres is markedly diverse. Many supernatural beings are named but
if there is any Navaho classification it remains almost completely implicit except to the degree that it merely echoes the ceremonial system.
Categories within the myths are also reflections of the ceremonials save
for the very loose segregation of emergence myth, ceremonial myths,
clan legends, and folktales. A plausible guess is that this divergence

rests upon a quite pervasive theme of Navaho culture: action. The cases where the Navaho are least equivocal on their classifications involve operations of the observation of action. A ceremonial either does or does not employ rattles (chant or non-chant). Prayer ceremonials are extremely reminiscent of Blessing Way, but there is a simple operational test: no singing. The presence of certain features immediately places certain ceremonials by ritual or subritual, chant subgroup, or chant (e.g. passing through hoops signifies a ceremonial according to Ugly Way ritual). Navahos categorize ceremonials (there are Navaho terms for each category below) as well as ceremonials, and here again they resort to observation of behavior. A *chanter* is one who sings with a rattle[27] *and* knows a ceremonial of at least five nights' duration. A *curer* may sing wth a rattle but is never observed to carry on more than an excerpt of a ceremonial. Curers who specialize in certain excerpts are named according to a primary activity (e.g. "blackeners"). *Apprentices* and *helpers* are designated on the basis of the functions they are noticed to perform. A diagnostician is known and referred to on the basis of the technique he is seen to carry out.

The Navaho are interested in words insofar as they categorize events with some precision. They are not interested in words just as expression of belief. The words of a chant myth must be just right because they prescribe a course of behavior that must be followed with minute exactness. But the test of correct behavior for a Navaho invariably stresses what is to be done and exactly how it is to be done. No unacculturated Navaho could possibly comprehend the Christian controversies over, say, the Arian and Monophysite heresies unless he were shown that accepting one or the other position inevitably involved different ritual practices. Hence, I suspect, the intricate classification of all ceremonial behaviors. A Navaho wants to know minutely where he stands here. Myths and beings are important only insofar as they affect ceremonial action, and there is little probability of error here so long as rites are correctly classified.

The Inanimate World

As already indicated, this title is really a misnomer from the Navaho point of view, though artifacts (in general) and some other inanimate phenomena are not held to have "inner forms." It will not be possible

to review this sphere at such great length. I shall content myself with some general remarks, with one example in some detail, and with the introduction of material illustrating somewhat different principles of classification.

Within the natural world there is a strong tendency to classify into "male" and "female" (rains, winds, mountains, mesas, etc.). Actually, as Reichard points out (1950, p. 176), the distinction is in no simple sense the literal one of sex but rather that between "coarser, rougher, and more violent" versus "finer, weaker, and more gentle." So far as some types of artifacts and some mineral and (dead) biological forms, there are broad classes deriving from the classificatory categories of Navaho verb stems. Particularly common are "hard goods," "soft goods," and "woven goods."

The Navaho speak of "the upper regions" which include sun, moon, constellations, individual stars, rains, clouds, and thunders. (There are a number of publications on Navaho starlore, the most comprehensive being Haile, 1947d.[28] Representations of constellations and of stars of the first magnitude may be found in Navaho drypaintings, on gourd rattles, on prayersticks, and on masks. The Big Dipper, Cassiopeia, Cervus, Pleiades, Hyades, Scorpio, Orion, and the morning and evening stars are generally known, but more detailed knowledge is esoteric. Translations of the Navaho names in Haile's list follow:

> Man with his feet ajar (Cervus)
> Big first one (Scorpio)
> Rabbit tracks
> Butterfly
> Big white stars in the east and west (morning
>   and evening stars)
> Big red star
> Pronged star
> Fire Supernatural
> Monster Slayer and Born for Water
> Black Big Star
> Blue Big Star
> Yellow Big Star
> Igniter of Flash Lightning
> Igniter of Thunder
> Monthless (Coyote's) Star (Canopus?)
> Dawn's Star
> Porcupine
> Horned Rattler

Slim First One (Orion)
Pinching Stars (Hyades)
Cornbeetle
Bear
Thunder
Flash Lightning
Male Revolving One (Ursa Major)
Female Revolving One (Cassiopeia)
Red Heavens
Dawn
Skyblue
Evening Twilight
Darkness
Trails of the Sun
Milky Way
Big White Star
Big Yellow Star

As is evident, the nomenclature is primarily descriptive, secondarily mythological. "Male" and "Female" appear once again. Many constellations are conceived as having human or animal form, and individual stars or groups of stars in them are designated as their body parts: legs, knees, hips, body, liver, kidney, arms, head; or appurtenances such as head feather or cane; each has an "igniter" which illuminates the entire group. A very few of the constellations are held to be interrelated in some way. The Pleiades, Hyades, and Orion form a central group.

Winds and directions.[29] Winds are differentiated by color: dark, white, yellow, blue-spotted; or by their manner of travel: left-handed, running sunwise, running sunward, and so on. We also get "small wind," "inaudible wind" ("which in summer at times blows inaudibly with a cool breeze, even in hot weather"), and "smooth wind" ("when it is cold and there is a warm breeze even in cold weather"). Then there are "whirlwind" and "big-jumping wind" (cyclone). Each of these has, of course, its supernatural linkages. The last two named are associated with witchcraft. Supernaturals "without meanness" have two souls of "inaudible and smooth wind." Dawn Woman and Talking God "breathe by means of white wind." Dark Wind became the "soul" of First Man, Blue Wind the soul of First Woman. Earth-surface People and Supernatural People alike get their being from one or more winds.

The cardinal directions are ultimately referable to the points where sky horizon edge and earth horizon edge meet. One can also refer to "upper regions" and "dark upper." Popular conception assigns color to the cardinal points and in this sequence: white to sunrise or east; blue to south; yellow to sunset or west; dark to north. The phenomena assigned to these cardinal points are: dawn in the east; horizontal blue in the south; horizontal yellow (evening twilight) in the west; darkness in the north. The corresponding "inner forms" are Dawn Man; Evening Twilight Woman; Horizontal Blue Man; Darkness Woman.

In interpersonal communication, in addition to distinguishing left and right, sunward and sunwise, the Navaho use many variations upon the theme of "this side of" (a specified point) or "the other side of." The language possesses many suffixes which divide space into zones and circles or into lines and directions with some precision. "Near me" and "nearer me than you" are refined by adding "at a point away from me and from you," "at a point distant from both you and me"; "way over there where he is," "away from where we are," etc.

Artifacts. There is considerable terminology—mainly descriptive— attached to weaving, silversmithing, pottery, basketry, ceremonial objects, and to the equipment used in the respective technologies. Only the first two reveal much typology. The Navaho, for example. distinguish only three types of pots (Tschopik, 1941, p. 7), two on the basis of function. Navaho treatment of artifacts does bring out particularly clearly one frequent feature of Navaho categorization: that of inclusiveness rather than exclusiveness, designating a whole or any of its parts by the same term. For example, the same word is used to refer to "medicine bundle with all its contents," "contents of medicine bundle," or "any separate item of these contents" (Reichard, 1950. p. 8).

Property. Haile (1954) has discussed such Navaho concepts as goods which could be bartered at will (pp. 8, 48-49); this concept included slaves; "hard goods" and "soft goods" (pp. 20-21); "labor by arm" (p. 44—to work out the value of a gambling wager); wife-asking and gifts to the bride's mother (pp. 13-14, 46-47); exchange gifts (p. 50). They illustrate the familiar Navaho combination of inclusiveness and fine distinctions.

Biological Phenomena

Here again Navaho categorization intergrades with that in the supernatural sphere. But, as Haile (1943, p. 67) says:

anthropomorphism may be said to be applied with a slight difference to plants and animals, than it is to natural phenomena proper. Thus, a study of ceremonial usage and popular practice reveals that plants and animals are conceived as existing... "in man form," and that they can remove their plant and animal form at will.... This man form is indestructible, and there is some evidence, though not conclusive, that plant and animal forms likewise are indestructible.

The basic contrast is between "one who speaks" (human beings) and "nonspeaker" (plants and animals). The latter category is broken down into vegetation, trotting beings (i.e. quadrupeds), flying beings, and crawling beings. The last three are subdivided into "night travelers" and "day travelers." There are also "Travelers on the Earth Surface" and "Travelers in Water."

The only thorough study of Navaho biological classification thus far published is that by Wyman and Harris (1941).[30] On Wyman's major study of Navaho entomology one preliminary communication (Wyman and Bailey, 1952) has appeared. Wyman, however, permits me to quote the following from his forthcoming monograph:

A few striking species from well outside the Navaho country... were shown to informants to test their reactions. They did not hesitate to equate them with species which somewhat resembled them, and they named them appropriately. Therefore, it is evident that although Navahos may be confused by certain types of insects found within their own domain, they react with assurance when confronted with species which bear a clear resemblance to their own valid Navaho genera.

Wyman and Harris say (p. 9):

The Navajo classify plants in at least three separate ways... first, plants are male and female. Another relation is that various groups are used for curing the same disease or for the same purpose, or are used in the same way. Still another is that they have similar characteristics, such as being prickly or sticky, and within these groups there are large, medium, and small or slender kinds. These three types of category are independent, except that when plants are named according to size the larger one is likely to be "male," while the smaller one is "female." They form, however, classifications within classifications, physical characteristics or "sex" being used to distinguish plants within a usage group.... There is an extraor-

dinary similarity between the names for supposedly allied plants in the works of the pre-Linnean herbalists, such as Gerarde's herbal of the sixteenth century, and many of the Navajo names for plants.

Of the 456 uncultivated plant species collected in the area, there were only three for which no Navaho name was given when shown to two or more informants, and for one of these a use was known. This does not mean that every plant is well known, but it does mean that the people are observant of their plant surrounding and can readily distinguish between plants of major, secondary, or minor importance, in their lives. . . . There is great variation in the names which may be applied to a particular plant unless it is a commonly used species, and even then the name given may vary with the informant and how he uses that plant. One informant explained this variation as follows: "most plants have at least three names, the real name, the way-in-which-it-is-used name, and a descriptive name." . . . Certain informants were inclined to give long descriptive names, while others have only the briefest names.

Wyman and Harris remark in a later study (1951, p. 55) that the complete or partial correspondence between materials from the eastern and far western portions of the Navaho territory, gathered about a generation apart,

is eloquent testimony for a rather remarkable uniformity in fundamental native botanical nomenclature over a wide expanse of territory, which exists along with enormous individual variation in the use and application of the nomenclature, and ingenious inventiveness in manufacturing new descriptive names when occasion demands.

Navaho propensity for being a little fussy about categories is reflected in the fact that there is not just a single term for "white man." They distinguish: "Anglo white man," Mexican, Mormon, and Texan. As a result of the Second World War, the English are "islanders"; the French "those of 'crazy' speech"; the Germans "metal hats"; the Russians "lawless ones." Asiatics are termed simply "slant-eyed ones." Negroes are "black Mexicans."

Ceremonial lore (as usual) supplies much information on the identification and classification of animals, both real and mythological. We find, for example (Haile, 1947a, pp. 5-7), the following "travelers on the earth surface": pig, chicken, cat; blue, gray, rock, white, gliding, and digging lizards; the horned toad; snakes; rattler, bull, garter, water, malpais; bear, porcupine, badger, black squirrel, white squirrel, long-tailed rock squirrel, chipmunk, weasel; and the following "travelers in water": toad, frog, armadillo (!), duck, "water lizards" (salamander), box turtle, otter, beaver. The land turtle is also assigned to this group. Many more animals are identified by the Navaho than those listed above. Reichard (1950, pp. 396-8) lists about a hundred. She notes that birds of different genera are sometimes classified as "male" and "female" of the "Navaho species" (e.g. cowbird is given as the female of Brewer's blackbird).

The famous Navaho "Big Fly," although apparently mythological, has recently been identified biologically by Wyman (Reichard, 1950, p. 390). The most interesting of the mythological animals are the "enemy monsters" or "enemy terrors," who include: Bony Bear; Throwing Monster, Kicking Monster, Horned Monster (Burrowing Monster), Crushing Rocks, Cutting Reeds, Eye Killers, Tearing Cactus, Water Monster, Traveling Rock. Psychoanalysts will please note that all of these are the fruits of the self-abuse of the wives of the chiefs in the lower worlds and of various kinds of sexual misbehavior on the part of certain Supernatural People.

Reichard (1948) has published a little on Navaho ornithological taxonomy. She notes (pp. 11-12):

the tribal scheme of classification—analogous, religious—should be kept in mind. It includes male and female divisions, some of which may separate genera, although too they may be rationalized so as to bring subspecies, species, or genera together. The categories will certainly be set up to include birds believed to contribute similar powers to ritual; to differentiate large and small, perhaps intermediate sizes; other classes may be determined by calls, colors, marking, odor, and habits.

In the same paper she has made (pp. 7, 9) some useful observations on Navaho categorization in general:

Navajo categories are inclusive, complementary, analogous, rather than distinctive, exclusive and homologous—they are more religious than scientific. . . . For instance, myth relates that the first world was inhabited by insects specifically mentioned, and the group includes bat. The Navajo know perfectly well that bat is not an insect, but they have established a connection between insects and a so-called 'helper'—bat is believed to have been a supernatural power of deliverance. Wolf, mountain lion, bobcat, and lynx are associated as predatory animals but their group also includes badger "because," as the Navajo explain, "he is their friend."

· · · · ·

All natural objects are divided by the Navajo into male and female, meaning, in addition to sex, that there are contrasting types: aggressive and compliant,

active and passive, kinetic and potential; coarse, rough, severe compared with fine, gentle, mild. Plants are so classified, the smaller varieties often being female. Plants are grouped also because they purport to cure the same diseases, that is, they fulfill a similar purpose; and because they have the same character—prickly, spiny, hairy, sticky ... such or similar categories dominate in all Navajo classifications.

Social Organization [31]

In principle, this subject ought to be treated at as great length as the supernatural world, but there is not enough space nor has this topic yet been worked out as fully as ceremonialism. I must limit myself to some definitely established categories, showing how the familiar categorizing principles of duality, sex, overlapping circles, syncretism, and description repeat themselves in this area.

In the old days—and to a considerable extent still—Navahos meeting each other for the first time would very quickly communicate their respective positions in the social world by stating their clan affiliations. But this would always be done for both sides of the family. A Navaho is a member of his mother's clan but is "born for" his father's clan. As a matter of fact, the exchange of information takes place in stereotyped phrases which result in the establishment of one of the following positions:

"The two of us are of one clan."
"He [she] is the one for whom I am born" (i.e. he belongs to my father's clan).
"He is born for my clan, [as] I belong to his father's clan."
"We two are born for each other" (i.e. our fathers and mothers are clan brothers and sisters).
"We started out together in birth" (i.e. our fathers are of the same clan).
"He [she] is not my relative."

From the position reached, there emerge immediately many specifications of interactive behavior: kinship terms, the kind of joking that can properly be carried on, mutual obligations. Marriage or sexual intercourse is permissible only for men and women finding themselves in the last category.

. There are somewhere between fifty and seventy Navaho clans, varyingly distributed in Navaho country, but most local groups will include representatives of about twenty clans, though membership is likely to be concentrated primarily in four to six clans. Clan names refer to places, origin (e.g. Ute or Chiricahua Apache), mythology (e.g.

Two Visited Water). In certain instances individuals who agree that they belong to the same clan will use different names, invoking the clan story. In other cases it is reasonably certain that as the Navaho tribe grew larger and spread out over wider territory a clan differentiated into two or more parts which gradually adopted different names while continuing to regard themselves as closely related.

This, in part, was presumably the origin of the "linked clans" or "clan groups." These cannot be designated as "phratries," for the Navaho do not name the various groups of associated clans. They refer to them merely as "partner clans." In theory, the prohibitions and mutual reciprocities prevailing among clan members are extended —with some diminution of intensity—to all associated clans. In recent practice the linked clans have played a minor role, particularly as far as those on one's father's side are concerned. Most adult, relatively unacculturated, Navahos will mention with some positiveness at least two or three "partner clans" into which they are forbidden to marry and toward the members of which they owe certain obligations. But the specification becomes vague and uncertain so far as the clan "for which I am born" (i.e. father's clan) is concerned.

Some alleged clan groupings would also appear to exhibit the syncretistic tendency. In general, Navahos welcome affiliation and secure placement in the world of social organization. The legends give a number of examples of this sort (Reichard, 1950, p. 12). The People-of-the-large-yucca-place affiliated with the Moving Mountain clan because their red arrow holders looked alike. Similarly, Base of the Mountain and Poles Strung Out clans recognized "partnership" because of similarities in headdress and equipment.

Into the intricacies of Navaho kinship terminology, some details of which remain to be worked out satisfactorily, I can enter only briefly. Relatives ("my kin") are distinguished from affinal relatives ("Those for whom I carry burdens"[32]). There are few affinal terms and relatively little discrimination by sex of speaker and relative designated: daughter-in-law; brother-in-law and sister-in-law (one term); "one married into [my, your, his] clan"; "he is married with him" (men who are married to women of the same clan but otherwise unrelated). Another term means both son-in-law and father-in-law, but ordinarily mother-in-law and son-in-law refer to each other by a word meaning "one whom he [she] does not see or look at."

Either parent may designate all children, regardless of sex, "my children." In general, however, the sex of the person speaking or referred to is taken into account. Mothers and fathers use distinct terms for their sons and daughters. An individual of either sex distinguishes "my brothers" from "my sisters." A male cross-cousin is "with me he goes around"; a female cross-cousin is called by another word which has not been etymologized. Relatives of the same order (e.g. "uncles") on the two sides of the family are differently designated because they belong to different clans. In some cases, reciprocal terms are utilized, sometimes with slight variations in the pair.

Ordinal as well as classificatory principles are employed: older brother, younger brother; older sister, younger sister. Parents differentiate (not in address but in reference) the ages of their children: "with whom birth started" or "the starting born one" or "who was born in the lead"; "the one in next position"; "the one between"; "one in position three" (four, etc.); "the concluding born." Generational lines are in some cases indicated by prefixes. Thus we get "twice daughter's children again" (i.e. a niece's children's children, both on the brother's and sister's side).

Language[33]

Here the categories exist in quite clear-cut form and are followed with great consistency by unacculturated Navahos, but are not, with two exceptions, named by the Navaho themselves. The Navaho do refer to a "respect language" which involves the use of a certain form of the third personal pronoun prescribed for speech to specific classes of relatives and persons of superior status. There also is, or was, a "war language," used by warriors. This was largely a matter of special vocabulary, though certain special inflectional forms were apparently involved also. In fact there is also an esoteric ceremonial terminology, but the Navaho do not call this a special "speech."

There are three major form classes in Navaho: particles, nouns, and verbs. "These differ mainly in the amount and kind of grammatical inflection they undergo." Particles (pronouns, numerals, modifiers, conjunctions, and other "relaters") are not inflected, though they often take one or more proclitics and enclitics. There are a number of nice discriminations that are typically Navaho with respect to pronouns. Thus "it" as the object of a verb has several different forms, depending upon whether "it" is thought of as definite or indefinite or as a place. The third person subject pronoun indicates whether the subject is ordinary or a place or what Sapir called "person of preferred interest." The latter designates the hero of a story as opposed to others, a Navaho as opposed to a member of another tribe, and so on. Possessive pronouns distinguish "my milk" in the sense of "milk owned by me" from "my milk" in the sense of "milk that came from my breasts."

There are few Navaho "nouns" in the sense of the "free forms" called nouns in Indo-European tongues. These Navaho nouns are not inflected save for an occasional plural. Other "nouns" or complex phrase-like constructions that function as nouns are really verbal forms which are inflected. No Navaho nouns have gender.

Each verb "consists of a theme—composed of a stem or set of stems with or without a thematic prefix—which may occur alone or with one or more non-thematic prefixes." The stem, though this must be selected in accord with categories discussed below, conveys an image which remains constant. Otherwise, meanings in Navaho (for communication is overwhelmingly by the verb) are derived from the assembling of elements that are generalized and colorless in themselves. Navaho might be called a chemical language: the basic process is that of utilizing the varying effects of small elements in different combinations.

Verb themes never occur as free forms and are usually provided with from three to seven or more distinctive stems, with or without a thematic prefix. Non-thematic verb prefixes are of two kinds, derivational and paradigmatic. The former are mainly adverbial in function, while the latter denote concepts of aspect, mode, tense, number and the pronouns for the subject, object, and indirect object. . . . Most verb themes . . . require one or another set of derivational prefixes in addition to the appropriate paradigmatic elements. Such derivations (i.e. verb themes plus derivational prefixes) are called verb bases. Many themes appear in several bases and some, like the theme "one round object moves," in more than a hundred bases. . . . Verb bases fall into two major categories, neuter and active. Neuter bases are conjugated for person and number in only one paradigm (the stem is invariant throughout the paradigm), but active bases have seven required paradigms: imperfective, perfective, progressive, future, iterative, customary, and optative.

In addition, both neuter and active verbs may have transitive and intransitive forms. Many verbs have separate stems for singular, dual, and plural. The dual is an important category in the Navaho verb, as

are paired forms in the various spheres previously surveyed. Then there are the classificatory forms of transitive verbs referred to at the beginning of this chapter. Most of these bear a fairly obvious relationship to the perceptual world, but others are conventional. Who, for example, would guess that "sorrow" is in the round object category?

Next to "neuter and active," the primary emphasis would seem to fall upon "aspect." This category defines the geometrical character of an event, stating its status with regard to line and point rather than its position in an absolute time scale or in time as broken up by the moving present of the speaker. Thus the interest is in completion or incompletion of action (perfective vs. imperfective) rather than in tense (past or present). Certain Navaho locutions supply, roughly, the functional equivalent of the tenses of Western languages, but Hoijer doubts that even a true future exists in Navaho (". . . the future, so-called, is better interpreted as an inceptive progressive—that is, as an aspect rather than a tense category").

Navaho verb categories center very largely about the reporting of events, or better, "eventings." These eventings are divided into neuters, eventings solidified, as it were, into states of being by virtue of the withdrawal of motion, and actives, eventings in motion. The latter are further subdivided into imperfectives, eventings in process of completion; perfectives, eventings completed; progressives, eventings moving along; and iteratives, eventings repeated over and over again. The customary reports eventings repeated by force of habit or custom; the optative, a desire that an eventing take place; and the future, the expectation that an eventing will occur.

But this is not all. A careful analysis of the meanings of Navaho verb bases, neuter and active, reveals that eventings themselves are conceived, not abstractly for the most part, but very concretely in terms of the movements of corporeal bodies, or of entities metaphorically linked with corporeal bodies. Movement itself is reported in painstaking detail, even to the extent of classifying as semantically different the movements of one, two, or several bodies, and sometimes distinguishing as well between movements of bodies differentiated by their shape and distribution in space.

. . . in three broad speech patterns, illustrated by the conjugation of active verbs, the reporting of actions and events, and the framing of substantive concepts Navaho emphasizes movement and specifies the nature, direction, and status of such movement in considerable detail. Even the neuter category is relatable to the dominant conception of a universe in motion; for, just as someone is reported to have described architecture as frozen music, so the Navaho define position as a resultant of the withdrawal of motion.

Summary

I have reviewed some of the evidence on what Navahos group together, how they do so, and in accord with what principles. The Navaho attain to many genuine concepts: i.e. not arbitrarily labeled classes to which a common response is made on the basis of rote memory but rather identifications of new instances on the basis of defining properties. In some instances only one or two attributes are sufficient for the Navaho to identify a category. For example: a ceremonial where singing takes place to the accompaniment of a rattle is immediately identified as "chant"; ceremonials without singing and featuring drypaintings made of pollen rather than sand and minerals are classified at once as prayer ceremonials; stories about "trotting coyote" and told only in winter are assigned to one and only one class of "myths"; a ceremonial context where color and other symbolism occurs in an "improper" way will unhesitatingly be classified as "witch-craft."

In more instances there are overlapping classifications based upon the three criteria specified by Wyman and Harris (1941):

Duality by sex. This criterion appears (though not consistently) in the classification of ceremonials), supernatural beings, stars and other natural phenomena, plants and other biota, kinship terminology, and language. Sometimes it is associated with another attribute that is also utilized independently in other connections: size.

Use or purpose: ceremonials, plants, artifacts, witchcraft.

Descriptions according to perceptible or symbolic similar characteristics. This principle of classification appeared to greater or lesser extent in every sphere examined.

In some cases these concepts are definitely disjunctive: i.e. one or another of the attributes is used in identifying or categorizing. Such overlapping classifications are not in conflict in the Navaho mind. They are merely different and correspond usually either to varying contexts of discourse and/or to varying knowledge of the speakers.

Some other recurring tendencies in Navaho categorization need mention in review. There is a marked tendency for all systems (with the exception of language?) to be referable at one or more points in the final analysis to Navaho theology and to the associated terminology

thereof. The supernatural system appears in many ways to be the ultimate paradigm for all systems.

There is also a strong tendency for entities to be segregable into aspects. Natural phenomena have their "inner forms." Human and divine nature is never portrayed as either completely good or completely evil: both elements are always present, though in varying proportions. Every ceremonial must have "its Blessing Way part." The most respected chanter must know something about witchcraft—"else he would go dry." Lightning comes as zigzag, forked, and flash. The segregations of Supernatural People appear to be largely by "aspects of personality": either in the form of complementary facets (as in the case of Changing Woman and Changing Bear Maiden) or of manifestations varying by context (cf. various names for the Hero Twins and for Changing Woman).

As a matter of fact, the personal dimension is prominent throughout much Navaho categorization. The language seems to organize both the natural world and the mechanical world in terms of direct bodily reference. Navaho avoidance of completion and overdoing relates back to the body and emotional experience. Most perceptual decisions have a personal reference. Reichard remarks (1950, p. 3): "Navaho dogma is based upon a cosmogony that tries to account for everything in the universe by relating it to man and his activities." And (ibid., p. 148), "the universe is conceived as a place for man, and all natural phenomena are interpreted as his allies or enemies."

Finally, there is a pervasive difference between Navaho categorization and ours about which I have not yet succeeded in being articulate. Reichard characterizes this as "inclusive rather than exclusive." She writes (ibid., p. 5):

for one purpose or another Navaho culture is divided into categories most elements of which have some features in common, but in order to make a category "complete" in the Navaho sense, it should contain at least one feature of an opposed or related category. In other words, categories are inclusive rather than exclusive.

Some of the phenomena do fall along these lines. Yet I am not quite comfortable with the phrasing because of syncretistic and other tendencies that have been noted in the evidence.

· NOTES

[1] Specific citations will be made only on central and controversial issues or where there are additional details quite relevant to this chapter but too involved to recapitulate here. Recordings of the terms in Navaho will be found only in this technical literature.

[2] Two frequently heard forms refer, respectively, to a whole ceremonial and to a single one of the component ceremonies.

[3] Haile (1951, p. 46) renders the basic term as "to restore by ceremonial."

[4] Two Navaho enclitics are translated "way." One means more precisely "in the direction of" or "on the side of." The other may be literally rendered as "by means of" or "with." Another enclitic (used with slightly different intent) means "if ritual [or Way] is directive" (Haile, 1947b, pp. 6-7).

[5] It is convenient, following Haile, to use "ceremonial" for all organized religious activities "on the good side"; "chant" for the corresponding Navaho term; and "rites" for "ceremonial which is not a chant." However, Navaho gives us here only one clear-cut term—that for chant.

[6] Could perhaps more correctly be rendered as "Supernatural" (see section below on Beings). But "Holy Way" is enshrined in the literature.

[7] Has also been rendered as "evil" and "ghost."

[8] Haile (1947b, p. 9) thinks we may regard Life Way ritual as merely a subdivision or phrase of Holy Way. This definitely does not appear to have been the native point of view—at least during the last twenty years. There are, however, some slight indications making it conceivable that Life Way ritual is an offshoot of Holy Way. Earlier (1938, pp. 650, 652) Father Berard tended to regard Life Way as a separate ritual.

[9] Also rendered as Fighting Way and Injury Way (cf. Wyman and Bailey, 1946, p. 214).

[10] Perhaps these two chants should be considered a separate group, governed by Life Way ritual. The evidence is conflicting. See Wyman (1944, p. 365), Wyman and Bailey (1945, p. 358), and Haile (1947b, p. 7).

[11] Some data indicate that this is simply a variant of the Female Branch, named in terms of an etiological factor.

[12] Navaho opinion is not clear-cut as to whether these belong in II or in I.

[13] May be only a special prayer rather than a distinct chantway. No information is available on actual performance.

[14] These first three may all be the same branch with the different names designating the ye-i of different localities as etiological factors.

[15] The Navaho do, however, regularly use a term "partner chants" for these groupings. The same Navaho word meaning "partner" is used in designating linked clans.

[16] See Wyman (1951).

[17] The forms without public exhibition are referred to as "just-visiting-here-and-there chants" or as "inside" or "interior-way chants" (Haile, 1938, p. 647).

[18] Striped Side may refer to a subritual rather than an etiological factor—specifically, the term may designate Navaho Wind Way, Male Branch, Injury Way (Kluckhohn and Wyman, 1940, p. 111). However, there are many other etiological factors. Wyman and Bailey (1946, p. 214) think that Deer's Wind Way, Scolder Wind Way, and Hail Wind Way refer to etiological factors rather than branches. Father Berard (1938, p. 644) lists: Bear-does-it-Way: Thunder-

does-it Way; Big Snake-does-it Way; Horned Toad-does-it Way; Changing Bear Maiden-does-it Way.

[19] He may, for instance, simply name the ritual or an etiological factor or specify the chant without mentioning the branch.

[20] In the main, this is to correct omissions (Haile, 1947b, p. 5). Father Berard to the contrary notwithstanding, there are grounds for regarding Blessing Way both as an independent rite and as a ritual analogous to Holy Way, Life Way, and Ugly Way.

[21] Little is known about the Gesture Dance, and what has been recorded is conflicting.

[22] Bead Way and Eagle Way which are concerned with the ritual trapping of eagles are today considered chants. Ritual bear hunting had strong connections with the various Mountain Top Way ceremonials.

[23] Some accounts (see Reichard, 1950, p. 390) associate Breast-Grabber similarly with the moon, but I suspect syncretism here—a tidying up of the system by Navaho intellectuals.

[24] There are some indications (Reichard, 1950, pp. 407, 431) that Earth and Changing Woman are equivalent, but this is not nearly as explicit as the three forms of Sun.

[25] Also known as White Shell Woman, although occasionally White Shell Woman is considered the sister of Changing Woman (Reichard, 1950, p. 482).

[26] Usually rendered into English as "Holy People."

[27] In a few cases present practice is not completely consistent (Kluckhohn and Wyman, 1940, p. 40).

[28] My summary is taken from Wyman's (1948) review, much of it word for word.

[29] The section (except for the final paragraph) is taken exclusively from Haile (1943) and often in the same words. This publication is little known in the United States.

[30] Cf. G. Dieterlen, "Classification des végétaux chez les Dogon," *Journal de la Société des Africanistes,* 22:115-58 (1952).

[31] This section is based primarily on materials in Haile, 1941.

[32] The reference is to the obligation of the husband to work for the wife's family.

[33] This section is based largely on Hoijer, 1951. Unless otherwise indicated, passages in quotation marks are from this article.

REFERENCES

Goodwin, Grenville. 1945. "A Comparison of Navajo and White Mountain Apache Ceremonial Forms and Categories," *Southwestern Journal of Anthropology,* 1:498-506.

Haile, Berard. 1938. "Navaho Chantways and Ceremonials," *American Anthropologist,* 40:639-52.

——— 1941. Learning Navaho. Vol. I. Saint Michaels, Arizona, Saint Michaels Press.

——— 1943. "Soul Concepts of the Navaho," *Annali Lateranansi,* 7:59-94.

——— 1947a. Navaho Sacrificial Figures. Chicago, University of Chicago Press.

Haile, Berard. 1947b. Prayer Stick Cutting in a Five Night Ceremonial of the Male Branch of Shooting Way. Chicago, University of Chicago Press.

—— 1947c. Head and Face Masks in Navaho Ceremonialism. Saint Michaels, Arizona, Saint Michaels Press.

—— 1947d. Starlore among the Navaho. Santa Fe, Museum of Navajo Ceremonial Art.

—— 1951. A Stem Vocabulary of the Navaho Language: English-Navaho. Saint Michaels, Arizona, Saint Michaels Press.

—— 1954. Property Concepts of the Navaho Indians. The Catholic University of America, Anthropological Series No. 17.

Hoijer, Harry. 1945. "Classificatory Verb Systems in the Apachean Languages," *International Journal of American Linguistics,* 11:15-23.

—— 1951. "Cultural implications of some Navaho linguistic categories," *Language,* 27:111-20.

Kluckhohn, Clyde. 1938. "Navaho Women's Knowledge of Their Song Ceremonials," *El Palacio,* 45:87-92.

—— 1939. "Some Personal and Social Aspects of Navaho Ceremonial Practice," *Harvard Theological Review,* 32:57-82.

—— 1956. "Some Navaho Value Terms in Behavioral Context," *Language,* 32:140-45.

Kluckhohn, Clyde, and Leland C. Wyman. 1940. An Introduction to Navaho Chant Practice. Memoirs of the American Anthropological Association 53.

Oakes, Maud. 1943. Where the Two Came to Their Father. New York, Pantheon Books.

Reichard, Gladys A. 1943. "Human Nature as Conceived by the Navajo Indians," *Review of Religion,* 353-60.

—— 1948. "Navaho Classification of Natural Objects," *Plateau,* 21:7-12.

—— 1950. Navaho Religion. 2 vols. New York, Pantheon Books.

Tschopik, Harry, Jr. 1941. Navaho Pottery Making. (Papers of the Peabody Museum of Harvard University 17.) Cambridge, Mass.

Vestal, Paul A. 1952. Ethnobotany of the Ramah Navaho. (Papers of the Peabody Museum of Harvard University 40.) Cambridge, Mass.

Wyman, Leland C. 1944. Review of *Origin Legend of the Navaho Flintway* by Berard Haile, *American Antiquity,* 9:363-65.

—— 1945. Review of *The Story of the Navajo Hail Chant* by G. A. Reichard, *Review of Religion,* 380-83.

—— 1948. Review of *Starlore among the Navajo* by Berard Haile, *The American Indian,* 4:45-7.

—— 1951. "Notes on Obsolete Navaho Ceremonies," *Plateau,* 23:44-48.

—— 1957. Ed. Beautyway, A Navaho Ceremonial. New York, Bollingen Series 53, Pantheon Books.

Wyman, Leland C., and Clyde Kluckhohn. 1938. Navaho Classification of Their Song Ceremonials. Memoirs of the American Anthropological Association 50.

Wyman, Leland C., and Stuart K. Harris. 1941. Navajo Indian Medical Ethnobotany. University of New Mexico Bulletin 3.

—— 1951. The Ethnobotany of the Kayenta Navaho. University of New Mexico Publications in Biology 5.

Wyman, Leland C., and Flora L. Bailey. 1945. "Idea and Action Patterns in Navajo Flintway," *Southwestern Journal of Anthropology,* 1:356-77.

Wyman, Leland C., and Flora L. Bailey. 1946. "Navajo Striped Windway, an Injury-Way Chant," *Southwestern Journal of Anthropology*, 2:213-38.
———— 1952. "Native Navaho Methods for the Control of Insect Pests," *Plateau*, 24:97-103.

ACKNOWLEDGMENT

I am grateful to Dr. Leland C. Wyman for careful criticism of an earlier version of this paper.

CONCERNING THE CONCEPT OF "PRIMITIVITY"

By Kurt Goldstein, M.D.

NEW YORK

THE USE of the word "primitive" in the literature about human behavior is very confusing. Its application to the ways of "uncivilized" people, at face value so different from those of civilized man, originated in the popular assumption that these ways were expressions of an inferior mentality. This opinion seemed to find scientific confirmation, particularly in the results of the research of Levy-Bruhl, who spoke of a prelogical mentality of primitive people whose life is supposed to be determined by the law of participation, a concept which he had taken over from Durkheim. The members of these societies do not experience themselves as separate individuals; they and the objects in their world appear to them sometimes as the same, sometimes as others.

Paul Radin has, on the basis of unbiased consideration of reported phenomena, taken a definite critical stand against the correctness of Levy-Bruhl's interpretation, so that it may seem no longer necessary to mention the latter in our discussion of the problem of primitivity— this the less as Levy-Bruhl later abandoned some of his concepts. However, we are induced to refer to his concepts because they had and still have a great influence on the interpretation of a number of abnormal mental phenomena of cultured and "uncultured" people, as, for instance, the behavior of children or of patients with mental diseases, of dreams, and the like. This situation demands our consideration not only because the assumption that these and other phenomena are experiences of a similar "primitive" mental state was one of the main origins of the confusion concerning the term primitive, but also because, as we shall see, it is based on a wrong interpretation of the mentioned phenomena. To illustrate the role Levy-Bruhl's ideas still play in this field, I would like to quote some remarks by a scientist who plays a considerable role in spreading the concept of the so-called prelogical mind and the similarity between the inferior mentality of primitive people and the other conditions I pointed to. He writes:

"The paleologician expresses himself in egocentric speech habits, for his thinking is predicative, and he has regressed to the egocentric speech of the child" (Domarus, 1944, p. 112). "We know that the child's speech has some elements of the speech of the primitive people . . . . . Therefore we are once more driven to the conclusion that the specific paleological thought and speech processes of the schizophrenics are in essence those of primitive people . . . the specific laws of language in schizophrenics show that they are the same as those of primitive people or even those of higher animals."

Another author tells us that if we accept this concept of paleological thinking it means that from the evolutionary point of view in biology, and correspondingly a comparative developmental approach in psychology, we also have to assume "the notion that intermediary stages once existed between some apes or ape-like species and the races of man who live today. Presumably these intermediary races of man thought paleologically" (Arieti, 1955, p. 269).

Heinz Werner has tried (Werner and Kaplan, 1956) to bring order into the chaos concerning the concept of primitivity by clarifying the various conditions to which the term has been applied. He wishes to reserve it—in relation to his concept of developmental psychology—for the lower level of behavior in the increasing differentiation and hierarchic integration characteristic for development. He writes: "It is empirically true that the processes emerging in the actual time sequence frequently conform to the developmental sequence; what occurs earlier in time often involves a greater lack of differentiation than what occurs later." Indeed, he does not want to be misunderstood as assuming that "primitive" means simply that which chronologically comes first. "The empirical relationship does not entail the proposition that temporal order of emergence and developmental sequence are of the same logical character." If I understand his reservation correctly, he wishes to avoid giving the impression that he believes in the generally relinquished "biogenetic Grundgesetz" of Haeckel. What he wants, it seems to me, is merely to state that the various behavior forms in different stages represent observable facts which can be considered similar or different expressions of degrees of differentiation. Indeed it seems to me doubtful whether, from this point of view, findings in the ontogenetic development of human beings could be compared with those in phylogenetic sequences; it seems particularly doubtful that childhood phenomena could be put parallel to those in "primitive" people. I have the impression that his studies have the intention of making such comparisons. I may or may not be correct on this, but I I do think that Werner did not pay enough attention in this comparison to *an aspect* which seems to me of essential significance for any comparison of phenomena observed in different organisms or in different stages of development: we should never consider phenomena isolatedly, and we should never compare phenomena observed in isolation. What we observe is *embedded in the activity of the total organism,* and all its activity is an expression of the coming to terms of the particular organism with the outer world in its tendency to realize its nature as much as possible (Goldstein, 1939). Any phenomenon can be correctly interpreted only if one at least considers it from this point of view too.

Developmental psychology considers phenomena in isolation insofar as it is interested in their formal structure; thus it often neglects the contents as unimportant. But when we want to understand a phenomenon, i.e., interpret it as a means for the organism's self-realization, we must also take the contents into consideration. Particularly is this the case when we want to decide whether we are dealing in a phenomenon with the effect of one definite capacity or the lack of another —in our example the lack of a higher mental activity. Or, when we want to know whether the organism possesses a capacity but it does not become effective in a definite situation—that is, in a definite relationship between organism and world—because the intention of the organism's activity can be fulfilled equally or even better without it.

It is not my intention to discuss concepts of the so-called primitive mind critically. Rather I prefer to analyze some phenomena often considered primitive which I have studied intensively, and to see whether this analysis gives us possibly a better interpretation of the behavior of "primitive" people than the assumption of prelogical thinking—an interpretation which, as I would like to show, is in principle in accordance with the results of the studies of Paul Radin.

It was particularly experiences with patients which taught me what erroneous interpretations of behavior one can arrive at when the conclusion is based on consideration of isolated phenomena, and how wrong one's results can be if one compares them with others which appear similar, even equal, at face value (Goldstein, 1946).

Before describing the behavior of certain patients with greater or lesser damage of the higher mental functions, I want to make some remarks concerning the concept of the organization of the human mind to which I came through studies of personalities with such damage.

We can distinguish in the behavior of normal human beings two kinds of approach to the world; we call these *concrete* behavior and *abstract* behavior (Goldstein and Gelb, 1925). Before I characterize both in more detail, I would like to illustrate the difference of the two approaches by a simple example. When we enter a darkened bedroom and switch on the light we act concretely, often without being aware of what we are doing; we experience only a desire to have light. The reaction is based on the aftereffect of previous equal situations. One can say we are given over somewhat passively to the world and bound to the immediate experience of the very things or the situation.

If, however, we reflect that by switching on the light we might awaken someone sleeping in the room and therefore do not switch it on, we approach the situation abstractly. We transcend the immediately given specific aspect of sense impressions; we detach ourselves from them and consider the situation from a conceptual point of view and react accordingly.

The two approaches are specific for all behavior organization of the human being (Goldstein and Scheerer, 1941) but one should not consider them as the effect of two different, separate capacities; they are rather two levels of the capacity of the human being. Each approach constitutes one definite behavioral range of performance, but they are always effective together as a unit which determines the organization of the performance. The participation of one or the other approach in a performance differs according to the different significance of one or the other approach for the fulfillment of the task.

All performances of the organism have the structure of a *figure-ground organization,* i.e., we have to distinguish in the unitary activity which every performance presents that one part which fulfills the task directly from another one which represents the activity in the "background" on which the correct performance is based (Goldstein, 1946, p. 109). We call the first activity the figure, the other one the ground. What is meant by figure and ground becomes immediately obvious in visual experiences, for instance, in the difference between a picture and the ground on which it is presented; here one can also see that figure and ground are *dependent on each other* and that the phenomena in one influence the other. Like visual performances, all other performances of the organism show the same figure-ground organization, all motor actions, feelings, thinking, speaking, and the like.

Which capacity level becomes figure and which ground depends upon the way in which the task can best be fulfilled. In some tasks this will be by virtue of one level of activity, in others by the other level. It is very important to be aware that the *starting* of any performance *presupposes the abstract attitude*. Also, in performances which have to be executed in concrete behavior, for instance motor automatisms, the situation has to be prearranged in such a way that concrete behavior is set in motion; the ground has to be prepared so that it can run smoothly, independently. To achieve that, the abstract attitude is necessary. Furthermore, if for any reason anything goes wrong in the concrete activity, we need the abstract attitude to correct the mistake and to induce the continuation of the interrupted task.

In many situations of normal life the ground is prepared for concrete behavior in general, so that concrete behavior can be elicited immediately. That is the case in the organization for special work activity in industry, similarly in social life by organization according to customs.

In such situations we may be inclined to assume that the concrete approach *alone* is determining behavior. Patients with impairment of abstract attitude may not appear to deviate grossly from normal persons in everyday behavior because many routine tasks do not require the abstract attitude once activity has been set in motion and the situation in which it must occur is given. But otherwise they show definite failures, we can say, in all situations to which one can come to terms only by the abstract approach.

From an analysis of the behavior of a great number of such patients in various situations in everyday life and in special test situations, we learned, on the one hand, the different modes of behavior in which the abstract attitude is necessary, and on the other hand, what characterizes the structure of concrete behavior. I would like to mention some of the modes of behavior where the patient *fails:* when it is necessary to give an account to himself for acts and thoughts; when he has to keep in mind various aspects of a task or any presentation simultaneously; therefore the same object may appear as something different when considered by chance from another aspect or in another situation. The patient cannot break up a given whole into parts to isolate and so synthesize them. He cannot form concepts, symbols, and does not understand them; therefore his language has lost the character of being used in a symbolic way (Goldstein and Scheerer, 1941; Goldstein, 1948). The patient is not able to detach the ego from the outer world or from inner experiences; the relationship between different objects, different events, persons, words, may be determined by their accidentally appearing in the same place or at the same time. Syllogisms may be based on the similarity of parts of the premises—or, better said, on what appears so to the patient. Under certain conditions the predicate may determine the conclusion while under normal conditions it is determined by the subject. But, under other conditions, experience of similarity of other parts of the two sentences which the premises represent determines this. One has to be aware that the patient is not even able to realize what is demanded of him; he is unable to understand the structure of a syllogism and the procedure to solve the problem.

The concrete behavior does not imply conscious activity in the sense of reasoning. We surrender to experiences of an unreflected character; we are confined to the immediate apprehension of a given thing or situation in its particular uniqueness, which is never mediated by discursive reasoning. Our thinking and acting are directed by the claims which one particular object or an aspect of it or a situation makes. I want to stress that the concrete attitude exists also in respect to ideas, thoughts, and feelings.

The concrete behavior of the patient with defect of abstraction shows *characteristic differences from concrete behavior of normals*. The normal person is induced to behave concretely in special situations, but his reaction does not occur passively—there is some intention to do it. The individual is not forced to perform it. Even when some reaction runs automatically, we have in the background the feeling of its significance, embedded in a wider, more or less aware realm of experiences. When we make a mistake we are able to correct it by switching to the abstract attitude which, one could say, is always hovering around. The patient is forced to react to the object, to the situation. His doing is not an activity of himself as a person; one should rather speak of a reaction of an apparatus to a stimulus to which it is bound. The object is a "sign," by which the reaction is elicited. But not even that is fully correct. Not everything can become a sign; the sign has always some relation to the subject who can use it. For the patient everything can become a "sign"—a stimulus, a word, an object, a situation, a feeling—which for any reason comes to the fore and becomes connected with something else, for instance, when it occurs at the same time or place or otherwise. This connection becomes determining for future activities. What is connected remains so until some other "stronger" stimulation takes place. Everything that occurs gets the character of "evidence."

The patient cannot easily detach himself from definite objects and the like; it is difficult, sometimes impossible, for him to realize other potential functions of the same object. He appears fixed, rigid. On the other hand, he may be particularly suggestible to any connections which are induced to him by other people, if they are presented in such a way that he can grasp them with the concrete behavior. He may not be able to evoke images voluntarily, but they may come passively to the fore and even overwhelm him in such a way that he cannot get rid of them. He may not be able to distinguish them from real experiences.

Because of the difficulty of producing reasonable relations, often what is normally on the "fringes" of our experience but usually is eliminated from use in our reactions may become effective and produce connections difficult to understand, but understandable from this point of view.

We have till now referred to the phenomena in concrete behavior in everyday life, in practical work. But there are other normal reactions and experiences which belong to concrete behavior: physiognomic experiences, emotions, religious experiences and activities in different forms, from the rites, mythical experiences and activities, to the highest forms—the rituals in the "highest" religions.

Where these behavior forms appear in primitive people they are often considered as a special expression of an inferior mind. They represent, in opposition to the experience mediated by the intellectual approach, a more *immediate concrete relationship* between the individual and the world, especially the world of living beings, but also what we call the physical world: landscapes, mountains, the ocean, the sky, the sun, the stars, clouds, thunder, and the like. These play a considerable role in the life of man. The same phenomenon which can be experienced as an object in the ordered outer world in which things are going on, and in which we act on the basis of abstract attitude or in concrete activity, appears from this point of view something totally different. These experiences are the basis of people's awe, admiration, devotion; conversely, of the feeling of helplessness and anxiety. They are the cause of a great number of activities which are strictly in opposition to rational understanding but have for them reality and influence the people.

Even highly educated people cannot escape from these influences. As much as one tries to eliminate these "disturbing" experiences which we have in all man's different realms, to eliminate them by interpreting the phenomena as illusions, they appear again and again, sometimes in very complex systematic forms in cosmic theories, religious interpretations, myths, social customs, individual habits. These immediate experiences in relation to other human beings give rise particularly to assumptions about what is going on in the experiences of the "other." They are the basis of mutual understanding among human beings. The thinking underlying these experiences does not follow the laws of logical thinking. It shows similarity with the organization of concrete behavior.

I have come to the conclusion that man always lives in two spheres of experience: the sphere in which the subject and object are experienced as separate and only secondarily related, and another one in which he experiences oneness with the world (Goldstein, 1958).

Because we observe these experiences in normal human beings, we must say they and the world in which they appear belong to man's nature. When we then see that they cannot be understood by logic, we are inclined to consider them as aberrations, i.e., pathological phenomena or manifestations of an inferior mentality. It is particularly these phenomena which induced the assumption that the primitive has a prelogical mind.

Are we right to make such an evaluation? One may think so if one neglects the differences between normal and pathological concreteness. Here particularly the *isolatedness* of the experiences and actions of the pathological person is in opposition to the relatedness of the normal concrete behavior to the individual in its totality and the general condition in which it occurs. What is described as prelogical is more like the pathological than the normal concreteness. Is not the case the same concerning the mentality of the primitive people? Is their mentality not more similar to our normal concreteness than to the concreteness of the patients? The study of patients with missing abstract attitude who can use only the concrete capacity level shows that they can live in an ordered way if their *fellow men prepare the conditions* (by their abstract behavior) in such a way that the patient can do justice to demands in a concrete way. The positive result of their activities is therefore the effect of the influence of both capacity levels in cooperation. The same is the case when normal individuals are involved in concrete activities. The difference is that the latter can *prepare the conditions themselves* (with their own abstract capacity) in an appropriate way.

From my experience with the behavior of patients, I guessed that the *people in primitive societies may not be inferior, but that their behavior may correspond to what we have characterized as concrete behavior.* If that can be assumed, we come to the further question: *how can these people exist with their concrete level of behavior alone?* and I pondered whether their *existence may not be guaranteed by the abstract attitude of fellow men.*

Authors who assume that the behavior of primitive people shows inferior mentality, that it is an expression of a prelogical state of mind came to the conclusion that people with this mentality could not survive, for example, the "ape-like ancestors of man" who possessed only this capacity. Arieti asked "how these primitive races were able to survive or evolve into others ["higher" ones] if their actions were determined by a system of thinking which is so unrealistic...," and he comes to the conclusion that "eventually the races which could not sufficiently overcome this type of thinking perished" (1955, p. 272). I could agree with him that human beings with such an inferior mentality could not survive—but only if one assumes that they were really human beings. If they were not that, why should living beings of another kind not have other conditions of existence? Now it is really only a hypothesis that these "predecessors" of man have lived. Arieti is interested in this problem of the possibility of the existence of a prelogical individual because he ascribes the same mentality to the living "primitive" men. He attempts to explain their existence by assuming that it is made possible through the "support of the authority" (the tribe); "therefore they may be able to indulge in the ritual with a certain facility" (1955, p. 227).

But how does this *support of the authority originate?* Does this not presuppose the existence of people of another, "higher" mentality in the society than the "primitive" man? I think that such an assumption would be necessary, not only as an explanation of the "concern" of the "authority" with their fellow men but particularly as explanation of the insight into the reason why the primitive man is not able to handle the difficulties of the world. Only then could the support occur in the correct way. If one assumes that the authority consists not of men but of rules of organization which guarantee the life of the tribe, then the problem is: *How could these rules grow out of a society of such inferior mentality?* I think only if one assumes that the inherited regulations were created by *men of higher mentality.* But that would mean that such men existed at least sometimes in the tribe. If that was the case, why not assume that one may have overlooked the fact that they exist also in present primitive society? Anyway it must induce us to study whether this may not be the case. This seems not improbable because rules can only be transmitted in history and remain effective later if there are men behind them who understand them and make them work.

With that, the not very plausible assumption of the existence of ape men as predecessors of men who perished would not be necessary. One would only have to assume that men with the higher mental capacity have always existed and may exist now in primitive tribes, although the great number of these people may live on a lower level of capacity, or, as I prefer to say, do behave concretely. When we speak later about Radin's concept of primitive societies, we shall see that this *seems really to be the case.* Such an assumption would make it unnecessary to explain how from the prelogical being the logical man "evolved." Without discussing this very delicate problem, I would like to say that I personally believe that there is no proof that such a development took place, and I do not see how it would be possible. How could (which it would mean) the symbolic function—so characteristic for man—develop from a capacity level which gives only the possibility for thinking and acting in "sign" relations?

Returning to the problem of how people who possess only concrete behavior can exist, again the observation of patients has brought us important information. As an example I would like to refer to the condition of the brain-damaged individuals we talked about before. We saw that patients with severe impairment of the abstract capacity level are not able to fulfill those tasks which we mentioned as depending on the use of this capacity. Therefore in the first period after the injury they are not able to come to terms with many demands of our —their previous—world and they therefore come easily into catastrophes and anxiety. Because of the disturbing aftereffects of the catastrophes, they are not even able to actualize fully their preserved concrete capacity. We could show that after a certain time mechanisms develop which protect them against the anxiety. How this occurs I cannot discuss here, but it is certainly not within their consciousness (Goldstein, 1939, pp. 42 ff.). But by these protections their life becomes more ordered, if even more restricted. They would have to live in a very reduced condition if they did not have the help of the people around them. *What does this help consist of?* What we observe is that after a certain time the patients come into better relations with the environment and are more able to use concretely what they had previously learned. One can easily get the impression that they are improved in respect to their defect. Examination of their capacities, however, shows that the defect exists as before. They can very easily come into catastrophes if confronted with tasks which cannot be fulfilled in concrete behavior. What brought the "improvement" was the organization of an environment from which such tasks do not, or only rarely, arise. Now they can live without difficulties in the way they are alone able to live, i.e., in an absolutely concrete form of behavior. This organization is the effect of the use of the abstract attitude of the people around them. Their behavior can be understood only as an effect of the *interaction of the abstract behavior of their fellow men and their own concrete behavior.* In this way their existence is guaranteed in spite of their being able only to behave concretely.

With that we came to the conclusion that living with the *concrete behavior alone is not possible*; human existence presupposes the influence of both capacity levels.

Another example which illustrates our viewpoint is the existence of the infant in the first year of life. The infant comes into the world as a very imperfect, very helpless organism, particularly because his abstract capacity is not yet developed. He escapes the immediate danger of death by the operation of some inborn mechanisms which immediately come into action. But as important as that is for survival, he would come again and again into disorder and dangerous catastrophes, he would not even be able to use his inborn capacities to come to terms with the world or to develop if he were not protected against these states of disorder by the people around, the prototype of whom is represented by the mother.

This protection consists in building up an *environment corresponding to the state of the infant's maturation.* Organization of this adequate "world" presupposes insight into the physical and psychological needs of the infantile organism and its changes during maturation. This insight and the tendency to use it in the interest of the infant is an effect of the application of abstract behavior. Certainly the mother does not always invent the adequate organization of the environment; she takes over many old customs she has learned from her mother or other people. But it cannot be said that her activities grow out of so-called instincts; they are the result of the abstract attitude of the mother and of the ancestors.

At about the end of the first year of the infant's life, the first signs of the development of abstract attitude become visible. Now more and more, but in very slow development, the behavior of the child shows the influence of the unity of the concrete/abstract capacity levels. The mother's influence has to change correspondingly. There is a time when the cooperation of the mother's abstract attitude with the not fully developed capacity of abstraction of the child represents a very complex problem, which is not always correctly solved by the mother and so may have an ill effect on the further development of the child. In this relationship between mother and child, the capacity of the mother to understand also the psychological needs of the child is of greatest significance. Because the concrete behavior of the child prevails for a long time, the structure of his behavior may show similarities with other conditions where concrete behavior is in the foreground—with the behavior of patients and primitive people. Therefore a comparison may be easily at hand. But the differences should warn us against assuming equal states of "development" in the various conditions. What for us at the moment is important is that the development of the behavior of the child shows clearly that it is the effect of *abstract and concrete behavior,* that the existence and development of the infant is guaranteed by the effect of the capacity of abstraction in the behavior of others until he has developed his own abstract attitude.

From my analysis of the behavior of persons lacking the use of the abstract attitude and showing correspondingly abnormal concreteness, I was inclined to assume that the people living in "primitive" societies may not have an inferior mentality but that they possess, like all human beings, the concrete-abstract unity of the human mental capacity. The impression of an inferior mentality might have arisen from the predominance of the concrete level in their behavior, by which they come to terms with the demands of the special world in which they live. I further assumed that they could exist only if their life was guaranteed by other people of the tribe, who have organized the world in such a way that people can come to terms with it with the concrete attitude. This in turn would make it necessary to assume that there are in the tribe people who have and use the abstract capacity. If that were true, then we would find here the same organization of their behavior as in our patients and in infants, insofar as it would represent the effect of the activity of themselves and of other people too. If this could be proved for primitive societies, then the question would arise: Do not the "primitive" people in these societies show under some conditions signs of abstract capacity also? It is not probable that a society consists of two groups of people mentally so different.

I was very much pleased when I realized that my conjecture seemed to be in agreement with the analysis of the mentality of "primitive" people by Paul Radin, and that his conclusions enforced my concept of the organization of human behavior in general.

I would like in this respect to refer to some statements by Radin in his book *Die religiöse Erfahrung der Naturvölker,* and to some of the reports by which he documents his conclusions. Radin stresses that the assumption of an inferior mentality of primitive people originated, on the one hand, from a generalization of the experiences with single or very few individuals. If a greater number had been investigated, it would have been realized that primitive people are not so passive, not such rigidly acting persons, but individuals; further—what is of particular significance—their individualities differ considerably. One can distinguish in all primitive societies two types of people, those who live strictly in accord with the rules of the society, whom he calls the "nonthinkers," and those who think, the "thinkers." The number of thinkers may be small but they play a great role in the tribe; they are the people who formulate the concepts and organize them in systems, which are then taken over—generally without criticism—by the nonthinkers. When one wants to understand the many peculiarities of the customs, rituals and the like, one must further pay attention to the fact that average people frequently misunderstand the formulations of the thinkers and distort them. There is another point in his remarks which is important, namely, that it is self-understood for these societies that the thinkers are so closely connected with community life that they also more or less participate in the certainly nonrational activities of the groups. This may give the impression that their mentality also is "primitive." Radin adds here that the same is the case also in civilized societies. He concludes: "Primitive societies differ in many respects essentially from ours, but not in that they have not the capacity of reasoning or in that they are not individuals." I would like to point out concerning his documentation for this opinion particularly the reports about conversations which Rasmussen had with the Eskimos. The comparison of the two reports given in detail leaves no doubt about the difference of the people in respect to thinking and not thinking, and about the existence of people with high mental capacity in the tribe, not essentially different from those in civilized societies. The latter makes it understandable, according to Radin, that the religious experiences of the primitive people show exactly the same differences that we find in the historical high religions—we find mystics, rationalists, conformists, revolutionaries, pragmatists.

When we read (Radin, 1950, p. 23) the remarks of the old Iglulik Eskimo, Ana—an Eskimo of the nonthinking type—in relation to the difficult life of the Eskimos, we recognize the realistic and concrete attitude toward the world; but the man seems not to be satisfied with simply pointing to the many difficulties and dangers of the life of the Eskimos but adds repeatedly the question: "Why is it so?" Further, "Why must there be storms which hinder us in looking for meat for ourselves and our beloved ones?" Why must the women he mentions suffer from pain and sickness without any guilt? Why must human beings suffer at all? And he adds to Rasmussen: "You also cannot answer our question—why is life as it is? And so it must be. We have no explanation." He adds then some remarks that are of particular significance in relation to the discussion of our problem about the capacity level of primitive people in comparison to our own. "We have anxiety . . . therefore our fathers tried, as their forebears taught them, to protect themselves by all those instructions and customs which grew out of experiences and the knowledge of generations. We do not know how and why. But we follow them so that we can live in peace. And with all our angacoqs and their secret knowledge, we know so little that we fear everything."

The report of Rasmussen concerning this Eskimo has, as Radin mentioned, induced Levy-Bruhl to assume the inferior mentality of the people. For him, Radin continues, the man's remark, "We have no explanation," represents the characteristic mental attitude of all primitive people, of each individual in every tribe. Is it justified to assume that such a man has a "*prelogical* mind"? In this respect I would like to stress that his behavior *is not like the behavior of our patients*. It does not show the deviations, the compulsiveness, by which the patients differ from normal concrete people. The remarks of the man show definitely a relationship of his activities and experiences to his total personality; this corresponds to the *concreteness of normal civilized people* but is in *opposition to the behavior of the patients, who have no "personality," no "world," only more or less isolated experiences.*

What might have brought the people of the primitive societies to this kind of organization of their culture to which concrete behavior is adequate? I cannot enter into a discussion of this problem. I do not feel at all competent for such a task. But I would like to say something about the role which *anxiety* plays in this respect. There is no doubt—again according to the remarks of the mentioned Eskimo —that the people know what anxiety is. On the other hand, they seem to have little anxiety. Radin says that Ana does not show in his behavior that he is in an emotional state when he speaks about the misery of their life and about their fear—at least not as if he experienced much anxiety. He mentioned that they live peacefully. If they were to be stricken by much anxiety that would not be possible, because as people living concretely they would not have the ability to escape anxiety. We know in general that anxiety cannot be overcome by concrete behavior. Thus the absence of anxiety must have another reason. *It is not eliminated; it does not occur,* because they live in a condition—due to their following the rules of the society—in which conflicts and anxiety usually do not arise. One could say also that they have no anxiety because they have the possibility of living in proportion with the demands on them.

This may not be so for the thinking people. To build up this adequate culture they must be aware of the anxiety and its danger and think about the way to avoid it. That would correspond again to the description of these people by Radin. They are aware of the difficulties of their own psychic disequilibrium and try to escape this by building up religious concepts and behavior. Their primary problem is to avoid anxiety and suffering and restore a normal psychic state of their own. With the awareness of this goal is connected another one, namely, to help the others to be able to live in physical and psychic health. It seems that this activity is based on altruistic feeling, even if other tendencies may be effective—the desire for power, reputation and wealth (Radin, 1950, p. 40). Be that as it may, *this goal would explain why they organize the society in such a way that physical and psychic health can also be reached by the nonthinking people.*

So it would be quite correct to say that people escape anxiety, but even better to speak of avoidance of the occurrence of conflict and anxiety by the structure of their culture. The nonthinking people may in their activity not be aware that the culture lets them avoid anxiety; in the same way as in civilized life, people who act concretely when menaced with anxiety are not aware that they are avoiding anxiety by acting concretely. The *nonthinking primitive people have no anxiety, because in the structure of their culture they are induced to act concretely and so do not come into conditions where anxiety could arise.* They know that there is anxiety; better, they are afraid of a great number of events. The thinker knows the reason for the occurrence of anxiety—as Radin has so clearly described in his discussion of the origin of their religion and organization of the rites to overcome their psychic disagreeableness—and so organized the culture in this way. This lack of much conflict and anxiety—also of guilt feelings—may explain why primitive people do not seem to suffer from compulsive neuroses. I think it is meaningless to say, as has been said, that the individuals have no compulsive neuroses, rather the whole culture is compulsive. There are mental states reported which look at face value like catatonia. What they represent is unclear. I would guess they represent severe shock reactions.

When the nonthinking Eskimo speaks of the significance of their culture as means to avoid anxiety, he may not be referring to his own experience of anxiety, but he is trying to explain how, by means of their culture, anxiety is avoided. That would show again how he is able to use his reasoning under certain conditions. When in his usual life in doing and thinking that is not the case, this would be explainable because it is not necessary. He behaves concretely because thereby he is able to achieve the best result. The application of abstract attitude may even disturb his successful concrete activities in the same way that the abstract attitude generally interferes in an activity which could be performed best in concrete behavior. The nonthinking man would then come into physical, particularly mental, disequilibrium which he would not be able to handle as the thinking man does and he would experience anxiety.

The concrete behavior of the primitive man consists particularly in the rituals, so-called magical experiences and religious and mythical activities. When we look at them isolated from the whole structure of the primitive culture, they may appear abstruse, irrational. They do not originate in the nonthinking people but are the produce of the religious concepts of the "thinking" religious man. They are the expression of the religious man's attempts to fulfill his needs, to find order in his life, particularly in respect to psychological difficulties, by assuming the existence of something outside himself which is more powerful than he and determines what is valuable in man's life and restores his psychic equilibrium (Radin, 1950, p. 28). What we observe in the nonthinking man are those parts of these concepts which can be grasped in a concrete way and may be modified, even distorted, by misunderstanding; but they play in the totality of his life the same role as for the thinking man, i.e., they stabilize his psychic life. They belong to the second sphere in which man lives in relation to the world, to which I have directed attention before (Goldstein, 1958). These phenomena may play a greater role in primitive life, but they are not essentially different from what we observe in the "thinking" man and the "nonthinking" man in civilized societies.

So we would come to the conclusion, in both civilized and primitive societies, acting and thinking are not the result of the concrete behavior alone. The abstract attitude is always effective in the organization of the "world" by the thinkers in such a way that the people can fulfill the task in a concrete way. This participation of the abstract attitude finds its expression in primitive society in the formation of a permanent structure of the society, in civilized life in certain formations under special conditions. This may give the impression that the abstract capacity of the individual is in the latter always somewhat in action—not so in the activities of primitive people. If one then overlooks the difference between normal concrete behavior and the behavior of patients with defect of abstraction, one may get the impression that the primitive people have an inferior mind, particularly because the "primitive" person appears more unfree, compulsive, which is the effect of the greater regularity of his life. Indeed, they are hardly comparable to the patients; they are much more able to shift from one activity to another when the situation demands it.

I know only too well that my little essay, which touches upon so many controversial problems, is not at all sufficient to clarify the concept of primitivity. However, it may stimulate consideration of the factors underlying the assumption of an inferior human mind, and may make us hesitate in comparing the behavior of children and patients with that of preliterate people. I hope the peculiarity of these people may come to be characterized by a more adequate term.

Paul Radin has said: "No progress in ethnology will be achieved until scholars rid themselves once and for all of the curious notion that everything possesses history, until they realize that certain ideas and concepts are ultimate for man." That is the same idea which grew out of my studies of the behavior of brain-damaged individuals in my attempt to acquire from these observations a concept of the nature of man.

REFERENCES

Arieti, S. 1955. Interpretation of Schizophrenia. New York, Brunner.

Cassirer, E. 1953. Philosophy of Symbolic Forms. New Haven, Yale Univ. Press.

Domarus, E. 1944. "The Specific Laws of Logic in Schizophrenia," in Language and Thought in Schizophrenia, ed. by J. S. Kasanin. Chicago, Univ. of Chicago Press.

Goldstein, K. 1939. The Organism. New York, American Book Co.

—— 1943. "The Significance of Psychological Research in Schizophrenia," *Journal of Nervous and Mental Diseases,* 97:261.

—— 1946. "Naming and Pseudonaming," *Word,* Vol. 2.

—— 1948. Language and Language Disturbances. New York, Grune & Stratton.

—— 1951. Human Nature in the Light of Psychopathology. Cambridge, Harvard Univ. Press.

—— 1958. "The Smiling of the Infant and the Problem of Understanding the 'Other'," *Journal of Psychology,* 44:115-91.

Goldstein, K., and A. Gelb. 1920. Psychologische Analysen hirnpathologischer, Fälle I. Leipzig, Barth.

—— 1925. "Uber Farbennamenamnesie," *Psychologische Forschung,* 6:127-86.

Goldstein, K., and M. Scheerer. 1941. Abstract and Concrete Behavior: An Experimental Study. Psychology Monographs, Vol. 53.

Radin, Paul. 1950. Die religiöse Erfahrung der Naturvölker. Zurich, Rhein-Verlag.

Rasmussen, K. 1915. The Intellectual Culture of the Iglulik Eskimo. Copenhagen.

Werner, H., and B. Kaplan. 1956. "The Developmental Approach to Cognition: Its Relevance to the Psychological Interpretation of Anthropological and Ethnolinguistic Data, *American Anthropologist,* 58:No. 5.

PLATO AND THE DEFINITION OF THE PRIMITIVE

By Stanley Diamond

BRANDEIS UNIVERSITY

IN THIS LITTLE PAPER, conceived, I trust, in Paul Radin's free and challenging spirit, I propose to place certain aspects of Plato's *Republic* in anthropological, and critical, perspective. The origin and nature of the state is a subject peculiarly appropriate to cultural anthropology, for states first arise through the transformation and obliteration of typically primitive institutions. Thinkers of the most diverse backgrounds and intentions have, throughout history, grasped this cardinal fact of state formation. Lao-tzu, Rousseau, Marx and Engels, Maine, Morgan, Maitland, Tonnies, and many contemporary students of society have understood that there is a qualitative distinction between the structure of primitive life and civilization. Moreover, they have, more or less explicitly, sensed the contradictions inherent in the transition from kinship, or primitive, to civilized, or political, society. This momentous transition, this great transformation in the life of man, this social and cultural trauma, if you will, has led to a passionate, and ancient, debate about the merits of primitive existence as opposed to civilization, to the state. Indeed, the debate has frequently been waged in utopian terms; some utopias face backward to a sometimes fantastic image of the primitive, others face forward to the complete triumph of the rational state. Although I have no intention of engaging in this debate, it seems to me that it is the opposition to the primitive which lies at the root of Plato's utopia,[1] and that is the theme I intend to pursue here. In opposing the primitive, Plato helps us define both it and the state.

I

The *Republic* can be considered a projection of the idealized, total city-state, conjured out of the ruins of fourth-century Athens, and

---

The author's recent field work among the Anaguta of the Nigerian Middle Belt supports many of the more intricate details of the argument set forth here, but, for obvious reasons, amplification of the article would have been inappropriate.

influenced by the Spartan oligarchy. But, in its perfection, it transcends these local boundaries and becomes a classic model of the state to which Western scholars have turned for centuries in debating the good life and its relation to political society. This tension between the local and the universal is evident in all utopian constructs, whether merely literary, or socially realized; it is preeminently true of the *Republic*. Plato maintains certain landmarks of the city-state, but he takes us as he says, on a "journey of a thousand years." This span of time is reckoned, perhaps, too modestly, for all subsequent political societies commanded by a permanent, self-proclaimed, benevolent élite, and all élitist social theory, are adumbrated in the *Republic*.

The *Republic*, of course, is more than a political tract. It is also a psychology, an aesthetics, and a philosophy, but it is all these things within a political context. There is hardly any facet of Plato's vision, however abstruse, nor any action he believed imperative which is not colored or dictated by political considerations. The *Republic* is, in short, a work of enormous scope, but it is saturated with politics, with ideology. This point deserves emphasis because Plato has traditionally been considered the very image of the pure philosopher, and the *Republic* has been extolled as the masterwork, in which most of his major ideas appear, impressively interwoven. As Emerson put it, "Plato is philosophy and philosophy Plato...." The New England Platonist goes further, ceding to Plato Omar's "fanatical compliment" to the Koran: "Burn the libraries, for their value is in this book."[2] The phrase sticks, it is an appropriately Platonic sentiment, and it is a political remark.

What then are the political assumptions underlying the *Republic*? To begin with, Plato's personal political bias is clear. He was an aristocrat, who experienced the decay of the Athenian "democracy." He was a philosopher in a society that put Socrates to death. He avoided the rough-and-tumble of politics and shrank from any actual political role for which his birth and training may have qualified him. Yet he seems to have been obsessed with the idea of politics; the political problem for Plato seems to have consisted in how to abolish politics.

It is possible, therefore, to view the *Republic* as the idealization and rationalization of Plato's personal motives. His ideal state is, after all, a utopian aristocracy, ruled by philosophers who have become kings, and the political problem has ceased to exist. But this is too close an exercise in the sociology of knowledge. Plato's personal motives are unquestionably important; they help fix the precise form of the republic, but they do not determine its broader cultural-historical meaning. In Cornford's words,

The city-state was a frame within which any type of constitution could subsist; a despotism, an oligarchy, or a democracy. Any Greek citizen of Plato's day, rich or poor, would have been completely puzzled, if he had been told that he had no interest in maintaining the structure of the city-state. The democrat, in particular, would have replied: "Do you really think that an oriental despotism, where all men but one are slaves, is a higher and happier type of society? Or would you reduce us to the level of those savages with all their queer customs described by Herodotus?"[3]

Plato's oligarchic inclinations, then, cannot be considered contradictory to the basic structure of the city-state; the exact form of his republic is less significant than its over-all statism. Returning to the theme set above, the political assumptions underlying the *Republic* are simply the assumptions of political society, of the state, writ large and idealized. We must remember that classical Greece could look back to its own archaic and primitive past; moreover, it lived on the fringe of a "barbarian" Europe. Thus, the forms and usages of primitive society, even when these were being transformed into organs of the state or abolished in favor of state institutions, were by no means strange to the Greeks, as Fustel de Coulanges, Engels, Morgan, Bury, and others, in varying contexts, have emphasized. Bury, for example, in tracing the early history of Greece, speaks of the authority of the state growing and asserting itself against the comparative independence of the family, and he remarks further that "in the heroic age . . . the state had not emerged fully from the society. No laws were enacted and maintained by the state."[4]

It seems likely, then, that Plato had ample opportunity to react against concrete primitive elements in Greek society and cultural tradition while envisioning his utopian state. Only the classical scholars, with the aid of a more fully developed classical anthropology, can establish the degree to which this was possible, but it is not essential to my argument. Plato could have been acting out of sheer political instinct, logically constructing the perfect political society, and rejecting those institutions and modes of behavior which could not be coordinated with it, that is, the primitive modes. In any case, the fact of opposition to the primitive is clear in the *Republic,* as is Plato's sure sense of the strategy of political society. And this, I believe, is the larger cultural-historical meaning of his work, conceived, as it was, in the morning of European civilization.

II

Although the themes that will concern us in the *Republic* are very subtly interwoven, and sometimes lack precise definition, I shall consider them separately, without trying to reconstruct Plato's full argument.

There is, first of all, the suggestion that Socrates makes about the initiation of the republic:

> They will begin by sending out into the country all the inhabitants of the city who are more than ten years old, and will take possession of their children, who will be unaffected by the habits of their parents; these they will train in their own habits and laws, I mean in the laws which we have given them: and in this way the State and constitution of which we were speaking will soonest and most easily attain happiness, and the nation which has such a constitution will gain most.[5]

The republic is to begin, then, by severing the bonds between the generations, and by obliterating the primary kinship ties. This is, of course, an extreme statement of the general process through which states arise, that is, by releasing the individual from kinship controls and obligations and thus making him subject to the emerging civil laws. There is, however, a remarkably exact parallel to Socrates' suggestion in native Dahomean usage, as reported by Norris, one of the early chroniclers of the Slave Coast. In the Dahomean proto-state, "children are taken from their mothers at an early age, and distributed to places remote from their village of nativity, where they remain with little chance of being ever seen, or at least recognized, by their parents afterwards. The motive for this is that there may be no family connections or combinations, no associations that might prove injurious to the King's unlimited power." [6]

But we must never forget that Plato has no intention of outlining the process of state formation per se; he is, in our view, idealizing that process, hence the purpose of setting up the republic in the manner described is seen as beneficent.

I might add, parenthetically, that the attempt to weaken or sever the ties between the generations is also a typical utopian and quasi-revolutionary aim. The most recent instance is the Israeli Kibbutz, wherein the collective rearing of children is motivated by the desire to produce a generation quite different in character from the parental image of the Shtetl Jew.[7] As a matter of fact, wherever a massive shift in political power and structure is contemplated, or wherever a radical rearrangement of public loyalties is demanded, the family, the psychic transmission belt between the generations, tends to be attacked not merely in terms of any particular form, but as a primary social unit. This is evident, in rather different ways, in the work of many reformists, in early Marxist literature, and in Nazi theory and practice.

Plato's modest proposal for initiating the republic, then, can be seen in both a "revolutionary" and cultural-historical perspective. The *Republic* begins, appropriately enough, in opposition to the antecedent kin and generational ties. And we shall see below that this imperative is extended to the rearing of the guardians within the republic. That is, state and family, echoing the old antagonism between political and primitive organization, are seen to be antithetical, even after the establishment of the ideal polity.

III

Primitive societies that are not in transition to one or another archaic form of the state, that is, that are not proto-states, may function through rank and status systems, and always function through kin or transfigured kin units, the latter being associations whose members are not necessarily reckoned as kin, but which pattern themselves on kin forms. They are, however, devoid of class or caste. Further, primitive societies do not manifest the highly specialized division of labor which is one of the major determinants in the rise of class and caste systems. In these related respects, Plato's republic represents the reverse of primitive usage, and is the state brought to its highest power. To clarify, let us begin with his vision of an absolute division of labor.

In the republic, no man is to engage in more than a single task. Indeed, the ultimate definition of justice, which Socrates pursues as perhaps the major aim of the entire dialogue, consists in each person doing the work "for which he was by nature fitted," within the class to which he constitutionally belongs. And "at that [occupation] he is to continue working all his life long and at no other."[8] Later on, Socrates elaborates this point as follows: ". . . in our State, and in our State only, we shall find a shoemaker to be a shoemaker, and not a pilot also, and a soldier a soldier, and not a trader also, and the same throughout." He emphasizes: in ". . . our State . . . human nature is not twofold or manifold, for one man plays one part only."[9]

In other words, it is imagined that the identity of the individual is exhausted by the single occupation in which he engages. The occupational status, so to speak, becomes the man, just as his class position is, in a wider sense, said to be determined by his nature. In this way, the existence of the state is guaranteed, but the life of the person is constricted and diminished. I do not evaluate this, for the division of labor is, even under ideal political conditions, an expression of the available technology. The point is that Plato not only sensed the congruence of the elaborate division of labor with state organization, but carried it to its furthest reach, and then gave it the name of justice.

The contrast with primitive usage could hardly be more striking. Primitives learn a variety of skills; a single family unit, as among the Hottentot, Anaguta, or Eskimo, may make its own clothing, tools, and weapons, build its own houses, and so on. Even in a transitional society such as the Dahomean proto-state it is expected that every man, whatever his occupation, know three things well: how to cut a field, how to build a wall, and how to roof a house.[10] Moreover, the average primitive participates *directly* in a wide range of cultural activities, relative to the total available in his society, and he may move, in his lifetime, through a whole series of culturally prescribed statuses. He plays, in short, many parts, and his nature is viewed as manifold. The relevance of this to Plato's conception of the drama will be considered below, but, it is first necessary to examine the class structure of his republic, and its implications.

The republic is to be divided into three classes: the guardians, or ruling élite; the auxiliaries, including, apparently, the soldiers; and the lowest class, consisting of all those engaged in economic production, particularly the artisans and farmers. We see, at once, that the manual laborers are at the base of the social hierarchy, being considered constitutionally unfit to rule themselves. This is, of course, a quite typical attitude, however rationalized, and we find it associated with the rise of civilization almost everywhere. In early states, the intellectual gradually emerges from the class of scribes or priests; his connections with the ruling groups are primary. The artisans and farmers grow out of the submerged primitive community, which is transformed into a reservoir of workers for the state through direct conscription of labor, taxation, slavery, or related means.

But, whatever the details of the process, and they vary in different areas, the subordination of primitive artisan and cultivator is a function of state formation. An Egyptian document dating from the New Kingdom is pertinent, in that it reflects this state of affairs, long consolidated:

Put writing in your heart that you may protect yourself from hard labor of any kind and be a magistrate of high repute. The scribe is released from manual tasks; it is he who commands. . . . Do you not hold the scribe's palette? That is what makes the difference between you and the man who handles an oar.

I have seen the metal worker at his task at the mouth of his furnace with fingers like a crocodile's. He stank worse than fish spawn. Every workman who holds a chisel suffers more than the men who hack the ground; wood is his field and the chisel his mattock. At night when he is free, he toils more than his arms can do; even at night he lights [his lamp to work by]. . . . The stonecutter seeks work in every hard stone; when he has done the great part of his labor his arms are exhausted, he is tired out. . . . The weaver in a workshop is worse off than a woman; [he squats] with his knees to his belly and does not taste [fresh] air. He must give loaves to the porters to see the light.[11]

This process and the attendant attitudes are, I believe, ideally reflected in the *Republic*. They develop in Plato's cave, so to speak, in the turmoil of history, but they are presented to us in a purified, philosophic, and ultimate form.

Now the classes in the ideal state are relatively fixed; they tend to be castes, rationalized on a eugenic basis. But Plato provides for both a modicum of social mobility and the predominant freezing of the entire structure through the medium of a "royal lie," that is, through "propaganda," a term that Cornford considers more appropriate,[12] and a condition which we shall take up later in connection with the exile of the dramatist. Socrates states:

Citizens. . . . God has framed you differently. Some of you have the power of command, and in the composition of these he has mingled gold, wherefore also they have the greatest honor; others he has made of silver, to be auxiliaries; others again to be husbandmen and craftsmen he has composed of brass and iron; and the species will generally be preserved in the children. But . . . a golden parent will sometimes have a silver son, or a silver parent a golden son. And God proclaims as a first principle to the rulers, and above all else, that there is nothing which they should so anxiously guard . . . as the purity of the race . . . if the son of a golden or silver parent has an admixture of brass and iron, then nature orders a transportation of ranks and the eye of the ruler must not be pitiful towards the child because he has to descend in the scale and become a husbandman or artisan, just as there may be sons of artisans who having an admixture of gold or silver in them are raised to honor, and become guardians or auxiliaries. For an oracle says that when a man of brass or iron guards the state, it will be destroyed. Such is the tale; is there any possibility of making our citizens believe in it? [13]

The class structure of the republic is, then, based on a theory of human nature, assimilated to Plato's doctrine of essences.[14] Here we confront a perfect example of the convergence of characteristic Platonic concepts to an immediate political issue, a technique that weaves throughout the dialogue, and accounts, in part, for its great dialectic density. The final nature of the individual is viewed as unambiguous, since human nature is a matter of distinct and single higher and lower essences, subdivided further into occupational essences. That is to say, the division of labor and class in the *Republic* is reflected in the division into essences, or, vice versa, if you will. The important point is that the whole structure is guaranteed by human nature, watched over by the guardians, justified by philosophy, and sanctified by God, as the allegory states.

At the peak of the pyramid stand the guardians. They are said to have a pure intuition of the good; they live in the place of light above the cave and are, in a sense, divine; or, they have, at least, intimations of divinity. Shall we call them divine kings? It matters little, for all kings have been considered holy since the primary differentiation of the king from the local primitive chief. The holiness of the king is the sanctification of civil power, as opposed to the common traditions which are symbolized in the person of the local chief and may thus render *him* sacred. The ultimate other-worldliness of the guardians, or philosopher kings, is, I believe, a reflection of the process through which civil power was first sanctified as the primitive community was transformed into political society. We should recall that Plato was impressed by the Egyptian theocracy and actually visited Egypt, where the concept of divine rule was as old as the state itself. In any event, the élite tradition of the guardians is the opposite of the communal tradition of primitive peoples.

Yet neither the divinity of the kings, who shape the end of the republic, nor the sterling quality of their auxiliaries is sufficient to ensure their devotion to the state. This can be achieved most readily through a completely collective life and training. Socrates says: ". . . the wives of our guardians are to be common, and their children are to be common, and no parent is to know his own child, nor any child his parent." [15] The children are to be reared collectively by special nurses who "dwell in a separate quarter." The mothers will nurse them but "the greatest possible care" will be taken that no mother recognizes her own child, nor will suckling be "protracted too long." The mother will "have no getting up at night or other trouble, but will hand over all this sort of thing to the nurses and attendants." [16]

Further, the guardians and their helpers, under a regime of spartan simplicity, are to live in common houses, dine in common, and hold no property; and they are not to engage in economically productive work. The obvious aim is to disengage them from all connections and motives which might diminish their dedication to the state. As noted above, Plato clearly sensed the antagonism between state and family, and in order to guarantee total loyalty to the former, he simply abolished the latter. Moreover, his distrust of kin ties in the ideal state leads him to invoke the aid of a "royal lie," possibly the first half of the propaganda-myth quoted above. Socrates, simulating embarrassment, says:

. . . I really know not how to look you in the face, or in what words to utter the audacious fiction, which I propose to communicate gradually, first to the rulers, then to the soldiers, and lastly to the people. They are to be told that their youth was a dream, and the education and training they received from us, an appearance only; in reality during all that time they were being formed and fed in the womb of the earth, where they themselves and their arms and appurtenances were manufactured; when they were completed, the earth, their mother, sent them up; and so their country being their mother and also their nurse, they are bound to advise for her good, and to defend her against attacks, and her citizens they are to regard as children of the earth and their brothers. [17]

This is, of course, a direct statement of the conflict between kin and political principles. The territorial state is to receive the loyalty previously accorded the kin group, and this can only be done by personifying the state, an essentially impersonal structure. Plato remarks that the fiction is an old Phoenician tale of "what has often occurred before now in other places." [18] Certainly, the myth is precisely of the type we would expect in societies in transition from kin to civil structure, that is, in societies engaged in a primary kin-civil conflict.

There is a peculiar parallel with Dahomean usage here, not in the form of myth, but in actual social convention. In Dahomey, every important official in the emerging state structure had a female counterpart within the king's compound. This woman, termed his "mother," had precedence at "court," acting as a sort of buffer between the official and the king and personalizing the purely material relationship involved.[19] The bureaucrats were mustered from the local villages, the conquered and subordinate areas; they had no kin ties with the royal clan or dynastic lineage. The system of "civil mothers" thus symbolized the new connections that had begun to develop in distinction to the old kin loyalties. The idea of the motherland, or fatherland, then, although expressed in kin terms, seems coincident with the rise of the state, at the point where the *problem* of political loyalty begins. This, I believe, is the meaning of Plato's fiction, concretely revealed in Dahomean usage.

It should be noted that Plato apparently confines the fiction of the "earth-born heroes" to the guardians and auxiliaries. The ordinary people, composed of brass and iron, are to live under ordinary family circumstances. No extraordinary behavior of any kind is expected of them, certainly no unusual loyalty to the state. Their worldly concerns, their emotional ties, and their inferior natures are conceived as making such behavior impossible. The soldiers guard the city, the guardians rule it; acquiescence and temperance, a living up to their own limited possibilities, are the demands made on the mass of people. That, and the labor which supports the upper classes. The economic producers are, of course, deprived of political means; in the ideal state this was visualized as the solution to the political problem. Yet Plato seems uncertain. He speaks of the soldiers selecting a spot "whence they can best suppress insurrection, if any prove refractory within," [20] and also of their maintaining "peace among our citizens at home . . . [that they may not] have the power to harm us." [21]

One further point is worth consideration. The selectively bred, but family-less, upper classes are to refer to all peers as brothers and sisters and to the members of the older generation as father and mother, seemingly congruent with extended family or clan usage. However, the upper classes represent what can be technically termed a collective, not a community, that is, the relational forms are retained, but the substance is lacking.[22] What we confront here is a rather interesting politicization of kin terminology, as in the case of the Dahomean "civil mothers," in direct opposition to primitive behavior. The latter is always based on concrete and complex family relationships which may then be extended outward to include remote relatives, strangers, or even natural phenomena. But, as we have seen, the mothers of the upper classes are not to know their own children.[23] They are to be relieved of all domestic and maternal responsibility, and thus converted into ideal instruments of the state, fully equal, in this respect, to the men.

The above, then, is a rough outline of class structure and function in the *Republic*. In general, and in the particulars considered, it is the antithesis of what Kroeber, for one, has called "primitive democracy." [24]

IV

There is, I believe, a keystone in the soaring arch of Plato's argument, an imperative on which it must inevitably rest. In this imperative, the statism of the republic culminates, as does its opposition to the primitive.

The dramatists, the makers of tragedy and comedy, the "imitative poets," as Plato calls them, are to be exiled, and their works are to be abolished or heavily censored. Socrates says:

When any one of these pantomimic gentlemen, who are so clever that they can imitate anything, comes to us, and makes a proposal to exhibit himself and his poetry, we will fall down and worship him as a sweet and holy and wonderful being; but we must also inform him that in our State such as he are not permitted to exist; the law will not allow them.[25]

Plato has already given us a reason for this, quoted above in connection with the division of labor: ". . . [in] our State human nature is not twofold or manifold, for one man plays one part only." The "pantomimic gentlemen," Homer or Aeschylus, for example, have no place in the class and occupational structure of the republic, assimilated, as it is, to the doctrine of essences or ultimate forms. Socrates makes this clear to Adeimantus: ". . . human nature appears to have been coined into yet smaller pieces, and to be as incapable of imitating many things well, as of performing well the actions of which the imitations are copies." [26]

But before pursuing Plato's theory of art, which emerges so logically out of the dialogue, let us examine some of the simpler reasons for establishing a "censorship of the writers of fiction" [27] and the implications thereof.

The poets are perceived as impious, and corrupters of youth. They misrepresent the nature of God, which is absolutely good, by spinning tales of rage and ribaldry in heaven. If at all possible, children in the ideal state should be told that conflict is unholy, and has never existed among the gods or between citizens. The wicked must always be represented as miserable, "because they require to be punished, and are benefitted by receiving punishment from God," but God must never, in verse or prose, be considered the author of evil, for such a fiction would be suicidal in "any well-ordered commonwealth." The poets, such as Euripides, must not be permitted to say that suffering is the work of God, or if it is of God, they "must devise some explanation . . . such as we are seeking." The task of the poet, then, is to justify the ways of God to man, to buttress morality in the republic. And the ultimate impiety is to speak, with Homer, of "Zeus, who is the dispenser of good *and* evil to us." [28]

Moreover, the poets are inappropriately emotional. They portray death and the underworld in lurid terms; they lament the fallen warrior, and rail against fortune, whereas, in the republic, "the good man . . . will not sorrow for his departed friend [or son, or brother], as though he had suffered anything terrible, [since he] is sufficient for himself . . . and therefore is least in need of other men." [29] What is worse, the poets portray famous men, heroes, even the gods themselves, in undignified postures of grief or frenzy. Nor can Homeric laughter, whether indulged in by men or gods, be tolerated; in men it leads to "violent reaction[s]," and it is a falsification of the nature of God. Hence, such verses from the *Iliad* as "inextinguishable laughter arose among the blessed gods, when they saw Hephaestus bustling about the mansion," must be excised. [30]

Finally, the heresy of the poets is expressed in the conception of

God as a magician, "and of a nature to appear insidiously now in one shape, and now in another—sometimes himself changing and passing into many forms, sometimes deceiving us with the semblance of such 'transformations.' " [31] For, "the gods are not magicians who transform themselves, neither do they deceive mankind in any way." [32]

Thus far, then, there are three related reasons for Plato's antagonism to the poets. First, they ascribe a dual nature to the gods, that is, the gods are the authors of good *and* evil. Second, they portray the gods as extravagantly emotional, sometimes obscenely so, as in the case of Zeus, who, at the sight of Hera, "forgot . . . all [his plans] in a moment through his lust." [33] Third, they present the gods in a variety of shapes and deceptive appearances.

I submit that Plato's objections converge to a direct antagonism against the transformer, or trickster, image of the gods, projected by the poets, but, in fact, "one of the oldest expressions of mankind," as Paul Radin has conclusively shown. [34] The Trickster is an authentically primitive figure, appearing in his sharpest form among primitive peoples, a bestial, human, and divine being, knowing "neither good nor evil, yet . . . responsible for both." Trickster "is at the mercy of his passions and appetites," is devoid of values, "yet through his actions all values come into being." At the same time, all figures associated with Trickster, for example the "various supernatural beings" and man, possess his traits. Thus, Plato says the poets must not be permitted to "persuade our youth that the Gods are the authors of evil, and that heroes are no better than men"; for "everybody will begin to excuse his own vice when he is convinced that similar wickednesses are always being perpetrated by 'The kindred of the Gods, the relatives of Zeus.' " He gives as an example "the tale of Theseus, son of Poseidon, or of Peirithous, son of Zeus, [who went forth] to perpetrate a horrid rape." [35]

In his never ending search for himself, Trickster changes shape, and experiments with a thousand identities. He has enormous power, is enormously stupid, is "creator and destroyer, giver and negator." Trickster is the personification of human ambiguity. He is the archetype of the comic spirit, the burlesque of the problem of identity, the ancestor of the clown, the fool of the ages.

Inevitably, Trickster must be banished from the republic, wherein identity is a matter of pure, ideal, unambiguous forms, and where men are to be totally and strategically socialized. The poets who have created or inherited Trickster's image of the world are, it follows, to be silenced. Once again, Plato's opposition to the primitive is clear, if not necessarily conscious.

It would be possible to claim that Plato's negative image of the poets themselves is that of the trickster, for has he not called them "pantomimic gentlemen" and "imitators"? And may we not add that Plato sensed and distrusted the old connection between art and magic? This is a sensible, if superficial, interpretation; to deepen it we must explore Plato's theory of art and its implications.

Plato regarded the art of the tragic and comic dramatists, along with that of the painters, as essentially imitative, as dealing with appearances only. The painter, for example, paints a bed, but this image is "thrice removed" from the truth. The ideal form or essence of the bed is created by God; this is the eternal bed which the philosopher kings can intuit; it is the bed in truth and goodness, of one nature, essentially inimitable and complete. At a second remove from the truth is the tangible bed created by the artisan, the particular bed, which is a "semblance of existence," [36] but not existence entire as manifested in God's bed. But the bed of the painter is sheer imitation, being neither useful nor ideal. In no sense can it be considered a *creation*. Further, all artists, save those who echo the needs of the state by composing "hymns to the Gods and praises of famous men," [37] are deceivers who, in effect, presume to create but cannot.[38] The painter, for example, does not know how to make a bed nor does he know anything of the work of the cobbler or carpenter whom he may represent. Socrates states: ". . . the imitator has no knowledge worth mentioning of what he imitates. Imitation is only a kind of play or sport, and the tragic poets, whether they write in Iambic or Heroic verse, are imitators in the highest degree." [39] Nor can the artist-imitator have any knowledge of good or evil, "and may be expected, therefore, to imitate only what appears good to the ignorant multitude." [40] Plato seems to mean here that the intuition into pure existence aided by the study of mathematics, a basic subject for the guardians, is also the apprehension of the good, or at least a prerequisite to it. The artist reproduces appearances only, and these vary; pure essence cannot be reproduced, only intuited. Since the artist has no knowledge of the good, he can have no knowledge of evil, nor does he possess any understanding of the useful for he is once removed from the particulars that he copies, hence thrice removed from the truth.[41]

Now, whether or not we accept the terms in which it is couched, this is an argument of extraordinary power and beauty. Plato expressed completely what many who have subsequently shared his attitudes have only dimly perceived; the artist is dangerous, as life is dangerous; he sees too much, because that is all he desires to do, and he presumes to create, to erect man into the role of the creator. But his vision is incomplete, he cannot penetrate to the objective order of the universe, the handiwork of God. And to men of Plato's temperament that objective order, the pure anatomy of reason, is as essential as breathing. Yet if the artist would accept the eternal order, and thus learn humility; if he could convert his art into a public strategy in behalf of an abstract idea of the good, the state would find a place for him. Let the protagonists of Homer, and of poetry in general, prove their worth and they will be returned from exile. Moreover, there is a passionate tie between the artist and the "ignorant multitude," the artist deals, not with intellectual, but with felt and ordered emotional ideas. Emotions ebb and flow, they are an unstable medium in which to work, the artist himself may be unstable, and this is a threat to any establishment. Thus Plato is entirely consistent. He was, it seems, a man of a certain type, incapable of tolerating ambiguity, positive in his conviction of an objective, superhuman good. He believed in God with the cool passion of a mathematician, and he believed, at least abstractly, that the perfectly just city could be established, through perfectly rational and perfectly autocratic means. He began as a poet, and so he must have understood in his own being the old argument between poetry and philosophy to which he occasionally refers. In evicting the dramatist, Plato reveals himself, the nature of the republic, and the functions of art; his motives, of course, are above suspicion.

The poets, then, are to be exiled from the ideal state. There is simply no room for them; they are the first superfluous men. The philosopher kings intuit the universal, ultimate forms, God creates them, and the multitude lives among, and constructs, their particular manifestations. Hence, the class structure of the republic reflects, or is reflected in, the doctrine of forms or essences. It descends from the superior, that is, from the abstract, created by God and grasped by the guardians, to the inferior, that is, to the particular, grasped by the craftsmen, and ordinary citizens, who live in a world of ordinary, useful, sensuous things. Here we encounter platonism enthroned, a political hierarchy perfectly mated to a conceptual one. The "fleshly" Homer, who also presumes to create, is a threat to this structure, and cannot be tolerated.

The class division between the universal and particular, between the institutionalized intellectuals and the economic men reflects, as noted above, a condition that develops with ancient civilization as opposed to the primitive. This is not to say that temperamental distinctions do not exist among primitives, for they do, as Radin has brilliantly shown in his analysis of the thinker and man of action.[42] The point is that among primitives such distinctions complement each other, the concrete and the abstract interpenetrate, "thinker" and "man of action" are tied together; sometimes, as Radin points out, they meet in the same individual, and, in any case, such differences are not politicized. Just as soon as the latter occurs, in early states or as idealized in the *Republic,* there is both an impoverishment and a denial of the sources of human creativity. Further, in early states in the real world, the differential worth often ascribed to people in the various occupations within the broader classes is a political rationalization, generated from the top down. For, not only did accidents of birth and training determine social fate, but the *point of view* from which evaluations were made was that of the scribes, the priests, the nobility. In the *Republic,* in the ideal world, Plato's division of labor and conceptual capacity is said to be genetically determined, the social accident is nullified, yet the division remains artificial because it isolates the abstract from the concrete, the intellectual from the emotional, and considers the crafts-man and the farmer useful but inferior beings, not from the perspective of the priest or noble, but from that of Plato's philosophy.

I submit, further, that the Platonic definition of the abstract has become so entrenched in Western thought that the frequently encountered attitude toward primitives, that they are incapable of or deficient in this capacity, is a manifestation of it. Conversely, the attempt to prove that primitives are capable of abstracting too often centers on the types of abstraction emerging out of the history of Western culture, which would seem quite irrelevant. While it is true that no primitive group is made up of Platonists in the technical sense of that term, for primitives tend to live, as Radin has put it, "in a blaze of reality," and the various politico-conceptual divisions generic to the state have not yet been established, this does not mean that they do not think abstractly. In the basic sense, every linguistic system is a system of abstractions; each sorting out of experience and conclusion from it is an abstract endeavor; every tool is a symbol of abstract thinking; indeed, all cultural convention, all custom, is testimony to the generic human capacity for abstracting. But such abstractions are indissolubly wedded to the concrete; they are nourished by the concrete, and they are, I believe, ultimately, induced, not deduced. They are not, in short, specifically Platonic abstractions, and they do not have the politicized psychological connotations of the latter.

V

Plato's opposition to the drama and dramatist is directly associated with the class and ideational structure of the *Republic*. At its root, this is also an opposition to the primitive, not merely with reference to the trickster, or the old tie between artist and magician, but, more comprehensively, in connection with the form and meaning of the primitive ritual drama.

In the ritual drama, art and life converge, life itself is seen as a drama, roles are symbolically acted out, dangers confronted and overcome, anxieties faced and resolved. Relations among the individual, society, and nature are defined, renewed, and reinterpreted. There is no theater containing these performances, ancestral to the civilized drama; the world is a stage and, at one time or another, all the people are players.

I am, of course, defining the primitive ritual drama in the broadest possible way, that is, as comprising those ceremonies which cluster around life crises or discontinuities, either of the individual or of the group at large. Generally speaking, the latter are concerned with crises arising from the group's relation to the natural environment, while the former are concerned with personal crises, that is, with the individual's relation to himself and the group. In all ritual dramas, however, despite the relative emphasis on the group or the individual, there is an apparent continuity from the individual's setting in the group to the group's setting in nature. Moreover, the problems of identity and survival are always the dominant themes, and it is for this reason that we can, I believe, term these primitive ceremonials, dramas.

To clarify, let us consider those ceremonials which devolve upon personal crises, such as death, marriage, puberty, or illness. These can be considered "existential" situations; that is, people die, marry, sicken, become sexually mature and economically responsible in all societies. In primitive societies, such ordinary human events are rendered extraordinary, that is, they are made meaningful and valuable, through the medium of the dramatic ceremonies. Here we confront man raising himself above the level of the merely biological, affirming his identity, and defining his obligations to himself and to the group. The ritual drama, then, focuses on ordinary human events and makes them, in a sense, sacramental.

At the same time, the ceremonials we are speaking of enable the individual to maintain integrity of self while changing life roles. The person is freed to act in new ways without crippling anxiety, or becoming a social automaton. That is, the person discharges the new status but the status does not become the person. This, I believe, is the central psychological meaning of the theme of death and rebirth, of constant psychic renewal, which is encountered so frequently in primitive ceremonials. It is an organic theme; what one is emerges out of what one was. There is no mechanical separation, only an organic transition, extending, characteristically, over a considerable time, often crowded with events, and never traumatic, but modulated and realistic in its effects.[43]

Hence, the ceremonies of personal crisis are prototypically dramatic in two related ways. They affirm the human struggle for values within a social setting, while confirming individual identity in the face of ordinary "existential" situations such as death or puberty. These ceremonial dramas, then, constitute a shaping, and an acting out of the raw materials of life. All primitives have their brilliant moments on this stage, each becomes the focus of attention by the mere fact of his humanity; and in the light of the ordinary-extraordinary events, his kinship to others is clarified. Moreover, these ritual dramas, based on the typical crisis situations, seem to represent the culmination of all primitive art forms; they are, perhaps, the primary form of art, around which cluster most of the aesthetic artifacts of primitive society —the masks, poems, songs, myths, above all the dance, that quintessential rhythm of life and culture.

Ritual dramas are not automatic expressions of the folk spirit. They were created, just as were the poems, dances, and songs that heighten their impact, by individuals moving in a certain cultural sequence, formed by that tradition and forming it. Whether we call these individuals "poet-thinkers," "medicine men," or "shamans," terms used by Paul Radin,[44] seems unimportant. Plainly, they were individuals who reacted with unusual sensitivity to the stresses of the life cycle and were faced, in extreme cases, with the alternative of breaking down or creating meaning out of apparent chaos. Let us call them primitive dramatists. The meanings they created, the conflicts they symbolized, and sometimes resolved in their own "pantomimic" performances, were felt by the majority of so-called ordinary individuals. There was, of course, magic here too; but, more deeply, there was a perception of human nature that tied the group together. The primitive dramatist served as the "lightning rod" for the commonly experienced anxieties, which, in concert with his peers and buttressed by tradition, the primitive individual was able to resolve. This is not to say that the primitive dramatist simply invented meanings promiscuously. It was always done within a given socio-economic and natural setting. But he shaped dramatic forms through which the participants were able to clarify their own conflicts and more readily establish their own identities.

There was an organic tie, then, between the primitive dramatist and the people at large, the tie of creation and response, which is, in itself, a type of creation. The difference was that the dramatist lived under relatively continuous stress, most people only periodically so. Thus the dramatist was in constant danger of breakdown, of ceasing to function, or functioning fantastically, in ways that were too private to elicit a popular response. In this prototypical primitive situation, we can, I think, sense the connection that binds the psychotic to the "shaman" whom we have called a dramatist and the dramatist to the people at large. The distinctions are a matter of degree. The very presence of the shaman-dramatist is a continuous reminder that life often balances on the knife edge between chaos and meaning, and that meaning is created or apprehended by man coming, as it were, naked into the world.

VI

The Greek drama is the direct heir of the primitive ritual drama, as

Cornford, Murray, and Harrison have helped establish. Indeed it retains various technical ritual elements: the chorus, the conscience of the play, was a vestige of group participation; the plays of Sophocles were watched with an air of "ritual expectancy," [45] Aristophanes was performed at the Dionysiac festivals, and the themes of Greek drama had the style of ritual.

Thus we can begin to apprehend why Plato found it necessary to exile the dramatist, as the very prototype of the artist, from the republic. The dramatist is tied to the "ignorant multitude," he presumes to create meanings and reveal conflicts, he senses in his own being the ambiguity of man, and he is concerned with the ordinary-extraordinary things, with values as a problem and the common human struggle for personal identity. Such men are dangerous precisely because they view life as problematical in the best of states; they clarify what others feel. Hence, they must either be confined to composing "hymns to the Gods and praises of famous men," or exiled.

We must remember that in the republic the problem of identity is presumably solved in terms of a political interpretation of higher and lower human natures. Such an institutionalized human identity is entirely contrary to the dramatist's perceptions; it is equally foreign to the mind of primitive man. The dramatist, as a dramatist, cannot believe in such stark and ultimate separations between men or within the individual man. When Shakespeare writes his tragedies of kings, he plays out their conflicts against a specific socio-economic background, but in the end he tells all of us about ourselves, and the "multitude" in the pit responds. And was not Shakespeare, in a sense, all the characters he constructed, what Plato would call a gross "imitator"?

Nor can the dramatist deny the sensuous, earthy things, since his plots are based on the "existential" situations: marriage, death, the coming to maturity, sickness of mind and body, the recurring issues in the inner relations among men, the very themes that served as the occasions for the primitive drama of personal crisis. Let me put it as plainly as I can. In the end, the dramatist must either become an antagonist to Plato's perfectionist God, or he must cease being a dramatist. Within his own lights, the philosopher was right.

VII

If the dramatist is a tragedian, then he is grimly concerned with the problem of identity, self-definition, integrity; for tragedy is no more than the dissolution of personal identity and social value through behavior to which the hero is compelled, and of which he is, sooner or later, aware. *The civilized tragic drama is, then, a free elaboration on the theme of identity, celebrated in the primitive ritual.*

If the dramatist is a comedian, then he burlesques the problem of identity, he laughs it out of court, he stands aside and lets men make fools of themselves; men, he tells us, with Aristophanes, are everything but what they presume to be. *The civilized comic drama, then, is based on the trickster's primitive image of the world, on identity, as it were, turned inside out.* It is a celebration of the failure of identity.

Among primitives, the most serious rituals, those ancestral to the modern tragedy, and the ancient comic spirit of the trickster are often mingled. In Wintun, Pueblo, and Kind ceremonials, for example, "in nearly every instance it is the very thing which is regarded with greatest reverence or respect which is ridiculed," as Steward states.[46] The Dionysiac tradition of the satyr (or trickster) play following the tragic trilogy echoes this primitive usage.

It should be clear, then, that on every major count Plato's exile of comedy and tragedy was inevitable; for the dramatist, in his elemental—or, better, primitive—nature, would have worked havoc with the structure of the ideal state, and its ideology of identities.

But if one exiles or diminishes the artist, who, then, helps discover and dramatize the people to themselves; and if the people are considered incapable of attaining to real understanding, a view obviously not held here but essential to the *Republic,* how, then, are value and meaning to be transmitted to them? Plato answers this question, although he does not ask it. The royal or noble lie, the manufactured or applied myth filtering down from above, that is, official propaganda, is to provide the popular *raison d'être* of the republic. The youth are to be told, in morality tales, that they live in the best of all possible worlds. We have already quoted the fictions which justify the class structure. These "lies," these political, as opposed to primitive, myths are the means for fixing personal and social identity for the majority of people in the ideal state, in the absence of the artist, both as a specialized figure and as an inherent aspect of the personality of every man.

But if the philosopher kings can lie in the name of the public good, and in the interests of a higher truth accessible only to them, the common people cannot. Socrates says: "It seems that our rulers will have to administer a great quantity of falsehood and deceit for the benefit of the ruled." [47] And further, "for a private man to lie to them in return is to be deemed a more heinous fault than for the patient or the pupil of a gymnasium not to speak the truth about his own bodily illnesses to the physician or to the trainer, or for a sailor not to tell the captain what is happening about the ship and the rest of the crew." [48]

VIII

Plato was a sober, shrewd, sometimes witty, but hardly comic, idealist; he constructed his heavenly city, brick by brick, with great care and impeccable intentions. When he has finished—and what a craftsman he was—we confront a shining, impervious structure, a luminous monolith, a society with no problems, no conflicts, no tensions, individual or collective. As the *Republic* approaches its end of perfect justice and harmony, it becomes perfectly inhuman. It is so abstractly and ruthlessly wise, so canny and complete an exercise in statecraft, that were we to disregard Plato's temperament, we should have to consider him one of the most skilled totalitarian thinkers in history, the first state utopian, as opposed to the primitive utopians. His historic fault, that speaks to us across millennia, is not merely in his anthropology, it is certainly not his intoxication with God, abstract though that was, but rather that he, who so fastidiously shunned politics, should have insisted upon the politicization of his faith. Even Cornford, an eloquent defender of Plato,[49] sees him finally as president of the Nocturnal Council, an inquisitor. His prisoner, of course, is Socrates.

NOTES

[1] Although Plato makes a passing reference to a kind of idyllic rusticity which some of his interpreters have called "primitive" life, it bears no resemblance to the latter at all and serves merely as a foil for his developing rationale of the state. See *The Republic of Plato*, trans. by B. Jowett (Oxford, Clarendon Press, 1925), p. 53.

[2] Ralph Waldo Emerson, *Representative Men: Seven Lectures* (Boston and New York, Houghton, Mifflin and Company, 1903), pp. 39-40.

[3] F. M. Cornford, *The Unwritten Philosophy and Other Essays* (Cambridge, The University Press, 1950), p. 129.

[4] J. B. Bury, *A History of Greece to the Death of Alexander the Great* (London, Macmillan, 3d ed., 1956), p. 56.

[5] *The Dialogues of Plato,* trans. by B. Jowett (New York, Bigelow, Brown, 1914). Vol. II, *The Republic,* p. 303. All citations, unless otherwise indicated, are to this edition.

[6] Although the details of the chronicler's observations are, in all likelihood, distorted, his conclusion is sound. Stanley Diamond, *Dahomey: A Proto-State in West Africa* (Ph.D. Dissertation, Columbia University, 1951), p. 26. Microfilm. This is a study of a society in transition from kin to civil structure and involved in a kin-civil conflict that ramifies throughout the culture.

[7] Stanley Diamond, "Kibbutz and Shtetl: The History of an Idea," *Social Problems,* V (Fall, 1957), 71-99.

[8] *Republic,* p. 68.

[9] *Ibid.,* p. 102. Compare this with the famous passage from *As You Like It:* "And one man in his time plays many parts." Shakespeare would have been excluded from the republic on the double score of being both a tragedian and a comic dramatist.

[10] Melville J. Herskovits, *Dahomey, An Ancient West African Kingdom,* I (New York, J. J. Augustin, 1938), p. 30.

[11] V. Gordon Childe, *Man Makes Himself* (New York, New American Library, 1955), p. 149.

[12] Cornford, *Unwritten Philosophy,* p. 134.

[13] *Republic,* p. 129.

[14] However, Plato's philosophy could, today, be characterized as both transcendental and essentialist.

[15] *Ibid.,* p. 187.

[16] *Ibid.,* pp. 191-92.

[17] *Ibid.,* p. 129.

[18] *Ibid.,* p. 128.

[19] Diamond, *Dahomey,* p. 91.

[20] *Republic,* p. 130.

[21] *Ibid.,* p. 128.

[22] For a recent, and rich, analysis of the distinction between collective and community, see Erich Kahler, *The Tower and the Abyss* (New York, George Braziller, Inc., 1957).

[23] Plato's educational psychology is what we would probably term "mechanically behavioristic." The attenuation of immediate kin ties among the élite, and the emphasis on morality tales, would tend to diffuse emotional-intellectual growth; the tensions that provide leverage for such growth can hardly be generated by institutions and abstractions. Further, the collective rearing of élite children would probably have defeated itself in the end by not producing enough emotion to secure loyalty. See, for example, the writer's remarks on collective rearing in the Israeli Kibbutz. "Kibbutz and Shtetl," *Social Problems,* V (Fall, 1957), 88-93.

[24] A. L. Kroeber, *Anthropology: Race, Language, Culture, Psychology, Prehistory* (New York, Harcourt, Brace, rev. ed., 1948), p. 281.

[25] *Republic,* p. 102.

[26] *Ibid.,* p. 98.

[27] *Ibid.,* p. 73.

[28] *Ibid.,* pp. 75-78.

[29] *Ibid.,* p. 86.

[30] *Ibid.,* p. 88.

[31] *Ibid.,* p. 78.

[32] *Ibid.,* p. 82.

[33] *Ibid.,* p. 91.

[34] Paul Radin, *The Trickster, A Study in American Indian Mythology,* with commentaries by Karl Kerenyi and C. J. Jung (London, Routledge and Kegan Paul, 1956), p. ix.

[35] *Republic,* p. 93.

[36] *Ibid.,* p. 380.

[37] *Ibid.,* p. 396.

[38] As Joyce Kilmer confessed, "Poems are made by fools like me, but only God can make a tree."

[39] *Republic,* p. 389.

[40] *Ibid.*

[41] For a perfectly antithetical view of the artist, written by a great artist, see Goya's statement in the catalogue to *Los Caprichos:* "Painting, like poetry, selects from the universe the material she can best use for her own ends. She unites and concentrates in one fantastic figure circumstances and characters which nature has distributed among a number of individuals. Thanks to the wise and ingenious combination, the artist deserves the *name of inventor and ceases to be a mere subordinate copyist.*" (Italics added.)
The absolute, reciprocal antagonism of the true artist and Platonism could not be more pertinently expressed. But this antagonism, it must be said, on the artist's side, is not necessarily directed against a belief in God or religiosity as such, only against the removal of God from the concretely human, i.e., against the turning of God into an abstraction. All religious art of any stature, and all religious artists worthy of the name, from the Byzantines and Giotto through Michelangelo to Blake and Rouault (confining the example to a fragment of the "Western" tradition), inscribe their vision in the flesh and see God either as an aspect of man's nature or as a perception to which every man is capable of attaining, usually out of his agony. Hence God may be apprehended by the artist as objectively real, yet always in the most ordinary, unexpected, various, but human guises. The institutionalized and abstract God of the church and the philosophers is never the God of the artist, though called by the same name. The human distance between Plato's God and Blake's is infinite.

[42] Paul Radin, *Primitive Man as Philosopher* (New York, Dover, 1957).

[43] I use the term "traumatic" here in the sense of deep, psychic trauma. This is not to deny the pain and suffering often involved in primitive rituals, but the personal and traditional meanings infusing them, the conventional structuring of the situation, strip these experiences of the unwitting, and pathological, ramifications of trauma.

[44] Paul Radin, *Primitive Religion, Its Nature and Origin* (New York, Dover, 1957).

[45] Francis Fergusson, *The Idea of a Theater* (New York, Doubleday, "Anchor Books," n.d.), p. 40.

[46] J. H. Steward, "The Ceremonial Buffoon of the American Indian," in *Papers of the Michigan Academy of Science, Arts, and Letters,* XIV (1930), 187-207.

[47] *The Republic of Plato,* trans. by A. D. Lindsay (New York, E. P. Dutton, "Everyman's Library," 1940), p. 148.

[48] *The Republic,* trans. by Jowett, p. 89.

[49] Cornford, *Unwritten Philosophy,* p. 67.

PART II

Approaches to Culture

EMPATHY, OR "SEEING FROM WITHIN"

By Robert H. Lowie

THE GENERAL PRINCIPLES of empathy and of individual differences have been enunciated many times by many people in many different connections. Yet, neither seems as yet to have permeated ethnological thought in all its ramifications. It has seemed to me a good idea to review the development of these principles and to apply them in fields where they are often disregarded. Modern man is still intolerant, and he still fails to see his own culture "from within." It is somewhat difficult to classify the phenomena that I am envisaging, and there may be some overlapping from one section of this paper to another, but for purposes of convenience, I will group the data under "Empathy in Evaluating Cultures," "Empathy in Language," "Empathy in Politics," and "Empathy in Religion."

Empathy in Evaluating Cultures

As soon as ethnologists began seriously to study primitive cultures, they became aware of the problems involved in understanding what they saw as contrasted with merely describing it. Thus, Spencer and Gillan, when observing Central Australians endeavored—whether successfully or not—"as best we could to enter into their feelings." R. R. Marett, commenting upon this procedure remarked: "It still remains a rare and almost unheard-of thing for an anthropologist to be on such friendly terms with a savage as to get him to talk intimately about himself and reveal the real man within." Karl von den Steinen, celebrated for his geographical and ethnographical studies in Brazil, put the case by warning against looking at primitives through the spectacles of civilization. As a matter of fact, Johann Gottfried von Herder had already in the eighteenth century taught that every people and every epoch must be judged in accordance with local and temporal conditions, not by any extraneous standards.

The late Dr. Lowie was Emeritus Professor of Anthropology at the University of California.

An important aspect of this point of view is that a scientist's business is never to pass moral judgment. As Henry Sumner Maine wrote in the second half of the last century: "It is not the business of the scientific engineer to assert good or evil of any particular institution. He deals only with existence and development." But this enlightened view was far ahead of many of Maine's scholarly contemporaries. As a consequence of evolutionist enthusiasm many otherwise estimable writers naïvely assumed that the Western nations of Europe and the United States had reached the acme of progress, and that other peoples were to be judged by the distance that separated them from the author's compatriots in, say, 1870. They paid no attention to the context of a given practice and continually assessed the moral value of a given custom without any attention to what was really going on in the minds of indigenous or exotic peoples.

Sir John Lubbock, later Lord Avebury, furnishes a glaring example. A banker by profession, a naturalist by avocation, he was a versatile writer on finance, animal psychology, prehistory, and ethnology; and on particular topics he made genuine contributions. Yet by way of supporting his general thesis, he is forever delivering ethical pronouncements that would be irrelevant if correct, and that often rest upon the flimsiest of evidence. The Damara are said to have "no perceptible notion of right or wrong"; the Yoruba "are wholly deficient in what the civilized man calls conscience." He does not consider how such sweeping generalizations could be established even after a prolonged acquaintance with the tribes in question.

As soon as we learn the circumstances of what at first may seem revolting callousness, the acts that have shocked us often lose their sinister character. Take two cases of infanticide recorded by Egede, an early missionary to Greenland. He is of course appalled, but by giving the concrete setting he enables us to see more clearly what was involved. Here is an entry from his diaries in 1725:

A mother had died three days after the delivery of a child. Since no other woman capable of nursing was willing to accept and bring up the child, pretending that otherwise she would have nothing for her own children, the man found himself obliged, having no food for so tender an infant, to put it into the mother's grave, where it found a pitiable death.

Ten years later a corresponding incident was reported by the same witness:

A widower committed the atrocity of throwing his newborn child down a high cliff; he did it with closed eyes in order not to look at his child's death. His excuse was that the mother had died and there was nobody able to nurse the infant, thus it would have had to die slowly, and, he added sadly, in this way everything was over quickly.

It is not astonishing that Egede characterizes these deeds as "inhuman," but he gives us the information to assess them fairly according to our own standards. The Eskimo fathers were evidently *not* acting from brutal callousness; in the absence of substitutes for the mothers and of nursing homes, they acted as seemed best in the children's interest. One of them shut his eyes because he could not bear to see his little one dashed to pieces.

Similarly, the supposedly cruel abandonment of aged persons in the Arctic by their sons and daughters assumes a quite different aspect when one understands the background. In his realistic story *Eskimo,* Peter Freuchen graphically describes how an old woman no longer able to keep up with her family *herself* requests that she be left behind. Her son vehemently protests and persuades her to make another effort. Only when it turns out that in the long run she simply could not keep up with the rest—and would therefore endanger everyone's food supply —her son, sick at heart, consents to abandon her. To take note of such emotional concomitants of acts is what we mean by "seeing from within."

"Infanticide" and "abandonment of aged parents" turn out to be blanket terms, each covering diverse phenomena, and it is the ethnologist's duty to demonstrate that often they are not at all what a superficial reader might assume. He does not need to defend the native's reactions; in fact, he would do better to omit moral judgments altogether.

As a final example, let us consider cannibalism, which is popularly believed to be a mark of extreme bestiality. Actually, it is an ethnographic commonplace that the aborigines who are crudest in their general mode of life generally do not eat human flesh at all, whereas those who most greedily indulge in it are comparatively advanced by almost every criterion commonly used to estimate progress. Georg Schweinfurth, botanist and explorer of the upper Nile, noted this fact in what is now the Belgian Congo as early as about 1870. The Manbettu, he discovered, "were in a far higher grade of culture than many savages who persistently repudiate the enjoyment of human flesh." He describes them as "a noble race of men," men of intelligence, and, in the judgment of their neighbors, faithful in friendly intercourse, and praiseworthy for "the order and stability of their national life." Yet, these people sometimes ate human flesh.

Let us scan some of the varieties of anthropophagy from the point of view of the motives that underlie the practice. The most obvious classification rests upon whether the flesh is eaten for primarily dietetic or for ritualistic reasons; of course, there may be a combination of the two. To take the bull by the horns, we must admit that some primitives ate human flesh because they thoroughly relished it as food. On this aspect of the question it is well to quote the late Sir Peter Buck, himself a half-Maori, and also a British-trained physician. Though in recent times the Maori, Cook Islanders, and Marquesans have been the only Polynesians to admit earlier cannibalism, Buck regards the denial of fellow-Polynesians as due to the horror of the practice imported

by foreign teachers who came from countries abounding in beef, mutton, and other flesh foods. Their ancestors had no lack of different animal foods to give them variety in their diet. It is, perhaps, natural for those who never felt the physiological need to condemn a practice without considering it from a purely dietetic standpoint. The acceptance of modern ideas beclouds the issue and leads to the forgetting of things now regarded with disfavor.

The Batak of Sumatra, who preferred human flesh to pork, were sometimes fiendishly cruel from our point of view in torturing the victim of a feast, but they rarely if ever indulged in wholesale slaughter just to satisfy the craving of their palates. Like various other aborigines in different regions of the globe, they had as the dominant motive the acquisition of the victim's magical powers; for them as for other Indonesians, cannibalism was a way of increasing their store of *spiritual* energy. Further, the Batak ate fellow-tribesmen by way of inflicting the maximal penalty and ignominy for such capital crimes as treason or adultery with a ruler's wife.

Radically different again is the Brazilian practice dubbed "endo-cannibalism," because it was directed against the deceased of one's own tribe. Thus the Tapajó preserved the bodies of their dead in a bone-house. When the flesh had decomposed, the bones were pulverized and mixed with the fermented beverage regularly drunk at feasts. In other words, the people consumed the bones of the dead—obviously, a ritualistic procedure with magical purposes.

Whatever we may think of such customs, they are widely different in import from the original Polynesian practice described by Buck; and neither can be put into the same category with Batak cannibalism as a legal device for the punishment of criminals. In these several instances the conscientious ethnologist must try to stick to his principles and to see the true inwardness of what he is describing. To bemoan the depravity of cannibals would be nowadays as much of an anachronism as it would be for a textbook in physics to introduce comments upon the benevolence of God into an exposition on gravity.

The ethnologist who has mastered Maine's proposition when dealing with the world of aborigines has gone a long way toward professional insight, but he has not yet arrived. The proposition has a corollary that constitutes a test for entrance into a higher grade. For all experience shows that while many learn to look with tolerance, if not with active sympathy, at the quaint ways of exotic peoples there are few of us who can look at practices of which we disapprove in our own culture without voicing the prejudices drilled into us from early childhood. The average ethnologist I have known is, I fear, no superman and differs little from his untutored neighbors. He will merrily give lip service to current theories of his guild and at the same time allow free rein to his biases. A disinterested student of human nature may learn a good deal about his colleagues by treating them with the complaisance he accords to an aboriginal shaman. Never contradicting, he can merely listen, at most interjecting an occasional word of sympathy; thus he is likely to disarm suspicion and not to check the outpouring of his interlocutor's true sentiments. If the student should have any qualms of conscience on the score of insincerity, he may console himself with Alexander von Humboldt's dictum: "In life one owes truth only to those whom one deeply respects."

Empathy in Language

Presumably every language has a number of dialects, and usually those who speak any given dialect have a highly emotional attitude towards it. These variations in speech show a lamentable tendency to become associated with different social levels; thus, dropping "g's" in the United States or "h's" in England immediately degrades the speaker to a lower social caste. In general, the popular assumption seems to be that any particular language has a "pure" or "standard" form, which has been corrupted into its many dialects. Historically, the reverse is unquestionably true. It is the several dialects of Italian, French, and German that are basic; the "standard" language of a country is simply one of the dialects that for some specific reason, political or cultural, has gained ascendancy. Thus, for instance, a Saxon dialect, which was used by Luther for his translation of the Bible, became the foundation of modern "standard" German.

Three specific cases deserve a few words of further explanation: the Judeo-German (Yiddish), the Norwegian Landsmaal, and the Swiss Schwyzerdeutsch. As Edward Sapir, among others, has shown, Yiddish is simply Middle High German developed in various countries in relative isolation from other German dialects. It underwent the changes expected under similar circumstances in any form of speech. That is, it adopted new words from languages spoken by neighbors and it suffered alterations in phonology and grammar. Some distinctive words are simply good German words that have become obsolete among Germans. Yet the revulsion of German speakers against Yiddish has been disproportionately violent. My own prejudice against the "jargon" and derivatively against its users, was the last bias that I had to overcome, and I was well into my sixties before I succeeded in doing so.

The Norwegian conflict over the proper national language can be understood only in the light of history. Norway was for a long time a province or mere dependency of Denmark, not only politically but also culturally. Her peoples appeared to the Danes as uncouth backwoodsmen, and specifically Norse words were treated as vulgarisms. In the early nineteenth century three main currents of speech could be distinguished. There was the Danish language, obligatory for authors who wished to see their writings in print, since the only outlets were publishers in Denmark. There were the despised rustic dialects, different in each mountain valley. Finally, there was "Dano-Norwegen," the urban tongue of the educated, based on Danish yet inevitably different from it, since no form of speech is static.

With the rise of European nationalism in the last century, Norway was profoundly affected, and in some quarters a veritable Danophobia sprang up. Not only were folklorists enthusiastically studying the traditions of the peasantry, but the people generally felt themselves to be a unique nation, with a need for a national language. As in other countries the dialects proved to be, not corruptions of a "standard" cultivated form of speech, but natural indigenous growths. They were, in fact, descendants from ancient Norse. The dialect investigator, Ivor Aasen (1815–96) combined several of what he considered the oldest of these dialects into a synthetic tongue that came to be known as "landsmaal" in opposition to the "riksmaal" that was in use for literary purposes.

There resulted a violent dispute over the legitimacy of the innovation. Ibsen vehemently derided landsmaal as the gibberish of monkeys, while others hailed it as a symbol of liberation from the Danish yoke. In any case, the new language maintained itself, so that by 1899 a chair for it was created at the University of Christiania, and some thirty years later over a quarter of the elementary schools used the synthetic peasant tongue as a medium of instruction.

Still another instance of the same category is offered by Alamannic Switzerland. The German Swiss does not speak German but one of the regional varieties of Schwyzerdeutsch; and this is spoken by all classes of society and on all educational levels, even though newspapers are printed in standard German and the latter language is used for university lectures. What at least some influential Alamannic organizations resent is the defilement of the *dialects* by standard German. From this angle it has seemed essential to compose dialect primers, not as a technical linguistic task, but as a "guide to good dialectal speech."

In all three of these instances the outsider is struck by the emotional values that have become attached to a strictly linguistic matter. Also, he is likely to consider the whole business as much fuss about nothing. Why should the Jews cling to their Yiddish? Why should the Alamannic Swiss not rid themselves of their dialects and merge in a pan-German language group? Why should the Norwegians attach so much importance to a synthetic language? Such practical considerations are secondary when it comes to a renunciation of the vernacular. The issue becomes one of honoring traditions and the unique value of a particular national or regional character. Looked at from without, all these and comparable attitudes are meaningless. But viewed from within, they present a different picture. When the Swiss insists upon speaking his regional dialect, when the Norwegian repudiates Danish, when the Israeli establishes Hebrew as a national language or the European Jew continues to speak a dialect that he knows will put a brand upon him among many of his fellow-countrymen, they are not being merely stubborn and unprogressive; they are setting up standards of major value—of liberty, independence, and the right to individual living. In short, to understand these puzzling phenomena and to evaluate correctly the emotionalism with which they are surrounded, one must see them from within, as the native sees them.

Empathy in Politics *

Nazism furnishes a capital test of ethnological maturity. Admittedly, horrible deeds were perpetrated under the Nazi regime, and a natural reaction on the part of the sufferers and of generous sympathizers is to blame everything on the German national psychology. In trying to get a clearer notion of what went on inside the German people—as a group or individually—during the crucial years we shall be helped by sticking to two elementary professional principles: the dynamic approach to social phenomena and the variability of individuals within a group.

The dynamic approach at once precludes our treating Nazism as being from the first what it became at the end. Let us consider the party program as launched in the early twenties and the situation of the fatherland at that time. Germany had been bitterly humiliated, and in the wake of defeat came inflation and widespread misery. Toward the well-intentioned but feeble republican government the Allies assumed and preserved a uniformly forbidding attitude. In this period of despair Adolf Hitler appeared with a gospel of hope that a German sociologist compared at the time with the messianic cults of aboriginal tribes. It is irrelevant whether or not the leaders of the movement were sincere; for the present purpose we are concerned with the effect of their message upon a despondent, downtrodden, starving population. The party program, which was declared to be immutable,

---

* It should be noted that in this section of his paper Dr. Lowie gives an illuminating example of his fundamental thesis: that it is possible to understand the attitudes and motives of people who live or have lived in a culture to which one is hostile—as he was to the Nazi regime.—*Editor.*

contained little to repel an average, well-meaning reader. The same holds for the officially sanctioned exposition of National Socialist aims as printed in the supplementary volume of *Der Grosse Brockhaus* (1935), the principal encyclopedia, soon after the party was in the saddle. There were indeed ideas that any Western liberal would reject, notably the leader principle, racialism, and the suggestion of a controlled press, but even these concepts were then presented in a moderate form. The leader professed to embody the popular will, to suppress not personal liberty but merely personal arbitrariness. Jews were not to be exterminated, but to be relegated to the status of unassimilable aliens. As Jews they might live in the Reich in accordance with their special needs, might fly the Zionist (though not the German) flag, and maintain their distinctive cultural life.

Further, some of the policies proposed and in part executed were rather advanced, even by Western standards. Who could reasonably oppose the denunciation of the spoils system, the promotion of industry, the elimination of war racketeering, the establishment of large old-age pensions, or a far-reaching land reform? The program included such eminently advanced notions as aiding the talented offspring of poor parents and the banning of child labor. In the earlier years of Hitler's rule some of his adherents drew parallels between his policies and President Roosevelt's New Deal. The party was pictured as being not only nationalistic but also, as its name implied, highly socialistic.

To welcome this program, then, implied no innate tendency to sadism; even the features less appealing to democratic tastes were not phrased in a revolting form, and others could easily arouse the enthusiasm of the progressively minded. That a people groaning under unemployment and constantly rebuffed in the most mortifying manner by the victors of the First World War should welcome the only visible way out of their slough of despond was perhaps politically naïve, but it was psychologically intelligible.

Actually, we are understating the case, for the promises were, in the earlier period, in appreciable degree followed by fulfillment. Unemployment seemed to vanish as though by magic, in the twinkling of an eye. As the bitterest enemies of Hitler concede, there was also initially a good deal done on behalf of the poorer classes, educational advantages were extended to them, and persons who would never normally go traveling were sent on recreational tours to Norway and the

Italian lakes. Spiritually, any normal, patriotic German thrilled at Hitler's diplomatic successes; the same powers that had hectored and browbeaten the Weimar government now came crawling in appeasement of the Austrian lance corporal.

But what of the popular reaction to the later excesses of the Nazis, to their tacit neglect of earlier promises? According to weighty evidence, many Germans experienced a change of heart and felt thoroughly disillusioned. It is absurd to suppose that any considerable number approved the pogroms of 1938 and later. Hans Driesch, the biologist-philosopher, and a severe critic of the Nazi regime, vigorously denies that the people as a whole favored the atrocities ordered by those in control. Contrary to the leaders' claims, there was no spontaneous uprising against the Jews; the riots were organized from above and were at times deprecated even by members of the SS. Notwithstanding the danger of being sent to concentration camps for criticizing the official acts of cruelty, men strongly condemned them in Driesch's hearing, and his observations are borne out by neutral Swiss observers.

Our second anthropological principle, individual variability, is bound up with the first. Not only did attitudes toward the regime change, but at every stage personal differences came to the fore. The large mass of any population tends to be opportunistic, and as the Second World War brought privation many took a less rosy view of leadership; and as early successes were followed by setbacks there were further misgivings and ultimate defections. To what extent a particular German was affected at a particular stage of developments would depend upon his individual character. The range of variation need only be hinted at. At one extreme were the fanatical worshipers of the leader and the sadists who allowed their vicious impulses to run riot as long as they could. At the other extreme were those who consistently opposed the underlying doctrines of the regime and bravely combated it from the start, regardless of the cost to themselves. The carping critic asks how many there were of these humanitarian fighters, and in the nature of things there can be no statistical answer. But with great assurance we can state that there were far more than the Germanophobes have been willing to concede. The "generals'" revolt, culminating in the attempt to assassinate Hitler on July 20, 1944, has been much publicized, but it is of far less significance for us than innumerable inconspicuous deeds of less melodramatic character. In this category belongs the revolt of the students in Munich in 1943;

since they distributed handbills against the government, they came to suffer the extreme penalty in consequence of their convictions. As the Swiss Réné Schindler bears witness, "many Germans who refused to participate in the persecution of the Jews had to undergo the penalty of transplantation into concentration camps." From the beginning "Aryan" Germans had been imprisoned and executed for opposing the rules, e.g. by aiding Jews and political dissidents to escape.

Lacking reliable statistical data we must fall back upon the statements of individual sufferers, who are certainly not likely to gloss over the treatment to which they were subjected during Hitler's supremacy. One of the most revealing of these documents is Else Behrend-Rosenfeld's book, *Ich stand nicht allein* (1945, 1949). The author in no way slurs over the cruelties of the regime, but from this single record the following facts stand clearly forth: To a considerable extent the common folk—maids and railroad porters, for example—displayed much sympathy with the author and in times of stress offered aid in the form of food and other necessities. The nuns of a convent in which a group of Jewish women were billeted went out of their way to supply the sufferers with food and other gifts; they also arranged for surreptitious visits of friends, contrary to governmental regulations. These nuns inspired their unsolicited guests "with the consciousness of not being hated and despised, but of being viewed with sisterly affection." Some German soldiers apologized to Mrs. Rosenfeld for having to do their duty; the inspector in a factory himself urged her to take sick leave before an inspection was due; the head of a state library spontaneously contrived a way by which she could take out books for her husband, in contravention of the law. Finally, when the danger of liquidation arose, Aryan friends helped Mrs. Rosenfeld to escape across the Swiss border, at the risk of their own lives.

When the wearing of a badge was imposed as obligatory on all Jews there were doubtless some Germans who rejoiced at now being able to recognize at once any member of the "Jewish rabble," but others were affected in precisely the opposite way from that presumably expected by the Nazis. Thus, a soldier presented an elderly Jewess with a week's bread-ration stamps; a gentleman on a streetcar offered his seat to a badge-wearing woman; butchers and grocers gave Jews preferential treatment; people from all walks of life extended countless small courtesies to the wearers of the yellow badge.

Confirmation of such observations comes from other sources. Dr.

Eugen Kogon, a liberal Catholic, spent six years in a concentration camp, escaping liquidation only by a lucky chance. He is a severe critic, not only of the Nazis but of the apathy of the people at large, who—out of a population of eighty million—produced only some thousands of heroic rebels. Yet in his realistic and graphic account of life in a camp (*Der SS-Staat*, 1947) he speaks of the numerous and death-challenging fighters of inner opposition against the regime, who in foreign countries still remain unknown. And although his general picture of the camp officials is devastating, he singles out one SS man at Buchenwald who, without any expectation of reward, aided the inmates whenever he could and who at the end risked his life to save the victims.

It would be too much to expect those who suffered directly or indirectly from the Nazis to assume an air of detachment or to discriminate nicely between Germans and Germans. We have, however, seen that some of the victims do draw distinctions between good and bad Germans and even between good and bad Nazis. At all events, the ethnologist's duty is to see the facts discriminatingly, which means seeing the Nazis "from within"—precisely as he sees Polynesian cannibals and Eskimo infanticides.

Empathy in Religion

When the Portuguese explorers found the African Negroes doing reverence to their own handiwork in the form of human effigies, their worship of inanimate objects was naïvely taken as a sign of savage degradation. Tylor already detected the underlying error in this interpretation: the natives did *not* worship the products of their craftsmanship, he argued, but the *spirits* believed to be associated with them. Everything learnt about fetishes since then supports the essentials of this view. An African sculpture remains a mere work of skill without any religious significance to its creator, unless it is supposed to embody a spirit or is consecrated by a sacred chant or some magical substance credited with supernatural power.

My Plains Indians furnish many parallels. Admittedly, the matter is somewhat blurred when the native shifts his ground, now treating an object merely as a token of a sacred reality, now addressing it as though it were a person possessing power in its own right. But the evidence is overwhelming that when a Crow prays to his shield or a feather or an odd-looking rock, he is not worshiping the tangible object but a mysterious being that in a vision granted him the right to treasure the object as a symbol of the superhuman power itself. Long since, it has become a foregone conclusion that the ethnologist will look below the surface and discover what is going on in the votary's mind.

Oddly enough, scholars who enter sympathetically into the attitude of West Africans find themselves quite unable to extend the same tolerance to members of different religious faiths within their own culture. Further, it is amazing how little Protestants and Catholics, for instance, know of one another's beliefs. Thus, the average Protestant seems to suppose that the Immaculate Conception and the Virgin Birth are the same thing. And Catholics can be just as ignorant and prejudiced. I knew one Catholic university professor who taught a course on the Protestant Reformation without ever reading a word written by a Protestant author, because he believed he would risk his immortal soul if he read the works of a heretic. In considering this matter, it is well to recall what Ernst Mach, the physicist-philosopher and long a leader of positivism, had to say about the Catholic Church in his *Mechanik* (7th ed., 1912):

It is popular to describe the conflicts of science with theology or, to put it better, with the Church. And as a matter of fact this is an ample and rewarding theme. On the one hand there is an impressive register of ecclesiastical sins against progress, on the other a considerable series of martyrs, including no lesser figures than Giordano Bruno and Galileo; even so pious a man as Descartes escaped only through the most favorable of circumstances. However, these conflicts have been sufficiently described, and if only these conflicts are stressed, one represents the issue one-sidedly and unfairly. One thereby easily gives the opinion that science has been held down *only* through ecclesiastical pressure and would have risen to unimaginable grandeur if only that pressure had been absent. It is true enough that the struggle of investigation against alien, external powers was not insignificant. In this struggle, furthermore, no means was too bad for the Church if it was able to insure victory, and it proceeded herein more selfishly, ruthlessly, and cruelly than any political party. But the scientists also had a not inconsiderable conflict with their own traditional ideas, especially with the prejudice that everything was to be treated from a theological point of view.

Mach illustrates by quotations from Napier, Pascal, Guericke, Newton, and Euler, stressing the point that they were saying what they did not under compulsion, but from the urge to give vent to their innermost personal convictions. "They felt no pressure from theology. In a city and at a court that harbored Lamettrie and Voltaire, there was no reason for one to conceal his convictions."

Contrary to widespread belief the Catholic Church is not on principle opposed to the teachings of modern geology or evolutionary biology. In 1907, addressing a group of women teachers, Cardinal Faulhaber declared: "Even in the smallest village school it should no longer be said that the creation of the world took place during a span of 6 times 24 hours." In a thorough article on human evolution the late Monsignor John M. Cooper, with exemplary caution, argued that the paleontological evidence supports the derivation of man from an animal form insofar as his physical characteristics go, but that science has by no means removed the barriers between man and the ape as regards human mentality. This proposition is not, however, unscientific; it literally represents the present status of the problem. An unbridged gap still yawns between man's psyche and that of the highest animal. If some assert that the gap will be closed, this statement is precisely as much an expression of faith as the Catholic doctrine that every human soul is implanted by a divine act of creation. There is no proof on either side.

As for illiberal representatives of any faith, there is not much to choose between Catholic and Protestant. Edward B. Tylor, later the foremost of British anthropologists, was not allowed to attend Cambridge or Oxford because he was a Quaker. Norway, nearly 100 percent Lutheran, cruelly discriminated against Quakers in the early part of the nineteenth century and constitutionally excluded Jews from the country until the 1850s. In the United States the ministers of Norwegian immigrants opposed the public school system as unchristian. About a century ago one of them declared: "We must rejoice when we are condemned as being hard-hearted, intolerant, and unchristian . . . . Truth must be exclusive over against darkness." When Björnsen visited Norwegian-American settlements, he came away convinced that their people were priest-ridden bigots.

In order to forestall the charge of a partially pro-Catholic argument, I will close this section with a quotation from a clever Catholic writer that is a prize example of offense against the law of empathy. Mr. Arnold Lunn writes, when contending against Westerners who have exalted Hinduism: "Both Mr. Joad and Professor Haldane have drawn attention to the spiritual values of Hinduism, that refined religion which prescribes for the faithful a diet of cow-dung, which offers little girls of five to become official prostitutes of the temple priests." Irrespective of whether Mr. Joad and Professor Haldane are well or ill informed about Hinduism, Mr. Lunn is here engaging in cheap pettifoggery. For, whatever the merits of their contention, the two gentlemen are not exalting Hinduism *because* it prescribes a diet of cow-dung or *because* little girls become temple prostitutes. In the statement quoted there is no attempt whatever to understand what the author's opponents had in mind. He has made no effort to "see from within."

By and large ethnologists have learned the lesson that alien cultures must be approached objectively and empathetically. Being human, the individual scholar will have his preferences; he may, for instance, prefer the Pueblo Indians to those of the Plains, but he will not seriously erect his personal tastes into absolute norms. Nowadays it is rare for an ethnologist to impose moral evaluations upon his readers. Mindful of Maine's caution, he does not assert good or evil of the subjects of his inquiry.

But there is a corollary to Maine's postulate that is not so generally accepted in practice. If head-hunters and cannibals demand understanding, what of our own political, ethnic, racial, and denominational groups, what of civilized opponents in the arena of international affairs? If the Crow worship of a medicine bundle can be understood, why should one condemn as the worship of idols the innumerable shrines that dot the Bavarian countryside? Is it reasonable to suppose that the two opponents in the "cold war" have made any real effort to see each other's virtues?

The test of the mature ethnologist is the extent to which he can extend the axioms of his professional creed to cover cases in which he is emotionally involved. The pitfalls are innumerable, and hardly anyone will succeed in avoiding all of them. But the ethnologist worthy of his salt will make a determined effort to rise above the partisan level, to project himself into the minds of others—even if they are his fellow-citizens—and to view his own culture from within.

THE ANTHROPOLOGIST AND THE QUESTION OF THE FIFTH DIMENSION

By Gene Weltfish

UNIVERSITY OF NEBRASKA

FOR THE ANTHROPOLOGIST, as well as for the rest of humanity, the human mind still remains the greatest unexplored area of the universe. The anthropologist's dilemma is doubly acute for not only does he encounter fellow minds in his own cultural milieu, but also as his special province he seeks out mankind in his least familiar settings with a view to setting up "contrast situations" to better understand our own lives.

Some anthropologists, especially in times past, have conceived of the material objects produced by native peoples as the most reliable indices of the exotic mind (Graebner, 1911; Perry, 1923; Smith, 1916). But the more thoughtful modern investigator has had a different opinion.

The field of material culture study does seem to offer special opportunities for considering native ways of thinking because of the greater opportunity for "verifiability" and "experiment" or for the exercise of "recognized scientific methods," but when the study is undertaken the investigator discovers a great many unresolved problems in his basic theoretical outlook. Attempting an inventory of the entire material culture of a northern Athabascan people, Osgood (1940) states:

The material culture has been divided into three hundred and thirty-nine items. Using the same data, there might have been a good many more or considerably less. How can one decide what should be considered a variation and what a separate item? One can select as arbiter the form or the function or a number of equally applicable aspects and proceed with great singleness of purpose, but the segmentation seemingly must in the end be arbitrary even allowing for the choice of a primary criterion. I have not found the rational answer to the problem. (p. 56)

Ford (1937), whose essay preceded Osgood's and was read by him, raises the question in the following terms:

If recognized scientific methods are applicable anywhere to the data of sociology and anthropology, the field of material culture would seem to offer the greatest likelihood of success. When considered as one of the many intricate phases of culture, man's material adjustment appears to be comparatively free from the perplexing difficulties which seem so characteristic of other segments of culture. When however, material culture is inspected in relative isolation, the apparent simplicity is transformed into complexity, and the problems encountered become so involved it is even difficult to indicate clearly what is meant by "material culture."

I believe the question is deeply involved in our own dilemma of how man and material are related. It is with this level of discourse that the paper deals.

From another perspective, M. J. Herskovits (1952, pp. 298 ff.) comes to the same impasse as Ford and Osgood. The economic problem he raises is this: Man is *par excellence* the tool-using animal. As such, tools are made to take care of future needs and for the most part, in a sense, represent accumulated capital. How is this type of capital formation to be described and assessed? However simple, there is no culture in which some material of this type is not to be found. Herskovits states:

The question of capitalization of resources in nonliterate societies has ... been given little attention ... because of the direction of anthropological interests toward other aspects of group life than its economic phases. Especially important, again, is the absence in these societies of any ready measure of value. Lacking this, almost any approach not wholly qualitative presents ever-present problems of method which are formidable in scope and have, as far as detailed analysis is concerned, yet to be solved. Our discussion here, therefore, will be focussed essentially on problem. (p. 302)

The inadequacy of the data concerning capital goods in nonliterate societies thus remains to plague the student. (pp. 306-7)

Under the circumstances, Herskovits makes a plea for further research:

There is little point in reproducing here any of the numerous listings of material goods, instruments of production, and public works such as can be found in almost any ethnographic work, inasmuch as, lacking their economic setting, relatively little would be gained by doing so.

But even were this done, we should then only be enlightened on the very general points just mentioned, while of the many further important problems arising out of the presence and use made of these goods and the manner of their control, such an exercise would tell us almost nothing.

At some future time, it is to be hoped students who stress the economics of capitalization in nonliterate societies will turn their attention to these tribes whose technological basis of production and whose material equipment is well known. Building on these essential data, they may then proceed to investigate the problems arising from the fact that these folk have invested their labor power in more or less long-lived goods. Until this is done, however, the incidence and significance of capitalization in non-literate societies can be discussed only in terms of problems to be studied and of possible procedures to be followed.... This much, nevertheless we can say: once such data are collected and made available, there is little doubt that they will provide comparative materials that will enrich our understanding of comparable processes in our own economy.   (pp. 308-9)

Bronislaw Malinowski, in the light of his personal bicultural experience delved deeply into the problem of the cultural significance of exotic material culture in his studies of the Trobriand Islanders of Melanesia. In his preface to his two-volume work, *Coral Gardens and Their Magic* (1935), he states:

Once again I have to make my appearance as a chronicler and spokesman of the Trobrianders, the Melanesian community so small and lowly as to appear almost negligible—a few thousand "savages", practically naked, scattered over a small flat archipelago of dead coral—and yet for many reasons so important to the student of primitive humanity.

The manner in which the so-called savages produce their primary sustenance, store it and handle it, the way in which they surround it with magical and religious beliefs, open problems of the relation between man and environment of some importance to economic philosophy.

Although the name of Malinowski is most commonly associated with the theory of functionalism in anthropology and with his special studies of law, sex habits, and magic and religion of the Trobrianders, his most solid and extensive works deal with their material life. *Argonauts of the Western Pacific* (1922) deals with trading practices, and *Coral Gardens* with horticulture, which, despite the heroic appeal to us of the seagoing life in *Argonauts,* has the highest value in the Trobriand mind. To be a good gardener (*tokwaybagula*), is the greatest aspiration of a *man* (I, 62).

In his preface, Malinowski states of *Coral Gardens* (p. xii): "I believe it is the best I have produced or am ever likely to produce." In attempting to probe the "native mind" through material culture study, Malinowski has made a unique contribution in this work, exploring thoroughly the linguistic aspect of gardening which marks it as one of the most conclusive comparative studies of epistemology extant, a phase of anthropology with which Malinowski dealt more generally in his widely read essay "The Problem of Meaning in Primitive Languages" (1936).

A second major feature of *Coral Gardens* is Malinowski's extensive self-critical comments throughout the study and especially in the second ethno-linguistic volume and its appendices. Adherence to a "functionalist approach" has been taken by some anthropologists as a mandate for underplaying the theoretical significance of technological subjects. In this connection, Malinowski's self-critical estimate of his field work is instructive (I, 460):

... a lack of competence in one aspect—technology—has not perhaps resulted in an inadequacy within its own domain. By dint of hard work I succeeded, I think, in giving a fairly accurate description of the structure of the storehouse. It is rather the relation between the technical description on the one hand, and native theory of stability, foundations and ventilation on the other, which has suffered. As a sociologist I have always had a certain amount of impatience with the purely technological enthusiasms of the museum ethnologist. In a way I do not want to move one inch from my intransigeant position that the study of technology alone and the fetishistic reverence for an object of material culture is scientifically sterile. At the same time, I have come to realize that knowledge of technology is indispensable as a means of approach to economic and sociological activities and to what might be adequately called native science. A thorough grasp of how natives construct a yam-house would have enabled me to judge why they construct in that way, and to discuss with them as between equals, the scientific foundations of their manual systems. It would have also enabled me to assess more rapidly the sociological implications of technological and structural details.

The criticism here is of the study of technological processes and their material products in isolation of their conceptual matrix. The question being posited is, "What are the implications of the technical process and material product for the whole cultural context in all its many ramifications?" rather than an emphasis upon the mechanics of technical production alone.

In the field situation, as was the case with Malinowski, the anthropologist finds observation of technical processes and material production the most ready to hand. And the obtaining of native names for common objects is a simple way of gaining an introduction to an entirely unfamiliar way of life. This reliance on native naming has its pitfalls. Technological operations as such may be fairly obvious to someone who has personal experience of craft procedures, and these do represent a certain level of common knowledge between observer and observed, but when it comes to classification on a psychocultural level, linguistic terms seem to be the most obvious data to be obtained. As examples of this level we might consider Malinowski's comments on such a commonplace object as a "stone axe." The stone axe is used by the Trobriand man in garden work to cut the roots found in the soil, preparatory to planting his seed yams. The axe is called *kema.* Quoting Malinowski (*Coral Gardens*, 1935, Vol. II):

When we translate *kema* by 'axe' we have to be ... on our guard, because here we are dealing with an object which also exists and functions in our culture and it is very important not to assimilate the uses, the form and the material of the native implement with those of our own. In so far as the axe is used in gardening, I have described most of its technical functions and also its magical role. And the meaning of the term *kema* is in the last instance to be derived not from substitution of 'axe' for the native word, but from our knowledge of the role which it plays within native culture, here more specifically within native gardening.   (p. 18)

Of the word 'stone,' viz. the material:

There is no abstract word for 'stone.' A coral stone, a rock, the material of which it is composed are all designated by the term *dakuna.* The natives do not lump these meanings together; but dead coral is the most familiar of this group of objects and, as it is little used for practical or technical purposes, anything made of it can be described without confusion.

The word for stones of plutonic origin imported from the South is *binabina. Binabina* covers rocks of various type and composition, stressing only their alien origin and the non-coral character of their substance; for the significant characteristic of these is that they are not procurable in the Trobriands, but in the D'Entrecasteaux Archipelago. They are not more exactly specified because they do not play a very important part in Trobriand technology, but are mainly used for certain magical purposes.
                    (p. 71)

The axe is made of neither of these materials, but of volcanic tuff. On the word *kema*, which we have translated 'axe,' the following is stated:

In the word *kema, utukema*, ... the material is stressed—the word being applicable to all objects made of volcanic tuff out of which the stone implements were made in the olden days. Here the word covers the rock in the mass, chips or lumps detached from it, the implement made out of it in process of manufacture, the finished blade, and the axe ready for use. This variety of meanings does not create confusion when the word is used within a pragmatic context. On the other hand similarities of the term introduce the necessary unity and gives the familiar element within the situation.   (p. 72)

As an example of such a usage in a pragmatic situation, the case is given of a group of people in a native village (p. 69). One of them is plaiting a bunch of fiber and as the others join him they begin to discuss what he is doing. He has no need to point out that he is holding a bunch of fiber which is derived from the context of the situation. In fact there is no term for 'fiber' or 'bunch of fiber' in Trobriand. What is important is the material which cannot be inferred from the appearance of the bunch; different materials are prepared in different ways and differ in quality and in the purpose for which they will be used. The verbal content of the conversation, therefore, will contain such terms as 'pandanus,' 'ficus,' or 'hibiscus,' calling the bunch by the same name as the whole plant, the flowers, or the fruit. The distinctions made are those which are not contained in the context of the situation, and only that which is not clear in the objective context and necessary for further action is verbally stressed.

Another common object of the planting complex is the basic staple, the yam. Observing a Trobriand gardening family, it would be normal investigative procedure to ask them the name for the yam which they would give as *taytu*. On this word Malinowski gives us the following data (II, 68):

... it is characteristic of the Trobriand language that the more important the term, the more pronounced is the tendency to use it over a wide range of meanings. *Ka'i*, for example, means anything from 'tree,' 'plant,' 'vegetable,' 'wood as material,' 'shrub,' 'magical herbs,' 'leaves,' 'stick,' to the abstract concept 'made of wood,' or 'long object'; in this latter sense it also functions as a classificatory formative. The words *megwa*, 'magic'; *taytu*, 'yam'; *kaulo*, 'crops,' all correspond to capital concepts and are all used in a variety of meanings, some of which are remarkably far-fetched and figurative.

The extension of the word *taytu*, which primarily means the plant (yam) and then the food derived from it and the year in which the crops ripen, is another example.   (p. 69)

The value of naming the year after the most important object in the principal economic activity is readily understandable. The word *taytu* underlines the most crucial aspect of the sequence of the seasons, and its theoretical, emotional and even pragmatic value is clear.   (p. 70)

Malinowski's study has provided us with a clear insight into the many nuances and subtleties with which the human mind approaches the material world, not only in that aspect of it that is an object of contemplation, but that which is intimately tied with man's daily life and survival. Every people that has survived has evolved a unique way of life of which the various aspects form an intricate connected network. A consideration of any one part implies the whole.

Group life is a universal condition of human survival. Grace de Laguna (1927) has made a definitive analysis of the connection between speech and man's adaptation to the external world in the course of group life. Malinowski's work gives us a functioning example of these observations. He has pointed out how speech functions in a concrete situation. In the ordinary coordination of activities, verbal comments and evaluations play an indispensable role. The words remembered will then be denotative of the one or more familiar situations in which they have functioned. For us to arrive at a translation of a native word it is necessary that we approximate the range of situations in which it has commonly functioned.

The evolution of speech and language in man's dealing with the material world, and its relation to the development of the thinking process as expounded by Grace de Laguna stresses a more general characteristic of human thought. The conversations that occur within the context of practical situations described by Malinowski serve the function of cross-checking our individual sense perceptions and evaluations, acting as a corrective of individual misjudgment, or a complementing of sense-perceived qualities, pooled and thus more complete than those observed within the limitations of one person's purview. As De Laguna points out, the more intricate the group life, the richer will be the complement of perceptions available to the individual who participates. At the same time, the outlook of such an individual will be strongly conditioned by his special group experience. The special matrix of the culture in which words or objects function or have functioned is therefore indispensable to any kind of cross-cultural communication. To derive an insight into the native view of the objective world, words and objects can only be evaluated in culture-contextual terms. Malinowski in his ethnolinguistic volume of *Coral Gardens* (II, 14–15), has clearly stated the problem of cross-cultural translation:

The translatability of words or texts between two languages is not a matter of mere readjustment of verbal symbols. It must always be based on a unification of cultural context. Even when two cultures have much in common, real understanding, and establishment of a community of linguistic implements is always a matter of difficult, laborious and delicate readjustment.

When two cultures differ as deeply as that of the Trobrianders and the English; when beliefs, scientific views, social organization, morality and material outfit are completely different, most of the words of one language cannot be even remotely paralleled in the other.

In this situation, Malinowski points out that our only recourse is to use a word or expression in our own language which we do not conceive as a translation, but as a mnemonic device by which we can refer to the native word or expression, which in turn can only be understood if we refer it to its whole cultural context. The mere denotation of a common object with a native word gives us no real insight into its ethnic significance.

We have no way of deriving a generalized designation out of *our* experience for a native word, for the combination of situations in which this one word or its homonyms is used has no equivalent in our lives. If our study of material culture is to open up for us another world-view, the exposure of our ethnically-limited viewpoint upon common objects and material can be a more demanding discipline than most of us have realized. It can also be highly rewarding, for an understanding of many different vistas on the material world can open the way to our supercession of our own ethnic limitations, and give us new insights into our ordinary activities. I think the major difficulty of anthropologists who have studied material culture so far has been their oversimplification of the problem.

Yet apart from its verbal designations and its ethnic significance, the material culture object does have a discrete identity and its anthropological classification has been of great importance to the science. Tribally and geographically arranged, direct observation of material culture objects in terms of form, color, and texture have yielded important culture-historical results. To cite a case from my own experience ancillary to a problem in aesthetics: In 1925 I undertook a study of the basketry techniques of North American Indians. The work was carried out in two phases—first in the museum and then in the field. In the museum phase of my study, the baskets were tribally and geographically arranged in order to control ethnic identity and the factor of borrowing of traits. As a result of this comparative study, I classified the basketry techniques of the North American continent into three broad categories in accordance with what I felt to be contrasting mechanical principles, *viz.* coiling, wicker-twining and plaiting. Tribally compared, within each of these technical categories, a large number of independently variable mechanical features appeared, each of which, entering into different combinations, gave the basketry of every tribe a technologically distinctive character (Weltfish, 1930; 1932; 1940; 1953, pp. 243–81).

In the field investigation an attempt was made to find out what kind of technical activities and concepts these detailed mechanical variables represented. Moving from tribe to tribe in the Southwest, I found it possible to get the basket-maker to vary her technical procedure by substituting one of the detailed mechanical variables of another tribe, while retaining the rest of her own technical complex. The basketmakers were also conscious of the fact that these detailed features could and did vary tribally, based on their observation of basket-making in other tribes. I found a similar situation in pottery techniques.

The most conspicuous result of this analysis was the detailed nature of the mechanical variables within the single technique. This would appear to be another manifestation of the extraordinary complexity of approach to the material world that is characteristic of the simplest peoples, reflected conceptually in language and mechanically in these basketry techniques. To add to this detailed variability of mechanical features, the basket-making activities of each of the tribes I studied were characterized by a conventionalized set of postures and motions that varied independently of the mechanical tasks they were designed to accomplish. A more familiar example from our own industry is the field of time and motion studies, and the special studies of motion and posture in sports, habits of posture and motion often being reorganized to accomplish the same result.

The fortunate circumstance of the preservation of certain archaeological materials, mainly in the Southwest, Great Basin, and in Oregon due to the dryness of climate, furnished the opportunity for developing a stratigraphic time dimension. Over a period of at least 1500 years in the Southwest, the basketry techniques had remained clearly identifiable, the technique in all its distinctive mechanical features remaining stable into modern times. On these baskets with identical technique over this period, there had been four major shifts in design style (Weltfish, 1953, pp. 153–56). A similar finding as to the comparative stability of technical styles was made by Margaret Mead (1928) in her comparative study of Polynesian material culture. The more stable character of technological features over other aspects of culture makes them available for a special role in anthropological studies, *viz.* as indicators of tribal and temporal connections. While analysis of archaeological specimens at times appears minute, my discovery in the field that the detailed mechanical features of basketry techniques identified in the museum were valid mechanical variables in practice, signifies that such archaeological analyses are likely to represent techni-cultural facts rather than arbitrarily distinguished qualities. A pot, a basket, an arrow-head—as a discrete and integral object—gives us assurance that this complex of conventionalized techni-cultural traits was within the minds of single individuals within a group at a given time, and thus has psychological reality as a cultural complex. This finding also validates the study of the material culture object, considered within its tribal setting and geographical distribution, as a means of establishing cultural continuities over time and space.

Material Culture Study as a Focus for
Arriving at a Unified Field of Anthropology
through a Synthesis of Epistemological
and Ethno-historical Approaches

The significance of the material culture object to the anthropologist, whether in an ethnological or archaeological context rests ultimately on its function as an index of a people's thought and emotion. The problem of arriving at these significances is one of our most profound dilemmas. In the words of Ogden and Richards:

Though with the growth of knowledge we have become much less certain than our ancestors about what chairs and tables are, physicists and philosophers have not yet succeeded in putting the question entirely beyond discussion. Everyone agrees that chairs and tables are perfectly good things—they are there and can be touched—but all competent to form an opinion are equally agreed that whatever we see is certainly not them. (p. 77)

The problem is compounded when we turn our attention to the

material culture of peoples intentionally selected for the extent to which their lives and thought are in contrast to our own, as is the case in most anthropological study.

Malinowski has conclusively demonstrated that without a knowledge of the "Context of Situation" (*Meaning of Meaning,* pp. 306–9) the attempt to use names or words to derive cultural significance is sterile. And yet resemblances among objects and their common uses, analogies of technical processes and ways of dealing with the material world, prove that there is, on some level, a universal *lingua franca* in which this communication over space and over time has taken place. The archaeological object and its counterpart in the modern ethnological product of native technology manifests this time and space continuity. What are the common elements of man's life in the material world of which these continuities are an expression? Survival is conclusive proof of the success of man's transaction.

Man has everywhere met the challenge of the physical world in groups. Every "tribe" or "group" that has survived has been or is a "going concern." By whatever criteria we may choose to delimit or identify this group, there is an order to their on-going that can be delineated. In the round of the seasons through the course of the year, there is a coordinated sequence of activities, followed out in terms of a given body of traditions through which a people develop a characteristic rhythm of life. With this rhythm of life as a framework, a context of culture can be developed. Certain features of this rhythm of life are so common to man that they can be categorically generalized. The coordinated activities that cluster around eating, viz. *provisioning,* occupy a primary place as the irreducible minimum of individual survival. Second to eating is *population maintenance* around which center activities that are basic to group survival (family and social relations, administration, shelter, clothing, utilities). Meaning and direction in group life is given in *recreation and celebration,* a broad area of activities that includes religion, ceremony, and the arts. And finally the group itself is defined and maintained only in terms of its relations with other groups—*external relations*—in trade, travel, war, and diplomacy.

As a portrayal of a round of life in a complex society, I was particularly impressed with the thinking of Wassily Leontief in his approach to the economics of our own society. His view is summarized in an article in the *Scientific American:* "Input-Output Economics, concerning a new method which can portray an entire economy and its fine structure by plotting the production of each industry against its consumption from every other." Leontief's concept of "industry" is a far broader one than appears in common usage at the present time. It includes not only the processes of reconversion of materials into industrial objects, but agriculture, foreign countries, government and households. This approach refers to the integral character of the economy as a system; since Quesnay devised his *Tableau économique* (1758), the idea of a general interdependence among various parts of the economic system has become the very foundation of economic analysis. Leontief (1951) states his objective as an attempt to achieve a closed or homogeneous system:

The economic activity of the whole country is visualized as if covered by one huge accounting system. Each business as well as each household is treated as a separate account unit, . . . each with an expenditure and revenue account.

He recognizes that at the same time, there are certain factors that so materially affect the economic system that the ideal of a self-checking homogeneous whole cannot be attained. For instance, certain administrative decisions may radically alter interrelationships. In a native community this may be just as true as in our own sociopolitical context, *viz.* a decision to war, trade, the death of an important person, a natural catastrophe, may precipitate such alternative administrative decisions that there would be major effects on the material-economic balance sheet.

In a later publication (1953), Leontief describes his plan as follows:

Considered from the point of view of the input-output scheme, any national economy can be described as a system of mutually interrelated industries or—if one prefers a more abstract term—interdependent economic activities. The interrelations actually consist in the more or less steady stream of goods and services which directly or indirectly link all sectors of the economy to each other.

The whole system has been sub-divided into fifty sectors comprising agriculture, various extractive and manufacturing industries, electric public service industries. Foreign countries are treated as a separate industry. Households and government, the latter comprising all public institutions not engaged in regular productive activities, constitute the two large non-industrial sectors of the system.   (p. 8)

The inclusion of these two large non-industrial sectors—government and households—as well as "foreign countries," makes this system particularly adaptable to anthropology. Of households, Leontief states:

No other field of economic inquiry can suffer so much from theoretical over-simplification as the study of household behavior. The structure of the consumers' tastes is less articulated than that of the more or less rationally organized productive processes. It cannot be easily approached "from below" via economic psychology or quantitative sociology for the simple reason that neither of these disciplines does yet actually exist. Thus analysis of the input-output structure of households has to fall back on the methods of indirect statistical inferences. The indirectness of such an approach can, however, be considerably reduced through the formulation of relevant qualitative information, i. e. far-reaching stratification of the available qualitative data.   (p. 15)

In an economy in which major attention has been given to the productive industries involved in the conversion of materials, one other factor in addition to administrative expediency and household behavior involves a dynamic aspect outside the productive scheme: technological innovation which "affects directly and nearly simultaneously a great number of apparently different industries, because behind the variety of products there is often concealed a similarity or rather identity of basic productive processes."

I think it is to these aspects of the economic problem that the anthropologist has something important to contribute through the insights gained from comparative and culture-historical perspectives. It is a new integrative approach to our field which I feel can be a decidedly creative one.

In Leontief's statement concerning households the need for the organization of qualitative data is to be noted. Note also Herskovits' reference to this problem. Much that we deal with in anthropology which perforce includes motivations and psychological aspects in a cultural matrix demands organization on a qualitative level.

Thus the question of the charting of qualitative data is a challenging one not only for the anthropologist, but also for the analysis of life in more complex societies. Verbal entities which constitute our most effective symbol system for representing qualities should comprise the basic element of the charting. Verbal entities must refer to the "Context of Situation" and this in turn to a presentation of the whole culture context. In order to fill the requirement of 'Context of Situation' all analytical charts should have parallel verbal charts, *viz.* the word-referent items categorized and elaborated in their semantic and linguistic aspects. As background for this, in the body of the integrated account of "culture context" the verbal usage should be interspersed in their relevant situations. I have already referred briefly to the "rhythm of life of a people" and suggested four general categories under which the integral picture, seasonally portrayed, might be subsumed.

A precedent for such charting as I am suggesting exists in Malinowski's *Coral Gardens and Their Magic* (1935) where the two volumes give a seasonal description of gardening activities, including all phases of life within one context, not omitting verbal expressions (see I, 50–51, fig. 3), and gardening and ethnolinguistics (Vol. II). In the first volume there is a "Chart of Magic and Work" showing the organizing function of Trobriand Magic (pp. 435–44, fig. 14) which is particularly valuable for the general problem of mapping such qualitative data. In addition to cross-referencing the columns, three different printing types are used to distinguish such categories as economic activities, noneconomic activities, and taboos or abstentions from work. This chart could well serve as a model for charting such as I am suggesting. In some cases, motivations, for instance, might be substituted for magic or other categories on a psycho-social level.

To be sure, the anthropologist will find himself hard put to fill this entire prescription. Whether he attempts to organize already-existing ethnological materials or to gather it in the field, the bulk of the material is likely to prove forbidding, especially until we develop new methodological devices. In the very limited scope of the Trobriand Island culture, for instance, Malinowski published two volumes on gardening, and one on external trade activities (*Argonauts*). His plan, which he never realized, for portraying the material life of this small and obscure group was to write one or more volumes on fishing, industries, and internal trade (1922, p. 7n). The greatest obstacle to the work, therefore, is loss of patience in carrying it through, or as in Malinowski and Boas' case, the limitations of the life span of a single investigator. Nevertheless I think such studies are of major importance to behavioral science. Only by realizing the universally complex character of man's approach to the material world can we refine our own dealings with it. As coordinate symbol systems, word and object are peculiarly pertinent to the question.

I have not yet touched upon the question of charting industries in a technicultural context. For this phase we have no adequate precedent. Malinowski did not include this in his work, although as noted, he did project it. I have made fragmentary attempts to devise partial charts of the industries of various tribes in this way, but have not yet attempted an integral approach to the life of one people. I shall in a later work make such an attempt. For the present the following considerations form the basis of a projected plan. For purposes of developing a body of comparative economic material referable to industrial economies, this aspect of culture is a main avenue of comparison.

Taking material objects as the focus of our analysis, our own analytic conceptions with relation to them probably rest largely on the four categories or "causes" of objective experience developed by Aristotle 2300 years ago. To begin with we can utilize these as a working hypothesis, subject to whatever revisions our changing concepts of the material world and comparative experience may direct.

Now let us consider the various classificatory qualities of our ethnological object:

Its form or shape aspect lies within the range of shapes of other objects of use and manufacture in a given culture, and the dynamic of this feature may well lie within those dimensions. Similarly with the color or texture of its material—a phenomenon within the range of this quality of used or manufactured things in the culture we are considering.

The process of manufacture has a two-fold aspect: the range of mechanical knowledge, and that of "body" knowledge of posture and motion. To elaborate on this latter factor—in my field experience I found that connected with each industrial pursuit there were a whole series of conventionally stylized postural and motor procedures which could vary independently of the specific mechanical tasks they were designed to carry out. (In our own industrial experience, similar material has appeared in the field of time and motion studies, and to some extent in sports.)

And finally, there are a whole range of social and mental-conceptual constructs of which the material culture object is one focal aspect.

The material object, therefore, as here conceived, represents the convergence of these different systematized approaches to experience.

To all of these, as I have already indicated, there is a parallel system of linguistic approaches which correspond, but which are not delimited in terms of the material categories as we analyze them.

Roughly summarized, the four primary material categories comprise form, material, process, and use or purpose. The work of charting the industries should begin with a series of subcharts correlating these features. One chart, for instance, could utilize *form* and *materials* as major coordinates, the latter perhaps classified as mineral, vegetable, animal; and *form,* in a manner related to the range and context of the forms that prevail in the culture. Another chart could be developed in an analogous manner with *materials-mechanical processes* as co-ordinates; another, *mechanical processes-motor procedures and postures*; still another, possibly a summary of these, with *form-materials,* the major coordinates and others more generally categorized than in the detailed tables, and subsumed under the major headings.

The other major phase of material culture study which embodies roughly the area of the needs and wants that the materials and industries fill, could be handled under the four tentatively suggested major categories. Initially, sub-charts treating families, or other sub-groupings could be consolidated into a tribal chart. Without going into detail on the needs-wants question, these, as above stated, are as follows:

> Provisioning
> > food
> Population Maintenance
> > family and social relations
> > administration
> > shelter, clothing, utilities
> Recreation and Celebration
> > including religion, ceremony, and the arts
> External Relations
> > trade, travel, war and diplomacy
> > communications

The major coordinates in this chart could be *materials* as one, and *need-wants* as the other. Through the materials category, the industrial charts could finally be coordinated with the need-want set. For any interrelationships of special interest, separate charts could be made with the relevant factors of either category as coordinates—the materials constituting the most general frame of reference. In man's dealing with the physical world, the material aspect is of course the most primary.

Conclusion

We return now to one of the most difficult of the problems involved in the question we are treating here. The classification "materials" covers an area of our lives today that is moving forward at an astronomical pace. As a major coordinate of our analysis of material culture, how are we to deal with it? We must face the fact of multiple systems of approach. Perhaps some of our initial classification will have to be on Aristotle's terms and some in the 200-year old outlook of Isaac Newton. As Sir James Jeans (1951) has observed:

The two schemes of Einstein and Newton are poles asunder in their physical interpretations but it would be a mistake to think of the Newtonian scheme as nothing but an accumulation of errors. The quantitative error in Newton's law of gravitation is so small that nearly two hundred years elapsed before any error was discovered, or even suspected. . . . And when we come down from the heavens to the earth, we find a science of everyday life which is still entirely Newtonian; the engineer who is building a bridge or a ship or a locomotive does precisely what he would have done if Einstein's challenge to Newton had never appeared, and so does the computer who is preparing the *Nautical Almanac,* and the astronomer who is discussing the general motion of the planets.   (p. 300)

Even in a native cultural context, the anthropologist will find at least two parallel systems of approach to the material world—the one mechanical, derived from the successful results of mechanical-technological experience, and the other magical or supernatural which serves to coordinate processes and also to explain the margin of what is mechanically unexplained in the technological process (see Malinowski, 1935, I, 444).

Today at the frontiers of our investigation of the physical world, arriving at a realm where his senses can no longer reach, the physicist utilizes metaphor to project his given experience into the unknown. A considerable number of these metaphors are derived from manufactured objects and physical features of his gross experience. Referring to this process as expounded in Einstein and Infeld's book, *The Evolution of Physics,* elevators and trains, tubes and strings are used to illustrate a point of new physical principle, and finally Einstein's photons or discontinuous units of light are likened to "light arrows"—

an interesting archaism. Wave mechanics were derived from observation of the action of rubber tubing and the attached strings of a violin:

WAVES OF MATTER

It has often happened in physics that an essential advance was achieved by carrying out a consistent analogy between apparently unrelated phenomena . . .

The association of solved problems with those unsolved may throw a new light on our difficulties by suggesting new ideas. It is easy to find a superficial analogy which really expresses nothing. But to discover some essential common features hidden beneath a surface of external differences, to form on this basis, a new successful theory, is a typical example of the achievement of a successful theory by means of a deep and fortunate analogy.[1]

Einstein does not consider that mathematics as quantification should take the primary role as a major instrument in the advance of physical thinking over the more general analogical method (p. 291):

Fundamental ideas play the most essential role in forming a physical theory. Books in physics are full of complicated mathematical formulae. But thought and ideas, not formulae, are the beginning of every physical theory. The ideas must later take the mathematical form of a quantitative theory, to make possible the comparison with experiment.

In the course of development, the question of wave and particle as terms for the ultimates in the nature of nature failed to fit the observed facts. The physicists then jokingly coined a word, "wavicles" and at last abandoned the old process of analogy and metaphor, probability becoming the bed-rock of physical theory, a fact that very much disturbed Einstein. Quoting from Lincoln Barnett's book to which Einstein himself wrote a foreword (*The Universe and Dr. Einstein,* 1956, p. 39):

. . . the twentieth century physicist tends to avoid metaphors. He knows that electricity is not a fluid, and . . . "waves" and "particles," while serving as guideposts to new discovery must not be accepted as accurate representations of reality. In the abstract language of mathematics he can describe how things behave though he does not know—or need to know what they are.

Yet there are present day physicists to whom the void between science and reality presents a challenge. Einstein has more than once expressed the hope that the statistical method of quantum physics would prove a temporary expedient. "I cannot believe," he says, "that God plays dice with the world."

With the work of Einstein and the proof that physical and mathematical systems develop within a limited field of experience, Euclidean geometry, applicable to the world and world view of Euclid, gave way to other geometric systems. Our time and culture-bound concept of number has also been fundamentally challenged. In an article entitled "Goedel's Proof," Nagel and Newman state:

He [Goedel] confronted mathematicians with proof that the axiomatic method has certain inherent limitations which rule out any possibility that even the ordinary arithmetic of whole numbers can ever be fully systematized by its means. What is more, his proofs brought the astounding and melancholy revelation that it is impossible to establish the logical consistency of any complex deductive system except by assuming principles of reasoning whose own internal consistency is as open to question as that of the system itself.

One important conclusion that emerged from this critical examination of the foundations of mathematics was that the traditional conception of mathematics as the "science of quantity" was inadequate and misleading. For it became evident that mathematics was most essentially concerned with drawing necessary conclusions from a given set of axioms (or postulates). It was thus recognized to be much more "abstract" and "formal" than had been traditionally supposed: more "abstract" because mathematical statements can be construed to be about anything whatsoever, not merely about some inherently circumscribed set of objects or traits of objects; more "formal" because the validity of a mathematical demonstration is grounded in *the structure of statements* [italics mine] rather than in the nature of a particular subject matter.   (pp. 71-91)

Thus one of the pillars of our conceptual world in relation to the material is shaken, and we are again thrown back upon the necessity of always continuing to examine the processes of our thinking. The attempt here proposed to parallel and cross-reference our material culture study with the relevant linguistic contexts may have a broader scientific connotation than we can now visualize. Number and word as symbols function only with reference to the substantive matrix they represent. The material culture object is also a focal aspect of a larger context which in an ultimate sense includes the whole of human knowledge and custom.

I do not think that this renders our material world, the human mind, or the transaction between them more, but rather less mysterious. Man possessing a material nature makes his transactions with the physical world in his own terms, terms that correspond to a true reality of which man is an integral part. Of all the "dust" that exists in the universe, the human mind is the most complex kind, equipped to include within its scope all the rest. Human culture in which man's cumulative knowledge is summarized is a major dimension of our universe, and it is one of the primary tasks of the anthropologist to search for it and to determine its common basis.

NOTE

¹ It is interesting here to compare Einstein's description of the process of advance in thinking in the realm of modern physics with Grace de Laguna's (1927) analysis of the evolution of speech and thought with relation to the external world. Speech is in her view, primarily and originally part of the social process of action and observation in the external world, the interaction of persons furnishing a method of checking individual perceptions and values. This process of action and observation of the external world enters the mind in part in terms of "internalized speech" as denotative of the remembered external situation. From this stage, "internalized speech and conversation," furnishing a temporary respite from external limitations, opens the way to new and previsioned experimental actions and discussions.

REFERENCES

Barnett, Lincoln. 1957. The Universe and Dr. Einstein. New York.

de Laguna, Grace A. 1927. Speech: Its Function and Development.

Einstein, Albert, and Leopold D. Infeld. 1938. The Evolution of Physics. New York.

Ford, Cleland S. 1937. "A Sample Comparative Analysis of Material Culture," in Studies in the Science of Society, ed. by Geo. P. Murdock. New Haven.

Graebner, F. 1911. Die Methode der Ethnologie. Heidelberg.

Herskovits, M. J. 1952. Economic Anthropology, Vol. XIII. New York.

Infeld, Leopold. 1938. See Einstein, Albert.

Jeans, Sir James. 1951. The Growth of Physical Science. Cambridge, England.

Leontief, Wassily W. 1951. The Structure of the American Economy 1919–1939: An Empirical Application of Equilibrium Analysis. New York.

———— "Input-Output Economics," Scientific American, Vol. 195, No. 4 (October, 1951).

———— 1953. Theoretical and Empirical Explorations in Input-Output Analysis (Research Project on the Structure of the American Economy). New York.

Malinowski, Bronislaw. 1922. Argonauts of the Western Pacific. London.

———— 1935. Coral Gardens and Their Magic. 2 vols. New York.

———— 1936. "The Problem of Meaning in Primitive Languages," in C. K. Ogden and I. A. Richards, The Meaning of Meaning. London. Supplement I, pp. 296-336.

Mead, Margaret. 1928. An Inquiry into the Question of Cultural Stability in

Polynesia. Columbia University Contributions to Anthropology, Vol. IX. New York.

Nagel, Ernest, and James R. Newman. 1956. "Goedel's Proof," *Scientific American*, June.

Ogden, C. K., and I. A. Richards. 1936. *The Meaning of Meaning*. London.

Osgood, Cornelius. 1940. Ingalik Material Culture. Yale University Publications in Anthropology, No. 22. New Haven.

Perry, W. J. 1923. The Children of the Sun. London.

Richards, I. A. 1936. *See* Ogden, C. K.

Semper, Gottfried. 1878–79. Der Stil in den Technischen und Tektonischen Künsten. 2 vols. Munich.

Smith, G. Elliot. 1916. "The Influence of Ancient Egyptian Culture in the East and in America," *Bulletin of the John Ryland's Library*, January–March.

Weltfish, Gene. 1930. "Prehistoric North American Basketry Techniques and Modern Distributions," *American Anthropologist*, N.S. 32, No. 3, 454-95.

———— 1932. "Problems in the Study of Ancient and Modern Basket-Makers," *American Anthropologist*, N.S. 34.

———— 1932. "Preliminary Classification of Prehistoric Southwestern Basketry," *Smithsonian Miscellaneous Collections*, 87, No. 7. Washington, D.C.

———— 1940. "Cave Dweller Twill-Plaited Basketry," Appendix to *Report on the Archeology of Southern Chihuahua*, by Robert M. Zingg, University of Denver, Center of Latin American Studies. Denver.

———— 1953. The Origins of Art. Indianapolis.

———— 1956. "The Perspective for Fundamental Research in Anthropology," *Philosophy of Science*. Vol. XXIII (January, 1956).

———— 1957. "The Ethnic Dimension of Human History: Pattern or Patterns of Culture?" *Selected Papers, Fifth International Congress of Anthropological and Ethnological Sciences*. Philadelphia.

———— 1958. "The Linguistic Study of Material Culture," *International Journal of American Linguistics*, Vol. XXIV (October, 1958).

———— 1959. "The Question of Ethnic Identity, An Ethnohistorical Approach," *Ethnohistory* (Fall, 1959).

HUMOR AND SOCIAL STRUCTURE
IN AN ORAL LITERATURE

By Melville Jacobs
UNIVERSITY OF WASHINGTON

THE SEGMENTS of a heritage which many anthropologists are now terming cultural phenomena, such as religious ideology, oral literature, and humor, are in a general way outlets for or expressions of feelings which can be traced to and connected with the manner of functioning of a social structure. Such outlets can be understood only by inclusion of statements about psychological processes.

As anthropology moves toward a system of scientific theory which covers both social structure and cultural expressions, structure will loom as primary, cultural items as secondary. The former can be treated without psychological statements to cover primary causal factors. To be sure, British social anthropology has lately dealt heavily with gross societal structuring and lightly with so-called cultural phenomena, maybe correctly so, at the current point in the development of anthropological theory and methods. I therefore believe that recent criticism of the disinterest in cultural systems exhibited by many British social anthropologists, and American anthropologists' strictures about British neglect of cultural expressions such as oral literature, plastic art, and psychological manifestations, are both accurate and unfair. Anthropology cannot advance very far in the direction of building a system of scientific theory for oral literature, another for plastic art, another for psychological processes, or another for humor among non-Western peoples, without initial possession of structural descriptions and a system of theory about societal structure which accounts for the causation of the principal components of such a structure. First things should come first.

On the other hand, even where anthropology has some incomplete knowledge about a socioeconomic system it ought to proceed, without interminable procrastination, to devise and evaluate methods for handling the cultural segments and expressions that are present. Anthropologists could try to perceive and select, as soon as possible, the units of which such cultural segments are composed. Anthropologists could then portray the webs or fabrics which such units display, and venture statements about the causes of such things if there is enough ethnographic material to help out. I have tried to do just this for humor in Clackamas Chinook literature, and in a society whose content and form can never be fully limned because scientific studies in the group began when it was long since shattered.

Some facets of culture contain few meaningful units and exhibit easily perceivable fabrics. I refer, for example, to phonemics, linguistic morphology, adult games, numeral systems, color constructs, musical rhythms, and the components of humor. Other facets of culture contain comparatively many meaningful units and show exceedingly complex fabrics. It is therefore much more difficult to analyze their contents and forms. Here I refer to personality structures, religious behavior, oral literature, values, world-view, children's play, dreams, and dance and musical heritages as wholes. It is understandable then, that anthropology possesses more knowledge of the items and their structuring in phonemics and numeral systems than of analogous units and their integration in personality types, oral literatures, or systems of value-ideals. I believe that we have not realized that our ability to perceive what transpires in humor is as great as our success in phonemics.

If we look back over the past generation of anthropologists we find, I think, that the constructs and methodological devices which they resorted to for analysis of culture and parts of culture, rather than of social structure, were ineffective. Some anthropologists operated in the manner of subjective impressionistic criticism in literature. Others deluded themselves in the belief that they were scientific when they employed a catalogue methodology which ignored the meaningfulness, for any system of scientific theory, of the cultural units which they listed. And I do not recall that a single one of the culture element lists contained a solitary item about humor, which all non-Western peoples employ incessantly.

Ruth Benedict's superconstruct of a "pattern of culture" contrasted almost sensationally with the lists of traits of culture which her contemporaries were compiling. But her contribution toward a system of scientific theory for culture was so generalized away from the components and webs of items in any one facet of a sociocultural system, that no one has found a usable place for it in advances in methodology or theory. Opler's theme-construct which urges descriptive statements of lesser generality seems to be only less removed from utility. I think that he has neither shown neatly how to employ such formulations as methodological tools, nor explained satisfactorily where they may be placed in a system of theory about society and its cultural manifestations. He has not weighted themes as to relative decisiveness. The units or constructs which sociocultural anthropology needs must still be sought. I suggest that the search for them may be managed by specific excursions into functional analysis of smaller segments of sociocultural systems, after the fashion of the profitable recent studies of phonemics and kinship.

My preference, in the present state of anthropological science, is to commence by maintaining a rough line between social structure and features or facets of culture. And I would wish for the latter, to regard them as largely projective expressions of social systems and to work upon them piecemeal, one segment of culture after another. That is, to select and arrange probably meaningful units within each facet of culture such as oral literature content, oral literature style, dreams, dance content, dance style, and humor. Once we have tentatively selected and identified a great many units within a cultural segment such as humor, and have arranged the units in classes or types, we may go on to ventures which indicate their likely origins, causes, the reasons for their maintenance, and factors which reinforce them. This has been my procedure in analysis of humor which I found in one oral literature. First, I attempted to segment all the recognizable examples of humor into a small and manageable inventory of minimal units, which I term fun-generating stimuli. Secondly, I tried to arrange such stimuli into types. Then I determined the frequencies of the types. Lastly, I attempted to trace such types back to common human behavior responses on the one hand, and to responses to specific strains and stresses in one social system, that of the literature's authors, on the other hand.

Humor is an important aspect of conversations and formalized verbal expressions of people the world over. It is important not merely because of its omnipresence but because of the services it renders. One may wonder why a century of anthropological methods, theories, and descriptions has fastened upon some aspects of social structure, religion, and technology as subjects which deserve scrutiny and scientific statements, and has almost wholly ignored a kind of behavior which any resident among a non-Western people encounters all day long and far into the night. There can be no doubt that like any other topic of anthropological investigation, humor can be analyzed in terms of its component parts, their structural integration, functionings, and causation.

Since humor appears in combinations of recurrent discrete traits which are in goodly numbers, there is potential for employment of an arithmetical, and therefore especially rigorous, approach to its analysis. Each humor situation, whether in chitchat, oral literature, or in a special stylization as in Western civilization's joke form, can be broken into many fun stimuli or elements. Minimal units such as these must be identified before anything else is done. Once ascertained and then classified, they can be manipulated arithmetically, notwithstanding the fact that they are always woven into fabrics of many strands. When the units, their types, and their variable patternings have been located, scientific work may proceed to display their causation and functions in terms of the social structure and the personalities of the people.

Each fun situation is really a package or fabric which is at once so complicated and so unique that little or nothing significant may come out of a typology of whole fun situations. Typing should deal with contrastable classes of the unit components identified in such situations. These units and types of units appear in varying frequencies. Some groups of units tie in strikingly with features of social structure and are largely caused by them. Other types do not relate closely to social structure.

I found over one hundred humor situations in myths which I had recorded in one of the Chinook languages, that of the Clackamas group which once lived in the vicinity of Portland, Oregon. Such humor contained, I suggest, sixteen or more types, some of them overlapping to a degree, of fun-generating stimuli. Five of these sixteen types are, I believe, common-human. One of the five may be captioned slapstick or practical joke. A second type is the skillful or incongruous use of pantomime, mimicry, or vocal mannerisms. A third type comprises instances of employment of onomatopoeia and special linguistic forms such as, in Chinook, diminutive and augmentative consonant changes. A fourth type is the use of incongruous language errors. And the fifth includes instances of repetition, progression, saturation, or suspense.

These five categories of humor stimuli found in the oral literature are relatively nonsocial or noncultural, in the sense that they do not arise in idiosyncratic features of a Chinook sociocultural heritage. They do not relate significantly to Chinook societal structure.

Another type of humor stimulus which certainly appeared in casual Chinook speech is surprise or the unexpected. It is of course common-human. It did not normally occur in Chinook oral literature because a Chinook audience attending to a raconteur-recitalist was acquainted with the myths and tales through annual formal repetitions and year-round citations and discussions of their content. Items of surprise were principally by identification with story actors who were surprised.

The remaining eleven types of fun stimuli which I identify in the oral literature tend, I think, to eventuate from and express feelings which are peculiar to Chinook and other Pacific Northwest Indians. I estimate that from six to seven-ninths of all the unit stimuli to Chinook amusement in literature recitals, and I counted about one thousand stimuli, are not common-human. They are generated by specific characteristics of the region's sociocultural features and personalities. I arrange stimuli of such kinds in eleven types.

The first and largest contains ten or more kinds of anatomical and physical reference. The type involves responses some of which appear to be regressive and connect with feelings established in early childhood conditionings. Other responses relate in part to feelings created in physical situations that are peculiar to the adult way of life of Chinooks. The anatomical and regressive responses include anality with some specific mentions of dysentery; orality, and also specific mentions of vomiting; going unconscious or falling asleep; concern about diminutiveness; anxiety at heights; and mutilation, maiming or physical pathology. Responses which tie in to a greater extent with attitudes and experiences of adult life include burning, drowning, and physical unattractiveness such as lack of beautiful long hair. Another group of responses, which may be captioned as references to sexual items, has roots which may be traced to Chinook social factors in both child and adult relationships.

A second class of sociocultural factors in Chinook humor flows from attitudes about pomposity, vanity, stupidity, gullibility, incompetence, immaturity, timidity, and lower-class status. The Chinook heritage placed such great emphases upon intelligence, competence, skill and high rank, and there was such intensity of feeling about them, that anyone, especially a man or actor in the oral literature who did not measure up to them was at once mocked.

A third class of socioculturally generated factors in Chinook villages includes narcissism as opposed to community-mindedness; penuriousness and greed rather than generosity; and doing forbidden, eccentric, or incorrect things. In Northwest States Indian villages community-mindedness was regarded as necessary for security and survival. The incongruous opposite was sufficiently provocative of anxiety to have to be relieved in laughter.

A fourth class of socially determined factors arises in pleasure in smart fakery or trickery, resourcefulness, or cleverness in relationships. Especially significant is the circumstance that Chinook society expected children and men to be tricky and clever. It smiled when they were. It was tense if lack of such talent or potential was evident. Adult females were supposed to be no more than competent and prudent. Only men should take initiative, be bright, and resort to trickery. Amusement at an adult female's cleverness was absent, at least in the oral literature, because her lack of mental alacrity hardly threatened village or lineage security. A Chinook town therefore lacked concern about absence of shrewdness in women. In their myths Chinooks did not indicate that a woman, before the menopause, would ever display so masculine a virtue as canniness. As for children, the need was that they socialize early and be intelligent, in order that at puberty they be competent in adult participations. Hence the smiles and pleasure when preadolescents exhibited precocious maturity. A similar response appeared when men did the smart things that resulted in wealth or other security-giving and aggression-satisfying consequences.

A fifth class of fun responses in Chinook related to the great value and intense concern in acquisitions of spirit-power relationships. Feeling about them was so strong that when a supernatural relationship of likely menace was manifested and it generated behavior which Westerners would regard as insanity in the recipient, people might drain off in laughter their horror, fear, or worry that everyone was endangered.

A sixth and important class of responses comprises laughter at all elders, and those other occasionally inadequate and often demanding persons who were hereditary headmen. Their power to control and exact constituted continuing irritation. Therefore elders and headmen were scapegoats. Hostile feelings toward them were resolved in laughter at their expense. Further, any older woman tended to be laughed at except in situations where her competency and passivity were stressed. Perhaps no other category of fun factors displays more clearcut a connection with Chinook society and culture.

A seventh class is laughter when a person is subjected to humiliation or depreciation. The humiliation complex of the entire Northwest Coast is involved here. It relates to values and feelings, among them much pent-up aggression, in potlatches, gift exchanges, ranking and other features of the social system. Everyone aspired to rise in rank. Everyone feared a social slight. Everyone needed to be far above those who were of slave class. Villagers channeled into laughter the anxiety they felt when they, or myth actors with whom they identified, were subject to depreciation.

An eighth and related type of fun-generating stimuli comprises instances when a dangerous person or story actor is defeated or comes to grief. The villain's frustration and abasement relieves everyone.

A ninth category is dishonesty which, in coastal Northwest States societies, usually relates to social climbing, cleverness and resourcefulness. It might be included with the latter. The prevalence of dishonesty and the rewards for successful cheating, whether in claims about supernaturals or in doctoring or mundane transactions, made villagers anxious. They took care of their uneasiness by laughing at instances of it.

A tenth type includes any successful vengeance or victory at the expense of nonvillagers or malefactors, who were of course equated. A victory in intervillage gambling games or feuding was the wished-for opposite of defeat and humiliation. One laughed when winning, because anxiety was being relieved.

An eleventh class is both common-human and woven from social factors found in Northwest peoples. It contains numberless instances of irony, satire, sarcasm, understatement, or overstatement.

An example follows of identification of unitary components in a fabric which I term a humor situation. This one was uproariously funny to Chinook and other Northwest States Indians. In a Clackamas Chinook myth the principals are incompetent and periodically starving bachelors named Skunk and Coyote. Coyote persuades Skunk to pretend that he is succumbing from a lethal supernatural. Since a person must not be permitted to die inside a house, Coyote summons a naïve man of the hinterland, who comes to help carry Skunk outside. When Skunk is being lifted out he discharges his musk at the unfortunate man and the effort makes him faint. The visitor also becomes unconscious and is then clubbed by Coyote, who promptly devours him and leaves the bones for Skunk to gnaw upon when he revives. I perceive many components in this fun situation. I suggest that common-human items in it include a practical joke and vocal mannerisms in recital of the principals' words. Socioculturally fashioned stimuli include Skunk's anality; Coyote's orality; Skunk's fainting and the doomed visitor's unconsciousness; Skunk's and the visitor's credulity; Skunk's lower rank, for Coyote represents both a headman and an older brother; Coyote's greed; his resourcefulness or trickery; Skunk's pretense at having a spirit-power ailment; Coyote's high rank coupled with wholly incongruous incompetence as a hunter; Skunk's inability to hunt; his shameful resort to anal sadism—it humiliates its victim; Skunk's humiliation when he finds only bones to eat; Skunk's and Coyote's dishonesty; and the elimination, following shaming, of a person who comes from elsewhere. Another possible fun-generating item is the sibling-like relationship wherein the actor who stands for an older brother commands and exploits a younger sibling. This fun situation, like most others, amounts to an exceedingly complex packaging of socioculturally generated stimuli, together with some components which perhaps all peoples enjoy. Northwest States Indians quickened in distinctive ways to portions of its content because of special Northwest characteristics of childhood upbringing, familial relationships, attitudes toward headmen, older brothers, and strangers, and feelings about social slights. Items which have been woven into the situation point to strong feelings in the Northwest States about spirit-power ailments, humiliations, and a number of social relationships.

Analysis of a people's literary or everyday humor may never yield depictions of their kinship, lineage, rank or political structurings. But it can point to some values in their social system the attainment of which are marked by uncertainties. Failures or possibilities of inability to actualize values, or to maintain status, or to ascend in the social order were upsetting to the point of being handled by laugh responses. The components of Chinook humor, like the actors, themes and plots of their mythology, can be employed as indicators of those parts of the social structure which creaked or often failed to grant security. Laughter covered over or resolved disapproving or anxious feelings which Chinooks had about those many characteristics of their way of life which did not measure up to wishes and ideals. Laughter also expressed satisfactions when aggressive wishes, shaped by the social system, received fulfillment. Examination of the occasions when Chinooks laughed assists in revealing a number of the stressful situations which were created by that society. Such analysis spotlights a number of the deficiencies in the structure and functioning of the social system. A simple arithmetical computation of the frequencies of the various types of laugh stimuli points serviceably to the relative weights of some stresses and strains in the social structure. However, not all of the causation of humor can be accounted for in terms of social structure and its functioning.

I suggest that an analogous method of analysis, wherein a segment of a cultural heritage such as dreams or religious ideology is split into presumably indivisible units which are then arranged in classes or types, may also grant results in the direction of building a system of scientific theory about the causal connections between societal structure and its cultural expressions. These segmental analyses, based largely upon oral literature text materials, offer the best means we have at present for advancing our comprehension of the functioning of earlier forms of societies, such as Chinooks and others of the Northwest, which are moribund or about to disappear.

THE NATIVE DOG IN THE POLYNESIAN
SYSTEM OF VALUES

By Katharine Luomala

UNIVERSITY OF HAWAII

THIS ARTICLE will discuss the position of the domesticated native dog in the Polynesian system of values during the period of major European discovery, mostly from the early seventeenth century to the mid-nineteenth century, by which time European influences had greatly modified native culture and the status of the dog. The native attitude toward the dog was ambivalent. On the one hand the dog was a symbol of prestige, a desired accessory for human beings which improved their status. On the other hand the dog was a symbol of the social outcast, a despised and often comic hanger-on of human society. Such a dual position is not unique for the dog; it is clearly evident elsewhere in the world from far back in time into the present. The problem here is to inquire into what specific ways Polynesians used the dog to define people in terms of status and rank, and to discuss the ideological background of the functions that the dog served in certain Polynesian islands.

Among the many functions of the Polynesian dog that made it a prestige symbol was the use of its flesh as a taboo food for honored classes of people and as a sacrifice to gods and spirits. Combined with magical acts, its blood and flesh provided medicine. Fishhooks and occasionally other artifacts were made from the bones. Teeth were fitted into mouths of idols, or bored and strung for necklaces and fashioned into elaborate anklets. Tufts of dog hair with attached pieces of hide ornamented the weapons of chiefs, the aprons and cloaks of nobility, and the wands of dancers and gaming directors, and also warriors' fringed breastplates. Fishhooks, balls, and other objects sometimes carried a tuft of dog hair. Pelts were shaped into war cloaks or sewn in strips on dress cloaks. Movements of living dogs and, after slaughter, their entrails had divinatory significance. A living dog could transmit messages from spirits, it was believed, and, when possessed by a spirit, act as a medium for a magician. The dog was also a companion, a pet, a scavenger, a sentinel and guardian, and an aid in hunting and war. Its figure appeared in carvings and petroglyphs; often it had a role in various forms of poetry and prose. It was a convenient medium of economic exchange. As a gift it strengthened bonds of peace and friendship. Every island with the dog in pre-European times did not use the dog for all purposes mentioned. However, this introductory summary indicates the range of uses. No Polynesian island with the dog used it in transportation, either as a draft or a pack animal. With the pig and the fowl the dog formed a triumvirate of the only domesticated animals in Polynesia. Not every island had all three, some had two of three, some only one, and still others none.

Descriptions by earliest European visitors to Polynesia suggest that Polynesia had more than one variety of dog. It may be sufficient to note, since canine zoology is not the purpose of this paper, that the most frequently used adjectives are small, long-bodied, short-legged, bushy-tailed, small-eyed, prick-eared, pointed-nosed, and large-headed. They tend to conjure an image Darwin might have put in a classification with his "humbug." To this image add characteristics like stupidity, laziness, shyness toward strangers, a poor sense of smell, and ability to howl but not to bark. Colors were black, white, and brown, in various shadings and mixtures. That different varieties occurred is evident from Maoris of New Zealand and Tuamotuans having, in addition to short-haired dogs, some highly prized long-haired dogs. Society Islanders imported them from the Tuamotus for their hair but concentrated, as did Hawaiians, on raising large numbers of short-haired dogs for food. Regional inbreeding even within an island probably produced local variations, for a range in size and other traits is occasionally noted in addition to differences in length of hair. A zoological survey by me, with illustrations, is scheduled to appear in Pacific Science late in 1959.

Most data about the dog, and, as concerns this paper, its value as a symbol, come mainly from the Society Islands, Hawaiian Islands, and New Zealand, with the last-named the best represented. These large, populous, and fertile high islands had abundant food and many comforts which attracted explorers to stop long and write much in their journals. Captain Cook's prestige and his enthusiastic evaluation made dog meat a respectable but exotic delicacy that crews long without fresh food wished, like the great explorer, to sample, and to compare their opinions with his. Later the flavor declined, they reported, as interbreeding increased between native and European dogs. The epicurean interest led to further observations about the dog than might otherwise have been made. Also because the dog functioned in numerous cultural situations it attracted enough attention to be mentioned often. This reflects the presence of the dog in these three island groups long enough before their reported discovery for them to have adapted it to a variety of uses and to have integrated it deeply into native values.

When the first known European discoverers arrived at these three archipelagoes, the dog was unquestionably already present. Wallis (Hawkesworth, 1773, 1: 451), discoverer of Tahiti, saw it there in 1767. Bougainville (1772, p. 249) soon confirmed the fact. The Cook and the Boenechea expeditions in the next few years saw dogs not only in Tahiti but in Meetia, Raiatea, and Huahine (Hawkesworth, 1773, 2: 152; Parkinson, 1773, p. 81; Cook, 1777, 1: 161; Corney, 1913, 1: 295; 1915, 2: 191, 287). These expeditions started the custom of giving islanders their ship dogs, some native, others foreign, and still others mixed. Tasman, who in 1642 discovered New Zealand but did not land, recorded nothing about the dog. However, the next visitors, Cook (Hawkesworth, 1773, 2: 313) and Surville (Crozet, 1783, p. 281), who happened to anchor in Doubtless Bay at the same time in 1769, independently established the presence of dogs in New Zealand. No doubt exists of dogs having been there in 1642, and more important, perhaps hundreds of years earlier, because artifacts of dog bone have been excavated in the Wairau Moa-hunter site of South Island, New Zealand (Duff, 1950, p. 93). In 1778 the dog was reported for the Hawaiian Islands by Cook, their discoverer (Cook, 1784, 2: 228). Dog bones occur too in the oldest Hawaiian sites studied by archaeologist (Emory).

A fourth archipelago, the Tuamotus, also unquestionably had dogs when the first known Europeans arrived. However, little has been written at any time about the Tuamotuan dog. The tantalizing references to Tuamotuans raising a dog with long white hair, which Tahitians eagerly sought in trade to trim their warriors' gorgets, come from the Society Islands (Parkinson, 1773, p. 70; G. Forster, 1777, 2: 40; J. Forster, 1778, p. 455). The gap in Tuamotuan information is unfortunate because the first three references to the Polynesian dog are from these low islands. In 1606 the Quiros Expedition (Quiros, 1904,

1: 200; 2: 337) saw a little white or speckled dog on a Tuamotuan atoll, perhaps Anaa. A strange fact is that the little dog, the first that Europeans reported for Polynesia, belonged to an elderly woman who was wearing a most un-Polynesian ornament, a gold and emerald ring. The Spanish coveted the ring but could not get it from her finger. She refused to exchange it for their brass ring. The dog ran away. Although the woman may not have received the ring and the dog from the same source, the ring at least points to an earlier, but unreported, European contact of some kind, perhaps through wreckage, with Polynesia. One wonders what else came with the ring. The next report comes from the opposite, the eastern, periphery of the Tuamotus in 1616 when the Le Maire and Schouten Expedition (Callander, 1766–68, 2: 236) named an atoll, now known by its native name of Pukapuka, Honden Eylandt for its dogs. In 1765 John Byron (who went on to discover that other Pukapuka, which is in the Northern Cook Islands) gave evidence about the dog for Napuka, Tepoto, Takaroa, and Takapoto (Callander, 1766–68, 3: 709). In less than a decade the Spanish added names of other Tuamotuan atolls which had the dog (Corney, 1913, 1915, 1918).

No evidence that the dog was present appears in journals describing the discovery of Polynesian islands other than the Tuamotus, Society Islands, Hawaiian Islands, and New Zealand. Negative reports will not be listed, but two possible exceptions will be mentioned. One is Gente Hermosa, thought to be Swains Island. When De Torres (Quiros, 1904, 2: 458), second in command of the Quiros Expedition, went ashore in 1606 at this western Polynesian island he "found no birds nor animals, except little dogs." This is clear enough. Doubt arises because Quiros' secretary (Quiros, 1904, 2: 215), who did not go ashore, wrote that he had heard that "certain white hairs were seen, which appeared to be those of an animal." Did the secretary hear a more conservative report than the one De Torres wrote for the king of Spain? Perhaps the white hairs were those of human beings; Marquesans, for example, used old men's white beards and hair for decorating artifacts. The other possible exception is Samoa. Archaeology would be important in establishing whether or not Samoans had dogs in pre-European times. The two earliest visitors, Roggeveen in 1722 and Bougainville in 1768, who mentioned neither presence nor absence, had little more contact with Samoans than Tasman did with Maoris.

The dog was not reported in Samoa until 1787, sixty-five years after Roggeveen's visit and fourteen years after Cook had introduced it on Tongatabu. At Tutuila La Pérouse (La Pérouse, 1798, 2: 161, 168, 196, 201), who bartered for two dogs for eating purposes, found them as plentiful as other foods.

Some Polynesian islands without dogs recognized what animals the dogs aboard European ships were and occasionally called them by the common Polynesian word for dog, *te kuri*. Tongans had no dogs in 1773. Neither Le Maire and Schouten in 1616 nor Tasman in 1643, who were in the region, said anything about them. However, a chief visiting Captain Cook, on seeing a Tahitian dog on deck, "could not conceal his joy, but clapped his hands on his breast, and turning to the captain repeated the word *goorree* near twenty times" (G. Forster, 1777, 1: 459). The explorers concluded that Tonga and other Polynesian islands, like the Cook Islands, which recognized the dog though they had none at the time, may once have had and lost them (Cook, 1777, 1: 215; Cook, 1784, 1: 177, 183). Complete loss may have resulted, as is known to have occurred later in other islands, from slaughter for food during famines or as part of village cleanup campaigns, natural destruction by hurricanes, droughts, or other disasters, and canine diseases (Martin, 1817, 1: 265; Dillon, 1829, 2: 94, 131; Emory). Perhaps, too, these islands bypassed pre-European opportunities to get more dogs until they saw how much Europeans prized them. The dog, though still recognized, had apparently not been possessed or known long enough to have left traces in myths or traditions, or, except for Tonga, in the vocabulary. Polynesian archaeology has so far established the pre-European presence of the dog only in New Zealand and the Hawaiian Islands. The expedition of Harry L. Shapiro, American Museum of Natural History, to the Marquesas has recently reported finding dog bones in what are regarded as pre-European sites.

When Europeans arrived, Polynesians were eager to get dogs whether or not their particular island had any, and whether they had ever heard of, or seen, them before. Acquiring a dog from Europeans gave the lucky owner prestige in his island. That anything belonging to a European had value for the native fortunate enough to acquire the exotic item, honestly or not, explains in part the pilfering, so enraging to foreigners, of anything removable, even if of no discernible practical use to the native. However, the display of courage, cunning, and boldness, with the object as proof of success, had real enough value, and moreover provided something to laugh and talk about for generations to come. Satisfaction of curiosity about European possessions was obviously an important objective too.

The best example of a dog as a removable object whose sole value was that of a symbol of prestige comes from Pukapuka, Northern Cook Islands (Beaglehole and Beaglehole, 1938, p. 399). Byron, the discoverer in 1765, could see nothing of what was ashore, but apparently dogs were absent and unknown until about 1850 when a foreign ship arrived on which the captain had a pet dog. When native canoes reached the ship, the people of each lineage bargained to try "to get as many European goods as possible in order to increase its prestige." A man, whose name and lineage are still remembered, saw what looked like a large rat near a swinging scupper located just above his moored canoe in which his people waited. When no one was looking, he pushed the dog through the scupper into his canoe where the passengers hid it under mats. The thief then jumped in, and his canoe left. The captain, missing his pet and suspecting a canoe had it, fired at the fleet now speeding toward land. All arrived safely except for one man who was killed and another who was wounded. The cause of the trouble, being a strange creature identified either as "rat" or "animal," for not even the word for dog existed, interested the people greatly. The lucky lineage took it as "a sort of prestige symbol," installed it in their principal god house and sacred enclosure, decorated it with flowers and leaves, and fed it the best food the island had. The people of this lineage "never tired of boasting of their prowess and bravery in stealing this animal from the white man's boat. The dog was honored thus until it died of old age. Other lineages tried later to get strange objects as prestige symbols, but none were so sensationally successful as this Muliwutu (lineage) 'rat.' "

The Pukapuka example suggests that Beechey (1831, 1: 147, 154, 185), discoverer of Mangareva in 1825, who found that nothing on board displayed to his native guests made them "so completely happy" as his two dogs, misjudged the motive for Mangarevan pleas that he give them a dog. If he had had a pair, he said, he would have granted their request, but since both dogs were males he thought that the people would only make a meal of the gift dog as they did of rats, the only quadrupeds on the island except for lizards. One Mangarevan had to be forcibly restrained from taking ashore Beechey's terrier that he solicitously fondled; the Newfoundland, because of its size and bad temper, he left alone.

Desire for fresh meat was also obviously not the motive for the attempted thefts of ship dogs at Rurutu and Hivaoa. In 1817 at Rurutu (none of the Australs or Rapa were reported as having dogs at the time of discovery), a native tried to steal the large ship dog until he found that it was chained to a kennel (Ellis, 1853, 3: 367). His attempts then to steal dog, chain, and kennel were frustrated by the kennel having been nailed to the deck. Noticing a kitten, he sprang on it "like a tiger upon its prey" and swam ashore with it where he exultantly displayed it to Rurutuans who immediately clustered about him. Meanwhile the ship dog recovered its courage and bit a native left on board.

In 1595 in the Marquesas, the first Polynesian islands reported as discovered, "four very daring natives" at Hivaoa stole a small dog aboard a ship of the Mendaña expedition (Quiros, 1904, 2: 21, 23), jumped with a shout and "great courage" into the water, and swam to the canoes. At Tahuata, a crew member happily announced that natives had fed his dog well. Nothing suggests, however, that the Marquesans were permitted to keep either dog. No dogs were reported as present or left behind, so far as I can determine, by subsequent visitors, until Captain Porter (1815, 2: 131) in 1813 reported some on Nukuhiva, two the pets of Americans stranded there and one or two, not seen and of unknown origin, on the other side of the island. Nukuhivans "were much afraid of the dogs, particularly the two large mastiffs" on the ship, and appeared not to hold "in any kind of estimation" either dogs or cats. The latter Porter thought might have been left by Cook and not reported. The variety of terms listed in later years for the dog and the conflicting attitudes about eating dog meat may point toward multiple introductions (Christian, 1910, pp. 82, 86).

Predominant motives in the Marquesas, Pukapuka, Australs, and Mangareva for attempting to acquire a dog were apparently desire for risky adventure and consequent admiration for the feat; curiosity about foreign possessions, especially an unfamiliar living creature so friendly to man; and acquisition of a unique prestige symbol. Interest in eating dogs came later, probably not until they were numerous, and was not inevitable. Marquesan tribes, for example, though eaters of pork, fowl, and human flesh, disagreed about whether or not dogs were suitable for human consumption (Christian, 1910, pp. 124, 127, 133, 142). Such conflicting attitudes were also present in other islands where the dog was introduced after discovery. Only the islands which had the dog before discovery took for granted the eating of dog meat when opportunity permitted.

That Captain Cook noted more than once that a dog or a pair of dogs was a highly valued gift to his peers ashore further emphasizes how great was the prestige of owning a dog acquired from Europeans, and how indifferent the recipients were at first to what other values it might have. Whether the dog was of native or foreign breed did not matter to islands without dogs.

In Tongatabu Captain Cook's adopted father, of course a man of rank, eagerly desired a dog. Cook's gift of a pair, one from Raiatea, the other from New Zealand, put the chief into "an ecstacy of joy" (G. Forster, 1777, 1: 460). Dogs still belonged only to chiefs four years later on Cook's return in 1777 when the pair had multiplied and had been supplemented with Fijian imports (Cook, 1784, 1: 333, 375). Not until twenty years later was Tongan use of dog flesh reported. Natives in 1793, bringing Labillardière (1800, p. 128) a small, fallow-colored, Pomeranian-like dog, informed him it was very good eating. Other reports of the custom in Tonga occur later (Turnbull, 1813, p. 396). It had probably begun well before 1793 as Cook perhaps informed Tongans of the edibility of the meat, and Bligh (1792, p. 151) in 1789 bartered at Nomuka for dogs for his own food, perhaps the offspring of a pair of puppies, Cook's gift in 1774 (Cook, 1777, 2: 21) to a man and a woman there. That usually only chiefs owned dogs at first and customarily tabooed all highly prized foods for themselves would insure dog meat being reserved, if they so wished, only for their meals. However, neither Tongans nor Samoans appear ever to have been very enthusiastic about dog meat.

Calling in 1777 at Mangaia and Atiu, two of his discoveries in the group bearing his name, Captain Cook (1784, 1: 177, 183) again observed how ardently dogs were wanted. The archipelago had no dogs, but Mangaians and Atiuans, who said they had never seen them before, knew that other islands had them. An Atiu chief, Cook's first

guest, left the *Resolution* bitterly disappointed, the captain learned
later, because, judiciously selected as his gifts had been, a dog had not
been included, and the chief had wanted a dog more than anything
else. The next day, the visitors prepared to barter for their heart's
desire. Demanding a dog, they refused everything else offered for a
hog and other supplies. Short of dogs and disappointed in getting rid
of a troublesome pair owned by a gentleman aboard, Cook accepted
Omai's offer of a pet dog, sex and breed not stated, which the Society
Islander had got in England on his voyage there with Cook. The
successful traders, delighted with their dog, were so much the center
of curious admirers on shore that the landing of representatives from
the *Resolution* was ignored for a time. Subsequently Atiuans composed
a drama about Omai's and Cook's ship (Gill, 1894, p. 262). "The
crowning present of all," the dog, was never forgotten. Even the
elusiveness of its fleas was remembered. Spirits of dead white men in
the dog's homeland is what the wise men deduced about the origin and
nature of fleas which had never been seen before, and what mortal can
catch a spirit? (Gill, 1876, p. 317.) Riddles tell what charmed Atiuans
about a dog. "Who shows his joy behind?—A dog wagging its tail,"
and "Who beats a drum at one end and dances at the other?—A dog
barking and wagging its tail" (Gill, 1885, pp. 219, 220).

Dogs spread as slowly through the Cook Islands and Tonga as
through the Marquesas. As long as dogs were scarce in the island
where they had been introduced, their value as a symbol of prestige
for that island remained high. Only unusual circumstances would lead
to another island getting one of these dogs, let alone a pair. In 1777,
when dogs still belonged only to chiefs on Tongatabu, none had spread
from there to other islands even though the island now had "a good
many" dogs (Cook, 1784, 1: 328). Atiu long gloated over its neighbors
in its exclusive possession of a dog or in the memory of having had
one, a gift of the great men, Omai and Cook. Rarotongans, wanting
the distinction and treasures resulting from Cook's visit of which they
heard, petitioned their gods for weather that would force Cook to their
island, but they still had no dog in 1823, when officially reported as
discovered (Williams, 1838, pp. 152, 201, 409). Aitutaki, which had
no dog in 1789 and still had none thirty-four years later, finally got
one under unexplained circumstances from Atiu, which since Cook's
visit must obviously have acquired a mate for Omai's dog (unless it

were a gravid bitch) or a new breeding pair (Bligh, 1792, p. 147; Williams, 1838, p. 69; Gill, 1876, p. 317). The role of whalers and native crewmen in introducing foreign culture traits to islands is little documented.

Even in islands which had the dog at the time of discovery, chiefs regarded any dog, whether of foreign or native breed, from a European ship as a highly acceptable gift. A foreign breed outranked a native breed, however. Its usually having been an officer's pet increased its prestige. Mutual affection of giver and recipient for the dog and interest in its welfare made the gift heartwarming and strengthened good relations. A Tahitian chief Tu (Otoo) asked for and was given the spaniel, "a fine dog," of J. R. Forster, who with his son George were naturalists on the second voyage of Cook and extremely devoted to their pet dogs. Tu, delighted with the dog, assigned it to the special care of a "lord-in-waiting," who by royal command "ever after carried the dog behind his Majesty," as George Forster, obviously pleased, wrote in his journal (G. Forster, 1777, 1: 334).

Between chiefs and, by extension of native custom, between a chief and a European officer, a live native dog was part of traditional, conventional gift exchanges, formal and informal, in the Society Islands. In these exchanges, the dog, although intended not as a pet but as a food, nevertheless had the special role of being a symbol of friendship. When, as in the Society and the Hawaiian Islands, an archipelago had both the dog and the hog, the hog outranked the dog as a gift either to human beings or to gods. As a conventional gift often consisted of several items, both animals might be given at the same time.

Once when Cook arrived ashore at Huahine, a highly formal exchange of gifts following native ritual pattern occurred (Cook, 1777, 1: 162; G. Forster, 1777, 2: 375). The welcoming party and the arriving party exchanged gifts. Each item was accompanied by a plantain stalk; like an olive branch elsewhere, it symbolized peaceful intent. Certain items were specifically designated by each party for the gods. Each set of gifts had a name and ritual significance. Forster caught the term *no te Toura* ("from the Rope") for the rite in which the hosts presented a dog to the guests. The significance was not comprehended then, but the dog symbolized, with the meaningful name of the rite, the tie of friendship, the bond of union, between the two parties (Ellis, 1853, 2: 336). The ceremony over, Cook and the resident chief embraced each other, and the people approached with dogs, hogs, and fowls to barter for foreign goods. Bligh (1792, p. 127), when on the *Bounty* at Tahiti, participated in a less elaborate greeting ceremony; chanting, orating, and weeping accompanied a point-for-point exchange of a puppy, a chicken, and two plantain stalks.

Dogs also figured in formal conciliation rites after quarrels when individuals or war parties wishing to make peace wove jointly as an offering for the gods a wreath of maile (a Tahitian fern) or ti leaves (*Cordyline*) and exchanged puppies (Henry, 1928, p. 319; Ellis, 1853, 1: 318). Tahitians made a more elaborate conciliatory gift to Wallis (Hawkesworth, 1773, 1: 451) after a misunderstanding. On the beach across from the ship they deposited plantain stalks, hogs and dogs with their legs tied, and other gifts. When the dogs, forelegs tied over their heads, tried to hop away, Wallis, watching from a distance, thought them a strange new animal. On discovering what they were, he released them as of no use to his expedition.

At Huahine after a misunderstanding, Cook (1777, 2: 360) received "the usual peace offering" from two chiefs, who each brought a pig, a dog, and plantain trees to present ceremoniously one by one. Earlier had occurred the most famous instance of a placating gift, when the Tahitian chieftainess Purea (Oberea) gave to Captain Cook (Hawkesworth, 1773, 2: 152–53) a gift made up of a dog, a hog, plantains, and other items. When Cook turned the very fat little dog loose, Purea protested so convincingly that it was good to eat that he kept it. After tasting roasted dog meat soon after, he had Purea's gift dog slaughtered and prepared in the native style in an earth oven for himself and officers to judge the taste. The detailed account led to dog meat becoming a socially acceptable addition to many a South Sea adventurer's meal and not something eaten only, as by Bougainville's party (Bougainville, 1772, p. 313), to stave off starvation. Cook, who received many dogs, hogs, and other items as informal gifts from chiefs, also noted more than once that the chief Tu also was given dogs and other things as gifts by his peers (Cook, 1784, 2: 57, 64). On leaving the Society Islands for Tonga on the second voyage, the *Resolution* had aboard through purchase and gifts, 209 live hogs, 30 dogs, and 50 fowls; the *Adventure* had about the same number (G. Forster, 1777, 1: 387).

The use of dogs between Europeans and Polynesians both in gift exchanges and barter reflected pre-European native custom. Two examples will show the dog in a more formal economic role and as a medium of exchange in systematized barter between natives. Meetia, an isolated island south of Tahiti, was a trading portal, an exchange center, for lively bartering of goods between Society Islanders and Tuamotuans (Emory, 1933, p. 109). The former imported Tuamotuan pearl shell, dogs with long white hair, and other items. Another exchange center was on Hawaii (Ellis, 1853, 4: 324). Until the native revolution of custom in 1819, fairs were held "at stated periods" along a shallow rocky ford in the Wailuku River. The most elaborate and systematized markets reported from early Polynesia, they may have been a casual native custom as in other islands until institutionalized perhaps in the time of Kamehameha I. People from Hilo and Hamakua districts displayed and shouted their wares on the north bank to people from Puna and Kau similarly gathered on the south bank. Preliminary dickering over, traders carried their sales to a large square rock in midstream. Officials, for a fee, stood on each side of the rock to act as arbiters and keepers of order. The regular duty of these men was to collect toll from all crossing the stream at the ford. They fixed the charge and based it usually on the rank and number of travelers, who then put the toll on a board laid across the square rock. The toll would be from whatever permanently valuable goods the trader or traveler had—a dog, a hog, fowls, packages of poi, dried salt fish, tapa, pandanus mats, and after European contact, tobacco.

Hawaiians, because of their more tightly organized and autocratic political and religious hierarchy, were more systematically and efficiently exploited than other Polynesians. Terms like fees, rents, taxes, and tolls seem more appropriately used here than in the less business-like atmosphere of the southern and southwestern high archipelagoes. Dogs were one of the standard means of payment and a source of wealth. A man whose wife had been abducted went to the king with a dog as a "gift," with the hope of recovering his wife (Malo, 1951, p. 58). Often not one or two dogs, but tens and hundreds of dogs, might be paid in other transactions. A ceremony to discover who had magically caused a man's death required a fee of about forty dogs and twice as many fowls from an ordinary person and four hundred dogs and as many more fowls from a man of higher rank; additional animals were needed for the ceremony itself (Malo, 1951, p. 103). In the

winter Makahiki period, a highly institutionalized elaboration of an
older, simpler, first-fruits and fertility ceremony with offerings to gods
and their earthly representatives, dogs were part of the rents and
tribute regularly collected. Taboos kept people at home until tax
collectors had made their rounds. Then followed merrymaking, also
directed by the political and religious hierarchy, perhaps to ease the
pain of extraction. (Ellis, 1853, 4: 347, 416; Fornander, 1916–19, 6:
Part 1: 38; Malo, 1951, p. 141.)

Neither the eating of dog flesh, nor, as in Hawaii, the commercial-
ization of dog raising, precluded Polynesians from treating some dogs
as pets. Of course, the dogs stolen, borrowed, or received as gifts from
Europeans were treated as cherished objects of affection as well as
symbols of prestige. One of the most outstanding values of dogs was
their use as pets. In 1773 at Huahine, George Forster (Forster, 1777,
I: 377) wrote, "The dogs in spite of their stupidity were in high favor
with the women who could not have nursed them with a more ridiculous
affection, if they had really been ladies of fashion in Europe." Either
because they had lost a child or simply because it was the custom,
lowerclass women in the Society and the Hawaiian Islands, who, with
their husbands, had much of the care of domestic animals, occasionally
selected puppies and pigs to feed at the breast. The custom is not
reported for New Zealand. Called *iliopoli* by Hawaiians who regarded
them as the best eating, these dogs sometimes became such pets that
their nurses surrendered them only with reluctance and great sorrow,
like the Hawaiian woman whose husband insisted she sell for a nail
one of the two puppies she was nursing, one at each breast (Portlock,
1789, p. 188; Remy, 1868, pp. 17, 54). Affection and desire to protect
valued and cherished property led Maoris to take their dogs with them
whenever they were going to be long away from home, and Hawaiian
men and women, particularly the latter, to carry them in their arms or
on their backs to social and religious gatherings (G. Forster, 1777, 1:
219; Colenso, 1877, p. 144; Ellis, 1853, 4: 218 ff.; Thurston, 1882,
pp. 52, 75).

Affection for selected pets is part of a marked Polynesian trait,
namely, the desire to own pets, to pamper them, albeit inconsistently,
and to train some of them. Western Polynesian pigeon fanciers and
Tahitian cockfighters are among devoted pet owners who immediately
come to mind. Besides whatever kind of domestic animal an island

had, any creature of land, sea, or air might become a favorite. A popular theme in storytelling is the attachment, sometimes described as mutual, of a human being and a creature.

The love of pets was projected into the world of gods, goddesses, and lesser supernatural beings who had pets, in addition to those creatures in which they manifested themselves or whose domains they ruled. The sea god Tinirau's devotion to his pet whale Tutunoa, his extreme and poetically expressed grief when the priest Kae killed it, his revenge, and its magical and happy restoration to life, constitute highlights of one of many narratives about anthropomorphized creatures and their human companions that find a ready response in Polynesian hearts (Luomala, 1955, chap. 6). Kupe, the putative native discoverer of New Zealand, left Hawaiki in pursuit of an octopus, another chief's pet that had annoyed him. The chase led him, his crew, and a couple of pet dogs to New Zealand (Smith, 1913, 1915, Part 2: 56).

The mystical, or were the word not so meaningless now, the totemic, relationship often present in these attachments, with the creature's spirit, sometimes believed to be a kinsman, acting as advisor, guardian, and magical medium, rises like a peak from a very broad, rich matrix of man's day-to-day association with nonhuman members of the animal kingdom in his environment. The association leads to anthropomorphism and to the selection of individuals as favorites. Their response to human caresses and offerings of food is sufficiently emotionally satisfying to encourage the human being to continue the relationship. Polynesian love of pets is too large and ramifying a subject to consider except as part of the background against which affection for selected dogs can be appreciated.

Devotion to a dog or other pet consists of a network of emotions difficult to disentangle or to weight as to relative importance. Men, women, and children, of all social ranks, fondled, pampered, and talked to their pets, named them, and grieved when death or other circumstances separated them. When dogs infested Turnbull's Tahitian premises in the early 1800s, the chief Tu permitted him to shoot trespassers. When Turnbull happened to kill the favorite dog of Tu's sister and the little dog of another chief's wife, the deaths caused "great lamentations" among the women and Turnbull (Turnbull, 1813, p. 281) fell into disgrace.

Grief over a dog was revealed through tears and poetical eulogies.

About 1831 a minor Maori chief, reluctant to surrender his pet, the only dog in the neighborhood, wept and grieved when it was almost forcibly seized from him to provide the sacred taboo food required by a tattooer working on a person of rank (Colenso, 1877, p. 151). Dog fat or excrement from a dog fed on fat birds was processed for use in the tattooing pigment, another use for a dog in tattooing (Colenso, 1891, p. 450). A chieftainess, the tattooer's subject, presumably outranked the dog's owner. The tattooer's exceptional ability and status are evident from his customer's rank and the food provided him. His assistant, who ate some of the meat and told the story, does not intimate what other emotions than sorrow might have caused the chief's tears. Perhaps he was angry and frustrated at having a status that forced him to submit without hope of revenge to the loss of a treasure, a unique possession that had set him off even from those of higher rank than himself.

A pet dog was sometimes given special burial, a further indication of its owner's esteem. Hawaiian graveyards reveal mingled bones of children and dogs. A baby received a dog as a plaything, a guardian, and an object of economic value. A mystical link, if any, between the two has not been reported. If the dog died, its teeth were made into a necklace for the child. If the child died first, the dog was killed and buried with it. Affection for a pet motivated its inclusion with some human burials, for adults occasionally asked to have a pet dog buried with them. Burying a dog alive with a human corpse was reported as late as 1862 (Daniels, 1862). Food for the spirit of the dead person was also a motive; another was the necessity for destroying a creature that had become taboo through contact with a corpse (Buck, 1957, p. 570). Thus a dog stubbornly remaining beside its dead master would be taboo and have to be destroyed. Only parts of a dog, as also in the case of a chief, might be ceremonially buried or hidden after serving for a while as sacred souvenirs of the dead; a dog's leg bones wrapped in stiff varnished tapa have been discovered in a Kauai Island burial cave (W. Bennett, 1931, p. 27; Malo, 1951, p. 98; Buck, 1957, p. 568).

Memorials might be established in the form of woodcarvings, petroglyphs, boulders, and perhaps special *maraes,* to honor individual dogs or dogs as a class. An undescribed Raiatean marae called *marai no te Oore* was a burying place for dogs (*uri*), according to Forster, "but, I think," wrote Cook (Cook, 1777, 1: 365), "we ought not to look upon this as one of their customs; because few dogs die a natural death, being generally if not always killed and eaten, or else given as an offering to the gods." He added, and his suggestions accord with later ethnographic accounts, "It might have been the whim of some person to have buried his favourite dog in this manner," or the *marae*, he noted, might have been where this type of offering was made. He meant, probably, since he knew that many *maraes* received a variety of offerings, that dogs were here the only, or the preferred, offering. Sometimes a *marae* was used for ceremonial feasts of only one kind of food which was offered to gods for whom it had peculiar significance (Emory, 1947, p. 10). To'ahiti, a deity created by Ta'aroa in the shape of a dog but with other manifestations also, was sometimes honored by a special *marae*; he protected not only thieves and woodsmen but travelers who journeyed in canoes made of wood from his domain (Henry, 1928, pp. 379, 383; Luomala, 1955, p. 172). Hawaiians named an Oahu *marae* for a legendary dog Kuilioloa (Ku-long-dog), a man-eater able to change his size at will (Beckwith, 1940, p. 348).

Honor to dogs as a class might have been the function of the *marae* that the Boenechea Expedition (Corney, 1913, 1915, 1918, 1: 295) in 1772 visited at Meetia. The Spanish, after passing some women who had a pointed-eared, black and tan puppy of "ordinary" size, came to a large, fenced *marae* avoided by islanders. Inside was a stepped stone platform "adorned with some posts on which were carvings or characters among which the figure of a small dog was pre-eminent in every place." Wallis (Hawkesworth, 1773, 1: 485) in 1765 saw dogs portrayed on similar posts in a Tahitian marae. "Several sheds," he wrote, were "enclosed within a wall, on the outside of which were several uncouth figures of men, women, hogs, and dogs, carved on posts that were driven into the ground." Carvings often exaggerated sexual characteristics. Of uncertain purposes, these carved posts were imposing decorations, boundary markers, and memorials to people of rank buried in the *marae*; that they indicated the type of offering accepted at the *marae* is doubtful (Emory, 1933, p. 15).

Hawaiian petroglyphs, some which depict the cow being obviously post-European, include sticklike figures of dogs with flopped-over ears, long pointed snouts, and extremely long tails, erect and curved at the end. Some on Lanai and Maui, but none on Oahu, connect by a line a human figure and a dog, or a woman and a child, obviously to symbolize a bond between connected figures. Numerous dog petroglyphs in Nuuanu Valley, Oahu, may have placated or honored a ghost dog that roamed there. (Emory; McAllister, 1933, p. 23.)

Rocks and rocky islets are interpreted either as memorials of dogs or as their transformed bodies. Part of Kuilioloa, defeated in a battle of magic with a supernatural hog-man, became a rocky islet, Mokolii, near Oahu (Fornander, 1916–19, 5: Part 2: 332, 370; Beckwith, 1940, p. 347). Near Honaunau, Hawaii, is another rock interpreted as a transformed dog; also on Hawaii is a lava tube named for a dog that crawled through to find water at the other end (Emory). At Tahaa, Society Islands, the legendary chief Hiro transformed an unnamed man-eating dog into rock (Henry, 1928, p. 545).

Maoris believe in a great many transformed dogs. Kupe's pair, Tauaru and Hurunui, who went with him to chase the octopus that led them to New Zealand, are pointed out at Hokianga as rocks (Smith, 1913, 1915, Part 2: 59, 64). Either they are the transformed dogs or Kupe's carvings of them, left to guard his newly discovered land. They were transformed, some say, to keep them from following him after he had left them behind on his return to Hawaiki. When they came back to shore after having strayed inland to hunt ground-dwelling birds, they found Kupe gone. He heard their woeful howling and from his canoe he chanted across the sea to transform them. Kupe's and Tauaru's footprints are pointed out in the same region as the doglike rocks. Some rocks are regarded as transformations of dogs that came with families in canoes in the legendary Great Fleet to colonize Kupe's discovery. Near New Zealand when a chief and his dog, Mohorangi, fell overboard, the dog's struggles stirred up great waves that wrecked the canoe; dog and canoe drifted ashore and turned into stone. When a chief and his daughter arriving on a later canoe stopped to perform rituals, the daughter, on passing the stone dog, did not cover her face as a woman should before sacred things, and was turned to stone. Now women refuse to visit the island for fear of the same fate, and strangers avert their eyes near the dog-shaped stone whose spirit guards the island (White, 1887–91, 2: 190, 192).

Despite these varied memorials to cherished individual dogs or dogs as a class, Europeans sometimes questioned, as did George Forster and Captain King of Cook's expeditions, whether the stupid and dull pets had any value as companions. Perhaps the Forsters questioned less. The Tahitian dog that the Tongatabu chief saw running across deck and inspired his excited identification was probably one of the Forsters' unconfined and indulged pets that later was killed and made into broth for Captain Cook when he was ill (G. Forster, 1777, 2: 3). Captain King (Cook, 1784, 3: 118), after a year of intermittent contact with Hawaiians, could not in 1779 "recollect one instance in which a dog was made a companion in the manner we do in Europe." The custom of eating them, he thought, was "an insuperable bar to their admission into society; and, as there are neither beasts of prey in the island, nor objects of chase, it is probable that the social qualities of the dog, its fidelity, attachment and sagacity, will remain unknown to the native."

Some Maori dogs probably should be excluded from blanket condemnation of the intelligence of Polynesian native dogs. While other Polynesians also tell about brave and bright supernatural dogs, only Maoris have supporting evidence that their stories are not completely post-European in attributing positive traits to dogs. Forster and King would probably have respected Ihenga's dogs, rated them as companions by their definition of the term, and wondered what real-life models inspired their traditional description.

A man already well placed in Maori society might gain further glory, like Ihenga, through his supernaturally intelligent and loyal hunting dogs, who hold a mirror to his own character (Shortland, 1882, pp. 64–77). When Ihenga, on going to his father's younger brother for assistance in a ceremony to honor his dead father, wore two dog-skin cloaks and other finery suitable to a chief, he so impressed his uncle that the welcoming meal included meat "from a dog of the breed of Irawaru," the god of dogs. Ihenga received not only a food of great prestige but the best of it available. He was also given his cousin as his wife. When she became pregnant, Ihenga went with his dog Potaka-tawhiti, named for a famous ancestral dog, to hunt kiwis (*Apteryx australis*), flightless birds, needed in the pregnancy rituals. When Potaka ran off to find water he killed kiwis as he went along but left them on the trail. One bird led him a chase that ended at a lake where he caught it. As he drank his fill, he also swallowed many small fish. On the way back he retrieved his birds to lay them at Ihenga's feet. His master, who was thirsty, had just decided to wait until after his meal to search for water when Potaka began to roll about, belly upward, and then to vomit fish. Thus having informed his master that he had found both water and fish, he guided him to the lake. Thanks to Potaka, Ihenga caught many fish and birds for his wife's ceremony. Later when master and dog were looking for new land for the expected child, a falling tree killed Potaka. Ihenga, after rescuing the corpse by magically commanding the tree to stand upright, sent Potaka's spirit to live in a tall tree, there to echo travelers' words in dog language. Ihenga lost his other dog Ohau while exploring the land he and Potaka had discovered. When Ohau drowned in crossing a river, Ihenga named the river in his memory.

The narrative of these extraordinary dogs who enhanced the fame of their already respected owner implies that Ihenga was extraordinary too in having these loyal and well-trained companions. He was a good chief whose devotion and responsibility to both his family and his dogs during life and after death are revealed in the narrative. Potaka symbolized the ideal Maori hunting dog—courageous, patient, loyal, and intelligent. He lacked only speech but Ihenga gave him eternity to learn to imitate human sounds.

Meriting mention are two other Maori dogs, Kohau and Maioha, pets of the wife of Tamatea, captain of the Takitumu canoe of the Fleet (Smith, 1913, 1915, Part 2: 242). After the woman, homesick for Hawaiki, had died in a snowstorm on a Maori mountain which she had climbed to look longingly toward home, her two dogs "would not follow other people, but ever rested by the side of their mistress, howling." Tamatea ordered a servant to remain with the dogs and the body.

Although ordinary dogs did not approach the standard of Potaka and other legendary dogs, the Maoris, to judge from these narratives, had formulated an ideal, however impossible of realization, for a good dog. The ability to do so suggests that not all of their dogs were stupid or spiritless. Individual variation existed, and people perhaps by asking for offspring of a locally renowned dog unconsciously carried on selective breeding for admired qualities. In 1772 Crozet (1783, p. 165) whose Maori dogs were always "treacherous," "impossible to domesticate . . . like our dogs," and frequently bit his crew members, considered that they would be as dangerous as foxes around poultry.

Only Maoris among Polynesians used and trained dogs for hunting, or, as Best qualified, as much as these dogs were capable of being trained (Best, 1942, pp. 176, 205–18; Smith, 1895, p. 152; Dieffenbach, 1843, 1: 232). Although developed after arrival in New Zealand, the custom is typically projected back to the arrival of the legendary Fleet, and the dogs show a post-settlement standard of intelligence. Te Paki, caretaker of his commander's dog or dogs, immediately on reaching shore, took his charges, later turned to stone, hunting for kiwis and other ground birds (White, 1887–91, 3: 96, 100). A dog needed skill, courage, and experience to hunt kiwis successfully because they defended themselves with a very long bill and powerful, clawed feet. Before going hunting for kiwis at night, a man recited many spells and studied omens, some being interpretations of his dog's twitchings and crying in its sleep. Dogs were sometimes muzzled to keep them from uncontrolled hunting of ground game. A necklace of wooden or bone rattles around the dog's neck enabled the hunter to locate his dog if it wandered off the leash in the forest, and imitated, so it is said, the sound of a creeping worm, the kiwi's favorite food. The hunter led his dog by a cord attached to a stick; the other end of the stick was fastened to another cord that passed around the dog's body. After decoying a kiwi by imitating its cries and bewildering it with blazing torches, the hunter, squatting beside his dog, released it, or enough of the cord to enable the dog to attack the bird. The first bird killed was dedicated to the gods; after reciting chants, the hunter roasted the heart and ritually fed it to the dog, a good training technique.

A curious use of the Maori native dog was for hunting large caterpillars in sweet potato vines. The dog was taught to thrust its nose into the vines, turn them over, and expose the caterpillars. Dogs were said to eat caterpillars, and, if not watched, kumaras (Thomson, 1922, p. 66).

In European times an occasional native dog, but mainly its hybrid relatives, ran wild and destroyed birds, preyed on introduced pigs which had gone wild, and attacked corralled domestic animals (Thomson, 1922, p. 68). Other islands also found the hybridized dog very destructive. Hybridization with foreign dogs, not all of which came from Europe but were picked up in various ports by voyagers, probably began in Polynesia by the time of Cook's first voyage.

Watchdogs and war dogs appear in Maori traditions and chants, but, so far as I know, no reports of actual usage exist. Presumably if native dogs could be trained for hunting they could serve in other situations requiring courage and intelligence. Three famous traditional packs will be mentioned. Uenuku, distinguished adventurer, one of several with that name, sent ashore from his canoe his pack of dogs against his enemies (White, 1887–91, 3: 9). The fate of the dead is shown in the name of the successful battle, The Food of the Dogs (Te mau-a-te-kararehe). The term *kararehe* is sometimes used to designate an adult dog, and the term *kuri* then reserved for a puppy. A pack of war dogs was loaned by Tama-i-waho, a god in the topmost heaven, to the great chief Tawhaki to help him in revenge against his father's slayers (Best, 1925, pp. 914–16). Maoris could kill a man-eating ogre who had kidnapped a Maori woman only because his pack of ten two-headed hunting dogs was absent (White, 1887–91, 3: 124, 189). A lament (Best, 1897, p. 29) calls upon "the descendants of Irawaru" to spring forth, worry, and tease a dead chief's slayers. Human, and, according to a late reference, dog sentinels guarded fortified villages and war camps (Buddle, 1912, p. 178). Man-hunting dogs did not always find their quarry; a tradition tells of a blind priestess who fruitlessly sent dogs to hunt down a man who had tricked her (White, 1887–91, 2: 55). A Society Islands war chant (Henry, 1928, p. 307) admonishes a warrior to be like a "great savage dog that is fleet of step" and Hiro killed and transformed into stone a monstrous dog; nothing else, however, points toward central Polynesians having anything but small, passive dogs in pre-discovery times.

Though J. R. Forster (J. Forster, 1778, p. 189) in his type description considered the native dog to have a poor sense of smell, the Maori proverb (Fletcher, 1922, p. 32), "A dog's nose, a man's legs," likens a dog sniffing from side to side of a track to a man's frequent turning aside at every village that cries welcome, and narrators tell of at least four legendary dogs that acted as guides (White, 1887–91, 3: 176; 4: 91, 107, 109; Grey, 1885, p. 142). How much post-European invention is involved is hard to tell. The most famous guide was the dog belonging to Manaia, a captain in the Great Fleet, that scented land before it was visible, also a whale stranded on the beach. When the dog jumped overboard and swam off, the canoe followed its guiding cries all night until land—New Zealand—was reached, and a feast of whale meat.

The tradition recalls to mind Hahn's (Hahn, 1896, p. 53) eulogy of the dog as "the truest companion of man," and the oldest of domesticated animals, one that attached itself to man more as a free-willed independent companion than as something converted by man to the status of slave. It has spread with him over the whole earth, Hahn observed, and has been doing so since the most ancient times, serving man in a wonderful variety of forms and colors in all zones, in all continents, in the most different kinds of service, and under the most different relationships. Sometimes it is the pampered darling, sometimes the watchful comrade. And, Hahn continued, among the many remarkable circumstances under which this "most loyal companion of man" has served and accompanied man was its presence in the great war canoes that carried the first Maoris over the broad expanse of the sea to their new home in New Zealand.

Hawaiians, unlike Maoris, used the terms "watchdog" and "war dog" metaphorically for vassals who fought for their masters and were mythologized as supernatural dog-men. By the same process vassals engaged in stone construction became mythologized as Menehunes, miniature wonder-workers. This class of dog-men, one Hawaiian thinks, is mentioned in the creation chant, the Kumulipo, in a line about the birth of "the wagging tails" who "had no fixed line of descent" (Beckwith, 1940, p. 343). Carelessness among commoners about intermarriage led them to be metaphorically equated with dogs. People of rank carefully arranged their formal liaisons with genealogical succession in mind. Other islands with the dog in pre-European times also likened indiscriminate human mating to that of dogs.

Hawaiian dog-men are described as hairless and human-looking, but dog-tailed or dog-headed, demigods who lived in dunes and formed the armies of their masters (Beckwith, 1940, p. 343; Beckwith, 1951, p. 89). They might also be bandits and even cannibals who prowled nightly for victims. On certain nights they joined a ghostly procession. Cloud forms identified as dog-men and other traditional dog characters were used in divination. A taboo on eating hairless dogs stemmed partly from their identification with those dog-men who were professional wrestlers and plucked off their body hair to prevent opponents from getting a hold. Legendary watchdogs who rescued women and others in distress sometimes lost ears and tail for their chivalry. Poki, a name still used for dogs, was said to be derived from Boss, the

English name of the favorite dog of Kamehameha I. Deified after death and worshiped, its spirit is even yet believed to roam clouds and earth. On Kauai a dog of the same name was believed to have owned land (Pukui and Elbert, 1957, p. 311).

Other archipelagoes also tell of man-slaying dogs, pigs, and other creatures, including plants. Usually they have no masters. Partly because these islands like Hawaii did not use the native dog in hunting either men or ground game, most of these narratives of clever or man-slaying dogs have always struck me as predominantly based on familiarity with large European dogs. Native dogs and pigs were scavengers eating corpses on the battlefields in New Zealand, Hawaiian Islands, and Society Islands (Ellis, 1853, 4: 160; Henry, 1928, p. 313; White, 1887–91, 4: 9). However, except for New Zealand, nothing indicates that native dogs would attack an able-bodied person. While little was reported of diseases of native dogs, symptoms of rabies were not mentioned.

Numerous European motifs in narratives about man-killing dogs further suggest their late post-discovery origin. According to Tongans, Fulupuputa, a dog "as large as a horse," lived in a magically closing cave in Fiji until slain either by Maui or Muni before he could eat his next victim, a princess; Maui finally died of sorrow for his father, slain by the dog (Gifford, 1924, pp. 121, 136; Collocott, 1921b, p. 51). A Samoan variant has Maui himself killed on a wind-catching expedition when a cave-dwelling red dog, perhaps an incarnation of Salevao, god of Maui's offended paternal aunt, attacked him (Stuebel, 1896, p. 65). Most obviously European-inspired is a Samoan story of a hero who, in tests to win a god's daughter, battled a dog and had other adventures involving a lost ring and a Magic Flight (the only clear-cut example, with a Niue variant, of this motif in Polynesia) with a comb becoming a thicket of thorns, a bottle of earth a mountain, and a bottle of water a sea (Turner, 1884, p. 102). Stories of supernaturally clever Hawaiian dogs like Kuilioloa, Poki, and others, which do not accord with descriptions of traits of the native dog, perhaps represent exaggerations of foreign dogs mingled with activities of mythologized dog-men. Puapualenalena, for instance, is a yellow dog, a clever thief, who saved his master's life and his own by stealing for a chief they had offended a shell trumpet that blown every night by spirits had been keeping the chief awake (Beckwith, 1940, p. 349). Cerberus-like

Kuilioloa guarded the road to the gods Kane and Kanaloa until he was torn to pieces with the result that dogs now are small (Fornander, 1916–19, 4: Part 3: 524; 5: Part 2: 364, 370).

That beliefs about relationships between dogs and the spirit world pervaded Polynesian ideology is evident. The wide distribution of certain beliefs, such as that dogs by eerie nocturnal howling or barking warn people of ghosts and of impending death and disaster, makes it difficult to determine whether pioneer Polynesians brought these beliefs with the dog into the eastern Pacific or adopted them from Europeans as being compatible with existing ideas. Hawaiians and Society Islanders muzzled animals to keep them quiet during ceremonies. Obviously adopted after Tongans got the dog in 1773, although whether directly from Europeans or through other Polynesians is unknown, was the notion that nocturnal barking or howling revealed the presence of ghosts (Gifford, 1929, p. 336). Maori dogs tended to be class-conscious in their warning systems. A certain dog-spirit living in a lake warned only chiefs of their impending demise (Tregear, 1904, p. 169; Best, 1925, p. 973). A god of evil and death used dogs to communicate his intentions, and a goddess took dog form to send warnings (Tregear, 1904, p. 169). Hawaiians and Tahitians were most apprehensive about warnings from black dogs.

Maori dogs had their own path to the afterworld (White, 1887–91, 2: 165; Tregear, 1904, p. 169). When the husband of Pare, a legendary chieftainess who had difficulty in finding a husband, deserted her, she committed suicide. Her remorseful husband asked the goddess of death to show him the human path to reach Pare but she showed him only the dog path until he bribed her. The Kumulipo (Liliuokalani, 1897) refers to the birth of a dog-child who being hairless will be sacrificed, but only after a speckled bird has first been offered; then the little dog will not sorrow as it goes naked on the road to Malama, the afterworld, by the easiest path, that used by children. Spirits of the dead, particularly of stillborn children, might enter dogs, Maoris believed, and become mediums for magicians to use in communicating with spirits. Maoris and Hawaiians (Fornander, 1916–19, 6: Part 1: 70) used dogs among other creatures to test magic and as an intermediate in magical practices. A Maori man (Smith, 1906, p. 140), to win back his estranged wife, sent her their dog over which he had chanted spells. Calling it by her husband's name, the woman greeted it by pressing her nose against its muzzle. The dog, having magically captured her breath, returned to the husband. With the captured breath he performed other magic to make his wife fall in love with him again. Tinirau, as famed for his fickle treatment of women as for his loyalty to his pet whale, in Tonga used his estranged wife's dog as an intermediary to win back his wife (Gifford, 1924, p. 190).

Combined with magical spells, blood from a dog's ear was boiled and used externally or internally by Maori sorcerers to cure spear wounds (Tregear, 1904, p. 18). Tahitians used, so it is claimed (Henry, 1928, p. 146), dog brain to repair a damaged human brain.

To'ahiti of the Society Islands and Salevao of Samoa, as stated above, could assume dog form at will. Samoans who, after discovery, acquired taboos against anyone eating dog meat rationalized them by declaring that dogs were sacred to gods (Turner, 1884, p. 113). One Tongan god hated dogs, but to another, Bulotu Katoa, dogs were so sacred that one always lay at the side of a priest in the worship of the deity; a proverbial expression reminiscent of the European "Let sleeping dogs lie" was said to have been first applied to Bulotu Katoa's dog (Gifford, 1929, pp. 310, 325; Collocott, 1921a, p. 162). Marquesans like Tongans fitted dogs smoothly into their beliefs in European times. Angry female spirits assumed the shape of a dog, cat, or cow, but a dog hung up near a dead body drove off evil spirits (Handy, 1923, pp. 110, 250, 256). Obviously European-influenced too was the Nukuhivan belief that on the third night after a certain chief's death his spirit took the form of a dog that howled until a priest ordered men with rifles to drive it away (Williamson, 1923, 2: 43, from Radiguet).

The dog, or any creature, on whom man projects his way of life, recreates him in turn. Both must adjust to each other if their partnership is to continue. Emotionality about the creature arises. "Love me love my dog," which implies preferences and values, reveals the dependence, whether sentimental, economic, or both, and the extension of self and personal and cultural values into a nonhuman part of society. In the relationship man has different levels of identification with the animal according to circumstances. At one level, an insult, mistreatment, or degradation of the pet by other than the owner is intolerable and is interpreted as a substitute or indirect means of treating the owner in the same way. To steal a Maori dog was to steal valuable material property and some of the owner's prestige. The distinction that the property had conferred was lost with the item. Moreover, the theft implied that one could steal from the owner without fear of punishment. A self-respecting man retaliated with aggression to recover his lost prestige, if not his lost property. Because dogs were few and the sole domestic animal in New Zealand, only people of rank owned them. Traditions recount how owners of a lost dog searched for it from village to village until at last some peculiar incident betrayed the guilty people who had eaten the dog and perhaps even staked out the hide to cure.

Numerous Maori traditions tell how wars started over dogs. The strong sentimental attachment to the pet and concern for its welfare often seemed overshadowed by the owner's anger at the insult to his status. Best (1924, 2: 225; Tregear, 1904, p. 37) wrote that "almost anything might lead to intertribal fighting," and no cause was "more prolific than the extreme sensitiveness of the rangatira (chiefly) class. The belittling of prestige or authority . . . has started many intertribal wars, as has also ridicule." Anderson in Cook's journal (Cook, 1784, 1: 160), also wrote, "No people can have a quicker sense of injury done to them, and none are more ready to resent it. But, at the same time, they will take an opportunity of being insolent when they think there is no danger of punishment; which is so contrary to the spirit of genuine bravery, that, perhaps, their eagerness to resent injuries is to be looked upon rather as an effect of a furious disposition than of great courage."

Before Maori departure from Hawaiki, feuds over dogs so exhausted some tribes, Maori traditions claim, that they decided to leave for newly discovered New Zealand (White, 1887–91, 2: 47). A famous feud between kinsmen over a dog started when Uenuku and Toi killed and ate the dog Potaka-tawhiti for violating Uenuku's sacred tapu by licking a sore he had (Grey, 1885, p. 76). The owner's two sons searched for Potaka from village to village. One was later captain of the *Arawa* in the Fleet and grandfather of Ihenga whose dog was also named Potaka. At Toi's village the two brothers on calling for Potaka heard it howl "Au, au," in Toi's belly. Toi's remark is now proverbial. He said, as he vainly tried to hold back the sound by clapping his hand over his mouth, "Hush, I thought I had hid you in Toi's big belly, yet there you are, howling away." The two brothers retaliated by stealing fruit from Uenuku's trees. When one brother was captured, the other rescued him. Toi and Uenuku, then attacking the brothers' village, were defeated. Because the conquerors ate the conquered, though close kinsmen, one brother's line became extinct and the other went to New Zealand.

Trouble over dogs continued in the new homeland. Two men by killing another Potaka-tawhiti owned by another Uenuku set off a great battle (Grey, 1885, p. 124). Another tradition tells of men related through marriage having trouble when a dog strayed (Gudgeon, 1895, p. 31). The owner, searching for it, asked two men and a woman near a village if they had seen it. Though they said no, a sneering aside convinced the owner that they had slain it. He killed the men but the woman fled for help. The pursuing band failed to catch him, however, and was embarrassed to learn later that he was the distinguished husband of one of their chieftainesses. A tribe that had protected a strange woman nevertheless got into trouble with her family and had their speech changed because they killed and ate her pet dog which in very rough country had guided her to safety (White, 1887–91, 4: 107, 112, 114). The god-power of the slain dog made the tribe speak in a dialect containing many sounds likened to a dog's howl of "Au, au." Marukukere, another tradition states (Smith, 1893, pp. 245, 250), for years sent his dog with a wooden spade in its mouth to an inferior chief Kahu as a silent messenger that Maru required his aid and that of his people in harvesting kumaras. Kahu, finally deciding that the sending of a dog as messenger degraded him and questioning perhaps if Maru really outranked him, had his people kill the dog. When Maru came for his missing dog he was killed too. Then Maru's nephew arrived looking for Maru. Eventually Kahu's tribe, worn out with feuding, split up and scattered. This story, the translator commented, "shows how slight a cause gave cause to a war in former times," and "also throws some little light on the intelligence of the Maori dog about which we know so little."

Although most Maoris prohibited women from eating dog meat, a husband respected his pregnant wife's food cravings. It is a common motif in narratives (Luomala, 1955, p. 163). Sometimes the wife craves dog meat and orders her husband to kill a dog though they own none (Smith, 1893, 2: 269–70). She may even specify one by name. All too often it belongs to her brother-in-law. The husband, though fearful of antagonizing his brother, gives in to his wife's craving and nagging, reluctantly kills the dog, and may even help eat it. When his brother, searching for his dog, asks the woman if she has seen it, she denies it. However, her belching, the resulting smell of dog meat, and the sight of the dog hide outside the hut, betray her. Or she boldly declares that her child is more important than the dog. The result is war and eternal separation of the two families. One woman, when her children were full grown, prolonged the active feuding by provocatively and evilly telling her sons that their elder relatives across the river were a "sweet food."

The level of identification of owner with animal shifts sharply if the owner is disparagingly likened to the animal in any way. A most effective Polynesian insult was just that. Except perhaps in Hawaii, Polynesians rarely likened a person to any kind of nonhuman being with favorable intent. Fundamentally, regardless of whatever positive values a culture ascribes to it, an animal is regarded as inferior to a human being. A person may voluntarily raise an inferior, animal or human, to his level. The act is often accompanied by a double satisfaction to the ego, for with that power one can anticipate that the inferior can be lowered again at will. It is another matter, however, to suggest that a person belongs on the level of this inferior being or is identical with it. "To liken a man to an animal or inferior was a curse" and an insult to Maoris into modern times (Tregear, 1904, pp. 170, 206).

Facetiously but guardedly out of a traveler's hearing, to illustrate how status declines away from home, a Maori might quote the proverb, "A dog, a traveler," meaning "A man is a man at his home; when traveling abroad both (he and his dog) are dogs" (Best, 1942, p. 37). It could mean too that for a traveler as for a dog any food was good enough. However, to call a man a dog was "a very deadly insult" to Maoris and "about the strongest" epithet there was to Tahitians, Tubuaians, and Tuamotuans (Tregear, 1904, p. 206; Aitken, 1930, p. 111; Emory). Even worse was to call him a "sacrificial dog," a euphemism for a human sacrifice (Henry, 1928, p. 197). "A little sneaking dog" identified a Hawaiian as the lowest kind of servant (Fornander, 1916–19, 6: Part 3: 391).

The most famous Maori example (White, 1887–91, 3: 135) concerns Apanui, a chief, who, noticing that his father's younger brother's son, his cousin, Kahukuranui, had white hair like a dog's, called "Moi,

moi," to him as to a dog. Kahu brooded and bided his time for revenge. It came when his son married Apanui's daughter. Apanui doubtless relaxed his vigilance then. Customarily if the insulted man could not wipe out an insult, he would establish marriage bonds with the insulter's family. Courtesy, it was hoped, would prevent the insult being mentioned or repeated again. Kahu who had built a fine carved house for the occasion prepared the wedding feasts that custom required the husband's kinsmen to give to the bride's kinsmen. However, at the second feast, Kahu set rubbish and filth, the food of dogs, before the wedding guests and killed them. Kahu could have had no comfort from knowing that Maoris greatly valued white dog hair. In an insult the part serves for the whole, whether the part is the call to the dog or the setting of filth before guests. The insulter's intent is clear to all; the victim has been shown, as a reflection of his status, the black phase of the dog's ambivalent position in society. The loss of prestige from the insult was as great as if a material object had been stolen. Revenge had to be as bold and spectacular as the original insolence.

In this context, identifying a man as a dog or as being in any way like one presented the creature most dramatically as the symbol of the pariah, the degraded outcast of human society. That the dog is nonhuman is relatively unimportant, for the line between human and nonhuman beings was tenuous in native philosophy and religion. The comparison damaged the ego because Maoris believed that the dog originated from a human being whose social misbehavior was punished by his human appearance being modified into that of a dog's, his power of speech removed and replaced by a howl, and his status reduced to that of a social inferior of the group which then granted him occasional favors and let him indulge, as best he could, the traits which had led to his social rejection. In Maori ideology the dog was not a gregarious, wild animal which had flatteringly attached itself to human society. It was a transformed human being ostracized by human society and tolerated as a hanger-on of its lowest fringes.

The custom of identifying a man with a dog to insult him gained effectiveness by being projected back to the beginnings of Maori culture and the universe, when Maui, the demigod, trickster, and culture hero, gave the insult its first and perfect form by transforming a man who had humiliated him into the first dog known to the world.

He taught it to fawn on man, to howl "Au, au," when it heard people call "Moi, moi," and to eat filth such as Kahu set before the wedding guests to show silently that he ranked them with dogs. Maui's favorite victim, his sister's husband Irawaru, was the Maori type-character of the social boor who gorged on his host's choicest foods, ate the fishing bait, imitated Maui's inventions, refused to carry his share of supplies on a journey, and slept in the sun instead of cultivating the fields. Irawaru was put outside the social pale except as a half-tolerated pariah. Hawaii and the Tuamotus have variants with Ri or Li instead of Irawaru.

As I have analyzed the story at length elsewhere, I shall merely point out the general nature of the plot (Luomala, 1958). Maui, humiliated sexually or in regard to food by a woman (his wife, mother, sister), who favors another man (her husband, lover, another son or brother), takes revenge for his damaged self-esteem on the man, and thereby on the woman too, by transforming him into a dog. The woman, ignorant of the transformation, is told that if she calls "Moi, moi," her loved one will come. She then publicly though unwittingly acknowledges the lowly nature of her favorite. The Maori female character sometimes commits suicide; the Tuamotuan temporarily at least takes a subservient attitude toward Maui. The story rationalized the taboo against Maori women eating dog meat.

So demeaning is the call of "Moi, moi" with its implications of inferiority that the aristocracy of dogdom could not be so addressed. Dogs also have their pride. Supernatural dogs of the Mohorangi breed, whose bodies are of stone, haunt Lake Taupo, New Zealand, where, with a glance, they turn to stone travelers unfortified by magic (Tregear, 1904, p. 171). They can send storms to kill the ignorant or skeptical who, hearing their voice, call "Moi, moi," to them as to ordinary dogs. Another Maori supernatural dog slew a family of brothers because one of them took fish from its forest storage-platform (Smith, 1913, 1915, 2: 185).

The dog-origin myths refer directly or indirectly to the favorite's gluttony, thievery, slothfulness, incest, and other socially condemned behavior. These traits, which appear in other Polynesian beliefs and proverbs about the dog, add to the seriousness of insulting a man by calling him a dog. Maoris called a lazy person "an oft-singed tail" after the lazy dog that slept by the fire and was the first to be eaten;

"a tail drawn from beneath" ("tail between the legs") was a "very severe saying" to a coward (Colenso, 1891, p. 452). Hawaiians (Pukui and Elbert, 1957, p. 93) likened a gossiper and tale-bearer to a dog. Maoris likened incestuous behavior to that of dogs, to Irawaru in particular. Of course, to trace a person's descent from a dog was a quick way to start a fight. Perhaps the Tubuai hero who could cut five hundred timbers a day and kill five thousand people in less time than that would have lived longer had he not enraged a man by accusing him of being of dog descent; the furious man, with his mother's advice, laid a trap that killed the loose-tongued warrior (Aitken, 1930, p. 111). Polynesian approximations of the dog-husband motif of folklore occur in the dog-origin myths and in tales about Kuilioloa and other dog characters.

A person or a tribe might honorably be named Dog without reference to ancestry, except when enemies wished to provoke bloodshed with jibes about the name. A Maori tribe (Tregear, 1904, p. 447) renamed itself Ngati Kuri, Dog Tribe, because it attributed the success of a war party to its dogs. To eliminate noise while the entire village marched on a surprise attack against a neighboring settlement, the chief ordered the killing of all dogs, of which there were many, both fat and beautifully furred. The women, although mourning over the slaughter, were consoled by the large amount of choice food available. The inference is that this tribe did not taboo dog meat to women. On the march the women carried both the meat and the dogskins. The latter, shaped into a huge bag stuffed with ferns, was then laid on the beach below the hostile village. Scavenging sea birds flying over the strange shape led the enemies to think a whale had stranded. Only after they had rushed down the hillside to cut up the meat did they discover the hoax. Returning to their palisaded village they were slain by the invaders who had meanwhile taken possession. After this the conquerors took the name of Ngati Kuri.

Followers of a Maori chief named Te Kuri killed and ate in 1772 Captain Marion du Fresne and some of his party (Dillon, 1829, 1: 185). The tragedy led Crozet (Crozet, 1783, p. 66) who took charge of the vessel to write that Maoris ate among other things "dogs, rats, and finally . . . their enemies." A chief in Maori tradition (White, 1887–91, 3: 234) was named The-Tail-of-a-Dog (Te rapa-a-te-kuri). A Tongan family closely associated with the worship of the god Bulotu

Katoa to whom the dog was sacred often used the word dog in names for their family members (Collocott, 1921a, p. 162).

Because a person's name was considered part of himself, to give his name to any animal was an insult. It identified the person as identical with the animal. When Omai, the Society Islander, accompanied Cook to England, he was indignant because the English named favorite horses and dogs for princes and princesses (Cook, 1784, 2: 170). In his home it would have meant death for the offenders; if a high chief took as a personal name the word for any object, the latter had to be renamed. A Maori chief in post-discovery times, insulted by his angry son naming the village pigs for him after a quarrel, seemingly ignored his son's contempt and maneuvered the situation to his advantage in a way that Maoris enjoyed (Firth, 1929, p. 338). The father, supported by warriors, seized and killed seventy pigs and carried them off. He followed the principle of *tapatapa,* according to which anything that had been in direct association with him belonged to him, and his name like his material property was a projection of his ego. His son had favored him, he implied, by setting the principle profitably into operation. The pigs with his name were his; had anyone eaten them it would have been like eating him.

An adult would not name an animal for himself or an elder, even a relative, except as an insult. However, he might name a dog for his child who then owned the dog. In 1949 a man in Tabiteuea, Gilberts, was pointed out to me as having given his son's name to a pet dog, not an unusual practice in the past, I was told, but rare enough now to be mentioned as part of the village curiosities. I find no record of Hawaiians naming dogs for their young owners, for themselves, or for other people. Maoris, however, have a famous example (White, 1887–91, 3: 36). Kahutia-te-rangi, son of the chief Uenuku by a highborn wife, named his pet dog for himself. Ruatapu, Uenuku's son by a slave wife, killed the dog. Grief-stricken for his pet, Kahutia complained to his father. Uenuku, although aware that the act was a substitute for killing the human bearer of the name, did not kill Ruatapu for the insult to the heir but harshly scolded him and reminded him that he was not the prized child but one born with little or no consideration of genealogical succession on his father's part. He added, "It is not seemly for you to kill that which is named after your elder brother." Wanting to use the same comb that his father had used for

Kahutia was another of Ruatapu's insolent acts of defiance which aroused his father's harsh criticism. The scolding stung Ruatapu so deeply that later he plotted and carried out the annihilation not of dogs owned by first-born sons but of the first-born youths themselves; only one in the village escaped. Ruatapu is the Maori type-character of the low-ranking son who bitterly resents his humbler origin, seeks to acquire privileges not his by rank, and finally succeeds in killing those who outrank him.

Food was one of the principal means by which Polynesians defined status and granted privileges to individuals high in the ranking order. Religious and social sanctions maintained prized foods as sacred or taboo. Their consumption was a privilege limited to certain social groups and usually only to the men in them. The right to eat these foods helped, in conjunction with other factors, to set the men off as of superior rank. Prized foods, no matter by whom raised or obtained, belonged to high-ranking people who had them collected from the producers, the commoners, both informally, according to fancy, and systematically, as in Hawaii during the Makahiki, and redistributed according to the ranking order of the society.

Among meats, pork, dog, fowl, turtle, large white fish, and, in New Zealand, wild birds, rated as delicacies. These prized foods were further rated among themselves. Of the four archipelagoes which definitely had the dog at discovery, Tuamotuans placed dog meat below turtle in prestige; after they got pigs they put dog meat below pork. Turtle, of great prestige throughout Polynesia, tended to develop a special niche for itself. As between pork and dog, Hawaiians and Society Islanders ranked pork above dog. New Zealand, having neither hogs nor fowls, rated dog very high. It was "not numerous enough to form an important item in the native bill-of-fare, but its flesh was highly esteemed" (Best, 1902, p. 47). It was served only on important occasions as when a distinguished visitor arrived; and when people approached death it was served for a "food for the death journey." Islands with chickens usually ranked them below dog and pork. In Easter Island the importance of the chicken, the only domesticated animal, so pervaded the culture that even the significance of the dog to Maoris pales by contrast.

Certain parts of favored meats, not necessarily the largest or tastiest portions, outranked other parts in prestige. Maoris rated a dog's hindquarters as best for eating. Hawaiians, at those feasts where most of the food was eaten in company instead of distributed and eaten at home, gave the highest chief present the head or the brains of a pig; the carver, a commoner, got the backbone and the tail; the priests got other undesignated parts (Ellis, 1853, 4: 346). Society Islanders frugally assigned enough prestige to the head or tufts of hair and another extremity like the tail to be able to give these parts to gods on occasion. Slaves and servants of chiefs usually received entrails of animals killed for secular feasts.

Because gods in Polynesia formed the highest ranking group and led all others in power and prestige, sacrifices and offerings of foods to gods cannot be separated functionally from foods consumed by people. Gods were ever present in the thoughts, emotions, activities, and behavior of subsidiary groups, and visible in material possessions and symbols. Deities had first claim to food as to amount, most desirable kinds, and most valued parts. They received these foods as sacrifices during formal rites and as offerings at communion feasts that concluded ceremonies.

Maoris made few blood sacrifices compared to Hawaiians and Society Islanders who, perhaps not long before discovery, began to sacrifice large numbers of people and animals, with human beings outranking hogs and dogs as sacrifices. Tongans, according to Cook (Cook, 1784, 1: 405), did not make offerings of hogs, dogs, and fruit as in Tahiti "unless it be emblematically," meaning perhaps that fewer were sacrificed. Western Polynesians, so far as I can determine, made few, if any, dog sacrifices. At least one Marquesan tribe added dogs acquired after discovery to their list of sacrifices. Among the first dogs reported were two sacrificed with human beings, pork, fish, and vegetables before images in a Nukuhivan sacred place (Stewart, 1831, 1: 272, 332). Killed and dressed as for eating, one dog hung by the neck from a pole, the other from a post in a coconut-leaf basket. Nothing indicates whether tribes abhorring dog meat thought gods felt the same way and did not sacrifice it. The first reported Polynesian dog sacrifices were seen in 1765 at Napuka and Tepoto, Tuamotus, by Byron (Callander, 1766–68, 3: 709) who wrote, "A rude but very agreeable avenue opened to a spacious area, in which was one of the largest and most spreading cocoas we saw in the place, before which there were several large stones, which were probably altars, and from the trees hung the figure of a dog adorned with feathers."

Cook's journal (Cook, 1784, 2: 32, 35) described a dog sacrifice at

Atahuru, a large Tahitian *marae,* that illustrates a ritual pattern. Although reported specifically only for Tahiti, dog sacrifices were probably general throughout the Society Islands. Purea's *marae* on Tahiti had skulls of "a great number of dogs" and of fifty pigs; another had remains of six dogs and twenty-six hogs (Hawkesworth, 1773, 2: 168; Cook, 1777, 1: 185). The dog sacrificed at Atahuru had been picked up earlier at a little island. It was killed and dressed as for eating. The entrails were burned up in the fire. Heart, liver, and kidneys, quickly broiled, were given, with the carcass, which had been smeared with blood collected in a coconut shell and dried over the fire, to the loudly chanting priests, who continued to pray as two men beat two drums and a boy screamed three different times. The priests, prayers ended, had the carcass put on a six-foot-high scaffold. To end the ritual, all present shouted together. On a nearby scaffold were remains of two dogs and two pigs that, sacrificed earlier, now emitted "an intolerable stench." The ceremony was part of several days of rites in which men and hogs were also sacrificed to win the god Oro's help in war against a neighboring island.

Maori gods received dog sacrifices when canoes in the legendary Fleet prayed for good weather, when aristocrats' children were tattooed or had their schoolhouse dedicated, and when a war party prepared to take revenge for a chief's death (White, 1887–91, 1: 9; Tregear, 1904, p. 172). A dog, but preferably a person, was sacrificed. The roasted dog was eaten only by gods or their representatives, priests and important laymen. Dog sacrifice was an old part of their culture, Maoris believed. When Turi's canoe en route from Hawaiki stopped near New Zealand at a little island to refit and to sacrifice a dog to get good winds, the island was named to commemorate the day of sacrifice (Smith, 1893, p. 218; Colenso, 1877, p. 152). A priest cut up the raw meat (the dog was named Tangakakariki) and laid it on pillars for the gods. After prayers and invitations to the gods to eat, this meat or that of another named dog was roasted; again spirits were invited to partake of the essence of the meat. No one is mentioned as eating this meat. Dog sacrifice was particularly dear to Maru, a war god, and when the *Ririno,* a companion canoe to Turi's *Aotea,* was lost, one explanation was that the captain irregularly ate dog meat dedicated to Maru, the most powerful god of the expedition.

Narrators state that before a certain war party to avenge a Maori chief's slain brother a dog caught along the way was sacrificed (White, 1887–91, 3: 224). The priest held up the heart, which had been removed and roasted, offered it to the dead man's spirit and the gods, and then gave it to the oldest man in the party to eat. Later on the journey, after challenging the enemy, the priest cooked the hind leg, offered it as before, but ate it himself. As the preferred type of sacrifice, an enemy, was captured the next day, nothing more is said of the dog meat. The same tribe had a chief who before a war party ate a whole cooked dog without cutting it up (White, 1887–91, 3: 170, 173). Perhaps this is a variant of the central Polynesian custom of a warrior trying to eat an entire animal himself before battle; to be unable to do so was a bad omen. In general it was bad manners and unlucky not to consume all consecrated food.

In the Hawaiian Islands, Captain King (Cook, 1784, 3: 17, 160) of Cook's expedition reported numerous sacrifices of dogs and stated that a pig or a dog, together with red feathers and vegetables, was customarily laid on a scaffold before an image decorated with red cloth and other ornaments. In 1804 Lisiansky (Lisiansky, 1814, p. 121) saw on Hawaii what appeared to be roasted hogs and dogs interspersed with human sacrifices but another observer differed on the nature of the offerings. "Vast offerings of fruit, hogs, and dogs" and no less than eleven people were sacrificed, said the Reverend William Ellis (1853, 4: 98), when Kamehameha's principal war god was installed on Hawaii in a specially built shrine. The island of Hawaii did not sacrifice dogs until the time of Kalaniopu'u (Tereeboo of Captain King's account), according to a Hawaiian whose grandfather had served in a temple, but "this may not hold true for other islands," Beckwith remarked (1951, p. 90). Perhaps the most certain value of this Hawaiian's claim relating to events nearly two hundred years ago is to indicate that the dog had less prestige in Hawaiian religion than, for example, the pig. Pork was so sacred that a boy of high birth could not eat it until he had gone through rites of passage that permitted him for the first time to eat in the men's house, the only place where pork could be eaten. Never again would he eat with women. The men's house, being the family shrine where images and the other sacred objects were kept, was taboo to women, who as one consequence could not eat pork (Malo, 1951, p. 94).

Hawaiian magicians used baked or broiled dogs in rituals (Malo,

1951, pp. 101-3, 108; Ellis, 1853, 4: 294). Two were ceremonially baked for an important man who was ill. He and other men ate one dog in the men's house; women in the common house offered the other dog to healing goddesses and presumably ate the meat. The ceremony was repeated if the ailing man were removed to another hut. A magician might also cut open, disembowel, and lay the body of a dog on the fire near the invalid and study the broiling food for omens. After eating a bit he let the rest burn to ashes and hoped the eaten portion would produce a dream revealing the identity of the sorcerer who had caused the illness. If the patient died, the magician stuffed parts of the liver of the dissected corpse into the mouths of dogs and chickens to help him to discover and punish the sorcerer who had caused the death. The patient's family paid large numbers of dogs, chickens, and other goods for the ceremony. Chanters to purify individuals who had handled corpses called for the blood of dogs and pigs to be sacrificed (Ellis, 1853, 4: 98, 164).

Ranked after gods in prestige, power, and privileges were their closest male descendants, hereditary high chiefs and high priests. They were free to eat highly valued foods at any time except during cere-monial periods when one or more prestige foods were taboo even to them. Restricted periods occurred during rites of passage for a chief and his family or during rites of intensification like the Hawaiian Makahiki from October into January. In December, 1788, at a feast on Hawaii, the only meat eaten by the king and his party was fish (Meares, 1790, pp. 278, 338). Lower-ranking chiefs, sitting some distance away, ate roasted dog. No one ate fresh pork or chicken; the taboo on pork applied during the Makahiki from the king to the lowest chief, that is, to those who ate it customarily. The taboo on the king eating even dog meat at the feast just mentioned doubtless derived from specific religious duties required of him at this time. High priests, to protect his sanctity upon which the welfare of society depended, might for other reasons at other periods, for varying lengths of time, restrict his diet and behavior. Six years later in January, Vancouver (1798, 3: 24) attended a feast at which "the more common productions, such as fish, turtle, fowls, and dogs" were completely absent because the pork taboo had just been lifted and sacred foods like pork, plantains, and coconuts, "consecrated for the principal chiefs and priests," were served. At a feast given by Kamehameha the next month, dog meat, fish, and fowls, but no pork, were served; the reason for the omission is not stated (Vancouver, 1798, 3: 36). Subsequently Vancouver gave a feast at which, in a scene reminiscent of Captain Cook, the guests informally voted on whether dog or mutton (the latter European, of course) was tastier; King Kamehameha himself broke the tie by rating his host's mutton above dog (Vancouver, 1798, 3: 61).

Ranking below high chiefs and high priests in hereditary or ascribed status were inferior nobles and inferior priests. Among the latter were individuals who had acquired considerable status because they were technological experts whose success required knowledge of magic and religion. The Maori tattooer who received the only dog in the village as sacred food when he tattooed a chieftainess illustrates how an individual achieved exceptional honor through occupational skill; his assistant who helped eat the dog illustrates the advantages accruing to those affiliated with such a man. Rebels like Ruatapu, who killed his elder half-brother's dog, often challenged hereditary status in a struggle to acquire more prestige and authority. Class lines, which tended to be clearer among Society and Hawaiian Islanders than among the less crystallized Maoris, blurred between lesser nobility and commoners. Slaves scarcely counted as human beings. Dedicated servants in *maraes* and favorite attendants of chiefs benefited from propinquity to leaders in food distribution. In the Society Islands those whose talents qualified them to join the Ariois, a stratified society of entertainers serving the gods, enjoyed privileges otherwise reserved for important chiefs, including the right to eat all delicacies both in this world and in the special afterworld reserved for them (G. Forster, 1777, 2: 130).

At those Hawaiian and Society Islands feasts which were occasions for redistributing food and goods, the highest chief allotted shares according to the rank of his lesser chiefs (Ellis, 1853, 4: 346; Malo, 1951, p. 143). They took home their share to redistribute it among dependents. The bottom man who actually tended the dogs and pigs got little or nothing. When a Society Islands chief killed a pig he divided it with his dependents, who were usually so numerous no one received much. Cook's party (Cook, 1784, 2: 49; Hawkesworth, 1773, 2: 196) saw just the entrails divided into eleven portions with each containing a bit of everything and given to servants. Producers had the privilege of openly eating scraps left from these secular feasts.

Pork, the most prized food, was especially taboo to commoners except as remnants of feasts. At a feast in Huahine that Cook (1777, 1: 176) attended, many of the commoners, as soon as guests had risen, "rushed in, to pick up the crumbs which had fallen, and for which they searched the leaves very narrowly. This leads me to believe that, though there is plenty of pork at these islands, but little falls at any time to their share." Earlier he had noted that "dogs and fowls fall somewhat more frequently to the share of the common man" (Hawkesworth, 1773, 2: 196), but later decided even these were restricted (Cook, 1777, 1: 185).

The Tahitian national atonement ceremony, at which hogs, dogs, and other foods were sacrificed to the gods in the hope of removing evil and trouble from the world, illustrates phases of social and religious niceties (Henry, 1928, pp. 131-77). Dogs and hogs were dressed differently for sacrifice according to whether they were labeled "petitions with food" or "peace offerings." The entire pantheon was invited to attend to receive sacrifices, which, to judge from references to the stench from scaffolds, were not eaten by people except when ceremonial procedure required the high priest or high chief to consume ritually a portion. Remains not eaten by birds, rats, and other creatures regarded as divine manifestations were finally removed and buried in special garbage pits on *marae* grounds. Food for the feast that concluded the week-long ceremony was specially prepared and consecrated with parts offered to gods before even the high chief removed his share from the *marae*. He did not eat in the *marae* with the other men eligible to share in the feast. The high priest and all the lesser priests and professional temple attendants sat down in special sheds to eat. Any haste, greediness, or other misbehavior in eating lowered a man's prestige and angered the gods. The feast was a communion, not an orgy. Theoretically all food should be eaten or thrown into the pits. However adjustments had been made. After asking divine permission, high priests felt free openly to take home to their wives and children some of the meat but not the most sacred parts. Lesser participants did not have this as an openly recognized privilege but secretly carried home leftovers to their families. Thus individuals who would under no circumstances be entitled to taste these delicacies at either secular or religious feasts nonetheless shared in them.

Women who were first-born children in important families tracing their ancestry to gods had privileges not permitted women of low rank, but even rank did not lift taboos on certain foods reserved for men. Dog meat was reported taboo to all women in two or three Maori tribes; how general the taboo actually was is not clear. Pregnancy cravings for dog meat, it will be recalled, were respected; were defense needed, a woman argued for the welfare of her unborn child, who might of course be male. Regulations seem to have been as flexible in the Society Islands as in New Zealand. Wealth and rank probably determined indulgence, for Purea seemed to speak from personal acquaintance with dog meat when she told Cook how good it was. Women, according to Cook's journal (Cook, 1784, 2: 156), were "excluded from a share of most of the better sort of food . . . and it is very seldom that even those of the first rank are suffered to eat pork." Yet expedition members themselves saw high ranking women at a secular feast given portions of pork to eat apart from men. Forster echoes Bougainville's statement (Bougainville, 1772, p. 251) that children and young girls never ate flesh. Women eagerly ate restricted foods if circumstances, like invitations to eat aboard European ships, seemed outside their taboo area psychologically and spatially. Society Islands women visiting Cook's ships even ate pork without apparent anxiety about the fact becoming known ashore.

Such was not the case in the Hawaiian Islands where even a queen (Campbell, 1816, pp. 187-88) asked that her dietary indulgences not be reported and Cook's party (Cook, 1784, 3: 295) told of a girl who was beaten when it was learned ashore that she had eaten pork with them. Women would not eat turtle and certain plantains, however; apparently these taboos women strictly enforced upon themselves because they regarded them as harmful to their physiological welfare as women. In 1809 "dogs' flesh and fish were the only kinds of animal food lawful for them to eat" (Campbell, 1816, pp. 187-88). However, a missionary wife, who arrived five months after the overthrow of the taboo system in 1819 by the king, the dowager queen, and the high priest, declared that dog meat was taboo to women "in the days of idolatry" (Thurston, 1882). Overthrow of the taboo was marked by the king's eating with women for the first time since childhood, and moreover eating food prepared in the same oven; the women ate for the first time, in public, foods formerly taboo to them. The list of foods reported tends to vary. Opinions conflict, it will be noted, on whether women were permitted to eat dog meat before the overthrow. According to Rev. William Ellis (Ellis, 1853, 4: 387), ". . . almost anything offered in sacrifice, was tabu to the use of the gods and the men; hence, the women were, except in cases of particular indulgence, restricted from using them." He does not state what the situation was in regard to dog meat. Later writers state that for nourishment before childbirth and for purification afterwards a Hawaiian chieftainess ate dog broth, but a brown dog must not be used (Malo, 1951, p. 139; Fornander, 1916–19, 6: Part 1: 2, 18, 28, 36, 40), and that during Makahiki ceremonies the king offered female divinities ten baked dogs while at the conclusion of Makahiki rites men prepared ovens of pork while women prepared ovens of dog meat.

At discovery Polynesians had a simple pattern of livestock care, most marked in islands where high-ranking people delegated the care to servants (J. Forster, 1778, p. 371), and perhaps too where a dog was particularly prized, like a Maori dog with a fine pelt which was given clean sleeping mats and kept from getting even its feet wet. Experts, later-day writers add, shaved the long hair off the tails in such a way as not to injure the dog or prevent regrowth of hair; and some dogs were castrated (Colenso, 1877, p. 150; Tregear, 1904, p. 167).

Three modes of shelter for dogs occurred, namely, a place in the Tuamotuan or Hawaiian family hut (G. Forster, 1777, 2: 42; Arago, 1823, p. 64; Lisiansky, 1814, p. 107); a special hut in New Zealand and Hawaii which might have a fence around it (Ellis, 1853, 4: 347; Dixon, 1789, p. 274; Dieffenbach, 1843, 1: 199); or a natural shelter like the Society Islands tree which was "old and jagged, the abode of rats and the shelter of pet dogs" (Henry, 1928, p. 548). Probably all three forms were present at discovery in all islands with the dog and other domestic animals.

Dogs that were systematically fed were predominantly vegetarian, leading to their being called "poi dogs" in Hawaii, but they also got some fish and scraps. Less well-attended dogs were scavengers. Breast-feeding of selected puppies has been mentioned. Forced feeding hastened the fattening process. Hawaiian dogs were thrown on their backs to stuff fish, and doubtless vegetable paste also, into their mouths (Fornander, 1916–19, 6: Part 3: 380); at Huahine George Forster (1777, 1: 377) saw a woman stuffing breadfruit poi into a reluctant

pig. Tinirau, according to a western Polynesian story, asked his estranged wife to chew up vegetables for her pet dog that she had left
with him. Vegetables were believed to give the meat a delicate flavor
that some natives prized above pork. Cross-breeding with European
dogs and a less selected diet caused the flavor to deteriorate (Dieffenbach, 1843, 2: 45). Hawaiians, it is said, maintained the standard
long after discovery (F. Bennett, 1840, 1: 86, 216, 246).

A dog to be eaten was usually suffocated, either by pressure with
the hands, with the aid of a stick, or a cord around the muzzle, or
sometimes with its head pressed into the chest. Before being baked
in an earth oven the dog was disemboweled, the body washed and
singed, and sometimes smeared with blood caught in a coconut shell.
Where the dog was not present or not reported at discovery but noted
later, it is specifically reported as being eaten at Futuna, Uvea, Pukapuka, Tonga, Samoa, Marquesas, and Easter Island; nothing is stated
about the practice at Tokelaus, Ellices, Cook Islands, Manihiki-
Rakahanga, Tongareva, Rapa, and Australs.

How many dogs Society Islanders and especially Hawaiians raised
is indicated by the numbers reported for feasts and other purposes.
In 1820 for a feast on the anniversary of Kamehameha's death, one
hundred to two hundred dogs, forelegs tied over their backs and mouths
bound, were collected and thrown in groups in a pen to be killed for
a feast (Thurston, 1882, p. 40). A few years later, nearly two hundred
dogs were cooked at one time; another feast had four hundred baked
dogs (Ellis, 1853, 4: 346). The large numbers of dog teeth, preferably
canines, used in ornaments also indicate the extent of Hawaiian dog
raising. Far from rare in museums today are dancers' anklets made of
canine teeth fastened in rows about nine inches deep on strong netting.
The thirteen of fifteen in Bishop Museum which are complete have a
total of 11,218 canine teeth from 2,805 dogs. Enough dogs were
raised to permit the ornament maker to be selective, for the teeth are
usually matched in size (Buck, 1957, p. 553; Cook, 1784, 3: 27;
Vancouver, 1798, 3: 39). Idols had double rows of dog fangs (Cook,
1784, 3: 17; W. Bennett, 1931, p. 89; Buck, 1957, p. 504); necklaces
and wristlets also used them (Buck, 1957, p. 545; Cook, 1784, 3: 139;
Fornander, 1916–19, 6: Part 1: 208).

Hawaiians used more dog teeth than did the Maoris who also had
dog-tooth necklaces (Hawkesworth, 1773, 3: 457) and earrings

(Hawkesworth, 1773, 3: 53), but they did not reserve these artifacts for aristocracy. Hawaiian abundance probably depreciated the prestige value and both Hawaiian men and women in the lower ranks wore dog-tooth ornaments. Dog bone was less used, although Hawaiians cut hair with a shark tooth set into the forepart of a dog jawbone (Cook, 1784, 2: 239) and both Hawaiians and Maoris used the bone for fishhooks (Malo, 1951, p. 79; W. Bennett, 1931, p. 83). Nothing has been reported of any Tuamotuan artifacts made from parts of a dog. Society Islanders, it will be recalled, trimmed their warrior chiefs' spectacular breastplates with white dog hair, and also used it on fishhooks, and perhaps wigs too (Cook, 1777, 2: 193; Parkinson, 1773, p. 70, Pl. XI; Henry, 1928, p. 299). Maoris also trimmed fishhooks with white dog hair, usually from the tail (Hawkesworth, 1773, 2: 218), and contrarily narrated that before he had created the first dog Maui used such a hook to fish up New Zealand and borrowed his mother's dog-hair trimmed apron for a disguise. Such a garment was usually worn only by men of rank (Hamilton, 1896, p. 289). White hair from a dog's tail ornamented a bulrush ball used in dances (Tregear, 1904, p. 62). Some types of staffs and clubs that chiefs carried both as weapons and symbols of authority bore tufts of white dog hair and red feathers; a thong of dog hide or flax attached a short weapon to the wrist. Hawaiians used little dog hair, but tufts of dog hair decorated wooden wands. Men wore short ones in their hair, and carried wands five to six feet in length in games, dances, and ceremonial processions (Cook, 1784, 2: 232, 236; 3: 5).

Even more spectacular as a class symbol than the Tahitian breastplate was the Maori dogskin cloak worn only by chiefs and perhaps the most prized of the various types of cloaks developed in this colder archipelago of Polynesia (Hamilton, 1896, p. 286). The cloaks, a local Maori invention, were of several different types, each named. Variations consisted largely of how, and in what color arrangements, men had attached long, hairy strips of dog hide, or tufts of long white tail hair, on the flax foundation closely woven by women. The scarcity of dogs gave cloaks rarity value and accounted in part for the more frequent use of strips rather than the entire pelt which was used only in a certain type of battle cloak named Irawaru for the god of dogs.

A dogskin cloak was a symbol of high rank, authority, dignity, mature age, wealth, and luxury. It was an heirloom that a father passed on at retirement or death to his eldest son, his customary successor to the chieftainship. While the son shared other inherited property with close kinsmen, he kept the cloak for himself. It was a treasure that was the pride of the individual entitled by rank to wear it and of all his kinsmen, who would have been ashamed if their leader had not been as elegantly outfitted as other chiefs. It was one of the most significant gifts that a kinship group could give in a gift exchange with another group to strengthen what were hoped would be lasting bonds of friendship. Added to its personal prestige and mana was the knowledge, perpetuated by tradition, of its characteristics and history. Each outstanding cloak, besides being identified as to type, had a personal name; and remembered too might be the names of the female weavers, the male processors of the pelt, the dogs whose pelts were used, and any previous owners of the cloak.

Observers mention only chiefs as wearing cloaks but a narrative refers to a chieftainess who had one. An Orpheus-type love story about Pare, a chieftainess of such high rank that no man was eligible to marry her, describes her way of living (White, 1887–91, 2: 163). It sounds like a Maori dream-wish. Her food had to pass through four different hands before being fed to her; her beautifully carved house was surrounded by three sets of palisades and perfumed with greenery; among her many named types of fine mats was one of dogskin which besides having strips of fur on the foundation was bordered at the top with long white hair from the dog's tail. Another legendary chieftainess owned fifty dogs and had as servants twenty-five men and as many women (Smith, 1913, 1915, Part 2: 248).

Early European visitors realized the value of these cloaks, usually admired them, and recognized that only chiefs wore them. Cook's remarks are typical. He immediately realized that the men with the fine clothing were chiefs, and that the "great pride of their dress" was the dogskin cloak, of which they took excellent care and tried to display to best advantage at ceremonies. When a chief traveled by canoe he either did not wear his cloak enroute or he turned the fur inside to protect it from salt water and other damage, and reversed it on arrival at his destination. Cook (Hawkesworth, 1773, 3: 466) noted that at "about a cable's length from the ship, they (canoes) used to stop; and the chiefs, rising from their seat, put on a dress which seemed appropriate to the occasion, generally of dog's skins, and holding out

their decorated staff, or weapon, directed the rest of the people."
Crozet (Crozet, 1783, p. 72) and a member of D'Urville's expedition
also admired the handsome appearance of the chiefs in their cloaks,
but a later observer regarded it as a "gaudy show" (Black, 1922).

Although Maoris waved greenery and dogskins at De Surville
(Crozet, 1783, p. 281), Cook's expedition apparently never got a cloak.
At least twice chiefs led the British to believe that they would barter
their cloaks for European cloth (Parkinson, 1773, pp. 94, 104), but
each time the chief took the cloth passed down to his canoe and
paddled away without giving up his cloak. One chief, who sold one
after the other all his garments until only the dogskin cloak was left,
was shot and killed for his trickery; the European cloth, native narrators
state, became his shroud. A cloak had too much prestige to be crassly
bartered for cloth. If a cloak were to be surrendered it would be in
connection with ceremony, as for De Surville. Usually two Maori
groups exchanged treasures as equal as possible in sentimental associations, mana, and quality. Each having given the other a cherished
part of himself hoped to create a binding link of friendship and peace.
Usually one party initiated the exchange by asking for a valued object.
Naturally the request came only from someone who considered himself
of equal status with the owner. To refuse would be an insult leading
to revenge. It meant that the asker was inferior to the owner and not
the kind of person with whom an important chief wished to initiate
a series of gift exchanges. One example of a tradition in which the
request was granted and one involving both a refusal and a granting
will be cited.

While still in Hawaiki, Turi, having asked his father-in-law for the
canoe *Aotea* and received it, sent his wife with an *utu matua*, "a return
gift for the parent," consisting of a double dogskin cloak named Potaka-
tawhiti and made from eight named dogs, one being Potaka himself
(Smith, 1900, p. 217). One fabulous gift was exchanged for another;
of the two the cloak was more fabulous because the Maoris did not
have such cloaks until they colonized New Zealand and the *Aotea*
was one of the canoes in the legendary Fleet.

The other tradition is about ambitious Tuahumahina, jealous of
another chief Kawaharu (White, 1887–91, 4: 101). He attacked him
but was defeated, for Kawaharu had the aid of his father-in-law, Toa-
rangatira. A dogskin cloak, the direct incitement to the attack, was

merely a counter in determining the relative status of the family led by Tuahumahina and that led by his rival and rival's father-in-law. That Toa, as the laconically told tradition states, received many gifts from other tribes of luxury foods like preserved birds, eels, mussels, shark, and dog's flesh is evidence that he was engaged in many inter-tribal gift exchanges. He would not have received so much if he in turn had not given much. That "like a father" he shared the gifts with his tribesmen who were devoted to him meant that they then whole-heartedly aided him in assembling return gifts. Toa's aid to his son-in-law reflects his generous nature and the good rapport between two men who knew what a good chief should be. Tuahumahina, who had decided that he wanted a noted dogskin cloak named Korongakahura, sent his messenger to request it of the tribe owning it. He was refused. When Kawaharu's old father, apparently retired, heard of the refusal he made up his mind to ask for it. His son, rhetorically, no doubt, asked how he thought he would get it if Tuahumahina did not. Said his father revealingly, "Does Tuahumahina ever give anything to the tribes? He is a greedy man, as is proved by the fact of the mat not having been given to him, but it will be given to me." He departed, saying that if he received the cloak he would blow his trumpet on his return. The trumpet was blown. When the rival heard of the incident his hostility flamed into "malicious hatred." That Kawaharu's family got the cloak showed that it was more respected than Tuahumahina's. Angrily the chief attacked not the givers who had made the evalu-ation but the recipients who had both the prestige and the cloak. Maui similarly took revenge not against the woman who discrimi-nated against him but against the man she had favored. Incidentally the respectful relations between a man and his father-in-law are illus-trated in the traditions about Turi, Kawaharu, and Ihenga.

More than one tradition tells of a dogskin cloak being thrown over a prisoner of war whose life was then spared because the cloak of the chief having touched the prisoner made him his property. It is the principle of *tapatapa* again. Another common theme regarding dogskin cloaks has to do with abduction of wives. The next story illustrates both themes. A chief named Turangitamau, whose wife and children had been abducted by a chief Moki, secretly slipped into Moki's house at night to talk with his wife (White, 1887–91, 3: 219). Hearing that Moki had treated her well, he threw his dogskin cloak over the sleeping chief and asked his wife to tell Moki he had spared his life. Moki was greatly humiliated on hearing of the visit and seeing the cloak. No warrior should be caught asleep, but since he had been caught he should not have been treated like a common prisoner to become Terangi's tabooed property which no one of lesser rank than his captor would dare injure. Eventually the two made peace. Perhaps the grandeur of Terangi's gesture and Moki's appreciation of the coup helped cancel the trouble.

That Maoris admired the ability to rise grandly to an occasion and then to soar above it is also evident in another story of a dogskin cloak and an abducted wife (White, 1887–91, 3: 137). When a superior chief carried off Tuhauanu's wife, Tu followed his wife's litter to say a last farewell and to throw over her his dogskin cloak. Tu, the narrator states, did "two noble deeds; he gave up his wife and his valuable dogskin cloak." Tu's inability to take revenge is rationalized into a grand gesture by his voluntary surrender of his wife and the symbol of his chieftainship; his lack of military support probably prevented him from taking revenge so that the principle of *tapatapa* would not apply.

A woman who once tried on a great chief's cloak thereby contaminated it; the chief's family killed in revenge a servant of the woman's family, and this set off a war between tribes (White, 1887–91, 3: 267). Rarity of a treasure might be a disadvantage sometimes. A husband needed no detective to deduce who had abducted his wife from near their kumara pit; on the upper sill were white doghairs; the only chief in the region who had a dogskin cloak was obviously the abductor (White, 1887–91, 4: 192).

Any domesticated animal has a peculiar situation in a culture. Its domestication and the traits forming part of the complex of domestication are determined by the existence of culture. Particular forms assumed by elements of the complex are fixed by the peculiarities of each culture. The appearance, habits, and comings and goings of an animal are altered by the culture adopting it. The animal, however, does not thereby become a passive figure in the cultural scene. It also modifies its human owner's superficial appearance, habits, and comings and goings. Animal and human being reciprocally influence each other's way of life. Man in a sense becomes as much a servant of his domesticated animal as the animal is his servant. While the direction of Polynesian culture was not fundamentally modified by the presence of domesticated animals, the major archipelagoes whether they had only one or two or all three would have had a much less rich culture in every way.

This article has described how one element of culture, one domestic animal, the dog, served those Polynesians who clearly had it at the time of discovery in a multitude of ways, utilitarian, emotional, and symbolic. Through the cultural values Polynesians associated with the dog, it served, in combination with other traits, to rate people in status, either positively or negatively. Some of these values placed on the dog were directly contradictory to each other in different facets of culture. To insult a dog was to insult its master, but to identify the master with his dog was to insult the master. To sacrifice a dog to a god was creditable, but to call a man a sacrificed dog was to discredit him. In communicating with each other, people well understood in which context to interpret an experience.

REFERENCES

Aitken, Robert T. 1930. Ethnology of Tubuai. B. P. Bishop Museum, Bulletin 70.

Arago, Jacques. 1823. Narrative of a Voyage Round the World ... (1817–1820). London.

Beaglehole, Ernest, and Pearl Beaglehole. 1938. Ethnology of Pukapuka. B. P. Bishop Museum, Bulletin 150.

Beckwith, Martha. 1940. Hawaiian mythology. New Haven.

—— 1951. The Kumulipo, a Hawaiian Creation Chant. Chicago.

Beechey, Frederick W. 1831. Narrative of a Voyage to the Pacific and Beering's Strait ... (1825–1828). Vols. 1-2. London.

Bennett, Frederick D. 1840. Narrative of a Whaling Voyage Round the Globe ... (1833–1836). Vols. 1-2. London.

Bennett, Wendell C. 1931. Archaeology of Kauai. B. P. Bishop Museum. Bulletin 80.

Best, Elsdon. 1897. Waikare-Moana, the Sea of the Rippling Waters. Wellington, N.Z.

—— 1902. "Food Products of Tuhoeland," New Zealand Institute, *Transactions* and *Proceedings*, 35:45-111.

—— 1924. The Maori. 2 vols. Polynesian Society, Memoir 5.

—— 1925. Tuhoe, the Children of the Mist. Polynesian Society, Memoir 6.

—— 1942. Forest Lore of the Maori. Dominion Museum, Bulletin 14.

Black, G. J. 1922. "A Maori Dog-Skin Cloak (kahu kuri)," *Polynesian Society Journal*, 31:59-63.

Bligh, William. 1792. A Voyage to the South Sea ... in the Bounty. ... London.

Bougainville, Louis Antoine de. 1772. A Voyage Round the World ... (1766–1769). Trans. by John Reinhold Forster. Dublin.

Buck, Peter H. 1957. Arts and Crafts of Hawaii. B. P. Bishop Museum, Spec. Pub. 45.

Buddle, Roger. 1912. "Contributions to South Island (N.Z.) Maori History," Polynesian Society Journal, 21:173-80.

Callander, John, ed. 1766–68. Terra Australis Cognita: or, voyages to the Terra Australis, or southern hemisphere, during the sixteenth, seventeenth, and eighteenth century. 3 vols. Edinburgh.

Campbell, Archibald. 1816. Voyage Round the World, from 1806 to 1812. Edinburgh.

Christian, F. W. 1910. Eastern Pacific Islands, Tahiti and the Marquesas Islands. London.

Colenso, W. 1877. "Notes, Chiefly Historical, on the Ancient Dog of the New Zealanders," New Zealand Institute, Transactions and Proceedings, 10:135-55.

———— 1891. "Vestiges: Reminiscences; Memorabilia of Works, Deeds, and Sayings of the Ancient Maoris," New Zealand Institute, Transactions and Proceedings, 24:445-57.

Collocott, E. E. V. 1921a. "Notes on Tongan Religion," Polynesian Society Journal, 30:152-63, 227-40.

———— 1921b. "Legends from Tonga," Folk-Lore, 32:45-58.

Cook, James. 1777. A Voyage towards the South Pole, and Round the World ... in ... 1772–1775. 2 vols. and atlas. London.

———— 1784. A Voyage to the Pacific Ocean.... 3 vols. and atlas. London. (Vol. 3 by James King.)

Corney, Bolton G. 1913, 1915, 1918. The Quest and Occupation of Tahiti by Emissaries of Spain during the years 1772–1776. 3 vols. Hakluyt Society, Ser. 2, Vols. 32, 36, 43. London.

Crozet. 1783. Nouveau voyage a la Mer du Sud ... rédigée d'après les plans et journaux de M. Crozet, by Alexis Marie de Rochon. On a joint a ce voyage un extrait de celui de M. de Surville dans les mêmes parages. Paris.

Daniels, W. P. 1862. In Hawaiian Ethnological Notes, Vol. 1, pp. 3136-3240 (No. 620, p. 3144). Trans. by M. K. Pukui from Ka Hoku o ka Paipika, Jan. 16, 1862. In Bishop Museum Library.

Dieffenbach, Ernest. 1843. Travels in New Zealand. 2 vols. London.

Dillon, Peter. 1829. Narrative and Successful Result of a Voyage in the South Seas.... 2 vols. London.

Dixon, George. 1789. A Voyage Round the World ... (1785–1788). 2d ed. London.

Duff, Roger. 1950. The Moa-Hunter Period of Maori Culture. Wellington, N.Z.

Ellis, William. 1853. Polynesian Researches. 4 vols. London.

Emory, Kenneth P., personal communication.

———— 1933. Stone Remains in the Society Islands. B. P. Bishop Museum, Bulletin 116.

———— 1947. Tuamotuan Religious Structures and Ceremonies. B. P. Bishop Museum, Bulletin 191.

Firth, Raymond. 1929. Primitive Economics of the New Zealand Maori. New York.

Fletcher, H. J. 1922. "A Few of the Maori Wise Sayings from Lake Taupo," Polynesian Society Journal, 31:29-36.

Fornander, Abraham. 1916–19. Collection of Hawaiian Antiquities and Folklore.

B. P. Bishop Museum, Memoirs 4, 5, 6.

Forster, George. 1777. A Voyage Round the World ... (1772–1775). 2 vols. London.

Forster, John Reinhold. 1778. Observations Made during a Voyage Round the World. . . . London.

Gifford, E. W. 1924. Tongan Myths and Tales. B. P. Bishop Museum, Bulletin 8.

———— 1929. Tongan Society. B. P. Bishop Museum, Bulletin 61.

Gill, William Wyatt. 1876. Life in the Southern Isles. . . . London.

———— 1885. Jottings from the Pacific. London.

———— 1894. From Darkness to Light in Polynesia. London.

Grey, George. 1885. Polynesian Mythology. 2d ed. Auckland, N.Z.

Gudgeon, W. E. 1895. "The Maori Tribes of the East Coast of New Zealand," *Polynesian Society Journal*, 4:17-32.

Hahn, Eduard. 1896. Die Haustiere und ihre Beziehungen zur Wirtschaft des Menschen. Leipzig.

Hamilton, Augustus. 1896. The Art Workmanship of the Maori Race in New Zealand. Dunedin, N.Z.

Handy, E. S. Craighill. 1923. The Native Culture of the Marquesas. B. P. Bishop Museum, Bulletin 9.

Hawkesworth, John. 1773. An Account of the Voyages ... for Making Discoveries in the Southern Hemisphere, by Commodore Byron, Captain Wallis, Captain Carteret, and Captain Cook. 3 vols. London.

Henry, Teuira. 1928. Ancient Tahiti. B. P. Bishop Museum, Bulletin 48.

Labillardière, Jacques Julien de. 1800. Voyage in Search of La Pérouse ... (1791–1794). English trans. London.

La Pérouse, Jean François de Galaup de. 1798. The Voyage of La Pérouse Round the World ... (1785–1788). English trans. 2 vols. London.

Liliuokalani, Queen (trans.), and Keaulumoku. 1897. An Account of the Creation. . . . Boston.

Lisiansky, Urey. 1814. A Voyage Round the World. . . . London.

Luomala, Katharine. 1955. Voices on the Wind. Honolulu.

———— 1958. "Polynesian Myths about Maui and the Dog," *Fabula*, 2:139-62.

McAllister, J. Gilbert. 1933. Archaeology of Oahu. B. P. Bishop Museum, Bulletin 104.

Malo, David. 1951. Hawaiian Antiquities. B. P. Bishop Museum, Spec. Pub. 2, 2d ed.

Martin, John. 1817. An Account of the Natives of the Tongan Islands. Compiled and Arranged from the Communications of Mr. William Mariner. 2 vols. London.

Meares, John. 1790. Voyages Made in the Years 1788 and 1789. . . . London.

Parkinson, Sydney. 1773. Journal of a Voyage to the South Seas. London.

Porter, David. 1815. Journal of a Cruise Made to the Pacific Ocean ... (1812–1814). 2 vols. Philadelphia.

Portlock, Nathaniel. 1789. A Voyage Round the World ... (1785–1788). London.

Pukui, Mary Kawena, and Samuel H. Elbert. 1957. Hawaiian-English Dictionary. Honolulu.

Quiros, Pedro Fernandez de. 1904. The Voyages of Pedro Fernandez de Quiros. Trans. and ed. by Sir Clements Markham. Hakluyt Society, Ser. 2, Nos. 14-15; Vols. 1-2. London.

Remy, Jules. 1868. Contribution of a Venerable Savage. . . . Trans. by William T. Brigham. Boston.

Shortland, Edward. 1882. Maori Religion and Mythology. London.

Smith, S. Percy. 1893. "Coming of Te Arawa and Tainui Canoes," *Polynesian Society Journal*, 2:220-52.

———— 1895. "Ancient Methods of Bird-Snaring amongst the Maoris," *Polynesian Society Journal*, 4:143-52.

———— 1900. "The 'Aotea' Canoe," *Polynesian Society Journal*, 9:200-33.

———— 1906. "An Explanation of Certain Maori Customs of Old," *Polynesian Society Journal*, 15:137-46.

———— 1913. The Lore of the Whare-wananga, or Teachings of the Maori College. Part 1: Te Kauwae-runga, or "Things Celestial." Polynesian Society, Memoir 3.

———— 1915. The Lore of the Whare-wananga, or Teachings of the Maori College. Part 2: Te Kauwae-raro, or "Things Terrestrial." Polynesian Society, Memoir 4.

Stewart, Charles S. 1831. A Visit to the South Seas . . . (1829 and 1830). 2 vols. New York.

Stuebel, O. 1896. Samoanische texte. Königlichen Museum für Völkerkunde, Veröffentlichungen, Vol. 4, parts 2-4. Berlin.

Thomson, George M. 1922. The Naturalization of Animals and Plants in New Zealand. Cambridge, England.

Thurston, Lucy Goodale. 1882. Life and Times of Mrs. Lucy G. Thurston. Ann Arbor, Mich.

Tregear, Edward. 1904. The Maori Race. Wanganui, N.Z.

Turnbull, John. 1813. A Voyage Round the World . . . (1800-1804). 2d ed. London.

Turner, George. 1884. Samoa, a Hundred Years Ago and Long Before. London.

Vancouver, George. 1798. A Voyage of Discovery to the North Pacific Ocean . . . (1790-1795). 3 vols. and atlas of charts. London.

White, John. 1887-91. The Ancient History of the Maori. 6 vols. Wellington, N.Z.

Williams, John. 1838. A Narrative of Missionary Enterprises in the South Seas Islands. . . . London.

Williamson, Robert W. 1923. Religious and Cosmic Beliefs of Central Polynesia. 2 vols. Cambridge, England.

A VIEW FROM THE FAR SIDE

A DOCUMENT IN ACCULTURATION

By *Walter Goldschmidt*

UNIVERSITY OF CALIFORNIA, LOS ANGELES

RARELY are we provided with a direct glimpse of first contact between a native people and the complexities of modern civilization. For that reason, I think it is worth recording the speech of Mr. Wanambwa, a Mugisu official speaking to a gathering of Sebei shortly after his return from an official visit to England.

The occasion was not long after I arrived among the Sebei in 1954. The Sebei are a Nilo-Hamitic people living on the slopes of Mt. Elgon in Eastern Uganda; they share the basic Nandi cattle-herding culture, but are somewhat more given to agriculture and less to aggressive warfare. Western civilization was first brought to them by the Baganda in the early years of this century, when a Muganda military leader headed an expedition against the "wild tribes" of the northern territories and subjected them to a harsh *pax Buganda* which was soon replaced by British authority. The Sebei remained remote to Europeanization, having had a regular local official for only about a generation and a road up the mountain for only about a decade. The tribe is still viewed as wild and unruly by more acculturated Africans, a reputation based, so far as I can see, upon nothing more than the fact that they still perform female circumcision. Few Sebei have ever left their narrow territory; some go regularly to the nearest European settlement (and district capital) of Mbale, and a handful have gone to Jinja and Kampala in Uganda or Kitale in Kenya. Though a good many outside things have come to them, their knowledge of the outside world is slight.

The Bagisu are their nearest neighbors, located immediately to the west of the Elgon massif. This is a Bantu-speaking, plantain-growing people, boasting one of the densest populations in Africa. Many Bagisu have moved into Sebei territory, seeking unused land. Mbale lies in this territory, and while the Bagisu do not pretend to the cultural heights of the Basoga, who lie between them and the Baganda (and much less to that of the Baganda themselves), they do manage to dominate the politics of the Mbale district. Wanambwa, whose hastily translated words I record, is a Mugisu.

Let me first set the stage. We gathered at the headquarters of Gombolola Binyinyi, one of the four that made up Saza Sebei. It will be helpful to realize that Uganda has been divided into provinces and these into districts, and that the Sebei share a district with the Bagisu. The districts are divided into counties, for which the Luganda word Saza is used, and Sebei territory forms a Saza with its own Sebei chief. Each Saza is divided into Gombolola of which Saza Sebei had four at this time; the Gombolola in turn are divided into Miruka, and these in turn into small semi-official Mitongole. There is a corresponding hierarchy of officials and councils, except for the lowest of these. The officials serve as administrators and tax collectors, and preside over a court of jurisdiction.

Binyinyi Gombolola headquarters is housed in a large rectangular building with a deep-pitched thatch roof and a dunged floor. Most of the building is an open pavilion, about 25 by 40 feet, with a raised dais at one end on which a battered oaken table stands in front of a few chairs. Walls reach part way to the eaves on two sides, and enclose the other two. Behind the dais a door gives into a couple of dingy offices. I spent many an hour in this building, listening to court cases held according to Baganda patterns. But today there was no court. The Secretary General was to talk to the people, who were seated on benches or standing outside the pavilion. I was seated next to my interpreter, Richard Bomet Chilla, who translated the remarks from Luganda, in which Mr. Wanambwa spoke. Wanambwa is the elected African official of the district, directly serving the District Commissioner and the district council which elected him. No European officials accompanied him on this trip, and there are no Europeans in Saza Sebei (except for a Catholic mission station at the far end). It will be recognized that this extemporaneous speech is rendered without the niceties of translation that one might wish for.

There was banter among the men before the meeting got under way. It had to do with the tendency of some modern fathers to be too ready to support their daughters in divorce cases: this was bad. Soon Wanambwa was introduced. He is a tall, loose-jointed man with an air of authority. His talk had the same moralizing tone that European officials used when they spoke to gatherings of Sebei, the kind of words that a parent might use to a group of children quarreling in the nursery. His speech opened with reference to rumors that the late Binyinyi Gombolola Chief had been a victim of black magic, which he disparaged, and an announcement of the replacement. He then spoke of his visit to Kabruron (a village in the Binyinyi Gombolola), and from here my notes can be quoted directly:

The Binyinyi people have enough food [Wanambwa said], but they need to plant cash crops. People should work hard for food for their homes and more as surplus for selling. In Bukwa I saw people going ahead. They are working hard and planting for sale and not only for making beer. The Binyinyi people have room for more crops.

Some people here are very lazy. They are satisfied with one granary. They don't think of the future. Coffee trees could do well here, but I saw people with only two or three to five trees. Does coffee do well? [The general reply was, "Yes, it does well."] The bananas are not well cared for in this area. I have gone to some homes and seen only one coffee tree like the stick that a witch doctor orders.

[This is a nice local figure of speech. Various magic ceremonies are held around a stick of hardwood placed in the ground, along with herbs, roots, and other items of ritual significance.]

Do you think that one tree like a devil will make you rich? Perhaps some have many cattle and don't care about fields, but for others it is only laziness.

I saw good things too. Children aren't drinking beer as in parts of Bukwa. In Bukwa, people have been badly beaten in beer fights and don't even try to go to a hospital. All over Sebei, drinking is becoming worse. At Bukwa school, the teacher reports even children are coming to school bringing beer, and some stay home drunk. Do you prevent the children from drinking beer? [General reply of "Yes, yes."] Well that's better.

The councilors should help the Muruka Chiefs to prevent this giving beer to children. If a full-grown man drinks too much, does he think of lying in bed or does he think of working? [There was the proper response.]

Very few men help their wives in planting, cultivating, or clearing homes. People should work in the morning and until one or two in the afternoon, and then go after beer. Drinking is good but only if it is done in the right way. It is the worst to give beer to children below eighteen years, because their brains are still tender. The government is now putting more and more departments in our hands, so we must stop the children from drinking beer, or we won't have educated boys to take over the work of the government. The Saza Council passed a resolution that beer making should be stopped in Sebei, but people get a permit to make three pots of beer, and then they make twenty.

I want to talk about fireplaces. The Council passed a resolution that fireplaces should be raised up.

[The Sebei hearth is on the ground. A campaign to build up a clay hearth was currently under way.]

It tried to encourage people to raise their hearths. Deep ones—that is, ones that are below the floor level—are dangerous to children who are crawling. We see many children who have been burnt. Which kind of hearth do you like? [The people replied, "Raised ones."] Some object to these raised hearths. They say that they are not as warm in the house. How many councilors have a raised hearth? [Only one raised his hand.] How many chiefs? [Only one.] Have you no blankets for cover? Think of the children's lives, not of getting warm. The child's nurses may be careless. People go to beer parties and they leave their children at home.

[Nurse here refers to older siblings or other children, who are given major responsibility for child care.]

The Sebei Council passed a resolution not to destroy a hardwood tree by hewing. Especially this Gombolola has good forest. Some of these trees are being cut for useless purposes instead of for good timber. The district council will mark off these forests. The Gombolola Chief must remove the man who has built his house in the forest.

[There is a forest reserve within which Sebei are not supposed to live.]

If a person needs timber, he can ask permission, but he must pay the African Local Government. In this way, people who want to improve life will be asking to cut by hand saws.

Are there any Kikuyu in this district? [Responses: No.]

[Mau Mau were still active at this time.]

If there are any Kikuyu, they should report to the chief. If a Kikuyu wants to stay, he should be known, and not settle without the knowledge of the government. Some of the Kikuyu who have caused deaths in Kenya are hiding here, but you must not think that all Kikuyu are bad.

The Council resolved that we should get rid of the Mitongole Chiefs. There are too many and there's too small pay, and we would rather have fewer with more pay. The present system is expensive. We want money for good buildings for government servants. We leave it to you to decide if the Mitongole are too small. Also to decide if Sebei Gombolola are too big. We can divide them if they are. If the Sebei Council agrees, they should have a new Gombolola combining Tyesoweri and Kabruron and another east of Sipi. We want you to ask the councilors to advise us how to divide the Gombolola.

[A redivision took place later in the year. Presumably this decision had already been reached at headquarters. It is doubtful whether rank and file Sebei cared one way or another, though those with political ambition might have been concerned.]

Now I want to talk about my visit to England. In England the councilors are the rulers. We are now being taught the system of government they have in England. The Miruka Council in England sits twice a year.

[Wanambwa is apparently speaking of village and district government in England. Miruka is a subdivision of a Gombolola.]

They don't have chiefs but only appoint one chairman. They decide about the health, roads, schools, etc.

From these they send representatives to a place like a Saza Council. They appoint representatives according to the population. If they find the village is big, it may have two rather than one. The Saza Council deals with what their county needs. They have dressers and also health officers to fight plagues.

[Dressers are partly trained medical orderlies.]

Also veterinarians and agricultural instructors and teachers. They have headquarters in the county. But some of you will be surprised to know that there are no Mitongole Chiefs, Miruka Chiefs, or Saza Chiefs—only councilors. All the work is done by councilors who work hard, and therefore they don't need rulers. If a person suffers from disease or rinderpest, he must report it—not hide it as people do here. Here the chief has to go around and say "Mr. So-and-so has a cattle disease." But there everybody knows to report every disease, land erosion, etc. Any man knows in England that he cannot make beer unless he has a license. In England people know when it is time for drinking beer and when it is time for working—not like here. There each person knows if they do wrong, they will get imprisoned or punished, so they don't do these things. In England a person is rich if he has fields, but a man who has been a Provincial Commissioner or a District Commissioner in Africa can't buy these things and is not so rich. There the people regarded as poor are those who have been Provincial Commissioners or District Commissioners in Africa; there they are like ordinary people.

[It must be remembered that these are about the highest-ranking and most powerful people a Sebei is likely to have seen. A Nigerian student once told me that when a native governmental official was brought to England, he inquired everywhere about the family of his District Commissioner and found it was not known to anybody. When he returned to Nigeria he joined the nationalist movement.]

The work of the County Council is to establish the graduated tax according to the income and according to land and fields.

[The discussion here must be appreciated in the context of current events in this part of Uganda. The Sebei had long paid a standard head tax, but a graduated tax had been established the previous year, placing a higher levy on the more wealthy. There was a very natural resistance to paying these excess amounts, and apparently some reluctance on the part of the chiefs to assess the higher figure, which fell upon the more influential members of the community. Aboriginal culture sanctions a person's refusal to let others know how many cattle he has. It is practically taboo to ask the question, and as a man places cattle out in other men's herds, it is not easy to find out for oneself.]

Even if he doesn't work his fields, he is taxed on it. They also tax depending upon the house the people live in. If a man has a very good building, every year they have to lower the tax on his house, because they know the owners are taking care of the repairs.

[Referring, presumably, to the tax credit for repairs.]

In England they are in need of very much poll tax. They have to charge five pence for each shilling of a man's salary. The man who has no house or land pays tax from his salary, but if he has a house and fields, he pays three different taxes—one on the house, one on his fields, and one on his salary. For example, we pay 15 shillings minimum. There the lowest is 400 shillings. The rich man pays 2,000 or 3,000, depending upon his income. He has to pay higher tax to help the country. The rich people who have shops must have government askaris to take care of them.

Those rich in cattle report stolen cows and need askaris, and that is why the rich person pays more than the poor one. Here if a cow gets stolen, the owner goes to the chief. The rich men pay more because the government helps them more.

[That is, the rich must pay more because they require more services. Wanambwa wisely puts this in terms of protecting livestock. Cattle raiding was endemic in aboriginal East Africa, and is still a problem to the Sebei.]

In England, once a person is in a tax bracket, he doesn't protest. Also, if the government has money, they think what to do for the people.

[That is, the money is spent in the public welfare.]

Some of the people can't afford to build houses and have no fields. In England, the people may take tax money and build houses for poor people to live in, and these will just pay a little rent. Sometimes growers may raise the price of food and the government will pay for part of the food for the poor man. For example, a bag of flour may cost 50 shillings but the poor man can't afford that, so the government pays 30 shillings and the poor man 20. They want all the people to live a good life. They don't want some of them to be miserable. If there is a famine in the country, it is up to the government to help. If the government brings food for starving people, they will charge the lowest prices.

In England the country is cold. I haven't been on the mountain to compare.

[Binyinyi is in a temperate climate at 6,500 feet above sea level, but higher on the mountain freezing weather is common. Wanambwa is native to the tropical zone at a 3,500-foot altitude; he knows of the temperature at greater heights only from others.]

A river like this one will freeze so a man can walk over it like on rocks. Sometimes people die from the cold, but the government may provide coats to poor people. That is why the government needs more taxes. The government controls prices to help the poor man buy clothes, etc. Many things need government help: hospitals, schools, etc. Children should be educated free without any fee. We should do those things here. Children in England are educated by tax money. Any man unwilling to send a boy to school is accused in court, because school is free. All boys and girls go to school, not as here where we send our boys to school because maybe they will become a chief, but leave the girls at home. In England you see girls doing what men do—acting like a chairman. Secretaries and clerks are only women; hospital attendants, teachers, especially in the primary schools, are mostly women; in factories where they are making wirelesses and gramophones and airplanes and automobiles, most are women—especially in the clothes factories.

The government collects money to build big buildings to care for old people who have nobody to care for them. Sometimes they live there without payments. The arrangements are made by councilors and not by rulers. There may be children who have lost their fathers. The government has a place for them until they are old enough to work.

Here pensions are only for the ex-chiefs. There they have pensions of 10 or 15 shillings weekly for all after they are sixty years of age. That is why men who pay taxes are given a pension. That's why we are trying to have graduated poll tax, to do things like England. But it is still new here. That is why many people are grumbling that cases are not solved. We have only one Saza chief for all Sebei, and he has too much work to do. That is why he needs an assistant. A man needs a good salary, a house, and cars for traveling. Unless we pay graduated taxes these things cannot run well. The road from here to Bukwa requires money.

[At the time, the road up the mountain went along the escarpment only part way. The far side of Sebei territory (Bukwa) could be reached by car only from the Kenya side, a trip of more than a hundred miles around the mountain.]

We need to get Kenya things here. Sebei county is big and needs a big hospital in the center. Now they are deciding to have an ambulance so if a person dies in the hospital, they can get the corpse back free and not have to pay Indians 300 or 400 shillings. The chiefs and the askaris need better buildings. You enrich your chiefs now, you enrich your country. It is the chiefs, and the askaris, and the clerks who are the people's servants. Whenever there is some trouble, these are the ones who serve you.

In England, they have Colonial Grants.

[Colonial Development and Welfare Grants, a form of aid to the colony which Wanambwa knows will cease when Uganda gains independence.]

Here too we need a treasury to have money. Later on these people will stop sending Colonial Grants. I am sorry that most people here have been given such a low tax. People fear the higher tax. All people complain of things in the county. There are 1,542 taxpayers and only 86 paid 60 shillings. In Bukwa, there are over 2,000 taxpayers and 23 paid 60 shillings. Here 50 shillings was paid by only 49 persons; in Bukwa by 92. In percent, you beat Bukwa because you have a bigger amount in the 40 shilling group. One hundred sixty-four paid 40 shillings. The remainder, 1,160 persons, paid 30 shillings. This is not very different from last year, when only 270 paid higher and the rest paid as usual. If you want the government to do things, you must pay more taxes. I expect about 1,000 next year to pay the graduated tax. [Someone from the floor said that the reason that people didn't pay graduated tax was because it was imposed on them from the outside. The man was reminded that he was himself a member of the council.] We can't have everybody present in these decisions. That is why the Mitongole Chief appoints a man to speak for his area. That is the reason for the group representative to tell the people what is happening and to find out what they want. There are representatives from different parts to tell what the people need. [A local leader asked the rhetorical question: "Do councilors appear for their own sake or for everybody at home?"] The representative does not pass on a matter automatically, but knows what the people in his district feel. You should appoint the right man who has the right things in his head. Therefore, people shouldn't argue. What the council decides is right. In England everybody tries hard to get more money to pay higher taxes. Chiefs are like companies which can go everywhere and get the things that are needed by the people.

[Trading companies serve as purchasers for local producers.]

Also, all the English farmers work hard to get what they live on. Each man tries his best to get money. Every man here thinks that the richest man here is the chief, but in England it is the farmer. It is not like here, because here people apply to become Mitongole Chief. There they work at different kinds of factories, making cars, repairing cars, clothes factories, factories for trains, gramophones, stoves, and many other things. For all the things we use here, you see many factories. It is not like here that people are forced to work. There they are not. People dig natural charcoal from the ground. It is about two miles deep. They go down in a chair two miles into the ground. Inside they can walk two miles. Above this are rivers and houses. Yet the people who work in these holes are happy to be working there. There are farmers outside the township, who grow crops and keep cattle like Europeans in Kitale. Each man has many plots; he puts up fences, rotates crops, and uses each field differently. They grow wheat and vegetables like cabbage and tomatoes. They work from early morning to evening, resting only for lunch. Unless they work hard, how would those factory workers get food? That's why the farmers work so hard. Some keep pigs and chickens in order to feed people in the factory. Cattle keepers are divided between those who keep them for milk and those for beef. Those who keep cattle for milk, may get a debby a day.

[A debby is the universal oil tin, holding five (U.S.) gallons.]

Farmers who keep cattle raise enough to feed the servants, etc., but also enough for those who are in other kinds of work. Not like here where one man does different things: farms, keeps cattle, keeps shop, etc.

The cattle are grazed inside fences; they are not allowed to roam about. Feeding is better so they produce more milk. The farmers keep cattle to make him rich and does not keep poor cows and bulls that produce poor cattle. Not like here, keep every old cow, but there they sell them. Here a man may have 60 head of cattle but only 5 will be good ones. Is there anyone here who had a cow to produce a debby of milk in a day? [Incredulously: "No, never!"] A man will keep the number of cows according to the size of his fields, but they will all be the best cows, of the kind that will make them rich.

[Grazing land is open in Sebei, so that the size of a man's herd is not determined by available grazing land.]

Each man has instruments for weighing the milk and records it so that he knows which cows are giving him a profit.

Also they have special barns for bulls, cows, and heifers. They are not mixed together, as with us. They are anxious to get the bull from the cow who has produced more milk. The price of a bull in England is very high. They use rubber for serving cows and don't let the bull water its sperm. They use sperm kept in a bottle and that will serve like an ordinary bull. If they let the bull go about with the cattle, they will have the calves all the same time, but they want to control them.

Other men only sell calves for beef. Others have only pigs. The bacon is the best meat for the whites than any other. Some keep sheep. Whites like mutton as much as the meat of pigs. Also get wool. In order to keep only chickens, one man may have as many as five thousand. He gets money by selling eggs. So the people who are working in the factories and in the charcoal can support one another.

City people need food from the farms, so the farmers won't be lazy. Now our towns of Mbale, Tororo, and Jinja are expanding and need more milk. They are looking to Sebei for meat and milk because they don't have enough cattle down there. People on the upper side should grow more vegetables and bananas for the people of the towns. The people of the plains should keep better cattle for feeding the people of the towns. They should change their ways of grazing cattle, because now they let their cattle run alone. They should start fences for grazing in fields. They should separate their cattle which give good milk from those which give poor milk. The man who wants to become a cattle man should do that. The man who wants coffee should do that, like in England. The veterinary department will help people who want to do these things. Nowadays the farmers are rich people, not the chiefs. In England, they have some men who grow potatoes and they unite together in societies. They think of ways to get wire for fence, good seeds, good bulls, or whatever they need. The officers will instruct them. They will send their milk, etc., where they can sell it. They also have societies for keeping chickens and they bring the eggs to the societies' stores. One man couldn't find a way to sell them. Now we have a coffee cooperative and the people get the cash instead of the Europeans, because people are united instead of each man sending his own crop. The Cotton Ginning and the Maize Cooperative in Bugisu are examples. We are better off than when we were sending these things to the Indians. But with unions, we can send these things to the world markets.

Health is important. People try to have a good house according to health instructions. They don't sleep in one house with the chickens and the sheep. A man can only become rich if his health is good. Who cares more for health than riches? In Sebei many people sell cows but only a few build houses. People should consider health to be an important thing. [The meeting concluded after a discussion of local issues.]

The processes of acculturation in the modern world are rapid. It is my great regret that Wanambwa did not include Los Angeles in his itinerary in a subsequent trip to this country, for I would like to know how his impressions of the Western world have filled out. Meanwhile, the Chief of Saza Sebei has himself gone to England.

The world moves rapidly, with its emphases on pecuniary aims, specialization of labor, and rationalized operations. The Sebei, remote on the slopes of Mt. Elgon, will soon be engulfed in this inexorable trend, of which on this day they were being told for the first time.

THE LIVELIHOOD OF THE ORDINARY PEOPLE OF THE PORTUGUESE ALGARVE

By Dan Stanislawski

UNIVERSITY OF TEXAS

IT WOULD BE DIFFICULT to find a more attractive place in which to make a living than the southern coast of Portugal. Seeing it for the first time, one is struck by the gay appearance of the polychrome scene; on the roads are brightly painted carts drawn by sleek mules, their harnesses decorated with metal and colored designs. Even the rope which reaches under the mule's forequarters to hold down the shafts is of brightly dyed henequen fiber, and as if all this were not quite enough color, long red and green tassels are hung on either side of the animal's head. As a background for this traffic, the roads are bordered by white rock and plaster walls, carefully maintained and frequently calcimined. Behind the walls, or facing directly upon the roads, are immaculately kept houses, painted in one or more of a great variety of colors, and topped by the pride of the Algarvians—fretted, lacelike chimneys.

This man-made color is set among the variegated rocks of several geological periods, from the grey schists of the Carboniferous at the north, through the red sandstones, conglomerates, and limestones of the Triassic, the white or sometimes orange dolomites and limestones of the Jurassic, to the grey sediments of the upper Tertiary and the Quaternary at the south. Through the year, these rock colors are seasonally embellished by the tints of both the spontaneous and culti-vated vegetation. The area of the grey schists, with a vegetation cover including cistus, heather, broom, and gorse[1] is lovely in the spring, when purple, pink, yellow, and great white flowers appear, to blend with many shades of green. In the limestone area, the colors of the vegetation are largely those of the differing greens of the fig, carob (*Ceratonia siliqua*), almond, and olive, brilliantly enlivened in January and February by the pink and white blossoms of the almonds and largely underlain by the green of planted grains. In the autumn, the drying grains make a tawny contrast to the green of the trees. The littoral of Tertiary and Quaternary materials, where the spontaneous vegetation has been largely eliminated, shows the colors of the large number of different crops, planted in small, irrigated plots.

The climate could hardly be better designed to display the colorful well-being of the Algarve. The rainfall that is received on the mountains to the north, in sufficient amounts to feed the streams and to maintain the subsurface water level of the littoral, falls on comparatively few days of the year—an average of about seventy for the coastal stations. The quick storms are followed by long periods of bright skies and warm sun. Furthermore, rainstorms are confined almost entirely to the winter season. A six-month drought period (less than an inch of rain per month) is to be expected in most lowland stations. So the summer is warm and glistening, with little wind and with bright, blue daytime skies. The nights are not uncomfortably warm, as the counter-radiation is considerable.

Beyond any of their predecessors, the Moslems recognized the potential of the Algarve, and the landscape is still, at least partially, a tribute to their skills in irrigation and garden combinations. To them this was the westernmost end of Moslem lands, hence called simply Al-Gharb (the west), a term which has emerged, slightly corrupted and with a redundant article, as the Algarve.

Compared to other parts of Portugal and Spain, there is well-being here. There is no shoelessness.[2] Most women seen on the country roads are not walking, but are riding donkeys; most men are driving mule-drawn, two-wheeled carts. Women are ordinarily not burden carriers. Burdens are carried either by the numerous donkeys or by the mule-drawn carts. However, prosperity is a relative matter, and to most Americans the life of the Algarvian as described below may seem harsh.

Land Systems

There are no baronial estates in the Algarve. A prosperous Algarvian landowner may have fifteen to thirty acres of good, irrigated land. Properties larger than thirty acres are exceptional. Although absentee ownership does exist, it is mostly by Algarvians whose absence from their properties would not usually be longer than a few days at a time. Typically, such owners live close by their farms. Association with the land, concern with it, and supervision of it are continuous.

Farm laborers may be divided into three categories. First, there is

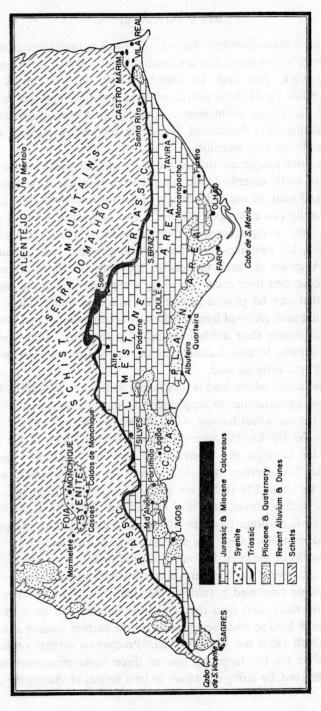

PHYSICAL REGIONS OF THE PORTUGUESE ALGARVE

a group of landless laborers. Second, there is a considerable group of farm owners whose properties are insufficient to support their families and who work, part time, for others. Third, another considerable group is made up of those people whose properties supply at least a minimum for family maintenance. This group is not always clearly distinguishable from the second, for at the border line between them necessities blend into amenities.

Of the three categories, that of the self-sufficient small farm owner is the most easily described. He will probably own less than ten acres of land, and with the aid of his family can work it without other labor. Such a family can exist upon a farm of two and a half acres of good irrigated land or eight acres of unirrigated land. However, units of size—acres, for example—may be misleading where unit production varies. A group of small farmers in the limestone area of central Algarve described their needs in *géiras*,[3] a term relating to the amount of land that can be plowed in one day with one mule. They said, further, that such *géiras* of land should have a certain minimum productivity. Expressing their needs in terms of man-hours, animal power, and land fertility is more realistic than the use of size units irrespective of quality and form of land.

For the farmer whose land is insufficient to support his family, there are various opportunities to supplement his income. Some go into the Alentejo for the wheat harvest, when wages and the demand for labor are high. As the harvest there does not fall at the time of the peak demand for labor in the Algarve, the farm at home need not be neglected. The average "take-home pay" for such a season would normally be about $35 (U.S.), not an inconsiderable sum to an Algarvian. Or such a farmer may hire himself out for limited periods of time to work on other farms in the Algarve itself, during the period of peak demand for labor. He also may hire himself out in the commercial towns of the coast for one of several tasks paying daily wages.

There are several arrangements through which persons who own no land at all are employed to cultivate the land of well-to-do owners who either have more land than they and their families can work or who have enough land so that they can live on the surplus income after the contract with labor has been fulfilled. Prosperous owners ordinarily secure labor for the farms by one of three basic arrangements: by renting the land, by hiring day labor, or by a system of sharing the crop.

Renting is not common in the Algarve, although it can be found in virtually all parts. More than in any other section it is found in the eastern coastal plain area near the city of Tavira. In such an arrangement the renter pays a predetermined figure per year for the use of the land, house, and sheds, and keeps the total usufruct. The surplus kept by the renter, although not great, is somewhat larger than that which would be received by the share-farmer or the day laborer, but the renter may be badly pinched in years of poor harvests.

In the two geographical extremes of the Algarve, day labor is the typical arrangement. On the east, beyond Tavira and within two miles of the border city of Vila Real de Santo António, an area is now given over to the production of early vegetables for the city markets as far away as Lisbon. In the early months of the year there is a great demand for labor here, but through long periods of time aside from those few months there is little demand. Much of this labor is hired by the day. At the other end of the Algarve, between the city of Lagos and the Cape, is an area devoted largely to wheat. The labor requirements are concentrated within a few weeks of the year. The daily wage is usually about 18 *escudos* (60 cents U.S.) for men, although it may be something less than that but with added perquisites. One group of laborers reported that their wage was 13 *escudos* (45 cents U.S.) but that they were given a daily ration of flour, olive oil, and a bit of pork as well. For women's work the scale is lower—usually from 35 cents to 45 cents U.S. a day. This is arrant discrimination, as women ordinarily do as much work as men. Although plowing and handling of animals (except for donkeys) is always the work of men, and although it is considered to be heavier work, it simply is not. The labor that women accomplish is in many cases heavier than that done by men.

Most men who work land belonging to others do so under a system of shares which differ according to the product. In the cultivation of any of the small grains, sharing is usually half and half. The owner furnishes the dwelling, the animals, the seed, and elaborate tools, if they are needed. The worker furnishes simple tools, including, in most cases, the plow.[4] The worker takes half of the crop, after the seed grain for the following year has been set aside. He shares equally with the owner any increment from the animals—the calves, lambs, pigs, and the like. As cow's milk is of almost no interest (it is "not exploited," they say), it can be used by the farmer as he wishes. Extraordinary expenses, such as terracing and chemical fertilization, are the responsibility of the owner.

Almost invariably there will be more than one system of sharing in any farm, for the specialized grain farms are really found only in the extreme west, where a system of daily wages is standard. Although all other farms will plant grain, it will be but one of several crops planted on the same property. Typically and almost universally, not only is there mixed planting in all seasons, usually with both trees and grain or leguminous crops in the same field, but also there are at least two major crop seasons and combinations in any one year. In some of the favored localities, and under certain systems of rotation, three crops within one year are possible.

The division of the other crops has been determined by long custom and is fairly standard, even though there may be variations from the norm by individual arrangements made between the owner and the farmer. From the fig harvest, there will usually be one part for the farmer and six for the owner of the fig trees. The latter in such case has planted the trees; the farmer picks the figs and lays them out to dry for fifteen days, caring for them during this process. The owner may pay for the trimming of the trees or the farmer may do it and keep the trim—a valuable economic item. Three other unirrigated trees are important in the Algarve: the almond, the carob and the olive. The harvest from them is usually divided one part to the farmer and four parts to the owner. In the case of olives, one of several special arrangements may be made to alter the division. Picking is troublesome and the picker may demand a higher percentage of the harvest than is ordinary, if labor is in demand at the time. In some cases the picker receives one-third of the product. If the division is made in terms of olive oil, the share will depend upon the place of pressing. As much as half of the product may be taken by the press owner as his share. In all cases, the owner of the land pays for the planting, and usually for the grafting, of the trees. If irrigation is necessary during the first or second year, as in the case of almonds, for example, the owner is also responsible for this.

Crops of the Algarve

Except for the small, recently specialized area near the mouth of the Guadiana River, virtually all farms of the Algarve plant one or more of the small grains. Probably during any half dozen years wheat and perhaps some rye will be raised for human consumption, as well as barley and oats for fodder. A large part of the cereal production, however, is that from grains planted under the unirrigated trees. Only one area—that between Lagos and the Cape—could be called a specialized grain area. It is, in fact, called "the granary of the Algarve." The title is proper in terms of specialization, but hardly so in volume of production. Planting would hardly be worth the effort, local laborers say, if chemical fertilizers were not applied.

A sickle is the harvesting implement. Hauling is done with mule carts in the lower country (ox-carts to the west of Lagos) and with pack frames for carrying grain on the backs of animals in the hills. Threshing is ordinarily done by driving mules, or occasionally donkeys or cows, over the grain piled on a threshing floor. Now however, even in the mountain area one may see some threshing machines. Many farmers dislike them, saying that the straw from animal threshing is preferable for feeding and bedding livestock.

Also widespread are the four important unirrigated trees of the Algarve. Figs, most extensively grown of the four, reach virtually from the Cape to the Guadiana River. Olives are more limited in distribution, the best of them being near Tavira and Monchique. Unfortunately, the local product does not have a good reputation even among the Algarvians themselves. Carobs appear sporadically almost everywhere upon the lowland, but the main concentration is upon the hilly calcareous area lying between the schist mountains to the north and the coastal plain to the south. They do not reach the Cape, owing to fogs. The almond appears from somewhat to the west of Lagos eastward to the Guadiana. It is not as rugged or as coarse a feeder as the carob and does less well in the limestone area. It is at its best in the area lying to the east of Faro and stretching past Tavira, both on the coastal lowland and somewhat into the limestone area.

Interplanting of grains with the almond and fig is virtually always successful. On the best soils, interplanting is advisable with figs, as without it their development is so precocious that it attracts the Mediterranean fruit fly. The worst of this condition is obviated by interplanting, which has the effect of retarding development.

While interplanting is common with the olive and not uncommon even with the carob, in neither case is the crop notably successful, for each tree is demanding of the soil. This is especially true of the carob, which diminishes the amount of moisture and soil nutrients available to the associated crops. Where the soil is barely adequate for olive and carob growing, interplanting of grain is not possible.

Chick peas are widespread, although not occupying the extent of land devoted to the small grains. They are found on both the littoral and the hilly limestone area across almost the full width of the Algarve, usually on what the Portuguese peasants term "strong land," and wherever possible in alluvium. Here they thrive and make a good return for the land and time devoted to them.

Horse beans are planted mostly for fodder—a high protein addition to the straw which makes up the bulk of the animal food. Barley, oats, and horse beans, and at times small amounts of other legumes, are given to ailing animals or to cows just before and after calving. Horse beans are excellent for human fare in February, when they are green. Some country people toast and eat the dried beans, which make nutritious, if unattractive, food. Horse beans may be planted separately, or, like the grains, may be found interplanted with trees and even occasionally with vines.

By far the greater part of the Algarvian product comes from irrigated fields (90 percent in the Faro area), and wells are the most important source of water. The commonest water-lifting device is the Arab-introduced *nora*, an endless chain of pots or buckets lifting water from the shallow well. For power, an animal (donkey, mule, horse, or cow) is hitched to a long, horizontal pole and treads the circle around the mouth of the well. In the less prosperous areas the *picota* or *cegonha* is common. This is a pole balanced between two uprights, with rope and bucket hanging from the long side and a weight on the other.

Vegetables are a standard part of the diet of the Algarvian. Green string beans are harvested from early April through October. Peas are less common, but are a part of the diet during January, February, and March. Cabbage is grown in all parts of the province and during all months of the year. It is fundamental to the soups and stews. Maize is planted usually in irrigated land, often in small plots between the rows of potatoes. The potatoes are planted in January. In March, at the time of the weeding and cultivation of the top soil around the potatoes, maize is planted. The potatoes are hilled-up by this time, and the maize rows are planted in the trenches between hills. In the western Algarve, at the time of the stripping of the leaves of the maize, a second crop of potatoes is often planted, or perhaps a crop of cabbages. The seed potatoes for the second planting are taken from the crop harvested earlier on the same ground. However, the second crop of potatoes is less productive than the first, and new seed potatoes must be brought in from the cold mountains of the north or from Belgium or Holland for the potato crop of the following year.

In the east of the Algarve, the plot which has yielded a harvest of potatoes and maize is commonly planted in August to green string beans or to cabbage.

Maize often enters into the scheme of rotation, not because it is worth more than wheat but because it fits better seasonally. In the east of the Algarve, wheat actually pays more on irrigated land than does maize, but planting wheat would eliminate the vegetables which fit so neatly into the rotation with maize. There is also the fact that the maize plant is totally used. The tassel is stripped first and then the leaves, both being considered good for cattle fodder, leaving the stalk bare except for the ears. After they are gathered, the stalk is used as bedding for cattle. Mixed with animal excretion, the stalk is ultimately worked back into the land.

Some rotations, however, may include the growing of both wheat and maize on the same land over a period of years. One such plan is to plant potatoes in the first year, then maize, then either green string beans, cabbage, or the second crop of potatoes. This will be followed in the second year by wheat and then by sweet potatoes and beans.

The above crops by no means complete the list of agricultural products of the Algarve, for in smaller amounts a large number of things are grown. On the unirrigated lands, legumes may be planted for fodder (ordinarily of the genera *Melilotus, Trigonella* and *Lathyrus*). On the irrigated land, there may be tomatoes (in the east mainly as a commercial crop, but elsewhere grown for local use), pimentos, melons, cucumbers, watermelons, squashes, and peanuts. Oranges do well in premium locations; peaches, apricots, plums, and apples are widespread.

Grapes deserve mention, for although the Algarvian wine is sweetish and too high in alcohol to make a good table wine, some is made for local consumption. One area is especially important—that extending from Lagôa toward Silves. More grapes are produced in this area than in all of the rest of the Algarve. Elsewhere, small vineyards can be seen between Sagres and the Guadiana, but the total acreage is not great and has been decreasing during the last several years.

Grapes are never irrigated and are planted on the bottomlands as well as on low slopes. The lowlands produce a better crop, but the attack of mildew is more serious. Also, much of the lowland is underlain by impermeable clays less than a yard from the surface, and the roots have inadequate room for development.

The construction of agricultural terraces is limited in the Algarve. It is unnecessary on the littoral and unjustified, economically, in the schist mountains. A few scattered terraces are found in the limestone area. Some have horizontal floors, but mostly the stone walls support a slope behind them. The exact degree of slope that can be successfully used depends upon the local condition of soils. However, it is in the Monchique area and on the slopes of Foia, wherever water is available from the permeable syenite, that the construction of terraces is a dramatic accomplishment. Here some terrace walls are over twelve feet high; this means a wall at least six feet thick at the bottom, which supports a flat terrace floor of an average of fifteen to twenty feet in width. Such terrace lands cost up to $2,000 (U.S.) an acre.

Gathering

To maintain themselves and their families, farmers in the Algarve must be concerned with many activities not directly connected with farming or even within the ken of American farmers. Time, and rather a good deal of it, must be spent in gathering fuel, fodder, food, and, to complete the alliteration, for fabrication. One cannot go far along any one of the roads without seeing a cart or a donkey laden with green or dried shrubs, trimmings, or leaves from trees.

A notable fuel is the gum cistus (*Cistus ladaniferus*), which grows in profusion upon the schist mountains and can be burned green (although fifteen days of drying improves its combustibility). Piled high upon mule carts, it is a common sight on the roads, being brought into the bakeries, its chief market. Occasionally, it is used for home fires, but this is not common, as it is a valuable source of cash income. A large load of gum cistus sells for 100 *escudos* ($3.50 U.S.). Cutting, gathering, loading, and delivery usually involves the time of one man for three to four days. After the expense of the cart is paid the return for labor probably comes to the almost universal Portuguese figure for unskilled labor, 18 *escudos* a day (approximately 60 cents U.S.).

In the homes of country people[5] roots, other wild growth, and the trim from cultivated trees are used for fuel. Olive trim and fig branches are preferred.

In the eastern section of the hilly limestone area, another cistus (*C. monspeliensis*), a bush oak (*Quercus coccifera*), and a species of mint (*Phlomis purpurea*) are often burned green, although they make better fuel when dried. If one can afford the root of the heather (*Calluna vulgaris*) he uses it for fires in the kitchen, forge, or fireplace, for, as the forgemen say, it is a "clean fuel." The root of the heather burns steadily for a long time. It also makes a fine charcoal, although it is not used commonly for this purpose. Although it is of spontaneous growth, it is not free to the gatherer. Owners of the land from which it is gathered charge from 1½ to 2 *escudos* (5 to 7 cents U.S.) an *arroba* (32 pounds) for it.

Charcoal is made in the mountains. In the summer, wood from the two evergreen oaks (*Quercus suber* and *Q. ilex*) is put into pits with branches of gum cistus, of the strawberry tree (*Arbutus unedo*), and of heather and lavender (*Lavandula stoechis*). It is covered with earth, and after being ignited a full-sized mound smoulders for about fifteen days. Although the oaks make what is considered the best charcoal for general use, wood or roots from the strawberry tree or the olive are considered next best. Whatever the original wood, however, charcoal is expensive and is used only in the cities for special purposes or in homes for cooking by relatively well-to-do people.

Various small factories or cottage industries have traditional fuel preferences. The little candy factory in Faro buys heather root from the country people to burn under the vat in which the sugar is melted for coating almonds. In the same room, charcoal made from the cork oak is used exclusively for the fires under the mixer in which the almonds are tossed with the melted sugar. The plant owner was quite positive that the fuels could not be changed without harm to the product. Pine is bought for fuel for the pottery ovens outside of Loulé if it is available, but otherwise branches of the *Erica australis* are used or a load of mixed lavender, *Cistus monspeliensis* and *C. ladaniferus*, is substituted. The fuel for the little stills in the mountains that make a liquor distilled from the fruits of the strawberry trees is usually cistus or heather, as both can be burned green. Wood of *Pterospartum tridentatum* has been used traditionally to burn the hair off the carcasses of pigs, because it makes a quick, hot fire.

For uses other than fuel, many things are gathered. The slender, straight rods of gum cistus are used as stalks to support pea vines. Only the straightest of the branches can be selected, and a gatherer sells them for 8 *escudos* (28 cents U.S.) per hundred. Each branch will serve for three to four years if carefully gathered and stored after use. For drying figs, the farmer gathers fennel stalks (*Foeniculum vulgare*, Miller) which he binds together with agave fiber to make the mats upon which the figs are laid to dry in the sun. Where available, a rush (*Juncus* sp.) is gathered from nearby streams for tying the sheaves of wheat.[6]

For fodder, not only fig leaves but several wild plants are gathered by the Algarvians. *Narcissus bulbocodium* and *Malva* spp. are gathered to be mixed with straw. *Dactylis cynosuroides,* a marine grass, is sometimes gathered from the shallow sea water, or the cattle are allowed to wade into the sea to graze upon it. In the latter case, the animals need careful watching, for they are apt to swallow too much water and become bloated. The above are among the most important of the fodder plants that are gathered, but countless others are known to the frugal Portuguese husbandmen through long experimentation and observation.

In this region, with its long, warm, rainless season, salt evaporation is simple and profitable. Small flat basins are made along the sea front, separated from each other by low earth barriers. Such basins are to be seen in many areas, but especially near Lagos, Portimão, Montes de Alvôr, Faro, Tavira, and Castro Marim. Collection is a simple matter of scraping up the crusts of salt after the water has evaporated.

Cork beehives of ancient derivation are in present use. The hive is a tube of untreated bark, just as it comes from the tree, about three feet high and twelve to fifteen inches in diameter, with crossed sticks inside to hold the combs of honey. Removal of the honey comb is simple, and the further processing consists merely in squeezing the mass between the hands. Imported sugar is expensive, and honey is a valuable addition to the diet. It is either eaten as it comes from the squeezing process or used in cooking.

The gathering of raw materials for use in crafts is diminishing with the decreasing number of craftsmen, but to some extent it continues. Chestnut has long been used. Trees still grow in a few groves near the Vila de Monchique, where they grew abundantly until stricken by the blight which has reduced them to a small part of their former extent. Besides chestnut branches, craftsmen gather oleander branches (*Nerium oleander*), cane stalks (*Arundo donax*), and varieties of willow (*Salix* spp.). A few people gather agave (the remnant of a once larger industry), wood from the strawberry tree (*Arbutus unedo*), the quince (*Cydonia oblonga*), the roots of the heather, and, from the swampy areas, cattail (*Typha angustifolia*). Eucalyptus is sometimes used as a substitute for chestnut, although it makes a poor one.[7] *Esparto* grass (*Stipa tenacissima*) and the leaves of the dwarf palm (*Chamaerops humilis*) are gathered occasionally in the Algarve, but the fabrication of useful articles from them is mostly based upon imports of these fibers from Spanish North Africa.

Fishing

Commercial fishing is probably the most ancient of Portuguese industries, harking back in time to several centuries before the birth of Christ, when Carthaginian fishermen were catching and salting fish at many places along the Algarvian coast. Tuna were important then, as now, and caught in the same type of fixed nets as those presently being used. Probably the Carthaginians also caught the other varieties of fish that are now important.

Sardine fishing takes place from early June through December and makes its heaviest demands upon labor during July and August.[8] The tuna migrations take place eastward in May and June and westward in July and August. Four of the five Portuguese fixed nets take tuna in both movements. Only the most western of these nets, that at Cape Santa Maria, is ordinarily limited to fishing only the eastward passage.

The specialized fishermen, who supply the fish to be canned, work at the great fixed nets (now located only on the eastern half of the coast) where the tuna are taken, or with the purse seiners which catch sardines, anchovies, mackerel, and a miscellany of other species. These are highly capitalized and seasonal operations. The laborers have long periods of idleness. There are about a dozen settlements on the shore, aside from the packing centers, where specialized fishermen may be found. Some, as is the case with the towns of Albufeira, Quarteira, Fuzeta, and even the capital city, Faro, supply relatively small amounts of fish to the factories. Other men fish to supply local needs. But aside from the specialized fishermen there are the somewhat "amphibious" men, working part time on their farms and part time in fishing.[9]

The fish that are caught and the methods used to catch them, by either the farmer-fishermen or the specialized fishermen of the group supplying local needs, are varied. For the most part, the fishermen use sail- and oar-propelled boats and traditional gear. They may use nets or lines or one of the special devices that have been employed since antiquity. For example, a rectangular net called the *sacada* is stretched between two boats, with bait and a light at the center. Another device, the shore seine, is anchored at one end on shore, leaving the other free so that a great arc can be made with a small boat reaching shore at another point. Both ends of the seine are then drawn in with the catch. Some of the tidal streams are blocked with nets to catch any fish that enter. Many other types of nets are used, including several different trammels. Line fishing is accomplished with several different types of equipment, mostly differing in terms of weight and length of line, but also in design. A single, heavy line with one hook is used for the large maigre (*Sciaena aquila*) and a relatively heavy line with two hooks (or two sharpened pieces of metal fastened transverse to the line) for two species of the conger eel. Commonly used is the long line, up to eight hundred meters in length, with short lines out from it about a meter apart, with a hook on the end of each. A large variety of fish are caught with this line, including bass, sole, seabream, hake, and others.

Among the miscellaneous devices used are two common types of traps (now made of wire, but formerly of willow), one for lobsters and a smaller, narrower relative used for catching eels. A lead weight of about three inches in length and with a crown of brass barbs turned backward to a forty-five degree angle with the shank is used to catch squid. The *alcatruz*, a long line connecting narrow-necked clay pots at about one meter intervals, serves to trap octopus. Shellfish are gathered on the beach at low tide or from small boats—or (in the west) even by lowering men by means of ropes over the edge of the cliffs.

A great variety of fish are sold fresh in the daily markets: bass, mullet, bream, sole, hake, horse mackerel, Spanish mackerel, gilthead, eel, drumfish, sardine, anchovy, and many others. All these must be sold at auction, under the eye of a governmental official, with the quotations starting at a price well above that which anyone supposes will be paid and then quickly reduced until some individual signifies his willingness to buy.

Although fish are an essential part of the diet of the Algarvians, the amount consumed is now decreasing because of the "boon" of transportation that makes the Lisbon market available to Algarvian fishermen and raises prices beyond the capacity of some local incomes. For those who can still afford to buy them, newly caught fish are sold each weekday morning in the markets of most of the towns of the littoral and even in some of those of the limestone area.

For some immemorially old and presently unexplained reason, fishermen in the Algarve, as in the rest of Portugal, wear plaids. Also, with the exception of the cod fishermen of Fuzeta, the average fisherman is somewhat more depressed economically than the population at large. Although figures for this comparison are not available, it would seem to be so from the appearance of their villages, houses, and personal dress, as well as by general agreement of non-fishing people. The latter agree that the fisherman is in a bad way economically, but they are apt to attribute it to his lack of thrift.

Grist Mills

A striking object in the landscape is the windmill, with its circular form and conical roof. The twenty-foot arms for the canvas sails are supported by the great shaft, which is connected within the millhouse by a cog and slot device with the vertical shaft which turns the millstone. The conical top of the mill with its great shaft and sails can be turned to face the wind. Grain, fed into the center of the stone, drifts out from the sides as flour. The miller takes 10 percent of the flour as his payment. The millhouse itself is of stone and plaster; almost all of the working parts of the mill are of wood. The great shaft is usually made of an especially hard wood. One shaft, for example, was made of "brazilian wood" (the kind was not determined) which had been in service since 1856, as attested by the date carved into it at the time that the mill was built. The other working parts are usually made of the holm oak (*Quercus ilex*), except for relatively small metal parts. For example, the smaller shaft turning the millstone is now always of metal and the wheel with slots to receive the large cogs is bound with it. In most mills there would be no other metal.

In the Algarve, millstones are always made of limestone. A millstone is about forty inches in diameter and, when new, about sixteen inches thick. At the place of making, one is sold for about $10.50 (U.S.). If it is delivered, the price depends upon distance. The cost of transport within the Algarve may amount to as much as the value of the stone, for each stone weighs about a ton and a half when new. A stone will last from three to fifteen years, depending upon the amount of work done with it. There is a busy season during and just after the wheat harvest, when a mill will probably be kept busy through most of the twenty-four hour day for several weeks. In Albufeira, one miller said that he worked throughout the year whenever the wind blew. Following the maize harvest is another, but lesser, peak of activity. Ordinarily only these two grains are ground.

With long work days, the stones must be scarified about every two days (some millers prefer to do it as often as once each twenty-four hours of work). To accomplish the task of scarification, the upper stone must be lifted off by means of a crow bar and slipped onto a table or frame with rollers, where it can be incised with radial lines one-quarter to one-half inch apart at the outer edge. This is done with a heavy sledge and a four-inch wide blade. After incising, the stone of an average mill will grind over sixty pounds of flour per hour. The amount declines with the succeeding period prior to the next time that the stone is reworked.

The only other costly and deteriorating part of the mills is the sail. Most mills have four. The canvas for one sail now costs about $25.00 (U.S.). Because of their value the sails are carefully tended, furled around the arms, and tied with ropes when temporarily out of use. When the mill is idle for a longer period of time, they are removed, to be carefully stored.

Narrow-necked pots are attached, sometimes in large numbers, to the great arms of the mill, "just for music" when the arms sweep through the air, the millers say. However, the sound does announce the movement of the arms—or the lack of it—and it may be an indication to the miller that the wind has shifted in direction.

The large, modern mill across the Guadiana River from Mértola is responsible for the abandonment of numerous windmills to the south and west of it. Some folk still cling to their preference for flour ground by the windmill, however. The less efficient and less "clean" grind is preferable, they say, for the particles of husks that remain in the flour are no trouble to sift out and are fine for chicken feed. At least one windmill was in construction in 1955, in the Serra do Malhão, about fifteen miles north of São Braz, testifying to this traditional taste.

In areas where water can be channeled for water mills, the windmill may not be used until about June first, when the water supply has dwindled. Water mills are more dependable than windmills until early summer; that is to say, good streams in the early part of the year are dependable and wind is capricious. However, during the last several weeks preceding summer, the water mills can only work part time, as the streams are usually not full enough to turn the wheels directly and must be fed into storage tanks about fifteen to twenty feet above the level of the wheels. When the tanks are full, the water is released into a flume or tube directed at the wheel. Algarvian tanks store enough water to run a mill for two hours on the average.

A typical water mill of the Algarve is built with a vertical shaft. The grinding stones are at the upper end of the shaft and at the other end are horizontal blades against which the force of water is directed through a six to eight inch tube. It is a simple and effective device, less complicated than the wind-driven mill. The great cog and slot wheels are not required, nor are the large sail arms with their costly canvases. Only slightly more complicated are the water mills with a horizontal shaft. These mills have a large vertical wheel, with slots around its periphery that are struck by the water from a tube. The power of the horizontal shaft must be converted by 45-degree angle cogs to turn another shaft fastened to the mill stone. Although one step more complicated than the water mill with a vertical shaft, it is also considerably less trouble to build than the wind-driven mill. In constructing either type of water mill, no metal is ordinarily used, except for the bearing at the water wheel end of the shaft. Hard wood must be used, and for the parts that are drenched with water not only must it be hard but resistant to the deterioration affecting most woods under such circumstances. Millers say that the wood of the olive is incomparably the best to meet these requirements.

One other type of water mill, formerly more important than at present, but still with a few representatives left, is the tidal mill. The shaft is turned by the force of tidal water, channeled into an artificial type of bore, striking against blades. Although this type of mill offers the advantage of use throughout the year, it requires a more elaborate structure, with channels and control gates to make use of the tides. Perhaps for this reason, its use has waned even more than that of the other traditional types.

Craft Materials

Most of the crafts that still exist use materials close at hand. Sturdy baskets for shipping fruits and tomatoes are made in the Vila de Monchique, from chestnut growing on nearby slopes. The long branches of the wood are used for ox goads, for the long-handled spatulas used to push unbaked dough into the bread ovens and to pull out the cooked loaves, for tool handles, and for beaters to knock down the olives, almonds, and carobs from the trees. It is still used to make occasional sets of knives, forks, and spoons, and for decorated walking canes. In some places, where cane grows along the streams, basket makers pay owners of the streamside land 8 *escudos* (28 cents U.S.) for each hundred canes. Sitting by the waterside they make the baskets, and when a load is ready they take it into the towns for sale. Oleander grows in the canyons of the dry mountains. In bloom, it is a handsome addition to the otherwise bleak landscape, and its larger branches serve for the strong framework of some types of baskets, while the smaller branches are plaited for the sides and ends. Pieces of the larger branches also serve as broom handles. Willow (*Salix viminalis*) is planted and gathered along the streams near Monchique to be made into excellent baskets and, in Faro, into tables and chairs. Agave was formerly of commercial importance, but only traces of such importance now remain. The leaves of the sparsely scattered plants may be gathered now without payment, yet only a few men do so. They remove the pulp by pounding and scraping and then hang the fibers in the sun to dry. It is difficult to understand the present neglect of the plant and fiber, as Algarvians agree that the best ropes, bridles, and animal muzzles are made from it. Cattail is used in some places to make sleeping mats. Flax is still grown for a small and decreasing use.

Algarvian clay seems to be less good than that from other provinces, as local pottery, although made in several locations, is not held in great esteem. Stone workers depend upon two sources, the syenite of Monchique and the limestone of the central region.

Brandy-making is common in the mountains. Most commonly, the fruit of the strawberry tree is the base. The still is a simple device that produces a colorless liquid of about 13 degrees of alcohol by the first distillation. A second run through the still yields the *aguardente* with 20 degrees of alcohol. At the still, a litre costs from 5 to 8 *escudos* (roughly 20 to 30 cents U.S. per quart). Occasionally, figs are made into brandy, but this is not a fundamental industry of the people. In the first place, the cottage industry of brandy-making belongs to the mountain folk, who have few fig trees; and second, according to the mountain people, figs do not make as good a brandy as does the fruit from the strawberry tree.

Craft Location

No region of the Algarve stands out because of its crafts, although the limestone area, in general, has preserved more remnants of earlier craft skills than either the mountain or the coastal plain regions. In Loulé, there are dealers in pottery, copper goods, articles of agave fiber, saddles, and baskets of palm and *esparto*. Much of the work with palm and *esparto* grass is not done in Loulé but is contracted, or rather arranged, with the country women, who buy the leaves of the dwarf palm or *esparto* grass from the store owners there. The merchants, in turn, have bought it from traders in Faro who imported it from Spanish Morocco. The Algarvian women take the palm leaves to their homes, where they plait them into strips to be returned and sold to the store from which they bought the material. According to demand, they may stitch the strips together to make baskets or panniers for packing the donkeys, or similar containers for a multiplicity of uses. In Loulé, copper is made into finely done pieces, for both utility and decoration. Here also is a factory, where brooms are made from the fronds of the dwarf palm, bound to a short handle of oleander wood with agave cord.

Relict crafts are still to be found in scattered locations, producing such articles as cane, willow, chestnut, or *esparto* baskets (two places of importance are Monchique for baskets of chestnut and Odeleite for those of cane, both sending their product to the truck farms of the coastal plain), ropes of *esparto* (Salir) and rugs of *esparto*, palm or corn husks (the latter for use in bedrooms). The little town of Alte reflects its earlier copper mining industry by a remnant of the former copper craft (but no longer based on local supply). Pottery, in limited amounts, is made in such settlements as Loulé, Lagôa, and Moncarapacho, but there is no production center of importance. In fact, the best pottery used in a large part of the Algarve is imported from the Alentejo. In both Monchique and Marmelete, the remnants of a linen craft remain. Small fields of flax can be seen on the mountain sides, which supply a few isolated looms. Maria Dias, in the remote village of Marmelete, makes rugs of strips of rag worked through a warp of linen thread, and in Alferce, outside of Monchique, rugs are also made on a linen warp. Back of Casaes, on the slopes of Monchique, the mountain women make highly colored saddle bags for use by family or close friends (they are not made for sale, they say).

Masonry is a continuing craft of importance, especially in and around Monchique with its rock-walled terraces. Masons there draw good wages, for they are in demand both for terrace walls and for the construction of houses made from the syenite of Monchique. Stoneworkers, less well paid than the construction workers, shape the syenite "bricks" used for highways (not widespread, however, in the Algarve as they are in north Portugal) and make the large conical rollers for the olive presses. These cones are nearly five feet from apex to base and have approximately the same dimension across the base. They are worked at the place where the syenite block has been blasted from the mountainside. Other stone workers fashion various articles from the limestone of the Algarvian central region; near the settlements of Paderne, Lagos, and Silves millstones for grist mills are made. An itinerant worker makes limestone basins to contain water and feed in pigpens, also the small querns which within this century were part of the dowry of every peasant girl of the Algarve.

Now appearing in the cities are evidences of the transition from traditional craft ways to those of modern production. For example, in Portimão is found a shoe shop which not only repairs but makes new shoes with primitive methods. Its tools are few and simple: hammers, pliers, awls, and needles, but an attempt is made to make a product similar to that of modern factories. The little cart plant of Portimão is an-

Monchique terraces

Algarvian chimneys

Fishing boats and netmaker at Alvôr

Tamped earth
construction

Cork beehive with honey

Windmill for grinding wheat and maize

Plaiting the fiber
of the dwarf palm

Maria Dias making a rag rug
Marmelete

Shaping stones for an olive press

Basketmaker with willow

Wheat stalks used as binder for sheaves

Circular structures in the eastern mountains

Watercart and wheelbarrow

other example. Strips and rounds of steel and rough lumber are the basic materials from which everything for the cart is made. The bolts are made by forge, hammer, and anvil, plus threading dies. The nuts also are pieces cut from the strip, plugged, and tapped. The axles are shaped and threaded from steel rounds. The boards for the wagon sides are planed and mortised with simple tools, as is the frame of the wagon. The spokes for the wheels are shaped with a draw knife. Three men are employed in the shop, each of whom is metalworker, carpenter, and painter. It is hardly a modern shop, yet its product bears comparison nicely with that of modern factories.

Houses

There is nothing more characteristic of the lower Algarve than its white houses and fences—of African provenience. Typical houses are made of stones set in clay mortar and plastered over. They always look—and are—immaculate, as the women clean them fastidiously and calcimine them twice a year. Occasionally the trim is painted with colors. Mountain houses have a different appearance, as many are not calcimined. The grey schist has streaks of rust color through it so it does not make a completely bleak scene, but these houses are less attractive than those of the lower Algarve. In shape and interior design the mountain houses are similar to those of the lower area with one interesting exception, the circular houses of the mountains of the east. These, however, are not now used as dwellings, although some are still of service for housing sheep. This ancient, perhaps Hamitic, type of house may indicate several thousand years of African influence on construction in southern Portugal.

Both in the mountains and in some areas of the lowland, another type of house is built, the house of tamped earth which was common in Iberia at the time of Roman domination. It is not as common as formerly and in many areas is branded as old-fashioned, but it is still common in the settlements of the hills around Monchique as well as those of the schist mountains to the east. In the lowlands of at least one area, that of Albufeira, such houses are still commonly built and the people there firmly maintain that they are superior to any other type and last virtually forever. They say that it is a good house for a man of modest means, if he builds in an area with a good limy soil. Certainly there is little expenditure for construction equipment. To contain the earth to be tamped, one needs boards and cords sufficient to put together a frame about fifteen inches high, twelve inches wide, and from two to five feet long. As two men usually work together, there will be required two tampers, club-like pieces of wood, each with a bulbous end and a four- to five-foot handle. These, with *esparto* grass baskets to carry the earth, make up the total equipment necessary.

A foundation of stone is usually made. Upon this the frame is placed. A carrier brings the slightly damp mixture of clay and sandy soil, usually mixed with small stones, and dumps it into the frame. The tampers pound it down until it is firm. When the frame is full, the boards are removed and set up again on the next length of wall until the level is completed. Another level is built upon this and so on, until the wall is of the desired height. Not only are the exterior walls made in this way, but the interior separating walls as well.

Houses may have only an earthen floor; in the mountains this is usually the case. In the lowlands, a prosperous farmer may have a floor of tile or concrete. The dirt floor is always hard packed and cleanly swept. Although it may be uneven, it is never untidy. Rooms are clean, even with the sooty ceilings of those many houses which do not have chimneys. Most rooms have a small window and perhaps a door, although this is less true of the houses of the mountains, where rooms without any opening to the outside are not uncommon. In the houses of the less prosperous people, the windows are not glazed, but covered with wooden shutters. These people say that glass windows are only for the rich. The equipment of houses is meager, usually consisting only of a simple table, a few chairs, a chest for blankets and clothes, wooden frame beds, and a few shelves against the walls.

Chimneys are the special pride of the Algarvians. Of Moorish influence in design, they are carefully made in a great number of shapes and patterns. Particularly in the limestone area they are distinctive. On some houses they are put merely for ornament, even though there is no fireplace within.

Fences of stone, with a cover of plaster and calcimine, parallel the Algarvian roads. Partly they represent a taste inherited from the Moors. Sometimes they serve to clear the land of excess stone; there are fences in the limestone area six to eight feet high and ten to twelve feet across. Tamped earth fences are common in parts of the west and scattered remnants appear in the eastern Algarve, attesting to a former importance greater than that of the present. People in the east say that no more of this type are now being built, whereas in the west such fences are still being constructed.

Animals

The donkey and the mule are basic to transport. A woman commonly has her donkey to carry the materials she takes to the market or brings from it. Commonly, one sees several women in single file riding their donkeys along the road, each facing to the right as it is the custom to mount from that side. Occasionally, a man can be seen riding a donkey, but almost invariably it will be an old man or an ailing young one, for the vigorous, working males drive mule carts.

Oxen, of a reddish brown breed typical of the Alentejo, are commonly used for plowing. They are the best animals for heavy work, although mules and even donkeys are frequently seen hitched to the plow.

Each family that can afford it has a pig or two, always kept in a pen close by the house and fed with scraps from the house or from the harvest (occasionally horse beans and, near Monchique, sweet potatoes). In a minimum diet, an Algarvian family would average the consumption of one pig a year.

Sheep are usually kept in small flocks. A farmer may own two or three, or if he is more prosperous, up to a hundred or more. In the first case, unless the small boy of the family is available for herding, he will make an agreement with other neighbors owning a few sheep to have them herded in common. (It is not unusual to see a small boy watching two, or even one, sheep grazing.) When the sheep of several families are herded in common, the herder will be hired by salary (15 escudos a day [53 cents U.S.] would be an average figure in the limetone area), or an arrangement made by which he will receive a share of the young and of the ewe's milk.[10]

Although arrangements must be made with the owner of the land, usually no charge is made for grazing, as long as the sheep are moved so that the manure is spread over the land. Most landowners are more than willing to allow the sheep to graze upon the remnants of harvest in order to gain the fertilizer for their land.

A good ewe will produce about two-thirds of a pint of milk a day for two to two and a half months in the spring, when there is good pasturage. All surplus above that needed for the lambs is made into cheese to be sold. Cheese is not difficult to make, and not only keeps better but sells for a higher price than milk. For example, five litres (almost nine pints) of milk worth about 44 cents (U.S.) makes one kilo of cheese which sells for $1.15 (U.S.).

The dominant sheep in the Algarve is the long-legged, hairy, Roman-nosed species, pied with black blotches on white background, originally from the west of Africa and far older in the peninsula than the merino. It is found in the Algarve from Sagres to the Guadiana River. The Algarvians say that it fits into their land system and economy better than does the merino. The latter needs more care and wider spaces in which to roam, so it does not thrive under the intimate arrangements necessary in the crowded landscape of small properties in the Algarve. The farmers say that it is not so *rustico*, that is, it doesn't adjust itself well to the general conditions and needs more attention. The hairy sheep, less specialized, demands less care. It is a large animal, weighing up to two hundred pounds. It becomes fertile earlier and produces considerably more meat than the merino. The fibers that it yields are coarse and not of much use for textiles but are used for mattresses and some heavy blankets. The Algarvians, of course, are not in great need of wool for clothing. In the climate of the region, a meat sheep and a milk producer offers more advantages than a wool sheep.

In the east of the Algarve, with its more highly developed and profitable agriculture, the hairy sheep is more confined, and more attention is given to its feeding. Many owners feed them oats, barley, and carob pods, plus maize leaves and leaves of the broad bean. Often the animal sleeps in sheltered places, such as compounds made of nets placed under trees. In the west, in general much less care is given to it, and the animal exists mainly upon wheat stubble and the native vegetation.

Although the merinos are relatively few in the Algarve, they are not entirely absent. At the extreme east—that is, east of Tavira—one sees occasional flocks. They are there due to influence from beyond the Guadiana; many Spaniards have moved into this area in times past, when lands were cheaper in Portugal than they were in Spain.

There are three other types of sheep, which are found in small numbers. One, called the *feltroso*, is smaller and hairier than the merino. It produces a relatively small quantity of wool of very ordinary quality. Almost all the sheep of this type are found around the city of Silves and somewhat to the west of there. In the mountains adjacent to the Alentejo, a sheep produced by the mixing of the Alentejo wool sheep and the hairy sheep of the Algarve is found. It is not valued highly, as its wool is not considered to be of good quality, and the animal is small. Another mixture that is found in various parts of the Algarve, but never in great numbers, is the cross between the Algarvian hairy sheep and the merino. These sheep are not valued highly.

Goats are to be seen frequently, but they are much fewer in number than sheep. Mostly they are to be seen in the mountains or in the uncultivated parts of the limestone area. Like sheep, one or two goats may be guarded by a small boy, or a professional herder may care for a flock of one hundred. Goats graze on virtually all shrubs, including the gum cistus and heather of the mountains. They also graze, as do the sheep, on the edges of the roads and sometimes in the stubble of the harvests. As in the case with the sheep, the herder may be hired by the day or he may take his wage as a percentage of the kids and the milk. His one tool, the sling, he makes of agave fiber. With this, he throws rocks to guide and control the flock.

Of the mules, the best is thought to be the *eguariço*, which has been born to a mare, with a donkey for a sire. The *macho* is said to be preferred as being gentler than the *mula*. The *asneiro*, with a donkey mother and a horse for sire, is rejected by some people because of its ugly head, shorter stature, and coarser appearance. The poorer people prefer the *asneiro* however, perhaps because it is cheaper, but also because it is more *rustico*, taking care of itself better and eating a wider assortment of fodder.

Transport

The *carinha* is a two-wheeled gig, handsomely made, light and elegant. Only a prosperous land owner, or one of similar economic status, can afford one. The work cart, the *carroço*, may be open or hooded. Larger and sturdier than the *carinha*, it is designed for heavy hauling. An older type, the *carro canudo* with heavy wheels and a heavy, low bed with upright stakes at the sides, demountable in case the load must project beyond the edges of the bed, is not commonly used now. All carts, except the *carros* for work in the fields, are brightly decorated with geometric designs or designs of flowers or fruits. The hooded *carroços* have brilliantly painted designs on the semitubular canvas tops. Water carts, and pack animals with water on their backs, are a common sight on the roads, especially between Portimão and Caldas de Monchique in the west. The water of Monchique, like so many of the mineral waters of Europe, is famous for "curing" a multitude of ills. It is not only the sick who buy it, however, for purchase of water for ordinary drinking is not uncommon. In the small towns where water is not piped to the houses, the water cart or wheelbarrow is also common. The wheelbarrow is a common device of transport in the west for diverse small loads as well as for water. The bicycle has become a rather important transport vehicle. With a cross-pole supported on a carrying frame above the rear wheel and a large basket hung near each end of the pole, considerable tonnage in total is carried each year.

Carrying on back or head is seldom seen. Both men and women carry parcels with their hands. Occasionally one sees a woman (and even a man) with a load upon his head, but the carrier is either from outside the Algarve or has learned the technique from outside; it is strange to the Algarvian. Goods brought to market or bought there to be taken back to the country by the women are packed in the large, shapeless, palm panniers straddling the backs of their donkeys. Larger and heavier loads are hauled by men in the mule carts.

Factory Labor

The largest factories are those concerned with the packing of fish. Portimão dominates the sardine industry, with its neighbor Lagos operating similar plants but running a weak second. Vila Real de Santo António dominates the tuna packing industry, with its neighbor Tavira being, as in the case of Lagos, greatly overshadowed by the more important packing center.[11] Olhão leads in the anchovy industry, but with a more balanced production than that of the other packing centers, including considerable amounts of sardines and horse mackerel.

With the long continued importance of fishing, there are the expectable ship-building yards for little fishing boats in various towns of the coasts. Ships up to 65 tons in size are built in two plants in Portimão.

Portimão has a tannery for sheep and goat skins which are used for the *albarda*, a Portuguese saddle. The tannery now uses imported chemicals and part of the cork oak. Other small factories in Portimão include a marble and breccia polishing plant, a tile factory, and a small plant for making jute sacking.

The plants for pressing and processing Algarvian olive oil—mostly to be used in the packing of the lower quality sardines—are to be found in various places. There is one, for example, in the Vila de Monchique and another outside of Monchique, near the settlement of Alferce. The olive press at Monchique is made of a base of four pie-shaped stones of syenite, with four slightly truncated cones on their sides as crushers. The olives are put in whole. Another press in the same establishment uses solid syenite wheels on edges instead of the cones.

Silves, the former capital of the Moslems in the Algarve, is now largely devoted to the manufacture of articles of cork. It does not make the full list of articles that are made in other parts of Portugal but chiefly cuts corks for bottles, most of them being the simple, tapered type or that with the flange on top. Much of the work is done by hand operation, rather than by automatic machines. Each cork is handled by several people; an average would be eight times for the ordinary cork, from the time that the large pieces of bark are cut by a table saw, through the punching, beveling, and grinding operations. Then it must be dried in the sun or oven, washed, rotated, dried again, and sacked. The refuse from these various processes is sent to other parts of Portugal to be made into agglomerated cork, or sent in power propelled barges down the Arade River to be loaded onto boats in the harbor of Portimão for shipment to the United States and other parts of the world to be used as insulation.

Outlined above are the most important activities of the Algarvians in supporting themselves. Living in the Algarve demands care and frugality difficult for Americans to understand, and involves habits, techniques, and the use of materials that ordinarily would be completely foreign to us, in our more favorably endowed environment. A foreign observer can hardly make sound judgment as to the virtues or demerits of the general conditions and methods. Obvious improvements could be made; but also damage might be done to a relatively thriving and seemingly happy community if radical change were involved. If great frugality and the absence of a large number of our amenities indicates substandard living, then the average Algarvian is to be pitied. If, however, friendly, generous, smiling, and seemingly contented people are an indication of successful living in their environment, then the Algarvian may be a person to be envied.

NOTES

[1] Several species each of the genera *Cistus, Erica, Genista* and *Ulex,* respectively.

[2] However, shoelessness may be a cultural matter and does not always indicate poverty. The women of Barcelos and its vicinity in north Portugal walk barefooted, but their bodies are bedecked with heavy gold jewelry.

[3] The term is derived from an ancient Roman word and concept. The Latin word described that amount of land which could be plowed in one day by a yoke of oxen.

[4] That is, the Mediterranean wooden plow with a steel point.

[5] On dry days, an outside, beehive-shaped oven is used. In rainy weather, baking, if any, is done inside the kitchen, where there may be a chimney to funnel off the smoke or it may simply be allowed to filter through the tiles of the roof.

[6] Where it is not available, as in parts of the coastal plain, the men are skilled in using the wheat itself as a binder. Two bunches of about fifteen stalks each are put end to end with the seed heads overlapping. Just below the heads, six to ten other stalks are wound round and twisted. This gives a length almost twice that of the length of the wheat stalk. A sheaf of wheat is bound with this improvised binder and the ends of it are twisted to hold it firmly.

[7] It has been planted by the government in many places in Portugal and its colonies. As a fuel it has some value, although in the Algarve it is never used to make charcoal. The foresters are now protesting that it is not only of little use, but that it takes so much water that it eliminates other vegetation around it, thus aggravating the problem of erosion on the hills.

[8] The three months at the beginning of the year are idle months for the sardine packing plants, as the government has forbidden fishing during this period of time. These months, as well as April and May, are poor fishing months in any event; April is apt to be stormy, and in May the scabbard fish (*Lepidopus caudatus*) may drive the sardines away from shore.

[9] Farmers in villages near the sea often fish when the demands of their crops are not pressing. However, specialized fishermen do not farm. There is a long record of fishermen going to nearby cities to beg when they are in need, rather than turn to possible employment in agriculture. This has been noted by Raquel Soeiro de Brito in her article "Um pequeno porto de pesca do Algarve: Albufeira," *Comptes Rendus de Congrès International de Géographie* (Lisbon, 1949), III, 232-44 (see p. 233).

[10] A half-and-half division proves to be better than payment of 10 *escudos* (35 cents U.S.) a day, informants agreed. They also said that a small boy might be hired to guard two or three sheep for 10 *escudos* a month; that a larger boy could herd up to fifteen sheep. Apparently larger flocks are put in charge of grown men.

[11] In both of these cases the older and historically more important city has been eclipsed.

ANTHROPOLOGICAL PERSPECTIVES ON THE MODERN COMMUNITY

By Maurice Stein

BRANDEIS UNIVERSITY

SOCIOLOGICAL THEORIES about community development usually contain historical assumptions as to the character of earlier communities. If the theory aims at encompassing the broadest sweep of human history, the theorist has to include anthropological materials. In the best tradition of social-political theorizing starting perhaps with Hobbes and Rousseau and moving through Marx, Spencer, Comte, Maine, Tönnies, Veblen, Durkheim and Weber, there is a serious effort to come to terms with available ethnographic materials. The classical theorists have been eminently responsible in this connection; for example, Maine's status-based social order, Tönnies' Gemeinschaft, or Durkheim's mechanical solidarity all offer conceptions of primitive social structure which constitute important contributions to the development of both anthropology and sociology.

In this connection, Robert Park's sociological theory of urbanization contains many important leads for anthropologists. While his own work focused on the modern city against the background of the rural community, his analysis of city life recognized the importance of folk cultural elements as a basis for important urban sub-communities and as a source of cultural vitality. Park's essays in *Race and Culture* written throughout his long, active career reflect an enduring concern with the effects of acculturation on the folk culture of American Negroes.

Robert Redfield recently employed Park's distinction between the technical and the moral order in community life as the central structur-

This essay, originally written for this volume, appears in slightly different form in *The Eclipse of Community: An Interpretation of American Studies* (Princeton, 1960), which goes further into the themes presented here to show hoy they clarify important aspects of modern American community life. Stanley Diamond helped me to grasp the significance of the anthropological perspective set forth in this paper, and Paul Radin patiently answered questions about his own work. I want to thank them both for introducing me to a conception of anthropology that differs considerably from those to which I had previously been exposed.

al concept in his synthetic work, *The Primitive World and Its Transfor-mations*. Redfield's later volumes, *The Little Community* and *Peasant Society and Culture*, advance our understanding of this distinction considerably and point the way toward developing concepts for ana-lyzing intermediate types on the folk-urban continuum. The importance of these books for sociological students of communities can hardly be overestimated. They will be discussed later, since their full significance can only be grasped in light of the anthropological tradition to which they are closely related.

There are signs that modern anthropologists are beginning to find more to admire in the folk societies they study than has been fashionable over the past few decades. The recent series of BBC lectures published as *The Institutions of Primitive Society* containing contributions from several leading British social anthropologists reflects this trend. It is by no means a form of primitivism or eulogy of any "noble savages," but rather proceeds with full consciousness of the special virtues of modern civilization. It seems to be a complex reaction on the one hand to the urgency of the immediate difficulties of that civilization, coupled with awareness that these difficulties can be illuminated when studied against the background of primitive societies where they do not appear. Anthropologists now seem increasingly willing to let their research throw light on the crises of our own civilization. They no longer feel that this necessarily entails abandoning scientific objectivity or choosing between primitive and modern ways of life.

Edward Sapir in a classic essay, "Culture, Genuine and Spurious," first published in the early twenties used his familiarity with primitive society as a baseline for commenting on contemporary culture. While there is much that can and has been justly criticized in his effort, it certainly does block out some of the main considerations:

. . . a genuine culture refuses to consider the individual as a mere cog, as an entity whose sole raison d'être lies in his subservience to a collective purpose that he is not conscious of or that has only a remote relevancy to his interests and strivings. The major activities of the individual must directly satisfy his own creative and emotional impulses, must always be something more than means to an end. The great cultural fallacy of industrialism, as developed up to the present time, is that in harnessing machines to our uses it has not known how to avoid the harnessing of the majority of mankind to its machines. The telephone girl who lends her capacities, during the greater part of the living day, to the manipulation of a technical routine that has an eventually high efficiency value but that answers to no spiritual needs of her own is an appalling sacrifice to civilization. As a solution of the problem of culture she is a failure—the more dismal the greater her natural endowment. As with the telephone girl, so, it is to be feared, with the great majority of us, slave-stokers to fires that burn for demons we would destroy, were it not that they appear in the guise of our benefactors. The American Indian who solves the economic problem with salmon-spear and rabbit-snare operates on a relatively low level of civilization, but he represents an incomparably higher solution than our telephone girl of the questions that culture has to ask of economics. There is here no question of the immediate utility, of the effective directness, of economic effort, nor of any sentimentalizing regrets as to the passing of the "natural man." The Indian's salmon-spearing is a culturally higher type of activity than that of the telephone girl or mill hand simply because there is normally no sense of spiritual frustration during its prosecution, no feeling of subservience to tyrannous yet largely inchoate demands, because it works in naturally with all the rest of the Indian's activities instead of standing out as a desert patch of merely economic effort in the whole of life.[1]

This quote does not sum up Sapir's whole argument, though it reflects the strengths and weaknesses of his position. His aspiration towards individual fulfillment *through* rather than despite community roles stands as a philosophic contribution of the very civilization which denies its realization. Contemporary existentialist critiques like those of Karl Jaspers and Gabriel Marcel elaborate these same points with similar emphasis on the fragmentation and despiritualization of modern life. Unfortunately, their grasp of the phenomenology of this experience remains as impressionistic as the "sense of spiritual frustration" and "subservience" that Sapir imputes to his telephone girl. Yet all three point to an important problem for the community sociologist requiring historical or anthropological perspective to conceptualize properly.

Running through this essay as well as Sapir's later articles on the interplay between culture and personality, is his profound emphasis on the requirement that any society should provide its members with meaningful life activities through which they can grow and express their full individuality. It is this emphasis that distinguishes him from most recent "objective" students of the relation between culture and personality, and which gives his writing on this subject much greater depth than this later work. Ruth Benedict, ardent exponent of cultural relativism though she may have been, frequently adopted a similar perspective. Her familiar article, "Continuities and Discontinuities in Cultural Conditioning," which is probably as widely known among sociologists as any other single piece of anthropological writing is an important case in point. Here she shows that our society forces sharply contrasting roles over the life cycle progression from child to adult as regards responsibility, authority, and sexuality without providing any significant transition rituals to bridge these discontinuities.

Her main thesis is in itself rather obvious, but it gains its special force from the brilliantly chosen illustrations of contrasting instances among non-literate cultures where these role disparities are either rendered continuous throughout the life cycle or bridged by elaborate rituals. It is hard to forget her description of the Papago grandfather's respectful patience while his three-year old granddaughter closes a heavy door, or the reciprocity expressed in primitive kinship terminology where the same term applies to father and son as our term "cousin" applies to equal participants in a paired relationship. Her comments on comparative sexual training deserve mention:

If the cultural emphasis is upon sexual pleasure the child who is continuously conditioned will be encouraged to experiment freely and pleasurably, as among the Marquesans; if emphasis is upon reproduction, as among the Zuni of New Mexico, childish sex proclivities will not be exploited, for the only important use to which sex is thought to serve in his culture is not yet possible to him. The important contrast with our child training is that although a Zuni child is impressed with the wickedness of premature sex experimentation he does not run the risk as in our culture of associating this wickedness with sex itself rather than with sex at his age. The adult in our culture has often failed to unlearn the wickedness or the dangerousness of sex, a lesson which was impressed upon him strongly in his most formative years.[2]

This commentary on the origins of sexual disturbances throws out a real challenge to conventional psychoanalytic theories dealing with the same problem.

Benedict goes on to observe that some primitive societies do make discontinuous demands, but that resultant strains are experienced collectively through the "solid phalanx of age mates" and supported by graduation into traditionally prestigeful secret societies with elaborate initiation rituals interdicting previous behavior and sanctifying new role expectations. Our own difficulties then appear in new light:

It is clear that if we were to look at our own arrangements as an outsider, we should infer directly from our family institutions and habits of child training that many individuals would not "put off childish things"; we should have to say that our adult activity demands traits that are interdicted in children, and that far from redoubling efforts to help bridge this gap, adults in our culture put all the blame on the child when he fails to manifest spontaneously the new behavior or, overstepping the mark, manifests it with untoward belligerence. It is not surprising that in such a society many individuals fear to use behavior which has up to that time been under a ban and trust instead, though at great psychic cost, to attitudes that have been exercised with approval during their formative years.[3]

So this seemingly simple thesis conceals a double criticism of a culture which both creates immense discontinuities in vital areas of life, and ignores the necessity for providing transition rituals when major strains arise. This double failure leaves the members of such a society eternally tied to their childhood regardless of chronological aging, even as the necessities of adult role-playing entail suppression of these childish "fantasies" lest they interfere with adult tasks. There are two main outcomes of this double failure: Insufficient suppression of fantasy can lead to inability to distinguish it from reality and consequent mental breakdown. Too firm suppression shrivels effective life to the point where spontaneous fantasy or perception becomes impossible. In either event, childish experience and experiential modes are not assimilated and therefore adult life remains significantly impoverished.

Far more comprehensive work has been done on the ways whereby primitive societies guarantee their members a full life. The whole corpus of Paul Radin's work is directed at this problem. His interpretation of primitive social structure and culture as summarized in *The World of Primitive Man* documents in great detail the defenses of individuation embedded in primitive social organization. It is unnecessary to trace his long dispute with the proponents of theories about the insufficiences of "the primitive mind," except to point out that this dispute was part of his larger aim in that it entailed elucidating the exceptional balance between reason and emotions which distinguish the socialized primitive from his civilized brethren. Here his convergence with Jung strengthened both their positions though no one has yet systematically explored the full implications of their common discoveries. Jung uncovered among his patients a twisted need for the same life syntheses that Radin found to be the cherished core of primitive social structure.

There is no point in trying to reproduce Radin's dense picture of this social structure. Doing so is as difficult as paraphrasing a poem and indeed, doing so would entail paraphrasing the many poetic and philosophic expressions with which his work is studded as it points at essentials of primitive life. Who can condense the saga of Trickster without doing serious injustice to it? Jung, Kerenyi, and Radin himself do try in the volume *The Trickster* but the story itself remains, like all works of art, immune to a final paraphrase. It is this literary quality in Radin's work, the acceptance of the finality of poetry and philosophy, that leads him to describe the primitive world-view by quoting examples with only slight analytic adumbrations, and that accounts for both its depth and its elusiveness. He asks us, by exercising our imaginative faculties, to see through the primitive's eyes; and if we are not ready or able to do so, both Radin and the world-view he strives to recapture remain beyond our reach.

But there is more of science in his work than this. He actually does provide an abstract conception of institutional functioning in primitive society which can stand with the best anthropological and sociological theorizing. His interpretation of primitive economics seems far closer to the facts as ethnographers have reported them than many of the interpretations of these same ethnographers. If one accepts his central thesis that primitive economies exist to insure each member of the society an irreducible minimum of adequate food, shelter, and clothing on the ground that "... Being alive signifies not only that blood is coursing through a man's body but that he obtains the wherewithal to keep it coursing,"[4] then his interpretations of primitive ownership, exchange, and distribution are indisputable. In this context, the inter-mixed utilitarian and non-utilitarian concerns in primitive economies can be explained in their own terms as products of a fundamental purpose utterly different from that underlying both our economy and our economics. So, his seemingly slight shift in emphasis when interpreting the flow of goods in primitive society clarifies a broad variety of specific manifestations:

In general, the tendency has been to speak of all aspects of primitive economics connected with transfer, barter and purchase, as if their main function was to serve as an outlet for the expression of specific human motions and as if there was not a rigorous restriction of purely personal activity in such matters.

.. What apparently Fortune, Malinowski and Thurnwald seem to have failed properly to understand and stress is that one of the primary roles, if indeed, it is not actually the primary, of a transfer and exchange is to visualize, dramatize and authenticate the existence of certain fixed relations subsisting between specific people and that this relationship has a "monetary" value. The actual reaffirmation of this relationship may take an exceedingly short time and the non-material emoluments flowing from it a very long time. That is, after all, true of every type of exchange and transfer. It is an unjustifiable procedure to relegate the utilitarian aspect of a transfer among primitive peoples to a secondary position because of the richness and the duration of its non-utilitarian accessories, just as unjustifiable as it would be to do the same in our own civilization.[5]

By hewing to his conception of primitive life as balanced between utility and ceremony rather than viewing it as being as lopsided in the direction of the latter as we are towards the former, he is able to comprehend the deeper "utilities" underlying property transfer and illuminate the brilliant ethnography contained in Malinowski's description of the "Kula" without imposing alien categories on it.

It is hard to leave Radin's analysis of primitive economics without reporting his neat conception of the function of "wealth" and "ceremonial property destruction" or to omit the brilliant disentangling and realignment of economics, magic and religion in Chapter Six of *The World of Primitive Man*; but space forbids this. Let it be noted, however, that he takes account of the exploitative manipulation of magic and religion when the fundamental purpose of the primitive economy has been perverted by the emergence of a surplus and a ruling class. Underlying this is a vital distinction between socially creative ceremonial magic which enhances living, and socially destructive magic which renders men subject to unnecessary exploitations.

With this distinction in mind, Radin's treatment of the crises of life and their rituals becomes immensely revealing. He starts by recognizing, as does Benedict, that growth from childhood to adulthood entails a major transition at puberty. But he recognizes that resolution of the strains accompanying this transition is always accomplished in such a fashion as to preserve the vested interests of the older people. This "subjection and domination" is only transformed into exploitation when the benefits are reaped and accumulated by individuals as such, rather than consumed immediately and ceremonially so that the person enjoying them sanctify the rights of all to their irreducible minimun and to their private life cycle. It is hard to keep attention focused on this vital distinction, and Radin does not always help as much as hi own firm capacity to do so indicated that he might have. Perhaps i is so clear to him that he never understood the difficulty others migh have with the distinction. One almost has the feeling here that on thes matters Radin is so sympathetic with the movement of the primitiv mind as to almost forget how remote this is from the spontaneou movement of civilized minds.

For that reason perhaps, useful as his chapter on the crises of lif and their rituals may be, too much is left for the untutored imagination Here, we need the help of other students like Stanley Diamond and Meyer Fortes to clarify the mysteries of the ritual dramas that Pau Radin inducts us into. But even here his first words, though not the last, remain indispensable:

... puberty, became not simply the recognition that an individual ha reached the age of sexual maturity; it became dramatized as the period o transition par excellence: the passing of an individual from the position of being an economic liability to that of an economic and social asset. . . Two distinct sets of circumstances, one physiological, the other economic social, thus conspired to make of puberty an outstanding focus which wa to serve as the prototype for all other periods interpreted as transitional It was certified and authenticated by magic and subsequently sanctifie and sacramentalized by religion. Its social and economic significance an evaluation are attested by the fact that the simplest tribes, the food gatherers and fishing-hunting peoples, have already developed intricate an complex initiation rites around it. These puberty rites are the fundamenta and basic rites of mankind. They have been reorganized, remodelled and reinterpreted myriads of times and, on their analogy, have been created not only new types of societal units, such as secret societies, but nev ideological systems as well.[6]

He goes on to place the puberty rites at the central and vivifying focal point from which rites and observances celebrating birth and death radiated so that the phases of human life were knit together, perhaps as the poet would have it, "bound to each other by natural piety." Separation and reintegration were accomplished through the social-biological formula involving death in one status with subsequent re-birth in another on a higher level. Underlying all of the great ritual dramas is the impulse:

... on the one hand, to validate the reality of the physical, outward world and the psychical inward world and, on the other, to dramatize the struggle for integration, that of the individual, the group and the external world. This is done in terms of a special symbolism which is expressed in actions and in words, a symbolism which represents the merging of images coming from within and from without. This validation, finally, is articulated artistically and creatively by individuals peculiarly qualified, emotionally and intellectually, that is, by the thinker and the religious formulator.[7]

So the old prestidigitator leads us to the periphery of the mystery by juggling inner and outer symbols, leaving those of us who are at least as peculiarly qualified as primitive "men of action" to pick them up ourselves when he drops them. That this is no easy task, all who have tried will testify.

Understanding these ritual dramas in the context of the part they play in protecting the primitive life cycle can be enhanced by closer inspection of the social and psychic mechanisms through which their effects are achieved. In order to show that anthropologists are still thinking about this problem, some comments by Meyer Fortes will be quoted at length:

Primitive people express the elementary emotions we describe by terms like fear and anger, love and hate, joy and grief in words and acts that are easily recognizable by us. Some anthropologists say that many non-European peoples are sensitive to the feeling of shame but not to guilt feelings. I doubt this. One of the most important functions of ritual in all societies is to provide a legitimate means of attributing guilt for one's sins and crimes to other persons or outside powers. In many primitive societies this function of ritual customs is prominent and it leads to the impression that individuals have a feeble sense of guilt, by comparison with Europeans. The truth is that our social system throws a hard and perhaps excessive burden of moral decision on the individual who has no such outlets for guilt feelings as are found in simpler societies. This is correlated with the fragmentation of social relations, and the division of allegiances and affectations in our society. I am sure it has a great deal to do with the terrifying toll of mental disease and psychoneurosis in modern industrial countries. We know very little about mental diseases in primitive communities. What evidence there is suggests that those regarded by many authorities as of constitutional origin occur in the same forms as with us. But disturbances of personality and character similar to those that cause mental conflict and social maladjustment in our society seem to be rare. I do not mean to imply that everybody is always happy, contented, and free of care in a primitive society. On the contrary, there is plenty of evidence that among them, as with us, affability may conceal hatred and jealousy, friendliness and devotion enjoined by law and morals may mask enmity, exemplary citizenship may be a way of compensating for frustration and fears. *The important thing is that in primitive societies there are customary methods of dealing with these common human problems of emotional adjustment by which they are externalized, publicly accepted, and given treatment in terms of ritual beliefs; society takes over the burden which, with us, falls entirely on the individual.* [Italics are mine.] Restored to the esteem of his fellows he is able to take up with ease the routine of existence which was thrown temporarily off its course by an emotional upheaval. Behavior that would be the maddest of fantasies in the individual, or even the worst of vices, becomes tolerable and sane, in his society, if it is transformed into custom and woven into the outward and visible fabric of a community's social life. This is easy in primitive societies where the boundary between the inner world of the self and the outer world of the community marks their line of fusion rather than of separation. Lest this may sound like a metaphysical lapse, I want to remind you that it springs from a very tangible and characteristic feature of primitive social structure, the widely extended network of kinship. The individual's identification with his immediate family is thus extended outward into the greater society, not broken off at the threshold of his home.[8]

This lengthy passage is quoted in full because its profound comparison of primitive and civilized situations contains enough leads for further exploration to keep a crew of social scientists profitably occupied for a long time to come. It points toward a breakdown of the boundaries between sociology, anthropology and psychiatry along lines designed to ensure their collective reconstitution as a genuine science of man in which the problems of healthy and pathological human functioning will emerge as central. Because of the dependence of ritual drama on the state of the arts, the humanities would necessarily play an important role in filling out this reconstituted science of man. As one indication of this, Francis Fergusson in *The Idea of A Theatre*, working in the tradition of Jane Harrison, develops an interpretation of drama that beautifully complements the anthropological contributions. His interpretation of *Oedipus Rex* as ritual encompasses the insights of Freud but avoids psychoanalytic reduction, by showing how the play functioned in the context of its place within the Greek Festival of Dionysos where it acted on the developed "histrionic sensibilities" of the audience. They were able to experience the rhythms and impulses behind tragic action without actually undergoing its disasters.

Paul Radin's synthetic view of primitive institutions includes a detailed interpretation of their political-legal structure and patterns of personal and social status. This is far too complex to be summarized here but the main links to the earlier discussion might be suggested. Primitive government consists of extended kin organizations like the clans with tribal chiefs serving to symbolize authority, while clan leaders actually wield authority over their kin when necessary. In all instances, authority carries as many duties as prerogatives. It is never personalized but must always be exercised in the name of the group. Custom hedges in persons wielding authority as much or more than it does their subordinates. Legal codes rarely appear until the kin authority system begins to give way to state forms. These are usually imposed by emerging national authorities and opposed by the tribal system. All important statuses in primitive society are kin statuses so that marriage becomes essentially the uniting of two kin groups. Individuality is status so that status ceremonies become vehicles whereby the primitive expresses his individuality at the same time that he reaffirms his social existence and the social existences of his relatives.

Primitive social order, as conceived by Radin, rests on a dramatic synthesis in which everyday life is imaginatively transformed and saturated with meaning. Individuality depends on the capacity to participate imaginatively in the experiences and satisfactions of the whole community. Men and women, old and young, weak and powerful, all have their place in the tribal order so that status guarantees the privilege of participation as well as assurance of the irreducible minimum required to sustain it. Western thought patterns interfere with sympathetic appreciation of this kind of individuation. In a sense, it is the deterioration of this same imaginative faculty so central to primitive life that renders us incapable of apprehending the fashion in which it releases human potentialities. In an essay on aesthetics, the British social anthropologist E. R. Leach comments on the symbolic powers of primitives expressed in daily life:

Whereas we are trained to think scientifically, many primitive peoples are trained to think poetically. Because we are literate, we tend to credit words with exact meanings—dictionary meanings. Our whole education is designed to make language a precise scientific instrument. The ordinary speech of an educated man is expected to conform to the canons of prose rather than of poetry; ambiguity of statement is deplored. But in primitive society the reverse may be the case; a faculty for making and understanding ambiguous statements may even be cultivated.

In many parts of Asia, for example, we find variants of a courtship game the essence of which is that the young man first recites a verse of poetry which is formally innocent but amorous by innuendo. The girl must then reply with another poem which matches the first not only in its overt theme, but also in its erotic covert meaning. People who use language in this way become highly adept at understanding symbolic statements. This applies not only to words but also to the motifs and arrangements of material designs. For us Europeans a good deal of primitive art has a kind of surrealist quality. We feel that it contains a symbolic statement, but we have no idea what the symbols mean. We ought not to infer from this that the primitive artist is intentionally obscure. He is addressing an audience which is much more practised than we are at understanding poetic statement.[9]

It is this trained imagination that allows the primitive to participate in the status dramas of daily life. Similarly, it allows him to dramatize the natural world so as to see in it regularly what only our painters and poets can see and they only sporadically.

This is a far cry from Levy Bruhl's conception of "participation mystique." In no sense does imaginative symbolization preclude logical thought or separation of self from the symbols or the objects symbolized. Our tendency to see it so is probably a cultural reflex arising from the deep split between logic and emotion in our own daily lives. Primitive life entails no such split so that duty, will, and impulse are imaginatively apprehended rather than explained logically—and imaginatively apprehended in a manner that admits the claims of all three even as the requirements of status are fulfilled. Here is where Radin's contribution to our understanding of primitive life is most important as well as least susceptible to paraphrase. *Primitive Man as Philosopher* reveals abundantly the complex perceptions of human nature and the human condition embodied in primitive folklore, mythology, and religion. These perceptions however, like the "obscure" character of primitive art referred to by Leach, require a symbolically imaginative response for comprehension. Anything less is likely to convert them to "parables" or explain them in one or another reductive frame of reference.

When Radin tells us that the Winnebago narrative about Trickster, which he so carefully preserved, contains a profound moral regarding the dangers of instinctual, non-socialized behavior, he is providing us with a clue for grasping the meaning of the story. The point here is that no Winnebago would ever have needed any such clue. The meaning of the story was directly and symbolically apprehended and its relevance to his imaginative reconstruction of his own experiences clarified as he assimilated the symbols and symbolic events in the story. Here is art functioning to modify consciousness directly, as it only occasionally does for us. Until we are able to feel its rhythms, even Radin's sensitive interpretation leaves us outside the story. Only when we let it infect our inner life, that is, experience it imaginatively, can we see how it could affect behavior. For we have to feel the Trickster in ourselves as the primitive does—quite spontaneously— before we can appreciate its tragic consequences or conquer it. Being told that the narrative ridicules Trickster's blind striving can hardly take the place of the wisdom that comes from sensing the folly in unguided instincts, both our own and those of our fellow men, any more than maturity can come from memorizing theories about human growth. The wonderful Winnebago philosophic tale, "The Seer," reproduced in *The World of Primitive Man* tells us more about human limits and the tragedies of human over-reaching than many books on ethics. But it speaks first to the ear of the heart and only when that ear listens can the ear of the head hear what is being said.

The combination of artist and philosopher in the role of the primitive thinker as distinct from the man of action is not as removed from civilized actuality as many would contend. Poetry and philosophy are intimately interrelated as diverse figures like George Santayana, T. S. Eliot and Wallace Stevens have argued and exemplified. But the conception that these activities *must* be interrelated is alien to our specialized civilization. And even more alien is the relation between primitive thinkers and men of action which rests upon the thinker's ability to sense crises of the community and cope with resulting strains by symbolic and ceremonial acts. While men of action live in a "blaze of reality," there are strains in their relation to their impulses, to the community and to the external world. Thinkers who perform properly feel these strains first and express them symbolically. Religious men, shamans and priests, cooperate in this endeavor and indeed are occasionally themselves the artist-philosophers of the tribe. Radin's complex interpretation of primitive religion denies the theories of "mystical participation" without denying that the bulk of primitives who are non-religious still have their experience illuminated by their relation to the authentic religious men of the tribe. Actually there is always a possibility that the tribal intellectuals will become exploitative, but prior to state development the larger context of tribal status should keep this tendency within limits.

In terms of a perspective on the modern community, the distinctions between men of action and thinkers or between religious and non-religious men must be seen as entailing important points of contact and even fusion between the distinctive groups. Primitive artist-philosophers articulate the symbolic-ceremonial web of the tribe, while religious men authenticate this web by inspiration and the evidence of their "seizures." Both are more sensitive to strains and tensions than ordinary members of the community and in their different ways both react to these strains in order to cushion their impacts on the less introspective members. But all remain tied to each other in the larger network of kin statuses and the experiences are shared insofar as they can be symbolically communicated. The revelations of the shaman are the property of the tribe.

Unfortunately modern counterparts of these primitive creators are hard-put to find a similar context for their own activities though many of them do indeed search for it. The turn toward magical doctrine and Celtic fables by a great poet like Yeats is one such manifestation. But the modern artist, mystic, or philosopher rarely breaks through to community experience, nor does he help to authenticate communal symbols. Modern men of thought are segregated from the everyday world and the people who live in it by barriers of sensibility and language. Our artists are therefore forced to record their private responses to the strains of civilization without any assurance that the meaning of their expression will carry much beyond a small circle of similarly inclined creators and critics.

More fundamentally, the role as celebrants of the major life transitions has been taken over perfunctorily by impersonal social agencies, the schools, churches, city halls, and newspapers of the modern city. Indeed these life transitions are often passed over in comparative silence. Adults have to a large extent lost control over their changing communities and so are neither inclined nor equipped to initiate succeeding generations. On the face of things, more distress is aroused over threats to job security than over the assumption of masculine or feminine duties. Social roles and role transitions are occasions for anxiety rather than vehicles for human fulfillment. The very lack of communal ties makes pursuit of substitutes mandatory. Insofar as the substitutes always whet the appetite further without satisfying it significantly, the individual finds himself back on the status treadmill no matter how badly he might have wished to get off.

There is an unfortunate inner dynamic in modern "spurious" community life wherein the very spuriousness creates anxiety which propels the climb to new levels of status in the hope that the gnawing will cease, yet this upward movement only leads to further anxiety aroused by the insufficiencies at the new level. The people involved soon lose their capacity for distinguishing status anxiety connected with important life transitions from the myriad status threats that daily life presents. There are no communal rituals to help discriminate the real from the trivial nor are there any close kin capable of providing guidance through stormy passages. The intellect is a weak crutch, since the complexity of modern existence demands broader perspective than most people can attain, while emotions are even more unreliable so long as childish impulses reign.

It almost seems as if community in the anthropological sense is necessary before human maturity or individuation can be achieved, while this same maturity is, in turn, a prerequisite for community. This is an over-simplification since we know that some people achieve integrity in spite of anomic community experiences. The real problems of life and its transitions have a way of breaking through even where appropriate ritual occasions are absent, and some people manage to lead fairly genuine lives in a spurious culture. Sociologists must search out such people to study the conditions that made their achievement possible. This could lead to further understanding of community patterns arising within our complicated civilization with potentialities for releasing true individuality.

There is little to be gained by sentimentalizing about primitive life or advocating a return to it in any form. We are far too deeply committed to urban-industrial civilization even to think of abandoning it now. Nor can we artificially incorporate outposts of "folk culture" within our own context since they quickly deteriorate into "pseudo-folk" forms when ripped from their proper setting. Folk music written on Tin Pan Alley or jazz produced by classical musicians, whatever its intrinsic merits, is hardly a satisfactory solution. Instead, the image of primitive society supplied us by Radin, Redfield, and Sapir, in which integral human functioning through an intelligible life cycle where major human needs are assured of satisfaction and major life transitions directly confronted helps us to formulate norms for human community life.

Anthropologists also provide a good many specific clues about the circumstances of life in a genuine culture even though these circumstances cannot be directly reproduced in a civilized community. Redfield's most recent book, *Peasant Society and Culture*, deals with peasant communities, which he regards as an intermediate type falling between folk or primitive society, on the one hand, and urban society on the other. He develops theoretical models for studying the linkages between urban and peasant social patterns co-existing within the same national framework. Sociologists are familiar with this problem. Most of the sub-cultural diversity of which Park and the Chicago sociologists during the twenties were so fond, stemmed from the presence in the city of first generation immigrants, many of whom retained peasant values and social patterns. Redfield's sensitive distinction between the great or sophisticated-urban tradition and the little or peasant tradition reformulates the time-worn division between high and low culture.

Community sociologists would be well advised to ask themselves why the most important book on methods of community study in recent years should have come from an anthropologist. This is, of course, Redfield's exemplary handbook, *The Little Community*, which contains far more than technical aids. It presents a number of alternative complementary conceptual frameworks as well as a highly sophisticated philosophy of research. It is as applicable to the study of cities or urban sub-communities as to peasant or folk societies, so that the outworn distinction between anthropological and sociological field methods is here exploded in the most convincing fashion possible. Even more striking, however, is Redfield's ability to combine methods for studying social structures from outside with techniques for exploring the inner perspectives of participants so that his battery of approaches ranges from ecology to life histories and the delineation of typical world outlooks. Here the "insight" of the humanist is combined with the "objectivity" of the scientist to present a richer conception of social science than one confined to either alternative.

Sociologists then can fruitfully turn to contemporary anthropology for perspectives on all phases of community life. Our whole interpretation of the structure of folk society, on which so many of our concepts rest, must be modified according to the theories and findings developed by Radin, Sapir, Redfield and the British anthropologists quoted earlier. These concepts and findings acquaint us with unique community systems in which important human potentialities are fulfilled in a fashion peculiarly alien to present-day America. It is exactly our collective commitment to ever-receding status goals that makes the contrasts provided by primitive peoples unusually apt. By cutting through the confusion between "success" defined in marketing terms and the achievement of integrity as a human being, these studies shed light on a dark aspect of American life.

NOTES

[1] Edward Sapir, *Selected Writings of Edward Sapir,* ed. by David G. Mandelbaum (University of California Press, Berkeley, 1949), pp. 315-16.

[2] Ruth Benedict, in *A Study of Interpersonal Relations,* ed. by Patrick Mullahy (Hermitage Press, Inc., New York, 1949), p. 305.

[3] *Ibid.,* p. 308.

[4] Paul Radin, *The World of Primitive Man* (Henry Schuman, New York, 1953), p. 106.

[5] *Ibid.,* pp. 126, 130.

[6] *Ibid.,* p. 152.

[7] *Ibid.,* p. 172.

[8] Meyer Fortes, *The Institutions of Primitive Society; A Series of Broadcast Talks by Evans-Pritchard, et al.* (The Free Press, Glencoe, Illinois, 1956), pp. 89-90.

[9] E. R. Leach, *The Institutions of Primitive Society, A Series of Broadcast Talks by Evans-Pritchard, et al.* (The Free Press, Glencoe, Illinois, 1956), pp. 29-30.

REFLECTIONS ON
THE ONTOLOGY OF RICE

By Jane Richardson Hanks

BENNINGTON COLLEGE

IN A SMALL, rice-growing community of central Thailand,[1] when a supply of the new rice for the family's meals is first withdrawn from the bin, the mother selects an auspicious moment, then lights the candles and incense of her offering. Every step in the growth of the grain—plowing, planting, transplanting, and harvesting—has been accompanied by rituals shared or monopolized by women. Ordinarily a woman boils the milk-white grains over a wood fire in the kitchen and brings them in the big pot to the eating-space of the house for the elders, the men, and the children. The individual plates are buried under great mounds of rice. Each person dips with his fingers or a spoon into the heap before him, after mixing a portion of it with a few bits of spiced fish or vegetables from one of the little dishes in the center. The cook tends to the needs of others before she serves herself. At the end of the meal, each person may make a little gesture of thanks before leaving.[2]

Rice itself is considered drearily tasteless, and the hot and spicy fish and vegetables are only to add flavor to help one consume as large a quantity of rice as possible. In privation rice may have to be eaten alone, but "famine" in this abundant land consists in going without rice, even when fish and vegetables abound. What makes these people gorge themselves on this admittedly vapid food? We also ask about the woman's role. Women all over the world cook and serve others before themselves. But, when ordinarily field work and rites in agricultural societies are delegated to men, why do women in Thailand assume such an important role?

Let us consider what a person is. A human body is but the perishable harbor of a *khwan*,[3] that indestructible soul-stuff which is born, eon after eon, as man, animal, insect, or other, until at last, by reaching *Nibbhan* ('Nirvana'), it is freed from the cycle of rebirth. Just as a man must be fed and cared for by a woman throughout life, so must this separable entity that is the (or his) *khwan*. *Khwan* are delicate and flighty; many are the ceremonies to restore them. At rites of passage, or on return from a long, debilitating ordeal like military service, a candidate is given a large ceremony (*tham khwan*) to strengthen his *khwan*. Delicious food is offered, on which the *khwan* is known to linger and feed. The candidate also eats bits of this food for the benefit of his *khwan* as well as his body.

Between earthly existences, the tiny *khwan* lives in a tree under the care of a female spirit, *Maeae* ('Mother') *Syy*. Like a "fairy god-mother" she continues her protection for a short time after the *khwan's* birth, until it is well incorporated in its human frame. Food is meager in the tree, for the only sources are the occasional offerings by people "to the ancestors," as at a water libation ritual (*truad nam*), at a wedding, or a funeral. Since there is more food during a human existence, the *khwan* is eager to be reborn. A woman alone can implement its reincarnation. She has no obligation to do this, for every *khwan* is an independent entity, unrelated to all others, responsible for its own fate. Yet in mercy alone a human mother begins a role of lifelong care by receiving the *khwan* into her womb at conception. To raise it she subjects herself to tedious food taboos and endures the pain of child-birth. After birth, she nurses with her milk "which is her own blood, purified to a pure white color." Thus, though the *khwan* of her child is not related to her, its body is part of her body. Some women have this female capacity to nourish to an unusually large degree. Their character (*nitsaj*) and ample milk supply enable them easily to bear and raise child after child. They are known for and as *liang dii* ('feed [another] well').

Thus the *khwan* is sustained by, and its incarnation grows from, the physical nourishment of a woman's body. What is to sustain it after a woman's milk gives out? Rice, because rice, too, is nourishment from a maternal figure. "Every grain is part of the body of Mother Rice (*Maeae Posop*) and contains a bit of her *khwan*." When weaning is to rice, there is no break in female nurture for body and *khwan*. Actually there is a cluster of female deities "concerned with our bodies," including *Maeae Thorani* ('earth'), *Maeae Nam* ('water'), and the Mother of the Fish. Mother Rice is the most important of these to the rice farmer, yet he is indebted to all of them to produce the sustaining grain.

A cardinal tenet of Thai life is that for every gift there must be a return, and so the nurture of a mother must also be reciprocated. A human mother is accorded lifelong obedience and respect, and, in her old age, food and care. Similarly one must reciprocate the care of the Rice Mother with gifts of food and feminine luxuries, and a place in the farmer's house during the hot, dry season. Women alone conduct these rituals because the men are said to be too easily captivated by the Mother's beauty, and might elope with her.

The idea that to nourish is to give life has been socially translated to a general feeling that a gift of food is especially acceptable, important, and appropriate. On a multitude of occasions foods are prepared, arranged with care, and offered to others. Most of the activity on any occasion of ceremony revolves around food preparation and serving. There is tremendous satisfaction not only in giving a feast, but in serving one's family the daily meals. A reputation for generosity with well-cooked foods is an integral part of leadership. Buddhist precepts have reinforced the importance of food giving. A major source of merit[4] is to give the priests their daily meals as well as to feed others, especially the poor. Offered food may not be refused lest one sinfully deny to the donor the opportunity of acquiring merit.

What are the interrelations of merit and rice? If a person has a store of merit he is successful in all his undertakings. For a woman, there is no merit in merely having a child, but she knows she has merit if she has an easy time in childbirth. A fine crop of rice is viewed by the farmer as indirect evidence of his merit. Merit allows a *khwan* to enter a rich instead of a poor family and a person to be skillful, wise, and lucky in life. If he is wisely attentive to the Rice Mother, she is pleased and gives him a large crop which is a means to acquire more merit. The less wise, less courteous get a smaller crop. But frequently Mother Rice manifests her mercy by giving a good crop to persons of apparently less merit, such as the poor and the wicked. In this sense, the mercy of the Rice Mother may mitigate the inexorability of the moral law that governs an individual's approach towards *Nibbhan*.

What, then, is the ontology of rice in Thailand? As each person partakes of rice, he demonstrates that he (or at least someone) has reciprocated his obligations in the past, and by eating it contracts new obligations to reciprocate. Rice nourishes his soul, which is eternally dependent on feminine mercy.

NOTES

[1] This data comes from Bang Chan, a community in central Thailand now under study by the Thailand Research Project of Cornell University, to which I am indebted for the opportunity of field research.

[2] The gesture, a *waj*, was not observed at meal-time in Bang Chan. It is reported by Praja Anuman Rachadhon in southern Thailand.

[3] To be sure, the complete person is recognized to have other aspects than body and *khwan*, e.g. *winjaan, cetaphud, phii,* but these aspects need not concern us here.

[4] Merit, acquired by good works and beliefs, raises an individual successively nearer to his goal of *Nibbhan*. A *khwan* also desires rebirth so as to increase its store of merit.

WINE, WOMEN, AND SONG

ROOT PLANTING AND HEAD-HUNTING
IN SOUTHEAST ASIA

By Edwin M. Loeb

IN CONNECTION WITH a discussion of some primitive planting cultures this paper offers an opinion that will, I hope, be a starting point for further discussion. The opinion is that the powers which presided over the birth of civilization were man's vices rather than his virtues. Indeed civilization may be said to have been ushered into the world by wine, women, and song, although no gala occasion celebrated its coming. To make the meaning of these remarks clear, it will be necessary to restate some of the known facts and more or less widely accepted assumptions about the earliest cultures.

According to the latest geographical and anthropological theories, civilization did not begin and progress in a series of "revolutions"—the Neolithic, the Bronze, and the Industrial revolutions, for example— rather, it has been a gradual process, accelerated from time to time by favoring circumstances. Looked at in this light, the evolution of human culture is comparable to the evolution of the higher, or more complex, forms from the lower, or less complex, forms in the biological realm. In particular, it may be added, the evolution of culture has resembled the evolution of plants and animals in that it has depended on a long series of mutations which, if successful, have been transmitted from one culture to another (Wissmann, 1957, p. 83). Here I shall emphasize certain of these mutations or inventions, including pottery, rice wine, and head-hunting. Sauer has said that agriculture started in the tropical rain forests along the banks of small rivers, specifically along those flowing into the Bay of Bengal (Sauer, 1952, Pl. 1). If so, the movement of progress was ever northward from this focus, and at the same time it spread like an opening fan to East and West: through the highlands of Southwest Asia, to the banks of great rivers such as the Tigris, the Euphrates, the Nile, the Indus, the Hwangho; then on to Greece and Rome, to Europe and the New World, and now, perhaps to Russia and even to the South Pole![1]

At the moment we are concerned with tropical Southeast Asia. Both

Sauer and Wissmann have been especially struck by the idea that southern Bengal was the original "Garden of Eden." Sauer writes: "No other area is equally well situated or equally well furnished for the rise of a fishing-farming culture" (1953, pp. 24-25). Perhaps few other regions in the tropics have as many fertile river banks. By farming, Sauer means the growing of taro, yams, and other root crops by the women. I have seen exactly this sort of farming carried on in the Mentawei Islands off the west coast of Sumatra, where along the banks of innumerable small rivers the women grow their taro under water, and moving about in outrigger canoes dig up rootstocks with their digging sticks. They also fish with their throwing nets. The men hunt and fish and grow coconut and banana trees. Both men and women have many working songs; the women especially, working together, sing in unison as they plant and dig and carry home their crops. Working songs appear first in a planting culture where workers must labor together and their movements, continually repeated, fall naturally into a rhythmic pattern. The University of California South African expedition of 1947–48 to the Kuanyama Ambo Bantu tribe collected many such songs which were used by these early seed agriculturists. The women sang as they reaped, harvested, and threshed the grain.

Most writers on the subject believe that the early root-planting culture was essentially a woman's world, since it was the women who performed the main work. A reconstruction of the culture on the basis of such evidence as is available indicates that the people lived on the banks of small rivers and lakes in elongated plank houses set on piles, each family having its own room in a communal house and its own fireplace for cooking. The inhabitants of a house were a matrilineal lineage, and several such houses formed a mother-right clan. The oldest woman in a house was the matron, but her eldest brother together with the other mature men of the house formed the village council. A mother, her brother or brothers, and her children, all inhabiting one room and using a single fireplace, made up the nucleus of the family. A man's nephews, not his sons, inherited his personal possessions, such as weapons and boats. Daughters inherited household goods from their mothers. Husbands came secretly at night to visit their wives, and frequently wives changed husbands without ceremony.

This form of society and manner of living are believed to have been decisive in the history of mankind. Except for the outrigger canoe and the blowgun, women were responsible for most of the inventions of the period including the use of bamboo utensils for cooking and holding liquids, the steeping and beating of tapa to make cloth, the cultivation of root plants, and above all, the domestication of small animals as household pets. Early in the period the children caught young wild dogs and pigs and brought them home to the women to be nursed. Chickens and other fowl were added later to the list of household animals. Eventually chickens were used in divination and also in sports as fighting cocks.

At least two questions arise regarding the validity of these assumptions. First, we may ask why we should assume a stage of culture in Southeast Asia for which we have little archaeological proof, compared to the great amount of archaeological evidence of early cultures that exists in Southwest Asia. We have already mentioned the fact that it is illogical to suppose that civilization suddenly burst upon the world when most of the plants and animals were domesticated in Southwest Asia. Certainly there was more than one "creative hearth" (Wissmann, 1956, p. 283) from which the earliest forms of culture were diffused, and Southeast Asia did have the requisites for such a center. Moreover the typography of the region suggests that much evidence has disappeared. As Wissmann says, "Shell mounds (kitchen middens), with their world-wide distribution, seem to have been in many places destroyed either by the surf during the eustatic drowning of coasts of the postglacial age of increasing temperatures or by the tectonic sinking of coastal areas. The result is that those areas of shell mounds remaining must represent only a fraction of their former extent and distribution" (*ibid.*). Then again there is proof that certain features of the root-eating period persisted into the Neolithic age, as is demonstrated by the long house of the Tripolje culture on the Dnieper River in southwest Russia (Hančar, 1955, p. 54). This form of house extends from the mainland of Southeast Asia, through Indonesia, into Micronesia. It almost always houses a lineage, and in Indonesia and Micronesia the lineage is usually matrilineal (Loeb and Broek, 1947, pp. 414-25; Loeb, 1947, pp. 168-72). The long house built on piles was also the form used in the Central European lake dwellings. Here too the Southeast Asiatic pig, *Sus vittatus*, was among the domesticated animals (Sauer, 1952, p. 37). Presumably the Southeast Asiatic root planters migrated to Central Europe in pre-Neolithic times.[2] On the other side of the world the Mentawei Islanders preserved many traits of early Asiatic root planters.

A second question arises as to whether or not the early root planters were matrilineal, and if so whether they had the custom of the husband's nocturnal visit. The first part of the question may clearly be answered in the affirmative. The early Malaysians in Champa were matrilineal, and the long house still exists there (Loeb and Broek, 1947, p. 422). Wissmann believes that the Malaysians received part of their early culture from the Gondid race of southern India, and that these proto-Caucasians migrated before the Malaysians to the island areas (Wissmann, 1957, Fig. 89). To answer the second part of the question is more complicated since only the more advanced matrilineal people of Southeast Asia had the custom of secret nocturnal visits by the husband. This custom probably existed at some time on the Malabar Coast of India; it still persists to some extent in Minangkabau on the West Coast of Sumatra. Plutarch, in his life of Lycurgus, mentions it as practiced in ancient Sparta, which, perhaps under early Cretan influence, is said to have preserved some indications of the mother-right. As we shall see, traces of the husband's nocturnal visit still are found in the Pageh islands of Mentawei.

Thus, the early planting cultures of Southeast Asia provided the song and the women complexes, two thirds of the trilogy of wine, women, and song. Now we may proceed to the all important invention of wine—again, we believe, a female discovery. Probably it was made late in the root-planting period, for the Mentawei Islanders like other primitive Indonesians had no intoxicants, although they had other traits of Southeast Asian culture.

There can be no doubt that the use of narcotics preceded the use of intoxicants among primitive peoples, such as those of the North American continent, Australia, and the islands of the Pacific. A single exception, pointed out to me by Edward Gifford, is the use of eucalyptus wine by the former aborigines of Tasmania. The manufacture of this wine, however, was taught to the natives by the early white settlers. Before the whites came the native women had been in the habit of climbing eucalyptus trees to shake out opossums for the men waiting below to kill. In order to climb the tree, the women cut notches in the trunk. From these notches the *Eucalyptus resinifera* dripped a slightly saccharine liquid which the natives gathered and used for

KAMCHATKA WINTER DWELLING
From Stellers, 1774.

UNDERGROUND ALEUT HOUSE, UNALASKA ISLAND, 1778
From Cook, 1784.

sweets. The first white men settled in Tasmania in 1807. Fifty years
later Bunce, noting the use of eucalyptus wine by the natives, wrote:
"At the proper season they grind holes in the tree, from which the
sweet juice flows plentifully. It is collected in a hole at the bottom

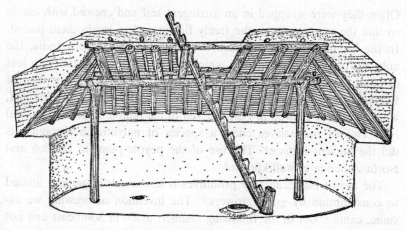

KIATUTHLANA PIT HOUSE RECONSTRUCTION,
EASTERN ARIZONA, A.D. 900
From Roberts, 1931.

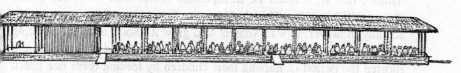

MEETING HALL IN TENGANAN, BALI,
APPROXIMATELY 185 FEET LONG
Loeb, 1955.

near the root of the tree. These holes are kept covered with a flat stone, apparently for the purpose of preventing birds and animals coming to drink of it. [Actually, the stone also prevents the liquor from turning sour.] When allowed to remain any length of time, the liquor ferments and settles into a coarse kind of wine or cider, rather intoxicating if drunk to excess" (Bunce, 1857, p. 47). It may be added that the whites also taught the natives to smoke tobacco. In other places where palm wine was used in early days by very primitive peoples it was always introduced by seafarers or neighbors of higher culture (Loeb, 1943, pp. 392-93), as, for example, was mead among the Bushmen of South Africa.

Narcotics, however, must have diffused very early in human history.

Often they were wrapped in an astringent leaf and chewed with chalk, so that the enzymes from the freely flowing saliva made them potent. In the list of narcotics we have the betel nut of southern India, the kola nut of West Africa (from which we get Coca Cola), the kadi leaf of South Arabia, the pituri nut of Australia, the kava pepper plant of Polynesia; and, in the New World, the coca and then the tobacco leaf, which was first chewed in Peru.[3] Even in the remote regions of central New Guinea the natives chew a species of narcotic mushroom,[4] as did the ancient Aztecs.[5] The use of the peyote plant in Mexico and North America is well-known.[6]

The use of intoxicants by primitives is less usual, in general limited to consumption by grain growers.[7] The invention of brewing we assume, came about in the following manner, again in Southeast and not Southwest Asia, and presumably in the region bordering the Bay of Bengal. Sauer writes: "Rice was originally a weed in underwater taro fields; in weeding, it was [accidentally] replanted elsewhere and a grain crop was produced, with partial retention of the vegetative planting habits"; that is, it could be transplanted rather than sown like grains (Sauer, 1952, p. 28). This then was the first grain ever grown by man; actually, however, is was women who grew it. Soon after the planting of underwater rice became customary, women found that they could shorten the period of nursing their children by feeding them rice gruel. Before this time a woman had to nurse her child for two to four years. Being in the habit of chewing narcotics, some woman chewed the rice before spitting it into her waterproof basket or coconut shell. But when the liquid was cooked and cooled it turned sour. If, however, the basket was lined with clay before being put over the fire and covered with a clay-lined lid, the liquid remained sweet when it cooled. This gruel was not good for the baby, but when it was strained it was hugely enjoyed by the men. Thus pottery and intoxicants were both discovered at the same time, for without pottery the women could neither make nor keep intoxicants, and the two traveled together. Sometimes pottery traveled a great deal farther, as for example, to Fiji, but occasionally, as in the case of Pueblo pottery, only a little farther. From the time rice wine was discovered, it was believed to be godlike in nature, and rice wine became sacred, to be drunk only on religious occasions. Heine–Geldern writes of the mountain people of Southeast Asia: "Rice beer plays a tremendous role in their customs and religion. When it is drunk the women must obey all kinds of superstitious rules and taboos. At no feast, marriage, or funeral may it be missing. It is also much used in sacrifice" (1923, p. 814). Rice now in Southeast Asia usually is malted by sprouting, and it is not chewed. Devereux recounts that when he visited the Sedang Moi, a mountain tribe of Indo-China, he was forced to take part in their rice-drinking orgies. Upon these occasions, not only was every male and female inhabitant of the village, young and old, compelled to drink to the point of insensibility, but the rice bran was thrown to the pigs and chickens, so that they too waddled around the next morning with evident hang-overs.[8] Beer was made from millet chewed by women in Neolithic North China (Bishop, 1942, p. 9), and is still made from millet chewed by the young women of the Taiyal mountain tribe of Formosa.[9] Among the Cham and the Indonesians, the cult of Shri, the Rice Mother, has taken the place of the religious drinking of rice wine (Loeb, 1943, p. 389). The Mentawei Islanders grow no rice and make no pottery. Their sacred drink is an unfermented fruit juice called *djurut*. Primitives are ignorant of the fact that bacteria cause wine and beer to become sour if the pottery used in their preparation is imperfect. The village people of Japan believe that evil spirits enter the pot through its cracks.

The invention of pottery was one of the most important ever made by men (by women). When the art of pottery spread to the Indus valley, the pots and bricks used in construction were kiln baked (Piggott, 1950, p. 154), but in Southwest Asia at the beginning of the Neolithic, mud houses and mud walls were hardened in the sun. Pots, however, must be kiln baked if they bear painted designs. With the coming of bricks to Mesopotamia and bricks and stone work to pre-dynastic Egypt, civilization was on its way.

The sacred wine of Southeast and Southwest Asia spread to the West long before the cultivation of rice. It was taken up in Ancient Egypt where barley, not rice or millet, was the first grain food. Judging from my African studies,[10] the grain to be used was malted by being moistened, placed under the sand, and allowed to sprout. Then it was boiled and strained. The liquid was a crude kind of beer. Just as rice became the god Shiva in the Orient, barley became the god Osiris in Ancient Egypt.[11] As the god was buried but sprouted and came to life again, so in symbolic repetition did the participants in the mysteries of Osiris, who ceremonially ate his flesh (the grain) and drank his blood (the beer). Thus the mystery cults of the Occident arose, superimposing themselves on primitive secret societies (Loeb, 1929, p. 283). The idea of immortality then spread eastward with the beverages which gave immortality to both gods and men: the *ambrosia* (without death) of the Greeks, the *haoma* of the Persians, and the *soma* of the Indo-European Caucasian invaders of northern India. These drinks were made from crushed plants, and were worshiped as gods.

Kipling's dual division of the world into East and West is more or less taken for granted, although it is difficult to explain. Yet there does exist a vital difference in both the outlook on life and the outlook toward the hereafter between the Near East, which is our ancient West, and the Far East; and this difference started perhaps eleven thousand years ago. The Far East, which is the Orient, remained on the root-planting level of civilization considerably longer than the Near East. It represented a stable, feminine, conservative outlook toward life. It is, on the whole, nonaggressive and non-warlike. Philosophically there is nothing to look forward to in the Oriental culture, and the best that can be hoped for in the future is a cessation of the cycle of existence —that is the hope that the transmigration of souls will have a termination. This philosophy of Nirvana is non-Indo-European in origin and may be derived from native totemism. Western Asia, however, modeled its thinking after a culture which malted its grain underground. The grain god died but came to life again, and so would the participator in the mysteries of the god. Here then there developed the idea of hope and room for individual existence (the worth of the individual) and an idea of the immortality of the soul. Here, to use Spengler's term, was born and nourished the Faustian man, restless and enterprising. Warfare gave him rich rewards in this life, for the most part in the coin of adventure. If he fell in battle, he had always a Valhalla to look forward to in the next life. The Occident became a man's paradise. The West was transformed into a man's world, while the East was still ascetic and feminine. Yet the East, perhaps owing to the fact that it was feminine, was the mother of the earliest of civilizations.

The Mentawei Islands

The best-known traces of the original root-planting and fishing culture of Southeast Asia are to be found in the Mentawei Islands off the west coast of Sumatra. Engano, "the Island of Women," was even more primitive, but there the original customs along with most of the population had been exterminated before the customs were adequately recorded. The Mentawei Islanders had an early root-planting culture without rice, pottery, or intoxicants. I now believe that, like the neighboring Enganese, they originally had a matrilineal society. This, however, all but disappeared under the influence of the warlike and patrilineal people of Nias from the north, and of the fantastic development of their own taboo (*punen*) system. The *punen* system made marriage a virtual sacrament, and the husband a household priest.

The Mentawei Islands are divided as follows. To the north is the island of Siberut, then comes Si Pora, and finally the North and South Pageh Islands. Siberut is most influenced by Nias, and perhaps even has patrilineal clans in the process of formation. All the Mentawei Islanders build their villages on the same plan. Each village is divided into hamlets with a long house or *uma* (Malay *rumah*) serving as the communal house for the entire hamlet. At its head is a priest or *rimata*. Individual families live in private houses or *lalep*. Unmarried young men and women also own small houses without altars, where they may sleep but may not eat. These are called *rusuk*.

Remains of a mother-right society are to be found in the premarital customs of the Pageh Islanders. A young couple will secretly meet in a *rusuk* for a number of years. It usually is only after several children are born that a young couple marries and builds a *lalep*. The proposal always comes from the woman. Marriage is matrilocal, since the woman owns the taro fields.

Head-Hunting in the Root-Planting Culture

Both head-hunting and human sacrifice are common accompaniments of the root-planting culture. Either one of these may lead to local cannibalism, especially when flesh from the head is eaten for magical reasons. Warfare itself among the early planters is always of a magical nature; these people have little of value to be seized by an enemy. Mentawei warfare illustrates these points. I shall quote in some detail from my book on Sumatra.

Wars are fought [in Mentawei] when a human sacrifice is needed for a new *uma* or for a large *punen*. In Siberut the head of an enemy is obtained as well as the arms and legs. The flesh of these members is eaten. The head is placed under the center post of the new *uma*.—The people of Sipora take the head, but not the members.—the people of Pageh never took heads. Some years ago, when they still were in the habit of going to Sipora or Siberut on war expeditions, they conducted the affair in the following manner. They first lay in ambush and shot at those who went fishing. The hostile *uma* was neither burnt nor attacked. If the warriors succeeded in killing one or more of the enemy, they hacked the bodies and decorated their own heads with plants and flowers. If not, they shot their arrows into the bushes and went home. Instead of a head, sacred flowers and leaves were placed under the center post of the new *uma* to appease Teteu, the earthquake god.

Head taking is (or was) very important in Siberut and there are many taboos connected with the custom. The women at home have to remain quiet, and cannot cook. They spend their nights in the *uma*. They abstain from fruits and certain fish. If they disobey these injunctions their men will come to harm.

When the warriors return with their trophies they utter a war whoop at the mouth of the river. The parts are hung up in the *uma* for two days while the warriors dance around them. Then the parts are buried, and the heads hung up in the bushes. The seers waft the ghosts of the slain away with sacred leaves, and a taboo period of two months follows.

(Loeb, 1935, p. 172)

Usually a people will have either head-hunting or human sacrifice, but not both. Thus the Naga of Assam and the Dyaks of Borneo formerly were noted for head-hunting, while the Gonds of India specialized in human sacrifice in connection with their agriculture. It seems probable that the Lake Dwellers of Central Europe practiced head-hunting and that their dwellings were built over water not only for the sake of sanitation but together with their long platforms to give protection to the inmates. According to R. Heine–Geldern the Greek story of the Gorgons' heads is a recollection of former European head-hunting. It will be remembered that the three Gorgon sisters had snakes on their heads instead of hair, and that their terrifying aspect turned the beholder to stone. Perseus killed Medusa, the mortal sister, by averting his gaze. He then put the head in a bag and brought it home in order to slay his enemies.[12] The magical potency of an amputated human head certainly reminds one of the concepts of primitive head-hunting.

Conclusions

There is as yet no agreement among scientists regarding the single or multiple origins of the root-planting cultures of the world. I have tried to establish the connection between this early planting culture, mother-right societies, the use of narcotics, and the long house. As Sauer writes, "The *Kulturkreis* school seems to have a valid generalization in equating the 'Old Planter' complex with matrilineal societies, and in linking to them multifamily houses, large, rectangular, gabled structures, providing living and storage space for the extended household, and often built on platforms set on posts" (1952, p. 28).

I believe that head-hunting also belongs to this "Old Planter" complex, but that intoxicants spread with grain culture. The complex is found in all quarters of the world, including Oceania, West Africa,[13] and North and South America. It has not been clear, however, how this complex diffused to the New World. Wissmann dates the beginning of the root planting as early as 13000 to 9000 B.C. in order to allow time for its diffusion (1956, p. 285). In a later article Wissmann writes: "The planting of tubers and the domestication of dog, pig, and fowl seem to have had their origin amongst a population of fishers and shellfish gatherers in humid southern Asia (at least some time before 10000 B.C., i.e., prior to the Two Creeks or Alleröd interval" (1957, p. 81). The latter was a substage of glaciation. Now we are informed about not only the place but also the time at which our first stage of civilization (hearth of culture) was founded. Both Wissmann and Sauer believe that there was only one hearth of root-planting culture (as well as one hearth each for later forms of culture) and that each culture in turn spread to the New World. The root-planting culture is thought to have come across Bering Strait, losing the tubers on the way. Sauer writes: "Numerous resemblances in customs between the Indians of our Northwest coast and peoples of Indonesia are familiar. In Kamchatka, the Alaskan Peninsula, Kodiak, and on the coast of British Columbia, there were matrilineal societies, living in multifamily houses with notions of property, prestige, and art forms which are about what might be left of Southeast Asiatic culture from which an adverse environment had eliminated certain possibilities, in particular agriculture" (Sauer, 1952, p. 55). Actually, the Indonesian long house extends in a continuous line from Japan (Loeb and Broek, 1947, p. 419), where it was brought in prehistoric times by Indonesians, to Kamchatka,[14] to Unalaska in the Aleutians (Collins and Walker, 1945, Fig. 3), to Kodiak, to Alaska, and even to the American Southwest Pueblo culture (Roberts, 1931). (See illustrations.) From Japan north this culture was carried by shell mound peoples who built their long houses underground, and who carried on a matrilineal form of society. It is interesting to note that tobacco was smoked everywhere in the New World where it was known, except on the northern Northwest Coast where it was only chewed with lime (Driver and Massey, 1951, p. 262). Evidently tobacco here took the place of an earlier narcotic. Head-hunting usually is replaced by scalping in North America, but often remains unchanged in South America, as with the Jivaro, who closely resemble in their head-hunting customs the natives of Southeast Asia. Stirling writes that ". . . in this respect, they have merely retained a custom and a war pattern that was widespread in northwestern South America at the time of the conquest."[15] In addition, as Sauer has pointed out, the state of Venezuela derives its name from the long houses on piles which reminded the Spanish of Venice (Sauer, 1952, p. 42).

Until we have further evidence of the migration of cultures between the Old and the New World,[16] American anthropologists will probably be mainly interested in the terms "hearths of culture," "root-planting culture," and "seed-planting culture." So far as Southeast Asia is concerned "root-planting culture" is a preferable term to "Mesolithic," since bamboo was more important to the region than stone implements. "Neolithic" was never a satisfactory term, for no people in the early seed-sowing age had polished stone implements. Perhaps our minds have been too concentrated on stone implements to be able to differentiate clearly the main steps in cultural evolution.

There is an old German proverb which I saw as a student on the walls of a German tavern in New Haven:

Wer weisst nicht Wein, Weib, und Gesang,
Der bleibt ein Narr sein Lebenslang.

It may contain a kernel of truth.

NOTES

[1] Griffith Taylor advanced this theory. He did not, however, start with the tropical rain forest of Southeast Asia, nor did he end with the South Pole (Taylor, 1946, p. 107).

[2] This would conform to Griffith Taylor's theory of the migration of round-

headed Asiatic people into Central Europe to form the Alpine-race (Taylor, 1937, p. 10).

3 The wild *Nicotiana tabacum* is found in Peru and Bolivia, and the wild *N. sylvestris* is found in northern Argentina. Domesticated *N. tabacum* is a hybrid of these two (Driver and Massey, 1957, p. 260).

4 Information from Professor R. F. Salisbury.

5 A narcotic mushroom has been used in central Meso-America since before the time of the Conquest. The Aztecs also ate tobacco leaves (Driver and Massey, 1957, pp. 275, 262).

6 The principal narcotics in aboriginal North America were tobacco, peyote, jimsonweed, "the black drink," and the mescal bean (Driver and Massey, 1957, p. 260).

7 "The distribution of alcoholic beverages falls almost wholly within the bounds of agriculture. But there is an area in northern Mexico without agriculture where wine is made from wild plants. For the world as a whole there is a correlation between agriculture and alcoholic beverages" (Driver and Massey, 1957, p. 266; see also Loeb, 1943, p. 392).

8 Information from Dr. George Devereux.

9 Dr. G. F. Ruey of Formosa tells me that millet and not barley is used by the Taiyal. In my article of 1943 (p. 394), I quoted Wiedfeldt as saying that barley was used. Wiedfeldt was mistaken. Wiedfeldt also must have been mistaken when he claimed that a hollow tree stump was used for the brewing. If the beer were not covered, it would have soured in fermenting.

10 The Kuanyama Ambo Bantu of Southwest Africa had many other pre-dynastic Egyptian traits besides this method of brewing beer.

11 Herodotus (II.171) mentions that the mysteries of the barley god were brought from Egypt by the daughters of Danaus to the Pelasgic (pre-Indo-Europeans) women of the Peloponnese. Rawlinson adds that the uninitiated in Egypt believed the Nile to be the god Osiris.

12 From a lecture given in 1945 by Heine-Geldern.

13 Dittmer (1954, Plate IX) shows a picture of a clan long house in South Cameroon.

14 Stellers (1774) shows an underground winter dwelling with entrance through a central opening and down a notched pole near the fireplace; the walls are lined with low platforms.

15 Stirling, 1938, p. 41. The Jivaro are a typical root-planting people, living in long houses. Interestingly enough, these people use narcotics (*datura arborea* or *banisteria caapi*) in order to obtain visions or acquire courage for head-hunting (Karsten, 1923, pp. 2, 3).

16 Sauer, 1952, p. 54. Sauer believes that we already have sufficient evidence. He writes that the case for the adherents of parallel invention between the Old and New worlds rests "not on evidence, but on authority." I believe that most European geographers and ethnologists agree with Sauer.

REFERENCES

Bishop, C. W. 1942. Origin of Far Eastern Civilizations. Smithsonian Institution, War Background Studies, No. 1. Washington, D.C.

Bunce, D. 1857. *Twenty-three Years Wanderings in the Australians and Tasmania.*

Geelong. Quoted in H. Ling Roth, *The Aborigines of Tasmania.* Halifax England, p. 94.

Collins, H. B. Jr., A. H. Clark, and E. H. Walker. 1945. The Aleutian Islands Their People and Natural History. Smithsonian Institution, War Background Studies, No. 21, Washington, D.C.

Cook, James. 1784. A Voyage to the Pacific Ocean.... London.

Dittmer, K. 1954. Allgemeine Völkerkunde. Braunschweig.

Driver, H. E., and W. C. Massey. 1957. "Comparative Studies of the North American Indians," *Transactions of the American Philosophical Society,* N.S., 47:Part 2. Philadelphia.

Hančar, F. 1955. Das Pferd in prähistorischer und früher historischer Zeit. Vienna.

Heine-Geldern, R. 1923. "Südostasien," in G. Buschan, *Illustrierte Völkerkunde.* Vol. II. Stuttgart.

Herodotus. History, ed. by Rawlinson.

Karsten, R. 1923. Blood Revenge, War, and Victory Feasts among the Jivaro Indians of Eastern Ecuador. Smithsonian Institution, Bureau of American Ethnology, Bulletin 79, Washington, D.C.

Loeb, E. M. 1929. Tribal Initiations and Secret Societies. University of California Publications in American Archaeology and Ethnology, 25:No. 3.

——— 1943. "Primitive Intoxicants," *Quarterly Journal of Studies on Alcohol,* 4:No. 3.

——— 1947. "Social Organization and the Long House in Southeast Asia and Micronesia," *Far Eastern Quarterly,* 6:No. 2.

Loeb, E. M., and J. Broek. 1947. "Social Organization and the Long House in Southeast Asia," *American Anthropologist,* 49:No. 3.

Loeb, E. M., and R. Heine-Geldern. 1935. Sumatra, Its History and People. Vienna.

Piggott, S. 1950. Prehistoric India. New York.

Roberts, F. H. H., Jr. 1931. Report of the American Bureau of Ethnology.

Sauer, Carl O. 1952. Agricultural Origins and Dispersals. New York.

Stellers, G. W. 1774. Beschribung von dem Lande Kamschatka. Leipzig.

Stirling, M. W. 1938. Historical and Ethnographical Material on the Jivaro Indians. Bureau of the American Ethnological Society, Bulletin 117, Washington, D.C.

Taylor, G. 1937. Environment, Race, and Migration. Chicago.

——— 1946. Our Evolving Civilization. Toronto.

Wissmann, H. von. 1956. "On the Role of Nature in Changing the Face of the Dry Belt of Asia," in *Man's Role in Changing the Face of the Earth,* ed. by W. Thomas Jr. Chicago.

——— 1957. "Ursprungsherde und Ausbreitungswege von Pflanzen und Tierzucht und ihre Abhängigkeit von der Klimageschichte," *Erdkunde,* Band XI, Heft 2.

CLASSICAL AND INDO-IRANIAN ANALOGUES IN SOUTHEAST ASIA AND PACIFIC ISLANDS

By Wilson D. Wallis

ANNHURST COLLEGE

ONE CAN FIND similar culture traits almost anywhere if one seeks them indiscriminately. It hardly bears repetition that diffusion is not necessarily implied even when there are many similarities in the cultures of two areas, for example, in ancient Egypt and Middle America. It is, however, pertinent to emphasize resemblances in the culture traits of areas remote from one another if the cultures are known to have had direct or indirect contact with one another, if such contact is suspected, or if the resemblances are so numerous or detailed, or both, that a common origin becomes a probable—though not inevitable—explanation of the resemblances.

John Loewenthal[1] lists many parallels in Graeco-Roman and Oceanic cultures, but he does not include any of the traits specified in the following account. The resemblances which he mentions are principally in material culture or technology; he does not, however, include the almost unique *amentum*, or thong, used in throwing the Roman javelin, which has an analogue in New Zealand. Tylor calls attention to the fact that the "whip-like instrument . . . in New Zealand . . . used for spear-throwing" has its "nearest approach [in] the classic *amentum*, a thong attached to the middle of the shaft of the javelin to throw it with."[2]

The distribution of the traits to which Loewenthal calls attention is erratic, and none of them is limited to classical and Oceanic cultures. Hence they do not imply specific relations between these two culture areas. A similar observation applies to Graebner's interpretation of similarities between the Germanic concept of Thor and the Polynesian concept of Maui.[3] The fallacy in such generalized inferences was indicated in 1890 by H. Ling Roth.

"Similar customs," he said, "such as smearing the hair with red ochre and grease, the violent dancing and vociferous singing, and hunting as a chief amusement, are customs too widely distributed among savages and barbaric peoples in general to bear any specific significance in a comparative study. . . . Distinct races in various parts of the world follow the custom of couvade, marriage by capture, circumcision, and cannibalism."[4]

The account which we here offer indicates specific similarities in traits which have not been reported for other areas, or have a very limited distribution outside the compared areas. Others have called attention to some of these traits. Tylor finds "reasons which may make us hesitate to consider the whole Polynesian mythology as independent of Asiatic influence."[5] Some of those "reasons" we shall specify as we examine a fraction of the data in some detail.

Cosmology

In the Indian concept, Pravati divided or broke into halves the egg in which the Sun's charioteer was hatched. A man, or semi-giant, came forth, elevated half the shell with his head, and with his body cast the other half into the deep. The halves became base and cover of the universe. Hence the celestial sphere, because it is egg-shaped, is called Brahma's Egg. The cosmic egg concept occurs in Burma, Borneo, Hawaii, and Tahiti. Origin of mankind from an egg, a concept in the Admiralty Islands, Fiji, and the Torres Straits, suggests the cosmic egg of Indo-Iranian belief.

Sir John Rhys comments on the similarity between Greek and Maori myths regarding the separation of Heaven from Earth, husband from wife. He finds "no reason to suppose that the Maori borrowed their myth from the Greeks, or the Greeks from the Maori," but he traces the similarity to "a common origin, or . . . to the independent workings of the human mind under similar circumstances." The myth was "known in modified form to the Hindus and . . . is . . . found in the Norse Edda; . . . it is possible to detect traces of it in Celtic."[6]

H. J. Rose remarks upon "the resemblance to the Polynesian story of how Rangi (Earth) and Papa (Heaven) were separated by their children, led by Maui" in the Greek account of the Titans led by Kronos. "If the two stories are not of independent origin, we may perhaps suppose that the myth originated in very ancient times . . . in Asia and spread in both directions."[7]

Forceful separation of the spouses Heaven and Earth appears in both areas; in both areas dew and rain are said to be the tears of

Heaven, caused by sorrow over the separation from Earth. The Lakher of Assam also depict Sky and Earth as husband and wife.

In India, man was created by God from a drop of sweat; in Vaitupu, woman was created out of man's sweat. In Tongan cosmogony there were four pairs of primeval twins. Each twin, with the exception of one pair, married its twin sibling, and they begot progeny. This, in character, is Hindu, and Hindus have four cosmic epochs.

There is close resemblance between Maori and Greek concepts of creation in their abstractness. Also, both cultures have the concept of the god (among Maori the goddess) swallowing and later disgorging his children. The Maori god Uta, who knew that his wife Houmete had swallowed their two boys, compelled her to disgorge them—none the worse for their experience. In the Maori account the Greek roles of the spouses are reversed; otherwise the incidents are almost identical.

The killing, in Polynesia, of a supernatural giant, or evil god or goddess, by pitching red-hot stones into his or her mouth under the pretext that they are food, suggests the giving of the swaddled stone to Kronos, who is deceived into believing that it is his child. The former motive occurs in Hawaii, Tahiti, Melanesia, Indonesia, India, Indo-China. In a south India Kota tale, a woman throws chili into a jackal's open mouth, after showing the beast a strip of dried meat which she held in the other hand. In a central New Guinea Kukukuku myth, a spirit-woman is killed by having a white-hot stone thrown into her mouth.[8] Borneo tribes and the Khasi of Assam relate that after a snake had become friendly and had learned to open its mouth to receive a lump of flesh which from time to time a man threw into its jaws, the man, acting under advice from a god (in some accounts the god was the agent), threw into the serpent's mouth a lump of iron, red-hot from the furnace, and thus killed the reptile. Phases of these motives suggest the feeding of the dog Cerberus in Hades.

Personification of nature and natural forces is elaborated in Greece and in Polynesia. Maori have a god of, respectively, earthquake, rainbow, comet, lightning, and other impressive natural phenomena. Perhaps an older concept of the tides underlies the description in the *Odyssey* (Book XII) of Charybdis, who "blackly sucks down the sea. Three times a day she sucks it down and three times she spews it out: an awful sight. May you not be there while she sucks it in. No power, not the Earthquaker's own, could then deliver you from ruin." This concept is strongly reminiscent of interpretations in India, the Andaman Islands, the Malay Peninsula, northwest Australia, and among the Ainu. In northwest Australia a serpent sucks in and spews out the water, and thus causes the tides. The Maori attribute the ebb and flow to Te Parata, a monster which lives in the deep waters of the ocean.

Tylor indicates another similarity in the myths of Polynesia and Greece, but he does not interpret it as implying diffusion of the motive. He remarks:

The Tahitians tell tales of their sea-god Hiro, whose followers were sailing on the ocean while he was lulled to sleep in a cavern in the depths below; then the wind-god raised a furious storm to destroy the canoe, but the sailors cried to Hiro, till, rising to the surface, he quelled the storm, and his votaries came safe to port. So in Homer, Poseidon the sea-god, dweller in caves of ocean, sets on the winds to toss the frail bark of Odysseus among the thundering waves, till Ino comes to his rescue and bids him strip and swim for the Phaikian shore. Both tales are word-pictures of the stormy sea told in the language of nature-myth, only with different turns. The New Zealanders have a story of Maui imprisoning the winds, all but the wild west-wind, whom he cannot catch to shut into its cavern by a great stone rolled against its mouth; all he can do is to chase it home sometimes, and then it hides in the cavern, and for a while dies away. All this is a mythic description of the weather, meaning that other winds are occasional, but the west wind prevalent and strong. These New Zealanders had never heard of the classic myth of Aeolus and the cave of the winds, yet how nearly they had come to the same mythic fancy, that it is from such blow-holes in the hill-sides that the winds come forth.[9]

There is striking analogy in the Greek myth about the Pleiades and concepts in Indonesia and Australia. In the Greek myth the seventh star of the Pleiades, the mother of the other six stars, fled the group when Troy fell. In the Malay Peninsula and in Borneo it is related that one Pleiad fell to earth. The Malay says:

> Seven stars, six only now remain.
> One has fallen into Manjapahit.

The Dyak describe the Pleiades as six chickens which an invisible hen follows. Formerly, before men had rice, there were seven. One of the chickens came down to earth and subsequently was taken aloft by Orion. In Australia there are accounts of a seventh star now married to a mortal or hiding behind her bolder sisters.

To my knowledge, the only (partial) analogue to this concept in the

New World is the Cherokee account that seven boys departed for the sky to form the Pleiades; one was pulled back by his mother, and only six arrived at their celestial destination. Some astronomers have suggested that the, to them, "apparently discontinuous" distribution of this motive suggests independent observations of a diminishing Pleione, the "number 7" of the Pleiades.

Professor Willem Luyten states: "Possibly there is evidence that it has been diminishing; but I do not think many people accept it as proved." [10] The difficulty often occasioned in identifying this feeble star in the cluster may in some instances have independently given rise to this basic motive. The Naga of Assam, for example, say that there are seven stars in the Pleiades, but that the ordinary man can see only six.

The motive of the lost Pleiad is, however, confined almost entirely to the Old World, and there to contiguous areas through which many culture influences have passed. Its distribution implies diffusion from a common source, or certainly few independent origins.

The Hawaiian motive that Golden Cloud was born from the head of Hina suggests the Greek account of the origin of Minerva. In the most commonly accepted Hindu story Brahmin were born out of Brahma's head. There is a suggestion of the motive in the Tibetan tale that on the head of a certain king grew a soft tumor, resembling somewhat a cushion of cotton or of wool. When it was ripe it broke, and there emerged a shapely and handsome lad.

Marquesans pay divine honors to Echo, a female spirit or goddess, who speaks to the worshiper out of the rocks. The Maori say Echo existed before the Creator, in as much as it sent his voice back to him. One recalls the Greek personification of Echo, and the Roman version that Echo was one of the Oreades, who connived at the amours of Jupiter and was changed by the jealous Juno into a lovesick maiden who pined with grief over her unrequited love for Narcissus until only her voice remained.

The Maori story of Maui's visit to his mother in the underworld suggests the Greek myth of Demeter and the association of the underworld with vegetation. There Maui found the people engaged in planting crops. He transformed himself into a small bird, perched on the upper part of a digging implement, and sang the song which since that time has been sung by those who plant.

This is only remotely suggestive of the Greek motive; but where, outside realms touched by Greek influences, does one find association of vegetation with an underworld god or goddess?

A common motive in Polynesian myth, common elsewhere in that form only in Melanesia, Australia, and Indonesia, describes the antagonism and contests between certain species of animals, especially between birds and fishes. A Tonga myth recounts the adventure of Rat when carried over the water on the back of Octopus. There is a partial analogue in the Greek story of the contest between Frogs and Mice. In the Greek story Frog says: "The Son of Kronos has given us Frogs the power to lead a double life, dwelling at will in two separate elements; and so we both leap on land and plunge beneath the water. If you would learn all these things, 'tis easy done; just mount my back and hold me tight lest you be lost, and so you shall come rejoicing to my house.' So said he and offered his back." Mouse climbs on, is carried by Frog, and drowns. During the ensuing battle, Zeus takes pity on the Frogs; the Crabs, which he sends to help the Frogs, rout the Mice.

Hawaiian tradition regarding Lono, or Rono, the culture hero whose return is expected, declares that he instituted games to commemorate his deceased wife. This sounds more Greek than Oceanic or Asiatic.

The Tahitian story of Maumea, mother of Tuture, who is told to bring water from a distant spring in gourds pierced with holes, suggests the Greek motive of carrying water in a sieve. In a Maori story, Honoura pierces a gourd and in jest sends his brother to bring him a drink of water in it. The motive of giving a demon a container with a hole in it with which to dip water from a stream occurs among Bougainville Siuai. In a Malay story, a girl abducted by a monkey pierces a hole in the bottom of a container and sends the monkey to fill it with water. Among the Bulu of Cameroons, Tortoise is asked to carry water in a basket, whereupon he requests a carrying-strap of smoke.

The Ainu goddess of fire, inherent in the household fire, sees and hears all that happens, is a witness to the words and actions of each member of the family, and on the day of judgment will appear for or against each of them.

This has a pronounced Iranian and Burmese Buddhist ring; and Ainu belief in a realm of six regions below the surface of the earth and as many above suggests Buddhist concept, perhaps introduced in recent centuries, but now accepted by Ainu as having existed from the beginning. Their dualism is emphatic. A struggle between a principle of good and a principle of evil rages incessantly. Always they have been antagonistic to one another, and so will they be forever.

Oaths

In Samoa, to smoke out a thief, grass is laid on the sacred village stone, each person places his hand on it, and says: "I lay hand on the stone. If I stole the thing, may I speedily die."

This is almost identical with early Greek custom, and with a practice which persisted in Albania until the last century, that of laying the hand on a certain stone when taking oath. A similar procedure is or was widespread in Europe, South Asia, Indonesia, and northeast Negro Africa. An accused Samoan holds a piece of grass in his hands, symbolizing a silent imprecation that if he swears falsely his entire family may die and grass grow over their habitation. In the Old World the areas in which formal oath is taken have a continuous distribution, and I do not know of the existence of this type elsewhere except in East Africa, where there is much Indonesian influence.

A form of Greek oath was: "So long as the grass shall grow and the tides flow." Similarity with the Samoan oath is striking. Samoans say: "Touch your eyes, if what you say is true," a conditional curse which suggests the Roman custom of swearing by eyes and ears.

Riddles, Songs, and Ceremonies

The riddle, a motive in Homeric cyclic literature, occurs also in India, Papua (Kiwai), and Polynesia, and infrequently in other preliterate cultures.

Polynesians have a rhyming contest which suggests a Greek motive. The *Contest of Homer and Hesiod*, which in the earliest preserved document dates from the time of Hadrian but apparently is based on an earlier version by the Sophist Alcidamas, about 400 B.C., contains verse competitions which savor strongly of Polynesian rhyming contests. Following is an example from the Greek contest:

Hesiod. "Then they dined on the flesh of oxen and their horses' necks...."
Homer. "They unyoked dripping with sweat, when they had had enough of war."
Hesiod. "And the Phrygians, who of all men are handiest at ships...."
Homer. "To filch their dinner from pirates on the beach."

Malays hold contests in which one side gives the first two lines of a stanza containing a hidden meaning. The contesting side must quickly offer a suitable solution in another two lines. Often a long contest ends without either side scoring a victory.

The Nepalese have a comparable custom which one infers is historically related to the preceding. It is

... a spontaneous entertainment ... when large numbers of pilgrims have gathered together for a sacred occasion. In the evening, some individuals may produce musical instruments, and a *zuwari* may get under way. ... Sometimes ... an unmarried boy and girl become *zuwari* rivals. The boy sings a song, concluding it with a question which she must answer.

The girl sings a reply, ending with a question for him.

So it goes, back and forth, until one of the two contestants breaks down, unable to improvise quickly enough. If the girl wins the contest, the boy must bow before her and present her with a bottle of wine and some money. If the boy wins, he may make her his bride. ... This form of marriage is quite rare.[11]

The Japanese *Kojiki*, the composition of which postdates the introduction of Buddhism into Japan contains several examples of verse contests. They were common then and long thereafter. The objective was to fit a suitable second hemistich, a half-verse or half-line, to the first hemistich of a standard poem of thirty-one syllables. In the Muramachi period (1392–1573), this matching of verses "had become ... a popular game, ... a craze and a serious business, with elaborate rules and a complicated system of marking, embodied in a tremendous literature of codes and commentaries. There grew up a class of professional teachers and judges (*tensha*, markers), and they were in great demand at social gatherings. A contemporary satirist said: 'Everywhere a jumble of Kyoto and Kamakura, ill-assorted parties of mock poets and self-appointed judges.' Diaries and other contemporary records indicate that almost all classes indulged in these contests."[12]

The Hawaiian so-called riddle contest, which is very similar to the Greek verse contest, is actually a combined riddle and verse contest. For example, the riddlers chant:

> The moon of Kaulua,
> The moon that bore the first breadfruit of Lanai ...
> The fruit of the taro swells down below,

The fruit of the sweet potato swells down below,
The fruit of the yam swells down below,
The fruit of the *pia* swells down below,
The fruit of the *ape* swells down below,
Down, down, down to Milu and below that!

The boy answers:

The moon of Kaulua,
The moon that gave birth to the great turtle and placed it,
The fruit of the seaweed swells below,
The egg *(hua)* of the fish swells below,
The egg of the turtle swells below,
The egg of the chicken swells below,
(At) the foundation of the house of Milu below,
The foundation of the house of Milu, laid below,
below, away below.

The men then name the fruits that ripen above ground—bananas, breadfruit, mountain apple, and a half-dozen others—and conclude:

The coconut *(nui)* puts forth fruit above,
Up to the flying clouds and above that.

The boy answers:

Kaulua is the moon,
The moon gives birth to a great turtle,
At Po-niu-lua [punning on the word coconut] on
Lanai is my fruit,
The fruit is the sun that hangs above,
The fruit is the moon that hangs above,
The fruit is the stars that hang above,
The fruit is the cloud that hangs above,
The fruit is the wind that hangs above,
The fruit is the lightning that hangs above,
Up, up above the flying clouds and above that!

The men jeer and say that their fruit still hangs above. The boy continues:

There it is, there it is,
There hangs the great wind cloud,
The south wind is blowing,
The wind that goes roughly,
Beating the leaves of the trees,
Pushing against the trunks of the trees,

Making them fall below,
The trunk, the branches,
The leaves, the fruit,
Brushed off till they lie bruised and fallen below,
The breadfruit bears fruit above,
Struck by the south wind it falls below....[13]

In the Basque village of Sare (Labourd) *bersulariak* compete in verse-making, one answering the other on a given subject.

A comparable verse contest, and one stemming, it seems, from classical antiquity, is carried on today by Brazilian cowboys. Thus one sings:

In God's good time, amen!
   I am not jesting, no!
I defy the entire world
   In singing at this show!

To which an adversary will reply in some such lines as the following:

In singing at this show,
   My friend and comrade true,
The one who accepts your challenge here
   Is the *fame* of this land, you know!

The contest continues until a contestant, entangled in a difficult rhyme, falters, strums his banjo nervously, and amid laughter from bystanders acknowledges defeat.

The "Big Toe" Motive

An Iranian parallel in Indonesia and Oceania is the concept that the soul enters or leaves the body through the big toe. The Zoroastrian *Vendidad* prescribes the means of ridding one of uncleanness by driving the demon from one part of the body to another until finally it escapes from the left great toe and rushes off with a buzzing noise.

The big toes and thumbs of a Brahmin corpse are tied with a small piece of cloth. This custom may be historically related to the Iranian belief about the place of exit of the soul. A Hindu saint who visits the house of a Lingayat to solicit alms dips the big toe of his right foot into water; and after a birth or a death this water is used for purification. Each Lingayat householder keeps some of it on a stand in the house; the water rids the house of insects—a further compliment to the potency of a Brahmin's big toe.

In the funeral rites of the Birhor of Chota Nagpur, each member of the party touches the ceremonial fire with his left great toe.

In a Bombay treatment to relieve the effects of evil eye, the patient breaks with a toe of the left foot a figure which represents the person who has sent the evil eye.

In a ceremony of the Kunbi of Marathi, India, designed it seems to rid one of a troublesome ghost, the bridegroom kicks off a betel nut with his right big toe.

The Lakher of Assam, to ensure the health of a young child, anoint the right big toe with the blood of a sacrificed fowl and with water. And at their funeral feast for a man the big toe of each relative of the deceased is anointed with the blood of a sacrificed fowl. This ceremony is prescribed, for it is essential that the souls of the deceased's family be at peace. If a Rengma Naga can move his big toes during a dream in which an evil spirit attacks him, he can free himself from the aggressive spirit; for these spirits have no big toe, and hence can not hold the big toe of a man whom they wantonly attack.

Probably historically related to Iranian concept is the Burmese belief that during the week the center of vigor shifts downward in the body. On Sunday it is in the head; on Monday, in the forehead; on Tuesday, in the shoulders; on Wednesday, in the mouth, chin, and cheeks; on Thursday, in waist and hands; on Friday, in chest and legs; on Saturday, in abdomen and toes.

The Kheng, in Arakan, Lower Burma, tie a dead fowl to the big toe of the deceased to terrify the worms which guard the portals of paradise, and thus ensure the soul easy entry into the next world.

In Siam, to exorcise the evil spirit which possesses a man, the sorcerer applies a metal nail to the point of the big toe of the victim, and later drives the nail into a piece of wood. The Siamese believe, also, that a vampire which resembles a black monkey, and lives in the jungle, sucks the lifeblood from the big toe of a sleeper; and another vampire has a similar penchant. Hence a man who sleeps in the jungle at night is well advised to keep hold of his feet, and thus ward off these toe-suckers.

In the Malay peninsula, to abduct a person's soul, a sorcerer stands with big toe of the right foot resting on big toe of left foot.

In a Parsi religious ceremony one of the officiating priests faces south, the right great toe over the left.

Among the Menik Kaien, the Lanoh, and the Kintak Bong, Negritos in the Malay peninsula, the soul, as in Iran, leaves the body by the big toe. Semang (Negrito) souls must cross a flimsy rope bridge which spans a boiling sea. At the farther end is a horrible monster. The sight of it so frightens the timid and wicked that they fall from the bridge and swim in agony in the boiling waters until a god graciously lowers his great toe to enable them to get out.

The Maori rite of sealing a peace pact includes tying a cord of native flax to the great toes of the opposing chiefs, thus symbolizing the union of the two gods. A Maori transmits his mana to his son by having the latter bite the great toe of the father's left foot. Before a student begins a course of instruction in the Maori House-of-learning he must bite the scalp or the big toe of the teacher, in order that, by this physical contact the knowledge of the teacher shall flow to the pupil.

In the Society Islands a demon which has entered one's body and caused sickness is driven out by applying a heated stone to the afflicted part, drawing it toward the arm or the leg of the patient, then down the limb to its extremity, where the demon is expelled.

In Hawaiian belief, Kiku catches the soul of Kawelu, which in the form of a butterfly had attempted to escape, and compels it to enter the body by a hole which he makes in the great toe of the left foot. These Society Islands and Hawaiian concepts suggest ultimate Iranian inspiration.

In Japan, to relieve a woman of the pains of childbirth, three spots on the little toe of her right foot are burned with mugwort; a practice possibly indebted to Iranian concept that the soul leaves through the big toe of the left foot.

Australia Murngin declare that the soul of a man enters the body of his killer between the big toe and the adjacent toe—at which spot the spear-shaft has been grasped—pushes its way upward into the leg of the killer, then into the body, "like an ant," until it enters the man's stomach and closes it.

A New Guinea Mountain Arapesh man places his big toe on his bride's big toe at her first menstruation ceremony.

We know of no precisely equivalent concepts in other preliterate areas; a passage in Plutarch's account of Pyrrhus (*Lives*), however, indicates a Greek concept similar to Iranian and perhaps derived from it. "It was," Plutarch says, "a general belief that Pyrrhus could cure the spleen by sacrificing a white cock and gently pressing, with his right foot on the spleen of the persons as they lay down on their backs, nor was anyone so poor or inconsiderable as not to be welcome, if he desired it, to the benefit of his touch. He accepted the cock for the sacrifice as a reward, and was always much pleased with the present. The large toe of that foot was said to have a divine virtue; for after his death, the rest of the body being consumed, this was found unhurt, and untouched by fire."

Plutarch tells us also that when Cimon was sacrificing to Bacchus ants took up congealed particles of the blood of the victim and laid them about Cimon's great toe. The context indicates that this was an omen of death. The behavior of the ants, "was not observed for a good while, but at the very time when Cimon spied it, the priest came and showed him the liver of the sacrifice imperfect, wanting that part of it called the head. But he could not then recede from the enterprise, so he set sail." Subsequently, "they understood that Cimon was dead; and computing the time of the oracle, they found that his death had been signified, he being then already with the gods."

Plutarch states also that in ancient Rome healing was practised by passing the sacred royal great toe over the affected part.

In Exodus 29.20 the blood of the ram, with which Aaron's sons were to be purified, was placed on the thumb of the right hand and the great toe of the right foot. Aaron was treated similarly (Leviticus 8.23; see also 14.14, 17, 25, 28).

Among medieval Jews it was believed that a man could banish sensual thoughts by pressing the big toes firmly into the ground and resting the weight of the body on them, without leaning against a wall.

In Tangier, itching of the big toe indicates that a member of one's family who is ill will die; and in Aglu, itching of the big toe of the left foot portends news of death. In a Moroccan Mohammedan treatment the husband dips his big toe into a basin of water, climbs three times over his wife, and she drinks a few sips of the water which has absorbed his vitality.

In Serbian folklore an old woman turned animals into ashes by touching them with the little toe of her left foot.

Dance Motives

In India, Java, and Bali, there are dances with characteristic hand and arm movements. Comparable ones, though not with identical patterning, are typical of Polynesia. There are many similarities between the hand gestures used in dances in India and in Hawaii. The movement flows from shoulder to wrist to curving fingers.

In five gestures of about two thousand in India and about four hundred in Hawaii, identical meaning is associated with the same respective gesture. In India, when the fingers are straight and are brought together so that the tips touch, the gesture means "flower bud." When conveyed to the mouth and thrust outward, it means "speech." In Hawaii this gesture means "flower"; or, if made at the mouth, it means "talk" or "song."

A gesture involving the two hands, the hand bent down from the wrist with fingers released means, in India, "rain," or "rain clouds." In Hawaii, the hands falling "flutteringly down" means "rain."

Thumb and index finger stretched out, the other fingers bent and touching the palm, means, in India, "moon"; when placed at the ear, "listen to me." In Hawaii, both hands, fingers slightly less bent in an otherwise identical gesture, means "moon"; a hand placed at the ear means "listen." In both areas, slightly cupped hands held at the level of the chest, fingers together and tips touching, means "house"; a hand stretched out in front, the other hand on it, palms down, thumbs extended and moved up and down, means "fish."

Some of these similarities, granting the existence in both areas of a similar mimetic dance pattern, might easily be due to independent origins, notably so in the representations of "moon" and of "house." However, similarities in the basic dance patterns of the two areas suggest indebtedness of one to the other or of both to an ultimately common source.

Similarity of certain other pantomimic elements is not unusual, since movements depicting common emotions such as fear, admiration, rage tend to converge, despite differences in dance techniques. In India the two palms are brought together, the fingers pointing down; this means death. In Hawaii the downward push means death or nothingness.

The idea of entwining the fingers to express unity or marriage is found in both areas.... Hindu hand movements are found throughout Indonesia in the Srimpis of the Javanese—where "the fingers tremble as if they had a life of their own," and in dances of Bali, which have become extremely stereotyped. We can not yet trace a definite development of dance technique from India through Indonesia to Hawaii.

But the ... many similarities ... encourage the belief that Hawaii owes a great deal of its dance fundamentals to Indonesia.[14]

Conclusion: Historical Evidence

Many traits of Greek, Roman, or Indo-Iranian provenience appear in Pacific islands—most of them, it seems, more prevalent in Indonesia and Polynesia or some portions of these areas than elsewhere. The character and the quantity of the similarities suggest historic relations, however indirect, between Greek, Roman, or Indo-Iranian cultures and certain Oceanic ones. How these Classical or Indo-Iranian traits diffused into the Pacific islands we do not know, but that they did so seems probable.

Historical sources acquaint us with possibilities for such diffusion. In the second century A.D., Ptolemy, utilizing information obtained from traders and explorers, depicted a world that extended from the coastline of China and the Malay peninsula to the Atlantic. Hindu civilization and political control were entrenched in southeast Asia.

In the early fifth, and possibly in the fourth, century Hindu power was established in Java, and soon thereafter in Bali, where, indeed, Hindu influences, especially in language and religion, still predominate. From about 650 to about 1300 a great empire, its capital in Palembang, Sumatra, included Sumatra, most of Java, Malaya, large portions of the Lesser Sunda Islands, and part of India. In Palembang, during much of this period, a great Buddhist university flourished. A Chinese, Yi Tsing, states in 671–695 that he studied Sanskrit in Palembang, where he lived in a community of more than a thousand monks; it was, he asserts, one of the best places in the world in which to study that language. In 860 a Sumatran ruler, Balaputra, founded a cloister at Nalanda, on the plains of the Ganges. A world traffic converged on that region, and the pilgrims became acquainted with intellectual and religious movements from almost all parts of east Asia.

It would not be surprising if some of these movements or fostered concepts seeped into Pacific Islands; and possibly "remoter historical roots of very many Ifugao religious conceptions *are* in India," as Barton states.[15]

Javanese records which date from 1365, after the Hindu capital had been removed to Java, reveal that the island's dependencies extended from Achin, in Sumatra, to New Guinea.

Later, Mohammedans conquered much of the Malay peninsula, Sumatra, Java, southern islands of the Philippines, and parts of other east Indies islands. Arabic civilization took to Europe many classical influences which were important factors in the Renaissance; it could have carried classical influences into Indonesia. Indonesia lies across wide seas from most of Micronesia and Melanesia; but culture traits have spread through these great spaces. We should recall that most of the languages are Austronesian (Malayo–Polynesian), a family of languages spoken, though not by every people, from the Malay peninsula to Formosa, Polynesia, and Melanesia.

These great culture areas are contiguous, and several fundamental phases of the cultures concerned overlap. Given sufficient time, a trait which enters Indonesia can find its way into any portion of Oceania. Precisely how "exotic" traits have spread through the areas we do not know and presumably never will know. There is comparable ignorance with regard to practically all portions of the preliterate world.

NOTES

[1] "Alteuropaisch-altozeanische Parallelen," *MdAGiw*, 59:1-8 (1929).

[2] Edward B. Tylor, *Primitive Culture* (1871), I, 66-67.

[3] Fr. Graebner, "Thor and Maui," *Anthropos*, 14-15:1099-1119 (1919–20).

[4] *The Aborigines of Tasmania* (London, Kegan Paul, Trench, Trubner, 1890), p. 224. Roth gives other examples as well.

[5] Edward B. Tylor, *Researches into the Early History of Mankind* (New York, Holt, 3d ed., 1878), p. 115.

[6] *Lectures on the Origin and Growth of Religion as Illustrated by Celtic Heathendom* (London, Williams and Norgate, 1888), pp. 113-14. (Hibbert Lectures, 1886.)

[7] Herbert J. Rose, *Primitive Culture in Greece* (London, Methuen, 1925), pp. 157-58.

[8] Beatrice Blackwood, "Folk-stories of a Stone Age People in New Guinea," *Folk-Lore*, 50:224-25 (1939).

[9] Edward B. Tylor, *Anthropology* (London, Macmillan, 1881), pp. 392-93.

[10] Personal communication.

[11] Victor Barnouw, "Eastern Nepalese Marriage Customs and Kinship Organization," *Southwestern Journal of Anthropology*, 11:22-23 (1955).

[12] Sir George Sansom, *Japan: A Short Cultural History* (New York, Appleton-Century, 2d ed., 1943), p. 383.

[13] Martha W. Beckwith, *Hawaiian Mythology* (New Haven, Yale University Press, 1940), pp. 457-58.

[14] Philippa Pollenz, "The Puzzle of Hula," *American Anthropologist*, 50:653-55 (1948).

[15] R. F. Barton, *The Religion of the Ifugaos*, American Anthropological Association Memoir No. 65, 1946.

THE SUDAN
AN ETHNOGRAPHIC SURVEY

By E. E. Evans-Pritchard
ALL SOULS COLLEGE, OXFORD

IT APPEARS to be worth while from time to time to take stock of our knowledge of the peoples of one or other region of the world. This serves two purposes. It gives the student indication of the sort of ethnological material he is likely to find should he consider including the region in his area of comparative research, an indication required the more as specialization increases and it becomes difficult to be thoroughly conversant with more than a very limited portion of the globe. Secondly, it shows the gaps in our knowledge and hence where new field studies are needed, and where, in the light of existing knowledge, they would be most profitable.

The Sudan is a political, and not an ethnological or geographical unit, but then anthropological research is often dependent on official encouragement and support, and an assessment of it is sometimes best made within politically defined areas. What is known as the Southern Sudan comprises those southern regions of the Republic of the Sudan (till recently the Anglo-Egyptian Sudan) occupied by pagan Negroid peoples in contrast to the Islamic, Caucasian, Semitic, and Hamitic peoples of the Northern Sudan.

It is just over fifty years since the first ethnographical expedition to the Southern Sudan was undertaken. Much about the peoples of that region of Africa had, one need hardly say, been recorded by travelers, and much of what was recorded was of a high quality. I mention the names of a few: Baker, Heuglin, Piaggia, Miani, Poncet, Schnitzer (Emin Pasha), Marno, Schweinfurth, Junker, Petherick, Beltrame. The first ethnographical expedition to be carried out as such was Dr. A. MacTier Pirrie's survey of the peoples of southern Dar Fung in 1906–7. He died shortly after his return to England. In 1909 the famous anthropologist Dr. W. H. R. Rivers made a short excursion up the Nile from Khartoum. Professor and Mrs. C. G. Seligman made surveys in the Southern Sudan in 1909–10 and in 1921–22, the results of which were embodied, together with information collected by others (including myself), in their important work *Pagan Tribes of the Nilotic Sudan* (1932). Professor Seligman was my teacher, and it was he who made the arrangements for me to continue the work of his wife and himself. In all, between 1926 and 1936 I carried out six expeditions, and I also served in the Sudan during the campaign in Ethiopia in 1940. The researches of the Seligmans and myself were done at the

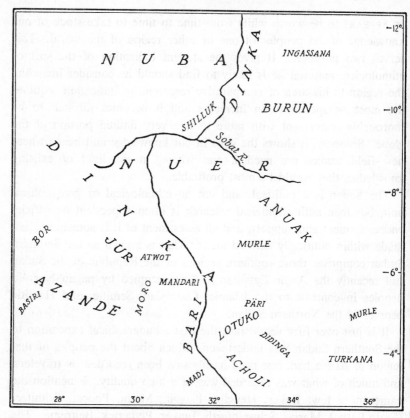

GEOGRAPHIC DISTRIBUTION OF PEOPLES OF THE SOUTHERN SUDAN

request of, and for the most part at the expense of, the Sudan government. From 1939–40 the Sudan government employed Dr. S. F. Nadel, whose early death was deplored by all his colleagues, to make a study of some of the peoples of the Nuba Mountains in Kordofan province. In 1933–34 Dr. Renato Boccassino, an Italian ethnologist, working under the auspices of the International African Institute, made a study of the Acholi, who live mostly in Uganda but extend across the frontier into the Sudan. In 1938 Muhammad Eff. Galal, an Egyptian student of Professor Marcel Mauss, the distinguished French sociologist, carried out some research in the Southern Sudan, chiefly among the Madi, also a Uganda people whose territory stretches into the Sudan, but he died shortly afterwards and, as far as I know, none of his research has been published. Between 1948 and 1954 Dr. R. G. Lienhardt made five expeditions to the Southern Sudan, making studies of the Dinka and Anuak peoples. Further research, referred to again later, has recently been conducted among Southern Sudan peoples by Dr. J. F. M. Middleton, Dr. Jean Buxton, and Mrs. Philip Mansfield (Elinor Mac-Hatton).

In addition to this professional research, much information has been recorded by missionaries and administrative officers, and with this supplementary material we have, or are likely soon to have, as good accounts of some of the peoples of the Southern Sudan as we have of any of the simpler peoples in any other parts of the world. They may be briefly reviewed under five headings: Nilotics, Nilo-Hamites, Sudanics, the peoples of the Nuba Mountains, and the peoples of Dar Fung. This is an *ad hoc* classification, not a scientific one, since the first three are defined by linguistic criteria and the last two by geographical provenance.

The Nilotics form a solid block on the Nile and its tributaries the Bahr al-Ghazal and the Sobat, consisting of the Shilluk, the Dinka, the Nuer, the Anuak, and the Atwot. There are also some small scattered Nilotic communities, mostly in the Dar Fung and Bahr al-Ghazal provinces, and a spill-over of the Acholi people in the south from Uganda.

The largest Nilotic people, both in numbers and in territory, in the Southern Sudan are the Dinka, but they are as yet the least known of the more important representatives of the Nilotic group. There are some useful papers on them in *Sudan Notes and Records,* and Professor and Mrs. Seligman devoted two chapters of their classic work to them. It is only recently (1948–50), however, that an intensive study of them has been made, by Dr. R. G. Lienhardt, whose first book about them, on their religion, is soon to appear. When his researches have been published we will possess a full ethnographic description of this people.

The Shilluk have attracted much attention, chiefly on account of what has been described as their "divine kingship." Here again, there have been some valuable papers written, especially those in *Sudan Notes and Records,* by Dr. P. P. Howell and others, and, again, Professor and Mrs. Seligman have devoted two chapters of their book to them. But in the case of the Shilluk there are also two monographs: Father W. Hofmayr's *Die Schilluk* (1925), a remarkable study for the time it was written, and Professor D. Westermann's *The Shilluk People* (1912), mainly a linguistic study. Nevertheless, neither of the two men was an anthropologist, and I believe that it would still be worth the while of an anthropologist to make an intensive study of the Shilluk. It is surprising how little is known about their social structure and some of their activities, and they have been relatively unaffected by government, missionaries, and traders.

The Nuer are now one of the most written-about African peoples, though almost nothing was known about them before Mr. H. C. Jackson, an administrative officer, published a lengthy article in *Sudan Notes and Records* in 1923 which was later reprinted with an appendix by Mr. P. Coriat as a book: *The Nuer of the Upper Nile Province.* In 1931 Miss Ray Huffman of the American Presbyterian Mission published a very short general account, *Nuer Customs and Folk-Lore.* Father J. P. Crazzolara of the Verona Fathers supplied Pater Wilhelm Schmidt with much information about Nuer religion, which appeared in Volume 8 of Schmidt's *Der Ursprung der Gottes-idee* (1949) and was later (1953) republished by Father Crazzolara in a monograph entitled *Zur Gesellschaft und Religion der Nueer.* I began my own research among the Nuer in 1930 and continued it in 1931, 1935, and 1936, spending about a year in all among them. The material gathered on these expeditions has been almost entirely presented in a trilogy: *The Nuer: A Description of the Modes of Livelihood and Political Institutions of a Nilotic People* (1940); *Kinship and Marriage among the Nuer* (1951); and *Nuer Religion* (1956). Dr. P. P. Howell, an administrative officer who had earlier taken the Anthropological Tripos at Cambridge and carried out research from that university among the Shilluk before joining the Sudan Political Service, made a special study of Nuer law as it had developed through the institution by the Sudan government of courts in their country, and this study appeared in *A Manual of Nuer Law* in 1954. There are thus no less than seven books on the Nuer, apart from articles in journals, so they may be said to be one of the best documented primitive peoples.

To the east of the Nuer live the Anuak. I made a short survey-study of their political institutions, especially of their royal house, a subject of quite unusual interest, in 1935. I wrote up rather hastily, in view of what was then happening in Europe, the results of my inquiries in a short book in 1940: *The Political System of the Anuak of the Anglo-Egyptian Sudan.* When acting in a military capacity in Anuakland in the same year I collected further information which appeared in an article in *Sudan Notes and Records* in 1947. I mention this article because it forms an appendix to the book. Both book and article dealt mainly with political affairs, and what was recorded about other aspects of social life was negligible. Dr. R. G. Lienhardt has since made a further, and more detailed, study of the Anuak during something over a year's residence among them in the years 1952–53 and 1953–54. He has already published several articles on them and has a book in preparation. When it appears we shall be able to say that four out of five of the larger northern Nilotic peoples are ethnographically well covered, though the Shilluk still await a deeper and more comprehensive study. Of the fifth, the Atwot, we know almost nothing.

In the extreme south of the Southern Sudan live part of the Acholi people. They have been mainly studied in Uganda, by Professor Boccassino, Father Crazzolara, and Dr. F. K. Girling. Father Crazzolara has incorporated much of his material on the Acholi in his *The Lwoo* (1950–54), and Professor Boccassino has contributed various papers on them in different journals. They still await, however, monographic treatment, though Dr. Girling's Ph. D. thesis (1953) on them may, it is to be hoped, be published without much further delay.

We know very little about the other Nilotic peoples of the Southern Sudan—almost nothing of the Burun and very little about the smaller Shilluk-speaking peoples of the Bahr al-Ghazal (Luo, Bodho, Thuri, Bor, etc.) and the Päri of Lafon Hill.

Surveying the whole field of Nilotic studies and the ethnological problems they raise, I would say that the study likely to pay the highest dividend would be that of the Päri, a small people speaking a dialect of Anuak, for a knowledge of their culture and social organization, besides being valuable in itself, might answer what seem at present to be unanswerable questions about the Anuak, the Shilluk, the Mandari, and other peoples of the region. Then I would suggest a study of the Atwot, for, here again, apart from the intrinsic value of such a study, it would shed a revealing light on the complex ethnological problem of the relationship of the Nuer with the Dinka. My third choice would be a study of one of the Shilluk-speaking communities of the Bahr al-Ghazal—perhaps the Bor—or of one of the so-called Burun peoples of Dar Fung.

The Nilo-Hamites of the Southern Sudan have recently been the subject of several ethnographic studies. The Jie and Turkana were studied, on the Kenya side of the Sudan-Kenya frontier, by Dr. P. H. Gulliver between 1948 and 1951, and he has published an account of them in *The Family Herds* (1955). Dr. Jean Buxton has made an admirable study of the Mandari of west bank of the Nile during fifteen months' residence among them in 1951–52, and there is every reason to expect that the results of her field research will soon appear in print as monographs. Mrs. Philip Mansfield made an intensive study of the Lotuko to the east of the Nile in 1951–52 and 1953–54, and she is now preparing the information she collected for a Ph. D. thesis and for eventual publication. Mr. B. A. Lewis, at one time a member of the Sudan Political Service, has made a study of the Murle people; first when he was their administrator, and afterwards, by grace of his government, on an ethnographical expedition. He is preparing a book on the Murle. It seems to me that what now most needs to be done in the field of Nilo-Hamitic studies in the Sudan is intensive research among the Bari and the Didinga.

The Sudanic-speaking peoples to the west of the Nile, other than the Azande—Ndogo, Bongo, "Jur" peoples, Baka, Avokaya, Moro et al.—are numerically small groups about whom we have only the scantiest information. This is true also of a number of peoples in varying degrees subject to the Azande and culturally assimilated to them—Basiri, Huma, Babuckur, and others (some of whom speak Bantu tongues). The only one of these peoples who can be said to have been the subject of an intensive study is the Lugbara (to whom the Madi, Kaliko, and Logo are closely related), a few of whom live in the Sudan. Dr. J. F. M. Middleton made a detailed study of them in the years 1949–52, and a volume by him will shortly be in the press. A study of any other of these scarcely known peoples would be well worth while, for the numerical size of a population is in no way related to its scientific interest. Apart from the intrinsic value of such a study, it would help us to solve some of the linguistic, historical, and anthropological problems of this ethnically most complicated region of

Africa. If a suggestion has to be made, I would select one of the so-called "Jur" peoples (Beli, Sofi, etc.) for the first of these studies.

One of the best known peoples in the Southern Sudan is the Azande of the Nile-Congo Divide, most of whose territory, however, lies outside the frontiers of the Sudan in the Belgian Congo and French Equatorial Africa. Much was written about the famous "Niam-Niam," as they used to be called, by early travelers in central Africa. Even to have seen a Zande was once regarded as something of a distinction. Their history has been written by a Belgian administrator, A. de Calonne-Beaufaict (*Azande*, 1921), and by a Belgian officer, A. Hutereau (*Histoire des peuplades de l'Uele et de l'Ubangi*, 1922). The latter also wrote a lengthy description of them in *Annales du Musée du Congo Belge* (1909). Articles which almost comprise a small book were written by Major P. M. Larken in *Sudan Notes and Records* (1923, 1926, 1927), and two long chapters are devoted to the Azande in J. Czekanowski's volumes in *Wissenschaftliche Ergebnisse der Deutschen Zentral-Afrika Expedition* (1907–8). In 1926 Monsignor C. R. Lagae, a Belgian Dominican, published his excellent short monograph *Les Azande ou Niam-Niam*. Twenty years later (1946) another Dominican, Father M. H. Lelong, published a further volume on the Azande (*Mes Frères du Congo*, Vol. II). In 1927 I commenced an intensive study of the Azande of the Sudan, concluded in 1930. So far, apart from a number of articles in journals, I have published a monographic account of only one side of their life, *Witchcraft, Oracles and Magic among the Azande* (1937). Other duties have prevented me from publishing the rest of my material. I have, however, returned to this interest, and I am preparing a volume on Zande history and political institutions, which will, I hope, be published in 1960. I hope that at least one, and possibly two, further volumes will eventually be completed and all the information I was at such pains to collect be recorded in print. A lengthy study of Zande agricultural methods by Mr. P. de Schlippe (*Shifting Cultivation in Africa*) has recently appeared (1956). The Azande, it will be granted, are a well documented people.

The peoples of the Nuba Mountains, about 300,000 souls, belong to over fifty different ethnic groups and speak languages of Sudanic type, Bantoid type, and Nubian type. Professor Nadel studied some of these communities—ten in all—for over two years, but only three (Heiban, Otoro, and Tira) with any degree of thoroughness. His account of the Nuba societies falls in between intensive studies and general surveys, and it may therefore be said that (at any rate apart from the three peoples mentioned above) any of the Nuba Mountains societies, particularly the Southern Nuba, would repay an entirely new and intensive study. I have not myself, however, any first-hand knowledge of the area and literary guidance does not adequately make up for this, so I am unable, in this case, to suggest where I think that research might best be begun. I can only say that it is everywhere most urgently required.

There are a number of small communities other than those of the Nilotic or semi-Nilotic Burun, to which reference has already been made, living on or at the foot of hills in the Dar Fung area of the Sudan: Berta, Uduk, Ingassana, etc. We have very little knowledge of these peoples beyond the brief and quite superficial survey I made of them in 1926. Here then is a virgin field for an anthropologist, and I would have little hesitation in directing his first attention to that fascinating people, the Ingassana of the Tabi Hills, among whom I did my first research. An intensive study of them would be an important piece of research, and it might also yield, especially in the study of religious beliefs and ritual, valuable ethnological evidence about Meroitic influences in the Negro Sudan.

We can therefore report much progress in the study of the peoples of the Southern Sudan, but it is little compared with what remains to be done. Any program must be to some extent a matter of personal choice, but over thirty years of research in this region give me the privilege to suggest what might be the most fruitful pieces of research and to list them in what may seem to be, but is not entirely, an arbitrary order. I would therefore ask indulgence in presenting them as follows: (1) the Päri, (2) the Ingassana, (3) the Bor, (4) the Didinga, (5) the Atwot, (6) one of the so-called "Jur" peoples, (7) the Shilluk, (8) one of the peoples of the Nuba Mountains, (9) the Basiri, and (10) one of the Burun peoples.

The government of the Republic of the Sudan is sympathetic to anthropological studies within their territories, and it is to be hoped that those who control research funds will be equally sympathetic towards the continuation of research in the Southern Sudan before it is too late.

OBSERVATIONS ON THE FUNCTION OF THE MUSEUM IN ANTHROPOLOGY

By J. Alden Mason

UNIVERSITY OF PENNSYLVANIA

ANTHROPOLOGY is the only social or behavioral science having any concern with material objects or with very fundamental visual and tactual approaches to education. Dealing thus—at least in certain phases—with objects, it requires museums to preserve, conserve, and display them, which of necessity brings it into rapport with some non-social sciences, especially the natural-history ones such as geology, botany, zoology, and paleontology. This involves specific problems in common with these sciences and with their teaching. Anthropological museums also have some common problems—though fewer and somewhat different—with museums of art and history.

When shown in a museum of natural history as one of its divisions, ethnological exhibits tend to give the visitor the impression that cultures—especially aboriginal ones—are as static as geography, fauna, and flora. Unless accompanied and expanded by exhibitions illustrating cultural development and evolution, those depicting the typical traits and fundamental aspects characteristic of a certain period give the visitor no concept of the universality of cultural change. No people has a constant, unchanging culture. Nor is there any inherent correlation between culture and environment.

Anthropological exhibits in an art museum suffer a like miscomprehension. Here they are shown as art objects, generally individually and spotlighted. The visitor conceives of them in the same category as modern or classical paintings and sculptures, non-utilitarian objects made for a purely esthetic purpose. He compares the latter with aboriginal products according to current or recent esthetic standards, and his prejudiced opinion of the inferiority and exotic nature of primitive peoples is thereby perpetuated: we have nothing in common with them. But in most aboriginal societies objects were seldom made purely for their esthetic appeal; they were purposeful objects ornamented and decorated. Since the awakening of artists' interest in the art of aboriginal peoples—which not long ago most of them despised as not being true art—exhibitions of primitive art have attained their merited place in art museums. But their appeal is limited to persons with art appreciation; they tell nothing of the life of a people. Strange arts should be viewed in their own terms before we pass judgment upon them.

Museums—especially anthropological and natural history museums —began in the sixteenth and seventeenth century as private cabinets of curiosities secured in that great period of exploration. However, they very soon were united into larger museums under public auspices, and by the close of the eighteenth century modern museums had begun. From early days they fell into two classes, municipal museums for the public, and college or university museums as instructional aids.

In recent years the distinction between the college and public museum has tended to disappear, as the colleges found that the public flocked to their museums while the great majority of the busy and uninterested students ignored them. Moreover their financial problems became similar. Yet only seventeen years ago (1942) Laurence V. Coleman, in his book, *College and University Museums,* stressed his own contention and belief that these should confine their interests to the education of the student, and not imitate the public museums in adult education. This point of view is held by few museum administrators today.

The primary purposes of a museum are twofold, to preserve and conserve, and to educate. The first function is the older one and the museum's *raison d'être.* Many small museums have not progressed beyond this stage of being merely storage, and the preservation of unique objects and those no longer being made is in itself a desideratum. The museum's educational method uses the visual approach, primarily on the adult level. Visual education is being more and more stressed and appreciated as a pedagogical method; its effects are more impressive and longer lasting than education by lectures or books, though a combination of all is, of course, better. This holds true for persons of all ages. Our large museums are thronged by school classes, but the exhibits are—and should be—aimed primarily at the adult. Special children's museums are certainly better for school classes, and many museums have special children's departments. Research and publication also are functions that the large museum shares with other scientific institutions.

In the generation from about 1890 to 1920 the centers of anthropology in this country were in museums, and the great anthropologists of that era were museum men. They formed the core of the anthropological faculties of the universities that had these departments, generally in the great metropolitan centers near the large museums. As museum men their interests were primarily empirical and historical, in material culture, technology, and archaeology. They developed and documented the concept of the culture area. Their museum exhibits reflected their interests; these were arranged by culture areas—often with emphasis on linguistic stock—or by chronology. The humanistic aspects, cultural evolution and the functional approach were almost neglected. Too often they emphasized the research interests of the professional curator, and were too erudite, with little popular appeal. The halls were generally crowded with too many uniform cases in monotonous regularity, and the cases were too crowded with objects that differed only slightly; it was practically "open storage." There was a maximum of specimens and a minimum of interpretation.

In recent years the centers of anthropological education and research have migrated to the universities, and many—probably most—anthropologists today have little or no concern with, or interest in, museums, seldom visit them, can teach and do without them, and tend to depreciate their value in anthropology.

Progress is ever like pendulum swings: innovations and tendencies are carried too far, and later swing too far backwards. The trend in anthropology in the last few decades has been away from studies of ethnography, material culture, and technology, which played such a large role in anthropological research a generation or two ago. Very few men of the type and caliber of William H. Holmes, Walter Hough, and Otis T. Mason remain. They were museum men. The great majority of younger anthropologists have little interest in descriptive ethnography, material culture, historical problems, or technology. Social and psychological anthropology with their manifold ramifications are now in the ascendency. Of the some 250 papers given at the 1957 meeting of the American Anthropological Association not one was primarily on technology, and less than five were concerned in any degree with material culture.

Universities training for a professional career in anthropology are stressing more and more the interdependence of all branches of the science. No matter what his research specialty, the student must know the basic principles of all other phases, among which material culture and technology still play a large role. The student of material culture, past (archaeology) and present, must have an acquaintance with the actual objects that in large measure document these cultures. He must, perforce, have access to a museum, not only to view, but also to handle and to study the specimens.

The primary function of the museum in anthropology is, has been, and doubtless always will be, in education and research in the fields of material culture and technology, in ethnology and archaeology. Physical anthropology also has its place. Museums are the organizations best suited to pursue field research among primitive peoples in material culture and technology, and in archaeology. The resultant objects are properly cared for, stored, and made available to students in storage or exhibition; and, if of sufficient educational or artistic value, they are welcomed by the trustees. They would be considered a space-consuming nuisance in a university without ample storage space. Photographic and sound records also find best storage and ready access in a museum. A broad research program can best be carried out by a large museum through its integrated staff, and in a natural history museum through collaboration between several departments.

The particular interest of the anthropological museum in material culture and technology implies that the curators should be men primarily interested in these subjects and specialists in some of them. This is doubtlessly true of the great majority of museum curators today, and all of them must be well-informed and competent in these fields, but there are a number whose hearts lie, as regards research, in non-material fields, somewhat to the detriment of their curatorial effectiveness.

It is one of the most important functions of the anthropological museum to maintain and foster interest in the presently neglected but very important field of material culture and technology, and to carry on until there is a reawakening of interest in these subjects.

The primary scheme of anthropological exhibition should be the portrayal of the life of other peoples and cultures and the restoration of past cultures. Their fundamental aspects and typical traits should be visually shown. The geographical and culture-area approach—and to some extent the chronological—are still the best. The exhibits should be accompanied by charts, maps, photographs and labels giving a better picture and placing the culture in its proper setting. The labels should be mainly of a general nature, with slight attention to points of minor and professional interest. Life-sized groups, dioramas, and miniature groups give a visual impression that can be achieved by no other means, but are expensive, and the first of them very space-consuming. Objects should ordinarily be shown in their natural milieu and, except in special or temporary exhibitions of primitive art, not shown as objects of art.

With the present paucity of technologists and the lack of interest in technology there has resulted a corresponding absence of exhibits illustrating technological points such as basketry, weaving, and other manufactures, and the development and evolution of such arts as fire-making, tool-making, illumination, etc. I feel that such synoptic exhibits are most instructive and interesting and should be included in all anthropological museums, permanently if there is sufficient room, temporarily and in rotation if not.

However, the modern museum is not—and should not be—satisfied with culture-area exhibits alone. Exhibits illustrating cultural evolution, diffusion, comparisons of culture, relations of culture to environment, acculturation, and many other important aspects of human culture bring these subjects vividly to the visitor's attention. Physical anthropology, racial differences and peculiarities, human biology and evolution have long been considered fit subjects for visual presentation in most scientific museums. Even the non-material phases of human culture, such as social organization, religion, linguistics, and folklore are to some extent susceptible of visual presentation, especially in the form of charts and maps.

Effective visual education by museum exhibition is a very specialized and non-scientific subject in which the problems of anthropology differ little from those of other natural-history disciplines. It is in this respect that museum anthropologists are least trained and effective and have least interest. They are generally chosen—and properly so—for their reputations as research scientists, and tend to neglect their exhibits and to let them remain old fashioned and static. The observation that "the better the anthropologist the poorer the curator" has more than an element of truth in it. They need to collaborate with specialists in the field of exhibition who must learn the special requirements of anthropology while teaching the curator the tricks of technique of museum installation.

In addition to the major questions of the arrangement of cases and of objects in them to best effect, the use of models, groups and dioramas, photographs, maps, and charts, must be considered, as well as the more technical problems such as daylight versus artificial illumination, interior lighting of cases, best use of color backgrounds, type of labels, and the like.

Of course under the topic of technical and non-scientific problems comes the most important one of museum architecture itself—the modification of older buildings to museum requirements, the necessity for much more storage area than is usually planned by architects, the advisability of blocking windows for permanent artificial illumination, and similar questions.

Today there are several institutions that offer specialized training in museum work, not only in the above-mentioned technical problems but also in those of radio and television, lectures, school and adult classes, extramural exhibits, as well as in the non-exhibitional technical questions of cataloguing, the storage and preservation of specimens, and, on a higher level, problems of administration and finance.

Standards of museum installation are today in a very unsettled state. Halls and exhibits arranged but a few years ago are already considered "dated" and *passé*. As an example, up until a short time ago long vistas often covering several halls were normal. A few years ago the fashion prescribed the erection of some block at the entrance to a hall to prevent a view of its interior from outside. This vogue, it seems, is already outdated. In education there should be no fads or fashions; surely there must be some best way, and eventually some standard criteria will be agreed upon.

Gone are the days of the exhibition of "open storage," with too many cases set too close together and crowded with too many objects differing only in slight details. Only the student and the specialist are interested in minor differences, and only they need to inspect and handle objects. The average visitor tires of such plethora and generally gets a more lasting impression from one—or a very few—typical objects than from a great many. We except, of course, the amateur collector of such "relics" as Indian arrowpoints and basketry; he wishes to see as many of these as possible to compare them with his own. However, to my mind, the pendulum has swung too far in this direction. In overzealousness to avoid crowding, too many important and instructive objects are relegated to storage and attention is centered on a few. Exhibits are too often arranged for their over-all esthetic effect; individual objects are spotlighted and emphasized, and often much more space than necessary is given to lounges and vacant floor spaces.

The larger museums—and especially the public ones—have always considered public education their primary purpose. The great number of people flocking to museums these days proves that the public is intensely interested in what museums have to offer. This seems to be especially true of archaeology. The necessity of appeal to and education of the public on the part of museums has become a vital matter in recent years. Rising costs have far outstripped income from endowments, and the number of wealthy benefactors has diminished tremendously. Most museum administrators have come to the realization that in order to continue they must appeal for public and legislative appropriations. To secure these they need to obtain support and good will by proving their value and service to the public. The motto of the modern museum has become "Bring the museum to the people and the people to the museum."

There are three types of visitors to a museum: the specialist, the interested person of some education, and the casual newcomer. The good museum will educate many of the last-named group into the second class. The older museum made little distinction between layman and scholar and tended to direct its exhibits at the latter. While not slighting research for the few, the modern museum must stress education for the many.

There is slight difference between the needs and desires of the educated layman and that of the student. The exhibit that is good for the former is also good for the latter, though he and the specialist should be given facilities for closer acquaintance with the larger number of objects in storage. The exhibit prepared primarily for the student or the expert is a waste of space, time, and money.

The modern museum therefore makes its exhibits and its halls attractive and educational. By means of lectures and popular guidebooks it encourages adult education, and fosters the formation of study groups. The director is a public relations man with a sound scientific background and point of view. He encourages the use of the museum as a civic center for many community activities.

But possibly the most important function of the anthropological museum in these parlous times is its liberalizing influence in combating racism and racial and national prejudice, in showing the essential unity of mankind and the interdependence of all cultures, the contributions that each has made to produce our modern civilization, and the lack of correlation between culture and physical type. If the lay visitor leaves with a more open mind and less prejudice, with a better appreciation of the accomplishments of other peoples and a deflated concept of the uniqueness, independence, and superiority in all respects of his own culture, the anthropological museum will have justified its existence and proved its value.

PART III

Ritual, Religion, and Myth

FOUR WINNEBAGO MYTHS
A STRUCTURAL SKETCH

By Claude Lévi-Strauss
COLLÈGE DE FRANCE

AMONG THE MANY TALENTS which make him one of the great anthropologists of our time, Paul Radin has one which gives a singular flavor to his work. He has the authentic esthetic touch, rather uncommon in our profession. This is what we call in French *flair:* the gift of singling out those facts, observations, and documents which possess an especially rich meaning, sometimes undisclosed at first, but likely to become evident as one ponders the implications woven into the material. A crop harvested by Paul Radin, even if he does not choose to mill it himself, is always capable of providing lasting nourishment for many generations of students.

This is the reason why I intend to pay my tribute to the work of Paul Radin by giving some thought to four myths which he has published under the title *The Culture of the Winnebago: As Described by Themselves.*[1] Although Radin himself pointed out in the Preface: "In publishing these texts I have only one object in view, to put at the disposal of students, authentic material for the study of Winnebago culture," and although the four myths were each obtained from different informants, it seems that, on a structural level, there was good reason for making them the subject of a single publication. A deep unity underlies all four, notwithstanding the fact that one myth, as Radin has shown in his introduction and notes, appears to differ widely in content, style, and structure from the other three. My purpose will be to analyze the structural relationships between the four myths and to suggest that they can be grouped together not only because they are part of a collection of ethnographic and linguistic data referring to one tribe, which Radin too modestly claimed as his sole purpose, but because they are of the same genre, i.e., their meanings logically complement each other.

The title of the first myth is "The Two Friends Who Became Reincarnated: The Origin of the Four Nights' Wake." This is the story of two friends, one of them a chief's son, who decide to sacrifice their lives for the welfare of the community. After undergoing a series of ordeals in the underworld, they reach the lodge of Earthmaker, who permits them to become reincarnated and to resume their previous lives among their relatives and friends.

As explained by Radin in his commentary,[2] there is a native theory underlying the myth: every individual is entitled to a specific quota of years of life and experience. If a person dies before his time, his relatives can ask the spirits to distribute among them what he has failed to utilize. But there is more in this theory than meets the eye. The unspent life-span given up by the hero, when he lets himself be killed by the enemies, will be added to the capital of life, set up in trust for the group. Nevertheless, his act of dedication is not entirely without personal profit: by becoming a hero an individual makes a choice, he exchanges a full life-span for a shortened one, but while the full life-span is unique, granted once and for all, the shortened one appears as a kind of lease taken on eternity. That is, by giving up one full life, an indefinite succession of half-lives is gained. But since all the un-lived halves will increase the life expectancy of the ordinary people, everybody gains in the process: the ordinary people whose average life expectancy will slowly but substantially increase generation after generation, and the warriors with shortened but indefinitely renewable lives, provided their minds remain set on self-dedication.

It is not clear, however, that Radin pays full justice to the narrator when he treats as a "secondary interpretation" the fact that the expedition is undertaken by the heroes to show their appreciation of the favors of their fellow villagers.[3] My contention is that this motive of the heroes deserves primary emphasis, and it is supported by the fact that there are two war parties. The first one is undertaken by the warriors while the heroes are still in their adolescent years, so they are neither included in, nor even informed of it; they hear about the party only as a rumor,[4] and they decide to join it uninvited. We must conclude then that the heroes have no responsibility for the very venture wherein they distinguish themselves, since it has been instigated and led by others. Moreover, they are not responsible for the second war party, during which they are killed, since this latter foray has been initiated by the enemy in revenge for the first.

The basic idea is clear: the two friends have developed into successful social beings;[5] accordingly, they feel obliged to repay their fellow tribesmen who have treated them so well.[6] As the story goes, they set out to expose themselves in the wilderness; later they die in an ambush prepared by the enemy in revenge for the former defeat. The obvious conclusion is that the heroes have willingly died for the sake of their people. And because they died without responsibility of their own, but instead that of others, those will inherit the unspent parts of their lives, while the heroes themselves will be permitted to return to earth and the same process will be repeated all over again. This interpretation is in agreement with information given elsewhere by Radin: i.e., in order to pass the test of the Old Woman who rids the soul of all the recollections belonging to its earthly life, each soul must be solicitous not of its own welfare but of the welfare of the living members of the group.

Now at the root of this myth we find—as the phonologist would say —a double opposition. First there is the opposition between *ordinary life* and *heroic life,* the former realizing a full life-span, not renewable, the latter gambling with life for the benefit of the group. The second opposition is between two kinds of death, one "straight" and final, although it provides a type of unearthly immortality in the villages of the dead; the other "undulating," and swinging between life and death. Indeed one is tempted to see the reflection of this double fate in the Winnebago symbol of the ladder of the afterworld as it appears in the Medicine Rite. One side is "like a frog's leg, twisted and dappled with light-and-life. The other [is] like a red cedar, blackened from frequent usage and very smooth and shiny."[7]

To sum up the meaning of the myth so far: if one wants a full life one gets a full death; if one renounces life and seeks death, then one increases the full life of his fellow-tribesmen, and, moreover, secures for oneself a state composed of an indefinite series of half-lives and half-deaths. Thus we have a triangular system:

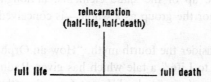

reincarnation
(half-life, half-death)

full life _____ full death

The second myth, entitled "The Man Who Brought His Wife Back from Spiritland," is a variation on the same theme, although there is a

significant difference involved. Here too, we find a hero—the husband
—ready to sacrifice his unspent life-span; not, as in the first myth, for
the benefit of the group, but rather for the benefit of only one individual, his beloved wife. Indeed, the hero is not aware at first that by
seeking death he will secure a new lease on life for both his dead wife
and himself. Had he been so aware, and this holds equally for the
protagonists in the first myth, the essential element of sacrifice would
have been missing. In both cases the result is similar: an altruistic loss
of life means life regained, not only for the self-appointed victim, but
also for the one or more persons to whom the sacrifice was consecrated.

The third myth, "The Journey of the Ghost to Spiritland, as Told
in the Medicine Rite," belongs, as the title suggests, to a religious
society. It explains how the members of the Medicine Rite, after death,
undergo (as do the protagonists of the other myths) several tests in
Spiritland, which they overcome, thus gaining the right to become
reincarnated.

At first sight this situation seems to differ from the others, since
nobody sacrificed his life. However, the members of the Medicine
Rite actually spend their lives in symbolic sacrifice. As Radin has
shown, in *The Road of Life and Death* and elsewhere, the Medicine
Rite follows the familiar pattern of letting oneself be "killed" and then
"revived." Thus the only departure consists in the fact that whereas
in the first and second myths the heroes are willing to die once and, so
they anticipate, permanently, the heroes of the third myth (the members
of the Rite) repeatedly, though symbolically, have trained themselves
to self-sacrifice. They have, so to speak, mithridatized themselves
against a full death by renouncing a full ordinary life which is replaced, in ritual practice, by a lifelong succession of half-lives and
half-deaths. Therefore we are entitled to assume that, in this case too,
the myth is made up of the same elements, although Ego—and not
another person, nor the group as a whole—is conceived as the primary
beneficiary.

Let us now consider the fourth myth, "How an Orphan Restored the
Chief's Daughter to Life," a tale which has given Radin some concern.
This myth, he says, is not only different from the other three, its plot
appears unusual relative to the rest of Winnebago mythology. After
recalling that in his book *Method and Theory of Ethnology*[8] he sug-

gested that this myth was a version, altered almost beyond recognition, of a type which he then called village-origin myths, he proceeds to explain in *The Culture of the Winnebago*[9] why he can no longer support this earlier interpretation.

It is worthwhile to follow closely Radin's new line of reasoning. He begins by recapitulating the plot—such a simple plot, he says, that there is practically no need for doing so: "The daughter of a tribal chief falls in love with an orphan, dies of a broken heart and is then restored to life by the orphan who must submit to and overcome certain tests, not in spiritland but here, on earth, in the very lodge in which the young woman died."[10]

If this plot is "simplicity itself," where do the moot points lie? Radin lists three which he says every modern Winnebago would question: (1) the plot seems to refer to a highly stratified society; (2) in order to understand the plot one should assume that in that society women occupied a high position and that, possibly, descent was reckoned in the matrilineal line; (3) the tests which in Winnebago mythology take place, as a rule, in the land of ghosts occur, in this instance, on earth.

After dismissing two possible explanations—that we are dealing here with a borrowed European tale or that the myth was invented by some Winnebago radical—Radin concludes that the myth must belong to "a very old stratum of Winnebago history." He also suggests that two distinct types of literary tradition, divine tales on the one hand and human tales on the other, have merged while certain primitive elements have been reinterpreted to make them fit together.[11]

I am certainly not going to challenge this very elegant reconstruction backed by an incomparable knowledge of Winnebago culture, language, and history. The kind of analysis I intend to offer is no alternative to Radin's own analysis. It lies on a different level, logical rather than historical. It takes as its context the three myths already discussed, not Winnebago culture, old or recent. My purpose is to explicate the structural relationship—if any—which prevails between this myth and the other three.

First, there is a theoretical problem which should be noted briefly. Since the publication of Boas's *Tsimshian Mythology*, anthropologists have often simply assumed that a full correlation exists between the myths of a given society and its culture. This, I feel, is going further than Boas intended. In the work just referred to, he did not suppose that myths automatically reflect the culture, as some of his followers seem always to anticipate. Rather, he tried to find out how much of the culture actually did pass into the myths, if any, and he convincingly showed that *some* of it does. It does not follow that whenever a social pattern is alluded to in a myth this pattern must correspond to something real which should be attributed to the past if, under direct scrutiny, the present fails to offer an equivalent.

There must be, and there is, a correspondence between the unconscious meaning of a myth—the problem it tries to solve—and the conscious content it makes use of to reach that end, i.e., the plot. However, this correspondence should not always be conceived as a kind of mirror-image, it can also appear as a *transformation*. If the problem is presented in "straight" terms, that is, in the way the social life of the group expresses and tries to solve it, the overt content of the myth, the plot, can borrow its elements from social life itself. But should the problem be formulated, and its solution sought for, "upside down," that is *ab absurdo*, then the overt content will become modified accordingly to form an inverted image of the social pattern actually present to the consciousness of the natives.

If this hypothesis is true, it follows that Radin's assumption that the pattern of social life referred to in the fourth myth must belong to a past stage of Winnebago history, is not inescapable.

We may be confronted with the pattern of a nonexistent society, contrary to the Winnebago traditional pattern, only because the structure of that particular myth is itself inverted, in relation to those myths which use as overt content the traditional pattern. To put it simply, if a certain correspondence is assumed between A and B, then if A is replaced by $-A$, B must be replaced by $-B$, without implying that, since B corresponds to an external object, there should exist another external object $-B$, which must exist somewhere: either in another society (borrowed element) or in a past stage of the same society (survival).

Obviously, the problem remains: why do we have three myths of the A type and one of the $-A$ type? This could be the case because $-A$ is older than A, but it can also be because $-A$ is one of the transformations of A which is already known to us under three different guises: A_1, A_2, A_3, since we have seen that the three myths of the assumed A type are not identical.

We have already established that the group of myths under consideration is based upon a fundamental opposition: on the one hand, the lives of ordinary people unfolding towards a natural death, followed by immortality in one of the spirit villages; and, on the other hand, heroic life, self-abridged, the gain being a supplementary life quota for the others as well as for oneself. The former alternative is not envisaged in this group of myths which, as we have seen, is mostly concerned with the latter. There is, however, a secondary difference which permits us to classify the first three myths according to the particular end assigned to the self-sacrifice in each. In the first myth the group is intended to be the immediate beneficiary, in the second it is another individual (the wife), and in the third it is oneself.

When we turn to the fourth myth, we may agree with Radin that it exhibits "unusual" features in relation to the other three. However, the difference seems to be of a logical more than of a sociological or historical nature. It consists in a new opposition introduced within the first pair of opposites (between "ordinary" life and "extraordinary" life). Now there are two ways in which an "extraordinary" phenomenon may be construed as such; it may consist either in a *surplus* or in a *lack*. While the heroes of the first three myths are all over-gifted, through social success, emotions or wisdom, the heroes of the fourth myth are, if one may say so, "below standard," at least in one respect.

The chief's daughter occupies a high social position; so high, in fact, that she is cut off from the rest of the group and is therefore paralyzed when it comes to expressing her feelings. Her exalted position makes her a defective human being, lacking an essential attribute of life. The boy is also defective, but socially, that is, he is an orphan and very poor. May we say, then, that the myth reflects a stratified society? This would compel us to overlook the remarkable symmetry which prevails between our two heroes, for it would be wrong to say simply that one is high and the other low: as a matter of fact, each of them is high in one respect and low in the other, and this pair of symmetrical structures, wherein the two terms are inverted relative to each other, belongs to the realm of ideological constructs rather than of sociological systems. We have just seen that the girl is "socially" above and "naturally" below. The boy is undoubtedly very low in the social scale; however, he is a miraculous hunter, i.e. he entertains

privileged relations with the natural world, the world of animals. This
is emphasized over and over again in the myth.[12]

Therefore may we not claim that the myth actually confronts us
with a polar system consisting in two individuals, one male, the other
female, and both exceptional insofar as each of them is overgifted in
one way ($+$) and undergifted in the other ($-$).

	Nature	Culture
Boy	$+$	$-$
Girl	$-$	$+$

The plot consists in carrying this disequilibrium to its logical extreme; the girl dies a *natural* death, the boy stays alone, i.e. he also
dies, but in a *social* way. Whereas during their ordinary lives the girl
was overtly above, the boy overtly below, now that they have become
segregated (either from the living or from society) their positions are
inverted: the girl is below (in her grave), the boy above (in his lodge).
This, I think, is clearly implied in a detail stated by the narrator which
seems to have puzzled Radin: "On top of the grave they then piled
loose dirt, placing everything in such a way that nothing could seep
through."[13] Radin comments: "I do not understand why piling the
dirt loosely would prevent seepage. There must be something else
involved that has not been mentioned."[14] May I suggest that this detail
be correlated with a similar detail about the building of the young
man's lodge: ". . . the bottom was piled high with dirt so that, in this
fashion, they could keep the lodge warm."[15] There is implied here, I
think, not a reference to recent or past custom but rather a clumsy
attempt to emphasize that, relative to the earth's surface, i.e. dirt, the
boy is now above and the girl below.

This new equilibrium, however, will be no more lasting than the
first. *She who was unable to live cannot die;* her ghost lingers "on
earth." Finally she induces the young man to fight the ghosts and take
her back among the living. With a wonderful symmetry, the boy will
meet, a few years later, with a similar, although inverted, fate; "Although I am not yet old, he says to the girl (now his wife,) I have been
here (lasted) on earth as long as I can. . . ."[16] *He who overcame death,
proves unable to live.* This recurring antithesis could develop indefi-

nitely, and such a possibility is noted in the text, (with an only son surviving his father, he too an orphan, he too a sharpshooter) but a different solution is finally reached. The heroes, equally unable to die or to live, will assume an intermediate identity, that of twilight creatures living under the earth but also able to come up on it; they will be neither men nor gods, but wolves, that is, ambivalent spirits combining good and evil features. So ends the myth.

If the above analysis is correct, two consequences follow: first, our myth makes up a consistent whole wherein the details balance and fit each other nicely; secondly, the three problems raised by Radin can be analyzed in terms of the myth itself; and no hypothetical past stage of Winnebago society need be invoked.

Let us, then, try to solve these three problems, following the pattern of our analysis.

1. The society of the myth appears stratified, only because the two heroes are conceived as a pair of opposites, but they are such both from the point of view of nature *and* of culture. Thus, the so-called stratified society should be interpreted not as a sociological vestige but as a projection of a logical structure wherein everything is given both in opposition and correlation.

2. The same answer can be given to the question of the assumed exalted position of the women. If I am right, our myths state three propositions, the first by implication, the second expressly stated in myths 1, 2 and 3, the third expressly stated in myth 4.

These propositions are as follow:
a. Ordinary people live (their full lives) and die (their full deaths).
b. Positive extraordinary people die (earlier) and live (more).
c. Negative extraordinary people are able neither to live nor to die.

Obviously proposition c offers an inverted demonstration of the truth of a and b. Hence, it must use a plot starting with protagonists (here, man and woman) in inverted positions. This leads us to state that a plot and its component parts should neither be interpreted by themselves nor relative to something outside the realm of the myth proper, but as *substitutions* given in, and understandable only with reference to *the group made up of all the myths of the same series.*

3. We may now revert to the third problem raised by Radin about

myth 4, that is, the contest with the ghosts takes place on earth instead of, as was usually the case, in spiritland. To this query I shall suggest an answer along the same lines as the others.

It is precisely because our two heroes suffer from a state of *under-life* (in respect either to culture or nature) that, in the narrative, the ghosts become a kind of *super-dead*. It will be recalled that the whole myth develops and is resolved on an intermediary level, where humans become underground animals and ghosts linger on earth. It tells about people who are, from the start, half-alive and half-dead while, in the preceding myths, the opposition between life and death is strongly emphasized at the beginning, and overcome only at the end. Thus, the integral meaning of the four myths is that, in order to be overcome the opposition between life and death should be first acknowledged, or else the ambiguous state will persist indefinitely.

I hope to have shown that the four myths under consideration all belong to the same *group* (understood as in *group theory)* and that Radin was even more right than he supposed in publishing them together. In the first place, the four myths deal with extraordinary, in opposition to ordinary, fate. The fact that ordinary fate is not illustrated here and thus is reckoned as an "empty" category, does not imply, of course, that it is not illustrated elsewhere. In the second place, we find an opposition between two types of extraordinary fate, positive and negative. This new dichotomy which permits us to segregate myth 4 from myths 1, 2 and 3 corresponds, on a logical level, to the discrimination that Radin makes on psychological, sociological, and historical grounds. Finally, myths 1, 2 and 3 have been classified according to the purpose of the sacrifice which is the theme of each.

Thus the four myths can be organized in a dichotomous structure of correlations and oppositions. But we can go even further and try to order them on a common scale. This is suggested by the curious variations which can be observed in each myth with respect to the kind of test the hero is put to by the ghosts.

In myth 3 there is no test at all, so far as the ghosts are concerned. The tests consist in overcoming material obstacles while the ghosts themselves figure as indifferent fellow travelers. In myth 1 they cease to be indifferent without yet becoming hostile. On the contrary, the tests result from their overfriendliness, as inviting women and infectious merry-makers. Thus, from *companions* in myth 3 they change to *seducers* in myth 1. In myth 2 they still behave as human beings, but they now act as *aggressors*, and permit themselves all kinds of rough play. This is even more evident in myth 4, but here the human element vanishes; it is only at the end that we know that ghosts, not crawling insects, are responsible for the trials of the hero. We have thus a twofold progression, from a *peaceful* attitude to an *aggressive* one, and from *human* to *nonhuman* behavior.

This progression can be correlated with the kind of relationship which the hero (or heroes) of each myth entertain with the social group. The hero of myth 3 belongs to a ritual brotherhood: he definitely assumes his (privileged) fate as member of a group, he acts with and in his group.

The two heroes of myth 1 have resolved to part from the group, but the text states repeatedly that this is in order to find an opportunity to achieve something beneficial for their fellow tribesmen. They act, therefore, for the group. But in myth 2 the hero is only inspired by his love for his wife. There is no reference to the group. The action is undertaken independently for the sake of another individual.

Finally, in myth 4, the negative attitude toward the group is clearly revealed; the girl dies of her "uncommunicativeness," if one may say

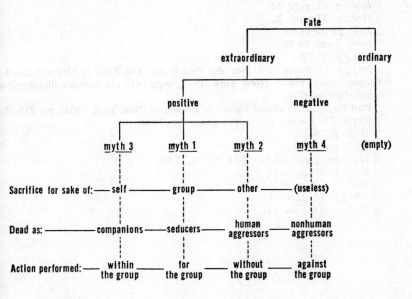

so. Indeed she prefers to die rather than speak; death is her "final" exile. As for the boy, he refuses to follow the villagers when they decide to move away and abandon the grave. The segregation is thus willfully sought on all sides; the action unrolls against the group.

The accompanying chart summarizes our discussion. I am quite aware that, in order to be fully convincing, the argument should not be limited to the four myths considered here, but include more of the invaluable Winnebago mythology which Radin has given us. But I hope that by integrating more material the basic structure outlined has become richer and more complex, without being impaired. By singling out one book which its author would perhaps consider a minor contribution, I have intended to emphasize, in an indirect way, the fecundity of the method followed by Radin, and the lasting value of the problems he poses for the anthropologist.

NOTES

[1] Paul Radin, *The Culture of the Winnebago: As Described by Themselves* Special Publication of the Bollingen Foundation (also published as Memoir 2 of the *International Journal of American Linguistics,* 1949, pp. iv, 1-119).

[2] *Ibid.,* p. 41, para. 32.

[3] *Ibid.,* p. 37, para. 2.

[4] *Ibid.,* paras. 11-14.

[5] *Ibid.,* paras. 66-70.

[6] *Ibid.,* para. 72.

[7] *Ibid.,* p. 71, paras. 91-93; see also Paul Radin, *The Road of Life and Death,* Bollingen Series, Vol. V (New York, 1945), especially the author's illuminating comments on pp. 63-65.

[8] Paul Radin, *Method and Theory of Ethnology* (New York, 1933), pp. 238-45.

[9] Radin, *The Culture of the Winnebago,* pp. 74 ff.

[10] *Ibid.,* p. 74.

[11] *Ibid.,* pp. 74-77.

[12] *Ibid.,* see paras. 10-14, 17-18, 59-60, 77-90.

[13] *Ibid.,* p. 87, para. 52.

[14] *Ibid.,* p. 100, n. 40.

[15] *Ibid.,* p. 87, para. 74.

[16] *Ibid.,* p. 94, para. 341.

PAUL RADIN AND THE PROBLEM OF PRIMITIVE MONOTHEISM

By David Bidney

INDIANA UNIVERSITY

THE PROBLEM of primitive monotheism is intimately connected with the problem of the origin and evolution of religion in general. Modern ethnologists and folklorists from the time of Tylor have adopted a naturalistic and humanistic approach in dealing with the problem of primitive monotheism and generally have sought to explain the evolution of religion as part of the natural evolution of human culture as a whole. Paul Radin has taken an active part in the controversies which have developed in connection with the ethnology of religion during the past forty years and has put forward a number of significant hypotheses. I propose to examine briefly the course of Radin's thought on the problem of primitive monotheism against the background of evolutionary cultural anthropology.

According to Tylor the primitive form of religion and the source of all later developments was "animism," the belief in spiritual beings envisaged as ethereal likenesses of bodies and as the source of life and activity in all things. There was a gradual evolution of religion from belief in ghosts, demons, and nature spirits to polytheism and finally to monotheism. Tylor doubted on principle that savages were capable of originating the idea of a High God and attributed all alleged instances of savages possessing the idea of a supreme being to the influence of missionaries or to contact with civilized peoples (Tylor, 1871, 2: 333-34).

His theory of linear evolution of culture called for a gradual evolution of religious thought. Therefore, he doubted the origin among savages of the idea of a supreme being and accounted for its presence by the supposition of historical diffusion and acculturation.

Andrew Lang challenged Tylor's theory of animism and the whole evolutionary theory of religion which it presupposed. He was prepared to accept the ethnographical evidence of a primitive belief in a High God as indicating the prevalence of primitive monotheism. He adduced evidence (1898) that the belief in a supreme being was found precisely among the rudest savages and not among advanced preliterate peoples. As against Tylor's theory of the progressive evolution of religion, he advanced the hypothesis of degeneration according to which archaic culture began with a rational belief in a supreme deity and then degenerated into a belief in demons and spirits owing to aboriginal man's irrational, mythological imagination. By a process of degeneration man's original religious insight was overpowered and contaminated by his superstitious, animistic beliefs.

According to Lang the idea of a supreme being was a natural product of primitive man's intellectual reflections on the order of nature. The deity was conceived as a magnified non-natural man whose creative power transcended that of all natural phenomena. Primitive man was said to be capable of rational, philosophical thought and to have originally conceived of a first cause or maker of the cosmos in anthropomorphic form, only to be overpowered later by his own irrational, mythopoeic fancies. According to Lang, "a notion of a good, powerful Maker, not subject to death, because necessarily prior to death, seems easier of attainment than the notion of Spirit, which, *ex hypothesi,* demands much delicate psychological study and hard thought" (1901, 1: 328-29).

Lang's theory of primitive monotheism and subsequent degeneration has found strong champions in Father Wilhelm Schmidt and Father Wilhelm Koppers. They differ, however, from Lang in one important respect: Whereas Lang's theory is polygenetic and is based on the assumption that the idea of a supreme being originated many times independently among aboriginal societies (since the concept does not seem to lie beyond early man's mental faculties), the Schmidt-Koppers position tends to be monogenetic and presupposes the aboriginal unity of human history. Archaic society is thought to have consisted of a single unit with a common culture prior to the dispersion of that society to all parts of the globe. Only this archaic society is said to have held the idea of a supreme being clearly and consistently (Schmidt, 1931, p. 255). It should be noted, further, that none of the extant primitive peoples is said to possess this monotheistic belief in its pure form but the rudest savages, such as the Congo pygmies and the Andaman Islanders, show traces of this aboriginal monotheism. The concept of the archaic culture and monotheistic religion of mankind is, therefore, a historical reconstruction and does not correspond precisely to any known historical culture (Schmidt, 1931, p. 285).

Koppers's thesis is that the uniformity of monotheistic beliefs among the oldest peoples leads to the conclusion that this belief must have originated in a primeval, divine revelation prior to man's dispersal over the globe. The folkloristic, mythological evidence seems to point to "the conclusion that there really had been something like a Paradise and Fall in the early ages of mankind, and that consequently some (direct or indirect) revelation of God to early man must actually have taken place" (Koppers, 1952, p. 181). Koppers is not dogmatic on this point but suggests that the data warrant such a hypothesis and that we may one day have sufficient evidence for a new historical proof of the existence of God (1952, p. 184).

American anthropologists have, on the whole, been rather wary of accepting the theory of primitive monotheism even in the rationalistic form suggested by Lang. It is rather significant that Robert Lowie did not accept the theory in the first edition of his *Primitive Religion* (1924) but granted the point in the revised edition (1948, p. vi) that "the high-god concept occurs among very rude tribes." Lowie conceded even earlier that in principle "monotheism in essence is possible even among the simplest tribes" (1934, p. 328). However, some contemporary American anthropologists still maintain that "the concept of a single, all-powerful deity is apparently lacking among all nonliterate peoples" (Beals and Hoijer, 1953, p. 484).

The outstanding exception among American ethnologists has been Paul Radin. As early as 1915 he acknowledged the fact of primitive belief in monotheism while noting that "the belief in a single supreme deity is not very common in America" (Radin, 1915, p. 292). "If," he continues, "we take the belief in a single God to mean the belief in a mildly benevolent creator, who may or may not be the creator of all deities and spirits, to whom offerings are made similar in nature to those made to other spirits, the conception, though not common, is found among the Californian tribes, the Bellacoola, the Central Algonkin, the Woodland-Plains, some of the Plains, and some of the Southwestern tribes" (1915, p. 292). The idea of a single deity, Radin explains, probably arises from the older belief in Good Spirits and Bad Spirits and represents the complete displacement of the latter. The single deity was never popular and was mainly a shamanistic construction (1915, p. 293).

Already in this early essay Radin distinguished three psychological types of individuals, namely, the truly religious, the intermittently religious, and the indifferently religious people (1915, p. 262). The shaman is the type of individual who possesses a true religious feeling and it is he who influences the religious experiences of the other two types. The shaman is the thinker, the one who systematizes religious thought and ritual, and it is he primarily who conceives the idea of a supreme God. The rest of the people in a given society may come to accept some of his beliefs but they usually confuse them with less abstract, animistic beliefs and magical practices.

In his essay "Monotheism among Primitive Peoples" (1924), Radin developed the thesis of primitive monotheism still farther. Here he distinguishes sharply between the two main concepts of primitive religion, the Creator and the Transformer. The Creator is the supreme deity, beneficent and ethical, not directly approachable and taking but little interest in the world after He has created it. The Transformer is the one who has established the present order of things; He is non-ethical, incidentally and inconsistently beneficent, and intervenes often and directly in the affairs of the world (1924, p. 8). The concept of the Supreme Being is said to be the construct of the shaman-priest, while the image of the Transformer or Trickster is the product of the ordinary, pragmatic layman. According to Radin, the so-called degeneration to which Lang and others refer is nothing but "the projection of the image of the transformer upon that of the supreme creator and vice versa." We are dealing with two distinct concepts formulated by different types of individuals and not with a single idea subject to degeneration.

Radin's essay is noteworthy for its clear presentation of his theory of psychological types and for his anti-evolutionary thesis. He assumes that there is the same more or less fixed distribution of ability and temperament in every group of approximately the same size; the devoutly religious, the intermittently religious, and the indifferently religious types are to be found in all societies. Each type tends to react and think in a similar manner regardless of the state of culture and society. The devoutly religious man, whether he be poet, philosopher, or shaman, always tends to picture the world as a unified whole and to postulate some first cause. No evolution from animism to monotheism was ever necessary in his case. All the monotheists have sprung from

mong the eminently religious individuals (Radin, 1924, p. 25). The
act that monotheism is an expression of an intellectual-religious tem-
erament explains why the Supreme Being is said to be unapproachable
nd to lack cults. The layman, the pragmatic realist, on the other
and, tends to convert the Supreme Being into a cult-deity, making
Him one among many and converting monotheism into monolatry.

Radin's theory of the recurrence of the basic psychological types
haracterized by similar modes of thought leads him to reject the
volutionary theory of culture in general and that of the evolution of
eligion in particular. "The cardinal error," he observes, "is, and always has been, the assumption that every element in culture must have
an evolution . . . . There is no reason whatsoever for supposing that
certain concepts require a long period to evolve" (1924, p. 27). Thus
we find him arguing against C. Buchanan Gray that Hebrew religion
did not develop from monolatry to implicit monotheism and finally to
explicit monotheism. Instead we may assume that among the Hebrews,
as among other peoples, there were from the outset two antithetical
attitudes towards the deity held by different types of individuals (Radin,
1924, p. 22). Similarly he is critical of N. Söderblom's Tylorian approach, which denies any form of monotheism to primitive peoples.
Radin assumes instead that "a limited number of explicit monotheists
is to be found in every primitive tribe that has at all developed the
concept of a Supreme Creator" (1924, p. 29). There is no difference
in temperament and in capacity for logical and symbolical thought
between civilized and primitive men and hence we must not deny to
the latter the ability to originate the concept of a Supreme Being.
Monotheism, he argues, does not depend upon extent of knowledge
but rather upon type of temperament, upon the "purposive functioning of an inherent type of thought and emotion" (1924, p. 30).

Radin here comes close to maintaining a theory of *Elementargedanken* reminiscent of Bastian. "Certain ideas," he writes, "and certain concepts are as ultimate for man as a social being as specific
physiological reactions are for him as a biological entity" (1924. p. 30).
The idea of God, including explicit monotheism, is an example of an
"ultimate idea" which tends to be conceived in specific forms by the
various types of temperament. Radin's phenomenological analysis of
fixed psychological types and their corresponding modes of thought is
the antithesis of the historical, evolutionary approach of Tylor and

Frazer which assumes the transformation rather than the fixity o types and the evolution of human intelligence and capacity for rationa thought.

In his *Primitive Man as a Philosopher* (1927) Radin reiterate essentially the same views as in his earlier essay. Indeed, the chapte entitled "Monotheistic Tendencies" (xviii chap.) appears to be largely a verbatim reprint of the earlier paper.

With the publication of *Primitive Religion: Its Nature and Origir* (1937) Radin began to modify his views seriously. He now assumed an evolutionary approach reminiscent in certain respects of Herber Spencer and Sir James Frazer. Probably under the influence of Marxis thought, which was extremely popular at the time, he stressed the "economic determinants" of primitive religion and the function of economic factors in the development of religion in general.

Especially noteworthy is Radin's evolutionary approach to primitive religion. Like Frazer, he now assumes that magic constitutes the oldest substratum of religion. "In the beginning," he writes, "there was magic and magic was with God and God was magic" (Radin, 1937, p. 60). In the evolution of religion the task of the religious interpreter is now said to be "the transformation of the coercion into a willing acquiescence" (*ibid.*, p. 71). The shaman is the one who is primarily responsible for the transformation of magic into religion of an animistic type. Radin is certain that "magic very definitely preceded religion" and identifies magic with the "preanimistic" state postulated by Marett (*ibid.*, p. 75).

Radin is, however, inclined to accept Spencer's theory that the dead and the ghosts of the dead were the materials out of which the notion of spirits actually developed (*ibid.*, 72). Religion, he explains, may be regarded as having been originally differentiated from magic by the extension to the dead of all the attributes that had been characteristic of the living (*ibid.*, 74). The dead became transformed into supernatural beings and served as prototypes for the personification and deification of the powers of nature.

Corresponding to the evolution from magic to religion there is the personal evolution of the religious thinker from magician to priest (Radin, 1937, p. 132). Thus, contrary to his earlier thesis, Radin now maintains that the psychological type, the introvert "thinker-artist," remains constant but the mode of expression tends to vary with change in culture. Motivated by economic and social considerations, such as the desire for wealth and the craving for power, and affected by his emotional sensitivity and instability, the shaman-magician was gradually led to separate himself from the ordinary world (*ibid.*, p. 108). He became a professional in the diagnosis and treatment of disease and elaborated a belief in spirits and deities together with a "technique of obstacles" (*ibid.*, pp. 135, 145). Thus the spirits and deities are originally the specific constructs of the shamans and priests, whereas formerly these same spirits and deities were said to be the constructs of the ordinary laymen (*ibid.*, p. 150). The dualism of magic and religion is never overcome, as is demonstrated by the ritual dramas centering about the "rites of passage" and the myths of origin (*ibid.*, chaps. 5, 14).

In the process of the evolution from magic to religion the shaman plays the dominant role after death as well as during his life. The ghost of the shaman remained for a long time one of the basic constituents in the necessary formation of the whole concept of the spirit (Radin, 1937, p. 196). "Man created spirits and deities originally in the image of the shaman" (*ibid.*, p. 197). But this, Radin is careful to note, is not equivalent to saying that spirits and deities are deified shamans or kings (*ibid.*). In view of Radin's professed acceptance of the euhemerism of Spencer and the thesis that "the dead thus became easily transformed into supernatural beings and served as the prototypes for that personification and deification of the external world that play so fundamental a role in primitive religion," (Radin, 1937, p. 74), I find it rather difficult to see how he can disclaim any connection with "our modern euhemerists."

Furthermore, in agreement with Frazer, Radin views the evolution from magic to religion as manifested subjectively by the gradual adoption of a ritual of conciliation and propitiation of the supernatural instead of the earlier ritual of coercion (Radin, 1937, chap. 9). The first link in this development was the concept of taboo, and the practice of taboo is regarded as an incipient form of the conciliation of the supernatural (*ibid.*, pp. 174, 175). There is a comparable evolution from spell to prayer (*ibid.*, p. 185). The prayer-wish is said to antedate religion and to be contemporaneous with magic (*ibid.*, p. 186).

When he comes to consider again the problem of primitive monotheism Radin's conclusion appears to be quite similar to that of the cultural evolutionists, even though he professes to disagree with them. After an interval of some thirteen years Radin now finds himself in substantial agreement with Buchanan Gray and speaks of primitive monolatry rather than of primitive monotheism. He states: "Monotheism, strictly speaking, is, in other words, extremely rare. What we have is monolatry, and this is essentially merely a form of polytheism. Even the monotheism we find is not the expression of a religious faith but of a philosophical drive. It would be just as legitimate to call Socrates or Seneca a monotheist. Monotheism in its strictly religious connotation implies that it is the official faith of the whole community. That is never found among primitive people" (Radin, 1937, pp. 259-60).

Monotheism, it now appears, is not a religion at all but a form of philosophical speculation, at least so far as primitive culture is concerned. The Supreme Being is an abstraction not meant to be worshipped (Radin, 1937, p. 266). The moment such a Supreme Being is worshipped He becomes transformed into the highest god of a polytheistic pantheon. There is no ground for speaking of primitive monotheism if by the latter term we refer to the faith of a society.

In view of the ethnographical evidence cited by Schmidt and Koppers, and Radin's own admission that true monotheism is to be encountered among the Polynesians, the Ewe of Africa and the Dakota, (Radin, 1937, p. 259), I find no basis for his sweeping statement that "these Supreme Beings are not meant to be worshipped." Even though such worship be limited more or less to the priestly groups it is still true religion and is not to be excluded as mere "philosophical speculation." It is indeed legitimate to call Seneca or Socrates a monotheist, since in addition to being philosophers they were also religious believers who were prepared to live and die for their faith. Radin tends to treat philosophical speculation and religious faith as if they were entirely independent of one another in contrast to his earlier approach wherein the philosopher was regarded as the type of the truly religious individual. I do not see why primitive monotheism need necessarily be the faith of a whole community in order to be regarded as a religion. Even if the minority of any given community accept and profess it this would be sufficient to justify our speaking of primitive monotheism as a form of religion. Furthermore, if it be granted, as Radin himself granted in his earlier work, that the thinker influences the other psychological types, then there is ground for assuming that monotheistic belief is not limited exclusively to the philosophers who may have originated the idea. It seems quite arbitrary to speak as if the only religious people and "true believers" are the adherents of magic and animism. On the latter assumption, degeneration is explained away on the ground that primitive monotheism never attained to the status of a folk religion and that hence the alleged "degeneration" never took place.

It is of interest to note that Radin himself later granted that in East and West Africa we do find a religion of a primitive High God with a highly developed priesthood. In *Die Religiöse Erfahrung der Naturvölker* (1951, p. 108), he writes: "Wohl gibt es Volksstämme, wie etwa die politisch und sozial hochdifferenzierten Gemeinschaften in West- und Ostafrika, bei denen sich die ganze Gruppe zum Glauben an einen Hochgott zu bekennen scheint. Hier haben wir es aber mit einer hochentwickelten Priesterschaft zu tun und gewissermassen mit einer Art 'Staatsreligion.'" Radin denies, however, any native primitive monotheism among American Indians and, like Tylor, attributes any such beliefs to the influence of Christianity (*ibid.*, p. 108). The Pawnee may be the one exception among American Indians because of the highly developed priesthood found there.

In this German monograph Radin once more refers to the two basic psychological types, the thinker and the nonthinker, but his description differs from the one to be found in his *Primitive Religion* and resembles in some respects that of his earlier work. He now states:

Der Denker aber ist bei den Naturvölkern fast immer ein Medizinmann, Schamane oder Priester. Mit anderen Worten, wir haben es dort mit Denkern zu tun, die entweder selbst religiös sind oder zum mindesten sich mit religiösen Dingen beschäftigen. Die meisten Schamanen dürfen wir mit Sicherheit ausschliessen. Ihr Erfahrungstyp geht nicht auf objektives Denken aus; gerade dieses aber ist, wie wir sehen werden, die Voraussetzung für die Idee eines Hochgottes. Wir sehen uns also lediglich auf zwei Menschentypen beschränkt: diejenigen, die ihrer Veranlagung nach zur Wakan-Erfahrung befähigt sind, und die wesenhaft nichtreligiösen Menschen, die Denker sind und Medizinmänner und Priester wurden. Beide Typen hat es schon-so behaupte icht-seit Beginn der menschlichen Kultur gegeben. Aus diesem Grunde dürfen wir nicht überrascht sein, wenn wir überall, sowohl in den einfachsten wie in den differenziertesten Primitivkulturen, den Glauben an einen Hochgott vorfinden. (Radin, 1951, p. 108)

Here we see that the thinker in primitive culture is also religious or is occupied with religious matters. The majority of shamans may be excluded as nonintellectual and are not concerned with objective thought. We are then limited to two types of thinkers, namely, those capable of a Wakan type of experience and those, essentially nonreligious people, who become medicine mén and priests. Hence we must not be surprised to find in primitive cultures of all stages of development a belief in a High God.

Radin proceeds to explain that the idea of a High God, in its purest form, is scarcely more than a philosophical concept and that is why the High God seldom becomes the object of a cult. However, this construct never remains merely a philosophical concept without functional value. For the thinker-priest this functional value is conceived in universal terms and has a moral significance since the High God is understood as the giver of justice; the nonthinker and average man imagines this function in terms of special activities. This explains the disparate notions of the High God in primitive cultures (Radin, 1951, pp. 111-12).

Thus, contrary to his position in *Primitive Religion,* Radin is here reaffirming, in part, the position maintained in *Primitive Man as Philosopher*. The thinker-priest tends to originate the idea of a High God and when conditions are favorable, as in Africa, this may lead to an institutionalized worship. The idea of a High God never remains a philosophical concept without religious significance but the religious value attributed to the High God by the thinker-priest and by the nonthinker layman differs considerably. Monotheism, therefore, never remains in its pure form and tends to be confused with animistic beliefs and magical practices.

In the Preface to the reprint edition of his essay on *Monotheism among Primitive Peoples* (1954) Radin reiterates the position taken in the German monograph: "On the whole," he states, "I feel that pure monotheism in the late Hebraic, Christian and Mohammedan sense of the term is rare. It is clearly encountered in certain parts of Africa, especially West Africa, and in Polynesia. Its occurrence in aboriginal America and Australia, it seems to me, is more than doubtful. As an essentially philosophic belief entertained by a few deeply religious individuals and connected with origin myths it may, however, appear everywhere." In the 1951 publication Radin still regarded the Pawnee as perhaps an example of American primitive monotheism, but even this one exception is not granted in the later publication. What passes for monotheism in the reports of priests and missionaries is usually some form of monolatry or henotheism.

Finally, in *The World of Primitive Man* (1953) Radin, it seems, has reverted in part to the position of his *Primitive Religion* (1937). In his latest work there is no discussion at all of primitive monotheism and the term does not appear in the index. Instead there is a lengthy discussion of psychological types, in which Radin now differentiates four types, namely, the man of action and the thinker as well as the religious and the nonreligious man (Radin, 1953, chaps. 3 and 4). To understand primitive religion we must begin with a description and analysis of the religious experience as manifested through the different types of human temperament (Radin, 1953, pp. 103-4).

The two main types are the man of action and the thinker. The man of action predominates in primitive as in civilized society and is characterized by a pragmatic interest in objects and their results or effects. The thinker is primarily interested in the subject and his states and tends to coordinate and unify his experiences. In matters of religion the man of action tends to be concrete and to judge objects by their effects; hence he regards *mana* as an impersonal power which works in an extraordinary manner. The man of thought tends to be systematic and abstract and to envisage objects as static and permanent; hence he regards *mana* as the generalized essence of a deity residing in an object or in man (Radin, 1953, p. 54).

The religious and nonreligious types correspond, on the whole, to the thinker and man of action. The thinker is the truly religious type of man but appears in two forms, namely, as the shaman and as the logical poet-thinker. Radin speaks of two types of religious temperament, the one manifesting acute psychical unbalance of the neurotic-epileptoid type associated with the shaman (Radin, 1953, p. 94). The other type of religious temperament is philosophic and is sensitive to the limitations of man and the importance of what is beyond human power. The shamanistic type of religious man is dominated by feeling, and the objects of his belief are secondary. The philosophic type of religious man is dominated by the idea of the divine object, and his feelings are secondary. The nonreligious type and the intermittently religious type are characteristic of the majority of people in primitive society as in our own society, though many find it expedient to behave as though they were truly religious. In times of economic and mental crises the indifferently or intermittently religious type tends to approximate the religious type. On the whole, Radin's theory of fixed psychological types is reminiscent of his earliest thought but the distinctions have now been worked out in more detail.

Radin recognizes that religion involves "the fusion of a particular feeling and attitude with an interconnected series of specific acts and beliefs" (1953, p. 68). But, with the social anthropologists, he stresses the point that "religion has had a primary social function, namely, the validation of the life-values of man" (1953, p. 69). With Tylor he admits that religious belief is "most inextricably" connected to a *something* outside of man which may be called a spirit and which is thought to exercise control over man's life values (1953, p. 70).

It is of interest to note especially that religious feeling is said to be characterized by "a far more than normal sensitiveness when in the presence of certain external objects." The idea of the holy, which Rudolph Otto has described as the distinctive emotion connected with the religious object, is not mentioned. Instead, religious feeling is described as comprised of sensations of exhilaration and mild euphoria, as well as of terror, fear, helplessness, bewilderment, and self-rejection (Radin, 1953, p. 71).

Religious belief and emotion are evoked especially at times of crisis or unbalance either in the order of nature or in one's self. Any interference with this balance is attributed to the interference of supernatural spirits (Radin, 1953, p. 72). The shaman, who is by temperament an unbalanced person given to epileptic fits and seizures, becomes the obvious spokesman and interpreter of religious experience. While the shaman proclaims that the spirits are coercing and constraining him, he is, in fact, being constrained by his own desperate psychical needs (Radin, 1953, p. 84). Radin is here obviously introducing his own psychological interpretation of the shaman's beliefs (1953, p. 85). The breakdown of aboriginal cultures in contact with European civilizations tends to promote collective hysteria and psychical disorganization even among the intermittently religious individuals (Radin, 1953, p. 96).

As in his *Primitive Religion*, Radin stresses here "the economic utilizations of magic and religion" (1953, chap. 6). Fear is the subjective correlate of economic and environmental insecurity, and this in turn brings about the dominance of magic with its coercive rites. Because the shaman is in control of the rituals of magic, the fear of the shaman hangs over the ordinary individual (1953, p. 140). The shaman tends to utilize magical rites to enhance his own wealth, power, and prestige, often in alliance with the chief. Contrary to the usual psychological interpretation of functionalists such as Malinowski and Raymond Firth, Radin maintains that witchcraft and magic persist even in complex primitive cultures because they are utilized for economic and political exploitation by the shaman and chief and those closely associated with them. Though faith in magical rites is psychologically justified by its pragmatic success, the primary reason for their persistence is economic exploitation (Radin, 1953, p. 150).

The question may well be raised at this stage: What led Radin to alter his views on primitive monotheism? Was it the discovery of new ethnographic data or was it rather a reevaluation of the old data in terms of some conflicting principle? The answer which emerges from our survey is that the change is due primarily to his adoption of an evolutionary point of view, that of Frazer and Spencer in particular, and that this approach led him to modify and disavow his earlier adherence to the views of Andrew Lang and the supporters of the theory of primitive monotheism.

In *Primitive Man as Philosopher* Radin adhered to a phenomenological theory of psychological types which he opposed to the evolutionary theory of the gradual development of primitive thought. Primitive man, like civilized man, is said to be capable of rational, philosophic thought, and some individuals of genuine religious temperament were bound to conceive of monotheistic ideas. Primitive monotheism does not depend on the evolution of knowledge but solely upon the existence of a special kind of temperament which is conducive to a certain timeless mode of thinking. It seems to me that at this point Radin's views approximated those of Bastian and his *Elementargedanken,* since both approaches are anti-evolutionary.

Radin explained the actual prevalence of magical rituals and animistic beliefs in primitive cultures as indicative of the dual origin of religious beliefs. The philosophic-religious type of individual tends to conceive a monotheistic deity but the pragmatic, fact-minded type of individual tends to imagine a world of spirits and especially the image of the culture-hero or Trickster who intervenes directly in the affairs of men. Thus what appears as degeneration to Lang and the Catholic ethnologists is, for Radin, a fusion of two antithetical modes of thought deriving from two different types of individuals—a fusion which results in the projection of the image of the Trickster upon that of the Supreme Creator. The truly religious individual is the primary source of monotheistic religion and ethical ideals. Radin's theory of the dual origin of religious beliefs may be compared with the similar thesis of Henri Bergson's *The Two Sources of Morality and Religion*, which also contrasts the intuitive, genuine religion and ethics of the philosophical mystic with the group mores and compulsive rites of primitive society.

In *Primitive Religion* Radin interprets the significance of the basic types of temperament in a radically different way. The religious formulator, it now appears, is really a shaman and magician, rather than a philosopher motivated by the quest for a logically coherent religious belief, and it is he who formulates the ideas of supernatural spirits as the source of his magical powers. The shaman is characterized by an unbalanced mental and emotional temperament and by epileptic seizures which he interprets as spirit-possession. In agreement with Freud, Radin now regards religion as "a neurosis" in the sense that it "perpetuates an interpretation contrived by a neurotic individual of man's relation to the world outside himself" (Radin, 1937, p. 160).

Radin now imagines the "hypothetical evolution" of religion as having occurred in four stages: (1) a magical stage wherein the relation between the ego and the objective world is completely coercive and unmediated; (2) a modified magical stage which is incompletely coercive and where a measure of volition is imputed to the object; (3) a further modification wherein volition is imputed to both the ego and object so that both are reciprocally coercive; (4) a noncoercive stage wherein the ego is regarded as being in conscious subjection to the object (*ibid.*, pp. 7-8). This outline is in basic agreement with the position of Frazer and Freud and assumes the evolution of religion from magic. In the case of the shaman this evolution was motivated primarily by economic considerations, by the desire for wealth, power, and prestige, and this "economic utilization of religion" has remained its fundamental characteristic (*ibid.*, p. 8). According to Radin, Rudolph Otto, being a theologian and mystic and not an anthropologist, completely misunderstood in his *The Idea of the Holy* the nature and economic origin of religious feeling (*ibid.,* p. 9). In view of Radin's arguments, however, I find it difficult to accept at face value his assertion in the Preface to the new edition of his *Primitive Religion* (1957) that while he stresses "the economic determinants" of religion he "at no time regarded it as determining, in any primary sense, the actual nature of the basic religious beliefs."

Once it is granted that the neurotic shaman, motivated by the desire for wealth and power, is the real formulator of animistic religious beliefs, it is easy to understand why Radin disclaims the existence of primitive monotheism. It would certainly be out of character for the shaman-magician to postulate a Supreme Being who could not be coerced by the ritual of magic. Nevertheless, Radin does assume that some shamans, though by no means all, do arrive at the notion of a Supreme Being (*ibid.,* p. 256). In more developed cultures, among agricultural tribes, the figure of the Supreme Deity is a construct of the dominant priestly class, as for example, among the Dakota and Winnebago Indians, or among the Polynesians and natives of West Africa (*ibid.,* p. 257). Thus, the "religious thinker" is introduced again, and it is he who is said to entertain the philosophic idea of a Supreme Being. In fact, however, monotheism is thought to be extremely rare; what we have in fact is monolatry which is essentially a form of polytheism.

Insofar as Radin regards magic as the essential substratum of religion he even denies that animism, in the Tylorian sense, is the universal characteristic of primitive religion. Animism is said to be a philosophy; "animism is not a religion at all" (*ibid.,* p. 198). Some shamans may have a philosophical theory of souls but the layman has no such theory. Similarly, monotheism is a philosophical theory developed by a minority of thinkers but is not characteristic of any society as a whole. If, then, neither animism nor monotheism as a speculative belief is essential to primitive religion what may be said to remain?

The answer appears to be, in accordance with Radin's theory of psychological types, that primitive religion is in fact an incoherent synthesis of magic and religion derived from the animistic philosophy of some shamans and the pragmatic magic of the layman (*ibid.,* p. 199). In those cultures where the shaman-thinker has conceived the idea of a Supreme Deity the actual religion of the majority of the people is

usually some form of polytheism mixed with magic. The Supreme
Being conceived by the primitive philosophers, as in Polynesian society,
is really not meant to be worshipped because there is nothing in the
social, economic and political structure of even the most complicated
of primitive civilizations which demands it (*ibid.*, p. 266).

Finally, it should be noted that Radin's theory of psychological types
may be understood from an evolutionary as well as from a nonevolutionary point of view. The basic types are the thinker and the man
of action, the former being an introvert and the latter an extrovert.
The thinker is fundamentally religious; the man of action tends to be
nonreligious or intermittently religious. From a nonevolutionary point
of view, the thinker in all cultures is the one who, in his quest for
coherent thought and intelligibility tends to arrive at the notion of a
Supreme Deity, or at least at polytheistic beliefs. From an evolutionary
perspective, the thinker is exemplified by the shaman, a neurotic of
unbalanced mind, who constructs an animistic theory to fortify and
enhance his magic rituals and economic exploitation of the people. To
this extent Radin agrees with Freud that religion is a special kind of
neurosis.

In *The World of Primitive Man* Radin differentiates the shaman-
thinker from the philosopher-thinker who is not a neurotic of unbalanced mentality but rather a very rational person who is extremely
conscious of the causal nexus of things. The philosopher as thinker
speculates about the order of nature and formulates myths of origin
to account for the evolution of man and nature. Thus, unlike the
shaman, the philosopher-thinker does not seek to validate magical
rituals in the interest of economic life-values, but is motivated instead
by wonder and the quest for intelligibility. It is precisely for this
reason that the practical type of man, the nonreligious type, fails to
follow him and seeks for a form of religious expression which he can
imagine and which has direct relevance to his functional needs.

I find in Radin's writings an ambivalent attitude towards the position
of the thinker in primitive culture. On the one hand, he is said to be
a fixed type and an essentially religious type of man who is responsible
for the formulation of religious beliefs in all forms of culture. That is
why Radin speaks of man as from the beginning *homo religiosus* (*The
World of Primitive Man,* p. 69). On the other hand, to the extent that
Radin follows Frazer's scheme of evolution and assumes the primacy

of magic in the evolution of religion, he tends to separate the religious man and the philosopher. The unbalanced shaman becomes the type of the religious man and the philosopher, whether he believes in animism or monotheism, and tends to be separated from the mass of religious believers. The philosophy of primitive man and his magical-religious rituals tend to be put in separate categories. I find no coherent synthesis in Radin's works of primitive man as philosopher and primitive man as *homo religiosus*.

REFERENCES

Beals, R. L., and H. Hoijer. 1953. An Introduction to Anthropology. New York, Macmillan.

Bidney, David. 1954. "The Ethnology of Religion and the Problem of Human Evolution," *American Anthropologist*, 56:No. 1:1-18.

Frazer, Sir J. G. 1942. The Golden Bough. 1 vol., abridged ed. New York, Macmillan.

Koppers, W. 1952. Primitive Man and His World Picture. London and New York, Sheed & Ward.

Lang, A. 1898. The Making of Religion. New York, Longmans, Green and Co.
——— 1901. Myth, Ritual and Religion. 2 vols. New York, Longmans, Green and Co.

Lowie, R. H. 1924. Primitive Culture. Revised ed. New York, Liveright, 1948.
——— 1934. An Introduction to Cultural Anthropology. New York, Farrar & Rinehart.

Marett, R. R. 1909. The Threshold of Religion. Revised ed. New York, Macmillan, 1914.

Radin, Paul. 1915. "Religion of the North American Indians," in *Anthropology in North America*, ed. by Franz Boas. New York, G. E. Stechert & Co. Pp. 259-305.
——— 1924. Monotheism among Primitive Peoples. Reprint, Ethnographical Museum, Basel, 1954.
——— 1927. Primitive Man as Philosopher. New York, Appleton-Century.
——— 1937. Primitive Religion. New York, Dover, 1957.
——— 1945. The Road of Life and Death. New York, Pantheon.
——— 1951. Die Religiöse Erfahrung der Naturvölker. Zurich, Rhein-Verlag.
——— 1953. The World of Primitive Man. New York, Schuman.
——— 1956. The Trickster: A Study in American Indian Mythology. London, Routledge and Kegan Paul.

Schmidt, W. 1926. Der Ursprung der Gottesidee. Münster.
——— 1931. The Origin and Growth of Religion. London, Methuen & Co.

Spencer, Herbert. 1910. The Principles of Sociology. 3 vols. New York and London, D. Appleton & Co.

Tylor, E. B. 1871. Primitive Culture. 2 vols. London, John Murray, 1913.

PRIMITIVE MAN AS METAPHYSICIAN

By Joseph Campbell

> *"The name of the song is called 'Haddocks' Eyes.'"*
> *"Oh, that's the name of the song, is it?" Alice said,*
> *trying to feel interested. "No, you don't understand,"*
> *the Knight said, looking a little vexed. "That's what*
> *the name is* called."
>
> LEWIS CARROLL

"THE METAPHYSICAL NOTIONS of man may be reduced to a few types which are of universal distribution," Franz Boas declared in the first edition of *The Mind of Primitive Man* (New York, 1911, p. 156); in the second edition, prepared a quarter of a century later (1938), this observation did not appear. In American anthropology a tendency to emphasize the differentiating traits of primitive societies had meanwhile developed to such a degree that any mention by an author of common traits simply meant that he had not kept up with the fashion. Recently, however, the tide has turned. In the encyclopedic inventory of problems and theories, prepared under the chairmanship of A. L. Kroeber and published as *Anthropology Today* (University of Chicago Press, 1953), we find a substantial article by Clyde Kluckhohn on "Universal Categories of Culture," as well as references by a number of the other authors to the present need for comparative evaluations. No one, however, appears to have brought forward again the idea developed by Paul Radin thirty years ago, when his work on *Primitive Man as Philosopher* offered a formula by which the two points of view successively represented by Boas might have been reconciled and brought together in a single general theory. His observation that among primitive as well as highly civilized peoples the two types of man are to be found that William James long ago characterized as the tough-minded and tender-minded [1]—and that the myths and symbols of all societies are interpreted in differing senses by these two—has apparently been forgotten by the representatives of a science, which, in the words of Boas himself, "does not deal with the exceptional man." [2]

"From the man of action's viewpoint," wrote Dr. Radin, describing the attitude of the tough-minded type, "a fact has no symbolic or static value. He predicates no unity beyond that of the certainty of continuous change and transformation. For him a double distortion is involved in investing the transitory and ceaselessly changing object with a symbolic, idealistic, or static significance." The thinker, on the other hand, the tender-minded type, "is impelled by his whole nature, by the innate orientation of his mind, to try to discover the reason why there is an effect, what is the nature of the relation between the ego and the world, and what part exactly the perceiving self plays therein. Like all philosophers, he is interested in the subject as such, the object as such, and the relations between them.... An original, moving, shapeless or undifferentiated world must be brought to rest and given stable form.... Philosophers have always given the same answer to this problem and predicated a unity behind these changing aspects and forms. Primitive philosophers are at one with their European and Asiatic brothers here." [3]

It appears to me that any science that takes into consideration only or even primarily the vulgar, tough-minded interpretation of symbols will inevitably be committed to a study largely of local differentiations, while, on the other hand, one addressed to the views of thinkers will find that the ultimate references of their cogitations are few and of universal distribution. Anthropologists, by and large (or, at least, those of the American variety) are notoriously tough-minded. (There is a Haitian proverb, I am told: "When the anthropologist arrives, the gods depart!") They have tended to give reductive interpretations to the symbols of primitive thought and to find their references only in the particularities of the local scene. In the following pages I should like to suggest an amplification of this view.

I

The first problem to be confronted by anyone wishing to deal with the metaphysical notions of mankind is that of distinguishing between symbols and their references—between what we may term the *vehicles* and their *tenor*. For example, the three or four instances of "metaphysical notions" enumerated by Dr. Boas in his chapter on "The Universality of Cultural Traits," are not metaphysical notions at all. They are simply images, symbols, or vehicles, which by a tough-minded individual might be interpreted physically, as references not to any metaphysical realization whatsoever, but to remote facts, realms or lands much like our own—whereas the term "metaphysical" refers to no place, no time, no thing, no fact: not even wonders of such stuff as dreams are made of. "Belief in a land of the souls of the deceased," for example,[4] "located in the west, and reached by crossing a river": this is not in itself a metaphysical notion, though it may be given a metaphysical reading. Nor can we call metaphysical "the idea of a multiplicity of worlds,—one or more spanned over us, others stretching under us, the central one the home of man; the upper or lower, the home of the gods and happy souls; the other, the home of the un-happy."[5]

Such images are not the final terms of our subject, if it is of meta-physics that we are treating. They have often served, indeed, as vehicles of metaphysical expression, and part of our problem, certainly, is to collect, compare, and classify them; but we miss our proper point if we rest with them as they stand. For an image may signify various things in various contexts and to various minds. Furthermore, where an image has disappeared, it need not follow that the tenor of its reference has disappeared: this may be lurking under another image entirely. Nor in cross-cultural comparisons can we safely assume that because the symbolic figures differ from culture to culture the tenors of their references must differ also.

Let us consider, therefore, a brief series of mythological images culled from a number of cultures, which may be discovered to be the vehicles of a single metaphysical tenor.

II

Natalie Curtis, in *The Indians' Book* (Harper and Brothers, 1907), years ago published a remarkable origin myth that was recounted to her by an aged Pima chief, Hovering Hawk:

In the beginning there was only darkness everywhere—darkness and water. And the darkness gathered thick in places, crowding together and then separating, crowding and separating until at last out of one of the places where the darkness had crowded there came forth a man. This man wandered through the darkness until he began to think; then he knew himself and that he was a man; he knew that he was there for some purpose.

He put his hand over his heart and drew forth a large stick. He used the stick to help him through the darkness, and when he was weary he rested upon it. Then he made for himself little ants; he brought them from his body and put them on the stick. Everything that he made he drew from his own body even as he had drawn the stick from his heart. The stick was of grease-wood, and of the gum of the wood the ants made a round ball upon the stick. Then the man took the ball from the stick and put it down in the darkness under his foot, and as he stood upon the ball he rolled it under his foot and sang:

> I make the world, and lo!
> The world is finished.
> Thus I make the world, and lo!
> The world is finished.

So he sang, calling himself the maker of the world. He sang slowly, and all the while the ball grew larger as he rolled it, till at the end of his song, behold, it was the world. Then he sang more quickly:

> Let it go, let it go,
> Let it go, start it forth!

So the world was made, and now the man brought from himself a rock and divided it into little pieces. Of these he made stars, and put them in the sky to light the darkness. But the stars were not bright enough.

So he made Tau-mik, the milky-way. Yet Tau-mik was not bright enough. Then he made the moon. All these he made of rocks drawn forth from himself. But even the moon was not bright enough. So he began to wonder what next he could do. He could bring nothing from himself that could lighten the darkness.

Then he thought. And from himself he made two large bowls, and he filled the one with water and covered it with the other. He sat and watched the bowls, and while he watched he wished that what he wanted to make in very truth would come to be. And it was even as he wished. For the water in the bowl turned into the sun and shone out in rays through the cracks where the bowls joined.

When the sun was made, the man lifted off the top bowl and took out the sun and threw it to the east. But the sun did not touch the ground; it stayed in the sky where he threw it and never moved. Then in the same way he threw the sun to the north and to the west and to the south. But each time it only stayed in the sky, motionless, for it never touched the ground. Then he threw it once more to the east, and this time it touched the ground and bounced and started upward. Since then the sun has never ceased to move. It goes around the world in a day, but every morning it must bounce anew in the east.[6]

It is impossible to read this story without thinking of the far flung Old World theme of the primordial giant out of whose body the universe proceeds, and who, until the end of time, remains within the forms of the universe as the "self of all."

"In the beginning, this universe was only the self, in a human form," we read in the Sanskrit *Brihadaranyaka Upanishad.*

He looked around and saw nothing but himself. Then, at the beginning, he cried out, "I am he!" Whence came the name, I. That is why, even today, when a person is addressed, he first declares, "It is I," and then announces the other name that he goes by.

He was afraid. That is why people are afraid to be alone. He thought, "But what am I afraid of? There is nothing but myself." Whereupon his fear was gone. . . .

He was unhappy. That is why people are not happy when they are alone. He wanted a mate. He became as big as a woman and man embracing. He divided this body, which was himself, in two parts. From that there came husband and wife. . . . Therefore this body [before one marries a wife] is like one of the halves of a split pea. . . . He united with her; and from that were born men.

She considered: "How can he unite with me after producing me from himself? Well then, let me hide myself." She became a cow; but he became a bull and united with her: from that were born cattle. She became a mare, he a stallion; she a she-ass, he a donkey and united with her; from that were born the one-hoofed animals. . . . She became a goat, he a buck; she a ewe, he a ram and united with her: from that were born goats and sheep. Thus did he project everything that exists in pairs, down to the ants.

Then he knew: "Indeed, I am myself the creation, for I have projected this entire world." Whence he was called Creation. . . ." [7]

Sometimes, as here, the projection of the world is pictured in Brahmanical mythology as voluntary; sometimes, as in the *Kalika Purana,*[8] where the gods spring spontaneously from the yogic contemplation of the demiurge, Brahma, the creation is a succession of surprises even to the creator. In the Icelandic Eddas, it will be recalled, the cosmic hermaphrodite, Ymir, gives off Rime-Giants from his living hands and feet, but is attacked during a later age by the young gods, Wotan, Wili, and We, to be cut up and transformed into the entire theater of the cosmos.[9] Comparably, in the celebrated Babylonian "Epic of Creation," the young god Marduk kills, cuts up, and fashions the universe from the body of the primal chaos monster Tiamat. Ovid, in the first chapter of his *Metamorphoses,* states that a god, in the beginning, brought order out of chaos.[10] And we learn from the ancient Egyptian Memphite theology that Egypt, the universe, and all the gods, came forth from Ptah, "The Great One," "Him-with-the-lovely-face."[11]

In the Indian metaphysical system of the Vedanta, which purports to be a translation of the metaphorical imagery of Brahmanical myths into abstract philosophical terms, the primordial entity out of which the universe proceeds is described as a fusion of Pure Consciousness (Brahman, vidya) and Ignorance (Maya, avidya), where Ignorance (Maya) is compared to the female of the mythological pair, furnishing at once the womb and the substance of creation. By virtue of her obscuring power she occludes the Absolute Brahman, and by virtue of her projecting power she refracts the radiance of that Absolute in the forms of the world mirage, somewhat as a prism breaks the white light of the sun into the seven colors of the rainbow—for, as Goethe has phrased the same concept in his *Faust:* "Am farbigen Abglanz haben wir das Leben." [12] In the fifteenth-century *Vedantasara,* this marriage of Ignorance and Consciousness, Illusion and Truth, Maya and Brahman, is described as at once the efficient and material cause of all things. "Consciousness associated with Ignorance (and the latter possessed of the two powers) is both the efficient cause and the material cause of the universe . . .; just as the spider, when considered from the standpoint of its own self, is the efficient cause of the web, and, when looked upon from the standpoint of its own body, is also the material cause of the web." [13]

Translated into Kantian terms, Ignorance as here interpreted corresponds to the *a priori* forms of sensibility (time and space), which are the inmost and outmost boundaries and the preconditions of all empirical experience: these *a priori* forms occlude the metaphysical realm of absolute reality and project the universe of phenomenality. But what the "true being" of the ultimate reality, dissociated from our modes of experience, might be, we shall never know; for, as the "great Chinaman of Königsberg" phrases it: "Was es für eine Bewandniss mit den Gegenständen an sich und abgesondert von aller dieser Receptivität unserer Sinnlichkeit haben möge, bleibt uns gänzlich unbekannt." [14]

Thus Hovering Hawk, the *Brihadaranyaka Upanishad,* the *Kalika Purana,* the Eddas, the Babylonian "Epic of Creation," Ovid, the Memphite theology, Vedantic philosophy, Kant, and Goethe, through varieties of metaphor, have stated and stated again a single thought— and what would appear to be an easy thought to state, namely: the One, by some sleight of hand or trick of the eye, has become the

Manifold. Yet, instead of stating this thought directly, they have employed allegorical vehicles, now of pictorial, now of abstract character, and, curiously, though each of the vehicles succeeds in conveying at least a hint of the tenor of the message, none actually elucidates it— none really explains, or even directly represents, the mystery of the coming of the Manifold out of the One. And in this respect Kant's formulation is no more satisfactory than Hovering Hawk's.

But the problem, again regarded, is seen to be not susceptible of outright elucidation; for it is a problem of the relationship of a known term (the universe) to an unknowable (its so-called source): that is to say, it is, strictly speaking, a metaphysical, not an empirical problem. Whether such a problem be presented for contemplation in the picture language of the myth or in the abstract of philosophy, it can only be presented, never elucidated. And since it is thus finally ineffable, no single metaphor, no combination of metaphors, can exhaust its implications. The slightest change of standpoint, and the entire conception undergoes kaleidoscopic transformation, as do likewise the correlative vehicles of imagery and communication. The primordial One, for instance, may be represented as masculine (as in the case of Brahma), feminine (as in the World Mother), hermaphrodite (as in the cases of 'I' and Ymir), anthropomorphic (as in most of the above presented examples), theriomorphic (as in the Persian myth of the dismembered World Ox), botanomorphic (as in the Eddic image of the World Ash, Yggdrasil), simply ovoid (as in the stories of the World Egg), geometrical (as in the Tantric yantras), vocal (as in the cases of the Vedic sacred syllable OM and the Kabbalistic Tetragrammaton), or absolutely transcendent (as in the cases of the Buddhistic Void and Kantian Ding an sich). But even the notion of the Oneness of the primordial is finally only a metaphor—referring past itself to an inconceivable term beyond all such pairs of opposites as the One and the Manifold, masculinity and feminity, existence and non-existence.

III

Kant, in his *Prolegomena zu einer jeden künftigen Metaphysik, die als Wissenschaft wird auftreten können*,[15] supplies an extraordinarily simple formula for the proper reading of a metaphysical symbol. What he offers is a four-term analogy (*A* is to *B* as *C* is to *X*), which points not to an incomplete resemblance of two things, but to a complete resemblance of two relationships between quite dissimilar things ("nicht etwa, eine unvollkommene Ähnlichkeit zweier Dinge, sondern eine vollkommene Ähnlichkeit zweier Verhältnisse zwischen ganz unähnlichen Dingen"): not "A somewhat resembles B," but "the relationship of A to B perfectly resembles that of C to X," where X represents a quantity that is not only unknown but absolutely unknowable—which is to say, metaphysical.

Kant demonstrates this formula in two examples:

1. As the promotion of the happiness of the children (A) is related to the parents' love (B), so is the welfare of the human race (C) to that unknown in God (X) which we call God's love.

2. The causality of the highest cause is precisely, in respect to the world, what human reason is in respect to the work of human art.

He then discusses the implication of the second of these examples, as follows: "Herewith the nature of the highest cause itself remains unknown to me; I only compare its known effect (namely, the constitution of the universe) and the rationality of this effect with the known effects of human reason, and therefore I call that highest cause a Reason, without thereby attributing to it as its proper quality, either the thing that I understand by this term in the case of man, or any other thing with which I am familiar."

Mythological, theological, metaphysical analogies, in other words, do not point indirectly to an only partially understood empirical term, but directly to a *relationship between two terms,* the one empirical, the other metaphysical; the latter being, absolutely and forever and from every conceivable human standpoint, unknowable.

If this be so then we shall have misread the series presented in section II, if we suppose that we have fully caught its tenor in the simple statement, "the One, by some sleight of hand, has become the Multiple." Such a statement furnishes, indeed, a terse summary of the vehicular aspect of the analogous metaphors but leaves unclarified their metaphysical tenor; that is to say, it summarizes only the first two terms of an implied four-term analogy, which would read, fully rendered, as follows: "As many (A) proceed from one (B), so does the universe (C) from God (X)." But the term X, it must be insisted, remains absolutely unknown and unknowable. Oneness can no more be a quality of this X than can Love or Reason. Hence, as Kant has declared, it is only by analogy that we speak of Love or Reason as of God.

X remaining unknown, then, the precise nature of its relationship to C must likewise remain unknown. Magic, simple fissure, sexual pro-creation, violent dismemberment, refraction, effusion, and delusion are among the relationships suggested—suggested, not as proper to the mystery of creation itself, but as vehicles to carry the analogy. And there are no end of possible vehicular relationships; no end of possible A terms and related B terms; for instance: as Earth Maker (B^1) is related to the things drawn from his body (A^1); as All-father (B^2) is related to the creatures that he has begotten (A^2); as meditating Brahma (B^3) is related to the visions of his meditation (A^3); as occluded light (B^4) to its refractions (A^4); the spider (B^5) to its web (A^5); etc., etc., etc., *ad infinitum* $(B^n: A^n)$; so is God (X) related to creation (C).

IV

Unless the myths can be understood—or felt—to be true in some such way as this, they lose their force, their magic, their charm for the tender-minded and become mere archaeological curiosities, fit only for some sort of reductive classification. And this, indeed, would appear to be the death that the heroes of the myths themselves most fear. Continually, they are pointing past and through their phenomenal to their universal, transcendental, aspect. "I and my Father in Heaven are One," declares the Christ, for example. And Shri Krishna, in the *Bhagavad Gita,* shows that all the forms of the world are rooted in his metaphysical essence, just as that essence itself, reciprocally, is rooted in all things:

Neither the hosts of gods, nor the great saints, know my origin, for in every way I am the source of all the gods and great saints. He who knows Me, birthless and beginningless, the great Lord of worlds—he, among mortals, is undeluded, he is freed from all sins... I am the Self existing in the heart of all beings; I am the beginning, the middle, and also the end of all beings. Of the gods, I am Vishnu; of luminaries, the radiant sun; ... of bodies of water, I am the ocean; ... of measures, I am time; of beasts, I am the lord of beasts; of birds, I am the lord of birds; ... of fishes, I am the shark; of streams, I am the Ganges; ... I am the gambling of the fraudulent; I am the power of the powerful; I am victory, I am effort, I am the harmony of the harmonious; ... of punishers, I am the scepter; of those who seek to conquer, I am the statesmanship; of things secret, I am silence, and the knowledge of the knowers am I....[16]

Comparably, Killer-of-Enemies, the hero of the Jicarilla Apache tribe of New Mexico, declares, when he is about to depart from the people:

This earth is my body. The sky is my body. The seasons are my body. The water is my body too.... The world is just as big as my body. The world is as large as my word. And the world is as large as my prayers. The seasons are only as great as my body, my words, and my prayer. It is the same with the waters; my body, my words, my prayers are greater than the waters. Whoever believes me, whoever listens to what I say, will have long life. One who doesn't listen, who thinks in some evil way will have a short life. Don't think I am just in the east, south, west, or north. The earth is my body. I am there. I am all over. Don't think I stay only under the earth or up in the sky, or only in the seasons, or on the other side of the waters. These are all my body. It is the truth that the underworld, the sky, the waters, are all my body. I am all over. I have already given you that with which you have to make an offering to me. You have two kinds of pipe and you have the mountain tobacco.[17]

Or once again, in the words of Aeschylus:

> Zeus is air, Zeus is earth, Zeus is heaven;
> Zeus is all things and whatsoever is higher
> than all things.[18]

"We should understand well," said an old Sioux medicine man, Black Elk, the Keeper of the Sacred Pipe, "that all things are the works of the Great Spirit. We should know that He is within all things: the trees, the grasses, the rivers, the mountains, and all the four-legged animals, and the winged peoples; and even more important, we should understand that He is also above all these things and peoples. When we do understand all this deeply in our hearts, then we will fear, and love, and know the great Spirit, and then we will be and act and live as He intends." [19]

Wherever myths still are living symbols, the mythologies are teeming dream worlds of such images. But wherever systematizing theologians have appeared and gained the day (the tough-minded in the gardens of the tender) the figures have become petrified into propositions. Mythology is misread then as direct history or science; symbol becomes fact, metaphor dogma, and the quarrels of the sects arise, each mistaking its own symbolic signs for the ultimate reality—the local vehicle for its timeless, ineffable tenor.

"But he who is called Krishna," said the nineteenth century Indian teacher, Ramakrishna, "is also called Shiva and bears the names Shakti, Jesus, and Allah as well—the one Rama with a thousand names. . . . The substance is one under different names and everyone is seeking the same substance; nothing but climate, temperament, and names vary."[20]

V

And so now we have to ask whether mythology can have originated in the camps of the tough-minded and only later have become sublimated and sophisticated into metaphysical poetry by the broodings of the tender-minded; or whether its course of development must not have been in precisely the opposite direction, from the poetical imagery of the tender-minded to the clumsy misreadings of the ungifted many. Dr. Boas appears to have been a champion of the former view. In his article already referred to, on "The Ethnological Significance of Esoteric Doctrines," he wrote:

It may be said that the exoteric doctrine is the more general ethnic phenomenon, the investigation of which is a necessary foundation for the study of the problems of esoteric teaching. It is, therefore, evident that we must not, in our study of Indian life, seek for the highest form of thought only, which is held by the priest, the chief, the leader. Interesting and attractive as this field of research may be, it is supplementary only to the study of the thoughts, emotional life, and ethical standards of the common people, whose interests center in other fields of thought and of whom the select class forms only a special type.[21]

Dr. R. R. Marett, on the other hand, in his article "Mana," in the *Encyclopaedia Britannica* (14th ed.), appears to take the opposite view. "By the very virtue of his profession," he writes, "the medicine man or the divine king must hold himself apart from those who by status or by choice are *noa*, laymen. The latter may live in brutish contentment; but to the end they lack enlightenment, participating in the highest mysteries at best from without. Every member of a primitive society is in some degree versed in experience of the occult, though for the most part some better qualified person is present to help him through it."

Whether primary or secondary in temporal terms—that is to say, in terms of "Which came first?"—the tender-minded, esoteric view is clearly the one that has played the chief role in the significant shaping of traditions, since it is everywhere the priests and shamans who have maintained and developed the general inheritance of myths and symbols. Dr. Radin, I observe, like Dr. Boas, regards the role of the intellectual as secondary in primitive societies.[22] He gives due recognition to the force of philosophical thought in the shaping of their cultural inheritance, however; and since we cannot go back, even hypothetically, to the moment when a metaphysical insight first dawned in a human mind, to learn whether myths, rituals, and symbols had already given shape to the society in which the first genius lived who thought like a philosopher, perhaps Dr. Radin's balanced recognition of the dialogue of the two types in the continuance and development of primitive traditions is about as far as we can go. "How are we ever to trace properly the development of thought and, more specifically, that of our fundamental philosophical notions," he asks, "if we begin with false premises? If it can be shown that the thinkers among primitive peoples envisage life in philosophical terms, that human experience and the world around them have become subjects for reflection, that these ponderings and searchings have become embodied in literature and ritual, then obviously our customary treatment of cultural history, not to mention that of philosophical speculation, must be completely revised."[23]

For myself, however, I believe that we owe both the imagery and the poetical insights of myth to the genius of the tender-minded; to the tough-minded only their reduction to religion. As far as I know, in the myths themselves the origins of their symbols and cults have always been attributed to individual visionaries—dreamers, shamans, spiritual heroes, prophets, and divine incarnations. Hovering Hawk, for example, when asked how his people made their songs, replied: "We dreamed them. When a man would go away by himself—off into solitude—then he would dream a song."[24]

In any case, the time has certainly come—as Paul Radin told us long ago—for the collectors and classifiers to regard the pretensions of their materials to a deep significance. From every corner of the globe they have gathered images, tales, and myths; yet the science of interpreting the materials can hardly be said to have broached even the first outposts of the psychology of man's approach to and experience of the metaphysical; for up to now the interest of the scholars has been almost exclusively ethnological and historical. They have analyzed from many points of view what may be termed the stylistic variations of the vehicles. Yet, what such stylistic variations signify it will certainly be impossible to say until the tenors of clusters of analogous metaphors have been established and understood. For the bed rock of the science of folklore and myth is not in the wisps and strays of metaphor, but in the ideas to which the metaphors refer.

NOTES

[1] *Pragmatism* (Longmans, Green and Company, New York, 1907), Lecture I, "The Present Dilemma in Philosophy."

[2] *Race, Language and Culture* (The Macmillan Company, New York, 1940): "The Ethnological Significance of Esoteric Doctrines" (1902), p. 314.

[3] Paul Radin, *Primitive Man as Philosopher* (D. Appleton and Company, New York and London, 1927), pp. 247-52.

[4] Boas, *Race, Language and Culture,* p. 156.

[5] *Ibid.,* p. 157.

[6] Natalie Curtis, *The Indians' Book,* pp. 315-16.

[7] *Brihadaranyaka Upanishad* I.iv, 1-5.

[8] See also Heinrich Zimmer, *The King and the Corpse* (Bollingen Series XI, Pantheon Books, New York, 1948; 2d. ed. with index, 1956), pp. 239 ff.

[9] *The Prose Edda,* Gylfaginning IV-VIII.

[10] Ovid, *Metamorphoses* I, 21.

[11] Cf. Henri Frankfort, *Kingship and the Gods* (University of Chicago Press, Chicago, 1948), pp. 25 and *passim;* see Index under "Ptah."

[12] Goethe, *Faust,* Part II, 1.1, last line.

[13] *Vedantasara* 55-56.

[14] Immanuel Kant, *Kritik der reinen Vernunft,* I.8.i.

[15] Immanuel Kant, *Prolegomena zu einer jeden künftigen Metaphysik die als Wissenschaft wird auftreten können,* paragraphs 57-58.

[16] *Bhagavad Gita,* chap. x abridged.

[17] Morris Edward Opler, "Myths and Tales of the Jicarilla Apache Indians," *Memoirs of the American Folklore Society,* XXXI (New York, 1938), 133-34.

[18] Aeschylus, *Heliades,* frag. 70.

[19] Foreword to Joseph Epes Brown, *The Sacred Pipe: Black Elk's Account of the Seven Rites of the Oglala Sioux* (University of Oklahoma Press, 1953), p. xx.

[20] *The Cultural Heritage of India* (Advaita Ashrama, Mayavati, India, 1936), II, 518-19.

[21] Boas, *Race, Language and Culture,* pp. 314-15.

[22] Radin, *Primitive Man as Philosopher,* pp. 211-12.

[23] *Ibid.,* p. 386.

[24] Curtis, *The Indians' Book,* p. 314.

RITE AND CROP IN THE INCA STATE

By John V. Murra

VASSAR COLLEGE

AS ONE READS the sixteenth-century European sources on Inca cere-monialism one becomes aware of a curious and unexpected discrepancy: the ritual crop calendar reported does not reflect either the agricultural realities of that period or the modern patterns of expressing concern over the fate of the crops. The chroniclers of the European invasion and early settlement fill many pages describing peasant- and state-sponsored ceremonies and sacrifices accompanying the planting, irri-gating, weeding, and harvesting of maize; they report little if any ritual connected with the many Andean root crops.

Such a discrepancy in reporting focuses attention on the botanical and ecological differences between the two sets of crops: one a locally domesticated, high-altitude series of frost-resistant tubers, of which the potato is only the most celebrated; the other a warm weather grain, of Pan-American distribution, maize. I hope to show that the chroniclers' discrepancy is also a hint to important cultural and social differences.

At the upper levels of the Andean *Altiplano* the alpine root crops—the potato, the *oca,* the *ulluco*—are the only ones at home. Juzepczuk found one wild species of potato blooming at 16,400 feet (5,000 meters) in an 18-degree frost,[1] and many of the cultivated varieties bear tubers regularly at 14,000 feet. Without them human occupancy in this area would be impossible; "half the Indians do not have any other bread." [2] In pre-Columbian times they were the mountain peas-ant's staple food crops, so common in the diet that time was measured in units equivalent to a potato's boiling time.[3] In the cold, high steppe known as the *puna,* around Lake Titicaca, the chroniclers were sur-prised to find no grains; they report the area's dependence upon alpine crops.[4] This does not condemn this area to culture-historical margi-nality: long before the Tiahuanaco and Inca expansions, the Collao made the most basic contribution to the possibilities of civilizational development in the Andes through the domestication of the llama and the alpaca as well as the tubers.

In our time, LaBarre collected over 220 named varieties of potatoes in the Collao alone; most of the names, after four hundred years of European occupation, show no trace of European influence.[5] While some diploid varieties, which botanists consider the more primitive, stick to the *quišwa,* the protected slopes of Andean valleys, most of the domesticated varieties are true *puna* specimens—hardy, frost-resistant and closely dependent on man. In fact, the most frost-resistant, the bitter *luki,* are sterile triploids which will not grow below 8,200 feet (2,500 meters) and cannot propagate themselves without human intervention.[6] The large number of these hybrid, high-altitude varieties would indicate that throughout most of the history of human occupancy in the Andes, the pressure has been on taming the high *puna;*[7] the steep, lower slopes, which would seem more inviting on first glance, can seriously be utilized only when large-scale public works provide terraces and irrigation.

Elsewhere in the world, root crops cannot usually be kept for any length of time.[8] Some of the Andean varieties keep seven, ten, and twelve months under *puna* conditions, which have a mummifying effect not only on vegetables but also on llama meat and other tissues. In addition, several processes were developed here which took advantage of the climate to increase storing capacity. Most potatoes could be made into *chuñu,* a substance derived from tubers alternately frozen and dried soon after harvest. The slow-ripening, bitter, high-altitude varieties are grown exclusively for *chuñu,* which can be kept for much longer periods than the potatoes themselves. Unfortunately, it has not been possible to determine exactly how long *chuñu* could be kept, though Cobo talks of "many years."[9] The process itself is closely dependent on *puna* conditions: cold nights, warm days, and a dry climate. There is no *chuñu* in Ecuador, which lacks a true *puna,* nor was Sapper able to make it experimentally in Germany.[10]

While potatoes have this neat zonal distribution, maize is found on both highland and coast. This has masked the essentially warm climate character of maize; it requires a good deal of humidity and warmth and has a relatively long growing season. The Andean highlands are dry and given to frequent frosts, and it is only on the *quišwa* slopes, and then not everywhere, that maize can be found as a field crop.

We still do not know when maize reached the highlands; there is no reason to doubt that it was long before the Inca conquest, though it probably was after the domestication of alpine tubers. Even on the coast it was relatively late; archaeology shows that it appears there only after a thousand years of root-crop, bean, and cotton agriculture.[11] According to Carbon 14 dates, corn was introduced *ca.* 900-700 B.C. in the Chicama valley.[12] It is hard to think of it ripening here without irrigation, although archaeologists tell us that artificial watering does not begin till considerably after the introduction of maize. It is possible that corn was first grown in *pukios*, the sunken cultivation plots which use some of the subsurface seepage.[13] This early association, or lack of it, between maize and irrigation on the coast, needs additional investigation.

As one moves from coast to highlands, the situation becomes clear-cut: in the Andes maize and irrigation were closely correlated. Despite the adaptation of certain varieties in the Callejón de Huaylas and the Urubamba valley, maize in the Andes is a handicapped plant: it cannot grow in the hot valley bottoms, where the desert has a way of reaching up to 5,000 and even 8,000 feet in the Apurimac valley, nor can it grow above 9,000 feet in northern Peru and 11,500 feet in the south, since above these altitudes frost can be expected any month of the year[14] with disastrous effects on the corn crop. In both Inca and modern times, irrigation was considered highly desirable wherever maize was grown,[15] even where there was no acute shortage of rainfall.[16] Garcilaso de la Vega tells us that "not a single grain of maize was planted without irrigation," and that given steady watering and the use of fertilizers corn fields "were like a garden."[17] Irrigated fields need no crop rotation, nor must they be left to lie fallow.[18]

There is some indication that the famous Andean terraces so laboriously constructed on the *quišwa* slopes were meant to produce maize. The terrace of Collcamapata, the garden of the Sun, was planted to corn and Garcilaso had seen it worked in his youth. He is also specific when discussing terraces in general: "this is how industrious the Inca were in expanding the lands for maize planting."[19] Pedro Pizarro, an eyewitness to the invasion, claims that "all were planted to maize."[20]

While irrigation is one of the factors making it possible to raise the upper limit of corn cultivation, it was rarely applied to potatoes and other alpine crops. In part, this is due to the topographic characteristics of the *puna*, a high plateau, with the rivers flowing in deep gorges far below it. As Garcilaso puts it, where irrigation did not reach "they

planted grains and vegetables of great importance . . . potatoes, *añus,
oca.*"[21] Cieza de León saw no irrigation in the Collao within twenty
years of the European invasion,[22] and most of our chroniclers similarly
make no mention of alpine crops when discussing irrigation.[23] In
modern times, the geographer Schwalm, who did considerable field
work in the area, reports that irrigation and fertilizers were applied to
maize, while potatoes were grown *de temporal,* depending on rain.[24]
LaBarre tells us that in Bolivia the high-altitude *luki* varieties receive
no irrigation or fertilizers, although some of the others apparently do
get assistance today.[25] Such rainfall cultivation means that lands must
rest between crops; Schwalm reports for Titicaca that a field was cultivated for four years and lay fallow for seven.[26] This matches what
Garcilaso tells us of sixteenth-century conditions: alpine crops had to
be rotated, and lands left fallow, every year or two.[27]

Despite their adaptation and probable domestication in high altitudes,
even these alpine crops failed frequently through hail, frost, and
drought. Polo de Ondegardo, who was for many years an administrator
in the *puna,* claims that three years in five saw crop failures, but it is
unclear which of the crops he is talking about; the chances are he
means maize.[28] Even so, the subsistence margin was quite narrow; in
the nineteenth century Tschudi reports that one good harvest in three
is normal for the *puna.*[29] Cabello Valboa, an independent sixteenth-
century source, indicates that famine stalked the land in years when the
potato crop failed.[30] At such times the peasants ate wild roots or grasses.
Fasting, sacrifices, and scapegoating were all employed in an effort to
mitigate frosts and water shortages.

In such circumstances we note again how little potato or other alpine
crop ritual has been recorded by our chroniclers. As indicated, their
ceremonial calendars deal almost exclusively with maize. In our time
there are elaborate ceremonies to protect and encourage the potato crop;
these have been described in some detail by contemporary observers.[31]
Of course, it could be that such practices are post-Columbian; the
absence of recorded sixteenth-century alpine crop rituals may indicate
lack of anxiety over a local, well-adapted crop.[32] However, this is
unlikely since the ecclesiastic writers and idol-burners like Avila, Arriaga, and others who turned their attention to the Andean peasant
community after 1600, report numerous instances of ritual concern
over highland crops, quite similar to modern ceremonialism. Such

parallels are also present in the unique early report to have broken through the chroniclers' disinterest: only fifteen years after the invasion a priest gave in to the urging of his communicants and allowed a potato planting ceremony in his village. There was music and dancing with digging tools and some competitive behavior between the two moieties. A llama was sacrificed, and selected large seed potatoes were dipped in its blood. At this point the priest intervened and stopped what had apparently gone too far. Soon after Cieza de León came through the area and recorded the priest's story,[33] but it took the chronicler consistently most sensitive to ethnographic detail to get it.

The rarity of potato rituals in our sources may perhaps be due to the fact that the Andean crops, while they may have been staple, were also low status food. In the legends from Huarochiri collected by Avila in the early seventeenth-century, potato-eating was considered evidence of low status; a raggedy beggar was known as Huatyacuri, potato-eater.[34] In another story, recorded by Cabello Valboa, the hero is hiding from his enemies among "very poor herders" who cultivate "potatoes, *ulluco,* other roots and grasses." [35] In describing the *puna*-dwelling Colla, Huamán Poma[36] calls them "Indians of little strength and courage, with large bodies, fat and tallowy because they eat only *chuñu*" and contrasts them with the Chinchaysuyus (northern and coastal Peruvians), "who, although small in stature, are brave, as they are fed on maize and drink maize *chicha,* which gives strength."

Despite such attitudes, from all we can gather potato ceremonialism was early and general in the Andes. Why then should our sources miss it?

There is no likelihood that our chroniclers would ignore maize. Grain eaters themselves, familiarized with corn in the Caribbean and Mexico, they reported early and in detail the Pan-American distribution of this crop. Its absence in any given area was noted.[37] Some of them thought of maize as the Andean staple,[38] which is clearly erroneous given the ecologic picture; as Sauer has pointed out, "nowhere south of Honduras is maize the staple foodstuff it was further north." [39] In most of South America it was grown primarily for beer-making and ceremonial purposes.[40]

The chroniclers communicate the feeling that in the highlands maize was a desirable, special, and even holiday food as compared with potatoes and *chuñu*. Maize was offered at village shrines.[41] The Andean writer Huamán Poma gives us the text of a lament recited by the villagers "during frost or hail if it [the crop] be maize, when no water comes from the sky."[42] At harvest time the corn was brought home amidst great celebration; men and women came singing, begging the maize to last a long time. The villagers drank and ate and sang and for three nights kept vigil over Mama Zara, Mother Maize, a shrine erected in "every house" by wrapping the best cobs in the family's best blankets.[43]

At the village level, corn is also an integral part of life cycle rituals, even if it is not locally grown. At the initiation of a peasant youth, when his hair was ceremonially cut and his name changed, maize, llamas, and cloth were among the gifts offered by his kinfolk.[44] At marriage, the families of the couple exchanged "seeds" along with cloth, spindles, pots, and ornaments.[45] Murúa, the sixteenth-century writer with the best information about women in the Andes, specifies corncobs as gifts to the bride. At death, corn meal was sprinkled around the deceased. On the fifth day, the widow and other survivors would wash at the meeting point of two rivers[46] where sacrifices were also offered after sowing.

The real contrast between the two crops and their associated ceremonials emerges as we move from the peasant community, where both are known though differentially valued, to the state, Inca level.

A considerable effort, both technologic and magic, was made by the state and its various agencies to ensure the propagation and harvest of corn. The Inca state origin myth gives credit to the royal lineage for the introduction of this grain into the Cuzco basin and refers to it as "the seed of the [Paqaritampu] cave" from which the dynasty was supposed to have emerged.[47] Mama Wako, the wife of the first (legendary) king, is reported to have taught the people how to plant it;[48] ever after, a plot near Cuzco called Sausero was devoted to the production of maize to feed the queen's mummy and her retainers. The annual cultivating cycle was ceremonially inaugurated by the king himself, who on the appropriate date during August-September[49] went to Mama Wako's field to break the ground for the planting, with the help of the royal kin. Poma illustrates this inauguration: the king is working, assisted by three relatives to form the usual Inca quartet; an equal number of royal women are kneeling, facing the men, to break the clods, much as peasant women are shown doing it elsewhere. A hunchbacked retainer is bringing refreshments to the royal workers.[50] The king's contribution was accompanied by vigorous singing of digging songs, on a triumphal, military refrain.[51] The national church and its priesthood, whose top hierarchy belonged to the same royal lineage, also had many duties in and about maize agriculture. Each year the gods were asked if crops should be planted that year; "the answer was always affirmative." Priests were assigned to watch the movements of the shadow at a seasonal sundial near Cuzco to determine the right time for plowing, irrigation, or planting[52] and to notify the peasantry of the approaching chore. If one missed the proper moment, the maize crop was in danger.[53] Priests also kept *khipus,* knot records of past seasons showing the succession of wet years and dry.[54] One group of clerics fasted from the moment maize was planted until the shoots were finger high. Cobo reports that the priests gathered at the sundial observatory and "begged the Sun to get there on time."[55] Processions were organized, the participants armed, beating drums, and shouting war cries to scare away drought and frost which threatened the maize more than any other crop.[56] The official state harvest began with the year's royal initiates going to reap on Mama Wako's terrace; then came the fields of the Sun, those of the king and queen. Sacrifices of llamas, fasting, thanksgiving offerings, and requests for future favors were all part of the harvest.[57]

A perceptive observer, Polo noted that there were many more observances and anxious rituals in "advanced" areas, where the population was dense and state exactions numerous, than there were in marginal territories like Chiriguanas or Diaguita.[58] At the symbolic center of the state, at Intiwasi, the House of the Sun, the priests had planted among the living cornstalks golden reproductions, complete with leaves and cobs, to "encourage" the maize.[59]. The temple's harvest was kept in heavy silver storage jars. Such attention and "nursery" care made it possible for the priests to cultivate maize at 12,700 feet, at the shrines near Lake Titicaca. They did not do as much for Andean crops; virtually all references to Cuzco ceremonials are about maize; there are none to potatoes in this context.[60]

The existence and survival of a sociopolitical structure like the Inca state depends technologically on an agriculture capable of producing systematic surpluses beyond the subsistence needs of the peasantry. Under Andean ecologic conditions the anxiety of the state is understandable, and the solution devised is not always ceremonial. The irrigated coast was a major producer of maize and probably supplied an important and worry-free quota to the state warehouses. Unfortunately, we lack many details about the special features of coastal land alienation under Inca rule and the extent of maize-growing corvée.[61] But most everybody has heard of the *mitmaq* colonists resettled by the Inca for what are usually considered security reasons. I have elsewhere presented some evidence that a major function of this population transfer was actually the expansion of the maize-growing area.[62] Bernabé Cobo tells us that wherever populations lived too high up on the *puna* they were "provided" with maize lands on the coast or in the *montaña*. Colonists and their families took up permanent residence in the new maize country. Such transplanted settlements remained within the jurisdiction of their traditional ethnic leader and provided their kin with corn, peppers, fruit, and other tropical produce in exchange for llamas, jerked meat, and *chuñu*.[63]

Terracing of the steep *quišwa* slopes, irrigation works, and coastal fertilizer delivered to the highlands were all similar measures, providing revenues of all kinds but with an emphasis on corn. Potatoes and the other root crops may have produced the necessary surpluses, and *chuñu* may have allowed their storage. However, the keeping qualities of maize are superior to those of *chuñu*; so is its higher prestige. Grains and stockpiling and the redistribution of status are basic state preoccupations everywhere. In the Inca state many factors made stockpiling a major necessity: a growing court made up of ten to twelve royal families and their thousands of retainers, a bureaucratic and ecclesiastic hierarchy, the military needs of the numerous campaigns which expanded the kingdom from Ecuador to Chile within barely a century. And the army also "preferred" maize to other rations.[64]

It is clear that in the minds of those who encouraged the production of corn there were also those other, redistributive considerations: the higher, semi-ceremonial status of maize, inherited from pre-Inca times, would add to the state's eagerness to obtain this commodity in the highlands. An issue of the rarer corn porridge would mean more than a dish of potatoes to a conscript soldier, and a mug of crown corn beer was a morale-building dispensation in a society where patterns of reciprocal generosity were still operative.

It is my contention in this article that in dealing with Inca times in the Andes we find not only two sets of crops grown in different climatic zones, but also actually two systems of agriculture. The staple crop and mainstay of the diet is autochthonous[65] and earlier in the highlands; grown by Andean mountaineers, it consists of plants domesticated locally, laboriously adapted to alpine conditions, grown on fallowed land and dependent on rainfall. The other crop is newer, imported; its culture is of holiday significance and centers around maize, an essentially warm weather crop, clinging to the lower and protected reaches of the highlands, handicapped though highly valued in Andean circumstances.[66]

It is my further contention that tuber cultivation was essentially a subsistence agriculture practiced by lineage (*ayllu*) members who became peasants after the Inca conquest. Maize was undoubtedly known, in a ceremonial way, to the peasant *ayllu* for many hundred of years before the Inca, but its large-scale, economic field cultivation in the highlands becomes feasible only when the emergence of a state makes possible such public works as irrigation, terraces, fertilizer from the faraway coast, and gingerly priestly concern. In Inca times maize was a state crop.

The original under-reporting of Indian highland crop ritual, which prompted this inquiry, has become under the circumstances a hint to cultural and structural matters way beyond the actual rites.

The bulk of sixteenth-century writers associated with few Andeans beyond the royal families, the bureaucracy, the Quisling palace guards. These informants emphasized inevitably the recently obliterated glories of the past, particularly the state machinery; in the process they ignored the Andean village and *ayllu,* and their lack of interest matched that of most of the chroniclers. Only the most inquisitive, men like Cieza and Polo, tried to get beyond this idealized statement of bureaucratic claim. It is only later, when Andean writers begin to comment directly on their own past and when village descriptive material becomes available, that we get a glimpse of what agricultural ritual reveals: not only two systems of agriculture, but significant differences between two ways of life, one of which—the power-wielding Inca state—was in the process of incorporating and transforming the other, a process far from completed when the European invasion arrested its course.

NOTES

NOTE. For an explanation of the bibliographic system followed below, see Appendix to John H. Rowe, "The Origins of Creator Worship among the Incas," pp. 424-25 in this book.

[1] LaBarre, 1947, p. 102.

[2] Cobo [1653], IV.VIII. Acosta reports one variety "accustomed" to coastal heat ([1590], IV.XVII; 1940, p. 270), and Salaman quotes Russian botanists who found wild varieties in the lowlands (1949, p. 34). While potatoes are known on the coast and are reproduced in coastal art (Salaman, 1949, pp. 15, 19; Yacovleff and Herrera, 1934, p. 299), there is no indication that they were a significant element in the food supply or the economy.

[3] Cobo [1653], XII.XXXVII; 1890-93, p. 295.

[4] P. Pizarro [1570], 1844, pp. 279-80; Cieza [1550], I.XCIX; 1862, p. 442; R.G.I., 1881-97, II, 14, 21, 41, 59; Polo [1571], 1916b, p. 63; Garcilaso [1604], V.I, IV; 1943, pp. 226, 233-34.

[5] LaBarre, 1947. For additional details on potato cultivation see Muelle, 1935, pp. 137-39.

[6] Latcham, 1936, pp. 81-82, 167; LaBarre, 1947; Salaman, 1949, pp. 54-55.

[7] On botanical grounds, Troll anticipated the current expansion of Andean chronology. In 1931 he already felt that the chronologies of Uhle and Means did not allow enough time for the development of Andean agriculture. See p. 271.

[8] Troll, 1931, p. 268; Sapper, 1936, p. 64.

[9] The best description of *chuñu*-making will be found in Cobo [1653], IV.VIII. Additional details in Schwalm, 1927, p. 186; Yacovleff and Herrera, 1934, pp. 297-98; Mejia Xesspe, 1931, p. 17; Latcham, 1936, pp. 175-77; LaBarre, 1947, pp. 91, 96 ff; Valcárcel, 1943-48, pp. 85-86; Salaman, 1949, pp. 11, 35; Sauer, 1950, pp. 514-16.

[10] Troll, 1931, p. 268; Sapper, 1936, p. 64.

[11] Bennett and Bird, 1949, pp. 29, 114-20, 126; Strong and Evans, 1952, pp. 22-45, 353.

[12] This is the Cupisnique period when Chavín influences are strong on the north coast (Junius Bird in Bennett, 1948, p. 27). The suggestion has been made, after Tello, that maize, like the feline deity characteristic of this era, is of ultimate *montaña* derivation (Strong and Evans, 1952, p. 237; Valcárcel, 1945, pp. 66-71).

[13] Strong and Evans, 1952, p. 9; Willey, 1953b, pp. 16-17, 367, 394, Plate 54.

[14] James, 1942, p. 150. In the protected bowl of Lake Titicaca, maize was grown in Inca and modern times even above the 12,540 foot level of the lake.

[15] Schwalm, 1927, p. 180; Quelle, 1931, p. 163; Latcham, 1936, pp. 115, 139-40; Cutler, 1946, pp. 265, 281, 286; Sauer, 1950, pp. 490-91.

[16] Schwalm, 1927, p. 176; some varieties of quick-ripening maize, not requiring irrigation, were known even before the European invasion: Poma talks of *cochaca* or *michica sara*, rainfall maize ([1615], 1936, p. 1164; see also pp. 260, 1137-38; Garcilaso, [1604], II.XXII; 1943, p. 112; see also Latcham, 1936, pp. 139-40). Cutler found one modern variety that went from seed to silk in forty-four days (1946, p. 265), and Sauer reminds Mangelsdorf that in the rainy Urubamba valley, east of the Andes, irrigation is not required (1950, p. 493). See also Mejia Xesspe, 1931, pp. 13-14.

[17] Garcilaso [1604], V.I, III; 1943, pp. 226-27, 229-30; Avila [1608], chap. XXXI; 1942, fols. 104r-105r.

[18] B. Ramirez [1597], 1936, p. 38; see also Latcham, 1936, p. 295.

[19] Garcilaso [1604], V.i; 1943, p. 226. See also III.xxv; 1943, p. 183.

[20] P. Pizarro [1570], 1844, pp. 291-92.

[21] Garcilaso [1604], V.i; 1943, p. 226.

[22] Cieza de León [1550], I.xxix; 1862, p. 442.

[23] See the highly revealing legend collected around 1600 by Avila in Huarochiri: Collquiri, a local *waka* connected with maize and irrigation, tried to reward his affinal relatives by emerging as a spring near their fields. But there was too much water; it threatened to flood their fields and all their *oqa* and *kinowa* which had been laid out to dry. Everybody was very mad, shouting "We are used to little water!"; his wife's folk begged him to stop. Collquiri finally stuffed some of his clothes in the spring to stop it (Avila [1608], chap. xxxi; 1942, fols. 103v–104r).

[24] Schwalm, 1927, p. 184. See also C. M. Rick and Edgar Anderson, 1949, p. 406. This may not check with reports that artificial watering was used in pastures (Garcilaso [1604], V.i, xxiv; 1943, pp. 225-26 and 276-77; Poma [1615], 1936, p. 944) which were usually located at potato-growing altitudes. See also Quelle, 1931, p. 165 and Schwalm, 1927, pp. 186-87.

[25] 1947, pp. 94-95, but see also p. 91.

[26] 1927, p. 186. See also Bandelier, 1910, p. 80; McBride, 1921, p. 7.

[27] Garcilaso [1604], V.i; 1943, p. 226.

[28] Polo [1571], 1916b, p. 156; [1561], 1940, p. 168.

[29] Tschudi, 1918, L, 222.

[30] Cabello Valboa [1586], III.v; 1951, p. 223.

[31] See Bandelier, 1910; Paredes, 1936; LaBarre, 1948; Salaman, 1949; Karsten, 1949; Tschopik, 1951.

[32] Malinowski, 1948, pp. 30-31; see also Homans, 1941.

[33] Cieza de León [1550], I.cxvii, ci; 1862, pp. 454, 444.

[34] Avila [1608], chap. v; 1942, fol. 67r.

[35] Cabello Valboa [1586], III.xxxi; 1951, pp. 451-52.

[36] Poma [1615], 1936, p. 336.

[37] Cieza de León [1550], I.lxxxiii; 1862, p. 431; see also Latcham's compilation from R. G. I. reports, 1936, p. 151.

[38] Valverde [1539], 1865, p. 98.

[39] Sauer, 1950, p. 495.

[40] Willey dates the beginning of the "Peruvian co-tradition" from the "advent of maize agriculture" (1953a, p. 374). This may indicate some support for my proposed separation of alpine crops from corn agriculture, which is likely to seem culturally artificial to some, particularly North American archaeologists who have done most of their field work on the coast and who tend to think of maize and potatoes as part of a single "complex of traits" (Bennett, 1948, pp. 2-4).

[41] Avila [1608], chap. xxxi; 1942, fols. 102v, 105r; Arriaga [1621], chaps. ii, iv, ix, xv; 1920, pp. 19, 46, 83, 193.

[42] Poma [1615], 1936, pp. 190-91; see also Arriaga [1621], chap. v; 1920, pp. 52-53; Cobo [1653], XIII.xxi; 1890–93, p. 77.

[43] Polo [1559], 1916a, pp. 20-21; this passage has been frequently copied by our other sources. Poma [1615], 1936, p. 245.

[44] Arriaga [1621], chap. vi; 1920, p. 58.

[45] R.G.I., 1881–97, II, 60; Murúa [1590], III.xxxii; 1946, pp. 240-41.

[46] Poma [1615], 1936, p. 297; Arriaga [1621], chaps. v, vi; 1920, pp. 51, 59-60.

[47] Betanzos [1551], chap. iv; 1880, p. 15; Molina [1575], 1943, pp. 66-67; Cabello Valboa [1586], III.ix, x; 1951, pp. 260, 269-70; Cobo [1653], XII.iii; 1890-93, p. 121; Montesinos [1642], II.i; 1882, p. 6.

[48] Women, and particularly the queens are credited throughout the Inca version of history, with the invention of onerous, new obligations to the state . . .

[49] Garcilaso [1604], V.II; 1943, p. 228; Cobo [1653], XIII.xxvIII; 1890–93, pp. 112-13.

[50] Poma [1615], 1936, pp. 250, 1153, 1156.

[51] Valera or the Jesuita Anonimo [?], 1945, pp. 49-50.

[52] King Pachakuti (see John H. Rowe's article, this collection) is credited by most sources not only with reforming the ceremonial calendar but also with the erection of Intiwatana, the seasonal sundial in Cuzco (Polo, 1940, pp. 131-32; contrast with dating by Cabello Valboa [1586], III.xIx; 1951, p. 136, who assigns it to Pachakuti's son, Thupa). It is likely that such sundials are pre-Inca; see Avila's text which reports that villages in the Huarochiri area had men assigned to watch the sun's shadow and notify the inhabitants. Pachakuti may have set up a *state* observatory which could ignore the different planting times varying according to altitude and ecology. In the Cuzco valley August-September was "right," and it thus assumed the special features of a national event, much as the seeds and tubers from Cuzco enjoyed special prestige in the provinces. Garcilaso [1604], III.xx; 1943, p. 171.

[53] Poma [1615], 1936, p. 1152.

[54] Roman [1575], II.xvI; 1897, p. 68; Murúa [1590], III.xxv; 1946, p. 225.

[55] Cobo [1653], XIII.xIII; 1890–93, p. 19.

[56] Murúa [1590], III.xIx; 1946, p. 210; Poma [1615], 1936, p. 285.

[57] Betanzos [1551], chap. xv; 1880, p. 102; Trimborn's Anonimo [?], 1934, fol. 457v; Román [1575], I.xxI; 1897, pp. 226-30; Poma [1615], 1936, p. 243; Avila [1608], chap. xIII; 1942, fol. 78r.

[58] Polo [1559], 1916a, pp. 36-37.

[59] P. Pizarro [1570], 1844, p. 266; Cieza de León [1550], II.xxvII; 1943, pp. 107-8; *Relación de muchas cosas acaecidas en el Perú* [after 1552], 1943, p. 37; Garcilaso [1604], III.xxIv, VI.II; 1943, I, 179, and II, 9; Cobo [1653], XIII.xII; 1890–93, p. 9. Gold and silver were ceremonial metals in the Andes.

[60] Though it may be significant that Garcilaso de la Vega does mention *kinowa*, the alpine grain, as being reproduced in the golden botanical garden of the Sun ([1604] V.I; 1943, p. 227) which matches his assertion that maize and *kinowa* were grown in the same fields.

[61] This point is discussed in Chapter II, "Land Tenure," of the author's unpublished dissertation, "The Economic Organization of the Inca State," the University of Chicago.

[62] See *ibid.*, Chapter VIII, "From Corvée to Retainership," pp. 288-303.

[63] Cobo [1653], XII.xxIII; 1890–93, pp. 226-27; see also Sancho [1534], 1917, p. 196; Cieza de León [1550], I.cIII–cIv; 1862, pp. 445-46; [1550], II.xvII; 1943, p. 63; P. Pizarro [1570], 1884, p. 280; Morales [?], 1868, p. 467 n. 1; Polo [1571], 1916b, p. 156; [1561] 1940, p. 177; Poma [1615] 1936, p. 852. One wonders if such contacts and trade in corn with the coast did not exist before the Inca conquest; it is likely that the kings took over the institution by expanding the maize-growing colonies and by incorporating the earlier trade within their redistributive apparatus.

[64] Garcilaso [1604], VII.I; 1943, pp. 86-87. In contrast Latcham states that the army ate *cocavi*, a kind of *chuñu*, but indicates no sixteenth-century references (1936, p. 176).

See indications of content in Inca warehouses: of 287 references to storage by 28 chroniclers, 86 deal with food. (The actual percentage is lower, as not every one of these is an independent source; several also list more than one crop. It was nevertheless assumed that the actual naming of a particular crop was significant.) Nine are rather general; of the remaining 77, 29 deal with maize and 7 with maize beer, 36 in all. Seven more list *chuñu*, and one mentions scarcity of maize but abundance of "vegetables and roots." There is only one specific reference to potatoes in the warehouse context. Of course, potatoes as such do not keep well and cannot be stored at the state level, but 7 *chuñu* references to 36 for maize when describing the state warehouses, is suggestive.

⁶⁵ Similar views of this historical relationship, based on different criteria, can be found in Tello, 1920; Valcárcel, 1925a, pp. 74, 90; 1925b, pp. 164-65; 1937–41, I, 27-28, and II, 23, 76-80; 1945, pp. 38, 68; 1943–48, II, 97-101; Trimborn, 1928.

⁶⁶ One should not confuse ceremonial limits, such as achieved by the priests at Titicaca (12,700 feet) with altitude of effective cultivation. The upper limit of any given crop, and particularly maize, is affected by many factors not all of which are ecological; the dryness of the southern Andes raises the upper limit at which annuals will grow; topographic features like protection against winds or good exposure to daylight may have a good deal to do with the effective upper limit, but none of these compare with cultural motivation; if tended like a rose, maize will of course grow anywhere. See Weberbauer, 1945, p. 624; Bowman, 1916, pp. 52-54; Schwalm, 1927, p. 183; Troll, 1931, p. 270.

REFERENCES

Acosta, José de la. 1940. Historia natural y moral de las Indias... [1590]. Mexico.

Arriaga, Pablo José de. 1920. Extirpación de la Idolatria del Perú [1621]. Colección de libros y documentos referentes a la Historia del Perú, Series 2, Vol. 1. Lima.

Avila, Francisco de, ed. 1942. De Priscorum Huarochiriensium Origine et Institutis [1608]. Ed. by Hipólito Galante. Madrid.

Bandelier, A. F. A. 1910. The Islands of Titicaca and Koati. New York.

Bennett, Wendell C., ed. 1948. A Reappraisal of Peruvian Archaeology. Memoir, American Antiquity, Vol. 13, No. 4, Part 2.

Bennett, W. C., and Junius Bird. 1949. Andean Culture History. American Museum of Natural History, Handbook No. 5. New York.

Betanzos, Juan de. 1880. Suma y Narración de los Incas... [1551]. Biblioteca Hispana-Ultramarina, Vol. V. Madrid.

Bowman, Isaiah. 1916. The Andes of Southern Peru. New York.

Cabello Valboa, Miguel. 1951. Miscelánea antártica [1586], una historia del Perú antiguo.... Universidad Nacional Mayor de San Marcos, Facultad de Letras, Instituto de Etnología. Lima.

Cieza de León, Pedro de. 1862. Primera parte de la crónica del Perú... [1550]. Biblioteca de autores españoles, Historiadores primitivos de Indias, Vol. 2. Madrid.

Cobo, Bernabé. 1890–93. Historia del Nuevo Mundo [1653], ed. by Marcos Jiménez de la Espada. Sociedad de Bibliófilos Andaluces. Seville.

Cutler, Hugh C. 1946. "Races of Maize in South America," *Botanical Museum Leaflets,* Harvard University, 12:No. 8:257-91.

Garcilaso de la Vega. 1943. Comentarios Reales [1604], ed. by Angel Rosenblatt. Buenos Aires.

Homans, George C. 1941. "Anxiety and Ritual: The Theories of Malinowski and Radcliffe-Brown," *American Anthropologist,* 43:No. 2:164-72.

James, Preston. 1942. Latin America. New York.

Jiménez de la Espada, Marcos, ed. 1881–97. Relaciones Geográficas des Indias. 4 vols. Madrid.

Karsten, Rafael. 1949. A Totalitarian State of the Past. Societas Scientiarum Fennica, Comentatione Humanarum Litterarum, Vol. 16, No. 1. Helsinki.

LaBarre, Weston. 1947. "Potato Taxonomy among the Aymara Indians of Bolivia," Acta Americana, 6:Nos. 1-2:83-103.

Latcham, Ricardo E. 1936. La Agricultura pre-Colombina en Chile. Santiago, Chile.

McBride, George McC. 1921. The Agricultural Indian Communities of Highland Bolivia. American Geographical Society, Research Series, No. 5. New York.

Malinowski, Bronislaw. 1948. Magic, Science and Religion. Glencoe, Illinois.

Mejia Xesspe, M. Toribio. 1931. "Kausay: Alimentación de los Indios," Wira Kocha, 1:No. 1:9-24.

Molina, Cristóbal de. 1943. Relación de las fábulas y ritos de los Indios [1575], ed. by F. Loayza. Los Pequeños Grandes Libros de Historia Americana, Series I, Vol. 4. Lima.

Montesinos, Fernando de. 1882. Memorias Antiguas Historiales del Perú [1642]. Colección de Libros Españoles Raros y Curiosos, Vol. XVI. Madrid.

Morales, Luis (?) de. 1868. Letter in Colección de Documentos inéditos del Archivo des Indias, ed. by Torres de Mendoza. Madrid. Vol. 7, pp. 467-68.

Muelle, Jorge C. 1935. "Restos hallados en una tumba en Nievería," Revista del Museo Nacional de Lima, 4:No. 1:135-82.

Murra, John V. 1956. "The Economic Organization of the Inca State." (Unpublished Ph. D. dissertation, University of Chicago.)

Murúa, Martin de. 1946. Historia del origen y de la genealogía real de los Incas [1590], ed. by Constantino Bayle. Madrid.

Paredes, Manuel R. 1936. Mitos, Supersticiones y Supervivencias Populares de Bolivia. 2 vols. La Paz.

Pizarro, Pedro. 1844. Relación del Descubrimiento y Conquista de los Reynos del Perú [1570]. Colección de documentos inéditos para la historia de España, Vol. V. Madrid.

Polo de Ondegardo, Juan. 1916a. Errores y Supersticiones; Linaje de los Incas; Ceremonias y Ritos. . . . Colección de Libros y documentos referentes a la Historia del Perú, Series 1, Vols. III-IV. Lima.

———— 1916b. Relación de los fundamentos acerca del notable daño que resulta de no guardar alos Indios sus fueros [1571], Colección de Libros y documentos referentes a la Historia del Perú, Series 1, Vols. III-IV. Lima.

———— 1940. Report to Briviesca de Muñatones [1561], ed. by Carlos Romero. Revista Historica, Vol. XIII. Lima.

Poma de Ayala, Huamán. 1936. Nueva Corónica y Buen Gobierno [1615]. Institut d'Ethnologie. Paris.

Quelle, Otto. 1931. "Künstliche Bewässerung in Süd Amerika," Ibero-Amerikanisches Archiv, 5:No. 2.

Ramirez, Baltasar. 1936. Descriptión del Reyno del Pirú [1591], ed. by H. Trimborn. Quellen zur Kulturgeschichte des präkolumbischen Amerika; Studien zur Kulturkunde, Vol. 3. Stuttgart.

———— 1943. Relación de muchas cosas acaecidas en el Perú [after 1552]. Los Pequeños Grandes Libros de Historia Americana, ed. by F. Loayza. Series I, Vol. IV. Lima.

Rick, C. M., and Edgar Anderson. 1949. "On some Uses of Maize in the Sierra of Ancash," Annals of the Missouri Botanical Gardens, 36:No. 4:405-42.

Román y Zamora, Jerónimo. 1897. Repúblicas de Indias [1575]. Colección de

Libros Raros o curiosos que tratan de America, Vols. XIV-XV. Madrid.

Salaman, Redcliffe N. 1949. The History and Social Influence of the Potato. Cambridge, England.

Sancho de la Hoz, Pedro. 1917. Relación de lo Sucedido en la Conquista [1534]. Colección de Libros y documentos referentes a la Historia del Perú, Series I, Vol. V. Lima.

Sapper, Karl T. 1936. Geographie und Geschichte der Indianischen Landwirtschaft. Hamburg.

Sauer, Carl O. 1950. "Cultivated Plants of South and Central America," in Handbook of South American Indians, VI, 319-45. Bull. 143, Bureau of American Ethnology. Washington, D.C.

Schwalm, H. 1927. "Klima, Besiedlung und Landwirtschaft in den Peru-nord Bolivianischen Anden," Ibero-Amerikanisches Archiv, 2:17-74, 150-96.

Strong, W. Duncan, and Clifford Evans, Jr. 1952. Cultural Stratigraphy in the Virú Valley. Columbia Studies in Archaeology and Ethnology, Vol. IV. New York.

Tello, Julio C. 1920. Introduction to Peruvian translation of C. R. Markham's The Incas of Perú. Lima.

——— 1942. "Origen y Desarollo de las Civilizaciones Prehistoricas Andinas," Papers, 27th Congress of Americanists. Lima.

Trimborn, Hermann. 1928. "Die kultur-historische Stellung der Lamazucht," Anthropos, pp. 656-64.

Trimborn, Anónimo. 1934. "A Letter to the King [?]," with facsimile reproduction. Published by H. Trimborn in Zeitschrift für Ethnologie.

Troll, Karl. 1931-32. "Die geografische Grundlagen der Andinen Kulturen und des Inka-reiches," Ibero-Amerikanisches Archiv, 5:258-94.

Tschopik, Harry, Jr. 1951. The Aymara of Chucuito, Peru: Part I, Magic. Anthropological Papers, American Museum of Natural History, 44:2. New York.

Tschudi, J. J. 1918. Kulturhistorische und sprächliche Beitragungen [1891]. Vienna. Peruvian translation in Colección de Libros y documentos referentes a la Historia del Perú. 2 vols. Lima.

Valcárcel, Luis E. 1925a. De la vida Incaica. Lima.

——— 1925b. Del aillu al imperio. Lima.

——— 1937-41. Mirador Indio: Apuntes para una filosofía de la cultura incaica. Lima.

——— 1945. La Ruta Cultural del Perú. Mexico.

——— 1943-48. Historia de la Cultura Antigua del Perú. 2 vols. Lima.

Valera, Blas (also known as Jesuita Anónimo). 1945. Relación de las Costumbres antiguas [?]. Los Pequeños Grandes Libros de Historia Americana, ed. by F. Loayza. Lima.

Valverde, Vicente. 1865. "Letter to Carlos V [1539]," in Colección de Documentos Inéditos del Archivo de Indias, 3:pp. 92-137. Madrid.

Weberbauer, August. 1945. El Mundo Vegetal de los Andes Peruanos, Lima. Peruvian translation of Die Pflanzenwelt der Peruanischen Anden (1911, Leipzig).

Willey, Gordon R. 1953a. "Archaeological Theories and Interpretations: New World," in Kroeber et al., Anthropology Today, pp. 361-85.

——— 1953b. Prehistoric Settlement Patterns in the Virú Valley. Bulletin, Bureau of American Ethnology. Washington, D.C.

Yacovleff, Eugenio, and F. L. Herrera. 1934. "El Mundo Vegetal de los Antiguos Peruanos," Revista del Museo Nacional de Lima, 3:No. 3:241-322.

THE ORIGINS OF CREATOR WORSHIP AMONG THE INCAS

By *John Howland Rowe*

UNIVERSITY OF CALIFORNIA, BERKELEY

BEFORE the Spanish invasion of 1532 introduced the doctrines of Catholic Christianity in Peru, the Incas worshiped a Supreme Being of their own whom they also regarded as the creator of all things. It has been assumed repeatedly by modern scholars that Creator worship was a traditional feature of native religion in the Andean area which the Incas inherited along with the rest of their culture from immemorial antiquity. The statements made by the Incas themselves when they were questioned by Spanish investigators do not support this assumption. The Incas said that the worship of the Supreme Being was invented by the great Inca conqueror, Pachakuti 'Inka Yupanki (1438–71), as part of a general reform of Inca religion which Pachakuti undertook at the time he organized the Inca imperial administration. This Inca tradition of the origin of Creator worship is consistent with other Inca traditions and is supported by internal evidence in the Inca myth of creation. Furthermore, a search of the surviving evidence for the native religion of the Lake Titicaca basin, where the Incas believed that the creation of mankind took place, reveals no indication that there was a Creator who was regarded as a Supreme Being in that area before the Inca conquest.

The Supreme Being of the Incas was most commonly called Teqzi Wiraqochan, a name which means roughly "fundamental god." He was also called Pachayachachi, "creator of the world." He was regarded as the maker and ruler of the universe, and lesser divinities, including the Sun, were his agents and assistants. He was represented as having human form, but the Incas did not know where he lived. He had no wife or family, although some of the lesser gods were spoken of as his "sons." He was believed to be compassionate and affectionate toward men, and he could be prayed to directly. It was considered appropriate to ask the Supreme Being chiefly for general favor, for peace and safety, for prosperity and the increase of the people, for long life and for victory. Requests for specific help were customarily addressed to the appropriate lesser divinity. The Inca government made regular sacrifices to the Supreme Being for the general welfare of the empire.[1]

In investigating the origins of the worship of this remarkable god it will be convenient to begin by analyzing the Inca myth of creation. Then we shall investigate the names by which the Supreme Being is referred to, and finally we shall see what the Incas themselves had to say about the history of their Creator worship.

The Inca Myth of Creation

In its final form, the Inca myth of creation ran somewhat as follows: Teqzi Wiraqochan, the Creator, made a world in darkness, without sun, moon, or stars. He then decided to make men to inhabit it, and he began by carving some giants in stone to see how they would look. After they were finished the Creator decided that the giants were too big, so he left them in stone and made men of his own size. After a while, the men displeased him, and he turned some to stone and sent a great flood to destroy the rest. He saved three helpers from the flood: T'oqapu Wiraqocha, 'Imaymana Wiraqocha, and Tawapaka Wiraqocha. Then he decided to renew his creation and to begin by furnishing the world with light. He created the sun, the moon, and the stars and caused them to emerge from the Island of Titicaca and mount up into the sky. The moon was created brighter than the sun, but the sun was jealous and threw a handful of ashes in the moon's face just before they went up into the sky.

The Creator established himself at Tiahuanaco and there created birds and beasts and snakes and insects and men. He made the men of clay, modeling and painting them with the style of hair dress they were to use and the clothes they were to wear. He gave them life and then told them to go down under the ground and emerge in the places where he had decided that they should dwell.

During the creation Tawapaka Wiraqocha proved himself to be a trouble maker, doing everything contrary to the Creator's instructions instead of helping. Therefore, the Creator ordered his other two assistants to tie Tawapaka Wiraqocha in a reed boat and cast him into Lake Titicaca. The winds and currents carried the boat to the shore at Chakamarka with such force that it burst through the land, making the Desaguadero River. Tawapaka Wiraqocha was carried down the river, cursing. Later on he came back and pretended to be the Creator, but he was discovered and went away again.

After the creation was complete Teqzi Wiraqochan sent out his two remaining assistants to summon the newly created people out of the ground and to teach them how they should live. He sent 'Imaymana Wiraqocha north along the edge of the *montaña* and T'oqapu Wiraqocha along the coast. The Creator himself set out between them along the line followed by the main Inca road.

Teqzi Wiraqochan found the people at Pucara disobedient, so he turned many of them to stone. Further along at Cacha, in the territory of the Canas, the people came out to stone him when he began to give his instructions. He called down fire from heaven upon them, and the fire consumed the hill on which they stood, making the stones light like pumice. From Cacha he went on to Urcos where he sat on a high hill and summoned the people to come out of the ground. Then he went on by Cuzco and Jauja until he reached the Pacific coast in the neighborhood of Manta. There he was rejoined by his two assistants, bade farewell to the people, and set off across the ocean, walking on the water.[2]

As I pointed out in an earlier study, this creation myth is obviously a late compilation. Many of the key episodes take place in areas, like Tiahuanaco and Manta, which were far distant from Cuzco and unknown to the Incas before the reign of Pachakuti 'Inka Yupanki, the ninth Inca king.[3] Since the episodes are so specifically localized, it seems probable that they represent bits of local mythology selected and combined by the Incas to provide a connected story of the general creation.

This conclusion carries with it the implication that in earlier times the Incas had no creation story of their own and hence no creator of the world. As we shall see, there is other evidence confirming the inference, and it seems to be a sound one. What the Incas did have was a myth which explained their own origin and the origin of a number of their traditional shrines and ceremonies. This origin myth told how the ancestors of the Incas emerged from a cave at a place called Paqaritampu, a few miles southwest of Cuzco, and how they migrated to the Cuzco valley via the sacred hill of Wanakawri.

Almost every village in the Andean area had its own origin story of the same sort as the one the Incas told, describing how the ancestors of the people living there had emerged from some hill, cave, rock, or spring. The places of origin named in these stories were called generically *paqarina* (literally, 'means of origin') and became important local shrines. The diversity of origin myths posed no difficulties as long as the villages were independent politically and in their religion, but it was bound to become a source of concern to any reformer who undertook to construct a comprehensive general theology for the whole area. The later Inca general creation myth provides an ingenious explanation for all of these local origin myths, including the one told by the Incas themselves, and it looks like a deliberate attempt to do so.

The key episodes of the Inca creation story, including the creation of the heavenly bodies and of all living beings, took place in the basin of Lake Titicaca, an area of Aymará rather than Inca speech. The Island of Titicaca, where the sun emerged, is in the lake itself; Tia-huanaco, where living beings were created, is in the territory of the Pacasas; Pucara is in Colla territory; and Cacha in the land of the Canas, as we have already noted. All three of these peoples spoke Aymará dialects in Inca times. These facts suggest the possibility that the Incas might have borrowed the whole idea of a Supreme Being who created all things from Aymará mythology, along with the stories describing the creation itself. Before we can look for any other source for this idea the possibility of an Aymará origin must be dealt with.

The information which survives on ancient Aymará religion is very scanty, but what there is suggests clearly that the Aymará did not believe in a Supreme Being or tell any general creation story. There are a number of points to be considered.

1. Ramos Gavilán gives an account of how the Inca prince, Wayna Qhapaq, attempted to introduce the worship of a new god into the Titicaca basin about 1491–92. Because of the immense local prestige of the wak'a or shrine of Titiqaqa, the attempt was not very successful. The new god was called in Aymará, Yatiri, 'he who knows, or has supernatural power.' After an unsuccessful attempt to establish the cult of the new god on the Island of Titicaca itself, Wayna Qhapaq moved his worship to the small island of Apinguela. This island came to be known as Wilaqota, 'lake of blood.' Ramos Gavilán gives a far-fetched explanation of this name, but the word looks suspiciously like an Aymará loan translation of the Inca word Wiraqocha, a common designation of the Inca Supreme Being. Although *wira* means

'grease' in Inca, while *wila* means 'blood' in Aymará, the correspondence of Inca *r* to Aymará *l* is common enough so that one of these terms might suggest the other. There is no question about the equivalence of the last part of the words, for Inca *qocha* and Aymará *qota* both mean 'lake.' Ramos Gavilán's story apparently reflects an Inca attempt to introduce Creator worship into an area where it was unfamiliar and where the people had other deities with which they were quite satisfied.[4]

2. The figure in Aymará mythology whose deeds the Incas appropriated for their story of the creation by Teqzi Wiraqochan was a god called Thunupa. Bertonio says of him:

These Indians had as god a being whom they called Thunupa of whom they tell innumerable tales, some unworthy not only of a god but of any sensible man, others which have some resemblance to the mysteries of our holy faith. It would be very useful to explain to the Indians the tricks of Thunupa, so that they would see clearly that everything they tell about him is fabulous and be disillusioned.[5]

Bertonio tells us nothing further about Thunupa's powers as a deity, and no other Colonial writer is any more informative. In modern Bolivia, however, Thunupa is worshiped as the Thunder God.[6] His role is an important one, since the Aymará believe that lightning, which is identified with thunder, is the source of magical and curing power.[7] This complex of belief is very likely ancient. The evidence cited does not prove that Thunupa was never worshiped as a creator god by the ancient Aymará, but it certainly does nothing to suggest such a possibility.

3. None of the Aymará words which the lexicographer Bertonio gives as divine titles in ancient times has any reference to creation. He lists *yoqaniha* 'my father,' *huskuriha* 'my generous provider,' and *qamiriha* 'my wealthy one,' identifying them as "terms which they used to worship their idols, Creator, Father, etc."[8] Speaking of the first two of these terms, he says: "They are ancient words with which they designated the giver of life and goods, that is, their idols."[9] Bertonio lists no Aymará title which might be a prototype for the Inca term Pachayachachi, 'Creator of the world.'

4. One of the most curious features of the Inca creation story is that the Creator is said to have caused the sun, moon, and stars to emerge from the Island of Titicaca. The heavenly bodies thus originated

in the same way that the ancestors of the Incas did, by coming out of the ground at a place which later became a shrine. This episode evidently stood alone before the Inca Creator God was inserted into it as an explanation. As Ramos Gavilán says, "The whole basis of [the shrine of] Titiqaqa and its remarkable prestige was the story, believed as fact by the ancients, that after they were without light for some days they saw the sun emerge from the rock there."[10] There is nothing to indicate that the Creator was originally part of this story.

5. The Incas described the creation of living beings, including mankind, as having taken place at Tiahuanaco, also in Aymará territory. There was a special reason why Tiahuanaco was an appropriate place for this event. It was an imposing archaeological site with many stone statues of heroic size. Placing the creation there provided a mythological explanation for both the buildings and the statues. According to this explanation, the buildings had been built for the Creator's use, and the statues represented unsatisfactory models which the Creator had made while deciding on the characteristics of the new human race. There is no positive evidence that the legend of the creation of living beings at Tiahuanaco was of local origin. Cieza de León, the only chronicler who asked such questions at Tiahuanaco itself (in 1549), reports:

I asked the natives in the presence of Juan Vargas, who has the *encomienda* over them, if these buildings had been built in the time of the Incas. They laughed at this question, asserting, as I have said, that the buildings existed before the Incas reigned, but they were unable to say who made them, except that they had heard from their forefathers that what there is to see there appeared suddenly in a single night.[11]

It is a striking feature of Inca and Aymará mythology down to our own time that a prominent place is given to explanations of the origins of prominent archaeological remains, especially statues and burial towers. The Incas were much impressed by the ruins at Tiahuanaco and needed no local tradition to see the place as an appropriate scene for mythological activity.

To sum up the argument about Aymará religion: We have seen that there is no reason to suppose that the Aymará worshipped a Supreme Being in the Inca sense before the Inca conquest. Thunupa, the great hero of Aymará mythology, was probably a thunder god, corresponding to the Inca 'Illap'a. Wayna Qhapaq met with considerable difficulties when he tried to implant the Inca state cult of the Supreme Being at Titiqaqa. There is likewise no indication that the Aymará had a general creation myth, in spite of the fact that several episodes of the Inca story probably had their roots in Aymará traditions. Thunupa seems to have been a kind of miracle-working culture hero. Bertonio's remarks about him, and the fact that he is also confused with the disreputable Tawapaka of the Inca story, suggest that he may have been a trickster-type hero in Aymará mythology.

Although none of the key episodes of the Inca creation myth suggests a source anywhere in the Andean area outside the Titiqaqa basin, there was an area in what is now the Department of Lima where general creation stories were told independent of Inca influence. At Pachacamac on the coast, for example, there was a myth that the universe had been created by a being named Cons who made everything, including mankind, by his breath alone. Later on, his creation was overturned by a local deity whom the Incas called Pachakamaq ('creator of the world'). Pachakamaq turned the people Cons had created into monkeys and banished them to the forest, making room for a new population.[12] A being closely parallel to Cons appears in the mythology of the neighboring province of Huarochirí. His name was Kuniraya, and he was likewise described as the first of all beings and the creator of everything. After the Incas penetrated the area, Kuniraya was explicitly identified with the Inca Creator. Kuniraya was also the protagonist in several trickster-hero stories.[13]

The creation myths of Pachacamac and Huarochirí could not, for chronological reasons, have inspired the Incas to develop their myth of a general creation. The Inca state religion was organized by Pachakuti 'Inka Yupanki, according to Inca traditions, and it was only much later, in the reign of Pachakuti's son, Thupa 'Inka, that the Incas occupied the area in question.[14] The creation myths of Pachacamac and Huarochirí became important to the Incas in later times, after the Inca conquest, precisely because, belonging as they did to an independent tradition, they conflicted at several points with the Inca story. How the Incas attempted to deal with this theological problem, however, is beyond the scope of the present paper.

The evidence of mythology may be summarized as follows. The Inca creation myth is clearly a late compilation, since it locates important episodes in remote places with which the Incas only became familiar in the reign of Pachakuti. Certain of the episodes associated with creation itself, notably the origin of the sun and the story of Tawapaka, were adapted by the Incas from Aymará myths current in the Lake Titiqaqa basin. Other elements, including the ideas of a Supreme Being and a general creation, appear to have been Inca inventions. At any rate, there is no known Aymará precedent for them. There was an area in the Department of Lima where myths of general creation were found, but it was conquered by the Incas too late to have served as a source of inspiration for Inca religious reformers.

The Names of the Creator

The Incas used a variety of titles and descriptive expressions to designate their Supreme Being. The variety of terms used in addressing this deity is best documented in the prayers which are preserved in Inca text. Only twelve prayers addressed to the Supreme Being have come down to us, but they include the following terms of address:

Wiraqochan	respected Wiraqocha
Wiraqochaya	oh Wiraqocha!
teqzi Wiraqochan	fundamental Wiraqocha
qaylla Wiraqochan	nearby Wiraqocha
t'itu Wiraqochan	generous Wiraqocha
wallpaywana Wiraqochan	diligent Wiraqocha
pachach'ulla Wiraqochan	Wiraqocha unique in the world
'ukhuch'ulla Wiraqochan	Wiraqocha unique within
kamaq	creator
kay pacha kamaq	creator of this world
ruraq	maker
runa ruraq	maker of man
churaq	placer, establisher
llut'aq	molder
runa wallpaq	former of man
wallparillaq	skil ful worker
teqzi qhapaq	fundamental king[15]

There are several points of interest in this list. In the first place, nearly half of the terms include the word *wiraqocha*, and this word occurs at least once in every prayer addressed to the Supreme Being. I have not attempted to translate it in the list but will discuss its meaning further on. In the second place, the word *wiraqocha* never occurs unmodified. At the least it has a respectful suffix, *-n* or *-ya*.[16] This usage suggests that *wiraqocha* was considered to be a designation of the class of beings to which the Supreme Being belonged, like our word "god," which we generally capitalize out of respect when applying it to our own deity. In the third place, there are a variety of terms referring to creation but few which emphasize the power of the god prayed to. The Incas seem to have regarded the Supreme Being as, in a sense, above all competition, so that it was not necessary to emphasize his power. Perhaps they felt at the same time that creation was the highest manifestation of power. Finally, there are no terms suggesting fear. The Incas believed very strongly that the gods punished sin, but they did not mention this role in their prayers.

A much shorter list of terms was used by the Incas in talking about the Supreme Being. Only the following were in common use:

Wiraqochan	respected Wiraqocha
Teqzi Wiraqochan	fundamental Wiraqocha
Pachayachachi	creator of the world

The first two of these terms occur also in the prayers; the third does not, although there is no obvious reason why. It should be noted that corresponding forms without the respectful *-n* suffix, i.e., Wiraqocha and Teqzi Wiraqocha, occur in the chronicles written by Spaniards or under heavy Christian influence. The two chroniclers who reflect best the reverence of Inca worshipers, T'itu Kusi Yupanki and Pachacuti, always use the *-n* suffix with the name of the deity.[17]

All of the terms applied to the Supreme Being in these lists are unquestionably Inca words and are transparently descriptive, except for Wiraqocha. The origin and meaning of this word have an important bearing on the problem of the origin of Inca Creator worship. So many mistaken ideas about the term Wiraqocha have found their way into the modern literature that it is high time to establish the facts.[18] These are as follows:

1. *Wiraqocha* is not a borrowing from Aymará but a native Inca word. Bertonio's Aymará dictionary lists it as an Inca word ("it means a wise man, according to the Incas . . .").[19] The episode of the burning of the hill at Cacha in the Inca creation myth took place in Aymará speaking territory, and its protagonist is called Thunupa by the chroniclers who drew on Aymará sources.[20] On the other hand, the ones

who drew their information from Inca sources ascribe the burning of the hill to Wiraqochan the Creator.[21] In other words, in the one case where an Aymará equivalent for Wiraqochan is mentioned, he has another name. Finally, as was pointed out earlier in this paper, when Wayna Qhapaq attempted to introduce the cult of the Creator in the Lake Titiqaqa area the shrine he built was called Wilaqota. This word appears to be an Aymará loan translation of the Inca word *wiraqocha*. If *wiraqocha* were itself an Aymará word, no loan translation would be necessary.

2. The Incas themselves regarded the word *wiraqocha* as unanalyzable. What makes this belief particularly interesting is that, to any outside observer, *wiraqocha* appears to be a complex word made up of two common shorter words: *wira*, 'lard' or 'grease,' and *qocha*, 'body of water, lake.' By the rules of Inca word formation, such a combination should mean 'lake of grease.'[22] This meaning, however, makes no sense in terms of any of the uses to which the word *wiraqocha* was put in historic times. When the Incas were asked its original meaning, they said it meant something like "god."[23] Bertonio's statement, quoted above, that *wiraqocha* "means a wise man, according to the Incas" is not inconsistent with the reports of the other chroniclers, for "wisdom" in both Inca and Aymará meant primarily supernatural power.

3. The word *wiraqocha* was not simply the name of the Creator, but it designated all members of a class of beings. We have already noted that the use of the respectful suffix -*n* with the word *wiraqocha* when it refers to the Creator suggests that there was a class of beings called *wiraqocha*. Further evidence to the same effect is furnished by the Inca myth of creation in which the Creator's three helpers were called T'oqapu Wiraqocha, 'Imaymana Wiraqocha, and Tawapaka Wiraqocha. Other *wiraqochas* are mentioned as attendants of the Creator in one of the Inca prayers preserved by Cristóbal de Molina.[24]

After 1532 the Incas called the Spaniards *wiraqochas*. This usage is significant because it also suggests that the word was considered appropriate to designate individual members of a large class. The new usage was, in fact, an extension of the older one in which *wiraqocha* could mean one of the Creator's assistants. The logical connection is explained in greatest detail by Cieza de León (1550) and Polo de Ondegardo (1561). At the time of the Spanish invasion the Inca

Empire was torn by civil war. A prince named 'Atawallpa had revolted against Waskhar, the ruler in possession, and after some months of fighting 'Atawallpa's generals had captured Waskhar and taken the Inca capital. Thereupon the surviving leaders of Waskhar's party made a great sacrifice to the Creator, begging him to help them in their extremity. Immediately afterwards word came that a small number of strange people had appeared in the northern part of the country and had taken 'Atawallpa prisoner. The partisans of Waskhar concluded that their prayers had been answered, and that the Creator had sent some assistants (*wiraqochas*) to help them.[25] Polo de Ondegardo adds that 'Atawallpa's partisans, who had no reason to be thankful for the arrival of the Spaniards, called the newcomers simply *zunkha-zapa*, 'bearded ones.'

It is possible that the fact that the Spaniards had light skins and wore beards encouraged Waskhar's followers to identify them as wiraqochas. At any rate, several of the chroniclers report that the Creator and his ancient helpers were described as light skinned and bearded, a fact which led some pious Spaniards to identify them as apostolic missionaries.[26]

We conclude from this discussion that *wiraqocha* is an unanalyzable Inca word designating the members of a class of supernatural beings. The greatest member of this class was the Supreme Being, Teqzi Wiraqochan. Not all supernatural beings were called *wiraqocha*, however. One other important class was that of the local divinities, some of them very powerful, called generically *wak'a*. There was some overlap between these classes, for some *wiraqocha* were also *wak'a*.[27]

The History of Creator Worship

We have two methods available to us for reconstructing the religion and mythology of the early Incas. One is to strip away all elements which can be shown to have had a later origin and see what is left. The other is to examine the Inca legends about early times for indications as to what elements were probably present. For example, the two great local divinities (*wak'a*) of Paqaritampu and Wanakawri are so intimately woven into the fabric of the Inca origin myth that it seems very probable that their worship is among the oldest elements of Inca religion. The worship of the sun is evidently ancient also, since the Inca tradition was that the development of Creator worship relegated the sun to second place.[28] There is, as we might expect, no sound evidence for Creator worship in early Inca times.

The name Wiraqocha first appears in the Inca traditions in the reign of Lloq'e Yupanki, the third Inca ruler, who must have flourished about A.D. 1300. Sarmiento de Gamboa and Cabello Balboa say that Lloq'e Yupanki enjoyed friendly relations with Waman Samu, lord of Huaro, and with Pachach'ulla Wiraqocha, a "person" of good judgment and prudence. The Inca ruler asked Pachach'ulla Wiraqocha's advice as to where he should seek a wife.[29] Cieza de León, referring to the same occasion, says that Lloq'e Yupanki consulted an oracle as to where he should seek a wife.[30] When we consider that the name Pachach'ulla Wiraqocha occurs as a divine title in one of the surviving Inca prayers, as noted in the previous section, it becomes evident that the prudent "person" who figures in the Sarmiento de Gamboa-Cabello Balboa version of the story was, in fact, a deity who gave oracles. We can even locate the oracle with a high degree of probability. There was a shrine at Urcos where a being called Wiraqocha was worshipped before the reform of Inca religion by Pachakuti 'Inka Yupanki. Urcos is the next settlement beyond Huaro.

Betanzos has preserved the legend of the origin of the shrine at Urcos in the form in which it was incorporated into the Inca myth of creation:

When the Creator reached a place which is now called the tampu of Urcos, six leagues from the city of Cuzco, he climbed a high hill and sat down on the summit of it, whence they say that he ordered the natives who live there today to emerge from the hill. Because this wiraqocha had sat down there, they built him a rich and ornate wak'a in which the builders placed a bench of fine gold, and on the bench was seated the statue of this wiraqocha. The statue was of fine gold, and in the division of the wealth of Cuzco which the Christians made when they took the town it was valued at sixteen to eighteen thousand pesos.[31]

The high hill referred to by Betanzos is still known locally as Wiraqochan. It is a very imposing hill, standing in an isolated position with the towns of Urcos and Huaro on one side of it and the Vilcanota River on the other.

Further information about the shrine at Urcos is provided by Cristóbal de Molina:

Hatun Wiraqocha ("great wiraqocha") is in the wak'a of Urcos. In this shrine there were stone images of an eagle and a falcon at the door of the wak'a, and inside there was a statue of a man with a white tunic reaching to his feet and hair to the waist. The images of the eagle and the falcon chirped every day at noon as if they were alive. The attendants said that they chirped because the wiraqocha was hungry, and they brought food and burned it.[32]

It is clear from these accounts that the shrine at Urcos was dedicated to the worship of a *wiraqocha* who was also a local divinity or *wak'a*. The mythological reason for his cult was that the *wiraqocha* of Urcos had brought forth from a hill the ancestors of the people of that place. He was thus a creator in a local sense. Later on, when the Inca myth of a general creation was put together, the *wiraqocha* of Urcos was identified with the Supreme Being.

No myths dealing with other ancient *wiraqochas* are preserved, so we cannot tell whether local creation activities were characteristic of other supernatural beings of this type. It seems likely that they were, however, because all the *wiraqochas* who figure in Inca mythology had something to do with creation. Another interesting question is whether other *wiraqochas* were generally worshiped. Again the surviving evidence does not permit an answer.

The word *wiraqocha* next appears in Inca history early in the fifteenth century as the name of the eighth ruler, Wiraqocha 'Inka. Sarmiento de Gamboa explains the origin of this name as follows:

Once, when this Hatun Thupa 'Inka [the prince's original name] was at Urcos, a town which is a little over five leagues distant from Cuzco to the south-south-east where the magnificent wak'a of Teqzi Wiraqocha was located, Wiraqocha appeared to him at night. In the morning he assembled his nobles and among them a certain Wallpa Rimachi, his governor. He told them how Wiraqocha had appeared to him the previous night and had announced that great good fortune awaited him and his descendants. In felicitating him upon the vision, Wallpa Rimachi saluted him, saying "Oh Wiraqocha 'Inka!" The rest followed him and made much of this name Wiraqocha; he kept it all the rest of his life. Others say that [the prince] took this name because, when he was armed knight [i.e., went through the men's initiation ceremony] and had his ears pierced, he took Teqzi Wiraqocha as the sponsor of his manhood.[33]

Apart from the fact that the first of the explanations which Sarmiento de Gamboa gives seems inherently more likely, the story of Wiraqocha 'Inka's vision is confirmed in general terms by Betanzos and Acosta.[34] Cieza de León's Inca informant told him that Wiraqocha was simply the eighth ruler's name.[35] The other chroniclers do not discuss the name at all.

It is worth emphasizing that this second occurrence of the word *wiraqocha* in Inca historical traditions again associates it with the *wak'a* of Urcos. The adoption of the name by the Inca ruler again suggests that it was not considered the exclusive designation of a single deity.

Wiraqocha 'Inka intended to leave his kingdom to a son named 'Inka 'Urqon, but during the crisis accompanying the Chanca invasion about 1438, the government was usurped by another son, Kusi 'Inka Yupanki, who distinguished himself in the last ditch defense of Cuzco. This new ruler was the real founder of Inca imperial power and was the organizer of the Inca state as well as a successful conqueror. He later took the well-deserved title of Pachakuti ('cataclysm') by which he is best known to history; we have called him Pachakuti 'Inka Yupanki earlier in this paper.

Before the crucial battle with the Chancas, Pachakuti had a vision in which he saw before him a resplendent figure of a man with snakes twined about his arms and a puma on his back. The vision told Pachakuti to fear not, that he would conquer many nations.[36] Molina identifies the figure in the vision as the sun, and Casas supports the identification.[37] On the other hand, Polo de Ondegardo says that it was the Creator who appeared to Pachakuti.[38] A key to the disagreement is provided by Betanzos, the earliest chronicler to mention the incident. Betanzos says first that Pachakuti prayed to Wiraqocha Pachayachachi, the Creator, and that the Creator appeared to him. Several chapters further on, however, he says that the figure in the vision did not identify himself, but that Pachakuti took him to be the sun because the figure addressed the Inca prince as "my son."[39] Sarmiento corroborates Betanzos' second version by saying cautiously that the vision was "like the sun."[40] In line with the evidence to be cited next—that Creator worship was not instituted until after the Chanca war—I suggest that the figure in Pachakuti's vision did not identify himself; that Pachakuti supposed at the time that it was the sun who had appeared to him, and that the story that it was the Creator arose later when people who were accustomed to pray to the Creator rationalized the whole episode.

Some years after the Chanca war, when Pachakuti had conquered all the territory around Cuzco and had turned to the problem of organizing an imperial administration for it, he decided that a state religion was also needed. To provide this religion he regulated existing cults, built new temples, established public ceremonies, and decreed regular sacrifices. The project raised theological problems, however, and Pachakuti gave due thought to them. As Molina tells it:

This Inca was so intelligent that he set himself to consider the respect and veneration which his ancestors accorded the sun, worshipping it as god. Yet the sun has no rest or relaxation but goes around the world every day. He discussed the matter with the members of his council, arguing that it was not possible that the sun was the god who created all things, because, if it were, a small cloud passing in front of it would not be sufficient to prevent its radiance from giving light. Furthermore, if it were the Creator of all things some day it would rest and give light to the whole world from one place, commanding whatever it wished. Hence, it was not possible; rather, there was another being who ruled the sun and gave it orders. This being was the Pachayachachi, which means Creator. On the basis of this conclusion and decision he gave orders for the construction of the temple buildings of Kiswarkancha which is above the houses of Diego Ortíz de Guzmán, going toward the main square of Cuzco where Hernán López de Segovia now lives. There he set up a golden statue of the Creator the size of a ten year old boy. It was the figure of a man standing with his right arm raised, the hand almost closed, and the thumb and index fingers raised in the gesture of a person giving commands.[41]

Essentially the same story of Pachakuti's theological argument is told by Cabello Balboa, Acosta, and Cobo. Cobo's account is taken from Molina, and there is a possibility that Cabello Balboa's may be also, but Acosta's is probably independent.[42]

There is no reason to question the general accuracy of Molina's report, though details of wording might have been modified in the transmission of the story over a period of more than a century by oral tradition. The Inca myth of creation is so obviously late that it provides strong evidence for a theological revolution not earlier than the reign of Pachakuti. In fact, if we did not have the story of Pachakuti's theological discussion, we would still have had to infer that some argument like it had been put forward at Pachakuti's court.

Pachakuti's argument becomes more intelligible if we remember that Inca mythology, and indeed Andean mythology in general, is primarily concerned with explaining origins. In terms of this interest in origins, the most satisfactory explanation of the present day movement of the sun is an account of why it began to move that way in the first place. It would not be enough to say that there exists a Supreme Being who orders the sun across the sky every day; the Supreme Being must also be the Creator who put the sun there in the beginning. A similar train of thought has been followed in much Christian philosophy.

Pachakuti's theological argument reflects the concept of imperial power he was developing. A being who is bound by rules to keep a regular schedule is the servant of the being who makes the rules. Only a being who is free to be capricious, yet able to make rules for others, has real power. Furthermore, such a being will demand respect and will not permit aimless clouds to interfere with its business. The argument tells us much, not only about Pachakuti's views on religion, but also about his views on his own position in the new Inca state.

Pachakuti's argument, as reported by Molina, led him to postulate the existence of a Supreme Being who was also a Creator (Pachaya-chachi). This much was purely logical and demanded no antecedents other than a traditional worship of the sun. There was nothing in the argument, however, which required that the Creator be visualized in human form or that he be called Wiraqocha. Nevertheless, both of these elements became important features of Inca Creator worship. These elements must have had their origin in another argument, not preserved, by which one of the class of supernatural beings called *wiraqocha* was identified with the newly postulated Creator God. The fact that *wiraqochas* were associated with creation activities would have made such an identification easier.

The particular *wiraqocha* who became identified with Pachakuti's new Supreme Being must have been the deity of Urcos, respected by the Incas for generations as a source of helpful advice and closely associated with the fortunes of their royal house. There is no other possible candidate.

Inca Creator worship began, as the Incas said it did, with the great religious reforms instituted by Pachakuti 'Inka Yupanki. The religious reforms were a necessary part of the effort made by the great organizer to provide new and coherent central institutions which might integrate the diverse peoples over whom Pachakuti had recently extended Inca rule. The new cult of the Creator was not simply a copy of something which the Incas had found among their new subjects. The fundamental idea was original and daring. Secondary details were then added to it from a variety of traditional sources. The name Wiraqocha and the idea that the Creator had human form came from an old Inca belief in a class of supernatural beings who had something to do with local origins; the particular one who was important enough to suggest this identification was the local deity of Urcos. Several of the episodes in the new creation myth were derived from local origin legends, as for example the origin of the sun on the Island of Titicaca and the burning of the hill at Cacha. The combination of elements in the new myth was also highly original, however, because it provided an ingenious rationalization for all the diverse origin tales of the common Andean type in which the ancestors were said to have emerged from the ground somewhere in the territory where their descendants lived. Our story epitomizes the position of the Incas in the Andean cultural tradition, heirs of centuries of earlier efforts which their best minds reinterpreted with creative originality to meet the new conditions created by their successful conquests.

APPENDIX

PROBLEMS RELATING TO THE SOURCES

Many of the most important chronicles of ancient Peru were not published at the time they were written but remained in manuscript until modern times. The date of publication of the text, therefore, bears no necessary relationship to the date of the information it contains. In order to clarify the chronological relationships, I have added the date of composition in brackets, following the author's name or the title of his work, at each reference in the notes and bibliography. When more than one chronicler is cited in the same note, the references are arranged chronologically by date of composition.

In two cases the dates of composition given in this paper differ from those usually found in studies of the chronicles. The dates [1561-66] given for Casas' *Apologética historia* refer only to the period when the section dealing with the Incas was written. Other parts of this great work are probably older. The date of [1548] assigned to the chronicle of Gutiérrez de Santa Clara is likewise the date when the section on Inca history and customs was written. The author went on for decades making additions and corrections to some of the other sections. The evidence for a date as early as 1548 is a statement in the section on the Incas which mentions Pawllu Thupa as still living; this collaborationist leader died in 1549.

I have cited two chronicles by title instead of author to indicate that the author's name is not known. Both of these chronicles have been cited by an author's name in most earlier works, including my own. However, further study indicates that the attributions were premature. The *Relación de muchas cosas acaecidas en el Perú* has usually been attributed to a certain Cristóbal de Molina ("of Santiago"), a contemporary of the Cristóbal de Molina who wrote on Inca religion. Raúl Porras Barrenechea has shown that there is somewhat greater likelihood that the chronicle was written by Bartolomé de Segovia, but the evidence is not conclusive (see his note on the subject following the 1943 edition of the *Relación*, pp. 91-92). The Inca chronicle which begins with the words *Runa yn.° ñiscap machoncuna* has been attributed by both the scholars who have edited it to Father Francisco de Avila; it is consequently usually cited under Avila's name. However, nothing is more certain than that Avila is not the author of the Inca text. The Inca text was written by some literate native of Huarochirí, probably at Avila's request. Avila intended to translate it into Spanish, but he never got beyond chapter 8.

Although in most cases I found it sufficient to cite the best modern edition of a chronicler, it proved necessary in three cases to cite the original manuscript as well. In these three cases the published texts have so many errors and injudicious emendations that they are misleading in a study in which the exact spelling of Inca words may be crucial. The original manuscripts are cited on the basis of microfilm copies made for me in Spain through the good offices of the distinguished Colombian historian, Juan Friede. It is a pleasure to express my thanks to Señor Friede and to the authorities of the Biblioteca Nacional in Madrid who were kind enough to authorize the copying.

The worst of the published texts is unquestionably that of the chronicle of Cristóbal de Molina—the most important single source on Inca religion and mythology. A critical edition of this work is very much to be desired.

All translations are my own. They are as literal as possible, except that long, involved sentences are broken up, and the subject is repeated where necessary for clarity.

NOTES

[1] Rowe, 1946, pp. 293-316; 1953, esp. p. 95.

[2] The Inca creation myth is told most systematically by Betanzos [1551], chap. i-ii; 1880, pp. 1-8; and Sarmiento de Gamboa [1572], chap. 6-7; 1947, pp. 100-110. Cieza de León gives only the episodes of the creation of the sun and of the Creator's journey through the land (Cieza de León [1550], part 2, chap. v; 1880, pp. 5-12). Molina recounts most of the episodes of the story individually, rather than as parts of a single narrative (Molina [1575], MS, f. 2 vta-4 vta; 1943, pp. 7-15). The episode of Tawapaka Wiraqocha is referred to by Sarmiento de Gamboa, but told in detail only by Casas [1561-66], chap. cxxvi; 1909, p. 334. Calancha gives a summary of the whole myth, taken from a lost report by Juan de Balboa written before 1586 (Calancha [1633], book II, chap. x; 1639, pp. 366-67). Cobo incorporates the whole of Molina's account in his discussion of Inca

426   JOHN HOWLAND ROWE

creation myths, together with material from other sources (Cobo [1653], book xiii, chap. ii; 1956, Vol. 2, pp. 149-53).

3 Rowe, 1946, pp. 315-16.

4 Ramos Gavilán, part 1, chap. xxx; 1621, pp. 151-55.

5 Bertonio [1612], 1879, part 1, p. 192; cf. part 2, p. 99.

6 La Barre, 1948, p. 170.

7 Tschopik, 1946, pp. 560, 564.

8 Bertonio [1612], 1879, part 2, p. 396.

9 *Ibid.*, p. 168; *see also* p. 35 and part 1, p. 149.

10 Ramos Gavilán, part 1, chap. xix; 1621, p. 98.

11 Cieza de León [1550], part 1, chap. cv; 1922, p. 327.

12 Gutiérrez de Santa Clara [1548], book iii, chap. lvi; 1904-29, Vol. 3, 1905, pp. 493-95. Cf. López de Gómara [1552], chap. cxxi; 1554, ff. 159-59 vta. López de Gómara's account is taken from that of Gutiérrez de Santa Clara.

13 *Runa yn.° ñiscap machoncuna* [1608], chaps. 1, 2, 14, 15; cf. 1942, pp. 311-17; 363-67.

14 Cieza de León [1550], part 2, chap. lviii; 1880, p. 220; Cabello Balboa [1586], part 3, chap. 18; 1951, p. 338; Calancha [1633], book i, chap. xxxvii; 1639, p. 234.

15 Nine Inca prayers to the Creator are preserved by Cristóbal de Molina [1575] (see Rowe, 1953); two by Pachacuti [early 17th century], MS, ff. 140 vta. and 147 vta.; 1879, pp. 248 and 265; and one by Guaman Poma de Ayala [1615], 1936, p. 54 [54].

16 The use of a suffix -n to indicate respect is a little known feature of Classic Inca morphology. It occurs in examples in the grammar of Domingo de Santo Tomás [1555]—for example, *yayan* 'sir,' from *yaya* 'father,' f. 6 (1951, p. 27). It is probably the same suffix described by González Holguín, 1607, f. 108.

17 T'itu Kusi Yupanki [1570], 1916, pp. 13, 30, etc.; Pachacuti [early 17th century], 1879, p. 236.

18 The modern literature is summarized by Lehmann-Nitsche, 1928, pp. 85-103. It contains nothing of any real value.

19 Bertonio [1612], 1879, part 1, p. 226.

20 Pachacuti [early 17th century], MS, f. 135 vta.; 1879, p. 237; Ramos Gavilán, part 1, chap. viii; 1621, p. 34.

21 Cieza de León [1550], part 2, chap. v; 1880, pp. 8-11; Betanzos [1551], chap. ii; 1880, pp. 5-7; Sarmiento de Gamboa [1572], chap. 7; 1947, pp. 108-9.

22 There is a good discussion of this point in Garcilaso de la Vega [1604], part 1, book v, chap. xxi; 1723, p. 158.

23 Betanzos [1551], chap. xvi; 1880, p. 114; Cabello Balboa [1586], part 3, chap. 14; 1951, p. 296; Garcilaso de la Vega [1604], part 1, book v, chap. xxi; 1723, p. 158 quoting Blas Valera, *Historia occidentalis* [1596].

24 See Rowe, 1953, p. 88 (prayer 3).

25 Cieza de León [1550], part 2, chap. v; 1880, pp. 10-12; Polo de Ondegardo [1561], 1940, p. 154.

26 *Relación de muchas cosas acaecidas en el Perú* [after 1552], 1943, p. 32; Cabello Balboa [1586], part 3, chap. 14; 1951, p. 297; Pachacuti [early 17th century], MS, f. 134 vta.; 1879, p. 236; Cobo [1653], book xii, chap. xix; 1956, Vol. 2, p. 99; cf. Cieza de León [1550], part 1, chap. lxxxvii and cv; 1922, pp. 283-84 and 327.

27 The Inca prayer preserved by Molina which gives a list of various *wiraqochas* is entitled "A prayer to all the *wak'a*" (Rowe, 1953, p. 88, prayer 3). The *wiraqocha* of Urcos, discussed in the following section, was also a *wak'a*.

[28] See, further on in this section, the account of the theological argument dvanced by Pachakuti 'Inka Yupanki.

[29] Sarmiento de Gamboa [1572], chap. 16; 1947, p. 137; Cabello Balboa [1586], art 3, chap. 12; 1951, p. 283.

[30] Cieza de León [1550], part 2, chap. xxxii; 1880, p. 129.

[31] Betanzos [1551], chap. ii; 1880, pp. 7-8.

[32] Molina [1575], MS, f. 16; 1943, pp. 39-40.

[33] Sarmiento de Gamboa [1572], chap. 24; 1947, pp. 156-57.

[34] Betanzos [1551], chap. v; 1880, pp. 18-19; Acosta [1590], book 6, chap. 20; 940, p. 492.

[35] Cieza de León [1550], chap. xxxviii; 1880, p. 146.

[36] Molina [1575], 1943, pp. 20-21.

[37] Casas [1561-66], chap. ccl; 1909, p. 656.

[38] Polo de Ondegardo [1561], 1940, pp. 153-54. Acosta's account of this incident s taken from Polo de Ondegardo; Acosta [1590], book 6, chap. 21; 1940, pp. 93-94.

[39] Betanzos [1551], chaps. viii, xi; 1880, pp. 35-36 and pp. 64-65.

[40] Sarmiento de Gamboa [1572], chap. 27; 1947, pp. 166-67.

[41] Molina [1575], MS, f. 6-6 vta.; 1943, p. 19. The Inca gesture of command ppears frequently in the illustrations of the manuscript of Guaman Poma de Ayala [1615], 1936, pp. 261 [263], 398 [400] and passim.

[42] Cabello Balboa [1586], part 3, chap. 15; 1951, pp. 307-11; Acosta [1590], ook 5, chap. 5; 1940, p. 361; Cobo [1653], book xii, chap. xii; 1956, Vol. 2, p. 78-79.

REFERENCES

Acosta, José de la. 1940. Historia natural y moral de las Indias . . . [1590], edición preparada por Edmundo O'Gorman. Fondo de Cultura Económica, Mexico.

Bertonio, Ludovico. 1879. Vocabulario de la lengua Aymara [1612]. Publicado de nuevo por Julio Platzmann. Edición facsimilaria Leipzig. 2 vols.

Betanzos, Juan de. 1880. Suma y narración de los Incas . . . [1551]. Publícala Márcos Jiménez de la Espada. Biblioteca Hispano-Ultramarina, Tomo V. Imprenta de Manuel G. Hernández, Madrid.

Cabello Balboa, Miguel. 1951. Miscelánea antártica [1586]; una historia del Perú antiguo, con prólogo, notas e índices a cargo del Instituto de Etnología (Seminario de Historia del Peru, Incas). Universidad Nacional Mayor de San Marcos, Facultad de Letras, Instituto de Etnología, Lima.

Calancha, Antonio de la. 1639. Coronica moralizada del orden de San Avgvstin en el Perv, con svcesos egenplares en esta monarqvia [1633]. Pedro Lacavalleria, Barcelona.

Casas, Bartolomé de las. 1909. Apologética historia de las Indias [1561-66], in Historiadores de Indias, por M. Serrano y Sanz, Tomo I. Nueva Biblioteca de Autores Españoles, Tomo 13. Bailly-Baillière é Hijos, Editores, Madrid.

Cieza de León, Pedro de. 1880. Segunda parte de la crónica del Perú, que trata del señorío de los Incas Yupanquis y de sus grandes hechos y gobernación [1550]. La publica Márcos Jiménez de la Espada. Biblioteca Hispano-Ultramarina, Tomo V. Imprenta de Manuel Ginés Hernández, Madrid.

428   JOHN HOWLAND ROWE

———— 1922. La crónica del Perú [primera parte. 1550]. Los Grandes Viaje Clásicos, No. 24. Calpe, Madrid.

Cobo, Bernabé. 1956. Historia del Nuevo Mundo [1653], in *Obras del P. Bernab Cobo de la Compañía de Jesús*. Estudio preliminar y edición del P. Francisc Mateos. Biblioteca de Autores Españoles (continuación), Tomos 91-92. Edicione Atlas, Madrid. 2 vols.

Domingo de Santo Tomás. 1951. Grammatica o arte de la lengua general de la indios de los reynos del Peru [1555]. Edición facsimilar publicada, con u: prólogo, por Raúl Porras Barrenechea. Ediciones del Instituto de Historia de 1 Facultad de Letras en el IV Centenario de la Universidad Nacional Mayor d San Marcos, No. I. Lima.

Garcilaso de la Vega ("El Inca"). 1723. Primera parte de los commentario reales . . . [1604]. Segvnda impresion, enmendada . . . . En la Oficina Real, á costa de Nicolás Rodriguez Franco, Impresor de Libros, Madrid.

González Holguín, Diego. 1607. Gramatica y arte nueva de la lengva genera de todo el Peru, llamada lengua Qqichua, o lengua del Inca. Francisco del Cantc Lima.

Guaman Poma de Ayala, Felipe. 1936. Nueva corónica y buen gobierno (code péruvien illustré) [1615]. Université de Paris, Travaux et Mémoires de l'Institu d'Ethnologie, XXIII. Paris.

Gutiérrez de Santa Clara, Pedro. 1904–29. Historia de las guerras civiles del Per (1544–1548) y de otros sucesos de las Indias [1548]. Colección de Libros Documentos referentes a la Historia de América, Tomos II, III, IV, X, XX XXI. Librería General de Victoriano Suárez, Madrid. 6 vols.

LaBarre, Weston. 1948. The Aymara Indians of the Lake Titicaca Plateau Bolivia. Memoirs of the American Anthropological Association, No. 68 Menasha, Wisconsin.

Lehmann-Nitsche, Robert. 1928. "Coricancha; el Templo del Sol en el Cuzco las imágenes de su altar mayor," *Revista del Museo de La Plata,* 31:1-260.

López de Gómara, Francisco. 1554. La historia general de las Indias . . . [1552 Juan Steelsio, Anvers.

Molina, Cristóbal de. [1575]. Relación de las fábulas i ritos de los Ingas. Biblio teca Nacional, Madrid, MS3169, ff. 2-36.

———— 1943. Fábulas y ritos de los Incas. Anotaciones y brevísimos comentario por Francisco A. Loayza. Los Pequeños Grandes Libros de Historia Americana Serie I, Tomo IV, second paging, pp. 1-84. Lib. e Imp. D. Miranda, Lima.

Pachacuti, Juan de Santa Cruz. Relacion de antiguedades deste reyno del Pirι [early 17th century]. Biblioteca Nacional, Madrid, MS3169, ff. 131-74.

———— 1879. Relacion de antigüedades deste reyno del Pirú, ed. by Márco Jiménez de la Espada, in *Tres relaciones de antigüedades peruanas*, pp. 229-328 Ministerio de Fomento, Madrid.

Polo de Ondegardo, Juan. 1940. "Informe del Licenciado Juan Polo de Ondegard al Licenciado Briviesca de Muñatones sobre la perpetuidad de las encomienda en el Perú [1561]," *Revista Histórica,* 13:125-96. Lima.

Ramos Gavilán, Alonso. 1621. Historia del celebre santvario de Nvestra Señor de Copacabana, y sus milagros, é inuencion de la Cruz de Carabuco. Geronym de Contreras, Lima.

Relación de muchas cosas acaecidas en el Perú. 1943. Relación de muchas cosa acaecidas en el Perú en suma, para entender a la letra la manera que se tuv en la conquista y población de estos reinos . . . [after 1552]. Anotaciones brevísimos comentarios por Francisco A. Loayza. Los Pequeños Grandes Libro de Historia Americana, Serie I, Tomo IV, first paging, pp. 1-78. Lib. e Imp. D. Miranda, Lima.

Rowe, John Howland. 1946. "Inca Culture at the Time of the Spanish Conquest," in *Handbook of South American Indians*. Bureau of American Ethnology Bulletin 143, Vol. 2, pp. 183-330. Washington.

——— 1953. "Eleven Inca Prayers from the Zithuwa Ritual," *Kroeber Anthropological Society Papers*, Nos. 8-9:82-99. Berkeley.

Runa yn.° ñiscap machoncuna ñaupa pacha quillcacta yachanman carca . . . [1608]. Biblioteca Nacional, Madrid, MS 3169, ff. 64-114.

——— 1942. Francisci de Avila, De priscorum Huaruchiriensium origine et institutis, ad fidem mspti n.° 3169 Bibliothecae Nationalis Matritensis edidit Hippolytus Galante. Consejo Superior de Investigaciones Científicas, Instituto Gonzalo Fernández de Oviedo, Madrid.

Sarmiento de Gamboa, Pedro. 1947. Historia de los Incas [1572]. Tercera edición. Edición y nota preliminar de Angel Rosenblat. Biblioteca Emecé de Obras Universales, Sección X, Historia y Arqueología, No. 85. Emecé Editores, S.A., Buenos Aires.

T'itu Kusi Yupanki. 1916. Relación de la conquista del Perú y hechos del Inca Manco II [1570]. Notas biográficas y concordancias del texto por Horacio H. Urteaga; biografía de Tito Cusi Yupangui por Carlos A. Romero. Colección de Libros y Documentos referentes a la Historia del Perú [Serie 1], Tomo II. Lima.

Tschopik, Harry, Jr. 1946. "The Aymara," in *Handbook of South American Indians*, Bureau of American Ethnology Bulletin 143, Vol. 2, pp. 501-73. Washington.

MAM RESIDENCE
AND THE MAIZE MYTH

By Suzanne W. Miles

BRANDEIS UNIVERSITY

IN WESTERN GUATEMALA, southern Huehuetenango, and San Marcos departments, the most precipitous rugged mountain terrain belongs to the Mam-speaking Highland Maya Indians. Mam is a poorly known language with several dialects that has been recently classified by McQuown (1956, p. 195) as the most conservative of the Maya. Two modern Mam towns, Todos Santos and Santiago Chimaltenango, have received rather careful study, the former from Maud Oakes, the latter from Charles Wagley. There is, therefore, a small body of information available about the present people and their country. But the history of the Mam is virtually unknown. No great native documents like the Quiche *Popul Vuh* and the Cakchiquel *Annals* have been found. In sharp contrast to the Dominicans and Franciscans of the mid-highlands, who were prolific producers of reports, dictionaries, and lexicons, the priests of the Order of Merced in the northwest kept their counsel. These missionaries communicated next to nothing for publication or archive deposition about the Mam, Chuj, and Jacalteca to whom they ministered. For late pre-Conquest times only the broadest outlines of Mam affairs can be pieced together. A few fragments in the accounts of the late wars of the Quiche and Cakchiquel and the archaeological work at Zaculeu, Huehuetenango (Woodbury and Trik, 1953), provide the information that Mam speakers were pushed westward by Quiche expansion toward the areas of Quezaltenango and Sacapulas and that, culturally, the late occupation of Zaculeu shows that the general features of architecture and artifacts of the Highlands were shared. Nearly all

---

One of the first anthropological books I owned was Professor Radin's *The Sources and Authenticity of the History of the Ancient Mexicans,* published in 1920 as Volume 17 of the University of California Publications in American Archaeology and Ethnology. In that volume Professor Radin discusses the historical value of myths and tradition; so that it is with particular pleasure that I offer this brief paper involving myth and time depth in an area which has long been of interest to him. I should point out, however, that my conclusions may fall within a category of rash interpretation, against which Professor Radin rigorously warned!

modern Mam towns are located on or very near archaeological sites of unknown characteristics and depth. It is appropriate to associate the modern towns with the sites, but in the absence of excavation and careful examination we have no idea of the length of Mam occupation.

There is, fortunately, another line of inquiry for exploitation that provides strong indication that the Mam peoples are very ancient inhabitants of the Cuchumatanes and San Marcos mountains. The material is drawn from botanical studies, place names, and myth.

Mangelsdorf and Cameron (1942, pp. 217–52) found that there are more varieties of maize grown in a small part of western Huehuetenango than in all the United States. The plants have a tremendous range of characteristics which suit them to the great variety of conditions under which they are grown. These characteristics are imparted by admixture with tripsacum, which grows wild and abundantly in the region, and with teocinte, the dominant plant cover for thousands of acres in the Huista and Trapachillo drainages near the border with Chiapas. Most of the types of maize show varying amounts of crossbreeding with these wild relative grasses, but a small amount of nearly pure maize is grown at very high altitudes. These findings brought Mangelsdorf and Cameron to the conclusion that this small area of northwestern Guatemala was certainly the area in which most of the Mexican and North American types of maize were developed, if not, indeed, the area in which maize was first brought under cultivation.[1]

The great myth histories of the Quiche and Cakchiquel relate that the gods finally chose maize as the material of which to make men. They looked for it and located it at last:

From Paxil, from Cayalá, as they were called, came the yellow ears of corn and the white ears of corn. These are the names of the animals which brought the food: *yac* (mountain cat [actually fox]), *utiú* (the coyote), *quel* (a small parrot), and *hoh* (the crow). These four animals gave tidings of the yellow ears of corn and the white ears of corn, they told them [the gods] that they should go to Paxil and they showed them the road to Paxil.
                                            (Recinos, Goetz, and Morley, 1950, pp. 165-66.)

The gods then made man of corn and Paxil was found to be a paradise of food plants of all sorts.

The Cakchiquel story differs only slightly:

Only two animals knew that there was food in Paxil, the place where these animals are found which are called the Coyote and the Crow. The Coyote animal was killed, and in his remains, when he was quartered, corn was discovered. (Recinos and Goetz, 1953, p. 46.)

Paxil (the place) has been discussed and sought by several translators and interpreters of the Quiche and Cakchiquel stories; it has been dismissed as mythological and impossible to find,[2] although a very large number of the places named in the myth histories have been accurately located. Very recently, however, the Mam provided the information that Paxil exists and indeed was, from their point of view, the birthplace of maize cultivation. In the course of a field trip in 1945–47, Oakes (1951, p. 244) was given the following story at San Pedro Necta:

Corn was obtained by the *naturales* from the sources created by God. One of the sources is here in San Pedro Necta.[3] It is a mountain called Xepaxa.[4] It is to this mountain the people sometimes go to make offerings, if the season is poor for corn. No one has ever worked the land there. The corn grows on this mountain alone [i.e., without cultivation]. It produces ears which dry and then fall on the earth. No one takes them, for no one visits this place except to make offerings.

The *naturales* who lived near it used to eat roots and fruit before they knew of corn. It is said that, one day, a *natural* went to this mountain for food. While he was setting traps to catch birds he came upon a corn plant which was still green. This man did not know what corn was, and when he saw the grains he thought that possibly one could eat them. So he carried this corn to his family and they all talked about how to eat it: boiled, roasted on the coals, or raw? "How should we eat it?" they asked. "We will put it on the fire," said the wife, and as it was young corn, it turned out very well.

Thereafter the man went every day to carry back more corn to his house. . . . He removed the leaves, and dried the kernels in the sun. Then, when a time, however, it became necessary for him to go quite a distance. So the man thought to himself, "Each day I have to go farther and farther. The mountain is covered with clouds and there are many animals who could devour me. It is better, therefore, if I look for the seed and plant it on my land. I had better not keep going to the mountain, I might not return; an animal might kill and devour me."

Thereupon he went to the mountain and found dry corn and carried it back to (his house). The rain came; he planted it. Very contented indeed was this man when he saw the plants grow; and when he saw that it was really so, that the plants produced ears, he worked hard on his land. It was worth it. Every year he planted and other people do the same right up to the present day.

In 1955, at Todos Santos Cuchumatan, several miles from Necta, I asked about the plants in the Necta story, and friends told me:

Paxa is far away. No one lives there; no one works the land. Xepaxa gives corn, holy maize. It is very dangerous, entirely forest and mountain; it is a place of priests. I lived in Necta for three years with my father when I was a little girl and Xepaxa is the other side of the river (the Selegua). It is huge. In other towns they call it Tui Xián[5] or K'man Xián[6] also. Those of Chumbal (Santiago Chimaltenango, a town nearby) say "Paxil," but it is all the same. It might take five days to get there.

An old man sitting and listening said, "When the world was born long ago, maize was born at Paxa. And there it was, in the ground, of the soil. And then man began to eat it."

The next day a friend who had been present and heard these statements came to me with an expanded story:

He said it was in very early times; for a long long time people had nothing, no machetes, no knives of iron, only their hands, a stick and stones. They were very poor. There was little food, just wild things and animals. Then the mouse took maize from the mountain Xepaxa, and men found it in his burrow and tried to eat it. They found it good. Then they sought and planted it and soon there was holy maize. There is another story of other people that says that the cave gave the maize, that the crow brought corn from the mountain. So say some people.

An old religious official who heard that I was planning to go to Paxa (the mountain) said:

It is good to know the road of Xepaxa. It was not necessary to go when I was alcalde.[7] It is the place of ceremonies when there is trouble for the milpas. My grandfather told me that high in Xepaxa there is a water. On its borders grow many strange plants and there are birds and animals. And if a man goes and looks into the water and sees money, it means that there will be a very bad year for the corn fields, and no maize, and the people must buy their food. But if it is purely yellow, then there will be a good year for corn. It is the source, the origin place, the "owner" of corn— so said my grandfather. The whole world knows that Paxa gives corn. If there is trouble for the fields go to Xepaxa with an offering.

When we were on the trail and nearly at Paxa, my guide, who had claimed no knowledge of any stories, offered this information: "There is a cave in Paxil. It is from there that corn first came. My father and my grandfather told me that a mouse or perhaps a bird took no more, perhaps, than a few grains, and from that men have maize fields. When a candle is placed at Paxil, it rains."

The mountain, Paxil, is almost the geographical center of the Mam area—two days ride from Todos Santos Cuchumatan. It is the highest spot in the great ridge between the Rio Selegua on the north, and the Rio Cuilco to the south. The peak rises to at least 12,000 feet in old limestone. About fifty years ago the town of La Libertad, of which my informants knew nothing, was started on a rich little table a thousand feet above the Selegua, and the lower slopes of the mountain are now fields of corn and grass. The cave and the water (a large spring) are another fifteen hundred feet up the mountain on its northern side. There was much evidence in their vicinity of steady worship for the benefit of the corn fields. Local farmers said that the most frequent visitors to the sacred place came from Necta, San Juan Atitan, Colote-nango, and Chumbal—all Mam towns.

It is scarcely coincidence that the place named by the Quiche and Cakchiquel stories, recorded in the sixteenth century, is identified by the modern Mam as the source of maize and is located in the midst of the area defined by botanical study as an ancient center of origination of many types of domesticated maize. The Mam are also the only Middle American people known to attribute the discovery of culti-vation of maize to *men*. Other maize stories relate either that certain gods located it, or that the people got corn from some earlier, older people.[8] These are clearly secondary and later developments.

In the case of the Quiche-Cakchiquel myth histories there is further internal confirmation of the antiquity of the Mam story and Mam residence in western Guatemala. Not only do the Quiche and Cakchi-quel heroes encounter the Mam as settled people early in their wan-derings, but some of the names of gods in the *Popol Vuh* were apparently names of Mam towns and peoples.

Although I inquired with great care in 1955, I could find no migration story among the Mam, excepting the brief information that certain clans had come from Chiapas at about the time Cumanchum (the archaeological site above Todos Santos) was last rebuilt, perhaps *ca.* A.D. 1100. There are a number of Mam towns in Chiapas directly across the border. The few sixteenth-century Mam suits and land titles that have turned up demonstrate a similar absence of migration story, an item inserted in even short *titulos* of other Guatemalan peoples (Crespo, 1956, pp. 11-12).

Thus, the Mam were, in all probability, very ancient inhabitants of the western mountains, and, perhaps, agricultural innovators.

NOTES

[1] At the time Mangelsdorf prepared this paper he felt that maize probably had a South American origin. Recently, however, he has expressed the thought that wild maize may have been widespread in the great north-south cordillera in the New World, and may have been brought under cultivation in more than one center.

[2] Nineteenth-century writers thought it might have been in Chiapas, near Palenque, or in Tabasco, on the migration route from Mexico.

[3] The territory of San Pedro Necta probably formerly actually included the mountain Paxil, but it is now in the *municipio* of La Libertad.

[4] Xepaxa means "below, in the soil of Paxa," or "under the feet of Paxa."

[5] "The mountain Xián."

[6] "Our lord, ancestor Xián."

[7] The religious *alcalde,* often called Chief Prayermaker, is responsible for rituals for the benefit of the crops and the town on appropriate days in the native calendar for one year. See Oakes, 1951, for a full discussion.

[8] Fuentes y Guzman (1933, p. 392), draws on a manuscript now lost, which related that the wandering Quiche had lost their maize seed but found three stalks of corn at Pambilil from which they obtained seed for planting. "Pam" means "within" or "at"; Bilil is a small town in northwestern Huehuetenango. Also, Robert Burkitt (1920, pp. 193-227) persuaded a Kekchi Indian to confer with others and write out a local story about corn. It involves a fight between two mountains for possession of the corn, inappropriately hidden away from the rightful owner-mountain, Xucanéb, otherwise known as the "Mam" (see Zuñiga). ("Mam" is a term widespread in Maya languages with the general meaning "ancestors.") Neither men nor gods, beyond the mountains themselves, are mentioned. The eastern mountains of Guatemala are botanically uninvestigated, but teocinte, the close relative of corn, grew in Alta Vera Paz in the sixteenth century. According to Zuñiga, *Diccionario,* Part II, "Quina—es nombre de una yerva que en hoja, caña y flor parece a la del maize. es de tierra caliente. el Mexicano la llama teocintli. ay mucha en Tucurub." The place is just east of Xucanéb. Thus, the conditions Mangelsdorf found in western Guatemala may also have been present in the eastern highlands.

REFERENCES

Burkitt, Robert. 1920. "The Hills and the Corn," *The University Museum Anthropological Publications,* 8:No. 2:183-227. University of Pennsylvania.

Crespo, Mario. 1956. "Titulos Indigenas de Tierras," *Antropologia e Historia,* 8:No. 2:10-16. Guatemala.

Fuentes y Guzman, Francisco Antonio. 1933. Recordacion Florida, discurso historial y demonstracion natural, material, militar y politica del Reyno de Guatemala, Part II. Biblioteca "Goathemala," Vol. 7. Guatemala.

McQuown, Norman A. 1956. "The Classification of Mayan Linguistics," *International Journal of American Linguistics,* 22:No. 3:191-95.

Mangelsdorf, Paul C., and James W. Cameron. 1942. "Western Guatemala: A Secondary Center of Origin of Cultivated Maize Varieties," *Botanical Museum Leaflets,* 10:No. 8:217-52. Botanical Museum of Harvard University.

Oakes, Maud. 1951. The Two Crosses of Todos Santos. Bollingen Series, Vol. 27. New York.

Recinos, Adrián, and Delia Goetz. 1953. The Annals of the Cakchiquels and Title of the Lords of Totonicapan, trans. by Dionisio José Chonay. Norman, Oklahoma.

Recinos, Adrián, Delia Goetz, and Sylvanus G. Morley. 1950. Popol Vuh. Norman, Oklahoma.

Woodbury, Richard B., and Aubrey S. Trik. 1953. The Ruins of Zaculeu, Guatemala. Richmond, Va.

Zuniga, Diego de. [ca. 1600]. Diccionario Pocomchi—Castellano y Pokomchi de San Cristobal Cahcoh, MS, pp. 145 ff. Photographic copy of MS, by William Gates, in Peabody Museum Library, Harvard University.

SOCIAL PERCEPTION AND SCRIPTURAL THEORY IN INDIAN CASTE

By David G. Mandelbaum

UNIVERSITY OF CALIFORNIA, BERKELEY

THE SCRIPTURAL THEORY of caste which lays down that there are four main, ranked divisions of society is known throughout India. Students of caste have frequently pointed out the shortcomings of this classification as a true picture of any Indian society, but in the course of a study of caste as system it became clear to me how very useful for societal purposes this theory, however inadequate, has been.

The main groups in an Indian village are the hereditary, endogamous units which we may call jatis. Each jati is represented in a number of villages of an area. The members of each jati are all assigned, by local opinion and action, to the same level of the local social hierarchy. In the villagers' formal theory, the rank of a jati depends on the ritual pollution and purity of its members as a corporate group. In practice, the ritual considerations set certain limits for a group's rank; within these limits there is considerable leeway for variation according to local considerations of the group's secular wealth and power.

In practice there also is frequent disagreement as to the precedence of particular jatis, especially in the middle echelons of a local social system. Even those whose jati is generally considered to be lowest of all in the vicinity, are generally adamant in the belief that there is at least one other jati in the locality whose people are lower still. Just as the other villagers avoid close contact with them, so do they avoid contact with those whom they deem to be beneath them.

Each villager adjusts his relations with his neighbors according to his perception of their position in the local social order. That order is not viewed in quite the same detail by all in a local system. A villager tends to make finer social discriminations about his own jati and those close to it than he does for jatis which are socially distant from his own.

Thus the Badagas of the Nilgiri Hills comprise several endogamous groups, each self-consciously different from the others, though all speak the Badaga language and are culturally similar. A Badaga villager refers to himself, in his conversations and dealings with other

Badagas, by the name of his endogamous group, such as Wodeya. This is his main unit of self-identification among the cluster of jatis collectively known to outsiders as the Badagas. It is a unit of paramount importance to him not only for marriage purposes, but also because much of his work and worship is carried on with his jati fellows rather than with any others who may be Badagas in name and culture.

But the Kotas and other neighboring peoples are little concerned with these distinctions among Badagas; they tend to view the Badagas as all of a piece and refer to them as one. Kotas are sensitive to individual differences in wealth among the Badagas with whom they have dealings, and they may shift their outward deference accordingly. But the ritual gradations among Badaga jatis are of little concern to Kotas. Similarly, Kotas label all immigrant squatters in their lands as "lowland folk" and deal with them as one subservient grouping, though the squatters are of different jatis and diverse origins.

A main reason why one sees finer social gradations in his own than in other jatis lies in the difference between an insider's and an outsider's view. A person has his most intense and intimate relations within his jati. Therefore he is more aware of differences among his jati fellows and is more sensitive to the ritual and social implications of these differences. An outsider has more casual relations with people of that jati and he need be concerned only with the services they render and with the general category of the social order to which they belong.

Within a large, widespread jati, finer social distinctions can be made in several ways. One is by the practice of hypergamy, a qualified kind of endogamy in which the jati itself is divided into ranked, hereditary sections. A man may marry a woman from a section lower than his own, but a woman may marry only into her own or into a higher section. Full choice of potential spouses is retained only for the men of the highest section of the jati.

Among the Pātidārs, an agricultural jati in Gujarat, each section is made up of the Pātidārs living in a particular circle of villages. Between the highest, most exclusive village circle, called Six Villages, and the circles which are larger and are inferior in status, there is considerable difference in ritual practice and in secular power. But by using the very name of Pātidār a low section includes itself with the highest village circles. "Since in the eyes of an outsider belonging to another caste the Pātidār caste is a unity, such a claim endangers the status of

the highest levels and consequently of the caste as a whole in the area."
(Pocock, 1957, p. 28.) Presumably not just anybody can call himself
a Pātidār, but some villagers have recognized claim to the name yet
are of markedly inferior practice than are other Pātidārs. The superior
circles manifest their superiority by refusing full endogamy, by marking
out inferior sections among those whom they recognize as fellow
Pātidārs but to whom they will not give their daughters in marriage.

Conversely, Pātidārs find it useful to ignore differentials in status
among the Bāriās, another large cultivator jati of Gujarat which is
lower than they are in the local hierarchies. In one village, Pocock
notes, certain Bāriā families are superior in their ritual practices to
some Pātidār families. But this does not disturb the Pātidār villagers
who "*include* the higher levels of the Bāriā with the lower levels of the
Bāriā and so *exclude* them from any claim to equality." While several
Bāriā families of the village are more strictly vegetarian than are some
Pātidārs, their Pātidār neighbors "refer to them simply as Bāriā and
include them in the general statement: 'The Bāriā eat meat.'" (*Ibid.*)

This gross, oversimplified classification is very useful; dealing with
people of other jatis is much simplified by it. One does not have to
calculate and adjust to all the actual gradations of ritual practice among
members of large and varied groups. All are Bāriā or Badaga (or some
other inclusive term) and are so treated.

Useful, even necessary, as such classifications are for villagers, they
present difficulties for students of caste, because the inside view of the
parts of the social order often varies according to which insider is
interviewed. Hence the terms which have been used by outside observers to describe the parts of village organization have often seemed
inconsistent and incomplete. Not lacking in ambiguity is the word
"caste" itself. It is an outsider's term in origin, first applied by the
Portuguese,[1] and it has been used to refer to differing social entities
and to quite different levels of social structure. Some writers have
found the shifting usages a hindrance to clear analysis. H. N. C.
Stevenson puts the trouble succinctly when he comments, "It is difficult
to pin the term 'caste' to any sociological reality." (1954, p. 49.) One
difficulty is that it has been pinned to too many social entities. It is
commonly used to mean an endogamous group, or some category of
endogamous groups, or a form of social organization—or all three.[2]

It is well to use the word "caste" to refer to a form of social organization, as the caste system of Indian civilization, and to the local social systems of caste within that civilization. The principal parts of a caste order are best specified by other terms.

The basic social unit in every local system is the family. Some are nuclear families, consisting only of parents and their unmarried children living in a single household. Some are joint families—and this is the ideal though not necessarily the more common type in a village—in which the parents, their sons, the son's wives and children, perhaps other relatives, share a single household and domestic economy.

Families group themselves in several ways, commonly into lineages and clans, exogamous groupings like the family itself. These are considered by villagers to be constituent parts within the larger orbit of the jati. Whatever term a villager uses for his endogamous group, whether jati or some other, he is, typically, keenly aware of that set of people to which all his relatives belong, from which his spouse must come, and among whom all his descendants will marry. And against these are all the others, who are neither actual kin nor potential affines.

A jati is thus a grouping *for* interaction, in that marriage inter-relations must take place within it. The units *of* interaction in an Indian village, the actual groups of cooperating people, are often made up of members of the same jati. Not only in the intimacy of the household, but in work and worship and recreation, a person's closest and most intense relations tend to be concentrated among his jati fellows in the village. Should his be the only family of its jati in the village, a man must perforce rely more on jati fellows in other villages and on fellow villagers of other jatis. But for many villagers, their whole jati-group forms a cooperating unit.

The term "jati-group" designates those of the same jati who live in a single village and therefore may have more frequent day-by-day contacts than they can have with others of their jati who live in many scattered places. It is what villagers often call "the brotherhood," using such terms as *biradari* or *bhaiband*. (See Blunt, 1931, p. 10; Hutton, 1946, p. 86; Bailey, 1957, p. xv.) Some jati-groups are far from being harmoniously cooperative; in Rampur village, near Delhi, the domi-nant jati of landowners is divided into several antagonistic factions, the major splits following clan lines. (Lewis, n.d., pp. 7-18.) A man's opponents here may be from his jati, but his closest friends and cohorts are also of his jati.

There are, to be sure, important cooperative groups in a village which must be made up of people from different jatis, as a set of associates in the traditional, jajmani, exchange of foods and services, or the participants in a village-wide ceremony. Many a man has trusted friends of other jatis, many participate in games or hymn singing or trade without giving much attention to the jati status of their associates in these activities. Yet the nature of a villager's participation in such multi-jati enterprises is, at least in some part, controlled by his jati status.

To the individual, his jati membership determines or delimits many of the functioning groups in which he operates and affects the roles which he may take in village enterprises. As Mrs. Karve states, "the endogamous units are the ultimate social realities, both from the point of view of the historical development of Indian society as also from the point of view of ultimate elements of the social organization of India." (1958, p. 133.) But when the individual villager refers to others outside his own jati, he often glosses over the jati divisions and lumps people of different jatis under one label.

One kind of label refers to several jatis whose members have close social relations and similar practices; other names class together jatis which have some cultural similarity but little or no social contact among all who are so classed; still another kind of label groups under one heading an array of jatis among whom there may be little special similarity beyond the similar treatment, by others, of all who are so classified.[3] We can distinguish these three kinds of grouping by using the terms jati-cluster, jati-set, and jati-category.

A jati-cluster is exemplified by the Badagas of the Nilgiris; the people of the several Badaga jatis have ceremonial and economic links and share many cultural traits distinctive of Badagas.

A jati-set is exemplified by the various jatis of Maharashtra which are called Kunbis. There are some common cultural traits, but no necessary social relations among those known as Kunbis. The common cultural characteristics are not many; the various groups of this name are tillers of the soil, they speak Marathi, there seems to be general agreement in the region that a jati called Kunbi ranks below the farmer-fighter jatis called Maratha. Beyond these similarities there are wide differences among Kunbis in such matters as kinship arrangements, dress, and economic functions. People of that name live in disparate

geographical parts of the region in which Marathi is spoken and one
group may not know of the existence of their namesakes. (Karve, 1958,
pp. 126-27.)

A jati-category is even more inclusive, embracing jatis, jati-clusters,
and jati-sets, or various parts of them. Jati-categories are used for the
ranking of groups of jatis. In any local system, the blocs into which
jatis are assigned are jati-categories. These blocs are fitted by villagers
into another set of jati-categories, the scriptural and India-wide table
of the four varnas.

Each varna is a reference category, a taxonomic device which does
not denote a functioning group of cooperating people nor much in the
way of cultural homogeneity. A varna is one of the four divisions of
society which are specified in certain scriptures; Brahmans as learned
men and priests are at the head of the order, Kshatriyas as warriors
are next in rank, Vaishyas as merchants and agriculturalists follow,
and Sudras as workers are last. (See Dandekar, 1953.)

The defects of this scheme as a true model of Indic society have
often been pointed out in the literature on caste. It omits those who
rank below Sudras, who are important to caste orders, and who are
organized according to the standards of caste. In some parts of the
land, as widely in South India, Kshatriyas and Vaishyas as defined in
scripture were only sporadically represented. Moreover, the varnas
mentioned in the earlier Rigvedic texts seem to have been more like
open classes than fixed, hereditary social strata. (Dutt, 1931, pp. 58 f.;
Ghurye, 1950, pp. 54-56; Prabhu, 1954, pp. 290-342.)

A villager, however, can use the fourfold division to sort out the
principal parts of society and to place a jati—especially one with
which he is not very familiar—in a general scheme. Typically, he
knows that Brahmans are ordained to be the highest of four social
layers: that usually fits with what he finds in his village, the Brahman
jatis are commonly topmost in the ritual hierarchy. It does not worry
him overmuch that a jati claiming to be Kshatriya is far from warrior-
like, or that no jatis claiming to be Vaishyas appear in his locality.
The four divisions, in popular view, were ordained in the beginning,
are presently maintained, and are found in all parts of the land.

The four varnas provide the basis for other classifications. Boys of
the upper three varnas may undergo a sacrament of initiation in which
they are invested with the sacred thread which each one thenceforth
wears over his left shoulder. The ceremony is deemed a second birth,

and those who have the right to wear the thread are *dvija,* twice-born, in contrast with the Sudras and those even lower who cannot undergo a ritual second birth. This ceremony is usually carried out more meticulously in the Brahman jatis than among other eligible jatis of a locality. In general, the Brahman jatis tend to have more cultural and functional similarity than do jatis of other varnas because they are the exponents of and are supposed to share knowledge in the Sanskrit scriptures.

Sudras are classified into clean Sudras, from whom men of the higher varna categories may, under stipulated circumstances, accept water, and unclean Sudras, from whom those of the twice-born varnas may, under no circumstances, accept water. The distinction between clean and unclean Sudras is generally an important one and demarcates one bloc of jatis from the next higher bloc. The line of demarcation is differently drawn in various places and in some there is disagreement among local villagers as to just where it should be drawn.

The varna categories serve several purposes. The scheme provides a simple way of indicating the sector of the hierarchy into which a particular jati can be fitted. Thus Mayer notes that in Ramkheri village, Madhya Bharat, the varna grading can "be seen as the best assessment of a caste's various rankings." Perhaps it is more of a handy and summary evaluation than it is a considered assessment. Because even in Ramkheri, the varna divisions do not quite fit the facts of social organization as is shown by a note following the listing of caste rank in the village, "The Vaisya *varna* has been placed below the Kshatriya in the traditional manner. In Ramkheri, however, the vegetarianism of the former is said by many to make the Vaisya equal to, if not superior to, the Kshatriya." (Mayer, 1956, pp. 138, 141.) Such discrepancies are not taken as serious objections to the four-part classification.

Just as the varna outline is a useful index of rank within a local system, so also is it convenient for assessing jatis of different geographic and linguistic regions. A stranger who comes into a village and encounters a batch of jatis unfamiliar to him, can make quick distinction among them by asking about their positions in the scale of four. In this way, somewhat paradoxically, the four divisions are useful for classifying jatis throughout the land even though these categories may not fit well with the facts of a particular local system.

Another function of the four-part scheme is to help legitimize changed social status. For those who are trying to raise their jati status, the next higher varna category can provide a goal for their ambitions. (See Srinivas, 1955, p. 224; 1956, p. 492.) When a group which has been known as Sudras can get their neighbors to call them by a title indicating Vaishya or Kshatriya status, and if they can receive the respect and precedence which go with the title, they have then succeeded in their efforts. (That the effort is always phrased, by those of the aspiring jati, as only a restoration of their ancient and proper due, is another matter.)

The varnas provide a clear-cut hierarchical pattern for a social arrangement which villagers may like to think of as neat and hierarchical, but which characteristically includes recalcitrant parts, overlapping jurisdictions, and fuzzy judgments. Thus Mayer comments on the function of varna in Ramkheri: "More important, perhaps, it helps to distinguish the hierarchy in the area of greatest obscurity, the middle reaches, where statements about varna membership are almost the only verbalizations of general status." (1956, p. 143.)

In like vein, Srinivas comments: "It is necessary to stress here that the many small castes in any local area do not occupy clear and permanent positions in the system. Nebulousness as to position is of the essence of the system in operation as distinct from the system in conception. . . . It is not only that the hierarchy is nebulous here and there, but the hierarchy is also to some extent local. The *varna* scheme offers a perfect contrast to this." (1954, p. 357.)

Students of society are familiar with theorists who, often unwittingly, shape their reports of a people's behavior to fit their theory. In this case, the people have provided the theoretical conception and have not been abashed by the lack of fit between fact and theory. That theory, we should note, has served its purposes for a long time. Varna is frequently mentioned in Sanskrit scripture, jati less often. "All ancient Indian sources make a sharp distinction between the two terms," Basham comments (1954, p. 148). But N. K. Dutt states that in the foremost code of all, "Even Manu . . . has confused varna with jati." (1931, p. 4.)

Émile Senart also warned that the two terms are confused in the literary tradition, which, he wrote, "is less concerned with the faithful record of the facts than with their arrangement in systems conforming to the tendencies of a strongly biased group." (1930, p. x.) More recently, K. M. Panikkar has developed this theme, writing (the italics are his) about the varna category that ". . . this four-fold division *is only ideological* and is not in any manner based on the facts of the social system. It is, as we shall try to show, only a schematic arrangement by theorists . . . what Hindu sociologists wanted their society to be—a theory of caste-idealism unrelated to actual practice." (1956, p. 7.)

Panikkar, an historian-statesman long and successfully engaged in practical political affairs, may underestimate the influence which a theory can exert. The varna scheme may not have been well based on social facts, but it certainly has influenced the facts of Indian society. Yet we must agree with Srinivas that "The *varna* model has been the cause of misinterpretation of the realities of the caste system." (1954, p. 362.) This model is commonly an important factor in a local system, and villagers find good use for the imperfect model, but students of caste have gone astray when they have mistaken the model for the reality.

The reality is that certain descent groups may change their relative positions in the system over time, that there frequently are disagreements about the exact place of some groups in the social order; that there are considerable differences among local systems. Moreover, the member of, say, the local Brahman jati may be accorded differing status in different contexts of behavior. They may be given all due precedence and respect in ritual affairs and be very little consulted on questions concerning crops or business or government. All of which is unlike the clear, immutable, and India-wide varna prescription. While the reality is not as neat and simple as is the varna model, it is also not as chaotic as the disorganized catalogues of caste practices make it out to be. There is the reality of the basic tenets of caste throughout village India; there is also the reality of the local caste systems operating according to these tenets across the land.

Each group within a local system, in certain (not necessarily all) of its relations with villagers of other groups, acts according to the systemic tenets and patterns. Thus the people of any village jati, whatever disagreements they may have with their neighbors about rights and privileges, do not abandon endogamy, or ignore the rules of ritual pollution, or flout the idea of social hierarchy. The very conflicts about a jati's place show how important social hierarchy is to villagers;

those who engage in a struggle about status are apt to be all the more convinced, by their exertions, that higher rank is worth the struggle.

These common conflicts about rank do not disintegrate a local system; neither do the differing perceptions about rank groupings make the system unfeasible. In a way, the grosser classifications make it feasible for the villager to comprehend and handle his social system. For example, a farmer of Gujarat knows that a local shopkeeper is likely to be a Bania, that Banias are in the third of the varnas, and he deals with him accordingly. Were the farmer to be fully informed about the shopkeeper, he would know, for example, that he is of the Sarta jati, of the Visā subdivision of that variety of those Vaniās (Banias) who are supposed to have originated in Desawāl. (Thoothi, 1935, p. 125.) Not only is it unnecessary for the farmer to know all this, it would be impossible for him to adjust his relations with all his neighbors on the basis of such finely discriminatory knowledge.

For the shopkeeper, these details are supremely important. By them he maintains bonds of kinship; from his jati he recruits most of his business assistants; with his jati-fellows he fulfills his religious duties. By the activities and relations which are so bounded, he helps maintain a firm social unit within the local caste system and upholds the caste standards according to which the social system is operated.

He, in turn, is quite uninterested in the precise social position of his farmer customer. All he needs to know is the general bloc in which the customer ranks; for it will not do to address a sweeper customer as though he were a Brahman and, still less, a Brahman as though he were a sweeper.

This kind of differential perception of social status is commonly found in complex societies and is a necessary condition in them. To cite only one example, in the study of "Old Town" in the Deep South of the United States, it was found that a person generally recognizes finer distinctions of class in his own range of the social scale than he does in the distal ranges. (Davis and Gardner, 1941, pp. 71-73.) The finer perception about one's own social circle contributes to the economy of the whole system. The grosser perceptions about the position of others enables the individual to deal economically with many kinds of other people.[4]

In this way, the differing views about social groupings which can be found in a single village do not disrupt the social system. Conversely, the general consensus about varna is a consensus about a theory which does not fit the facts. Nevertheless the varna concept has helped villagers in organizing their mutual relations within a local social system.

NOTES

[1] The word Hindu was also a foreigners' gross classification, originally applied by Persians to the people living along the Indus River and then, by extension, to all inhabitants of the sub-continent. Professor A. R. Wadia remarks of the word "Hindu": "Etymologically it had no religious significance, but when a strong aggressive religion like Islam found a home in India, there was a tendency to lump together all non-Muslims in India as Hindus whether they were caste Hindus or the so-called untouchables." (Wadia, 1955, p. 7.)

[2] The term "subcaste" has been used by some writers as a more precise label to mean an endogamous group. But its sharpness of definition tends to be blurred if "caste" is concurrently used in several different senses. As used in several of the direct quotations which follow, "caste" refers to what we term jati, an endogamous group.

[3] To be sure, a common label and common treatment (especially if felt to be mistreatment) can promote social solidarity and joint action among peoples who had shared neither. With improved communications, such coalescing increasingly occurs.

[4] A social system entails some system of communication about social relations. In any communication system there is a certain amount of "noise," irrelevant or accidental transmission. Differential perception and understanding about social groupings in a system contribute "noise" to social communication. But it is not necessary that all noise be eliminated. What is necessary is that enough mutually understood information be transmitted so that, aided by a general *gestalt* perception, reciprocal action can be carried through.

REFERENCES

Bailey, F. G. 1957. Caste and the Economic Frontier: A Village in Highland Orissa. Manchester, University Press.

Basham, A. L. 1954. The Wonder That Was India. London, Sidgwick and Jackson.

Blunt, E. A. H. 1931. The Caste System of Northern India. Madras, Oxford Press.

Dandekar, R. N. 1953. "The role of man in Hinduism," in *The Religion of the Hindus,* ed. by Kenneth W. Morgan. New York, The Ronald Press Company.

Davis, Allison, Burleigh B. Gardner, and Mary R. Gardner. 1941. Deep South: A Social Anthropological Study of Caste and Class. Chicago, University of Chicago Press.

Dutt, Nripendra Kumar. 1931. Origin and Growth of Caste in India. Vol. 1. London, Kegan Paul, Trench, Trubner.

Ghurye, G. S. 1950. Caste and Class in India. Bombay, The Popular Book Depot.
Hutton, J. H. 1946. Caste in India: Its Nature, Function, and Origins. Cambridge, The University Press.
Karve, Irawati. 1958. "What is caste? (1) Caste as extended kin." *Economic Weekly* (Annual Number), 10:125-38.
Lewis, Oscar. n.d. Group Dynamics in a North-Indian Village, a Study of Factions. Prepared for D. G. Karve, Head Programme Evaluation Organization, National Planning Commission, New Delhi. Mimeographed.
Mayer, Adrian C. 1956. "Some Hierarchical Aspects of Caste," *Southwestern Journal of Anthropology*, 12:No. 2:117-44.
Panikkar, K. M. 1956. Hindu Society at Cross Roads. Rev. ed. Bombay, Asia Publishing House.
Pocock, David G. 1957. "Inclusion and Exclusion: A Process in the Caste System of Gujerat," *Southwestern Journal of Anthropology*, 13:No. 1:19-31.
Prabhu, Pandhari-Nath. 1954. Hindu Social Organization. Bombay, The Popular Book Depot.
Senart, Émile. 1896. Caste in India. Trans. by Sir E. Denison Ross. London. Methuen and Company, Ltd, 1930.
Srinivas, M. N. 1954. "Varna and caste," in *A. R. Wadia, Essays in Philosophy Presented in His Honour*. Bangalore.
―――― 1955. "Village Studies and their Significance," *Eastern Anthropologist*, 8:Nos. 3–4:215-28.
―――― 1956. "A Note on Sanskritization and Westernization," *Far Eastern Quarterly*, 15:No. 4:481-96.
Stevenson, H. N. C. 1954. "Status Evaluation in the Hindu Caste System," *Journal of the Royal Anthropological Institute of Great Britain and Ireland*, 84:Parts I–II:45-65.
Thoothi, N. A. 1935. The Vaishnavas of Gujarat. Bombay, Longmans, Green and Co., Ltd.
Wadia, A. R. 1955. "Working Paper," in *Report of the Seminar on Casteism and Removal of Untouchability*. Bombay, Indian Conference of Social Work, pp. 1-10.

BEZIEHUNGEN ZWISCHEN DEM ALTEN TESTAMENT UND DER NILOTISCHEN KULTUR IN AFRIKA

von Ad. E. Jensen

JOHANN WOLFGANG GOETHE-UNIVERSITÄT

DIE BEHAUPTUNG eines direkten Kultur-Zusammenhanges zwischen den Juden des Alten Testamentes und ost-afrikanischen Hirtenvölkern ist am nachdrücklichsten von dem deutschen Schutztruppen-Offizier M. Merker vertreten worden, der bereits im Jahre 1904 *Die Masai* als eine Abspaltung von den semitischen Völkern bezeichnete. Zum Beweis dieser These führte er eine ganze Reihe von hauptsächlich religionswissenschaftlichen Parallelen an, die von anderen ebenfalls sehr zuverlässigen Forschern wie z.b. dem Missionar Fokken nicht bestätigt werden konnten. So veröffentlichte Merker Berichte der Masai, die ausserordentlich an die entsprechenden Bibelstellen erinnern und die Verkündung der 10 Gebote durch einen Engel von einem Berge herab oder eine genaue Parallele zu dem Erbbetrug Jacobs an Esau (Merker, 1904, S. 274) beinhalten. Diese Thesen Merkers sind teils freudig aufgenommen, teils heftig kritisiert worden. Seine Arbeit ist aber von vielen Fachgenossen bis auf diese engen religionswissenschaftlichen Bibel-Parallelen als eine vorzügliche Monographie über die Masai anerkannt worden. Offensichtlich hat er einzelne Auskunftspersonen gehabt, die bereits stark von der christlichen Mission beeinflusst waren und die deshalb die Urgeschichte der Masai im biblischen Sinne umbogen. Vielleicht war er auch von seiner Theorie so stark fasziniert, dass er selbst diese Parallelen in die Geschichten der Masai hineingehört hat. Das ist — wie gesagt — bereits von den Kritikern Merkers hervorgehoben worden.

Ohne diese Fragen nochmals berühren zu wollen, möchte ich im folgenden den Versuch unternehmen, die Idee von Merker wieder aufzugreifen, wenn auch mit ganz anderem Material und ohne seine These von der direkten Abwanderung der Masai von den Semiten aufrecht zu erhalten. Die Juden, wie sie uns das Alte Testament schildert, sind ein Hochkultur-Volk, während es sich bei den Masai um ein in vieler Hinsicht besonders primitives Eingeborenen-Volk handelt, so dass beide kaum miteinander zu vergleichen sind.

Dagegen ist ein Vergleich zwischen dem Alten Testament und den kuschitischen Völkern sehr wohl möglich — ein Vergleich, der letzten Endes zeigen wird, dass das Alte Testament zwar die Kultur eines schriftbesitzenden Volkes schildert, dass aber trotzdem diese Kultur nur eine der Spielarten der kuschitischen Kulturen darstellt. Bei der Ur-Verwandtschaft zwischen den semitischen Sprachen einerseits und den kuschitischen Sprachen andererseits wäre ein solches Ergebnis auch nicht besonders verwunderlich. Aber nicht dieser Vergleich soll Gegenstand dieser Zeilen sein, obgleich er bei der Fülle der vergleichbaren Elemente sehr vielversprechend sein würde, sondern eben die Merkersche Idee eines Vergleiches der Masai, eines Volkes mit einer nilotischen Sprache, mit dem Alten Testament.

Vergleiche zwischen kulturellen Gegebenheiten, wie sie uns im Alten Testament geschildert werden, und denen afrikanischer Völker — besonders südafrikanischer Völker — sind immer wieder — auch in neuester Zeit — gezogen worden. Am nachdrücklichsten hat wohl Von Sicard die Parallelen zwischen dem Alten Testament und den Sitten südrhodesischer Völker, wie den Karanga und Lemba, in seinem Buche *Ngoma lungundu* (1952) hervorgehoben. Die Ähnlichkeit der Lemba oder Remba mit den Juden des Alten Testamentes war schon vor langer Zeit aufgefallen und wurde unter anderem von Frobenius (1938) in einer Monographie geschildert. Brown (1926) sagt auch von den Tschwana, dass viele ihrer Zeremonien "a close relation to the levitical code" aufweisen. Der Gedanke ist also nicht neu. Er scheint sich vielen Autoren geradezu aufgedrängt zu haben.

Wie erklärt man sich nun aber diese vielen Hinweise auf alttestamentarische Einflüsse in Afrika? Die meisten Autoren haben zweifellos — ausgesprochen oder unausgesprochen — an die Einflüsse der hamitischen Kultur gedacht und dabei angenommen, dass diese hamitische Kultur auf irgendeine Weise vom Alten Testament her beeinflusst worden ist. Man hat aber zweifellos diesen Einfluss der hamitischen Kultur auf den afrikanischen Erdteil erheblich überschätzt. Besonders Frobenius hat beispielsweise den ganzen Viehzüchter-Komplex auf die Hamiten zurückführen wollen. Tatsächlich braucht man die Kuschiten nicht zur Erklärung des Viehzüchter-Komplexes in Afrika heranzuziehen, denn es finden sich alle Elemente dieses Kom-

ɔlexes in konzentrierter Form bei den Niloten. Es wäre sogar merk-
würdig, wenn diese Ausbreitung tatsächlich auf die hamitischen
Kuschiten zurückginge, ohne dass einige Elemente dieser Schicht die
„hamitische Wanderung" mitgemacht hätten. Ich erwähne nur die von
den Kuschiten angebauten Körnerfrüchte, Weizen und vor allem Gerste,
der wahrscheinlich ein beträchtliches Alter zugesprochen werden muss,
wohingegen im übrigen Afrika — vom Mais abgesehen — eigentlich
nur die Hirse verbreitet worden ist.

Nun hat viel zu diesem Irrtum von der hamitischen Wanderung die
Behauptung Meinhofs von hamitischen Spracheinflüssen in der Hotten-
otten- und Masai-Sprache beigetragen. Heute ist auch dieses Hindernis
durch Greenberg ausgeräumt. Nach Westermann (1952, S. 255):
"Greenberg refutes the view of Meinhof who included Hottentot in his
Hamitic family, a view which has never found real acceptance."

Ich neige also zu einer Auffassung, die früher schon einmal von
Childe in mehreren Aufsätzen — wenn auch mit Vorbehalten — an-
gedeutet wurde, wonach die nilotische Kultur — und damit eine ältere
und primitivere Schicht — einen weit grösseren Einfluss auf den
afrikanischen Erdteil ausgeübt hat, als wir bisher angenommen haben
und dass sie für die Verbreitung sehr vieler Kulturgüter in Afrika,
insbesondere — wahrscheinlich — für die erste Ausbreitung des Rindes
als Haustier, auf jeden Fall aber für die Verbreitung des sogenannten
Grossviehzüchter-Komplexes verantwortlich gemacht werden muss.

Die nilotische Kultur im engeren Sinne die sich ostlich und westlich
des oberen Nils ausgebreitet hat und zu der auch die Masai als süd-
lichste Gruppe gehören, bildet auch sprachlich und rassisch (nach Von
Eickstedt) eine Einheit. Die nilotischen Völker stellen in ihrer Gesamt-
heit eine Kulturprovinz dar, die in ihrer Geschlossenheit kaum von einer
anderen afrikanischen Kultur-Provinz erreicht wird. Es ist in der
Literatur eine bisher viel diskutierte, aber natürlich nicht eindeutig zu
entscheidende Frage, ob diese Kulturprovinz, die heute den Körner-
frucht-Anbau neben der Viehzucht deutlich zeigt, nicht eine ursprünglich rein pflanzerische Kultur gewesen ist, die die Viehzucht erst
sekundär von den Kuschiten übernommen hat, oder eine ursprünglich
rein viehzüchterische Kultur, die den Pflanzen-Anbau erst später nach
einer Verschmelzung mit Bauernvölkern oder ob sie von Anfang an
Viehzucht- und Körner-Anbau gemeinsam gehabt hat.

Es würde zu weit führen, Gründe dafür zu nennen, weshalb ich die zuletzt angedeutete Möglichkeit für die weitaus wahrscheinlichste halte. Es würde auch vom eigentlichen Thema abführen. Überhaupt ist die reine Grossvieh-Zucht ohne gleichzeitigen Bodenbau nach meiner Meinung eine Sonder-Entwicklung einer Wirtschaftsform, die ursprünglich sowohl den Körner-Anbau wie die Grossvieh-Zucht kannte; diese gemischte Wirtschaftsform ist für alle Niloten typisch und ist sehr wahrscheinlich auch im west-asiatischen Raum — und damit für die alt-testamentarischen Juden — einst bestimmend gewesen. Die in beiden Räumen sehr ähnlichen klimatischen Bedingungen, mit weiten Trockengebieten, die für den Bodenbau ungegeignet sind, haben die Entwicklung der Spezialform der reinen Grossvieh-Zucht begünstigt. Dabei leben diese Viehzüchter-Nomaden in einer Art Symbiose mit den Bodenbauern, sei es mit einem benachbarten Volk wie bei den Masai (Merker, 1904, S. 30) oder seien es zwei Teile ein und desselben Volkes wie bei den Murle oder Beir (Tucker, 1952, S. 99), von denen der eine Teil in den Bergen vorwiegend den Bodenbau, der andere im Tiefland vorwiegend die Viehzucht betreibt.

Von dieser nilotischen Kultur möchte ich nun im folgenden zeigen, dass sie auch für die vielen Übereinstimmungen zwischen afrikanischen Völkern und dem Alten Testament verantwortlich zu machen ist. Dabei ist es nicht verwunderlich, dass bei der Spärlichkeit der für diesen Vergleich zur Verfügung stehenden Nachrichten es nicht immer dieselben Vergleichsmomente sind, die von den Feldforschern herangezogen werden. Meiner Meinung nach genügt es, zu zeigen, dass auch die Niloten solche biblischen Elemente aufweisen, um es hinreichend zu erklären, dass überall, wo nilotische Kultur-Einflüsse hingelangt sind, sich solche biblischen Einflüsse — wenn auch andere — ebenfalls finden. Dabei sind es auffälligerweise gerade die älteren in der Bibel nur beiläufig erwähnten Formen, die zum Vergleich mit den Niloten oder den nilotisch beeinflussten Negern herangezogen werden können.

Wir versuchen es so zu erklären, dass nicht etwa die alt-testamentarische Kultur nilotisch gewesen sei — wie Merker es gemeint hat — sondern dass der biblischen Kultur eine Substrat-Schicht zu Grunde liegt, die sich in der heutigen nilotischen erhalten hat. Mit anderen Worten, es müsste in relativ alter Zeit, die auf jeden Fall vor der Herausbildung der ägyptischen Hochkultur gelegen hat, in den sehr ähnlichen Räumen in West-Asien und Nordost-Afrika eine einheitliche

Kultur verbreitet gewesen sein, die grosse Ähnlichkeit mit der heutigen nilotischen Kultur gehabt haben muss.

Unter den zahlreichen Opfern, die aus beiden Räumen berichtet werden, befindet sich eine Zeremonie, die aus dem allgemeinen Rahmen herausfällt und die wahrscheinlich einer altertümlichen Schicht des Alten Testamentes zuzurechnen ist. Im I Mose 15 wird erzählt, wie dem Abraham von Gott versprochen wird, dass er eine zahlreiche Nachkommenschaft erhalten und dass er das Land besitzen werde, in das ihn Gott aus Ur in Chaldäa geführt hat. Abraham bittet Gott um ein Zeichen, dass die göttliche Verheissung verwirklicht wird. Darauf machen die Beiden einen regelrechten Vertrag, d.h. Gott verpflichtet sich zu dem von ihm Verheissenen und bekräftigt sein Versprechen durch ein Opfer. Auf Gottes Geheiss bringt Abraham eine dreijährige Kuh, eine dreijährige Ziege, einen dreijährigen Widder, eine Turteltaube und eine junge Taube. Alle Tiere mit Ausnahme der Vögel zerteilt er in zwei gleiche Teile, die er einander gegenüber legt. Gegen Abend, als tiefe Finsternis eingetreten war, geht eine Feuerfackel zwischen den Fleischstücken der Opfer hindurch und Gott wiederholt sein Versprechen.

Dass diese Flamme Gott symbolisiert und dass er sich wirklich feierlich verpflichtet hat, erfahren wir aus Jeremia 34.17 ff., wo dieses besondere Opfer noch einmal erwähnt wird. Es handelt sich dort um das jüdische Gesetz, nach dem ein hebräischer Sklave im siebenten Jahre seiner Sklaverei frei zu lassen ist. Jeremia beanstandet, dass das Gesetz nicht mehr eingehalten wird und erwähnt dabei, dass die Oberen Judas, die Kämmerer, die Priester und das gesamte Volk des Landes sich feierlich dazu verpflichtet haben, indem sie zwischen den beiden Hälften eines zweigeteilten Kalbes hindurch gegangen sind.

Von den Nuer, einem nördlichen Niloten-Stamm, berichtet Seligman (1932, S. 207) genau dasselbe Opfer. In der Ursprungs-Mythe dieses Volkes heisst es, dass das erste Menschenpaar zwei Söhne und mehrere Töchter hatte und dass daher jeder der beiden Söhne mit mehreren Schwestern eine Ehe eingehen musste. Um die unangenehmen Folgen dieses Inzestes zu vermeiden, vollzog der Vater dieses besondere Opfer. Er teilte einen Ochsen der Länge nach durch und verpflichtet (durch dieses Opfer?) seine gesamte Nachkommenschaft, sich an eine festgelegte Heiratsordnung zu halten, die bestimmte, dass die Nachkommen der beiden Söhne sich stets nur gegenseitig heiraten können. Von Wichtigkeit ist noch die Angabe, dass der älteste Sohn die rechte Hälfte des geopferten Ochsen erhielt und als Häuptling eine ranghöhere Stellung einnimmt als der jüngere Bruder, dem die linke Hälfte des Opfertieres zugewiesen wurde. Er erwähnt dieses Opfer noch einmal (S. 237) bei der Totenzeremonie der Nuer, wo die Längsteilung einer Ziege offenbar dazu dient, alles Üble von der Familie abzuwehren.

Von den Nuer erwähnt auch Evans-Pritchard (1949, Nr. 96) dasselbe der Länge nach geteilte Opfer, jedoch diesmal im Rahmen der Befriedungszeremonien nach einem Kriege.

Von den Bari berichtet Seligman (1932, S. 246, 264) ein ganz ähnliches Opfer, das sowohl mit Rindern wie mit Ziegen vorgenommen werden kann. Auch hier ist der Sinn des Opfers ganz ähnlich, nämlich die Vermeidung der Üblen Folgen eines Inzestes.

Auch von den Nuba (Dilling) beschreibt er (S. 395) eine Zeremonie, bei der ein Rind getötet und dann zweigeteilt wird (down the middle line). Die Zeremonie wird ausgeführt, um zu verhindern, dass eine Seuche unter dem Vieh ausbricht oder um Unglück vom Vieh fernzuhalten.

In einer anderen Arbeit von Seligman (1932) erwähnt er diese Opfer mit mehr Einzelheiten (S. 198 ff.) die uns aber in diesem Zusammenhang nicht interessieren. Jedoch gibt er in dieser Arbeit (S. 200 ff.) eine Information von Evans-Pritchard über die Azande wieder, wonach hier eine Kalebasse gespalten wird, um die gefürchteten Gefahren eines Inzestes abzuwehren.

Auch erwähnt er dort einen Bericht von Rattray (S. 177), wonach dieselbe Zeremonie mit dem Zerbrechen einer Kalebasse bei den Stämmen im Ashanti-Hinterland vorkommt, wenn beispielweise das Sterben der Kinder in einer Ehe anzeigt, dass möglicherweise eine unbeabsichtigte inzestuöse Heirat geschlossen worden ist. Die beiden Eheleute fassen beide die Kalebasse, "each retaining half."

Schliesslich erwähnt er noch in seinem Beitrag unter dem Stichwort "Dinka" (Hastings, IV, 712a) ein Opfer eines Schafes bei den Shish Dinka, das ihrem Gott "Dengdit" geweiht ist; auch hier ist wieder die Längsteilung des Tieres in zwei Hälften zu beobachten. Die Hälfte, die der Erde abgewandt ist, wird in kleine Stücke geschnitten, die zum Himmel geworfen werden. Wenn sie auf die Erde fallen, werden sie von Menschen nicht berührt und von Hunden und Vögeln gefressen. Die andere Hälfte wird von den Menschen gekocht und gegessen.

Ist in diesen von Seligman berichteten Beispielen von Niloten, Nuba und anderen Völkern das Motiv für die Ausführung des Opfers nicht einheitlich und auch nicht vergleichbar dem des Alten Testaments, so habe ich auf einer Expedition nach Südwest-Äthiopien (1950–52) eine weitere Schilderung erhalten, in der wieder die feierliche Verpflichtung zweier Parteien im Vordergrund steht. Möglicherweise enthielt auch einst die mythische Erzählung der Nuer die Verpflichtung der Nachkommenschaft zur Einhaltung einer besonderen Heiratsordnung. Bekanntlich siedelt ein Teil der Niloten hier im Südwesten diesseits der Grenzen des äthiopischen Kaiserreiches auf äthiopischen Gebiet. An der östlichen Grenze ihres Wohngebietes erhielt ich die Schilderung einer Friedens-Zeremonie zwischen den Male und den Baka. An der Grenze zwischen beiden Völkern treffen sich die beiden Häuptlinge begleitet von ihren Haupt-Priestern. Sie haben jeder einen Schild und ein Schaf mitgebracht. Die Schilde werden einander gegenüber aufgestellt. Dann werden in dem Raum zwischen den Schilden die beiden Schafe mitten durchgeteilt und in dem entströmenden Blute waschen sich die beiden Priester ihre Hände. Darauf werden die Schafe verzehrt, indem Male und Baka von beiden Opfertieren essen. Darauf werden auch die Schilde in der Mitte durchschnitten und der Friede feierlich beschworen.

Fast genau die gleiche Friedens-Zeremonie beschreibt Tremearne (1912, S. 159) von den Kagoro * in Nord-Nigerien, wo ebenfalls die beiden Parteien je eine Ziege — "except for the head" — der Länge nach durchteilen und gemeinsam verzehren.

Eine Tötung eines mythischen Schlangenkönigs, der mit der Stadtgründung und dem Dualismus zwischen der westlichen und östlichen Hälfte zusammenhängt, und der nach seinem Tode der Länge nach zweigeteilt wird, erwähnen Lebeuf und Detourbet (1950, S. 49) von der Stadt Makari im Südosten des Tschad. Paques (1956, S. 214 f.) berichtet aus dem Fezzan die traditionelle Form der Fleischverteilung bei einem Opfer: "Puis [le bélier] est d'abord divisé, en deux dans le sens de la longueur de manière à obtenir une moitié à l'Est et une à l'Ouest."

---

* Diese und mehrere andere Angaben verdanke ich der Freundlichkeit von Dr. Hildegard Klein.

Bei dem Bergvolk der Amarro, das auf der Ostseite der süd-
äthiopischen Grabenbruches siedelt, der westkuschitischen Sprach-
familie angehört und ein ausgeprägtes Zweiklassensystem besitzt, ist
gleichfalls die rituelle Längsteilung der Opfertiere anzutreffen. Im
Verlauf der Begräbniszeremonien wird die rechte Seite des Opfertieres
vom Sohn des Verstorbenen, die linke Seite aber vom Schwiegersohn
des Toten enthäutet. Während dem Sohn das Fleisch der rechten Hälfte
zusteht, nimmt der Schwiegersohn, der der korrespondierenden Heirats-
klasse des Verstorbenen angehört, das Fleisch der linken Hälfte des
Opfertieres an sich. Die symbolische Teilung der Tiere wird verständ-
lich, wenn man das Totenritual durch die Aussagen der Ursprungs-
mythe ergänzt, die von der Teilung der Nachkommenschaft des Stamm-
vaters der Amarro in die zwei exogamen Heiratsklassen berichtet
(Straube, 1958, S. 350-51). Das Opferritual und die Ursprungsmythe
der Amarro entsprechen vollkommen der mythischen Tradition der
Nuer (Seligman, 1932, S. 207) und lassen erkennen, dass auch hier
die Längsteilung der Opfertiere mit der Einsetzung der beiden Heiratsklassen und der Beseitigung der Inzestgefahr in Zusammenhang zu
bringen ist.

Bei den Kikuyu ist die Kaste der Schmiede anscheinend weniger
verachtet, als im allgemeinen in Nordost-Afrika. Wenn jemand in die
Gilde der Schmiede aufgenommen werden will, so muss er eine Zeremonie durchlaufen, von der uns Hobley (1938, S. 168) eine Schilderung
gibt. Bei dieser Zeremonie wird ein Widder zerteilt from neck to tail,
"the right half being eaten by the smiths and the left half by the
villagers present."

Eine ähnliche Zeremonie wie bei den Baka und Male wird in einer
Arbeit von De Cocker (1950, S. 277 f.) über den "Parallelisme Biblico-
Congolais" erwähnt. Dort wird aus Anlass einer Allianz die zwischen
zwei Dörfern geschlossen wird, ein Sklave getötet (heute eine Ziege),
in zwei Teile zerlegt und gemeinsam verzehrt.

Das erinnert wiederum ausserordentlich an einen Bericht über einen
Ritus, den wir Frobenius verdanken (wiedergegeben bei Vatter, 1926,
S. 107 f.), der mit einem sehr auffälligen Maskentyp der Kongo-Völker
(Abb. 47 bei Vatter) zusammenhängt. Nach Fertigstellung der Maske
durch den sogenannten Zauberpriester kann sie nur ihre volle Wirk-
samkeit erhalten, wenn der Eigentümer einen Sklaven tötet, ihn der
Länge nach zerschneidet, die beiden Hälften einander gegenüber und

lie Maske zwischen diese Leichenteile legt. Schilde (1937, S. 157), der
auch bereits die Bibelstellen und die Quellen von Seligman erwähnt,
nennt dann noch weitere Vorkommen dieser besonderen Art des
Opfers, aber leider ohne jede Quellen-Angabe. Nach ihm kommt es
bei den Lumbwa, Dschagga, Kikuyu, Nyamwesi und Asu im nordost-
afrikanischen Raume vor, ferner bei den Bara auf Madagaskar und
bei den Kagoro in Nigeria (das wir möglicherweise oben schon erwähnt
haben). Alle diese Völker kennen die Halbierung der geopferten Tiere.
Bei den Gabun-Pygmäen, den Egap in Kamerun und Malinke und
Bambuk wird von ihm die Halbierung eines Huhnes erwähnt.

Einen weissen Hahn opfern auch die Schmiede der Fouta in West-
Afrika den Geistern, die den Ort bewohnen, wo Eisenerz abgebaut
werden soll. Durand (1932, S. 49) schildert uns, wie der Älteste das
Opfer darbringt. Dabei wird der Hahn "partagé dans le sens de la
longeur."

Für die Verbreitung in West-Asien sei schliesslich noch ein Volks-
brauch der Hethiter erwähnt, von dem Gurney (1952, S. 151) schon
selbst die Ähnlichkeit mit dem biblischen Bericht hervorhebt: Bei einer
militärischen Niederlage machten die geschlagenen Truppen folgenden
Ritus "hinter dem Fluss." Man tötet einen Mann, eine Ziege, einen
kleinen Hund und ein kleines Schwein, indem man sie durchschneidet
und die beiden Hälften einander gegenüber legt. Davor macht man
ein Tor aus Holz, und die Truppen marschieren durch dieses Tor und
werden am Fluss mit Wasser besprenkelt.

Alle Berichte scheinen mir in Bezug auf die Anwendung dieses
Opfers eine gewisse Gemeinsamkeit aufzuweisen: Meistens ist dabei
eine besondere feierliche Verpflichtung, eine erhöhte Wirksamkeit oder
die Abwendung einer grossen Gefahr im Spiele. Im übrigen bin ich der
Meinung, dass die zahlreichen Beispiele, in denen ein Zusammenhang
mit (exogamen) Zweiklassen-Systemen belegt ist, zu den (ethnologisch)
ältesten Vorkommen dieses Opfers zählen. Das Vorhandensein von
zwei Gruppen, die allerdings auch bei den Friedens-Zeremonien gegeben sind, legt die absolut gleiche Zweiteilung, die nur durch die
Längsteilung zu erreichen ist, nahe. Dass die linke Hälfte dabei der
geringeren, die rechte der führenden Gruppe zufällt, gehört ebenfalls
zu den Dual-Systemen, in denen die eine Gruppe meist als linke,
weibliche einer anderen rechten und männlichen gegenübersteht.

Ein anderes Vergleichs-Merkmal zwischen der nilotischen Kultu und dem Alten Testament ist die Stätte, an der das Opfer dargebrach wird. Auf der bereits erwähnten Expedition nach Südwest-Äthiopie besassen alle Völker von nilotischem Kulturgepräge das Tor als di heilige Stätte, an der sowohl Opferungen von Tieren als auch ander heilige Handlungen stattfanden. Es handelte sich entweder um das To des Viehkrals oder des Gehöftes oder um frei in der Landschaf stehende Tore, die dieselbe Bedeutung besassen. Diese ganz allei stehenden Tore sind meistens die Reste früherer Gehöfte, von dene eben deshalb die Tore stehen bleiben, weil sie diese heilige Bedeutun haben. Oft wird das Tor mit einem oder mehreren Gräbern in Ver bindung gebracht, in denen verstorbene Vorfahren des Inhabers diese Tores liegen.

Die Tore nun sind die Stätte, an der die blutigen Opfer für di Ahnen oder für die Abwehr von Krankheit, was vielfach in der Vor stellung dieser Völker dasselbe ist, ausgeführt werden, oder es werde andere heilige Handlungen, wie beispielsweise der Ohrenschnitt an Vieh, an ihren durchgeführt. Die aus dem nilotischen Kulturgebie stammenden Nachrichten über das Tor als heilige Stätte sind spärlic Sie reichen aber aus, um die Bedeutung des Tores sichtbar werden z lassen. So bildet Peristiany (1939, S. 21) in seinem Buche über di Kipsigis (Lumbwa), eines südlich wohnenden, den Masai unmittelba benachbarten Niloten-Stammes, ein frei stehendes Tor ab, das in eine Zeremonie eine Rolle spielt. Ob die Lumbwa oder Kipsigis als ei Teil der Masai anzusehen sind, obgleich sie auch Ackerbau treiben oder einen selbständigen Stamm bilden, wird in den Berichten leide widerspruchsvoll dargestellt. Auch bei den Masai findet die Beschnei dung der Jünglinge am right-hand door-post des Viehkrals statt (Hollis 1905, S. 297).

Von den benachbarten Nandi berichtet Hollis (1905, S. 47) ein Ernte-Dank-Zeremonie, für die ebenfalls ein Tor errichtet wird, a dessen Pfosten die alten Männer stehen und die jugendlichen Tänze mit Milch und Bier segnend bespucken.

Auch von den Madi in Uganda hebt Williams (1949, S. 209) di Bedeutung des Tores als "guardians of moral" hervor. "Frequentl at the entrance to a compound it is possible to see a small structur simply made from one or more stones and occasionally with a fram work of sticks." Auch dieses Tor wird offensichtlich als heilige Stätt angesehen, denn jemand, der etwas Unrechtes getan hat, darf es nicht durchschreiten und wird, wenn er dem Verbot zuwiderhandelt, mit Krankheit geschlagen.

Von den bantu-sprechenden Küstenstämmen in Kenya, die unter starkem nilotischen Einfluss stehen und unter dem Namen der Nyika zusammengefasst werden, berichtet Joy Adamson (1957, S. 253) ebenfalls von solchen freistehenden Toren auf Kultplätzen.

Ausserhalb des nilotischen Siedlungsraumes, aber wahrscheinlich als ein Niederschlag ihrer finden wir das Tor bei verschiedenen afrikanischen Stammen wieder. Eine besondere Betonung hat es bei den Nyakyusa (Wilson, 1957, S. 69, 85, 105, 206); es wird als Eigentum der Verstorbenen bezeichnet. Sodann kommt es auf dem Plateau von Nord-Rhodesien vor. Gouldsbury und Sheane (1911, S. 92) bilden ein solches freistehendes Tor ab, das sie den "foundation stone" eines Dorfes nennen, der dort meistens in Gestalt eines Hornes in den Grund gesteckt worden ist. Wenn aussergewöhnlich viele Todesfälle im Dorf vorgekommen sind, wird dieses Horn befragt und die nötigen Sühne-Opfer angeordnet (S. 27). Weitere Angaben über das Tor finden sich bei Gouldsbury und Sheane (S. 55, 186). Von den rhodesischen Tonga berichtet Torrend (1910, S. 163) das Opfer eines Ochsen am Türeingang und fügt in einer Fussnote hinzu: "the doorway is the Tonga altar." Sogar bei den Herero in Südwest-Afrika findet sich das Tor in dieser hervorgehobenen Bedeutung: Köhler (1956, S. 88) berichtet, dass beim Opfer ein Teil des Fleisches beim Kraltor zubereitet wird und dass von diesem Fleisch nur die verheirateten Männer essen dürfen.

Ich erwähnte soeben den Ohrenschnitt am Vieh als eine heilige Handlung, die ebenfalls oft am Tore ausgeführt wird. Man liest meistens in der Literatur, dass dieser Ohrenschnitt eine Eigentumsmarke sei, um dem Besitzer des Viehs das Erkennen seines Eigentums zu erleichtern. Dem steht an sich schon entgegen, dass die am Ohr angebrachten Marken innerhalb eines Klanes meist einheitlich sind. Alle Argumente sprechen für die Auffassung, dass der Ohrenschnitt mindestens früher und wahrscheinlich ursprünglich als eine Ersatz-Herero in Südwest-Afrika. Dort erhält der Vater bei der Geburt von schon mehrfach erwähnte Expedition nach Südwest-Äthiopien bei den Tsamakó festgestellt, dass an Tieren, die eigentlich getötet werden müssen, der Ohrenschnitt als vorläufige Handlung durchgeführt wird, der dann erst später die eigentliche Tötung zu folgen braucht. Noch deutlicher wird es in einem Bericht von Irle (1906, S. 98) über die Herero in Südwest-Afrika. Dort erhält der Vater bei der Geburt von Zwillingen so viele Ochsen von den anderen Stammesangehörigen, dass es inopportun für ihn ist, sie alle gleich zu schlachten, weil Fleisch genügend vorhanden ist. Statt der Tötung schneidet er dann den Ochsen die rechten Ohrlappen ab, röstet diese und lässt sie von den Festgenossen duch Berührung mit dem Munde beschmecken. Hernach werden die Ohrlappen auf Riemen aufgereiht und um seine Milch-Kalebasse gebunden.

Wir haben auch auf unserer Expedition vielfach von Opfern gehört, bei denen es von Wichtigkeit ist, dass das Tier beschnittene Ohren hat und von anderen, bei denen es darauf ankommt, dass die Ohren des Tieres noch nicht beschnitten waren. Jedoch waren diese Angaben nicht ausreichend, um einen vernünftigen Sinn darin zu finden. Nur die Angabe, dass der Ohrenschnitt beim Opfer von Wichtigkeit ist, deutet ebenfalls darauf hin, dass er ursprünglich keine Eigentumsmarke war. Darauf kommen wir sogleich bei den Beispielen des Alten Testamentes zurück.

Zunächst ist darauf hinzuweisen, dass das Tor im Alten Testament sehr häufig erwähnt wird, und zwar immer als Stätte, an der sich für die Gemeinschaft wichtige Dinge vollziehen. Man gewinnt den Eindruck, dass das Tor, insbesondere das Stadttor, in späterer Zeit die Gerichtsstätte schlechthin ist. Als besonders bedeutsam erscheint mir eine Fussnote (2 Mose 21.6) von Holzinger in der Ausgabe des Alten Testamentes von Kautzsch, nach der die Zelttür oder der Hauseingang heilig waren. In alter Zeit, bevor es ein zentrales Heiligtum gab, wurde an ihnen geopfert. Am überraschendsten ist aber die Parallele zum Ohrschneiden am Tor, die im 2 Mose 21.5 f. (oder 5 Mose 15.16 f.) berichtet wird. Es ist da von Sklaven die Rede, die im 7. Jahr freizulassen sind. Wenn aber dem Sklaven während dieser Zeit ein Weib vom Herrn gegeben worden ist, das Söhne oder Töchter geboren hat, so sollen diese in der Sklaverei verbleiben. "Wenn jedoch der Sklave erklärt: Ich habe meinen Herrn, mein Weib und meine Kinder lieb und mag nicht freigelassen werden, so soll ihn *sein Herr vor Gott bringen und soll ihn an die Tür oder an den Türpfosten* bringen; da soll ihm sein Herr das Ohr mit einem Pfriemen durchbohren, und er soll dann für immer sein Sklave sein."

Das Tor ist darüber hinaus auch bei anderen Völkern, z.B. in China und Südost-Asien (vgl. Hudspeth oder Kaufmann) von heiliger oder hervorgehobener Bedeutung. Ich halte es auch für wahrscheinlich, dass die meisten Berichte darüber in einen kulturhistorischen Zusammenhang gebracht werden können. Aber dieser Frage nachzugehen würde hier zu weit und vom Thema ab führen. In Nordost-Afrika und im Alten Testament scheint mir aber die Bedeutung des Tores als der Opferstätte schlechthin oder für andere heilige Handlungen — darunter die Ohrbeschneidung oder Durchbohrung — für einen engen Zusammenhang zu sprechen.

Neben der Opfer-stätte und einer besonders feierlichen Form der Verpflichtung durch ein Opfer liessen sich noch mehr mit dem Opfer zusammenhängende Elemente für den Vergleich anführen, aber dies scheitert an der mangelnden Präzision der Angaben und besonders daran, dass der Sinn dieses Rituals nicht zu enträtseln ist. Warum das Opfer zu einer feierlichen Verpflichtung wird, wenn man das Opfertier in zwei Teile zerlegt, wissen wir zwar auch nicht, aber die Beschreibung dieses Opfers ist doch so eindeutig, dass es wohl zum Vergleich herangezogen werden kann. Ganz anders verhält es sich mit weiteren Elementen des Opfers.

Beispielsweise wird die Sonderstellung der Ziege als Opfertier sowohl im Alten Testament wie bei den Niloten durchaus nicht deutlich. Man spürt zwar fast bis zur Gewissheit, dass in Bezug auf die Bewertung der Ziege etwas Vergleichbares sowohl bei den Niloten wie im Alten Testament vorliegt. Aber aus Mangel an Deutlichkeit müssen wir dieses Argument fortlassen.

Ein weiteres Element wäre die Behandlung des Blutes. Den Juden ist jeder Genuss von Blut untersagt, während die meisten Niloten den Aderlass beim lebenden Vieh kennen, also den Blutgenuss durchaus schätzen und auch das Blut des geopferten Tieres meistens geniessen. Jedoch beim Opfer ist dann wiederum eine sehr ähnliche Haltung der beiden Völkergruppen zu beobachten. Sowohl bei den Juden sprengt der Priester das Blut des getöteten Tieres auf den Altar, wie auch bei den Niloten ist dieses Blutsprengen in das Haus beim Hausbau oder auch einfach in alle vier Himmelsrichtungen bekannt. In 3 Mose 17.11 wird die Haltung der Juden damit begründet, dass das Blut als des Leibes Leben bezeichnet wird, durch das die Menschen sich Sühne verschaffen sollen, eine Haltung, die durchaus der der Niloten entsprechen könnte. Es passt beispielsweise gut dazu, dass schwangere Frauen bei den Niloten vielfach besonders mit Blut ernährt werden (weil des Leibes Leben sich eben darin befindet). Aber auch dieses Argument wagen wir nicht anzuführen aus Mangel an Deutlichkeit.

Aber einigermassen sicheren Boden betreten wir wieder, wenn wir das Verbot, Schweinefleisch zu essen, anführen; dieses Tabu gilt auch für alle kuschitischen Völker. Dass sich dieses Speiseverbot selbst bis in die drei grossen Religionen des Orients erhalten hat, spricht durchaus nicht gegen sein hohes Alter. Ich möchte die Vermutung aussprechen, dass dieses Verbot jener alten Kulturschicht zugehört, die wir in Afrika als die "nilotische" zu bezeichnen pflegen.

Zu diesem Zwecke müssten wir uns die Kultur der Menschen, die vor der nilotischen Überlagerung diesen Raum bewohnten, etwas näher ansehen, als es im Rahmen dieses Aufsatzes möglich ist. Es soll aber wenigstens andeutungsweise geschehen auf die Gefahr hin, dass diese hypothetischen Ausführungen noch hypothetischer wirken.

Es ist das Verdienst von Grottanelli (1948), darauf hingewiesen zu haben, dass eine Gruppe von Völkern zwischen Weissem und Blauem Nil eine von der nilotischen sehr verschiedene Kultur besitzt, zu der unter anderem auch das Hausschwein (das ebenfalls in den Nuba-Bergen vorkommt) und Hunde-Opfer gehören. Er nennt diese Bevölkerung Prä-Niloten. Nun gibt es unter den Kuschiten und ebenfalls unter den Niloten eine verachtete Kaste, die endogam ist und die vermutlich eine ältere Bevölkerung darstellt. Auch unter den Masai gibt es sehr wahrscheinlich diese älteren Volksgruppen; denn Merker (1904, S. 32) erwähnt, dass die Töpfe von "ansässigen Volksstämmen" angefertigt und von den Masai gekauft würden. Leider erfahren wir nicht mehr über das Verhältnis dieser "ansässigen Volksstämme" zu den Masai. In Äthiopien sind sowohl bei Kuschiten wie bei Niloten die verschiedenen Namen für diese ältere Bevölkerungsschicht stets gleichbedeutend mit "Töpfer."

Ob nun diese Töpfer-Schicht ursprünglich dieselbe Kultur hatte wie Grottanellis Prä-Niloten wird sich wohl niemals mehr mit Sicherheit erweisen lassen, da die heutige Kultur dieser Unterschicht viel zu sehr an die der Herrenvölker angeglichen ist. Es ist aber in diesem Zusammenhang von Interesse, dass allgemein in Äthiopien die Absonderung dieser Bevölkerungsgruppe damit begründet wird, dass sie "unrein" ei. Ihre mythischen Vorfahren sollen "Unreines" gegessen haben, lämlich Wildschweinfleisch auf der Jagd. Verschiedene dieser Gruppen pflegen noch heute — unbekümmert um das Vorurteil der Oberchicht — Wildschwein-Fleisch zu essen. Das Wildschwein ist hier vermutlich an Stelle des Hausschweines getreten, weil dieses in Äthiopien so weitgehend ausgerottet ist, dass den Eingeborenen selbst der Begriff des Hausschweines unbekannt ist.

Andererseits kommt es ebenfalls bei den Baka vor, dass diese Absonderung mit einer Zeremonie begründet wird, bei der ein mythischer Stammesführer zwei Töpfe mit Hundefleisch und einen Topf mit Schaffleisch für sein Volk zubereiten lässt. Aufgefordert zwischen den beiden Töpfen zu wählen, essen darauf einige vom Hundefleisch und einige vom Schaffleisch. Anschliessend wird die Bestimmung getroffen, dass diejenigen, die Hundefleisch gegessen haben von den anderen nicht geheiratet werden sollen und sie alle niederen und unreinen Arbeiten verrichten sollen.

Bei den Sidamo und Darassa gibt es eine Mythe, wonach die verachteten Töpfer von einer Hündin abstammen, die sich in einen Menschen verwandelt hat.

Hieraus darf man vielleicht schliessen, dass mindestens in der Schweinehaltung und in den Hundeopfern eine Verwandtschaft der Prä-Niloten Grottanellis mit den verachteten Kasten, die unter Kuschiten wie Niloten leben, bestanden hat.

Wir glauben daher mit einer gewissen Berechtigung von den Prä-Niloten und von den verachteten Töpfer-Kasten als von einer archaischen Schicht sprechen zu können, die grosse Teile Nordost-Afrikas inne hatte, bevor die Niloten mit einer ganz anderen Kultur — und sehr wahrscheinlich auch mit einer ganz anderen Rassen-Zugehörigkeit — in diesen Raum einbrachen. Obgleich diese Vorbevölkerung die Töpferei bereits kannte, fiel sie der Verachtung der Eroberer anheim und mit ihnen ihr Haustier, das Schwein.

Nun bedürfte es einer genaueren Kenntnis des west-asiatischen Raumes, um diese hypothetisch ausgesprochene Ansicht auch dort als den wahrscheinlichen Ursprung des Verbots des Schweinefleisch-Essens zu erhärten. Ich fühle mich dafür nicht kompetent. Auf jeden Fall muss es auch zu Christi Lebzeiten Bevölkerungsteile in Palästina gegeben haben, die das Hausschwein kannten. Wie hätte es sonst in dem Gleichnis vom verlorenen Sohn heissen können, dass er schliesslich bei einem Manne sich verdingte, der ihn die Säue auf dem Felde hüten liess (Lukas 15).

Dass das Verbot des Schweine-Essens mit der nilotischen Kultur verknüpft ist, dafür mag nur die Mitteilung von Gouldsbury und Sheane (1911, S. 96) aus Nord-Rhodesien angeführt werden, nach der der ganze Wemba-Stamm kein Wildschwein isst und ähnliches auch für die Wabisa und Wamambwe gilt. Bei den Wiwa darf kein Mitglied der königlichen Familie Schwein essen, während es für das gewöhnliche Volk nicht verboten ist.

Dass man die Unterworfenen nicht heiraten soll, dass sie unrein sind, man sich unrein macht, wenn man sie berührt, dass man überhaupt unrein werden kann, überwiegend im Zusammenhang mit dem Geschlechtlichen, und dass man durch Zeremonien — meistens Opfer — wieder rein werden kann, das alles sind Zusammenhänge, die wir soeben berührt haben, die uns auch vom Alten Testament bestens vertraut sind.

Endlich ist noch das absolute Erstgeburtsrecht zu erwähnen, das in beiden Gebieten sowohl im Alten Testament (5 Mose 21.16) wie in Nordost-Afrika vorherrscht. Bei den Niloten ist es so, dass meist nur der älteste Sohn erbt und alle jüngeren Brüder auf seine Gnade angewiesen sind. Vor allem erbt der älteste Sohn die heilige Stätte, das Tor, an dem allein Tiere getötet werden dürfen und folgerichtig kann auch niemand von den jüngeren Brüdern selbständig ein Tier töten, sondern ist auf seinen älteren Bruder angewiesen, der das Opfer für ihn vollziehen muss. Auch kann nur der Inhaber der heiligen Stätte einen Segen aussprechen. Das absolute Vorrecht des männlichen Erstgeborenen ist auch bei den Juden des Alten Testamentes belegt. Besonders ist das Recht, Segen zu verteilen, anscheinend ebenso an den jeweils Ältesten in der Familie gebunden.

Dieses sind vielleicht alles in allem sehr wenige Elemente, aber sie scheinen mir doch charakteristisch genug, um daraus zu folgern, dass ein Vorläufer der Kultur des Alten Testamentes mit der nilotischen Kultur Nordost-Afrikas verwandt gewesen ist. Daraus ergibt sich eine Erklärung dafür dass überall dort, wohin die nilotische Kultur gekommen ist, insbesondere nach Süd-Afrika, Einflüsse alt-testamentarischer Art beobachtet werden können.

LITERATURANGABEN

Adamson, Joy. 1957. "Kaya und Grabfiguren der Küstenbantu in Kenya," *Paideuma*, 6:Heft 5.
Brown, J. T. 1926. Among the Bantu Nomads. London.
De Cocker, M. 1950. "Essai de Parallelisme Biblico-Congolais," *Zaire*, S. 277-98.
Durand, Oswald. 1932. "Les industries locales au Fouta," *Bulletin du Comité d'Etudes historique et scientifique de l'Afrique occidentale Française*, 15:42-77.
Evans-Pritchard, E. E. 1949. "Two Nuer ritual concepts," *Man*, Nr. 96.
Fokken, H. 1917. "Gottesanschauungen und religiöse Überlieferungen der Masai," *Archiv für Anthropologie*, N.F. 15.
Frobenius, Leo. 1938. "Die Waremba, Träger einer fossilen Kultur," *Zeitschrift für Ethnologie*, 70:159 ff.
Gouldsbury, X., and H. Sheane. 1911. The Great Plateau of Northern Rhodesia. London.
Greenberg, Joseph H. 1949-54. "Studies in African Linguistic Classification," *Southwestern Journal of Anthropology*, Vols. 5, 6. 10.
Grottanelli, Vinigi L. 1948. "I Pre-Niloti," *Annali Lateranensi*, Vol. 12.
Gurney, D. R. 1952. The Hittites. London.
Hastings, James, ed. 1908-21. Encyclopaedia of Religion and Ethics. 12 vols. Edinburgh.
Hobley, C. W. 1938. Bantu Beliefs and Magic. London.
Hollis, A. C. 1905. The Masai. Oxford.
——— 1909. The Nandi: Their Language and Folk-Lore.
Hudspeth, W. H. 1922. "The cult of the door," *Folklore*, 33:406-10.
Irle, J. 1906. Die Herero: Ein Beitrag zur Landes-, Volks- und Missionskunde. Gütersloh.
Jensen, Ad. E. 1959. Altvölker Süd-Äthiopiens. Stuttgart.
Kaufmann, Hans E. 1955. "Die Bedeutung des Dorftores bei den Angami-Naga," *Geographica Helvetica*, 10:Nr. 2:84-95.
Kauttsch, E. 1909. Die Heilige Schrift des Alten Testaments. Tübingen.
Köhler, Oswin. 1956. "Ahnenkult der Herero," in *Afrikanischer Heimatkalender*. Windhuk.
Lebeuf, J.-P., und A. M. Detourbet. 1950. La civilisation du Tchad. Paris.
Meinhof, Carl. 1912. Die Sprachen der Hamiten. Hamburg.
Merker, M. 1904. Die Masai. Berlin.
Paques, Viviana. 1956. "Le bélier cosmique." *Journal de la Société des Africanistes*, Tome XXVI.
Peristiany, J. G. 1939. The Social Institutions of the Kipsigis. London.
Rattray, R. S. 1932. The Tribes of the Ashanti Hinterland. Oxford.
Schilde, W. 1926. "Beiträge zur Hamitenfrage," in *Tagungsberichte der Deutschen Anthropologischen Gesellschaft*. Augsburg.
——— 1929. "Ost-westliche Kulturbeziehungen im Sudan," in Otto Reche, ed., *In memoriam Karl Weule*. Leipzig.
——— 1937. "Beiträge zur Kulturgruppierung in Negerafrika," in *Tagungsberichte der Deutschen Gesellschaft für Völkerkunde*. Leipzig.
Seligman, C. G. 1932. "Anthropological Perspective and Psychological Theory," in *Journal of the Royal Anthropological Institute*, Vol. 62.
Seligman, C. G., and Z. Brenda. 1932. Pagan Tribes of the Nilotic Sudan. London.

466 AD. E. JENSEN

Sicard, Harald von. 1952. Ngoma Lungundu. Uppsala.

Straube, Helmut. 1958. "Das Dualsystem und die Halaka-Verfassung der Dorse als alte Gesellschaftsordnung der Ometo-Völker Süd-Äthiopiens," *Paideuma,* 6:Heft 6:350-51.

Torrend, J. 1910. "Likenesses of Moses' Story in the Central African Folklore," *Anthropos,* 5:54 ff.

Tremearne, A. J. N. 1912. The tailed head-hunters of Nigeria. London.

Tucker, A. N. 1952. "Notes on Murle," *Afrika und Übersee,* Band 36.

Vatter, Ernst. 1926. Religiöse Plastik der Naturvölker. Frankfurt a.M.

Westermann, Diedrich. 1952. "African Linguistic Classification," *Africa* 22: 250 ff.

Williams, F. R. J. 1949. "The Pagan Religion of the Madi," *Uganda Journal,* 13:202-10.

Wilson, Monica. 1957. Rituals of Kinship among the Nyakyusa. London and New York.

MYTH AND HISTORY
IN ISRAELITE-JEWISH THOUGHT

By George Widengren
UPPSALA UNIVERSITY

History and Myth are almost inextricably mixed.
PIETER GEYL

THE PROBLEM of myth and history in their mutual relation according to Israelite-Jewish thought is of primary importance to the understanding of many questions in the Old Testament and Jewish religion and spiritual life. Thus far, however, this problem has not received a modern, comprehensive treatment in the light of our knowledge of ancient Israelite-Jewish thought in general, and of myth and history especially.[1] Nor does the present article aim at such an ambitious task, which would require much more space than is at my disposal here. The intention is only to present some general views on this difficult complex of ideas, at the same time trying to correct some wrong opinions which have been long accepted in a more or less articulated manner and have thus gained the position of long established scientific truths.

It is quite obvious that we must start with a definition of myth. What is myth? Or rather, what does modern research understand by myth? In Great Britain much effort has been spent on the attempt to give an adequate description of what myth means, and for all practical purposes I think we can accept the definitions given us by the so-called "myth and ritual school," which, it should be pointed out, is no school at all in the traditional, especially the German, meaning of the word but can be more adequately defined as a certain trend in British Old Testament and oriental research work. Professor Hooke, the leader of this "school," has defined myth on many occasions. The following definition is fairly representative and may be adopted here:

The ritual consists of the part which was *done*, for which the Greeks had the name *dromenon*, and the part which was spoken, to which the Greeks gave the name *muthos*, or myth. In the ritual the myth was the spoken part which related the story of what was being done in the acted part, but the story was not told to amuse an audience, it was a word of power; the repetition of the magic word had power to bring about or re-create the situation which they described.[2]

Adopting this definition I should like to emphasize not only the magical but also the *symbolical* aspects of the words of the myth as recited in the actual ritual. Symbolical words and actions were probably no more foreign to the ancients than to us.[3]

Myth, as just stated, was a repetition, a repetition in ritual of what once had happened. Myth accordingly includes both past and present time, but not only that: myth as relating constantly repeated, ever recurring events also includes the future. Time will ultimately bring back what once happened in the beginning, an important aspect of myth that we shall have to consider in the following. With reference to the time aspect then, myth includes both the past, the present, and the future.[4]

The Hebrews did not possess any special word for myth, but the thing was there, for in the beginning of their history in Palestine they had a rich store of myths, as we have tried to show in another connection.[5]

The definition of the term "history" presents greater difficulties, chiefly because our word "history" is taken in various meanings. History means to us what has happened and is happening as well as the knowledge and story of what happened, without any limitations whatsoever to a special subject.[6] But, in a more narrow and articulated sense, the word "history" refers to events in the world of mankind. As it came from the Greek term ἱστορία, the word originally possessed the meaning of inquiry and then of knowledge based upon inquiries, thus the aspect of intellectual curiosity is very prominent.[7] "History" also means the science of history, that department of humanistic research devoted almost exclusively to the investigation of what happened and happens in the world of mankind.[8]

In this article I shall have to deal with history in all these various meanings, but will try to define each time, as far as possible, the particular notion of history which is of concern.

I

As has been correctly observed, the Hebrew language does not possess any indigenous, Semitic name for "history" in our scientific sense of the word.[9] But in this case too the thing was there, as we shall see.

The double meaning of the word "history" has attracted the attention not only of historians but also of Old Testament scholars. Thus an American exegete, when speaking of the religion of the Hebrew prophets, has some very interesting observations to offer. He says:[10]

When we use the word "history" we may mean either events happening in time, or the record of those events. In the former sense, everything that has ever occurred either in nature or in human life is a part of history, but no human mind can ever record or comprehend even a small fraction of that total. Nor is it important that one should. Much of history in this sense is trivial and worthy only of oblivion.

Most of us would surely accept this statement without further comment. But what he then goes on to say is likely to meet opposition in some quarters.

History in the second sense may be either objective or subjective. Objective history is a mere narrative of events as they have occured, with no interpretation of their meaning. In spite of the pretensions of the modern historian, absolutely objective history is extremely rare, if not wholly impossible of attainment, and it is actually of little value and less interest. Subjective history seeks not simply to recover what actually occurred but to explain why it occurred and its meaning for man. Subjective history is internal history, remembered events bound together by a thread of interpretation. It may include tradition, and tradition often is of deeper meaning for man than purely objective history. We should not think, however, that when one is concerned with history all critical faculties must be suspended. Everyone interested in the writing and interpretation of history must, because of the compelling curiosity of the human mind, search for objectivity; but he must remember that objective fact alone is of little value.

I do not in this place intend to enter upon a discussion of the principles of historical research; I wish only to point out that the declaration just quoted runs counter to the main principle of all historical investigation since the days of the great Leopold von Ranke, who declared its aim to be to ascertain "wie es eigentlich gewesen ist."[11]

Of course all historians—and I myself write here as an historian—are grateful for the permission granted us to make use of some critical faculties. At the same time, all professional historians would probably claim the right to use as many critical faculties as possible and they would also most probably contend that even if in some cases objectivity obviously is difficult to attain, the situation isn't as bad as our American colleague wants us to believe. Further, the fact that objectivity is hard to reach does not liberate us from the duty to do our research work in the most objective way possible. "That objective fact alone is of little value" is also a sentence the truth of which is not easily seen, because history as a science recording events in the world of mankind is wholly dependent upon the conscientious recording of single objective facts.[12]

Still more interesting is the position taken by our American colleague when treating of the time aspect of history, for now he says:

> We have thus far considered history as if it included only past occurrences. But an adequate definition of history must include both present and future as well as past. The past is only a small fragment of time, and history cannot contain a sense of destiny and purpose unless the present and future are comprehended within its scope ... to some degree the future is latent within the past and the fleeting present to him who has eyes to see.

The last sentence is taken over from Berdyaev's well-known work on the meaning of history.[13]

Leaving aside some doubtful contentions, such as the one that to this author history as a science also ought to possess a sense of destiny and purpose—a contention likely to meet with a most violent opposition, e.g., among Scandinavian historians[14]—we turn our attention to that special idea of history advocated by our American authority. The quotations given to illustrate his position afford us excellent examples of what may be called a prescientific, nonscientific, or mythic view of history. For this American conception of history can well serve as a modern illustration of the ancient Hebrew notion of history.

The conception of history among the Hebrews, indeed, had nothing to do with modern, scientific ideas of history as they are accepted by all real scholars occupied with research in various historical subjects. When the modern American scholar just quoted—who, however, is no historian—and Berdyaev, Toynbee, and a few other people take a different view they exhibit a most remarkable agreement with the view taken by the ancient Hebrews. The reasons for this rather astonishing agreement cannot be dwelt upon here.[15] We wish only to point to *one* single important factor: the idea of time, for we remember the striking statement that "to some degree the future is latent within the past and the fleeting present to him who has eyes to see." Here the historical past, the present wherein we live, and the future yet to come are fused into a mystic totality. Let us see then what the aspect of time has to teach us about the Hebrew notion of history, for it goes without saying that for our understanding of the meaning of history among the Israelites and Jews it is necessary to know what the notion of time meant to Israel.

Then it should first of all be noted that time to the Hebrews was no abstract idea, not "a neutral and abstract frame of reference but rather a succession of recurring phases, each charged with a peculiar value and significance" as H. and H. A. Frankfort once put it.[16] Now, it should be expressly stated that this insight is due above all to Pedersen, whose name is casually mentioned in a note to the passage just cited. Actually, Pedersen's words deserve quoting. He says: "For the Israelite time is not merely a form or a frame. Time is charged with substance or, rather, it is identical with its substance; time is the development of the very events."[17]

To the Hebrews, then, time was filled with content. Each epoch possesses its special substance, and vice versa; every thing has its special time, an idea known above all from Ecclesiastes 3.1 ff.: "All things possess their time, all things that are done under the heaven possess their own time ... God ... hath made all things good in their time."[18]

Not only that, but time in this manner always is a repetition of what once has passed. As Ecclesiastes says (3.14-15): "I know that whatsoever God doeth, it shall be forever; nothing can be put to it, nor anything taken from it ... That which happeneth hath been (already), and that which is to be hath (already) been. God establisheth anew that which is past."

Against this background we understand that "times of the same substance are identical." The Israelite can say: "When this time again becomes alive," meaning "at the same time next year."[19] Time is conceived of, then, as an infinite cyclical repetition. The year comes back again in springtime, when the so-called "return of the year" takes place.[20]

Time, accordingly, is felt to be something experienced, not something to be merely measured. You find the same distinction also in modern conceptions of time, where on the one hand you have what the

Germans call "die messbare Zeit," and on the other hand the so-called "erlebte Zeit."[21] The second of these two conceptions corresponds precisely to the Hebrew idea of time.

Time then, according to the Hebrews, was filled by important events, but the peculiar Israelite conception of time with its strong cyclical aspect forbids history as a series of happenings to be conceived of as "a long chain of events, divided into special periods."[22] This does not mean that there was no idea of special periods. On the contrary, there was, and such ideas played an important role in Israelite thought. But characterically enough such a period was no abstract idea. The term used for it was *dōr,* and in Pedersen's definition which is adopted here it denotes "a time with the events distinguishing it, and first and foremost the people who create it and its substance, or, as it is usually rendered: generation."[23]

History, then, is made up of various *dōrōt,* "each with their special stamp."[24] All *dōrōt* together form ᶜōlām, a complex notion, conventionally rendered "eternity" but properly meaning "the most distant time,"[25] and this both in the past and in the future.[26]

When speaking of the Hebrew conception of history we should of course not forget to mention the fact that there also was a Hebrew presentation of history in a sense more akin to our modern, scientific meaning of the word. This Israelite writing of history is famous, as we all know, and deservedly so. But it should nevertheless be noted that the O.T. presentation of history in our scientific meaning of this term does not provide us with a simple account of Hebrew history, but with a peculiar *interpretation* of this history, as has been duly recognized, e.g. by North.[27]

II

In the ancient Near East there was no factual distinction between myth and history as far as quality was concerned. Actually the distinction that immediately presents itself to us as soon as there is a question of the immediate character of reality is not to be found between the spheres of myth and history in the ancient Near East. This has repeatedly been contended by Hempel, and there are very good reasons for doing so.[28] Thus the great historical work in O.T. literature called "conventionally and conveniently" "J," the work of probably the first outstanding Hebrew "historian," started its compre-

hensive history of Israel not with the oldest period from which real
historical traditions were still kept living in memory, but with the
creation of the world—an act, according to our way of historical
thinking, belonging to the sphere of myth and not to history.[29] That
such stories in fact belonged to myths as ritual texts is shown also by
the fact that Yahweh's activity as a creator was glorified at the great
annual festival, the New Year festival. Moreover, it has been argued
with some good reasons that a story of creation, though not that of
"J," was read by the priests at the New Year's festival.[30]

Next comes the Flood story, of which we will soon have to speak
more. The mythical character of the story of the Great Flood cannot
be doubted, for in this case we are able to trace its wanderings back
to remote Sumerian times in Mesopotamia where still more of its
original mythic character is preserved.[31] Now it also is of considerable
interest to see that in the hymns, where Yahweh's deeds are glorified,
no distinction is made as to his sphere of activity, be it situated according to our views within the realm of myth or demonstrated in the
clear light of history. In fact, his act of creation is associated with his
active dealing with his chosen people Israel, e.g. in Psalm 95.5, 8 ff.,[32]
where we read:

> To him belongs the sea,
>   for he made it,
> and the dry land
>   which his hands formed.
>
> Harden not your heart as at Meribah,
>   as in the day of Massah in the wilderness.
> When your fathers tempted me,
>   proved me, and even saw my work.

In the same way Yahweh's selection of his servant David (in Psalm 89.
20 ff.) is celebrated against the background of Yahweh's fight with
the Powers of Chaos and his act of creation (vv. 10–13). Even if we
argue that the hymnal section (vv. 6–19) is an independent poem,[33] we
find nevertheless within these verses too the connection of mythical
and nonmythical elements, for the thoughts of the poet pass from the
great deeds of Yahweh over to his people Israel and its concrete
situation: Israel is happy because it knows the cry of jubilation,
terūᶜāh,[34] and walks in the light of Yahweh's face.[35] The word
terūᶜāh alludes to the joy and jubilation at the great festivals when the

memory of God's great deeds was kept alive—as we have just stated in the case of the New Year festival when his activity as a creator was celebrated in song.

In this way we meet with a connecting link, joining the great deed of creation in a mythical past with the present state of Yahweh's people and, ultimately, the actual desperate situation of Yahweh's Chosen and Anointed (vv. 39–46). Yahweh's promise to David (vv. 20–38) is given in immediate connection with the preceding sections of the psalm. In that way the introduction of the psalm, with its motif of Yahweh's faithfulness, is taken up in that part where his promise to his servant David is rendered. The psalm is skillfully built, one part meshing with the other. We get also a parallelism of thought: in the beginning Yahweh conquered Rahab and the Powers of Chaos, then he chose his servant David, before whom he will beat down his foes. Exhorting Yahweh not to forget his promise to David, the singer invokes Yahweh not to let the foes of his Anointed scornfully triumph over him and Israel.[36]

In Psalm 136 the poet passes with equal ease from the mythical to the historical sphere of thought. This liturgical hymn, after a short exhortation to thank Yahweh (vv. 1–3), passes to a glorification of Yahweh as the creator of the world (vv. 5–9), then, however, praises his great acts in Egypt and at the Exodus.[37]

The same interaction between Yahweh's mythical and historical deeds is found in Psalm 148, where in a majestic hymn Yahweh's creative activity is glorified by all his creations, nature and man alike. Only in the last verse (v. 14) does the singer pass over to the historical sphere, giving the reason for his exhortation to praise Yahweh: he has exalted the horn of his people.[38]

As we already may be able to see from these few illustrations in Israelite thought, myth in our sense of the word was, so to speak, added to history in our sense of the word. In the psalms just cited Yahweh's activity as a creator was mentioned at the same level as his guidance of the chosen people.

III

Chronology is always said to be the backbone of history. Let us therefore consider the Israelite system of chronology to see how Israel's conception of history works out in its special aspects.

First of all, we should note that the Hebrews possessed an elaborate system of chronology. This chronological system is easily discernible above all in that collection of traditions that literary criticism has labeled "The Priestly Code," abbreviated "P." The chronological scheme found there is intimately linked up with the genealogies of which this collection of traditions is so fond.[39] The key word of "P" actually is *tōledōt,* which may be translated "genealogy." The traditions the "P"-traditionist found before him he brought into a special order by introducing various genealogies.[40] This tendency of his finds its most important expression in the so-called "genealogical tree of Seth" (Genesis 5.1 ff.). Here we find the tradition of the Primeval Patriarchs:

Adam lived	930	years before the Flood
Seth	912	
Enosh	905	
Qenan	910	
Mahalalel	895	
Jered	962	
Henoch	365	
Methuselah	969	
Lamech	777	
Noah	600	

All in all, ten Primeval Patriarchs lived 8,225 years before the Flood.

These ten Primeval Patriarchs of Hebrew tradition long ago were for the first time compared to the ten Primeval Kings of Mesopotamian tradition, at that time known only from the history of Mesopotamia, written at the beginning of the Hellenistic age by the Babylonian priest Berossos,[41] but now found also in original Sumerian documents, the so-called "Kinglists."[42] The points in which both lists actually agree are so many and so striking that the conclusion was inevitable from the outset: Hebrew tradition in this case ultimately can be traced back to Mesopotamian historico-mythical traditions, being taken over from Mesopotamia as part of a complex of traditions, the other two parts of which are the Story of the Flood and the Story of Creation.[43]

In this connection it should be observed that even the chronology of these ten Patriarchs as used in Israel exhibits clear traces of mythical speculation, as is also the case with the Babylonian chronology of the ten Primeval Kings, which was based upon speculations on the great, so-called "world-year."[44]

Now, it cannot be doubted that "P" aimed at establishing a chronological scheme, serving what he imagined to be an historical purpose, "historical" in this case taken as belonging to the scientific department of history.[45] The chronological framework of these Patriarchal traditions served the purpose of establishing a chronology of the duration of the world.[46] For this reason the whole history of mankind from the First Man to appear on earth, Adam, to the time of the author or collector of traditions was estimated to comprehend a certain sum of years. It stands to reason that in this way were combined elements that *we*—but *not* the Hebrews—attribute to two different categories, i.e. myth and history. Thus the Primeval Patriarchs have nothing to do with real history; they owe their place in the chronological system to a Hebrew heritage from Mesopotamian mythical literature.

In order to create, so to speak, a world history, "P" accordingly mixes mythical and historical elements, seemingly without feeling any difference whatsoever between myth and history.[47] The same attitude is found in Mesopotamia.[48] In this connection it should be observed that genealogy renders immense service by linking up mythical and truly historical figures together in one single chain.

Next we have to consider the Story of Creation and the Story of the Flood. From the outset both stories are myths, as modern research has proved. But they have been adapted by the traditionist to his chronological scheme of world history. One reason for this interrelation of myth and history is to be found in the chronological aspect of myth, for myth, as we stated, is not only repetition and actualization of what once happened, in fact it also is a narrative of what happened at that time. We should not forget *that* very essential aspect of myth, i.e., to the believer it is a *true* story, it is always held by the community to relate truly and adequately what once happened.[49] A chronologically framed history of the world from its beginnings to the time of the author therefore must include both mythical and historical chronology —from our point of view.

But we should always remember that our view was not at all that of the ancient Israelites, because they considered the Story of Creation and the Story of the Flood as narratives of quite historical events, as we have stressed here, the word "historical" being taken in our modern sense of the word. We did hint at the fact that in this regard Israel was perfectly in agreement with the Mesopotamian manner of looking upon these things, since the Babylonian Epic of Creation ends its chronological exposition of the story of the beginning by telling how the city of Babel was founded, thus carrying the story from mythical events over to the oldest known real history. *Enūma eliš* accordingly relates not only a myth but also the beginnings of history and these follow immediately after the mythical story of the creation of the world.[50] This fact has been duly emphasized by Hempel.[51]

The collector of the traditions constituting what we are accustomed to call "the Priestly Code" used another principle of arrangement which also possesses a clear mythical background. He introduced four periods in the history of mankind, and of Israel as part of mankind, each period starting with a great bringer of revelation. In this manner we get the epochs of Adam, Noah, Abraham, and Moses, each of whom received from God his own revelation and was given a covenant as a visible sign of his special relation to God.[52] This doctrine of the four periods during which revelation is brought to mankind has an old Near Eastern background and has played a most important role in the history of the religions of the ancient Near East.[53]

The last of the four periods, the period in which Israel actually existed, was introduced by Moses. At this point the true historical period of the life of the Hebrew tribes is linked up with the foregoing —from our scientific point of view—entirely mythical periods. But once more it must be remembered that viewed with Israelite eyes the three foregoing periods were quite as "historical" as the fourth and last one.

Within this last period too we meet with special divisions of time, introduced by important bringers of revelation. When Josephus relates the story of the cult-reformation carried out by Josiah he says:

And when he had done thus in Jerusalem, he came into the country, and utterly destroyed what buildings had been made therein by king Jeroboam, in honour of strange gods; and he burnt the bones of the false prophets upon that altar which Jeroboam first built. And as the prophet Jadon, who came to Jeroboam when he was offering sacrifice, and when all the people heard him, foretold what would come to pass, viz. that a "certain man of the house of David, Josiah by name, should do what is here mentioned." And it happened that those predictions took effect after three hundred and sixty-one years.   *Antiq.* X.ɪv.4 (Loeb Lib. ed.)

However, this chronological observation is entirely wrong; the reformation of Josiah takes place only about 300 years after the accession of Jeroboam. But Josephus wanted to single out Josiah as introducing a new epoch. He—or his source—therefore used the number 361 years, because this number corresponds to that of a "great year," 360 or 361 being a number of mythic-astrological significance in ancient Mesopotamia.[54] Josiah, who in tradition is depicted as a new Moses, concluding a new covenant with his people and bringing a new law as the outward symbol of the divine revelation[55] is in this manner made to introduce a new "great year," a new Aion. Such numerical speculations are indeed highly characteristic of the mythical thought of the ancient Near East.

IV

More specifically characteristic of Israelite thought is the quite astonishing extent to which what we should call a "myth" has been interpreted "historically."

The outstanding example, recognized as such long ago, is the way in which the traditions of the Exodus and the victory over the Egyptians are treated.

The oldest allusion is found in the song of triumph in Exodus 15. 1, 4–5:[56]

> I will sing unto Yahweh for he is elevated,
>   the horse and his chariot hath he thrown into the Sea.
> Pharao's chariots and his host hath he cast into the Sea,
>   and the chosen officers[57] are sunk in the Red Sea.
> The deeps cover them,
>   they went down into the depths like a stone.

This glorification of Yahweh's deeds is kept within the borders of what we call "history," irrespective of how much the original and real event may have been exaggerated in Israelite tradition.[58]

Of great importance, however, is the fact that a text recording an historical event is recited, perhaps even enacted, in the cult.[59] Historical traditions, in this case, take the place of cult myths in the recital of rituals, constituting as it were the "agenda" of the ritual. As the text of the cult, history is the substitute for myth, both "history" and "myth" taken in the modern sense of the terms.

Passing over to psalm literature and prophetic oracles we find, however, another situation. In Psalm 87.4 it is said:

I will mention Rahab and Babel among them that know me,
    behold Philistia, and Tyre, with Ethiopia,
    "this is born there."

The parallelism between Rahab and Babel as well as the following
geographical names show that Rahab, which is properly the term for
the mythic monster, the Deep or Tehom, in this passage is an enigmatic
name for a purely geographical-political entity. How this is to be
explained is clear from Isaiah 51.9 f., where the prophet exclaims:[60]

Awake, awake, put on strength,
    oh arm of Yahweh!
Awake as in the ancient days,
    in the generations of primeval times.
Art thou not he that cut asunder Rahab,
    pierced through the Dragon?
Art thou not he that dried up the Sea,
    the waters of the great Deep?
That made the depths of the sea a way
    for the ransomed to pass over?

Because of verse 10b, "That made the depths of the sea a way / for
the ransomed to pass over," there can be no doubt about the prophet's
thinking of the passing of the Israelites through the Red Sea. The
perishing of Pharaoh and his Egyptian army is accordingly seen in
the mythical colors of Yahweh's victory over the Primeval Dragon,
the Deep of Chaos personified.[61]

In this manner Rahab may be used so to speak as the mythological
name of Egypt, as we found in Psalm 87.4. So it is used also by (the
first) Isaiah (30.7) when the prophet says:[62]

For Egypt, they shall help with vanity and emptiness,
    therefore I call it:
"Rahab, brought to silence."

Egypt is the Power of Chaos, raging in vain, brought to silence by
Yahweh.[63]

It is surely not sufficient to say that in these passages adduced here
Egypt has been painted in mythical colors, so that we may speak
of a "mythization" of history. No, the wording in Isaiah 51.10 clearly
shows that to the prophet Egypt really *was* the Primeval Dragon, the
actual representative of the Chaos-Deep, dried up and brought to
silence by Yahweh. The Red Sea in this case was the nature symbol,

Pharaoh and his host as it were "the helpers of Rahab," as they are called, the military forces put into action by the Power of Chaos. We may say that Egypt and Pharaoh are the actual historical representatives of the mythical forces let loose in the beginnings, but then we must remember that this is only our own way of looking upon these things, it is *not* the view of the Hebrews. For to them, as we repeatedly tried to make clear, our differentiation of mythical from historical events and persons did not exist. Hence the actual political enemies could be seen as the ever recurring mythical opponents of Yahweh; they were, we might say, the concrete visualization in present history of these foes.

This takes us to the much discussed problem of the enemies in the psalms. Who are these enemies? Political enemies of the ruler, personal enemies of the individual worshipper, or mythical enemies of the sacral king, acting in the ritual as the representative of Yahweh? [64]

Twenty years ago when I was occupied with this problem I tried with the help of Accadian parallel texts to demonstrate how one and the same expression might be applicable to all the three possibilities because of the vagueness of the texts.[65] I was also rather anxious to show how political enemies could be depicted more or less in mythical colors. The fact that they were seen as actual representatives of mythical forces was not altogether neglected by me, but I did not drive home this point with all necessary explicitness.[66] This being the case, I cannot but quote with approval the words of Birkeland, when he says: "Yahweh has once manifested his power through his victory over chaos and enemies, and he shows it again now and ever. The actual powers of chaos, therefore, are the foreign *'elīm* and their worshippers, the *gōyīm*, who disturb order, attacking and oppressing Yahweh's people." When, however, Birkeland argues that *all* enemies mentioned in the psalms must be political enemies of the Israelite ruler it is more difficult to follow him,[67] for in some passages we only find a purely mythical description of the enemies, who are depicted as demoniacal animals attacking the supplicant, e.g. Psalms 22.12–13, and 57.4.[68]

It would seem then, that just as the great Primeval Enemy, Rahab, or Tehom could be mentioned together with political, hostile powers, so also other mythical enemies, demoniacal beings of the Nether World and the like, could be alluded to along with external or internal, political or nonpolitical enemies.[69] This statement does not imply any general opinion on the question of the enemies in the psalms; it deals only with the special aspect we are interested in here.[70]

Before leaving the problem of this so-called "historification of myth" we may note that the prophets sometimes make use of a myth when describing or attacking contemporary persons, powers, or conditions. This is the case with the dirge of Isaiah on the fall of Babel (Isaiah 14), or with Ezekiel's description of the king of Tyre (chap. 28), both poems being written as mythical compositions and based on real myths, as especially emphasized by Hempel.[71]

V

There is another aspect of our main theme that I want to touch upon briefly, namely the importance of the feasts.

Modern research has proved—we may venture to say conclusively— that at least many of the ancient Israelite feasts, being seasonal festivals, originally were intimately associated with a cult myth.[72] So, e.g., the Sukkōt festival (the great annual Feast of Booths) in its Canaanite form obviously was connected from the outset with the marriage between God and Goddess, the leafy hut, *sukkāh,* serving as the place of the *hieros gamos.*[73] But, according to the accepted Israelite-Jewish tradition, this feast was associated with and inspired by the historical memories of the wanderings of the Hebrew tribes during forty years in the desert. Hebrew historical tradition had thus completely shifted the emphasis of this festival, connecting it with the nomad period in the history of the people, whereas popular tradition and custom still kept alive the memory of its original and *truly historical* setting in life within the framework of the Canaanite agricultural system of seasonal festivals, in that way also guarding something at least of its original *mythical* character. From our point of view there is an obvious clash here between myth and history, and I think that the traditionists who tried to connect this festival with the great national memories of Israel really felt something of this clash and were intentionally aiming at a "demythologization" of the annual festival. It must have been a clear intention and purpose behind their effort.[74]

Myth relates events which are repeated cyclically. History, on the contrary, is characterized by what the Germans call *Einmaligkeit,* for history never repeats itself in exactly the same manner.[75] Because of the special Israelite conception of time, however, history "through the annual festival . . . was made something still living and present," as Pedersen puts it, and in this way history was quite like what we call a myth.

History in this case is made a living present, and thus the difference between myth and history is eliminated, a process made possible because history here fulfills the role of myth in ritual. History is thus substituted for myth—according to our modern, scientific views.

VI

Eschatology is both the fulfillment of history and the realization of myth. Eschatology is the doctrine of the last things, *ta éschata*. The last things to happen mark the end of all history and therefore its fulfillment. Eschatology belongs to history, because the last things will happen on this earth, but at the same time it embraces mythical elements, chiefly because the time of end rejoins the time of beginning: end and origin meet each other, the end renewing the time of creation and beginning. As the Germans put it: "Endzeit wird Urzeit." [76] As Yahweh once created the world, so he will now create a new world; he will once more act as a Creator, bringing back the time of paradise.[77] At the same time, however, all eschatological speculation deals with purely historical entities, such as people, countries, political powers.[78]

Apocalyptical speculation about this time of end was much concerned with ideas of the change of time, when the present world period, *hā-ᶜōlām hazzæ*, will be substituted by the world period to come, *hā-ᶜōlām habbā*. But recent research has proved this special notion of ᶜōlām to be entirely foreign to original Israelite thought, and it can easily be shown that we come across in this case one instance of Iranian influence of late Hellenistic age.[79]

We cannot develop here at length the role historical and mythical elements have played in the Israelite-Jewish conception of the figure of Messiah. Suffice it to say that, on the one hand, he is associated with the mythic idea of the returning time of paradise but, on the other hand, as a descendant of David he also belongs to real, human history.[80]

VII

We have found that the Israelite-Jewish conceptions of what we would call myth and history are completely at variance with our Western scientific ideas of what is meant by these two terms. The Israelite notion often seems to move somewhere between myth and history. This is a most conspicuous feature in the so-called patriarchal legends and will perhaps explain our difficulty in interpreting them either as myth or as history. Pedersen, who in some passages speaks of these narratives of the fathers, prefers to define them as "the condensed history of many generations" or as "the history of the people in a condensed form." [81]

But he also prefers this expression when dealing with the special Israelite form of historical outlook. The Israelite people, he says, "still sought their history, so to speak in a condensed form, in the desert. . . . It is understandable that in this way an artificial element must creep into their conception of their history," he continues. [82]

I cannot discuss in this article the expression "condensed history" and its possible value, nor can I take up the idea of Yahweh as the God of history, as he is so often qualified in O. T. modern study, but it goes without saying that, if our viewpoints are correct, the implications in the last mentioned case are of considerable importance. [83]

The quite natural and free way in which to the Israelite mind the ideas and notions pass from a sphere that we call "historical" to what we think a "mythical" sphere and vice versa should warn us not to draw any fixed line of demarcation between myth and history in Israelite-Jewish thought. To Israelite thought Yahweh's interference in the history of Israel is clearly on the same level as his creative activity. For this reason exception is to be taken to the statement of Von Rad à propos Psalm 136: "Hier stehen also Schöpferglaube und Heilsglaube ganz unverbunden nebeneinander." [84] To my mind this is a typical example of the wrong way of interpreting O.T. conceptions, looking at them from the very narrow view of a Christian theologian whose dogmatic training leads him to distinguish sharply between "Schöpferglaube" and "Heilsglaube," and who is unable to place himself in a position subordinate to the texts and to learn how their originators saw things. To the Israelites the great deed of salvation wrought by Yahweh was just his act of creation following his victory over the Chaos Powers. This is really "Heilsglaube," it is the yēšaʻ given by Yahweh.

This deed of creation and all other miracles performed by Yahweh, both "mythical" and "historical," were glorified at the great festivals. At these feasts the Israelite in the present time looked back to the past, remembering Yahweh's deeds, but also looked forward, finding in the past a guarantee for the future, exhorting Yahweh to renew his miraculous deeds of old. Clearly the festival is of essential importance to our understanding of the Israelite-Jewish ideas of "history" and "myth." In the festival there is to be found the real forms of the Israelite interpretation of "history." It is here we find the wide range of themes going from the theme of creation to the theme of settlement in Canaan.[85]

As to apocalyptic speculation, Noth has shown that in the Book of Daniel there is a striking mixture of two ideas in the description of the four World Empires, these being conceived of as succeeding empires but, also, as contemporaneous at the world's end. We see here that the time aspect in our modern sense is completely absent. In that moment when the fate of the world is decided by God, the whole course of "history" is present. We can see then that "history" in our sense of the word is not present in these speculations.[86] Thus apocalyptic ideas confirm our views on the relation between myth and history in Israelite-Jewish thought.

APPENDIX

Some Remarks on Myth and History in the Babylonian Epic of Creation

Weiser says concerning the *Enūma eliš:* "Kann man somit an diese Form des Weltschöpfungsmythus eine Geschichte nicht einmal äusserlich anschliessen, so besteht noch weniger hier eine 'innere Verbindung' von Schöpfung und Geschichte, gegen Hempel, Gott und Mensch im Alten Testament."[87] For his opinion he finds support in the words of the concluding hymn on Marduk, where we read:

May he vanquish Tiamat,   may her life be strait and short.
Into the future of mankind,   when days have grown old,
May she recede without cease   and stay away forever.
Because he created the spaces   and fashioned the firm ground.

Enūma eliš VII.132–35

From these words[88] he concludes that the Babylonian Epic of Creation moves within the idea of a cyclical return of events. As he puts it: "Hier ist mit wünschenswerter Deutlichkeit der Weltschöpfungsgötterkampf nicht als Anfang einer 'Geschichte', sondern als 'Anfang und Ende' eines immer widerkehrenden Kreislaufes aufgefasst, der auf dem Boden des natur-mythologischen, kosmischen Denkens entstanden ist und diesen Boden an keinem Punkt verlässt."

In this case Weiser, however, would seem to have overlooked the fact that the epic has as its concluding event the foundation of the town Babel with its sanctuary (*Enūma eliš* VI.47 ff.). Not with the best will in the world can this event be said to be located within the sphere of the ideas of a cyclical return, for the foundation of Babel is not to be repeated every year; it is a fact once for all, and one cannot at all doubt its character of *Einmaligkeit*. Noth[89] and especially Hempel accordingly were quite right in their contention, and not even the most ingenious exegesis would be able to deny the fact that, in the Babylonian Epic of Creation, myth in our sense of the word is followed in the sequence of events by actions belonging to history in our sense of the word. In other words: myth is followed by history, without of course the Babylonians feeling any difference in the character of reality of "myth" and "history."

But even the interpretation of the passage quoted from the *Enūma eliš* needs some qualification. Weiser seems to have overlooked the fact—which is indeed conspicuous everywhere in the Epic but especially in Tablets VI and VII—that the Babylonian Epic of Creation is a cult text, intended to be recited at the New Year festival. The wish that Tiamat may be vanquished forever is of the same kind as that in the hymn in Habakkuk 3.2 ff., when the singer depicts Yahweh triumphantly proceeding to save his Anointed and his people. In the festival the great deeds of Marduk are experienced anew as they were in Israel in the case of Yahweh. We should note the allusion to Marduk's creative activity (*Enūma eliš* 7.135), a motif well known from Israel in connection with Yahweh's fight against the Power of Chaos.

Another viewpoint calls for notice. The Sumerian Kinglist[90] tells us that "when kingship was lowered from heaven, kingship was in Eridu." It then mentions all the kings ruling before "the Flood swept over [the earth]." The kingship again was sent down from heaven, and we get to know all the rulers reigning after that event, i.e. all the postdiluvian kings. Among them are to be found such figures as Etana, Dumuzi, and Gilgamesh, to mention but a few of these mythical rulers. The list then passes over to Mes-Anne-padda, a clearly historical figure because we possess historical inscriptions of his own. Thus the Kinglist passes from the "mythical" to the "historical" sphere with the same ease as we find in Israel. And this fact demonstrates that the same attitude is to be supposed also in *Enūma eliš*, where the creation of the world is linked to the foundation of Babel with its sanctuary.

NOTES

ABBREVIATIONS

ANET   *Ancient Near Eastern Texts Relating to the Old Testament*
BJRL   *Bulletin* of the John Ryland's Library
BZAW   *Zeitschrift für die alttestamentliche Wissenschaft.* Beihefte
ICC   *International Critical Commentary*
JNES   *Journal of Near Eastern Studies*
JSS   *Journal of Semitic Studies*
JThSt   *Journal of Theological Studies*
KAT   *Die Keilinschriften und das Alte Testament*
LUÅ   *Lunds Universitets Årsskrift*
MaR   *Myth and Ritual,* ed. by S. H. Hooke
RGG²   *Die Religion in Geschichte und Gegenwart,* 2d ed.
RHPhR   *Revue d'histoire et de philosophie religieuses*
SMSR   *Studi e Materiale della Storia dei Religioni*
StTh   *Studia Theologica*
UUÅ   *Uppsala Universitets Årsskrift*
ZAW   *Zeitschrift für die alttestamentliche Wissenschaft*

[1] The comprehensive article by Hempel, "Glaube, Mythos und Geschichte im Alten Testament," ZAW, 65:109-67, 1953, which will be quoted several times in the following and which anticipated some of my own conclusions, does not treat of all the aspects of our theme. The present essay is a development of some viewpoints found in my *Religionens värld,* 2d ed. (Stockholm, 1953), pp. 163 f., and reproduces the text of a lecture given at The University College of North Wales in January, 1956. I should like in this connection to thank Professor B. J. Roberts for his invitation and his kind hospitality. I remember also with pleasure my discussions with Professor C. R. North. In the text of my lecture some passages have been slightly expanded, and the notes have been added. I regret that lack of time and space forbids me a more detailed treatment of certain points, but I hope to be able to revert to this interesting theme.

[2] Hooke, *In the Beginning* (Oxford, 1948), p. 18; see also his *Myth and Ritual,* pp. 3 f.; Widengren, *Religionens värld,* pp. 132 f.

[3] The importance of religious symbols has been underlined by Widengren, "Evolutionism and the Origin of Religion," *Ethnos,* 10:90 n. 91, 1945, with reference to Bevan, *Symbolism and Belief* (London, 1938), and Dumézil, *Les dieux des indo-européens* (Paris, 1952), pp. 114-17.

[4] See Widengren, *Religionens värld,* pp. 149 f., with reference to Lévy-Bruhl, *La mythologie primitive* (Paris, 1935), p. 7.

[5] Widengren, "Early Hebrew Myths and their Interpretation," in *Myth, Ritual and Kingship,* ed. by Hooke (Oxford, 1958), pp. 149-203. In modern Hebrew the term for "myth" is the Greek loanword מיתוס

[6] Bernheim, *Einleitung in die Geschichtswissenschaft,* 4th ed. (Berlin-Leipzig, 1926, p. 5; cf. Kirn, *Einführung in die Geschichtswissenschaft* (Berlin, 1952), p. 8: "1. Geschehen, 2. Darstellung des Geschehenen, 3. Wissenschaft vom Geschehen."

[7] See Liddell and Scott, *A Greek-English Lexicon,* s.v. ἱστορία, and Powell, *A Lexicon to Herodotus* (Cambridge, 1938), s.v. ἱστορέω and ἱστορίη; see Herodotus VII.96.

[8] Bernheim, *Einleitung*, pp. 58 ff.

[9] Hempel, *Gott und Mensch im Alten Testament*, 2d ed. (Stuttgart, 1936), p. 86: "Dass das A.T. kein Wort für "Geschichte" hat—ebensowenig für "Natur"—, erschwert den Einblick in die Sachlage." In modern Hebrew in this case too we find a loanword, היסטוריה.

[10] Hyatt, *Prophetic Religion* (New York-Nashville, 1947), pp. 77 f.

[11] Ranke, *Geschichte der römischen und germanischen Völker 1495–1534*, Vorwort, in *Gesammelte Werke*, 1 Aufl.

[12] Cf. the weight attached in historical research to the criticism of sources in order to ascertain the objective facts so despised by our American authority; see, for the importance of source criticism, Bernheim, *Einleitung*, pp. 136 ff., and Kirn, *Einführung*, pp. 52 ff. Cf. Bernheim, p. 163: "... unwillkürlich begleiten wir die Güter, Ideen, Ziele, die wir für die erstrebenswertesten halten, überall mit unserer Teilnahme, wir bevorzugen die Parteien und Personen, welche für sie eintreten, die Epochen, wo sie herrschen und gedeihen, unwillkürlich vor anderen. Gegen die Einflüsse dieser subjektiven Parteinahme und der ihr zugrunde liegenden *Werturteile* auf unsere Geschichtserkenntnis müssen wir uns mit wissenschaftliche Bewusstsein soweit irgend möglich schützen. "Wir müssen uns vor allem klarmachen, dass es 'allgemein anerkannte', gleichbleibende Werte, Werturteile in der Wirklichkeit der Geschichte nicht gibt." After developing some principles of method Bernheim then continues, on p. 165: "Durchweg vermögen wir so mit unseren methodischen Hilfsmitteln Objektivität in einem Grade zu erreichen, der von subjektiver Auffassung himmelweit verschieden ist."

From Kirn, p. 85, we may quote the following passage: "Damit haben wir die Forderung anerkannt, dass der Historiker gerecht sei. Wir meinen, er muss auch sachlich sein, d.h. nach der viel umstrittenen *Objektivität* streben. Man drücke sich nicht um die Schwierigkeit mit Hilfe der banalen Behauptung, dass die volle Objektivität nie erreicht werden könne. Es geht ja zunächst darum, ob man sich ihr so weit als möglich nähern soll. Wer dies durch den Hinweis auf die volle Verwirklichung abzutun glaubte, gliche einem Schiffskapitän, der sagte: 'Es ist unmöglich, genau auf der mathematischen Linie des gewählten Kurses quer über den Ozean zu fahren. Also schleudern wir den Kompass ins Meer und steuern wild darauf los!' Die Unmöglichkeit der buchstäblichen Erfüllung eines Gebots entbindet nicht von der Pflicht der bestmöglichen Erfüllung."

Cf. also Geyl, *Use and Abuse of History* (New Haven, 1955), pp. 59 f., on the importance of recording of single objective facts ("specialized pursuits"). Geyl, of course, stresses that "the fact in history cannot be isolated. In itself it is meaningless; it can be made to show different aspects of meaning only as it is related to different parts of the circumstances in which it is embedded" (p. 61). It is obvious that this apparent truth is not what is in the mind of our American colleague who—as far as I am able to understand him—expresses his contempt for the recording of objective facts on which all historical research is based.

[13] Berdyaev, *The Meaning of History* (New York, 1936), p. 41.

[14] Landberg, *Historia* (Stockholm, 1954), pp. 12 ff.; cf. Geyl, *Use and Abuse of History*, p. 70.

[15] It is obvious, however, that the chief factor lies in the substitution of interpretation of history for real historical research. Such is the case especially with Toynbee, who bases his interpretation of history (a) on wrong data, (b) on distorted data, (c) on misinterpreted data. Toynbee's quite fantastic views have been exposed to a trenchant criticism by Geyl, who (as he himself says) "attempted to show

in detail the hollowness to its pretense of being based on empiricism and logical induction"; see Geyl, *Use and Abuse of History*, p. 65 n. 4, with reference to *Debates with Historians* (Groningen, 1955).

[16] See *The Intellectual Adventure of Ancient Man: An Essay on Speculative Thought in the Ancient Near East* (Chicago, 1946), p. 25, where "early man" in general is spoken of. I do not know how the Frankforts were able to speak with such assurance about this rather vague entity, "early man" (who is meant by this expression? Neanderthal man or people in the *historical* cultures of the ancient Near East?). It should also be observed that the title "The Intellectual Adventure of Ancient Man" is singularly misleading, as some critics have noted.

[17] Pedersen, *Israel*, I–II (Copenhagen-London, 1926), 487; see also *Scepticisme israélite* (Paris, 1931), p. 37: "Si nous ne parlons pas par figures, nous distinguons nettement entre le temps et les événements qui se passent dans le temps. C'est ce que ne font pas les anciens Semites. C'est particulièrement évident chez les Arabes. Naturellement, le temps pour eux représente également des moments et des périodes, mais toujours de sorte que le temps et son contenu soient identiques. Le temps est la somme de ce qui se passe." Accordingly, it was not Boman (*Das hebräische Denken im Vergleich mit dem Griechischen*, 1st ed. [Göttingen, 1952], pp. 120 ff.) who was the first to find that to the Semites (but in fact the same holds true also of many other people) the time and its content are identical, as Hempel would seem to believe (see ZAW, 65:134, 1953).

[18] Pedersen, *Scepticisme israélite*, p. 34f.

[19] Pedersen, *Israel*, I–II, 488.

[20] *Ibid.*, p. 489.

[21] RGG, 2d ed., V, 2090.

[22] Pedersen, *Israel*, I–II, 490.

[23] *Ibid.*, p. 490. When Pedersen (p. 549) says that a connection with Arabic *dahr* might be possible he thinks of the near relation between the roots *dwr* and *dhr*. See Gesenius and Buhl, *Handwörterbuch*, p. 159a.

The Hebrew word *dōr* belongs to the base *dr*, "surround" or "turn round." In Hebrew *dōr*, "circle" or "circuit" (of time), assumes the meaning of "generation," the cyclical period from birth to death in the life of an individual (Baumgartner and Köhler, *Lexicon*, p. 206b). In Arabic we have the corresponding word *dawr*, "period" (see Driver, *Problems of Hebrew Verbal System* [Edinburgh, 1936], p. 5, to which we are able to add Accadian *dāru*), which also as the *dawr* of a planet denotes the cyclical turn the planet makes until it comes back to the same point (see Dozy, *Supplément aux dictionnaires arabes*, I. 472b). In Arabic the verb *dāra* of the same root *inter alia* means "to happen," i.e., what comes back again or what turns around (see Orelli, *Die hebräischen Synonyma der Zeit und Ewigkeit* [Leipzig, 1871], p. 34). In Accadian we find the words *dāru* and *dūru*, "eternity," i.e., an ever recurring time cycle, an unlimited period. In Aramaic-Syriac we find correspondingly *dār*, "circle," "period," "generation," and in Ethiopic *dār*, "period."

Especially worth noting is the fact that Hebrew *dōr* < *dawr* is exactly formed as Arabic *dawr*, which denotes not only the period of time but also what it brings of destiny for man, thus "changed fortune," "fate" (see Driver, JThSt 36:403, 1935).

In view of all these facts, strong exception is to be taken to the following viewpoints of Boman (p. 115). He first admits that it is possible that *dōr* comes from the same base as *dūr*, "circle," "circuit" (but, as we have seen, there is not the slightest doubt possible in this case, hence this fact ought to be articulated in a much more affirmative way). But then he continues: "Damit ist aber nicht bewiesen, dass sich die Hebräer die Generation doch als einen Kreis vorgestellt haben. Es ist nämlich möglich und wahrscheinlich, dass sie umgekehrt den Kreislauf als einen ewigen Rhytmus von Anfang, Fortsetzung und Rückkehr zum Anfang gedacht haben." This supposed "rhythm" is unfortunately a purely gratuitous hypothesis, put forward by the author, who moreover knows from where the Hebrews possessed this rhythm—namely, from their dances in circuit! Here we have definitely left the firm ground of facts and embarked upon the frail ship of pure guesswork. Actually we have been able to ascertain that the Hebrew word for "generation," dōr, is entirely connected with the common Semitic base dr, "to turn round" and corresponds perfectly to the Arabic term dawr, the cyclical period. Hebrew dōr then is intimately bound up with the idea of a cyclical return, and means what recurs cyclically.

²⁴ Pedersen, Israel, I–II, 490.
²⁵ Jenni, Das Wort 'ōlām im Alten Testament (Berlin, 1953), esp. p. 50.
²⁶ Ibid., pp. 44 ff.
²⁷ North, The Old Testament Interpretation of History (London, 1946), p. xi. "The Old Testament in its present form contains, not a straightforward account of Hebrew History, but that history as viewed from the standpoint of the Jewish Church in the period after the Exile."
²⁸ Hempel, ZAW, 65:121 f.: "Dass zwischen dem, was wir Geschichte nennen, dem menschlich-völkischen Leben, in dem Menschen nach menschlicher Vernunft oder Unvernunft, nach dem, was sie über 'gut' und 'böse' wissen oder wider solche Erkenntnis, nach Gottes Gebot oder in sündiger Lust handeln und ihr Leben zum Guten oder Bösen wenden, und dem, was wir Mythos nennen, dem unmittelbaren Handeln Gottes unter uns Menschen, sei es zum Segen oder zum Fluch—dass zwischen 'Geschichte' und 'Mythos' ein qualitativer Unterschied, ein Unterschied des unmittelbaren Wirklichkeitsgehaltes besteht, ist ein dem antiken Schriftsteller fernliegender Gedanke.... Der Sündenfall ist ihm genau so ein einmaliges 'geschichtliches' Ereignis wie die Arche Noah oder der Turmbau zu Babel oder die Gottesstimme, die Abraham aus Chaldäa rief und in das gelobte Land geleitete." Cf. further Hempel, Gott und Mensch im Alten Testament, p. 61 f.; and Altes Testament und Geschichte (Gütersloh, 1930), pp. 12 f. I quote what Hempel says in his Gott und Mensch, p. 61 f.: "Ich habe in anderem Zusammenhang darauf hingewiesen und muss auch gegenüber neuester Bestreitung daran festhalten, dass die Verknüpfung von Schöpfung und geschichtlichen Grössen an sich noch kein spezifisch israelitischer Gedanke ist. Wie für den Babylonier die Formung der Welt aus den Hälften des erlegten Drachen in der Gründung der Stadt Babel und ihres Tempels gipfelt, so stehen in den Hymnen Deuterojesajas und späteren Texten die Offenbarung der Macht Jahves in der Schöpfung und in der Geschichte Israels aufs engste zusammen." The same example was adduced by me in Religionens värld, p. 163.
²⁹ See Hooke, In the Beginning, p. 28: "it seems clear that the Jahvist is using for his own purpose a myth which formed part of ancient Hebrew tradition."
³⁰ See Hooke, p. 36, where he obviously alludes to the article by Humbert, RHPhR 15:1-27, 1935, even though he does not expressly mention Humbert's name.
³¹ See my Early Hebrew Myths, pp. 162, 164 f., 168, 172 f., 174, 176, etc., for the general observation that myths have come from Mesopotamia to Canaan where they were taken over by the Hebrew tribes after the settlement. For the wandering of the Flood story and the intermediary role played by the Hurrians, see, e.g.,

Rowley, BJRL 32:36 f., 1949. That the Flood story as a living myth has been recited at the great Autumn Festival would seem to be evident from the role played in this feast by the coming of waters; see Pedersen, *Israel*, III–IV (Copen hagen-London, 1940), 749 f., where he refers to Lukianos, *De Dea Syria*, § 13.

[32] Hempel, *Gott und Mensch*, p. 105 with n. 6 (references to Is. 51.9 and to Gunkel and Begrich, *Einleitung in die Psalmen* [Göttingen, 1933], pp. 71 ff.).

[33] Cf. Kittel, *Die Psalmen*, 5th-6th ed. (Leipzig, 1929), p. 296. I cannot under stand Kittel when he says: "Sowohl der Anfang, als besonders das Stück 6-19 schliessen sich metrisch und inhaltlich nur lose an das Übrige an." As to the metrical character, we should note that v. 16 has 4 + 4, like the preceding verses whereas vv. 17–19 have 3 + 3, like the following section. This is quite the opposite of what Kittel alleges.

[34] For this important term see Humbert, *La "terou'a": Analyse d'un rite biblique* (Neuchatel, 1946).

[35] The meaning of באור פניך יהלכון is debated; see the commentaries.

[36] See Kittel, *Die Psalmen*, p. 296; Humbert, *La "terou'a"*, pp. 11, 20, 40 f., 45 Ringgren, in *Psaltarens fromhet* (Stockholm, 1957), p. 152, has been sensible to the interplay of myth and history in this psalm. I find myself in general agreement with him; see below, n. 67.

[37] Von Rad, BZAW, 66:139, 1936, says: "ab v. 10 geht der Psalm in scharfer Wendung zu der Aufzählung der geschichtlichen Grosstaten Jahves über. Hier stehen also Schöpferglaube und Heilsglaube ganz unverbunden nebeneinander.' For a criticism of such a view see p. 483.

[38] See also Psalm 114 where, according to the hymnal language of the poet, all nature, the Sea, the Jordan, the mountains, show their compassion in the Exodus of Israel.

[39] See Gunkel, *Genesis*, 3d ed. (Göttingen, 1910), p. xciv.

[40] *Ibid.*, pp. lxxxvi, xciv, 131 ff., 140 f., 152 ff., 262, 385, 493 ff.

[41] See Schnabel, *Berossos und die babylonisch-hellenistische Literatur* (Leipzig-Berlin, 1923), pp. 179 ff.

[42] Jacobsen, *The Sumerian Kinglist* (Chicago, 1939), esp. pp. 70 ff. Hooke (*In the Beginning*, p. 45 f.) referred not only to Berossos but also to the Sumerian kinglists. The older discussion is found in KAT, 3d ed., pp. 530-43.

[43] Gunkel, *Genesis*, p. 132.

[44] See KAT, 3d ed., pp. 538 f., 541 f.

[45] On "P" as an historian, see Millar Burrows, "Ancient Israel," in *The Idea of History in the Ancient Near East* (New Haven, 1955), pp. 124 f.

[46] Gunkel, *Genesis*, p. 133.

[47] Thus we can see how at a given point the exposition passes over from myth to history.

[48] The Mesopotamian kinglists in some cases start with entirely mythical figures like Tammuz or Gilgamesh and pass eventually into the purely historical realm. See Appendix.

[49] That the myth is felt by the worshipers and believers to be a *true* story has been emphasized, e.g., by Pettazzoni, SMSR, 21:104-16, 1947-48. Pettazzoni however, is of the opinion that the truth of the myths is not of an historical kind. This is correct in so far as the distinction between history and myth is absent on the "mythical" stage. Gaster, in Numen, Vol. I, 1954, contends that Pettazzoni in this case confuses truth with efficacy. If we stick to the fact that myth really is held by its believers to be *true*, to render a truth, no confusion is possible.

[50] The exposition in the mythical epic *Enūma eliš* accordingly corresponds to the passage in genealogy from mythic to historical times.

[51] See also the dictum of Hempel above, n. 28.

[52] See Gunkel, *Genesis*, pp. 264 f.

[53] Widengren, *Religionens värld*, pp. 350 ff., 364 ff. Gunkel (p. 265) was definitely wrong in assuming a Babylonian origin of this typically Indo-Iranian speculation. It is very interesting and important to find it in Israel already in the time of "P".

[54] We may put the accession of Jeroboam in the year 931 B.C., according to Montgomery, *The Book of Kings*, in ICC, 1951, pp. 58, 63, and the reform of Josiah in the year 621 B.C., also according to the chronology given by Montgomery. Other chronological systems, e.g. those of Albright and Begrich, present small deviations.
The number of 361 years is somewhat puzzling for we would expect 360 years. It may be explained by a special computation taking the actual year after the 360 years and adding it to the real mythical number; or, rather, as a Great Year, 354 years, plus a Great Week, 7 years. On the mythic-astrological number 360, see Meissner, *Babylonien und Assyrien*, II (Heidelberg, 1925), 415.

[55] Widengren, "King and Covenant," JSS, 2:2-5, 17-19, 29 f., 1957.

[56] For the poetical form of this song see Albright, *Archaeology of Palestine and the Bible*, pp. 145 f.; *Studies in Old Testament Prophecy*, ed. by Rowley (Edinburgh, 1950, p. 5); Cross and Freedman, JNES, 14:241 ff., 1955.

[57] For the proper meaning of the term *šālīš* see Baumgartner and Köhler, *Lexicon in Veteris Testamenti libros*, p. 977b; Cross and Freedman, p. 245a. The *šālīš* is the third man standing in the chariot.

[58] This exaggeration is of course due to the fact that a "mythization" of history in this case has exerted a great influence on the authentic traditions of the event; see, e.g., Pedersen, *Israel*, III–IV, 728: "The object cannot have been to give a correct exposition of ordinary events but, on the contrary, to describe history on a higher plane, mythical exploits which make of the people a great people, nature subordinating itself to this purpose. Östborn, "Yahweh's Words and Deeds," JUÅ, 7:15, 1951, also stresses the mythological traits in the story in Exodus 5.1–18. From the article of Cross and Freedman we may quote the following statements: "It seems most reasonable to suppose that the poetic styles and canons of Canaan have affected strongly the structure, diction, and, on occasion, the actual phraseology of the poem. Certain clichés concerning the anger and might of Yahweh, and conversely, the heaving of the sea, may be derived secondarily from mythological cycles, or rather the lyric poetry and psalmody of Canaan. . . . It seems necessary to conclude that we do not have a mythologically derived conflict here. It is dubious in the extreme to suppose that we have the result of the 'historicizing' of myth ... Rather we have 'history' shaped by familiar clichés, motifs and literary styles, and even these influences are remarkably restrained" p. 238a). "The situation, both historically and in regard to the problem of mythological relationships, is far more complex in vss. 16b-18. . . . It is in these verses that we feel the strongest influence of mythological motifs" (p. 240a). We miss, here, however, an insight into the fact that to the Hebrews at this time there was no contrast between history and myth. As to the traditions of the Exodus, I hope to be able to return to this subject, the character of these traditions being a very complex one as is generally recognized.
Hempel, *Gott und Mensch*, p. 65, contends that in Israel history never was mythicized ("in den Bann des Mythus gezogen"), but the Exodus tradition would seem to point in the opposite direction.

[59] On the Exodus tradition as the cult legend of the Passover, see Pedersen, ZAW, 52:161 ff., 1934. Mowinckel, StTh, 5:66 ff., 1952, has disputed the inter-

pretation of this complex of traditions as given by Pedersen, but he too admit
that as we now have it it is built upon traditions possessing a "cult-legendary
character. I cannot enter here upon a discussion of this problem but must postpon
it for the future. I shall say only that even Mowinckel does not deny that we ar
entitled in a way to speak of the Exodus tradition as the cultic myth of the Passove
festival: "In diesem Sinne darf man mit Pedersen von der Exodustradition al
Kultmythus des Passahfestes sprechen" (p. 86). We should not overlook the fac
that still in the Mishnah, Pesachim x.5b, there is a quotation from Exodus 13.
giving the whole feeling of the festival. The Passover is experienced as an actua
izing of the Exodus tradition; see the pertinent remark in Beer, *Pesachim* (Giesser
1912), pp. 195 f. The Exodus story would accordingly serve the same purpose a
the Passover festival as the Flood story at the Autumn festival (leaving aside th
major problem of whether the Exodus too may have been associated with th
Autumn feast). Hence, even in this case, a perfect parallelism between mythica
and "historical" texts.

[60] For the general interpretation see Gunkel, *Schöpfung und Chaos*, 2d ed
(Göttingen, 1921), pp. 30 ff.; Widengren, *Early Hebrew Myths*, pp. 169 ff.

[61] See Gunkel, *Schöpfung*, pp. 31 f.: "Indess bleibt die Frage bestehen, wi
denn hier der Untergang Pharaos als die Vertilgung eines grossen Ungeheuer
geschildert werden könne. Solche Bilder werden nicht willkürlich erfunden
sondern sie treten nur als eine nachträgliche Umdeutung und Aneignung de
Tradition auf,—man beachte, dass Rahab ein Name ist. Das ist hier um so
sicherer, als das Bild von Rahabs Zerschmetterung nicht als eine deutliche, von
Dichter erfundene Allegorie begriffen werden kann; denn wer soll Rahab sein—
Pharao und Ägypten oder das rote Meer?—Unleugbar ist also, dass hier ein Mythu
von Rahabs Überwindung in der Urzeit vorausgesetzt ist, mit dessen Farben a
dieser Stelle Pharaos Untergang ausgemalt wird. Das eigentümliche Schiller
aber, dass Rahab zuerst Rahab und dann ein Bild für Ägypten ist, ist dem Stil
des Dtjes charakteristisch."

[62] For this passage see, in general, *ibid.*, pp. 38-40.

[63] Text: ‏ומצרים הבל וריק יעזרו‏
‏לכן קראתי לזאת‏
‏רהב המשבת‏

The interpretation of ‏הם שבת‏ as ‏המשבת‏ has been proposed by Gunkel (p. 3
n. 1) with a reference to a proposal advanced by Hensler in Dillmann's commentary
on Genesis. All interpreters seem to agree that we have here a clear case of false
word division; see, e.g., Delitzsch, *Die Lese- und Schreibfehler im Alten Testamen*
(Berlin-Leipzig, 1920), p. 4 § 5a (where, however, another reading is adopted)
The new MSS from the Dead Sea scrolls in this passage bring the same division
of the word as *Textus Masoreticus*. Baumgartner and Köhler, *Lexicon*, p. 947
reads ‏רָהְבָה מָשְׁבָּת‏. Why?

[64] See Widengren, *The Accadian and Hebrew Psalms of Lamentation as Religious Documents* (Stockholm, 1937), pp. 238 ff.; Birkeland, *Die Feinde des Indi-
viduums in der israelitischen Psalmenliteratur* (Oslo, 1933), and *The Evildoers i
the Book of Psalms* (Oslo, 1955).

[65] Widengren, *Accadian and Hebrew Psalms*, pp. 197 ff.

[66] *Ibid.*, pp. 208 f., 236 f., 240 f., 242 f. For this reason there is undoubtedly
some justification in the criticism directed by Engnell against my position; see
Studies in Divine Kingship in the Ancient Near East (Uppsala, 1943), p. 49 f. Bu
Engnell in his turn exaggerates the "mythical" interpretation of the actual text o
both Accadian and Hebrew psalms of lamentation.

[67] Birkeland, *Evildoers in the Psalms,* pp. 77, 89 f. Ringgren, *Psaltarens from-*
et, p. 179 n. 13, has exploded Birkeland's hypothesis in just four lines.
[68] Widengren, *Accadian and Hebrew Psalms,* pp. 122, 242 f.
[69] Cf. above pp. 479 ff. and note that my conclusions in *Accadian and Hebrew*
salms, pp. 250 f., ought to be supplemented in a corresponding manner.
[70] It is my intention to treat of the description of misery in the Hebrew psalms
ı another connection, where I hope to be able to revert to the problem of the
ıemies in the psalms.
[71] Hempel, ZAW, 65:111-13, 1953.
[72] Widengren, "Early Hebrew Myths," in *Myth, Ritual and Kingship,* pp. 175 f.,
78 ff.
[73] *Ibid.,* pp. 181 ff.
[74] It is still valuable to quote what Wellhausen once had to say on the asso-
ıation of festival and history in Israel: "Eine Gegenprobe für die behauptete
ıenaturierung der Feste im Priesterkodex liegt darin, dass die schon von der
ːhovistischen Tradition vorbereitete geschichtliche Deutung derselben hier ihre
ɒitze erreicht hat. Denn sind dieselben ihres ursprünglichen Inhalts verlustig
ɛgangen und zu vorgeschriebenen Formen des Gottesdienstes herabgesunken,
ɔ steht nichts im Wege, die leeren Schläuche nach dem Geschmack des Zeitalters
ɛu anzufüllen. So werden nun auch die Laubhütten (Lev. 23) ein historisches Fest,
ıngesetzt zum Andenken an die Obdächer, unter denen sich das Volk während
ɛs vierzigjährigen Wüstenzuges behelfen musste. Bei Ostern wird über die bereits
ıı Deuteronomium und in Exod. 13, 3 ss. sich findende Motivierung durch den
ˌuszug aus Ägypten noch ein Schritt hinaus getan. Im Priesterkodex ist nämlich
ɪes Fest, das gerade wegen seines eminent geschichtlichen Charakters hier als
ıs bei weitem wichtigste von allen gilt, noch mehr als bloss-Nachhall einer
ɔ̈ttlichen Heilstat, es ist selber Heilstat. Nicht *weil* Jahve die Erstgeburt Ägyptens
ɛschlagen, wird in der Folge das Pascha gefeiert, sondern vorher, im Moment
ɛs Auszugs, wird es gestiftet, *damit* er die Erstgeburt Israels verschone. Die Sitte
ʾird also nicht bloss geschichtlich motiviert, sondern in ihrem Anfange selber
ıı einem geschichtlichen Faktum verdichtet und durch ihren eigenen Anfang
ɛgründet.... Einzig beim Pfingstfest zeigt sich noch kein Ansatz zur historischen
)eutung; hier ist dieselbe dem späteren Judentume vorbehalten geblieben, welches
ˌarin, auf grund der Chronologie des Buches Exodus, eine Erinnerung an die
ˌnaitische Gesetzgebung erkennt. Man sieht aber, wohin der Zug der späteren
ˌeit geht." *Prolegomena zur Geschichte Israels,* 6th ed. (Berlin, 1905), pp. 97-98.
It is highly regrettable that Kraus did not digest these passages in Wellhausen's
ˌassical work. His own rather uncritical position takes Old Testament studies
ˌack to the pre-Wellhausen period. See Kraus, *Gottesdienst in Israel: Studien*
ˌr *Geschichte des Laubhüttenfestes* (Munich, 1954).
[75] That history never repeats itself in the same manner is stressed by, e.g.,
ˌandberg, *Historia,* pp. 85 f. See further Renier, *History, its Purpose and Method*
ˌondon, 1950), pp. 224 f.
[76] Van der Leeuw, *Phänomenologie der Religion,* 1st ed. (Tübingen, 1933),
. 87.5; Gunkel, *Schöpfung und Chaos,* pp. 366 ff.; Bousset and Gressmann, *Die*
ˌeligion *des Judentums im späthellenistischen Zeitalter,* 3d ed. (Tübingen, 1926),
ɒ. 283 ff. The German dictum "Endzeit wird Urzeit" is quoted by Frost, *Velus*
ʾestamentum 2:73, 1952.
[77] Emphasized by Hempel, *Gott und Mensch,* p. 248: "Jahve wird sich abermals
ˌs der *Schöpfer* betätigen, die neue Welt schaffen."
[78] *Ibid.,* p. 248: "Die israelitische Religion aber ist so stark geschichtsgebunden,

dass auch dort, wo wirklich der Glaube an die *Endzeit* lebendig wird, die Gröss. der *Geschichte,* Volk, Land, Feinde, mitgesetzt sind. Auch die Endzeit rechn mit *geschichtlichen* und damit mit universellen Grössen." Frost (p. 75) emph sizes by rights the fact that there was an old Israelite "eschatology in the O Testament which is not expressed in the terms of myth." By "myth" we und stand in this case the notion we have defined above in our introduction. But is not a legitimate method simply to blot out Jeremiah 4.23–26 from the authent oracles of this prophet (using as his "method" a vicious circle). The same qui gratuitous operations are undertaken (pp. 78 f.) with the prophet Isaiah. For the reasons his conclusions cannot be accepted, for they are based first on the abov mentioned amputations of the texts of the pre-exilic prophets, second on a fal assumption of a contrast in Israelite thought of "history" and "myth."

79 Jenni, *Das Wort 'ōlām,* esp. pp. 86 f. For the idea of the two Aions see Vol *Die Eschatologie der jüdischen Gemeinde im neutestamentlichen Zeitalter* (T bingen, 1934), and Bousset and Gressmann, *Religion des Judentums,* pp. 243 : The hypothesis of Iranian influences in this special case was put forward Bousset and Gressmann (p. 509), but above all by Reitzenstein, *Das iranisc Erlösungsmysterium,* pp. 231 f., and by Von Gall, *Basileia touthrou* (Heidelber 1926), p. 275.

80 For Messiah as associated with the return of paradise, see Gressmann, *D Messias* (Göttingen, 1929), pp. 149 ff., 278 ff.; for Messiah as a descendant David, see the material presented by Gressmann on pp. 232 ff. (where, howeve the interpretation suffers from the wish of the author to interpret—*à tout prix* every Messianic oracle as alluding to the returning David (a highly dubious id in view of the fact that David may be only the regnal name of the ruler) not the Davidic king as a sound exegesis demands. The same idea is developed Schmidt, *Der Mythos vom wiederkehrenden König im Alten Testament* (Giesse 1933). See also Volz, *Eschatologie der jüdischen Gemeinde,* pp. 203 ff., a Bousset and Gressmann, *Religion des Judentums,* p. 230.

81 See Pedersen, *Israel,* I-II, 275, 476, 491; III-IV, 656 ff.

82 *Ibid.,* III-IV, 657.

83 For the general opinion in this case see Lindblom, LUÅ, 31:43, 55, 72, 193 In the first of these passages the author says: "Och då för Mose Jahve visat s makt på historiens område, blev han från den stunden i första hand en historie levande gud, som såsom personlig vilja handlade i historien, och det efter etis' principer." The second passage reads: "Genom att Jahves verksamhet förlad till historien kom hans egenskap att vara en personlig vilja på ett så domineran sätt till uttryck att naturbestämdheten i princip övervanns." We should like ask: on what Old Testament passages are these statements based? It cannot too strongly emphasized that in this case "history" does not at all mean the sar thing as in modern historical research. It is history in the Hebrew sense that v have analyzed above. However, Mowinckel, *Psalmenstudien,* II (Christiana, 192 54, would seem to have been sensible to our problem.

84 See above, n. 37.

85 The importance of these various themes for the growth of the Pentateu has been seen in a most meritorius way by Von Rad, *Das Formgeschichtlich Problem des Hexateuchs* (Stuttgart, 1938).

86 Noth, *Das Geschichtsverständnis der alttestamentlichen Apokalyptik* (C logne-Opladen, 1954), pp. 24 ff.

87 Weiser, *Glaube und Geschichte im Alten Testament* (Stuttgart, 1931), p. : n. 86.

[88] It is only fair to observe that Weiser had to rely on a text that was inferior to the recension we possess today, though of course I do not know if he would change his views when confronted with the text quoted above. I have quoted from the translation given by Speiser, ANET, p. 72a.

[89] Noth, "Die Historisierung des Mythus," *Christentum und Wissenschaft* (1928), p. 267.

[90] On the Sumerian Kinglist see above, n. 42.

THE DIALECTIC OF CHRISTIANITY

By Stanley Edgar Hyman

BENNINGTON COLLEGE

I HAVE BEEN STUDYING the history of Christianity, in connection with a course I give in the Bible, and one of the books I have found most useful as a theoretical approach is Paul Radin's *Primitive Religion.* Christianity is far from a primitive religion, although it is built on primitive foundations, but so much of Radin's theory seems relevant that he may be dealing with universal constants in the religious experience. (The other possibility—that his ideas have been unconsciously shaped by the dominant Christian pattern of our culture and that my application of them is thus entirely tautological—is one I prefer to reject.)

The three ideas of Radin's that I find particularly applicable have in common the recognition of dialectic process, considering the results with which we are confronted to be the synthesis of oppositions. The first sees religious doctrine, dogma, or orthodoxy as a precarious compromise between the opposed needs and temperaments of the two religious types into which Radin divides societies: the extroverted lay mind (in our terms, this group would include many clergymen) craving material satisfactions and security; and the introverted religious formulator craving less tangible things, among them power. The second sees the motivations of the religious formulator himself, priest or prophet or shaman, as a tension between his genuine neurosis, expressed in disorientation and suffering, and the practical manipulations and sly self-aggrandizement of "priestcraft." The third sees notions of deity, ranging from the simplest name to the most complex theology, as a synthesis of ambivalent impulses of love and hate, originally directed elsewhere. Radin is not the inventor of these dialectic concepts—the first is in a general way familiar to all our thinking about religious history; the second is implicit in Bogoras, Jochelson, and others on the Siberian shaman; and the third comes from Freud, and has been elaborated as an approach to religion by such Freudians as Theodor Reik—but in combination, as a general dialectic of process in the study of religion, they represent a substantial theoretical contribution on Radin's part.

It has been customary to see the history of Christian dogma or belief as a series of great debates: St. Athanasius against Arius on the Trinity; St. Augustine against Pelagius on Original Sin and the need for Grace; St. Thomas Aquinas against Duns Scotus on the Immaculate Conception of the Virgin Mary; Luther against the Pope or his spokesmen on Faith and Works; Arminius against Calvin, or such Calvinists as Gomar, on Free Will. In this simplistic view, one argument won out, the loser was stigmatized a heretic like Arius and Pelagius, or became a minority line of thinking in the church like Scotus and Arminius, or founded a schismatic church of his own like Luther and Calvin.

In a less simplified view, orthodoxy does not win out over heresy, but emerges as a tension between two heresies. A clear-cut example is the Council of Chalcedon, which convened in 451 and formulated the orthodox doctrine of the Incarnation, the Christian paradox that Christ was both fully God and fully man. The Church Fathers of Alexandria, principally Clement and Origen, emphasized His divinity to the point where their Incarnation resembled Theophany and the Monophysite denial of Christ's humanity; the Church Fathers of Antioch, among them St. John Chrysostom and Theodore of Mopsuestia, emphasized His humanity to the point where their Incarnation resembled Inspiration and the Adoptionist denial of Christ's divinity. In the words of the *Oxford Dictionary of the Christian Church,*[1] "It was these two opposite tendencies which the Chalcedonian formula sought to hold in proper balance." Yet the real opposition the Formula resolved was not between the extremist theologians of Alexandria and Antioch; but between Alexandrian theology and the body of Christians, including many of the five hundred bishops present, unconcerned with the abstractions of Incarnation but rallying in defense of the suffering human Jesus of the Synoptic Gospels; and between Antiochene theology and the same body of Christians, rallying in defense of the divine Jesus of St. John's Gospel and St. Paul's Epistles. The Council of Chalcedon, in other words, was not a compromise between opposed religious formulators, but a double compromise between formulators and the body of laymen with a vested interest in Scripture (and its securities in this world as well as the next). As the example shows, the Chalcedonian formula reflects an earlier compromise of precisely the same sort by the Synod of Carthage in 397, when it fixed the canon of the New Testament.

Let us look at another contribution of Clement of Alexandria and Origen, the doctrine of Apocatastasis—that all share in salvation—attacked by St. Augustine and stigmatized a heresy by the Council of Constantinople in 543. We see it developing in the Old Testament as a denial of the exclusive salvation of the Chosen People: it extends the Covenant to the Moabite Ruth and to the heathen of Nineveh to whom Jonah is sent: it is formulated by "Deutero-Isaiah" in Isaiah 49. 6, "I will also give thee for a light to the Gentiles," and Hosea 2. 23, "And I will say to them which were not my people, Thou art my people." The universality of the glad tidings of redemption is the central message of the New Testament: it is the point of the descent of the Holy Ghost on the apostles at Pentecost, giving them the gift of various tongues (thus neatly reversing the Tower of Babel story) in Acts 2. 4; and it is the essential Pauline message, typically in Galatians 3. 28, "There is neither Jew nor Greek, there is neither bond nor free, there is neither male nor female: for ye are all one in Christ Jesus." Yet from the sixth century on it is Christian heresy, held only by a few Anabaptist and Arminian sects and the small Universalist church, while predestined damnation for many becomes the central tenet of Calvinist Protestantism, which proceeds to divide the modern world into sheep and goats.

Clearly when the interest is evangelical, as in the optimistic stages of Judaism when Jonah and Deutero-Isaiah were written, or the early days of Christianity when it was attempting to break out of the limiting confines of Judaism and spread through the whole Roman world, the emphasis is on universality. When the interest is consolidation, and a going church needs the power to punish by withholding salvation, the emphasis suddenly returns to a Chosen People or a predestined Elect. The exclusivist religious formulator, whether the compiler of the Pentateuch or John Calvin, rediscovers the doctrine of limited salvation, the laymen defend their material and spiritual stake in it, and the religious thinker out of step with the times is anathematized if he is lucky and burned to a crisp if he is not.

We get a dialectic taking in both church and state in the great Arian controversy. The heresiarch Arius, early in the fourth century, taught a position somewhere between the Trinitarian and the Unitarian, in which the Son was subordinate to the Father but created by him "of like substance," *homoiousios*. Against him, Athanasius argued the doctrine of the Trinity later formulated in the Nicene Creed, that Father and Son were equal and "of one substance," *homoousios*. The Emperor Constantine, not much concerned with theology but very much concerned with Christianity, which he had made the official religion of the Roman Empire, wanted to unify it instead of disuniting it, and convoked the Council of Nicaea in 325. It decided in favor of Athanasius, and Arius and the bishops who supported him were banished. A few years later, the Emperor, somewhat persuaded of Arianism by his sister Constantia, asserted his new role of Pontifex Maximus by himself banishing Athanasius, by that time Bishop of Alexandria, and restoring Arius to favor. Soon after Constantine died in 337, his son and successor Constantius openly embraced Arianism, and Athanasius fled to Rome. Constantius had been a joint emperor with his brothers Constantinus and Constans until their deaths, and he did not like power-sharing for either God the Father or himself. During the next two decades, the influence of Arianism grew. Its high point was the adoption by a double council of Eastern and Western bishops at Sirmium in 359 of a compromise formula that Father and Son were *homoios,* similar. St. Jerome, who was seventeen at the time, commented, "The whole world groaned and marvelled to find itself Arian." Two years later Constantius died, the conservative semi-Arian bishops lost their nerve, and the pendulum swung back. Despite everything a later Arian emperor of the East, Valens, could do, orthodoxy was reestablished at the Council of Constantinople in 381, although Arianism continued among the Teutonic tribes in Europe for a long time after.

Here we have the party of the laymen, led by Constantine and his successors, and the party of the religious formulators, whether the ascetic and saintly deacon Arius or the equally ascetic and saintly deacon Athanasius, locked in complicated combat. The final decision, by which the Nicene Creed was reaffirmed orthodoxy, and Athanasius became bishop and saint, and Arius the chief of heresiarchs, was determined neither by their arguments nor by the cabbalistic magic of the iota of difference between *homoousios* and *homoiousios,* but on the basis of considerations of imperial polity, imperial whim, and the accidents of imperial survival.

Or we might consider the history of Antinomianism, the doctrine that Grace or Faith frees from the Law. Its roots are again in the Old Testament, in the protests of the Prophets against the priestly ritual of sacrifices in Deuteronomy and Leviticus. The protest is most eloquently stated in Micah 6.8, insisting that the Lord asks not burnt offerings "but to do justly, and to love mercy, and to walk humbly with thy God." It flowers in St. Paul, in the idea of a New Covenant that frees from the Old Covenant, the Pentateuch or Torah, particularly in the Epistle to the Romans 3.28, "Therefore we conclude that a man is justified by faith without the deeds of the law," and 6.14, "For ye are not under the law, but under grace." Developed by the heretic Marcion in the second century, it becomes the doctrine that Love (Christian love, Paul's *Agape* of I Corinthians 13) frees from the Law, and with an irony that has sometimes accompanied Christian love in history, it led to violent anti-Semitism. Marcion rejected the entire Old Testament and anything in the New that seemed to him under Jewish influence or to be inspired by the despotic Jewish God of Torah as against the new Christian God of Love, so that Marcion's Scripture contained only ten Pauline Epistles and a de-Judaized Gospel of St. Luke. Marcion was excommunicated—what in Paul's milder form was a necessary relaxation of Jewish rigidities to facilitate extensive proselytizing of the Gentiles, in Marcion's more extreme form was the subversion of Church authority and a denial of its claim to traditional ancestry—although his followers continued to be a problem for several centuries.

Antinomianism took other forms among the Gnostics and Manichaeans in the early Christian centuries, and was strongly revived in the Reformation by Luther's return to Romans 3.28 and the doctrine of justification by faith alone, without works. As the Protestant churches developed their own bureaucracies, it became the property of such smaller protesting groups as the Anabaptists. In our own day neo-Marcionism, as represented by such a writer as the Jewish-born Simone Weil, has an intellectual currency in fashionable literary circles but pure Antinomianism is widespread in England and America, if one can judge by the popularity of Graham Greene's novels or James Gould Cozzens' *By Love Possessed* (in which Love frees from the Law in the most literal sense).

The Donatist heresy is equally instructive. Donatus and his fol lowers in Numidia in the fourth century refused to recognize a new bishop on the grounds that he had been consecrated by an apostate, and that sacraments conferred by the unworthy were invalid. Other factors, among them personal rivalries, African nationalism, and economic unrest were involved, and the Donatists eventually split off from the Church and took to marauding. The doctrine that the efficacy of sacraments depends on the worthiness of the minister survived them, however, as it survived St. Augustine's argument that the true minister of sacraments is Christ, the priest only his vessel. Julian the Pelagian, in controversy with St. Augustine in the fifth century, argued that St. Augustine was himself an unworthy minister, whose concept of Original Sin was based on his Manichaean youth. In the Middle Ages, the monk Henry of Lausanne revived the argument that the sacraments have no objective efficacy, but depend on the worthy character of the priest. His preaching had no effect beyond getting him periodically jugged for heresy, but when another monk, Martin Luther, preached the same Donatist doctrine four centuries later, it tore the Church apart. Here corruption among the clergy (still Radin's easygoing laymen) would be thesis, protest by rigorist reformers (his formulators) antithesis, and the synthesis the sudden miraculous transformation whereby corruption puts on incorruption, to become in turn the new Protestant thesis and begin to corrupt. (It is amusing to note that those rigorist Protestants, like Barth and Niebuhr, who preach against the worldliness and secularity of their Church in our time, do so not in the name of Donatus, their true progenitor, but of his antagonist St. Augustine.)

With the Reformation, the alliance between church and state, Christ and Caesar (what cynical historians call "the Chi and the Kappa"), took radically new forms, as well as continuing some of the same old Catholic forms. At their simplest, they are the alliance for extortion that Radin (quoting Gayton) shows in *Primitive Religion* between chief and shaman among the Yokut. At the other extreme they are the great events of history. Luther, advocating the merciless extermination of the Lutheran peasants in the Peasants' Revolt, lost a considerable part of his mass following, but from then on the German princes were devoted Lutherans, and the safety of Protestantism against Catholic armed repression was assured. Calvin, if no more bellicose than Luther in temperament, managed by one symbolic action to make the point even more vividly than did Luther's stand on the peasants. When Michael Servetus denied the Trinity and the divinity of Christ, arguing a very modern-looking Unitarianism, one of Calvin's people denounced him to the Catholic Inquisition; he fled to Geneva for safety, and there Calvin had him burned.

The princes were thus assured that no dangerous revolution was in the saddle, while the real Calvinist revolution, social and economic, went on invisibly, the oxidation of rust rather than burning. Where Luther still condemned the lending of money at interest, the old Catholic sin of Usury, Calvin approved it, and the *Institutes* developed a new ethic for the rising class of burghers who constituted Calvin's chief support. "While a natural consequence of belief in election might be expected to be to weaken or destroy moral effort," the *Oxford Dictionary of the Christian Church* remarks ingenuously, "history in fact does not bear out this deduction, even in the case of those holding an extreme form of the doctrine." From the work of Weber, Sombart, and Tawney, we have learned the relation between the Protestant ethic and the new society. Tawney explains in *Religion and the Rise of Capitalism*:

In their emphasis on the moral duty of untiring activity, on work as an end in itself, on the evils of luxury and extravagance, on foresight and thrift, on moderation and self-discipline and rational calculation, they had created an ideal of Christian conduct, which canonized as an ethical principle the efficiency which economic theorists were preaching as a specific for social disorders.

Here the shaman-figure, John Calvin, speaks for the practical laymen in a rarely efficient synthesis.

Radin defines as "the fundamental trait of all shamans and medicine men everywhere," emphasizing it with italics: *"They must be disoriented and they must suffer."* "Solitude and suffering open the human mind," a Caribou-Eskimo shaman told Rasmussen. In the simpler societies, Radin generalizes, "neurotic-epileptoid individuals predominate among the medicine men." He defines the traits of the shaman:

his ability to fall into a trance state involuntarily and to put himself into one voluntarily; his capacity to transform himself into an animal; his power to travel through space and time and to journey to the spirit-world; and, finally, the fact that he is possessed by some spirit either unrelated to him or an ancestor. To this we may add his dual character: unconscious at one moment, and not only conscious at the next moment but the most practical of men.

If we discard the shape-shifting into an animal (and even here there are analogues), we get a remarkable description of the priest-prophet figure in Christian history. In the Old Testament, the prophets are called *nebi'im,* which seems to mean something like "ravers," and are obvious shaman types; Jeremiah 29.26 makes the flat equation, "For every man that is mad, and maketh himself a prophet." In the New Testament, the shaman figure runs from John the Baptist (robed in camel's hair, crying in the wilderness) early in the Gospel story, to St. John the Divine (with his ecstatic visions of journeying to the spirit-world, full of animal transformations) in the last book.

The most fully developed shaman figure in the New Testament is of course St. Paul, glorying in his infirmities, with his epileptoid conversion like that of the Ashanti priests whose initiation is described by Rattray, "They hear the voice of some god or fall down in a fit or, it may be, go into a trance." Radin might be writing of Paul when he says of the shaman: "His projections, his hallucinations, his journey through space and time, thus became a dramatic ritual and served as the prototype for all future concepts of the religious *road of perfection.*" Yet at the next moment, Radin reminds us, the shaman is not only conscious but the most practical of men. Here are the conflicting tasks of the religious formulator in the more highly-organized primitive societies, as Radin defines them:

As a thinker, for instance, he is impelled to transform coercion into willing consent; yet, as one who has most to gain by accentuating the difficulties of the approach to the spirits and the gaining of their help, he must insist on attention to minutiae which play right into the hands of the very magical practices he wishes to displace. As a theologian he must give the deities real definiteness and separate them, as far as he can, from the turmoil of life; as a medicine-man or priest whose power depends on the ordinary man he must, on the contrary, emphasize their closeness to this average man by indicating their relationship to his food supply and his life values. Finally, to satisfy his own artistic-intellectual temperament he must elaborate the attitudes of humility, reverence, other-worldliness, and willing subjection to divine control. Yet these are apt to lead him to a subjectivism which, precisely among those primitive societies where the medicine-man or priest is politically dominant, is regarded as definitely anti-social.

It is almost a synopsis of the Pauline Epistles.

In early Christian history, the shaman pattern is obviously continued in the waves of hysterical martyrs, who die crying: "I am the wheat of Christ! I am going to be ground with the teeth of wild beasts!" and their successors, the mad anchorites and stylites. We find it less obviously in the ascetic early fathers of the church: St. John Chrysostom who ruined his health by his austerities as a hermit, or Origen who castrated himself on the strength of Matthew 19.12 ("There be eunuchs which have made themselves eunuchs for the kingdom of heaven's sake"). A few saints have had attested powers of bilocation, the ability to be in two places at the same time, among them St. Alphonsus Liguori, St. Anthony of Padua, and St. Philip Neri. Others, beginning with St. Francis of Assisi in the thirteenth century, have been granted stigmata, the five wounds of Christ on the Cross, which do not become septic and resist ordinary treatment, but are liable to periodic bleedings, mostly on Fridays and during Lent and Passion Week. There have been three hundred and thirty known stigmatics since St. Francis, about sixty of whom have been beatified or sanctified. In addition to stigmata, they sometimes have powers of levitation, bilocation, and telepathy, symptoms of hysterical lameness or blindness, and the ability to abstain from food and sleep. St. Gemma Galgani, an Italian stigmatic who lived into the twentieth century, enjoyed frequent ecstasies and marks of scourging in addition to her stigmata. The *Oxford Dictionary* concludes blandly: "Apart from her conviction of occasional diabolic possession, her spiritual life was normally peaceful." Therese Neumann, a stigmatic apparently still alive in Bavaria, is said to have taken no solid food since 1922, and since 1927 no nourishment whatsoever but daily Communion. She has visions during which she is able to read consciences and discern the authenticity of relics, and her home has become a place of pilgrimage.

The Church has varied in its attitude toward the insane. In the early Church, they were admitted to Communion but barred from ordination. In the medieval Church a surprising number of them attained to the priesthood, and some founded orders and were eventually canonized. Under Henry VIII in England, Foxe's *Acts and Monuments of the Christian Martyrs* reports, an insane man named Collins saw a priest holding up the host over his head. He held up a little dog over his own head in mimicry of the action. For it he was tried, condemned, and burned; and the dog with him. (This suggests two different treatments of the insane, that they were burned for heresy and that they sat in judgment.) At least two of the stigmatics, St. Francis and St. Catherine of Siena, were outstandingly rational and practical in other phases, adept organizers and shrewd power-manipulators.

Radin identifies the curing techniques of primitive shamans as projections of their own "neurotic-epileptoid mental constitution." Christian healing has not been without its shamanistic features. In the first seven Christian centuries, recovery from illness was regularly expected from the sacrament of Extreme Unction, and in the Roman Catholic church Unction is still given "for the health of soul and body." The possession of a gift for healing was regarded in the early Church as a recommendation for holy orders, and the curative miracles of saints, their relics, and their shrines have continued in Roman Catholicism to the present. The Reformation rejected all Christian healing as Romish superstition, but the tradition continued in tiny splinter sects like the Plumstead Peculiar People of London, who reject medical aid and heal each other with oil and prayer, on the basis of James 5. 14 ("Is any sick among you? let him call for the elders of the church; and let them pray over him, anointing him with oil in the name of the Lord."). The great recent flowering of Christian faith healing has been the Christian Science church, founded by Mary Baker Eddy after her own miraculous recovery from a variety of apparently hysterical ailments, in the classic pattern of the shaman.

The primitive priest-thinkers' descriptions of religious phenomena, Radin explains, are "often specifically conditioned by economic-social considerations, such as, for instance, the validation and justification of their authority, the maintenance of their rights and their privileges, and the justification of their desire for prestige." Sometimes in Christian history these religious conceptions, however disoriented and suffering, seem to have been designed primarily to advance the conceiver's privileges and prestige. This has been the traditional Protestant view of Catholic miracles, that they are, to quote Foxe, "feigned and forged of idle monks and religious bellies, for the exaltation of their churches, and the profit of their pouches." Like healing, however, this sort of visionary careerism has had a Protestant apotheosis in recent history. In the eighteenth century in Switzerland, two brothers named Christian and Hieronymus Kohler founded the sect of the Bruegglers, claiming that they and a girl named Elizabeth Kissling were Father, Son, and Holy Ghost, and that certain remarkable sexual freedoms followed from it. At the end of the century, in England, Joanna Southcott announced that she was the Woman of Revelation 12 ("Clothed with the sun, and the moon under her feet, and upon her head a crown of twelve stars"), and that she was to give birth to the Prince of Peace in 1814. She sealed thousands of believers into the company of the elect for fees ranging from twelve shillings to a guinea. Always a loyal member of the Church of England, she left a box of prophecies to be opened after her death only by the Archbishop of Canterbury, and well into the twentieth century her followers were pestering successive Archbishops to open the box, "to save England from ruin," employing for that purpose a press agent and sandwich men in the streets. A few decades after Joanna's death, H. J. Prince, who had been a curate in the Church of England, and his rector, Samuel Starky, seceded to found the Church of the Agapemone. They announced at various times that they were the Holy Ghost, the Prophet Elijah, and the Two Witnesses of Revelation 11 ("These have power to shut heaven"), acquired a body of followers, and went in for varieties of scandalous wrongdoing until (Marcion having been wrong) the law caught up with them. The thinly-veiled claims of Father Divine to be God in our own time and country are too well-known to need comment.

On the subject of primitive ambivalence toward deity, Radin presents some extraordinarily suggestive material. Among the Baila of Northern Rhodesia, according to Smith and Dale, the high god Leza is called by a variety of names. In Radin's view, the oldest are those concerned with his ambivalent character: He-Who-Besets-Anyone, He-Who-Persecutes-Anyone-with-Unremitting-Attentions, He-Who-Stirs-Up-to-Do-Good-or-Bad-by-Repeated-Solicitation, He-Who-Trades-on-a-Person's-Good-Name, He-Who-Asks-Things-Which-He-Has-No-Title-to-Ask-For. Radin sees the second group, the praise-names, as created by the priest-thinkers to offset the popular ambivalent names: The Creator, The Moulder, The Constructor, The Everlasting-and-Omnipresent, He-from-Whom-All-Things-Come, The Guardian, The Giver, Deliverer-of-Those-in-Trouble. "But the answer of the lay realist was devastating and mordant," Radin says of the third group: Dissolver-of-Ant-Heaps-but-the-*Maumbuswa*-Ant-Heaps-Are-Too-Much-for-Him,

He-Can-Fill-Up-All-the-Great-Pits-of-Various-Kinds-but-the-Little-
Footprint-of-the-*Oribi*-He-Cannot-Fill, and The-Giver-Who-Gives-Also
-What-Cannot-Be-Eaten. Among the Ewe of West Africa, Radin says
(crediting Spieth) that the high god Dente "had no less than twenty-five
epithets associated with him," such as:

I am the king of the cave; I am he who drags the cliff; When you serve
Dente, you are serving a real king; Dente is the great *tro* of Kratsi; Dente is
the owner of the town; Kwasi died in vain, for it is I, Dente, who killed
him and took possession of his things; Bestower of gifts; Dente is bad
because the people of Kratsi are bad; I am he who sees the occult; I seize
the sinner in his sin; I confuse the people; If you see anything beautiful,
give it to your guardian-deity; I break without reason; I break certain things
and I destroy others; If your grandfather gives you nothing, do you believe
that your guardian-deity will give you something?; I, who adorn myself with
trifles, visit the people at night; I am the great liar of the world; I am the
tro of the tribes; I am he before whom the great kings kneel; I am the
great hunter who gives nourishment to those who wish me to be with them;
If you will not give it to me, I will take it from you; I am the great pot;
I send the rain; Do not forget him who helps you; If no other *tro* can help
you, I, Dente, can do so.

Radin concludes "The whole history of religion, primitive and civilized,
is epitomized in these names."

It would be a useful project to go through Scripture culling names,
descriptions, and attributes of deity exactly comparable, but it is not
feasible in these pages. It is possible, however, to note a few of the
wilder heresies that have appeared in Christian history, most of them
in the first fanatic centuries, showing similar ambivalence. Some are
patently priest-thinkers' excesses, some lay realists' counterstatements,
some an ambiguous tension of the two. The Adamites advocated
undoing Adam's Fall and returning to Eden by going naked. The
Cainites held the God of the Old Testament responsible for all the evil
in the world, worshipped those who withstood him—Cain, Esau,
Korah, etc.—and had an apocryphal Gospel of Judas Iscariot. The
Collyridians, in Thrace in the fourth century, worshipped the Virgin
Mary and sacrificed cakes (Greek *kollyris*) to her. The Ophites worshipped the Eden Serpent as the Liberator and Illuminator of Mankind,
and held the Fall to be a progress from ignorance to knowledge and an
advantage to mankind. Their branch, the Naasenes, called the Serpent
by his Hebrew name, *nahash,* instead of the Greek *ophis.* The Mige-
tians, in Spain in the eighth century, held that God had revealed himself

successively in David as Father, Jesus as Son, and St. Paul as Holy Ghost. The Stercoranists (from the Greek *stercor*, excrement) in the twelfth century, held that God embodied in the Blessed Sacrament is digested and evacuated by the recipient, thus carrying the orthodox doctrine of Transubstantiation to its logical end.

It seems unlikely that many Christians in our day believe that Elizabeth Kissling was the Holy Ghost, or Judas the Savior, or H. J. Prince the Prophet Elijah, but it also seems unlikely that they believe most of the traditional theology of their churches. The evidence suggests that if most practicing Christians in the United States believe in the divinity of God the Father, they are Arian or Adoptionist regarding the divinity of Jesus and the reality of the Holy Ghost. Where their churches are Augustinian and Calvinist, they are Pelagian, Arminian and Origenist, assuming natural innocence, free will, and that Hindus and agnostics are about as apt to be saved as they are. If they believe in an afterlife they give no sign of it in this life. The last word in the American synthesis seems to be that of Radin's lay realist: the shamans have filled the Good Book and the Creeds with their fancy ideas, but a Christian is a man whose wife takes the children to church on Sunday.

NOTE

[1] *The Oxford Dictionary of the Christian Church* is edited by F. L. Cross (London and New York, 1957). Most of my references can be found in this volume. I have noted its High Church Anglican bias in a review in *Commentary* (September, 1958), but its factual information is detailed, reliable, and invaluable.

THE GOTR CEREMONY
OF THE BORO GADABA

By Karl Gustav Izikowitz

ETHNOGRAPHICAL MUSEUM, GÖTEBORG

DURING MY VISIT to India in 1952 I was fortunate enough to observe the so-called Gotr ceremony among the Gadaba on the Koraput plateau in Orissa. These ceremonies had supposedly disappeared and until now there existed only a description of them written down according to the narration of various informants.[1] As this ceremony is considered the most important among the Gadaba and only seldom takes place, it was indeed an unusual opportunity for me to have been able to witness it with my own eyes.

The Gadaba are often spoken of as a single tribe, but actually the name covers several tribes on the Koraput plateau and its eastern slopes in Orissa. These tribes resemble each other and dress alike, but they do not speak the same language and it is possible that they do not have the same form of society. In a recently published work Bhattacharya[2] shows that the language of one of the Gadaba tribes, Ollari, belongs to the Dravida group. There are several other Gadaba, but these have not been investigated. The tribe with the most members speaks the Munda language; they are the so-called Boro or Moro Gadaba, i.e. the big Gadaba or, as they call themselves, the *Gutob*. For the sake of simplicity I shall use the term Gadaba to cover also Boro Gadaba.

In addition to the Munda-speaking tribe there are others in the vicinity, the Pareng, who are neighbors of the Gadaba to the south. As an example of how the names of the tribes can vary we can mention that the Poya Gadaba who live at Salur sometimes call themselves Gadaba, sometimes Pareng, though they do not speak the Munda language. These two names very likely include groups which live in a similar way in spite of differences in language. To the southwest the Gadaba have as their neighbors the Bondo, also Munda-speaking, who in their turn are neighbors of the Didayis in the Machkund valley. While the Bondo have been described by Elwin, there has as yet been no research done on the Didayis.³ These two tribes are the southern-most representatives of the Munda-speaking peoples.

In addition to these tribes there a great number of different kinds of peoples on the Koraput plateau. The Joria and other Gond tribes have many members, as is also the case with the Oriya-speaking Doms and Hindus of different castes. The Gadaba inhabit a larger part of the plateau but are concentrated round Nandapur Taluk.

The Koraput plateau itself is practically without forest. Only on the hills and the steep slopes is there any woods left. But the Gadaba say that this is a recent phenomenon. The old men assure us that as recently as in their youth there was still plenty of forest. The last of it is supposed to have been cut down around the time of the First World War, when there was still valuable timber here. Therefore the peoples of the Koraput plateau nowadays have a great deal of trouble in collecting fuel. Very likely there has also been a considerable migration of people to the plateau, and this would naturally make the fuel shortage still more acute.

The Gadaba are mainly farmers, but they also have herds of buffaloes, cows, and goats. On dry land they raise mainly *ragi* (Eleusine coracana) as well as a number of other cereals. Because of the lay of the land they can only irrigate the canyon-like, deepened river beds, which they widen as far as possible. Here they raise only rice. As this river-bed section is limited, they can obtain only a relatively small quantity of rice. This is eaten only at more important feasts. The rest of the rice, as is the case with the valuable oil-plant seeds, *niger* (Guizotia abyssinica), is a money crop. Thus the Gadaba live mainly on a gruel made of *ragi* flour and water.

Since the rice is already sown and set before the monsoon comes, the irrigated fields with their fresh green color down along the river bottoms form a sharp contrast with the dried red-brown landscape in general, giving the appearance of a land of green rivers.

The villages are arranged rather irregularly. In the center there is usually an open place and in the middle of this a big *bo* tree (Ficus religiosa) under which there is a *sodor*. It consists of stones, both standing upright and lying flat, and it is here that the village council meets with the members seated on the stones. These have been placed here in memory of the descendants of the village founder. Each pair of stones (one upright and one flat) has been placed here on the

occasion of the great Gotr ceremony in memory of the parents of the
dead chieftain, because the leadership here is inherited and comes in
a direct line from the village founder. Sometimes the *bo* tree has
become so old and big that it has actually grown over a part of the
stones. One could probably determine the age of a village by the
number of such stones.[4]

The larger villages are often divided into sections, each of which
contains one sib. Only one biological family lives in a house, but the
married sons prefer to have their houses near their fathers'.

In a Gadaba village there are seldom only Gadabas. Often there
are also Doms, who constitute a section of their own, and some Hindu
families as well. On the other hand one can find Hindu villages where
there are a minority of Gadabas who apparently have joined the
village at a later period.

In addition to the chieftain there can be assistant chieftains, and
every village has also a *barrik* (herald) who is always a Dom and who
stands ready to serve the chieftain. In larger villages there are also the
dissari (shaman) and several other functionaries.

The Gadaba are divided up into a number of patrilinear, totemistic,
and exogamous clans which for the most part are spread over the
whole territory. Only in a few villages does the majority belong to
one clan, this being the case especially in the southwestern section.

The clans are divided into sub-clans, often many in number, all of
which consider themselves not only related but also originating from
the same village. The name of such a sub-clan sometimes indicates
its local origin; in other cases it can also indicate special occupations
they have had in ancient times, but often the names cannot be explained. One such sub-clan is called *kuttum,* and it is a part of this
group from the same village who join in the Gotr ceremony.

The sub-clans are furthermore divided into sibs; these in turn are
divided into groups of relatives from the same village, which frequently form their own sections. It is therefore a segmented community.

Apart from this there are friendship relationships of several different
degrees. These contribute to the formation of groups of families which
constantly exchange services and things with each other. We shall here
mention two of these: The relationship with the *panjabhai* and the
moitur, which may be considered sacred bonds of friendship. Families

which have made such sacred compacts may not intermarry. Consequently they form together an exogamous group. *Panjabhai* is actually an Oriya term and means originally one of the five brothers who make up the *panchyat,* the group which governs the village. The Gadaba have no such group. The proper term among the Gadaba is really *dissel,* but this word is rarely used. A *panjabhai* is the one who is to take over the buffaloes containing the spirits of the deceased at the Gotr ceremony. But he has other functions as well. *Moitur* (originally a Sanskrit term) is a kind of a general sacred friend who even in other situations plays an important role. During his lifetime a Gadaba goes through a succession of different kinds of friendship relationships, from more playful ones in childhood to the sacred ones of adult life beginning at the time of his marriage.

The year is divided into two main seasons. When the rainy season comes, it is time to begin the sowing on the dry lands, that is, about the middle or end of July.

During the rains the people are wholly occupied with their farming; not before January, when the crops have been harvested, does a new season begin. First of all they make preparations for weddings, and it is not unusual for a large number of couples to marry at the same time. During the dry period there is plenty of food and leisure and it is then that all the big feasts take place. But the same ceremonies are not repeated every year.

One can divide their life into a production cycle and a life cycle. In the former there is a complicated system of ploughing, rotation of crops and fallowing. This cycle covers several years before the rotation of its components begins again. Connected with production are a series of ceremonies, in part related to farming and in part to other things which are repeated every year. Many of these ceremonies are identical with the more important Hindu feasts.

The life cycle, which extends from birth to the final death feast, Gotr, follows its own rhythm and its own continuity. It begins with birth, the shaving feast, marriage, and certain lesser ceremonies, but by no means ends with one's death and cremation. To the physical phenomena are added the social factors. Ten days after the cremation there is an important ceremony, and several years after that, perhaps after a generation or more, the cycle ends with Gotr. This final feast of life is, according to the Gadaba, the greatest and the most significant of them all, and to arrange such a feast is "the highest" Gadaba activity.

One can throw light on the motivation of the Gotr by examining more of the beliefs of the Gadaba about the spirits of the dead. They believe that these spirits wander about restlessly and can, sooner or later, cause trouble. "If one is rich and does not hold a Gotr, the cattle will die and the harvest will be poor," is a usual explanation. "One can also become sick. Many kinds of illness are caused by *goigigi*" (spirits of the deceased), they say. This is a sure sign that the deceased relatives are angry. If anyone becomes seriously ill one can be sure that the spirits of the dead have caused this because no Gotr was held.

It is then advisable to make a serious promise on one's oath. To do this they take two reeds from the plant *Sátreng*. They cut off one ear of a calf, whereupon they let the calf pass between the two reeds as they drink the blood of the calf's ear. They say: "I let the calf pass between the *Sátreng* reeds. Do not be angry from this day on for I shall hold a Gotr and you shall be honored." "When one has held a Gotr the harvest is generally good," they say.

But these rhythms or cycles are interwoven, and therefore the ceremonies of the life cycle are placed at that time of the year when food, leisure, and place are most available. On the other hand the production cycle surplus is "pumped into" the different feasts of the life cycle. The two cycles together form a life stream in time, and all actions float along through the canals which are made by the relationships, that is, by the structure.

One may well ask the question: how can we say what is important and what is less important when it is a matter of ceremony? But one can measure the amount of work that is done, the economic efforts that are made, and the relationships which are involved, all based on statements from the people themselves. Since a number of social factors are implied in the different ceremonies and rites, it is important to determine their significance. This varies a great deal in the different communities, and a determination of a ceremony's rank is a very important method.

Everyone emphazises the fact that it is only the great men, the so-called Morolok, that is, those who are rich, who can arrange a Gotr. It is not sufficient that one person be rich; preferably the whole sib (*kuttum*) should be wealthy. As a matter of fact, it can be said, that the largest part of a Gadaba's savings go into the Gotr feast and that one must save all his life in order to be able to arrange such a feast. It is probably for this reason that they wait so many years before giving the feast for all the relatives who have died. The Gadabas can even leave their entire fortune to be used for a Gotr. I have run into several such cases, where it was said that the man had made a will according to which his property after death was to be used for a Gotr. This is called *Saraigú,* which means "how to spend money." It is no doubt also the Gotr which motivates the Gadaba to do extra work, for example on the Assam tea plantations, to make extra money.

I have obtained some information on what a Gadaba thinks a Gotr should cost, but the figures can not possibly be correct. Probably there is a good deal of exaggeration in these figures because of the social importance of the feast. One must buy or raise a certain number of buffaloes since, as we shall see later, a buffalo is given away for every deceased member of the family. In addition, one must have a certain supply of buffaloes to be used as gifts at similar feasts as well as at weddings and the like. Since these animals are not used in ploughing or other work among the Gadaba but are an investment, it is obvious that they also eat up a considerable part of the poor pasturage which the people have for all their animals. This is capital which does not draw interest until after a very long time and which in the long run becomes rather expensive to keep.

Only a few people actually have these resources, and it is usual that now and then one must borrow animals from relatives and friends. What this can imply I shall show later when I describe the feast. Along with buffaloes one should also have a certain number of cattle and goats ready for slaughter for the meals which are to be served. But often one receives these animals as gifts at the different feasts, a debt which one must later pay back.

At most of the important feasts it is necessary to cook the food in new pots which are bought especially for the feast in the Hindu pottery-making villages. Also used are quantities of rice, salt, eggs, and vegetables, especially chilis and turmeric. Unfortunately I cannot give the cost for a family with a given number of members, but I would imagine that the foodstuffs involved would surely run to as much as a whole year's income for a very well-to-do family. But this is certainly only a minimum. In addition there are certain services which must be paid for, such as chopping and carrying wood, husking rice, making leaf bowls, and all the other work, most of which however is done by the members of the *kuttum*. When it comes to gathering wood the *kuttum* membership is generally not sufficient, so other people in the village must be called upon to help.

The first Gotr which I had the opportunity of witnessing took place in a little village or hamlet, Kammarguda, and it began immediately after the *pus porob* feast, on the 10th of January, 1952. Long before —the villagers said three years before—they had begun to buy up the buffaloes that would be needed. The final preparations followed. This meant, first of all, husking the rice and making bowls of leaves, which are often used in this area. Husking rice takes considerable time and from morning till night the women of the Gotr-celebrating families are busy husking the rice with their heavy pestles. The mortar itself is simply a little hole in the earth which has been hardened with cow manure. In Kammarguda the high point of the feast is reached a month later, that is, the first Friday after the full moon of the month of *magh*. This day was supposed to bring good luck, and in this particular case it was a *dissari* from a neighboring village who had decided on the day.

Searching for all the fuel which is needed for the cooking of the food means a great deal of trouble for the Gadaba, since nowadays it is quite a distance to the forest. Formerly the custom was to suspend this matter until the last moment but they then had a better supply of fuel than at present.

Around two o'clock A.M. after the first day, they took two stones and placed them where the *dissari* had decided, not far from the house belonging to the Kirsani family. One of the stones was laid flat on the ground and the other was placed upright behind it. The *dissari* then placed an egg on the flat stone and mumbled something. Simultaneously with this act he decided when the actual final ceremonies would be held. At the same time two big poles or branches of a *simili* or red silk cotton tree (Salmalia malabarica) were taken into the village and driven into the ground on each side and just behind the upright stone. This was followed by the beating of drums all throught the night.

The next morning a buffalo was taken into the village and tied to he two *simili* poles. The people explained to me that this buffalo one of the finest I have seen in this region and with enormous horns) was the *raja bongtel,* the king of buffaloes, and that it contained the deceased spirit of Kulia Kirsani. Kulia had died five years before and had been chief of the Kirsani families.

Women belonging to the families celebrating the Gotr then fed this buffalo with rice and other food while they wept loudly. Eventually all the older inhabitants of the village joined in the chorus of wailing. Then nothing happened for a while except that the husking of rice and other preparations for the feast continued. The buffalo however was taken in every day for ceremonial feeding.

A week or so before the high point of the feast the *panjabhai,* who in this case was Duaro Kirsani from Alungpada, the nearest neighboring village, arranged a feast for the Gotr families.

On the eighth day before the final day of the feast the actual Gotr ceremonies begin. The first day all the Gotr families and all the relatives from other villages who were invited gather together. They now make a larger fence of *simili* branches and all the buffaloes which are meant to be given away at the Gotr are now taken in and fed ceremonially every day. Besides rice and curry, which are served in fine leaf cups, they are given beer to drink. The people pat the buffaloes and wail their lamentations, and I even saw a number of women claw their cheeks with their nails so that the blood ran, while they beat themselves on the head and wept uncontrollably. The buffaloes, which contain the deceased spirits of the families, that is to say, the spirits of all those who have died since the last Gotr feast, are now washed with lukewarm water just as one does when there are important guests in the village, and then they are rubbed with oil. One now hears the drums night and day, and the wailing songs fill the whole night. The men dance in front of the row of buffaloes, dances which may be described as a kind of war dance, for the men have weapons in their hands. They yell and whistle wildly, and some of them wear rows of brass bells. When this twenty-four-hour period is over, the relatives go home, and during the following day only the inhabitants of the village feed all the buffaloes, in this case nine, twice a day.

In addition to the special place, *gotr munda,* where the buffaloes are tied, there are two other places of importance. One of these is the family's own stone place (*nggom munda*) which on this occasion was in the immediate vicinity of the huts of the Kirsani family. The other one is a bit outside the village, not far from the area where the deceased are cremated. Characteristically a number of big stones stand there in memory of earlier Gotr ceremonies. This place is called *gotr langbo,* that is to say, gotr "out in the fields," and each *kuttum* has its own stones there. In a Gadaba village one can usually point out the different stone places for each family.

At this point a decision is made concerning which members of the family on both sides, *bongso* and *somdi,* are to contribute animals. *Bongso* is the patrilineage and *somdi* the female relatives who have married into the family. They then ask who will give buffaloes and who will give oxen, goats, and the like. They must keep their promises and not substitute any other animals. The *bongso* give buffaloes and the *somdi* oxen. But these animals must later be paid back at weddings or other important feasts.

The following day, the seventh day before the final ceremony, they carry, with the help of the inhabitants of the village, a large stone to *gotr langbo,* and place there also a branch of the *simili* tree for each deceased person. The seventh night the buffaloes remain in the village, while the Gotr families and the other inhabitants sing and dance the whole night through. In the morning and evening the buffaloes are fed. If they refuse to eat, force is used. The important people among the guests are invited to have a bath in warm water and those who bathe give from two to five rupees to each of the people who help them. They spend this money at the next market where they buy dried fish and share it in the village. This happens one day before the final day. Of the two families in Kammarguda who were arranging a Gotr ceremony only the Kirsani family had a *nggom munda,* because only rich people can acquire one. Both of these stone places later become permanent.

The feast had been set by the *dissari* for the first Friday after the full moon, but at the last minute he changed this so that the final stage began on Sunday, the 3d of February, at eight o'clock in the morning. At that time they tied all the buffaloes, numbering twelve, to the poles of *gotr munda.* They fed them with both cooked and uncooked rice and gave them beer to drink.

The relatives came about ten o'clock. They too fed the buffaloes. They then bathed themselves in hot water and consumed a dinner prepared by both of the Gotr families for all the guests. They then danced in front of *gotr munda,* before the buffaloes, at which time all the men were anointed with rice beer and turmeric. After this the relatives went home.

On Monday the only ceremony was the feeding of the buffaloes. There was wailing and dancing and, of course, an endless beating of drums, which during the last days continued both night and day.

The buffaloes stood in their places until Tuesday morning, and after being fed again they were driven off. At about two o'clock they were brought back and were once more tied at *gotr munda*. Later in the afternoon a cow was slaughtered in order to make a feast for the chief of Alungpada, who is the *panjabhai* of the Kirsani family. The Alungpada people arrived late in the afternoon with a cow as a gift, a couple of stones for *gotr munda,* and bunches of banana leaves. After this came a *moitur* with his followers from Devulpada, also bringing stones. These people placed the stones on the *nggom munda* of the Kirsani family. Then the groups from both villages gathered and ate together.

On Tuesday evening additional groups from Tikkirapada joined the celebration, bringing with them two bulls, a basket of rice, and a pot of beer. The people from the village of Sankai came also, and they brought along two small cows as well as rice and beer. The eating and dancing continued all night.

Wednesday was the last day and the climax of the feast. After a ceremonial feeding early in the morning the buffaloes were decorated with mirrors and combs which were placed on their horns. A piece of cloth of *kereng* or other material was draped over their backs.[5] The buffaloes were then rubbed with turmeric. Later, about eleven o'clock, to the music of drums and shawms (oboes) and the noise of loud wailing they were led, at the front of a procession of all the relatives, out to *gotr langbo*. At the same time they also carried food to the family's cremation place, where it was offered as a sacrifice. At *gotr langbo* they had made a fence similar to the one within the village at *gotr munda*. They also set up another stone, as at *gotr munda*. Even in this case it was placed there by the Alungpada people. But of the original twelve buffaloes there were now only nine left, for three had been taken away. Of these nine, five were to be taken by the Alungpada, the *panjabhai* of the Kirsani family, and one was to go to the Kirsani's *moitur* in the village of Lugum. The three remaining came from the Pujari families and were to go to Kangarapada, the Pujari's *panjabhai*. Of the three buffaloes which were taken away from the village before the nine were led out, the Alungpada chief took one, which was at once taken to his village and slaughtered the night before the big feast. The third was allowed to remain in the village for the time being, since it limped and had difficulty in walking. It was to be taken by the Kirsani's *moitur* in Lugum.

This division of the animals was made known officially on Wednesday morning. The buffaloes containing the spirits of the deceased had thus been carried away from the village, and the first phase of the rites was completed; that is, the spirits of the deceased had been removed from the actual village region.

Within the village and just outside it tremendous crowds of people had now gathered. It seemed as if the people of the whole territory had come to witness the spectacle, and one could now feel an intense excitement in the air. The men were naked except for a breech cloth which had been drawn tight around the hips and between the legs. The breech cloth was as short as possible, so as not to hinder movement. The men stood in groups and waited for what was going to happen, looking like fighters or athletes ready for a contest. It was clear that they now waited impatiently for the climax of the drama. But they could concentrate and control their feelings.

Suddenly there could be heard music and whistling, screams and yells from the hills round about. From different directions came processions of men, armed with axes, knives and spears, and every kind of weapon they could get. They came towards the village like troops to an accompaniment of music. Those who first arrived at the village were the people from Sankai, who turned out in great numbers. They all carried weapons which they waved in the air as they danced. As soon as they came within the boundaries of the village they had to surrender all the dangerous weapons to an especially appointed policeman, a man who was considered sober and responsible. But this was, as fas as I could understand, an exception. There was some fear of bloodshed and fighting on such occasions; thus as a substitute for their weapons the men were given long sticks or clubs with which they later danced.

When the Sankai people came in leading a buffalo, they brought it to the Kirsani's house for display. As soon as that was done, they led the buffalo out of the village. The custom is that the buffaloes contributed by relatives and friends are to be taken outside the village on the last day and torn to pieces. But, instead of turning it over to the waiting crowd, the Sankai people ran off with the buffalo toward their own village. The situation was that the Kirsani had once borrowed a buffalo from the Sankai, so the Sankai gave this buffalo as a present but then took it back at once as payment for the debt.

But the Alungpada people would not stand for this, and soon there was a terrible quarrel which turned into a real fight. The Alungpada and Sankai men beat each other with clubs, and the women screamed and tried to separate them. Some of the women hung on to the clubs to prevent the men from using them. The fight got hotter. Several men were struck on the head and the blood ran in streams. This episode lasted a long time, but it was not the end of the drama.

One troop after another marched in to the accompaniment of drums and shawms. People came from several villages leading one or more buffaloes, first to the Kirsani's house, then to the Pujari's. Those who brought several buffaloes sometimes took one back, in this way taking care of an old debt. One person gave the Gotr families several buffaloes, but took back the number which was owed. At once, certain Gotr men ran off beyond the village with the remaining buffaloes, usually stopping in the shade of a tree. All the men followed and it did not take long for them to knock a buffalo to the ground and throw themselves over it. Soon there was a tangled mass of fighting men all over the buffalo, and each one tried to tear out the animal's entrails with his bare hands. Some crawled over the pile of men and others tried to wedge themselves underneath. Those who got hold of a piece stuck it inside their belts.

There was a stench of entrails, excrement, and blood, and everyone was more or less covered with the same. It was impossible to say whether the men were drunk or simply intoxicated with emotion. There was battle in the air. People quarreled, and the fighters had constantly to be separated. Outside the village an enormous crowd had gathered. Men, women, and children from the whole region had come to see the brutal spectacle, and some women had set up stands with food and drink for the hungry and thirsty. It was like a big market, and everyone was festively dressed. But the atmosphere was charged in the extreme, and the excitement increased every time a new buffalo was thrown down and torn to pieces by the wild mob. Each one wanted to assure himself of a bit of the entrails for it is in the entrails that the buffalo's enormous strength resides, according to the Gadaba. The men explained that the piece they succeeded in grabbing they would later bury in their fields, thus insuring a good harvest. No less than twelve buffaloes were torn to bits within a few hours; not until this was accomplished and the heat began to be intense was the spectacle over. Then, each village group gathered in the shade of a tree to rest and eat the food they had brought with them.

During this time Kammarguda's own men cleaned up the field of battle and one saw heads, forelegs, and hind parts of the buffaloes dragged into the village where they would again be divided up.

About two o'clock the intermission was over and the whole crowd went to the *gotr langbo,* where the original buffaloes containing the spirits of the deceased were standing. The bereaved families came, wailing their lamentations; they stroked the buffaloes, and finally removed from them the mirrors, combs, and pieces of cloth with which they were decorated. When this was done the *panjabhai* of both the Kirsani and Pujari families rushed to the buffaloes, then took them and disappeared with them in the direction of their villages as fast as the buffaloes could go. This was the end of the ceremonies in Kammarguda and the spirits of the deceased had now been carried away by the families' helpers, the *panjabhai,* who later slaughtered them in their own villages, one after another at great feasts, and finally devoured them all. With this, the deceased relatives of the Kirsani and the Pujari were considered "finally dead," to use the Gadaba's expression. The dangerous spirits, *goigigi,* had at last been killed.

But the actual feast was not yet over. The market was in full swing and the men demonstrated their cleverest sword dances. A team of fencers composed of young boys from Tikkirapada was especially outstanding. They had their teacher and their own music with them. To the delight of the crowd they did a certain kind of sword dance which simulated fencing between two opponents. The whole thing was very formal and acrobatic. They made brilliant stabs at each other and parried them with a kind of wooden shield made for the occasion, rectangular in shape and with a spike sticking out from the upper edge. They fenced from a sitting position and wrestled and threw each other over their shoulders. All the fighters were painted with turmeric and rice flour and had a black cross on their faces. It was apparently a very skillful team, as the audience was most enthusiastic.

Later on in the afternoon the crowds separated and went to their homes, but a great number of guests remained in the village. The idea was that the evening should be concluded with a dinner for the invited guests who had brought gifts of animals and other things, but unfortunately the fuel had given out. This, however, did not matter so much, because the Alungpada people had already slaughtered a couple of buffaloes and some of the participants in the Gotr ceremony were therefore invited to their village. The celebrants came back to Kammarguda late at night, quite intoxicated and very noisy.

The next morning the people were out early gathering fuel so that a dinner could be given. Thus far in the feast only one cow had been slaughtered, but now so many cows had come as gifts that ten could be slaughtered at once. The pink haunches were set up in a row on the fence as if they were on exhibition; they were later to be given away.

The guests then gathered for the festive dinner, which lasted far into the night. When they left next morning their departure was accompanied by many formalities. The people were especially ceremonious towards the *panjahbai* and *moitur,* whom they embraced and whose feet they touched. Several of the guests took with them a haunch of beef or at least a leg.

The following day there was another dinner, but it was only for the officials of the village. The guests were the chief of Devulpada, the village of which Kammarguda is a part, and the *barrik,* the herald of Kammarguda, the *dissari,* and a number of the closest relatives in the village. At the end of the dinner there was the presentation of the so-called *moali,* or obligatory gifts. Sukra Kirsani's mother's brother (*māmung*), Budda of the village Tukum, had contributed a buffalo for the Gotr. He received a brass bowl and a brass pot. Kulia Kirsani was one of those for whom the Gotr was given. His sister received a *moali* from Sukra Kirsani's wife. Kulia is Sukra's father; his mother is dead. Sukra's wife thus gave a *moali* to her father-in-law's sister that is to say, to her husband's aunt. Sano Pujari held the Gotr in memory of his father Somo. His mother's brother, Angra Bordenaik of Tikkirapada, who gave a buffalo, also received a *moali* in the form of a brass pot. Thus, in the family who gives a Gotr, the husband gives a *moali* to his mother's brother, from whom he has received a buffalo, and his wife gives a *moali* to his father's sister, in case her husband's mother is dead.

As is usual among the Gadaba, there was a quarrel that lasted for hours involving the gifts. The phrase "It is not sufficient" and the insistence upon additional gifts with the bargaining and haggling that follows recurred again and again. It seems to be taken for granted that one is never to be contented but should try to get as much as possible. The Gotr was now finally finished, and the guests left with the remains of the slaughter as presents. Only the old *dissari* who had been constantly occupied and had been given too much to drink, did not get farther than a few meters beyond the village, where he fell down, dead drunk, and at once went to sleep.

This is a description of what I observed in Kammarguda. One might ask what happened in the villages before the people left for Kammarguda and what happened in the friendship villages. This, of course, I can not say, since Kammarguda was my point of vantage. However, during the same spring I was able to witness several other Gotr ceremonies, and I shall try to describe what happened as seen from the other side, that is, how the preparations were made among the *moitur*. I observed such a case at a Gotr between two different villages. In one case there was a family involved whose chief was Sida Muddili, of the village Kinchop, which strangely enough is not a Gadaba village but one inhabited by the Pareng. This man's *moitur* was, however, a Gadaba, the second chief in the village Godi Honjaro, Kanja Muddili. These villages are only three or four kilometers apart. As a *moitur,* Kanja brought with him no buffaloes but two large stones, one of them for a seat and the other to be stood upright. These had been fetched long before I came to the village, and in order to carry them, the people had made a structure of bamboo poles. The day of the final phase, the procession was started by a majority of Honjaro's male inhabitants. They also carried a number of *simili* poles with them. The women were to come the next day. Among the inhabitants of Honjaro village was another *moitur,* Sukro Bordenaik, who had no animals with him. He received two buffaloes on the Gotr day from his friend in Kinchop, and later he received two more. These were not counted in with the Gotr but were taken care of informally. At the actual Gotr, fourteen buffaloes were led away and torn to pieces. But later on, when Sukro arranges his Gotr, he will pay back the four buffaloes to Sida or his relatives. Sukro gave a special *moitur* feast for his friend in Kinchop immediately after the Gotr ceremony.

It was the *barrik* of Honjaro who called the people together and organized the march. Before they started the women came forth and pressed rice and turmeric on the stones and on the foreheads of the people who carried them. Then they marched off in single file, with music being played at the head of the line. When they had come a bit beyond the village they stopped and there groups of men began a sword dance. One pair of skillful dancers after the other swung their sabres above and at each other. One got the impression that this was a way of showing their skill. But why they do this and what its meaning is I was not able to discover. The march continued with several pauses to allow the bearers of the heavy stones to rest. In the discussion between the men I heard that they were wondering how Sida of Kinchop was going to divide up his animals. Discussions about such division of property is very usual among the Gadaba. It must be difficult for them to remember and keep straight all the debts from the past. Upon their arrival in the village the music started up and there was a general mêlée, the men dancing with drawn swords and swinging axes. The guests were greeted more formally in the Pareng village than in other places where I had been. The stones were placed according to ritual and the celebration of the Gotr followed the same general lines as in the feast described above.

In this short study I shall not dare to try to explain each and every phase of the Gotr feast. That would require a more general and thorough analysis of the Gadaba community than I am prepared to make here and also considerably more material than I have been able to collect during five short months. The Gotr ceremony is a kind of *rite de passage,* and, according to Van Gennep's scheme, these rites are a transition from one to another of life's phases.[6]

All these ritual actions are a kind of "social transformer," which mark the transition not only in life but from one kind of action to another kind: for instance, the transition from a magic or religious action to one of productive-technical character, or the reverse. Such a social transformation, at least when it concerns the life-rhythm, is composed of a number of different elements of which the physical change is one. An emptying phase, or an eliminating of dangerous or wicked elements, is the second; and the preservation of the good is the third. This takes place through the collecting of economic means, and through solemnization, in which religious, magic, and dramatic means come into use.

In the Gotr the physical factor is someone's death. And with this in mind a person can also make preparations, in this case a will. Later there is a succession of other actions, but this order of events, which applies especially to Gotr and perhaps also to other death feasts, does not necessarily apply to all kinds of *rites de passage* among all peoples. The order can vary. One needs only to contrast the child marriage of India, which long afterwards is followed by consummation, with what is usual in Europe. In the former case the solemnization comes much earlier than the living together. Among many peoples on the earth the reverse is true.

In the Gotr, the final ceremony after death comes after a very long time, perhaps ten years, perhaps a generation or more. As has been indicated, a Gotr implies tremendous economic effort for a family and their relatives and a really impressive accumulation of wealth. In earlier times when money did not exist it was still more difficult. The herds of buffaloes must be increased, as well as everything else, and the longer one delayed the more buffaloes and other goods were consumed. The life span was relatively short for these peoples, and it was not always certain that they could collect all that was necessary during a lifetime. If one knew all the factors it would probably be possible to make an equation for economic growth or accumulation in relation to mortality and thus figure out the time for a Gotr, or the interval between two Gotr ceremonies.

Among many peoples where the burial rites are of greatest importance they often wait a very long time before carrying out the final ceremony. This is so, for example, among the Muong tribe in Tonkin, where I myself have seen coffins containing the bodies of prominent people now dead which have lain on the beams inside the house for years, awaiting a respectable funeral. This was surely related to the economic surplus and the accumulated means which were available. A Gotr is actually a sort of social measure of one's success in life. It is without any doubt the Gadaba's most expensive feast, absorbing the greater part of their surplus. Thus it is rather obvious that the Gotr is connected with social prestige or at least with the respectability of the donor of the feast. On the other hand, one might say that the Gotr is only a means for prestige between relatives and individuals.

It would be interesting to know what the connection is between certain dominants within the life cycle and the production cycle, that is, the time organization on the one side and the structure on the other. One does not need to go further than the Hindus to find an example, for among them marriage is without a doubt the dominating life feast. In order to clear up this problem a series of similar investigations would have to be made in different communities.

The stones and the two poles made from the *simili* tree, which are erected at the beginning of the ceremony, are very important. Apparently, this is a kind of isolation of what is holy, just as one sets up an entrance or gateway to an altar. The promise, under oath, to arrange a Gotr when one makes use of two reeds may be considered a parallel phenomenon.[7] The essential thing in the Gotr ceremony seems to be the people's wish that the dangerous spirits of the dead (*goigigi*) should definitely disappear for good, which is accomplished by driving them out from the village to the "final place"—even here there are *simili* poles—where they are taken over by the *panjabhai*, the helper-in-time-of-need. He and his people eat up the buffaloes; a kind of analogy to this funeral custom exists in South America and is there called *endocannibalism*.[8]

This idea that the spirits of the dead reside in an animal and are later carried away is nothing other than the old motive of the scape-goat. Frazer[9] mentions several examples among the Todas and another tribe in southern India, but the whole concept resembles to an even greater degree the Juggernaut cult, which nowadays is centered in the Puri temple in Orissa. Even here the dangerous gods are carried off on a cart to be kept outside the region during the perilous rain period in a special temple building. I have seen a similar phenomenon in the Koraput section, where the people make a small model of a cart drawn by oxen, containing some kind of illness demons, which, following a ceremony, are thrown out of the village.

It is this ceremony which represents the elimination of the dangerous elements. But how is the good element preserved? The spirits of the dead are one thing and life power[10] is another and it is the latter that is to be preserved. I think I may assume here that the bringing of stones by relatives and friends is involved. The Gadaba say that by seating themselves on the *sodor*, the stones which are erected at the Gotr ceremony to the memory of the descendants of the founder of the village, the council members are in some way influenced by these ancestors so that their deliberation will benefit the people. The life power of their forefathers would thus supposedly be bound by these stones and influence those who came after. It seems therefore that they bless the descendants who stand on the newly placed stones, and it is indeed considered more important to bring a couple of stones than anything else to a Gotr. This is certainly no unusual phenomenon; the Koya, the neighboring tribe erect a stone for a certain person before he leaves for the tea plantations in Assam.[11] I think we may assume that this is done so that the traveler's life power will be bound to the village and can return home if he should die.

Perhaps the most difficult thing to explain is why certain people bring buffaloes which are later torn to pieces by the crowd. One thing has already been mentioned, that is, that the buffaloes' entrails are credited with great power and that they increase the fertility of the fields. I would imagine that this has something to do with a sort of general strengthening of the life power or power in general. The buffalo is known to be one of the strongest animals in the area and this is true particularly of the wild buffaloes, which still exist rather near the Gadaba territory. It is therefore possible that the buffaloes are a symbol of power and strength. But that is something which requires a thorough study. It may also be possible that there is some connection between this and the Khond tribes' so-called *meriah* sacrifice. When they were forbidden to tear a human being to pieces, they began using buffaloes.

In a ceremony there is often an intensifying element, and this finds expression in certain aesthetic actions, such as the Gotr songs, drum-beating, dances, and the like. It would also be of interest to try to analyze the dramatic elements in the Gotr feast. That they are not significant here is perhaps because the Gotr in its entirety is enormously dramatic and it is unnecessary to add extra elements. The actual fights and the tearing of the buffaloes are dramatic enough.

We thus see in the Gotr ceremony an example of a "social trans-former" and its different elements among the Boro Gadaba. It is not until one begins to understand the Gotr and all that it implies for these people that one can gain any understanding of their life and activity. They produce, carry out magical acts, pray, make sacrifices and work hard in order to get a surplus which they can put aside for the future. Years and years go by while they struggle over bits of earth. At the same time they want to show that they are respectable. There are even faint trends towards *potlatch*, which is, however, hindered because of lack of means. Instead one tries to get at one's neighbor by making him ashamed, by calling out in front of the crowd that his gifts are not sufficient. But a Gadaba is forced to save and to be stingy for the final goal, Gotr. Into this ceremony is pumped whatever is left of his savings after the expense of other ceremonies and gift-giving. The result is the availability of the good life power along with increased prestige. The life power of the ancestors can not be seen, but it influences the harvest and health and it appears again in the production rhythm and closes the circle exactly as in the grounding of an electric circuit. In this way, security is obtained in everyday life. It is through the Gotr that the valuable things are carried on, "Gotr is the highest," say the Gadaba.

In this paper I have preferred to use the term "social transformer," which is a somewhat broader concept than Van Gennep's "scheme." A "social transformer" is an institution which contains elements in a certain standardized order. This institution is a part of the life cycle, thus a *rite de passage*. It has a physical basis, whether it be birth, puberty, marriage, death, or some other of life's elements. The main principles and the meaning of it are to protect against or annihilate the evil and to preserve the good in life.

In order to accomplish this there must be a separation, or seclusion, from everyday life. At the climax of the feast intensifying elements come in, in the form of aesthetic or dramatic means. It may also be necessary to strengthen the good with various magic rites.

In such a "transformer" three different systems are interwoven. As a part of the life cycle the feast carries the individual over from one status to another. An element of prestige is also implied in this process. The life cycle absorbs the accumulation from the production cycle. The production cycle brings in a material result and gives out a religious result. This influences in its turn the good will of the powers, and this again has its effect on the production cycle, there to be again strengthened with more rites for a maximal result.

We have also to determine the relationships between individuals and groups. Here we have the exchange of gifts, friendship, and the like, and the structure forms channels for such transformations which often occur at feasts. But such exchanges form their own cycle, which is bound to the other two. Through this interaction the structure also creates feed-back systems.

Through the dominants in the life and production cycles we obtain the "main leads" for the currents between these cycles, to use the analogy of the electric circuit, and the less dominant elements (as, for instance, hunting in the production cycle, where agriculture is the dominant) can be looked upon as auxiliary "leads."

Of great importance for the individual are the actual principles that the evil shall be "emptied out" and that the good shall be preserved or increased. For examples of this one certainly does not need to go to primitive communities. There is, for instance, the well-known scheme for the Inquisition's "educational" process, which consisted of emptying the mind, acknowledging evil, and "filling up" with the good. This phenomenon surely has its parallel also in modern "brainwashing."

It may seem bold after an analysis of a single feast to draw such general conclusions. But they must be taken as they are meant: as ideas suggested for further research in the rites of the life cycle. For my part, I tend to believe that in a community everything does connect, but that it does this in a very definite way, in a sort of system of closed interlocking loops, the different items of which—institutions, rites, actions—are complementary to each other.

NOTES

[1] C. von Fürer-Haimendorf, "Megalithic Ritual among the Gadabas and Bondos of Orissa," *Journal of the Royal Asiatic Society of Bengal,* Vol. 9, 1943.

[2] Sudhibhushan Bhattacharya, *Ollari, A Dravidian Speech* (Department of Anthropology, Government of India. Memoir No. 3, 1956).

[3] Verrier Elwin, *Bondo Highlander* (Bombay, 1950).

[4] In the village of Alungpada there are 15 *sil birrel* (upright stones) and 31 flat stones. If we assume that they erected a stone for the headman of the family every generation, about 25 years to the generation, this *sodor,* and thus the village also, must be at least 300 years old. There are, however, other villages which have definitely larger *sodor,* and by counting the stones in these one could obtain a chronology of Gadaba villages. In some of the villages the *bo* tree is so old that the stones have been enclosed in the trunks.

[5] *Kereng,* or *kisalop,* is a fiber which comes from the bark of a bush, Calotropis gigantea. It is allowed to decay, and is then pounded and spun into thread.

[6] A. van Gennep, *Les rites de passage* (Paris, 1909).

[7] *Ibid.,* p. 25.

[8] S. Linné, "Darien in the Past," *Göteborgs Kungl. Vetenskaps- och Vitterhets-samhälles handlingar*, Femte följden, Ser. A, Band 1, No. 3 (Göteborg, 1929), pp. 227 ff.

[9] J. G. Frazer, *The Scapegoat*, Part VI of *The Golden Bough* (London, 1913).

[10] I have not found evidence of any definite concept of an individual soul among the Gadaba, but rather a belief that each person has within him a certain "life power" (*birrel*). Apparently the stone binds the life power. I have developed this point in "Fastening the Soul," *Göteborgs Högskolas årsskrift*, 47:14 (1941).

[11] C. von Fürer-Haimendorf, "Megalithic Ritual," p. 173. It is probable that the stone "fastens" the life power of the person in question so that it comes back to the village in case the person should die.

THE GRAPE TRICK

By Richard G. Salomon

MAGIC PRACTICES, *maleficia*, divination, *sortilegia*, and similar arts
have from early times aroused the mistrust and disapproval of the
Church.[1] As early as the fourth century some synods formulated
canons against magic practices,[2] and the early medieval Penitentialia
are full of provisions against occult arts.[3] Gregory the Great gave sharp
orders against *incantatores* and *sortilegi*; his namesake Pope Gregory II
(715–31) instructed his legates to take action against all kinds of
maleficia.[4] The Church authorities believed unquestionably, as everybody else did, in the reality and efficiency of magical practices. It has
often been pointed out that clergy participated in large numbers in
these forbidden activities. Even popes have been credited with magic
capacities or accused of unholy magic practices; especially those distinguished by unusual scientific talents, like Silvester II (999–1003)
and John XXI (1276–77), or controversial figures like Gregory VII
(1073–85) and Boniface VIII (1294–1303).

Papal legislation or administrative action in the high Middle Ages
shows little interest in the prosecution of magic arts. Pope Gregory
IX's law code, the *Decretales* of 1237, the so-called "Liber Extra,"
deals briefly with *sortilegia*.[5] Two orders of Alexander IV, issued in
1258 and 1260, directed the courts of the Inquisition to prosecute
divinatores et sortilegi only if their practices showed evident connection
with heresy and to leave all other cases of, we might say, ordinary or
commonplace magic practices to the jurisdiction of the *iudices ordinarii*,
the bishops.[6] There is no indication that magic was considered important enough to be dealt with by the central administration of the
Church, the Pope himself, or the judicial authorities of the Curia
Romana.

In the following century however the attitude of the popes changed.
Popes John XXII (1316–34) and Benedict XII (1334–42) proceeded
to take action in the prosecution of magic practices, as witnessed by a
great number of orders and missives[7] concerning the judicial treatment

of occult practices like nigromancy, geomancy, *envoûtement*, or other *maleficia*. John XXII personally took part in the trial of Bishop Hugo of Cahors, who was accused of a murderous attempt of *envoûtement* against the Pope and was executed in 1317. *Envoûtement*, if this technical term needs explanation here, is a long-distance method of murder: a treatment of mutilation, perforation, or burning applied to a wax or leaden statuette of the victim, which, if practiced with adequate magic ritual, would cause death.

The belief in such practices was general; they have been tried against many people, high and low. Matteo Visconti, the Signore of Milan and leader of the Ghibellines in Lombardy, was suspected in 1320 of having planned and encouraged an attempt of such kind against John XXII.[8] Some years later the Pope ordered a committee of cardinals to investigate a similar attempt against King Charles IV of France;[9] again, in 1331, the Bishop of Paris received an order to investigate a group of regular and secular clergy, among them a Benedictine abbot and a Dominican friar, suspected of *maleficia*—probably *envoûtement* practices again—undertaken against Charles IV's successor, King Philip VI,[10] and his entourage.

The most important step in this direction undertaken by Pope John XXII is a legislative act, a papal law against magic practices: the constitution "Super illius specula" of 1324.[11] Its text complains of the growing use of magic arts by "name-Christians who ally themselves with Death and make a pact with Hell, sacrifice to demons and adore them, and, using magic techniques, make images, a ring or a mirror or a vial or something else to enclose demons"; it threatens excommunication *ipso facto* to all practitioners of such arts and the penalties of heretics to all those who do not reform at once. There is also a papal order of 1330 by which the bishops of the provinces of Narbonne and Toulouse and the courts of the Inquisition in Southern France are requested to send all their material concerning trials of magicians to the Pope for further disposition. Although there is no saying how far such matters were handled by John XXII himself or by any office at the court under delegated power, it seems certain that the Pope took a strong personal interest.

Under Benedict XII the picture is very similar. A papal order[12] directs a Cistercian abbot to start an investigation of a secular priest and several monks of his own monastery suspected of having searched for a hidden treasure with the help of a wax statuette which was to be blasphemously baptized for this purpose. Or, to quote only one other case: in 1338 Count Gaston de Foix-Béarn reported to the Pope that he had arrested a priest and a layman under suspicion of *sortilegia, factiones, maleficia, magicae artes*.[13] The answer was a request to extradite the prisoners. Two papal officers, a chief doorkeeper and a sergeant, were especially sent in order to transport the two men under strict custody to Avignon, *ut de ipsis melius et plenius iusticia fieri valeat*. In this case we know that the further investigation was entrusted to a special commissary,[14] but the fact of the special report made to the Pope and the demand for extradition clearly indicate how much Benedict himself must have been interested in such cases.

Considering the strict attitude against magic arts taken by the two popes, it is with some surprise that one will read the following story recently found in the diary notes of one Opicinus de Canistris, a *scriptor* in the service of the Poenitentiaria Apostolica in Avignon, written in 1337 and conserved in the Vatican Library in the autograph MS Vat. lat. 6435 f. 58v.[15]

Audivi quendam cardinalem album in magica arte peritum de mandato pape semel iocose contra naturam temporis secundum apparentiam produxisse vitem cum racemis maturis et precepisse unicuique presenti, ut apposito cultello super racemum non ultra precideret. Quo facto phantastica vel magica visione cessante illisque repertis tenere cultellos super virilia sua se cognoverunt fuisse delusos. . . .[16] Similiter de predicto vel alio mago audivi, quod cum navigaret per mare cum aliis metuentibus impetum piratarum, precidit virgulam vel festucam in truncos minutos, qui proiecti in mare apparuerunt in similitudine multitudinis navium munitarum: quo hostibus effugatis trunci reversi sunt ad suam naturam. . . . Sapientissimus iste magister et iudex cum denudaverit magicam artem coram deo et hominibus erit laudabilis nec ullum imputabitur sibi peccatum. Propter obedientiam summi pontificis optime fecit cardinalis albus ad maiorem revelationem glorie dei et ad discretionem veri a falso. . . . Nunc unus idemque magister et iudex . . . a minoribus ad maiora promotus cum denudaverit utrosque phantasticos ludos, omnis metus et sollicitudo discedit et . . . tristitia in risum et gaudium convertetur.

Translated as verbally as possible into English, the story reads as follows:

I have heard that one cardinal, called the White Cardinal, an expert in magic arts, once by order of the Pope, and as a joke, produced the unseasonable appearance of a vine with clusters of ripe grapes. He ordered each one present to put his knife over the grapes, but not to cut. Then he made an end to the fantastic or magic vision; and the audience found themselves holding their knives over their own *virilia* and saw that they had been duped.

I also heard another story about the same magician or another one: he was traveling on board ship together with people afraid of an attack by pirates. He took a rod or stick and whittled it into tiny pieces, threw them into the water and they appeared transformed into a fleet of armed ships; but when the enemies had been chased away by this they changed back into little pieces of wood.

So this wise master and judge unmasked the magic art before God and men; he will deserve praise for it and it will not be imputed to him as a sin. Being obedient to the order of the Pope the White Cardinal has done very well for the higher glory of God and for discrimination between true and false. Now the same master and judge has been promoted to a higher station, and since he has unmasked both these fantastic tricks, we have nothing to fear any more, and sadness may be changed into laughter and gaiety.

The identification of the persons mentioned in this strange report is easy. "Cardinalis albus" is one of the popular pseudonyms often used for cardinals in the later Middle Ages, such as "cardinalis Anglicus" for an English-born member of the Sacred College, "cardinalis Ruthenensis" for one who had been bishop of Rodez before, and the like. "Cardinalis albus" appears several times as a name for cardinals from the Cistercian order, referring to the white habit of the Cistercians. But in the early 1330s there was only one member of the order in the College, Jacobus Fournier, cardinal since 1327.[17] That he is meant here is proved by Opicinus' remark at the end of his tale that the wise master "has now been promoted to a higher station." In 1334 Cardinal Jacobus Fournier became Pope Benedict XII. Nothing else can be meant by this "promotion." To refer the story to the only other Cistercian who ever was pope, Eugene III (1145–53), is impossible because of the "now."

Thus we have here the surprising statement that Benedict XII, one of the most consistent persecutors of magic art on the papal throne, was at least credited with magic experiences and practices himself—practices carried out in the presence and at the command of his peer in hostility to magic: Pope John XXII.

Whether the story is true, whether Benedict ever tried his hand at such tricks, perhaps to be classified as white or parlor magic,[18] is another question. "I have heard," says our author, and he is as cautious in the wording of his tale as is advisable for a lowly scribe in papal service when speaking of the Pope, evidently anxious to avoid giving umbrage and to prevent unfavorable conclusions.

The scene which he describes in the first sentences is, however, so irresistible that for a moment we might postpone the question of true or not and allow our imagination some liberty: a company of distinguished persons—certainly dignitaries of some rank high enough to rate an invitation—is assembled in the old papal palace of Avignon, the former episcopal residence which was not yet replaced by the huge pile now dominating the city. They may have been invited for a social gathering or for a serious discussion of measures against magic practices; we do not know which. The Pope himself is present and one of the Cardinals produces a magic trick with a slightly indecent turn, either to entertain the company or to teach them a lesson, at any rate an amusing stroke of color that we would like to add to the often-painted picture of life at the papal court. But can we rely on the source?

Professor Lynn Thorndike, when discussing the prosecution of magic arts at the papal court at Avignon, remarks that one may suspect Benedict XII of "a certain amount of personal curiosity" about such practices.[19] He gives no reasons for this assumption; but the story as told by Opicinus, if true, would bear it out brilliantly.

I regret not to be able to present the tale as proof for the validity of Professor Thorndike's hypothesis, although I share the suspicion. We have to be careful. Rumors and questionable stories played a large part in the life of the papal residence; witness, e.g., the stories which the most famous of all the inhabitants and gossips of Avignon, Petrarch, perpetuated in his letters. And besides, there is another reason and a stronger one for mistrust.

When my old friend Paul Radin has read so far, he will already know why I am not inclined to believe a word of the story. He, the friend and connoisseur of classic literature in all languages, knows very well that the first part of the tale, the grape story, appears with only a slight variation over four hundred years later in Goethe's *Faust*. What we have before us is a *Wander-Anekdote*.[20]

The *Faust* passage which comes to mind is the scene in Auerbach's Cellar at Leipzig in which Faust and Mephistopheles appear at a party of drunken students. Mephistopheles entertains them with the famous "Song of the Flea," and Faust shows his magical capacities by tapping wine out of the wooden table. One drop spilt produces an infernal flame; the students draw their knives to attack the sorcerer, but he quells the excitement with a new trick. The text is given here in the original form of the "Urfaust," of which the Cellar scene is one of the oldest parts, probably written in or about 1771.[21]

> *Siebel.* . . . . Stosst ihn nieder! (*Sie ziehn die Messer.*) Ein Zauberer ist Vogelfrey. . . . (*Sie wollen über Fausten her, er winckt, sie stehen in frohem Erstaunen und sehn einander an.*)
> *Siebel.* Was seh ich! Weinberge!
> *Brander.* Trauben um diese Jahres zeit!
> *Alten.* Wie reif! Wie schön!
> *Frosch.* Halt, das ist die schönste! (*Sie greifen zu, kriegen einander bey den Nasen, und heben die Messer.*)
> *Faust.* Halt! —Geht und schlaft euern Rausch aus! (*Faust und Mephistopheles ab. Es gehen ihnen die Augen auf, sie fahren mit Geschrey aus einander.*)
> *Siebel.* Meine Nase! War das deine Nase? Waren das die Trauben? Wo ist er?
> *Brander.* Fort! Es war der Teufel selbst. . . .

> *Siebel.* . . . . Knock him down! (*They pull knives.*) A magician is an outlaw. . . . (*They try to seize Faust, he waves his hand, they stop in happy astonishment and stare at one another.*)
> *Siebel.* What's this! Vineyards!
> *Brander.* Grapes at this time of year!
> *Alten.* What ripe ones! What beauties!
> *Frosch.* Whoa, here's the best one! (*They make a grab, take one another by the nose and raise their knives.*)
> *Faust.* Stop! —Go and sleep it off! (*Faust and Mephistopheles exeunt. The students come out of their trance and scatter yelling.*)
> *Siebel.* My nose! Was that your nose? Is that what the grapes were? Where is he?
> *Brander.* Gone! It was the devil himself. . . .

The definitive version (*Faust, Der Tragödie erster Teil,* 1808) has Mephistopheles, instead of Faust, doing the magician's tricks; the tricks themselves remain unchanged.

    The identity of Opicinus' tale and Goethe's scene is evident without any further explanation, and so is the slight difference at the end.

    It is a long way from Avignon to Leipzig, and a long space of time between the fourteenth-century tale and Goethe's masterpiece. German *Goethe-Philologie* has of course thoroughly investigated the sources from which Goethe took the material for his scene. In the extensive *Faust* literature since the late sixteenth century the grape trick story appears dozens of times. The oldest version known so far appears in Augustin Lercheimer's "Christlich Bedencken und Erinnerung von Zauberey," first printed in Heidelberg in 1585.[22] The story reads here as follows:[23]

Hie erinnere ich mich eines solchen gesellen der am hofe zu H. war, und eins mals seinen gesten ein seltzam schimpflich gauckelwerck machete darin auch eine besondere teufels krafft gemerckt wird. Nach dem sie gessen hatten, begerten sie... dass er jnen zum lust ein gauckelspiel machte. Da liess er auss dem tisch ein reben wachsen mit zeittigen trauben, deren vor jedem eine hieng, hiess ein jeglichen die seine mit der einen hand angreiffen und halten, und mit der ander das messer auff den stengel setzen, alss wann er sie abschneiden wolte, aber er sollte bey leib nicht schneiden. Darnach gehet er auss der stuben, kommt wider, da sitzen si alle und halten sich ein jeglicher selbs bey der nasen und das messer darauff. Hetten sie geschnitten, so hette jm ein jeder selbs die nase verwundet. . . .

Here I am reminded of such a fellow who lived at the court of H. and once treated his guests to a jocose trick in which the devil's special art comes to light. After dinner they asked for entertainment. And the host let grow a vine out of the table with ripe grapes, one hanging before each of the companions, and he commanded every one to grasp and hold his grape with one hand and with the other to put his knife to the stem, but not to cut, not for the life of them. Then he went out, came back, and lo—there they were sitting, each one holding his own nose and the knife above it. If they had cut, each one would have wounded his own nose.

From Lercheimer to Goethe the story has been traced through a long series of curious old *Scharteken*—the English language has no word corresponding to this characteristic term for dusty literary trash—in solemn Latin[24] or in informal German and in French, English, and Italian, some of them quite entertaining and equipped with charming and very long baroque titles.[25] For two centuries one author copied the other, often verbally, and so the story was preserved unchanged in its essentials, until in the final version of *Faust* Goethe dispossessed the sorcerer and had the devil himself do the trick. Some minor variations appeared in this period. In Lercheimer's version the sorcerer is anonymous; but he became the Dr. Faustus almost at once: in an anonymous *D. Joh. Fausten Historia* published in 1587 and usually quoted with the name of the publisher, Spiess at Frankfurt. Since then the story has remained indissolubly connected with Faust's name. Another not very essential change appears in a comparison of Lercheimer's and Goethe's versions: in the old tale each of the table companions holds his own nose, in Goethe's each holds another's. As far as I can see this variation appears first in 1710 in a French translation of the story: in Laurent Bordelon's *Histoire des Imaginations Extravagantes de Monsieur Ouffle*.[26] From this work, which was translated into various languages, it entered into some German texts of the eighteenth century.

So the story of the grape trick, the *Traubenzauber,* as the Goethe specialists call it, is at least two and a half centuries older than hitherto assumed. Opicinus' tale is of course not Lercheimer's direct or even indirect source. His manuscript is an old property of the Vatican library, which Lercheimer never saw, and has never been used by anybody before Professor Almagià discovered it in 1944.[27] Opicinus and Lercheimer both are independent witnesses for the existence of the *Wander-Anekdote,* and it would be no surprise if a chance discovery should bring to light a version older than that of the fourteenth century, or one from the time between the two authors.

NOTES

[1] The literature on this subject is too large to be listed here even in selection. The essential material is to be found in Joseph Hansen's two works: *Quellen und Untersuchungen zur Geschichte des Hexenwahns und der Hexenverfolgung im Mittelalter* (Bonn, 1901), and *Zauberwahn, Inquisition und Hexenprozess im Mittelalter und die Entstehung der grossen Hexenverfolgung* (Munich, 1900); and in Lynn Thorndike's *History of Magic and Experimental Science,* Vol. III (New York, 1934), chap. ii: "John XXII and the Occult Arts."

[2] Those of Elvira (A.D. 306), Ancyra (314), Laodicea (375). Hansen, *Zauberwahn,* p. 40.

[3] There is a wealth of samples in J. T. McNeill and H. M. Gamer, *Medieval Handbooks of Penance* (New York, 1938). See index under Magic, Incantation, Trick, Superstitions, etc.

[4] Hansen, *Zauberwahn,* p. 47.

[5] *Decr. Greg.* I.v, t. 21.

[6] Hansen, *Quellen,* p. 1, note 1. The order became law by inclusion in Boniface VIII's *Liber Sextus* I.v, t. 2, c. 8.

[7] Hansen, *Quellen,* pp. 3-15, Nos. 3-22.

[8] The story has been told several times already and needs no repetition here. A survey of it is, e.g., in G. Mollat, *Les Papes d'Avignon* (7th ed., Paris, 1949), pp. 166-68; a broader presentation is in R. André-Michel, *Mélanges d'Histoire et d'Archéologie: Avignon; Les Fresques du Palais des Papes: Le Procès des Visconti*

(Paris, 1920), pp. 149-84. The source material concerning the investigation, especially interesting and much discussed in the Dante literature because it mentions "magister Dante Aleguiro de Florentia" as an expert in such matters, is published by C. Eubel in the *Historisches Jahrbuch der Görres-Gesellschaft*, XVIII (1897), 609-25. Some additions may be found in André-Michel, pp. 184 ff.

[9] Hansen, *Quellen*, pp. 671 f.; cf. pp. 447-49.

[10] *Ibid.*, p. 7, No. 7 and note 2.

[11] Raynaldus, *Annales ecclesiastici*, A. 1327, No. 44. Extract in Hansen, *Quellen*, p. 5, No. 5.

[12] Hansen, *Quellen*, p. 14, No. 22.

[13] *Ibid.*, pp. 9-15, Nos. 12-16, 18.

[14] *Ibid.*, No. 18: The two men were kept in prison for 140 days "de mandato domini G. Lombardi commissarii ad hoc specialiter deputati par dominum nostrum papam." The case seems to have ended in acquittal.

[15] See R. G. Salomon, "A Newly Discovered Manuscript of Opicinus de Canistris," *Journal of the Warburg and Courtauld Institutes*, XVI (1953), 45-57. The older literature on Opicinus is listed there, p. 45 notes 1-4.

[16] Some digressions in the text both here and below have been omitted.

[17] A second White (Cistercian) Cardinal, Guillelmus de Curte (or Curti) was promoted to the College only in 1338. So he cannot be meant in this text which was written in 1337. See Steph. Baluzius (Baluze), *Vitae paparum Avenionensium*, ed. by G. Mollat, II (Paris, 1927), 321: "Nam duo tantum per ea tempora cardinales reperiuntur Albi cognominati, Jacobus nimirum de Furno et Guilelmus Curti, ambo ita dicti quia erant monachi albi, id est, Cistercienses." C. Eubel, *Hierarchia catholica medi aevi*, I, 16 No. 19, and 17 No. 4, gives the dates for both.

[18] Criminal magic, *sapiens heresim* (tasting of heresy), as in the cases mentioned above, would have been impossible in this setting anyhow.

[19] Thorndike, *History of Magic*, III, 36.

[20] I am not concerned here with the second story, that of the whittled stick. It might also be a *Wander-Anekdote*.

[21] I owe this information and the translation of the text to the friendliness of my colleague Dr. Bruce Haywood of Kenyon College.

[22] Lercheimer is a pseudonym for the Heidelberg professor of mathematics Hermann Witekind (1522-1603). The book, interesting as one of the earliest protests against the witch-hunts of the age, went through several editions. The enlarged edition of 1597 is reprinted in Carl Binz, *Augustin Lercheimer und seine Schrift wider den Hexenwahn* (Strassburg, 1888), which I have used. In Lercheimer, a pupil of Melanchthon, a stubborn belief in the devil and evil spirits blends strangely with his advocacy of tolerance and humane understanding. He does not doubt the reality of magic; but it is the devil's own work, witches and sorcerers are only his tools: "in magic the devil does everything, human beings nothing" (p. 75 ch. XV).

[23] *Ibid.*, p. 40.

[24] The oldest and often repeated version is that of Philipp Camerarius, *Operae horarum subcisivarum* (Frankfurt, 1602).

[25] A few abbreviated examples will suffice here: Bernhard Waldschmidt, *Pythonissa Endorea* (1660); Bartholomaeus Anhorn, *Magiologia, Christliche Warnung für dem Aberglauben und Zauberey.... Der fürwitzigen Welt zum Ekel, Schewsal und Unterweisung fürgestellet* (1674); Kristian Frantz Paullini, *Zeitkürtzende Erbauliche Lust* (1697; critical of Camerarius); *Petri Goldschmidt's Verworffener Hexen und Zauberey-Advocat* (1705; a masterpiece of obscurantism,

directed against Christian Thomasius). They all are excerpted in a work of love and wondrous industry, Alexander Tille's *Die Faustsplitter in der Literatur des sechzehnten bis achtzehnten Jahrhunderts, nach den ältesten Quellen herausgegeben* (Berlin, 1900), pp. 1221 ff.

[26] Tille, *Die Faustsplitter*, p. 409, No. 178.

[27] Roberto Almagià, *Monumenta Cartographica Vaticana*, I (Città di Castello, 1944), 95 ff. and Plate 48.

REMARQUES SUR LE "ROPE TRICK"

Par *Mircea Eliade*

UNIVERSITY OF CHICAGO

AŚVAGOṢA RACONTE DANS son poème *Buddhacarita*, XIX, 12-13, que le Bouddha, après l'Illumination, visitant pour la première fois sa ville natale, Kapilavastu, fit montre de quelques "pouvoirs miraculeux" (*siddhi*). Pour convaincre les siens de ses forces spirituelles et préparer leur conversion, il s'éleva dans les airs, coupa son corps en morceaux, et laissa retomber sur le sol sa tête et ses membres, pour les réunir ensuite sous les yeux émerveillés des spectateurs.[1] Ce miracle appartient si profondément à la tradition de la magie indienne qu'il est devenu le prodige-type du fakirisme. Le célèbre "rope-trick" des fakirs et des jongleurs crée l'illusion d'une corde s'élevant très haut dans le ciel et sur laquelle le maître fait monter un jeune disciple jusqu'à ce qu'il disparaisse aux regards. Le fakir lance alors son couteau en l'air—et les membres du jeune homme tombent l'un après l'autre sur le sol.

Le *Suruci-Jātaka* (No. 489) nous présente le récit suivant: pour provoquer le rire du fils du roi Suruci, un jongleur créa magiquement un manguier (l'arbre Sanspareil),[2] et jeta très haut en l'air une pelote de fil, qui resta accrochée à une de ses branches. En y grimpant, le jongleur disparut au sommet du manguier. Ses membres tombèrent ensuite à terre mais un deuxième jongleur les rassembla, les arrosa avec de l'eau—et l'homme ressuscita.[3]

Le rope-trick devait être assez populaire dans l'Inde des VIIIe et IXe siècles, car Gauḍapada et Śaṅkara s'en servent d'exemple pour illustrer plastiquement les illusions crées par la *māyā*.[4] Au XIVe siècle, Ibn Battūta prétend avoir assisté au miracle de la corde à la cour du roi de l'Inde. De son côté, l'Empereur Jahangir décrit un spectacle similaire dans ses *Mémoires*. Comme depuis Alexandre au moins, l'Inde était connue comme le pays classique de la magie, ceux qui la visitaient étaient censés avoir vu un ou plusieurs miracles typiquement fakiriques. Même autour d'un mystique aussi considérable que Al Hallâj, circulaient quantité d'historiettes laissant entendre qu'il avait été aux Indes pour apprendre la magie blanche, "afin d'attirer les hommes à Dieu."

L. Massignon résume et traduit un récit conservé dans le *Kitab āl 'Oyoûn*, selon lequel, Al Hallâj, une fois arrivé dans l'Inde,

se renseigna sur une femme, alla la trouver, [et] causa avec elle. Et elle le remit au lendemain. Alors, elle sortit avec lui au bord de la mer, avec un fil tordu pourvu de noeuds, comme une véritable échelle. Puis, la femme dit des paroles, et elle monta sur le fil, le pied posé sur le fil, et elle montait, si bien qu'elle disparut à notre vue. Et Al Hallâj, se retournant vers moi, me dit: "C'est pour cette femme que je suis venu dans l'Inde."[5]

Il est impossible de reprendre ici le dossier, assez volumineux, du rope-trick dans l'Inde ancienne et moderne. Sir Henry Yule et Henri Cordier en ont recueilli un certain nombre d'exemples dans la presse anglo-indienne du XIXe siècle.[6] R. Schmidt, A. Jacoby, et A. Lehmann ont enrichi le dossier et y ont ajouté de nombreux exemples extra-indiens.[7] Car ce miracle-type du fakirisme indien n'est pas limité à l'Inde. On le retrouve, par exemple, en Chine, dans les Indes néerlandaises, en Irlande, et dans l'ancien Mexique. Voici la description par Ibn Battūta d'une séance à laquelle il avait assisté en Chine. Le jongleur

prit une boule de bois qui avait plusieurs trous, par lesquels passaient de longues courroies. Il la jeta en l'air, et elle s'éleva au point que nous ne la vîmes plus.... Quand il ne resta dans sa main qu'un petit bout de la courroie, le jongleur ordonna à un de ses apprentis de s'y suspendre, et de monter dans l'air, ce qu'il fit, jusqu'à ce que nous ne le vissions plus. Le jongleur l'appela trois fois sans recevoir de réponse; alors il prit un couteau dans sa main, comme s'il eût été en colère, il s'attacha à la corde et disparut aussi. Ensuite il jeta par terre une main de l'enfant, puis un pied, après cela l'autre main, l'autre pied, le corps et la tête. Il descendit en soufflant, tout haletant, ses habits étaient tâchés de sang.... L'émir lui ayant ordonné quelque chose, notre homme prit les membres du jeune garçon, et les attacha bout à bout, et voici l'enfant qui se lève et se tient tout droit. Tout cela m'étonna beaucoup, et j'en eus une palpitation de coeur, pareille à celle dont je souffrit chez le roi de l'Inde, quand je fus témoins d'une chose analogue....[8]

Au XVIIe siècle, le voyageur hollandais Ed. Melton prétend avoir assisté à un spectacle similaire à Batavia, mais il s'agissait toujours d'un groupe de jongleurs chinois.[9] Des récits presque identiques se rencontrent chez plusieurs voyageurs hollandais des XVIIe et XVIIIe siècles.[10]

Il est remarquable que le rope-trick est également attesté dans le folklore irlandais. L'histoire la plus répandue se trouve dans la collection traduite par S. H. O'Grady.[11] Le jongleur projette en l'air un fil de soie, qui s'accroche à un nuage. Sur ce fil, il laisse courir un lapin suivi d'un chien. (Rappelons que le jongleur dont parle Jahangir dans ses *Mémoires* avait envoyé successivement sur la chaîne un chien, un cochon, une panthère, un lion, et un tigre).[12] Ensuite il envoya un jeune homme et une fille—et tous disparurent dans le nuage. Quelque temps plus tard, découvrant que par la négligence du garçon le chien avait mangé le lapin, le jongleur grimpa lui aussi sur la corde. Il trancha la tête du jeune homme, mais, à la prière du seigneur, il la lui remit en place et le ressuscita.

On a enregistré dans diverses régions européennes des légendes comportant, conjoints ou séparés,[13] ces deux thèmes spécifiques du rope-trick: (*a*) des magiciens se coupant en morceaux ou coupant les membres d'un autre individu pour les réunir ensuite; (*b*) des sorciers et sorcières disparaissant dans l'air à l'aide de cordelettes. Ce dernier motif nous retiendra plus loin. Toutes ces légendes européennes sont solidaires d'un milieu de magiciens; celles du premier type sont probablement d'origine savante. Voici comment le magicien Johann Philadelphia se produisit à Göttingen, en 1777: il fut coupé en morceaux et mis dans un tonneau. Mais, celui-ci ayant été ouvert trop tôt, on y trouva un embryon, et comme celui-ci n'avait pas pu évoluer, le magicien ne revint plus à la vie. Mais au Moyen-âge on racontait une légende similaire de Virgile, et Paracelse a rapporté des histoires semblables des Siebengebirge.[14] Dans ses *Disquisitiones magicae* (1599), Debrios relate que le magicien Zedechée le Juif, qui vivait au temps de Louis le Pieux, jetait des hommes en l'air, coupait leurs membres, et les réunissait par la suite.[15] Notons au passage que Sahagun rapporte des choses similaires chez les Huasteques du Mexique. Il s'agit d'une classe de magiciens nommés *motetequi*, litt. "ceux qui se coupent eux-mêmes." Le *motetequi* se coupait lui-même en morceaux et mettait les membres détachés sous une couverture; il pénétrait ensuite sous la couverture et ressortait un instant après sans montrer la plus petite blessure.[16] (Rappelons que Jahangir avait noté le même procédé chez les jongleurs du Bengal: l'homme coupé en morceaux était couvert avec un drap; un jongleur entrait sous le drap; et l'instant suivant l'homme sautait sur ses pieds.)[17]

On a proposé d'expliquer l'illusion du rope-trick soit par la suggestion collective, soit par l'art prestigieux des jongleurs.[18] De son côté, A. Jacoby avait attiré l'attention sur le caractère fabuleux, de *Sagen*, de la plupart des récits parallèles européens.[19] Mais, quelle que soit l'explication pour laquelle on penche—suggestion ou jonglerie—le problème du rope-trick ne nous semble pas encore résolu. Pourquoi a-t-on inventé ce type de jonglerie? Ou, pourquoi a-t-on choisi exactement ce scénario—ascension d'une corde, démembrement d'un apprenti suivi de sa résurrection—pour l'imposer, par suggestion ou autosuggestion, à l'imagination du public? Autrement dit, le rope-trick, sous sa forme actuelle de scénario imaginaire de récit fabuleux ou de jonglerie, a une *histoire*, et cette histoire ne peut être élucidée qu'en tenant compte des rites, des symboles, et des croyances religieuses archaïques.

Il y a lieu de distinguer dans le miracle de la corde deux éléments distincts: (1) la mise en pièces de l'apprenti; (2) l'ascension au ciel au moyen d'une corde. Les deux éléments sont caractéristiques des rites et de l'idéologie chamaniques. Analysons, pour commencer, le premier thème. On sait que, durant leurs "rêves initiatiques," les apprentis-chamans assistent à leur propre dépècement par des "esprits" ou des "démons" qui tiennent le rôle de maîtres de l'initiation: on leur coupe la tête, on met leur corps en petits morceaux, on leur nettoie les os, etc., et à la fin les "démons" regroupent les os et les recouvrent d'une chair neuve.[20] Nous avons affaire là à des expériences extatiques de structure initiatique: une mort symbolique est suivie d'un renouvellement des organes et de la résurrection du candidat. Il est utile de rappeler que des visions et des expériences pareilles ont cours chez les Australiens, les Esquimaux, les tribus américaines et africaines.[21] On est donc en présence d'une technique initiatique extrêmement archaïque. Or, il est remarquable qu'un rite tantrique et himalayen, le *tchöd*, comporte également le dépècement symbolique du néophyte: celui-ci assiste à sa décapitation et à sa mise en pièces par les *dakinis* ou par d'autres démons.[22] Revenons au rope-trick: on peut donc considérer le dépècement de l'apprenti et sa résurrection par le fakir comme un scénario d'initiation chamanique presque entièrement désacralisée.

Quand au deuxième élément chamanique que nous avons distingué dans le rope-trick, notamment l'ascension au Ciel au moyen d'une corde, il constitue un problème plus complexe. Il y a, d'une part, le mythe archaïque et extrêmement répandu d'un arbre, une corde, une montagne, une échelle, ou un pont qui reliaient, aux commencements du Temps, le Ciel à la Terre et qui assuraient la communication entre le monde des Dieux et des humains. A la suite d'une faute de l'Ancêtre mythique, cette communication a été interrompue: l'arbre, la corde, ou la liane ont été coupés.[23] Ce mythe n'est pas limité aux zones dominées par le chamanisme

stricto sensu, mais il joue un rôle considérable aussi bien dans les mythologies chamaniques que dans les rituels extatiques des chamans.

Le mythe de l'escalier ou de la corde qui reliaient le Ciel à la Terre est
assez connu dans l'Inde et au Tibet. Le *Dhammapada Aṭṭhakathā* III,
24, décrit le Bouddha descendant du Ciel Trayastiṃśa par un escalier,
avec l'intention de "battre le chemin des humains": du haut de l'escalier
on peut voir, au-dessus, tous les Brahmalokas, et, en bas, les profondeurs
de l'Enfer, car c'est un véritable *Axis mundi* dressé au Centre de l'Univers.[24]
Cet escalier miraculeux est figuré sur les reliefs de Bharhut et de Sañci,
et dans la peinture bouddhiste tibétaine il sert aussi aux humains pour
monter au Ciel.[25]

Au Tibet, la fonction rituelle et mythologique de la corde est encore
mieux attestée, spécialement dans les traditions pré-bouddhistes. Selon
le mythe, à l'origine, les dieux descendaient du Ciel sur la Terre le long
d'une corde. Après la chute de l'homme et l'apparition de la mort, la
liaison entre le Ciel et la Terre a été abolie.[26] Le premier roi du Tibet
serait, lui-aussi, descendu du Ciel au moyen d'une corde. Et les premiers
souverains tibétains ne mouraient pas, mais remontaient au Ciel.[27] Mais
depuis que cette corde a été coupée, seules les âmes peuvent monter au
Ciel, au moment de la mort; les cadavres restent sur la Terre.[28] Dans
beaucoup de pratiques magiques, spécialement Bon, on essaie encore
aujourd'hui de monter au Ciel au moyen d'une corde magique (Geister-
seil).[29] Et l'on croit également qu'à la mort, les pieux sont tirés au Ciel
par une corde invisible.[30] Les traditions Bon connaissent un clan, dMu,
qui prétendait détenir le pouvoir de guider les trépassés au Ciel parce qu'il
possédait une corde ou une échelle magiques.[31]

Ces croyances indo-tibétaines relatives à la corde mythique capable de
relier le Ciel à la Terre doivent être rapprochées d'un groupe assez
complexe d'images, de symboles, et de spéculations cristallisées autour
de l'idée que le Cosmos aussi bien que l'homme sont articulés grâce à
des cordes ou à des fils.[32] Les cordes cosmiques sont les vents, et comme
le dit la *Maitri Upaniṣad*, I, 4, lorsqu'à la fin du Monde, les cordes de
vents seront coupées, l'Univers se désintégrera. La *Bṛhadāraṇyaka-Up.*
III, 7, 2 rapporte qu'au moment de la mort, les membres de l'homme se
désarticulent parce qu'ils ne sont plus rattachés l'un à l'autre par l'air
(= la respiration) comme par un fil. C'est dans cette conception cosmo-
physiologique que l'on doit chercher le point de départ des spéculations
philosophiques sur le *sutrātman,* l'*ātman*-en-tant-que-fil. Et si l'on

consulte le dossier constitué par Coomaraswamy sur le *sutrāman* dans les textes pâlis, on se rend compte de la persistance, et donc du caractère pan-indien, de cette conception.[33]

Les images des Vents en tant que cordes cosmiques, de l'air qui tisse les organes et les tient ensemble, de l'*ātman* en tant que fil, sont solidaires d'autres conceptions archaïques, notamment celles du fil de la Vie, de la destinée en tant que tissage, des déesses ou des fées fileuses, etc. Le sujet est immense, nous ne pouvons l'aborder ici.[34] Un seul aspect intéresse notre propos: le rôle de la corde et du fil dans la magie. Non seulement les magiciens sont réputés ensorceler leurs victimes par des cordes et par des noeuds,[35] mais on rencontre également la croyance qu'ils peuvent voler dans les airs ou disparaître au Ciel à l'aide d'une cordelette. Nombre de légendes médiévales et post-médiévales racontent que des sorciers ou des sorcières se sont échappés de la prison, ou même d'un bûcher en flammes, parce que quelqu'un leur a jeté le bout d'un fil ou d'une cordelette.[36] Ce dernier thème folklorique rappelle étrangement le rope-trick indien.

Comme on vient de le voir, la corde n'est pas seulement le moyen exemplaire de communication entre le Ciel et la Terre; elle est aussi une image-clé, présente dans les spéculations concernant la Vie cosmique, l'existence et la destinée humaines, la connaissance métaphysique (*sutrātman*) et, par extension, la science secrète et les pouvoirs magiques. Au niveau des cultures archaïques, la science secrète et les pouvoirs magiques impliquent toujours la capacité de voler dans les airs ou de monter au Ciel.[37] L'escalade chamanique des arbres est, par excellence, un rite d'ascension au Ciel. Et il est significatif que dans l'imagerie traditionnelle indienne, l'escalade de l'arbre symbolise la possession aussi bien des pouvoirs magiques que de la gnose métaphysique. Nous avons vu que le jongleur du *Suruci Jâtaka* grimpe à un arbre à l'aide d'une corde magique, puis disparaît dans les nuages. On a là un thème folklorique, mais attesté également dans les textes savants. Le *Pañcaviṃśa Brāhmaṇa*, XIV, I, 12-13, par ex., parlant de ceux qui montent au sommet du Grand Arbre, précise que ceux qui ont des ailes—c'est-à-dire *ceux qui savent*—réussissent à voler, tandis que les ignorants, dépourvus d'ailes, tombent sur terre. On retrouve, ici encore, cette séquence: escalade de l'arbre, connaissance ésotérique, ascension au Ciel, c'est-à-dire, dans le contexte de l'idéologie indienne, la transcendance de ce monde-ci et la délivrance.

Il faut ajouter au dossier du rope-trick quelques documents moins connus, se rapportant aux medicine-men australiens. On savait depuis les études de Howitt que les medicine-men disposent d'une corde magique à l'aide de laquelle ils prétendent monter au Ciel.[38] Les recherches récentes de Ronald Berndt et du Prof. A. P. Elkin ont apportés des précisions sensationnelles sur cette corde magique. Voici la description qu'en donne Elkin.

During their making in S.E. Australia, a magic cord is sung into the doctors. This cord becomes a means of performing marvellous feats, such as sending fire from the medicine-man's inside.... But even more interesting is the use of the cord to travel up to the sky or to the tops of trees and through space. At the display at initiation time... the doctor lies on his back under a tree, sends his cord up and climbs up on it to a nest on top of the tree, then across to other trees, and at sunset, down to the tree again. Only men saw this performance, and it is preceded and followed by the swinging of the bull-roarers and other expressions of emotional excitement.... In the descriptions of these performances recorded by Mr. Berndt and by myself, the names of the doctors are given, and such details as the following: Joe Dagan, a Wongaibon clever man, lying on his back at the foot of a tree, sent his cord directly up, and "climbed" up with his head well back, body outstretched, legs apart, and arms to his sides. Arriving at the top, 40 feet up, he waved his arms to those below, and then came down in the same manner, and while still on his back the cord reentered his body.[39]

Il est remarquable qu'en Australie aussi la corde magique est l'apanage du medicine-man, c'est-à-dire, de celui qui possède la science secrète. On retrouve donc au niveau australien de culture la même séquence qu'est attestée dans l'Inde et dans le folklore médiéval européen: science, magie, corde magique, ascension des arbres, vol au Ciel. D'autre part, on sait que les initiations des medicine-men australiens présentent une structure chamanique, c'est-à-dire, qu'elles comportent la décapitation et le morcellement rituels du candidat.[40] Il suit de là que les deux éléments constitutifs du rope-trick—l'ascension au Ciel au moyen d'une corde et la mise en pièces de l'apprenti—sont attestés conjointement dans les traditions des magiciens australiens. Est-à-dire que le rope-trick ait une origine australienne? Non, mais il est solidaire de techniques magiques et de spéculations mystiques extrêmement archaïques, et le rope-trick n'est donc pas à proprement parler une invention indienne. L'Inde n'a fait qu'élaborer et vulgariser ce miracle fakirique, tout comme la spéculation indienne a organisé toute une cosmo-physiologie mystique autour du symbolisme des cordes cosmiques et du *sutrātman*.

Il existe un autre aspect, tout aussi important, du problème, mais il dépasse la compétence de l'orientaliste et de l'historien des religions : nous voulons parler des éventuelles expériences parapsychologiques qui ont pu inspirer la croyance dans une corde subtile rattachée au corps. Selon les expériences du Dr. H. Carrington et de Sylvan J. Muldoon, expériences récemment discutées par Raynor C. Johnson, dans son beau livre *The Imprisoned Splendour*,[41] il semblerait que certains êtres humains sont capables de sentir et, à la fois, de visualiser une sorte de corde, ou de fil, qui relient le corps physique au corps subtil (ce que l'on appelle en jargon pseudo-occultiste le "corps astral"). Nous n'avons pas à discuter l'authenticité de telles expériences. Nous constaterons, sans plus, que certains de nos contemporains occidentaux prétendent sentir et voir cette corde subtile. Le monde imaginaire, et le monde intermédiaire des expériences extrasensorielles, ne sont pas moins réels que le monde physique. Il n'est pas donc exclu que les croyances des medicine-men australiens et des autres magiciens dans une corde miraculeusement reliée à leur corps aient été suscitées, ou renforcées, par de telles expériences parapsychologiques.

Mais c'est surtout la fonction culturelle du rope-trick—ou, plus exactement, des scénarios archaïques qui l'ont rendu possible—qui nous intéresse. Nous, venons de voir que de tels scénarios et l'idéologie qu'ils impliquent, sont solidaires des milieux des magiciens. L'exhibition a lieu dans le but de dévoiler aux spectateurs un monde inconnu et mystérieux : le monde sacré de la magie et de la religion auquel n'ont accès que les initiés. Les images et les thèmes dramatiques mis en oeuvre, et notamment l'ascension au Ciel à l'aide d'une corde, la disparition et le morcellement initiatique de l'apprenti, n'illustrent pas seulement les pouvoirs occultes des magiciens ; ils révèlent, en outre, un niveau plus profond de la réalité, inaccessible aux profanes. Ils révèlent en effet le mystère de la mort et de la résurrection initiatiques, la possibilité de transcender "ce monde-ci" et de disparaître dans un plan "transcendantal." Les images libérées par le rope-trick sont susceptibles de déclencher tout à la fois l'adhésion à une réalité invisible, secrète, "transcendantale" et le doute quant à la réalité du monde familier et "immédiat." De ce point de vue, le rope-trick —comme, d'ailleurs, tous les autres exploits des magiciens—a une valeur culturelle positive, car il stimule à l'envi l'imagination et la réfléxion, en suscitant des questions et des problèmes ; en définitive, en posant le problème de la "vraie" réalité du Monde. Ce n'est pas par hasard que

Śankara utilise l'exemple du rope-trick pour illustrer le mystère de l'illusion cosmique; dès les commencements de la spéculation philosophique indienne, la *māyā* était la magie par excellence, et les dieux, dans la mesure où ils étaient "créateurs," étaient des *māyīn*, des "magiciens." Enfin, il faut également tenir compte de la fonction du rope-trick (et des exploits analogues) en tant que "spectacle." Le magicien est par définition un metteur-en-scène. Grâce à sa science mystérieuse, les spectateurs assistent à une "action dramatique" à laquelle ils ne participent pas activement, en ce sens qu'ils ne "travaillent" pas (comme il arrive dans les autres cérémonies dramatiques collectives). Durant les "tricks" des magiciens, les spectateurs sont passifs: ils contemplent. C'est une occasion d'imaginer comme les choses peuvent être faites sans "travailler," simplement par "magie," par la puissance mystérieuse de la pensée et de la volonté. C'est aussi une occasion d'imaginer la puissance créatrice des Dieux, qui créent, non pas en travaillant de leurs mains, mais par la force de leurs paroles ou de leur pensée. En somme, toute une affabulation de la toute-puissance de la science spirituelle, de la liberté de l'homme, de ses possibilités de transcender son Univers familier, est suscité par la découverte du "spectacle," c'est-à-dire par le fait que l'homme découvre la situation d'un "contemplatif."

NOTES

[1] Cf. Mircea Eliade, *Le Chamanisme et les techniques archaïques de l'extase* (Paris, 1951), pp. 379 sq.; Eliade, *Le Yoga; immortalité et liberté* (Paris, 1954), pp. 319 sq.

[2] Le manguier Sanspareil est identique au "manguier central" du roi Vessavaṇa, qu'un autre *jātaka* (No. 281) présente comme un *Axis mundi* (cf. *Jātaka*, texte pāli, II, 397 sq.; trad. de Fausboll, II, 271).

[3] Texte pāli, IV, 324; trad. IV, 204.

[4] H. von Glasenapp. *La Philosophie indienne* (trad. de A. M. Esnoul, Paris, 1951), p. 152 et p. 369, n. 36.

[5] L. Massignon, *Al Hallaj, martyr mystique de l'Islam* (Paris, 1922), I, 80-83.

[6] Sir Henry Yule et Henri Cordier, *The Book of Ser Marco Polo* (London, 1921) I, 316 sq.

[7] R. Schmidt, *Fakire und Fakirismus* (Berlin, 1908), pp. 167 sq.; A. Jacoby, "Zum Zerstückelung und Wiederbelebungswunder der indischen Fakire," *Archiv für Religionswissenschaft*, XVII (1914), 455-75, spéc., 460 sq.); A. Lehmann, "Einige Bemerkungen zu indische Gaukler-Kunststücken," *Jahrbuch der Museums für Völkerkunde zu Leipzig*, XI (1952), 48-63, spéc. 51-59.

[8] C. Defrémery et le Dr. B. R. Sanguinetti, *Voyages d'Ibn Batoutah* (texte arabe accompagné d'une traduction, Paris, Société Asiatique, 1822), IV, 291-92. Nous avons déjà reproduit ce passage dans *Le Chamanisme*, p. 380, n.i; *Le Yoga*, pp. 319-20.

[9] Yule et Cordier, *Marco Polo*, I, 316; Jacoby, "Zum Zerstückelung," pp. 460-62, d'après E. D. Hauber, *Bibliotheca, acta et scripta magica* (1740), pp. 114 sq.

[10] Jacoby, "Zum Zerstückelung," pp. 462-63.

[11] *Silva Gadelica* (London, 1892), II, 321-22. Jacoby, "Zum Zerstückelung," p. 470, cite une variante identique, d'après *Erin, Eine Sammlung irisches Erzählungen*, VI, 130 sq.

[12] *Memoirs of the Emperor Jahangir*, p. 102, reproduit par Yule et Cordier, *Marco Polo*, I, 318: "They produced a chain of 50 cubits in length, and in my presence threw one end of it towards the sky, where it remained as if fastened to something in the air. A dog was then brought forward, and being placed at the lower end of the chain, immediately ran up, and reaching the other end, immediately disappeared in the air. In the same manner a hog, a panther, a lion and a tiger were successively sent up the chain, and all equally disappeared at the upper end of the chain. At last they took down the chain and put it into a bag, no one ever discovering in what way the different animals were made to vanish into the air on the mysterious manner above described."

[13] Cf. les exemples réunis par Jacoby, "Zum Zerstückelung," pp. 466-67, 472-73.

[14] Jacoby, "Zum Zerstückelung," p. 464. Sur les légendes rapportées par Paracelse, cf. W. Mannhardt, *Germanische Mythen*, pp. 64 sq.

[15] Jacoby, "Zum Zerstückelung," pp. 464-65.

[16] Eduard Seler, "Zauberei im alten Mexico," *Globus*, 78 (1900), 89-91, reproduit dans *Gesammelte Abhandlungen zur Americanischen Sprach- und Altertumskunde*, II (Berlin, 1904), 78-86, spéc. p. 85.

[17] *Memoirs of the Emperor Jahangir*, p. 99, reproduit par Yule et Cordier, *Marco Polo*, I, 318.

[18] A. Lehmann, "Einige Bemerkungen zu indische Gaukler-Kunststücken," *Jahrbuch der Museums für Völkerkunde zu Leipzig*, XI (1952), 48-63, rejette l'hypothèse de la suggestion, et explique le rope-trick par la prestidigitation.

[19] Jacoby, "Zum Zerstückelung," pp. 464, 474, et passim.

[20] Voir notre livre *Le Chamanisme* pp. 47 sq. Cf. aussi H. Findeisen, *Schamanentum* (Stuttgart, 1957), pp. 50 sq.

[21] Eliade, *Le Chamanisme*, pp. 55 sq.

[22] Eliade, *Le Chamanisme*, pp. 384 sq.; Eliade, *Le Yoga*, pp. 320 sq.

[23] Cf. Eliade, *Le Chamanisme*, pp. 419 sq.; Eliade, *Mythes, rêves et mystères* (Paris, 1957), pp. 88 sq.

[24] Ananda K. Coomaraswamy, "Svayamātṛṛṇā: Janua Coeli," *Zalmoxis*, II (1939), 1-53, 27, n. 8, 42, n. 64.

[25] Giuseppe Tucci, *Tibetan Painted Scrolls* (Roma, 1949), II, 348, et *Tanka*, No. 12, plaques 14-22.

[26] Mathias Hermanns, *Mythen und Mysterien, Magie und Religion der Tibeter* (Köln, 1956), pp. 42-43. Cf. aussi H. Hoffmann, *Quellen zur Geschichte der tibetischen Bon Religion* (Wiesbaden, 1951), p. 246.

[27] Cf. Eliade, *Le Chamanisme*, p. 381 et n. 3; Tucci, *Tibetan Painted Scrolls*, II, 733-34; Hoffmann, *Quellen*, pp. 141, 150, 153, 245; Hermanns, *Mythen und Mysterien*, pp. 37 sq.

[28] Hoffmann, *Quellen*, p. 246.

[29] Hoffmann, *Quellen*, p. 154; Hermanns, *Mythen und Mysterien*, p. 42.

[30] S. H. Ribbach, *Drogpa Namgyal* (München-Planegg, 1940), p. 239, n. 7; Hermanns, *Mythen und Mysterien*, p.42.

[31] Tucci, *Tibetan Painted Scrolls*, II, 714 sq.; Eliade, *Le Chamanisme*, pp. 381 sq.

[32] Voir à ce propos l'article de A. K. Coomaraswamy, "'Spiritual Paternity' and the 'Puppet-Complex,'" *Psychiatry*, VIII (1954), 25-35, spéc. 29 sq.; cf. Eliade, "Le

'Dieu Lieur' et le symbolisme des noeuds," *Revue de l'histoire des religions* (1947), pp. 5 sq., étude reproduite dans le volume *Images et symboles* (Paris, 1952), pp. 120-63).

[33] Coomaraswamy, "Svayamātrṇṇā," p. 31.

[34] Cf. notre étude "Le 'Dieu Lieur' et le symbolisme des noeuds."

[35] Cf. "Le 'Dieu Lieur' et le symbolisme des noeuds," pp. 23 sq. (*Images et symboles*, pp. 146 sq.).

[36] Voir quelques exemples dans Jacoby, "Zum Zerstückelung," pp. 467 sq.

[37] Cf. Eliade "Symbolisme du 'Vol Magique,'" *Numen*, III (1956), 1-13, reproduit dans *Mythes, rêves et mystères*, pp. 133 sq.

[38] A. W. Howitt, *The Native Tribes of South-East Australia* (London, 1904), pp. 400 sq.; cf. aussi Eliade, *Le Chamanisme*, pp. 133 sq.

[39] A. P. Elkin, *Aboriginal Men of High Degree* (Sydney, 1946), pp. 64-65.

[40] Cf. Elkin, *ibid.*, pp. 31, 43, 112 sq.; Eliade, *Le Chamanisme*, pp. 55 sq.

[41] Sylvan J. Muldoon, *The Projection of the Astral Body*, with a preface by Dr. H. Carrington (London, 1929); Muldoon, *The Case for Astral Body* (1936); cf. aussi Raynor C. Johnson, *The Imprisoned Splendour* (London, 1953), pp. 230 sq.: "He (i.e., S. J. Muldoon) says that there is an astral cable or cord linking together the heads of the physical and astral body—of great elasticity. This exerts a considerable pull or control up to a variable range of about 8 to 15 feet. Once outside this range there is a feeling of freedom, but the cord is always present, even though quite thin, and it retains the same thickness indefinitely.... Once the astral body has moved beyond cord-activity range... the cable diminishes to a fine, thread-like structure and, as might be expected, the flow of energy from the astral to the physical body is greatly reduced.... Death of the physical body is presumably caused by the severance of the astral cord." Remarquons en passant les similitudes avec les croyances indiennes concernant les "fils" et les "cordes" qui articulent le Cosmos et l'homme.

RELIGIOUS ASPECTS OF THE WIND RIVER SHOSHONI FOLK LITERATURE

By Åke Hultkrantz

UNIVERSITY OF STOCKHOLM

THE STUDY of primitive folk literature has hitherto been concentrated mainly upon analysis of the literary form, in which connection the influence of the narrator and of the milieu upon the structure and form of the narrative has also been treated in detail. It is here worth remembering Paul Radin's contributions in this field of research, perhaps best manifested in his essays "Literary Aspects of North American Mythology" (1915) and "Literary Aspects of Winnebago Mythology" (1926). The folklorists in the narrower sense have exploited the primitive literature as source material for studies on diffusion, whereas the anthropologists have to an increasing extent occupied themselves with the study of culture reflexes in the oral narrative tradition. The psychologists, finally, have deduced the personality structure in different peoples by analyzing their literary treasures.

There is, however, one angle from which primitive folk literature has not often been approached: that given by the study of its religious significance and, in connection therewith, its classification from the standpoint of religious belief.[1] Yet, it is a fact that a large number of the prose traditions among primitive peoples everywhere refer to the world of religious belief, to fictive figures and events in a supernatural milieu. It has more than once been emphasized that such a classification is not easy to make; the classifications applied by different peoples and tribes differ widely and often clash with one conceived along the lines here indicated. The objection is perhaps justified when the question is that of distributing the literary material among the three classical categories of comparative religion: myths, legends, and fairy tales. But probably no one will deny that among primitive peoples both narrator and listener may draw a distinction between what for them are true and untrue stories. Even though individual variations in belief and attitude toward belief are not uncommon, there do nevertheless in most societies seem to be (or to have been) common bases for the assessment of the value of the tales as religious truth. Further, in the majority of cases these tales can, independently of the classificatory pattern of the natives themselves, be roughly sorted according to our schema—drawn up, admittedly, in conformity with European criteria—of myths, legends, and fairy tales.

Such a classification should be made, moreover, that we may exploit the rich literary material among primitive peoples to get a more comprehensive and detailed idea of their religious belief. The strict boundary between religion and folklore in the sense of mythology that is maintained in so many works is artificial and strange. As a field researcher, one often finds that to illustrate their religious conceptions one's informants refer to or cite tribal traditions, not infrequently of the type of migratory narrative that some writers have in this connection found so suspect. It is not possible to understand a people's religion if one does not take its mythology into account.

The following exposition is an attempt at a classification on the lines adduced of the folk tales among the Wind River Shoshoni in Wyoming.[2] For the sake of completeness it should be mentioned that the primitive literature of these Shoshoni has already been subjected to a detailed analysis by Shimkin, though from quite other points of departure.[3] Shimkin tried to elucidate their "main forms of unwritten literature." He divides the traditional material into myths (in which connection he distinguishes between "the heroic novelette" or travel and adventure narrative and "the incidental story or personality sketch," which concentrates mainly on throwing into relief the character of the chief personage), anecdotes (to which, curiously enough, he also refers mythological and legendary fragments and European fairy tales), poetical songs, prayers, and minor invocations. This, however, is a classification according to literary forms, and as such it is instructive. Only in passing does Shimkin deal with the question of the alleged value as truth of the tales, and he does not compare the different categories of narrative from this angle.

We shall here leave the poetry and the prayers on one side, and instead discuss the prose tales to which Shimkin refers, perhaps a little arbitrarily, as myths and anecdotes. Considered in relation to the scale of religious values, prayers and songs present no problem; the prayers always have a religious character, and the songs acquire such a character if they are included in a religio-cultic context. Far more interesting to ascertain are the boundaries between play and entertainment and sincere religious expression in the comprehensive genre of Shoshoni folk literature commonly referred to as folk tales, or tales, or (unfortunately!) myths.

The classifications of this traditional material adopted by the Shoshoni themselves give us no direct clues. As is to be expected, they do not classify their tales in accordance with the criteria of religious or historical reality; nor do they arrange them by literary forms. The great majority of Shoshoni do not define any boundaries at all between different tales— they are all *nareguyap* 'stories'—but at least the elders have a tacit understanding of a definite cleavage or line of demarcation between tales whose action takes place in the mythical primeval era and tales whose action relates to a later period. This division, which, as Boas has observed, is that generally adopted among the majority of North American Indian tribes, seems to constitute the tacit underlying assumption of all storytelling, but I have never found it clearly expressed, not even among what Radin calls the "religious formulators," the medicine men and other persons with visionary gifts. These distinguish instead different types of narrative according to the peculiar character of the main personages, grouping them practically according to their entertainment value and theoretically according to a fictive "historical" sequence, though here the definite difference in kind between primeval tales and later traditions falls away. Only as a secondary consideration do we find a valuation of the supposed truth of the narratives. And it would never strike any Shoshoni to classify them according to such a criterion.

It may be as well, however, to give here the Indians' classification schema in somewhat greater detail, since it must form the background to our discussion in the sequel. I shall in the main base my account on the pronouncements of the intelligent medicine man J.T. His view is shared, as far as I have been able to ascertain, by the majority of the older Shoshoni. Where this is not the case, it will be pointed out.

As has been mentioned, the tales are grouped according to the character of the chief persons. Thus, for example, a distinction is drawn between *tïndzo:anareguyap*, which deal with cannibalistic forest and mountain trolls; *haivonareguyap*, turtle-dove stories; *kucunareguyap*, buffalo tales; *tïanareguyap*, horse stories (including tales of horse stealing and the like). An important group is constituted by *ižapönareguyap*, coyote stories, called after Coyote, *ižapö*, "because he was the head of all animals," but also includes the adventures of the mythic Wolf ("Wolf and Coyote, they always go together"). These are the tales of the so-called trickster cycle;

Coyote, but in some measure also his brother Wolf, is the trickster of the Shoshoni. A special position is accorded to *taivonareguyap*, white men's stories, inasmuch as their names do not refer to the main personages, but to the provenience of the tales.

A classification like this of the Shoshoni takes into account in the first place the value of the tales as literature of entertainment. Those animals which naturally occupy the foreground of interest among a hunting people become characters in fables at least in their typical traits and in their actions imitate human beings, in part, on a grotesquely distorted scale. They thus have everything that is needed to make this literary genre well-liked and popular. This is not, however, to say that these tales originated solely for entertainment.

Without doubt the Coyote tales occupy first rank among these stories. Interest attaches in the first place to the amoral joker Coyote, whose character tallies in all essentials with the figure in the Winnebago mythology that Radin has so splendidly drawn in his book on the Trickster. The Coyote stories make up about half of that part of the Shoshoni prose literature whose action takes place in the mythic primeval era. In consideration of the frequency with which these tales are recounted, they are predominant in the total traditional prose material. It is worth emphasizing that their importance is in direct proportion to their entertainment value. It is no sacral consideration that has determined the prominent position occupied by these stories.

Another very much appreciated narrative genre is constituted by the stories of the cannibalistic monsters (*nïmïrïka, pandzo: aβits, tïndzo: aβits*). If the Coyote stories form in the first place amusing, droll entertainment, the cannibal stories introduce an element of excitement and horror that holds the listeners, and especially the small children, in a firm grip.

Tales of a more realistic kind, such as warpath narratives and narratives of visions and medicines, may command interest, but not in an equally high degree (at least not in our times). In J.T.'s classification of tales these are included as it were by chance. Other narrators, above all those who are not shamans but who nevertheless try to keep up the contact with the past, have a good many more war stories to tell. The tales of visions always find an audience, but there are few who are able—or willing—to retail them. We shall revert to this point.

While J.T. thus classified the tales according to their popularity, their value as entertainment literature, he could also arrange them in chronological order. But he got tangled up if he had to repeat the procedure after a short interval of time: the individual narratives then exchanged places in a number of cases. Obviously, the order was approximative, although, in order to give the chronological sequence authority, J.T. strove to be exact. Certain it is that the actual idea of the chronological order was not his own invention, for on the whole the chronology adduced by him recurred in pronouncements by other Shoshoni. That is to say, not the position of the individual tales, but certainly the place of the types of narrative, was precisely determined in a relative time scale:

1. Tales of the creation (creation of the animals, creation of man).

2. Coyote's adventures (in this connection J.T. referred especially to those tales which deal with Coyote's interventions in nature and culture, whether these were profitable or not).

3. The experiences of other "ancient" animals (Owl, Skunk, and others).

4. Tales of cannibal monsters.

5. White men's stories; and tales of people and heroes with a visionary gift or supernatural powers, and war stories. It should be added that only J.T. adduced white men's stories in this connection, they were altogether omitted by other informants.

It is at first glance hard to draw any definite boundary in time between the different groups. Coyote, who belongs primarily in the primeval era—the period when animals were human beings—and who in several tales is said to have died or to have become a star, actually appears in all five groups, even in the last (he occurs, for example, in a tale concerning the hero kïnyaguiⁿagant 'chickenhawk-owner'). The cannibal monsters certainly belong to the primeval era. Thus my informant G.W. said of one of these beings, pandzo:aβits, that formerly he was to be found almost everywhere, but he is now extinct. Nevertheless, the Indians seemed to fear that he might come if his name were mentioned.

But—and this is the important point—in principle both Coyote and the cannibal monsters belong to the mythic primeval era. As divine primeval beings they have, certainly, actuality also in our times (see below), but their real historical appearance belongs to that period when living beings, the order of nature, and the constituent parts of culture were designed. For this reason one can glimpse a decisive boundary between categories 4 and 5, the boundary between the mythic primeval era and the historical present. Over the first four categories floats the atmosphere of a world, long since lost, which was an arena for beings with miraculous supernatural powers. The last narrative category has to do with human beings, furnished, it is true, with supernatural power, but not themselves supernatural beings nor able to change the world as Wolf and Coyote could.

In other words, behind the narrative chronology of the Shoshoni Indians we divine the fundamental, consciously or unconsciously understood, distinction between primeval tale and ordinary tale that Franz Boas perceived among so many Indian peoples. Boas was of the opinion that the primeval tales should be classified as myths, other narratives as "folk tales."[4] He was right in his intention, but his definitions must be modified. In the first place, "folk tale" is a very wide designation which should also include the myth. In the second place, the reference to the primeval action is only one of the characteristics of the myth; the myth must first and foremost be believed.

We can, however, constate that the Shoshoni chronological classification of the narrative material affords a certain, even if faint, clue to the solution of our problem. In order to get a firmer grip of this we must arrange the Indian divisions in a larger whole, where functional points of view can be decisive. The types of narrative as they have been organized by the Indians themselves must be arranged in relation to one another according to their effect upon the listeners. The latter's mode of reaction must be the criterion.

Now it is inevitable that one and the same tale cannot always evoke the same responses in all the members of a circle of listeners. What is from our point of view most troublesome is, of course, the fact that a tale which is by some regarded as a true relation of events which actually took place on the natural or the supernatural plane is by others not accorded anything else but entertainment value. We may be assured, however, that such a reaction was not so common formerly as it is now. The negative attitude is above all a product of the ideological decay that sets in when different ideologies and notions of value clash. And this process is acute in an Indian milieu in the North America of our times.

Here we must abstract from such negative reactions, and we shall do this best by relying on the way in which older informants and the conservative elements experienced the traditions of the tribe. Even when we draw a distinction between "primeval tales" and "present-day tales" we are endorsing a conservative view of the narratives, for in the eyes of the younger Shoshoni with the more American attitude all tales except the war stories belong to the category of entertaining fairy tales, and the differentiation between them is therefore unclear.[5] We have seen, however, that to a certain extent the old designations also reflect a religious valuation of the traditional material, and for us there is therefore every reason to hold fast to them. In this connection it should be borne in mind that "present-day tale" is not a completely adequate designation for a large group of narratives (and types of narrative) whose action may as well refer to our own time as to a period tens of generations back. However, for lack of a better term we must keep the designation, since it contrasts meaningfully with the term "primeval tale," and its import is that the scenes described belong to a period when the present world order has been definitively fixed and people of present-day form have stood in the foreground of developments.

Tales

A classification of the Shoshoni prose traditions according to their import and their effect upon the listeners will turn out as follows.

Primeval tales. These coincide with the groups 1-4 in the foregoing schema, and thus have to do with the adventures of the primeval beings in animal shape. Their function is threefold. In the first place, as we have found, they constitute a very popular literature of entertainment: the tales about Coyote are droll, amusing, especially for men (some storytellers do not wish to have women present when narrating tales from the trickster cycle); the stories about the cannibal beings are exciting. In the second place, several of these tales, particularly those about cannibal giants and cannibal owls (*wo:ka⁴mumbic*), have a pedagogic value: to keep the children quiet in the evenings the parents are in the habit of telling them of the cannibal owl that carries off small children who are troublesome, who shout and cry. It is not here a matter of incidentally invented tales, but of old narratives from the rich treasure of tradition in the tribe. In the third place, finally, the primeval tales have an explanatory function. They tell how natural and cultural phenomena once arose, and they do this in two ways: either this explanation is added loosely and incidentally to the narrative, as an appended conclusion—we have then to do with the etiological narratives in the narrower sense—or else the narrative in its entirety constitutes the explanation of a natural phenomenon, a custom, an institution.

Now it is quite certain that all the stories mentioned here have and have had in the first place entertainment value. And from this point of view it is of no concern to the narrator whether his hearers believe in the present or earlier existence of the persons active in the narrative. Even the explanatory narratives may pass as amusing examples of the narrators' inventive powers. If a number of the narratives constitute—to use the term launched by a Swedish researcher, C. W. von Sydow—"frightening ficts" for children, this does not necessarily imply that they have been believed true by the adults.

But nonetheless, the suspicion creeps in that at least some of the primeval tales were received as true. We do not here need to seek support in the well-known fact that imaginative persons cannot always distinguish between a fictive character in a novel and a historical personality. The important point is that so many of the tales under discussion are adduced as evidence of the way in which natural phenomena and cultural institutions have arisen. Time and again my informants reverted to the content of the primeval tales when the solution of the origin of certain cultural institutions was to be sought. It was never a matter of attempting to dupe or ridicule me; the informant who made the somewhat surprising reference commented on it in detail, doubted it, or tried to find a satisfactory explanation that might obtain credence for it. Thus the previously mentioned medicine man, J.T., referred the use of the menstruation hut and couvade[6] to orders from Coyote at the dawn of time, and in this connection he particularly emphasized that the spirits (*puha*) were dissatisfied with the arrangement.

As a possible further confirmation of the tendency to regard the tales as true accounts of actual happenings from the past, it may be mentioned that the narrators often confine their train of events to definite areas. They like, moreover, to adduce earlier narrators from whom they have heard the tales. In one such instance, after having told the story of how the animals were distributed in different regions, the narrator, W.E., made the following remarks: "This is a really true story, told to me by my grandmother, and the place it tells about is in Nevada. There is a well there, and Coyote, still petrified, southwest of Reno." The reference to older narrators is intended to affirm that the tale is properly repeated, without additions or subtractions—many presumptive storytellers do not dare to relate their tales for fear of relating them wrongly. The contempt for a storyteller who cannot memorize correctly is great, especially among other storytellers.[7] One may ask oneself whether this unwillingness to accept changes and new combinations of motifs does not stem from the feeling that the tales in any case *may* reflect a past reality. The argument is not strong, but it should be tentatively put forth.

If we have so far tried to solve our problem indirectly, we shall now tackle it more directly by reproducing some pronouncements of the Shoshoni themselves in this question. For the sake of completeness, it should be pointed out that these pronouncements sometimes took the form of replies to questions that I posed, sometimes of marginal notes, reflections after the communication of one of the old tales, and without my having introduced the subject with the slightest indication. In both cases the pronouncements were rather similar: they left no doubt that in at least the older and more conservative generations the Indians still had, in any case, half a belief in the truth of the primeval tales.

This is what I was told concerning the truth of the Coyote tales.

L.S.C. (middle-aged, a defender of the old cultural tradition and a believer in the sun-dance and in the spirits), has never bothered about the native tales, as he does not regard them as true. He argues against the notion that God—*tam apö*—should have been able to dress himself in Wolf's clothes (according to the tales, Wolf is the creator); "Wolf is a killer," and God might have chosen a better character. L.S.C. most definitely repudiates Coyote's role as culture hero: "Everything that we have learned we have received through visions in the sun-dance; Coyote has not given us anything, it is only invention."

S.N. (middle-aged): "God created Wolf and Coyote and equipped them with powers so that they could act as creators." It does not, however, emerge clearly whether this, according to S.N., is what the old Indians believed or whether it was perhaps his own view.

G.W. (younger than S.N., an ardent peyotist, who tries consciously, however, to preserve the old religion, at least in part): Wolf is God and is called *pia apö* 'great father,' while Coyote is *tei apö*, 'little father.' All the animal primeval beings, who were first people but afterwards became animals, are dead, but their progeny live today. G.W. does not, however, understand how God could have died.

P.W. (upper middle-age, knows a number of tales): "Coyote was a kind of god." According to P.W., he belonged to a series of primeval beings that no longer exist.

P.C. (old woman, old believer): Coyote helped God to create life on the earth, together with Bear, Wolf and other "ancient animals." In other words, P.C. considers that the tales of Wolf's and Coyote's creative activities are true.

T.R. (old medicine man): "There is such a being as God. He had a young brother, that is Wolf. But later on there was another brother, Coyote. Wolf and Coyote are dead now. Wolf did not create the world, but he gave it the ruling" (i.e., instituted the seasons, weather conditions, and so forth, as described in the trickster cycle).

J.T. (elderly medicine man, who, however, through contact with the whites has modified his otherwise traditionalistic attitude), does not know for sure whether the tales about Wolf and Coyote are true, and asserts that the Shoshoni do not as a rule think about this question, still less discuss it. On one occasion J.T. says that the tales are "just stories," and he continues: "I think it is more a man's story than anything. But the way they [Wolf and Coyote] created the wild game sounds like true." After having recounted this tale, however, J.T. says: "But I don't know how true this is." On the other hand, J.T. is more positive in his comments on the tale in which we are told how winter was restricted to four months —a story in which Coyote plays the chief role. "It seems like it is true, for there are four winter months—November, December, January, February." On another occasion J.T. declares that "all stories sound true to me"—with one exception, ordinary joke stories. He asserts that all the tales he heard the old people tell are true, they report events that occurred at the time "when Coyote ruled the world." J.T. blames his brother-in-law because the latter (now deceased) did not believe that the Coyote tales were true. Perhaps the following judgment by J.T. concerning these tales gives his attitude in a nutshell: "It sounds true, and in another way you take it, it's a story." That is to say, the tales have a genuine basis in reality, but they serve chiefly as entertainment.

One arrives at a similar result if one investigates the truth value of the other animal tales for the Shoshoni. In my opinion there can be no doubt but that the majority of the primeval tales were in former times regarded as true narratives of what once took place in our world before it had been definitively regulated. In consequence of the change in culture during the past century the tales have for many Shoshoni lost their old import and have only survived as entertaining stories. An investigation of the provenience of the different tales shows that many of them derive from other tribes, usually from groups belonging to the Shoshonean language family (Ute, Paiute, Paviotso, and so on). This must not be taken as proof that the native mythological tradition has been broken down and transformed into pure entertainment literature. The Wind River Shoshoni have made room for these alien stories because in well-known turns of phrase they have thrown light upon the same theme as have their own inherited narratives. One may confidently assume that the exchange of oral traditions has been going on for a very long time.

Present-day tales. The present-day tales fall into two large categories, the religious and the profane traditions.

The religious traditions tell of visions and auditions that heroes in a past or more recent time have had (in a number of cases their names and the historical figure concealed behind the name are known). They also tell of wondrous meetings with supernatural beings, of the transformation of people to spirits or animals, and so forth. All these tales were included in an older period among the "true stories" that were told to a younger by an older generation to impress ideals of living and right behavior in different situations, or to give instruction concerning the origin of ritual or other behavior in visionary experiences. By the side of this didactic value the tales naturally also had a function as entertainment, even if in practice this was of subordinate importance.

In those circles in which the old belief still has a firm anchorage the religious traditions are naturally regarded as true. The tales dealing with visions, especially, are held in great esteem, but one seldom hears them related. The one who has been vouchsafed the vision often does not venture to speak of his supernatural experiences, or else he relates no more than their external details; the secret itself goes into the grave with him. Many medicine men, moreover, refuse to divulge their colleagues' visions in so far as they may be aware of them (which is not always the case). Above all, the Indians avoid mentioning the visions that recently deceased persons have had. Precisely this caution testifies to the intimacy of the connection between these traditions and the religious sphere. One may even state that the whole Shoshoni religion is built up on visionary experiences.

A particular category within the group of religious traditions is constituted by the tales deriving in the last analysis from the whites. In their original milieu they functioned, at least within surveyable time, as fairy tales without any value as truth. It is characteristic that in the Indian milieu these stories should have been integrated with visionary motifs and to a certain extent revaluated. Two Indian informants told me the story of St. George at the same time, assisting each other, and one of them made the following comment: "We both heard this story since we were small; our grandparents told us. This story could be true." But then the informant in question was convinced that the story was Indian from the beginning, and he adduced it to illustrate the popular belief about *pandzo:aβits*—this monster, here with seven heads, has in the narrative taken the place of the dragon.

The profane traditions may be divided into historical narratives and joke stories. The former are told rather frequently and tell as a rule of war-like campaigns and ambushes. Sometimes one also finds super-natural elements in them, such as powerful war medicine, or meetings with ghosts. Formerly these tales constituted a species of moralizing descriptions for young people intended to show model examples of social action, a way of impressing social ideals (cf. above concerning the religious traditions!). In our days they are exciting entertainment and at the same time provide escape from the straits and humiliations of the present, a return to "the good old times." The tales are not historical in the proper sense of the term; they tailor the events ethnocentrically and leave room for supernatural actions, but they are generally understood by the listeners as true descriptions from the past, unless the narrator's way of reproducing them is disapproved.

The joke stories or anecdotes have this in common with the Coyote tales, that they give mirth-provoking entertainment; but otherwise the two narrative groups diverge. The joke stories are recognized to have a fictive background unless, like the tales of the Shoshoni *pandzïta:ŋgö* ('Bare Spot') and his fantastic experiences, they are associated with a known person.[8] J.T. distinguished between the tales of Wolf and Coyote, which are "true stories," and ordinary joke stories, which need not be true. An intermediate position between the two groups is occupied by a number of animal stories (of the type of the primeval tales) with a jocular etiological conclusion.

If we now take a survey of the collected material of folk tales among the Wind River Shoshoni, it is striking to what an extent the tales are regarded as true descriptions of a natural or supernatural past reality. In a particularly high degree, of course, does this apply to the genuine native tales. As the believers belong to the older and more conservative levels of the present population, it may be considered probable that in older times practically all stories, with the exception of a few joke stories, were regarded as true—*in so far as this problem was consciously approached at all.* Many tales, e.g. the Coyote stories, were probably told now as pure entertainment, now as edifying or warning examples, and again as motivation for existing conditions. Only as origin tales have they actualized the question of their truth. One may also express the matter thus: that this problem has been relevant in certain situations, but has been irrelevant in other situations.

It was mentioned by way of introduction that in its religious aspects the primitive oral prose traditions may be classified in the categories—myth, legend, and fairy tale—so often used in comparative religion. Also the Shoshoni narratives may be classified on these lines. Before I make an attempt at such a classification I shall define briefly what I mean by myth, legend, and fairy tale. I have given a more detailed characterization and motivation elsewhere.[9] The myth, as I understand it, is a narrative of gods and divine beings, whose actions take place in the period when the present world was formed (in principle, their actions are not bound by time). The myth is often sacred in itself, and it is always an object of belief. The legend deals with human beings, preferably heroes, and their supernatural experiences, and it is regarded as a true description. The fairy tale (*Märchen*), again, makes use of the milieu and the personages of the myth and the legend, but without the dramatic action in which these are involved being considered true. There are, naturally, also profane *Märchen*, but these are without relevance in the present connection.

Let us now see how far the Shoshoni tradition categories we set up above are compatible with this new classification. Even a hasty comparison is sufficient to convince us that a collocation does not seem unnatural. The primeval tales correspond most closely to what we have here referred to as myths, while the present-day tales, in so far as they have a religious character, may be designated as legends. It is, on the other hand, extremely problematical whether the fairy tale (in the sense used here) has at all been represented in the Shoshoni folklore in older times.

Seen from the point of view of comparative religion, the religiously colored prose tradition among the Wind River Shoshoni seems to be distributed in the following way.

Myths

Almost all the primeval tales, in so far as their aim has been to give expression to religious belief, may be considered as myths. On account of their entertaining character they risk gliding into a category lying outside every religious classification. But, as has been pointed out above, many of them have also a sanctioning, explanatory, or etiological function. In the following the Shoshoni myth material is differentiated in different groups. In order to bring out its peculiar character our short survey will be introduced with a myth group which is *not* represented, but which in other cultures plays a very prominent role.

Sacred myths. These constitute among the Shoshoni a myth category that is conspicuous by its absence. By sacred myths I refer to those whose recitation takes place in a solemn, perhaps ritually fixed, way, and whose content inspires a devotional mood. They may be cult myths, i.e. the text to a cultic act, but they may also occur independently of any cult. Real cult myths are not found among the Wind River Shoshoni, and this for natural reasons. The culture of these Shoshoni, before the influence from the Plains tribes dwelling to the east had made itself felt, was of a primitive Basin structure. In the simple Shoshoni hunting and gathering society, with its individualistic stamp, common cultic enterprises could find no soil.[10] It was only with the spreading of the genuine Plains culture to the Shoshoni, and with the appearance of a firmer sociopolitical organization, that a real cult system arose, concentrated on the powerful sun-dance. The Shoshoni have a tradition concerning the origin of their sun-dance. But as the introduction of the sun-dance took place at a comparatively late period (the end of the eighteenth century) and the memory of this persists, the origin tradition does not belong to the remote world of the myth.[11] It has its place among the legends (see below).

Sacred myths which have not had a cultic background probably have not existed either. The trickster mythology has certain points of contact with this category (see below concerning the myth of the origin of death!) but differs, otherwise, in its present form in a striking way from the sacred myths we know from other peoples. In my opinion, however, it constitutes a relic of an older sacral mythology (see below). I have also noted down an extremely fragmentary version of the old myth of the great flood, and this myth *possibly* constitutes a relic of an older series of sacred myths.

Origin myths with serious intention (so called in contradistinction to playful etiological tales). Among the Shoshoni these myths occupy the foremost place and come nearest to the sacred myths. These tales do, certainly, generally belong to the trickster cycle, but through their serious import they diverge from the majority of Coyote stories and should therefore not be judged exclusively as such. To the category of origin myths we may probably in the first place refer the tales of how the living beings, humans, game, and fish, were created (note that the focus of attention is occupied by those animals that are economically important to man). To the same category belong the stories of how the animals acquired their present appearance, and how they were distributed over the country; also the tales of how the seasons were determined, how the medicine men appeared, how the course of childbirth was established, and how death was introduced into the world. It is more doubtful whether the numerous tales with an appended etiological conclusion may be referred to the same category, e.g. the tales with astral ending; they ought preferably to be referred to a category of their own (cf. below).

The Coyote stories mentioned here are real myths in so far as they are regarded as true, deal with the divine beings of the primeval era (Wolf and Coyote) and have a serious intent. Their value as truth and their relation to the events of the primeval era have been discussed above. As regards Wolf and Coyote, they undoubtedly were originally exalted divine beings, even if their connection with the subsequent supernatural beings of the Shoshoni religion has fallen into oblivion.[12] We cannot here elucidate this question in detail; I hope to be able to revert to the matter on a later occasion. My standpoint may shock American anthropologists and folklorists, but it is based upon two important pieces of evidence. First, testimony from the Shoshoni themselves, both at Wind River and at the reservations west of the Rocky Mountains. Second, the result of an investigation of the composition of the trickster cycle. It proves that the origin narratives in which Wolf and his "younger brother," Coyote, figure, constitute parts of the brother and twin myths associated with the conception of the culture hero. It may be added that Coyote's character of divine being has also been noted by European researchers.[13] For my own part, then, I incline to the view that several of the Coyote stories are earlier myths, which—undeniably in consequence of Coyote's trickster character—have degenerated more and more and become entertainment literature bordering on the fairy tale, to which at the same time a number of new, humoristic motifs, created by the narrator or taken from other narratives, have been added.

In the origin myths one discerns behind the description of Coyote's pranks a serious meaning which is easily lost if one is prepared to regard these tales only as amusing entertainment. The clash between joking and earnestness may seem alien to us, but two things should here be borne in mind. In the first place, that over large parts of North America, and especially on the Plains and in the Southwest, ritual solemnity is quite deliberately disturbed by clownish, even obscene elements.[14] In the second place, that the Shoshoni oscillate in a very labile way between moods of grief and gladness. They can break out into unrestrained weeping on occasions which are otherwise stamped with harmony and great happiness; and they can turn to jokes and laughter during a funeral. We shall not here attempt to explain these extremes of mood; we merely record them.

That the Coyote stories do not always release responses of gladness and a mood of irresponsibility is certain. The tale of the origin of death is told, as I have remarked in an earlier connection, by no means to the accompaniment of the same mirth and merriment as other trickster narratives.[15]

Astral myths. The astral myths are also to a certain extent origin myths, but in contradistinction to the foregoing category they cannot be assessed as such in their entirety, as the explanatory element is appended at the end of tales with a content that does not naturally or directly correspond to what follows. Several constellations of stars have a mythologic background (the Great Bear="the jackrabbits," Orion="the three buck mountain sheep" or "Coyote's daughters," and so forth), but in the actual narrative the etiologic element constitutes a transient final episode, more forced than natural. Otherwise expressed, the astral myth is constituted by the final episode in the narrative.

Of more indefinite religious value are the other animal tales in the category of primeval tales. In so far as a comparative religious classification is to be applied they must be regarded as myths—perhaps declassed myths that have lost their direct anchorage in the world of religious reality. Today, at all events, it is difficult to realize what religious function the beings mentioned in these myths once had.

Legends

To this class of tales we must refer all the present-day traditions of a religious character, first and foremost the important tales of meetings and experiences with spirits in visions. A number of these narratives are of recent date and derive from persons who are still alive; but others of them date further back, and among these are to be noted in the first place the origin legend of the sun-dance. We have already mentioned that this is not a cult myth, and we may add here that it is also not a "cult legend." It functions in no way in connection with the actual ceremony. Its only aim is to tell us how the latter originated. The tale has, however, a peculiar sacral character: it has, according to what I was told, been passed down as a secret tradition in one and the same family.[16] When it was told to me it had been divulged to an outsider, who was no longer so particular about secrecy. As far as I am aware, this is the only Shoshoni narrative that has had a secret character and that has been "owned" by a certain family. The prototype is probably to be sought in the narrative privileges of the more easterly Plains tribes.

It is interesting to observe that the Supreme Being—*tam apö* 'our Father'—is not with certainty represented in the myths,[17] whereas he does, on the other hand, occur in the legends. Thus there are legends about the way he reveals himself as a bright light or a voice that warns humans when they are in danger.

Fairy Tales

As has been mentioned, it is difficult to indicate with any assurance tales which in older times dealt with religious material but were at the same hme regarded by the Indians themselves as fictive. It is only in our day mat the Shoshoni myths have tended to become fairy tales, and in this connection we may find an interesting parallel in a corresponding process to Europe: the fairy tale appeared when the content of the narrative iasuld no longer maintain its connection with the cultural and religious tasumptions of the listeners. The fairy tale is, among the Shoshoni as ticnong he Europeans, a degenerated folk tradition.

We may hus summarize our results as follows: in older times the Shoshoni in tall probability attached to those tales which convey religious content a religious value. And the forms in which these tales have occurred have been the myth and the legend, as defined above. The fairy tale, the fictive "supernatural" story, has presumably not belonged to Shoshoni folk tradition. It is only in our day that certain religious narratives have come to be regarded as fairy tales.

NOTES

[1] See also, for the following, W. R. Bascom, "Four Functions of Folklore," *Journal of American Folklore*, 67:333-49 (1954), pp. 335 f.

[2] I was in the field with these Shoshoni in the years 1948, 1955, and 1957. "Wind River Shoshoni" is, as I pointed out in a lecture at the Americanist Congress in Copenhagen in 1956, an ethnic concept which corresponds only to the conditions obtaining during the reservation period. Before this the Wyoming Shoshoni were divided into three different culture groups with different economic activities: *kucundïka* or buffalo-eaters, *tukudïka* or eaters of big-horn sheep, and *haivodïka* or "dove-eaters" (a nickname for the commercialized Indians about Fort Bridger). As regards the folk literature, it was probably in older times common to all the groups.

[3] D. B. Shimkin, "Wind River Shoshone Literary Forms: An Introduction," *Journal of the Washington Academy of Sciences*, Vol. 37, No. 10:329-52 (1947).

[4] Franz Boas, "Mythology and Folklore," in *General Anthropology*, ed. by F. Boas (Boston, Heath, 1938), pp. 609 ff.

[5] The last living storytellers complain that the old tales have lost their grip on children and young people. The younger generation is now a stranger to the world of religion and culture reflected by the traditions.

[6] The concept of couvade is here used in a very restricted and special sense: the father of a newborn infant fasts for four days in connection with the birth, rises early in the morning and runs long distances every day, and scratches his hair with a stick.

[7] This does not prevent the Indians from admitting that one and the same story may be told in several different ways. They do not, for example, reject a Bannock version of a tale because it is presented in another form than the Shoshoni version.

[8] The Shoshoni mentioned "was no good, liked to lie, gave funny stories."

[9] See Å. Hultkrantz, *The North American Indian Orpheus Tradition* (Statens Etnografiska Museum, Monograph Series, Pub. No. 2, Stockholm, 1957), pp. 12 ff., 274 ff.

[10] The ghost-dance presents a special problem complex, which must here be passed over in silence.

[11] There is a Coyote story concerning the sun-dance of the mice; it is also found among other Plains Indians.

[12] Å. Hultkrantz, "Configurations of Religious Belief among the Wind River Shoshoni," *Ethnos*, 1956, pp. 208 ff.

[13] See, e.g., the following: R. Pettazzoni, "Die Wahrheit des Mythos," *Paideuma*, 4:1-10 (1950); Pettazzoni, *The All-Knowing God* (London, Methuen, 1956), pp. 364ff.; G. Kock, "Der Heilbringer," *Ethnos*, 1956: 194-215, pp. 118-29.

[14] V. F. Ray, "The Contrary Behavior Pattern in American Indian Ceremonialism," *Southwestern Journal of Anthropology*, 1:75-113 (1945).

[15] Å. Hultkrantz, "The Origin of Death Myth as Found among the Wind River Shoshoni Indians," *Ethnos*, 1955: 127-36, pp. 133 f.

[16] This tradition is not identical with any of the short origin narratives that Shimkin adduces. *The Wind River Shoshone Sun Dance* (Washington, D.C., Bureau of American Ethnology, Bulletin 151, 1953), pp. 409 ff.

[17] We abstract here from the possibility that Wolf and *tam apö* are one and the same person.

SOME NOTES ON THE GREEK
ORPHEUS TRADITION

By Erland Ehnmark

IN THOMPSON's *Motif-Index of Folk-Literature,* entry F 81: 1 is headed "Orpheus. Journey to land of dead to bring back person from the dead." Under this heading we find, of course, first the well-known Greek tale, from which the name of the whole group is taken, and then, among various other instances, the so-called Orpheus myth found among North American Indians. This latter tradition has been analyzed in great detail by Gayton and, more recently, by Hultkrantz.[1] An interesting problem with this group of myths is whether there exists a historical connection between geographically distinct forms of the tale, or whether they originated separately in different cultures. Concerning the American tradition, Gayton and others are of the opinion that European influence in post-Columbian time must be out of the question.[2] On the other hand, the theory has been advanced that the Greek and American traditions are variants of one and the same tale. Rose, for instance, says about the Greek myth that it is a variant of "a very old tale, known apparently from Thrace to North America, of the man who went to the other world, to fetch his wife and (usually) lost her after all his efforts because he broke some tabu."[3] Hultkrantz concludes, after a careful investigation, that the arguments that can be advanced for diffusion are strong but not sufficiently convincing.[4]

It is not my purpose here to discuss these various opinions, nor the general question of diffusion or separate origin in the case of the American or other tales. The aim of this paper is only to point out some details in which the Greek story has a specific structure that distinguishes it from the commonest form of the American tale. This form is defined by Hultkrantz as "the narrative of a man who, driven by love for his deceased wife, seeks her out in the realm of the dead and tries in vain to restore her to life."[5] The same author has further called attention to the close similarity between the Orpheus tale and narrations of shamanistic experiences.[6] In both these respects the

Greek tale is different from the American. In its oldest form it regularly has a happy end, and the Greek Orpheus is no shaman, nor does he use magical means.

The Greek evidence is collected in Kern's *Orphicorum Fragmenta* (Test. 59 sq.). It has been made the object of a very thorough scrutiny by J. Heurgon,[7] who has been able to show that the whole literary tradition before Virgil, possibly with one exception, presents a version of the tale in which Orpheus was successful in bringing his wife back from the dead and where, moreover, there is no mention of a condition, a "taboo." There would be no reason to discuss the texts again if K. Ziegler in a learned and detailed article[8] had not criticized Heurgon's interpretations (in my opinion on very weak grounds), and if the exception mentioned above, when correctly interpreted, were not found also to presuppose the happy end.

The oldest text in which the story is mentioned is a passage in Euripides' drama *Alcestis* (vv. 337 sq.). Admetus—whose wife, Alcestis, has voluntarily died in his stead—is speaking: "If only I had Orpheus' voice and art of singing, I would bring thee back from Hades." Ziegler contends that Euripides adduces the example of Orpheus only as far as it fits his purpose. But this is no more than an *argumentum e silentio*. And the scholiast *ad loc.* is quite positive in stating that Orpheus brought Eurydice back from Hades. Moreover, the whole drama turns round the fact that Heracles really did what Admetus was too much of a coward even to attempt: he overpowered Death and brought Alcestis back to life again. That is, Heracles performed the role of Orpheus as Admetus could not, or dared not. Further support for this interpretation—that the poet had in mind a version of the tale where Orpheus succeeded—is found in the fact that Admetus after the quoted words goes on to say that neither Cerberus nor Charon should have deterred him (if he were an Orpheus): if Euripides had alluded to such a form of the tale as we find in Virgil and Ovid (with the unhappy end) he would rather have made Admetus say that he would not look back and break the condition (the "taboo") imposed upon him.

Other texts are even more positive. Isocrates (XI. 8) says that Orpheus brought "the dead" back from Hades (the plural is of course a generalization), and nothing is said about any failure. The poet Hermesianax, quoted in Athenaeus (XIII. 597b), has a detailed description which ought to be given in full (Orpheus' wife is here called Agriope):

Such was she whom the dear son of Oeagrus, armed only with the lyre, brought back from Hades, even the Thracian Agriope. Ay, he sailed to that evil and inexorable bourne where Charon drags into the common barque the souls of the departed; and over the lake he shouts afar, as it pours its flood from out the tall reeds. Yet Orpheus, though girded for the journey all alone, dared to sound his lyre beside the wave, and he won over gods of every shape; even the lawless Cocytus he saw, raging beneath his banks; and he flinched not before the gaze of the Hound most dread, his voice baying forth angry fire, with fire his cruel eye gleaming, an eye that on triple heads bore terror. Whence, by his song, Orpheus persuaded the mighty lords that Agriope should recover the gentle breath of life.

Hermesianax then proceeds to recount other myths dealing with love. It is to be noted that the poet twice, in the beginning and in the end, states that Orpheus succeeded.

Still another instance is found in the poet Moschus, in his *Epitaphios Bionos* (vv. 122 sq.): "Even as once she [Persephone] granted Orpheus his Eurydice's return because he harped so sweetly, so likewise she shall give my Bion back unto the hills; and had but this my pipe the power of that his harp, I had played for this in the house of Plutus myself." Ziegler comments on these last two texts: "Beiden Dichtern kommt es darauf an, die Macht des Gesanges und der Gattenliebe zu preisen; so schweigen sie von dem Rückschlag, der ja nicht durch einen Mangel an dem, was sie preisen, sondern durch andere Ursachen herbeigeführt worden ist, aber doch, erwähnt, das lichte Bild trüben würde." [9] This is nothing but a *constructio ad hoc:* how could the poets say that Orpheus succeeded if they really meant, and everyone knew, that he did not? There is, indeed, no apparent reason why all who have alluded to the Orpheus-Eurydice tale in the period before Virgil should have been so reticent about the unhappy ending of his expedition into Hades.

Yet it may be objected that there is one pre-Virgilian text in which Orpheus is said to have been unsuccessful. This is the earliest literary mention of an unhappy end of the adventure, but it remains to be proved that this version is parallel to Virgil's. In his *Banquet* (p. 179b) Plato refers to the story of Orpheus in the following words (Phaedrus is speaking):

Furthermore, only such as are in love will consent to die for others; not merely men will do it, but women too. Sufficient witness is borne to this statement before the people of Greece by Alcestis, daughter of Pelias, who alone was willing to die for her husband, though he had both father and mother. So high did her love exalt her over them in kindness, that they were proved alien to their son and but nominal relations; and when she achieved this deed, it was judged so noble by gods as well as men that, although among all the many doers of noble deeds they are few and soon counted to whom the gods have granted the privilege of having their souls sent up again from Hades, hers they thus restored in admiration of her act. In this manner even the gods give special honour to zeal and courage in concerns of love. But Orpheus, son of Oeagrus, they sent back with failure from Hades, showing him only a wraith of the woman for whom he came; her real self they would not bestow, for he was accounted to have gone upon a coward's quest, too like the minstrel that he was, and to have lacked the spirit to die as Alcestis did for the sake of love, when he contrived the means of entering Hades alive.

Heurgon is inclined to interpret this passage as showing that Plato knew the Orpheus tradition which we may call the "Virgilian." He has, Heurgon opines, reduced this tale to its essential elements: the gods did not give Orpheus back his wife.[10] Ziegler too takes this representation of the story as the oldest literary instance of the unhappy ending, although he recognizes its similarity with Stesichorus' recasting of the Helena tale.

It is true that the Platonic version differs from all the others before Virgil in that Orpheus does not succeed. But this is also the only point of connection with the "Virgilian" version. There is no question of a condition—a "taboo"—nor do we hear anything of his song or the power of his lyre. He "contrived the means" to enter Hades alive, but it is not said that he won the compassion of its rulers. What Plato says is that he was cheated: he went back without the real Eurydice, but evidently he was not aware of this before he was well out of Hades. When it is said that the gods did not give him the real Eurydice, it is obviously implied that they gave him something else, i.e. her image. Thus the background to Plato's version cannot be the "Virgilian" form of the tale (if he wished to represent Orpheus as a weak character he might as well have used this version), but a story according to which Orpheus really brought back his wife. So he did, Plato means, but not his real wife, only her image. It served him right, he being only a musician and a coward.

As has been remarked long ago,[11] this version of the story closely resembles that of the Helen tale given in the *Palinodia* of Stesichorus, which is also quoted by Plato (*Phaedrus* 243b; *Republic* 586c). Stesichorus there says that it was not the real Helen for whom they fought at Troy, but only her wraith (*eidolon*). Through "ignorance of the truth" they thought it was the real Helen (*Republic* 586c; Euripides, *Helen* 605 sq.). In both cases there is the question of an imposture. Orpheus was deceived, and so were Menelaus and the Greeks. The Platonic version of the Orpheus tale has no point whatsoever, if not seen against a current version according to which Orpheus really brought his wife back, just as Stesichorus' version of the Helen tale lacks point if not seen against the common tale about Helen's flight to Troy.

The result, thus, is that no literary version before Virgil has the unhappy ending which we find with him (*Culex* 268 sq., *Georgics* IV. 453 sq.) and with Ovid (*Metamorphoses* X. 1 sq.) as well as with other later authors. And nowhere is a "taboo" mentioned before Virgil. Even with a contemporary of his we find the version with the happy ending. Diodorus Siculus says (IV. 25) that Orpheus brought his wife back, *just as* Dionysus brought his mother, Semele, back from Hades.

On the other hand, the version including a condition and an unhappy ending is probably much earlier than Virgil, as is shown by the well-known relief in Naples which must belong to the fifth century—if the current interpretation, obviously based on Virgil and Ovid, is correct. How old this version is, cannot be decided, but very good reasons have been advanced for the theory that it belongs to the archaic period. But the evidence adduced above makes it certain that the other version was much more common down to the time of Virgil. Professor Nilsson summarizes his opinion thus: "If we accept it [the current interpretation of the Naples relief] . . . we have to admit that the myth of the unhappy ending existed in the fifth century B.C., but it is later than the tradition of the happy ending. This change of the myth is an outcome of the general Greek idea of the irresistible power of death and has a parallel in the Theseus myth and comes from the addition of the very widespread motif of the punishment of curiosity." [12]

Theseus is said to have carried off both Ariadne and Helen. Nilsson thinks that these tales are variations of the same pre-Greek myth, the abduction of the vegetation goddess, and that a third myth, in which Theseus attempted to remove Persephone, belongs to the same group. Regarding this last mentioned myth he writes:

It is highly improbable that this attempt was originally considered a crime; success would have been the crowning end of the hero's career, just as the victory over Hades or the fetching of Cerberus crowned the career of Heracles. But the attempt of Theseus failed; he and his friend Peirithous, whom he accompanied and on whose behalf he undertook the adventure, according to the current myth were magically held fast on their seats in the Underworld. The myth must be understood in a different way.—Persephone was identified with Kore, the vegetation goddess carried off by Pluto, who was identified with the Ruler of the Dead. Consequently Theseus appears here also in his old rôle as carrying off the vegetation goddess; but, as this goddess was identified with the Queen of the Dead, his deed appeared of course to be an attempt to vanquish the Empire of Death. This attempt was bound to fail according to current Greek ideas concerning the all-conquering and irresistible power of Death. The earlier and contrary conception of the victory over Death and the Empire of the Dead was preserved in the Heracles myth in traces only, and these were but half understood. Here the current conception won; the Vegetation Goddess was thought to be identical with the Queen of the Nether World, and thus Theseus was doomed to remain in the Underworld.[13]

To what is said here about Heracles might be added that in some versions of the Alcestis story it was not Heracles who rescued her; rather she was released by the powers of the underworld themselves. (See Plato, *Symposium* p. 179c; Apollodorus, *Bibliotheca* I. 9, 15.)

There exists a parallel to this reinterpretation in consequence of an altered view regarding human conditions and human possibilities in the face of death. Asclepius had restored dead persons to life and was therefore punished by Zeus, who slew him with his thunderbolt. Edelstein[14] has made a strong case for the supposition that in the oldest versions of the tale Asclepius was killed not because he transgressed the laws of the universe in raising up the dead, but because he revived those who had made themselves enemies of the gods, e.g. Capaneus and Hippolytus, the former having been slain by Zeus (Sophocles, *Antigone* 127), the latter brought to death by Aphrodite (Euripides, *Hippolytus* 1400). Stesichorus and other early sources[15] do not tell us that Asclepius was punished just because he raised the dead, but because he raised certain persons whose names are expressly mentioned—persons who were hated by one god or by all the gods.

But in later tradition the revivification itself is regarded as a crime. And so we hear Hades complain to Zeus that his power is diminishing in consequence of the activity of Asclepius, for the dead are continually growing fewer (Test. 4. 75; Diodorus IV. 71; Ovid, *Fasti* VI. 757).

What could be called an intermediate interpretation is found in Ovid (*Metamorphoses* II. 642 sq.): it was the privilege of Asclepius to revive men, but he was not allowed to interfere with the wishes of the gods.[16] The idea that a resurrection from the dead infringes the cosmic order is first found in Aeschylus and Pindar. Aeschylus says (*Agamemnon* 1019) that "man's dark blood, once it hath flowed to earth in death" cannot be called back by chanting spells. "Even him who possessed the skill to raise from the dead—did not Zeus put a stop to him as a precaution?" [17] Pindar, who relates the whole story (Pythian Odes III), has it that Asclepius was seduced by money to bring back one who was dead. Edelstein suggests that Pindar needed this motive in order to justify the conduct of Zeus, which otherwise would remain inexplicable to him.[18] Edelstein quotes, however (Testimony 1), only verses 1–58 in Pindar's poem, and he has not seen that Pindar's real motivation is different; it is the same as the one found in Aeschylus. For the poet goes on to say (vv. 59 sq.): "We must seek from the gods for such boons as best befit a mortal mind, knowing what lieth before our feet, and knowing of what estate we are. Seek not, my soul, the life of the immortals; but enjoy to the full the resources that are within thy reach." That is, immortality is only for the gods, and therefore it is a crime to try to raise up the dead.

The original myth thus seems to have been remodeled, and it is very tempting to see a Delphic influence here. According to Herodotus (I. 91), the Pythia answered Croesus that "none may escape his destined lot, not even a god." However, as Professor Nilsson suggests to me, we may see here the outcome of Homeric influence. To the rationalistic Homeric mind it was impossible that the gods should be able to rescue a man from death, when once his appointed hour had struck (*Odyssey* III. 236 sq.): "But of a truth death that is common to all, the gods themselves cannot ward off from a man they love, when the fell fate of grievous death shall strike him down." (Cf. *Odyssey* XXIV. 29; *Iliad* XXII. 209 sq.). On the mainland we find, as usual, different ideas, as shown by the myths. At the end of the archaic age, however, the Homeric view prevailed, e.g. in Pindar.

As to Orpheus, that myth has been recast in two different ways. The one is shown by the Naples relief and, later on, by Virgil. The other is instanced by the Platonic version, in which Orpheus was given only a "wraith" of Eurydice. Here we may compare a passage in

Homer (*Iliad* v. 445 sq.) where Apollo set Aeneas apart from the battle and "fashioned a wraith in the likeness of Aeneas' self and in armour like to his," around which they fought. This is a parallel to Stesichorus' Helen and may have influenced Plato when he retold the Orpheus tale.

It may be observed that the Heracles myths were not affected by this new tendency: he was venerated both as a god and as a hero. In the *Odyssey* (XI. 601), his phantom dwells in the Nether World, while he himself lives among the gods. (Cf. *Iliad* I. 1 sq.: the slain warriors were made a spoil for dogs and birds, while their souls [psychai] went to Hades.) And so his apotheosis by fire was invented, connected with the pyre on Mt. Oeta.[19]

I am much obliged to Professor Nilsson for these suggestions which seem to me to trace a very clear line from Homer downwards. I will add only this. In all the cases mentioned the "image" or "wraith" (eidolon, psyche, phasma) is opposed to man himself. This is in opposition to old Attic usage where the dead are never called "images" or "souls." Even the Attic orators never use the word "soul" of a deceased, but speak of him as "the dead man." [20] This shows the difference between Homeric ideas and those current on the mainland in ancient times.

Heurgon[21] has advanced the theory that the unhappy end of the Orpheus tale is to be ascribed to Pindar—in his view a resuscitation from death surely would be an affront to Fate. As we have seen, this is exactly what he says in the case of Asclepius. Pindar has, in fact, treated the Orpheus tale (Frag. 22 Puech), but unfortunately the fragment breaks off just where Orpheus is mentioned. According to Heurgon, the poet would have mentioned here the sufferings of Orpheus, that is the loss of his wife. Be that as it may, the remodeling of both the Orpheus and Asclepius tales fits in very closely with the ideas prevailing at the end of the archaic time, and it is perhaps no mere coincidence that Euripides has the old form of both tales in the *Alcestis*. He was not interested in justifying the ways of God to man.

The second point worth considering is that the Greek Orpheus does not use magic when attempting to liberate Eurydice.[22] He is no shaman. There is nothing in the Greek material which suggests that he compelled the powers of the underworld to let go their hold of his wife. On the contrary, the effect of his music lies in its beauty. Aeschylus says (*Agamemnon* 1629) that he charmed all nature with the *delight* of his music. When Guthrie describes Orpheus as "the musician with magic in his notes"[23] this is true exactly in the sense in which we too can speak of the "magic" of music. Norden[24] has very rightly stressed the fact that Orpheus is said to *persuade* the subterranean powers (the same expression is used by Hermesianax, Diodorus IV. 25, and Apollodorus I. 14); he has no power over them, but they are moved by his sorrow and his song. And this is exactly the reason why Ovid lets him make a veritable speech. In the (pseudo) Virgilian *Culex* it is said: "This same lyre availed to conquer thee, O bride of Dis [Persephone] and make thee of thine own will [*ultro*] restore Eurydice to be led away" (vv. 286 sq.). We may compare this with the well-known description in Ovid's *Metamorphoses* (x. 40 sq.) where even the Eumenids shed tears. Seneca says that Orpheus "had power to bend the ruthless lords of the shades by song and suppliant prayer" (*Hercules Furens* vv. 569 sq.; cf. *Hercules Oetacus* 1061 sq.) and if we turn to Virgil's *Georgics* (IV. 453 sq.), the accent is even here laid on his song and his sorrow which moved hearts not wont to give way to human prayers— *te veniente die, te decedente canebat.*

The result is that there are some very characteristic differences between the Greek tale and the American. Whether these differences are suffcient to make the diffusion theory impossible, so far as Greece is concerned, must be left to the consideration of the folklorists.

NOTES

[1] A. H. Gayton, "The Orpheus Myth in North America," *Journal of American Folklore*, 48:263 sq (1935); Å. Hultkrantz, *The North American Indian Orpheus Tradition* (Stockholm, 1957).

[2] See Hultkrantz, *Orpheus Tradition*, pp. 184 sq.

[3] H. J. Rose, *A Handbook of Greek Mythology* (New York, 1928), p. 255.

[4] Hultkrantz, *Orpheus Tradition*, p. 206.

[5] *Ibid.*, p. 20.

[6] *Ibid.*, pp. 240 sq.

[7] "Orphée et Eurydice avant Vergile," *Mélanges d'archéologie et d'histoire de l'école française à Rome,* 49:6 sq. (1932); cf. W. K. C. Guthrie, *Orpheus and Greek Religion* (London, 1952), pp. 31, 276; M. P. Nilsson, *Geschichte der griechischen Religion* (Munich, 1954), I, 681.

[8] In Pauly-Wissowa, *Real-Encyclopädie*, 18:Part 1:1272 sq. (1939).

[9] *Ibid.*, p. 1276.

[10] "Orphée et Eurydice," p. 33.

[11] O. Kern, *Orpheus: Eine religionsgeschichtliche Untersuchung* (Berlin, 1920), p. 13.

[12] "Early Orphism," *Harvard Theological Review*, 1935, p. 189; *Opuscula Selecta*, 2:638 (1952).

[13] *The Mycenaean Origin of Greek Mythology* (Berkeley, Calif., 1932), p. 173.

[14] E. Edelstein and L. Edelstein, *Asclepius* (Baltimore, Md., 1943), II, 47 sq. The first part of this work contains a complete collection of the testimonies, also in translation.

[15] See the testimonies pp. 69 sq. in Edelstein and Edelstein; Stesichorus is quoted by Sextus Empiricus I.260; Apollodorus III.10, 3; schol. in Euripides, *Alcestis* 1; schol. in Pindar, Pythian Odes III.96.

[16] Cf. Edelstein and Edelstein, *Asclepius*, II, 47 note 87.

[17] For the interpretation of the passage see *ibid.*, II, 46 note 84; I, Test. 66.

[18] *Ibid.*, II, 49 note 93.

[19] Cf. Nilsson, "Der Flammentod des Herakles auf dem Oite," *Opuscula Selecta*, 1:348 sq. (1951).

[20] H. Meuss, "Die Vorstellungen vom Dasein nach dem Tode bei den attischen Rednern," *Neue Jahrbücher für Philologie*, 1:805 (1889).

[21] "Orphée et Eurydice," p. 46, cf. p. 58.

[22] Cf. Ziegler in *Real-Encyclopädie*, 18:1262.

[23] *Orpheus and Greek Religion*, p. 39.

[24] *Sitzungsberichte der Berliner Akademie*, 22:668 (1934).

MYTH AS WORLD VIEW

A BIOSOCIAL SYNTHESIS

By Earl W. Count

HAMILTON COLLEGE

I

ABOUT a million years ago (it is the dimension of the time, not its precise point, that is relevant) some members of the primate order reached a level of brain organization, of corresponding psychic complexity, where the *representation of reality* not only could occur, but apparently was by nature of the case inevitable.

The meaning of "representation" actually will occupy all of this essay. It is a process of symbolization, of symbolopoea. Symbol has been declared the very "roots" of myth,[2] and it has also been denied to myth altogether.[3]

The contradiction lies less in the authors' conceptions of myth than in their definitions of symbol. We shall adopt Professor Bevan's use of the word, who in turn begins with Professor Whitehead:[4] "'The human mind' [says Whitehead] 'is functioning symbolically when some components of its experience elicit consciousness, beliefs, emotions, and usages, respecting other components of its experience' .... A symbol certainly, I think, means something presented to the sense or the imagination—usually to the sense—which stands for something else. Symbolism in that way runs through the whole of life."

For the purposes of this study, the statement gives us adequate definition of symbol; for we are concerned with the symbolic process as a creative social force, rather than with a philosophy of symbolism or a metaphysic; granted none the less that it is hardly possible to treat the one without reference to the other.

A science of mythology must pose the following questions:

1. In the evolution of man, when and under what circumstances did the capacity to symbolize come into being?

2. What symbolopoetic ingredients produced whatever we define as "myth"? Or, what are the sources of "myth"?

3. What shall we settle upon as properly includible under "myth"?

4. What place has mythopoea had in the building of cultural configuration?

5. As a cultural configuration is transformed (through elaboration, transmutation, dissolution), what happens to its myths?

The array of questions is enough to show why as yet there exists no science of mythology, but only discrete studies of myth materials by literary essayists, historians, psychologists, folklorists (taken in the broadest sense). Equally well the questions suggest the difficulty of bringing about an organized and comprehensive discipline of mythology —ranging as it must, at one end of its spectrum, over the operations of a peculiarly powerful mammalian brain, and at the other reaching the artist's appreciation and insight. But no less does the very scope and magnitude of such a proposed discipline urge its importance for a holistic appraisal of man. The present study (within the strictures of the circumstances that have elicited it) must remain but suggestive; it cannot even cover all of the aspects.

II

The capacity to symbolize is known certainly only at the human level of cerebral development. Possibly, however, it exists rudimentarily at the lesser levels of ape and even of other mammals. It is wholesome to keep this in mind; for it saves us from assuming too glibly that the capacity is some kind of unaccountable and mystical *tertium quid* which man completely refuses to share with his humbler fellow-creatures. Nevertheless, it is certain that in no society but man's is symbolopoea all-pervasive, all-important, a *sine qua non* for his very being.

A little farther along, we shall examine (though all too briefly) the organic seat of some of the activities that play into the symbolopoetic edifice. Suffice it here that the endocranial casts of the earliest and lowliest Hominidae permit us the respectable guess that the capacity to symbolize, to mythologize, to speak genuine language belonged already to those early levels of humanization and that they had had simultaneous and common origin and development. If so, then mythopoea is coeval with humanity and indeed an aspect of human morphology.

The problem of mythopoea has yet another naturalistic side. How an organism relates with its environment is the subject of ecology. But an organism is no passive *tabula rasa* whereon environment writes as it pleases. The organism—as biopsychologists in particular know full well—meets it in a very real way and to a very significant extent on the organism's own terms. That is to say, we may consider the universe as a vast system of energies; it is the peculiar constitution of the organism itself that converts energies into "stimuli." There is nothing intrinsic about a light-wave that makes of it the source of visual experience; it does not compel eyes into existence; the intrinsicality of vision resides in the organism. Nay more: organisms (and this is truer the more elaborate their neurological constitution) can "elect" to "ignore" or "give attention to" certain energies and phenomena which they are quite capable of perceiving. The energies called "light" are externally given; their mode of treatment by the organism is an autogenous matter.

Thus out of the natural surroundings an animal organizes a world within which it acts. This is what lies behind Von Uexküll's distinctions of *Umwelt* and *Merkwelt*. It follows that richness of *Merkwelt* is a function of neuropsychic elaborateness. It follows further that only a symbolopoetic neuropsyche can trace regularity in the courses of the stars because it is concerned about them somehow; only to such a psyche can it matter whether the universe is friendly or not. At this level of evolution, *psychoecology* becomes a very real and a tremendous province within the total life-activities of a certain organism's *Umwelt* and *Merkwelt*.

The Neuropsychic Basis of Symbolization

The endocranial casts of fossil Hominidae, fragmentary evidence though they be, are precious and tantalizing hints of a psychic life that vanished beyond recovery a million years ago. And it has been but a very few years since the brains of extant men were still refusing to give up to the minds of other extant men their secret for producing the life of the mind which the psychologists were seeking to probe. Symbolopoea declined to discuss with visitors its neurophysiological housekeeping.

All is no longer utter darkness, though full daylight is not yet at hand. Psychoanalysis brought insight into the interplay of the conscious and the unconscious, the rational and the irrational, the symbolisms of dreaming—forcing even a reexamination of those terms. From a diametrically opposite approach has come comparative neurology, and especially neurosurgery. The two expeditions do not yet walk arm-in-arm; but at least they are within hailing distance.

We shall assume the findings of psychoanalysis and other "depth" psychologies, since they are so readily accessible.[5] A treatise on brain architecture is far beyond our scope, nor is it even desirable. On the other hand, the "hailing distance" is pertinent to the naturalistic approach with which this study has begun.[6]

THE BRAIN AS PSYCHIC PURVEYOR

The central nervous system of all vertebrates receives information from both the external and the internal environments—from the physical surroundings and from the bodily systems. It processes both kinds conjunctively; it organizes and distributes a response; some of this is assigned to remain within the organism (such as, accelerated heartbeat, visceral tonus) and some of it to perform upon the external environment (such as, running). The messages which thus activate the internal environment are mediated by the "autonomic" nervous system. The messages which begin and end where the animal effects contact with the external environment are mediated by the "voluntary" nervous sytem. These two systems are brought into effective conjunction (to speak simplistically) in the diencephalon—one of the major and basic portions of the brain.

All this is neuropsychic process. Under proper conditions a portion of it—but never more than a small portion—can be "conscious." Another, and far vaster portion, never can rise to the level of "consciousness." Between the two lie matters that are more or less amenable to being summoned into consciousness. All levels are involved simultaneously in the symbolic processes, as will be brought out further, below. Mythopoea will remain largely a mystery until it has been accounted for on this multivalent basis.

The cerebral hemispheres are an adjunct to the brain which are possessed only by mammals. All vertebrates, on the other hand, possess those basic portions of brain which carry out the functions just outlined. This can mean only that, deep below the surface, below the obvious of the symbolopoetic processes, and therefore of the mythopoetic phenomena, there feed into these mechanisms neurologic energies that are more ancient even than the mammals, let alone the primates and the line of man. Whatever, then, be the function of the cerebral hemispheres, it must be in the nature of something added to an ancient base. It is necessary that we examine a little this more ancient base, which in the lower vertebrates is the total brain, but which at the mammalian level we may term, roughly, the "brain stem," or "archaic" brain. We shall pay special attention to its two anteriormost portions: the *telencephalon* and the *diencephalon*.

In all vertebrates, the telencephalon receives the olfactory stimuli; besides this, its "roof" contains tracts by which these and the stimuli received by other portions of the archaic brain become associated by interstimulation. In other words, stimuli become related, so that the animal may organize a response.

The olfactory region of the telencephalon is the rhinencephalon. But this region is not so simple as that would suggest. For the sense of smell is to be viewed as one element in a more complex mechanism; one which comprises taste and other oral sensations, and visceral sensations including sexual. The life-mode of an animal is a reflex of its psychoneural structuring; in the lowest vertebrates this olfactory-oral-visceral complex means that the animals move through a world of smell-taste-visceral sensations.

From fish to man this primitive mechanism is never lost. In the course of evolution others arise, they interpose connections with it, they come to overshadow it—but they never erase it. MacLean therefore has named it the "visceral brain." In psychosomatic health and disease it is fundamentally involved in the production of the elemental emotional tonus of a mental state. Both psychologist and mythologist will immediately appreciate MacLean's observations:[7]

In primitive forms the visceral brain provides the highest correlation center for ordering the affective behavior of the animal in such basic drives as obtaining and assimilating food, fleeing from or orally disposing of an enemy, reproducing, and so forth. . . . it will serve to point up the problems discussed . . . if it is first indicated how the primitive brain perhaps ties in with behaviour that has been so often described as primitive, or infantile, in patients with psychosomatic illness. Psychiatrists have resorted to these adjectives probably because so much of the information obtained from these patients has to do with material which in a Freudian sense is assigned to the oral and oral-anal level, or, as one might say all inclusively, the visceral level. In practically all the psychosomatic diseases such as hypertension, peptic ulcer, asthma, ulcerative colitis, that have been subject to fairly extensive psychiatric investigation, great emphasis has been placed on the "oral" needs, the "oral" dependencies, the "oral" drives, etc., of the patient. These oral factors have been related to rage, hostility, fear, insecurity, resentment, grief, and a variety of other emotional states. In certain circumstances, for example, eating food may be the symbolic representation of psychologic phenomena as diverse as 1) the hostile desire to eradicate an inimical person, 2) the need for love, 3) fear of some deprivation or punishment, 4) the grief of separation, etc. It will be useful to refer subsequently to the *excessive* oral manifestations of hostility and anger as "visceral aggression"; of insecurity and fear, as "visceral fear"; of a feeling of dependence, as "visceral need", etc. It is to be noted that many of the seemingly paradoxical and ridiculous implications of the term "oral" result from a situation, most clearly manifest in children or primitive peoples, where there is a failure or inability to discriminate between the internal and external perceptions that make up the affective qualities of experience. Visceral feelings are blended or fused with what the individual sees, hears, or otherwise senses, in such a way that the outside world is often experienced and dealt with as though it were incorporated. Thus the child looking at a leaf may say, "It tastes green." Or the primitive may attribute a feeling of anguish to a squirming animal in his stomach. . . .

The diencephalon, which lies immediately behind the telencephalon, is very complex. In one way or another it eventually receives the stimuli that enter the body via all portions of the nervous system other than the olfactive. Buried deeply within it is a major portion of the reticular system. In recent years this has come to be considered the very essential region where the animal's entire response is at last brought together and organized, and it is somehow very much involved in the production of the state of consciousness.[8] Penfield terms this great coordinating mechanism seated in the depth of the diencephalon, the "centrencephalic system." To and from the diencephalon run pathways connecting it with all other parts of the brain. It is reciprocally connected with the cerebral hemispheres, and its hypothalamic region contains the terminals of the autonomic system.[9]

The cerebral hemispheres have evolved out of the association area in the roof of the telencephalon. From fishes to reptiles there is a series of these developments (archicortex, paleocortex, mesocortex); from reptiles to mammals this development is climaxed by the relatively enormous neocortex. Some, but far from all, of the information that enters the archaic brain is transmitted to these hemispheres. Here it is subjected to a final and elaborate scanning; it is filed in the archives of memory, chiefly in the temporal lobes. Recent and remote experiences are synthesized; reasoning is applied. The product is passed back to the diencephalon for final organization into a total response. Intermediate between the neocortex and the diencephalon lie the portions of cortex that have evolved from fish to reptile. The micro-structure of all these several regions reflects the fact that both phylo-genetically and ontogenetically they present successive levels of de-velopment; their contributions to the total psychic recipe, as far as these have been identified, seem consistent with this fact. In his behavior as well as in his physical structure, man never gets away from his vertebrate family history.

In the temporal region of their cerebral hemispheres, the primates are particularly well developed; the brain swells into a pair of large temporal lobes. Here are the archives of memory. Furthermore the rest of the neocortex on the one hand and the visceral brain on the other are intimately tied up with them—in fact, the terminations of the visceral brain are incorporated into the base of the lobes.

For decades, experimental neurologists have exposed the cerebral cortex of various animals; and, by applying electrodes to different regions, they have mapped out something of what each contributes to the sum total of behavior. In more recent years, neurosurgery—particularly in the hands of Dr. Wilder Penfield—has been uncovering the psychic meaning of the temporal lobe in man. That the temporal lobe must contribute heavily to symbolistic activity, he has demonstrated dramatically.[10] He remarks, eventually:

One of my former patients once wrote to me asking whether at the time of operation I had been stimulating her subconscious mind when I produced in her a recollection of the past. I was amused for a moment. Then I was startled for these records become something like that. Perhaps her suggestion was not far from the truth. The great body of current experience seems to be forgotten but it is not lost, for the little strips of record that the electrode activates reproduce experiences that are clear and accurate in every detail. There is much evidence from other sources that we make subconscious use of them. Yes, the continuous strip of current experience is converted into a subconscious record and one might well say that it forms the neuronal basis of what has been called the subconscious mind.[11]

It should be clear by now that any symbol is a composite, in which archaic and highly evolved ingredients have merged: the symbolizations of everyday life, the fantasies of the waking state, the dreams of sleep, the tales and rituals of primitives and of sophisticates are blendings of the "rational" and the "irrational."

[The] "ancient brain"—much of which lies in the depth of the temporal lobe, with its dreamy states of psychomotor epilepsy and its body-memories

—has extensive relationships with both neopallium and hypothalamus. . . .
[It is] a crossroads or association for both *internal* and *external* perceptions
arising from the eye, the ear, the body wall, the apertures, the genitals, the
viscera. These reach the temporal lobe via the diencephalon. Smell reaches
it directly. Here, then, within the temporal lobe and its connections, is the
crossroads where the "I" and the "non-I" poles of symbol meet. It is impossible to overestimate the importance of this fact that the temporal lobe
complex constitutes the mechanism for integrating the past and the present,
the phylogenetically and ontogenetically old and new, and at the same time
the external and internal environments of the central nervous system. It is
through the temporal lobe and its connections that the "gut" component
of memory enters our psychological processes and the symbol acquires its
dual pole of reference. Thus in the temporal lobe and its deeper primitive
connections is the mechanism for the coordination and integration of all
of the data which link us to the world of experience, both extero- and
interoceptive. It is by means of this temporal lobe complex operating
through a bipolar symbolic system that we are able both to project and
introject. It makes of the temporal lobe and its intricate bilateral and
autonomic connections, which MacLean has called the "visceral brain,"
the central nervous organ which can mediate the translation into somatic
disturbances of those tensions which are generated on the level of psychological experience. It might even be called the psychosomatic organ.[12]

The meaning of symbol from the standpoint of a neuropsychology
may now be summarized in Kubie's words:[13]

(*a*) There is the symbolic function by means of which in thought and in
speech we represent abstractions from experience. Here the term "symbolic
function" is coextensive with all higher psychological functions, and especially with concept formation.

(*b*) There is the symbolic function with which we are all familiar in
figures of speech, metaphors, slang, poetry, obscenities, puns, jokes, and
so forth. Here the concept behind the symbol is translated into some other
mode of expression; but the relation between the original concept and the
symbol remains relatively transparent, except when it is obfuscated in
varying degrees for "artistic" purposes, as in the obscure realms of modern
art and modern verse. This use of the symbolizing capacity of the human
psychic apparatus characterizes that type of function which Freud called
preconscious or the *descriptive subconscious*. It reaches its most systematic
development of course in the intuitive processes of the creative artist and
scientist.

(*c*) Finally, there is the more limited psychoanalytic use of the term
"symbolic function" where the symbol is a manifest representation of an
unconscious latent idea. Here the link between the symbol and what it
represents has become inaccessible to conscious self-inspection.

For *symbol*, in the psychoanalytic sense, we might reserve some special term; but since all three are aspects of the symbolizing capacity which is the unique hallmark of Man, and since the three merge and overlap one with another, not to have one generic name for them would obscure the essential continuity of all "symbolic functions" from one end of the spectrum to the other. . . . it is important to recognize the continuity of these three kinds of symbolic function: since it is because of this continuity that every symbol is a multivalent tool. That is to say that simultaneously on conscious, preconscious, and/or unconscious levels every direct or indirect representation of any conceptual process will in all circumstances, if in varying proportions, be literal, allegorical, and also "symbolic" in the dreamlike or psychoanalytic sense. Consequently, in actual daily use symbols are simultaneously charged with meaning in all three ways and on all three levels. This makes of every symbol a chord with a potentiality of at least nine simultaneous overtones.

This continuity will be clear if we consider the various ways in which the symbol SNAKE can be used. First it can represent a real snake, or the species Snake as a whole. Here it does not matter whether the spoken word or the written word or drawing or model of a snake is used as the symbol. Secondly, the symbol SNAKE can be the snake of the Garden of Eden, or the traditional snake-in-the-grass of melodrama. Such an allegorical reference to external evil and to conscious conflicts over instinctual problems will be clear to everyone. Finally, however, there is the use of the same symbol as the manifest representative of some unconscious latent idea, of which "penis" would be a typical clinical example, plus all the urges and conflict-laden struggles which center around this latent idea. There can be no hard and fast lines between these three major types of symbolic usage; and whenever we use the symbol SNAKE at all, there will be a simultaneous excitation of all three levels of meaning in varying proportions. In other words, every moment of thought and feeling involves simultaneously the activation of a literal, an allegorical, and a dreamlike meaning of the symbolic representative of all of the percepts which are relevant to that amount of psychic activity.

A science of mythology is not yet equipped to deal with the myth-systems of the world to the very penetrating degree that this quotation suggests; regretfully, we are forced to leave the problem thus suspended. We can at least gather up the signposts of a biological approach to mythopoea thus:

1. Symbols are multivalent in any given instance.

2. The symbolic process is a very complex neuropsychic evolute; it is both symptom and reflex of an edifice that has been compounded both phylogenetically and ontogenetically of primitive materials that represent a succession of elaborations.

3. We may reasonably suppose that emergence of the symbolizing function is what has brought culture out of no-culture.

4. By corollary, technology and social regulation are presumably coeval with it, and their development is bound up with it.

5. We may not simply equate symbol with metaphor, with *pars pro toto,* or with any other substitutive procedure; although these complicated procedures can and do occur in symbolopoea. We must first see the symbol as a reifying integral, first as a means for contacting reality, and not as a device designed to shut out reality. It is extroversion quite as much as it is introversion, if not more so. Like the proverbial furskin of stone age man, it is intended first of all to make possible a coping with a demanding environment, one which could not otherwise be coped with; secondarily, it can of course be converted into an escape-mechanism. It depends not upon the garment but upon the wearer.

6. The focus must be upon the neuropsychic root of the symbolic process, and away from any classification based upon kinds of symbols or upon the sociocultural purposes they may serve.

7. Consequently it is the oneness of folktale, ritual, myth-tale, as products of a common symbol-making matrix, that must be grasped first; whereupon these several formal categories are seen as secondary, and even artificial.

8. Mythopoea is an activity of psychoecology.

9. World-view begins in psychoecology.

Toward a Definition of Myth

PROLEGOMENA—MYTH AND SCIENCE: EVENT TO PROCESS

A major contribution to our present-day perspective on man has come from cultural anthropology: the concept of culture itself.[14]

Cultural evolution may be read in terms of its success in finding regularities or dependabilities in the world it deals with. These regularities or dependabilities are the ground fabric of both personality development and cultural configurations. Recognition of this fact, whether conscious or not, has generated in the last quarter-century or so the discipline of Personality-and-Culture—the flourishing hybrid of psychology and cultural anthropology. A little thought will show that personality and culture actually are inseparable; world-views of a person and of his culture reciprocate. None the less, the hybrid discipline has not yet come to exploit the resources of the data of mythology; and such exploitation would be a department of mythology as a science.

However, the mythology of the person must in this essay be set aside. We shall deal only with that abstraction, culture. And we return to the question of dependabilities as they are envisioned by a culture.

To most, if not all, primitive cultures the universe is somehow numenal; it has been so likewise to many cultures that were not primitive. Now, in a given culture, not only do its carriers display a certain basic personality structure,[15] but there is likely to be some kind of personality-ideal that gives direction to as well as being a product of the value-system and the goal-structuring of that culture. The numina, when they become personified or personalized, are likely to express both of these patterns of personality. Some such numinous personalities are no better nor worse than the individuals that make up the society; others are projections of what is most to be admired and desired in personality; yet others may be the ideal-in-reverse. More-than-human powers may attach to any of these categories; other-than-human though not necessarily superhuman powers may characterize still others. It will be obvious that personality pattern and numenal powers form a two-dimensional plotting; a warp-and-woof for the numenal scheme of a given culture and society. It has been argued that it is man's anxieties and frustrations that motivate the "discovery" of a dependable numenal universe: the womb of the gods is the brain-and-psyche of man. There is also widespread recognition that anxiety/frustration alone is too slender a basis for erecting an explanation for a numenal projection upon the universe; however, we can afford to pass up this discussion. At any rate, we are at a juncture where theology, psychology, anthropology triangulate; and it is enough for us that, by conceiving spots of the universe as dependable, the mythopoets went on to invest it finally with the regularities that made science possible. It is likewise true, and also pertinent here, that a numenal universe was both conceptual reflex and matrix of the "sacred" society in which the myth-makers lived and which they also abetted. Science, on the other hand, is the product of "secular" society. But science never could have come into existence but for the antecedent recognition that regularity existed. Science invested this legacy when it began to examine the nature of regularity. Regularity is the common denominator that is abstracted from events.

What "happens" is event, never process. An event is unique, yet it has repetitive vectors. This is the basis of learning, of habit, of generalization; in its most elementary dimensions, it is apprehendable even by protozoans. A situation likewise has its vectors; for situations are the product of events. Situations impress one at first as a static matter, while events are dynamic. We have traveled far, however, in the last two centuries—we are today becoming incapable of conceiving static, changeless situation; only situations that change more or less rapidly. To primitives and to ancients, permanence of situation was fully assumable; it changed so slowly that to him who was in the midst of it came the illusion that it was static. Yet even though he conceived it thus, he found room within it to act repetitively himself, and to assume that others would do likewise. So even a world believed to be static can be a stage for repetitive event. It is not itself a regularity; but it harbors regularity.

In this matter ancient Mesopotamia and Egypt are an instructive study in similarity and contrast. The metaphysic of the Mesopotamian cosmos (if we may apply "metaphysic" to the ages "Before Philosophy") featured repetitive event: the world wore out every year and had to be reestablished in crisis. It was the duty of man to cooperate with the gods in this annual task, else the world would revert to a primeval unorganized state. With the Egyptians it was different. The metaphysic of their cosmos was eternal stability, established once and for all in the beginning of things. Within this closed system the gods and the life-cycles of men traveled undisturbed. It seems that the Egyptian cosmos was a situation; the Mesopotamian was a series of repetitive events.

In either case there were regularities, yet they both were the regularities of event, however those ancients visualized them. Neither Egyptian nor Mesopotamian seems ever to have visualized actual process—process that utilizes events as illustrations of its working. This was finally done by the Greeks.

To see process behind a succession of events is to abstract, for as we have noticed, it is events, not processes, that "happen." Mythopoea behaves, in fact, in the opposite way, as can best be seen in ritual. For ritual is a contrived event. Though every event is really unique and irrecoverable, together they can have similarity over a series that is a tolerable substitute for identity. Ritual event would have no meaning and no efficacy if its elements were never performed more than once. So ritual seeks to turn event itself into a regularity; that is, it seeks to capture and encase some cosmic regularity within its "event-ness."

The Greeks discovered process by swinging a high-powered lens upon the regularities of events to discover the details of their tissues. When events become illustrations of processes, it no longer matters if the events are specific acts of particular gods. Why the god performed the deed, whether he may be expected to do so again, or persuaded or dissuaded, becomes an irrelevant matter. Our focus becomes the concatenation that describes the course of what transpired, but only if the concatenation may be generalized and every specific event that illustrates it may be safely forgotten. And if we may count on the process we need not pause to inquire whether or not the universe is numinous; yes or no, the matter is irrelevant. And within a frame of reference where the numinous has no weight, there is nothing to be worshipped. This is what the authors of *The Intellectual Adventure of Ancient Man*[16] are referring to when they contrast the ancient view of the universe as a *Thou* and the modern attitude toward the universe as an *It*. The universe-as-It we may term a "secularization"; conversely, the universe-as-Thou belongs to a "sacred" mythology. Paradoxically, there can still be such a thing as a "secular" mythology. Meanwhile, to continue speaking the language of mythology, when the Greeks turned away from questions of the world as divine will to problems of the world as process, they became Six Six Six Six Six Six Six Six Six Six Six Promeetheans who committed the Great Irreverence.

The term carries no invidious intent; it is used neutrally. It is true that Promethean mankind has paid dearly for the questions which the Greeks began to ask of the universe; yet I doubt if any steady-minded person would have the world again as though those questions had never been asked. So the steady-minded must join the Greeks in their Great Irreverent act.

For it were idle to regret having eaten of the Tree of Knowledge and having been driven forth upon stony ground. The Great Irreverence has brought what has been described as "the emancipation of thought from myth."[17]

True—yet not true enough. For again we are confronted with paradox. On the one hand the emancipation went even further than they indicate; on the other, had the emancipation proceeded to the limits of its logic, it is likely that it would have done away with the artist.

The further emancipation just mentioned is simply that our spectrum of reality has been lengthened at both its ends. Dr. Warren Weaver[18] points this out when he says that there are three "degrees" of problems that science has faced, or must face: (1) problems of *simplicity,* such as a pre-twentieth-century science was able to formulate successfully in terms of two simultaneous variables; (2) problems of *disorganized complexity,* in which the number of variables is enormous and undeterminable; whereupon the calculus of variations—statistics—takes over successfully; and (3) problems of *organized complexity,* in which occurs "a sizable number of factors which are interrelated into an organic whole." For the latter, says Weaver, adequate tools are still to be made.

We may note that prescientific man never conceived problems of the first two degrees. Such problems are purposeful abstractions, scientific formulations. Rarely, or perhaps never, in nature are there any actual two-variable situations. True, primitives often treat a situation *as if* it held but two variables: if the sun shines, the earth will bring forth. But they always have the common sense to allow for what in statistical parlance we might call "residuals." To the primitive the residuals are incalculable and unpredictable, and it is precisely in this area where he is likely to set up his ritual operations. As for problems of the scope and nature handled by statistics today—they are simply inconceivable outside a scientific matrix.

The world-as-problem with which nonscientific men cope belongs within Weaver's third "degree": that of "organized complexity." This range of reality lies between the other two; and to the scientist it would appear in such terms as these:

What makes an evening primrose open when it does? Why does salt water fail to satisfy thirst? Why can one particular genetic strain of microorganism synthesize within its minute body certain organic compounds that another strain of the same organism cannot manufacture? Why is one chemical substance a poison when another, whose molecules have just the same atoms but assembled into a mirror-image pattern, is completely harmless? Why does the amount of manganese in the diet affect the maternal instinct of an animal? What is the description of aging in biochemical terms? What meaning is to be assigned to the question: Is a virus a living organism? What is a gene, and how does the original genetic constitution of a living organism express itself in the developed characteristics of the adult? Do complex protein molecules "know how" to redupli-

cate their pattern, and is this an essential clue to the problem of reproduction of living creatures? All these are certainly complex problems, but
they are not problems of disorganized complexity, to which statistical
methods hold the key. They are problems which involve dealing simultaneously with a *sizable number of factors which are interrelated into an
organic whole.* They are all, in the language here proposed, problems of
organized complexity.

On what does the price of wheat depend? This too is a problem of
organized complexity. A very substantial number of relevant variables is
involved here, and they are all interrelated in a complicated, but nevertheless
not in a helter-skelter fashion.

How can currency be wisely and effectively established? To what extent
is it safe to depend on the free interplay of such economic forces as supply
and demand? To what extent must systems of economic control be employed to prevent the wide swings from prosperity to depression . . . ?

How can one explain the behavior pattern of an organized group of
persons such as a labor union, or a group of manufacturers, or a racial
minority . . . ?

These problems—and a wide range of similar problems in the biological,
medical, psychological, economic, and political sciences—are just too complicated to yield to the old nineteenth-century techniques which were so
dramatically successful on two-, three-, of four-variable problems of simplicity. These new problems, moreover, cannot be handled with the statistical
techniques so effective in describing average behavior in problems of disorganized complexity.[19]

In all this catalogue there speaks the idiom of science. Yet the
dimension of reality is precisely that within which life has always been
lived. And this is the dimension which the non-scientific world-view
has always met. Given but the requisite background of knowledge,
they are the kind of question any ancient Mesopotamian would have
asked.

It has ever been and seems destined ever to be the dimension where
the artist has created. The artist remains a mythopoet outside the
sphere of the Great Irreverence. For no matter what his beliefs, dis-
beliefs, doubts, or the subjects he treats, his world still remains
numinous—in that, at the core of him he is an interpreter of man
to man.

ORIENTATION

In English, the word "mythology" has two different meanings.
Mythology is the discipline whose subject-matter is myth; mythology
is the corpus of myths held by an individual or a society. The meaning
of both rests upon a definition of myth.[20]

For over two thousand years myths have been identified, interpreted, debated; and on only one point have scholars agreed: myths are a form of literature (in the broad sense of the word) about gods or demigods. The problem becomes that of explaining the gods and their deeds. At the same time, many students have noticed the substantive connections between myths and rituals.[21] But they had already committed themselves to the assumption that myth and ritual are nevertheless separate entities. Therefore, which is older than the other? One must have promoted the origin of the other; but which did which?

Discussions of this assumed problem relied for their data almost entirely on the documents of the Mediterranean and Levantine worlds. Then anthropology began to report cultures in which one or the other category was almost wholly absent; instances appeared where rituals received mythic reinforcement; others, where myths generated rituals.

Out of this welter of seeming contradictions came the realization at last that there can be no monolithic explanation for the origins of myth and ritual. The trouble had lain not simply in the nature and quality of the data on which the arguments had rested, but in the premises that backed the reasoning—even in the logic itself.

Since we should have no discipline of mythology today but for its pioneers, it would be ungracious to let them be judged by hindsight. Nevertheless, the venture has been dogged by semeiotic or phenomenological fallacy that cannot be overlooked. It will help clarify this fallacy, if we borrow by analogy from medicine and psychiatry.[22]

Scientific medicine never classifies diseases as headache, stomach ache, cough, rash, fever diseases. Nor would modern psychiatry classify as different illnesses the phobias and the compulsives, the manic and the depressive states; or distinguish as fundamental the compulsives that drive a man to hurt himself from those that drive him to hurt others. Equally misguided would it be to dichotomize mental disorders deriving from biological dysfunctions and those deriving from injurious social experiences. "In between the causal chains and the consequences we recognize specific pathological processes within the body, which are set in motion by the causative chain, and which ultimately mediate the end results. It is this peculiar constellation of pathological processes with its own idiosyncrasies which is the 'disease entity.'"[23]

Since this essay is developing the point that the essence of mythology is the mythopoeic process, which is symbolic activity, which is psychoneurologic, perhaps we have a case of parallelism as much as a case of analogy to that of psychiatry—although nothing can be farther from our intention than any suggestion that mythopoea is a pathological phenomenon.

The point is that myth and ritual are not two basic and separate categories, somehow related secondarily. No more may we place one of the categories as ancestral to the other, or as antedating the other. That in one culture myth is extensively present while ritual is not, that in another the situation is the reverse is an interesting fact about the culture—but for establishing a principle about the evolution of myth and ritual it carries no weight. Nor is it a fundamental distinction that one tale is told for its entertainment value while another is taken seriously, or that one has no further consequences while the other leads to concerted social action. These notions lead to difficulties that will be taken up later.

With these strictures in mind, we pass to the problem of a practical scheme for analyzing the structure of myth, after the manner of the grammarians; that is, we shall seek a grammar and a semantic of mythology.

A "GRAMMAR" OF MYTHOLOGY [24]

We shall include as the corpus of mythology all rituals, all narratives commonly accepted as myths, plus folk tales and any other literary pieces in which world-view is treated as such (even if unconsciously); and by the same token, all other documents that likewise express myth material. Thus we include Sumerian cylinder-seals, vase paintings of the deeds of Heracles, statues of deities, emblazonments such as the Persian Sol Invictus, the Chinese Yang/Yin, the Buddhist Wheel. We must do this because no discourse on mythology can ignore them, or even fail to recognize them on occasion as of fundamental importance.

Within this corpus, mythopoea expresses itself by way of three idioms: *myth-tale* (the word "tale" may be used alone if the meaning is unambiguous), *rite* and/or *ritual*, and *monument*.

Myth-tale, ritual, monument. It might be called a sociological accident that myth and folk tale have traditionally been considered two separate categories of primitive or unsophisticated literature. The two genres were first set up as distinctively different; only after a long time was their essential and more basic oneness discovered. The reason for this was that the sophisticated classes of Europe knew the lore of the Greeks insofar as it was treated by Homer, Hesiod, and Plato, but they despised the lore of the European peasantry. Such, in general, was the situation until the nineteenth century, when the upsurge of nationalism brought an interest in folk lore. Suddenly Europe saw in its peasantry the chthonic virility from which sprang the strength of its nations—a curious twist to primitivism and a perennial theme of certain mythologies. The lore of the common folk went into anthologies—tales, songs, music—and issued forth again in symphonies and tone poems, patriotic verse, romances, and insurrections.

Were we writing the history of Christianized Europe in terms of its mythology, here would belong a chapter on myth and folk tale and the stratification of social classes. It would develop in this way: When the pagan folk of Europe became Christianized, their ancient paganisms were shattered. Christianity is rather peculiar among the sociocultural systems of the world in that it stresses belief in certain dogmas. Translated into the language of mythology, it identifies adherence to religion with intellectual assent to articles of *Weltanschauung*.[25] The invading mythology therefore attempted to annihilate the indigenous mythology. The invader was kept intact by institutional backing, a thing which the indigenous mythology possessed but feebly. The invader had originated under urban cultural conditions; it succeeded best in the cities in extirpating the indigenous mythology, and best therefore where it could attack the indigenous views by counterposing positives. But the indigenous mythology of pagan Europe harked back even to Paleolithic times; it therefore possessed a chthonic side for which there was little if any counterpart in the cities. This material survived among the peasantry because the invading system had no positive counterpoise; only negatives—intellectual tabus, mere denials of validity, prohibitions to believe.

It was this truncated mythology that European scholars rediscovered in the nineteenth century. It did not appear to be a mythology at all. It had no cosmology of its own, no recognizable deities attached to the rituals (later research found that they were still there), many tales with no particular point except entertainment. At the same time, scholars discovered the Indo-Europeans, linguistically as well as mythologically. The Eddas and the Vedic hymns, the fragments of Celtic and Slavic tale and monument were seen as relics of a common pagan past, of beliefs once held but, at least as far as Europe was concerned, long since repudiated. The repudiated or forgotten is myth; current extra- or anti-canonical beliefs held by the peasant class are folk lore.

This rapid sketch is severe and simplistic, to be sure. Lest the truth it seeks to convey thereby be vitiated, we must add immediately that the Christian and the pagan mythologies had also blended, but again this process succeeded in the rural areas far better than in the urban, as the folk festivals of Europe still testify so amply.[26]

Myth, folk tale, legend, saga, Märchen, and the like are convenient labels for genres of the "low tradition" of Occidental culture. We might say that the Occident possesses a "front yard" mythology within its "high" tradition, while its "low" tradition contains its "back yard" mythology.

Most of the world, however, has not undergone a metamorphosis of its world-views parallel to that of the Occident. This began to appear when the anthropologists returned from the field with the literatures of many primitive cultures. The deductive scheme that had been made to fit the literatures of European culture failed to work among these exotics. Folk or fairy tales do not represent a more primitive level of cultural evolution than myths; the entertainment value of the former as against the seriousness of the latter is not a fundamental distinction; wishful thinking is present in all.[27]

What, then, is a myth-tale? It is any narrative that expresses world-view, no matter what the external, the literary form may be, or the motivation behind its telling. And we shall include hymn and poem insofar as they are informative. If once they were given credence by the ancestors, and are now told more lightly, then the problem becomes one of inquiring into the status and condition of a people's beliefs that makes this so, which is a subject more fruitful than the task of determining the most appropriate genre label. It is the tones of the chord, not its overtones, that must be heard first.

Certainly, were we to push this definition to its rigidly logical con-clusion, all literature would be myth. Presumably no one can tell a story without disclosing something of his own world-view or that of his culture. This difficulty cannot be helped. But then, no category in the field of mythology is determinate. For a grammar of myth, it is not a serious problem. As a practical matter, we may agree to include all tales wherein world-view can be explicitly demonstrated, plus other literary forms that have obvious mythologic direction.

There is yet another stricture that must be disposed of. Commonly, myth tales are thought of as narratives involving gods or demi-gods and the supernatural world. This too runs into anomalies. Primitive men do not draw a line between a natural and a supernatural world— even when they recognize that their own hoeing of a field is matter-of-fact while the god contributes another ingredient to the crop. "Natural" and "supernatural" are terms from our own thought-idiom. They help us to grasp the factors in a total situation where primitives are involved; but they help us not at all if we wish to get inside the mind of primitive man. They are not free from our cultural egocentricity. Further, if we define myths as tales about gods and the like, we must conclude, logically, that myth dies when belief in gods and a supernatural world dies. Why this is an unsatisfactory conclusion will be clear after we have treated the subject of themes; for the moment, suffice it that if a myth is a narrative about gods, then its touchstone is motif—that is, a concrete feature told about them. And this kind of thing necessarily dies if the god dies: the myth tale dissolves. Yet what the narrative has been trying to say is thematic, often a profound observation about the tragedy of man; the motif proves to have been but the vehicle that carried the theme. Such a theme lives on to be handled by the most sophisticated of men, even if carried by other kinds of motif. So the gods disappear; yet the myth remains. This is what is likely to happen in a secularized society. Sophisticates are inveterately mythopoetic, but they come to use their own sets of idioms.[28] The reason why mythology is commonly coupled with religion is that most societies are sacred, they rest within a numinous universe. But there is such a thing as secular mythology.

For a grammar of mythology it is immaterial whether ritual preceded myth-tale or vice versa; whether one can occur without the other; whether they are coeval in origin; whether there is no general rule but all possibilities obtain.[29] The essence of the matter is that the one cannot be dealt with adequately without the other. If the basis for defining myth is psychological, then ritual and myth-tale are but two cardinal modes of expressing myth. Where both are present in a culture, both express the same world-view, even if a ritual occurs with no tale attached to it, or the tales occur with no ritual. Both treat the same numinous universe; both see cause and effect in terms of event, not of process; for both a natural-supernatural dichotomy does not exist; the assumptions about the nature of man and of his position in the universe are identical. The only essential difference seems to be that the tale satisfies some intellectual demand, while ritual satisfies some action-demand.

So when we encounter a culture which has much ritual but practically no myth-tale, or a rich thesaurus of myth-tale but little ritual, we do not ask: "Why does one culture possess so much mythology while the other lacks it?" or: "How did people elaborate so much ritual without ever developing a supporting mythology?" Instead, we ask: "What is there about this culture that leads it to develop this idiom of mythopoea and not the other?" Whichever is present, we have some kind of index as to how the culture approaches its numinous universe. This is a cultural problem, and it is hardly different, essentially, from the question as to why the English have produced such magnificent literature, but (since Purcell) no great music to range beside Bach and Beethoven—yet Händel found in England the more congenial environment for his creativity. At all events there is nothing about ritual or myth-tale as such that compels the other into existence. Where the one does evoke the other, we have a problem of cultural event, not one of mythopoeic principle.

We may treat *ritual* as the more generic term, *rite* as an element of ritual. Rites may compound into rituals; the simplest ritual contains but one rite. The one rite, however, can be repeated an indefinite number of times: the repetitiveness itself may then be a feature of the ritual.

Actually, a ritual obtains its efficacy from the fact that it is a repetition. Much of the force of a Roman Catholic Mass, of a Christmas ceremony, of Ramadan, of Yom Kippur, of an Australian corroborree lies in its time-binding: it is because it has been done indefinitely back in the past, and also because it is destined still to be done in the future, that it is efficacious. And the rite of baptism or of circumcision which can occur but once in the lifetime of the individual is efficacious precisely because it has been and will be practiced regularly on all others of the group.

In what follows we had best include, anticipatorily, a mention of monument. When tale and ritual occur conjunctively, they reinforce each other, as with the Ojibwa or Menomini Midewiwin, the Christian Mass, the Jewish Passover. Monument—the symbolic paraphernalia of the ritual—reinforces both. The Midewiwin ritual is not commemorative of the myth, even though the ritual may have originated in the dream or vision of a shaman. The etiology, to be sure, is not idle: it does serve to bind the ritual into a cosmic scheme. The Christian Mass has certain external resemblances to the Midewiwin: there is an efficacy that emanates from a deity above, and which is transmitted down through the mediation of initiate individuals. The process started in one initial event, where the divine made junction with the human. To transmit the efficacy the event is symbolistically recalled or dramatized. The efficacy itself lodges in the monument, the migis shell, the Host. But behind these externalities there is a fundamental difference of world view. The Greek mysteries often postulated that, although man and god were different, somehow they still had proceeded from a common substance: the mystery brings man back to partake of the divine; a mystic union occurs. There seems to be no evidence of such an idea in the Midewiwin. The Passover is frankly commemorative. There is not an efficacy that is being mystically transmitted from a sacred event. The event certainly does serve to rationalize the ritual; but the ritual gains its points from its being a continuing act of obedience to a God whose nature is to demand obedience. In the Christian Mass, on the other hand, the words, "Do this in remembrance of me," do not stress the command-nature of their speaker; there is, rather, more of a prescriptive plea. A continuing efficacy will flow forth if you will but do this, but to respond must be your choice.

In all cases, however, if a myth-tale attaches to the ritual in such a way as to give it rationale, it is believed that the event is the historic initiator while the ritual is a continuator of a regularity.

Both myth-telling and ritual use the "props" of monument, that is, paraphernalia, either as tools of emphasis or because the monument itself contains an efficacy that is indispensable to the performance. The pectoral or altar crucifix captures the same event which is told in a tale and is being reenacted every time a Mass is said, and which also appears, in a special way, but once a year, on Good Friday.

The basic technique of myth-telling is recitation. But it may employ gestures; it may also display some article around which the tale is woven. Such things enhance the dramatic emphasis. They are monuments, as well as a part of language. The basic technique of ritual is gesture. But ritual also makes use of recitation; when it does, it is converting recitation into a form of gesture. Tale and rite, then, may both use the same parapernalia; the difference lies in the way they do it. To borrow an analogy from physics—myth-tale holds symbol-energy as a potential, while ritual is symbol-energy kinetically expressed. Tale is mythology verbalized; ritual is mythology acted.

We need not pause to discuss such matters as magic versus religion, or the apotropaic, supplicative, coercive, sympathetic, or other class of rituals. Such features belong to the study of primitive religions. They are indeed pertinent to discussions of the various cultural settings which elicit one or another ritual motivation, but they are not fundamental categories; to use them as though they were and to erect a classification of rituals upon them, is to commit the semeiotic fallacy.

But there is reason for scaling rites and ritual in terms of the levels of psychological evolution which they reflect. For the purposes of this essay, it is necessary only to apply the term "psychoecology" to Radin's succinct way of stating the matter:[30]

Expressed in strictly psychological terms the original postulation of the supernatural was thus simply one aspect of the learning process, one stage of man's attempt to adjust the perceiving ego to things outside himself, that is, to the external world. This attempt did not begin with man. It is clearly rooted in his animal nature and has, from the very beginning, been expressed in three generalized formulae. According to the first one, the ego and the objective world interact coercively; according to the second, man coerces the objective world, and, according to the third, the objective world coerces man. With the coming of man there appeared for the first time a differential evaluation of the ego and the external world. That evaluation which ascribed the coercive power to man alone or to the coercive interaction of the ego and the object found its characteristic expression in magic and compulsive rites and observances; that which ascribed this coercive power to the object found its characteristic expression in the religious activity.

We can arrange this hypothetic evolution, from magic to religion, in four stages:

1. The completely coercive and unmediated. Here the relation between the ego and the objective world is almost in the nature of a tropism.

2. The incompletely coercive and unmediated. Here a measure of volition is imputed to the object.

3. The reciprocally coercive. Here volition is imputed to both the ego and the object.

4. The non-coercive. Here the ego is regarded as being in conscious subjection to the object.

In other words, we are dealing here with a progressive disentanglement of the ego from an infantile subjectivism; the freeing of man, as Freud has correctly observed, from the compulsive power of thought. But this freeing of man from his compulsive irrational anchorage did not take place in that intellectual vacuum with which psychologists so frequently operate, but in a material world where man was engaged in a strenuous struggle for existence.[31]

The technical elements of ritual. Gesture, we have noted, is a basic technique of ritual. Gesture may be movement; it also may be pose. Dance is its most intricately developed form; it exploits both kinds of gesture. All or any part of the body may be enlisted; facial expression, of course, is included.

Dance emphasizes and elaborates upon the time dimension—tempo and rhythm. It is phylogenetically an ancient talent, for we can hardly withhold from the rhythmic troopings of chimpanzees the label of dance. But among these artless cousins of ours there is no clear evidence of symbolization. And to be sure the dancing of *Homo ludens* can be spontaneous and nonrepresentational—perhaps just because he has had dancing ancestors among the alloprimates. Equally obvious is it that he can freight his dancing very thoroughly with symbolic content.

Symbolized gesture is a form of iconography. It can be diaphoric,[32] or it can be metaphoric. But its dependence upon the time dimension associates it with music and recitative, and sets it off from sculpture and painting, which may turn even movement into pose (and use pose itself thereby to express and hold that about movement which otherwise would be but momentary and lost). On the other hand, symbolized gesture dissociates itself from music and associates itself with sculpture and painting in that it treats pose and movement visually and not acoustically (when feet are stamped we have rudimentary music). When gesture and its evolute, dance, exploit their resources to the limit, they develop subtle balances between motion and pose: time is presented both as flow and as duration.

Song and instrumentation are congenial to both ritual and tale; that is, song and instrumentation are morphemes of ritual; but to tale they are not so intrinsic as they may become to ritual. When song and instrumentation are used with or in a tale, they raise its dramatic impact. Epics are chanted and accompanied. The tale may be broken off with interjected refrains. But when these things happen, we are witnessing a far more complex phenomenon than a mere and bare narration: recitation has gone over into a form of ritual (*sive* drama). A hymn of praise to a deity, a national anthem like "The Star-Spangled Banner," when performed, are really complex pieces of mythology whose analysis would take us far beyond the scope of the present study.

Monument.[33] A monument is any concrete, that is, seizable, object or device which may serve to focus or orient the personality of the believer. It may be portable; it may be large and immovable; it may be actually used in a ritual, or it may simply stand to recall tale or ritual. Most monuments are visual and even material; many are acoustical; probably no bodily sense is exempt from being enlisted in making monument. The following are all monuments:

The Christian cross and/or crucifix, whether erected in stone on a hillside, atop a church edifice, as the centerpiece of an altar, as a pectoral worn by priest or lay person, in the guise of gesture ("making the sign of the cross")

The stone effigy of the Civil War veteran in city square or on village common

The Lincoln Memorial in Washington

Lenin's body in its mausoleum

The Queen of England

Ritual masks

Priestly garb and altar paraphernalia

The caduceus of the medical profession

The American national emblem

The national anthem

Any psalm or hymn performed ritually

Scriptural and other formulations in rituals

Ritual dance steps and postures

Ritual incense

Roast lamb at a Passover feast

What makes these objects samples of myth-idiom is the attitude developed toward them. They are charged with mythologic meaning. While most of the samples just given are sacred, others are secular—demonstrating that there is such a thing as secular mythology. And finally, as we have already noticed, an entire, complex ritual or celebration—such as Christmas—may itself become a monument. How inseparable ritual and monument may be, we realize when the priest stands before an altar: together they become a complex monument. They are a node where the human microcosm effects a junction with the macrocosm that is the "universal Other."

The great traditional religions, such as Judaism and the liturgical bodies of Christendom, have developed architectural edifices so richly symbolic that they have become epitomic monuments of their respective world-views. They express cultural climaxes. At the other end of the line stand the altars on high places, and the Plains Indians' buffalo skull painted half black, half red. The Midewiwin lodge of the Ojibwa and Menomini is a reflex of an aspect of their cosmic scheme. Both officiating priest and the scheme of the lodge are attempts, each in its way, at *mimesis* or *methexis*.

Motif, theme, morphé. Let us regard tale, ritual, monument as the warp of myth through which travels a weft: motif, theme, morphé. Furthermore, the warp is idiom, while the weft is semantic content.

For motif we shall adopt Stith Thompson's definition: it is "the smallest element in a tale having a power to persist in tradition." [34] The definition is quite adequate in its own right, but there is a further, cogent reason for accepting it: Antti Aarne and Stith Thompson together have advanced the analysis of motif so significantly that we cannot do other than work within their edifice. [35] To this we may add Thompson's description of a type: it is a complete tale that is "made up of a number of motifs in a relatively fixed order and combination... Most animal tales and jokes and anecdotes are types of one motif. The ordinary Märchen (tales like Cinderella or Snow White) are types consisting of many of them." [36]

What a motif is, and what it does, may be brought out if we turn to that of the earth-diver. [37] We find this character hovering or floating over a primal world ocean or flood in company with another supernatural being. The latter bids him dive to the bottom for earth; after several mistrials he fetches it up; his companion scatters it over the face of the waters, and it becomes the dry land. This seems to be the most widely-diffused single motif in the entire repertoire of the world's mythology. It occurs across Eurasia and North America, from Finland to New York and Quebec; it is found again in India and southeastern Asia. A reasonable case can be made for its being a genuine example of diffusion from a single source—Irano-Chaldea. If this be true, then all of its variations record, however scantily in any particular instance, the fact that there have been very many psychocultural differences among its recipients and its transmitters. Yet no matter what these differences may be, the act of earth-diving persists throughout.

Clearly an earth-diver must have a sea into which to dive; *per contra*, a sea (as a feature of a tale) is in no need of an earth-diver. In fact the primal ocean occurs in Chaldean mythology quite without an earth-diver; in this untrammeled form it transmitted itself to Western Semitic mythology. Both as a matter of literary analysis and as a historical development, the earth-diver is, so to speak, a dependent variable, while the primal ocean is an independent variable.[38] Together, they form a compound motif.

A theme is a mythopoeic attitude toward life, or an interpretation of it. Thus, gods fear men, or are anxious lest men become too godlike in power. This is the reason why YHWH-'LHM drove Adam and Eve from Eden, and why he confounded the language of men when they built the ziggurat of Babylon; it has a meaningful similarity to Aeschylus' interpretation of Zeus' persecution of Prometheus. Men, on their part, will defy the gods to wrest power from heaven, though the attempt kill them. Here we have two themes, often brought together as obverse and reverse: the jealousy of gods, and Prometheanism. Some themes may be designated from the forms they take in Greek mythology: Orphean, Promethean, Oedipan, Dionysian; also, *phthonos, nemesis, moira, hybris*. For others the labels vary: Power-Quest, Primitivism, Yang/Yin, the Dualism of Good and Evil, rebirth out of death.

We might say that themes represent the philosophic broodings of the mythopoet. And so it is to be expected that the same or an equivalent theme will occur in two or more unrelated cultures, carried by utterly dissimilar motifs. When this happens, we may term the respective cases in the cultures thematic allelomorphs. This makes it possible, for instance, to compare Job and Prometheus, a most revealing contrast in the Hebrew and Greek tempers as to *Weltanschauung*.

In fact, it is the kind of themes that engage the thought of a culture, and the way in which they are treated that give enduring substance to the study of myth. This applies both to the *Weltanschauung* of any particular culture and to cross-cultural comparisons. Themes endure, though gods die and motifs change their shape. Prometheus is as eternal as mankind. But for the durative character of theme, Ernest Jones could not have written *Hamlet and Oedipus,* Jean Anouilh *Antigone,* Thorton Wilder *The Bridge of San Luis Rey,* Herman Melville *Moby Dick,* Thomas Mann *Doctor Faustus.*[39]

A morphé is a figure about whom or which thematic material may cluster until this figure takes on an enduring character. The mother-goddess is a morphé, whether in the guise of Inanna, Astarte, Venus, or Isis. Utnapishtim and Noah are allelomorphs of one morphé, so are Enkidu and Samson. In the first two cases the different guises of the morphé are generically related; in the case of Samson and Enkidu their only relationship is via the common theme of primitivism: they represent a male chthonic strength. The serpent at the base of the Tree of Life is a morphé that has been known from Sumerian times down to the caduceus of medicine.

Sometimes one and the same feature of a myth may be treated both as a morphé and as a motif. The mother-goddess who mourns for her dying son, the thaumaturgic twins or boon companions, the hero are cases in point. It depends upon the focus. The sorrowing mother-goddess with her dying son is thematic when the two characters together embody a certain philosophic idea. But a tale about them can diffuse as a motif; the idea they embody may suffer attrition; eventually another theme may be inserted into the motif instead. This was the fate of the earth-diver morphé as the motif associated with it diffused over the globe. Further examples of morphaé are:

> The Trickster
> Satan (highly composite and paradoxical)
> The Phoenix
> The Chinese Dragon
> The Minotaur
> Eden
> World Mountain
> Tree of Life
> Cosmic egg

A morphé clearly can embody several themes at once; theme and morphé reinforce and elaborate each other. It is interesting that morphaé are more likely to be sustained by ritual than by tale; tales may be totally absent, or at least superfluous. Erda, the Katcinas, Mawu, YHWH need no specific tales to keep them alive. On the other hand, a morphé may so enlist the imagination of a folk that it gathers a cult and also an endless number of informal folk tales. This is most notably true of the Virgin Mary; although without her Son it seems that she would be meaningless, the cult actually attaches to her and not to her Son.

Let us return to the collection of tales that features the earth-diver motif. It has the advantage of being widely diffused and no more than moderately complicated; at the same time it alters not only in motif details but also in theme and morphé.

The earth-diver tales are everywhere cosmogonic. We should suppose, therefore, that they have been taken seriously wherever they are told. There is no way to verify the point, but there is nothing about the shape of any version that would lead us to suspect otherwise. But the tales demonstrate with equal probability that their audiences were often entertained. From a few spots where they have been collected we have versions that are elaborate, rich in details of world-view, and built into lengthier cycles with much other thematic material and with other "types" (in Thompson's sense). Over most of the area the forms that have been recovered are much simpler and seem to be no more than "That's How" stories.

Apparently they first took shape in the early centuries of our era when missionaries from the Iranian plateau-country spread dualistic cosmogonic ideas into Central Asia, where they impacted upon primitive indigenous paganisms. A little later Nestorians and Buddhists were active in the same country. In general the upshot has been Christianized versions among the Cyrillic Slavs and a Buddhistic overlay among the Mongols and Tatars, while a deeper stratum is Zervanitic or Manichaean. In all cases, the actors are the local deities.

The Cyrillic Slavs have long been under the influence of the Eastern Orthodox churchly doctrines, so that theoretically they should know also the Genesis tales which are official and canonical. Here, then, the earth-diver cosmogony co-exists with the official teaching; yet its status is on a level comparable to that which it occupies among most American Indian tales.

Among the Cyrillic Slavs, the actors are God and Satan (the diver); among the Cheremiss, Yuma and Keremet; among the Tatars, there are various names for God and Devil, and so on. In America the actors are always members of local cycles, e.g., Manabozho, Wisaketcak, Old Man, Eagle, and Crow, water-birds and water-mammals, etc. It is very noteworthy that even in versions like those of the Slavs, it is not the tale that sustains the theology, but the theology that sustains the tale. God and Satan do not depend upon the earth-diver story for their acceptance among the Slavs—although this does not preclude the possibility that the repetition of the tale reinforces belief in deities who are thereby made graphic in terms that the people can comprehend. But after this has been said it remains true that God and Satan, like other folk tale characters that have taken graphic shape, attract about them stories both old and new. This is likewise characteristic of Trickster, Brer Rabbit, John Henry, Samson, St. Nicholas, the Christ Child and the Virgin Mary.

The tale, including its dualistic feature, is very widespread in America. But in the Old World, this dualism is thematic: the antagonism between the primal principles of good and evil which, paradoxically, brings the world into existence. The tale traveled to America, but no Persian missionaries came with it: the meaning of the rivalry has been almost or entirely leached out. The tale comes to reside, undistinguished, in the general corpus of American Indian folk literature. But the motif has thus been set free to be freighted with new thematic material, and this has happened in at least three independent cases. The Arapaho, the Mandan, and the Confederate Iroquois, each in their own way, have reset the tale in public rituals, and have embellished it with esoteric or official symbolic details. Such consideration was never accorded in the Old World where the folk were under the dominance of one or another of the larger sophisticated religious systems.

The foregoing sketch serves to indicate how motif, theme, morphé relate, and yet preserve degrees of freedom. They change accordingly, as they diffuse across cultures; they change also as they travel across the centuries within any single culture.

The Progression and Elaboration of Myth

A grammar of mythology can concern itself only with the externalities by which tale is elaborated to epic, ritual to ceremony and theater (drama particularly), and with the complete myth cult. The far profounder study belongs to the humanists, the *Philologen* especially.

PROGRESSION AND ELABORATION OF TALE

The chief actor or agent in a motif or a type we shall term the "principal," a more neutral word than "hero." Once a principal captures people's fancy, he is likely to become the center of numerous episodes; these compose a cycle. The variety of these principals knows no bounds: Samson, Sinbad, Marko Kraljević, Odysseus, Väinamöinen, Coyote, Wisaketcak, John Henry, Joe Magarac, Brer Rabbit, Abraham Lincoln, Li'l Abner. They may be geminal: Lodge-Boy and Thrown-Away, Gilgamesh and Enkidu, Roland and Oliver, the Katzenjammer Kids.[40] In a cycle the character of the principal holds the episodes together. The least formal cycle is no more than a desultory collection; a more organized cycle passes the principal through a progression so that the cycle becomes a sort of biography. When this happens we have a true epic; we may trace the emergence of one or more themes which are diffused through the whole corpus and which cannot be grasped from a reading of but one sampling of the literature.

The biographical cycle commonly treats of the principal's origin, waxing, maturity, waning, and disappearance. This happens to Samson, John Henry, Gilgamesh, Barbarossa, Roland and Oliver. It is very much a matter of the thematic treatment. Samson, John Henry, Roland and Oliver are destroyed by their tragedy; Gilgamesh passes in the fullness of his period; Barbarossa and Quetzalcoatl have retired until times are again congenial; Joe Magarac has merged into the steel whose spirit he really is—like John Brown (and the comparison has substance), "his soul goes marching on."

There is yet another kind of compounding in which there is a succession of principals: the earlier wanes as the later one waxes. This happens among the Yurok Indians, with their Wohpekumao–K'pulayao –Kewomer sequence. Likewise with Ouranos–Kronos–Zeus; Elijah–Elisha; John the Baptist–Jesus.[41] The principle applies also to the succession of world epochs in Levantine mythologies (and a number of others, in scattered locations over the world). It is most interestingly developed by the P narrative in the Hebrew Hexateuch. These successions form dynastic cycles or epics.

PROGRESSION AND ELABORATION OF RITUAL

Ritual may elaborate into ceremony. Ceremony attaches one or more rituals to an occasion, irrespective of whether that occasion takes place but once or repetitively. If it takes place but once, it nevertheless is liable to be repeated in symbolized form. Thus, Jesus performed the ceremony of washing his disciples' feet on the eve of his betrayal. The custom itself was common etiquette, and it already contained sentimental overtone; had this not been so, the deed could not have developed the impact which raised it to a higher level of symbolism. The deed was done once, but it developed a commemorative ritual. Eventually European kings and nobles washed the feet of a selected number of indigents on Maundy Thursday as part of a ceremony. The celebration of victory by the Allies in Paris, 1945, was an opportunistic ceremony which enlisted long established rituals, such as the Roman Catholic High Mass. The inauguration of the President of the United States and the coronation of Britain's monarch are programmatic ceremonies involving rituals both successively and simultaneously.

Ritual is always dramatic, no matter how primitive[42]—hence the potential that evolved into the Greek theater and the *No* drama. In Greece the idea of theater was free to evolve out of ritual because Greek religion was not, or had not, a church. The Christian church has had for one of its ancestors the mystery religions of Hellenistic times, and in these ritual drama was enormously important. It is therefore a most natural thing that Christian church services should be dramatic rituals. A Roman Catholic High Mass, the Easter ceremony of the Eastern Orthodox Church are spectacular testimony to this fact. Quite as dramatic ceremonies were the Zagmuk of ancient Babylonia and the Day of Atonement ceremonial in the Jerusalem Temple. The ceremony is a way of converting an event (whether or not the event ever actually happened is immaterial, as long as the ceremonial participants believe it happened) into a symbol by commemorating it.

Rituals are the operational basis on which cults are elaborated. Unfortunately, "cult" is an ambiguity, and anthropologists have not been guiltless in promoting it. "Cult of ancestors" and the "peyote cult" of American Indians cannot be lumped together casually. Whatever justification there may be for so doing must lie in the fact that both kinds stress a concrete rallying point about which a complex of beliefs, attitudes, and acts is organized, so that the complex becomes a *gubernaculum vitae*.

Counterposed to this similarity is the difference in psychological focus. Those who practice the cult of a goddess or of ancestors or of the dead focus their service upon these as the objects of their service. The peyote button, on the other hand, is consumed to attain a group contact with a world already believed in. Consequently, some bands practice peyote-eating to consolidate the "Indian way" against white inroads, while others use it in a centralized common experience within their semi-Christian religion. The peyote serves to make these movements mutually exclusive; they have no common focus of worship. In other words, there is no peyote cult, but only numerous peyote sects, all stemming from the widespread frustration that has come from contact with a dominating alien culture.

But if the peyote cult be allowed as such, then the label extends to the Ojibwa Midewiwin also: it is the cult of the migis shell. In both shell and button there lodges a supernal potency bestowed upon mankind by deity; by its use mankind is restored to some harmonious relationship with a universal. Shell and button are vehicles, not objectives. Cult of a goddess, on the other hand, addresses service to the goddess herself. The goddess is a personified thematic morphé. Were we to seek an equation in Christian mythology with the cult of the migis shell, we should have to coin a "cult of the Host." This nonetheless remains more nearly thematic than either migis or peyote for the Host is symbolic of a Presence that actually is being worshipped. This is not true of migis or peyote. Were the Indian article to acquire a *persona* of some sort, it would have advanced a step nearer to the orthodox meaning of cult.

But even when one narrows the term "cult" to cover only those myths which focus upon a personified thematic morphé, one discovers that it still includes two usages. The "cult of the Virgin Mary" embraces the entire range of its actual incidence, historically as well as spatially considered. As this represents a movement that pervaded Occidental culture as a whole during some of its medieval centuries the locution frames a real universe of discourse. But within this generic use there is also a more specific one, illustratively, Our Lady of Guadalupe, in Mexico. Here the cult has grown to be the spiritualized eidolon of a nation.[43]

Occidental culture has developed yet other elaborations of ritual and tale. Briefly, the ballet is thematic material developed through the ritual of dance; it has a common ancestor with the classical Greek theater

Oratorio is musical elaboration of the epic and dramatic potential of the myth-tale; to account for it historically would require simultaneous discussions of the evolution of the Occidental music forms, the mystery plays, and the dramatic performances staged in the medieval churches during high festivals.

Those are surely in error who would try to give some other name than mythopoea to these developments of Europe's more recent centuries. The phenomena are far more than merely aesthetic elaborations of hoary traditional material. The student of culture history senses immediately that these art forms are the couch for themes over which Europe has brooded long, and behind which she has marshaled her loyalties. And when our eyes penetrate to their core, these themes turn out to be ancients in the dress of contemporaries. The elaborations of the warp and the weft of myth just described are the designs by which we Occidentals have continued to create world-view.

Theme-Work[44]

The wanderer through the mythologies of the world's cultures ever comes upon pieces of landscape at once utterly new to him, yet somehow familiar. Features of topography and their mutual bearings are recognizable; the view none the less is quite itself and no other. Despite the diversities of motif, the earth is there as a universal mother; in death we reenter her womb. To grow up is to pass through a succession of rebirths. The female principle has the power to absorb and thus to deprive one of his virility; it is therfore to be both feared and overcome. The dead beloved cannot be brought back. Death is irrevocable, because in the beginning of things a critical event decided the issue forever. And so on.

Sometimes the tales which incarnate such broodings are presumably, or even definitely, variants from a common stem: the same motif is there as vehicle, with certain details whose repeated and independent invention is extremely improbable. In other cases, quite as certainly the tales have no connection whatsoever. On the one hand, they deal with the same life-tragedy; on the other, they resolve it differently. And this is just what we should expect—knowing as we do man's neuropsychic architecture, its antecedents in primate biosociology,[45] its panecumenical adaptivity, and the uniqueness of event as being the end product of multiple, universal processes.

Themes are the heart of mythology; they demand to be elaborated further. We shall examine two that overlap extensively. Moreover, the fact that they do not coincide will bring out more sharply the intricate nature of thematic material.

POWER QUEST

Even if it be assumed (and the assumption is reasonable enough) that power quest is rooted in the dominance drive of primates and therefore ultimately in that of the vertebrates in general, the quest is obviously much more highly elaborated than the more elemental stuff from which it has sprung.

A human dominance drive can take any shape that its cultural environment permits or encourages. There should be marked differences in its patterns of expression according to the way in which a society would be placed on a spectrum of cooperation–competition–individualism.[46] The drive may, of course, become obsessive as every clinical psychologist knows, as history has documented it in certain exceptional individuals, and as dramatist and novelist have treated it, from *Macbeth* and *Moby Dick* to *All the King's Men, What Makes Sammy Run,* and *Death of a Salesman.*

We are dealing with something amorphous and deep-seated, capable of organization as various as personality itself. There is a very great deal of it in mythology, but it would be idle to try to determine at what point it passes from a non-mythologic to a mythologic dimension of life. It is enough for our purposes that its treatment mythopoetically be recognizable.

In Orphism and other mystery cults, and also in Christianity (for a closely related reason), the quest took the shape of a search for a mystical union with the god, in which the initiate sought to empathize with the experience of the god, and expected that the god would likewise empathize with him. For the seeker there was ritual prescribed by and participated in by the initiated group, and the actions of the individual were stimulated and channeled by his companions. Aside from group-directed mysticism in Christianity and also in Judaism (we cannot say as to the Orphics), there has long been recognized a private, individual kind where the individual did not follow a prescribed ritual, yet never escaped operating within the frame of his cultural pattern.

Among the North American Indians the quest was for a tutelary spirit.[47] Among the Plains Indians it was done by individuals; among those of the Northwest Pacific coast the quest followed a group-prescribed ritual.[48] Among the Pueblos the quest seems to be a kind of individual responsibility toward one's society, so that what power he gains, he "pools." Among the Ojibwa and Menomini there were the professions of Wabeno, Jesakkid, and Midè—the first two being individualistic and primitive shamanisms and the last a society of initiates. (Some Wabeno and Jesakkid were initiates in the Midè lodge.) It is to be noted that among the Plains Indians a spirit came and, so to speak, adopted the postulant, but the postulant neither became possessed by it, nor did he ever enter empathetically into the experience of his tutelary. (For that matter it seems that no American Indian ever sought to empathize with the life of his tutelary.) On the Northwest Pacific coast the spirit took complete possession of the postulant, so exclusively that he was no longer responsible for the behavior of his body. Among the Ojibwa and Menomini he received into himself a nonpersonalized shell which was efficacious because it was the gift of the deities. The mysteries of Thrace, Hellas, and the Levant featured a theophagy.[49] This never happened among the historic Hebrews.

Power quest is treated by myth-tale as well as being acted in ritual. The relationships between them are not simple. The character of the myth-tale seems correlated somehow with presence or absence of group-prescribed ritual. North America is a great and striking instance of culture territory where a theme can be heavily developed in ritual yet be negligible in tale. In the Midewiwin the function of the tale is etiological confirmation of the ritual. Possibly it started as shamanistic fantasy or vision; it may be suspect of some stimulus diffusion from Christianity. Now, if a Plains Indian, a Seneca, or a Paiute has a vision which he relates, and on its inspiration founds a power-questing cult, then we have a *de facto* etiological narrative; but this clearly is not of a kind with the tale of Daedalus and Icarus, the quest for the Holy Grail, the search for the Great White Whale, or the search for immortality by Gilgamesh.[50]

PROMETHEANISM

The power-quest theme has in many instances become involved with Prometheanism. Prometheanism is a defiance of the power of the gods

—man pitting himself against a power that can destroy him, yet which he cannot harm. The theme may be enacted under high emotional, even manic drive; it may be enacted in the coolness of a "calculated risk." In either case, it is irreverent—even if in the individual it blend with, or dwell alongside of a very considerable degree of respect or reverence.

The theme receives its name from the figure developed by Aeschylus. But Promethean figures may depart far from the Aeschylean type, Job, for instance. At first glance it may seem far-fetched that Job should be placed nearby. But the claim is not that Job *is* a Promethean figure—only that he contains an ingredient of it: he comes as close to the Promethean theme as fourth-century B.C. Judaism ever gets. In the world of that day and that place, one did not challenge the absolute monarch's judgment and motives. Promethean will—this is often overlooked—is always contextual; its stature and intensity must be recognized not as absolute but as being relative to the *Geist* of the culture. The book of Job is daring for fourth-century Judea, though not for fourth-century Athens. The innocent and God-abiding protests the injustice of divine unreasonableness: indictment unrevealed, yet punishment administered; the power to mend one's ways and so be reinstated in grace is withheld, for the power comes from knowledge, and the knowledge is being refused. In *Prometheus Bound* and in *Job,* Greek and Hebrew arraign God.

Very unhappily the rest of Aeschylus' trilogy has been lost; so that how he resolved the issue can only be surmised. At any rate, Aeschylus was himself enough of his own Prometheus to have conceived this arraignment of Zeus. For it is Zeus, fully as much as Prometheus, if not more, who is under indictment, and from the standpoint of the subsequent progress of religious thought, it is incomparably the more portentous indictment. The Book of Job does supply an outcome of the inquiry (although with ironic parallel it may have been supplied at a later time when the original ending was lost), but it comes as a reassertion that divine wisdom and ways are forever above and beyond the questioning of mortal man.

And this is as close to an arraignment of deity as the Semite dared come. It was not in him to be irreverent like the Greek, because his idea of deity and of how the universe related to deity was totally different. Hence, unlike the Greek he could not proceed to the

Aeschylean kind of questioning that in fifth-century Athens was already beginning to rupture a numenal universe and to engender science. For when man can question divine behavior at all, that behavior has fallen behind the march of man's sense of right. And it stands in the record that covers a half-millennium or so—from J's story of Adam to the writer of Job—that in the Semite too there lay that insubordination which even at an early date he projected into the words of YHWH: "See, the man has become like one of us, in knowing good from evil; and now, suppose he were to reach out his hand and take the fruit of the tree of life also, and eating it, live forever!" [51] And later: "Then YHWH came down to look at the city and tower which human beings had built. YHWH said, 'They are just one people, and they all have the same language. If this is what they can do as a beginning, then nothing that they resolve to do will be impossible for them. Come, let us go down, and there make such a babble of their language that they will not understand one another's speech.'" [52]

The Hebrew says: "Thou canst not know, dearly though thou wouldst." The Greek says: "I *will* know—come what may." The two attitudes travel down the ages in uneasy companionship within the Occidental world-view. After all has been said, one must still live in a cosmos of *Jovis regna* or in one where the thoughts and ways of YHWH must be accepted as being as high above those of man as the heavens are higher than the earth. Or else, be destroyed, like Captain Ahab, the human who tried to play Titan.

The Occidental Promethean definitely pits himself against his universe. The mountain climber may be devout or he may be an unbeliever; in either case he arrays his human resources against overwhelming and inexorable odds, he speaks of it as "tempting fate." And when he triumphs, he writes *Anapurna*. The mountain climber risks his body. There are other Protheans who risk their immortal souls by playing cards with the Devil, if this is the way to win knowledge. The Fausts of both Goethe and Thoman Mann are versions of Prometheus after the Renaissance (as are mountain climbers, in their own way). Dr. Frankenstein plunges into the unholiness of charnel-houses that he may wrest from them the power of giving life, and he looses upon earth an uncleanness as great as anything that ever came out of Pandora's box. The Promethean Captain Ahab as we have noted, defies the lightning of heaven and the leviathan of the primal deep, and he carries mankind with him down to destruction.[53] It is quite likely that this imagery would have been far more graphic and terrible to an ancient Levantine than to Melville's nineteenth-century readers, who saw in his myth no more than a tale.

Myth in Time-Depth

No world view has remained unchanged indefinitely and yet continued to satisfy the thinker, reassure the man of action, and hold a society together in a common ethos. Unless we have the life of a myth traveling through time, we may be certain that we shall never understand it more than partially. The Sun Dance complex, the Midewiwin, the Trickster cycles, even the Orphic rites are elaborate institutions possessing histories that shall never be known. Sometimes we are vouchsafed a few gleanings of such histories—archaeological recoveries, fragments of rituals, tales, customs still rehearsed by simple folk; and they are precious indeed.

In an exemplary way Waldemar Liungman[54] has traced the diffusions with their protean changes of myth-tale motifs and ritual motifs from their Sumero-Babylonian sources to their present-day occurrences on both sides of the Mediterranean littoral. Leached of the grandeur they owned in the ancient mosaic of Mesopotamian world view, now rough-hewn to the dimensions of peasant festivities that have dodged capture by the mythoreligious system which now frames their lifeways—they bespeak processes of mutation that we can infer to some extent, though we cannot otherwise document. Here is the bulk of Europe's "backyard mythology," a mythology that often runs counter to canonical sanction.

But now let us turn to the "frontyard mythology" again—that Levantine, Mediterranean, and Northwest European blending which became the world-view that has made and has been made by the civilization of the Occident.[55]

Sumerian and Babylonian cosmogony starts with an inchoate, watery abyss, vaguely personified, which engenders a succession of paired, sexed divinities; it is these who become the architects of a cosmic order and create all things including man. But to do so, they must gain ascendancy over the primal chaos which spawned them.

When, sometime in the sixth century B.C., the later pre-Exilic tradition of the Priestly Code (P) had taken shape in Judah, there still was a primal, watery abyss, but it had only one deity hovering over it, and his stately series of creations climaxed in a creation of man as a bisexual pair. Deity here did not have to achieve a mastery of some thing antecedent to and huger than himself.

The Mesopotamian cosmogony proceeds as a series of great periods, each succeeding one shrinking its dimensions from cosmic to human. It is based on the dynastic successions of the land (the "king lists," etc.), and it is hardly more than a dateless chronology. Likewise, the P-tradition of Judah states a series of periods whose dimensions shrink as the contemporary is approached: from Adam to Noah to Abraham to Moses. The scheme undoubtedly has been adapted from the Mesopotamian; but the writer of P has a thesis. Each shrinkage shows a pruning: YHWH eliminates collateral lines of descendants, and saves a remnant from the earlier period with which to build the next; he starts a fresh covenant with the first man of the new dynasty. These are the deeds of YHWH, in the P-tradition, the only kind of stories told about him. He "speaks," he passes his breath over the earth, but that is all. And it dawns on us that here is creation and planned control of the affairs of the world by a single deity, so that the entire account actually is the *epic of YHWH*: his *gesta* are the events of history. Here is no mere chronology; here is history and philosophy of history—the discovery of the Judean mythopoets. It is not without significance that this epic interpretation of events of the centuries came at about the time when Judah disappeared under the neo-Babylonian flood: YHWH's pruning was continuing. The very fall of Jerusalem and the exile to Babylon became an operation in this cosmic process.

Judah and Israel never contributed anything to the science of astronomy. Their tradition accepted the astronomic findings of the Babylonians, but it rejected the Babylonian astrology that had been born of those observations, and substituted a different status of God and man in the cosmic scheme. Before the middle of the first millennium B.C. had arrived, Judah had asserted that its deity alone was creator of the universe and the arbiter of all men, and also that that deity was still operating to bring about a completed divine order. It was a number of centuries more before the Greeks arrived at anything comparable and they arrived along a different route. For Zeus and his companions had not created the universe; they had only seized it as loot in warfare. It and they remained under the rule of the *moirae*.

It took time for Zeus to gain control of Fate, and also to be recognized as a universal creator. But Zeus never matched the full stature of YHWH who did all this and more, for he also wrested out of his people a concentrated and exclusive dedication to himself. This Zeus never approached even remotely.

"Thy sons, O Zion, against thy sons, O Greece." During the half-millennium after Alexander the Great, one great body of world view, which we shall for convenience call Levantine, confronted another, the Occidental, then in the form of the Hellenic. Whenever great, matured cultures, each with a formulated world-view of its own, face each other and are forced to devise some *modus vivendi* between them, it is an Age of Cosmopolitanism. The first age of this sort is the one just mentioned. In an Age of Cosmopolitanism the world-view ceases to be identified with locale, to be coextensive with political boundaries, to possess ethnocentric deities. Instead values and principles transcend national boundaries because government and ethnos cease to be relevant—the principles are universalized. The meaning of the individual is reevaluated. The world-view carries a dynamism, so that its adherents dedicate their lives to winning followers to it. In the first Age of Cosmopolitanism, Iranian and Syrian and Buddhistic missionaries penetrated inner Asia at the risk of life and limb; Jewish Pharisees "encompassed heaven and earth to make one proselyte." An unknown seer wrote the Book of Jonah. The Bundahish was an ethical cosmology.

There has been since that time only one more, a second, Age of Cosmopolitanism. It has come upon the world in but the last four centuries or so. The symptoms are here again: matured cultures with profound world-views face each other, and are forced to a *modus vivendi* between them. The individual is reevaluated; world views bid for his allegiance; missionaries seek him out. The very assumptions on which evaluations are made are rescrutinized. An Age of Cosmopolitanism is not an age of faith, but an age of search for a faith.

The Intellectual Achievement of Mythopoeic Man[56]

As the capacity to symbolize emerged in a certain primate line, its members became committed—quite unwittingly—to an "intellectual adventure." Primitive men built themselves worlds which have become the foundations for all the worlds that have followed.

Out of their tales, rituals, monuments, their motifs, themes, morphaé, they condensed concepts which have never left us, which show no indications of ever leaving, and without which we should have no art, music, philosophy, science, or religion. A sample listing of these concepts will testify to their achievement:

"I" and the "Other"
Value (as such)
Space
Time
Nature as power, and as numinous; the "Holy"
Cosmos
Permanence and transcience; continuity, tradition
Regularity in the phenomenal world
Person
Ethic
Antithesis: the antagonism and balance of opposites
Event (as such)
Relatedness, and cause-and-effect
Relativity
Quest
Catharsis
Conscience (guilt)
Generation, germination, birth
The irrevocability of death
Knowledge as value
Credo as value
History
Tragedy

The story of how a primate has been humanized is that of un- utterably naive young men beginning to see visions, and scarcely less naive old men dreaming dreams. As long as young men shall see visions, and old men shall dream dreams, so long will mythopoea abide with us. And when and if ever they cease, we shall no longer have either poets or engineers. For to see and to dream is mythopoea; and it is the mark of being human.

NOTES

[1] "World view" is an attempt to translate the German *Weltanschauung*. Although I had been using this term before "discovering" Dilthey, I think I mean the same thing essentially as he does. It is described thus by H. A. Hodges (*Wilhelm Dilthey: an Interpretation*; p. 160): "Outlook. *Weltanschauung*. There is no adequate English equivalent, and I have often used the German word. In Dilthey it means a complex of ideas and sentiments comprising (*a*) beliefs and convictions about the nature of life and the world, (*b*) emotional habits and tendencies based on these, and (*c*) a system of purposes, preferences, and principles governing action and giving life unity and meaning. The Weltanschauung of a person or a society includes that person's or society's answer to the fundamental questions of destiny which Dilthey calls the *riddle of life*."
Although I certainly have no intention of divorcing the *Weltanschauung of* the individual from that of the society which provides him the matrix for his own, and concur that at any time a culture is embodied in its carriers, I must confine the efforts of the present essay to *Weltanschauung* in society or societies.
The anthropologist who in his definition of myth comes closest to Dilthey's conception of *Weltanschauung* is, I think, B. Malinowski. See his *Myth in Primitive Psychology*. This places me in substantial agreement with Malinowski—as far as he goes; I do not accept as narrow a definition of symbol as he seems to hold—as will appear in the main text; and I am at pains to demonstrate that to assume myth and ritual as separate entities before adducing their similarities and relationships is an inverted procedure. Malinowski, moreover, confines his exposition to the situation of primitive man, although he does indicate that the same processes are at work in high civilizations. In this I agree; but in a proper treatment of *Weltanschauung* we cannot afford to neglect the high civilizations, and they shall not be neglected in this essay.

[2] Susanne Langer, *Philosophy in a New Key* (Cambridge, Harvard University Press, 1942).

[3] Bronislaw Malinowski, *Myth in Primitive Psychology* (New York, W. W. Norton, 1926), p. 19.

[4] Edwyn Bevan, *Symbolism and Belief* (Boston, The Beacon Press, 1957), p. 11.

[5] For "basic readings," as they pertain to symbolization and mythopoea, consult: S. Freud, *The Interpretation of Dreams* (available, among other sources, in A. A. Brill, ed., *The Basic Writings of Sigmund Freud*, New York, The Modern Library; E. Fromm, *The Forgotten Language* (available now in paperback, New York, The Grove Press); C. Jung, *Psyche and Symbol;* P. Mullahy, *Oedipus: Myth and Complex* (New York, Hermitage Press, 1948).

[6] There is no literature in this field that is not purely technical; hence the synopsis in the main text which otherwise would be overly extensive for an essay of the present scope. The following are essential titles:
L. S. Kubie, "Instincts and Homeostasis," *Psychosomatic Medicine,* X:1(1948): 15-30; "The Distortion of The Symbolic Process in Neurosis and Psychosis," *Journal of the American Psychoanalytical Association,* I:1(1953):59-86; "Some Implications for Psychoanalysis of Modern Concepts of the Organization of the Brain," *Psychoanalytic Quarterly,* XXII(1953):21-68; "The Central Representation of the Symbolic Process in Psychosomatic Disorders," *Psychosomatic Medicine,* XV:1(1953):1-7; "The Fundamental Nature of the Distinction between Normality and Neurosis," *Psychoanalytic Quarterly,* XXIII(1954):167-204; "Influence of Symbolic Processes on the Role of Instincts in Human Behavior," *Psychosomatic Medicine,* XVIII:3(1956):189-208.

P. D. MacLean, "Psychosomatic Disease and the 'Visceral Brain'," *Psychosomatic Medicine,* XI:6(1949):338-53.

H. W. Magoun, "An Ascending Reticular Activating System in the Brain Stem," *A. M. A. Archives of Neurology and Psychiatry,* 67:2(1952):145-55.

W. Penfield, "Memory Mechanisms," *A. M. A. Archives of Neurology and Psychiatry,* 67:2(1952):178-98.

F. Schiller, "Consciousness Reconsidered," *A. M. A. Archives of Neurology and Psychiatry,* 67:2(1952):199-227.

[7] MacLean, "Psychosomatic Disease," p. 344.

[8] This statement, unfortunately, must remain purposely vague. Neither "consciousness" nor "integration of response" can be localized as simplistically as the remarks might imply. The point is, that there now exists real evidence that these regions are essential to the particular functions mentioned. In the mammal with its superaddition of cerebral hemispheres to the "archaic" brain, integration must also be viewed as a harmonious reciprocation between the centrencephalic system of the diencephalon and the cortical areas with which it is connected.

[9] See Magoun, "The Brain Stem"; Penfield, "Memory Mechanisms."

[10] See especially his "Studies of the Cerebral Cortex of Man," in *Brain Mechanisms and Consciousness; A Symposium* (Springfield, Ill., Charles C. Thomas, 1954). See pp. 294f.

[11] *Ibid.,* p. 303.

[12] Kubie, "Modern Concepts of the Organization of the Brain," p. 31.

[13] Kubie, "The Distortion of the Symbolic Process," pp. 67ff. Kubie also reproduces this passage in "Some Implications for Psychoanalysis," pp. 39ff.

[14] Paradoxically—even among anthropologists there is no universal agreement on its definition. The question is reviewed magnificently by A. L. Kroeber and C. Kluckhohn, "Culture: a Critical Review of Concepts and Definitions," *Papers of the Peabody Museum in American Archeology and Ethnology,* XLVII:1 (1952).

[15] For the meaning of this technical term, see A. Kardiner, *The Psychological Frontiers of Society* (New York, Columbia University Press, 1945).

[16] H. and H. A. Frankfort, J. A. Wilson, Th. Jacobsen, W. A. Irwin (Univ. of Chicago Press, 1946).

[17] *Ibid.*

[18] "Science and Complexity," *The American Scientist,* 36:4 (1948), pp. 536 ff.

[19] *Ibid.,* p. 539.

[20] A brief but excellent treatment of the history of mythology is that of Richard Chase, *The Quest for Myth.* See also Ernst Cassirer, *The Myth of the State,* Part I.

[21] See Clyde Kluckhohn, "Myths and Rituals: a General Theory," *The Harvard Theological Review,* XXXV:1 (1942), 45-79 for an excellent review of this question. See also "Myth," by Ruth Benedict, in *Encyclopaedia of the Social Sciences* (New York, 1933).

[22] Kubie has criticized psychiatry precisely for the same fallacy, and this has suggested the analogy. *See particularly* "The Distortion of the Symbolic Process," pp. 59 ff., and the references cited there; "The Fundamental Nature of the Distinction between Normality and Neurosis." This is a model of analytic and expressive clarity.

[23] Kubie, "The Distortion of the Symbolic Pocess," p. 62f.

[24] This attempt at a "grammar" is a purely empirical matter. It represents a system of categories which I first developed to aid my students in mythology to a workable architecture beneath a mass of inchoate data. It is hoped that the

system will help rather than hinder a science of mythology, but to such a science it pretends to do no more than supply a "prolegomenon." Dr. Claude Lévi-Strauss has been developing what seems a most promising method of analyzing the structure of myth-tales. He starts by breaking down a tale into the elemental movements of its motifs. These he sorts and rearranges in a kind of matrix, and from this pattern he apparently is able to force the emergence of the theme treatment. Thus he claims that he comes upon the essential meaning of the tale. (*See* "The Structural Study of Myth," in *Myth: a Symposium,* Thomas A. Sebeok, ed. ["Bibliographical and Special Series of the American Folklore Society, V."], Philadelphia, 1955.) In doing this, Dr. Lévi-Strauss has progressed beyond anything I have undertaken systematically. But his analysis is confined to myth-tales, and the tale seems to be coextensive with his definition of myth itself. We seem to be traveling different roads; and neither of us vitiates the work of the other.

The present "grammar" attempts to remain amenable to the humanistic approach while making way for a scientific approach. It is an article of the writer's faith that the very stature of cultural anthropology as a science requires it never to cease being a "humanity." With the possible exception of psychology, this makes it the only science of which this can be said. Of no part of cultural anthropology can this be truer than that which enters the land where dwells the psyche of man.

[25] Ruth Benedict has expressed this point with beautiful succinctness. See her article, "Myth," in the *Encyclopedia of Social Sciences.*

[26] An example of what can come of such mutual acculturations has been done into a charming book by Dr. Sula Benét: *Song, Dance, and Customs of Peasant Poland* (New York, Roy Publishers, n. d. [ca. 1952]). Here is the community's seasonal round, replete as its life is with ritual dramatization at every juncture, and also the ritual in the biography of the individual as he too passes through the drama of his own life.

[27] Fortunately it is no longer necessary to spend effort validating these assertions. They would be accepted by most anthropologists today, and, I believe, by most folklorists. The matter is adequately and effectively summarized by Stith Thompson, in "Myths and Folk Tales," in *Myth: a Symposium,* pp. 104-10.

[28] Not *categories* of idioms: these abide: tale, ritual, monument.

[29] For divergent views of this set of problems, *see* Lord Raglan, "Myth and Ritual;" and Stanley Edgar Hyman, "The Ritual View of Myth and the Mythic," both in *Myth: A Symposium.*

[30] *Primitive Religion* (New York, Dover Publications, 1957), pp. 7 ff.

[31] As long as we do not take "coercive" and "stages" in too rigid senses, this seems to me a most valid statement of the case. Dr. Radin himself is very free from such rigidity of thinking; hence the following strictures are *caveats* directed anywhere but at him. (1) The "stages" must be considered as but scale-markings along a continuum. (2) "Coercion" is but our own interpretive figure of speech; it does not necessarily portray the intent of the primitive who began exercising it. The raw act of seizing any living thing, whether plant or animal for the purpose of eating it is not a coercion on the human level any more than on that of any carnivorous or frugivorous animal. The making of the first knife out of a piece of flint is not a coercion of the material. Before we can have magic rite, just as before we can have a material technology, we have just technique. In other words—even back of Radin's stage one, there is a still more primitive and undifferentiated one. He seems to be suggesting it in his remark about "almost... a tropism."

[32] See Philip Wheelwright, "The Semantic Approach to Myth," p. 97, in *Myth: A Symposium*.

[33] This is the least fortunate of the three terms for idioms, but it must do *faute de mieux*.

[34] *The Folk-Tale*, p. 415.

[35] See esp. Antti Aarne, "Verzeichnis der Märchentypen," *FF Communications* No. 3 (translation by Stith Thompson, "The Types of the Folk-Tale," *FF Communications* No. 74); Stith Thompson, *Tales of the North American Indians* (Cambridge, Mass., 1929); *The Folk Tale* (see Appendix); "Motif-Index of Folk-Literature," *FF Communications* Nos. 106-9, 116, 117 (published also in *Indiana University Studies*, Nos. 96-97, 100-1, 105-6, 108-10, 111-12).

[36] See E. W. Count, "The Earth-Diver and the Rival Twins," in *Indian Tribes of North America: Proceedings of the 29th International Congress of Americanists, III*, Sol Tax, ed. (University of Chicago, 1952).

[37] *Ibid.*

[38] The primal-flood motif is probably continuous with both the biblical *tohu-bohu* of *Genesis* I and the deluge of *Genesis* VI, but collaterally so, in that the source of both the biblical and Eurasiatic-American branchings presumably is Mesopotamian-Iranian.

[39] Stanley E. Hyman, in "The Ritual View of Myth and the Mythic," in *Myth: A Symposium* (p. 93 f.) says: "What such modern writers as Melville or Kafka create is not myth but an individual fantasy expressing symbolic action, equivalent to and related to the myth's expression of a public rite. No one, not even Melville (let alone Moritz Jagendorf) can invent myths or write folk literature." If we define myth as a form of folk literature, then there is nothing more to be said. It is not at all clear what is meant here by Melville's not being able to "invent" myth. And if to "individual fantasy expressing symbolic action" is to be denied the label of mythopoea, then there are no myths at all. How else did Gilgamesh or the story of Adam come into existence? Shall we deny myth status to the initiatory tale of the Midewiwin, if we discover that it originated as a shaman's vision? Or to the vision that started the Ghost Dance? If we start with the premise that mythopoea is a process now dead in sophisticated culture, then the case is closed before its hearing. But thereupon we are faced with the task of explaining the phenomena generated in modern man from the same psychological wellsprings, and of finding new technical terms to fit; and all the while we are postponing a reckoning with the dictum that "plus ça change plus c'est la même chose."

[40] It hardly needs pointing out that some of these can be morphaé; others perhaps have not achieved that stature.

[41] See John 3:30.

[42] Dr. Lucile H. Charles has analyzed most ably the dramatic nature of ritual, in a series of papers published in the *Journal of American Folklore*: "Growing up through Drama": July-September 1946:274-82; "Regeneration through Drama at Death": April-June 1948:151-74; "Drama in First-Naming Ceremonies": January-March 1951:11-35; "Drama in Shaman Exorcism": April-June 1953:95-122.

[43] For an account of this phenomenon, at once philosophical and understanding, consult F. S. C. Northrop, *The Meeting of East and West* (New York: Macmillan Co., 1946), chap. II.

[44] The work of C. G. Jung and his followers—notably, C. Kerényi—in the field of mythology has been so vitally significant that virtual absence of its mention so far needs explaining, the more so, since this writer has profited greatly from these authors.

In *Essays on a Science of Mythology* ("Bollingen Series XXII," New York, 1949), Jung and Kerényi treat as "archetypes" the "Primordial Child" and "Kore." Maud Bodkin, in *Archetypal Patterns in Poetry* (Oxford, 1934; paperback edition, Vintage Books, 1958), applies "archetype" to discussions of "rebirth," "Paradise-Hades," the image of woman, and others. These labels include features which, in the present essay, in some cases would be identified as morphaé, in others as themes. The phenomena are real enough, whatever the method of analysis. But the writer is not at all ready to accept as valid Jung's concept of "archetype." Moreover, this essay does not attempt to explore points of divergence and similarity among different approaches, let alone attempt reconciliations between them.

[45] See E. W. Count, "The Biological Basis of Human Sociality," *American Anthropologist*, LX (1958): 1049-85; also *Eine Biologische Entwicklungs Geschichte der Menschlichen Sozialität* (Mainz), Homo IX (1958): 129-146; X (1959): 1-35; X (1959):65-92.

[46] Margaret Mead, ed. *Cooperation and Competition among Primitive Peoples* (New York: McGraw-Hill, 1937).

[47] See Ruth F. Benedict, "The Vision in Plains Culture," *American Anthropologist* 24:1(1922)1-23; *The Concept of the Guardian Spirit in North America* (Memoire No. 29, American Anthropological Association, 1923); Robert H. Lowie, *Primitive Religion* (Boni & Liveright, 1924; Liveright, 1948), chap. I.

[48] It will be noted that within mystery cults and Christianity, there has been room for both quest-with-group and individualistic quest; the Plains and Northwest Indian culture-areas together were a matter of either-or.

[49] Ghost Dance and peyote cults demand mention; they are peculiar and variegated hybridizations of nativism and nonliturgic Christianity. They represent the desperation of primitive cultures that are dying under the impact of Westernism, and they are messianic. Similar messianisms have occurred in South Africa and Melanesia.

[50] The theme, curiously enough, can be acted out epically instead of ritually, as instanced by Ponce de Leon, or by an entire people, in search for a Promised Land. This was exemplified by the United States during the nineteenth century. Not only were there writers who interpreted the westward movement as an epic with plenty of mythologic overtones, but the mythology itself became a *mystique* that was sometimes explicit and not at all subtle and that abetted the movement. See Henry Nash Smith, *Virgin Land* (Harvard University Press, 1950). Also paperback edition: Vintage Books, 1957.

[51] Genesis 3.22.

[52] Genesis 11.5-7

[53] In her *Ancient Myths in Modern Poets* (New York, 1910), Helen A. Clarke cites fifteen examples of Occidental authors in the seventeenth to nineteenth centuries who develop the Promethean theme. The fact is an interesting symptom in post-Renaissance Occidentalism. But she limits her cases to explicit treatments of Prometheus. Thus, that towering example of Prometheanism just cited she does not mention at all.

It would be unthinkable that an age should produce Promethean figures in its literature, yet none among its actual and living dwellers. One cannot study the life of Beethoven–particularly as it has been written about so sensitively by J. W. N. Sullivan (*Beethoven: His Spiritual Development*. New York: Knopf, 1927; Paperback edition: New York: The New American Library, 1949), without feeling that here is Prometheanism at its greatest and its profoundest.

[54] "Traditionswanderungen Euphrat-Rhein," *FF Communications*, Nos. 118-19 (Helsinki, 1937-38).

[55] A *caveat* none the less. The above statement is diagrammatic. Actually, as we know, the "high" and the "low" traditions of Europe are not thus easily sundered. See, for instance, Richard B. Onians, *The Origins of European Thought* (Cambridge, University Press, 1954).

[56] With appreciative apologies to H. Frankfort, H. A. Frankfort, J. A. Wilson, Th. Jacobsen, W. A. Irwin, *The Intellectual Adventure of Ancient Man.*

REFERENCES

MYTHOLOGY

Gaster, Theodore. Thespis. New York, Henry Schuman, 1950.

Harrison, Jane E. Prolegomena to the Study of Greek Religion. Cambridge, University Press, 1903.

——— Themis. Cambridge, University Press, 1912.

Murray, Gilbert. The Rise of the Greek Epic. New York, Oxford University Press, 1924.

Auerbach, Erich, Mimesis. German edition: Berne, A. Francke, 1946; English edition: Princeton, Princeton University Press, 1953.

Fergusson, Francis. The Idea of a Theater. Princeton, Princeton University Press, 1949.

Weston, Jessie L. From Ritual to Romance. Cambridge, University Press, 1957.

DOMINANCE/SUBORDINANCE

The literature covering dominance/subordinance is a large body in itself. Here a few leading suggestions must suffice:

Allee, W. C., in *Biological Symposia*, VIII (1942): 139-62.

——— and others. Principles of Animal Ecology. pp. 413ff.

Structure et physiologie des sociétés animales; Colloques internationaux du Centre National de la Recherche Scientifique. Paris, 1952. Papers by W. C. Allee, F. Bourlière, G. P. Baerends, F. Frazer Darling, C. R. Carpenter.

Maslow, A. H. A series of papers in *The Journal of Genetic Psychology*, XLVIII (1936): 261-77, 310-38; XLIX (1936): 161-98; *The Psychological Review*, XLIV (1937): 404-29; L (1943): 514-39, 541-58; *The Journal of Social Psychology*, X (1939): 3-39; XI (1940): 313-24; XVI (1942): 259-94.

——— with S. Flanzbaum. *The Journal of Genetic Psychology*, XLVIII (1936): 278-309.

Murchison, C. A series of papers in *The Journal of General Psychology*, XII (1935): 3-39, 296-312; *The Journal of Social Psychology*, VI (1935): 3-30; *The Journal of Genetic Psychology*, XLVI (1935): 76-102.

——— with C. M. Pomerat and M. X. Zarrow. *The Journal of Social Psychology*, VI (1935): 172-81.

Noble, G. K. *The Auk*, LVI (1939): 263-73.

Greenberg, B. *Physiological Zoology*, XX (1947): 267-99.

——— with G. K. Noble. *Physiological Zoology*, XVII (1944): 392-439.

The sociology of the phenomenon is treated most significantly in:

Simmel, Georg. Soziologie, Untersuchungen über die Formen der Vergesellschaftung. Leipzig, 1908-23. The relevant chapters of this work have been rendered into English by Kurt H. Wolff in *The Sociology of Georg Simmel*, Part III (Glencoe, Ill., 1950).

PART IV

History, Social Theory, and Law

MARX'S VIEW OF HISTORY

A STUDY IN THE HISTORY OF THE PHILOSOPHY
OF HISTORY

By Paul Tillich

HARVARD UNIVERSITY

The General Character of Marx's View of History

MARXISM *belongs to that mode of interpreting human existence in which the interpretation of history is decisive.* Marxism consequently denies the two main types of nonhistorical world view, the naturalistic and the mystical. The negation of the naturalistic type is clearly expressed in Marx's criticism of Feuerbach as a philosopher of *intuitive* materialism and in Marx's doctrine of *historical* materialism. In his *Historische Materialismus* we learn that nature is nature for man only through history:

The human character of nature is actual only for man in society ... only here nature has become ... nature for man. Society is the fulfilled unity of man with nature, the actual resurrection of nature, the perfect naturalization of man and the perfect humanization of nature. (Kröner ed., I, 297)

Social activity, industrial activity first of all, produces nature for man. The negation of the mystical type of nonhistorical world view is implied in the general criticism of religion by Marx: "Religion is the imaginary realization of human nature because human nature has no true realization. ... The religious misery is at the same time the expression of the actual misery and the protest against it" (Kröner ed. I, 264). It is obvious that this criticism meets the nonhistorical mysticism which seeks consolation and salvation of the individual above history. Man is a historical being, and every attempt to interpret him from nature or from supernature is a flight away from his distorted reality.

Marxism belongs to that mode of interpreting history in which the idea of three periods of history is the principle of an active interpretation. According to this mode the meaning of history is seen in its development towards a period of final perfection through a period of distortion after a fall from an original perfection. In Marxism the original perfection is characterized as original communism (*Communist*

Manifesto I, note), in a very cautious way, however. The second period is characterized as the period of class struggles in different forms and with different results. The third period is characterized as the period of classless society, in which man will have a really human existence.

The history of all past society is the history of class struggles: "The old bourgeois society with its classes and class contrasts will be replaced by an association in which the free development of every individual is the condition for the free development of all" (*Manifesto*). The idea of a universal goal of history, in which an original perfection is to be restored and an intermediate distortion is to be overcome, connects the Marxian interpretation of history with the prophetic one and separates it from all interpretations in which the universal direction of history is denied, such as those which find the meaning of history in the growth and decay of nations, races, and circles of culture. The negation of these ideas is implied in Marx's presupposition that all nations are or will be in an equal situation of class struggle, and consequently that it is not the individual character of nations and races that gives meaning to history, but the universal quality of historical mankind to live in class struggle. In this he agrees with Hegel, in whose philosophy of history the universal process of self-realization of the absolute mind is the meaning of history. Marx contradicts Hegel in so far as, according to the latter, the individual fates of nations are the embodiments of the absolute mind.

Marxism belongs to that mode of interpreting history as developing in three periods, in which the third period is not expected to be reached, i.e. Marxism belongs to the revolutionary type of the interpretation of history. The active man as well as the interpreter of history has the consciousness of standing between the second and the third periods, between the distortion of historical existence in the present and the new perfection in the future. The feeling of living at the end of the second and the beginning of the third period inspires revolutionary enthusiasm in acting and the impulse to interpret. The most striking example of this attitude is the *Communist Manifesto*. Its whole analysis of history has the purpose of elucidating the present transition; on the other hand, in the light of this transition from the bourgeois to the proletarian society, the whole of history gains meaning. Through this revolutionary interpretation of the three-period scheme Marxism belongs to that line of prophetic interpretation of history which was represented by the sects in opposition to the churches: by Joachim in opposition to Augustine, by the originally revolutionary bourgeoisie against feudalism, by the Young Hegelians against Hegel. Marx's criticism of Hegel's *Philosophy of Law* is the outstanding document of this contrast. While the conservative interpretation of the three periods presupposes that the third period has already begun, the revolutionary interpretation denies this assumption as reactionary ideology, which serves to protect the ruling class.

The Powers of History in Marx's View

Since, according to Marxism, history is the motion of human society, the moving powers in history are the powers implied in human social existence. Marxism denies that the historical powers may be sought above or below human social existence. Marx's criticism of Hegel contains the refutation of the idealistic attempt to derive the historical motion from logical process instead of from real human activities. The matter of fact, from which he starts, is not understood as "matter of fact, but as a mystical result . . .," namely of a logical motion (*Manifesto*, I, 26). "Reality becomes a phenomenon, but this phenomenon is the only content of the idea." This interchange of idea and reality, this mystical realism, is the mystery of Hegel's philosophy. Marx contradicts it by demanding the nominalistic method, which starts with the real man, i.e. with man in society. "Consciousness never can be something other than conscious being, and the being of man is his real life" (II, 73). But this criticism is opposed at the same time to the metaphysical materialism which seeks the historical power below man in a physical mechanism.

The main failure of every materialism (Feuerbach included) is, that reality . . . is described only from the point of view of intuition, as object, not as human activity, as practice, as subject.   (II, 3)

Only a radical humanism can overcome idealism as well as materialism and make history understandable (I, 332).

The moving powers in history, as implied in human social existence, are the social contrasts appearing with the rise of the division of labor (Arbeitsteilung) and gaining social reality in the growth of social classes.

We gain . . . the result, that these three elements: Productive power, social situation and consciousness can and must contradict each other, because the division of labor makes it possible, that mental and material activity, that pleasure and work, production and consumption belong to different individuals. (II, 23)

"Division of labor and private property are identical terms" (II, 23). The division of labor implies a division of individual and common interests in every individual through the general interdependence of all. The expression of this common interest is the rise of states. But, since states are controlled by individuals or individual groups, they are at the same time the expression of the individual interests of those individuals or groups, so that their first character as expressing the common interest becomes illusory. Therefore every class which wants to rule must conquer the state; even the proletariat must do so in order to abolish control and state. The class itself is a product of common interests of individuals in the division of labor:

The individuals become a class only insofar as they have to make a common struggle against another class .... On the other hand, the class elevates itself over the individuals so that these find their conditions of living preformed. (I, 59)

The most important cleavage between classes is the contrast between those who have private property and those who have not. A revolutionary change always occurs when a new class gains a new productive power through the development of technical improvement. In this case, the productive power and the social order contradict each other. "All clashes in history originate according to our analysis in the contradiction between productive power and the social relationship" (II, 56). Therefore two basic contradictions can be named, which create history: (1) an abstract one, productive power and social situation; (2) a concrete one, a ruling and an oppressed class. Both belong together, since a class gains historical importance only insofar as it represents productive power. Although Marx acknowledges the importance of the state for the class struggle, he denies that the state is an independent power in history: "All struggles within the state, e.g. between aristocracy and monarchy . . . are only the illusory forms in which the real struggles of the different classes are carried on" (II, 24). Therefore the political state must die after the end of the class society. The state is no genuine power in history, but only a transitory means.

The materialistic interpretation of history asserts that man, acting according to his passions and interests, is the material of history. Marx challenges mechanistic materialism as "hostile to man," as lacking the flavor of sensuality, as purely abstract for the sake of overcoming the abstract idealism. On the other hand, he emphasizes that kind of materialism which gives an impulse to provide man with true human existence. "If man is shaped by circumstances, circumstances must be shaped humanly" (I, 393). Man should be able to feel himself as man, and since he is a social being he must receive a social environment in which he can develop his individual interests in harmony with the group interest. Thus the materialistic interpretation of history pre-supposes freedom; not the negative freedom of avoiding this or that, but the positive freedom of self-development (II, 3). Thus Marx pragmatically justifies the idea of freedom without referring to meta-physical indeterminism. Political activity is the confirmation of this theory.

The best known idea of historical materialism is Marx's doctrine of ideology, i.e., his criticism of the idealistic interpretation of history.

Morals, religion, metaphysics and other ideologies and the categories which correspond to them lose their pretended independence. They have no history, no development, but men changing their material production and their material relationships change with their reality also their . . . thoughts. Not consciousness determines life but life determines consciousness. (II, 73)

This interpretation of history explains the actual process of producing, starting from the material production of life itself; it further explains the social relationships which are connected with and created by the process of production, thus describing the bourgeois society in its different degrees as the foundation of all history and also describing the activities of the bourgeois society with respect to the state as well as to the theoretical forms and products of consciousness, religion, philosophy, morals. At the same time this description gives the reason for the rise of those forms, and finally points to matter in its totality including the interdependence of those different sides on each other. (II, 37)

From this point of view it is obvious that pure ideas have no historical power. "The idea always failed and became ridiculous when it was separated from interest" (I, 379). It is without importance for the actual development that a revolutionary idea is often proclaimed even if there is no change in the material situation of a society and no revolutionary mass movement which attacks the existing social system as a whole. The materialistic interpretation of history does not attempt to derive the intellectual life itself from economic or physical causes.

It uses not the category "causality," but "condition." Otherwise Marx could not speak of the interdependence of all realms of human production; he could not believe in the objective truth of his theory and of the natural sciences. He could not develop a moral pathos of greatest power and introduce the idea of humanity. On the other hand, he really denies religion and metaphysics insofar as they assert transcendent objects. "It is the task of the historical process to establish the truth of the immanent world, after the transcendent truth has disappeared" (I, 264). In other words, this world has a truth which is not realized: "Realistic Humanism." "Ideology" means not only (1) the dependence of the mental ideas of a period on the material production of this period and (2) the special ideas of religion and metaphysics which transcend sensory experience, but also (3) the false ideas which a special period develops with respect to itself. "The ideas of the ruling class are the ruling ideas in every period. The class which represents the material power in society at the same time exercises intellectual power" (II, 37). Not all ideas of the ruling class are false. They are true insofar as they express adequately the real situation, of a society. But they become false—ideologies in a purely negative sense—if they are understood as eternal truths, independent of the concrete situation. In this case they pretend to be valid for the whole society and for every period; that means they protect the ruling class against criticism and change. Nevertheless, they disappear with the catastrophe of the ruling class through the real and therefore ideological power of a new class. Every interpretation of history should consider this relationship of real power and ideological power, although the majority of historians did not do so, thus failing to recognize the real power in history.

Marx's View of the Aim of History and Its Fulfillment

The aim of history for Marx is the liberation of man from his "self-estrangement" and the realization of real humanity. The estrangement is a structural necessity within the class society, especially within its last and most perfect form, the bourgeois society. Real humanity can be actual only in a society in which the natural interests of the individual harmonize with the natural interests of the society, i.e. in a "classless society." Consequently the classless society is the goal of history. Marx refused to give a utopian description of this society, because it would be merely an ideological attempt to describe a social situation for which not all the material foundations are in existence. Therefore "classless society," "kingdom of freedom," "realistic humanism," and "real democracy" must be understood as symbols rather than as concepts. Their content must be derived more or less from the meaning of the negative aim of history: liberation of man from self-estrangement. Estrangement is rooted in the division of labor. Since a society in which the production of goods is characterized by division of labor is called "bourgeois society," there has always been a bourgeois society in some sense, although the typical bourgeoisie as the destructive power of feudalism first appeared in modern times. To this double meaning of "bourgeois society" corresponds a double meaning of estrangement: the general estrangement connected with the division of labor, and the special and final estrangement connected with the victory of the bourgeois society and the rise of the proletariat.

The category of estrangement is taken from Hegel's *Phenomenology*, where it means the alienation of mind from itself through the creation of an objective world in which the mind finds itself a stranger. Marx turns the category from the epistemological to the practical sphere and describes by it the fact that the products of human labor gain an independence from man and even a control over him:

This consolidation of our own products as a power over us, which we are unable to control, which crosses our expectations, which frustrates our calculations is a main factor in historical development. (II, 25)

This insight implies many assertions through which the destructive character of self-estrangement becomes more obvious.

The estrangement appears (1) in the fact that my means for living are in the hands of another, that the object of my wishes are in the unapproachable possession of another, (2) in the fact that everything in itself is alienated, and (3) in the fact, which is valid also for the capitalist, that the inhuman power controls the human. (I, 326)

This means, first, that the human relationships in which the true nature of man is expressed are replaced by the mechanism of production and exchange. Second, things have become articles of commerce not in their quality of satisfying a need, but in their quality of bringing forth profit (the fetishism of the ware). Third, the highest expression of human self-estrangement is money. Money is the general perversion of human relationships: "What I am not, I can be by money." Money perverts "fidelity into infidelity, love into hatred, virtue into vice, vice into virtue . . ." (I, 359). "Money is the estranged power of man" (I, 358).

The quantity of money becomes more and more its only powerful quality; as it reduces everything to the abstract character of a quantity of money, so it reduces itself in its motion to a merely quantitative being.   (I, 374)

The last step in the self-estrangement of man is the transformation of man himself into an article of commerce. This happens when he is obliged to sell his working power and becomes himself only a quantitative reality calculable in quantities of money: the proletarian situation.

In the Marxian view of history the proletariat is the center of history, because it is at the same time the point of the most radical estrangement and the final victory of real humanity. The preparation of the existence of a proletariat is the history of the bourgeois society and the destruction of all human relationships. The description of this victory and these destructions is the most impressive and most prophetic part of the *Communist Manifesto.* The dissolution of personal relationships and personal dignity in the community, in family and nation, in profession and work, and their replacement by open, unveiled, direct exploitation is the presupposition of proletarian existence. The description of the proletarian existence takes its colors from the actual situation of the proletarians in early capitalism. The basic point is complete destruction of humanity in the typical proletarian existence. At the same time it is the turning point. The proletariat "being the complete loss of man can gain itself only through a complete restitution of man" (I, 278). "If the proletariat proclaims the dissolution of the existing world order, it only reveals the mystery of its existence, for it is the real dissolution of this world order" (I, 279). Marx describes the messianic character of the proletariat by calling it

A class . . . which has a universal character because of its general suffering, and which claims no special right because it has experienced no special wrong, but the absolute wrong—a class, therefore, which cannot aspire to a historical dignity, but only to the dignity of man.   (I, 278)

The messianic vocation is fulfilled through the proletarian revolution in which the negation of all conditions of the present society creates man in his true essentiality. Marx expresses this idea in the following words:

The head of this emancipation is philosophy, its heart the proletariat. Philosophy cannot be realized without the negation of the proletariat and the proletariat cannot be negated without the fulfillment of philosophy. (I, 280)

This means that philosophy anticipates human essentiality, which gains actuality only in the proletarian revolution. For the existence of the proletariat is the historical refutation of the idealistic philosophy of essence.

The purpose of the proletarian revolution is neither the victory of the proletariat in itself, nor communism, nor the conquering of the means of production by society, but the transition from "the realm of necessity into the realm of freedom." The victory of the proletariat is the condition for this revolution which frees even the capitalist from the objective power of estrangement. The communist party is the vanguard of the revolution because it possesses the radical will and the radical knowledge of the situation.

Communism is not the situation which is to be reached, not an ideal to which reality should be subjected. We call communism the real movement which abolishes the present situation. (II, 23)

Marx denies strictly the collectivistic consequences of some forms of communism. His ideal of man implies freedom and personality for everybody.

The question whether or not this ideal is utopian must find an ambiguous answer. It contradicts utopianism insofar as it denies a general development towards this ideal through persuasion, enlightenment, education, morality, and insofar as it connects the fulfillment of the aim of history with the interest and passion of a special social group.

On the other hand, there is a utopian element in this ideal, insofar as Marx considers neither the differences in the interests of the present proletariat and the communist movement nor the possible new contradictions within the classless society. The assertion that with the proletarian revolution the prehistory of mankind is finished and history begins contradicts the experience that the impulse of history is the contrast of powers. It contradicts the experience that human nature always has shown will to power and cupidity beyond every limitation. And even if it is supposed that in the classless society human nature is transformed, there is no reason for the assumption that the real proletariat acts according to the standards of the typical proletariat and real communism according to the standards of ideal communism. The transitory stage which the political power of the proletariat is supposed to represent can become a definite stage. From the point of view of this criticism, the religious interpretation of Marxism has denied the utopian element. "Religious Socialism" employs the concept of *Kairos* in order to explain that the classless society, although a phrophetic demand of today, cannot be considered the ultimate aim of history.

The Structure of the Historical Process in Marx's View

According to Marx, the historical process has a dialectical character; the self-estrangement in history is the necessary and understandable way towards self-realization. The point in which both are identical is the proletariat. The argument whether dialectical materialism is a scientific method or a real interpretation of history has to be decided for the latter assertion. Marx offers an actual interpretation of the whole of history by describing the course of mankind as passing from the periods of preliminary class struggles through the period of the final class struggle to the classless society. He embraces in this description all nations in their individual development till the rise of the world bourgeoisie, world commerce, and the world proletariat. That is not a methodological interpretation of history as neo-Kantian Marxists assert, but an ontological one. This, however, does not prevent the methodological use of dialectics in every special case of historical analysis. The most important example is the dialectical analysis of capitalism in Marx's chief work.

The ontological application of the dialectical method has a threefold background: (1) the Christian idea of providence according to which God leads history through an overwhelming amount of meaninglessness toward the fulfillment of meaning; (2) the rationalization of this idea in Hegel's doctrine of the "cunning of reason," according to which interest and passion serve the realization of reason, although they consciously contradict reason; (3) the idea of a preestablished harmony between idea and reality. The difference between Marx's use and the liberal use of this doctrine is that liberalism derives from it a harmonistic interpretation of past and present, while Marx uses it for the future, and for present and past only insofar as they prepare for the future through their radical disharmonies. Nevertheless a belief in the ultimate meaning of history is implied dialectical materialism—a belief in the fulfillment of man through self-estrangement of man.

The process of history has the character of dialectical necessity, i.e. of a necessity in which human activity is included. The bourgeoisie "produces first of all its own grave-digger. Its doom and the victory of the proletariat are equally unavoidable." (*Manifesto* I, end). The meaning of this word "unavoidable" has been the subject of many discussions and of great practical differences in the Marxist movement. The mechanistic interpretation, as given by many Marxists since the latter part of the nineteenth century, cannot be maintained as the genuine idea of Marx. In refuting mechanistic materialism, he also refutes mechanical necessity in history. Bolshevism has accepted the dialectical interpretation of history as genuinely Marxian in order to justify the communistic revolution in a country in which there was not even a dialectical necessity for its victory. German Social Democracy had accepted more or less the mechanistic interpretation and by this means lost its revolutionary power. Marx does not hesitate to suggest that not every attempt to overcome capitalism by a proletarian victory may be successful. He admits that he himself was in error about the imminence of victory. He does not even deny the possibility of a complete chaos as the consequence of the doom of capitalism, in case communism should not gain the victory. His political activities and the *Manifesto* itself, as an appeal to all proletarians, prove that he recognized the element of freedom in the dialectical necessity. Nevertheless it is obvious that he himself believed in the ultimate fulfillment of humanity, although he intimated that perhaps the whole development must begin anew (II, 26). The tendency toward realizing man by overcoming his self-estrangement is as unavoidable as human existence itself.

It is obvious that this belief of Marx is a paradoxical belief transcending every empirical experience. Moreover, it is clear that this belief in a meaning of history and in the fulfillment of this meaning gave the tremendous historical power to the Marxian interpretation of history.

MARXIAN THEORIES OF LAW
IN PRIMITIVE SOCIETY

By Stanley Moore

WHETHER to recognize the existence of law in primitive society is, in the first place, a question of definition. Yet, to the extent that conflicting answers not only formulate but defend the definitions they advance, this question raises some of the most radical and persistent issues of legal theory. Since the debates of Socrates with the Sophists, social theorists have disputed as to whether law is found or made. One tradition tends to identify as the laws of a society the minimal rules of conduct acknowledged by the members of that society. The opposing tradition tends to identify as the laws of a society the formal commands of the governing authority of that society. This central conflict finds expression throughout almost the entire range of legal theory, but usually in a form enormously elaborated by complicating issues and questions of degree. However, the topic of law in primitive society seems to raise the problem in a relatively simple and decisive way. A theorist of the first tradition, who argues that there is no society without law, must assert the existence of law in primitive societies. A classic example is Locke.[1] A theorist of the second tradition, who argues that there is no law without a sovereign power, must deny the existence of law in such societies. A classic example is Hobbes.[2]

It is generally recognized that the Marxian theory of law stands nearer to the second tradition than to the first, that it defines laws as rules of conduct sanctioned by public authority. And it might be expected that Marxian theorists would unanimously deny the existence of law in primitive societies. But examination of the texts reveals a division of opinion. Marx and Engels assert that law exists in some primitive societies. Lenin denies that it exists in any such societies. I propose in this essay, first, to establish in terms of textual evidence the conflict between these theorists on the question of law in primitive society, and second, to indicate in the light of this analysis the contrast in their general theories of law and public authority. Accordingly, statements of these theorists about primitive society will not be examined in the light of empirical evidence, in order to determine their truth or falsehood. Instead, they will be examined in the light of other statements, in order to clarify the general theoretical positions they imply.

For the purpose of this discussion the following definitions are adopted. A state is defined—in accordance with Marxian practice—as a public authority based on the coercive power of armed bodies separated from the people, such as police and standing armies.[3] A primitive society is defined as a society in which the state has not developed. It follows from these definitions that what are here called primitive societies are what Marx and Engels—following Morgan—call societies at the levels of savagery or barbarism.[4] It follows further from these definitions that to ask whether law exists in primitive society involves asking whether law exists without a state.

In *The State and Revolution* Lenin seems definitely to assert that there is no law without a state. Discussing the first stage of communist society (which he calls socialism as distinguished from fully developed communism), he writes: "Of course bourgeois law (*pravo*) with respect to the distribution of consumers' goods necessarily presupposes the existence of a bourgeois state, for law is nothing without an apparatus capable of compelling compliance with legal rules." [5] Yet his actual words are that law is nothing without an *apparatus* for its enforcement. In this context he identifies that apparatus with the state; but he is discussing here a specific situation, that of socialist society. It might be the case that in a socialist society the only apparatus capable of enforcing law is a state apparatus. It might also be the case that in another sort of society another sort of apparatus could be found. The degree of generality with which Lenin asserts this identity can be determined only by additional evidence.

In an early work, written more than twenty years before *The State and Revolution,* Lenin contends that in primitive societies there exists a coercive power which is not a state. He is combating Struve's view that the state exists wherever there is organization of order by some coercive power. Struve, he argues, "quite erroneously regards coercive power as the distinctive mark of the state. There is a coercive power in every human community. Such a power existed in the gentile organization and in the family, though the state did not exist there. 'An essential characteristic of the state', writes Engels in the same work which Mr. Struve quotes on this subject, 'is a public power separated from the mass of the people'. . . . And in an earlier passage, discussing the establishment of the *naukrariai,* Engels writes that this 'undermined the gentile constitution in two ways: first, it created a public power (*öffentliche Gewalt* . . .) which no longer simply coincided with the totality of the armed people'. . . . So the distinctive mark of the state is the existence of a special class of people in whose hands *power* is concentrated. Obviously no one could apply the term to a community in which the 'organization of order' is administered by *all* its members in turn."[6] It can be agreed that no Marxian theorist at least could use the term "state" in connection with the organization of order here described. But if that order included rules of conduct enforced by coercive power, why should he not use the term "law"?

In the work from which this passage is quoted Lenin does not commit himself upon this question. But twenty-five years later, in his lecture *The State,* he returns to the problem of order in primitive societies. There he speaks of "the rule of custom" and of "the authority, respect, and power accorded to the elders of the tribe." In a later passage he refers to "the force of habit, of tradition, and of the authority or respect accorded to the elders of the tribe."[7] Habit—custom—tradition. Respect—authority—power. But not a word about law.

This negative evidence, taken together with the assertion quoted from *The State and Revolution,* seems sufficient to establish Lenin's position on the question of law in primitive societies. I believe it confirms the common opinion that he denied the existence of law in such societies and asserted without qualification that there is no law where there is no state. But though this evidence is sufficient to establish his views, it is insufficient to establish his reasons for holding them. Nowhere does Lenin explain why varieties of public power other than the state cannot provide the necessary apparatus for enforcing legal rules.

An explanation can be found. But the clearest way of presenting it is to examine first the contrasting position of Marx and Engels.

In an early work, *The Condition of the Working Class,* Engels asserts that law is necessary only in class societies. "It is obvious," he writes, "that the primary purpose of all legislation is to protect the propertied against the propertyless. Laws (*Gesetze*) are necessary only where there are people without possessions."[8] Since according to Marxian theory all societies with classes are societies with states,[9] Engels asserts by implication that law is unnecessary in societies without states.

But in *Die deutsche Ideologie,* which Engels wrote with Marx slightly more than a year later, the authors assert that law is found in the earliest societies, before the development of class divisions. "The history of law reveals that in the earliest and rudest epochs law (*Recht*) is made up of factual relationships in their crudest form. With the development of civil society, and therefore with the development of personal interests into class interests, legal relations alter and become civilized in their expression. They are no longer grasped as individual but as universal. At the same time the division of labour assigns to a few people the reconciliation of conflicting individual interests, and barbarous methods of protecting rights disappear."[10] The last sentence in this passage asserts that law exists before the state.

Did Engels change his mind? Or do the two passages deal with different things—*Gesetz* being confined to class society, *Recht* being recognized in primitive society? However interesting in themselves, these questions are irrelevant for establishing Engels' mature views. At the time both passages were written, as he pointed out some forty years later, "the pre-history of society, the social organization existing previous to recorded history, was all but unknown."[11] In two works written in the eighties, *The Origin of the Family, Private Property and the State* and *The Mark,* Engels explicitly and repeatedly recognizes the existence of law in some primitive societies.

The German word *"Recht"* has sometimes a wider meaning than the English word "law." And it might be asked whether Engels, in using the term when describing primitive institutions, uses it in a sense which can properly be translated "law." The question is answered, I believe, by Engels himself. In *The Origin of the Family* he writes of Bachofen: "To denote recognition of descent through the mother exclusively and the lines of inheritance which in time resulted from this practice, he uses the term mother-right (*Mutterrecht*); and, for the sake of brevity, I retain it. The term, however, is incorrect; for at this stage of social development there can be no talk of right (*Recht*) in the legal sense."[12] The stage of development referred to in this passage is that of savagery or lower barbarism. But what about societies which Engels places at the upper stage of barbarism—such as those of the Greek tribes in the Homeric Age, the Italian tribes at the foundation of Rome, and the German tribes described by Tacitus?[13] If, in discussing these more developed primitive societies, Engels uses the term "*Recht*" without any such qualification, is it not clear that he is using it in the legal sense? This interpretation is strengthened by the fact that he uses the term "*Gesetz*" in connection with all three groupings of these relatively advanced societies. It is further strengthened by the fact that he asserts the existence of legislation in two of these groupings, and the existence of courts in all three. Only in the case of the Iroquois, whom he places at the top of the lower stage of barbarism, does he use the term "*Recht*" unsupported by unambiguously legal terms.[14]

It is easy then to decide whether Engels in his descriptions of advanced primitive societies means by "*Recht*" what we mean by "law." He clearly indicates that he does. It is more difficult to establish the identifying characteristics by which he recognizes the presence of law in these societies.

Ordinary usage has established for the term "law" no single, clear-cut sense but a cluster of related senses, uniting in a central area of agreement and diverging through a peripheral area of dispute. If a rule of conduct has been laid down by acts of legislative authorities, if it has been applied to particular cases by acts of judicial authorities, if individuals have been compelled to comply with such decisions by acts of executive authorities, and if all these acts have been carried out by properly designated persons in accordance with generally recognized procedures—then ordinary usage is unanimous in calling that rule a law. This was so when Engels wrote and it is so today. Disagreements arise in cases where not all of these elements are present or where they are present in different degrees. Can there be laws without legislation? Without adjudication? Without execution? And to what extent must the indispensable act or acts be carried out by determinate officials in accordance with formal procedures? The statements Engels makes about law in primitive societies, together with other statements he makes about these societies, add up to a clear-cut position on these basic questions of definition.

Legislation, according to Engels, takes place in some primitive societies—specifically, among the Germans and the Romans. In *The Mark,* for example, he writes of German communities before the emergence of the state: "Just as all the members of the group originally had equal portions of land and equal rights to use what was held in common, so they shared equally in legislation (*Gesetzgebung*), administration, and adjudication within the *Mark.* At fixed intervals and at such other times as were considered necessary, they met in the open air to conduct the affairs of the *Mark* and to judge the misdeeds and disputes of its members. . . . Laws (*Gesetze*) were made, though only rarely was this necessary. Officials were elected and their conduct in office controlled. But, above all, justice was dispensed. The presiding officer had only to formulate the questions: judgement was delivered by the entire assembly."[15]

Engels, however, does not assert that all laws found in primitive society are the results of legislative acts. A few are, but most are not. Primitive law consists of some statutes and a much larger body of customary law.[16] What unites its subdivisions is not a common origin but a common use. Adjudication, not legislation, is a universal concomitant of law.

Engels recognizes in the very earliest societies the existence of officials whose duties include effecting the settlement of disputes. "In each such community," he writes in *Anti-Dühring,* "it was necessary from the beginning to assign to individuals, though under control of the entire group, the protection of certain common interests: settlement of disputes; repression of individual encroachments upon propriety; control of water, particularly in hot countries; and finally, under the most primitive conditions, religious functions. Such offices are found in primitive communities of every period—in the oldest German *Mark* communities and in India even to this day. They are obviously endowed with a certain authority and the beginnings of state power."[17]

Settlement of disputes by such officials may or may not be a judicial process. It may be simply arbitration. Settlement of a dispute is effected by a *court* only if, in addition to being conducted by authorized officials, it follows standardized procedures and applies to the particular case established rules. Engels recognizes the existence of courts only in relatively advanced primitive societies—specifically, among the

Greeks, the Romans, and the Germans. He writes, for example, of Rome's gentile constitution: "The assembly of the *curiae* accepted or rejected all laws (*Gesetze*), elected all higher officials, . . . and, as the highest court (*Gericht*), decided on appeal from the parties concerned all cases involving a death sentence on a Roman citizen."[18]

Judicial process seems a necessary condition for the existence of law, but is it also sufficient? It may be true that wherever there is law there is adjudication. Is it also true that wherever there is adjudication there is law? The problem of enforcement is crucial for theories of law in primitive society.

Executive power, according to Engels, develops out of the office of chief military commander in primitive society. But though these officials acquire this power with the emergence of the state, they cannot possess it before that process takes place. The coercive apparatus essential to executive power does not exist in primitive society. Engels writes, for example, of Greek institutions in the Homeric Age: "The assembly was in the last analysis sovereign; for, says Schömann in his *Griechische Altertümer,* 'if a decision required the cooperation of the people for its execution, Homer reveals to us no means by which they could be coerced'. At this time, when every adult male in the tribe was a warrior, there was as yet no public power separated from the people which could be used against the people. Spontaneous democracy was still in full bloom; and this fact must be the starting point for judging the power and position of both the council and the military leader (*basileus*)."[19]

Are there other institutions in primitive society capable of serving as agencies of law enforcement? According to Engels, a public power exists before the state exists. The emergence of the state is not equivalent to the first establishment of public power, but to the replacement of one kind of public power by another. The state is distinguished from the gentile constitution that precedes it, first, by the organization of its members on a territorial rather than a kinship basis, and second, by the establishment of "a public power (*öffentliche Gewalt*) which no longer directly coincides with the population organizing itself as an armed force." State power is a public power separated from the people; the public power in a primitive society is identical with the adult male population, self-organized and self-armed.[20] State power functions as a law enforcing agency. Can the armed population perform that function in societies without states?

To the extent that the public power in a primitive society compels individual members of that society to comply with judicial decisions, it does not do so by force of arms. According to Engels, the armed population of such a society is capable of organized physical coercion only externally, against other societies. It is incapable of such coercion internally, against its own members. The gentile constitution, he writes, "had no means of coercion except that of public opinion."[21] But is this not equivalent to admitting that in primitive society no determinate agency of law enforcement exists?

In such societies, however, the absence of *agencies* for enforcement does not entail the absence of enforcement. The coercive power of public opinion is far stronger in classless societies than in societies torn by pervasive, enduring, and fundamental conflicts of interest. The attitude of individual members of a primitive society towards a public authority which directly represents the community as a whole is quite different from the attitude of individual members of a state towards a public authority separated and increasingly alienated from society. Describing the position of state officials, Engels writes: "In possession of the public power and the right of taxation, the officials now become organs of society standing *above* society. The free and willing respect accorded to the organs of the gentile constitution is not enough for them, even if they could obtain it. As representatives of a power alienated from society, they must have respect decreed for them in exceptional laws which endow them with a special sanctity and inviolability. The lowest police officer in a civilized state has more 'authority' than all the organs of gentile society put together; but the mightiest prince and the greatest statesman or general in civilized society might envy the humblest of gentile chiefs for the unforced and unquestioning respect accorded him. One stands in the midst of society. The other must seek to present himself as something outside and above it."[22]

According to Engels, then, law is enforced in primitive societies, but not by an executive power. In these societies there is no need for determinate officials, acting in accordance with standardized procedures, to compel compliance with judicial decisions. In the existing circumstances enforcement is effective without being formal.

The general position taken by Engels on the characteristics of law in primitive society can be summarized in three propositions. First, the rules of conduct recognized as laws are only rarely results of legislation. Second, these rules are applied to particular cases by courts. Third, these rules are enforced, but not by an executive power. In such societies, formal adjudication and informal enforcement are the universal concomitants of law.

There is less evidence for the views of Marx on these questions, since he did not live to write his projected work on primitive society. But the evidence that exists is sufficient to establish his agreement with Engels on the central issues involved.

Marx left in manuscript extensive notes on Morgan's *Ancient Society,* parts of which Engels incorporated in *The Origin of the Family.* The great bulk of Marx's work consists of extracts from Morgan, often underlined for emphasis, sometimes challenged by quotation marks, question marks, or exclamation points. A small portion consists of extracts from authorities not quoted by Morgan. An even smaller portion consists of critical or expository comments by Marx.[23] Both extracts and comments provide evidence for the views of Marx on various questions—negative and inconclusive evidence in those cases where he extracts without challenging or commenting, positive evidence in those cases where he indicates his own opinions.

Marx recognizes, both tacitly and explicitly, the existence of law in some primitive societies. Morgan refers to customary law and rights based upon this law in such societies. In one instance, where Morgan applies the expression "marital rights and privileges (*jura conjugialia*)" to societies at a stage of development "low down in savagery," Marx in an otherwise expository comment dissents by placing the term "rights" in quotation marks.[24] But he transcribes without comment passages in which Morgan asserts the existence of legal rights, customary laws, and even legislation in the more developed primitive societies of the Greeks and Romans. Morgan writes, for example, of the Roman *comitia curiata* in the period of the gentile constitution: "All laws were passed or repealed by this assembly; all magistrates and high public functionaries, including the *rex,* were elected by it on the nomination of the senate. The *imperium* was conferred upon these persons by a law of the assembly (*lex curiata de imperio*) which was the Roman method of investing with office."[25] The fact that Marx summarizes this passage, and others like it, without protesting makes it reasonable to suppose that his position on the question of law in these societies does not differ from that of Morgan. This supposition is confirmed by the fact that Marx explicitly recognizes the presence of courts in such societies.

Marx asserts that courts existed in some primitive societies—specifically, among the Greeks and Germans. Morgan, in discussing Greek institutions of the Homeric era, quotes Aristotle to the effect that the *basileus* was general, judge, and chief priest. Marx comments: "The judicial (*sudebnykh*) functions of the *basileus* must have been of the same character as those of the chiefs among the ancient Germans. There the popular assembly constituted the court (*sud*), at which the chief presided. He merely put the questions: he did not deliver the judgement." [26]

Marx denies the existence of executive power in primitive society. Engels quotes two of his comments contrasting the office of *basileus* in Greek society before the emergence of the state with that of king after the emergence of the state. And the passage Engels quotes from Schömann, to the effect that in Homeric society there was no way for officials to compel the people to cooperate against their will, is one of those extracts from authorities not quoted by Morgan which Marx added to his summary. [27]

Marx, then, agrees with Engels in recognizing, first, that law exists in some primitive societies, second, that it is applied by courts, and third, that it is not enforced by executive power.

The conflict between the views of Marx and Engels, on the one hand, and those of Lenin, on the other, concerning law in primitive society has now been established in terms of textual evidence. The next step is to indicate in the light of this analysis the contrast in their general theories of law and public authority.

In a survey of the theory of the state in Marx, Engels, and Lenin, I have attempted to formulate their definition of law in the following terms: "The laws of a society are those rules of conduct explicitly sanctioned by public authority, that is, by the public power of that society or by officials or voters whose decisions are supported by that power. 'With law', writes Engels, 'there necessarily come into existence organs entrusted with its support—public power, the state'. According to Lenin, there can be no law without a state to support it. According to Marx and Engels, there can be no law without a public power to support it: state power is the particular kind of public power characteristic of class society. According to all three, in societies with states laws are those rules of conduct explicitly sanctioned by the state." [28]

If this general definition is correct, then to ask whether law exists in primitive societies is equivalent to asking, first, whether a public authority exists in such societies, and second, whether that authority explicitly sanctions rules of conduct.

Marx, Engels, and Lenin agree that a public authority exists in primitive societies. This public authority, like that of any other society, includes a public power (*öffentliche Gewalt*) and public officials whose decisions are supported by that power. What distinguishes it from state authority is the fact that its public power is identical with the adult male population, self-organized and self-armed.

Does this public authority explicitly sanction rules of conduct? In order to answer the question it is necessary to clarify what is meant by sanctioning. The verb "to sanction" is ordinarily used in two senses, both of which are relevant to the Marxian account of law. In the first sense it means to authorize or confirm by some public act; in the second, to enforce by attaching penalties to transgression. The expressions Marx and Engels use in describing the relation of public authority to law cluster around two focal terms—"sanctify" and "support." [29] Their usage can be summarized in a definition by employing the verb "to sanction" in both its senses and qualifying it with "explicitly." The qualification serves to emphasize the fact that rules of conduct only tacitly or indirectly sanctioned by public authority are not called laws.

In some primitive societies, according to Marx and Engels, some rules are sanctioned in the sense of being authorized or confirmed by public acts. This follows from the assertion that courts exist there. These rules are also sanctioned in the sense of being enforced by attaching penalties to transgression, though these penalties are not applied by determinate officials in accordance with standardized procedures. The qualification follows from the denial that executive power exists there. The general definition covers the case of primitive law if "explicitly sanctioned" is given the minimal meaning of formally adjudicated and informally enforced.

Lenin differs from Marx and Engels at this point in adopting a narrower definition of law. For him law is nothing without an *appa-*

ratus capable of compelling compliance with legal rules. It must be sanctioned in the sense of being enforced by determinate officials acting in accordance with standardized procedures. Marx and Engels admit that such an apparatus of enforcement does not exist in primitive society. But they do not consider its presence a necessary condition for the existence of law. Lenin's disagreement with them does not turn upon a question of fact but upon the use of a word.

Is this *all* that is involved? As was pointed out at the beginning of this essay, often in the history of legal theory contrasting definitions of law have reflected basic theoretical differences. Is the contrast between Lenin's definition and that of Marx and Engels a case in point? Or is it an isolated and trivial divergence, without general theoretical significance? I believe the first answer is correct. And in the remainder of this essay I shall indicate, without establishing in detail, related divergences on two substantive questions of prime importance for Marxian theory. The first of these divergences concerns the content of law. It centers on the problem of establishing the common social function of those rules of conduct which receive the sanction of public authority. The second concerns the future of law. It centers on the problem of deciding whether law and public authority will continue to exist when the state has withered away.

Lenin's characterization of the content of law is that every law is an expression of the will of some ruling class. "But what is a law (*zakon*)?" he asks in a controversy with Plekhanov. "It is an expression of the will of those classes which have attained victory and hold in their hands state power."[30]

Nine years later, in a critique of Pyatakov, he reaffirms the connection between law and class. "A law (*zakon*)," he writes, "is a political measure; it is politics." According to Marxian theory, "Political power, properly so called, is merely the organized power of one class for oppressing another." Within the Marxian system, therefore, the assertion that every law is a political measure is equivalent to the assertion that every law is an instrument of some ruling class.[31]

Lenin's claim that every law expresses the will of some ruling class is even more restrictive than his claim that there is no law without a state. According to Marx and Engels, the state existed in societies at stages of development preceding the emergence of classes. What ruling class expressed its will in the laws enforced by Oriental despotisms? Or were there no laws in Asiatic society?[32] According to Lenin, the state will continue to exist, though in process of withering away, in societies at stages of development succeeding the elimination of classes. He writes in *The State and Revolution*: "The state withers away in so far as there are no longer any capitalists, any classes, and there is consequently no class which it is necessary to suppress. But the state has not yet completely withered away, since there still remains the protection of 'bourgeois right' (*pravo*), which sanctions actual inequality."[33] The Russian word "*pravo*," which Lenin uses here, like the German word "*Recht*," means either "right" or "law." If in this case it means "law," then Lenin has contradicted himself; for this law cannot express the will of a non-existent ruling class. But if it means "right," the situation is not much better. How could a state protect a system of right without using any laws?

Where class societies are concerned, Marx and Engels agree with Lenin that law is an expression of the will of the ruling class. "Your ideas themselves," Marx and Engels inform their critics in *The Communist Manifesto*, "are the outgrowth of bourgeois production and property relations, just as your law (*Recht*) is but the will of your class exalted into statutes (*Gesetz*), a will which acquires its content from the material conditions of existence of your class."[34] But the statement that capitalist law is an expression of the will of a ruling class does not imply the statement that *all* law is an expression of the will of some ruling class. In this passage Marx and Engels characterize the content of law in a particular class society. To discover their general characterization—applicable to law wherever it is found, in societies with states and classes, in societies with states but no classes, and in societies with neither states nor classes—it is necessary to look elsewhere in their writings.

In *The Housing Question* Engels writes of the origins of law: "At a very primitive stage in social development the need arises for a framework of generally recognized rules to regulate the daily recurring acts of producing, distributing, and exchanging products, so that individuals will limit their activities by observing the necessary conditions for production and exchange. This regulation, which is at first custom, soon becomes law (*Gesetz*)."[35]

In *Capital* Marx writes of feudal law: "It is clear, moreover, that here, as always, it is in the interest of the ruling section of society to sanctify existing practice as law (*Gesetz*) and to fix in legal form the boundaries given to that practice by custom and tradition. Aside from other considerations, this happens by itself when in the course of time the continual reproduction of the foundation of the existing state of affairs, and of the relations based on that foundation, takes on a regulated and orderly form. This rule and order is an indispensable element for any mode of production which is to attain social stability and independence from mere accident or arbitrary action.... If it lasts for some time, it establishes itself as custom and tradition; and finally it is sanctified as explicit law."[36]

In his address to the jury at Cologne, Marx says of capitalist law: "Society does not rest upon the laws (*Gesetze*). That is a juridical fiction. Law, on the contrary, must rest upon society: it must express, in opposition to the arbitrary wills of single individuals, the community of interests and needs arising from the existing mode of production. Here in my hand is the Napoleonic Code. It did not produce modern civil society. On the contrary, the civil society which arose in the eighteenth century and continued to develop in the nineteenth finds in the Code no more than its legal expression."[37]

All three of these statements antedate the discovery of Morgan by Marx and Engels; yet they agree in presenting a characterization of the content of law sufficiently broad to be applicable to both class and classless societies. In any society where law exists, the rules of conduct sanctioned by public authority are those considered necessary to protect against arbitrary actions the orderly functioning of that society. In a class society, the rules of conduct sanctioned by the state are those the ruling class considers necessary to protect against arbitrary actions the orderly functioning of that society. The statement that law is an expression of the will of a ruling class, which is for Lenin a characterization of the content of all law, is for Marx and Engels the application of a much wider characterization to an important sector of its total range.

It has previously been established that Lenin's definition of law is narrower than that of Marx and Engels. It has now been established that his characterization of the content of law is narrower than theirs. It remains to establish the disagreement of these theorists on the role of law and public authority in communist society when the state has withered away.

Would a fully developed communist society require laws to protect its orderly functioning against arbitrary actions? According to Marxian theory, with elimination of the basic conflicts of interest characteristic of class society and with replacement of an economy of scarcity by an economy of abundance, the number and variety of potential threats to social order will be sharply reduced. And it may be expected that the methods of dealing with such threats will be radically changed. But it does not follow from these considerations that anti-social actions will *completely* disappear or that those which remain will be dealt with by methods excluding *any* use of law.

Lenin admits that anti-social actions will occur in communist society, but he denies that such actions will be curbed by legal process. "We are not utopians," he writes in *The State and Revolution,* "and we do not in the least deny the possibility and the inevitability of excesses on the part of individual persons, or the necessity to suppress such excesses. But . . . no special machinery, no special apparatus of suppression, will be necessary for this task. It will be performed by the armed population itself, as simply and easily as any crowd of civilized people, even in contemporary society, parts two individuals who are fighting or interferes to protect a woman from assault."

Yet in the very same paragraph he proceeds to argue that "the fundamental cause of excesses, which are violations of the rules of social life, is the exploitation of the masses, their poverty and misery. With the removal of this chief cause, excesses will inevitably begin to 'wither away'. We do not know how quickly, but we do know they will wither away. With their withering away, the state also will wither away." [38] Here the complete withering away of the state is equated with the complete disappearance of anti-social actions.

Apparently Lenin regarded communist society with individual excesses as a transitional stage in a development toward communist society without any excesses. But this does not remedy the inconsistencies of his argument. In analyzing the second stage, he asserts that the state withers away to the degree that individual excesses wither away. But in analyzing the first stage, he claims a state is quite unnecessary for dealing with such excesses. In analyzing the second stage, he asserts that after the elimination of exploitation and poverty individual excesses will completely disappear. But in analyzing the first stage, he characterizes this view as utopian and disclaims it. Furthermore, his analysis of the second stage, communist society without excesses, rests on an invalid argument. Granted that exploitation and poverty are the *chief* cause of excesses, it does not follow that they are the only cause. And granted that with elimination of this chief cause the state will *begin* to wither away, it does not follow that this process will ever be completed.

In communist society as Lenin describes it, no legal machinery would be available for dealing with individual excesses in the event that any occurred. According to him, the disappearance of the state is equivalent to the disappearance of all organized public authority. "Only then," he writes of communist society in *The State and Revolution,* "will democracy itself begin to wither away, owing to the simple fact that . . . people will gradually become accustomed to observing the elementary rules of social life—which have been well known for many centuries and reiterated in copy-book maxims for a thousand years—without force, without compulsion, without subordination, without the special apparatus for compulsion which is called the state." Lenin does not restrict himself to asserting that the rules of social life will be observed without being enforced by the special apparatus for compulsion called the state. He asserts that they will be observed without any force and without any compulsion, which is equivalent, under the circumstances, to asserting that there is no place in such a society for organized coercive power of any kind. He asserts further that these rules will be observed without subordination. In Marxian theory, as in ordinary usage, authority involves control by some wills over other wills and presupposes as its counterpart subordination. Lenin's assertion that the rules of social life will be observed without subordination is equivalent, under the circumstances, to asserting that there is no place in such a society for organized public authority of any kind.[39] In this situation it is impossible for the rules of social life to take the form of laws. Where there is no public authority there can be no law.

For Marx and Engels, on the other hand, just as there was a public authority in primitive society before the emergence of the state, so will there be a public authority in communist society after the disappearance of the state. The state is a particular kind of public authority, based on a particular kind of public power. Its withering away does not involve the elimination of all organized coercion, but the replacement of a public power separated from the people by a public power united with the people. Nor does its withering away involve the elimination of all organized authority, but the replacement of a public authority effectively dominated by a ruling class with a public authority actually representing the entire community. Public authority in a fully developed communist society will include elected officials, however few, and a militia, however small.[40] And to the extent that this authority formulates the rules of social life, applies them to particular cases, and enforces compliance upon recalcitrant individuals, these rules will take the form of laws.

Another essay would be required to support in terms of detailed textual evidence this general summary of what Marx and Engels wrote on the withering away of the state. That task must accordingly be postponed. In the present essay I have attempted merely to outline the major differences between Lenin's position and that of Marx and Engels on the definition of law, the characterization of its content, and the question of its future. But even an outline should suffice to show that among Marxian theorists, as among their rivals, the problem of law in primitive society is a key that unlocks many doors.

NOTES

Wherever in the body of this essay I have quoted in English material originally written in German or Russian, responsibility for the translation is mine. Wherever in the following notes I have referred to a work originally written in German or Russian but available in English translation, the paragraph numbers refer both to the English translation and to the original text. Where the two diverge, the first reference is to the translation, and it is followed by a second in parentheses to indicate the corresponding paragraph of the original.

[1] Locke, *Second Treatise of Civil Government,* secs. 4-8, 87-89, 95-110.

[2] Hobbes, *Leviathan,* chap. 13, throughout; chap. 26, throughout.

[3] References are given in Moore, *Critique of Capitalist Democracy,* chap. 1, sec. 1, para. 1.

[4] Engels, *Origin of the Family,* chap. 1, throughout; chap. 9, paras. 14-18.

[5] Lenin, *State and Revolution,* chap. 5, sec. 4, para. 15.

[6] Lenin, *Economic Content of Narodism,* chap. 2, para. 71 (*Russian* 44). Compare Engels, *Origin of the Family,* chap. 5, paras. 22, 9.

[7] Lenin, *The State,* paras. 8, 10.

[8] Engels, *Condition of the Working Class,* chap. 11 (Attitude of the Bourgeoisie), para. 8 (*German* 10).

[9] References are given in Moore, *Critique of Capitalist Democracy*, chap. 1, sec. 1, paras. 4-7.

[10] Marx and Engels, *Die deutsche Ideologie*, part 2, div. 2, sec. 2, subsec. "Aneignung von Verbrechen und Strafe durch Antithese," note 3.

[11] Marx and Engels, *Communist Manifesto*, part 1, para. 1, note to English translation of 1888.

[12] Engels, *Origin of the Family*, chap. 2, sec. 2 (Punuluan Family), para. 6.

[13] Compare with the passage cited in the preceding note, Engels, *Origin of the Family*, chap. 1, sec. 2, div. 3, para. 1.

[14] For the Greeks, Romans, and Germans, references are given in notes 15, 16, and 18 below. For the Iroquois, compare Engels, *Origin of the Family*, chap. 3, paras. 10-11, 24 (*German* 22-23), 26 (*German* 25), 32 (*German* 30), 42 (*German* 40), 45 (*German* 43).

[15] Engels, *The Mark*, para. 20 (*German* 18). See also Engels, *Origin of the Family*, chap. 6, para. 25 (*German* 24). And compare Engels, *Origin of the Family*, chap. 4, para. 23 (*German* 21).

[16] Compare Engels, *Geschichte der Urgermanen*, part 2, sec. 2, para. 14: Engels, *The Mark*, paras. 10 (*German* 8), 15-16 (*German* 13-14), 19-20 (*German* 17-18): Engels, *Origin of the Family*, chap. 4, paras. 1, 5, 7, 9, 14-15, 18, 34 (*German* 29); chap. 5, paras. 3-4; chap. 6, paras. 4, 10, 11, 13, 25 (*German* 24); chap. 7, paras. 2-3, 9 (*German* 6); chap. 9, para. 15.

[17] Engels, *Anti-Dühring*, part 2, chap. 4, para. 13.

[18] Engels, *Origin of the Family*, chap. 6, para. 25 (*German* 24). See also Engels, *Geschichte der Urgermanen*, part 2, sec. 2, para. 14: Engels, *The Mark*, paras. 20-21 (*German* 18-19); Engels, *Origin of the Family*, chap. 4, paras. 23 (*German* 21), 37 (*German* 31); chap. 7, para. 23 (*German* 20). For the absence of courts in less developed societies see Engels, *Origin of the Family*, chap. 3, para. 42 (*German* 40).

[19] Engels, *Origin of the Family*, chap. 4, paras. 29-30 (*German* 27). Compare Engels, *Geschichte der Urgermanen*, part 2, sec. 2, para. 14: Engels, *Origin of the Family*, chap. 3, paras. 5, 27 (*German* 26); chap. 4, paras. 31-37 (*German* 28-31); chap. 6, para. 25 (*German* 24); chap. 7, para. 23 (*German* 20).

[20] Engels, *Origin of the Family*, chap. 9, para. 22. See also the same work, chap. 4, para. 30 (*German* 27); chap. 5, paras. 9, 22; chap. 7, para. 23 (*German* 20). But compare Engels, *The Mark*, para. 21 (*German* 19): Engels, *Origin of the Family*, chap. 3, para. 40 (*German* 38); chap. 5, para. 1.

[21] Engels, *Origin of the Family*, chap. 9, para. 18. Compare Engels, *The Mark*, para. 21 (*German* 19): Engels, *Origin of the Family*, chap. 3, para. 42 (*German* 40); chap. 5, paras. 5-8, 22; chap. 9, paras. 3, 13, 15.

[22] Engels, *Origin of the Family*, chap. 9, para. 24. Compare the same work, chap. 3, para. 45 (*German* 43).

[23] This work, originally written in English and German, has been available to me only in a Russian translation. I shall refer to it as *Konspekt Morgana*, and for each passage cited I shall indicate the relevant passage in Morgan's book.

[24] Morgan, *Ancient Society*, part 2, chap. 1, para. 2; Marx, *Konspekt Morgana*, part 2, chap. 1, para. 1. Compare Engels, *Origin of the Family*, chap. 2, sec. 1 (Consanguine Family), para. 1. But compare further the same works: Morgan, part 3, chap. 5, para. 14; Marx, part 3, chap. 5, para. 8.

[25] Morgan, *Ancient Society*, part 2, chap. 12, para. 26; Marx, *Konspekt Morgana*, part 2, chap. 12, para. 24. Compare Engels, *Origin of the Family*, chap. 6, para. 25 (*German* 24). See also the same works: Morgan, part 2, chap. 10, para. 5;

Marx, part 2, chap. 10, para. 3; Engels, chap. 5, para. 3: Morgan, part 2, chap. 11, point 4 (Obligation not to marry in the gens), para. 1; Marx, part 2, chap. 11, point 4, para. 1; Engels, chap. 6, para. 7: Morgan, part 2, chap. 12, para. 30; Marx, part 2, chap. 12, para. 28: Morgan, part 4, chap. 2, paras. 16, 18-19; Marx, part 4, chap. 2, div. 3, paras. 11, 13-15.

26 Marx, *Konspekt Morgana,* part 2, chap. 9, point 3 (Basilevs), para. 14. Marx does not name the office among the ancient Germans with which he compares that of *basileus* among the Homeric Greeks: both occurences of the term "chief" are my interpolations. These differ from those of the Russian translator, who has interpolated at the first gap "king" and at the second "king or chief of the tribe." In *The Origin of the Family,* chap. 7, paras. 10 (*German* 7), 23 (*German* 20), Engels asserts that "king" in its original sense was synonymous with "chief." But in *The Mark,* para. 21 (*German* 19) he seems to deny this. Since the whole point of the discussion is to contrast the functions of the *basileus* with those of a king in the sense of a monarch, it seems clearer simply to interpolate "chief." Compare Engels, *Origin of the Family,* chap. 4, para. 37 (*German* 31).

Ordinarily, in questions turning upon points of terminology, no translation is a reliable substitute for the original text. In this instance, however, it seems wholly unlikely that the Russian version is inaccurate with respect to the key terms. Compare Aristotle, *Politics,* Book 3, chap. 14; Tacitus, *Germania,* chaps. 11-12; Morgan, *Ancient Society,* part 2, chap. 9, point 3 ("Basileus"), para. 9; Engels, *Origin of the Family,* chap. 7, para. 23 (20).

On the question of courts, see also the same works: Morgan, part 2, chap. 2, point 5 (Reciprocal obligations), para. 3; Marx, part 2, chap. 2, point 5, para. 3: Morgan, part 2, chap. 9, para. 11; Marx, part 2, chap. 9, para. 9; Engels, *Origin of the Family,* chap. 4, para. 23 (*German* 21): Morgan, part 2, chap. 12, paras. 13, 26; Marx, part 2, chap. 12, paras. 12, 24: Engels, *Origin of the Family,* chap. 6, para. 25 (*German* 24).

27 Engels, *Origin of the Family,* chap. 4, paras. 29 (*German* 27), 32 (*German* 28), 36 (*German* 30); Marx, *Konspekt Morgana,* part 2, chap. 9, point 3 (Basilevs), paras. 2, 1, 9. In the latter work the quotation from Schömann precedes the summary of Morgan, *Ancient Society,* part 2, chap. 9, point 3, para. 3; the comment on Gladstone refers to Morgan's footnote to the same paragraph; and the comment on the *Iliad* refers to the succeeding paragraph.

See also the same works: Morgan, part 2, chap. 4, point 7 (Head-chief), para. 1; Marx, part 2, chap. 4, point 7, para. 1; Engels, chap. 3, para. 27 (*German* 26): Morgan, part 2, chap. 5, paras. 21-22, 51; Marx, part 2, chap. 5, paras. 17-18, 51; Engels, chap. 3, paras. 38-39 (*German* 36-37): Morgan, part 2, chap. 9, point 3 (Basileus), para. 9; Marx, part 2, chap. 9, point 3, para. 14; Engels, chap. 4, para. 37 (*German* 31): Morgan, part 2, chap. 12, para. 28; Marx, part 2, chap. 12, para. 26; Engels, chap. 6, para. 25 (*German* 24).

28 Moore, *Critique of Capitalist Democracy,* chap. 1, sec. 8, para. 3.

29 For "support" see the passage from Engels quoted in the second paragraph of this section. For "sanctify" see the quotation from Marx's *Capital* in the section following this section below. For other references see Moore, *Critique of Capitalist Democracy,* chap. 1, sec. 8, note 4. (In that note Marx, *On Nationalization of the Land,* is cited only in Russian translation. The English text can be found in Marx and Engels, *Kleine ökonomische Schriften* [Berlin, 1955].) For further references see Engels, *Condition of the Working Class,* chap. 8 (Labour Movements), paras. 8, 22 (*German* 14).

30 Lenin, *Agrarian Program of Social Democracy,* chap. 4, sec. 1, para. 9 (*Russian* 6).

[31] Lenin, *Caricature of Marxism*, sec. 4, para. 4; Marx and Engels, *Communist Manifesto*, part 2, para. 83 *(German* 85).

[32] References are given in Moore, *Critique of Capitalist Democracy*, chap. 1, sec. 1, paras. 4-5.

[33] Lenin, *State and Revolution*, chap. 5, sec. 3, paras. 19-20. Compare the same work, chap. 5, sec. 4, paras. 6, 15-16; Lenin, *Discussion on Self-Determination*, sec. 1, para. 9 *(Russian* 6).

[34] Marx and Engels, *Communist Manifesto*, part 2, para. 37 *(German* 38). For additional references see Moore, *Critique of Capitalist Democracy*, chap. 1, sec. 8, notes 4-5.

[35] Engels, *Housing Question*, part 3, sec. 2, para. 24.

[36] Marx, *Capital*, Vol. 3, chap. 47, sec. 2, para. 6 *(German* 5).

[37] Marx, *An die Kölner Geschwornen*, para. 14. Compare the other references in Moore, *Critique of Capitalist Democracy*, chap. 1, sec. 8, notes 4-5.

[38] Lenin, *State and Revolution*, chap. 5, sec. 2, para. 23 *(Russian* 21). Compare the same work, chap. 5, sec. 4, paras. 29-30.

[39] Lenin, *State and Revolution*, chap. 5, sec. 2, para. 18 *(Russian* 16); Engels, *Authority*, para. 1. Compare Lenin, *State and Revolution*, chap. 4, sec. 2, para. 6; sec. 6, para. 10: Engels, *Authority*, paras. 2-8.

[40] References are given in Moore, *Critique of Capitalist Democracy*, chap. 1, sec. 8, note 3, para. 4.

REFERENCES

In cases where a work written in German or Russian has been translated into English, both the translation and the original text are cited in the notes; both, accordingly, are identified in this bibliography.

Aristotle. Politics, trans. by Ernest Barker. Oxford, 1948.

Engels, Friedrich. Herr Eugen Dühring's Revolution in Science (Anti-Dühring). (Marxist Library, Vol. 18.) New York, 1939.
German text: Herr Eugen Dühring's Umwälzung der Wissenschaft, in Marx and Engels, *Gesamtausgabe*, Sonderausgabe. Moscow, 1935.

——— On Authority, in Marx and Engels, *Selected Works*, Vol. 1. Moscow, 1950. First published in Italian; original text unavailable to me.

——— The Condition of the Working Class in England in 1844. London, 1950. German text: Die Lage der arbeitenden Klasse in England, in Marx and Engels, *Gesamtausgabe*, Abt. 1, Band 4. Moscow and Leningrad, 1933.

——— The Housing Question. (Marxist Library, Vol. 23.) New York, n.d. German text: Zur Wohnungsfrage, in Marx and Engels, *Ausgewählte Schriften*, Band 1. Berlin, 1951.

——— The Mark, in *Socialism: Utopian and Scientific*. (Marxist Library, Vol. 2.) New York, 1935. German text: Die Mark, in Marx, Engels, Lenin, and Stalin, *Zur deutschen Geschichte*, Band 1. Berlin, 1953.

Engels, Friedrich. The Origin of the Family, Private Property and the State. (Marxist Library, Vol. 22.) New York, 1942. German text: Der Ursprung der Familie, des Privateigentums und des Staats, in Marx and Engels, *Ausgewählte Schriften*, Band 2. Berlin, 1952.

——— Zur Geschichte der Urgermanen II, in Marx, Engels, Lenin, and Stalin, *Zur deutschen Geschichte*, Band 1. Berlin 1953.

662   STANLEY MOORE

Hobbes, Thomas. Leviathan. Oxford, 1929.
Lenin, V. I. A Caricature of Marxism and "Imperialist Economism," in *Collected Works,* Vol. 19. New York, 1942.
    Russian text: O Karikature na Marksizm i ob "Imperialisticheskom Ekonomizme," in *Sochineniya,* Tom 23. USSR, 1952.
———— The Agrarian Program of Social Democracy in the First Russian Revolution, 1905–1907. Chapter 4 in *Selected Works,* Vol. 3. New York, n.d.
    Russian text: Agrarnaya Programma Sotsial-Demokratii v Pervoi Russkoi Revolyutsii 1905–1907 Godov in *Sochineniya,* Tom 13. USSR, 1952.
———— The Discussion on Self-Determination Summed Up, in *Collected Works,* Vol. 19. New York, 1942.
    Russian text: Itogi Diskussii o Samopredelenii, in *Sochineniya,* Tom 22. USSR, 1952.
———— The Economic Content of Narodism and the Criticism of It in Mr. Struve's Book. Chapter 2 in *Selected Works,* Vol. 11. New York, 1943.
    Russian text: Ekonomicheskoe Soderzhanie Narodnichestva i Kritika ego v Knige G. Struve, in *Sochineniya,* Tom 1. USSR, 1951.
Lenin, V. I. The State, in *Selected Works,* Vol. 11. New York, 1943.
    Russian text: O Gosudarstve, in *Sochineniya,* Tom 29. USSR, 1952.
———— The State and Revolution, in *Selected Works,* Vol. 7. New York, n.d.
    Russian text: Gosudarstvo i Revolyutsia, in *Sochineniya,* Tom 25. USSR, 1952.
Locke, John. Second Treatise of Civil Government. New York, 1937.
Marx, Karl. An die Kölner Geschwornen, in *Karl Marx vor den Kölner Geschwornen,* ed. by Engels. Berlin, 1895.
———— Capital, Vol. 3. Chicago, 1909.
    German text: Das Kapital, Volksausgabe, Band 3. Moscow and Leningrad, 1933 and 1934.
———— Konspekt Morgana, in *Arkhiv Marksa i Engel'sa,* Tom 9. USSR, 1941. Original text unavailable to me.
Marx, Karl, and Friedrich Engels. The Communist Manifesto, Centenary Edition. London, 1948.
    German text: Manifest der Kommunistischen Partei, in Marx and Engels, *Ausgewählte Schriften,* Band 1. Berlin, 1951.
———— Die deutsche Ideologie, in Marx and Engels, *Gesamtausgabe,* Abt. 1, Band 5. Moscow and Leningrad, 1933.
Moore, Stanley. The Critique of Capitalist Democracy: An Introduction to the Theory of the State in Marx, Engels, and Lenin. New York, 1957.
Morgan, Lewis H. Ancient Society. Chicago, n.d.
Tacitus. Germania. (Loeb Classical Library.) Cambridge, Mass., 1946.

THE DATA OF LEGAL THEORY

By Huntington Cairns

NATIONAL GALLERY OF ART, WASHINGTON, D.C.

LEGAL THEORY seeks to present an intelligible picture of the world it has selected for study; it attempts to clarify principles of order in terms of a jurisprudential subject matter. That subject matter is composed of data which are sorted out, subjected to examination, and interpreted. Behind all inquiries of this nature, whether in art, science, religion, philosophy, or history, is the impulse of dissatisfaction. Either the data of the world do not fall immediately into a clear pattern or they appear to be inimical. In the first situation, dissatisfaction with the apparent unintelligibility of data leads to the desire to understand the world as it is really constituted; in the cairns, it prompts efforts to improve the order of things. The desire to reach a clear and true idea of the world, and to improve it, are not usually distinct impulses, except perhaps in the higher reaches of inquiry; they are difficult to distinguish in the case of even our most apparently disinterested thinkers. Both impulses seem to be wholly good in the sense that the first leads to knowledge, which is valuable on its own account, and the second to a closer agreement of human institutions with the pattern of the world, without which man's own existence is in danger. But these remarks on dissatisfaction do not cover all the cases. Jeremy Bentham, as much as any man of the law, sought both to understand the legal process and to improve it. But was his dissatisfaction a product of his own thoughts, or was English law in the eighteenth century actually in the condition in which he saw it? To some of his contemporaries the causes of his dissatisfaction lay within himself, and were the result of his own basically wicked nature; Sydney Smith, for example, is reported to have said that Bentham thought people ought to make soup of their dead grandmothers. Legal theory's first task, therefore, in considering the data which constitute its subject matter, is to determine to what extent, if any, the nature of its data is dependent upon the legal theorist's own view of those data.

It seems reasonable to demand, however, that the data of the legal theorist should have an existence outside the legal theorist's mind. The society described in *Erewhon,* as it was imagined and before it was committed to paper, may be said to have existed only in Samuel Butler's mind; it now exists in the minds of all those who have read the book and remember it. But this is not enough to make it a datum in the sense in which science is concerned with data. If Samuel Butler maintained that *Erewhon* had an existence comparable to that of the objects seen through telescopes the traditional position of science would deny it, although philosophy, in some of its aspects, would say that Butler's position is correct. But science (and philosophy, for the most part) has always taken the existence of an external world as an assumption upon which its inquiries might be based, and thus the entertainment of an idea in the mind is not sufficient to give it the existence required of a scientific datum. It seems clear that for science the existence of an object in the external world is not dependent upon a scientist forming a conception of it. If there were no telescopes and the human race were suddenly afflicted with a degree of near-sightedness that made it impossible to see the stars at night, and there were no other clues to their presence, it is an extreme position to argue that the stars would therefore cease to exist. But a datum for science is rarely the exact equivalent of an object in nature; in the scientific process objects are transformed into data to become the material out of which theories are constructed.

It is therefore necessary to distinguish between the objects that exist in the external world and the ideas that are in the mind of the scientist. For legal theory, and scientific method generally, the initial step is to assume that the dissatisfaction that prompts the investigation is due to actual conditions and not alone to notions in the mind of the investigator. The issue here is not whether the investigator is suffering from mental disorder, for it is possible for an insane person to utter the truth. The issue is to what extent, if any, the datum of the scientist takes its character from the mental state of the inquirer. Astronomy is confronted with the circumstance that the planets exhibit slight deviations in their orbits. These perturbations are not anomalies, but are shown by observation to be in accord with astronomical theory. No method has yet been developed, however, of computing the perturbations with complete accuracy. It is assumed in astronomy that there is here an existing external state of affairs which calls for analysis and which can perhaps be straightened out by a study of its incidents, and not by a study of the minds of astronomers. In social thought the case is sometimes otherwise. Sydney Smith at first supported Bentham in his legal reforms and denounced Lord Eldon as a "noodle." When Bentham proposed religious reforms he then, in Smith's eyes, became a noodle, and the situation Bentham described was held to have no existence outside his disordered mind. In the customary processes of science, the dissatisfactions that arise in the minds of scientists are removed by the substitution of a more satisfactory account of an external situation than the one with which the scientists began, or by changing that situation. A pathological condition is sometimes improved or eliminated by the same procedure. In that case the situation that provoked the disturbance is either hallucinatory or has an actual existence, as in the case of Lear's insanity. The fact that treatment of Lear's mind might restore him to health does not eliminate the actuality of the situation that brought him to his state of disorder.

Scientific thinking thus appears to start with reflection on a subject matter whose elements at first sight do not seem to be in proper relation to one another. To the investigator the circumstances do not present a harmonious pattern, and his task is to eliminate the apparently inconsonant, and to discover an organization of data which is intellectually satisfying. There is here an unsolved and perhaps insolvable problem. Why is it that all minds do not react with equal positiveness to the discordant? Our present knowledge of psychic processes is too indefinite to be of help. As the following example shows, one investigator will perceive a problem where others will have no awareness of one:

Once I was returning home from the Salford Sessions, in company with two other constables, when within about three-quarters of a mile of Eccles a man passed us, apparently very respectably dressed. It was rather dark, but I could see that he was carrying something on his head. 'By jingo,' I remarked to the others, 'I believe that fellow has got some stolen property.' 'Oh, no, he has not,' they both joined in saying; 'the man is all right'; and ridiculed my suspicions. I determined, however, to see whether he had or not, so I turned back and ran after him as fast as I could. The moment he heard me he threw away his load and started to run at his utmost speed. I continued the chase for some distance till he suddenly stopped, and putting one arm around a lamp-post, aimed a tremendous blow at my head with the other; but I at once clenched my fist, and in place of receiving his stroke he received a blow from me which felled him to the ground. I took him back to see what he had thrown down and found it was nearly three-quarters of a hundredweight of lead. On searching his pockets I found part of an onion and a knife.

I made inquiries up and down, but could hear nothing of any lead being missing; but as it appeared to be very old lead, it occurred to me to go to Eccles Church and examine the roof. I went there and in the course of inquiries the sexton told me he had made an examination, but there was not a bit of lead missing. Not being satisfied with this statement, I got upon the roof of the church myself, and not only discovered that a large quantity of lead had been stolen, but I also picked up *part of an onion* corresponding with the piece I found in the prisoner's pocket. . . . At the sessions he was sentenced to seven years' penal servitude.[1]

So far as the matter has been investigated this example may be taken as typical. In the presence of the same circumstances the reaction of trained investigators may be different. The history of science is replete with instances of the failure of scientists to recognize problems in the matter under study, which, as later investigators became aware of them, opened fruitful avenues of inquiry.

Since the actual beginnings of scientific inquiry are thus concealed in the neuro-muscular organization of the individual scientist, scientific method as a matter of theory thus takes its departure from a problem.[2] Its starting point is not an assumed principle or hypothesis, inasmuch as principles of this kind are involved as working devices to aid in the answering of problems; a principle is logically subsequent to the perception of the problem. Neither is the starting point of science the "facts," since it is precisely the task of science to discover the "facts" that are relevant to the problem. The native guide on a high Andean plateau explains that the potatoes will not cook because of the fact that "the cursed pot," no doubt inhabited by a devil, "does not wish to cook potatoes"; the scientific traveler answers the problem in terms of the dependence of the boiling point upon pressure.[3] In law (to take a problem the solution of which is still in dispute), are the rules formulated in the M'Naghten case[4] with respect to a defense on the ground of insanity in criminal proceedings sound ones? A recent analysis from the legal point of view concludes that the rules are basically adequate for the purposes of the law, although the weight of psychiatric opinion is otherwise.[5] It is apparent from the more than hundred year's discussion of this problem that there are no simple brute facts to which it is possible to turn for an answer. It is also clear that if any "facts" are ultimately agreed upon as controlling they will be highly complex affairs containing a large admixture of theory.

In short, the problem—that is, the challenge presented to the in-inferences from data which are obviously given to a realm which is the point of beginning. As Leibniz observed, physical phenomena stimulate us to discover more than physical phenomena can in them-selves tell us.

We are thus led to the two principal problems which here confront the legal theorist: (a) how does he get before him the data which are related to his problems? and, (b) what is the significance of the data? Theories of scientific method, which customarily take as their model the practices of the natural sciences, treat the task of obtaining data as a matter of perception. This method of getting data is also utilized by the legal theorist, but to a limited extent; other methods are more commonly employed, and their reliability stands in need of appraisal. The problem of the significance of the data raises the problem of "reality." To what extent have the data employed by the legal theorist a "reality" of their own, and to what extent, if any, are their charac-teristics the product of the mind of the legal theorist? For example, does a corporation have an existential status, or is it solely a concept in the minds of lawyers and others? There is a further point of view which must also be considered. Contemporary philosophy of science associates the problem of the nature of reality with the legitimacy of inferences from data which are obviously given to a realm which is necessary in order to make the data intelligible.[6] Most data, even the obviously given, must in order to possess meaning be taken from the world of sense impressions and be transferred to another realm. Sense impressions tell us that a man is seated clothed in a gown on a chair in a room. That is the obviously given datum; but the important datum is that the man is a judge, or a priest, or a king, or some other object from which legal speculation may take its departure. Now the central point, in the view of the current philosophy of science, is not that legal speculation knows that a man in a gown is seated in a room, not even that it knows that the man is a judge, or a priest, or a king, but the significant aspect is *how* it knows that the man is one of those legal objects. This emphasis on our ways of knowing, rather than on what we know, may be an expression of the Alexandrianism of our age; even so, this does not eliminate the problem, and it must be met. Let us assume that we ask ourselves the not unreasonable question:

Is the state the source of law? There are six possible methods, taken singly or in combination, by which we can approach the problem. We can consult the views of those who are presumed to know something about the question, which is the method of authority. We can appeal to our own intuition, the method of mysticism. We can, on the basis of certain assumed premises, attempt to work out the answer logically, the method of rationalism. We can consult our own sensory experience, as by watching legislatures in action, the method of empiricism. We can consider whether the consequences of holding such a belief are beneficial or harmful, the method of pragmatism. Finally, we can adopt the negative position that the problem is insolvable, the method of scepticism.[7]

As a source of knowledge, we turn to the testimony of others because it represents the views of persons who have exhibited mastery of a subject, i.e., who are "experts," or because their testimony is the only possible basis of knowledge, as in the case of much of Livy's writings, and of Gregory of Tours' history of the Franks. However, the justification for reliance upon the opinion of experts it at bottom pragmatic. Either we must postulate the infallibility of expert opinion—a clear impossibility—or we must find its defense in its convenience and practicality. No one has exhibited more faith than Plato in the principle that we should commit to others that which they know how to do, and which we do not know; but in the *Charmides*, where the principle is directly challenged, Socrates concedes that there would be no great benefit to society if it were followed. Nevertheless, it is plain that the arguments of convenience and practicality are not without force. In the first place, in view of the brevity of life, we cannot personally examine into the validity of every item of information that is offered us; and in principle, unless we have cause for rational doubt there is no reason why we should. In the second place, inquiry starts from the already known. What is accepted as truth, it has been pointed out, is of immense importance; inquiry could not proceed a step without it.[8] If every new investigator were forced to reestablish the validity of all the propositions which previous workers in his field had put beyond reasonable doubt, he would never be in a position to begin his own inquiry. Authority is thus a valuable repository of knowledge, but at the same time, since it may be a source of error, it is always open to scrutiny. Peirce[9] once observed that to follow the method of authority

is to follow the path of peace, but that the greatest intellectual benefactors of mankind have never dared to utter the whole of their thought.
This suggestion might be difficult to sustain as a matter of proof, but
it is true that the great teachers of the world have usually professed
two doctrines, one for the public and a secret one for the initiated. To
this extent the observation is accurate, hence a shade of *prima facie*
doubt is cast upon every proposition which is considered essential to
the security of society.

In any legal system the appeal to authority serves at least two
functions. First, it may be simply an effort to ascertain knowledge.
We may want to know if a certain rule of law obtained in England in
the thirteenth century and we find in Bracton the only testimony that
it did. We may accept Bracton's statement as true, we may reject it as
false, we may regard it as partly true and partly false, or as indeterminate. The final estimate of Bracton's assertion must turn on the critical
methods which historical scholarship is able to bring to bear upon it.
It is equally arbitrary to reject him out of hand, as was done from the
fifteenth to the seventeenth century, as it is to accept him blindly under
the impulse of an historicism which overvalues the prestige of ancient
texts. Critical history weighs all the available evidence, from the trust-
worthiness of Bracton as a whole and in detail to the conditions which
surrounded the production of his book, and on the basis of such
factors, determines the degree of belief to accord him. The various
attempts of the courts to improve upon this approach have not proved
workable in practice. The rules that writers who had not held judicial
positions could not be cited as authorities, that only the works of dead
authors could be cited, that legislative debates could not be consulted
to determine the meaning of a statute, have all had to be abandoned
or drastically modified as they were gradually tested in the judicial
process. In its historical aspect legal scholarship is faced with the same
problems and employs the same methods as history generally.

In its other function authority serves as one of the sustaining elements of the legal system. From this point of view jurists have not
infrequently taken the position it is sometimes more important that
authority maintain the prestige of the law than that it be right. This
is a hard doctrine, and it has been frequently abused; however, it
contains an element of truth. Since legislators, including judges, are
not omniscient and cannot foresee the operations of their rules in all

the instances in which they will be applied, the probabilities are that injustices will result in the enforcement of rules in some cases. Properly to amend a rule may require the same degree of omniscience that was necessary to make it a just one at the time of its original promulgation. But since this prerequisite cannot always be satisfied, amendments should be postponed until experience with the application of the rule has disclosed what fallible legislators cannot foresee. A continued tinkering with a system of law to meet every apparent case of injustice promotes an instability that may be more injurious to the life of the community than the allowance of some cases of hardship. This in substance seems to be the thought behind Plato's[10] suggestion that only old men, ripe with experience, should be allowed to suggest amendments to laws; Aristotle's[11] argument that a readiness to change from existing to new and different laws will tend to weaken the general power of law; Maine's[12] belief that no durable system of jurisprudence can be produced if it is continually modified to suit transient notions of morality; and Holmes's[13] assertion that "weak cases must fall within any law which is couched in general words." The substance of truth in these contentions does not, however, amount to an endorsement of the scholium that it is better to trust Aristarchus rather than Hermappias even when the latter seems to be speaking the truth.[14] Courts[15] which insist upon following admittedly unsound precedents, when the element of legal stability is not materially involved, promote neither certainty nor a settled jurisprudence. They advance, on the contrary, such phenomenon as the free-law movement of Ehrlich and Isay, and no doubt, in the end, even a completely discretionary jurisprudence.

But the lawyers of the Middle Ages went even further and associated authority with the principle of justice. The warrant of authority is to maintain justice, not injustice. The authority of the lady or lord, say the Assizes of the Court of Burgesses of Jerusalem, is only an authority to do law or justice, they have no authority to behave unjustly.[16] This great principle had its roots in the antecedent Roman and Canon law, and was developed for English law by Bracton.[17] It represents the furthest point to which legal thought has carried the idea of authority. It is the whole purpose of the medieval legal analysis to show that authority itself is not a final arbiter. The king's authority, Bracton argues, rests on the fact that he governs well, not that he reigns. Authority serves many ends that are desirable and necessary, but the data it furnishes are always subject to independent scrutiny.

There is a conviction in Aristotle[18] that the authoritative insight of the expert is grounded in intuition. This view has its counterpart in the claim advanced on behalf of the mystical experience that it affords an insight into the nature of things which ordinary human experience and reason cannot attain. It is also a view which is not unknown to legal speculation. In both the Hellenistic and Classical periods of Roman law the doctrine was accepted that an eminent man, experienced in political and legal affairs, possessed an intuitive perception of law if he had devoted his mind seriously and conscientiously to the subject.[19] In contemporary theory we have the authority of Holmes that "general propositions do not decide concrete cases. The decision will depend on a judgment or intuition more subtle than any articulate major premise."[20] We have also the carefully worked out conclusion of Cardozo that the judge's insights are "not unlike the derivatives of the scientist. His experiments must be made significant by the flash of a luminous hypothesis."[21] Empirical psychology has little to tell us of the nature of the process by which intellectual vision discovers the great hypotheses and forms which have proved important in the departments of knowledge. We need not therefore be concerned with that aspect of intuition. But the idea of intuition as a source of knowledge raises the question of epistemological order. A basic distinction between jurisprudence and legal theory turns on the nature of the answer given to that problem.

Scientific theory now devotes itself in large part to an attempted reconciliation, or marriage, of empiricism and intuitionalism. If scientific theory takes empiricism as its starting point it quickly finds itself in an epistemological morass from which no exit has yet been discovered. We are even told we should be doubtful that it is a real policeman who directs us at the entrance to a museum to an interesting part of the exhibition. It is certainly clear that a lifelike wax policeman with a gramophone inside him could perform this task. However, we are entitled to say, "There is a noise making *polizoid* patch of color" and on the basis of this proposition, although it is still open to some doubt, since the experience may be occurring in a dream, we may endeavor to arrive at further knowledge.[22] On the other hand intuitionalism yields us sets of premises as starting points which may appear self-evidently true but which are impossible to verify. In the calculus of propositions rules have been developed to assist in the framing of premises—the premises must be consistent, they must be independent, they must yield completeness, and so on—but these rules have nothing to do with the truth or falsity of the premises. Again, in metaphysics intuition may tell us that the bedrock of perfect certitude is the realm of essence[23] but this insight is also, like that on which the premises of mathematical logic are constructed, a matter of faith. Still, these mathematical and metaphysical premises have resulted in great systems of thought which constitute part of our most precious store of knowledge. Inasmuch as empiricism also has enormous successes to its credit, and since it is less open than intuitionalism to the charge of inconsistency, there is now an effort to bring the two methods together. The problem is to relate the intuitively given premises, which Aristotle long ago saw were the starting points of knowledge,[24] but which are apt to yield only the most rarefied results, to the occasions of the empirical world. If that aim were achieved the sole ground for acceptance of the premises would not be merely a matter of faith.[25] Nineteenth-century empiricism managed to approach this problem backwards. Thus Mill[26] argued that "all numbers must be numbers of something: there are no such things as numbers in the abstract. *Ten* must mean ten bodies, or ten sounds, or ten beatings of the pulse." On this theory he was able to arrive at the erroneous conclusion that the premises of mathematics are generalizations from experience. Our premises are principles of possibility, and their validity is independent of any exemplification in actuality.

Meanwhile, with the relationship between intuition and empiricism still to be worked out, legal theory must take intuition as one of its starting points. It does this not in the mystical sense of a direct awareness of truth transcending both reason and sensory perception. Legal theory's intuitional starting point amounts to no more than the effort to formulate a set of premises which will guide an inquiry into the nature and character of law. These premises are hypotheses which are subject to all possible modes of verification. They are not deductions from particulars in any strict logical sense, nor are they self-evident; they possess, however, an initial credibility that persuades us to risk following out their loose implications. They are not applied with logical rigor, but as a framework within which to operate on a particular subject matter. How they arise it is impossible to say; they are the sudden insights that come to workers in all intellectual fields. Their final worth is their power to lead us to the proper ordering of legal relations, to the verification of those relations and to the discovery of their meaning.

All this is exemplified by the notable legal systems of the past, whether jurisprudential or juridical. Austin's premise is that the matter of jurisprudence is positive law, that is, law set by political superiors to political inferiors. This is one of the most pregnant insights in the history of jurisprudence, and its ramifications, as Kelsen has shown, are still far from their full development. But from all that appears in Austin's work it is an immediate apprehension; logically it is also a beginning *in medias res* with a vengeance. Neither of these characteristics is open to criticism on methodological grounds. Great hypotheses, as the history of science abundantly shows, are frequently unaccountable except on an intuitional basis; and since scientific inquiry is not omniscient it has never had an absolutely determinable starting point. Again, Marshall developed the powerful hypothesis that the Constitution is an ordinance of the people of the United States, and not a compact of states. It was an intuitional insight, impossible of empirical justification, but it gave Marshall's opinions the force and unity they possess.

In this context the initial focus of legal theory, as distinguished from jurisprudence, is upon the matrix in which law functions rather than upon law itself. It is an endeavor to discover the notions which underlie the legal order and in terms of which its ultimate explanation resides. Jurisprudence isolates and analyzes the operative concepts of legal systems; it seeks to bring them into a rational arrangement, it evaluates them, and it exhibits some of their implications; it tries to be deductive. The problems of legal theory arise before deduction is possible. They move in an amorphous realm aiming at the capture of elements which, when fitted into a structure, will tell us some of the secrets of law. The detection of those elements in the first instance is primarily a matter of intuition.

A third method of obtaining data is through deduction from a set of assumed propositions. The great impulse which the speculations of Descartes, Spinoza, and Leibniz gave to this approach made its inevitable impression upon legal thinking. In jurisprudential thought the method was developed with varying degrees of rigor, but the Anglo-

American courts for the most part applied it loosely and with no apparent awareness of the objections to the method disclosed by subsequent analysis. A classical account from the nineteenth century of the juristic attitude towards the method is given by Chief Justice Shaw in *Norway Plains Co.* v. *Boston and Maine RR.*:[27]

It is one of the great merits and advantages of the common law, that, instead of a series of detailed practical rules, established by positive provisions, and adapted to the precise circumstances of particular cases, which would become obsolete and fail, when the practice and course of business, to which they apply, should cease or change, the common law consists of a few broad and comprehensive principles, founded on reason, natural justice, and enlightened public policy, modified and adapted to the circumstances of all the particular cases which fall within it. These general principles of equity and policy are rendered precise, specific and adapted to practical use, by usage, which is the proof of their general fitness and common convenience, but still more by judicial exposition; so that, when in a course of judicial proceeding, by tribunals of the highest authority, the general rule has been modified, limited and applied, according to particular cases, such judicial exposition, when well settled and acquiesced in, becomes itself a precedent, and forms a rule of law for future cases, under like circumstances. The effect of this expansive and comprehensive character of the common law is, that whilst it has its foundations in the principles of equity, natural justice, and that general convenience which is public policy; although these general considerations would be too vague and uncertain for practical purposes, in the various and complicated cases, of daily occurrence, in the business of an active community; yet the rules of the common law, so far as cases have arisen and practices actually grown up, are rendered, in a good degree, precise and certain, for practical purposes, by usage and judicial precedent. Another consequence of this expansive character of the common law is, that when new practices spring up, new combinations of facts arise, and cases are presented for which there is no precedent in judicial decision, they must be governed by the general principle, applicable to cases most nearly analogous, but modified and adapted to new circumstances, by considerations of fitness and propriety, of reason and justice, which grow out of those circumstances. The consequence of this state of the law is, that when a new practice or new course of business arises, the rights and duties of parties are not without a law to govern them; the general considerations of reason, justice and policy, which underlie the particular rules of the common law, will still apply, modified and adapted, by the same considerations, to the new circumstances.

In this case the court passed upon the liability of a railroad for the destruction of goods by fire in its depot. The goods had been carried by the Railroad from Rochester to Boston and were in the terminal awaiting delivery to the consignee. As its premise the court assumed the general principle that the Railroad as a common carrier was liable, with exceptions irrelevant in the present case, for losses occurring to goods during transit. But, the court reasoned the transit in this instance had terminated and there was no liability, since a railroad's line of movement and point of termination are fixed. The case of goods transported by wagons would be otherwise inasmuch as the goods could be delivered at the house of the consignee.

However, the reasoning in this case is analogical rather than deductive. The result is reached, not as a deduction from a premise, but on the basis of a nominal definition of "termination of transit" arrived at through an analysis of the rules with respect to wagons and vessels. This is recognized in the leading case to the contrary which held that transit was not terminated by delivery to the depot, but persisted until the consignee had a reasonable time to remove the goods.[28]

This kind of rationalism in the law led in the end to what was denounced in the early years of this century as mechanical jurisprudence. This approach conceives of knowledge as a set of first principles, often *a priori* in nature, and known intuitively. It believes, on the model of mathematics, that from these principles rules can be deduced which will correctly dispose of legal issues. There is no doubt that the method as rigidly applied by many courts and textbook writers led to highly undesirable results, as in the failure to adapt the law of master and servant to the demands of an industrial society. Jhering and Pound were the leaders of the revolt against this approach and urged the salutary corrective that a preliminary question should always be, how will a rule or a decision operate in practice?

In truth, the rationalist method has severe limitations for a subject such as law, which should be more concerned with what goes on in the external world than with the relations of propositions. If the premises are set up carefully enough, deduction can tell us that the transit of goods on a railroad ends when they are unloaded from the freight car. But from the point of view of the liability which should be imposed upon a newly developed form of transportation for the loss of goods before delivery to the consignee, the conclusion may be completely at variance with sound trade practices. As a method of arriving at new knowledge, logic in its severe sense is ill-adapted to the empirical necessities of law. In order to rise above nominal definitions rationalism in the juridical and jurisprudential processes must take account of so many elements, that the achievement of rigor is almost an impossibility. The employment of the method can lead the courts to new knowledge in the sense that it guides them to positions which they have not heretofore taken. However, the method in such cases amounts to no more than a resolution to use words in a new way to express an idea known to the court before the deduction is initiated. The conclusion reached by the court is thus not comparable to a theorem in algebra reached by a long chain of reasoning from a few postulates. At the end of such a calculation the mathematician is in possession of knowledge heretofore unknown to him. It is the essence of rationalism in the legal process that the writer of a judicial opinion seldom finds himself in this situation.

Nevertheless, neither legal theory, jurisprudence, nor the judicial process can dispense with the method of rationalism. It provides one of the starting points of all inquiry, both pure and empirical. It furnishes some of the hypotheses on which investigations of the legal order are founded; they assist in bringing what is the case into some kind of organization. In an empirical science such as law the hypotheses are related to what goes on in the world; mathematical postulates may not refer to objective existence. The hypotheses of legal theory are plausible assumptions not at variance by immediate inspection with what is known of the facts. They are not self-evidently true in the sense that they may not be questioned; they are credible, but the possibility must always be allowed that they may be shown to be invalid. Sometimes the assumptions are of such a nature that it is only with great difficulty that satisfactory tests can be devised to determine their validity or invalidity. Thus Gény assumes a realm of objective truth, and a second realm open to juristic modification to the extent it does not run counter to the first realm. He postulates further that law-making must take account of such factors as geography, climate, the human personality, tradition, general beliefs, and religious and ethical ideals. Gény chose to base these hypotheses on an intuitive religious sanction, but they possess a sufficient empirical plausibility to regard them as methodologic postulates worth developing. In Gény's hands they led to some important insights with respect to the judicial process, but they did not generate a system that found any general acceptance. Empirical hypotheses are anticipations of the way the legal order functions, and the measure of their validity is their correspondence with that situation.

A fourth method of obtaining knowledge is through observation of the external world and of ourselves. In the modern analyses of scientific method no other doctrine has received greater attention, but so far it has proved impossible to make it completely intelligible. It seems to be true in some sense, though that sense can be stated precisely only with the greatest difficulty. If the doctrine is stated with technical exactitude in the form "All synthetic knowledge is based on experience" the idea gains in clarity but the multitude of problems remains undiminished.[29] In this latter form the doctrine is a universal proposition which cannot be verified by experience; thus if the doctrine is true it cannot be known, hence it is either false or unknowable.[30] But the more serious difficulty arises when we attempt to pass on the basis of experience from the known to the unknown. All empirical sciences begin with this simple type of generalization. We observe, for example, a number of societies and find that all of them possess legal systems. We then infer that all societies have legal systems. Even Bacon observed that "the induction which proceeds by simple enumeration is childish; its conclusions are precarious, and exposed to peril from a contradictory instance."[31] Nevertheless, this naive method is in practice a starting point of science and, however logically unsound, has led in countless instances to valuable generalizations. Simple enumeration as a method justifies itself through its power of being able to suggest generalizations that may be fruitful, but which must be validated by other means. However, simple enumeration marks the beginning of the real difficulty. A subject matter which has passed beyond the rudimentary stage, such as law, and has become organized exhibits the characteristics of a system. Many facts have been determined and many propositions have been established. Taking all that we know today about the elements necessary to constitute a society, we might make the inference that the existence of a society is impossible without some form of a legal system. This would not be a case of simple enumeration but an inference from the conditions of the system. If the system is an empirical construction, the problem here is to show that the particulars are related in such a way that inferences from one set to another are possible. This in turn necessitates a set of causal principles as grounds for such inferences, but experience by itself is not able to furnish them.

Although the logical difficulties that stand in the way of a justification of empiricism have not been overcome, it would be difficult to deny that the method is an immensely valuable one. But it is more than that. Coleridge, however inaccurate his summary of the two philosophies may be, was feeling for an important distinction when he observed that men are born either Platonists or Aristotelians. The true antithesis is between rationalism, in the form which takes the law of contradiction as its starting point, and all other philosophies; but the assumptions of empiricism raise the issue in an acute manner. That issue has two aspects: (a) are universals real? and (b) are the laws of nature necessary or contingent? The character of any theory of law, the domain that it will mark out for study, the problems it will consider, the answers it will find, will all be determined by the attitude taken at the outset towards those questions. The history of thought, including juristic thought, is the record of the effort to grapple with those issues. At one extreme is the opinion that the world consists of nothing but particulars and the scientific laws are shorthand expressions or fictions; at the other, that only universals are real and that the universe exhibits no contingency. In between are many compromises. Empiricism assumes that the world is disorderly; rationalism that it is orderly. One of the perplexities of the history of science is that the two methods working in combination, but basically irreconcilable at their extremes, have yielded the bulk of mankind's established knowledge.

Finally, there is the method of pragmatism which advises us that a source of knowledge is to be found in the consequences of our beliefs. If we take this proposition at its face value, it is innocent enough. Only when it is developed into systems of metaphysics and epistemology are we faced with the issues which have produced the loud battle cries and logic chopping which have marked its advance. If we recognize that it is totally inadequate as a system of metaphysics, or as a substitute for metaphysics, that as a theory of truth the difficulties that lie in its path seem insuperable, we may deprive the doctrine of much of its claim of eminence, but we are, at the same time, preserving something of value. To know the practical consequences of a theory is the least interesting thing about it philosophically; disinterested understanding is the supreme philosophical ideal. But in the jural world practical consequences cannot be ignored. Men do not act in a vacuum but for a purpose. To inquire into the purpose, to ask whether the action is likely to bring it about and whether it is desirable, is an inescapable task of legal study.

Legal theory is occupied not only with the natural order of events of the legal order but with the ends of that order. An analysis of those ends and of the most efficient means of reaching them cannot fail to disclose matters to us of which we would not be aware if we passed them over. One method of bringing those ends before us is to apply the pragmatic principle of clarifying propositions by working out their implications. The meaning of Euclid's definitions, postulates, and axioms is made evident by the statement of their consequences. That procedure does not establish their truth but only their meaning. Similarly the meaning of the Commerce Clause in the United States Constitution is to be found in the application by the Courts of the proposition it embodies to the numerous instances in which they have applied it. There is no implication in this principle that the applications are necessarily correct ones.[32] Even as thus limited pragmatism is closely associated with rationalism, empiricism and theology. It differs from the first two in that it is a theory of meaning rather than a method of arriving at truth, although as we have seen it must also be considered as a way of reaching new sources of information. Since it has a deep concern with consequences it stresses the teleological character of legal action. The desirability of this approach has been made evident by the contributions since the turn of the century of the sociological and realist schools of jurisprudence.

On these five sources—testimony, intuition, reason, sense-perception, and practice—rests all that we label "knowledge." They are rarely pursued singly in any inquiry, but in various combinations.[33] Since it is inescapable that all human knowledge springs from these sources, it is apparent that knowledge is at bottom scarcely more than a surmise. "All human knowledge," Russell[34] concludes at the end of the most severe analysis of the problem attempted in modern times, "is uncertain, inexact, and partial." This state of affairs was understood by ancient Greek thought and generated the movement known as scepticism. But absolute scepticism must either be arbitrary or be silent. If the sceptic makes an assertion other than an arbitrary one he is presupposing that the assertion is open to examination within the framework of the three so-called laws of thought. If he denies that he is making that assumption, then the contradictory of his assertion is equally valid, and it is impossible to continue the discussion except on the basis that all propositions are true (or false) including their opposites. However, systematic doubt, which assumes the validity of the laws of logic is a fruitful method of science. In mathematics the classical case is the construction of the non-Euclidean geometrics of Lobachevski and Riemann based on the doubt of the validity of Euclid's parallel postulate.[35] The same method, though far less rigorous, operates in the legal field. On the basis of the most carefully considered premises, and through a most exact analysis, Aquinas reached the view that law is an ordinance of reason. This position was sustained by one of the most powerful philosophies the world has known. Yet there have been many alternative conceptions of law, some of them leading to new insights. None of the conceptions, anymore than the Euclidean premises, may represent absolute truth, since they are founded ultimately on the shaky paths to knowledge open to man. But many of them supplement one another and contribute to the systematic growth of legal thought.

Closely associated with the act of getting data through the methods considered above is the problem of the rôle of the mind in that process. In general there are four positions with respect to this problem: (a) we can assume that physical objects have no existence apart from human perception; (b) we can assume that the physical object exists exactly as we perceive it; (c) we can assume that we have immediate perception of physical objects but that our interpretation is erroneous; (d) we can assume that we do not perceive the physical object itself but a mental representation of it caused by the object setting in motion sensory impulses. Grave difficulties stand in the way of the acceptance of any of these theories, and although logic is drawn upon heavily in current discussions, the problem at its roots seems to be a psychological one. At all events its analysis today is carried on largely in terms of speculative psychology. It is also apparent that psychology in this field has little to offer in the way of an accurate description of the mind's processes that could serve as a foundation for the establishment of the validity of the laws of physics. We can only tell how the mind works through an examination of the product, and whatever we may believe about the operation of the mind it cannot be introduced as a principle of physical explanation since it is not a principle of determination.³⁶ Legal theory and philosophy generally occupy the same position with respect to the epistemological problem: Both subjects must await the establishment of more information than exists at present before there is any hope of solution.

If there is little hope at present of solving the epistemological issue through the methods of literary psychology now in vogue, the problem of the validity of what we think we know still remains. To what extent may we rely upon the data furnished us by testimony, intuition, reason, sense-perception and practice? Now the datum does not record itself mechanically. A human mind for the purposes of science has to be aware of data in the first place, and in the second it must record them for communication. That process, as epistemology has shown, is an extremely fallible one. But it does not follow from this that data are personal. The Protagorean principle "man is the measure of all things" clearly does not hold for the laws of physics. What does hold is the principle that human beings vary appreciably in their abilities to estimate what is the case, and the causes for this are both inherent and environmental. Not everyone can follow a musical theme, not everyone can follow a mathematical argument; the temper of Galileo's time was such that his opponents refused even to look at Jupiter's satellites through his telescope on the ground that they could not credit their senses. But scientific method has many self-corrective devices which seem to have resulted in a view of the world which possesses a high degree of certainty. That view falls far short of the ideal of certainty entertained by current epistemology, but it has sufficient measure to at least suggest that we ought not to throw up all scientific inquiry in despair. We should recognize that the getting of data, their statement, their interpretation and their evaluation are all operations strewn with pitfalls, but also that there are many corrective aids available to help in that enterprise. We may admit that human limitation is a factor in scientific method, but not that the data because of that are personal and private, or that science's account of the world itself has the same characteristics. No reason suggests itself why science should not continue its inquiries on its present insecure formulations and with its logically uncertain methods while it watches for the dawn of an epistemologically sounder day.

When we are satisfied that we have achieved the data for which we

are looking, we put them in propositional form. That is to say, we give
utterance to an expression which we believe, or doubt, or deny, or take
other attitudes toward, e.g., "it is true that law is a command," "it is
doubtful that statutes are not law but only sources of the law," "it is
false that only the legislature makes law." In formal logic the theory
of propositions is far from settled, but for the present purposes we
need to go into the matter no further than to distinguish the proposition from the sentence, from the fact, and from the judgment.[37] We
can write either "omnia mutantur, nos et mutamur in illis" or "all
things are changing and we are changing with them." In both cases
the proposition is the same but the sentences are different. When we
say "it is true that law is a command" we believe what the sentence
means, and the use of the adjective is in reference to that meaning, not
to the words of the sentence or its grammatical form. Similarly, facts
are not true or false or doubtful; they simply are or are not. A judgment is the act of accepting a proposition as true or false, and it may
be correct or mistaken.

Propositions are judged true or false by their relationship to other
propositions. Legal theory formulates its propositions on the basis of
data furnished by any or all of the five methods discussed above, and
any such proposition, by whatever method it may have been reached,
may be measured against other propositions arrived at by the same or
different methods. If legal theory were a strict rationalist system this
would not be legitimate; a rationalist system would find the criteria of
the truth of its propositions in their coherence with other propositions
of the same system. But since legal theory is not confined to any
method in the construction of its propositions, it may consider their
degree of coherence with other propositions which it has warrant to
believe are valid. Thus the proposition "law is a command" is in
accord with many other propositions the validity of which we have no
reason to doubt. But its meaning also is in conflict with other propositions the truth of which we think is well established, e.g., "historically law is prior to the state," "many laws are obeyed because of the
hope of reward." Since Austin was attempting to construct a system
on quasi-rationalist lines he was free to regard the two latter propositions as false or otherwise account for them in relation to his aims.
But legal theory cannot assume this attitude. It is as much occupied
with the material truth of its propositions as with their strictly logical

implications. In short, for an inquiry such as legal theory there is no single criterion of truth, neither correspondence nor coherence, nor the pragmatic. It must test its propositions by all the means which carry the warrant of conviction.

The valid propositions of legal theory refer to an external state of affairs; that is to say, their reality it not purely mental. Hobbes's belief that truth is solely a matter of combinations of words has its counterpart in the contemporary legal doctrine that rules of law exist only in the minds of those who think them. But nearly all the words in the dictionary are universal and we use them presumably because they refer to something in the world. If universals were not real, scientific laws would have no application. When we say that "the historical school," "the positive school," "the sociological school," and "the philosophical school" all constitute "schools of jurisprudence" we are asserting that they have something in common, namely, that they are all occupied with the construction of general theories about law. If the proposition "schools of jurisprudence occupy themselves with the construction of general theories about law" is not actually the case, if it is only an idea in somebody's mind, then it is idle to examine the works of Maine, Austin, Pound, and Hegel to ascertain if they have constructed general theories about law. Similarly, the proposition "penal statutes should be strictly construed" refers to a class of objects —penal statutes—which possesses a real likeness; if it did not the rule would be meaningless. It is true that the rule finds its application in individual discussions, but it does not follow that the class of penal statutes is therefore nonexistent, or that the rule is merely a matter of language. Propositions and rules of law are formulated in words, but the components of valid propositions and rules are objective universals.

For legal theory the propositions that will be formulated will be of five different kinds:

Propositions concerned with particulars. These are the propositions that make assertions with respect to the single instances of the legal order, e.g., "Abrams v. U.S. was decided by the U.S. Supreme Court on November 10, 1919"; "*A* shot *B*."

Propositions which combine the particulars into wholes. These propositions emphasize the pattern into which the single instances may be combined, or the pattern of a single instance itself from the point of view of its legal significance. "*A* shot *B*" is the single instance, and it may or may not have legal meaning. But if a pattern is added the instance at once becomes a matter of legal concern: "*A*, a burglar, shot *B*, a householder, while in the act of robbing *B*'s house." The pattern consists of the circumstances which transform the particular into a legal object. The rules and definitions of the legal order represent an effort to state abstractly the patterns to which legal consequences attach. Thus it may be asserted: "Anyone who causes the death of another in the commission of a felony, whether accidentally or not, is guilty of murder." *A*, who is taking money from *B* at the point of a gun but who accidentally trips him and causes him to fall to his death is guilty of murder; *D*, who is taking money from *E*, but in a friendly way as a bill collector, and who trips *E* under similar circumstances, is not guilty of murder. The significance of this class of propositions is that it is applicable to situations which are repetitive in their general outline.

Propositions which refer to the persistent elements of the legal order. The rules and definitions of legal systems, the patterns which are meaningful, change from time to time. At one period an accidental death brought about during the commission of a felony is murder, at another it is not. But the proposition "All legal systems possess sanctions for homicide" is true of all known systems past and present. What these propositions gain in generality they lose in precision. The specific rules of the various systems of law contradict one another, and thus it is impossible to state a rule of homicide applicable at all times and everywhere. However, we do know that the killing of a human being by a human being is taken cognizance of by all systems, although the significant patterns are variable.

Propositions which assert relations of invariance. The laws of physics are the great prototype of this class, but to what extent there are comparable social laws, if any, we need not here stop to inquire. If there are any they would fall into this group.

Propositions which assert possibility. These are the propositions which refer to the hypothetical and to what ought to be, e.g., "if the American courts adopted the method of British criminal procedure, then more criminals would be brought to justice"; "the American legal system should have a ministry of justice."

These are the kinds of propositions legal theory will generate, and they are classified in this manner in order to achieve the widest generality. At bottom, it is a metaphysical classification and not one constructed from the special facts of historical systems of law. Our existing schemes of jurisprudence follow the latter course; but since material systems of law contradict one another, their classifications are forced and provide points of departure for analysis that yield nothing more than discussions of comparisons and differences. The traditional sociological classifications have the same limitations. If we start for example with the idea of the family, we run at once into the fact that the Roman and common law conceptions are entirely different, and the construction of even a subclassification with significant points of similarity is impossible. We stand in need of a classification that avoids these defects and that also points the way toward the development of a scientific system, that is, one in which the propositions are connected by principles rather than by historical events. No doubt it is difficult to construct a system in the social field that will compare favorably with the achievements of physical systems. Legal theory is concerned with human nature, the life of man in society, and the elements of the social process. Law itself is a means, and its end for man is the good life. Whether the multitudinous factors which make up this total picture, together with their many unforeseeable combinations, can be caught in any meaningful sense within the net of language is certainly more than doubtful. But the goal of scientific theory is clear enough, although it may be unrealizable in actuality, and if we do not keep it plainly before us legal inquiry will remain at the descriptive level.

NOTES

[1] Bent, *Criminal Life* (1891), p. 41, quoted in Wigmore, *Science of Judicial Proof* (3d ed., 1937), p. 148.

[2] This was recognized by Aristotle, *Topics,* 101b, 104b, but obscured by nineteenth-century positivism's emphasis on "facts."

[3] Nunn, *The Aim and Achievements of Scientific Method* (1907), p. 46.

[4] 10 Cl. and F. 200, 4 St. Tr. (N.S.) 847, 8 Eng. Rep. 718 (1843).

[5] Hall, *General Principles of Criminal Law* (1947), p. 479 *et seq.* By a problem I mean a question to which it seems possible to give an acceptable answer. A question is a propositional function, that is to say, an expression containing one or more undetermined constituents, and which becomes a proposition when the undetermined constituents are determined. F. Cohen, "What is a Question?" *Monist,* 39:350 (1929); Russell, "Philosophy of Logical Atomism," *Monist,* 5:192 (1919). "*X* is a contract" is a propositional function, and if we substitute "the

agreement made by *A* and *B* on July 18, 1955, etc.," then the expression becomes a proposition.

[6] Benjamin, *Introduction to the Philosophy of Science* (1937), p. 438.

[7] Montague, *The Ways of Knowing* (1948), p. 39 *et seq.*; Cohen, *Reason and Nature* (1931), p. 23 *et seq.*

[8] Dewey, *Experience and Nature* (1925), p. 154.

[9] *Five Collected Papers* (1934), p. 246.

[10] *Laws* 634 E.

[11] *Politics* 1269ᵃ 24.

[12] *Ancient Law* (1931), p. 62.

[13] *U.S. v. Officers, etc. U.S.S. Mangrove,* 188 U.S. 720, 725.

[14] See Schulz, *History of Roman Legal Science* (1946), p. 124.

[15] *In re* Carrington, [1932] 1 Ch. 1 (C.A. 1931); *In re* Fish [1894] 2 Ch. 83 (C.A. 1893). Cf. Bucher v. Cheshire RR Co., 125 U.S. 558 (1888).

[16] Carlyle, *History of Mediaeval Political Theory in the West,* 3:32 (1916).

[17] *De Legibus* III.9.3. For the contrary view of a modern writer see Stahl, *Die Philosophie des Rechts* (5th ed., 1878), p. 171, where it is asserted that the state's authority to bind its members rests on its mere existence as such.

[18] *Nichomachean Ethics* 1113ᵃ 29.

[19] *Op. cit. supra* note 14 at 61 and 124.

[20] *Lochner v. N. Y.,* 198 U.S. 45, 76.

[21] *The Paradoxes of Legal Science* (1928), p. 59.

[22] Russell, *Philosophy* (1927), p. 9; Russell, *An Inquiry into Meaning and Truth* (1940), p. 189. For a criticism see Chisholm, "Russell on the Foundations of Empirical Knowledge," in *The Philosophy of Bertrand Russell,* ed. by Schilpp (1944), pp. 421 *et seq.* For Russell's reply see *Ibid.,* pp. 710 *et seq.*

[23] Santayana, *Scepticism and Animal Faith* (1923), p. 110.

[24] *Posterior Analytics* 99ᵇ ff.

[25] Russell's *An Inquiry into Meaning and Truth* is devoted solely to the solution of this problem.

[26] *Logic* (1864), p. 167.

[27] *Norway Plains Co. v. Boston and Maine RR,* 1 Gray (Mass.) 263 (1854).

[28] *Moses v. Boston and Maine RR,* 32 N.H. 523 (1856).

[29] Russell, *Human Knowledge* (1948), p. 496 *et seq.*

[30] *Ibid.,* p. 506.

[31] *Novum organum,* Book I, Aph. 105.

[32] In his *Popular Science Monthly* article of January, 1878, "How to Make Our Ideas Clear," Peirce focused upon the consequences that belief in an idea have for conduct. Later in an article in the *Monist* in 1905, and in *Baldwin's Dictionary of Philosophy* (1901–5), he emphasized that pragmatism was a principle of meaning. He eventually coupled it with evolutionary doctrine and arrived at a logic and a metaphysics. The best exposition of pragmatism in jurisprudence, beginning with the influence of Peirce, is Patterson, *Jurisprudence* (1953), p. 465 *et seq.*

[33] See Montague, *The Ways of Knowing* (1948), pp. 211 *et seq.* for systematic consideration of their interrelations.

[34] *Op. cit. supra* note 29 at 507.

[35] Cohen, *Reason and Nature* (1931), pp. 86, 174.

[36] *Ibid.,* p. 223 n. 38.

[37] Eaton, *General Logic* (1931), p. 12.

THE EVOLUTION OF
POLYNESIAN SOCIETIES

By Irving Goldman

SARAH LAWRENCE COLLEGE

THE COMPARATIVE STUDY of Polynesian societies enables us to reconstruct some of the ways in which social structures based upon the unity of lineage and graded hereditary rank evolve into new social systems in which lineage has been replaced by a territorial-political organization and rank has given way to social stratification. As we trace this development through Polynesia, we see how these changes have been intertwined with readjustments in almost every sphere of social life to such a degree that we may conclude that it has been the pivotal process in Polynesian history (Burrows, 1939; Goldman, 1955, 1957, 1958a, 1958b). From this observation rises the question whether the processes of Polynesian cultural evolution have specific application to a general theory of cultural evolution. In all probability they have. In any event, we need not remain in the dark, since social structures similar in the main to those of Polynesia are found elsewhere in Oceania, as well as in other parts of the primitive world. We should expect to find that similar social structures tend to evolve in similar ways even in different cultural settings. Polynesian social structure has special interest for us because of its seeming "set" towards a sequence of changes culminating in social classes and in states. Further study should tell us whether this is true of corresponding types of social structure elsewhere. Thus, while this is a study of Polynesia, its findings are pointed towards a more general evolutionary theory.

The lineage that stands at the center of the prototype social structure in Polynesia is not a conventional unilineal descent group. It has two aberrant features, lack of exogamy and an associated bilateral kinship system of the Hawaiian type. These deviations from classic lineage form contribute markedly to lineage instability and evolution-proneness, although, in the final analysis, it is its hierarchical arrangement that determines its mode of evolutionary change. Because of its exceptional nature we may ask whether this descent group is a lineage at all. This question is of some importance if we are to consider testing our hypotheses by comparing Polynesian social structures with other uni-lineal descent groups. On this point there is some disagreement. Most writers on Polynesia have identified the descent groups as "lineages." Some (e.g. Burrows, 1936, 1937) have wavered between "lineage" and "kindred," and some have felt the need for a new term (Goodenough, 1955). Firth (1936), for example, had labeled the Tikopian *paito* as a "ramage" in recognition of its branching structure, but subsequently he reverted to "lineage" (1956). Sahlins, who also recognized the distinctive nature of the Polynesian descent group, has, however, retained "ramage" (1957). In simple fact, there are no hard and fast formal criteria by which to define the Polynesian descent group in an unequivocal fashion. Since these descent groups are unconventional, they need to be defined from the point of view of some clearly stated theoretical position. In this respect, what seems clear from the present study is that Polynesian societies and their descent groups are variants of a common type. This being so, it follows that the theoretical perspective must be a historical one which lets us focus upon tran-sitional features, something we would hesitate to do if we were dealing with structures that were historically discontinuous.

The comparison of variant forms must be recognized as a special kind of comparative analysis that involves the formulation of a hypo-thetical gradient along which the variations can be "measured." What this gradient should be depends upon one's interpretation of Polynesian society. Whatever that interpretation may be, it must come from a study of societies as a whole, and, in addition, it must deal with the area as a whole. If we are to maintain a historical perspective, we cannot deal with social structure in terms of scattered "diagnostic" traits such as descent, residence, types of kinship terminology, land-holdings, or forms of marriage. If we are dealing with variations, it is the total pattern that is important. By the same token, variations acquire meaning only if the entire area is studied. While these strictures apply with particular force to historical or evolutionary studies, they are pertinent to functional-structural analyses as well. To the extent that the structural-functional school has lacked historicity, it has over-looked what should have been a rich field for investigation, namely the study of variations within a historical continuum. Eggan (1937), in particular, and Leach (1954) are notable exceptions.

The viewpoint of the present study is that the dynamic center of

Polynesian society, speaking now of the area as a whole, is its mode of concern with social status. For this reason, I have identified the main Polynesian descent group as a "Status Lineage" (1958b), a term that appears to correspond to Fried's "ranking lineage" (1957). The term "status lineage" emphasizes its two distinctive features: (1) that linearity is primarily by status and only incidentally by sex, and (2) its hierarchical structure, by which member families and related lineage branches are all ranked. In its traditional and prototype form the status lineage has preferential patriliny, but persons affiliate to a lineage through the maternal side if that side offers a closer link to an ancestor of high status. Patriliny accords with the Polynesian doctrine that since men have higher *mana*—the mystical sanction of rank—than women, rank and the prerogatives of leadership descend more suitably through a line of males. As for ranking of family lines and lineages, this follows from standard lineage principles of seniority of descent and growth by branching. A lineage consists of related family lines whose genealogies are known and who are ranked by degree of genealogical relatedness to the senior line. As new lineages are formed, they retain their links with the parental stem and are also ranked by degree of genealogical relationship to the senior line of the founding lineage. Leadership positions follow the lines of male seniority, the head of a family being its senior male, the head of the senior family line being the lineage chief, and the head of the senior lineage being the tribal chief. Seniority also defines the rank of individuals, which follows a fine gradation from highest ranking chief, the descendant of a line of first born males (the ideal of highest rank), to the lowest ranking "commoners," a descendant of junior lines. In the prototype form all ranks are bound together by kinship ties; all share crop lands and take part in the common activities of group life.

From the point of view of general evolutionary theory, the Polynesian status lineage is to be regarded as one of the variant forms among the broader class of hierarchically structured lineages that are normally exogamous and supported by a unilaterally biased kinship system. The evolutionary significance of ranked lineages has been recognized by several writers (Fried, 1957; Kirchhoff, cited in Fried), although lack of interest in cultural evolution as a problem has continued to stand in the way of the detailed comparative study that they merit.

The lineage in its generalized form has been regarded as a structure of the "middle range of relatively homogeneous pre-capitalistic societies in which there is some degree of technological sophistication and value is attached to rights in durable property." (Fortes, 1953, p. 24.) According to this view, the lineage breaks down when modern economic structures are introduced. Kirchhoff was among the first to point to conical clan structures—homologous to hierarchical lineages—as lending themselves readily to evolutionary changes that lead to the formation of states. Kirchhoff did not undertake to elaborate on this hypothesis, but it may be said that even a casual survey of proto-states would seem to bear out his thesis.

The Polynesian status lineage, as a special form of the class of ranked lineages, may be expected to have a somewhat different historical fate than descent groups that are exogamous and truly unilinear. Perhaps the main difference is that the status lineage is "triggered" for change, whereas "normal" ranked lineages have greater inherent stability. Lacking exogamy, the Polynesian lineage is readily transformed under political pressure. By contrast, the "normal" ranked lineages may survive well after states have been formed. Ranking gives to all descent groups a potentially unstable character simply because human beings do not tolerate social inequality too well. As a consequence, no known hierarchical society has been able to devise more than temporary measures to insure its stability. All social structures, of course, must provide for constant readjustments in their patterned interpersonal relations. The question is whether these readjustments act to restore the original equilibrium, or whether they must constantly alter it. The suggestion from the Polynesian study is that hierarchical structures tend to restore stability only within a pattern that was unstable to begin with. They have the inertia, so to speak, of a body in motion and the adaptations that they make are corrections that maintain them in their generally set course. For the short run, at least, status inequality can evolve only new forms of status inequality.

In addition, then, to the dynamism inherent in ranking, the Polynesian status lineage is subject to the double pressures of agamy and of kinship bilaterality. These three forces do not necessarily push in the same direction. Agamy and kinship bilaterality undermine lineage structure by permitting flexibility of kin alignments. They sanction shifting lineage memberships so that, depending upon political and economic conditions, lineages grow weaker or stronger *vis-à-vis* one

another. New lineages rise and old ones fall as people regroup themselves around different leaders. Under such conditions, lineages may
survive for a while as fictional groupings, but in the end they give way
to outright political organization. The principle of ranking, on the
other hand, acts in the opposite direction. Male seniority stabilizes
the status lineage, and as long as the traditionalism of hereditary rank
through male primogeniture prevails, the status lineage is able to overcome the counterpressures from agamy and kinship bilaterality by
providing an orderly basis for leadership and for social status.

The status lineage then is highly dependent upon the traditional
status system, a system based on seniority of descent in the male line.
If this is so, we need to know how stable, in its turn, this traditional
status system is. The logic of hereditary rank speaks for stability, but
only in the abstract. The psychology of status is such that inequality
provokes rivalry, if not throughout the entire society then surely in its
upper status ranges. In Polynesia, status rivalry is given ample scope
by characteristics of structure as well as by the values of each society.
With respect to social structure, status rivalry is fanned by potentially
equal claims to chieftainship resulting from bilaterality. Concurrently
the significance of status rivalry is heightened because rank conveys
more than prestige; it confers leadership. Changes in prestige may
have only a formal significance for a society, but a change in the
pattern of leadership has the most far-reaching effects upon every
major aspect of social life. Finally, status rivalry is stimulated by the
value Polynesians place upon capability in war and in political leadership. *Mana,* an attribute of high birth, is, they believe, manifest in
deeds, with the result that outstanding accomplishment can always
challenge an inherited position. The holders of inherited rank must
demonstrate their worth. Whatever form Polynesian status systems
take, they provoke to some degree a conflict between hereditary rank
and achieved status. At the high status level of *ariki,* rank has a sacred
quality and conveys, therefore, relatively fixed and exceptional prestige.
Ideally, rank, privilege, political leadership, and power are combined
in Polynesia. Rank may lose power and privilege, but it will ordinarily
retain the prestige owed to its sacredness. Achieved status, on the
other hand, may allocate to itself power, privilege and prestige, but
lacking proper genealogical claims can never acquire the special prestige
that is the exclusive prerogative of the upper hereditary ranks. Hence,

newcomers to high social status have always tried to assume the mantle of respectability. Sometimes they have invented or distorted genealogies. In many cases intermediate social ranks were formed where lesser highborn and ascendant lowborn could mingle on an equal plane. Like *arrivistes* everywhere, the Polynesian newcomers to power were not rebels against the social order. They sought only for a place in it for themselves. If, in the meantime, they disturbed the social order, they did so inadvertently.

It is the various modes of interplay between hereditary and achieved status that give rise to the variations upon the traditional Polynesian status system. Since rank with its connotations of sacredness is more immune to change, the real issues in status rivalry converge on secular privileges, i.e., political power. In a real sense, status rivalry is a conflict for power, and it is through this conflict, primarily, and its resulting stresses and adaptations that Polynesian societies evolve. The most immediate effects of this conflict are upon the status lineage. Since the lineage is the axis of the social structure, changes in its form and function necessarily affect most aspects of social and cultural life. However, within the lineage itself the point of change is in leadership.

Variations in Polynesian status systems follow a hypothetical gradient that expresses the politicalization of status. At the "low" end of this gradient are societies where social status and political power are relatively undeveloped. At the "high" end are societies where status and political power have reached a peak. The criteria by which Polynesian societies have been placed along this gradient are imprecise, to be sure. However, the validity of the alignment is testable by comparison with variations in other components of social structure. If the theory that the status lineage is stabilized by the system of graded hereditary rank is correct, we should expect to find a reasonably close correspondence between variations in social status and variations in lineage structure. By the same token, the more general theory—that variations in the systems of social status govern the evolution of Polynesia as a whole—should lead us to expect further a general relationship between such variations and other pertinent aspects of society and culture.

In sum, we are dealing with three main questions. The first concerns variations in systems of social status and their probable line of evolution. The second refers to the evolution of the status lineage in its

Table 1
ECOLOGICAL AND DEMOGRAPHIC FACTORS IN POLYNESIA

Society	Terrain	Population (estimated)	Area (in sq. miles)	Productivity (estimated)
		TRADITIONAL		
Ontong Java	atoll	5,000	a	marginal
Tokelau	atoll	1,200	4.0	marginal
Pukapuka	atoll	630	2.0	marginal
Tikopia	high	1,300	3.0	marginal
Manihiki	atoll	873	3.5b	marginal
Maori	high	100,000	44,281.0c	high
Tongareva	atoll	2,000	6.0	marginal
Uvea	high	3,000	23.0	high
Futuna	high	2,000	25.0	high
Manu'a	high	2,200	18.5	high
		OPEN		
Niue	high	5,080	100.0	marginal
Easter	high	3,000	55.0	marginal
Mangaia	high	2,500	27.0	marginal
Marquesas	high	50,000d	400.0	marginal
		STRATIFIED		
Tonga	high	25,000	226.0	high
Mangareva	high	2,000	6.0	marginal
Tahiti	high	100,000e	637.0e	high
Hawaii	high	300,000f	6,412.0f	high

a Not available.
b Figure includes Rakahanga also.
c North Island only.
d Some estimates are as high as 100,000.
e For all Society Islands.
f For all Hawaiian Islands.

interaction with systems of social status. The third deals with evolution as a whole by examining the general social and cultural consequences of the concomitant changes in status and lineage. These questions do not by any means exhaust the many lines of inquiry that belong in a complete evolutionary study. But they do provide bases for a schematic presentation of main lines of change. While a schematic presentation has the inevitable defect of understating complexity, its aim is valid enough, and that is to call attention to what seem to be the main lines and processes of cultural evolution in Polynesia. A more detailed statement as to the multitude of factors that enter into the evolutionary process and of the variety of their interactions would enrich the picture but it is questionable whether it would change it.

This study draws upon all Polynesian societies that have been adequately described. There are eighteen such societies, and in Table 1 these have been arranged in a hypothetical evolutionary sequence based on variations in systems of social status using the criterion of politicalization. The sequence divides itself into three phases or types which I have labeled, in order, "traditional," "open," and "stratified."

The Traditional Societies

The ten societies in this group are those in which status conflict is minor as compared with the open and the stratified societies, and in which graded hereditary rank is most fully represented. They are by no means uniform with respect to status. Those at the center are the most "typical" and those at the ends the most aberrant. Ontong Java and Tokelau, for example, stress status by age rather than by seniority. Pukapukan traditions also tell that gerontocracy preceded seniority. Perhaps among these societies status by seniority of descent was in the process of evolving from status by age seniority. On the other hand, Tongareva, Futuna, and Uvea at the upper end of the scale have deviated from the traditional pattern, and among these the warriors have become politically and socially more prominent. Manu'a, at the very end, is a borderline case that stays on the traditional side because its mode of status rivalry lacks the aggressive and military character of the typical open society. The ideal type of traditional society is epitomized by Maori. Maori has the most fully developed system of graded hereditary rank as well as the classic form of status lineage.

We assume that the traditional societies are the prototypes of all other Polynesian status systems because their key traits are almost universal in the area. Moreover, variations in these key traits can be accounted for. It is significant that the term *ariki*, or cognates, is universal in Polynesia and that it has everywhere a connotation of sanctity. In Ontong Java, where there is no *ariki* office, the term *alii* refers to the sacred robes of the priest. Except for the honorific *tohunga* (skilled craftsman or expert) no other status term in Polynesia has a universal distribution.

The Open Societies

Among the open societies, status rivalry has intensified to the point where leadership depends more upon political prowess and force than upon traditional seniority. Except for Niue, which is an uncertain case, traditional rank does exist in all, but it no longer assures leadership.

In the open societies the warriors (*toa*) have assumed so much power that the status lineage has been regrouped around them or around political leaders and the traditional order of seniority has been broken. These leaders formed power centers of near and distant kin and strangers held together more by material considerations of safety and self advancement than by claims of genealogy.

Among the open societies, Mangaia is the most enlightening example. On this compact little volcanic island chronic warfare between two contending tribes led to the eclipse of the traditional *ariki* lines and produced the successful warriors as the real temporal authorities. These were awarded lands taken from the vanquished and were given command over districts. The poor, the weak, and the vanquished, on the other hand, had to accept voluntarily or otherwise the protection of the powerful. War was thus the principal source of status mobility; but once the more venturesome were admitted into the higher echelons of authority, rearrangements of the order of status and authority became common enough, even in peacetime. The traditional order was still recognizable, but as Buck remarked, "Seniority of blood though revered was somewhat theoretical as compared with the practical advantage of number." (1934, p. 10.)

In the Marquesas, on the verge of stratification because in some places chiefs had openly begun to expropriate tribal lands as their own, we encounter an interesting variant of the Mangaian model. Here, too, as in Mangaia, warriors received rewards of land and social status, but the chiefs who did not have to go to war advanced themselves by political adroitness rather than by military prowess. Respect for seniority prevailed throughout the Marquesas. On Ua Pou and on Nuku Hiva chieftainship followed seniority. Elsewhere in the islands a chief, to quote Handy, "arrived at his position of authority through social prestige and power resulting upon being the head of a large and wealthy family aligned with other powerful families ... a chief was one that was the head of a family whose members were very numerous and could perform much work for him." (1923, p. 45.)

As a type, the open societies do not break abruptly from the traditional pattern, but represent instead an intensification of power conflict that is present in all the traditional societies. Whether we think of them as a clear-cut type or not, they are transitional between the traditional and the stratified societies. In their histories are most clearly revealed the ways in which the traditional social order breaks down and the ways in which the stratified order comes to be formed. Although the open societies do not have economic stratification, they have achieved a social stratification of a type that in the traditional societies is only hinted at. Niue, for example, had a high-ranking class of servants (*hakahakau*) and "low people" (*lalo tagata*), referring to those that ran away in battle. Easter Island had honorable commoners (*hurumanu*) and a low class of servants (*kio*) or vanquished. Mangaia recognized a class of *rangatira*, or lesser "nobility," as well as a class of *'ao*, or "fatherless people," referring to those who had been defeated in war. The Marquesas, finally, recognized a chiefly class (*poi tiketike*), landlords (*anatia*), and commoners (*mata-ei-nana*).

The Stratified Societies

Stratification set into motion new forces and brought into existence or gave clearer expression to new motives. It created a social cleavage that the Polynesians themselves began to regard as unbridgeable and in some instances it made subsistence itself an issue in political conflict. Yet different as the stratified societies were from the traditional and the open, their unity with all of Polynesia is unmistakable. All the main Polynesian features were present; but they are in new contexts and hence have new meanings or they have been intensified and given new vigor or, in some cases, subordinated. Seen from the perspective of the contenders for power this means that all material and cultural resources available in Polynesia have been put to use for the demanding purposes of more climactic struggles. As a result, these societies synthesized the traditional and the open and emerged with a new form that retained roots in both. The key change was in land tenure—expressed socially in a clear distinction between landed and landless.

The four stratified societies are variations on the same economic theme. Tonga seems closest to the traditional system; Mangareva shows most clearly how the Mangaian pattern leads to the expropriation of land and the formation of landed and landless tribesmen; while Tahiti and Hawaii may be regarded as a culmination in Polynesian political evolution, in which administrative divisions have replaced the older and more traditional organization of lineage and tribe. The latter two, and Hawaii in particular, are noted for administrative specialization.

The position of Tonga in this evolutionary scheme is actually uncertain, because the system of land tenure has not been fully described. What little information on this subject we do have, tells that rulers, tribal or lineage chiefs, allotted lands to lesser chiefs who, in turn, granted holdings to low ranking kin who served them as "tenants." The commoner tenants were known as "*tua*," a derogatory expression meaning "weak" or "banana stalk." The "landlords," a gentry class, owed their superiors tribute as well as military and courtly services. The *tua*, it has been said, "were ground down" and "could not call anything their own." W. D. Alexander, an early observer, concluded that the Tongan land system differed from that in New Zealand and in Samoa and that it was "feudal" (cited in Gifford, 1929, p. 171). The history of Tongan lineages is similar to that we have noted for Mangaia and for the Marquesas. Under stress of war and status conflict they were constantly rearranged around strong leaders. Tongan genealogical traditions trace out clearly the decline of the traditional rank system as a principle of government and its replacement by a pattern of rule based more realistically upon political power. Thus, the history of the *Tui Tonga,* the sacred ruler over all the Tongan islands, reveals a process of gradual separation of sacred and secular authority and finally eclipse at the hands of newly risen warring chiefs.

Mangarevan traditions portray a ceaseless struggle for power that manifested itself in virtually every corner of social life, from the intimacy of the household to the broad arena of the tribe. Tribes fought tenaciously to assert their authority over the entire island. In the course of this struggle the seniority principle wavered, was overcome and reasserted itself, but never remained unchallenged. On at least two occasions, the traditions report, commoners had wrested authority from traditional chiefs. The traditions also tell how in these struggles for power the system of land tenure changed from the lineage type to a "feudal" type. Although the high chiefs, the *akaariki*, were expected to respect the rights of the people to land, they had, in fact, become predatory. After each war, victorious chiefs rewarded their allies with landed estates, and at the death of a chief, his heirs fought savagely to divide the lands, many becoming landless and others acquiring great estates. The most aggressive seized lands from their own kin. The lands of the vanquished were expropriated by the rules of war; while the weak gave up their lands voluntarily for the sake of protection. Eventually a few families came to "own" all the lands. These they leased to a middle class of lower gentry and ascendant commoners. Those who had no land at all either became fishermen or were "rats" who lived in caves and reportedly robbed graves for food.

The Tahitian social order was more stable than the Mangarevan and imbued, at the same time, with more deference for the ceremoniousness of the traditional societies. Tahiti had a class of chiefs, *arii*, who were the ruling aristocracy and a *raatira* middle class that was made up of lower-ranking "nobles" and of upward-moving plebeians. Land ownership was prerequisite for *raatira* status. At the bottom of the social scale were the landless *manahune*, the commoners and the majority of the population. Tahiti may very well have once been, as Polynesian historians believe, the very center of traditional aristocracy in Polynesia.

The general theme of Society Islands' genealogical traditions is the familiar one of growth of political power and of the dispersal of tribes and lineages by other aggressively expanding lineages and tribes. The best historical account of this is the chronicle of the *Arii Taimai* as related to Henry Adams (1947). Taimai, who was a high ranking chieftainess of the district of Papara in Tahiti, tells how the old aristocratic ruling lines were overcome by conquest and how lands taken from the vanquished were reallocated among the leading supporters of the victor chiefs. Rank, she noted, never lost its prestige, but it was no assurance of power either.

The traditions of hereditary rank persisted through all the vicissitudes of Tahitian history. Veneration for seniority was always signalized by an elaborate status symbolism that included the prominence given to genealogies. Power-derived status may, to all intents and purposes, have superseded birth, but even so, newcomers to high position were impelled to model themselves upon the traditions of the aristocracy.

Before unification under Pomare I, the largest political unit in Tahiti was the district which was ruled by a high chief (*arii nui* or *arii rahi*). In theory, but rarely in fact, the high chief represented the senior line among all the lineages in his district. The district was divided into subdistricts each ruled over by members of the *arii nui*'s family, usually his younger brothers. In each subdistrict some lineages were *raatira,* a hereditary land-holding gentry. The larger number of people were the *manahune,* not only landless, but to all intents and purposes a caste. At the time of the Pomare conquest, which established a unified kingdom, only one district on Tahiti was apparently kin-unified; the others had become political entities.

Features of social organization that appear vague in the Tahitian data are seen more clearly in the Hawaiian Islands. Since the two societies are historically very close, the stronger outlines of developments in the Hawaiian Islands bring out more distinctly those processes that are less clearly described for Tahiti. Even before Kamehameha had unified the islands, the smaller independent "kingdoms" in the islands had already brought to fruition the main forms of stratification. Supreme chiefs (*arii nui*) ruled over an island and held title to all the land which they allocated among their powerful supporters in return for tribute and taxes. Whereas the Tahitian gentry remained secure in their land-holdings, except for conquest, the Hawaiian recipients of land were subject to eviction with every overturn of the central authority. The commoner tillers of the soil were untouched by these upheavals, and they were free to leave an abusive landlord and join another. Only a few families held traditional rights; the rest were bound in a "feudal" tenure that embraced the entire political community in a pyramidal structure of wealth, power and status. An island was divided into districts each ruled over by descendants of the ancient families. Districts were subdivided into smaller units headed by lesser chiefs who in turn let out land to tenants, the common people. In addition to tenants, there were those who did farm labor for others and some, an outcaste group, who had no connection with the land at all. Overseers and administrators represented the supreme chiefs and saw to it that tribute and services were properly forwarded up. Apart from this "feudally" administered domain, the *arii nui* held certain districts in a personal tenure.

With this territorial administration, tribal organization had just about disappeared in the Hawaiian Islands. The fact that a tribal organization existed in the isolated region of Ka'u on Hawaii must surely be taken as a survival of an earlier system. Hawaiian historical traditions bear this out amply and the use in Hawaii of the term *makaainana*—a cognate for "tribe" in most parts of Polynesia—to mean "commoner" is a revealing bit of evidence along the same lines. In Ka'u, *makaainana* still means tribe.

Hawaiian political organization was centralized and, by Polynesian standards, elaborate, with a well-structured court—brought to its full development after unification—and a large and diversified administrative hierarchy that included a constabulary to enforce taboos and first fruit collections. The most important administrative official was the *kalaimoku,* a prime minister who was often a commoner and therefore not likely to be involved in palace intrigues. The *kalaimoku* gave administrative continuity to governments that were otherwise unstable.

As elsewhere in Polynesia, seniority gave prestige, and the rank of *alii* was sanctioned by genealogical claims. Long periods of conquest and civil disorder had disarranged, to be sure, the traditional lines of seniority, but the genealogical myth prevailed for the upper ranks, and genealogies were tampered with to give them a traditionalistic appearance. To accommodate the complex interrelations between their respect for traditional rank and their realistic regard for achieved power, the Hawaiian aristocracy gave free rein to bilaterality so that linearity of descent was strictly by status. Between commoners and nobility the breach was complete. The social organization of the common people was the *'ohana,* a fully bilateral kindred dispersed throughout an island division (Handy and Pukui, 1950–51). Members of an *'ohana* maintained a social unity that ran beneath the main political structure. An elder male of the senior branch of the *'ohana* in a district was its leader in minor social and economic functions. He was called a *haku,* a term that conveys no connotation of rank but means merely a "director," and he lacked, of course, the traditional prerogatives of leadership for land distributions. However, he represented the *'ohana* in its economic relations with the *alii,* and was responsible for delivering the annual *makahiki* tribute. (This was a "first fruits" payment in the traditional societies that in the stratified societies had become a formal tax.)

From historical traditions, as presented by Fornander (1916, 1919), can be traced the evolution of Hawaiian society from an early traditional phase, during which the power of senior lines grew steadily, through a long period of unrest beginning sometime in the fourteenth century, leading to an open phase during which the traditional lines were overcome, and culminating finally in the consolidation of political and economic power in the manner of the stratified societies.

This summary of Polynesian status systems has been presented to suggest an evolutionary sequence. Before proceeding further we need to consider more closely the nature of the evolutionary evidence. It is fair to say that my theory of Polynesian cultural evolution rests upon the demonstration that the status systems have, in fact, evolved in the sequence traditional-open-stratified. My evidence follows four main lines. First, and most important, is that of intergrading. The argument of intergrading assumes that the main differences in Polynesian status systems have resulted from variations in a common core of culture rather than by intrusion from foreign sources. Early interpretations of Polynesian history did, in fact, postulate successive waves of migrants, each bringing in new cultural levels. More recently, however, the burden of evidence from linguistics, archaeology, somatology and from careful cultural analysis has pointed more and more strongly to the indigenous character of Polynesian culture. The present study is a case in point. The recent work of Sharp (1957) adds still more weight to the argument of differentiation by variation for Polynesia. The rather extreme isolation of the Polynesian islands from main land masses and the nature of primitive seagoing would normally preclude active and large-scale migrations. An island area is, in fact, ideally located for evolutionary study. Our interpretation of the data has led to the conclusion that, apart from a few difficult cases, the traditional system of social status has been the prototype of all others. Not only have we seen traditional features represented in almost all Polynesian societies but we have been able to account in some detail for the processes by which the traditional order became successively transformed.

If the unity of Polynesian status systems is demonstrable, the case for intergrading is more complicated, if only because there are no hard and fast criteria for ranking societies by social status along a continuous scale. The procedure is subjective, but it is not haphazard. It involves, first, a theory as to the nature of the Polynesian status systems. Such a theory emerges readily from a reading of the ethnographies and from a study of structure and function of all status systems in the area. What is immediately clear is the inherent conflict between hereditary rank and achieved status. The logic of Polynesian culture dictates limited possibilities for the resolution of such conflict. If this conflict is closely contained, the traditional order survives. If achieved status wins out, an open society results. Among the open societies the issue of conflict for power has been fully joined. It may remain indeterminate, in which case the condition of "openness" continues or it reaches a resolution in consolidation of power and so results in a stratified society. To understand the logic of these sequences we must bear in mind that in Polynesia power depends upon wealth and upon control of land and basic resources. Control of land, however, is not an end in itself. Land is the source of political power because it allows chiefs to control people. The control over a territory and of the people in it is the prime objective of the leading men in all Polynesian societies. In the traditional societies the *ariki* were secure in their authority by virtue of respect for seniority and they ruled in behalf of their kinsmen. In the open societies, land holdings and kinship groupings were disarranged, and power displaced the sanctity of seniority as a basis for control over people. The theory of kinship, however, still prevailed, tribal membership alone giving land rights. In the open societies, chiefs had learned the political art of giving land as a reward for services. This new point of view about land reached its logical conclusion in the stratified societies so that only the worthy held land; the rest did not. Thus it may be said that the modes of controlling land resources, and of winning over and controlling people, governed the variations in the systems of social status and guided them within a narrow range of possibilities. At the same time, the complexity of changes provoked by the evolution of status systems made the process irreversible for all practical purposes. In a new location, colonists from open or stratified societies could revert to traditional forms as the Maori may have done when they left Central Polynesia. Once the restructuring of social structure has occurred, however, a reversion is unlikely. A society that has allowed its most aggressive members to taste new power and status finds it difficult to go back to the unity of lineage and rank.

The theory of intergrading may be verified by several other independent lines of evidence. The most direct of these is the information from Polynesian genealogical traditions. In using these traditions it is not genealogical accuracy that is the issue but rather the sequence in which the traditions depict major events. One would hesitate to build an evolutionary theory from Polynesian traditions alone, but their use in this limited way and as one of several lines of independent evidence is eminently justifiable. Actually, there is little need to be apologetic about Polynesian traditions. Most have rich circumstantial detail, and to a surprising degree they picture an evolution of society that corresponds to the sequence traditional-open-stratified. The traditional histories of the open and stratified societies narrate the decline of an established traditional order under the disorganizing impact of wars and internal disputes. This is not to say that the histories of the traditional societies have, by contrast, been peaceable. The histories of traditional societies may take us back to a period in which a dominant *ariki* line is established over an island, but the political centralism that arises in traditional societies is quite different from that in the open and in the stratified. The centralism of traditional societies comes from the rise to dominance of an *ariki* who has strong religious but limited economic powers over tribes and lineages. He does not, however, disturb their autonomy or the segmented character of the society. In the stratified societies, in particular, centralism, as we have seen, breaks lineage and tribe and creates a unitary society.

To draw upon the language of archaeology, we may say that the first line of evidence for the evolution of status systems was that of seriation embracing the area as a whole; the second line was that of stratigraphy in a specific culture. A third line is rather in between, within the compass of a relatively small subarea, and offers an even more precise approach to seriation. Thus, if we choose small clusters of Polynesian societies that, by independent trait-list analysis, are to be regarded as very closely related we find that these, too, show the characteristic forms of variation in status systems that mark the Polynesian area as a whole. In Western Polynesia, for example, Samoa, Niue, and Tonga show traditional, open, and stratified forms, although it is interesting to note that each of these is a marginal society within its type. However, if we add to these three other societies of Western Polynesia—Futuna, Uvea, and Tokelau—the distribution of variations is more ample. In Eastern Polynesia the Marquesas, Mangareva, and Easter Island show variations around the theme of openness, Mangareva being the most open of the stratified societies. If we add to these the Maori, the distribution of types is complete. Finally, Mangaia, Tahiti, and Hawaii illustrate still another line of connected variations. Ideally, we should be able to study variations of status systems among the even more closely related tribes of particular island complexes.

Here, however, the data fail us. Still there are hints that the major variations in status systems existed among separate tribes or districts in the Society Islands, the Hawaiian Islands, the Tongan Islands, the Samoan Islands, and in the Marquesas. New Zealand would also be a rewarding study along these lines.

Finally we come to the fourth line of evidence, one that we have already called attention to, that is, the close correspondence between status system types and other aspects of Polynesian culture. We are assuming, in this connection, that if the typology of status systems is a false one both as to type characterization and as to historical sequence, the correspondences would not occur. These correspondences are subject to a double check; they must fit the type and they must follow the logical historical sequence. Among all possible correspondences the most important is that between variations in systems of social status and variations in the form of the lineage. It is to this that we now turn.

In the traditional societies, to summarize what has already been brought out, descent groups formed themselves around a line of first born, preferentially males, and conducted all essential regulatory economic, social, political, and religious functions except that of exogamy. Community organization was of the village type, village councils representing the interests of households and of family lines as well as of lineages if several occupied a village. This generalized view of traditional society social organization applies more or less to all but Ontong Java and Tokelau at the "low" end of the traditional scale, and to Manu'a at its "high" end. The Ontong Javanese descent group, referred to in the literature as a "joint family," included all persons who could trace their descent back through males five or six generations to a common ancestor. In this respect it resembled a lineage. On the other hand, its headman, who was often the priest, was not a descendant of a senior line but only its eldest male. Residence was matrilocal, so that it was a group of women who owned the taro gardens and the houses in the main village. Residence, however, was ruled by economic status. If the wife's family was poor, residence was patrilocal. If both families were poor, it was matrilocal, and if both were wealthy it was bilocal. Economic status also regulated the degree of cohesiveness of the joint family. Poor joint families having no common economic interests were held together loosely, whereas the wealthy families were cohesive and had totems. The exceptionalism of the Ontong Java case underscores our thesis in two respects. One is that the weak character of the lineage seems related to the absence of well-established rank, and the other is that lineage cohesiveness depends upon economic status. In the fully formed status lineage, cohesiveness comes from the system of rank as well as from economic status.

The Tokelau exception is also instructive. Here the descent group has been called a "kindred." Although descent was patrilineal in the main, residence was largely matrilocal and property rights were determined bilaterally. The *ariki*ship, primarily a priestly office, descended, however, in the male line with a tendency towards seniority of descent. Again, the distinction between a kindred on the local level that regulated everyday affairs and a principle of linearity that transmitted the religious office of *ariki* conforms to the expectations of the theory.

Turning to Manu'a at the "high" end, we again find a close correspondence between form of descent group and the system of social status. The Manu'an *aiga* is a bilateral grouping in which the male line is the important land-holding group and is normally localized while the female lines are dispersed. Leadership and property rights move freely in either line, residence is ambilocal, one third of marriages resulting in matrilocal households. Manu'an bilaterality accords with the lapse of primogeniture and the decline of the formal system of senior rank. In Manu'a the traditional rank system was undermined by the growth of local and village interests. It is, in fact, on the local level that bilaterality is most effective in Polynesia. Mead's account (1930) makes it clear that bilaterality and local status mobility were closely linked. From Williamson's compilations (1924) it appears that the situation was essentially the same in Western Polynesia.

In the open societies, where the traditional forms of status and leadership had given way to a more mobile system, bilaterality became more strongly established. Attendant changes included the loss of village organization, growth in the importance of the tribe as a unit of social organization, and the formation of multitribe political units through conquest. Land holding tended to shift out of the lineage into the hands of smaller kin groups. Because information on descent groups is sparse for Niue and Easter Island, we must rely upon information from Mangaia and the Marquesas. But we may note first that the

Niuean *fagai* was a bilateral grouping with patrilocal residence and a rule of inheritance that gave most land to an eldest son. Whatever its past history, we do know that in recent times Niue had neither graded rank nor lineages. Métraux has reconstructed Easter Island history to suggest that paternal descent groups (*mata*) had, in the course of wars, become scattered and intermixed with one another. The *ariki-mau,* who had apparently once been a ruler, had become merely a religious leader while warriors took over the actual authority. The office of *ariki-mau* descended by the traditional mode of male primogeniture within a particular descent group. All other descent groups, on the other hand, formed themselves around military leaders and were, therefore, genealogically mixed.

In Mangaia, the formal social structure was of the traditional type. The *ariki*ship went by seniority in the male line; lineages and tribes were strongly patrilineal and patrilocal, and rank was graded according to degree of relationship to the senior line. Mangaian lineages and tribes were, for Polynesia, uniquely exogamous. However, as is brought out in their traditions, practice had moved far from this ideal. Descent lines were disrupted by wars in a number of ways. A man who feared for his safety in his own tribe took refuge with his wife's tribe and his descendants became incorporated into the mother's lineage. Similarly, a man who had lost his land in war domiciled himself and his children with his wife's kin. Men of defeated tribes sought protectors in the victor tribe and worked for them as menials until, having proven their loyalty, they were given a grant of land and so were incorporated into the tribe. Finally, the end of a war invariably led to a redistribution of lands among the outstanding warriors so that tribal territory, and with it tribal units and their component lineages, became dispersed. New groupings formed themselves around victorious leaders. Exogamy exerted some stabilizing influence but did not prevent absorption of a man's children into his wife's tribe. In Mangaia, too, the high-ranking families preserved strict patriliny and seniority, but the lower ranks did not. Since the *ariki* lines had lost their political authority they controlled in the main the fiction of a genealogical descent line but not necessarily an actual descent group.

Bilaterality was clearly developed in the Marquesas, where by all indications lineages did not exist at all. Tribes and subtribes were kindreds ruled by chiefs who had risen to their position by political maneuvering. As in Mangaia, popular and effective leaders established their own political centers, drawing to them the discontented from other tribes. Yet here, too, traditional rank persisted, and some families traced their genealogies back as far as twenty-five generations through a line of firstborn.

Turning, finally, to the stratified societies, we note the full emergence of two developments already foreshadowed in the open societies. One is the dissolution of lineage and tribe in Tahiti and in the Hawaiian Islands, and the other is the sharp break in kinship at the class line. Among the four stratified societies, Tonga has developed economic stratification, but the tradition of status lineage is still strong. Nevertheless, the dissolution of this system is quite evident. Gifford has noted:

Everything points to the necessity of a line of powerful chiefs for a nucleus about which the lineage groups itself. Without such chiefs it appears to wilt and die, and its membership gradually aligns itself with other rising lineages. This process of realignment naturally contravenes the rule of patrilineal descent, which theoretically and largely in practice determines lineage membership. (1929, p. 30)

In theory, all ranks in Tonga were connected by genealogical ties. In practice, the gulf had widened so greatly that chiefs felt privileged to treat their commoners with capricious cruelty.

The Mangarevan social structure has moved closer to the Tahitian-Hawaiian pattern. Essentially we may regard Mangareva as illustrating the further evolution of the Mangaian pattern. Here, too, a status lineage was drastically rearranged by wars and realignments around strong chieftains. Land holdings, as we have already remarked, went by leasehold, and commoners were dispossessed from the land altogether.

In Tahiti a district organization, a strictly political grouping, had become the dominant feature of social structure at the time of European contact. The districts were called *mataeinana* a term that connotes "tribe" elsewhere in Polynesia. They may have very well been tribes and there are suggestions that they had been divided into lineages.

The Hawaiian situation has already been described. Here the political system had fully replaced the lineage. To some degree linear principles regulated the prestige of higher ranks, but patriliny was altogether gone and the masses of the people lived in dispersed communities of kindred.

We have described the interaction between status and lineage in some detail because that seems to have been the focus of all the many forces and factors comprising the process of cultural evolution in Polynesia. Since the status lineage regulated all major aspects of social life, it was bound to follow that changes in its structure would cut deeply. We may now consider, briefly, those other aspects of social structure that interacted with the evolution of status and lineage. Since a social system evolves as a whole, all changes that emerge become new factors in the evolutionary situation so that the entire process of change is one of complex interactions. I have singled out the status system and lineage interaction as a particularly controlling one, without implying that this interaction was either simple or direct. The lineage responded to political and economic pressures, and, as its form changed, new political and economic possibilities were created. As these possibilities became, in fact, actual, they reacted upon the lineage still further, producing new changes. This is but a schematic view of interaction among components of social structure, which needs to be illustrated from a discussion of further components of social structure that correlated with changes in the systems of social status.

The first of these to be considered is that of community organization. Except for Tongareva, the traditional societies had a village organization, the stratified societies had dispersed communities, and the open societies were divided, with villages in Niue and perhaps in Easter Island, but none in Mangaia and in the Marquesas. The village organization reflected the more democratic and less power-centered political systems of the traditional societies, whereas the dispersed settlements were formed by groupings of people around the estates of leading chiefs and war leaders. If we think of the status lineage as a localized group, we can visualize the weakening effects of dispersal. Dispersal was due partly to the direct effects of war, but in the main to internal power conflicts that regrouped populations and so contributed to the weakening of the lineage. At the same time, the decline in the stability of the lineage hastened dispersal.

Land tenure, an aspect of social structure, is the most significant economic factor in culture change. We have seen how the control of lands and their productivity is the main source of political power. In fact, in the evolutionary picture, it is not so much the direct fact of conquest of one tribe by another that is significant in war, but rather those indirect processes that transformed land tenure from a lineage type to a "feudal" type. In the latter form, land was given in return for services and tribute. These "feudal" relationships developed in an atmosphere of war. This new system of land tenure involved, on the one hand, chiefs enlisting the services of warriors and, on the other, the weak submitting themselves to the authority of the powerful. Polynesian feudalism emerged from the disruption of the traditional order. The feudal relationship replaced that of the close kin ties of the lineage. At the same time, within the traditional system, those power and status relationships that eventually led to feudalism were already in evidence. In short, the conditions of status rivalry created latent feudal centers that weakened the lineage and finally replaced it. The feudal relationship dealt the lineage a double blow; one, political, replaced its hereditary leadership by a political leadership; the other, economic, replaced collective land holdings by individual family holdings.

Little more need be added to what has already been said about political factors. What bears emphasis is the steady way in which rank and power bifurcate, conflict, and become reconciled again; but reconciled in a new setting. The bifurcation between rank and authority was accompanied by the separation between secular and religious powers, although this relationship was not a clear-cut one. The political struggles represented, in sum, a host of factors that reacted against the lineage. Administrative simplicity coincided with the vigor of the status lineage, while the formation of a court and of an officialdom came with the decline of the lineage system.

Throughout these major changes in Polynesian social structure, the kinship system never changed in any substantial way. This is a tribute to the flexibility of bilateral kinship that can accommodate itself to virtually every level of organization. Bilaterality, however, contributed to the decline of the lineage because it was always in unstable equilibrium with it, giving constant legal sanction to status mobility through genealogical means. Kinship bilaterality and the lack of exogamy suited community dispersal for obvious reasons.

Among interactive factors must be included ecology. Polynesianists have always called attention to the fact that the more complex Polynesian societies were formed on the high volcanic islands and the simple ones on the low coral atolls. This generalization is, on the whole, valid. All the atolls were traditional societies, while the high islands contained all three types, as we might expect from the common dictum that environment limits but does not create. Nevertheless, it would be misleading to assume from the relationship between coral atoll and "simple" society that it is poverty or smallness of size that limits political evolution. In this connection, the case of Mangareva is instructive. A small island, it permitted the evolution of a social system equivalent in structure to that of Tahiti. The relative poverty of the island, however, did tell on the Mangarevans in that it endowed their political struggles with additional ferocity because land was so scarce and defeat could mean starvation. Perhaps a more significant factor than smallness or poverty is the differentiation of terrain into ecological zones of unequal productivity. Where the incentive for competition is present, such inequality becomes translated into political inequality and paves the way for conquest.

As we cannot make an axiom of the social consequences of scarcity, we cannot accept blindly the time-honored assumption that "surplus" provides the necessary basis for continued political evolution. A more significant approach is to examine the different ways in which differing political systems deal with their physical environments. The Polynesian data illustrated the point that economic efficiency was a major factor in political rivalry. The ability of a chief to organize production by constructing irrigation and terracing systems and fish ponds was a vital factor in his political success. In other words, it was the political incentive and the presence of a political organization that made public works possible rather than, as commonly believed, the other way around. The traditional societies on the atolls met scarcity by establishing community reserves; the open societies, and Mangareva among the stratified, utilized scarcity to promote inequality. As for abundance, we again find that the social order decides what to make of it. The Hawaiians, for example, were land hungry in a political rather than in a demographic sense. Thus, if we take gross population densities, we find that with only 47 persons per square mile the Hawaiians were expansionists, while Manu'a with 117 and Tikopia with 400 were, by contrast, peaceable.

The concept of adaptation to physical environment has been overstressed by evolutionists who have persisted generally in following too rigid and mechanical a biological model of adaptation. The assumption of such evolutionary theory is that societies are normally in equilibrium until they are acted upon by external forces. They then make the necessary adaptive accommodations. The point of the present study has been quite the opposite. I have tried to show rather that the dynamic element is in the social structure, particularly in its component system of social status. The concept of adaptation, important in evolution, has not been abandoned. What I have wished to demonstrate is the nature of internal adaptations to stresses that are produced by inherent features of the social structure. With social structure as the focus, the emphasis in evolutionary study shifts from the postulation of "stages" to the discovery of the modes of variability of particular social systems. Differentiation by variation, after all, is the very heart of evolutionary doctrine and not general laws, as Steward maintains in *Anthropology Today*, nor "temporal-formal" sequences as defined by White (1945). The study of differentiation by variation is truly an historical study in that it starts from the analysis of particular societies whose historical connections with one another can be established. For such studies the logical locus is the culture area. Within the context of the culture area we are no longer bound by the artificial distinctions between history, science, and evolution. All three become part of a unified approach to the elucidation of the fundamental characteristics of social systems.

REFERENCES

Note. For detailed bibliography consult Goldman, 1955, 1958b.

Adams, Henry. 1947. Tahiti, Memoirs of Arii Taimai. New York. (Scholars Facsimiles and Reprints.)

Buck, Sir Peter H. 1934. Mangaian Society. Bernice P. Bishop Museum Bulletin 122.

Burrows, E. G. 1936. The Ethnology of Futuna. Bernice P. Bishop Museum Bulletin 138.

—— 1937. The Ethnology of Uvea. Bernice P. Bishop Museum Bulletin 145.

—— 1939. "Breed and Border in Polynesia," *American Anthropologist*, 41: 1-21.

Eggan, Fred. 1937. Social Anthropology of the North American Tribes. Chicago, The University of Chicago Press.

Firth, Raymond. 1936. We, The Tikopia. New York, American Book Company.

—— 1956. Elements of Social Organization. London, Watts and Co.

Fornander, Abraham. 1916. Fornander Collection of Hawaiian Antiquities and Folklore. Memoirs of Bernice P. Bishop Museum No. 4.

—— 1919. Fornander Collection of Hawaiian Antiquities and Folklore. Memoirs of Bernice P. Bishop Museum No. 6.

Fortes, Meyer. 1953. "The Structure of Unilineal Descent Groups," *American Anthropologist*, 57:17-41.

Fried, Morton H. 1957. "The Classification of Corporate Unilineal Descent Groups," *Journal of the Royal Anthropological Institute,* 87:1-29.

Gifford, E. W. 1929. Tongan Society. Bernice P. Bishop Museum Bulletin 61.

Goldman, Irving. 1955. "Status Rivalry and Cultural Evolution in Polynesia," *American Anthropologist,* 57:680-97.

—— 1957. "Cultural Evolution in Polynesia: A Reply to Criticism," *Polynesian Society Journal,* 66:156-64.

—— 1958 a. "The Evolution of Status Systems in Polynesia," in *Selected Papers of the Fifth International Congress of Anthropological and Ethnological Sciences.* Philadelphia. University of Pennsylvania Press.

—— 1958 b. "Variations in Polynesian Social Organization," *Polynesian Society Journal* 66:374-90.

Goodenough, Ward H. 1955. "A Problem in Malayo-Polynesian Social Organization," *American Anthropologist,* 57:71-83.

Handy, E. S. C. 1923. The Native Cultures in the Marquesas. Bernice P. Bishop Museum Bulletin 9.

Handy, E. S. C., and Mary Pukui. 1950–51. "The Hawaiian Family System," *Polynesian Society Journal,* 59:170-90, 232-40; 60:187-222.

Leach, E. R. 1954. Political Systems of Highland Burma. Cambridge, Mass., Harvard University Press.

Mead, Margaret. 1930. Social Organization of Manu'a. Bernice P. Bishop Museum Bulletin 76.

Sahlins, M. 1958. Social Stratification in Polynesia. Seattle, University of Washington Press.

Sharp, Andrew. 1957. Ancient Voyagers in the Pacific. London, Penguin Books.

Steward, Julian. 1952. "Evolution and Process," in *Anthropology Today,* ed. by A. L. Kroeber. Chicago, University of Chicago Press.

White, Leslie A. 1945. "History, Evolutionism and Functionalism: Three Types of Interpretation of Cultures," *Southwestern Journal of Anthropology,* 1:221-48.

Williamson, Robert W. 1924. The Social and Political Systems of Polynesia. 3 vols. Cambridge, Cambridge University Press.

ON THE EVOLUTION OF
SOCIAL STRATIFICATION AND
THE STATE

By Morton H. Fried

COLUMBIA UNIVERSITY

> *The evolutionists never discussed in detail—still less*
> *observed—what actually happened when a society in*
> *Stage A changed into a society at Stage B; it was*
> *merely argued that all Stage B societies must somehow*
> *have evolved out of the Stage A societies.*
>
> E. R. LEACH, 1954, p. 283

TO SOME EXTENT E. R. Leach's charge, which relates to the evolution of political organization, is unfair. The climate in which pristine systems of state organization took shape no longer exists. The presence of numerous modern states and the efficiency of communications have converted all movements toward state level organization into acculturation phenomena of some degree. In fact, it seems likely that the only truly pristine states—those whose origin was *sui generis,* out of local conditions and not in response to pressures emanating from an already highly organized but separate political entity—are those which arose in the great river valleys of Asia and Africa and the one or two comparable developments in the Western Hemisphere. Elsewhere the development of the state seems to have been "secondary" and to have depended upon pressures, direct or indirect, from existing states. Where such pressures exist, the process of development is accelerated, condensed, and often warped, so that a study of contemporary state formation is a murky mirror in which to discern the stages in the development of the pristine states.

Further, the conditions of emergence of rank and stratification as pristine phenomena are similarly obscured when the impetus to change is the introduction of aspects of a market economy, money as a medium of exchange, rationalization of production, and the transformation of labor into a commodity. It would be extremely gratifying to actually observe societies in transition from a "Stage A" (egalitarian organization) to a "Stage B" (rank society) and from there to a "Stage C" (stratification society) and finally from that stage to a "Stage D" (state society). Indeed, some of these observations have been made, though no one has yet been able to follow a single society or even selected exemplars from a group of genetically related societies through all these stages. Instead a variety of unrelated societies are selected, each representing one or another of the several possible transitions. Mr. Leach himself has contributed one of the most valuable of the accounts dealing with this matter in his analysis of the movement from *gumlao* to *gumsa* organization among the Kachin of northern Burma.

Following leads supplied in the data of such accounts as that of Leach, just mentioned, of Douglas Oliver (1955), and others, it is our intention to discuss in detail the things which it seems to us must have occurred in order to make the previous transitions possible. Since the data are largely contemporary, the statements are to be viewed as hypotheses in their application to pristine situations beyond even archaeological recall.

Here then is what we seek to accomplish: (1) to suggest some specific institutional developments, the occurrences of which are normal and predictable in viable societies under certain conditions, and in the course of which the whole society perforce moves into a new level of socio-cultural organization; (2) to suggest some of the conditions under which these institutional developments occurred and came to florescence; (3) to indicate as a by-product, that the movement occurs without conscious human intervention, the alterations taking place slowly enough and with such inevitability that the society is revolutionized before the carriers of the culture are aware of major changes.

In approaching this task, it seems wise, if only to head off needless argument, to deny any intention of supplying a single master key to a lock that has defied the efforts of great talents from the time of the Classical civilizations to the present. It seems obvious that other sequences of events than those sketched here could, under proper circumstances, have had similar results. Indeed, the writer is eager to entertain other possibilities and hopes hereby to stimulate others to offer counter suggestions. It will also be obvious to the reader that substantial trains of thought herein stated are merely borrowed and not created by the writer. The recent strides in economic anthropology, and I refer primarily to the work of Polanyi, Arensberg, and Pearson (1957), the clarification of some basic concepts in the study of social organization, and the incentives provided by a seminal paper by Paul Kirchhoff (1935) have all been combined in the present effort.

The Non-Rank, Non-Stratified Society

Every human society differentiates among its members and assigns greater or less prestige to individuals according to certain of their attributes. The simplest and most universal criteria of differential status are those two potent axes of the basic division of labor, age and sex. Beyond are a host of others which are used singly or in combination to distinguish among the members of a category otherwise undifferentiated as to sex or age group. Most important of the characteristics used in this regard are those which have a visible relation to the maintenance of subsistence, such as strength, endurance, agility, and other factors which make one a good provider in a hunting and gathering setting. These characteristics are ephemeral; moreover, the systems of enculturation prevalent at this level, with their emphasis upon the development of subsistence skills, make it certain that such skills are well distributed among the members of society of the proper sex and age groups.

The major deviation from this system of subsistence-oriented statuses is associated with age. However, it makes no difference to the argument of this paper whether the status of the old is high or low since the basis of its ascription is universal. Anyone who is of the proper sex and manages to live long enough automatically enters into its benefits or disabilities.

Given the variation in individual endowment which makes a chimera of absolute equality, the primitive societies which we are considering are sufficiently undifferentiated in this respect to permit us to refer to them as "egalitarian societies." An egalitarian society can be defined more precisely: it is one in which there are as many positions of prestige in any given age-sex grade as there are persons capable of filling them. If within a certain kin group or territory there are four big men, strong, alert, keen hunters, then there will be four "strong men"; if there are six, or three, or one, so it is. Eskimo society fits this general picture. So do many others. Almost all of these societies are founded upon hunting and gathering and lack significant harvest periods when large reserves of food are stored.

There is one further point I wish to emphasize about egalitarian society. It accords quite remarkably with what Karl Polanyi has called a reciprocal economy.[1]

Production in egalitarian society is characteristically a household matter. There is no specialization; each family group repeats essentially similar tasks. There may be individuals who make certain things better than do others, and these individuals are often given recognition for their skills, but no favored economic role is established, no regular division of labor emerges at this point, and no political power can reside in the status (Leacock, 1958). Exchange in such a society takes place between individuals who belong to different small-scale kin groups; it tends to be casual and is not bound by systems of monetary value based upon scarcity. Such exchanges predominate between individuals who recognize each other as relatives or friends, and may be cemented by such procedures as the provision of hospitality and the granting of sexual access to wives.

Within the local group or band the economy is also reciprocal, but less obviously so. Unlike the exchanges between members of different local groups which, over the period of several years, tend to balance, the exchanges within a group may be quite asymmetrical over time. The skilled and lucky hunter may be continually supplying others with meat; while his family also receives shares from the catch of others, income never catches up with the amounts dispensed. However, the difference between the two quantities is made up in the form of prestige, though, as previously mentioned, it conveys no privileged economic or political role. There frequently is a feeling of transience as it is understood that the greatest hunter can lose his luck or his life, thereby making his family dependent on the largesse of others.

In all egalitarian economies, however, there is also a germ of redistribution. It receives its simplest expression in the family but can grow no more complex than the pooling and redisbursing of stored food for an extended family. In such an embryonic redistributive system the key role is frequently played by the oldest female in the active generation, since it is she who commonly coordinates the household and runs the kitchen.

The Rank Society

Since a truly egalitarian human society does not exist, it is evident that we are using the word "rank" in a somewhat special sense. The crux of the matter, as far as we are concerned, is the structural way in which differential prestige is handled in the rank society as contrasted with the way in which egalitarian societies handle similar materials. If the latter have as many positions of valued status as they have individuals capable of handling them, the rank society places additional limitations on access to valued status. The limitations which are added have nothing to do with sex, age group, or personal attributes. Thus, the rank society is characterized by having fewer positions of valued status than individuals capable of handling them. Furthermore, most rank societies have a fixed number of such positions, neither expanding them nor diminishing them with fluctuations in the populations, save as totally new segmented units originate with fission or disappear as the result of catastrophe or sterility.

The simplest technique of limiting status, beyond those already discussed, is to make succession to status dependent upon birth order. This principle, which is found in kinship-organized societies, persists in many more complexly organized societies. At its simplest, it takes the form of primogeniture or ultimogeniture on the level of the family, extended family, or lineage. In more complex forms it may be projected through time so that only the first son of a first son of a first son enjoys the rights of succession, all others having been excluded by virtue of ultimate descent from a positionless ancestor. There are still other variants based on the theme: the accession to high status may be by election, but the candidates may come only from certain lineages which already represent selection by birth order.

The effects of rules of selection based on birth can be set aside by conscious action. Incompetence can be the basis for a decision to by-pass the customary heir, though it would seem more usual for the nominal office to remain vested in the proper heir while a more energetic person performed the functions of the status. A strategic murder could also accomplish the temporary voiding of the rule, but such a solution is much too dangerous and extreme to be practical on the level which we are considering. It is only in rather advanced cultures that the rewards associated with such statuses are sufficient to motivate patricide and fratricide.

Whether accomplished by a rule of succession or some other narrowing device, the rank society as a framework of statuses resembles a triangle, the point of which represents the leading status hierarchically exalted above the others. The hierarchy thus represented has very definite economic significance, going hand in hand with the emergence of a superfamilial redistributive network. The key status is that of the central collector of allotments who also tends to the redistribution of these supplies either in the form of feasts or as emergency seed and provender in time of need. Depending on the extent and maturity of the redistributive system, there will be greater or lesser development of the hierarchy. Obviously, small-scale networks in which the members have a face-to-face relationship with the person in the central status will have less need of a bureaucracy.

In the typical ranked society there is neither exploitative economic power nor genuine political power. As a matter of fact, the central status closely resembles its counterpart in the embryonic redistributive network that may be found even in the simplest societies. This is not surprising, for the system in typical rank societies is actually based upon a physical expansion of the kin group and the continuation of previously known kinship rights and obligations. The kingpin of a redistributive network in an advanced hunting and gathering society or a simple agricultural one is as much the victim of his role as its manipulator. His special function is to collect, not to expropriate; to distribute, not to consume. In a conflict between personal accumulation and the demands of distribution it is the former which suffers. Anything else leads to accusations of hoarding and selfishness and undercuts the prestige of the central status; the whole network then stands in jeopardy, a situation which cannot be tolerated. This, by the way, helps to explain that "anomaly" that has so frequently puzzled students of societies of this grade: why are their "chiefs" so often poor, perhaps poorer than any of their neighbors? The preceding analysis makes such a question rhetorical.

It is a further characteristic of the persons filling these high status positions in typical rank societies that they must carry out their functions in the absence of political authority. Two kinds of authority they have: familial, in the extended sense, and sacred, as the redistributive feasts commonly are associated with the ritual life of the community. They do not, however, have access to the privileged use of force, and they can use only diffuse and supernatural sanctions to achieve their ends. Indeed, the two major methods by which they operate are by setting personal examples, as of industriousness, and by utilizing the principles of reciprocity to bolster the emergent redistributive economy.[2]

Despite strong egalitarian features in its economic and political sectors, the developing rank society has strong status differentials which are marked by sumptuary specialization and ceremonial function. While it is a fact that the literature abounds in references to "chiefs" who can issue no positive commands and "ruling classes" whose members are among the paupers of the realm, it must be stated in fairness that the central redistributive statuses *are* associated with fuss, feathers, and other trappings of office. These people sit on stools, have big houses, and are consulted by their neighbors. Their redistributive roles place them automatically to the fore in the religious life of the community, but they are also in that position because of their central kinship status as lineage, clan,[3] or kindred heads.

From Egalitarian to Rank Society

The move from egalitarian to rank society is essentially the shift from an economy dominated by reciprocity to one having redistribution as a major device. That being the case, one must look for the causes of ranking (the limitation of statuses such that they are fewer than the persons capable of handling them) in the conditions which enable the redistributive economy to emerge from its position of latency in the universal household economy, to dominate a network of kin groups which extend beyond the boundaries of anything known on the reciprocal level.

Though we shall make a few suggestions relating to this problem, it should be noted that the focus of this paper does not necessitate immediate disposition of this highly complicated question. In view of the history of our topic, certain negative conclusions are quite significant. Most important of all is the deduction that the roots of ranking do not lie in features of human personality. The structural approach obviates, in this case, psychological explanations. To be precise, we need assume no universal human drive for power[4] in comprehending the evolution of ranking.

It is unthinkable that we should lead a reader this far without indicating certain avenues whereby the pursuit of the problem may be continued. We ask, therefore, what are the circumstances under which fissioning kin or local groups retain active economic interdigitation, the method of interaction being participation in the redistributive network?

In a broad sense, the problem may be seen as an ecological one.

Given the tendency of a population to breed up to the limit of its resources and given the probably universal budding of kin and local groups which have reached cultural maxima of unit size, we look into different techno-geographical situations for clues as to whether more recently formed units will continue to interact significantly with their parent units, thereby extending the physical and institutional range of the economy. Such a situation clearly arises when the newer group moves into a somewhat different environment while remaining close enough to the parent group to permit relatively frequent interaction among the members of the two groups. Given such a condition, the maintenance of a redistributive network would have the effect of diversifying subsistence in both units and also providing insurance against food failures in one or the other. This is clearly something of a special case; one of its attractions is the amount of work that has been done upon it by another student of the problem (Sahlins, 1957, 1958).

It is possible to bring to bear upon this problem an argument similar to that employed by Tylor in the question of the incest taboo (Tylor, 1888, p. 267; White, 1948), to wit: the redistributive network might appear as a kind of random social mutation arising out of nonspecific factors difficult to generalize, such as a great personal dependence of the members of the offspring unit upon those they have left behind. Whatever the immediate reason for its appearance, it would quickly show a superiority over simple reciprocal systems in (a) productivity, (b) timeliness of distribution, (c) diversity of diet, and (d) coordination of mundane and ceremonial calendars (in a loose cyclical sense). It is not suggested that the success of the institution depends upon the rational cognition of these virtues by the culture carriers; rather the advantages of these institutions would have positive survival value over a long period of time.

We should not overlook one other possibility that seems less special than the first one given above. Wittfogel has drawn our attention on numerous occasions to the social effects of irrigation (see Wittfogel, 1957, for a summation of his latest thinking). The emergence of the superfamilial redistributive network and the rank society seem to go well with the developments he has discussed under the rubric "hydro-agriculture," in which some supervision is needed in order to control simple irrigation and drainage projects yet these projects are not large enough to call into existence a truly professional bureaucracy.

It may be wondered that one of the prime explanations for the emergence of ranking, one much favored by notable sociologists of the past, has not appeared in this argument. Reference is to the effects of war upon a society. I would like in this article to take a deliberately extreme stand and assert that military considerations serve to institutionalize rank differences only when these are already implicit or manifest in the economy. I do not believe that pristine developments in the formalization of rank can be attributed to even grave military necessity.

The Stratified Society

The differences between rank society and stratified society are very great, yet it is rare that the two are distinguished in descriptive accounts or even in the theoretical literature. Briefly put, the essential difference is this: the rank society operates on the principle of differential status for members with similar abilities, but these statuses are devoid of privileged economic or political power, the former point being the essential one for the present analysis. Meanwhile, the stratified society is distinguished by the differential relationships between the members of the society and its subsistence means—some of the members of the society have unimpeded access to its strategic resources[5] while others have various impediments in their access to the same fundamental resources.

With the passage to stratified society man enters a completely new area of social life. Whereas the related systems of redistribution and ranking rest upon embryonic institutions that are as universal as family organization (*any* family, elementary or extended, conjugal or consanguineal, will do equally well), the principles of stratification have no real foreshadowing on the lower level.

Furthermore, the movement to stratification precipitated many things which were destined to change society even further, and at an increasingly accelerated pace. Former systems of social control which rested heavily on enculturation, internalized sanctions, and ridicule now required formal statement of their legal principles, a machinery of adjudication, and a formally constituted police authority. The emergence of these and other control institutions were associated with the final shift of prime authority from kinship means to territorial means and describes the evolution of complex forms of government associated with the state. It was the passage to stratified society which laid the basis for the complex division of labor which underlies modern society. It also gave rise to various arrangements of socio-economic classes and led directly to both classical and modern forms of colonialism and imperialism.

The Transition to Stratified Society

The decisive significance of stratification is not that it sees differential amounts of wealth in different hands but that it sees two kinds of access to strategic resources. One of these is privileged and unimpeded; the other is impaired, depending on complexes of permission which frequently require the payment of dues, rents, or taxes in labor or in kind. The existence of such a distinction enables the growth of exploitation, whether of a relatively simple kind based upon drudge slavery or of a more complex type associated with involved divisions of labor and intricate class systems. The development of stratification also encourages the emergence of communities composed of kin parts and non-kin parts which, as wholes, operate on the basis of non-kin mechanisms.

So enormous is the significance of the shift to stratification that previous commentators have found it essential that the movement be associated with the most powerful people in the society. Landtman, for example, says: "It is in conjunction with the dissimilarity of individual endowments that inequality of wealth has conduced to the rise of social differentiation. As a matter of course the difference as regards property in many cases goes hand in hand with difference in personal qualities. A skilful hunter or fisher, or a victorious warrior, has naturally a better prospect of acquiring a fortune than one who is inferior to him in these respects" (Landtman 1938, p. 68).

If our analysis is correct, however, such is definitely not the case. The statuses mentioned by Landtman are not those which stand to make great accumulations but rather stand to make great give-aways. Furthermore, the leap from distribution to power is unwarranted by the ethnographic evidence.

There are unquestionably a number of ways in which secondary conditions of stratification can emerge. That is, once the development of stratification proceeds from contact with and tutelage by cultures which are at the least already stratified and which may be the possessors of mature state organization, there are many specific ways in which simpler cultures can be transformed into stratified societies. The ways which come quickest to mind include the extension of the complex society's legal definitions of property to the simpler society, the introduction of all-purpose money and wage labor, and the creation of an administrative system for the operation of the simpler society on a basis which is acceptable to the superordinate state. Often the external provenance of these elements is obvious in their misfit appearance. A sharper look may reveal, indeed, that the stratified system is a mere façade operated for and often by persons who have no genuine local identities, while the local system continues to maintain informally, and sometimes in secrecy, the older organization of the society. Put more concretely, this means that "government" appointed chiefs are respected only in certain limited situations and that the main weight of social control continues to rest upon traditional authorities and institutions which may not even be recognized by the ruling power.

An excellent climate for the development of stratification in a simple society can be supplied in a relatively indirect way by a society of advanced organization. Let us take the situation in which a culture has no concept of nuclear family rights to land. The economy is based upon hunting, trapping, and fishing, with the streams and forests being associated in a general way with weakly organized bands which have a decided tendency to fragment and reconstitute, each time with potentially different membership. Subvert this setup with an external market for furs and a substantial basis for stratification has been laid. This system, like the direct intervention of a superordinate state, also seems to have certain limitations for there is ample evidence that the development of private property in such a system as that just mentioned is confined to trapping lines and does not extend to general subsistence hunting and fishing in the area (see Leacock, 1958).

Another situation that bears study is one in which important trade routes linking two or more advanced societies traverse marginal areas in which simple societies are located. Certain geographical conditions make it possible for the relatively primitive folk to enhance their economies with fruits derived from the plunder of this trade or, in a more mature system, by extorting tribute from the merchants who must pass by. The remoteness of these areas, the difficulty of the terrain and the extreme difficulties and costs of sending a punitive force to pacify the area often enables the simpler people to harass populations whose cultural means for organized violence far exceeds their own. Be this as it may, the combination of the examples of organization presented by the outposts of complexly organized societies and the availability of commodities which could not be produced in the simple culture may combine to lay the basis for an emergence of stratification. Precisely such conditions seem partially responsible for the political developments described for the Kachin (Leach, 1954, esp. pp. 235, 247 ff.).

None of this seems to apply to the pristine emergence of stratification. As a matter of fact, it is not even particularly suggestive. There is, however, one particular ecological condition that appears in highland Burma which also has been noted elsewhere, each time in association with rather basic shifts in social organization paralleling those already sketched in the previous section of this paper. We refer to the shift from rainfall to irrigation farming, particularly to the construction of terraced fields. This is admittedly a restricted ethnographic phenomenon and as such it cannot bear the weight of any general theory. It is the suggestive character of these developments and the possibility of extrapolating from them to hypothetical pristine conditions that makes them so interesting.

In brief, the shift to irrigation and terracing is from swiddens or impermanent fields to plots which will remain in permanent cultivation for decades and generations. Whereas we have previously stressed the possible role of hydro-agriculture in the transition from egalitarian to rank society, we now note its possible role in the transition to stratification. This it could accomplish by creating conditions under which access to strategic resources, in this case land and water, would be made the specific prerogative of small-scale kin groups such as minimal lineages or even stem families. Through the emergence of hydro-agriculture a community which previously acknowledged no *permanent* association between particular component units and particular stretches of land now begins to recognize such permanent and exclusive rights. Incidentally, the evidence seems to indicate that the rank-forming tendencies of hydro-agriculture need not occur prior to the tendencies toward stratification: both can occur concomitantly. This in turn suggests that we must be cautious in constructing our theory not to make stratification emerge from ranking, though under particular circumstances this is certainly possible.

A point of considerable interest about hydro-agriculture is that it seems to present the possibility of an emergence of stratification in the absence of a problem of over-population or resource limitation. We need a great deal of further thought on the matter. Studies of the last two decades, in which a considerably higher degree of agricultural expertise on the part of the fieldworkers has been manifested than was formerly the case, have increasingly tended to show that hydro-agriculture does not invariably out-produce slash and burn and that, other things being equal, a population does not automatically prefer hydro-agriculture as a more rationalized approach to agricultural subsistence. Here we can introduce a factor previously excluded. The hydro-agricultural system invariably has a higher degree of settlement concentration than swiddens. Accordingly, it would seem to have considerable value in the maintenance of systems of defense, given the presence of extensive warfare. Here then, is a point at which military considerations would seem to play an important if essentially reinforcing role in the broad evolutionary developments which we are considering.

The writer is intrigued with another possibility for the emergence of stratification. Once again, the conditions involved seem a little too specific to serve the purpose of a single unified theory. It requires the postulation of a society with a fixed rule of residence, preferably one of the simpler ones such as patrilocality/virilocality or matrilocality/uxorilocality [6] and a fixed rule of descent, preferably one parallel to the residence rule. It further postulates a condition of population expansion such that, given slash and burn agriculture, the society is very near the limits of the carrying capacity of the system. Such conditions are very likely to develop at varying speeds within an area of several hundred miles due to obvious imbalances in reproductive rates and to microecological variation. Now, as long as there is no notable pressure of people on the land, deviation in residence and even in descent will be expectable though quite unusual and lacking in motivation. As the situation grows grave in one area but remains relatively open in another, there may be a tendency for a slight readjustment in residence rules to occur. For example, in a normally virilocal society, the woman who brings her husband back to her natal group transgresses a few customary rules in doing so but presents her agnates with no basic problems in resource allocation since she, as a member of the agnatic group, has her own rights of access which may be shared by the spouse during her lifetime. The complication arises at her death when her husband and all of her children discover themselves to be in an anomalous position since they are not members of the kin community. Where local land problems are not severe and where such breaches of the residence pattern are yet uncommon, it is not unlikely that the aliens will be accepted as *de facto* members of the community with the expectation that future generations will revert to custom, the unorthodox switch of residence fading in memory with the passage of time. Here we have a crude and informal *ambil-anak*. But as the local community enters worsening ecological circumstances and as the exceptional residence becomes more frequent, the residence and descent rules, particularly the latter, assume greater and greater importance. As the situation continues, the community is slowly altered, though the members of the community may be unable to state exactly what the changes are. The result, however, is clear. There are now two kinds of people in the village where formerly there was only one. Now there are kernel villagers, those who have unimpaired access to land, and those whose tenure rests upon other conditions, such as loyalty to a patron, or tribute, or even a precarious squatter's right.

The State Society

The word should be abandoned entirely ... after this chapter the word will be avoided scrupulously and no severe hardship in expression will result. In fact, clarity of expression demands this abstinence.

(Easton, 1953, p. 108)

The word was "state" and the writer, a political scientist, was reacting to some of the problems in his own field in making this judgment, but it does look as if he was pushed to drastic action by the work of some anthropologists in whose hands the concept of state lost all character and utility, finally ending as a cultural universal. E. Adamson Hoebel, one of the few United States anthropologists to make a serious specialization in the field of law and the state, formerly introduced students to this question by remarking that

where there is political organization there is a state. If political organization is universal, so then is the state. One is the group, the other an institutionalized complex of behavior.   (Hoebel, 1949, p. 376)

In a revision of the same book after a few years, Hoebel's treatment of the subject seems to indicate that he is in the process of rethinking the matter. His summary words, however, repeat the same conclusion:

Political organization is characteristic of every society.... That part of culture that is recognized as political organization is what constitutes the state. (Hoebel, 1958, p. 506)

This is a far cry from the approach of evolutionists to the state as exemplified in Sumner and Keller (1927, I, 700):

The term state is properly reserved for a somewhat highly developed regulative organization.... It is an organization with authority and discipline essential to large-scale achievements, as compared with the family, for example, which is an organization on the same lines but simpler and less potent.

Without making a special issue of the definition of the state (which would easily consume the entire space of this article, if not the volume) let me note one used by the jurist Léon Duguit which conveys the sense most useful to the point of view of this paper:

En prenant le mot dans son sens le plus général, on peut dire qu'il y a un État toutes les fois qu'il existe dans une société donnée une différenciation politique, quelque rudimentaire ou quelque compliquée et developée qu'elle soit. Le mot État designe soit les gouvernants où le pouvoir politique, soit la société elle-même, où existe cette différenciation entre gouvernants et gouvernés et où existe par là même une puissance politique.

(Duguit, 1921, p. 395)

The difference between Hoebel and Duguit seems to be in the clear statement of power. Reviewing our own paper in the light of this difference we note our previous emphasis on the absence of coercive economic or political power in the egalitarian and rank societies. It is only in the stratified society that such power emerges from embryonic and universal foreshadowings in familial organization.

The maturation of social stratification has manifold implications depending on the precise circumstances in which the developments take place. All subsequent courses, however, have a certain area of overlap; the new social order, with its differential allocation of access to strategic resources, must be maintained and strengthened. In a simple stratified society in which class differentials are more implicit than explicit the network of kin relations covers a sufficient portion of the total fabric of social relations so that areas not specifically governed by genuine kinship relations can be covered by their sociological extensions. The dynamic of stratification is such that this situation cannot endure. The stratified kin group emphasizes its exclusiveness: it erodes the corporative economic functions formerly associated with stipulated kinship and at every turn it amputates extensions of the demonstrated kin unit. The result of this pruning is that the network of kin relations fails more and more to coincide with the network of personal relations. Sooner or later the discrepancy is of such magnitude that, were non-kin sanctions and non-kin agencies absent or structured along customary lines only, the society would dissolve in uncomposable conflict.

The emergent state, then, is the organization of the power of the society on a supra-kin basis. Among its earliest tasks is the maintenance of general order but scarcely discernible from this is its need to support the order of stratification. The defense of a complete system of individual statuses is impossible so the early state concentrates on a few key statuses (helping to explain the tendency to convert any crime into either sacrilege or *lèse majesté*) and on the basic principles of organization, e.g., the idea of hierarchy, property, and the power of the law.

The implementation of these primary functions of the state gives rise to a number of specific and characteristic secondary functions, each of which is associated with one or more particular institutions of its own. These secondary functions include population control in the most general sense (the fixing of boundaries and the definition of the unit; establishment of categories of membership; census). Also a secondary function is the disposal of trouble cases (civil and criminal laws moving toward the status of codes; regular legal procedure; regular officers of adjudication). The protection of sovereignty is also included (maintenance of military forces; police forces and power; eminent domain). Finally, all of the preceding require fiscal support, and this is achieved in the main through taxation and conscription.

In treating of this bare but essential list of state functions and institutions the idea of the state as a universal aspect of culture dissolves as a fantasy. The institutions just itemized may be made to appear in ones or twos in certain primitive societies by exaggeration and by the neglect of known history. In no egalitarian society and in no rank society do a majority of the functions enumerated appear regardless of their guise. Furthermore there is no indication of their appearance as a unified functional response to basic sociocultural needs except in those stratified societies which are verging upon statehood.

The Transition to State

Just as stratified society grew out of antecedent forms of society without the conscious awareness of the culture carriers, so it would seem that the state emerged from the stratified society in a similar, inexorable way. If this hypothesis is correct, then such an explanation as the so-called "conquest theory" can be accepted only as a special case of "secondary-state" formation. The conquests discussed by such a theorist as Franz Oppenheimer (1914) established not stratification but super-stratification, either the conqueror or the conquered, or perhaps even both, already being internally stratified.

The problem of the transition to state is so huge and requires such painstaking application to the available archaeological and historical evidence that it would be foolish to pursue it seriously here. Let us conclude, therefore, by harking back to statements made at the outset of this paper, and noting again the distinction between pristine and secondary states. By the former term is meant a state that has developed *sui generis* out of purely local conditions. No previous state, with its acculturative pressures, can be discerned in the background of a pristine state. The secondary state, on the other hand, is pushed by one means or another toward a higher form of organization by an external power which has already been raised to statehood.

The number of pristine states is strictly limited; several centuries, possibly two millennia, have elapsed since the last one emerged in Meso-America, and there seems to be no possibility that any further states of the pristine type will evolve, though further research may bring to light some of the distant past of which we yet have no positive information. In all, there seems to have been some six centers at which pristine states emerged, four in the Old World and two in the New: the Tigris-Euphrates area, the region of the lower Nile, the country drained by the Indus and the middle course of the Huang Ho where it is joined by the Han, Wei, and Fen. The separate areas of Peru-Bolivia and Meso-America complete the roster.

If there is utility in the concept of the pristine state and if history has been read correctly in limiting the designation to the six areas just enumerated, then we discover a remarkable correlation between areas demanding irrigation or flood control and the pristine state. Certainly this is no discovery of the author. It is one of the central ideas of

Wittfogel's theory and has received extensive treatment from Julian Steward and others (see Steward, 1955, pp. 178-209; Steward *et al.,* 1955). The implication of the "hydraulic theory" for this paper, however, is that the development of the state as an internal phenomenon is associated with major tasks of drainage and irrigation. The emergence of a control system to ensure the operation of the economy is closely tied to the appearance of a distinctive class system and certain constellations of power in the hands of a managerial bureaucracy which frequently operates below a ruler who commands theoretically unlimited power.

It is an interesting commentary on nineteenth-century political philosophy that the starting point of so many theories was, of necessity, the Classical world of Greece and Rome. According to the present hypothesis, however, both of these great political developments of antiquity were not pristine but secondary formations which built on cultural foundations laid two thousand years and more before the rise of Greece. Furthermore, it would seem that the active commercial and military influences of the truly ancient pristine states, mediated through the earliest of the secondary states to appear in Asia Minor and the eastern Mediterranean littoral, were catalysts in the events of the northern and western Mediterranean.

Conclusion

The close of a paper like this, which moves like a gadfly from time to time, place to place, and subject matter to subject matter, and which never pauses long enough to make a truly detailed inquiry or supply the needed documentation, the close of such a paper requires an apology perhaps more than a conclusion.

I have been led to write this paper by my ignorance of any modern attempt to link up the contributions which have been made in many sub-disciplines into a single unified theory of the emergence of social stratification and the state. That the theory offered here is crude, often too special, and by no means documented seems less important than that it may be used as a sitting duck to attract the fire and better aim of others.

NOTES

[1] The reader may object to crediting Polanyi with the concept of a reciprocal economy. While it is true that Thurnwald and Malinowski earlier expressed

similar concepts, and Durkheim, with his distinction between segmental and organic societies, also foreshadows this development, it awaited Polanyi's analysis to place reciprocal economies into systematic harmony with other, more complex types of economy, such as the redistributive type discussed later on, and the market kind as well. For Polanyi's definitions of each of these types see Polanyi, Arensberg, and Pearson, 1957, pp. 250-56.

[2] For an ethnographic illustration of this point see Oliver, 1955, pp. 422 ff.

[3] These, of course, would be ranked lineages or ranked clans. Cf. Fried, 1957, pp. 23-26.

[4] As does Leach 1954, p. 10.

[5] Strategic resources are those things which, given the technological base and environmental setting of the culture, maintain subsistence. See Fried, 1957, p. 24.

[6] Our residence terms follow usage suggested by J. L. Fischer (1958).

REFERENCES

Duguit, Léon. 1921. Traité de droit constitutionnel. 2d ed. Vol. 1. Paris.

Easton, David. 1953. The Political System. New York.

Fischer, J. L. 1958. "The Classification of Residence in Censuses," *American Anthropologist*, 60:508-17.

Fried, Morton H. 1957. "The Classification of Corporate Unilineal Descent Groups," *Journal of the Royal Anthropological Institute*, 87:1-29.

Hoebel, E. Adamson. 1949. Man in the Primitive World. 1st ed. New York.

────── 1958. Man in the Primitive World. 2d ed. New York.

Kirchhoff, Paul. 1935. "The Principles of Clanship in Human Society." (Ms; cf. *Davidson Journal of Anthropology* 1 [1955]).

Landtman, Gunnar. 1938. The Origin of the Inequality of the Social Classes. London.

Leach, E. R. 1954. Political Systems of Highland Burma. Cambridge, Mass.

Leacock, Eleanor. 1958. "Status among the Montagnais-Naskapi of Labrador," *Ethnohistory*, 5:Part 3:200-209.

Oliver, Douglas. 1955. A Solomon Island Society. Cambridge, Mass.

Oppenheimer, Franz. 1914. The State: Its History and Development Viewed Sociologically. New York.

Polanyi, Karl, Conrad M. Arensberg, and Harry W. Pearson, eds. 1957. Trade and Market in the Early Empires. Glencoe, Ill.

Sahlins, Marshall. 1958. Social Stratification in Polynesia. Seattle.

────── 1957. "Differentiation by Adaptation in Polynesian Societies," *Journal of the Polynesian Society*, 66:291-300.

Steward, Julian H. 1955. Theory of Culture Change. Urbana, Ill.

Steward, Julian H., et al. 1955. Irrigation Civilizations: A Comparative Study. Social Science Monographs #1, Washington, D.C.

Sumner, W. G., and A. G. Keller. 1927. The Science of Society. New Haven, Conn.

Tylor, Edward B. 1888. "On a Method of Investigating the Development of Institutions; Applied to Laws of Marriage and Descent," *Journal of the Royal Anthropological Institute*, 18:245-69.

White, Leslie. 1948. "The Definition and Prohibition of Incest," *American Anthropologist*, 50:416-35.

Wittfogel, Karl A. 1957. Oriental Despotism. New Haven, Conn.

CARRIER ACCULTURATION

THE DIRECT HISTORICAL APPROACH

By Julian H. Steward

UNIVERSITY OF ILLINOIS

The Problem

IN 1940 there were 1,666 Carrier Indians on 23 reserves scattered in the general area of Stuart Lake and Babine Lake. The population of the reserves ranged from 5 at Black Water to 257 at Fort St. James on Stuart Lake, where the present research was carried out. These Indians still spoke their own language as well as English, retained a few native crafts, and were fairly orthodox Catholics. They subsisted partly by hunting and fishing, but more importantly they depended upon the fur-trapping in the area. Carefully mapped trapping territories were registered in the names of individuals with the Provincial Government of British Columbia (see map) and protected against exploitative trespass by the game warden.

A century ago these same people were divided into what Jenness and Morice call "phratries." "Phratry" is hardly the appropriate term, however, since the divisions were not strictly unilinear, exogamous, non-localized groups, and they were not subdivided into clans. Rather they were localized groups which carried titles of nobility that theoretically were inherited matrilineally but in practice were acquired in various ways. The titles were validated by potlatches supported by the wealth in fur and fish taken from particular territories.

Two centuries ago the Carrier were hunters and fishers who lived in some kind of simple bands and lacked any nobility or potlatching.

The research problem was, first, to ascertain the process of change from the hunting bands to the nobility and potlatches and, second, to understand how the latter broke down into individual families, each with its trapping territory.

The nature of the earlier change from hunting bands to a society of nobles and commoners is inferential, since it took place before whites entered Carrier country. There are interesting similarities and differences between the northern Carrier, herein discussed, and the Alkatcho Carrier to the south, who were studied by Irving Goldman. The Stuart Lake

Carrier derived their northwest coast patterns ultimately from the matri-lineal Tsimshian of the Skeena River who adjoined the Carrier of the Babine and Bulkley rivers, both tributaries of the Skeena, whereas the Alkatcho were influenced by their western neighbors, the patrilineal Bella Coola.

The breakdown of the "phratry" system during the last two or three generations and the division of territories of nobles into individual trapping territories are well documented. It was possible to begin with the Provincial British Columbian maps which showed registered trapping territories of 1939, and, by means of genealogies, to trace the inheritance of these back to the nobility holdings. These genealogies were especially well illustrated by the case of Kwah, the native chief of the Fort St. James village, whose grandson, the elderly and extraordinarily able "chief," Louis Billy Prince, was my main informant. The processes were also verified by tracing the genealogies and land tenure among holders of other trapping territories in the Stuart Lake region.

Hunting Bands

The nature of the early Carrier hunting bands can only be surmised. Throughout most of north central Canada, Athabaskan bands were "composite," that is, multifamily societies which subsisted mainly by hunting large caribou herds. The Carrier live on the Pacific watershed and had access to salmon as well as caribou and, later, to moose. While their fisheries were not comparable to those of the downstream Indians —e.g. on the Lower Skeena and Fraser rivers—they yielded perhaps 50 percent of the foods. This densely forested, mountainous area with its thousands of lakes and streams was also rich in fur-bearing animals, which, however, were important to the aboriginal people more for their meat than their pelts.

There is nothing in recorded or recent Stuart Lake ethnography that clearly indicates the nature of early Carrier band organization. Goldman believes that the Alkatcho Carrier bands may have consisted of extended and predominantly patrilineal families which controlled trapping terri-tories. Owing to the comparative scarcity of caribou, which later dis-appeared to be replaced by moose, and to the abundance of fish and nonmigratory small game, such localization may have characterized all the Carrier. These extended family units, however, should be distinguished from the nuclear families which held trapping territories in eastern

Canada and which today hold such territories among the Carrier. While
Cooper and Speck had argued that family territories were aboriginal,
the evidence seems pretty conclusive that they represent the breakdown
of hunting bands and the emergence of the family as the socioeconomic
unit in response to the fur trade. The eastern Algonkian family territories,
in other words, are the same as the registered Carrier territories of the
present day, and they developed for the same reasons.

The map shows the principal permanent Carrier villages known in
historic times. Probably the population was much more dispersed before
the era of fur trade than it is today. Fort St. James, established in 1806
at an Indian village at the outlet of the lake, became a major trading post
and religious center of central British Columbia by mid-century. In 1909
it had 198 persons, and in 1939 it had 257. That the function of village
chief remained distinct from that of nobles and that it was inherited
patrilineally, whereas the latter was in theory acquired matrilineally,
accords with Goldman's data in indicating strong patrilineality among

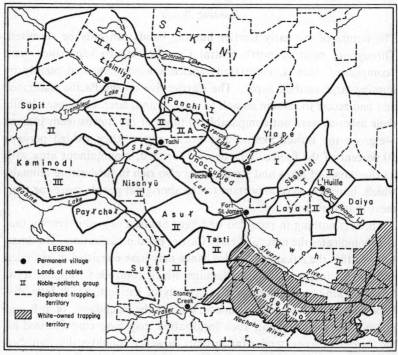

CARRIER TERRITORIES

the hunting bands. Possibly the smaller communities were actual patri-lineages.

From Band to Nobility and Potlatch

Since introduction of the northwest coast social and economic patterns to the Carrier probably took place two or three decades before the whites entered their country and without any change whatever in exploitative technology or local resources, this seemed to represent a case in which the cultural ecology or organization of society with respect to land use had considerable latitude for variation. If so, the change from bands to nobles and potlatching was caused by the fortuitous historic circumstance of contact with the coast.

As Goldman clearly implies, however, this interpretation is untenable. The fur trade reached important proportions on the northwest coast in the last two decades of the eighteenth century. The coastal Indians, acting as middlemen for the Indians living east of the Coast Ranges, created a new source of wealth in furs. Without any change in resources or pro-ductive technology (until steel goods began to filter in), the Carrier suddenly had a negotiable surplus.

In considering the processes by which the pattern of nobility spread inland to the Carrier, it is important to distinguish production of basic subsistence commodities—food, clothing, housing—from surplus goods, which were predominantly furs and secondarily fish. In a sense, two social arrangements for land use—two unlike cultural ecological adap-tations—coexisted.

At Stuart Lake, subsistence continued to follow the older pattern in that people could hunt food animals anywhere and, if in dire need, could kill fur-bearing animals for food provided they gave the pelt to the owner of potlatch rights. The village chief, *köyohodachum* ("village big tree"), had the duties of exhorting people to provide for their own needs, of arbitrating disputes over hunting boundaries (probably band boundaries regarding large game), and settling disagreements among villages. This position was strongly patrilineal, passing to the chief's brother or son or to someone chosen by the retiring chief for his ability. Later it tended to be elective, and in some cases the chief was appointed by government officials or Catholic missionaries.

A title of nobility might also be possessed by a village chief, but the two positions were separable. Thus, Kwah at Fort St. James was *köyohodachum* and held the highest potlatch title, *agetas*. But the title of *agetas* was passed on to Yuwani, his nephew (probably his sister's son, which accords with the theory of descent), while the village chieftainship was taken over by Prince, his own son. In part, this latter succession reflected or at least accorded with white interests, for the government officials had designated Kwah as "king" and his son, of whom they approved, as "Prince."

There was less conflict between the hunting band pattern and the potlatching pattern among the Alkatcho Carrier than among the northern Carrier. The former retained their patrilineal pattern as the basic economic, social, and potlatching unit, although it is not clear whether these units were localized. Through intermarriage with the Bella Coola and establishment of titles of nobility supported by the new surplus, the old could be transformed into the new.

The mechanisms of diffusion from the matrilineal Tsimshian to the northern Carrier are more complicated and more hypothetical. The Bulkley River and Babine River Carrier unquestionably first acquired the coastal patterns through intermarriage or other direct contact with the Tsimshian and passed them eastward to Stuart Lake. In theory, a title of nobility is transferred to the sister's son, and marriage, especially of the eldest son, is with the mother's brother's daughter. My recorded genealogies go back to the parents of Kwah, who died in 1840, but they show no case of cross-cousin marriage, and Carrier kinship terminology in no way suggests such marriage. The wide distribution of cross-cousin marriage among the Athabaskan-speaking peoples east of the Coastal Range, however, makes the early occurrence of cross-cousin marriage among the Carrier plausible.

It is quite possible, then, that the introduction of a nobility inherited from a man by his sister's son was initially facilitated by the marriage of his own daughter to his sister's son. Cross-cousin marriage may, therefore, have provided the mechanism for the addition of matrilineal principles of a class of nobles into an otherwise patrilineal hunting and fishing people.

But among the Stuart Lake and Babine Lake Carrier the system of nobility and potlatching involved individuals rather than groups. Consequently, the term "phratry" is inappropriate. Individual men held titles which gave rights to the surplus from certain tracts of land which they used to potlatch. The common people who subsisted on this land were required to contribute furs and certain foods to the nobles. They were said to be of the same "company," that is, "phratry," as the nobles, but this probably did not imply genuinely exogamous matrilineal kin groups. The commoners may in fact have been related through either parent to their nobles; for it was the title to nobility rather than land use for subsistence purposes that was theoretically inherited by a man's sister's son.

While the earliest genealogical data are from the latter part of the nineteenth century, a time when the Hudson's Bay Company, Catholic missionaries, and other outside influences were beginning to undermine the pattern of nobility, it seems clear that matrilineal principles never became as firmly rooted as among the Tsimshian or coastal people. At Fort St. James there were only two so-called phratries, while a third was represented only at the western end of Stuart Lake. Of the first two, Ltsəməshyu (II), was predominant at Fort St. James, where at least six of its nobles resided. Each of these nobles controlled the surplus of a tract adjoining the lake. The other group, Lasilyu (I), had one noble residing at Fort St. James and several others to the north and east. Each controlled a tract.

Toward Fraser Lake to the south, the Ltsəməshyu titles seem to have been very recently introduced from Fort St. James. Just to the east of Stuart Lake live the Sekani, who, according to Jenness, attempted fairly recently to adopt the nobility-potlatch system but had to give it up for lack of resources. My own data show that the Carrier nobles were pressing eastward, incorporating Sekani tracts.

The determining factor in the spread of this pattern seems clearly to have been potential surplus. The Bulkley and Babine rivers were not far from the coast and received salmon runs. Since feasting as well as present-giving was part of the potlatch pattern, fisheries were extremely important. At Stuart Lake, which is virtually the source of the Fraser River and is far from the coast, the salmon were reduced in numbers and much decreased in weight by their long travel. While the country afforded beaver, fox, and other fur-bearing animals, it did not provide the quantity of trade pelts realized by the coastal Indians in sea otter. The quantitative basis of potlatching was meager at Stuart Lake but even poorer among the Sekani, who lacked salmon fisheries. In their failure to maintain a nobility-potlatch pattern, the Sekani are more like the many Canadian Indians who, under the fur trade, changed from hunting bands directly into individual families with trap lines.

These interpretative remarks are illustrated by the map and by specific data of the genealogies and land use. A comparison of this information with that of Morice and Jenness indicates the fading of the pattern toward the east. The table shows the "phratries" recorded from west to east.

The division of the Bulkley River people into five phratries, four of which were subdivided into three clans each, certainly represents a strong coastal pattern. My own informants recorded five divisions for Babine Lake, three of which clearly correspond with Bulkley River groups. The other two names, Kwanpahoten and Grand Trunk (named from the railroad), do not correspond to the phratries on Bulkley River, but Kwanpahoten means "fireside" and may have been derived from one of the Bulkley River Laksilyu clans. Morice's five Stuart Lake groups may actually include people farther afield, for my informants were very definite that Fort St. James had only two. Correspondences are in I (Lasilyu), II (Łtəmǝshyu), and III (Tsayu). But the subdivision into clans breaks down, for Lasilyu was merely equated to frog, which Morice equated to Łtsǝmǝshyu, and Tsayu was identified as owl. Moreover, the Stuart Lake people considered Lasilyu the same as Kwanpahoten which was distinctive at Babine Lake; and they regarded Tsayu, which occurred between Stuart Lake and Trembleur Lake as the equivalent of Łtsǝmǝlshu, since it helped the latter potlatch.

While the significance of these divisions bears far more comparative study, it seems clear that as a status system spread eastward through intermarriage, control of surplus, and perhaps other factors, it became so simplified that Stuart Lake and Stoney Creek had only two main divisions and no subdivisions, and that nominal equivalents from one locality to another became confused. In fact they became so confused that such names as Grand Trunk and Japan were adopted in certain localities.

Within the framework of this somewhat erratic diffusion, most of the people of Fort St. James at Stuart Lake were brought into Łtsǝmǝshyu, shown on the map as II. The group II nobles at Fort St. James holding land were Kwah, Asuł, Təsti, Kədǝlcho, and Daiya, while Skǝlǝtjat of group I, (Lasilyu), also lived in this village. While each of these five nobles of II controlled the surplus of the territory indicated on the map and potlatched after their own fashion, they were subservient to Kwah, who held the title of *agetas* and was thus supreme over all group II nobles. The equation of IIA, Tsayu to the northwest, to II is based upon the former's obligation to assist in potlatching.

In other words, group II diffused into the Stuart Lake area, especially

NORTHERN CARRIER NOBLE-POTLATCH OR PHRATRY GROUPS

Bulkley River (Jenness)		Babine Lake (Steward)	Stuart Lake (Morice)	Stuart Lake (Steward)	Stoney Creek (Steward)
Phratry	Clans				
I. Laksilyu	Many eyes House On Flat Rock House Fireside House	I. Lasilyu	I. Yesilyu	I. Lasilyu =Kwanpahoten Frog	I. Nukkwiten =Lasilyu
II. Laksamshyu	Sun House Twisted House Owl House	II. Łtsemashyu	II. Łtsemashyu Frog	II. Łtsemelshu Owl = IIA. Tsayu at Trembleur Lake	II. Ta'chekten =Łtsemelshu
III. Tsayu	Beaver	III. Sayu	III. Tsayu		
IV. Gitamtanyu	Grizzly House Middle of many Anskaski	IV. Grand Trunk	IV. Təm'tenyu		
V. Gilserhyu	Dark House Thin House Bark House	V. Kwanpahoten	V. Kwanpahotene		

to Fort St. James, and its several nobles held tiny feudal domains while being subservient to the principal lord or *agetas*, Kwah. But the existence of strong hereditary principles, marriage rules, or group organization beyond the obligation to supply surplus to the noble is very questionable.

Of ten marriages of Ɫtsəməshyu nobles at Fort St. James, four were with local Ɫtsəməshyu women, four with local Lasilyu women, and two with Stoney Creek women who apparently belonged to no nobility group. Marriages of nobles elsewhere near Stuart Lake show a similar lack of consistent exogamy either by noble group or locality.

There was, however, a strong feeling about keeping the title within the group. In the case of exogamous marriage, the title passed to the sister's son; in the case of endogamy, it often passed to a man's own son or to a son-in-law. However, the title required land to support it, and land was the object of some jockeying. New lands at Stoney Creek and among the Sekani were being brought under the control of Fort St. James nobles, while local land might be exchanged in return for assistance in potlatching or even acquired forcibly. Kwah, the village chief and supreme noble at Fort St. James arbitrated land disputes, but he also came out the richer himself.

From Nobility to Individual Family

The nature of the land rights of the nobility and of the factors which destroyed this pattern are best seen in the case histories of the nobles indicated on the map. The undoing of the nobles had already begun during the lifetime of the earliest men in the genealogies. The principal factors were the trading companies, the Catholic Church, and the social and political effects of the Provincial Government and white settlers. The trading companies gave direct access to manufactured goods, the desire for which eventually overshadowed the importance of status. The interest in retention rather than ceremonial giving of material goods was enhanced as white trappers began to move into the country. In the course of time, new concepts of land rights came into conflict with and finally superseded the old; trap lines registered under Provincial law destroyed the domains of the nobles. (The territories indicated on the map by dotted lines were registered in 1926.) Meanwhile the Catholic Church, especially under the able missionizing efforts of the priest-ethnographer Father Morice, destroyed the religious sanction of the nobility and potlatch at Stuart Lake.

These processes had run their course more completely at Stuart Lake than elsewhere. In 1939, in certain isolated areas, the Carrier, though holding registered trap lines and nominally Catholic, had no resident priests and were still holding secret potlatches. This same year certain Skeena River Tsmishian, although largely deprived of their fisheries and other sources of wealth and still caught in the economic depression, were using relief money to potlatch. The long-run outcome of individualization of sources of wealth, however, is clear. And at Fort St. James, the dependence upon certain European foods, hardware, clothing, and most material essentials had reached the point where each individual had to trade his wealth in furs in order to support his family.

The case history of Kwah is the most interesting. Kwah was the son of a Lasilyu nobleman from Fort St. James and a Ltsəməshyu woman from Stoney Creek. That he acquired control of several main tracts around Fort St. James—those mapped as Kwah, Təsti and Asuł—suggests that his role as village chief was a main factor in gaining support for his title, *agetas*, which he inherited orthodoxly from his mother's brother. At some point Kwah shared the title with his brother, Howeapah. Later it passed to his nephew (his sister's son?) Yuwani, who seems to have acquired it by marrying Kwah's widow. Still later, Təsti, a possible relative of Kwah, who had trapped with him, acquired the title *agetas*. Meanwhile, Kwah's son, Prince, initiated the breakdown of nobility and their tracts. As village chief but not *agetas*, he forced Təsti back into the land shown on the map and in time divided the land mapped as Kwah's among his own sons and grandsons. During this time, white trappers pressing in from the east had preempted the former territories of Kwah which are shaded on the map, and they now have legal rights to them.

Kwah's brother's (Howeapah's) son, Kədəlcho, belonged to group II but was a minor noble. He married a Stoney Creek woman who probably belonged to no group and claimed land just south of Stuart River. This was lost to the whites.

The case of Asuł and Skələtjat also shows failure to follow a fixed rule. Skələtjat's sister's son, Tylee, born of a marriage to Asuł, inherited his uncle's land but passed it on to his own son by a marriage to a Stoney Creek woman. Asuł, however, gave his land south of Stuart Lake to his own son, Song (Tylee's brother), who gave it to his son, Bacome Song. Asuł is thought to have acquired this land from his first wife's family.

Layał, who lived in the village on the western shore of Great Beaver

Lake, obtained the land from his mother's brother, a member of the same village. In the absence of children he passed on a portion of it to the son of a part Cree, who in turn gave it to his stepson.

Daiya, of group II, married a woman of II and acquired from her father the territory east of Great Beaver Lake. Daiya took Asuł's potlatch name and was then called "nephew" by Asuł, although they were not related. Part of Daiya's land was given to Sagalon, his friend, and part to his wife's sister's son, Louie Mattess.

Summary

While the course of Carrier culture change is somewhat inferential in early times and confused in certain detail, its broad outlines can be seen in terms of two culminations which are closely paralleled elsewhere. Murphy and Steward have shown that the Munducurú of the Amazon and the Montagnais of Labrador acquired a new source of wealth in rubber tapping and fur trapping respectively. At first, the village chief of the Mundurucú and the band chief of the Montagnais acquired great power through assuming the new role or function of entrepreneur in the trade. In time, however, individual tappers and trappers preferred to trade directly with the whites, whereupon band or village organization disintegrated and individual families acquired rights to their own delimited territories.

Among the Carrier, too, the fur trade created a new wealth and local chiefs came into prominence. The specific pattern of wealth prominence, however, was dictated by contacts with coastal Indians. The formerly patrilineal Alkatcho Carrier bands exalted the position of their chiefs by reinforcing them with potlatch-sanctioned titles borrowed from the patrilineal Bella Coola. The northern Carrier were seemingly involved in a conflict that was never wholly resolved. Village chieftainship was a separable role from potlatch nobility, although the same man might hold both. There can be little doubt, however, that the power of the village chief enabled him to assume potlatch titles when the effect of the fur trade was felt and the Tsimshian matrilineal pattern began to spread. Since the Stuart Lake pattern was one of individual titles with rights to surplus from tracts of land rather than one of strictly exogamous groups, the feeling was that the titles should be kept in the "phratry" or "company." Inheritance by the sister's son served this end, but in the absence of exogamy it was not the only means to the end. Possibly inheritance by the sister's son was more strictly observed between 1800 and 1850. The present data, which relate mainly to a period beginning shortly after 1850, show such inheritance only when there was marriage between the two principal title groups. But they also show that marriages within the groups were equally frequent and that inheritance by the son or the daughter's husband occurred in these cases.

The fur trade brought about a concentration of the new surplus in the hands of a few men. The half dozen or so title holders among the Ltsəməshyu group living at Fort St. James helped one another potlatch, and especially they helped the holder of the principal title, *agetas*. Such concentration is fairly common among people who acquire a new source of wealth, even though there may be local mechanisms, such as fear of witchcraft as among the Navajo or ceremonial obligations as among the many corporate peasants of Latin America, for leveling the wealth. In fact, the dissipation of accumulated wealth in the *cargos* or ceremonies of the peasants has a certain resemblance to the potlatch, except that the *cargos* are rotated and do not affirm sharp status differences.

Following the culmination of the nobility-potlatch pattern, there appeared processes which are world-wide in general terms. Access to manufactured goods, desire to use the surplus of one's effort for personal benefit, contact with Europeans and the impingement of concepts of individual land use rights which are in conflict with traditional rights undermine the earlier patterns. In more specific terms, wealth afforded by nonmigratory, conservable, wild resources led to the particular pattern of the family-held trapping territory which is precisely like the Mundurucú family-held tapping territory.

The Stuart Lake Carrier in 1939 had lost most native and nobility-potlatch institutions. Their society, like that of the Mundurucú and Montagnais, consisted of individual families held together by common dealing at the trading post and by enforced association with one another owing to isolation on small reservations and strong race prejudice among the whites.

REFERENCES

Goldman, Irving. 1941. "The Alkatcho Carrier: Historical Background of Crest Prerogatives," *American Anthropologist*, 43:396-418.

Jenness, Diamond. n.d. The Indians of Canada. 2d ed. National Museum of Canada, Bulletin 65, Anthropological series No. 15.

Laut, Agnes C. 1918. The Conquest of the Great Northwest. 6th ed. 2 vols. New York.

Morice, A. G. 1890. "The Western Dénés," in Proceedings of the Canadian Institute, 3d ser., 7:109-74.

—— 1895. "Notes Archaeological, Industrial, and Sociological on the Western Dénés," in Transactions of the Canadian Institute, 4:1-222. Toronto.

—— 1905. History of the Northern Interior of British Columbia, formerly New Caledonia. 3d ed. Toronto.

Murie, Olaus G. 1935. Alaska-Yukon Caribou. North American Fauna, No. 54, U.S. Department of Agriculture, Bureau of Biological Survey, Washington, D.C.

Murphy, Robert F., and Julian H. Steward. 1956. "Tappers and Trappers: Parallel Process in Acculturation," Economic Development and Cultural Change, 4:No. 4:335-55.

THE PRIMITIVE PRESENCE IN PRE-CLASSICAL GREECE

By Thalia Phillies Howe

BRANDEIS UNIVERSITY

SINCE the pioneer work of Durkheim, Freud, and Jung, it has been recognized that the myths of a given people reflect its social history, its experiences both actual and imaginary. It is as though all the elements which are part of the original substance of a myth hover in suspension within the cultural atmosphere of a society; out of this atmosphere, from time to time, bits are extracted, isolated, and given verbal or bodily (ritual) expression or both. Eminent ethnologists such as Paul Radin and Bronislaw Malinowski have observed such processes among myth-makers of modern times.[1]

Now it is entirely possible that some Greek myths also had similar origins, as the work of superior poetic intellects who extracted a core of ideas, a mythic theme that was introduced initially as a simple spontaneous narrative before a single narrow audience. The further development of such a myth would then have become the work not only of the originator but also of a succession of poets reworking and enlarging the original theme to a more complex scheme and proportions. In an age of incipient art, where there do not as yet exist literary forms of specific structure, such as the drama or novel, and where individual authors' rights are transferable, a given theme may be left intact by the purists among the bards and thus transmitted unretouched; but, more likely it is taken up by restless, gifted spirits who transform it as their genius compels.[2]

As the materials for myth are selected and detached from the social atmosphere and are crystallized about a theme, protagonists are chosen to carry the theme who are usually not derived from historical figures but are, instead, generalized social prototypes. Normally these protagonists are given names which are integral to the core of the myth and which, by their descriptiveness, frequently indicate something of its subsequent development. For example, the name of Perseus is derived from the root which means "to cut," and Perseus can thus be designated as the "Cutter," an apt designation for the Gorgon's decapitator.[3]

But the analyst of myth, in addition to a thorough knowledge of linguistic techniques,[4] must also have a thorough and sympathetic grounding in the workings of literature, say that of a writer as extraordinarily sensitive to words as James Joyce, who writes inside out, deliberately, to show how the creative genius links and ties, loops and weaves his words and ideas together. It is precisely this Joycean interlacing and manipulation of the names that cluster about the Jason and Medeia myth that makes one realize, contrary to frequent assumptions, how important is the role of the individual creative mind in the formation of such a myth. While its form may be looser than that of epic for instance, in myth, too, one may find evidence of the proper selection, organization, and integration of imaginative and social materials, the work of genius.

As first observed in Hesiod's *Theogony* the Jason and Medeia myth reveals the mythopoeic process in embryo. On first analysis it is observable that the name of Iason, as the Greeks called that hero, suggests the simple reversal of the first syllable of his father's name, *Ai*son. Then, starting from line 956 in the *Theogony,* we hear how *Ai*etes (note again the phonetic reversal of *Ia*son) was born and how *Ai*etes begat *Mēd*eia. Then, after a few lines, the goddess, *Dem*eter (note here the phonetic reversal of *Med*eia) is coupled with a certain *Ia*sion, after which the poem reverts to the myth again and tells us how the son of *Ai*son led away from *Ai*etes the daughter of *Ai*etes, and how the son of *Ai*son, Iason by name, had as his son *Mēd*eios who was also trained by Cheiron like his father.[5]

Now if *Ai*etes, *Ai*son, and *Ia*son as father-in-law, father, and son had been actual people this similarity of names could only have been a coincidence.[6] But they were not actual people. In each case the myth-maker had free choice of names, and plainly he chose not to range very far. He stayed within the simplest kind of phonetic scheme, the sound *Ia* and its reversal *Ai*.

In a scholion under fragments from Hesiod's *Catalogue of Women,* this phonetic pattern recurs. It begins: "and of *Ai*son and Poly*mēde,* according to Hesiod, *Ia*son was born," and it continues, "whom Cheiron brought up in woody Pelion." This scholion, reporting what is the oldest tradition, gave a name that contains *mēd,* for its root, as the name of Jason's mother.[7]

The consistency of this scheme becomes more than phonetic, however, when we realize that the two sounds also separate according to the male and female genders—all the *Ia* and *Ai* sounds pertain to the males, and, with the apparent exception of *Mēde*ios, the son, the females revolve about the sound *med*. Now in addition to consistent phonetic patterns and separation of these according to gender, let us see whether these roots form consistent patterns of meaning as well. What do the names of these figures mean and how do their actions relate to these meanings?

When, at the end of the *Iliad* ancient Priam is fumbling his way into the Greek camp, to his great relief he meets Hermes disguised as a messenger. In blessing the messenger, Priam calls him *aisios,* 'auspicious,' 'sent by the gods as a good omen.'[8] Plainly it is this same root that forms part of such Homeric terminology as *aisymneter,* 'ruler, prince,' and *aisymnatas,* 'judge.' *Ai*son, then, suggests a personage who obtains his authority by his extraordinary skill in omens, by which he brings about judicious and fortunate decisions.[9] He is beyond the ordinary, he is "in the know."

Aietes himself, the father-in-law of Iason, is no less fortunately placed in the social terminology than Aison, for as Odysseus says: "we came to the island *Ai*a, where dwelt fair-tressed Kirke, a dread, divine enchantress, own sister to *Ai*etes of baneful mind."[10] Aietes, then, was brother to the greatest sorceress of antiquity, who dwelt in the "auspicious," "*omened* places," "*Ai*a," and was called by Homer "Aiaian Kirke." Aietes himself was *olophronos,* 'baleful,' a worker of "deadly evils," a concept we associate with sorcerers and the supernatural powers of the shaman. And, indeed, did not Aietes possess the brazen-hoofed, fire-breathing bulls by which he hoped to get rid of Iason and deprive him of the Fleece? Who could obtain and control such magical beasts except a wizard, or the wizard's daughter?

Aison > Aietes > Aia > Kirke—we begin to move in a world early- or even pre-Greek as these names grade backward in time from respectable and judicious augury to deadly sorcery. How deep into this territory, foreign or simply primeval, does Iason penetrate? At the least he was intended to set foot in it or else he would not have been chosen as the son and son-in-law of two such cultural figures of specific connotation.

His own name, Iason, probably derives from the verb *iasomai* which, both in its roots and its earliest Homeric usage, means 'to heal.' His name also appears under the word *iatrike*, 'medicine,' in ancient lexicons. And then there is the reference to his teacher, Cheiron, who taught the art of healing to Asklepios, the father of medicine himself.[11] Now Cheiron's methods of healing represented, as Jaeger describes them, "the forces of magic and spells which still passed for medicine in the old-fashioned Greek world of Pindar," where the old centaur cured "with soothing potions" and "kindly incantations."[12]

Thus there was always a suggestion of healing clinging to Iason's name. Observe also that the *iatroi*, the 'healers,' who bound up the wounds of Odysseus, like Cheiron "checked the black blood with a spell."[13] These *iatroi* are further described as "peerless" and "wise above many men," "the worth of many men," that is, as superior to others in the community by reason of their knowledge.[14]

Homer, however, also implies that his heroes, even while lending their ears to the Olympian gods who will help them institute a "well-ordered and meaningful world,"[15] at the same time continue to employ their lips and hands in the old ways:

Who, pray, of himself ever seeks out and bids a stranger from abroad, unless it be one of those that are masters of some public craft, a prophet, or a healer of ills, or a builder, aye, or a divine minstrel, who gives delight with his song. For these men are hidden all over the boundless earth.[16]

Now these men, professionals, bards, and builders alike, all combine their special technical knowledge with oral techniques. But one normally may not stop to realize that oral ritual probably also played an important part in preclassical times in the construction of large and complex public works, the building of a penteconter for instance. Homer, the poet, does not describe the building of the ships that assembled at Aulis. Malinowski, the technical observer, records the complex ritual with which the Trobrianders surround the constructing of their large and handsome canoes. These are great open boats that, like the Greek, held crews of up to sixty and more persons and crossed the open seas.[17] In the making of such craft, ritual is indispensable because the charm and incantation employed in it "builds in" the assurance that even the most mechanical skill cannot. Roes, in her work on Dipylon ships, points to certain wheel-shaped decorations on their prows which she interprets—how else?— as magical symbols to insure good fortune.[18] Though he began to pay more and more attention to Olympian powers, Geometric Greek man, for a while at least, no more neglected his former dependence on magic than he did any other kind of technical knowledge. For in the early period magic was still conceived of as an extension of practical knowledge, actually closer to science than to religion. How closely these old animistic and magical beliefs were kept functioning along with the advancing Olympian faith is best shown in the building of the Argo, Iason's ship. Because this magnificent ship was intended, like the Trobrianders' ships, for a venture both unusual and precarious, special care was taken to include in its construction a "divine" beam from the speaking oaks of Dodona. More than once on its voyage for the Fleece, the beam spoke up and saved the floundering crew of heroes and demi-gods. And who fitted this animistic beam of Dodona to the Argo?—the Olympian Athena herself.[19]

Iason, we shall find, is far more deeply enmeshed in this world of sorcery than his actions or his name would lead us to believe. There is an arresting statement in the Fourth Pythian Ode of Pindar in which the hero introduces himself to Pelias by stating that it was Cheiron, who, in addressing him, was *accustomed* to calling him by the name of Iason. An ancient footnote explains this odd circumlocution by stating that Iason was also known by the name of "Diomēdes," a fact corroborated by inscriptions on two vase paintings that were done within the same decade as the *Fourth* Pythian Ode (ca. 460 B.C.), and on which Iason appears and is labelled "Diomedes."[20] Thus we have for this myth the striking unification of names for the protagonists—Iason-Dio*medes*-*Med*eia.

Who then is Medeia really? If Iason be the hero as male, Medeia is his female aspect, with Diomedes as their intermediary link, while their son *Med*eios similarly shares their name.[21] But *Med*eia later bore yet another son, and his name was *Mēdos*. Him she bore after she broke with *Ia*son and had found a suitable substitute for *Ia*son in the king of Athens, named *Ai*geus.

We still have to consider the meaning of the name Medeia, to observe whether it has any bearing on the name Iason and whether she is truly his feminine counterpart. Her name it seems, stems from *mēdomai*, the meaning of which comes closest to the Old English word 'bethink,' which has not only cognitive connotations, but also sensory and emotional ones.[22] Then we note that this root *mēd* combines with descriptive prefixes to form the names of certain females who are all distinguished for their knowledge of drugs. In addition to *Mēd*eia there are Aga*mēde*, Heka*mēde*, and Peri*mēde*. In the Homeric epic these women mix magic potions by which men's spirits and lives are revived.[23]

Thus, it seems that early Greek culture recognized two kinds of dispensers of healing: females whose names were distinguished by the use of the stem *mēd* and who brewed drugs for internal use; men, *iatroi,* whose title stems from the same name as Iason's and who healed with external applications and sometimes with incantations. Among the *iatroi* named by Homer is Achilles, who was trained in medical skills by Cheiron, that same teacher of Iason, Medeios, and Asklepios.[24] Also, let us not forget the important Homeric fact that this hero was closely associated with other extraordinary supernatural powers, namely his horse which, like the oaks of Dodona, was gifted with human speech. To describe this animistic beast, Homer uses the same epithet that he does for Kirke, *audēëssa,* literally 'en-*chant*-ress.'[25] Moreover, it should be noted that there is a scholion to the effect that both the early lyric poets Ibycus and Simonides regarded Achilles as a "divinity of healing whom Medeia finally wedded in the underworld."[26]

This is a strange union, and, especially when viewed in isolation, might easily be dismissed as a later fanciful invention. But it is not so strange, really, when placed in its proper cultural context, for most of these figures are closely related by blood or intermarriage, and certainly by their magical capacities; where they are not conjoined by family they are united as a peer group by reason of their knowledge and their superiority to others, as Homer describes them.

Among the various other *iatroi* with supernatural powers of healing were Autolykos and his two sons, while his daughter Polymede was the wife of Aison.[27] There were also the sons of Asklepios, Podaleiros and Machaon.[28] Cheiron has given special training not only to Asklepios, but also to Medeios and to Iason and Achilles, both of whom eventually married Medeia.[29] Kirke, sister to Aietes, then became aunt to Medeia, and they in turn are related to Agamede through their common ancestor Helios.[30] In fact all these figures, male and female, form a closed in-group corresponding to the kind of relationship that Malinowski studied in the living situation:

Magic had to be handed over in direct *filiation,* from generation to generation. Hence it remains from earliest times in the hands of specialists, and the first profession of mankind is that of wizard or witch.[31]

Perhaps it was for this reason that even in the Classical Period there remained in Greece a class of physicians known as Asklepiads, described by Cohn-Haft as "some sort of guild oganization of the profession along family lines." In fact, "normally, medical knowledge descended from father to son as son followed father in the profession."[32] But this condition would hardly distinguish this profession from any other craft in general, except for two other factors which were part of the profession from the beginning: first, the continued high social status of the physician. Although he practiced a *technē*, a craft, the physician was not disdained as other craftsmen were.[33] Secondly, the secrecy normally surrounding this professional knowledge made it a craft apart. One of the solemn provisions of the Hippocratic Oath was that from the moment of admittance the pupil must keep secret this knowledge; from the beginning he was initiated into its mysteries as into a religious rite.[34] Thus, the original social traditions were retained intact even after the original primitive methods of practice had, for the most part, been superseded.

But the shaman was not only altered in time into the honorable physician, but eventually found new professional opportunities, as tribal chieftain or king.[35] This, in fact, was the ultimate fate of Aison, Aietes, and certainly of Aigeus, king of Athens. Also, among the second dynasty kings of Athens was *Mĕdo*s, the mythical ancestor of the *Mĕdo*ntidae, "whose name," says Hignett in his *History of the Athenian Constitution*, "seems derived from their kingly power." The Medontidae were, as they claimed, of the *genos basilikos,* and as late as the fifth century B.C. they owned land close to the Akropolis, the ancient residence of the Attic kings.[36]

Let us examine Medeia herself, as an individual figure. There is something so excessive and strange about her behavior that many have regarded her as of alien origin. Certainly her love for Iason was most unclassical and incontinent and involved her in all kinds of opportunistic maneuvering on his behalf. For him she murdered her own brother and charmed fire-breathing bulls and the dragon of the Fleece; she repeatedly saved the princely crew of the Argo; and, finally, she butchered old Pelias to regain Iason's lost heritage. Her costume, too, was certainly exotic with its elaborate eastern dress and tiara or Phrygian cap. And she frequently carried her box of magical herbs in her hands. But this extraordinary dress is to be expected, for the sorcerer or shaman in any society is usually distinguished by a bizarre costume.[37] Now in Medeia's case, since the social role of the shaman, which once marked her origins, had long since declined, there remained only the memory that she had once been unusual and different in the community. Such a figure, once familiar and different, gradually became unfamiliar and foreign.

When a people do not as yet have a strong historical, or even a well-developed chronological scale, memories and concepts which involve time not only telescope or expand, but may also suffer other, strange changes. The memory of the sorceress type remained vital and integral to this myth and its culture, while the actual figures and their dominant social role had virtually disappeared from the community. But in the case where there still remains hearsay knowledge of such figures, the primitive mind may argue that such things continue to exist, but not locally—only further off, among foreign peoples. Hence we may say that where chronological accuracy does not yet appear, then not only may events be made to telescope in time, but there may arise a *substitution* of space for time. This must happen throughout the development of myth, legend, and fairytales, and probably in part explains why it is that so many of the protagonists are exotic and the liveliest events seem to be taking place in the present yet in distant realms.[38]

In Medeia's case, however, more than historical or cultural misconception is at work to cause this transposition of time for space; what is at work is a mistrust of her extraordinary powers. There were those of her creators who expressed a perfectly human inclination to put a good physical distance, the edge of the world in fact, between themselves and the very idea of the Medeias of this world. So it is also that Aia, the island of the great sorceress Kirke, is set by Homer at the "risings of the Sun and the dwelling place of Dawn."[39] Hence there came to be a dual tradition in regard to Medeia's origins: for Pindar, for example, she was of Greek birth, a queen of Corinth even; for Euripides, a royal barbarian, a witch of Colchis, whose powers were of a kind that left men uneasy since they were very potent and arbitrarily used.[40] This was particularly true of her powers of rejuvenation, for according to early legend, she was regarded as having rejuvenated Aison and Iason at different times, and she was also entrusted with the rejuvenation of Pelias, though here she deliberately defaulted.[41]

What does rejuvenation mean in these cases? The answer is found in the kind of help Medeia rendered Aigeus as he passed through Corinth on his way to Delphi, a childless man, desperate at his own impotence. By her promise to cure this difficulty she was assured of sanctuary in Athens.[42] Hence the implications of rejuvenation are clear. But how does she come by this power? Medeia, as has been noted, was derived from *mēdomai,* but there is another noun with the same pronunciation as her name, though deriving from a quite different root, namely *medea,* which means 'genital organs.'[43] This verbal pun on her name was an inevitable connection for any myth-maker to make, so characteristically open is myth to verbal and phonetic possibilities. Thus Medeia, by reason of the sound of her name, was endowed with a gift of great, but arbitrary, power.

The ancient shamaness was relegated to the more comfortable distance of Colchis, partly to put at rest the psychological fears of Greek man, and partly because she had become outmoded. Yet she could be thus relegated because her social role had declined in importance, and not only in regard to healing and magic.

To understand this social decline, we need only recall that Medeia and the other women of supernatural powers plied their craft with the use of herbs and drugs taken from field, garden, and grove. Thus Medeia is rendered in paintings with her coffer of herbs, or holding a sprig. Sometimes she extends to Iason a wreath, the symbol of her magical powers which made his victories possible.[44] Thus, too, the women of Greek lands since Cretan times are depicted holding wreaths or dancing amid groves and plants, for the green growing things were their special area of knowledge, and by binding them the women exhibited their control over them.[45] What such females indicate is a familiar level of economy, in which the tending of gardens and a modest planting of a narrow field is commonly the work of women and children, while the men hunt or go off to war. At that point of domestic economy society depends on women, for they particularly possess the knowledge to make gardens grow. Thus their role as food-getters is important, and, by the same token, so is their social role. But as the population increases and agriculture rather than horticulture is predominantly practiced, a shift involving heavier labor in fields at a greater distance from home, the women retire to the care of the house. As their role as food-getter markedly declines, so in due proportion does their social role.[46]

This cultural concept of Medeia as a mistress, though not a divinity, of horticulture suggests that her beginnings extend back through Cretan times to the simple economy of a neolithic people. But it was a concept which still survived in popular memory, not as part of religious belief, but as myth with social-economic content. Medeia represents, not a goddess, but a particular aspect of fertile and gifted womankind. As Bouché-Leclerq has said, and considerably before Jung developed the concept of archetypes, it is not so much the question of whether an individual by the name of *Medeia* ever existed "as the fact that a certain set of attributes belong together, and cohere in a recurrent type."[47] While Iason stems from the archetypal concept of the *iatros,* Medeia *is* the archetype, and as such she antedates the Cretans; she is as old as the first green shoot planted by woman with a coaxing chant, half spell and half lullaby.

Lastly, it is this same fertile confluence of current and recurrent ideas that may well have made the *Theogony* draw Demeter and Iasion into contiguity with the Medeia and Iason myth. For the poet, immediately after the reference to the "neat-ankled Medeia," describes thus the goddess whose name *Dem*-eter suggests the reversal of *Med*-eia:[48] "Demeter, bright goddess, was joined in love with the hero *Ia*sion in a thrice-ploughed fallow in the rich land of Crete, and bare Plutus. . . ." Demeter, of course, is female fertility personified; while Iasion's name means the "Enlivener," the "Freshener," here, of the Earth. It was, then, not merely a fondness for alliteration or verbal play that caused the similarity of sounds in this quartet of names Iasion-Demeter, Iason-Medeia, to appear within these same few lines of the *Theogony*. It was primarily the connotations of fertility inherent in each name. We have, therefore, a group of names, tightly interwoven nuclei of sound and thought, that determine not only the immediate terminology of the myth, but can even temporarily attract other units similarly related in sound and thought but which have no direct connection with the myth.

It is my opinion that this core of names, with their interlocking sound patterns, their divisions into male and female genders, and their correspondence of meanings, all of which were originally culturally determined—that this core may well have been recognized and brought together by a single primitive Greek myth-maker, one with the verbal gifts of a James Joyce. It is certainly possible that such consistency arose within the psychological disposition and reaction of a single mind.

If so, no matter what else eventually accrued to the core of the myth—and a very great deal did—as the work of other minds, there would always have remained this individually and consciously conceived nucleus resting upon a shamanistic core and having male and female counterparts, in which the female prevailed and proceeded either to reinforce or deplete the male as the need might be. This was the center of the myth: Jason and Medeia as representations of two basic archetypal conceptions of a primitive stage. They are earlier materials that have been converted into myth at a turning point of an evolving society.

And that society? I would hazard it was Crete, as it shifted from a late neolithic to a more developed stage of culture, a culture which was in turn to form a basic part of the Greek. This later cultural fusion happened as Pausanias quite simply tells us: when Herakles came from Crete to found the Olympic games, that is, to mark the establishment of the classical Greek world, he brought with him four men: Paionios, Epimedes, Idas and Iasion.[49] Of these, Idas stands for Cretan Ida itself, while Paionios, like Paieon in Homer, was one of the *iatroi*; there was also near Athens the temple of Apollo Paionios and Athena Paionia, divine Healers.[50] Epimedes, too, is merely an eponym of primitive wisdom and medicine. And as for Iasion, it is hoped there is no need to identify him further.

NOTES

[1] P. Radin, *The Trickster* (1956) and *Evolution of an American Indian Prose Epic* (1954); B. Malinowski, *Magic, Science and Religion* (1948), pp. 83-84, 96 ff., *Argonauts of the Western Pacific* (1922), chap. 12, and *Myth in Primitive Psychology* (1926); H. J. Rose, "Myth and Pseudo-Myth," *Folklore* 46:10 (1935).

[2] Radin, *The Trickster*, pp. 122 ff.

[3] "The Origin and Function of the Gorgon-Head," *American Journal of Archaeology* 58:209 ff. (1954).

[4] Gustaf Stern's important study on semantic analysis is particularly recommended: *Swift, Swiftly and Their Synonyms* (1921).

[5] P. Mazon, in his edition of Hesiod's *Theogony* (Budé, 1928), is of the opinion that Hesiod concluded his work on this poem at line 964, and the remainder of the poem, lines 965-1022, is the appended work of an inferior poet. For a fuller discussion see F. Jacoby, *Hesiodi Theogonia* (1930) pp. 30 ff. The material under discussion is derived from both sections of the poem but remains unaffected by the textual problems of the dual authorship.

[6] Particular thanks are due here to the poetic insight of Eric Havelock who first pointed out to me in the course of conversation the striking similarity of

names in this passage, and who subsequently has made most helpful suggestions and corrections.

7 Scholion to Pindar, *Nemean Odes* 3.92; T. Gaisford, *Poetae Minores Graeci* (1823) I; Hesiodi fragmenta 32; Evelyn-White, *Hesiod* (Loeb ed.), p. 163 frag. 13. According to Pherekydes her name was Alkimēde.

8 *Iliad* 24.376.

9 As in *Odyssey* 2.231, 8.258, 22.46, 23.14; *Iliad* 24.347; Pindar, *Nemean Odes* 9.18; Plutarch, *Lives* 2774C.

10 *Odyssey* 10.135 ff.

11 Liddell and Scott, *Greek-English Lexicon* (1948); É. Boisacq, *Dictionnaire étymologique de la langue grecque*, 4th ed. (1950), s.v. *iasomai*; *Etym. Magnum*, ed. by Sylburg (1816), s.v. *iatrike*; cf. Pindar, *Pythian Odes* 4.115 ff. On Cheiron, see Pindar, *Nemean Odes* 3.53 ff. There is also Iaso, Goddess of Healing, of the cult circle of Asklepios, see Aristophanes frag. 21K and his *Plutus* 701 and scholion; Pausanias i.34.3; Hermippus frag. 73K. For Jason as healer, see also H. Usener, *Götternamen* (1896), pp. 156 ff.; O. Gruppe, *Griechische Mythologie* (1897-1906), pp. 544-45 and n. 1.

12 W. Jaeger, *Paideia*, III (1939), 5; Pindar, *Pythian Odes* 3.47-53; W. Jayne, *The Healing Gods of Ancient Civilizations* (1925), p. 283.

13 *Odyssey* 19.455 ff. For the word "spell," Homer here uses *epaoide*, literally 'a song,' 'sung to or over' (Liddell and Scott). Also Sophokles, *Ajax* line 581 "... 'tis not a skilfull leech [*iatrou sophou*] / Who mumbles charms [*epoidas*] o'er ills that need the knife" (trans. by F. Storr). This implies of course that by the time of the tragedian the surgeon had superseded the witch-doctor in professional esteem, if not completely in practice, for even in the *Agamemnon* Aeschylos still says (Loeb ed., lines 1020-21) "But man's black blood, once it hath first fallen by murder to earth—who by magic spell [*epaeidon*] shall call it back?" K. Marot, *Acta Antica. Magyar Tud. Academia.* I (1951–52), 277-79.

14 *Odyssey* 4.231; *Iliad* 4.194, 11.518.

15 B. Snell, *Discovery of the Mind* (1953), p. 21.

16 *Odyssey* 17.384.

17 Malinowski, *Magic, Science and Religion*, pp. 139 ff., and *Argonauts of the Western Pacific*, chaps. 4-6.

18 G. Kirk, "Ships on Geometric Vases," *Annual of the British School at Athens*, 44:39, fig. 1; pl. 40, fig. 1 (1949). A. Roes, *Greek Geometric Art* (1933), p. 45, sees the wheel-shaped decoration as a sun-symbol. Cf. also C. Hopkins, "Oriental Elements in the Hallstatt Culture," *American Journal of Archaeology*, 61:334 ff. (1957). But there seems no reason why it should not be regarded, instead, as deriving literally from a wheel, as the symbol of a people to whom the chariot was a new and revolutionary invention. Roes also stresses the fact that the objects most closely associated with wheels in Villanovan and Hallstatt art are horses and birds. The horse would demonstrate my point, while the bird was poetic expression of the fact that the chariot now made man a fleet as a bird. We also find birds frequently in relation to chariots and ships for the same reason, in Geometric Greek vase painting, as in the illustration above from Kirk. This might also explain the origins of the swastika, so frequently cited by Roes in relation to the wheel, as a four-spoked wheel with sections of the rim removed at intervals.

19 The beam from Dodona is mentioned in the account of the fifth-century B.C. mythographer, Pherekydes, as preserved in Apollodorus 1.9.16, in *The Library*, ed. by J. Frazer (1921). But there is a celebrated Geometric Greek vase

painting on a bowl from Thebes in which the beam is rendered in place; see
Journal of the Hellenic Society, Vol. 19 (1899), pl. 8; R. Hampe, *Frühe griechische Sagenbilder in Boeotien* (1936), pl. 22b; A. Koster, *Das Antike Seewesen*
(1923), pl. 19. Kirk, "Ships on Geometric Vases" #40, fig. 4. There were also
the supernatural ships of the Phaeacians (*Odyssey* 8.553 ff.) that had neither
rudders nor pilots, but knew "the mind and will of man."

[20] Pindar, *Pythian Odes* 4.119. Diodorus Siculus 4.15.3 also has a late glimmer-
ing of this notion when he speaks of a Diomedes who had bronze mares (cf. the
brazen bulls of Medea's father) who sailed with Jason to bring away the fleece.
Scholia Vetera in Pindari Carmina II, Pythian Odes 4.211, ed. by Drachmann.
Natalis Comes (pseud. of N. Conti), *Mythologiae* (1568), in the 1596 edition
gives the name as *Dolomedes.* See E. Braun, *Bulletin des Deutsches archaeologi-
schen Institut,* 10:13 (1838); E. Gerhard, *Auserlesene griechische Vasenbilder*
(1840–58) pl. 155; Vol. III, p. 23 and notes 18-21. These two vase paintings also
contain an arresting instance of symbolism in classical iconography: the focal
point of both scenes, which are virtually identical, is the altar with its sacrifice
of a ram's head. This is normally an undesirable portion to offer the gods,
but the curved horn of the beast presumably was used by the artist to suggest
the ram of the Golden Fleece. It may also suggest the curved prow of the Argo.

[21] Medeus, as Mazon remarks in his edition of Hesiod's *Theogony,* is otherwise not known in any other connection. But his role does gain significance
when he is viewed as the son of this healer and his magic-working wife, and as
the pupil of that physician's physician, Cheiron.

[22] Liddell and Scott, *Greek-English Lexicon,* s.v. *medomai*; É. Boisacq, *Dictionnaire étymologique de la langue grecque,* s.v. *medo.* As Snell notes in *Discovery
of the Mind* in his chapter on Homer, the physical and mental processes were
not regarded as the sharply demarcated functions that they were later. See the
New English Dictionary (1888), s.v. *bethink.* Something of this also is indicated
in the Prologue to Chaucer's *Wife's Tale,* line 772, "He spak moore harm than
herte may bithynke." Note also that Medeia's mother's name was *Idyia,* which
means 'knowledge,' or 'wisdom.' Hesiod, *Theogony* 958 ff. See Liddell and
Scott, *Greek-English Lexicon,* s.v. *oida,* 'to see with the mind's eye,' 'to know.'
Very closely related etymologically is the verb *mĕdomai,* 'be mindful for, con-
trive,' etc. (Boisacq, p. 619). In poetic connotation *mēdomai* and *mĕdomai* are
indistinguishable and are used so in the context of this paper.

[23] Usener, *Götternamen,* p. 163, was the first to note this connection between
medicine and Greek and Roman names containing the root *mēd.* He concluded
they referred to a goddess of medicine, perhaps Agamede (*Iliad* 11.740), "who
knew all drugs (*pharmaka*) that the wide earth nourisheth," or Perimede (Theocritus, *Pharmaceutria* 2.15.16). Propertius 2.4.8, ed. by Paganelli (Budé, 1921).
The scholiast on Theocritus (ed. by Deubner, 1849) remarks that Perimede is the
same as Agamede. J. Bacon, *The Voyage of the Argonauts* (1925), p. 132.
Another goddess of medicine is Hekamede (*Iliad* 11.624–41), who mixes for
Nestor a *kykeon,* from *kykao,* 'to mix thoroughly,' also 'to be mixed up, or
disturbed.' Kirke's drugged drink was also a *kykeon* (*Odyssey* 10.316). Poly-
damna may be included among these, as the phonetic reversal of *med.* (*Odyssey*
4.219 ff.). She was a "woman of Egypt" and one "who had taught Helen how
to brew drugs." Her name is derived from *poly,* 'much' and *damazo,* "to tame,
master, conquer: I. of animals, . . . III. the powers of nature" (Liddell and Scott).
From the several uses of this verb as they occur in the *Iliad* and *Odyssey,* one
also derives the notion that it meant mastery over the physical nature of man.

24 *Iliad* 11.832.

25 *Iliad* 19.407. The *Iliad* states that it was the goddess Hera who had given the beast this power of speech. But the Olympian etiology is unnecessary, for one could extract this line and lose nothing of the original meaning thereby. Horses, like the oaks of Dodona and other natural objects and creatures talked to pre-Greek man long before the Olympian hierarchy was conceived.

26 J. Edmonds, *Lyra Graeca*, II, 105, Ibycus frag. 42 = Bergk III, Ibycus frag. 37. Simonides, Bergk frag. 213. Scholion to Apollodorus Rhodius 4.815, ed. by C. Wendel, p. 293.

27 *Odyssey* 19.455 ff. Apollodorus, *The Library*, ed. by J. Frazer (Loeb ed., 1921), 1.9.16. Apollonius Rhodius in *The Argonautica*, ed. Seaton (Loeb ed., 1912) 1.233, calls her Alkimede, instead of Polymede.

28 *Iliad* 2.732; 4.194.

29 *Lyra Graeca* (*supra* n. 26) on the marriage of Medeia and Achilles.

30 Bacon, *The Voyage of the Argonauts*, p. 131.

31 Malinowski, *Magic, Science and Religion*, p. 88.

32 L. Cohn-Haft, *The Public Physicians of Ancient Greece*, (Smith College Studies in History No. 42, 1956). Jaeger, *Paideia*, III, 9 ff. Both Jaeger and Cohn-Haft are of the opinion commonly held by classical scholarship that even in the Homeric period the *iatros* was quite divorced from magic and spells. In contrast, others, such as Singer in his essay "Medicine" in Livingston's *Legacy of Greece* (Oxford, 1923) and Jayne in *The Healing Gods of Ancient Civilizations*, are of the opinion that there is ample evidence that the Greeks inherited, in common with other peoples of Europe and Asia, a whole system of magical pharmacy from remoter ancestry. The trained eye of the physician, anthropologist, and scientist recognizes and evaluates data which the best of philologists and scholars may underestimate or disregard.

33 Cohn-Haft, *Public Physicians of Ancient Greece*, p. 14 ff., 19.

34 *Ibid.*, p. 16, n. 27; W. H. S. Jones, *Hippocrates*, III (1923), 291-97; Jaeger, *Paideia*, III, 11.

35 Frazer stresses this point throughout the early part of *The Golden Bough*. See also J. Maddox, *Medicine Man* (1923) I, 143.

36 C. Hignett, *History of the Athenian Constitution* (1952), pp. 38 ff.; Pausanias 4.5.10; U. Wilamowitz-Moellendorf, "Die Lebenslaenglichen Archonten Athens," *Hermes* 33:119 ff. (1898). See also Liddell and Scott, s.v. *mēdomai*.

37 *Annali dell' Institut* (1848) Plate G; H. Heydemann, "Jason in Kolchis," *Hallisches Winckelmannsprogramm* No. 11 (1886), figs. 1-3; Maddox, *Medicine Man*, p. 95; G. Thomson, *The Prehistoric Aegean* 2d ed. (1954), p. 336.

38 As R. Lattimore has said in reference to this idea in his *Aeschylus Oresteia* (1953), p. 4 n. 3: "So Shakespeare drew on history and legend for his tragedies and romances, or, when these dealt with time not specifically antique, the place would be idealized by distance and the vagueness of his audience's information: Italy, Bohemia, Illyria, Arden." The myth-maker always depends so on the "vagueness of his audience's information."

39 *Odyssey* 12.3.

40 On Medeia as Corinthian in origin, the earliest known source is Eumelos of Corinth of the early eighth century B.C., as quoted in a scholion to Pindar, Odes 13.74 (ed. by Drachmann, I, 373). See also Pausanius 2.3.10; L. Farnell, *Cults of the Greek States* (1896–1909), I, 202 ff.; Preller-Robert, *Griechische Heldensage* (1920), II 1, 185 ff.

41 The earliest reference to this is from the *Nostoi*, as quoted in the scholion

to Euripides *Kn.* 1321 (ed. by F. Deubner, 1877), "She made good Aison lusty as a youth / Wiping old age away by wise devices / With simple seethings in a pot of gold." Bacon, *The Voyage of the Argonauts,* pp. 129 ff. One is also reminded of Shakespeare's *Merchant of Venice,* V.i.14: "Medea gathered the enchanted herbs which did renew old Aeson." Another instance of that poet's "less Greek"! See also L. Séchan, *Revue des études grecques* (1927), 40:235 n. 3, and his *Études sur la tragédie grecque* (1926), p. 408, n. 2; p. 467, n. 3.

[42] Euripides *Medea,* 1. 669 ff.

[43] Boisacq, *Dictionnaire étymologique de la langue grecque,* s.v. *madan.*

[44] The Theban bowl: see references given in note 19.

[45] For illustrations of Medeia see Cohn-Haft, *The Public Physicians of Ancient Greece,* p. 14 ff., 19. For Cretan examples, see A. Evans, *Palace of Minos* (1921–36), II, figs. 194, a, d, e, 483, 559; III, figs. 39, 91, pl. 18.

[46] A. S. Diamond, *Evolution of Law and Order* (1951), pp. 90 ff., 128, 178. V. G. Childe, *Man Makes Himself* (1955), p. 71. It is worth noting in this connection that even on the celebrated scene of Harvesters on the black steatite vase from Hagia Triadha three female choristers are included in the group of male threshers who march to work singing. These women are directly behind the priest, who leads them with his sistrum in hand (Evans, *Palace of Minos,* Vol. II, fig. 22, p. 47).

[47] A. Bouché-Leclerq, *Divination* (1879–82), II, 95 ff.

[48] Hesiod, *Theogony* 969 ff.

[49] Pausanias 5.7.6; Usener, *Götternamen,* pp. 152 ff.; *Odyssey* 4.231; Thomson, *The Prehistoric Aegean,* p. 292. Charles Picard, *Revue des études grecques,* 40:336 ff. (1927).

[50] Pausanias 1.34.3. J. Frazer, *Pausanias' Description of Greece* (1898), 2, p. 474, describes the temple as having one altar divided into parts, one of which was sacred to Apollo Healer and others to Aphrodite, Panacea, Iaso, Hygeia, and Athena Healer. Note Frazer's commentary on the origins of this epithet, *Paion:* "Prof. A. Bastian, like Macrobius [1.17.15 ff.] explains the word to mean 'the Striker' (from *paio*), and supposes it to refer to a primitive method of cure, which consists in beating the sick person in order to drive out the devil by whom he is supposed to be possessed (*Die Völker der östlichen Asien,* IV, 11). But this explanation of the epithet is at best extremely doubtful." There seems less reason to doubt this interpretation now, in view of the other evidence. It would seem, however, that it was not the sick person who was beaten, but rather that the witch-doctor or shaman struck his hands or feet in rhythmic beat and sang his incantation. This musical beating of time might well explain the meaning of the word *paean,* as chant or song of victory and possibly part war-dance as well. See in this connection M. Nilsson, *Griechische Festschrift* (1906), pp. 99 ff. Also K. Marot, *Acta Antica. Magyar Tud. Akademia* I (1951–52), 279. Further, Apollo's connections with Paionios might well have suggested the Olympian's dual role of God of Healing and of Music, because the two functions were, originally, inseparable. *Paeion,* the name as it appears in Homer (*Odyssey* 4.231 ff.) and Solon (frag. 13.43) etc., does not refer to an individual, but is a generic term for the divine skill of healing.

NEO-AZTECISM IN THE EIGHTEENTH CENTURY AND THE GENESIS OF MEXICAN NATIONALISM

By John Leddy Phelan

UNIVERSITY OF WISCONSIN—MILWAUKEE

ONE OF THE MOST STRIKING consequences of Spanish expansion in the New World was the emergence of societies characterized by racial and cultural heterogeneity. Spanish, Negro, and Indian were thrown together, and out of this mixture grew a new culture which was neither totally European nor predominantly indigenous. This development, of equal interest to the historian and the cultural anthropologist, was slow, painful, and sometimes demoralizing to the groups involved. The ultimate significance of this process has become apparent only in our time with the emergence of a dominant mestizo civilization in much of Hispanic America. This paper seeks to explore some of the attitudes of articulate Creoles toward the Indians. Out of this Indianist preoccupation the first glimmerings emerge of a Mexican national consciousness, based on the racially diverse character of Mexico's culture.

During the three centuries of the colonial period the Creoles (people of European blood born in the Indies) gradually adopted the Aztec world of pre-conquest times as the "classical antiquity" of Mexico. This proposition may sound historically incongruous for several reasons. First, Creoles had no racial affinity with the colonial Indians or their Aztec ancestors. Second, colonial society was rigidly caste-centered, with the Creoles near the top of the pyramid and the Indians forming its base.

The origins of neo-Aztecism in the eighteenth century go back to the sixteenth-century religious chroniclers. The early missionaries were animated by the conviction that the new Indian Church was a return to the spirit of the primitive Apostolic Church of Christ's time. Since the sixteenth-century Indian Church appeared like the primitive Church, the pre-conquest period in America became analogous to the pre-Christian era in Europe, that is, classical antiquity. Juan de Torquemada's *Monarquía indiana* (1615), for example, is saturated with analogies and comparisons, many of them of dubious pertinence, between the history of the Aztecs and that of the Greeks and the Romans. By these analogies, Torquemada clearly implied that Aztec society was the "classical antiquity" of Mexico.[1]

Torquemada's implication was made more explicit by succeeding Creoles. The notion received a literary expression in Valbuena's epic poem, *Grandeza Mexicana,* a powerful impetus in the erudite studies of Carlos de Sigüenza y Góngora, and a historical reaffirmation in Mariano Veytia's *Historia antigua de México.* The correlation of Aztec culture with Greek and Roman cultures reached its colonial culmination in the *Historia antigua de México* of Francisco Javier Clavigero.

The deities of the Aztecs were enveloped in an atmosphere suggestive of the gods of the Greeks and the Romans. The Aztec rulers took on the virtues of heroic Roman emperors. Each Aztec sovereign was thought to personify a classical virtue. The Council of the Republic of Tlaxcala became enfused with the aura of a Roman senate. In saluting the arrival of the viceroy, the Conde de Paredes, Sigüenza y Góngora urged that representative of the crown to seek inspiration in the classical virtues of the Aztec emperors.[2]

The Creoles' adoption of the Aztec world as their own American classical antiquity sprang from a yearning to secure roots that sank deep into the history of the New World. They felt the need for an American past, one totally disconnected from the Europe they had come from. The Creoles, of course, did have an American past of their own, something which began with Cortés. This tradition, however, was too brief in duration and too European in content to satisfy their need to identify themselves with a historical tradition indigenously American. To fill this same historical vacuum the Creoles warmly espoused the cult of the Virgin of Guadalupe. Their enthusiasm for the cult of Guadalupe was nationalist-inspired. She was an Indian, that is, an American, and not a European Virgin. Hence the Creoles claimed her as their own.[3] It was not fortuitous that Father Hidalgo proclaimed her patroness of the independence movement in 1810, for the brown Madonna was as popular with the Creoles as she was with the Indians.

It would be misleading to assume that the Creoles were adopting an attitude similar to that of the descendants of American immigrants, who claimed as their heritage all that had occurred in English America since the landing of the Pilgrims. For the American immigrant the English colonial and national past, which antedated his arrival, was a tradition that still continued to mold the cultural environment of the United States. In the eighteenth century the Aztec tradition had no such comparable influence on the colony, for the Spanish Conquest had terminated the cultural creativity of indigenous society. The dominant civilization of the colony, even for the Indians, was Spanish. The post-Conquest world was to the Creoles what the English colonial tradition was to the North American immigrant.

The Creole attitude toward the Aztec world also differed from the medieval ideal of the *renovatio imperii romanorum*. In the Middle Ages much of Antique culture had survived both in the Church and in the sphere of higher learning. The Creoles were not seeking any conscious restoration of Aztec cultural ideals similar in scope to the medieval program of the *renovatio*. Instead, they were feeling their way toward self-identity; their aim was to distinguish their culture from European culture. By claiming the Aztec world as their own American heritage they were accomplishing two objectives. First, they were beginning to break some of the ties which bound them to Europe. Second, they were laying the foundation for a rationale justifying their own assumption of political control over the Hispanic-American world. The nationalist and anti-Spanish implications of neo-Aztecism begin to become apparent in the historical investigations of Francisco Javier Clavigero.

Born in the city of Veracruz in 1731 of Spanish parents, Clavigero played a vigorous role in reforming the Jesuit educational curriculum in Mexico after 1750.[4] This movement aimed at replacing much of traditional Scholasticism with the rationalist philosophy of Descartes and Newton. These eclectic Jesuit reformers sought to introduce as much of the new philosophy of science as would not conflict directly with the dogmas of Catholicism.[5] On the ideological plane this movement represents the first stage in the dissolution of the Spanish imperial system, for Scholasticism had powerfully buttressed the hold of the Spanish crown over its overseas dominions.[6] Clavigero's pedagogical labors were cut short in 1767, when at the age of thirty-seven he found himself exiled to Italy, a victim of the Spanish crown's decision to expel the Society of Jesus from the Spanish dominions.

In the Papal States Clavigero spent the rest of his life completing his

Historia antigua de México, which was first published in Italian in 1780–81.[7] This work soon acquired a solid reputation for excellence both in Europe and in America. Clavigero's account, in reality, was a revision of Torquemada's earlier text. One basic difference between the two books is the contrast between the methodology of a Baroque scholar and that of a historian of the Enlightenment. Clavigero used his sources more critically. He had scant sympathy for Torquemada's penchant for the mythical and the fabulous. Although Clavigero shared the eighteenth century's scorn for the florid erudition of the Baroque age, he retained and expanded Torquemada's central thesis of the supposed parallel between the histories of the Aztecs and that of the Greeks and the Romans. What Clavigero did was to revise Torquemada, using a more up-to-date method.[8]

The outstanding feature of Clavigero's text is his contribution to the development of neo-Aztecism. He brought out for the first time its anti-Spanish implications, and he related the cult of Aztec antiquity to the social problems of the contemporary Indians.

Clavigero spent the last two decades of his life in an enforced exile in Italy, the victim of what he thought was the arbitrary and unjust act of the Spanish crown in expelling the Jesuit order from the Spanish empire. An articulate Creole and a political exile, he had an understandable grudge against the Spanish metropolis.

His American patriotism was further sharpened by his spirited reaction to the then widely read *Recherches philosophiques sur les Américains* (1768–69) of Cornelius de Pauw. That Dutch-born publicist claimed that all forms of physical and human nature in the New World were degenerate. A general inundation, which allegedly occurred a few centuries before the Conquest, was Pauw's explanation for the degeneracy of American nature. The Indians had such weak memories that they were unable to remember one day what they had done the day before. Their minds were so dull that they were incapable of arranging even the most simple ideas in any kind of orderly sequence. Their emotions were so frigid that they were unable to respond to the stimulus of love. Pauw also accused the Indians of drunkenness, sodomy, ingratitude, and suicide. Refusing to make any distinctions between the various Indian peoples, Pauw argued that the cultures of the Incas and the Aztecs bordered on brute savagery. Did they not lack minted money, iron, large vessels, arches, and an alphabet? The ease with which a mere handful of Spanish adventurers were able to overthrow these nations was convincing proof to Pauw of their lack of solid cultural progress.[9]

However unscientific, illogical, and ill-documented Pauw's reflections may now appear, he was a publicist of some repute in his own time. Hence Clavigero thought it necessary to add a one-volume appendix to the *Historia,* called the *Disertaciones sobre la tierra, los animales, y los habitantes del reino de México,* in which he set out to refute systematically Pauw's dismal portrait of the Aztecs.

On more than one occasion Clavigero exploded in wrath:

... European travellers, historians, naturalists and philosophers have made America into a warehouse for their childish fantasies. In order to make their works more delectable with the fantastic novelties of their alleged observations, they have attributed to all Americans that which they have observed in some or in none.... I do not pretend to maintain that the Americans are stronger than the Europeans. They can even be less strong than the Europeans without being positively weak and degenerate. The Swiss are stronger than the Italians; but we do not call them degenerate, nor even less do we blame the Italian climate.... If Pauw has seen, as I have, the enormous burdens that the Indians carry on their backs, he would not have had the insolence to hurl in their faces any accusation of physical weakness.[10]

Clavigero was reacting against the blatant Europe-centered attitude of Pauw. Clavigero's theme was that the "empire of reason" was not confined to Europe.[11] Other areas of the world in addition to Europe had made cultural achievements of note. In order to refute Pauw's galaxy of charges he was compelled to compare and to contrast in a systematic fashion the pre-Conquest world of America with other civilizations. What he did was to use a comparative historical method, one first suggested by Montesquieu in *L'esprit des lois.*[12] Several major spokesmen of the Enlightenment, including Leibnitz, Christian von Wolff, Montesquieu, and especially Voltaire, rejected the arrogant cultural parochialism personified by Pauw. Voltaire, for example, stressed the achievements of the Chinese;[13] Clavigero vindicated pre-Conquest America. This Mexican Jesuit participated in the Enlightenment's repudiation of a narrow, Europe-centered attitude toward the non-Western world.

Pauw claimed that the Aztecs had been vastly overrated by the early Spanish chroniclers. The colonial Indians were stupid, indolent, and alcoholic. How could their ancestors before the Conquest have made any respectable cultural accomplishments? Impossible! insisted Pauw. Clavigero admitted the demoralization of the colonial Indians. His quarrel with Pauw was about its cause. Pauw claimed that the backwardness of the Indians was a congenital condition. Clavigero rejoined that the cause was environmental. He added:

... I solemnly affirm to Pauw and to all Europe that the minds of the Mexican Indians are in no respect [congenitally] inferior to those of the Europeans: that the Indians are capable of learning all the sciences even the most abstract ones. If their upbringing were carefully supervised, if they were educated in schools by competent teachers, and if they were encouraged by rewards, one would see among the Indians philosophers, mathematicians and theologians who would vie with the most famous of Europe. But it is very difficult if not impossible, to make progress in the sciences in the midst of a miserable and servile life full of continual vexations. He who contemplates the present state of Greece could not convince himself that long ago that country produced those great men about whose existence we know, if he were not assured of the fact by the survival of the immortal works the Greeks wrote and by the consent of the ages. But the obstacles that the Greeks must surmount in order to acquire an education are small in comparison to the difficulties that the American Indians have always and still have to overcome.[14]

Today it is almost taken for granted that people are molded in some significant measure by their cultural environment. But in the eighteenth century this contention, which formed a cornerstone for the idea of progress, was a novel and revolutionary proposition. Montesquieu was one of the first to stress the central importance of environment. His conclusion was derived from John Locke's principle that human nature is plastic at birth and that it is molded by its surroundings (its sensory experiences). By demolishing the theory of innate ideas Locke challenged the traditional Christian notion of the innate depravity of man springing from original sin. The humanitarianism of the Enlightenment was built upon the belief that social evil was not the result of God's wrath and curse on mankind, but merely the consequence of conditions susceptible to rational criticism and improvement.[15] This environmentalist doctrine of the Enlightenment was clearly echoed in Clavigero's defense of the Indian.

Clavigero set out to defend the Indians against what he considered were the slanderous attacks of Pauw. He ended by affirming a faith (often voiced in the Enlightenment) in the capacity of any people to achieve distinction, provided they were given a favorable social milieu in which to develop their abilities. Not only did the environmentalist doctrine provide an answer to Pauw's charge about the congenital inferiority of the Indians, but it also gave Clavigero an opportunity to criticize Spanish colonialism. The analogy Clavigero made between Spanish rule over the Indians and Turkish enslavement of the Greeks was scarcely flattering to the Spanish empire. To suggest that the Greeks under Turkish rule had more opportunities for upward social mobility than did the Indians under Spanish dominion was a pointed charge. The Spanish authorities, who examined and postponed granting Clavigero's request for a Spanish edition, were not slow in catching the powerful anti-Spanish undercurrent of the Indian-Greek analogy.[16] In Clavigero's view the Conquest had imposed chains on the Indians. A vast portion of Spain's rule in America was implicitly condemned, for the colonial administration did not create social conditions which would encourage the Indians to develop their latent talents.[17]

Until Clavigero, the neo-Aztecism of the Creoles had little connection with the contemporary Indians. The latter were considered remote and rather brutish descendants of the "classical" Indians of Aztec antiquity. Such was the attitude of Valbuena, Sigüenza y Góngora, and Veytia. But Clavigero realized that the Creoles could not merely adopt the Aztec world as the classical antiquity of America and continue to ignore the social conditions of the descendants of the Aztecs. In Clavigero's view the Indians belonged to the Mexican nation as much as the Creoles did, and the latter's responsibility to improve the condition of the former could not be evaded. Platitudinous though this realization may sound today, it was then a novel thought for a spokesman of the Creoles, who as a class were notoriously unmindful of the plight of the Indians.

Not only did Clavigero condemn the colonial administration of the Indians, but also he attacked the race-caste system of the colony:

There is no doubt that the policy of the Spaniards would have been much wiser, if, instead of importing women from Europe and slaves from Africa, they had married the Indians so that the result of this fusion would have been a single and integrated nation. If the character of this work would permit, I could very easily demonstrate the incalculable advantages to the kingdom of Mexico and to the whole Spanish monarchy that would have resulted from this racial amalgamation, and I could indicate the grave ills that have been caused by its non-existence.[18]

Given his preoccupation to unite the Creoles and the Indians into one cultural community, Clavigero wistfully regretted that the ties between the Creoles and the Indians were psychological, geographical, and historical rather than biological. Envisaging Mexico as a nation of mestizos, Clavigero was a prophet who has found his vindication in the mestizo Mexico of the twentieth century.

It would be misleading to overemphasize the anti-Spanish innuendos of the *Historia antigua de México* without taking note of the fact that Clavigero on several occasions defended Spain's conduct in the New World. Clavigero sharply criticized contemporary European historians such as the vitriolically anti-Spanish *abbé* Raynal and the more objective William Robertson for exaggerating and in several cases inventing atrocities attributed to the Spaniards during the Conquest.[19] Cortés emerges as an inspired and resourceful leader—not, however, without a few blemishes of character.[20] In Books VIII-X Clavigero radically revised his "chains" metaphor. The oppressive servitude imposed on the Indians by the Conquest was a just punishment decreed by Providence to chastise the ancient peoples of America for the sins of their paganism. On this somber note Clavigero concluded his book.[21]

The ambivalence in Clavigero's attitude resulted from a conflict of loyalties. He felt himself both a Spaniard and a Mexican. As a Spaniard and as a priest he became the defender of the Conquest. As a Creole and as a Mexican patriot he was somewhat critical about several phases of Spanish activity in the New World. This conflict was resolved a generation later when several advocates of independence outwardly repudiated their Spanish inheritance. Clavigero died in 1787, two years before the outbreak of the French Revolution, which would begin a chain of events leading to the dissolution of the Spanish colonial empire.

Two leading publicists for Mexican independence—Servando Teresa de Mier and Carlos María de Bustamante—gathered up the threads of colonial Indianism and fashioned out of them a rationale for Mexican separation from Spain. They made explicit what had been largely implicit in the thought of Clavigero. Mier and Bustamante formulated the thesis that the justice of independence lay in the injustice of the Conquest. Their argument was that the Spaniards in 1519-21 had deprived the Mexican nation of 1810, which they identified with the pre-Conquest Aztecs, of her liberty by means of brute force and deception and that Spain had held the Mexican nation in an oppressive subjugation for three hundred years. Bustamante interpreted the War of Independence as a revenge for the alleged atrocities committed during the Conquest against the Mexican nation.[22] The fathers of Mexican independence were intoxicated with North American, British, and French constitutional theories which seemed a panacea leading toward political stability and economic prosperity. They proposed to repudiate their Spanish colonial heritage. In its place they proclaimed Aztec antiquity as the true origin of the nation which they intended to govern by the maxims of Anglo-Saxon and French constitutional theory.

The notion that the justice of independence lay in the injustice of the Conquest did not exist merely in the writings of Mier and Bustamante. This idea was a part of the climate of opinion of that era. Morelos's inaugural address to the Congress of Chilpancingo, delivered on November 6, 1813, was saturated with neo-Aztecism.[23] Morelos's conception of Mexican independence as the restoration and continuation of the Aztec empire can not be dismissed as an esoteric bit of romantic sentimentality. Of mestizo and mulatto background himself, he candidly recognized the new nation's responsibility to the Indians. His constructive program was stillborn as the result of his defeat by a coalition of Spanish royalists, clericals, and Creoles—the latter being afraid that Morelos's promised social revolution would jeopardize their privileged position.

These same forces which destroyed Morelos engineered the bloodless coup d'etat of 1821 carrying into effect Mexico's separation from Spain. The plan of Iguala envisaged a monarchy headed by a Bourbon prince. Such a program seemed to run contrary to the spirit of neo-Aztecism. Yet its current was running so swiftly that this same ideology, which influenced Morelos, also permeated the declaration of independence issued by the governmental junta in 1821: "Mexico at long last ends the three centuries of oppression under which she has lived, and is restored to all the rights that the author of nature conceded her."[24]

The fact that neo-Aztecism was discarded by the Creole oligarchy, who directed the affairs of independent Mexico in the nineteenth century, is no valid reason for minimizing the influence of this point of view. This pattern of ideas played a significant role in preparing the Creoles for independence, it provided a neat although historically dubious rationale for independence, and it foreshadowed a mature Mexican national consciousness based upon a recognition of the racially heterogeneous character of Mexican society. In terms of a program for sustained political action, the Indianist preoccupation of the generation of 1810 proved abortive. The Revolution of 1910, however, was to translate the stillborn aspiration of 1810 into a social reality.

NOTES

[1] See my *Millennial Kingdom of the Franciscans in the New World: A Study of the Writings of Gerónimo de Mendieta 1525–1604* (Berkeley and Los Angeles, University of California Publications in History, No. LII, 1956), pp. 42-55, 110-11.

[2] Ramón Iglesia, "La mexicanidad de don Carlos de Sigüenza y Góngora," in *El hombre Colón y otros essayos* (Mexico City, 1944), p. 133.

[3] Francisco de la Maza, *El Guadalupanismo mexicano* (Vol. XVII of *México y lo mexicano*, ed. by Leopoldo Zea, Mexico City, 1953).

[4] The most useful primary source for the biography of Clavigero is Juan Luís Maneiro, S.J., *De vitis aliquot mexicanorum aliorumque qui sive virtute, sive literis Mexici inprimis floruerant . . .* (Bologna, 1791–1792). The most comprehensive secondary source is Sara E. Lake and A. A. Gray's Introduction to *The History of [Lower] California of Francisco Javier Clavigero* (Palo Alto, 1937).

[5] Bernabé Navarro, *La introducción de la filosofía moderna en México* (Mexico City, 1948).

[6] Leopoldo Zea, "The Arcana of Spanish-American Culture," in *Interrelations of Culture* (Paris, UNESCO, 1955), pp. 284 ff.

[7] The first seven Spanish editions of the *Historia antigua de México* from 1826 to 1917 were based on Spanish translations of the Italian edition, *Storia antica del Messico* (4 vols., Cesena, 1780–1781). The original manuscript in Spanish, which Clavigero translated into Italian, was believed to have been lost until Mariano Cuevas found it in Mexico City. I have used Cuevas's text, *Historia antigua de México* (4 vols., Mexico City, 1945). Charles Cullen translated the Italian version into English and published it in London in 1787. It was reprinted in London in 1807, in Richmond, Virginia in 1806, and in Philadelphia in 1817. A German edition translated from the English version was published in Leipzig in 1790.

[8] Julio Le Riverend Brusone remarked on Clavigero's critical attitude toward Torquemada, "We are never so conscious of the limitations of a work when we owe to it a large part of our knowledge on the subject." Julio Le Riverend Brusone, *La Historia antigua de México del Padre Francisco Javier Clavigero*, in *Estudios de historiografía de la Nueva España*, ed. by Ramón Iglesia (Mexico City, 1945), p. 307.

[9] Cornelius de Pauw, *Recherches philosophiques sur les américains ou mémoires intéressants pour servir à l'histoire de l'espece humaine* (3 vols., Berlin, 1770), I, 4, 35, 113; II, 60-72, 74, 83-117, 153-56, 159, 163, 203. Pauw's thesis about the degeneracy of both physical and human nature in America was a popularization and an extension of Buffon's hypothesis that nature in the New

World was "green" and underdeveloped. Count George de Buffon (1707–88) was the leading zoologist of the Enlightenment.

10 Clavigero, *Historia antigua de México*, IV, 232-33, 235, 237.

11 *Ibid.*, II, 196.

12 Although Clavigero found in Montesquieu much illustrative data which he often cited (*Historia antigua de México*, IV, 136, 277, 279, 321, 340, 341, 343, 345, 348), his use of Montesquieu's comparative historical method was more significant.

13 Pauw's anti-Chinese prejudice aroused the ire of Voltaire. See Antonello Gerbi, *Viejas pólemicas sobre el nuevo mundo* (Lima, 1946), p. 91. In this book and in his more recent *La disputa del nuovo mondo: storia di uma polemica, 1750–1900* (Milan and Naples, 1955) there are illuminating discussions about the intellectual polemics concerning the physical and human nature of the New World in which Buffon, Pauw (to a lesser degree), and Hegel figured prominently.

14 Clavigero, *Historia antigua de México*, IV, 259; see also I, 165-72.

15 Carl Becker, *The Heavenly City of the Eighteenth-Century Philosophers* (New Haven, 1932), pp. 64-65.

16 For official and academic reaction in Spain to Clavigero's book see Lillian Estelle Fisher, *The Background of the Revolution for Mexican Independence* (Boston, 1934), p. 306. The Spanish authorities would not license the publication of a Spanish edition, for they took strong objection to the Greek-Indian analogy. The first Spanish edition was published in London in 1826 by a Spanish liberal émigré, Joaquín de Mora.

17 Clavigero, *Historia antigua de México*, I, 167; IV, 266.

18 *Ibid.*, II, 225-26.

19 *Ibid.*, III, 14-15, 88, 161.

20 *Ibid.*, III, 12, 40, 49, 154.

21 *Ibid.*, III, 313-14.

22 José Servando Teresa de Mier Noriega y Guerra, *Historia de la revolución de la Nueva España* (2 vols., Mexico City, 1920; 1st ed., London, 1813) II, 276-78; Carlos María de Bustamante, *Cuadro histórico de la revolución mexicana* (3 vols., Mexico City, 1843), I, 41-42. For a stimulating analysis of neo-Aztecism during the independence period see Edmundo O'Gorman, Prologue to his *Antología de Servando Teresa de Mier* (Mexico City, 1945), pp. xxxv ff. Bustamante's neo-Aztecism was more exaggerated and militant than Mier's.

23 For the text of Morelos's address see Bustamante, *Cuadro histórico de la revolución mexicana*, II, 391.

24 Lucas Alamán, *Historia de México* (5 vols., Mexico City, 1883), V, 287.

THE COLUMBIA INDIAN CONFEDERACY

A LEAGUE OF CENTRAL PLATEAU TRIBES

By Verne F. Ray

UNIVERSITY OF WASHINGTON

THIS PAPER is concerned with a remarkable confederation of Indian tribes which came into being in the Plateau of northwestern America in pre-white times and which persisted until the end of the nineteenth century.[1] Secondarily it is concerned with the greatest recent leader of this confederacy, a man known to the whites as Chief Moses. This man was a leader second to none among the many great chiefs of late times in northwestern Indian history. He is less well-known than Chief Joseph of the Nez Perce tribe, but the parts he played in both purely native affairs and in relationships with the whites were equally dramatic and more significant. Joseph was chief of but one sub-tribe of the Nez Perce, whereas Moses was executive and spokesman for the four tribes of the Columbia Confederacy.

The existence of the Columbia Confederacy became known to me in the course of early field researches with the constituent tribes: the Columbia, Wenatchee, Entiat, and Chelan. But it remained for ethno-historical research which I have conducted in recent years to provide the provocative leads which sent me back to the field for specific study of the confederacy so that the picture might be presented with reasonable fullness and detail.

The member tribes were all Salish speaking and occupied a contiguous block of territory on both sides of the Columbia River in what is now central Washington. Culturally they were close—especially the Wenatchee, Entiat, and Chelan. The Columbia tribe diverged somewhat in having a stronger tribal organization, more tendency to warring activities, and more frequent and prolonged ventures into the Great Plains for buffalo hunting.

It is not surprising that the significance of the Columbia Confederacy and the role of Chief Moses remained undiscovered for so long a time. The tribes involved occupied an area which was the last in the Northwest to feel the impact of white settlement. It was not until the 1890s that any considerable number of whites arrived in the area. Indeed, the present metropolis of Wenatchee, one of the first towns to be established, was not laid out until 1892. As late as 1910 nearly all the land in the vicinity of Manson, on Lake Chelan, was owned by Indian families.

The fur traders who were active in the Northwest during the first half of the nineteenth century gave almost no attention to the country occupied by the tribes of the Columbia Confederacy. A relatively inactive fur trading post was maintained at the confluence of the Okanogan and Columbia Rivers, opposite and a few miles distant from the northwest corner of Columbia territory, from 1811 to 1850, first by the Pacific Fur Company and later by the Northwest Company and Hudson's Bay Company. However, there was little contact between this post and the Indians to the south, and this was unidirectional. The Indians came to the post but the post officials seldom ventured out among the Indians. The Wenatchee and Entiat were too far away to have more than casual contact with the post, and the center of population for the Columbia was about 100 miles distant. Even the Chelan were approximately 30 miles removed. There was no trading post between Fort Okanogan and the mouth of the Walla Walla River, far to the south in the country of the linguistically different Sahaptin tribes.

Various fur traders, including Alexander Ross, Ross Cox, Alexander Henry, and David Thompson, traveled the Columbia River in the course of journeys, passing through the territories of all the tribes under consideration. Only Alexander Ross, however, gave enough attention to the Indians and their ways of living to provide more than a few words of information.

Lewis and Clark, in 1805–6, mentioned these tribes on the basis of information from Indians on the lower Columbia, but the explorers never came within many miles of their territory. The missions established by Whitman at Waiilatpu, near Walla Walla, and Spalding at Lapwai, Idaho, in 1836 did not touch these tribes directly in any way, but young Moses attended school at Lapwai for three years. His later relationships with the whites and the character of his leadership of his people were undoubtedly greatly influenced by his experiences there.

In connection with the Pacific Railroad Survey, and in negotiation of treaties of cession under Governor Isaac I. Stevens, George Gibbs made brief ethnographic inquiries among the Chelan, Entiat, and Wenatchee in the course of which he learned of the existence of the Columbia Confederacy and of its pre-white origin.[2]

Contacts between the United States government and these Indians were meager to the point of silence for most of the period prior to 1870. For the ensuing fifteen years, however, official relationships with Moses, already head of the Columbia Confederacy, were extensive and continuous. The records of these relationships are to be found in hundreds of documents preserved in the United States National Archives. These documents, together with many additional ones in the archives of the Bureau of American Ethnology, the Library of Congress, Yale University, Bancroft Library of the University of California, the Oregon Historical Society and the University of Washington, are the sources to which I referred earlier when speaking of the insights they provided and the stimulus to further field research.

That a great confederacy should have developed among central Plateau tribes is not surprising. Political organization was highly developed among all of the Plateau tribes—the offices, departments, and functions of government were laid out with precision, even though the overall structures were of the modest proportions appropriate to the characteristically small populations. The emphasis placed by such tribes as the Wenatchee, Entiat, and Chelan upon village autonomy in all local affairs made a larger organization either desirable or necessary for such purposes as the organization of buffalo hunting ventures into the Blackfoot country. Tribal organization might have served these purposes, but a league of all the tribes which traveled together was a more logical mechanism. Intertribal affairs of other sorts, for example the summer ceremonies, found the same group of tribes in cooperative association.

Among the tribes of the confederacy and to the south (but not to the north) there was another powerful incentive to intertribal cooperation and organization: chiefly intermarriage. This pattern was so strong as to constitute a rule in the choice of mates and it applied not only to the tribal officials but also, to a considerable extent, to the other members of chiefly families. The numerous chiefly genealogies which I have recorded, extending back five to seven generations, clearly show the extent to which this pattern of marriage linked the tribes of the confederacy and even those beyond.

The Columbia Confederacy was not, indeed, the only such league in the Plateau. A comparable organization existed among the tribes immediately to the south. This was the Yakima Confederacy, comprised of the following tribes and perhaps some others: Kittitas, Yakima, Wanapam, Klikitat, and Palus. Its greatest leader was Kamiakin, a

Palus-Yakima man whose name was most prominent in the treaty negotiations of 1855 at Walla Walla and in the so-called "Yakima War" which followed. But that is another story.

The first head of the Columbia Confederacy, regarding whom substantial information has been recovered, was a man whose chiefly name was Shooktalkoosum (*cktálqu'sam* 'broken sun'). He may, indeed, have been responsible for the formation of the Confederacy. His first remarkable feat was the acquisition of chiefly leadership over the Columbia Indians, despite the fact that his own ancestry was from entirely outside the tribe. His father was an Okanogan Indian from Tonasket; his mother (*cnaxo'mx*) belonged to the Chelan tribe. Since this is seven generations back from the present, memory does not provide details of his parents' lives. It is certain that Shooktalkoosum went to live with the Columbia Indians at an early age, but again the circumstances are obscure. Such a change of tribal residence was not unusual, but only the most remarkable man would have been able, under these circumstances, to place himself in the chieftainship. The Columbia tribal rules for succession to chieftainship were extremely rigid, providing that a deceased chief should be followed by his eldest brother, or, in the absence of brothers, by his eldest son. Normally there was no deviation from such a line of succession—save in the case of incompetency of the normal successor due to extreme dullness, insanity, or some such affliction. Among the tribes of the Northwest whose rules of succession to power were as these, only two exceptions are known. One is that of Shooktalkoosum, the other that of Kamiakin of the Yakima Confederacy. The cases are parallel in that both men achieved their positions as a consequence of their abilities and martial leadership. However, Shooktalkoosum's exploits occurred previously to contact with the whites and were principally concerned with warfare against the Blackfoot and other Plains Indians, while Kamiakin's prominence developed as a consequence of his leadership in the wars with the whites following the Treaty of 1855.

It seems probable that the Columbia tribe either lacked a proper successor to the chieftainship at the time when Shooktalkoosum took over, or that such a successor was a very weak man. We know, at least, that Shooktalkoosum was a very strong man. There are more accounts of his remarkable exploits in war and his bravery in all critical situations than for any other chief within memory. Furthermore, informants strongly emphasize the fact that he obtained guardian spirit aid to a degree superior to all contemporaries. His particular spiritual tutelary was, in addition, different from that possessed by anybody else. Not only were the Columbia Indians impressed by this supernatural help which never seemed to fail Shooktalkoosum in battle, but the enemy was equally respectful and most distraught by his power. The shamans of the Blackfoot were consistently at work attempting to counteract the effects of the Columbia chief's spiritual assets. In fact, it was an elderly medicine woman of that tribe who, according to Blackfoot accounts, succeeded in neutralizing these powers of Shooktalkoosum, thereby bringing about his downfall and death.

During many intervening years, however, Shooktalkoosum led large parties of Columbia, Wenatchee, Entiat, and Chelan Indians to the country of the Blackfoot each summer where the activities were twofold: hunting buffalo and fighting with the enemy. Shooktalkoosum and his Columbia warriors attempted always to take the initiative and to provoke battles with the Blackfoot. As soon as it was seen that the Blackfoot were making ready to retaliate, Shooktalkoosum put on a particular red blanket which he always wore on such occasions and which he felt would save him from any harm. Anecdotal accounts recite many instances in which bullets apparently hit the chief without having any effect. At long last, however—about 1840—he was shot in the arm and fell to the ground. His sons attempted to carry him from the field of battle but he ordered them to retreat and said that, finally being wounded, he had lost his honor and would fight no more. A Blackfoot warrior killed the fallen chief, cut off his head, and dismembered his body. This was not characteristic treatment of a fallen foe, to say nothing of a respected chief and battle leader. The reason it was done was because the feeling was so strong with respect to Shooktalkoosum's supernatural powers that it was felt that he would come to life again if merely killed in the ordinary manner.

Examining Shooktalkoosum's role as head of a confederacy of the Columbia, Chelan, Entiat, and Wenatchee Indians, we first note that members of all these tribes went to Montana for the buffalo hunting and warfare which has been mentioned. Coming from one of these other tribes to the chieftainship of the Columbia Indians probably caused Shooktalkoosum to have a broader perspective in tribal affairs than was the case with an ordinary chief. Furthermore, no warrior of such note could fail to be followed in the warring exploits by representatives of all friendly tribes. Also, there were many cultural ties among them. Despite the vigor with which warfare was carried out against the Blackfoot, there is no record or memory of any conflicts between or among the four tribes which came to form the confederacy. All four spoke a common language in contrast to some of their neighbors, particularly the Sahaptins to the south as represented by the Kittitas, Yakima and others. On the west, linguistically-similar Sanpoil and Colville tribes were not in the habit of making warring ventures against the Plains Indians. The Okanogan tribe, while always friendly with the four tribes of the confederacy, took pride in acting independently. The Methow, adjacent to the Chelan on the north, participated in some activities of the confederacy, but at other times they were under the influence of their northern neighbors, the Okanogan.

It was inevitable that the unity among the four tribes attending the warfare with the Plains Indians—single ventures of which sometimes were prolonged for two or three years—should be carried over into the less dramatic concerns of domestic and economic life in their home territories.

The ethnographers George Gibbs, Edward Curtis, and James Mooney, and the early settler and writer A. J. Splawn, all speak of the character and effectiveness of the confederacy under Shooktalkoosum.[3] For example, Gibbs wrote in 1854: The Columbia, Wenatchee, Entiat, Chelan (and possibly the Methow) are bands which "were formerly all united under one principal chief, Stalkoosum, who is said to have been a man of great note among them. He was killed a few years since in a fight with the Blackfeet since which there has been no head of the tribe." It is not surprising that Gibbs should make the mistake of assuming that the tribe was without a chief following the death of the great leader, because his immediate successor, Patsksteeweeya, lived only one year, most or all of which was spent in Montana, and his successor in turn, Kwiltninuk, lived during these years in areas which Gibbs never touched.

Curtis stated that, "the Skoahchnuh, at Rock Island Rapids opposite the mouth of Moses Coulee, were at one time the most important of the group, because of their Chief Sukutahlkesum, who was practically head chief of all the bands, as well as very influential among the Salishan tribes west of the Columbia.... Sukutahlkesum had always been victorious in his encounters with the Blackfeet, and believed himself invulnerable to bullets." Curtis continued, recounting the circumstances of Shooktal-koosum's death and a succession by Kwiltninuk. (He was unaware of the fact that the chieftainship was held by Patsksteeweeya for an intervening year.) "Qultninak gradually grew into the place left vacant by his father." Splawn wrote that, "about the year 1800, their [Columbia] chief Talth-scosum was the greatest chief and warrior in all the Pacific Northwest country. He made annual hunts into the buffalo country, into the Rocky Mountains where he met in battle the Blackfeet and other tribes who considered him and his bands trespassers. Oftimes his force was joined by the Flatheads and many battles were fought. He was a very large and strong man and a desperate fighter, and was thought to bear a charmed life. The mere sight of him often caused the enemy to flee; but he nevertheless seems to have been only human, for in his last fight a stray bullet found its mark, striking his heart and he fell."

Immediately following the death of Shooktalkoosum he was succeeded by his eldest son, Patsksteeweeya (*patsksti'wiya*), who was present in Blackfoot territory with other members of the family at the time of his father's death. He was a warrior but not one who was noted for daring exploits. Well liked by everyone, he was welcomed to the position which could never again, it was felt, be filled by a warrior and leader of the stature of Shooktalkoosum. Ironically, it was only a year later that a Blackfoot bullet cost Patsksteeweeya his life.

Again, by the rule of succession, Shooktalkoosum's next son came into the chieftainship. This was Kwiltninuk (*qwı'ltni'naq*), a man who held the positions of chief of the Columbia tribe and head of the Columbia Confederacy until his death in 1858. His role as head of the Confederacy was largely a matter of leadership in matters of war with the whites. The four tribes readily acknowledged Kwiltninuk's right to lead the Confederacy because they realized that no other person among them would or could stand against the whites with his determination and fearlessness. He was not well liked as an individual, and members of the various tribes of the Confederacy freely criticized him for his attitudes and acts upon occasion. Had this been a time of peace, it is doubtful that he would have succeeded in holding together the Confederacy but the strain o fwarfare and the threat of loss of their homelands made it possible for a strong character like Kwiltninuk to hold the reins firmly.

At this point certain statements made by George Gibbs must be corrected. In 1854 he wrote that the "Pisquouse," by which name he designated the tribes of the Confederacy, had been without a head since the death of "their noted leader, Stal-koo-sum." He added that

"Quil-tan-ee-nok, or Louis, was an aspirant for his father's throne, and came over to Katetas [Kittitas] to recommend himself to Captain McClellan's patronage." It was McClellan's decision, however, that an election should be held by these Indians "and their neighbors" to select a head chief. "When the election came off, however, he was beaten, and by a candidate whose name had never previously been mentioned."

The facts are these: In 1854 when "Quil-tan-ee-nok" was recommending himself to Captain McClellan, he had already been chief of the Columbia tribe and head of the Confederacy for about twelve years. His representations to McClellan could only have been for one or both of two purposes: first, to become a "white man's chief" as well as Indian chief; second, to become chief of several tribes rather than the Columbia only. Whatever his ambitions, he attained neither goal. We are not told the nature of the election decreed by McClellan, but the circumstances were such that the outcome might have been predicted. The Wenatchee certainly were not going to depose their chief in favor of the Columbia man. As for choosing him as a super-chief, his character was such that the Columbia Indians alone would doubtless have rejected him. Entiat or Chelan tribesmen would no doubt have voted against Kwiltninuk for the same reasons: They had their own hereditary tribal chiefs and they were not well disposed toward the rough and quarrelsome Columbia man. (It is interesting to note that the "newcomer" who was reported to have won the election is not named and nothing is heard of him thereafter.)

Another explanation or two are in order to clarify certain items in the Gibbs report. Louis was not, as reported, an alternative name for Kwiltninuk, but rather for Broken Sun's fourth son, Panekstitsa (*pınaqsti'tsa* 'bending robe'). The latter regularly accompanied his father, along with Kwiltninuk and Moses, on buffalo hunting ventures in Montana. He was so grieved by his father's death that he chose to remain in Montana, saying that he, too, might as well lose his life at the hands of the Blackfoot enemies. But the Blackfoot did not attack him and he stayed on to take a Blackfoot woman as his wife. Later he returned to Columbia territory and it may have been he who accompanied McClellan.

Gibbs further reported that the candidacy of Kwiltninuk or Louis for the chieftainship was favored by the Yakima chief Ow-hai [Owhi], "who seemed to be interested in his promotion." This is understandable regardless of whether the candidate was Louis or Kwiltninuk. Moses, their brother, was married to Owhi's daughter. Moses himself, of course, was not eligible for such a position so long as an elder brother was living, any more than Louis but, of the two, Louis might have had out-of-line aspirations while such would not have been in character for Moses.

Kwiltninuk was a prominent figure in the conflict between the Indians and whites which followed the Yakima Treaty of 1855. He and the people of the Columbia Confederacy were not primary participants in the affair but they could not keep out of it entirely. Kwiltninuk's quick temper and belligerent character drew him into the conflict and his bold and sometimes desperate actions made him a feared warrior. Taking the initiative, he undoubtedly protected his people from attacks which they otherwise would have suffered.

On July 11, 1858, John Owen, Special Indian Agent, reported to his superiors that "A party of miners, ninety strong, were attacked by the Isle-de-peiree [Columbia] Indians, fifty of whom were killed, and the balance retreated towards the Yakima country. I fear there is no life for them. The Indians lost seven, Quill-Te-Mina, the chief Owahi's son, and five others. The disparity in numbers of the fallen is great, *but it is Indian report*, and all believe it here." This is all that official records tell of the death of Kwiltninuk, a most significant event in the history of Indian-white relations in the Northwest. Had he continued in office the record of Indian wars in the region would undoubtedly have been more bloody.

Edward Curtis wrote an account of Kwiltninuk's death which is confused and erroneous, but he correctly identified Kwiltninuk as being married to a Wenatchee woman—she was, as a matter of fact, the daughter of Tookolookin (*tisa'qat*), the Wenatchee chief—and he rightly stated that Tookolookin (*tuqo'laxan*) was killed on the same occasion.

As a consequence of Kwiltninuk's death, his next younger brother, Moses, succeeded to the chieftainship. Unlike Kwiltninuk, Moses was a sober and even-tempered man who was opposed to war and expended his very considerable abilities as a leader and diplomat to keep the tribes of the Columbia Confederacy out of war during the thirty critical years during which he served as head of the Columbia tribe and of the Confederacy. His stature as an individual and his critical role in Indian-white relations justify giving his childhood and early years a glance before relating his activities as tribal chief and Confederacy leader.

Moses was born about 1825 in one of the villages of the Columbia Indians on the west side of the river above Vantage, Washington. He was the third son of Shooktalkoosum. His mother was Kanitsa (*q'a'ni'tsa'*), the first and favorite wife of Shooktalkoosum. Kanitsa had borne the chief his first child, the boy named Patsksteeweeya. Prior to Moses's birth, his father had married the second wife, Sipitsa (*si·pi·'tsa*). She had borne one son, Kwiltninuk. Both of these wives were from the Columbia tribe.

Subsequent to the birth of Moses, four other sons were born, all to other co-wives of Shooktalkoosum. In order of age they were: (1) Panekstitsa, whose mother, Nkiyapitsa (*nq'iyapi'tsa*) was one-half Columbia and one-half Spokane; (2) Paqin (*paqaxi'n*) whose mother was Sipitsa; (3) Kwayitsa (*qwɛi'i'tsa* 'green blanket') also a son of Sipitsa; (4) Shpowlak (*cpa'ula'q*) the son of a Columbia woman named Tohomatku (*toxoma'tqu*).

Moses and his oldest brother, Patsksteeweeya, were in an especially favorable position both in the family and in the tribe. Their mother was the head wife of the family by virtue of having been the first one taken by Shooktalkoosum in marriage. In addition, she was herself the daughter of a chief of the Spokane tribe. Furthermore, all evidence indicates that she was in her own right a powerful and capable woman. When the chief was away or otherwise occupied, the people looked to her for leadership. Although the Columbia tribe did not recognize women as chiefs—in contrast to the practice of several other Plateau tribes—they found it quite normal for Kanitsa to take this role in the light of her chiefly background and her personal characteristics. (At the present time there is talk among both Indians and whites of the central Washington area of erecting a monument in her honor in Moses Coulee.)

Moses and all his brothers were born to a setting in which they normally looked forward to the possibility of chieftainship in later years, and in any event, to being respected and responsible leaders of their people. Succession to chieftainship among the Columbia Indians provided that when a chief died, his eldest brother assumed the office, with further succession from brother to brother in this manner until none was left, or until the office was refused by virtue of old age or infirmity. Next in line of succession was the eldest son of the retiring chief. No brothers survived Shooktalkoosum; therefore his first-born son, Patsksteeweeya, succeeded. The next in line was his second son, Kwiltninuk. The fact that the latter was born of a woman who was other than the chief's principal wife made no difference. The knowledge that one or more of Shooktalkoosum's children might become chiefs naturally affected their training and their attitudes during early years. The concept of the "chiefly family" was strong. Not only did Shooktalkoosum's wife,

Kanitsa, have a position of leadership but the older boys were likewise expected to help lead the people and make decisions for the tribe, especially in the absence of their father.

When Moses was about twelve years old his father made a decision which was vitally to influence his life. An invitation had been extended by the Presbyterian Mission at Lapwai, Idaho, for Shooktalkoosum to send one of his boys to be trained at the mission. The same invitation was extended to some of the other chiefs of tribes of the area. Shooktal-koosum responded, choosing Moses as the one who should receive this training. Two other chiefs sent their sons at the same time. One was Chief Lot of the Spokane Indians who sent his son, Skwaiyamptkan (*sqwaiya'mtqın*), and a chief from Entiat, who sent his son named Tuskin (*tu'sqın*).

I have spoken of Moses's advantage in having Kanitsa as his mother. In addition, he was not only the son of one of the most powerful and respected chiefs known in the recent history of the region, but apparently he was a favorite as indicated by being chosen to receive the advantages of training at the mission center. The missionary in charge at Lapwai was Reverend H. H. Spalding, the churchman who accompanied Marcus Whitman to the West to establish the first contacts with the Indians. The man who actually taught the boys at the mission was probably Mr. Cornelius Rogers who, by all evidence from the historical sources, was an exceedingly competent teacher and a man who understood the Indians as well as could be expected at such a time.

Moses remained three years under the tutelage of the mission. During this time he not only received religious and educational instruction from Mr. Rogers, but he also had the opportunity to get acquainted with the ways of the whites, their modes of thinking, and their culture—at least as represented by this outpost. Of equal importance, perhaps, he learned from his playmates, the Spokane and Entiat boys, of their tribes and of their history. At the same time he became even better acquainted with Nez Perce Indians and Nez Perce culture because the Lapwai mission was located in their territory. Moses received fewer hours of formal training from the missionaries than did the other boys because he was an independent spirit and frequently wandered away to spend time in the nearby hills or in the camps of the Nez Perce. No doubt these experiences were equally as important as those at the mission proper in determining the course of his later life.

He learned the Nez Perce language, becoming fluent in this Sahaptin tongue. It was easier for him to learn the Spokane language, from his Spokane companion and others of the tribe who visited the mission, because this language was Salish, like his own. Earlier in his youth he had learned the rudiments of the Yakima language, the next-door tribal neighbors in his boyhood home, and the Colville language which was spoken by visitors that he met during those years. While at Lapwai he was able to perfect his control of these languages because of the opportunity there of meeting people who spoke the various languages. In addition, of course, he learned some English but his truancy kept him from becoming proficient. (Even though his control of the English language improved as the years passed, Moses used an interpreter to convey his ideas to the whites on his trips to Washington, D.C. It is of interest to note that he was never able to employ his native Columbia language, however, in these conferences. The only interpreters available to him on these trips were those who spoke the Yakima language and he therefore presented his ideas in this foreign tongue and his Yakima interpreter then translated into English.)

During most of the period that Moses spent at the Lapwai Mission his parents were absent in Montana on extended buffalo hunting ventures. It was not long subsequent to Moses's return to the family household that his father was killed. Prior to this time Moses had accompanied his family on their yearly economic rounds, had lived in the winter villages on the Columbia with them, and generally had lived the active and stimulating life of a member of a chiefly Columbia Indian family. During these years he exhibited two primary interests. He loved to raise fine horses, to train them and to enter them in races. One of the principal sporting activities of the Columbia Indians was the running of horse races and Moses had one or more horses in most of these contests. Sometimes he rode himself, but upon many occasions other boys of the tribe were selected to ride. Moses's second interest was hunting. He enjoyed the chase and became a talented hunter, bringing considerable amounts of game food to his family and his tribe.

During this time Moses exhibited numerous effects of his training at the mission school, not the least of which was a sincere and rather active interest in the Christian religion. He was given to "preaching" in an informal way and he tried to set an example for other young men by refusing to play cards, a new form of gambling which had recently been adopted by the tribe and was not only frowned upon by the missionaries because of their principles but also by the more sober members of the tribe because so much money was bet on these games.

Moses's social behavior at this time included a penchant for the proclaiming of Christian doctrines. He took a hand in regulating local affairs and entered into local interpersonal disputes in a manner which undoubtedly would have been resented in a person other than the son of a chief. This kind of behavior was to be even more prominently displayed later when his brother Kwiltninuk was chief.

When Shooktalkoosum was killed Moses undoubtedly began to think about the possibility that he might someday himself become chief. During the many years that Kwiltninuk was in the office, Moses became more and more critical of his brother's harsh policies. He often remonstrated with Kwiltninuk and insisted that his treatment be more humane and temperate. In fact, in some instances Moses took it upon himself to turn loose those prisoners who were, from his point of view, unjustifiably held by his brother. Moses always made it a point to be present, if possible, when some member of the tribe was being accused of a wrong doing. Often he spoke up in defense of the individual.

From his boyhood days, Moses was always present at the council meetings and assemblies of his tribe. At first he just listened, but when he had reached an age where he thought it appropriate for him to speak, he voiced his opinions on all matters that came up for discussion.

After Moses became chief, his treatment of the people remained equally lenient and sympathetic. He took positive action to assist members of the tribe whenever help was needed. However, when he thought a man guilty, he called firmly for punishment. His people paid him the compliment of saying, in colloquial English, that he was "never a mean man."

Although a strong pacifist, in deeds as well as words, Moses did fight and fight effectively when he saw no honorable and wise alternative. He was involved, as an ordinary soldier, in some of the sporadic fighting which took place between 1856 and 1858. He was, indeed, present in the party which attacked the miners and which ended with Kwiltninuk's death. Earlier, he had taken a minor part in the 1855 encounter at Union Gap with Major Rains. These two small episodes, and possibly another one or two, seem to have been his only activities in armed conflict at the time of the "Yakima War." The 1855 event was a military engagement but the 1858 encounter was merely a fight with trespassing miners.

In both of these affairs, together with any others in which Moses might have been implicated, he was acting under orders of his superior, Chief Kwiltninuk.

Moses, even before he became chief, feared that the Whites were intent upon taking away the lands of the Indians or of moving them to places other than their homelands. He was determined to oppose such action by any necessary means, but to him warfare was the last necessary means. He was an unwilling participant in the fighting between 1856 and 1858 because he did not feel that other remedies had been exhausted. The circumstances of these years, however, convinced him that it was unsafe and unwise for him either to continue the armed opposition to the Whites after his brother's death or even to remain in their presence. During the latter months of 1858 he appeared briefly in one and another place in the Northwest, mostly outside the territory of the tribes of the Confederacy, but he was taking no active role in events. He was, at this time, in partial hiding because he thought that the only sensible course for him to take, now that he was the heir apparent to the position which had been held by Kwiltninuk. He wanted the whites to have time to forget the details of conflict and to assume once more an objective view toward the problem of relationships with the native tribes. Furthermore, he feared for his own life because he was now the leader of the late belligerents and he did not want to die: he wanted to live to lead his people in a manner which would best protect their interests at this critical time. He remained in hiding, wandering from one to another place outside the territory of the tribes of the Confederacy, until 1861. By this time the members of his own tribe had given him up for dead but the various constituent groups were scattered due to their own uncertainties and fears, and they had not yet inaugurated a successor to Moses in the chieftainship. In fact, from the point of view of Columbia tribal practice, Moses was not yet officially the chief because no ceremony of inauguration had taken place.

When he considered the time was ripe, Moses went to a military camp located near the present Chewelah, Washington. This was during the days of Fort Colville, which was situated nearby, and the officer at the Chewelah camp was apparently a captain under Major Lugenbeel. He explained that he now intended to return to his people and he wanted the military to know the reasons for his hiding out and his attitudes toward the "Yakima War," and the whites generally. As recounted by his granddaughter,[4] his words to the captain were these: "It was not my decision to make war. I was not chief when the decision was made. It was not Chief Owhi's decision, either. It was the other chiefs who made this decision—my brother, who was chief of the Columbia Indians at that time, also Piopiomaksmaks, Selatasie, Tamayetsas, Swahwayu, and Kamiakin. I just went along with the chiefs' decision because everyone has to agree with the chief." (The chiefs named, except for Kwiltninuk, were all from tribes of the Yakima Confederacy.) Moses said much more in this vein during the period when he was briefly detained at Chewelah. The captain in command then told Moses: "All that you did was to follow your leader. That's the same way it is in the American Army. So, if it be true that you were merely following orders, we'll take you to Washington, D.C. so that you can tell your story to the officials there."

Moses was then permitted to return to his people. The time of the year was June and the people were gathered at the great ceremonial center near Moses Lake where they regularly came after the spring root digging season. When Moses rode in and made his presence known he was received with much enthusiasm and expressions of gratitude that he was still alive. By unanimous acclaim, he was immediately declared to be not only the hereditary successor to the chieftainship, but the popular choice of the people because of their respect for him as a person and as a leader. He had convinced them of his abilities by the roles he had already played in the native life and in relationships with the whites.

Until this time Moses had been known by the name given him as a child, Kwitalahan (*qwita'laxan*). When he officially became chief he was given the name of his father, Shooktalkoosum, by action of the people. During subsequent years he not only served his people well as chief of the tribe, but he also became the recognized head of the Confederacy of the Columbia, Wenatchee, Entiat, and Chelan tribes, as had been the case with his father. His immediate predecessor in the tribal chieftainship, his brother, Kwiltninuk, had held this position, too, but his role had been largely a martial one. The chiefs Shooktalkoosum, elder and younger, were leaders of the Confederacy in matters of peace as well as war.

After his inauguration, Moses remained with his people through the following winter, living in the village named Panko (*pá'nqo*) on the Columbia River. In the spring he is said to have been taken to Washington, D.C., in accord with the promise of the captain at Chewelah. This was Moses's first service in official capacity as leader of the Confederacy.

As a consequence of Moses's pacifism and the changed conditions in the Northwest, there ensued a period of relative quiet so far as Indian-White relationships were concerned, and Moses led his people in peaceful economic exploitation of their traditional lands and in petty inter-tribal affairs. All the while, however, he was conscious of the continuing problem posed by the presence of the nearby whites, even though they were not situated in any numbers within the territories of the four tribes. There was a continuing determination on the part of government officials, supported however only by feeble measures, to get all of the members of these tribes to go on to the Yakima Indian Reservation. When it appeared that this would be an extremely difficult feat to accomplish, the Wenatchee Indians, at least, were told by one or more officials that they might take homesteads in the same manner as the whites in their own Wenatchee Valley. This instruction came in 1875 and was acted upon by some of the Indians of that tribe before the order was rescinded and declared illegal. At the same time other tribes were acting in accordance with Moses's advice, not to say insistence, that they maintain themselves in their aboriginal territories.

It appears that the Chelan, Entiat, and Columbia tribes were not told that they, like the Wenatchee, might take homesteads in their own country. The only course open to them, as they were told in strongly worded orders from the Yakima Agency and other government offices, was to go on the Yakima Reservation. Again and again Moses stated that this they would not do, and all the members of the Confederacy supported him.

The reasons for feeling so strongly against such a move was that the area covered by the Yakima Reservation was entirely outside the aboriginal territory occupied by these tribes, the character of the country was quite different, and—most important of all—the Indians who had lived there and who were now situated there were of a language stock totally unrelated to that spoken by the members of the Confederacy and their ways of life contrasted sharply. One exception must be noted: the Kittitas and the Wenatchee whose territories adjoined, while linguistically different, were nevertheless fairly close to one another in culture and were considerably intermarried. The linguistic difference was not a barrier because virtually all Kittitas could speak the Wenatchee language and vice versa. The same could not be said of the tribes more distant from one another. But it should be emphasized that neither distance nor linguistic contrasts interfered in any way with the peaceful relationships among these tribes. The people of the Confederacy under Moses were perfectly friendly and traditionally had always been so with the tribes of the Yakima Confederacy. It was the strong feeling of homeland and the desire to be situated with others of their same tongue that led Moses and his tribes to hold so tenaciously to their determination to remain off the Yakima Reservation and on their own lands.

From 1870 forward Moses had almost continuous negotiations with military and Indian Service officials on and about the Yakima Reservation. Some of the Indian Service spokesmen, for example the Presbyterian missionary Wilbur, who was also Indian Agent, declared that it was their conviction that Moses would bring his people to the Yakima Reservation if friction between the whites and the Indians could be sufficiently minimized. However, the turn of events made these predictions meaningless.

For the actual course of history was such that Moses was placed in jail in Yakima City, manacled, held in custody for many weeks at Fort Simcoe, and accused of murders in which he had no part. During these years, the noted General, O. O. Howard, was the principal figure involved in negotiations with Moses and the documentary record provides abundant detail. Throughout his career, Moses made a point of dealing with military officials rather than Indian Service officials whenever possible and considered the Army to be a friendly agency of the government. In turn, General Howard praised Chief Moses as a great and talented leader: "the chief who kept his people out of war."

Despite incarceration and maltreatment Moses did not give up his fight for a home for his people in their own lands. Broken promises saddened but did not discourage him. He had to live the life of the hunted, but he succeeded in the extremely difficult task of keeping the tribes of the Columbia Confederacy from going to war against the trespassers who were trying to force them from their lands.

Moses achieved what he had been told again and again was the impossible. He succeeded in getting the United States to abandon the long standing and repeatedly declared policy of placing the tribes of the Columbia Confederacy on the Yakima Reservation. It is true that he failed to obtain for the Confederacy a reservation embracing the bulk of the aboriginal lands of the four tribes, as he had hoped, and as had been recommended by General Howard in consequence of the convincing arguments advanced by Moses. Of course, from the vantage point of the present day, we know that this hope of Moses's was really impossible of achievement.

However, during Moses's 1879 trip to Washington, D.C., the claims of the Columbia Confederacy and Moses's position as leader were recognized by the establishment of a large reservation partially within the lands of the Confederacy and wholly within the territory of Salish speaking peoples. This reservation extended from the Columbia and Okanogan Rivers to the Cascade ridge, and from Lake Chelan to the Canadian border. It was, therefore, adjacent to the Colville Reservation as established in 1872. Although set aside for the tribes of the Confederacy, permission was later given for Methow Indians and Okanogan Indians to live on this reserve which was in part cut out of their aboriginal territory.

Some time after the establishment of the Columbia Reservation the Entiat people, with the exception of Chief Silico and his family, moved to the reservation under pressure from the Army. They settled, for the most part, in the vicinity of what is now the town of Mallott, on the north side of Lake Chelan. Most of the Chelan Indians were already on the Columbia Reservation because their principal aboriginal villages, which they still occupied, were north of Lake Chelan, an area which had been incorporated into the reservation. The Columbia and Wenatchee Indians, on the other hand, remained in their old homelands, off the reservation, dissatisfied with the compromise.

Complaints were soon received by the federal government stating that the Indians for whom the reservation was set aside were not making use of it and that it was wrongfully being withheld from public settlement. An investigation was ordered, the result of which was the calling of Chief Moses to Washington, D. C., once more. At this time Moses agreed to give up the Columbia Reservation if the tribes for whom it was established, those of the Columbia Confederacy, were given rights on the Colville Reservation and assured protection. In addition, the agreement provided that a house be built for Chief Moses on the Colville Reservation, that he be paid a salary of $1,000 per year as long as he might live, and that he receive certain other privileges.

As a consequence of this agreement by Moses on behalf of his people the Columbia tribe voluntarily moved in 1884 to the Colville Reservation. Another provision of the Moses Agreement of 1883 allowed the Indian of the Columbia Reservation to take a homestead of one square mile rather than to go on the reservation. The following year Congress passed a bill known as the Indian Homestead Act. This provided that Indians might take homesteads of one square mile in the same manner as whites. Under these two acts the Indians of the Chelan, Entiat, and Wenatchee tribes were encouraged to take homesteads in the places in which they were living when it appeared that they were reluctant or adamant about going to the Colville Reservation, as they had been with respect to the Yakima Reservation. Some Wenatchee Indians availed themselves of this opportunity and descendants still live on the same grounds as did their forefathers. The Chelan Indians not only refused to go on the Colville Reservation, but also would not permit their lands to be surveyed. At a later date, however, the Chelan were forcibly placed on the Colville Reservation.

With this breakup of the tribes, the Columbia Confederacy can be said to have come to an end. Chief Moses died at his home near Nespelem, on the Colville Reservation, just at the turn of the century.[5]

NOTES

[1] For a general description of Plateau culture, see Verne F. Ray, *Cultural Relations in the Plateau of Northwestern America*, Publications, Hodge Anniversary Publication Fund (Los Angeles, 1939), Vol. 3.

[2] Report on the Indian Tribes of the Territory of Washington, in Reports of Explorations and Surveys... for a Railroad from the Mississippi River to the Pacific Ocean, 33rd Cong., 2nd Sess., H. R. Doc. 91, 1:402-36 (Washington, D.C., 1855). All quotations from Gibbs in the present paper are from this publication. I have also examined all of Gibbs's manuscripts in the archives of the Bureau of American Ethnology, Smithsonian Institution, Washington, D.C.

[3] Edward S. Curtis, *The North American Indian* (Norwood, 1911) Vol. 7. James Mooney, "The Ghost Dance Religion...," Annual Report, Bureau of American Ethnology, 14:Part 2:734-37 (Washington, D.C., 1896). A. J. Splawn, *Ka-mi-a-kin* (n.p., n.d.).

[4] My informants have included many direct-line relatives of Shooktalkoosum and Moses. The granddaughter here referred to is Lucy Covington, who was reared by Mary Moses, wife of Chief Moses. Mary Moses was herself one of my early and most valuable informants. Lucy Covington's mother, Nellie Friedlander, has also been an important informant; she died in 1959. Madeline Moses Covington, a daughter of Shooktalkoosum's son, Louis, has furnished me with invaluable data. George Friedlander, brother of Lucy, has also provided significant information. In making special mention of these lineal descendants of Shooktalkoosum I do not wish to minimize the worth and importance of information provided by many other excellent informants with whom I worked.

[5] This home in which Moses died was the one provided him in accord with the agreement of 1883. It was in this house that much of the field work for this paper was done. Since Moses's death it has been occupied by his widow, Mary Moses, Lucy and John Covington, and other relatives.

WINNEBAGO PROTOHISTORY

By Nancy Oestreich Lurie

UNIVERSITY OF MICHIGAN

IT WAS BELIEVED for many years that the historic Winnebago Indians were the descendants of the people who made the effigy mounds in Wisconsin. The error was an understandable one, based on sound logic but a paucity of data. The mounds are scattered throughout a territory occupied by the Winnebago well into the nineteenth century. Although no Winnebago could recall having seen his people building mounds, the mounds in many cases conform to shapes of animals which are totems of Winnebago clans. Traditional references to earth works could be easily construed to refer to the effigy mounds as well as to the linear and round mounds belonging to the same trait complex. Whether this association of ideas first occurred to the Winnebago and was transmitted to archaeologists, or whether archaeological interest in the mounds spurred development of such a reasonable explanation is no longer known.[1] The fact remains that a majority of the Winnebago people today believe that their ancestors made the Wisconsin mounds.

More recent archaeological research refutes this contention and assigns the Winnebago to a different prehistoric tradition, known as the Mississippi Pattern. Apparently an intrusive population from the southeastern area, the Winnebago in Wisconsin did not produce these effigy mounds nor did they build any truncated mounds typical of the Mississippi Pattern in its fullest representations in other regions. The proper prehistoric relationships of the Winnebago were ultimately revealed through study of village sites which had long been obliterated from casual view and were often discovered by mere chance. These archaeological manifestations did not cry out for explanation as did such obvious surface features as the effigy mounds.

However, the logic of the effigy mound reasoning remains persuasive unless the ethnological and historical materials relating to the Winnebago are reexamined in the light of present archaeological knowledge.[2] Basically, the prehistoric Winnebago lived in large villages which were occupied over relatively long periods of time. Although refuse pits disclose animal bones and dependence on hunting, the village sites show a necessarily heavy reliance on agriculture as well. Archaeological evidence of the prehistoric Winnebago furthermore confines the tribe to an area considerably smaller than that used and occupied by the tribe in historic times. Finally, the historic Winnebago, as known from ethnographic reconstructions and documentary materials of the eighteenth and nineteenth centuries, are a people differing in only minor details of culture from surrounding Algonkian speaking tribes of the midwestern region. The Winnebago are thus viewed as a sort of Siouan speaking anomaly in a woodland cultural setting shared by Menomini, Potawatomi, Ojibwa, and others.

It is obvious that either the Winnebago never differed significantly from their woodland neighbors, or they underwent a transition from sedentary village life to a more roving, Algonkian type of existence characterized by seasonal itineraries, small villages, and greater emphasis placed on hunting.[3] A review of well-known sources indicates that acceptance of the effigy mounds as authentic prehistoric evidence of the tribe obscured recognition of important data in the records available for analysis. Information exists concerning a revolutionary and rapid cultural transition; it can be dated fairly accurately, and the reasons for the shift are clearly apparent. The material derives from ethnographic and historic documents, but eye-witness accounts of the events in question are rare. Thus, the points at issue are here referred to as "protohistoric," and occur from about 1620 to 1670.

The Winnebago in Wisconsin and the French along the St. Lawrence River were aware of each other's existence at least a decade before any actual meeting occurred between the two groups. Ottawa traders journeyed to the Winnebago area as early as 1623; their visits were then first noted by Gabriel Sagard, a lay brother in the Récollet branch of the Franciscan order. Sagard's reference to the tribe did not appear in published form until 1632 when his general account of the Huron and Ottawa was issued under the title, *Le Grand Voyage du Pays des Hurons*.[4] Although this publication is generally considered more accurate than the later and elaborated edition of 1636, *Histoire du Canada*,[5] both versions are necessary to reveal the full substance and source of Sagard's knowledge of the Winnebago.

In the earlier edition Sagard speaks of the Huron language as useful not only in dealings with the Huron, but also with other tribes where the language was understood such as the "Tobacco Tribe, the Neutral nation, the province of Fire, that of the Stinkards [à celle des Puants] and several others."[6] The Puants are easily recognized as the Winnebago on the basis of internal evidence in Sagard's writings and later French accounts which consistently utilize the designation. In 1632 Sagard supplied the information that the Ottawa went "in bands into many regions and countries as far off as 400 leagues or more (or so they told me), and there they trade their goods and exchange them for furs, pigments, wampum and other rubbish."[7] It appears that Sagard learned of the Winnebago through the Ottawa rather than the Huron, since he amended the above passage in the later edition of his work to state that the Ottawa traveled as far as 500 leagues and specifically to the Puants.[8]

At the time Sagard's first publication appeared, another writer took cognizance of the tribe. In 1632 Champlain prepared a map of areas known to the French through exploration or dependence on Indian information. Whether Champlain's knowledge derived from Sagard is uncertain, but he also had direct access to the Ottawa traders and utilized their information in his journal accompanying the map. He noted "La Nation des Puants" as living all about the shores of a lake north of and between Lake Huron and Lake Superior. This small lake was depicted as lying some distance up a river which emptied into Lake Huron.[9] The map may be but a mistaken attempt to portray Lake Michigan, but the relative size of the Puant lake and clearly delineated river makes it highly probable that Champlain had heard of Lake Winnebago lying upstream of the Fox River. The presence of Lake Michigan, a great inland sea comparable to Lake Huron, was not clear to Champlain, possibly for the reason that the Winnebago were shifting their residence at the time they were reported to Champlain. Green Bay on Lake Michigan was long known as the Bay of the Puants, although by the late seventeenth century the tribe had removed further inland to the smaller lake up the Fox River which still bears their name. Although not comparable in size to Lake Michigan, Lake Winnebago is an impressive body of water, about the same size as the restricted tip of Green Bay.

Champlain's confusion about the geography of the Wisconsin area is further illustrated by his statement regarding the map in these particulars: "Riviere des Puants qui vient d'vn lac auquel il y a une mine Ciure de rosette." [10] Copper was known to exist in the Lake Superior region where Champlain locates the Winnebago, although neither archaeological nor historical data allow placing the Winnebago in the copper area. However, copper was transported to the region occupied by the Winnebago in prehistoric times, [11] and the tribe still retains traditions of having used copper prior to the time of European contact. [12] Reports of copper ornaments among the Puants may have given rise to the idea that the tribe resided in the immediate vicinity of a mine. These speculations would be of little interest except that the interpretation of Champlain's map as an effort to show Lake Winnebago and the Fox River conforms reasonably to later accounts which strongly suggest that the Winnebago had withdrawn westward from their traditional home on Green Bay as early as 1632.

The Jesuits provide the next references to the Winnebago, and their information can be correlated with the accounts by Nicolas Perrot and Claude Charles le Roy, sieur de Bacqueville de la Potherie. [13] The Jesuits came to Huronia to aid the Récollets, the two orders working side by side from 1625 to 1629 when the British acquired New France and forced both groups to leave. Upon the restoration of Canada to France, the Jesuits alone returned to the mission field. The *Jesuit Relations* covering the period after 1634 refer to the Winnebago as the "Gens de Mer," the people of the sea, and reiterate with monotonous frequency the explanation that the tribe derived its name, "Ouinipigou," from an Algonkian word meaning salt, brackish or sea water. [14] Hence the French term *Puant,* unhappily rendered "Stinkard" in English translations.

Data derived from Sagard, Champlain, and the *Jesuit Relations* have been drawn together into a romantic tradition purporting to be an early phase of Wisconsin history. It seems that Champlain was so entranced with accounts he had received of an unusual people, the Puants, who spoke a peculiar language, that in 1634 he sent a special envoy to visit them. During the seventeenth century the French and other Europeans entertained high hopes that a passage might be found through the American land mass giving access to the Orient. Jean Nicolet was thus dispatched to ascertain whether the people of the sea lived on the hither edge of Asia or were a colony from the fabled East. Such, at least, is the explanation for the Chinese robe donned by Nicolet when he was about to greet the Winnebago. Presumably he brought it along on the outside chance that he might meet representatives of the Grand Khan.[15]

Apart from the possibility that Champlain was primarily interested in laying claim to a copper mine, the only specific and recorded reason given for Nicolet's voyage is provided in the *Relation* of 1642–43, "To make a journey to the nation called the people of the sea, and arrange a peace between them and the Hurons."[16] Other documents indicate that the intercessions for peace probably extended to other tribes than the Huron, and that the Jesuit chronicler employed a common device of using the term "Huron" to refer to any tribes served by the mission station of Huronia.

After Nicolet's brief visit the Winnebago were disregarded for over twenty years due to hostilities of the Iroquois which kept the French fully occupied along the St. Lawrence. Therefore, the history of the tribe in the period before 1634 and immediately thereafter is based on much later sources. However, the Perrot and La Potherie narratives so convincingly fill a cultural and historical gap between archaeological and ethnological depictions of the Winnebago that they are worthy of detailed consideration. The general neglect of these data in regard to the Winnebago can be traced to several circumstances. First, John Gilmary Shea, a nineteenth-century historian, believed that Nicolet made his famous voyage in 1639 or 1640. He took note of the fact that the *Jesuit Relation* of 1669–1670 stated that about thirty years earlier the Winnebago were virtually annihilated by the Illinois. Shea surmised that the *Relation* was in error about the date of the battles between the Winnebago and Illinois, and that the extended description of these hostilities referred to a period antedating Nicolet's visit by many years. How else, Shea reasoned, could a people have recouped such losses in so short a time for Nicolet to describe them a year after the events as "populous?"[17]

Careful research by Benjamin Sulté led to a reliable correction of the date of Nicolet's journey as having occurred in 1634 rather than in 1640. Thus, there would have been time for Nicolet to have visited the tribe when it enjoyed its full strength and for the Illinois to have made telling inroads five or six years later. However, Sulté confined his interest to the arrival of Nicolet and did not consider the problem of warfare between the Illinois and Winnebago.[18]

As a result, Shea's original error was perpetuated in the work of

Publius V. Lawson, a Wisconsin antiquarian, who wrote the only extensive accounts of the Winnebago prior to the time that any serious ethnological research was devoted to the tribe. Lawson utilized Sulté's date of 1634 for the Nicolet visit, but also accepted the opinion of Shea that the Illinois affair derived from a much earlier period, if it occurred at all.[19]

At the time Paul Radin published his major work on the Winnebago, there was no reason to inquire further into the matter as set forth by Lawson. The territorial expansion of the tribe was conceived as a gradual movement from Green Bay to the West, and attested to by the presence of mounds attributed to the Winnebago beyond the Green Bay area. The events themselves were of interest ethnologically, even if merely folklore, and references to them discovered in the field were accordingly transcribed.[20] Radin's interests centered in general cultural reconstructions rather than in historical sequences. However, the accuracy and completeness of his work as an ethnographer have proved invaluable now that the archaeological situation is better understood. Radin's inclusion of given details and variant versions of particular information aid in clearing up the confusion promulgated by Shea and Lawson. Thus, it is possible at this time to reconstruct a logical chronology of historical events, along with the cultural changes peculiar to given eras.

The primary historical report about the Winnebago relating to the period prior to European contact is probably colored by the outraged views of enemy Indians. It is possible that Champlain was in possession of such information as early as 1632, along with other details available today only through archaeological and ethnological reconstructions. If this were the case, although we may question whether Asiatic affiliations were thereby suggested, we cannot avoid the impression that there was something unusual about the Winnebago that may have excited the curiosity of the French. La Potherie wrote of the tribe:

The Puans were masters of this Bay [Green Bay], and to a great extent of the adjoining country. This nation was a populous one, very redoubtable, and spared no one; they violated all the laws of nature; they were sodomites, and even had intercourse with beasts. If any stranger came among them, he was cooked in their kettles. The Malhominis [Menomini] were the only tribe who maintained relations with them, (and) they did not dare to even complain of their tyranny. Those tribes believed themselves the most powerful in the universe; they declared war on all nations they could discover, although they had only stone knives and hatchets.[21]

Radin's data correlate significantly with archaeological conclusions concerning the tribe. Although pottery was no longer produced when Radin began his research, it was possible to obtain a generalized account of its manufacture which conforms to Mississippi Pattern pottery.[22] The Winnebago sites are still not completely excavated, therefore no evidence concerning house types has been unearthed. It is generally known, however, that a square or rectangular floor plan is typical of the Mississippi Pattern. The historic Winnebago used the Algonkian style of domed wigwam with a circular or oval floor plan, but Radin's data indicated that the original Winnebago dwelling was more commonly a gabled lodge built on either the ground or a platform and thus agreed generally with expectations concerning prehistoric dwellings of the tribe.[23] The villages themselves were relatively large in comparison to historic villages, a point stressed in Winnebago tradition. Radin discounted descriptions of a single village so large that the people at one end did not know what was transpiring at the other, but such descriptions persist and can now be given greater credence in the light of archaeological data.[24] At least it is no longer necessary to expect traditional accounts to be compatible with the later historic fact of small, widely scattered settlements. Two Wisconsin informants born in the early 1860s said that they had often heard of old villages in the Lake Winnebago region where the gardens alone were alleged to have been several arrow-shots in length and breadth. A Bear Clan informant explained as late as 1944 that he understood that the "police force" function of his clan originated in a very early, pre-white period when the Winnebago lived together in villages of several thousand people. They thus required a powerful and highly formalized organization to maintain control over the group.

The entire concept of leadership is particularly interesting in connection with protohistoric traditions and historic practices. Radin's account of chieftainship based on mythological and legendary sources emphasizes the presence of a single head chief over large numbers of people. The chief had well defined duties and obligations to "all the different bands and groups of people that exist among the Winnebago."[25] He was a man of peace and conciliation, a leader rather than a ruler. Strong sanctions and actual force were available as social controls through the activities of the Bear Clan. These generalized views of chieftainship are still expressed by reliable informants. However, during the treaty period in the early nineteenth century, the Winnebago clearly practiced a system of leadership based on the local group. Each band chief exercised his sway over his own community. Cessions of land could be made only by agreement among these representatives. Nevertheless, even during the treaty period, there was a head chief and a succession of chieftainship in a particular family line, usually designated as the *keramani*.[26] Deference and respect were accorded this individual recognized throughout the tribe as the head chief, although the geographic dispersion of the population over a wide area rendered traditional exercise of the office impractical.

Radin also noted changes in religion in that his data supported the idea that the Medicine Rite among the Winnebago was modeled after another ritual within the culture, but reached its fullest development in response to crises posed by the inception of the fur trade. He derives the shooting ceremony directly from Algonkian sources.[27] A final note on religion is Radin's view that the historic importance of the Thunderbird may represent a replacement of the water spirit as a primary deity.[28]

The cultural alterations discerned by Radin can be related to documented historical materials which also provide reasons for certain changes. On the authority of Sagard, it is known that the Ottawa visited the Winnebago as early as 1623. Since Sagard makes no reference to overt hostilities on the part of the Winnebago at that time, it appears that the Ottawa returned to the tribe after 1623 when the events recorded by La Potherie occurred.

They did not desire to have commerce with the French. The Outouaks, notwithstanding, sent to them envoys whom they had the cruelty to eat. This crime incensed all the nations, who formed a union with the Outouaks, on account of the protection accorded them by the latter under the auspices of the French, from whom they received weapons and all sorts of merchandise. They made frequent expeditions against the Puans, who were giving them much trouble . . .[29]

The effects of the hostilities brought a division of opinion in the tribe:

. . . and then followed civil wars among the Puans who reproached one another for their ill-fortune, brought upon them by the perfidy of those who had slain the envoys, since the latter brought them knives, bodkins and many other useful articles of which they had had no previous knowledge. When they found that they were being vigorously attacked, they were compelled to unite all their forces in one village, where they numbered four or five thousand men.[30]

The term civil wars raises questions to which there are no answers. Curiously, La Potherie makes no mention of Nicolet in his account of the fortunes of the Winnebago. But, if La Potherie may be trusted, Nicolet must have put in his appearance at about this point in the narrative. The location of the huge village alluded to is undetermined, although by this time the tribe may have removed from the shores of Lake Michigan along Green Bay to the more protected region of Lake Winnebago. There remains the further question whether Nicolet visited the village mentioned in this connection or whether he visited any regular settlement of the Winnebago Indians.

Both the Nicolet and La Potherie narratives appear to refer to the same period of warfare. Nicolet may have arrived when the Winnebago still held the ascendancy in the hostilities. We do know that the primary purpose of his journey was to establish peace with the Winnebago. Unfortunately, even the Nicolet account was not transcribed until almost ten years after the voyage took place, and then it was reported by a second person, Bartelmy Vimont, S.J. However, fragments of data obviously obtained from Nicolet appear in the *Relations* prior to 1643. Although Nicolet's visit was brief, it deserves careful attention in the total sequence of events.

Nicolet set out from the St. Lawrence in 1634 with seven Indian companions. Upon traversing Lake Huron, he made the earliest recorded journey of a European beyond the Straits of Mackinac. It is logical to assume that Nicolet followed the western shore of Lake Michigan, but it is uncertain whether he crossed among the islands at the mouth of Green Bay and continued along the Door County peninsula. It is more likely that he skirted the mainland of Upper Michigan and Wisconsin into the Bay since he lists the tribes in the region as they would be encountered from north to south. Just where Nicolet landed cannot be determined definitely, for Vimont merely states:

When they arrived at their destination, they fastened two sticks in the earth and hung gifts thereon, so as to relieve these tribes from the notion of mistaking them for enemies to be massacred.[31]

What was meant by their destination and who the dangerous tribes were can only be matters for speculation. Certain it is, however, that Nicolet's first landfall was not among the Winnebago directly, for the story continues that when he was two days' journey from the Winnebago he sent out an envoy,

... to bear tidings of the peace, which word was especially well received when they heard that it was a European who carried the message; they despatched several young men to meet the Manitouiriniou—that is to say, "the wonderful man." They meet him; they escort him, and carry all his baggage.[32]

Lawson argued on the basis of the foregoing statement that Nicolet landed at the mouth of the Fox River, and that the Winnebago carried his baggage over the portage necessitated by the rapids in the Fox between its mouth and its juncture with Lake Winnebago. From this he drew the conclusion that the Winnebago were living in the vicinity of what is now the site of Neenah-Menasha in Wisconsin.[33] Lawson found few supporters for his theory, and the weight of historical opinion favors Red Banks on Green Bay as the place of Nicolet's landing because it is known to the Winnebago as their traditional homeland and point of origin.[34] In truth, it seems that Nicolet should have made some mention of the Fox rapids, had he passed by them; similarly, Lake Winnebago is of sufficient size to have merited some comment. Thus, it is doubtful that Nicolet traveled any distance inland. His remarks on the more westerly tribes bear this out, since he described them all as Algonkian speaking, including the Sioux and Assiniboin. The obvious misunderstanding of Indian information also points up an error on the part of Vimont, who inferred that Nicolet visited the tribes named.[35] Nicolet was familiar with Algonkian and Iroquoian dialects and would have noted the difference in Siouan speech had he heard it.

In respect to Lawson, however, Champlain's map of 1632 suggests that the Winnebago were indeed living in the vicinity of Lake Winnebago at the time of Nicolet's arrival, although the argument that Nicolet visited them remains weak. Nicolet may well have landed at the mouth of the Fox to be greeted by those Winnebago still residing on Green Bay or perhaps by those from Lake Winnebago who came out to meet him. He described the Winnebago as located in such a way that they formed "one of the most important openings for the Western tribes and somewhat more for the Northern." This reference is clearly to the

Fox-Wisconsin portage route to the Mississippi that was to figure so prominently in subsequent travels of the French. Its extent and direction were only vaguely grasped by the Jesuit chronicler who stated the case regarding Lake Michigan that, "Sieur Nicolet . . . assured me that, if he had sailed three days' journey upon a great river which issues from this lake he would have found the sea.[36] Surely Nicolet would not have let a matter of three days stand between himself and the discovery of the long sought Northwest Passage.

While it is doubtlessly true that Nicolet landed along Green Bay and probably near the mouth of the Fox River, the only support for the location being at Red Banks specifically is Winnebago tradition that this was their place of supernatural origin. But, wherever Nicolet did land, his arrival must have been spectacular:

He wore a grand robe of China damask, all strewn with flowers and birds of many colors. No sooner did they perceive him than the women and children fled, at the sight of a man who carried thunder in both hands— for thus they called the two pistols that he held. The news of his coming quickly spread to the places round about, and there assembled four or five thousand men. Each of the chief men made a feast for him, and at one of those banquets they served at least sixscore beavers. The peace was concluded; he returned to the Hurons.[37]

The robe may have been no more than standard equipment, along with the pistols, to impress newly encountered aborigines. If Nicolet really expected to find Chinese, he encountered only Indians at the end of his voyage. Perhaps it was disappointment that accounts for his terse observation that the Winnebago were sedentary and populous. However, this lack of detail, if we discount the China theory, underscores the question of whether Nicolet visited a Winnebago village at all. Since he made one of the outstanding journeys of his time to meet a specific tribe, it is strange that the record is so silent about that tribe. Nor does La Potherie mention Nicolet in connection with his account of Winnebago history. The seeming corroboration of Nicolet and La Potherie in reference to a gathering of four or five thousand men may concern two different groups and locations. The assembled Indians described by Nicolet came from the "places round about." Furthermore, we do not know if Nicolet's "chief men" were the leaders of several tribes or simply clan or family heads of a given tribe.

The familiar interpretation of Nicolet's landfall might be as easily construed to mean that he was greeted by a mixed group of Menomini and Winnebago and possibly other tribes who gathered at some indeterminate point on Green Bay for the occasion. For example, the word "Manitouiriniou" is patently Algonkian, while the earliest known and traditional Winnebago word for a French person is properly Siouan, *waxopini,* or spirit. This linguistic curiosity may be no more than Vimont's interpolation, since Nicolet did report that the Winnebago spoke a language entirely their own. There is the alternative explanation, however, that Nicolet was greeted by Menomini whose Algonkian dialect he could recognize even if unable to converse with them. If Nicolet transmitted more details of his trip to his superior, Champlain, no records of the matter have been found to date. Champlain died in 1635 and Nicolet might never have had the opportunity to convey his information fully and officially.

These details would be unimportant except that archaeological and ethnological evidence indicates that the Winnebago did differ significantly from the tribes familiar to the French in 1634. The uncritical acceptance of the Nicolet narrative has tended to negate these differences. When next encountered in the documents relating to the latter half of the seventeenth century, the tribe is greatly reduced in number and seems almost indistinguishable from the surrounding Algonkians, apart from a difference in language. Unfortunately, the tribe was of such small account when missionaries entered the area that they did not take the trouble to study the Winnebago language as they had studied Algonkian and Iroquoian dialects. Consequently, the *Jesuit Relations* are of little help in discerning non-material aspects of culture which might have remained in force from a prehistoric period. Since no mention is made of Nicolet in the account by La Potherie, it appears that the peace established was of short duration or that the Winnebago were far more affected by other events than Nicolet's intercessions. La Potherie stated that after the Winnebago formed their large village as a measure of defense,

maladies wrought among them more devastation than even war did, and exhalations from the rotting corpses caused great mortality. They could not bury the dead, and were soon reduced to fifteen hundred men. Despite all these misfortunes they sent a party of five hundred warriors against the Outagamis, who dwelt on the other shore of the lake; but all those men perished, while making that journey by a tempest which arose.[38]

The lake in question is probably Lake Winnebago, since the Fox supposedly left what is now the state of Michigan and migrated to eastern Wisconsin sometime between 1634 and 1650. According to La Potherie, the Winnebago were dauntless in their determination for revenge "to satisfy the manes of their ancestors." However, "the destitution to which they were reduced made it still more difficult for them to find favorable opportunities for their subsistence; the frequent raids of their enemies had even dispersed the game; and famine was the last scourge that attacked them."[39]

At this point the Illinois took pity on the tribe and brought them provisions. The Winnebago, in turn, entertained the Illinois with games and dancing, but during the festivities surreptitiously cut the bow-strings of their generous guests and slew them all. Fully aware that revenge would follow, the Winnebago took refuge on an island. They believed themselves safe since the Illinois did not use canoes. At length the Illinois came to investigate the reason for the protracted absence of the delegation, but found only an abandoned village and human bones which they surmised were those of their fellow tribes-men.[40] The Illinois waited a year to gather their forces and engage in a winter campaign in order to cross over the ice to the new Winnebago village. The Winnebago anticipated their arrival by a day and left in a body for their winter hunt, but the Illinois pursued them and managed to capture or kill almost the entire tribe apart from a few who escaped to the Menomini.[41] The Jesuit account of these events adds a dramatic detail differing from the Perrot version:

... all of the people of this Nation were killed or taken captive by the Illinouek, with the exception of a single man who escaped, shot through the back with an arrow, when the Illiniouetz had sent back his captive countrymen to inhabit the country anew, he was made a Captain of his Nation, as having never been a slave.[42]

When Perrot observed the Winnebago, more than thirty years after Nicolet's visit, he reported a population of only 150 warriors,[43] that is about 600 people in all by the reckoning generally used of one warrior for every four persons. Even if Perrot erred in his estimate, the Winnebago were obviously greatly reduced in numbers since the time information concerning them first came to the attention of the French. They evoked scarcely any comment from later travelers in the seventeenth century. The early maps retained the designation of

Green Bay as the Bay of the Puants, but the tribe as such was seldom noted in contrast to the careful plotting of neighboring tribes. Radisson, for example, merely mentioned them in passing as sedentary and agricultural. They are not included on Marquette's map of 1673–74, although Joliet's map of 1674 shows them on the lower Fox, east of Lake Winnebago but considerably west of Green Bay.[45]

The veracity of the narratives provided by Perrot and the Jesuits and the relative recency of the events recounted are underscored by the fact that recognizable features of the story may still be obtained among the Winnebago. Radin transcribed a version in 1910 which tended to merge all the occurrences as one continuous campaign against the tribe. The location is given as Red Banks where the Winnebago may have been living at the time the Ottawa first attempted to deal with them.

All this time the men of the tribe were being killed off. After a while they began to kill the male children too. Whenever they saw a child they raised up its dress and if it was a male child they killed it. However, there was a young mother who had a boy, and fearing that if the enemy discovered him they would kill him, she tied a string to the end of the child's penis and pulled the string back under its legs so that the child was given the appearance of a girl. From this woman and her child all the pure-blooded Winnebago living today are descended.

The final statement is curious since the above narrative concludes: "The war against the Winnebago was ended by a young Winnebago chief painting himself blue and surrendering himself to the other tribes."[46] The reference to pure-blooded Winnebago in this context probably reflects concern with the fact that after the hostilities a great deal of intermarriage with other tribes took place, as Perrot observed.[47]

Parts of the story were also collected in the field since 1950, both among the Wisconsin and Nebraska branches of the tribe. The disguise of the boy as a girl appears as an isolated incident, but in Nebraska several elderly men mentioned an old man, now dead but known to them personally, who was the last individual able to trace his genealogy directly to the boy in the story. In recent accounts the location of the final battle with the Illinois is either not made explicit or is described as in the region of Butte des Morts, just north of Lake Winnebago. The enemy is identified as either Fox or Illinois. One Wisconsin informant said that while many people tell the story of one man surviving uncaptured, his father and a number of other reliable old men always insisted that fifty men had thus escaped, forming a nucleus for re-establishing the tribe when the hostilities came to an end.

Apart from literary embellishments, the incidents set forth in the documentary and ethnographic sources leave little doubt that some great upheaval affected the tribe after 1634, leaving the Winnebago disorganized and greatly reduced in population. Subsequent observations, as well as reconstructions based on ethnographic materials, reveal that by the eighteenth century the Winnebago were quite similar in customs to their Algonkian neighbors and that they resided generally in the vicinity of Lake Winnebago. If, upon the cessation of warfare, the Winnebago attempted to regroup effectively according to their former habits, they were prevented from doing so. Hordes of Algonkian speaking peoples descended upon their country from east of Lake Michigan; Sauk, Fox, Potawatomi, Miami, Kickapoo, Ottawa, Ojibwa, Mascoutin, Illinois, and a remnant of the Iroquoian speaking Huron. The interloper tribes filtered into the Green Bay region and beyond, spreading out along the Wolf, Fox, Wisconsin and Rock Rivers as far west as the Mississippi, and north along the Black and Chippewa Rivers. It was reported in the *Jesuit Relations* of 1653–54 that:

All these peoples have forsaken their former country and withdrawn to the more distant Nations, toward the great lake we call "the Lake of the Stinkards." The devastation of the Huron country having made them apprehensive of a like misfortune, and the fury of the Iroquois having pursued them everywhere, they thought to find security only by retreating to the very end of the world, so to speak.[48]

Between 1669 and 1674, the accounts of the Jesuits Allouez, Dablon, and Marquette illustrate the rapid influx of population, swelling the numbers of Indians served by Allouez from his mission at Green Bay to twenty thousand.[49] Unable to withstand the invasion by strange tribes and former enemies, and all being in fear of the dreaded Iroquois, the Winnebago lived in peace and intermarried with the newcomers. In the process of recouping their strength by taking mates from the alien tribes, the Winnebago also borrowed many material traits from new kinsmen and neighbors. Culturally disordered, they reformed their socio-economic patterns around the pursuit of peltry animals. Thus, the first distinguishable phase of Winnebago acculturation was not to Europeans or to European goods as such, but to models of

Indian-white relationships and material syncretisms worked out by other tribes.

It is possible that the central Algonkian tribes were better able to accommodate themselves to the requirements of the fur trade than were the Winnebago when the Ottawa first appeared with goods of French origin. The Algonkians were already organized in terms of local bands and relied largely on hunting before the fur trade was introduced. The Winnebago, by contrast, were sedentary people, living in a few large communities, primarily dependent on agriculture. European goods and services available through concentration on the trapping of beaver may not have seemed worth the effort. Although it must be noted that even such semi-sedentary and agricultural groups as the Huron and Iroquois proper were deeply committed to the fur trade at an early period, the Iroquois and Huron-Algonkian factions were competing for ascendancy and thus recognized the utility of European arms and allies. The Winnebago at that time, according to La Potherie, were the unquestioned "masters" in their own region.

The initial rejection of the Ottawa as trading partners can also be understood in part by examining the actual conditions of contact. The eastern tribes eased into the fur trade gradually over a long period of years. They met the French directly and saw more than the few utensils and baubles offered in trade. To the Winnebago, the donor culture was merely Ottawa, not French. Despite the fact that they had only stone weapons, their demonstrated power up to that time could well have led the Winnebago to feel superior to the Ottawa traders. However, trade goods did pique Winnebago interest, and by the time the French arrived in the area, the Winnebago were in a more receptive frame of mind. This change had been conditioned by the overwhelming defeats suffered in warfare and the effect of decimating disease. Such crises doubtlessly brought home to the Winnebago that they were, after all, vulnerable to outside forces.

The subsequent history of the tribe shows an expansion toward the Mississippi River by way of the Rock and Fox-Wisconsin waterways. The gradual departure of alien tribes left vacant the area of southern Wisconsin and northwestern Illinois to supply the increasing needs of the expanding Winnebago population. Large villages gave way to scattered communities of several hundred people each, distributed over a wide territory. A general diminution of game throughout the eighteenth century contributed to a further scattering of local groups. The final result of events stemming from the protohistoric period led to the historic appearance of the Winnebago as a linguistic curiosity in a woodland, largely Algonkian, cultural setting.

NOTES

[1] Paul Radin, "The Winnebago Tribe," Bureau of American Ethnology, Smithsonian Institution, *Annual Report*, XXXVII (1915–16), 76-103, reviews the work of archaeologists who developed the theory of Winnebago relationships to effigy mounds, but points out that the mounds must then have been built in relatively recent times since the traditional home of the tribe was at Green Bay.

[2] See Will C. McKern, "Preliminary Report on the Upper Mississippi Phase in Wisconsin," *Bulletin of the Public Museum of the City of Milwaukee*, XVI (1954), 111-25. Will C. McKern and Robert Ritzenthaler, "The Upper Mississippi Peoples," *Wisconsin Archeologist*, XXVII, No. 1 (1946), 10-21. John Bennett, "Prehistory of the Northern Mississippi Valley," in *Archeology of the Eastern United States*, ed. by James B. Griffin (Chicago, 1952), pp. 108-23.

[3] It has been pointed out by Dr. James B. Griffin in personal communication that such a transition may have been under way prior to the time of European contact. Subsequent events as set forth in this paper then accelerated rather than initiated the shift.

[4] George M. Wrong, ed., *The Long Journey to the Country of the Hurons* (translation of the Paris ed., 1632 [Toronto: the Champlain Society, 1939]); the French text is also included.

[5] Edwin Tross, ed., *Histoire du Canada* (4 vols., Paris, 1866); this edition is considered a reliable republication of the very rare Paris edition of 1636.

[6] Wrong, *The Long Journey*, p. 9.

[7] *Ibid.*, p. 67.

[8] Tross, *Histoire*, I, 194.

[9] C.-H. Laverdière, ed., *Oeuvres de Champlain* (in 6 vols., Quebec, 1870), VI, facing page 1385. The Laverdière edition is used rather than the English edition of H. P. Biggar because of greater clarity of reproductions of illustrative materials.

[10] Laverdière, *Oeuvres*, VI, 1388.

[11] Robert Ritzenthaler, "Similarities between Copper Pendants Found in Wisconsin and Georgia," *Wisconsin Archeologist*, XXX, No. 3 (1949), 51-52. George L. Pasco and Robert Ritzenthaler, "Copper Disks in Wisconsin," *Wisconsin Archeologist*, XXX, No. 4 (1949), 63-64. Many copper artifacts have been found in Wisconsin but these articles have particular reference to Mississippi Pattern types; they are of Middle Mississippi Phase style compared to other regions, but found in Upper Mississippi Phase territory in Wisconsin.

[12] Field notes of N. O. Lurie; all ethnographic data not otherwise cited derive from this source.

[13] These accounts are contained in Emma Helen Blair (ed.), *The Indian Tribes of the Upper Mississippi Valley and Region of the Great Lakes* (in two volumes, Cleveland, 1911, 1912): Nicolas Perrot, "Memoir of the Manners, Customs, and Religion of the Savages of North America," I, 25-272, and Charles le Roy,

sieur de Bacqueville de la Potherie, "A History of the Savage Peoples who are Allies of New France," I, 275-372; II, 13-136. Although Perrot's work was written between 1680 and 1702, it was not published until 1864, in Paris, ed. by Jules Tailhan, S.J. Blair's selection of La Potherie is from the second and fourth volumes of his *Histoire de l'Amerique Septentrionale*, published in Paris in 1716. Perrot was a French agent and interpreter who was delegated to keep peace among certain of the Great Lakes tribes in the period 1665–80. La Potherie is believed to have had access to Perrot manuscripts other than those published by Tailhan, but which are now lost. Blair presents a translation of all of Perrot's published works and begins the La Potherie account where it ceases to duplicate Perrot.

¹⁴ Reuben G. Thwaites (ed.), *The Jesuit Relations and Allied Documents* (in 73 volumes, Cleveland, 1896–1901), XV, 155; XVIII, 231; XXIII, 275; XXXIII, 151; XXXVIII, 239; XLII, 221.

¹⁵ Louise Phelps Kellogg, *The French Regime in Wisconsin and the Northwest* (Madison, 1925), pp. 75-82. It is interesting that so sober a scholar as Dr. Kellogg was sufficiently impressed by the documentary material alone to suggest that the French supposed the people of the sea were something other than Indians. Nicolet's landfall has been the subject of several paintings, the most famous being that by Edwin W. Deming. It now hangs in the building of the State Historical Society of Wisconsin and was reproduced on a commemorative postage stamp in 1934 and reissued in 1935. One hesitates to fly in the face of such a cherished tradition that Nicolet landed among the Winnebago at Red Banks on Green Bay, under the impression that he would be greeted by Chinese.

¹⁶ *Jesuit Relations*, XXIII, 227.

¹⁷ John Gilmary Shea, "The Indian Tribes of Wisconsin," *Wisconsin Historical Collections*, III (1856), 137-38.

¹⁸ Benjamin Sulté, "Notes on Jean Nicolet," *Wisconsin Historical Collections*, VIII (1862), 188-94.

¹⁹ Publius V. Lawson, "The Winnebago Tribe," *Wisconsin Archeologist*, (O. S.) VI, No. 3 (1907), 93.

²⁰ Radin, *Winnebago Tribe*, pp. 55-59.

²¹ Blair, *Indian Tribes*, I, 293.

²² Radin, *Winnebago Tribe*, p. 119.

²³ *Ibid.*, pp. 104-5.

²⁴ *Ibid.*, p. 184.

²⁵ *Ibid.*, pp. 319-20, 209-10.

²⁶ Thomas L. McKenney and James Hall, *History of the Indian Tribes of North America*, ed. by Frederick Webb Hodge (in three volumes, Edinburgh, 1933–34), I, 146-55, provides an account of this family and a sketch of the *keramani* chief of the period in which many treaties were signed between the Winnebago and the Unites States.

²⁷ Paul Radin, *The Road of Life and Death* (New York, 1945) pp. 50-51, 74.

²⁸ A personal communication. The water spirit was usually envisioned as a serpent, a common enough form in the woodlands area, but its importance in myths, Radin believes, stems from a very early period and may have significance in connection with southeastern affiliations of the Mississippi Pattern.

²⁹ Blair, *Indian Tribes*, I, 293.

³⁰ *Ibid.*

³¹ *Jesuit Relations*, XXIII, 227.

³² *Ibid.*

[33] Publius V. Lawson, "Habitat of the Winnebago, 1632–1822," *Proceedings of the State Historical Society of Wisconsin,* LIV (1906), 144-66.

[34] Mr. and Mrs. Kenneth Lawson of Menasha, Wisconsin, kindly permitted the examination of the late Publius Lawson's correspondence and other papers which revealed the disputatious attitudes which existed between the Neenah-Menasha and Green Bay supporters. The personal exchanges helped to explain why the Nicolet narrative went uncriticized for so many years, once public opinion had swung to the Red Banks location for Nicolet's landfall as the final word in an old argument. Historic markers were eventually erected at both sites.

[35] *Jesuit Relations,* XVIII, 231-33.

[36] *Jesuit Relations,* XVI, 253; XVIII, 237. By 1653–54 (XLI, 185), the journey from Lake Michigan to the sea was estimated as requiring nine days although no European had yet made the trip. The continuing hope of finding a passage to the Orient is reflected in the observation that this route would probably lead to the "sea separating America from China."

[37] *Jesuit Relations,* XXIII, 279.

[38] Blair, *Indian Tribes,* I, 294-95.

[39] *Ibid.,* p. 295.

[40] *Ibid.,* p. 298. La Potherie noted that ruins of the "cabin" where the massacre occurred and the bones of the Illinois were still visible. This was doubtlessly based on Perrot's personal observation some time after 1665. Certainly no great length of time had elapsed for the structure still to be in evidence.

[41] Blair, *Indian Tribes,* I, 296-300.

[42] *Jesuit Relations,* LIV, 237. Pierre François Xavier de Charlevoix, *Journal of a Voyage to North America* ed. by Louise Phelps Kellogg (in two volumes, Chicago, 1923), I, 57, visited the tribe in 1720 and recounted substantially the same story. However, Charlevoix depended on the *Jesuit Relations* to augment his own information and thus may not have heard the account from the Winnebago themselves.

[43] Blair, *Indian Tribes,* I, 300.

[44] Gideon Scull, ed., *Radisson's Voyages* (Boston: the Prince Society, 1885), p. 246.

[45] These maps are reproduced in Sarah Jones Tucker, "Indian Villages of the Illinois Country," *Scientific Papers of the Illinois State Museum,* Vol. I, Part I, Atlas, 1942, plates V and IV respectively.

[46] Radin, *Winnebago Tribe,* p. 58.

[47] Blair, *Indian Tribes,* I, 201.

[48] *Jesuit Relations,* XLI, 79.

[49] H. Clyde Wilson, "A New Interpretation of the Wild Rice District of Wisconsin," *American Anthropologist,* LVIII, No. 6 (1956), 1061–62, reviews the influx of tribes into Wisconsin as related to flight from the Iroquois rather than attraction to the great stands of wild rice.

A HYPOTHESIS FOR THE PREHISTORY OF THE WINNEBAGO

By James B. Griffin
UNIVERSITY OF MICHIGAN

THIS PAPER will deal primarily with the archaeological evidence which has pertinence to the prehistory of the Winnebago, the tribe with which Paul Radin's name will always be associated. Archaeological knowledge in the eastern United States has changed considerably since Radin wrote his monograph and incorporated such information from prehistory as he felt was pertinent to the area within which the Winnebago lived.

One of the excellent results of the more recent archaeological work in the Upper Mississippi Valley is the clear recognition of distinctive prehistoric and early historic complexes which were Winnebago, Ioway, Missouri, and presumably Oto. Archaeological analysis also indicated that these complexes could be grouped together into a classificatory unit called the Oneota Aspect, which had such a high degree of correspondence in its essential characteristics that any attempt to explain the prehistory of one of the tribal groups involved necessarily includes the origins of the other three historical tribal units. Linguistic studies have shown the very close connections of Chiwere-Siouan and Winnebago, so that any hypothesis projecting the Winnebago into prehistory must also include the origins of Ioway-Oto and Missouri.

There is a variety of approaches which should be combined when an attempt is made to reconstruct the prehistory of a given group of people. One of these approaches is the legends and traditions of the group. Radin's informants asserted that the Winnebago prehistoric home was Red Banks, near Green Bay, and since this is the same general area as that of the early historic Winnebago we are not helped very much in our search for their earlier home by the Winnebago of Radin's time. It is unfortunate that the early French explorers or missionaries did not obtain an answer, or answers, to this question in the middle of the seventeenth century. Nancy Lurie has presented

The author is indebted to Mrs. James D. Hall, University Museums Illustrator, for Plates I-IX, and to Mr. Jerry Stilkind for the three maps.

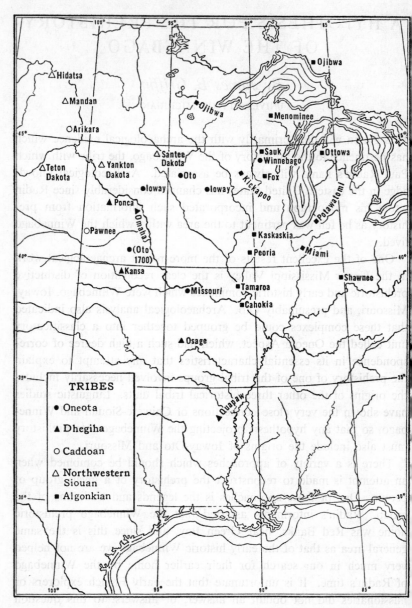

a modern interpretation of the early historic locations of the Winnebago
elsewhere in this volume. The Ioway were located to the west of the
Winnebago in the adjacent areas of Iowa, Minnesota, and Wisconsin

(see Map). According to J. O. Dorsey and Cyrus Thomas (1907), the Ioway chiefs claimed that their tribe, along with the Oto, Missouri, Omaha, and Ponca, "once formed part of the Winnebago nation." They are also said to have claimed that when they were so united "their priscan home" was "north of the Great Lakes." There is no archaeological evidence which would support such a location or movement of these tribes from north of the Great Lakes to their historic habitat. The historically recorded movements of the Ioway are reviewed by Mott (1938), but it is probable that during most of this period the Ioway had lost many of the material culture traits which are studied by the archaeologist.

As an indication of the difficulties of historic research and dependence on native tradition, I will present two views of the relations of the Santee Sioux with the Ioway and Winnebago (Miner, 1911, pp. 28–36). One missionary, the Reverend G. H. Pond, was informed before 1852 by "Takoha, the old war prophet, . . . that the Iowa Indian never occupied the country around the mouth of the Minnesota river. He affirms that it once belonged to the Winnebagoes who were long ago driven from it by the Dakotas—a few others of the Dakotas agree with Takoha. But Black Tomahawk, . . . says that in the earliest years of the existence of the Dakotas they became acquainted with the Iowa Indians, and that they lived in a village at the place which is now called Oak Grove, seven or eight miles from Fort Snelling, on the north side of the Minnesota river. The numerous little mounds which are to be seen about Oak Grove, he says, are the works of the Iowa Indians." Another missionary, the Reverend T. S. Williamson, obtained information before 1856, about the "Sioux" that led him to write: "Their common and most reliable traditions inform us, that when their ancestors first came to the Falls of St. Anthony, the Iowas . . . occupied the country about the mouth of the Minnesota river. . . ." These reports are somewhat contradictory. Their importance is that the extreme lower Minnesota Valley and the adjacent Mississippi Valley is one of the key areas for the study of the development and differentiation of the Oneota Aspect. Archaeologically it is more likely to have been the Ioway, rather than the Winnebago, who would have been in the area during the time referred to in the traditions of the Dakota informants.

The Oto lived west of the Ioway (see Map) and then moved into eastern Nebraska where they may have been responsible for sites like that of the Leary village (Hill and Wedel, 1936). The Missouri Indian tribe was placed on early maps made before 1750 in west central Missouri along the Missouri river (Chapman, 1946).

Considerable attention will also be paid in this paper to the Siouan linguistic group called Dhegiha by J. O. Dorsey. The tribes involved are the Omaha, Ponca, Kansa, Osage, and Quapaw. The Dhegiha are of interest here because of their linguistic, cultural, and geographical connections to the Chiwere-Winnebago, and also because various archaeologists have suggested that Dhegiha, or presumed Dhegiha, archaeological remains could be viewed as part of the Oneota Aspect.

Unfortunately there have not been systematic studies made of the skeletal material from sites involved in this problem, so that we do not have the aid of physical anthropology in evaluating the hypothesis of Chiwere-Winnebago origins. A study of modern or recent Winnebago populations might well give a misleading result because of the drastic decrease in Winnebago tribal size during the seventeenth century and the intermixing with neighboring Algonquian groups.

Linguistic Relations of the Winnebago

Unfortunately no one has prepared an estimate of the length of time which has elapsed since the separation of various Siouan speaking groups. The time would seem to be ripe for a glotto-chronological study of this nature. Two recent groupings of the Siouan languages are germane to this study. Voegelin (1941) stated that Catawba clearly was a distinctive unit and was markedly divergent from all other Siouan languages. He regarded Ofo-Biloxi of the Lower Mississippi Valley as extremely close, and saw them related to the Tutelo of the Virginia-Carolina piedmont region in such a manner that he called them a language group. This group, most unfortunately, he named the Ohio Valley group. In this he was following what I believe to be Swanton's erroneous allocation of Siouan "tribes" to the Central Ohio Valley in the early historic 1650–1700 period. In a more detailed study of Siouan languages, Wolff (1950) reaffirms the distinctiveness of Catawba in somewhat surprising words. "It is impossible for the writer to tell what place—if any—Catawba occupies in the Siouan linguistic family." Wolff also "proves conclusively" that Ofo, Biloxi, and Tutelo have a group reality, but that "from the standpoint of comparative phonology Tutelo and Biloxi are much more closely related, while Ofo shows a considerable number of phonological innovations." It is unfortunate that Quapaw material was not available, for on historical, geographical, and archaeological grounds Quapaw should be close to Biloxi and Ofo. It is difficult to understand the close connection between Tutelo and Biloxi on archaeological grounds. In any event, I would urge the linguists to rebaptize this linguistic group with another term which will not carry a historical and geographical implication that cannot be substantiated. As a stimulation to this end, I submit the coined term "Tubilo group." The "o" is placed last, for our knowledge of the Ofo language was obtained from one old lady (Swanton, 1952, p. 232).

Voegelin agreed that Dorsey "proved" that Ioway-Oto-Missouri and Winnebago were two separable linguistic units with very close connections. He suggested that the term "Chiwere" had been somewhat abused and was no longer valuable, and that it should be abandoned for the exclusive use of archaeologists to equate with Oneota prehistory. It is doubtful, however, if archaeologists will accept responsibility for such a term which, if conceived in error, is of no value to anyone for further investigations. Wolff emphasizes that Ioway-Oto-Missouri are mutually intelligible dialects and, as a "language," more archaic than Winnebago. He was more satisfied than Voegelin with the view that Winnebago and Ioway-Oto-Missouri belong together as a separate language group. Wolff separated Omaha and Ponca on the one hand from Osage within the Dhegiha group, while recognizing the "close relationship of the dialects which constitute the Dhegiha group of Siouan." Kansa and Quapaw are not sufficiently well-known to allow their allocation within the parent Dhegiha group. However, in a recent summary of Kansa culture the statement is made that "Their speech affiliations, as Lewis and Clark, Pike, Say, and others early pointed out were particularly close to Osage, and in somewhat lesser degree with the Quapaw" (Wedel, 1946, p. 3). Wolff also prefers to keep Crow, Hidatsa, and Mandan and Dakota as three distinct language groups. He thus does not, I believe, embrace Voegelin's desire for a large Mississippi Valley group, which would have included Chiwere-Winnebago, Dhegiha (?), Mandan (?), and Dakota (?).

Carl F. Miller has compiled early historic data on Virginia tribes called Siouan, including various manuscripts from the files of some of the Smithsonian personnel who were interested in and wrote about the

Siouan problem. Miller reaches the conclusion from his interpretation of the data at his command "that the Occaneechi, Saponi, and possibly the Tutelo, were a frontier group whose cultural and linguistic affiliations are of an Algonquian stock" (Miller, 1957, p. 207). It is safe to predict that this view will not meet with universal acceptance.

Some Ethnological Relations of the Chiwere-Winnebago and Dhegiha Tribes

In his comparison of ethnological group and environmental areas in North America, Kroeber (1939) placed the Winnebago in the Wisconsin or Wild Rice area along with resident Central Algonquian tribes as they were known in the latter half of the seventeenth century. He attributed the population density in this area to the subsistence value of the wild rice and to the favorable agricultural opportunities in the central Lake Michigan area. The concentration of Algonquian tribes in Wisconsin of the time chosen by Kroeber is probably, however, best interpreted as a historical "accident" caused by Iroquoian pressure from the east. The greater population density of the Wisconsin wild rice area in the eighteenth century (Kroeber, 1939, Map 18) over adjacent Illinois, Iowa, Michigan, and Indiana cannot be carried back into the late prehistoric period from say A.D. 1000 to 1600 when the archaeological evidence would certainly suggest higher population density in the southern two-thirds of Illinois than for the wild rice area. Kroeber also refers to the "legendary southwestward movement of the Dhegiha-Chiwere Siouans" out of the Ohio Valley (1939, p. 91). Later historical and archaeological studies have cast considerable doubt on this Ohio Valley Siouan homeland (Griffin, 1942, 1945, 1952b).

Kroeber placed the Ioway, Oto, and Missouri along with the Omaha, Ponca, Kansa, and perhaps Osage in his Southern Prairie or "Central Siouan" sub-area. He noted considerable cultural resemblance between these groups and the Wisconsin area and observed that this was "surprising" since the Dhegiha-Chiwere should affiliate with Illinois (1939, p. 85). The archaeological evidence indicates that Illinois is the better association, particularly if the Winnebago are included as a part of the Chiwere.

In his study of the Ioway Indians, Skinner (1926) made some interesting observations on the relationship between the Ioway and their neighbors. He felt that the Winnebago-Chiwere group had influenced their neigboring Algonquian tribes toward the more definitely organized Siouan social structure. The social system of the Ioway is interpreted as reflecting a strong caste and rank system based on birth and that these divisions are reflected in the mythology and folklore. The Ioway had a large number of societies and cults with prescribed paraphernalia and special clothing. Whitman (1937), in his study of the Oto, also emphasizes the relationship between the Oto, Ioway, and Winnebago in social organization. One of his interesting observations is that the Oto were more conscious of belonging to a gens which had its own privileges, institutions, and traditions, than they were of belonging to a discrete entity called the Oto tribe. Radin had earlier pointed out this strong orientation of the individual Winnebago to the smaller units instead of to the "tribe" (1923, p. 485). There is also considerable evidence of hereditary rank among the Oto, and while this was not emphasized by Radin for the Winnebago in his major paper, the chief of that tribe was from the Thunderbird clan and was "apparently restricted to certain families" (Radin, 1923, p. 209).

Recently, however, Radin has expressed himself as follows:

There is much more involved here than the simple distinction between the child of a chief and a person without any living close relatives and, conse-quently, one with no social prestige. Considerable internal evidence exists to show that the Winnebago, at one time, possessed a stratified society as did the southern Sioux when they were first encountered by Europeans. The insistence on this point by the mother represents, then, the survival, in this waika, of a feature of Winnebago social organization that must have been discarded centuries ago, probably before they had departed from such linguistically and ethnologically closely related tribes like the Oto, Iowa and Missouri. There are a number of other such archaic features in this waika —the power of the chief, the method of burial, certain stylistic details, etc. One might even hazard the guess that the unusual behavior of the heroine is a distorted reflection of this older structure of society, when the position of woman was much higher than it subsequently became and when, in all likelihood, descent was reckoned in the female line as it was among the western Siouan groups, Hidatsa, Crow, and Mandan. A number of waika, particularly such as have been secondarily reinterpreted as origin myths of the war-bundles and which bear every indication of great antiquity, have just these characteristic details.   (Radin, 1949, p. 99)

An examination of the ethnological accounts of the Winnebago-Chiwere and Dhegiha causes this archaeologist to wonder if they do not reflect a societal organization and orientation more in keeping with an archaeological complex like the Middle Mississippi sites. Perhaps a modern comparative study of these Siouan groups would show a significant relationship to southeastern social and religious forms. In a comprehensive study of burial customs Ermine Voegelin (1944, p. 372) reached the conclusion that ". . . the Eastern Plains people (the Dhegiha Siouan group) formerly occupied a more central position between the Woodlands and the Southeast, and that they removed westward from this location in the late prehistoric period."

The latest opinion on Siouan cultural resemblances by an ethnologist to be included in this paper are those of Eggan (1952) who points out that the Chiwere and Dhegiha tribes "were organized in terms of patrilineal clans grouped into exogamous moieties, with kinship systems of the Omaha sub-type; the Mandan and Hidatsa of the Village Area were organized in terms of matrilineal clans and moieties with kinship systems of the Crow sub-type." In spite of these differences he sees a similarity between the earth lodge using tribes of the Prairie area in their complex social organization centered in a well-defined village and the formal clan units with kinship systems of lineage type. Of especial interest is his feeling that the Dhegiha group is a likely one to have participated in the development of the Mississippi cultures (ibid., p. 44). I would only add that the Chiwere-Winnebago probably did also. To say that these peoples participated does not imply that they were the developers of the Mississippi archaeological culture.

Calendrical Emphasis upon Agriculture

One of the more important observations by early French explorers and missionaries is the reiteration of the view that the Winnebago were sedentary and agricultural, even though they still hunted in band groups during certain periods of the year. This emphasis upon agriculture is reflected in the Wisconsin Winnebago names for the fifth to eighth months, which are translated as "drying of the earth month, digging month, cultivating month and tasseling month." According to a member of the Bear clan, the major activity of his group during the sixth month was to plant corn, squash, and beans; in the seventh month there was a deer hunt away from the permanent villages; in the eighth month they dried the corn and stored it (Radin, 1923, pp. 124-25).

An earlier list published by Schoolcraft of "moon" names from the Winnebago lists as number five, drying of the earth; six, digging of the earth or planting time; seven, corn hoeing time; eight, corn tasseling time; and nine, corn popping or harvest time (Cope, 1919, p. 166).

In marked contrast to this emphasis upon agriculture in Winnebago month names is the prominence of wild rice in the names for the fall harvest period among the Ojibwa, Ottawa, Menominee, and Pottawatomi. The Dakota referred to September as the "ripe rice" moon, and October as the gathering or storing period for rice. Other accounts of Dakota Siouan groups give slightly variant meanings (Jenks, 1900, pp. 1089–90). The Algonquian tribes mentioned above also have many references to rice in their mythology.

The data in regard to the Winnebago strongly indicate that, while there was considerable dependence upon agriculture, there was also wild rice gathering and seasonal hunting and fishing activities. The Winnebago were definitely more closely associated with agriculture than the Menominee to the north and east of them, but they appear to have had about the same balance of economic pursuits as the Illinois and Miami to the south.

The Ioway referred to only the month of April by a term that suggests an agricultural emphasis. They called it the "Cultivating Moon" (Skinner, 1926, p. 294). The Oto term for April is translated literally "stick used" or "the time they dig the earth," while May is "the time they cultivate the earth" (Whitman, 1937, p. 14). There are also corresponding month names between the Ioway, Oto, and Winnebago. I have found no references to Missouri Indian moon names.

Historic and Prehistoric House Types

Another fact of considerable archaeological importance was the information obtained by Radin in regard to house structures. The Winnebago claimed to have had eight types of lodges. Most of these had a circular floor plan, and they were covered by reed matting, bark, or a combination of both. The older Winnebago informants said that:

... the earliest type of lodge used by the Winnebago was the ten-fire gable lodge, of which there were two types, rectangular in form, one built on a platform and the other on the ground. Poles of cedar, forked at the top, formed the sides. Through the forks transverse poles were laid to which the gable roof was attached. Three poles (naⁿji'k'ere) were arranged in the center of the lodge for the better support of the roof. Beds were placed along both of the long sides on a platform raised 2 feet (haza'tc). Frequently a platform 4 to 5 feet high was erected in the rear of the lodge and partitioned off. Here the favorite child of the family lived when he was fasting. In front of the lodge a spot was always kept carefully cleared (nowaxi'nera). There were two doorways to the lodge. Often the entrances were shaded with boughs. According to some informants, this was only done for the chief's lodge. According to another description of the gable lodge, there were only two central poles, one at each entrance; these were always painted blue to symbolize the day.

As far as can be learned at the present time, the platform lodges were merely gable lodges on platforms. What purpose the platform served is now difficult to determine, but most Winnebago questioned said that it was provided as a protection against the dampness of the ground and insects.

The ceremonial lodge was merely a large long bark lodge. The grass lodge seems to have been a roughly constructed round lodge with a covering of grass instead of bark. The sweat lodge was a round bark lodge having a framework of four poles. The tipi was of a simple type provided with a three pole framework.

All the evidence obtained points to the fact that lodges of these types were used synchronously. According to the myths and the oldest informants, in ancient times a village occupied for a considerable period consisted entirely of gable lodges, but these seem to have given way to the round and long type, probably borrowed from the Central Algonquian. The gable type seems to have held its own, however, among the more western villages of the Winnebago. The round bark lodges were used in winter and the reed matting lodges in spring and summer. In the spring those who still lived in bark lodges covered the roofs with reed matting, as that material shed water more effectually than bark. The tipi was generally used on the hunt, the grass lodge merely for a shelter overnight.

(Radin, 1923, pp. 105-6)

There is a natural tendency to correlate the rectangular gable house, believed to be the older Winnebago form, and the one most commonly erected in their permanent villages with the archaeological evidence for associating rectangular houses with the development and northward spread of the Middle Mississippi culture into the Upper Mississippi Valley. Houses of this form are associated with the Old Village and Trappist foci in the St. Louis area, with the Spoon River Focus in the Peoria area, with the Fisher Focus near Joliet, at Aztalan, and they are now known at the Carcajou site on Carcajou point of Lake Kosh-konong (a personal communication from Robert L. Hall). If my hypothesis for Winnebago origins is correct, the more substantial archaeological houses of the Lake Winnebago Focus and early Oneota Aspect as a group should be rectangular, with an excavated wall trench or single dug holes for wall posts, and there should be evidence of wattle and daub construction. Most of the earlier excavations in Oneota sites were not of a nature to permit obtaining evidence of house structures.

The first and only reference to a Chiwere wattle and daub house is contained in Skinner's study of the Ioway. He says that the Ioway "have retained an unusual number of house types, including the earth lodge, wattle and daub house, the square bark and oval mat houses, and the buffalo hide tipi" (Skinner, 1926, pp. 271-72). He points out that this indicates a mixture among the Ioway of the earth lodge and tipi which are normally associated with Plains tribes, of the bark and mat wigwams of the northern woodland (ethnographic term), and the wattle and daub house of the southern part of the Mississippi Valley and southeastern United States. He felt that perhaps all of these house types could be found in Wisconsin. Skinner recognized that the "Brickets" from Aztalan were the fired daub from houses of wattle and daub construction. He made the first valid statement of which I have any record that Aztalan was prehistoric Siouan. "Other indications show that one group of the occupants of this site, which was evidently a rendezvous for peoples of several cultures, were probably Siouan" (1926, p. 272). Skinner stated, "Ioway informants gave the size of their wattle and daub houses, from tradition, as thirty to forty feet long by twenty broad. The Ioways did not believe that either this type of lodge or the circular earth lodge was sunken in the ground by their ancestors, as is the case with the archaeological remains, but this may simply be defective memory and oral tradition. Of course further proof must come from the examination of known Ioway sites by archaeologists" (*ibid.*, p. 273). "This type of lodge (wattle and daub) was called *máhatci* and was rectangular in shape. It was about the same size as the bark house of the same form, that is thirty to forty feet long by twenty broad. The walls were made of split 'shakes' of wood about ten feet high set up some three inches apart, the shakes themselves being only four or five inches across. The cracks were then caulked or chinked with hay and clay. The roof, which was only slightly arched, was sodded" (*ibid.*, p. 276).

There is even less definite evidence of Oto house structures of the seventeenth or early eighteenth century, for the Oto were located in the Missouri Valley during the early 1700s. According to Whitman (1937, pp. 1-3), the Oto lived as family groups in villages of mud lodges, and by 1800 the circular semi-subterranean house with a covered entryway was the normal house form. Whitman speculates that "Originally, before they adopted Plains patterns and institutions, we may suppose that the villages themselves were groups of bark houses after the fashion of the Winnebago, and even today the Oto speak of such dwellings." When away from the villages and on hunting expeditions they erected tipis covered with skins. According to Möllhausen (Bushnell, 1922, p. 120), who visited an Oto village in 1842, in Nebraska they did erect bark lodges similar to those of the Upper Mississippi Valley.

There is not much information on the house types of the Missouri tribe and we must hope that future excavations will produce house forms.

The Northern Distribution of Pyramidal Mounds and Wattle and Daub House Structures

Pyramidal mounds are one of the more important features of the Middle Mississippi cultural complex, and the presence of three of them as far north as Trempealeau, Wisconsin, is of considerable significance. These mounds (Squier, 1905) were built on the bluffs overlooking the Mississippi River and made use of natural elevations as a part of the mound construction. The largest of these is 108 by 122 feet at the base and 65 by 80 feet on the top surface. It was raised some 6 feet above the highest part of the hill, and dirt had been placed along one side to a height of 18 feet to raise the area to a flat, level top. A smaller platform some 45 feet square was very close to the largest mound. The smallest platform was 30 by 45 feet in size and was located 70 feet away from the first two structures. Squier mentions finding a few fragments of pottery on the east side of the hill beneath the large mound, which he says had "a mere film of what appears to be red ochre, forming a glaze which reflects the light, the surface appearing to have been smooth as our common tableware" (ibid., pp. 30, 34). Squier also mentions incised pottery which is probably the shell tempered specimens described, but whether these were Old Village or Oneota is not known. In commenting on the archaeological features of this area McKern referred to the "truncated-pyramid or platform types" found here as evidence of the importance of the Mississippi River as a route of cultural spread (McKern, 1931, p. 194).

The Mills mound group of the Apple River Focus, Jo Daviess County, Illinois, to be discussed further on pages 834-38, is located on a wide flood plain on the east side of the Mississippi River. Of particular interest here is the square, flat-topped pyramidal mound which was about 80 feet in diameter, 8 feet high, and had a 35-foot platform on top (Bennett, 1945, pp. 131-34). Partial excavation of the mound indicates that it was composed of earth gathered from village debris and contained ten refuse pits. A house floor of hard yellow clay was identified 15 inches below the surface. While no postholes were recognized, the structure is said to have been burned. No mention is made of burned daub fragments from this mound or from the excavation in the Mills village site, although a house floor and postholes were identified in the latter area.

In the discussion below of Mississippi sites in the Red Wing, Minnesota, area there is mentioned the presence of a pyramidal mound on Cannon River and burnt daub fragments on Prairie Island, Goodhue County, Minnesota. L. H. Larson Jr., informs me that daub was found at the Cambria site in Blue Earth County. The best known site with pyramidal mounds and wattle and daub house construction is Aztalan, which was a primary focus of the Old Village migrants.

I am particularly indebted to Robert L. Hall for calling my attention to a reference to fired wattle and daub house remains in the area of Little Lake Butte des Morts on the Fox River near Lake Winnebago. "Among the articles discovered in the field near by, was some burnt clay in irregular fragments, with impressions of the leaves and stems of grass, precisely like those found at Aztalan. This had been a place of burial, and perhaps of well-contested battles; for the plough constantly turns up fragments of human bones and teeth, much broken and decayed. Arrow-points of flint, and pipes of the red pipestone and other materials, have also been brought to light" (Lapham, 1855, pp. 60-61). Perhaps from this same location are the finds briefly mentioned by Lawson. "From a pit near the 'Hill of the Dead' the author obtained, in 1882, a dozen sherds of shell-tempered earthenware, several fragments of carved bone and a number of bone awls." (Lawson, 1903, p. 53). If this is the same spot it would connect pottery of the Mississippi tradition with the wattle and daub house.

At Aztalan and the Mills village site the pyramidal mound is associated with Old Village pottery. At Trempealeau and the Cannon River site the association is with some type of Mississippi pottery

which is not clearly identified. Since Oneota sites do not have pyramidal mounds, Trempealeau and Cannon River should have been built
by a group who also made Old Village pottery. The same inference
applies to wattle and daub houses, although this form of house construction may have continued longer than the custom of building pyramidal mounds.

A Possible Climatic Factor in the Northern Spread
of the Old Village Complex

The movement of the Old Village Cahokia complex (see Map) to
the north is from approximately 39° north at St. Louis, to 45° north
in the Red Wing area, and is from a region of 210 frost-free days to
the region of 170 frost-free days. The archaeological evidence indicates
that agriculture was of considerable importance in the Old Village
complex, and it is somewhat surprising that a prehistoric culture with such
emphasis on agriculture would have gone so far north. It may be
that at the time of this movement, the climate in the Upper Mississippi
Valley and in Wisconsin was somewhat warmer. This hypothesis finds
comfort in and was stimulated by the historically recorded climate
change in southeastern Greenland (Brooks, 1949, pp. 356-58). When
the Icelanders moved to Greenland in the latter part of the tenth
century they found evidence of earlier Eskimo settlements, but the
Eskimo had retreated to the north. The pack ice and seals were not
along the coast, and the Eskimo depended upon the seals for much of
their food supply. This European colony prospered during the eleventh
and twelfth centuries raising cattle and hay, but between A.D. 1200 and
1300 the climate became increasingly colder, and the Eskimo moved
south. By A.D. 1400 the ground was permanently frozen, and effective
European colonization of the original type was impossible. There are
other indications of an amelioration of climate in Europe from around
A.D. 700 to 1000 and of a minor cooling which caused a readvance of
the Alpine glaciers by A.D. 1300. The Iceland glaciers are said to have
had their greatest expansion of the last 2,000 years between A.D. 1300
and 1350 (Brooks, 1949, p. 303), but Flint (1957, p. 484) places the
greatest recent expansion at about A.D. 1750. Flint has well expressed
a widely held view on the correlation of North American and European
climatic changes. "The similarity, in Europe and North America of
the sequence representing the last 15,000 years or more implies that

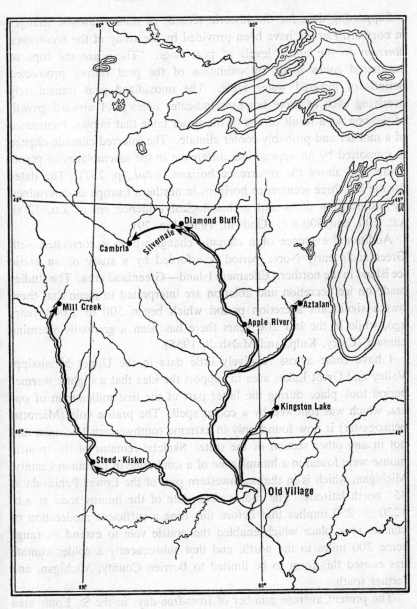

temperature fluctuations on both sides of the Atlantic, and probably throughout the northern hemisphere, have been contemporaneous" (*ibid.*).

Supporting data for the historic records of minor climatic changes in northern Europe have been provided by the study of the *recurrence horizons* in the upper levels of peat bogs. "These are the tops of weathered zones made by oxidation of the peat during protracted periods of lowered water table. The unoxidized peat immediately overlying each of these horizons indicates renewal of upward growth of the bog, as a result of rise of the water table that implies recurrence of a moister and probably cooler climate. The inferred climatic change is supported by an appropriate difference in the assemblages of plants below and above the recurrence horizon" (*ibid.,* p. 287). The dates for the last three recurrence horizons in northern Europe as determined by radiocarbon dates and archaeological evidence are at A.D. 1200, A.D. 500, and 600 B.C. (Godwin, 1956, Fig. 29).

Additional evidence of a climatic change which is correlated with Greenland's early Norse period is afforded by a study of an arctic ice island in the northern Ellesmere Island—Greenland area. The studies made on ice accretion and ablation are interpreted to mean that there was a significant accretion period which began 500 to 1,000 years ago, while in the last 200 years there has been a gradually warming climate (Crary, Kulp, and Marshall, 1955).

I have come across relatively little data in the Upper Mississippi Valley and Great Lakes area to support the idea that a slightly warmer period took place during the latter part of the first millennium of our era, which was followed by a cooler spell. The prairie vole (Microtus ochrogaster) is now found only in extreme southwestern Michigan and not in any other section of the state. Skeletal remains of this prairie mouse were found in a humus zone of a sand dune in Leelanau County, Michigan, which is in the northwestern part of the Lower Peninsula at 45° north latitude. The radiocarbon date of the humus zone at A.D. 1220 ± 250 implies that before this time a sufficient moderation of climate took place which enabled the prairie vole to extend its range some 200 miles to the north, and that subsequently a colder climate has caused this form to be limited to Berrien County, Michigan, and farther south.

The present average number of frost-free days in the St. Louis area is 210, in Peoria it is 188; in Madison and in Minneapolis it is 171. The average July temperature at Minneapolis is 73.3 degrees; at Madison it is 72.1; at Prairie du Chien it is 73.7; at LaCrosse it is 72.7;

at Peoria it is 76.4; and at St. Louis it is 80.6. From studies of temperature efficiences for plant growth we can see that the areas of southwestern Wisconsin and southern Minnesota are noticeably superior to northern and southeastern Wisconsin (Klages, 1942, Fig. 39). The area of St. Paul is near the northern border of modern efficient corn growing.

The northern distribution of Old Village-Aztalan cultural material and of the Oneota complex corresponds rather well to the northern border of effective corn agriculture. V. H. Jones has suggested to me that the eastern type corn which is primarily associated with the Mississippi cultures is probably a more effective type of corn than was available in pre-Mississippi times, and if grown under similar ecological conditions would produce more food than the earlier type associated with Hopewellian culture.

From the location of the Old Village-Aztalan sites in the north, it is clear that they preferred areas along the Mississippi flood plain and in the lower levels of the major streams in the Northern Mississippi Valley. In this regard they were merely following a prior settlement pattern established in the St. Louis area which was necessary for their agricultural practices. Even a minor climatic change toward more frost free days and toward warmer summer temperature would have had a significant advantage for the primitive agricultural practices on the Old Village–Aztalan level.

Earlier Interpretations of Winnebago and Chiwere Prehistory

In this section there will be presented some of the interpretations made by anthropologists of the archaeological complexes which are regarded as Winnebago or are closely related to Winnebago archaeology. This is designed to provide a background for the views presented in this paper and to show the gradual changes in archaeological thought. In doing this I am, I think, commenting on interpretations and not on persons.

Archaeologists now recognize three major prehistoric cultural periods in the eastern United States (Griffin, 1952a, pp. 352-64). The first of these is the Paleo-Indian period, which is identified as primarily a hunting economy with the fluted projectile points as a distinctive characteristic. This division, for purposes of this paper, may be said to end about 8000 B.C. The second major period is called the Archaic, and in Wisconsin the best-known cultural unit is known as the Old Copper Culture. With the introduction of pottery and other traits a significant new culture called Woodland develops about 1000 B.C., and in various forms this persists until the arrival of the French in the Wisconsin area. The last major chronological division of the Woodland pattern is called Late Woodland, which is—by and large—contemporary with the growth, development and spread of the fourth major prehistoric cultural unit, which is called the Mississippi Pattern. In Wisconsin the Lake Michigan Phase of Woodland is present during the Late Woodland period, and one of the subdivisions of Lake Michigan is the Effigy Mound Aspect (Rowe, 1956). The Effigy Mound division of Woodland may be said to begin in the Wisconsin area about A.D. 700-800, and it continues, probably, until well into the thirteenth and fourteenth centuries and probably later.

The Mississippi Pattern is a significantly different prehistoric complex from the Woodland pattern, and it had its center and probable area of origin in the south central part of the Mississippi Valley. It was predominantly an agricultural economy, and this is reflected in the size of the village sites, the amount of occupational debris and other evidences of increased population, and a more sedentary way of life than had been characteristic of the earlier Woodland peoples. The two recognized major divisions of the Mississippi Pattern in the Wisconsin area are called the Oneota Aspect of the Upper Mississippi Phase and the Rock River Focus of Middle Mississippi. The latter is primarily known from the Aztalan site in Jefferson county about half-way between Madison and Milwaukee (Barrett, 1933).

When Paul Radin wrote his monograph on the Winnebago he devoted a significant portion of it to a presentation of some of the salient features of Wisconsin archaeology obtained from published sources and from individuals in the state who had some familiarity with Wisconsin archaeology. For various reasons Radin suggested that the Winnebago and closely related tribes had built the effigy mounds and that the earth effigies were clan symbols. He also believed that the Winnebago had come into Wisconsin from the east and south and that this movement was not of any great antiquity, occurring shortly before the Winnebago became known to the early French explorers.

The archaeological culture known as the Oneota Aspect resulted from the work of W. C. McKern in Wisconsin and of C. R. Keyes in

Iowa during the late 1920s and early 1930s. W. C. McKern, in his active archaeological period, 1925–42, made the first adequate analyses, classification and interpretation of Wisconsin's prehistory. One of the phases of his work was the presentation of an archaeological complex called the Lake Winnebago Focus, which rather clearly was the prehistoric remains of some portion of the Winnebago tribe. His work also indicated that the archaeological complex called Lake Winnebago was not found in effigy mounds, nor for that matter in other types of burial mounds in Wisconsin. For these reasons he concluded that the Winnebago and their immediate ancestors did not build the effigy mounds. This view has recently been repeated by C. W. Rowe (1956).

McKern recognized three distinctive prehistoric complexes in southern Wisconsin which, in spite of minor differences, had a surprising degree of uniformity. He originally called these units the Lake Winnebago Focus, the Grand River Focus, and the Western Uplands Focus (see Map). Keyes had observed the very close connections between a number of sites in northeastern Iowa to which he gave the name of Oneota. He had found that this complex was intrusive into burial mounds of the Hopewell complex and that it was associated with a small amount of historic trade goods. Keyes, therefore, suggested that this Oneota of northeastern Iowa was Iowa and Omaha, while McKern attributed the Lake Winnebago Focus to the late prehistoric Winnebago and had determined that it was later than the Trempealeau-Hopewell and other Woodland complexes.

The Oneota complex was recognized by archaeologists as having its closest cultural connections to Middle Mississippi sites in the central Mississippi Valley and in the southeast, and it was regarded as a "foreign" complex in an essentially Woodland pattern archaeological area. For this reason McKern viewed the Oneota complex, particularly the Orr Focus, as a relatively late arrival in the Upper Mississippi Valley. He said that it "is basically of southeastern affinity rather than midwestern in character, having much in common with the divisions most typical of the former area and very little in common with the divisions most typical of the latter" (McKern, 1945, p. 171). McKern postulated a migration of the Chiwere and Winnebago "from the southeast of near vicinity to subsequent homes in the west" and that a study "of cultural remains illustrating the Upper Mississippi Phase," i.e. Oneota, would reveal the migration route (McKern, 1945, p. 173).

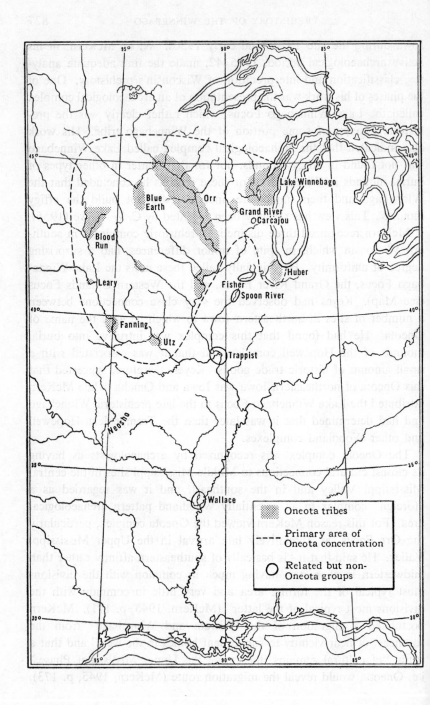

Lake Winnebago

Blue
Earth

Orr

Grand River
Carcajou

Blood
Run

Huber

Leary

Fisher
Spoon River

Fanning

Utz

Trappist

Neosho

Wallace

Oneota tribes

Primary area of
Oneota concentration

Related but non-
Oneota groups

There are a number of interesting views implicit in McKern's interpretation. One is the clear statement that the pre-northern Mississippi Valley sites of the Chiwere-Winnebago are to be identified as Oneota in culture type, and that the series of such earlier Chiwere-Winnebago sites would lead to the Southeast. Unfortunately McKern never specified which "Southeastern" archaeological material he had in mind. He also referred to the Rock River Focus (Aztalan) as "Southeastern" and recognized its basic connection with his Oneota sites. This connection was of such an order that it might "appear to warrant a correlation" of Aztalan and Wisconsin Oneota sites "within the same phase," but, in order to make clear "a sufficiently strong cultural divergence between the two manifestations," McKern believed that a classificatory separation was demanded "for the sake of convenience in handling cultural data, involving the only purpose of classification" (*ibid.*, pp. 160-61). He asserted that classification is arbitrary in dividing closely related cultures, and since there were only two "Mississippi phases," namely Upper Mississippi and Middle Mississippi, he felt that Aztalan was clearly of the latter phase and that, in spite of the demonstrated close connection between Aztalan and Wisconsin Oneota, the relationships of the two units were adequately expressed by being regarded as separate and discrete entities of the broad cultural division called the Mississippi Pattern.

McKern's interpretation of the connection between Aztalan and Oneota was handicapped, I believe, for a number of reasons. In the period during which he was actively concerned with the problem, archaeologists were employing a foreshortened chronology which placed the Hopewell culture roughly around A.D. 1200. This did not leave very much time for the Mississippi cultural development and for local cultural change which would allow distinctive archaeological complexes to shift from one culture type to another. In some ways probably McKern was handicapped by his concept of the Midwestern Taxonomic System (McKern, 1939), which did not allow him to recognize the possibility of the Rock River Focus of Middle Mississippi as a logical ancestor of the Oneota Aspect of Upper Mississippi. In other words, these two "phases" were regarded as relatively fixed cultural units within which additional foci might be found, or regroupings attempted, but one would not expect genetic or historic development from one phase to the other. Another hindrance was the lack of sound comparative data from the surrounding areas on related cultural units and particularly for the area to the south. Temporal relationships between distinctive archaeological complexes were just beginning to emerge, and the recognition of regional sequences was in an incipient stage.

One statement of McKern's concerning the question of the origin of Oneota and the connection to Aztalan appears in the *Wisconsin Magazine of History:*

All the available evidence conclusively indicates that the various groups classified within the Oneota aspect belong to the late prehistoric period. They were fairly recent arrivals in Wisconsin at the time of the white man's entry. Consequently, they must have come from somewhere, . . . whatever the history of the Upper Mississippi Phase of the more general Mississippi Pattern may have been, it is safe to say that its origin and seat of distribution was also toward the southeast from Wisconsin. Its introduction into our state was probably by way of the Mississippi, Rock and Wisconsin rivers.

Another, quite different invasion from the Southeast also features the late prehistoric period in Wisconsin. In fact the Oneota people may have been fully established here when these new arrivals first made their appearance. . . . We do not know the actual tribe or people responsible for this introduction of higher culture into Wisconsin; deep in the Southeast the Muskogians were the principal bearers of Middle Mississippi culture.

This particular band in all probability migrated north from the vicinity of the great Cahokia Mounds near East St. Louis, Illinois, which were built by their cultural brothers, and established a village on the Crawfish River, Jefferson County, the remains of which is widely known as the Aztalan site . . . little or no influence on neighboring people (Oneota or Woodland) is apparent, and since there is abundant evidence that the village was destroyed by fire, never to be rebuilt.   (1942, pp. 161-62)

Perhaps one of his unstated reasons for the priority in time of entrance in Wisconsin of Oneota over Aztalan, is the marked simplicity of the former, and the relative simplicity of other culture units then grouped with Oneota to form Upper Mississippi. It is also likely that the marginal northern position of Oneota compared to Middle Mississippi groups helped McKern believe they were earlier than Aztalan.

One of the most recent interpretations of Oneota origins is by Robert Ritzenthaler, of the Milwaukee Public Museum, who accepted McKern's view that Oneota had moved into Wisconsin in its developed and recognizable Oneota form from the south around A.D. 1000.

One group was in the east centering around Lake Winnebago, and it stayed into historic times when it was introduced to the white man as the Winnebago tribe. The other group settled in the western portion of the state along the Mississippi River, extending from the southern border to about half way up the state. The western group (Orr Focus) differed but slightly in culture from the eastern, and there is evidence that it later moved across the river into Iowa where it was known in historic times as the Iowa tribe.

(Ritzenthaler, 1953, p. 24)

He also recognized that the Aztalan site represented a migration from Cahokia and suggested that it took place roughly around A.D. 1200. His time estimates were based on then known and published radiocarbon dates of the age of the Mississippi Pattern. Ritzenthaler's confidence that the appearance of Oneota in Wisconsin preceded the Aztalan migration is his major difference from McKern's ideas.

In 1933–35, while I was working on the delineation of the Fort Ancient Aspect of the central Ohio Valley and its relationships to the northeast and northwest, I was able to study the Wisconsin-Iowa collections through the courtesy of McKern and Keyes. In the spring of 1936 I saw the collection from the Utz village site in Saline county in central Missouri in the U.S. National Museum, and it had a strong resemblance to the sites attributed to the Ioway and Winnebago. Since the Missouri, Iowa, and Oto were known to be closely linked by linguistic and cultural ties as a distinctive group, and in turn to the Winnebago, I became impressed with the possibility of demonstrating that the Oneota Aspect could be attributed to the Chiwere and Winnebago, and that it had had its beginning during the time when these peoples lived close to each other in the Upper Mississippi Valley (Griffin, 1937).

I also studied the Mississippi collections at the University of Illinois, the University of Chicago, and the Dickson Museum in Fulton County, Illinois. Particularly important in formulating a hypothesis regarding the origin of the Oneota Aspect were the collections from Cahokia of the Old Village (see Plate I) and Trappist complexes, the considerable amount of Spoon River Focus material from Fulton County with its clear indications of Oneota contact (Smith, 1951), and the collections from Jo Daviess County in northwestern Illinois made by Robert Adams. An analysis of this latter collection has been published by John Bennett (1945), and this reflects interpretations by both McKern and myself on the significance of the Mississippi material obtained by Adams. My 1938–39 views on Oneota were finally printed in 1943.

PLATE I. VESSEL SHAPES AND DECORATION FROM BENEATH POWELL MOUND No. 2, CAHOKIA SITE, ILLINOIS

These vessels are representative of the Old Village complex beneath the mound. Draw were made from University of Illinois photographs and are not to the same scale. This m was excavated for the University of Illinois by Gene M. Stirling in 1931. A, E: Ramey I jars; E has a cambered rim. B: Powell Plain cylindrical beaker, base slightly rounded, than flat. C: Powell Plain jar without handles. D: Powell Plain single handle jar with can rim. F: Two loop handles on Powell Plain jar. G: Powell Engraved vertical rir H: Powell Plain wide mouth bottle. I: St. Clair Plain with two loop handles and kn lower rim. J: Large Powell Plain pan. K: Small Powell Plain bowl. L: Mound Pla Incised bowl.

It is believed that both the Fort Ancient Aspect and the Oneota Aspect derived their Mississippian complexion from the Middle Mississippi. In part, the reason that they are considered as belonging to a phase distinct from Middle Mississippi is that they are marginal to and do not possess the cultural refinements evidenced by such sites as Cahokia. While Fort Ancient has many elements also found in early Woodland cultures this is definitely not the case with Oneota. Whether or not the Oneota peoples were genetically derived from Middle Mississippi peoples it is impossible to say, but that the culture was in direct descent appears highly probable. The most logical progenitors would seem to be the Old Village and Rock River foci. The distinctiveness of Oneota is probably as much a result of its geographical position in an area marginal to later Middle Mississippi groups as it is of its chronological position.   (Griffin, 1943, p. 302)

In 1939 I began formal preparation of a synthesis of eastern United States prehistory to present to the final meeting of the Indiana Historical Society's anthropology group in October. A version of this paper was read at the Society for American Archaeology meeting in Minneapolis in April, 1940, and at a meeting of the American Anthropological Society in Andover, in December, 1941. It was published some five years later due to world conditions (Griffin, 1946). In this paper I presented additional views bearing on the origin and connections of the Oneota Aspect.

The most likely hypothesis accounting for the origin of Oneota is that it developed from a pre-existing Mississippi culture, the most likely predecessor being the Old Village-Aztalan complex. Possible transitional stages are represented by material from northwestern Illinois obtained by University of Chicago expeditions. It would require no great ceramic shift to produce the Oneota series (of pottery types) from the Old Village series, and relative separation from the heart of the Middle Mississippi area might have aided the shift as well as the other changes in material culture.

(*Ibid.*, p. 90)

Another interpretation of the origin of Oneota was presented by Ford and Willey (1941):

Brief as have been the discussions of the various Temple Mound II cultures of the southeast, the treatment of the so-called Upper Mississippi culture must be even shorter. It will suffice to suggest that such cultures as that of the Iroquois, in New York (61); Fort Ancient along the Ohio River (56); Oneonta (sic) in Wisconsin, Iowa and Nebraska (62); were formed as a result of first Burial, and later Temple Mound influences. These tended to become merged along the northern periphery of their distribution and were firmly welded to the Archaic traits of the various localities. Most of the puzzling similarities between Upper Mississippian cultures had best be examined from the viewpoint of these features having derived from a common source. The "woodland" cultures found even farther away from the Mississippi Valley centers tend to show an even greater retention of the older trait complexes.

The various Upper Mississippian cultures probably began to be formed before 1500 but they all reached their peaks after that date and all lasted until historic times. (pp. 356-57)

Another major contribution to the definition of Oneota in the northern Mississippi Valley is that of Mildred Mott (1938) who concentrated on the Iowa collections gathered together by Keyes which were Oneota in type. She concluded that there was a high degree of homogeneity in the Oneota collections from Iowa, and their locations in the state coincided remarkably with the known distribution of the Ioway village sites. She suggested that perhaps the Correctionville site on the Little Sioux river in Woodbury County, northwestern Iowa might belong to a different focus and tribe than the Ioway. The hypothesis was presented that this might be Oto, for it resembles sites in north central Iowa and in the Blue Earth River area in Minnesota (*ibid.*, p. 308).

In 1936, a detailed paper was published on the Leary site in Richardson County in eastern Nebraska (Hill and Wedel, 1936). In this report Wedel recognized the Leary complex as a part of the Oneota culture and the fact that it was connected with Siouan-speaking people. In his discussion of the distribution of Oneota material he refers to sites in Nebraska and Kansas. Of particular interest here is the reference to the Glen Elder site in Mitchell County, Kansas. The Glen Elder Focus has connections to Oneota but is somewhat aberrant. It is in an area in which Kansa remains should be found, but it seems too far south and west to connect with either early historic Ponca or "certain northern Caddoan peoples" as Wedel (1948, p. 51) suggested. Further development of his views of Kansa prehistory will soon appear.

The Apple River Focus of Northwestern Illinois

A cultural division called the Apple River Focus has been proposed by Bennett (1945, pp. 127-58) to include three Mississippi sites in Jo Daviess County, Illinois, particularly the Mills, Chapman, and Savannah Village sites. Bennett concluded that the collection from the Mills village was a homogeneous one and that there were no significant

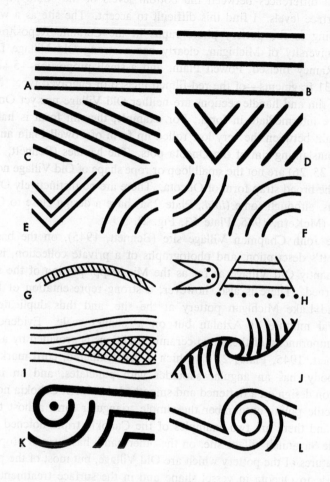

PLATE II. RAMEY INCISED, POWELL ENGRAVED, AND MOUND PLACE (?) DESIGNS FROM THE CAHOKIA SITE

H, J-L: Ramey Incised designs taken from photographs and pottery specimens in the
~m of Anthropology, University of Michigan. B: Mound Place (?) horizontal incised
~es on a bowl rim. I: Powell Engraved design on jar beneath Powell Mound No. 2.

cultural differences between the bottom levels of the strata pits and the surface levels. I find this difficult to accept. The site as a whole, according to the pottery photographs in the Ceramic Repository at the University of Michigan, clearly has a strong Old Village flavor with Ramey Incised, Powell Plain, and a small proportion—5 sherds of 2,431 fragments—of the red-filmed incised or engraved type. Many of the rim and handle sections are neither Old Village nor yet Oneota, but are intermediate in form. For example, the rim form is halfway in height between the very low rolled lip form of Powell Plain and the high outslanting rim of the Oneota pots. The handles (Bennett, 1945, Plates 25, 26) are not the small loop or rope shape of Old Village nor are they the broad strap form of Oneota. There are no distinctively Oneota designs, although some (*ibid.*, Plate 25a) have a design close to Grand River (McKern, 1945, Plate 63, Fig. 2).

The John Chapman Village site (Bennett, 1945), on the basis of Bennett's description, and photographs of a private collection, is predominantly Old Village as far as the Mississippi portion of the site is concerned. There is also, however, a strong representation of Effigy Mound–Lake Michigan pottery at the site, and thus duplicates the cultural mixture at Aztalan but on a smaller scale. Evidence for contemporaneity of these two ceramic traditions is provided by a sherd (Bennett, 1945, Plates 22 f.) which is grit tempered, cord marked on the body, has an angular shoulder with punctates, and an incised chevron design on a flattened and smoothed shoulder. Cahokia notched projectile points outnumber the simple triangular form almost two to one, and there are two examples of the Cahokia triple notched point.

The Savannah village site, on the other hand, has a small proportion of features of the pottery which are Old Village, but most of the pottery is close to Oneota in vessel shape and in the surface treatment. The designs, including a scroll, are still strongly curvilinear. This pottery complex is not quite Oneota but is only a short distance from it. The Savannah site should not be regarded as a component of a focus which would include the Chapman and Mills sites, nor should it be regarded as a part of an Orr Focus. It is a distinctive transitional unit. Bennett suggested that Apple River should be thought of as a single floating focus and felt that as such it was closer to Old Village than to Oneota. The interpretation made in this paper is that the three sites contain a developmental sequence from an Old Village level to a proto-Oneota

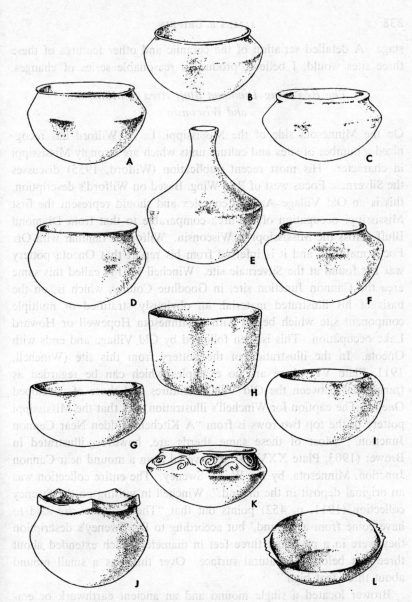

PLATE III. VESSEL FORMS AND SCROLL DECORATION FROM AZTALAN, JEFFERSON COUNTY, WISCONSIN

wings made from Barrett, 1933, and not drawn to same scale. A-D, F: Aztalan variant of
ell Plain jar. E: Rare bottle form at Aztalan of Powell Plain type. G-I: Varieties of bowl
as of Powell Plain type. J: Late Woodland cord marked jar of Effigy Mound–Tampico
style. K: Aztalan variant of Ramey Incised. L: Deep rim pan of Powell Plain type.

stage. A detailed seriation of the ceramic and other features of these three sites would, I believe, produce a reasonable series of changes.

The Red Wing–Diamond Bluff Area of Minnesota and Wisconsin

On the Minnesota side of the Mississippi, L. A. Wilford has recognized a number of sites and culture units which are strongly Mississippi in character. His most recent publication (Wilford, 1955) discusses the Silvernale Focus west of Red Wing. Based on Wilford's description, this is an Old Village–Aztalan complex and should represent the first Mississippi occupation of the area comparable to that from Diamond Bluff across the Mississippi in Wisconsin. Wilford is familiar with Orr Focus material, and it is inferred from his report that Oneota pottery was not found at the Silvernale site. Winchell (1911) called this same area the Cannon Junction site, in Goodhue County, which is, on the basis of his illustrated material, an obviously stratified or multiple component site which begins with a Minnesota Hopewell or Howard Lake occupation. This is then followed by Old Village and ends with Oneota. In the illustration of the pottery from this site (Winchell, 1911, Plate VI), there are no examples which can be regarded as transitional between the Old Village features and those of developed Oneota. The caption for Winchell's illustration says that the Mississippi pottery in the top two rows is from "A Kitchen-Midden Near Cannon Junction." Most of these same sherds are, however, illustrated in Brower (1903, Plate XXV) as "Recovered from a mound near Cannon Junction, Minnesota, by Dr. W. M. Sweney. The entire collection was an original deposit in the mound." Winchell in writing on the Sweney collection (1911, p. 452) points out that "These objects are said to have come from a 'mound,' but according to Dr. Sweney's description they were in a pit about three feet in diameter which extended about three feet below the natural surface. Over this was a small mound about three feet high."

Brower located a single mound and an ancient earthwork or embankment on Prairie Island, Goodhue County, Minnesota, which is halfway between the Cannon Junction group and the Mero–Diamond Bluff sites. This embankment he regarded as LeSueur's trading house built in 1695. Near these earthworks on the west side of Sturgeon Lake is a mound group. In the bank which was being washed by the

PLATE IV. DESIGNS FOUND ON VESSELS AT AZTALAN
TAKEN FROM BARRETT, 1933

Woodland vessel with cordmarked rim. B: Variant of Madison Cord-Impressed Late
Woodland jar. C-P: Rectilinear and curvilinear variants of Ramey Incised at Aztalan.

lake were "pieces of burnt clay that was plastered against reeds and round sticks. An ash heap and a pile of burnt debris, mostly of clay, was uncovered" (Winchell, 1911, p. 150). A more detailed description is given by Winchell on page 451 and it is quite apparent that he is speaking of burnt daub of the common Mississippi type wattle and daub. In writing of the long embankment with a squared projection, Brower says that it was "excavated and found to be an artificial earthwork which was undoubtedly executed as a defensive enclosure" (1903, p. 54). This is the first published reference I have found to such wattle and daub construction so far north and in apparent association with Mississippi pottery. Village debris gathered by Brower from this locality was briefly described by Winchell (1911, p. 449) who points out that there are 113 examples of shell tempered sherds and 57 grit tempered pieces, and thus resembled the proportion of grit to shell found at Cannon Junction. It is not known whether the pottery is Oneota or Old Village. Brower's report on the area (Brower, 1903, pp. 58-59) illustrates Woodland pottery of Howard Lake–Hopewell style, Old Village, and Oneota from Goodhue County. These are identified as "Dakota Indian Potsherds" in the illustration, which is the identification given by Brower to material collected from this area (*ibid.*, pp. 53-56).

One of a group of 64 mounds on Cannon River

is a flat-topped rectangular mound, having dimensions 48 feet by 60 feet, and 4 feet high. It is surrounded by ordinary tumuli, amongst which are a few broad-elongated mounds. This abrupt diversion from the usual shape of these mounds is remarkable, and this mound may have been used for a different purpose. Its size and shape suggest the type of communal house described by Morgan as characteristic of most of the aborigines, but its isolation from all others of that type and its close association with numerous others of the usual form create some doubt whether it was the base of a communal house. The dimensions of the flat top are 24 feet by 36 feet, and the ascent from the base to the top is 12 feet wide all around. Surveyed September 10, 1885. (Shown on page 153)   (Winchell, 1911, pp. 151-54)

One of the most northerly occurrences of Oneota pottery is a whole vessel which is slightly elliptical and has two handles which join the rim beneath a raised and bifurcated lip. The rim slants outward and is notched at closely-spaced intervals across the lip. There are visible in the photograph 9 wide and medium deep parallel vertical lines on the upper body which do not extend below the maximum diameter

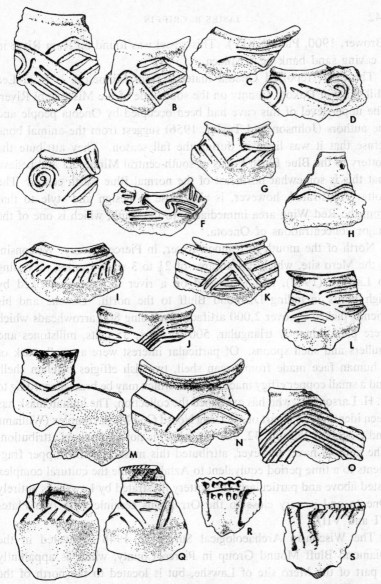

PLATE V. DRAWINGS OF DECORATION AND SHAPES OF
POTTERY FRAGMENTS FROM THE CAMBRIA SITE,
BLUE EARTH COUNTY, MINNESOTA

mens on loan to the Museum of Anthropology, University of Michigan, from the
esota Historical Society. A-I: Cambria Incised variants of Ramey style. J-Q: Cambria
d primarily rectilinear decoration placed on vessels with an angled rim approaching the
ta form. N: Cambered rim with three horizontal cord impressions. R-S: Handle forms
on low straight rim jars.

(Brower, 1900, Plate XXIV). This vessel was found on Rum River in a caving sand bank near Milaca.

The latest reported Oneota material from Minnesota is from Lee Mill Cave in Dakota County on the south side of the Mississippi River. The upper level of this cave had been occupied by Oneota people and the authors (Johnson and Taylor, 1956) suggest from the animal bone refuse that it was lived in during the fall season. They attribute the pottery to the Blue Earth Focus of south-central Minnesota and believe that this is somewhat northeast of the normal Blue Earth center. The pottery illustrated, however, is also close in design and style to that from the Red Wing area immediately to the south, which is one of the major concentrations of Oneota.

North of the mouth of Cannon River, in Pierce County, Wisconsin, is the Mero site, which has an area of $2\frac{1}{2}$ to 3 square miles, according to Lawshe (1947), and is located on a river terrace overlooked by high bluffs including Diamond Bluff to the north. Lawshe and his friends picked up over 2,000 artifacts, including 800 arrowheads which were predominantly triangular, 500 scrapers, 35 celts, millstones and mullers and shell spoons. Of particular interest were a small mask of a human face made from ocean shell, two fish effigies of clam shell, and a small copper effigy mace or baton which may be brass, according to L. H. Larson, Jr., who has examined the collection. The human mask has been identified as a part of the Long Nosed God Mask complex (Williams and Goggin, 1956, pp. 32, 38, 47), which is not an unlikely attribution. The authors have, however, attributed this mask and the copper fragments to a time period equivalent to Aztalan; while the cultural complex listed above and particularly the pottery illustrated by Lawshe is entirely Oneota and is very close to the Orr Focus ceramic style (see Plates VI and VII).

The Wisconsin Archaeological Survey in 1948 excavated in the Diamond Bluff Mound Group in Pierce County, which is apparently a part of the Mero site of Lawshe, but is located to the north of the main village area from which Lawshe and his friends collected (Maxwell, 1950). Traces of nearly two hundred mounds could be identified on the bluff and 48 of these were relatively untouched and in an unplowed field. Six of these were excavated in the survey as well as 150 square feet of a village area located at the edge of the bluff. Unfortunately a final report on this excavation has not appeared, but

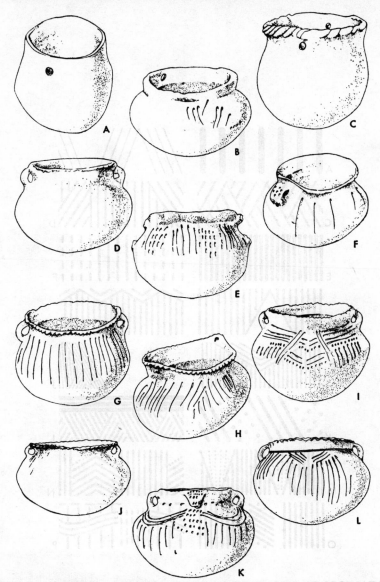

PLATE VI. VESSEL SHAPES AND DECORATIONS FROM VARIOUS
ORR FOCUS SITES IN IOWA, MINNESOTA, AND WISCONSIN

photographs in the Museum of Anthropology, University of Michigan, not drawn to
scale. A: Very small jar from Allamakee County, Iowa. B: Small straight rim jar from
akee County. C: Small funerary vessel from Midway village site, LaCrosse County,
nsin; dia. 6.7 cm.; Milwaukee Public Museum, Cat. No. 35660. D: Small funerary jar,
wo strap handles, from Allamakee County, Iowa. E: Vessel with two broken handles,
the Oneota Valley, Allamakee County, Iowa; hgt. 9.2 cm. F: Vessel from Upper Iowa
, Allamakee County. G: Vessel from Upper Iowa Valley, Allamakee County. H: Vessel
Tartt Farm Grave, Upper Iowa Valley, Allamakee County; hgt. 9.8 cm. I: Vessel from
Red Wing, Goodhue County, Minnesota; drawn from Winchell, 1911, Plate VII of
. J: Large restored strap handled vessel from Midway village site, LaCrosse County,
nsin; hgt. 29.9 cm., shoulder dia. 49.2 cm.; Milwaukee Public Museum, Cat. No. 34909.
ur strap handle vessel from northeast Iowa; hgt. 12.6 cm. L: Large jar with two strap
s, probably from O'Regan village site, Allamakee County, Iowa; hgt. 17.5 cm. Vessels
A, B, D-G, K, and L are in the Iowa State Historical Society Collection.

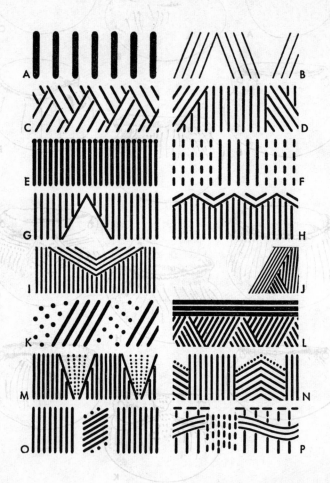

PLATE VII. ORR FOCUS DESIGNS FROM VARIOUS SITES

A, E, G, J, L, M, O: From Midway village site in LaCrosse County, Wisconsin. B: O'Regan village site in Allamakee County, Iowa. C-D, F, I, K, P: From sites in Alla‑ County, Iowa. H, N: From Shrake-Gillies village site in Trempealeau County, Wis‑

in addition to the brief report referred to above, there is a group of photographs in the Museum of Anthropology of pottery from this site. Dr. Maxwell has also allowed me to see the manuscript of his talk before the Society for American Archaeology in Norman, Oklahoma, in May, 1950. Mound 4, large and conical, was sampled by means of intersecting 5-foot trenches. Because of the mixture of organic material, pottery and other cultural debris in the soil of the mound it is clear that it was built of earth from a village occupation. The five burials, four very poorly preserved adults and a child, were in the upper portions of the mound, and did not have grave goods with them. There were 108 pottery fragments in the mound, of these, approximately one third were grit tempered primarily Late Woodland specimens almost certainly of the Effigy Mound Culture period. Less than one third were shell tempered, and a few of these were cord marked. Maxwell has interpreted all of the shell tempered rim sherds as typical of Old Village–Aztalan, and the photographs in our collection support this view. A little more than one third were grit tempered with Old Village features. A possible interpretation of this mound is that it was built from village refuse obtained from an occupied area—indicating association of Old Village–Aztalan people with Effigy Mound populations, and some degree of cultural admixture.

Mounds 6, 8, and 15 were small and had very little material in them. They are representative of Effigy Mound conicals. Mound 8 was almost barren, while Mound 6 had a cube of galena, 2 Woodland, and 2 plain Mississippi sherds. Mound 15 was Woodland and contained no Mississippi traits.

Mound 26 was a panther effigy with burial material in the shoulder region. There were two small vessels in this mound. One of these is a small handled jar suggestive of Oneota, while the second, which was associated with fragments of a twelve-year-old child, according to McKern and Maxwell, is close to the knobbed shouldered Grand River type (McKern, 1945, Plate 67, Fig. 2). There are incised concentric arches on the shoulder area above each of the 10 lobes on the vessel. Slightly beneath the original ground surface under the mound and near a subsurface burial pit was a rim sherd with a poorly incised Old Village decoration. This panther effigy, according to Maxwell, was erected at a time when Oneota ceramic material was in existence and was erected for Oneota burials.

Maxwell has emphasized that there is a considerable amount of Oneota Orr Focus debris in the village area as well as typical Ramey Incised and Powell Plain pottery of Old Village origin. So far no clear evidence of the temporal order of the Woodland, Old Village, and Oneota material has been presented, and further investigations of this area are of considerable importance. There are indications from the pottery of the contemporary existence of Old Village and Effigy Mound from the blending of these two traditions on vessels. There is also evidence of Oneota peoples burying in a panther effigy mound, which they presumably built. As yet there is no clear evidence of the contemporary existence of Old Village and Oneota, nor of a gradual shift from the former ceramic style to the latter from the evidence gathered by Maxwell—except for one sherd (Cat. No. DBVI $\frac{44}{2}$) from the village which is a rather high rim approaching the Oneota type and has a decoration of incised rectilinear lines.

Some thirty miles south of Diamond Bluff is the Armstrong site on the east side of Lake Pepin, in Pepin County, Wisconsin. The brief report on a surface and test pit excavation presents material which is very close to the Orr Focus sites further south (Johnson, 1949). None of the material illustrated or described is Old Village, and there are no specific Effigy Mound traits.

The Distribution of Oneota Sites in Eastern Wisconsin

In addition to the better-known Lake Winnebago Focus sites such as Karow, McCauley, and Lasleys Point in Winnebago County, the survey of Lawson (1903) suggests the village at Butte des Morts in Menasha, the village at Asylum Bay on Lake Winnebago north of Oshkosh (perhaps now in the city), and Manser Bay in the southern part of Neenah, were also Mississippi culture sites. They were probably Oneota and perhaps of the Lake Winnebago Focus. Some of the pottery from north of the Black River along the sandy beach of Lake Michigan in Sheboygan County is certainly Lake Winnebago Focus in type (Gerend, 1904, Plate III, Figs. 24, 28, 32, 34, 39). The same identification can be made of pottery from Green Bay between Red Banks and Point Au Sable (ibid., Plate V) and on the same plate from a site near the mouth of the Fox River. Mississippi pottery has been found as far northeast as Washington Island where on West Bay a village with shell tempered pottery is known (Fox, 1915, p. 75). Two

Mississippi vessels were obtained from a gravel pit near Calumet Harbor on the east side of Lake Winnebago. The incised jar is certainly Oneota, but the crude effigy vessel is a rare type for east central Wisconsin (Titus, 1915, Plate 10).

Recent excavations during 1957 at Carcajou Point on Lake Koshkonong by Robert L. Hall have produced an extremely interesting village complex which has not heretofore been reported in this area of southern Wisconsin. These excavations will provide a basis for his Ph.D. thesis. The complex at Carcajou does no violence to the proposed cultural change from a Rock River Focus assemblage to one which is Oneota. Hall has provided the radiocarbon samples which are reported in this paper.

The Cambria Complex in Minnesota

Another prehistoric complex in central Minnesota which clearly has Old Village–Aztalan as a part of its ancestry is the Cambria Focus (Wilford, 1945, 1955). The type site is located in Blue Earth County on the Minnesota River, and other sites attributed to this focus are located along the Minnesota river. Wilford recognized three distinctive ceramic types which he has labeled A, B, and C, and in his paper he implies that Cambria is a homogeneous complex and that all three types are contemporary. The initial reference to this site (Winchell, 1911, p. 742) however, indicates village site refuse and disturbed soil some 4 to 5 feet deep with a great variety of animal bone including bison and elk. The material referred to by Winchell is in the collection of the Minnesota Historical Society. Some of these specimens were photographed by Stephen Williams and the negatives are in the Museum of Anthropology of the University of Michigan.

Type C pottery is grit tempered, but has the distinctive Old Village shoulder, small loop handles and a predominantly curvilinear decoration featuring scrolls and wavy lines which are placed on the insloping shoulder area. The designs, however, show a rectilinear character suggesting a trend toward the Oneota style. The short handles are not circular in cross-section on the vessels of Old Village shape but are ovoid to somewhat flattened.

Type A pottery at Cambria has a developed high rim and usually slopes outward. The lip is flattened and when decorated will have closely spaced oblique or transverse gashes, or cross hatches. The decorated zone, as on type C, is the shoulder area, and some vessels have retained the marked angularity of shoulder which is a hallmark of Old Village jars. The decoration is primarily rectilinear of nested open base triangles, with the apex of the outer triangle at the base of the neck, and the lower ends of the triangles resting on the shoulder. Between the nested triangles (four to a vessel?) there are parallel horizontal lines done in the same broad incised style. Some rim sherds have nested arches instead of triangles. Handles apparently on vessels of this type are larger and broader than on type C, but they have not progressed to the broad, strap form of Oneota. As Wilford has observed, type A is a unique complex of ceramic characteristics not known from any other division. It appears to have developed from type C and, if so, this relationship should be found in a deep occupation such as the type site, or by means of seriation within the Cambria Focus. The designs and the style with which they are executed are clearly analogous to Oneota but are moving toward the appearance of a portion of the pottery of the Over Focus of southeastern South Dakota, and toward some of the Mill Creek sites of northwestern Iowa.

Other pottery from the Cambria site, apparently not included within Wilford's types, are examples identical or close to Over Focus types called Mitchell Incised, and Kimball and Mitchell Modified Lip, Foreman Incised Triangle, and Foreman Cord-Impressed (Hurt, 1953). These ceramic groups are also present in Mill Creek sites. In some of the Mill Creek sites there is a strong element of the Old Village tradition in every feature of the pottery, including the shape, decoration and handles of the Ramey Incised and Powell Plain types, as well as bowls with effigy heads and other bowl forms. A minor proportion of these are shell tempered. This close adherence to Old Village is not as strong in Over Focus sites of South Dakota nor in the Cambria Focus. Hurt's classification of Mitchell Broad-Trailed has merged a number of quite distinct ceramic units. There is a much more elaborated and varied pottery assemblage in the Over Focus and Mill Creek sites than is present at Cambria (see Plate V). A possible explanation is that the Cambria complex represents a time span which begins later than Aztalan, Silvernale, and early Mill Creek, and ends before Oneota has clearly developed, and before the more complex rim decorations and shapes have fully matured in the Over Focus and in the Mill Creek Complex. The latter stage of the cultural material at Cambria is more intimately connected with developments in the Middle Missouri basin to the west rather than those taking place in the northern Misisippi Valley which develop into Oneota. The early segment of the Mill Creek history should be on about the same time level as the shift from proto-Oneota to Oneota. The Old Village tradition of Mill Creek sites and the Over Focus fades out and is replaced by a complete reorientation of ceramic ideas.

Comments on Osage Archaeology

The Osage tribe, with its close linguistic connections to Kansa and as a unit of the Dhegiha group, should have an archaeological complex which is related to other Dhegiha tribes. Furthermore, there could well be indications of more distant connections to Chiwere-Winnebago. The Osage seem to have been located in the southwestern part of Missouri and adjacent Kansas, Arkansas, and Oklahoma at the beginning of the eighteenth century. The length of time they had resided in this area is not known. Archaeological remains almost certainly from Osage villages in Vernon County, Missouri, and well within the historic period have been regarded as a component of Oneota by most of the archaeologists in the state of Missouri (Berry, Chapman, and Mack, 1944; Chapman, 1946; and Chapman, 1952). While recognizing the strong resemblances of the ceramic complex of the Vernon County sites to the Missouri (Indian) Utz style pottery, I have been reluctant to equate early historic or proto-historic Osage archaeology with Oneota. This is because of the possibility that during the latter part of the eighteenth century the Missouri tribe became affiliated with the Osage, and the resultant admixture might be that found on the Vernon County sites. Furthermore, if Osage were prehistoric Oneota it would upset the perhaps too neat hypothesis of Oneota origins in the northern Mississippi Valley.

At the same time the archaeologists in Missouri were identifying Osage remains in that state, the Oklahoma archaeologists were concerned with the late prehistoric complex now called the Neosho Focus (Baerreis, 1939). Baerreis recognized that "the decorative complex bears a decided resemblance to the Oneota aspect." In May of 1940 I received a shipment of Neosho Focus pottery from the University of Oklahoma for study, and I sent them, in July, a type description which has, perhaps fortunately, never been published. The general statement on the Neosho pottery which I examined is given below.

The collection of pottery sent to the Ceramic Repository in May, 1940, from a number of sites in northeastern Oklahoma, belonging to the tentatively designated Neosho Focus, apparently constitutes an interesting example of cultural admixture. The shell tempered paste and globular, open-mouth vessels, with strap and loop handles and plain outer surface immediately suggest that this complex belongs in the Mississippi Pattern. The incised and punctate designs show a definite and in some instances a very strong connection with the techniques and designs on the pottery of the Oneota Aspect of Upper Mississippi. This is particularly marked in the examples which have punctates paralleling a series of incised lines. On the majority of these sherds, however, the punctates have their long axis parallel to the direction of the incised lines, whereas in the normal Oneota design, the punctates are placed at right angles. As on Oneota pottery the lip is decorated in a great majority of cases. The most typical single style for such treatment in the Neosho Focus is for the punctates to be placed directly upon the lip and paralleling its edges, while the minority were cut across at an angle. The use of horizontal bands of oblique punctates does not appear in any Oneota Focus, nor is there often found other uses of punctates alone as the decorative pattern.

There is a greater use of the loop handle in the Neosho Focus and this corresponds with certain other features of vessel shape and paste characteristics which strongly suggest that this pottery is basically Middle Mississippi and probably is derived from the eastern Arkansas and Missouri area. The wide-mouth, round-bottom jar, with a rounded but slightly constricted shoulder and a short, vertical rim is more characteristic of, or more closely related to vessel shapes from that area than they are to Oneota shapes which have a more strongly constricted mouth and highly characteristic angled rim. One of the sherds from the Neosho Focus is a bowl with small rim lugs and small mamilliform nodes on the body. Bowls are not characteristic of Oneota pottery. The shell temper of the Neosho pottery is finer, does not present a laminated appearance, and there is apparently a smaller amount than is characteristically found in the Oneota sherds. A rather high percent of this pottery has a hardness between 2.5 and 5, while some of the sherds run as high as 6.5. This is much harder than any Oneota pottery now described or of any Middle Mississippi wares. A few of the sherds which most strongly suggest eastern Arkansas vessels in shape and color are also quite soft, as they can be scratched by the fingernails.

It can be regarded as a definite possibility that this pottery was made by a people with a basic cultural connection in the eastern Arkansas area who had been influenced by contact with Oneota culture traits. Translated ethnologically one might advance the hypothesis that this pottery could be the remains of the Osage, who were a Dhegiha speaking division of the Sioux, and who are thought to have formerly lived farther east in the eastern Missouri, Arkansas area. This assumed contact of Middle Mississippi and Oneota could have taken place in the last mentioned area or while the migratory movement was in progress. A further guess might be made that the chronological period represented would be between 1675 and 1775.

During the last ten years the University of Missouri has been conducting an extensive series of excavations in the Ozarks of southwestern Missouri in the area where one might expect to find the remains of proto-Osage. If Osage is truly a segment of the Oneota Aspect then there should be a number of sites without European trade items in this area with a full and well-rounded Oneota complex. In scanning recent numbers of the *Missouri Archaeologist* I have not found such evidence, but there are many references to a late Mississippi component at a large number of sites. Where interpretations are hazarded as to the archaeological connections of this late complex, the suggestion is made that it is to the area from southeast Missouri to the Arkansas River (Bray, 1956, pp. 71-74). This may represent a "Marginal Mississippi" group who have received elements of the Mississippi complex from the east or an actual movement of people. If the traits listed by Chapman (1956, p. 41) are representative of the Mississippi complex in the White River area of Missouri, then the dominant late Mississippi complex does show strong connections to the northeast Arkansas area.

In a recent trip to the University of Wisconsin, David A. Baerreis kindly allowed me to examine some of the Neosho pottery again. One of the first specimens I picked up resembled a Wallace Incised rim (Phillips, Ford, and Griffin, 1951, pp. 134-36), but this was the only example of the type in the collection. My reaction to the Neosho pottery during this viewing was, again, that it is not Oneota although there are clear indications of Oneota influences. One of the marked differences is the flat base of Neosho jars. This type of base is not found in Oneota or, in general on Middle Mississippi jars. It is, however, the dominant type of base on the Great Bend Aspect of east central Kansas which is provisionally attributed to the Wichita (Wedel, 1942, 1949).

Conjectures on Quapaw Prehistory

The Quapaw are the southernmost Dhegiha tribe, and in the latter part of the seventeenth century they were located near the mouth of the Arkansas. In spite of a fair amount of historic contact between the French and the Quapaw, none of their villages of the 1670–1700 period has been definitely identified as a specific archaeological site. This identification problem was explored at some length by Phillips (Phillips, Ford, and Griffin, 1951, pp. 392-424). His conclusion was that there is some probability that Quapaw may yet be connected with a late archaeological complex of the lower Arkansas which we found at the Wallace site and on other related sites of the area. In this same publication the discussion of the pottery type Wallace Incised (*ibid.*, pp. 135-36) is somewhat more definite in attributing the Wallace site material to Quapaw. In my chapter in *Archeology of Eastern United States* on the prehistoric cultures of the central Mississippi Valley, I describe some of the late archaeological material from the lower Arkansas as "the Menard Focus" (Griffin, 1952a, pp. 237-38). This was simply an attempt to recognize a regional complex which was significantly different from sites to the north in the St. Francis and from the sites which I called "Walls-Pecan Point." It is now apparent that future studies of the materials from "the Menard Focus" should be able to differentiate a complex on about the A.D. 1500–1600 time level that should be distinguishable from the last prehistoric and historic complex of the Quapaw for which the name Wallace Focus is proposed. On the basis of recent excavations by Preston Holder for the National Park Service at the Dupree site (16-L-6) in Phillips County, Arkansas, I believe the Wallace Focus will be recognized as to some degree a degenerate phase of Walls-Pecan Point as it appears on sites such as Kent, Carson, and other late sites near the mouth of the Arkansas. If the Ofo were a functioning Siouan tribe of the 1600–1700 period, their villages sites might have been in the state of Mississippi near the mouth of the Arkansas. I would not move the Quapaw into their early historic location from any great distance, but would look for their cultural ancestry in the Middle Mississippi complexes of eastern Arkansas.

The Temporal Factor in the Present Hypothesis

The Hopewell or Hopewellian Phase in the Illinois-Wisconsin area had disappeared by approximately A.D. 500 (Griffin, n.d.). This culture stage is followed by Late Woodland complexes in the same area before Old Village is known at Cahokia. Radiocarbon dates from a number of sites of Late Woodland run from A.D. 700 $\pm$ 250 (M-398) at an

Effigy Mound site in Wisconsin (Wittry, 1956) to A.D. 690 ± 150 (M-512) at a site in Muskegon County, Michigan. There should not be a temporal break between late Hopewell and early Late Woodland for there is not a marked cultural unconformity. As indicated earlier in this paper Late Woodland sites in the northern Mississippi Valley will last well up into the Aztalan-Oneota period.

The proto-Oneota people left the Cahokia area after the Old Village complex had reached a high point of its ceramic development. We now have two radiocarbon runs on a charcoal specimen from Mound 34 of the Cahokia group (Crane, 1956) excavated by the University of Michigan in 1950. These two runs were 700 ± 300 and 900 ± 300, or 800 ± 200 years ago. The date of A.D. 1150 ± 200 is from a location which I believe is representative of Old Village culture either at the time of northern dispersal, or slightly later than the move to the north of the proto-Oneota. As I write these brave words, the radiocarbon laboratory is processing some specimens including additional examples from Mound 34 made by Gregory Perino in 1956–57, from a cremation in the northwest pyramid of Aztalan, and from Carcajou Point. If "science" bears out this archaeologist's interpretations, the Cahokia specimens should date between A.D. 1100 and 1200; Aztalan at about A.D. 1200–50; and Carcajou Point between A.D. 1300–1400. The results (without an apology) are given below.

M-642	Charcoal from Aztalan, Jefferson County, Wisconsin Material from the charred house in the northwest pyramid mound. Submitted by Robert Ritzenthaler, Milwaukee Public Museum.	320 ± 200 (A.D. 1638)
	Carcajou Point Site (Jev2) Jefferson County Wisconsin Submitted by Robert L. Hall, Rock County Historical Society, Wisconsin.	
M-747	Charcoal from Feature 17, Level 3. This is from a late occupation of the site which is predominantly Oneota in character.	430 ± 200 (A.D. 1528)
M-785	Charcoal from fill of center post of wall trench of rectangular house. This house is part of the earliest Mississippi occupation of the site and is regarded as later than Aztalan by the excavator.	930 ± 250 (A.D. 1028)
M-786	Charcoal from Feature 41, a cache pit located inside the above house. This pit is regarded by the excavator as the earliest pit at the site.	960 ± 250 (A.D. 998)
	Cahokia Site, Madison County, Illinois. Submitted by Gregory Perino and Dan Morse.	

M-635   Mound 34. Charcoal from ceremonial fire at ramp.   670 ± 200
Mound junction on west side of mound thus postdates   (A.D. 1288)
construction of ramp and mound. Material in association includes plain and serrated triangular, two-notched
and three-notched points, burnt arrowpoints and novac-
ulate flaring celts, a flint spade, seven pearl beads, a
flint effigy sharks tooth, wooden bowl fragments, a
negative painted sherd, an "Alba Barbed" point, and
two destroyed conch shell vessels. This complex is
about same age as the strong Caddoan connections with
Cahokia.

M-636   Charcoal from a refuse pit 150 yards east of Monks   660 ± 200
Mound which should equate with Mound 34.   (A.D. 1298)

M-670   Charcoal from small log on clay floor of burned house   960 ± 250
located about 100 yards east of northeast corner of   (A.D. 998)
Monks Mound. This is regarded as an "Early Trappist"
house.

M-672   Charcoal from a fire basin in floor of burned house   480 ± 200
located about 100 yards east of northeast corner of   (A.D. 1478)
Monks Mound.

M-33   Charcoal from Mound 34, University of Michigan Ex-   700 ± 300
cavation Unit 3, Test Pit 1, Feature 4 at a depth of   900 ± 300
4 feet 3 inches in the sub-mound village debris. This   average
level is a well developed Old Village Complex and is   800 ± 200
close to the period with indications of Caddoan con-   (A.D. 1152)
tacts. (This is a carbonblack date.)

An Interpretation of the Prehistory of the Winnebago and Their Cultural Brothers

The northward movement of an Old Village style culture from the
rich alluvial flood plains at Cahokia is perhaps to be explained on
cultural grounds. Since we really do not know why the movement took
place, the possibility of tribal conflict and competition for the more
favorable agricultural lands in the vicinity of St. Louis can be suggested,
but without much conviction. During the period of the development
of the Old Village complex at Cahokia there were Late Woodland
peoples in the same general area, but the sites are located primarily
on the bluffs and in the smaller stream valleys surrounding the American bottoms. There is some evidence of the adoption of Mississippi
culture traits into the Late Woodland complex. The Trappist Focus
which succeeds Old Village in time at Cahokia is, by and large a
development from it, but has some characteristics of the Woodland
tradition. There also seems to be a continuation of the occupation of

the bluff areas and smaller stream valleys with a clearly mixed Mississippi and Woodland complex closely related to "pure" Trappist at the Cahokia site. The most logical direct descendants of the Trappist Focus and its close relatives would be the resident Cahokia and Tamaroa tribes of the Illinois confederacy of the 1670–1700 period, even though satisfactory proof of this is still not available. We know on comparative and stratigraphic grounds that late Trappist material is the last prehistoric culture in the Cahokia area and that it was probably functioning during the seventeenth century. One of the private collections from a Trappist Focus site near Lebanon, Illinois, 12 miles east of Cahokia, has a possible association of a small amount of European trade material (Griffin and Spaulding, 1951, Plate 4, Fig. 1). What is needed, of course, is the clear association of early European trade material with late Trappist burials or houses, or a Trappist cultural complex at a definitely identified village location of the Cahokia or Tamaroa tribes. The latter possibility is not likely to be realized for there are not pre-1700 specifically identified villages of the Illinois tribes in the St. Louis area.

One of the dilemmas of this proto-Oneota migration hypothesis is that it requires the Chiwere-Winnebago to have been participating as a part of the Old Village complex at Cahokia at approximately A.D. 1000. They then move north to northwestern Illinois, Wisconsin, and eastern Minnesota. The Aztalan site with its fortification, platform mounds, and impressive village material implies a rather large, stable and cohesive social group to have built it and maintained it for x-period of years. Does this mean that Aztalan was a tribal unit to be equated with one of the historic Siouan tribes? Does it mean that Aztalan is a social unit from which one or several tribes subsequently emerged? Is Aztalan the first Middle Mississippi site in these latitudes, and did other sites with a similar complex appear after Aztalan was abandoned? The present comment on these questions is that we don't know. The other sites which have been mentioned which have Old Village-Aztalan materials, from Apple River to Diamond Bluff, may be interpreted as the remains of a number of other distinctive social units which are essentially contemporary with Aztalan. They would thus represent discrete social entities which either moved north as such or which splintered off from a major migrating whole, the largest segment of which moved to Aztalan. It is probably safe to say that there are no sites comparable to Aztalan in the north, but there should be a fair number of sites equivalent to Apple River and Silvernale.

A major question is, if proto-Oneota is Old Village at Cahokia and the group, or groups, move north, how can there be the continuity at Cahokia between Old Village and Trappist? The same type of question applies to the suggested connection between early Mill Creek and Old Village. Cahokia is one of the largest areas of Mississippi occupation in the East. Old Village type material has been found over a considerable area around St. Louis both east and west, and north and south. It is associated with a number of distinctive mound complexes within the Cahokia site. Fairly large social groups could have moved from Cahokia without breaking the strong evidence of continuity in the general Cahokia region. These could have been clan groups which were of sufficient size and strength to maintain themselves in their new northern environment and which then gradually became the historic Chiwere-Winnebago tribes.

Additional population movement from the Old Village center is postulated for the appearance in the Steed-Kisker site near Kansas City of specifically Cahokia area style pottery, and also for the appearance in northwest Iowa of Old Village pottery. I have several times proposed that this might represent the movement of the proto-Omaha-Ponca into the Missouri Valley, but this idea has not been sufficiently stimulating apparently, to provoke anyone to show either that it is definitely wrong or possibly correct. A few speculations have been made in this direction by Hurt (1953, pp. 10-11, 48-64), and more would be refreshing, particularly from Nebraska archaeologists. In any event, this relatively early movement from Old Village into the Missouri Valley was by a group or groups of people who had a highly similar culture to proto-Oneota in the Cahokia area, but their line of cultural development was modified into a significantly different direction from that taken by the Oneota. When the proto-Oneota or Old Village-Aztalan groups arrived in the Wisconsin region they found resident Woodland populations of the Lake Michigan Effigy Mound period occupying the land. Cultural materials of this northern Late Woodland type are found on all of the sites with the Mississippi complex, and in some cases it is certain that peoples of these two different traditions existed side by side with some resultant cultural exchange. At Aztalan this is clearly seen in the pottery where a fair proportion of Mississippi vessel forms and handles are grit-tempered, the rim shapes of Lake Michigan jars are modified towards the Mississippi mode, and Woodland cord marked bodies are smoothed to simulate the Mississippi surface finish. The Mississippi occupation at Aztalan does not seem to have lasted over any great period of time, and there are few, if any, indications at this site of the postulated culture change to Oneota. As a site, however, Aztalan must have been a fairly popular place for a considerable period of time. There are several varieties of Lake Michigan pottery which are probably not all contemporary with each other and with the Old Village complex. A small Hopewell occupation is obvious from the platform pipes and Hopewell pottery on the site. There are a number of items illustrated in Barrett (1933, Plate 98), such as the large projectile points, the grooved axes and two forms of bannerstones—implying one or more Archaic occupations.

The Old Village–Aztalan complex arrived in the north as a well-rounded Middle Mississippi culture and during the suggested transition to Oneota many of the distinctively Cahokia area traits were abandoned or modified.

Among the traits which so clearly link Aztalan to the Cahokia area are the five examples of large chipped flint spades found at Aztalan (Barrett, 1933, pp. 271-72) and which are said to be made from flint similar to that at Cahokia. These large digging implements are the only ones known from Wisconsin, but they are common in the St. Louis area. They are not found on Oneota sites in Wisconsin, Minnesota, or Iowa. In northwestern Illinois two spades have been found at the Mills village site, which has a strong Old Village representation as well as later material (Bennett, 1945, p. 144). A photograph of these specimens shows very clearly that they are of the expanded bit type and they very closely resemble Cahokia specimens in form and in the appearance of the flint (Bennett, 1945, Plate 33). These large flint spades do not normally appear as a part of the Spoon River Focus of central Illinois. One of them was found at the Kingston village site, Peoria County (Simpson, 1939) which has a strong Old Village component, as well as a later Spoon River complex, but it is not of the normal Cahokia forms.

At most of the sites in Wisconsin and Minnesota where Old Village pottery is present there is also a significant number of small triangular arrowpoints with side notches, or with side notches and one basal notch.

This form is rarely if ever found in an Oneota context in the northern Mississippi Valley. Both Old Village and Oneota have the simple triangle as the common arrowhead. Some of the other Middle Mississippi traits that tend to disappear are pyramidal mounds, wattle and daub houses, ear spools, perforated shell hoes, ocean shell columella pendants, and a considerable use of shell beads and stone discoidals.

The shifts in pottery shapes, surface finish, handle forms, painting and incised decoration are the best guide to cultural change. The Old Village-Aztalan peoples made a variety of vessel forms from large to small jars which have a very distinctive angle at the shoulder, an insloping shoulder area and a low, usually rounded, lip (see Plate III). The incised decoration is placed on the shoulder area and almost never on the body of the vessel. The designs are made in the soft clay by a rounded tool about the size of an antler tip. The designs are predominantly curvilinear meanders and modified scrolls particularly on Ramey Incised in the St. Louis home area. I believe that Aztalan has a significantly higher proportion of rectilinear patterns of horizontal, oblique, chevron, and line filled triangles than does Cahokia (see Plate III). This can be interpreted as the beginning of a shift of emphasis from curvilinear to the predominantly rectilinear designs on Oneota. This shift can be seen at Cambria and Apple River. Among the new designs are the concentric half circle arches on the shoulder area, and the wide arch on the shoulder with a group of vertical lines within the arch. The small cylindrical loop handle gradually changes to a strap which is wide and relatively thin. Intermediate forms tend to be ovoid in cross section. Some of the Aztalan loop handles have knobs on the upper section of the handle. The basic jar form changes from a shouldered vessel to one with a gradual curve as the greatest diameter is approached. The most striking change of the jars, however, is the development of a distinctive rim section which is set at a marked angle to the maximum constriction of the body and is normally, on Oneota vessels, angled outward (see Plates VII and VIII). The varieties of rectilinear patterns and punctates that form the several regional patterns of Oneota pottery are not found to the south and east of the specifically Oneota sites (see Plates VII and IX). I believe that this distinctive design complex developed in the northern Mississippi Valley area and that its appearance to the west and south in the Missouri Valley is the result of specific movement of Oneota people after the style had been set.

PLATE VIII. LAKE WINNEBAGO FOCUS VESSEL SHAPES
AND DECORATION

n from various photographs, not to the same scale. A: Restored small jar from Lasley's
site, Winnebago County, Wisconsin; Milwaukee Public Museum Neg. 420009 left.
all restored ladle from Lasley's Point; M.P.M. Neg. 419649. C: Small and rare bowl
from Lasley's Point; M.P.M. Neg. 42009 center. D: Small restored jar from Lasley's
M.P.M. Neg. 420009 right. E: Medium sized restored jar from Lasley's Point; M.P.M.
418579. F: Restored jar from Karow site, Winnebago County; lip dia. 24.9 cm., hgt. 20.3
M.P.M. Cat. No. 41192. G: Complete jar from Karow site; lip dia. 9.8 cm., hgt. 10.0 cm.;
M. Cat. No. 41168. H: Restored jar from Lasley's Point site; M.P.M. Cat. No. 420007.
stored jar from Karow site; lip dia. 17.1 cm., hgt. 15.0 cm.; M.P.M. Cat. No. 41169.
mplete jar from Karow site; lip dia. 15.7 cm., hgt. 13.6 cm.; M.P.M. Cat. No. 41167.
r from a site near Neenah, Winnebago County; M.P.M. Neg. 60896. L: Small Lake
bago Focus jar from Oshkosh, in the State Historical Museum, Madison, Wisconsin;
. 9.0 cm., hgt. 8.0 cm.; M.P.M. Neg. 406230. Vessels A-E, H, and perhaps K are in the
Oshkosh Public Museum.

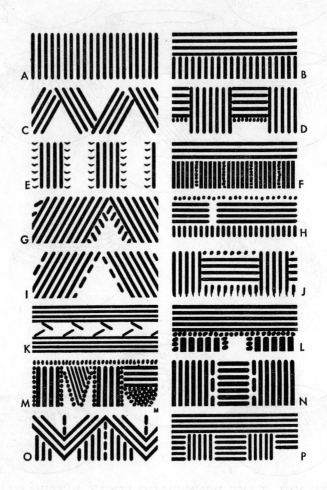

PLATE IX. LAKE WINNEBAGO FOCUS DESIGNS

A, H-I: From the Karow site, Winnebago County. B-D, F-G, K-N: From the Lasley's site, Winnebago County. E, J: From the Oshkosh area, Winnebago County. O: From the McCauley site, Winnebago County. P: From Winnebago County.

Bowl forms including effigy heads, seed bowls, and red filmed bowls are almost entirely discarded. There are a few bottles at Aztalan including a gourd effigy. These too do not continue into the Oneota period. In the Middle Mississippi ceramic complex the jar forms and other utilitarian vessels were made from a more coarsely tempered paste than many of the bowls, plates and bottles. In Oneota only the coarser paste ware is produced. All in all, the Oneota complex is a marked decline in quality and variety from its proposed ancestors.

Some of the ceramic changes and shifts which took place from Old Village-Aztalan in the jars also occur throughout the Middle Mississippi cultures to the south. This is particularly marked in the development of high rims, the location of incised designs and the shifts in the forms of handles. The Oneota changes are then a part of a broad cultural trend and are not unique to the northern Mississippi Valley, although the end result is not found in any other complex.

Because of the large number of flint scrapers and bone beamers in Oneota, there is postulated a considerable production of skin clothing and other artifacts. The bone awls and sewing needles could have been used in making rush mats. The shell fish lures, bone fishhooks, harpoons, and probably nets, added fish to their diet. There is a small amount of copper beads and pendants on the Oneota sites including what seems to be a "Thunderbird" effigy from a site in Fond du Lac County (McKern, 1945, Plate 45, Fig. 8). Small copper forms on the same illustration have been interpreted as replicas of the ceremonial mace of the southeastern ceremonial complex. A similar connection is also suggested for circular copper discs with a cross design. Two of these are from a Grand River site in Kingston Town, Green Lake County, Wisconsin (Pasco and Ritzenthaler, 1949a, 1949b).

The speculations, hypotheses, and interpretations which have been gathered together for this paper imply an alignment of the prehistoric Chiwere-Winnebago and Dhegiha tribes along the west side of the Mississippi River from northeastern Arkansas to the mouth of the Illinois at approximately A.D. 1000 where they were participating in the development of Middle Mississippi culture. The proto-Oneota people move north and eventually become the Chiwere-Winnebago. The proto-Omaha–Ponca move both north and west and eventually emerge as late Mill Creek in the area north of Omaha, Nebraska. The Osage and Quapaw are not a part of the specifically Old Village complex for they were to the south beyond the limits of the Old Village Focus. At a considerably later time the Osage moved west while the Quapaw remained in the lower Arkansas Valley. The proto-Dakota would be located in this reconstruction in essentially their historic area, where they formed a number of varieties of Late Woodland cultures at the time of the northward movement of their linguistic relatives from the south. The Siouan people on the west side of the Mississippi faced east to primarily central Algonquian groups in Wisconsin and Illinois. These Algonquian groups were also adopting the Mississippi archaeological culture and they finally appear at the 1650–1700 period as a number of varieties of the Mississippi complex. These varieties are Trappist, Spoon River, and Fisher.

REFERENCES

Baerreis, David A. 1939. "Two New Cultures in Delaware County, Oklahoma," *The Oklahoma Prehistorian*, 2:No. 1:2-5.

Barrett, S. A. 1933. Ancient Aztalan. Bulletin of the Public Museum of the City of Milwaukee, Vol. XIII.

Bennett, John W. 1945. Archaeological Explorations in Jo Daviess County, Illinois. University of Chicago Publications in Anthropology, Archaeological Series.

Berry, Brewton, Carl Chapman, and John Mack. 1944. "The Archaeological Remains of the Osage," *American Antiquity*, 10:No. 1:1-11.

Bray, Robert T. 1956. "Culture Complexes and Sequence at the Rice Site (23SN200) Stone County, Missouri," *The Missouri Archaeologist*, 18:Nos. 1–2: 47-134.

Brooks, C. E. P. 1949. Climate Through the Ages: A Study of the Climatic Factors and Their Variations. New York.

Brower, J. V. 1900. Mille Lac: Memoirs of Explorations in the Basin of the Mississippi, Vol. III. St. Paul.

—— 1903. Minnesota: Discovery of Its Area, 1540–1665. Memoirs of Explorations in the Basin of the Mississippi, Vol. VI. St. Paul.

Bushnell, David I., Jr. 1922. Villages of the Algonquian, Siouan, and Caddoan Tribes West of the Mississippi. Bulletin 77, Bureau of American Ethnology, Smithsonian Institution.

Chapman, Carl H. 1946. "A Preliminary Survey of Missouri Archaeology: Part 1, Historic Indian Tribes," *The Missouri Archaeologist*, 10:Part 1.

—— 1952. "Culture Sequence in the Lower Missouri Valley," in *Archeology of Eastern United States*, ed. by J. B. Griffin, pp. 139-51.

—— 1956. "A Résumé of Table Rock Archaeological Investigations," *The Missouri Archaeologist*, 18:Nos. 1–2:15-46.

Cope, Leona. 1919. "Calendars of the Indians North of Mexico," *University of California Publications in American Archaeology and Ethnology*, 16:No. 4: 119-76.

Crary, A. P., J. Lawrence Kulp, and E. W. Marshall. 1955. "Evidences of Climatic Change from Ice Island Studies," *Science*, 122:No. 3181:1171-73.

Dorsey, J. Owen, and Cyrus Thomas. 1907. "Iowa," in *Handbook of American Indians North of Mexico*, ed. by F. W. Hodge, pp. 612-14. Bulletin 30, Bureau of American Ethnology, Smithsonian Institution.

Eggan, Fred R. 1952. "The Ethnological Cultures and Their Archeological Backgrounds," in *Archeology of Eastern United States*, ed. by J. B. Griffin, pp. 35-45.

Flint, Richard Foster. 1957. Glacial and Pleistocene Geology. New York.

Ford, James A., and Gordon R. Willey. 1941. "An Interpretation of the Prehistory of Eastern United States," *American Anthropologist*, 43:No. 3:Part 1: 325-63.

Fox, George R. 1915. "Indian Remains on Washington Island," *The Wisconsin Archeologist*, 13:No. 4:157-76.

Gerend, Alphonse. 1904. "Potsherds from Lake Michigan Shore Sites in Wisconsin," *The Wisconsin Archeologist*, 4:No. 1:3-19.

Godwin, H. 1956. The History of the British Flora: A Factual Basis for Phytogeography. Cambridge, England.

Griffin, James B. 1937. "The Archaeological Remains of the Chiwere Sioux," *American Antiquity*, 2:No. 3:180-81.

―――― 1942. "On the Historic Location of The Tutelo and The Mohetan in the Ohio Valley," *American Anthropologist*, 44:No. 2:275-80.

―――― 1943. The Fort Ancient Aspect: Its Cultural and Chronological Position in Mississippi Valley Archaeology. Ann Arbor, Mich.

―――― 1945. "An Unusual Oneota Vessel from Minnesota," *American Antiquity*, 11:No. 2:120-21.

―――― 1946. "Cultural Change and Continuity in Eastern United States Archaeology," in *Man in Northeastern North America*, ed. by Frederick Johnson, pp. 37-95. Volume III of *Papers of the Robert S. Peabody Foundation for Archaeology*. Andover, N. H.

―――― 1949. "The Cahokia Ceramic Complexes," in *Proceedings of the Fifth Plains Conference for Archaeology*. Note Book No. 1, Laboratory of Anthropology, University of Nebraska, pp. 44-58.

―――― 1952a. Archeology of Eastern United States. Chicago.

―――― 1952b. "The Late Prehistoric Cultures of the Ohio Valley," *Ohio State Archaeological and Historical Quarterly*, 61-No. 2:186-95.

―――― 1958. The Chronological Position of the Hopewellian Culture in the Eastern United States. Anthropological Papers, Museum of Anthropology, University of Michigan. Ann Arbor, Mich.

Griffin, James B., and Albert C. Spaulding. 1951. "Valley Archaeological Survey, Season 1950: A Preliminary Report," *Illinois State Archaeological Society*, N.S. 1:No. 3:75-81.

Hill, A. T., and Waldo R. Wedell. 1936. "Excavations of the Leary Indian Village and Burial Site, Richardson County, Nebraska," *Nebraska History Magazine*, 17:No. 1:2-27.

Hurt, Wesley R. 1953. Report of the Investigation of the Thomas Riggs Site, 39HU1, Hughes County, South Dakota. Archaeological Studies Circular No. 5, South Dakota Archaeological Commission. Pierre, S. Dak.

Jenks, Albert Ernest. 1900. "The Wild Rice Gatherers of the Upper Lakes: A Study in American Primitive Economics," *Nineteenth Annual Report of The Bureau of American Ethnology*, Part 2, pp. 1013-37.

Johnson, Elden, and Philip S. Taylor. 1956. "Spring Lake Archeology: The Lee Mill Cave," *Science Bulletin*, No. 3:Part 2:1-31. The Science Museum of the St. Paul Institute.

Johnson, Thorley. 1949. "The Armstrong Site: An Upper Mississippi Site at Pepin, Wisconsin," *The Wisconsin Archeologist*, 30:No. 4:79-86.

Klages, Karl H. W. 1942. Ecological Crop Geography. New York.

Kroeber, Alfred L. 1939. Cultural and Natural Areas of Native North America. University of California Publications in American Archaeology and Ethnology, Vol. XXXVIII.

Lapham, Increase A. 1855. "The Antiquities of Wisconsin as Surveyed and Described by I. A. Lapham," *Smithsonian Contributions to Knowledge*, 7:i-xii, 1-95.

Lawshe, Fred E. 1947. "The Mero Site Diamond Bluff, Pierce County, Wisconsin," *Minnesota Archaeologist*, 13:No. 4:74-95.

Lawson, Publius V. 1903. "Summary of the Archeology of Winnebago County, Wisconsin," *The Wisconsin Archeologist*, 2:Nos. 2–3:40-85.

McKern W.C. 1931. "A Wisconsin Variant of the Hopewell Culture," *Bulletin of The Public Museum of the City of Milwaukee*, 10:No. 2:185-328.

——— 1939. "The Midwestern Taxonomic Method as an Aid to Archaeological Culture Study," *American Antiquity*, 4:No. 4:301-13.

——— 1942. "The First Settlers of Wisconsin," *The Wisconsin Magazine of History*, 26:153-69.

——— 1945. "Preliminary Report on the Upper Mississippi Phase in Wisconsin," *Bulletin of the Public Museum of the City of Milwaukee*, 16:No. 3:109-285.

Maxwell, Moreau S. 1950. "A Change in the Interpretation of Wisconsin's Prehistory," *Wisconsin Magazine of History*, 33:No. 4:427-43.

Miller, Carl F. 1957. Revaluation of the Eastern Siouan Problem with Particular Emphasis on the Virginia Branches—The Occaneechi, the Saponi, and the Tutelo. Bulletin 164, Bureau of American Ethnology, Smithsonian Institution. Anthropological Papers 49-56.

——— 1954. Pottery Types of the Over Focus, South Dakota. Prehistoric Pottery of the Eastern United States. Museum of Anthropology Ann Arbor, Michigan.

Miner, William Harvey. 1911. The Iowa. Cedar Rapids, Iowa.

Mott, Mildred. 1938. "The Relation of Historic Indian Tribes to Archaeological Manifestations in Iowa," *The Iowa Journal of History and Politics*, 36:No. 3: 227-314.

Pasco, George L., and Robert E. Ritzenthaler. 1949a. "Copper Discs in Wisconsin," *The Wisconsin Archeologist*, 20:No. 3:51-52.

——— 1949b. "Copper Discs in Wisconsin," *The Wisconsin Archeologist*, 20: No. 4:63-64.

Phillips, Philip, James H. Ford, and James B. Griffin. 1951. Archaeological Survey in the Lower Mississippi Alluvial Valley, 1940–1947. Papers of the Peabody Museum of American Archaeology and Ethnology, Harvard University, Vol. XXV.

Radin, Paul. 1915. The Social Organization of the Winnebago Indians, An Interpretation. Canada Geological Survey, Museum Bulletin No. 10. Anthropological Series, No. 5. Ottawa.

——— 1923. The Winnebago Tribe. Thirty-seventh Annual Report of the Bureau of American Ethnology, Smithsonian Institution.

——— 1949. The Culture of the Winnebago: As Described by Themselves.

Indiana University Publications in Anthropology and Linguistics, Memoir No. 2. Memoir of International Journal of American Linguistics.

Ritzenthaler, Robert E. 1953. Prehistoric Indians of Wisconsin. Popular Science Handbook Series No. 4. Milwaukee Public Museum.

Rowe, Chandler W. 1956. The Effigy Mound Culture of Wisconsin. Milwaukee Public Museum Publications in Anthropology No. 3.

Simpson, A. M. 1939. The Kingston Village Site. Archaeological Section of the Peoria Academy of Science. Peoria, Ill.

Skinner, Alanson. 1926. "Ethnology of the Ioway Indians," *Bulletin of the Public Museum of the City of Milwaukee,* 5:No. 4:181-354.

Squier, G. H. 1905. "Certain Archeological Features of Western Wisconsin," *The Wisconsin Archeologist,* 4:No. 22:25-34.

Smith, Hale G. 1951. The Crable Site, Fulton County, Illinois. Anthropological Papers No. 7, Museum of Anthropology, University of Michigan. Ann Arbor, Mich.

Steffens, D. R. 1947. "The Bear Creek Sites in Fillmore County, Minnesota," *The Minnesota Archaeologist,* 13:No. 3:52-55.

Swanton, John R. 1952. The Indian Tribes of North America. Bulletin 145 of the Bureau of American Ethnology, Smithsonian Institution.

Titus, William A. 1915. "Fond Du Lac County Antiquities," *The Wisconsin Archeologist,* 14:No. 1:1-27.

Voegelin, Carl F. 1941. "Internal Relationships of Siouan Languages," *American Anthropologist,* 43:No. 2:Part 1:246-49.

Voegelin, Ermine. 1944. "Mortuary Customs of the Shawnee and Other Eastern Tribes," *Prehistory Research Series,* 2:No. 4:227-444. Indiana Historical Society.

Wedel, Waldo R. 1942. Archeological Remains in Central Kansas and Their Possible Bearing on the Location of Quivira. Smithsonian Miscellaneous Collections, Vol. 101, No. 7.

——— 1946. "The Kansa Indians," *Transactions of the Kansas Academy of Science,* 49:No. 1:1-35.

——— 1948. Prehistory and the Missouri Development Program. Smithsonian Miscellaneous Collections, Vol. III, No. 2, Publication 3950.

——— 1949. "Some Central Plains Sherd Types from Kansas," in *Proceedings of the Fifth Plains Conference for Archaeology,* pp. 86-90. Note Book No. 1, Laboratory of Anthropology, University of Nebraska.

Whitman, William. 1937. The Oto. Columbia Contributions to Anthropology, Vol. XXVIII.

Wilford, Lloyd A. 1945. "Three Village Sites of the Mississippi Pattern in Minnesota," *American Antiquity,* 11:No. 1:32-40.

——— 1947. "A Brownsville Minnesota Collection," *The Minnesota Archaeologist,* 13:No. 2:26-32.

——— 1955. "A Revised Classification of the Prehistoric Cultures of Minnesota," *American Antiquity,* 21:No. 2:130-42.

Williams, Stephen, and John M. Goggin. 1956. "The Long Nosed God Mask in Eastern United States," *The Missouri Archaeologist,* Vol. 18, No. 3.

Winchell, N. H. 1911. The Aborigines of Minnesota. The Minnesota Historical Society. St. Paul.

Wittry, Warren L. 1956. "Kolterman Mount 18 Radiocarbon Date," *The Wisconsin Archeologist,* 37:No. 4:133-35.

Wolff, Hans. 1950. "Comparative Siouan," *International Journal of American Linguistics.* 16:61-66; 113-21; 168-78.

PART V

Language

LANGUAGE, EVOLUTION, AND PURPOSIVE BEHAVIOR

By Eric H. Lenneberg

HARVARD UNIVERSITY

Introduction

THERE IS a tendency, even among sophisticated social scientists, to regard language as a wholly learned and cultural phenomenon, an ingeniously devised instrument, purposefully introduced to subserve social functions, the artificial shaping of an amorphous, general capacity called "intelligence." We scarcely entertain the notion that man may be equipped with highly specialized, innate propensities that favor, and, indeed, shape the development of speech in the child and that the roots of language may be as deeply grounded in our biological constitution, as for instance our predisposition to use our hands. To demonstrate the logical possibility—if not probability—of such a situation is the purpose of this paper. It is maintained that clarity on the problem of the biological foundation of language is of utmost importance in formulating both questions and hypotheses regarding the function, mechanism, and history of language.

The heuristic method to be employed here will be analogous to procedures employed in studying processes too slow and inert to be amenable to laboratory experimentation, notably biological evolution. The reasoning of the argument may gain by a few general statements on this type of theory construction and by a review of the basic, modern principles evoked in current discussions of evolution.

In many scientific endeavors we are faced with the problem of reconstructing a sequence of events from scattered, static evidence. It occurs in the writing of geological, phylogenetic and cultural histories. But the treatment of geological and phylogenetic history differs from the treatment of cultural history when it comes to "explaining" the causal relationships that hold between the events.

In geology we may trace cycles of elevation of the continent, subsequent levelling by erosion, followed by sedimentation at the bottom of the sea and then recurrent elevation of the once submerged land, far above the level of the sea, resulting again in erosion and so forth. We cannot "explain" these sequences in terms of purpose, for purpose assumes a planned action, a preestablished end. Erosion, for instance, serves no more the "purpose" of establishing a balance, than the eruption of a volcano serves the purpose of making erosion possible. It is appropriate to speak about disturbed and reestablished equilibria; but the use of the word "purpose" has the common connotation of striving toward a goal and therefore, ought to be reserved for pieces of behavior that do indeed aim at a preestablished end without, however, being bound by nature to reach such end by preestablished means.

In our discussions of phylogeny we must be as careful to avoid teleological explanations as we are in the case of geological history. Yet the proverbial man in the street seems to have no small difficulties in living up to this ideal. It seems so reasonable to say that the "purpose" of his increased cranial vault is to house a large brain; and that the "purpose" of a large brain is the perfection of intelligence. We must take exception to this formulation because it implies finality in evolution or, at least, the assumption of a preestablished direction and end.[1] The geneticist looks at evolution as the interplay between a *random* process and certain constraining factors. The random process is the blind generation of inheritable characteristics, i.e., mutations, while all the constraining factors have to do with viability of the individual or the species as a whole. Of the many new traits that may chance to appear the great majority will have a lethal effect under given environmental conditions, and are thus of no consequence whatever for evolution. But occasionally there is one that *is* compatible with life and will result in perpetuation, at least over a limited period of time.

Attempts have been made to discover whether specific types of mutation could be regarded as adaptive responses of the germ plasma to environmental necessities, but I believe it is fair to say that results so far are not sufficient to conclude that there is a generally adaptive directionality in mutations. Dobzhansky states: "Genetics . . . asserts that the organism is not endowed with providential ability to respond to the requirements of the environment by producing mutations adapted to these requirements."[2]

If it is conceded that variability of inheritable traits due to mutation does not reflect direct responses to "needs," it is quite conceivable that we find characteristics compatible with life under prevailing conditions, but which have no heightened adaptive value and can therefore not be explained in terms of utility to the organism.[3] The differentiating characteristics of human races may be cases in point. The shapes of skulls or the textures of hair cannot be rated by usefulness, nor can those mutations resulting in new species without extermination or limitation of the older forms.

The problem is more complicated when we observe a long and linear evolutionary trend, for instance the more or less steady increase in the body size of a species. Such a trend is commonly explained in terms of natural selection which might be pictured in the following way: suppose the animal is so constituted that if mutations of size occur at all, a wide variety of sizes are generated randomly (there may be greater probability for certain sizes to occur than others, but we may disregard this variable in the present context since it does not alter the essential point of the argument); suppose further that the conditions of viability in this species' ecological space are such that to be below a certain size—say smaller than one standard deviation from the mean—is lethal, *sub specie aeternitatis,* because one falls victim to competing individuals. In this case there are environmental constraints on the random generation of sizes. The result is that only a limited variety of mutation is "allowed to remain"; by allowing larger individuals to occur, eliminating the smaller ones, the mean size of this species is raised and thus the ecological conditions are altered. This means that a given absolute size which some generations ago would have been "permissible" now falls into the lethal range. Other environmental changes may have a similar effect, e.g., slow changes in climate, the gradually increasing pressure of a predatory species, or the possibility of surviving on a hitherto unavailable diet.

When such a linear development occurs we say that the evolved trait is the result of adaptation to ecological conditions and in this sense we may say the trait is "useful" to the animal. I would like to stress, however, that the word "useful" (or reference to utility) must be employed with great care in this context and not without careful definition lest it be confused with purposiveness. In the example given an individual animal stays alive if it is of a certain size; it is killed (or its progeny is killed) if it falls short of the size that is criterial at the time it flourishes. Since it cannot alter its inherited size, it also cannot change its fate of being killed before maturation (or of reaching that age). Thus, no matter how "useful" it may be to be large, this state of affairs cannot be reached by the purposeful striving of an individual animal. Much less can we conceive of a super-individual entity (such as the species as a whole), to make use of this or that trait in order to "insure the continuation" of the species. Something can become useful after it has come into being by a random process; but to make systematic use of a trait, such as size, seems to imply foresight and providence not usually accorded to the driving forces of genetics.

The situation is quite different when we come to a discussion of cultural history. Here explanations in terms of purpose and utility often are in order because man indeed does have final ends in view which he strives to achieve by various means. Frequently there are even explicit criteria for usefulness in reaching a goal, such as reduction of physical effort, maximizing gratification, or introducing order and manageability into a certain situation. In the development of coin money, for instance, there may have been some trial and error in the course of history, but many changes were introduced by fiat with the explicit purpose of facilitating economic intercourse. In other words, the development of coin money is the direct result of a certain property of human behavior, namely purposiveness.

Purposiveness is a trait that is itself the result of evolutionary history, a phylogenetic development with rudimentary forms observable as far back as the invertebrates. It is the ability to strive toward a goal (say nest-building) by more than a single rigid action pattern. It is an ability to take advantage of specific environmental conditions, such as utilizing tiny shreds of newspaper in the nest-building activity. Purposiveness requires anticipation or expectancies together with flexibility in the choice of routes that lead to the goal.[4]

Man has inherited a high degree of purposiveness which is reflected in virtually all of his socio-cultural activities. In some instances he exercises this purposiveness in conspicuously creative behavior, that is, he occasionally acts in a way that is neither the result of specific conditioning, nor the direct reflection of innate mechanisms (e.g., the creation of the *Missa Solemnis*); but in many more instances man merely profits from the accumulated effect of purposive behavior of preceding generations.

It would be a mistake to think of behavior itself as either clearly instinctive and automatic or clearly purposive and varied; as either innate or acquired.[5] There are convincing data that show that innate predispositions and environmental conditions often interact so as to make it impossible to classify an action as either instinctive or learned. Beach has illustrated this beautifully. In a recent paper he states: "The maternal behavior of primiparous female rats reared in isolation is indistinguishable from that of multiparous individuals. Animals with no maternal experience build nests before the first litter is born. However, pregnant rats that have been reared in cages containing nothing that can be picked up and transported do not build nests when material is made available. They simply heap their young in a pile in a corner of the cage. Other females that have been reared under conditions preventing them from licking and grooming their own bodies fail to clean their young at the time of parturition." [6]

Many types of behavior are the result of an intricate interaction between innate predispositions and exogenous stimulation. For theoretical considerations it is often important to evaluate the role that each of these factors played in the elaboration of the final behavioral product. Such evaluation is facilitated if we have a set of criteria that will distinguish between behavior dominated by innate factors and behavior shaped predominantly under the influence of environmental factors. In an attempt to produce such criteria, we shall juxtapose two types of behavior of which we know intuitively that in the one case environmental influences are for all intents and purposes negligible, whereas in shaping the other, specific innate factors are minimal.

Bipedal Gait	Writing
Inherited. Bipedal gait cannot be taught or learned by practice if the animal is not biologically constituted for this type of locomotion.	*Acquired.* Writing does not develop automatically. It can be taught and must be learned. The biological predisposition lies in a general ability to produce and perceive iconographic representation.
No history within species. We cannot trace the development of bipedal gait from a primitive to a complex stage throughout human culture. There are no geographical foci from which cultural diffusion of the trait can be said to have emanated. All human	*Only history within species.* If we consider only those graphic symbols that serve the explicit purpose of communication, then we can arrange such graphic codes in order of efficiency. In fact, we might find cultures where even the most primitive

races have the same basic foot pattern. On the other hand, it is believed that the earliest fossil men may
have constituted an intermediary step
between the more common primate
locomotion and that characteristic of
modern man.

writing system is completely absent.
We can follow the development of
writing historically and can study the
distribution of writing geographically.
We can make good guesses as to the
area of invention and development,
and trace the cultural diffusion over
the surface of the globe.

No intra-species variations. The
species has only one type of locomotion; it is universal to all men.
(This is a special case of the more
general point that inherited traits
have poor correlations, if any, with
social groupings: Cf. black hair or
protruding zygoma.)

*Intra-species variations correlated
with social organizations.* A number
of unrelated, successful writing systems coexist. The distribution of
writing systems follows cultural and
social lines of demarcation.

*Presumption of specific organic cor-
relates.* In the case of gait we do not
have to *presume* organic correlates,
but we *know* them. However, behavioral traits that are regarded as
the product of evolution (instincts)
are also thought to be based on organic predispositions, in this case
merely on the grounds of circumstantial evidence and often in the
absence of anatomical and physiological knowledge.[7]

*No assumption of specific organic
correlates.* This point deserves
greater elaboration than is possible
in the present illustration. Of course,
we do presuppose organic development usually seen in the presence
of certain manual skill-potentials
and association-potentials.[8] However, we do not suppose that the
people in a society that does not
write lack the organic predisposition.
It is axiomatic in anthropology that
any normal human infant can develop all cultural traits in any society, given the specific cultural upbringing.

We have compared bipedal gait and writing in terms of the above
four characteristics because these seemed to be criteria capable of
revealing the fundamental differences between the innate and socio-
environmental factors. We shall now apply the same criteria to verbal
behavior in order to demonstrate that there are linguistic aspects which
might well be the result of innate predispositions, and constitute part
of our *biological* and not of our *cultural* heritage. Thus, their existence
must not be explained in terms of purpose any more than we can
explain our bipedal mode of locomotion in these teleological terms.

Phylogenetic and Sociocultural Factors in Language

The order in which the four characteristics were presented in the preceding section was dictated by theoretical importance. We shall now use the same characterizations, but this time in the order of their empirical ascertainability. It will be seen in the discussion of each characteristic that language developments always resemble in some respects our bipedal gait and in other respects the elaboration of writing. (Anthropologists and linguists are keenly aware of the role of sociocultural, environmental factors and, consequently, these will be discussed sparingly in this context.)

1. VARIATION WITHIN SPECIES. The apparently infinite variability in phonemic and syntactic structures needs no special mention. In the light of this diversification it is interesting to note that in some respects all languages are alike:

(a) *Phonology:* Speech is without exception a vocal affair and, more important, the vocalizations heard in the languages of the world are always within fairly narrow limits of the total range of sounds that man can produce. For instance we can faithfully imitate the noises of many mammals, the songs of a number of birds, the crying noises of an infant, yet these direct imitations never seem to be incorporated in vocabularies. There is onomatopoeia, to be sure, but onomatopoetic words are never faithful imitations but phonemicized expressions. This is precisely the point: all languages have phonemic systems, that is, the morphemes of all languages can be further segmented into smaller, "meaningless" components of functionally similar sounds. Words and morphemes are constituted in all languages by a sequence of phonemes. This is not a matter of definition or a methodological artifact. One can visualize a very complex language in which the symbol for 'cat' is a perfect imitation of that animal's noise (and so on for other mammals), for 'baby,' the infant's characteristic cries, for a 'shrew,' scolding yells; the size of objects could be represented by sound intensity, vertical direction by pitch, color by vowel quality, hunger by roaring, sex by caressing whimpers, and so on. In such a language we would have morphemes or words that could not be segmented into common sound elements. Most words, and perhaps all morphemes, would constitute a sound-gestalt *sui generis* much the way a Chinese character cannot be analyzed into a small set of letters.

A more familiar example of non-phonemic verbal behavior is furnished by talking birds. A parrot raised on Russian words during the first half of his life and then switched abruptly to English words is extremely unlikely to pronounce these with a Russian accent. The bird learns words like imitations of the sound-gestalt. He does not derive from his word habits an invariant phonemic system.

(b) *Concatenation:* This term denotes the phenomenon of stringing up morphemes or words into a complex sequence called phrases, sentences, or discourse. No speech community has ever been described where communication is restricted to single-word utterances, where the customary utterance would be something like "Water!" or "go," or "bird"; where it is impossible to give geographical directions by means of concatenated, independent forms. Man everywhere talks in what appears to be a "blue streak."

(c) *Syntactic structure:* We know of no language that concatenates randomly, that is, where any word may be followed by any other. There are contingencies between words (that is, languages have typical statistical structures)[9] but this in itself does not constitute grammar.[10] We can program stochastic processes into machines so that they generate symbols (e.g., words) with the same statistical properties as those noted for languages, yet these machines will not "speak grammatically," at least not insofar as they generate new sentences. It is usually assumed by linguists—and there are compelling yet intuitive reasons for this—that there must be a finite set of rules which defines all grammatical operations for any given language, and that any native speaker will produce sentences that conform to these grammatical rules, and are recognized as being grammatical by any speaker of that community. We are dealing here with an extremely complex mechanism and one that has never been fully described yet in purely formal terms for any language (if it had, we could program real or theoretical computers that could speak grammatically) and yet, we know that the mechanism must exist for the simple reason that every speaker knows and agrees with fellow speakers about whether a sentence is grammatical or not. (This has nothing to do with familiarity or meaning of an utterance. Chomsky demonstrates this convincingly by comparing the two sentences "Colorless green ideas sleep furiously" and "Furiously sleep ideas green colorless" where both sentences are meaningless and have never been heard before. Yet one is recognized as grammatical and the other is not.) Grammatical structures are as variable as speech sounds among the languages of the world, but the phenomenon of grammaticalness is absolutely universal.

(d) *Conclusion:* The importance of the universality of phonematization (evidenced by the universality of small and finite phoneme stocks); of the universality of concatenation; and of the ubiquitous presence of some grammar cannot be overestimated. Consider the vast differences in the forms and semantics of languages (making a common and focal origin of language most unlikely); consider the separation of some human races that must have persisted for many millennia; consider the physical differentiation into a number of different stocks and races. Yet everywhere man communicates in a strikingly similar pattern. There are only two kinds of conclusion that can be drawn from this situation. Either the similarities are due to the fact that by happenstance identical principles of communication have developed completely independently, over and over, hundreds of times—an extremely improbable supposition; or the universal phenomena reflect some trait related to the genetic mutation that has constituted the speciation of *homo sapiens* and are therefore of a venerable age. I should like to take the latter view and I feel strengthened in this position by the evidence that follows.

2. PRESUMPTION OF ORGANIC CORRELATES. It is generally believed that a normal child, regardless of radical background, can learn any language with which he has intensive experience, and no anthropologist, as far as I know, has ever described a speech community where children have not mastered their mother tongue by the age of four. It would appear, then, that man has the organic equipment to learn any language and that no one language calls for the presence of peculiar innate skills. No child is born to learn French rather than Chinese. Nor does it seems likely that a child who fails to learn the language of his native land, because it is too "difficult," could learn a "simpler" foreign language without trouble. So far, no one has offered objective measurements by which to rank languages in terms of absolute difficulty or complexity. Those aspects in which languages differ from one another cannot have any organic correlates. However, there is good evidence that the aspects in which all languages are alike do have an innate substratum.

(a) *Phonology:* No two languages have the same sound system, yet all languages have phonemes. Is there any evidence that the phonemic type of speech (as opposed to parrot-talk which is non-phonemic) is based on an innate mechanism? I should like to argue that there is.

Baby talk is a well established phenomenon in all western societies, and the basic phenomena seem to be the same in other cultures. (There is a conspicuous absence of reliable data on the subject; my superficial impressions have been checked with colleagues in anthropology and natives from other lands.) With the onset of speech there is a characteristic paucity of phonemes resulting in consistent "inaccuracies" for every word that is attempted. If an "l" is pronounced inaccurately it is done so for every word that contains that sound; if the distinction between "s" and "θ" is absent, there is either a demonstrably random vacillation between these sounds, or they are represented by phones that cannot be identified as one or the other adult phoneme. Jakobson and Halle[11] present evidence that the development of a phonemic system follows fairly strict developmental rules. The importance of their observations should not be underestimated. It leads us to a picture of phonemic development which is relatively independent of the acquisition of vocabulary. It is as if the child at a certain age had learned only a few phonemes with which he tried to repeat and learn any word that is worth the effort at that stage. As he learns more phonemes the repeated words approximate more and more adult English until, in the end, all phonemic distinctions are mastered and the speech exhibits adult phonemic characteristics. Note the difference between this type of speech acquisition and acquisition in the absence of phonemes à la parrot talk. The first few words that the parrot is heard to say are not baby-language. A parrot learns to pronounce one word completely and then another, and still another, and there is no gradual development of phonemic distinctions. If the development of phonemic systems were not intimately related to predispositions for neurophysiological organizations which mature gradually to a final and unalterable state, we would expect that a child could be taught to pronounce "correctly" any word in the earliest stage of word-repetition, or at least those of high frequency of occurrence, or words that are of great importance to the child would be pronounced "more correctly" than words heard less often or of no reward value. In short, there should be no consistent phoneme development that is invariable for all words at a certain stage, but in some words we should find sounds pronounced correctly that are not yet mastered in other words. If phoneme development correlates with the rate of maturation, but not with the rate of reinforcement, i.e., planned training, we may conclude that organic factors are of greater importance than "training" variables.

I would like to make a distinction here between "training" variables and environmental variables. In Beach's research on the rat's nesting behavior it was shown that maternal behavior could not be called simply "instinctive." It was necessary that some innate factors were acted upon by environmental conditions (the presence of things that could be picked up and transported) for the full blown nesting habit to develop. Thus, environmental variables entered the developmental history, but the animal was not trained in the sense the word is used in the animal laboratory.

It should be obvious that the development of a particular phonemic system depends on the language environment surrounding the child. However, the regularity and consistency (all words being pronounced by means of an invariant phonemic stock at one given stage) with which this system developed leads us to suspect that it is maturation that sets the pace, rather than reinforcement or any other training variable.

There is yet another line of evidence supporting the "organic" hypothesis of phonemic speech. There is the phenomenon of foreign accents which seems to correlate fairly well with the age during which a second language is acquired. The writer had to learn to speak Portuguese, in addition to his native German, at the age of twelve. Within a couple of years his enunciation in the second language was so close to standard Portuguese that native speakers frequently disbelieved his German origin. He was completely bilingual throughout this time. At the age of twenty-two, the writer had to switch languages once more, this time to English, and in contrast to the previous learning situation, he has spoken this new language almost to the complete exclusion of either German or Portuguese. The result is interesting. His ability to speak English has completely displaced his facility in Portuguese and even the availability of his German vocabulary seems to have suffered in the course of the years. Yet his pronunciation of English is marked by a gross and virtually insuperable foreign accent, while his German continues to sound like that of a native and his Portuguese, as evidenced in the pronunciation of isolated words, continues to have the phonological characteristics of perfect Portuguese. (Yet, the writer has heard and spoken more English during his life than either German or Portuguese.) The conclusion is that childhood and early adolescence are *physiologically* more propitious for the acquisition of phonemic structures than adult age.

As further evidence let us consider from a learning-theoretical viewpoint how, say, English pronunciation is acquired by the child. I think everyone will agree that the random babbling heard in the child of six months is quite different from the phonemes heard in the adult English speaker.[12] How did the mature speech sounds develop? Some authorities believe that adults reinforce the child's first randomly produced approximation to an adult sound, and that such reinforcement causes the child to repeat that utterance again and again; each further approximation to the adult norm is consistently rewarded, so the theory goes, and thus a perfect imitation is finally reached. Some psychologists who hold this view admit that the reinforcement is not done entirely by the training adults, but that the child soon learns to listen to his own sounds and that each time he hears himself utter sounds resembling those of the adult this constitutes an award in itself (secondary reinforcement) and he thus trains himself. But this model of speech acquisition does not explain to us why all children are for some time satisfied with an extremely inaccurate "imitation" of, for instance, mother's voice (whose speech is objectively quite different from their own) and why a child first speaks a language that is phonetically unlike anything he hears spoken around him. If the child's "final aim" were perfect imitation, why does no child ever strive to perfect *individual* phrases including intonation, timbre, and pitch pattern before going on to new speech items? It can be shown that by the age of three many a child speaks phonemically immaculate English, while not a single speech sound appears to have the same physical attributes as corresponding sounds in the adult. We have to conclude that the child must have an innate ability somehow to select out of the great variety of sounds he hears when listening to adult speech, those features or relationships that are in some sense "essential" for speech while he appears to be disinterested in the imitation of sound features that are accidental. We could hardly *teach* him speech "essentials" because we are completely unable to define, describe, or *ad hoc,* produce them. It is hard to see why a child who chose to practice completely accurate imitations of individual words, one by one, would get less reinforcement than the child who acquires a stock of speech units, each a rough approximation of the paradigm, with which he attempts to repeat any word he hears. There must be an innate predisposition for the latter strategy.

What I am saying here is actually not counter to at least one learning theorist's view. Skinner says: "Suppose we wish to teach a child to name the alligator in the zoo . . . we cannot wait till such a response appears spontaneously, and the method of progressive shaping (used by Skinner to teach a pigeon to run around a cage in a figure eight) may take too much time. If we can evoke the response as an assemblage of small echoic units never before arranged in this order, the behavior can be suitably reinforced. . . ." [13] While Skinner does not believe that the smallest unit is necessarily a phoneme (this is, after all is said and done, a purely empirical question and can only be answered by careful and sophisticated verification), it seems clear that we must assume a propensity in the child to analyze perceptually the word he hears in terms of small functional segments and to organize his own vocal behavior in terms of similar segments. The similarity is clearly not one of a sensory, acoustic nature, but has to do with phonemic function and structure. How different a child's articulation and view are from those of an adult becomes particularly obvious when we hear, unexpectedly, a child's speech over the telephone.

(b) *Concatenation:* It is well-known that at an early stage the child speaks utterances of one or two words only. He may have a vocabulary of fifty or more words before phrases of three or more consecutive words appear. There is nothing logically necessary about this. If the child can retain fifty words, it would be as logical to expect him to say ten five-word phrases; or one ten-word sentence, two five-word sentences, five three-word phrases and the rest one-word utterances. But the one-year old is unable to learn such utterances. Instead we see the phenomenon of concatenation unfold step by step, the complexity of concatenation being consistent for all utterances during that stage. A child of twelve months seems organically incapable of concatenating five words from his vocabulary, no matter how much reinforcement we give him. On the other hand, at three years this action seems to be performed in the absence of any training specifically directed towards this phenomenon. It is true that child psychiatrists are familiar with a condition known as delayed speech, often marked by monosyllabism, but the etiology of this state is usually not faulty speech training, nor does the therapy consist of systematic concatenation training. The conclusion is that a normal child begins to speak more or less automatically in longer and longer sequences.

(c) *Grammaticalness:* Unfortunately phenomena of grammar have never been studied systematically with respect to their ontogenesis. We are, therefore, reduced here to some common-sense observations. First of all, it is hard to see how syntactic operations could be the result of planned training inasmuch as the average adult speaker is completely unaware of grammatical rules. Language "training" consists of no more than to provide a language environment. The child hears a great number of sentences, some of which he may repeat and learn as stereotyped units. But even at an early stage he seems to be doing more than "play back" utterances in taperecorder fashion; he utters morpheme assemblies that he has never heard before and that are, in a sense, the expressions of correct grammatical rules (e.g., regularizing irregular verbs: I goed, buyed, swimmed; regularizing comparatives: gooder, littler, badder). Likewise, he will ask questions that he has never heard asked before ("What does blue look like from the back?"), makes statements never stated before ("This is a fire dog; I bought him for a grillion dollars"); and in general learns inadvertently to perform syntactic operations which, when formalized yield an extremely complex algebra.

Again, we have to repudiate any notion of an "instinct for grammar," particularly English grammar. There is no reason to believe that formalization of all the grammars of the world is going to yield a single algebra—at best one general form with as many special cases as there are languages. Nevertheless we must assume some general "grammatizing" ability. The fact that children can utter correct sentences, and even more, that they can "over-apply" the rules and introduce regularities that are not there, implies that they analyze heard sentences in much the same manner that the grammarian "abstracts rules" in a series of extremely laborious operations. Since no child remains at the level where only *heard* utterances are repeated, and completely automatically begins to grammatize, we may assume that the generalizing of grammatical rules reflects a constitutional propensity, which is, for instance, conspicuously absent in the parrot, and only develops in crude rudiments in severely retarded children.

(d) *Conclusion:* It is interesting to note that each of the phenomena that are characteristic of *all* languages, in spite of their formal differences, appears to have some correlations with organic maturation. Also the acquisition of these phenomena by the learning child can only be explained by assuming specialized, innate skills in addition to the socio-cultural environment.

3. INHERITANCE. The obvious experiments for testing the question, to what degree language is inherited, cannot be performed: we may not control the verbal stimulus input of the young child. However, pathology occasionally performs some quasi-experiments and, while anomaly frequently introduces untoward nuisance variables, it gives us, nevertheless, some glimpses into the immensely intricate relation between man's nature and his verbal behavior.

Just as we can say with assurance that no man inherits a propensity for French, we can say with equal confidence that all men are endowed with an innate propensity for a type of behavior which can be shaped into language with great ease (as compared to the effort needed to teach an animal to respond to an "artificial" sign, let alone to train him to emit a sign) and that this propensity is so deeply ingrained that language-like behavior develops even under the most unfavorable conditions of peripheral and even central nervous system impairment.

Language development, or its analogue, is not dependent either on the infant's babbling, or on his ability to hear. The congenitally deaf who will usually fail to develop an intelligible vocal communication system, who either do not babble or to whom babbling is of no avail (the facts have not been reliably reported), will nevertheless learn to write and to communicate efficiently through writing. Apparently even under these reduced circumstances of stimulation, the miracle of the development of a feeling for grammar takes place.

There is another important observation to be mentioned in connection with the deaf. I recently had occasion to visit for half a year a public school for the congenitally deaf. At this school the children were not taught sign language, on the theory that they must learn to make an adjustment to a speaking world, and that absence of sign language would encourage the practice of lip-reading and attempts at vocalization. It was interesting to see that all children, without exception, communicated behind the teacher's back by means of "self-made" signs. I had the privilege of witnessing the induction of a new student, eight years old, who had recently been "discovered" by a social worker who was doing relief work in a slum area. This boy had never had any training and had, as far as I know, never met with other deaf children. This newcomer began to "talk" sign language with his contemporaries almost immediately upon arrival. The existence of an innate drive for symbolic communication can hardly be questioned.

The case history of another handicapped child (soon to be published in detail) gives an illustration that true organic muteness in the presence of good hearing is no hindrance for the development of a speech comprehension ever so much more detailed than, for instance, a dog's capacity to "understand" his master. This was a five-year old boy who, as a consequence of fetal anoxia, had sustained moderate damage to the brain prenatally, resulting in an inability to vocalize upon command. When completely relaxed and absorbed in play he was heard to make inarticulate sounds which at times appeared to express satisfaction, joy, or disappointment (as when a tall tower of blocks would tumble to the floor). But the boy has never said a single word, nor has he ever used his voice to call someone's attention. I was once able, after considerable coaxing and promises of candy, to make him say "ah" into a microphone of a tape recorder. The tape recorder had a volumemeter with a large hand that would make excursions with each sound picked up by the microphone. The child had been fascinated by this and had learned to make the pointer go through an excursion by clapping his hands. After his first production of the sound "ah," he was able to repeat the sound immediately afterwards but when he came back the next day he tried in vain to say "ah," despite the fact that he seemed to be giving himself all the prompting that he could think of, like holding the microphone in both hands and approaching it with his mouth as if to say "ah." A series of examinations revealed that this boy had a remarkable understanding of spoken English; he could execute such complex commands as "take a pencil and cross out all A's in this book." "Look behind the tape-recorder and find a surprise" (this was a tape-recorded instruction delivered in the absence of the experimenter). "Point at all pictures of things to eat." He was able to distinguish pronouns ("touch my nose; touch your nose"), to show one, two, three, four, or five fingers; he could distinguish between a question and a declarative statement by nodding a yes or no answer to the question but not to the declarative sentence. He could even nod yes or no correctly when asked about situations that were spatially and temporally removed. This is discrimination learning, but on a plane that requires a much more intricate understanding and sensory organization than the simple association of an object and a sign.

These examples do not *prove* that language is an inherited phenomenon. But they do point to the degree of man's preparedness for speech, a preparedness which seems to be responsible for the universality of the speech phenomenon.

4. HISTORY WITHIN SPECIES. Languages, like fashions, have histories: but nowhere does the historical evidence take us back to a stage where the phonemic mode of vocalization was in its infancy; we have no records testifying to an absence of grammar; we have no reason to believe that there are places or times where or when concatenation had not been developed. Perhaps this ought to be attributed to the rather recent development of written records. Yet a lingering doubt remains: Writing can be traced back some five thousand years and while the earliest written records give us few clues about the language they represent, some of our linguistic reconstructions reach back to about the same era. This is a time span that comprises one tenth of the age of the earliest evidence of Levalloiso-Mousterian culture (some 50,000 years ago) and the appearance of fossil forms that may be considered to be the direct ancestors of modern man. Thus the oldest documented history of languages is short when compared with the palaeontological history of the races, but it would not be too short to demonstrate trends in the evolvement of, for instance, phonematization if this phenomenon *did* have a developmental or cultural history. We might expect that historical phonemic changes follow a general pattern, namely from a supposedly "primitive" stage to one that could be called "advanced." But the phonemic changes that we actually find—and they occur rapidly (within periods of ten to fifteen generations)—frequently, and continuously seem to follow no universal line and have, by and large, a random directionality; we cannot make predictions as to the qualitative changes that will occur in English two hundred years hence.

The concatenating phenomenon is, historically, completely static. Throughout the documented history there is evidence that concatenation must have existed in its present complex and universal form for at least some five thousand years and probably longer.

The history of syntax is the same as that of phonemes. Our oldest linguistic reconstructions are based on reliable evidence that there was an *order* in the concatenation of forms, that there were rules and regularities governing the sequences of morphemes which, from a formal point of view, cannot have been much different from grammatical processes of modern languages. We are not speaking here of specific grammars, but merely of the grammatical phenomenon as such. Syntax changes as rapidly and widely as phonemic structures but, again, we cannot discern any constant and linear direction. At the most, there is a certain cyclicity, one grammatical type perhaps alternating with another. The so-called analytical languages, such as Chinese and English, were preceded by synthetic types and there is reasonable evidence, at least for Indo-European, that the grammatical "synthesis" as evidenced in ancient Greek was preceded by a more analytic stage (inflectional endings having been derived from once independent words). We cannot be sure, however, whether synthesis *generally* alternates with analysis; indeed, the very polarity expressed by these two terms is not very well defined in grammatical theory and, therefore, not very meaningful. It is widely agreed today that no typology of modern grammars reflects stages of absolute, non-recurring grammatical development, unlike, for instance, the taxonomy of vertebrates which provides the basis for phylogenetic reconstruction. Nor do we have any means for judging one grammar as more primitive than another. In short, we cannot trace language back to an agrammatical, aphonemic, or simple imitative stage and there is, indeed, no cogent reason to believe that such a stage has ever existed.

The Role of Purposiveness in the Development of Language

We have questioned the theoretical necessity for assuming a gradual and historical development of phonemic, concatenating, and grammatical modes of communication. This does not force us into an absurd position where we have to assume an "instinct for language," let alone for specific languages. Obviously the child's acquisition of Chinese constitutes the acquisition of certain culturally evolved traits. But phonematization as such need not be thought of as a cultural achievement, need not constitute the summation of inventions, need not have resulted from a long series of trial and error learning in the field of communication. If it is said that man speaks in phonemes (i.e., automatically assigns physically differing events into a small number of functional classes), *because* this is the most efficient way of perceiving and responding, we must reply that it is "the most efficient" merely in virtue of man's biological constitution; this is equivalent to the naïve and tautological statement: "man's language is phonemic because he was made to speak in phonemes!"

To put my point more bluntly: the absolutely unexceptional universality of phonemes, the child-developmental considerations, the absence of historical evidence for the slow evolvement of phonemes lead me to propose that phonematization is a genetically inherited trait, is the reflection of an innate matrix which forces speech behavior to be of one and no other type. Similar statements may be made about concatenation and grammar.

Language development, seen in the light of modern genetics, does not call for an explanation in which each of its essential and universal traits must be considered the result of a gradual, selective, perfecting mechanism. Mutations are thought of today as sudden molecular reorganizations in the germ plasm, bringing about all at once, several simultaneous alterations in the gross anatomical structures and also in radical innate, neuronal reorganization manifested by unalterable behavioral patterns.[14] I am suggesting that genetic mutations might have brought about "in one jump" neuro-anatomical changes producing sensory and behavioral matrices for perception and communication patterns, and that these patterns are reflected in the linguistic universals that we have been discussing.

In culturally evolved and ontogenetically acquired traits purposiveness is easily detectable, particularly in man. But genetic traits transmitted by heredity are beyond the realm of purposiveness, except in vitalistic, teleological theorizing which it has been our maxim to repudiate. Language is a combination of both cultural learning and inherited predispositions and, thus, there are certain aspects of language that are the result of man's purposiveness, while there are other aspects that are not.

1. CLEARLY PURPOSIVE VARIABLES. Purposiveness is closely related to inventiveness and to the ability to introduce changes by fiat into a given behavior pattern. The most prominent area in which an individual can be an inventor and legislator with respect to language is the lexicon. He can introduce new words and outlaw others. He can change the length of words, their reference, or their meaning.

It may be possible, though there is no reliable evidence for it, that individuals may directly influence the phonetic quality of a language. It has, for instance, been said that the French and German *r* sound is the result of a fashionable affectation of the eighteenth century, particularly by the aristocracy who, supposedly, were mimicking a French monarch afflicted by an articulatory disorder. However that may be, it is certain that an individual can adopt various kinds of phonetic characteristics in order to achieve a certain end, such as creating an aura of interest about him. From this, however, it does not follow that he can alter characteristics of the phonemic structure of a language. Further, the adult has the greatest difficulty in eradicating the phonemic structure that had been "imprinted" upon him during his formative years. Nor can he increase the efficiency of phonemic transmission (for instance by extraction of redundancy and temporal compression).

Purposive behavior may also be called an individual's effort to learn a second language, or the parents' choice to teach a child this or that language.

2. DEVELOPMENTS THAT ARE CLEARLY NOT PURPOSIVE, BUT PROBABLY ARE EVOLUTIONARY PHENOMENA. First of all we must mention the impulse to talk or, in general, to communicate. From St. Augustin to Herder, language was discussed as if it were the product of invention. Some exceptionally bright individual "discovers" that his voice can serve such a purpose. Even today we find in the most sophisticated psychological treatment of language "explanations" of the ontogenetic beginning of language in terms of some pleasure-seeking or utilitarian principle. ("The child says 'dada' because this sound has become associated with the experience of mother's care"; or "he uses words in order to obtain an end"; or "he begins to use words because it reduces a feeling of helplessness.") These statements are as meaningless as a discussion of the "purpose" of bipedal locomotion.

Man is not the only communicating animal. Among insects we have the bee with an elaborate communication system with respect to locations where nectar may be gathered. Among vertebrates there are several species of birds who emit cries as territorial and warning signals. The noises of birds are particularly interesting because it has been shown that the young bird's "social" surroundings have a distinct influence on shaping his songs and cries in adulthood. Thorpe[15] has done some fascinating experiments on hand-reared Chaffinches who were visually and aurally isolated from all other Chaffinches and has demonstrated (by making and publishing spectrograms) that the innate and unlearned component of the song is of a primitive and monotonous nature, and that the typical modulations heard in the adult wild bird are variations superimposed upon the basic innate pattern. This is a somewhat analogous situation to a human infant's babbling patterns which are eventually modified by the language environment surrounding the child. But it would be a mistake to assume that the babbling is comparable to a dog's bark and that it becomes communication merely by dint of training.

There is a world of differences between the common vertebrate trait of making noises and those more specific noises that mature into communication systems. While the social influence on form and detail of communication patterns cannot be questioned, it is not at all certain —in fact it is quite improbable—that the impulse for communication itself is acquired *de novo* by each individual of the species. This thesis is not likely to be questioned in the case of bees and birds. Nor could it be seriously maintained that individuals of a species that does not innately communicate could be trained to communicate with *each other* in whatever rudimentary form we might wish. In the light of these considerations I see no need for explaining the child's first word as the result of reward or contiguity training—certainly not until the present speculative elaborations have been substantiated by empirical evidence. For the time being it seems more in line with other biological theories to regard the beginning of speech as the manifestation of an innate pattern, released and influenced by environmental conditions; and not as a purposive or pleasure-seeking piece of acquired behavior.

Phonematization, concatenation and grammatization are also beyond the realm of purposiveness. It would be foolish to say that any of these phenomena have been developed because they proved so useful. From many points of view phonemic systems are redundant and grammars cumbersome. But so far we have no means of planning and instituting more efficient languages with respect to phonology and syntax. This is not merely a social problem, it is primarily a biological one. It would be possible to decree that in a certain community every child has to learn an official language, either a *lingua franca* like Hindustani, or an artificial language like Basic English. But here we do not have departures from structure and basic nature that is common to all natural languages. For instance, the chances of succeeding in establishing a more efficient language in that "more can be said in a shorter time," are very slim because both the rate of speech production and of perception are almost certain to be controlled by deep central neurological factors. (One of the most common language disturbances in pathology is a very startling slowing down of speech and/or marked sluggishness in the perception of discourse.)[16]

3. DEVELOPMENTS THAT WERE NOT BROUGHT ABOUT BY PURPOSIVE BEHAVIOR BUT ARE NOT RELATED TO GENETIC CHANGES. Into this group fall the historical changes discussed before. Sound shifts—for instance Grimm's Law—or specific morphological trends, such as the gradual replacement of inflections by word-order cannot be discussed in terms of either purposiveness or evolutionary changes. They must be attributed to the peculiar properties of the human communication system, to inaccuracy in production of speech and limits of toleration for such inaccuracies by the listener. The exact reasons for historical change are not yet understood. Whatever they are, they seem to be quite independent of the biologically innate factors responsible for the existence of the universals discussed, because these aspects of language never seem to be affected or essentially altered in historical change.

Summary and Conclusion

The aim of this article was to distinguish between innate, biological factors on the one hand and cultural, training factors on the other which all together shape language into the mold of normal speech. It was pointed out that innate traits, both anatomical and behavioral, are evolutionary, genetic phenomena that must not be explained in terms of purpose because mutations, the basis of evolution, do not occur as a response to environmental needs or conveniences. It is of great importance to know—or to be able to make a good guess—which aspects in language are predominantly innate and which are learned, for such insight would allow us to ask appropriate questions about the significant variables in the learned aspects and would at the same time prevent us from offering unwarranted speculative explanations about the phylogenetic origin or ontogenetic beginning of speech.

In pursuit of an answer to the problem posed, the following method was employed. Two types of behavior were briefly compared with each other. One, bipedal gait, was intuitively said to be an evolutionary phenomenon; the other, writing, was regarded as cultural and learned behavior. The comparison was made in terms of four criteria which pointed out fundamental differences between the two types of behavior. When the same four criteria were applied to language it became apparent that there are at least three linguistic phenomena, phonematization, concatenation, grammatization, that have all the characteristics of inherited, innate traits and none of the learned type of behavior. The evidence used in partial corroboration of this thesis was derived from anthropological and developmental data and further support was found by considering some facts of historical linguistics and speech pathology.

As a general conclusion we may say that speech is learned in this sense: a child does not develop full-fledged language in the absence of an appropriate speech environment but even so there will be some rudiments of communication by means of symbolic representation. Under normal conditions there is a continuous interaction between innate mechanisms (or matrices for speech behavior) and the stimulating effects of the child's environment. By processes of maturation the child makes progressive use (in the sense this word is employed in genetic theory) of environmental stimulating or releasing mechanism, not because the child's "long range purpose is to speak like the neighbor" but because he is endowed with a complex series of innate, interacting behavior patterns that are elicited in a more or less automatic manner (i.e. unplanned by parents) by the speaking environment that surrounds him. The direction of speech development, the intrinsic assembly of the immensely complex speech act and speech perception, cannot, I feel, be the result of training as such, and I have tried to show we must assume some preestablished propensities, some innate patterns of organizing the speech heard, patterns that determine innately what shall constitute sensory similarity (phonemes), and patterns for coordinating the muscular activity involved in the production of speech.

This paper is in the nature of an hypothesis. No claim is made that the point is proven conclusively, but the belief is expressed that it is only through this type of consideration that a program of experimentation and empirical observations on the nature of language can be instituted and thus lead to a new approach to an age-old question.

NOTES

[1] For a philosophical treatment of this point see Herbert Feigl, "Notes on Causality," and Ernest Nagel, "Teleological Explanations and Teleological Systems" both reprinted in H. Feigl and M. Brodbeck, *Readings in the Philosophy of Science* (New York, 1953). For a bio-theoretical point of view see Ludwig von Bertalanffy, *Theoretische Biologie*, Vol. I (Berlin, 1932). For the geneticist's position see J. B. S. Haldane, *Causes of Evolution* (New York, 1932).

[2] Theodosius Dobzhansky, *Genetics and the Origin of Species*, 3d ed. (New York, 1951), p. 51. See also the same author's broad survey of the entire field, *Evolution, Genetics, and Man* (New York, 1955).

[3] See H. J. Muller, "Human Values in Relation to Evolution," *Science*, 127:625 f. (1958).

[4] W. H. Thorpe, *Learning and Instinct in Animals* (Cambridge, Mass., 1956). This is the most scholarly source on the subject of innate and acquired behavior. My entire article has been thoroughly influenced by this book.

[5] See William S. Verplanck, "Since Learned Behavior is Innate, and Vice Versa, What Now?" *Psychol. Rev.* 62:139-44 (1955), for an elaboration.

[6] Frank A. Beach, "The Descent of Instinct," *Psychological Review*, 62:401-10 (1955).

[7] For pertinent references see Anne Roe and George Gaylord Simpson, *Behavior and Evolution* (New Haven, 1958). For physiological and anatomical aspects of human locomotion see A. Steindler, *Kinesiology of the Human Body under Normal and Pathological Conditions* (Springfield, Ill., 1955), and D. J. Morton and D. D. Fuller, *Human Locomotion and Body Form* (Baltimore, 1952).

[8] See Arthur L. Drew, "A Neurological Appraisal of Familiar Congenital Word-Blindness," *Brain*, 76:440-60 (1956).

[9] George A. Miller, *Language and Communication* (New York, 1951), Chap. 10.

[10] Noam A. Chomsky, *Syntactic Structures*, in *Janua Linguarum*, ed. by C. H. v. Schooneveld (The Hague, 1957), and N. A. Chomsky, "Three Models for the Description of Language," *IRE Transactions on Information Theory*, Vol. IT-2, No. 3, pp. 113-24, n. d. I am also indebted to Chomsky for reading an earlier version of this article and for making valuable suggestions.

[11] Roman Jakobson and Morris Halle, *Fundamentals of Language*, in *Janua Linguarum* (The Hague, 1956).

[12] G. A. Miller, *Language*, pp. 144 f. presents O. C. Irwin's interesting tabular survey of the chronological emergence of consonants and vowels. The most common sounds heard in young children are rarely heard in adult English and some of the most common adult sounds are among the last to be acquired by the child.

[13] B. F. Skinner, *Verbal Behavior* (New York, 1957), p. 62 f. Despite the quoted statement, Skinner does not draw the conclusions that I have drawn. He would insist, I believe, that speech is an arbitrary modification of random babbling—an instance of operant conditioning.

[14] See Erwin Schroedinger, *What is Life* (Cambridge, 1944), Chaps. III and IV; also Haldane, *Evolution;* and Dobzhansky, *Genetics and the Origin of Species* and *Evolution, Genetics and Man.*

[15] Thorpe, *Learning*, Plates VI to IX, opposite p. 368.

[16] C. S. Sherrington notes in *Schafer's Textbook of Physiology* (London, 1900)

(!) that sectioning of the brain of a live monkey between the anterior and posterior corpora quadrigemina (this is the area of the mesencephalon, a short portion of brain between the upper brain stem and the cerebral hemispheres) abolishes reflex vocalization. Vocalization integrated at this level has a peculiar long drawn-out quality and is often accompanied by slowly executed reflex movements. There is no way of showing that the shortening of words, exhaustively discussed by George K. Zipf, makes a language more efficient or speeds the rate of communication. We can compute redundancy on a phonemic level but not on a semantic level and we shall, therefore, be unable to say whether one language communicates more "concepts" in less time than some other language, until we can quantify meaning into discrete and indivisible units. All attempts that have been made in this direction so far have been unsuccessful.

ON INTERHEMISPHERE LINGUISTIC CONNECTIONS

By Morris Swadesh

NATIONAL AUTONOMOUS UNIVERSITY OF MEXICO

General Considerations

IN THE COURSE of recent comparative studies of Amerindian languages, the author found himself not infrequently running across structural features and specific meaningful elements reminiscent of Indo-European and other Old World linguistic groups. This is not an unusual experience for an Americanist, nor was it new for the author. In the past, like many of his colleagues, he has set these similarities down as sheer coincidences, more amusing than significant, and has brought to mind various considerations to explain them in terms of chance. Of course many of the like forms involve divergent meanings which could be the product of differentiation from original identity but might also be attributed to the presence of synonyms in every language, which gives the comparativist a choice of elements among which to seek similarities. That is, if a word of one language does not match one of like meaning in a second language, one can look around among the synonyms, more or less approximate, and perhaps find one whose form is roughly comparable. Then again, when we are dealing with a number of languages on each side of the comparison, we have the combined vocabularies of all of them in which to seek supposed cognates. However, on this occasion we were engaged in a broad comparison of Amerindian linguistic stocks and had found evidence that quite a number of them may go back to a form that was common perhaps 15,000 years ago. It was striking then, that similarities with Indo-European were shown by elements and features that are very widespread in America and which seemed, because of their spread and their consistent phonology, to go back to the Ancient American protolanguage which we are reconstructing. Hence, if our reconstructions are

---

Abbreviations used in this article are as follows:

AA = Ancient American	IE = Indo-European
MP = Malayo-Polynesian	HS = Hamito-Semitic
CC = Caucassic	ST = Sino-Tibetan

Sources are listed in the section headed References. The principal sources used are Swadesh for AA, Pokorny for IE, Rivet for MP, and Trombetti for some of the others.

correct, at least in essence, these are not a mere collection of scattered coincidences from a variety of languages but similarities belonging to a single speech form. And their number seems to be too great to have resulted from the procedure of picking and choosing among synonyms. Still, this is only a tentative conclusion which we offer diffidently because the reconstruction of Ancient American is still in its beginning stages and comparable work in the Old World still more embryonic. The possible value of presenting it now is that it may stimulate the study of remote linguistic relations in both hemispheres and may add something to our orientation in an important problem of prehistory.

In the past there have been many proposals linking New World languages with certain ones of the Old World, particularly Hebrew, but also with various others. These ideas have been advanced often without evidence, sometimes with a few citations of supposedly similar words which were either too farfetched or too few to carry conviction to the critical scholar. On the other hand there have been a certain number of comparisons made by competent persons and supported by impressive bodies of data. Some of the more serious efforts are: attempts to link Eskimo-Aleutian with Ural-Altaic by various scholars, beginning with Rasmus Rask; Sapir's theory of Nadenean connections with Sino-Tibetan, backed by a large manuscript collection of comparisons though represented in print mainly by independent materials of Shafer and the present author; various comparisons of Nahua with Sanskrit and Indo-European; Rivet's attempts to relate Tsonekan with Australian and Hokan with Malayo-Polynesian. As will be seen, some of these theories can be assimilated to the one being offered here, while others would seem to represent later levels of affinity.

The reception of these theories in the scholarly world has ranged from confident acceptance to a flat refusal even to consider them based on the notion that such distant relations can never be scientifically proved. The present author does not share the pessimism of the ultra-skeptical, but on the contrary feels that if we make good use of available techniques of study and proceed systematically, in the main but not exclusively from the easier to the more difficult problems, we are certain to penetrate much farther back in time without loss of accuracy. All the published theories of interhemisphere relations, along with the present one, are not yet adequately supported, but they reaffirm the need for, and perhaps show the feasibility of, this kind of study. In time we will surely see satisfactory proof of these or other theories of interhemisphere linguistic relationships.

There is geologic and archaeologic evidence for various waves of immigration into the New World, beginning perhaps 30,000 years ago by the land bridge which connected America with Siberia when the glaciers were extensive and the sea level low; interrupted by the rising sea but renewed about 15,000 years ago with the new glaciation and the reappearance of the land bridge; again interrupted by the sea, and reopened some thousands of years later by the development of water travel. Each wave must have brought one or more languages, but not all of them survived. Some may have been swamped out by later arrivals, others lost in the face of languages already present; before disappearing they may or may not have left traces, principally in the form of loan words in other tongues. Those languages which were maintained must have in the course of time split up into dialects, which eventually developed into completely separate languages and groups of languages. All these divergent speech forms may be studied by the comparative method to reveal the number and nature of the earlier languages from which they stem.

Recent research seems to show that the great bulk of American languages form a single genetic phylum going far back in time. They show an intergraded relationship whose nature and geographic distribution are such as to suggest that the entire phylum developed out of a single speech community in America. The time depth of the complex is too great to be directly estimated by lexico-statistic methods. By noting actual measures of up to about 10,000 years in some of the component parts of the complex, we infer that the age of the group is considerably greater than this figure, and it seems possible that we are dealing with the languages derived from one brought in with the second great migration, about 15,000 years ago. Eskimo-Aleutian and Nadenean seem to stand apart, and may therefore represent later waves of migration; they would then be no more closely related to the remaining American languages than other languages still in the Old World. As for more recent movements, aside from the obvious case of Asian and Alaskan Eskimo, evidently based on a back migration from America within the last several centuries, there is no close interhemisphere linguistic relationship of the type that exists between, say, English and German, nor even one of moderate time depth, like that of English and Hittite. New languages probably came into America in the late millenia just before Columbus, but their speakers must have been absorbed into the earlier speech communities or returned to the Old World without leaving any language that has continued to modern times.

If we are dealing with a linguistic complex going back 15,000 years in America and represented by scores of distinct stocks today, it would be good to find a comparable entity in the Old World with which to compare it. However, remote comparative linguistics in the eastern hemisphere has not yet established any such ancient and far-reaching complex. There are various groups of up to about 6,000 years of time depth and various theories of more remote relationship which have not yet been sifted and coordinated. The various theories taken together may add up to the same thing as Trombetti's monogenetic explanation, whose age must be considerably more than 15,000 years. Just how much older we cannot say, but the total impression one gets from comparing modern linguistic stocks suggests that it probably does not go back to the dawn of human society and may be as recent as about 30,000 years. This would imply that the earlier development of human culture was achieved with a more primitive form of vocal communication, which may have eventually given rise to modern language but was notably different from it. The passage from elemental to true language may have spread from a single subarea within the range of the human species, carrying with it not only its structural innovations but also its specific vocabulary elements.

If proto-Indo-European stems from a dialect identical with or closely related to the one that entered the New World 15,000 years ago, it would be no farther removed from proto-Ancient American than stocks of similar time depth in America, for example Uto-Aztecan or Otian (Miwok-Costanoan). They would all be about nine or ten thousand years more recent than the common tongue. Yet to establish the connection in the Old World would be harder because in America we can go back step by step, involving each time the next most closely related groups. Some day, when the order of relationships is determined in the Old World, the stepwise comparison can be achieved there in the same way. Under present circumstances, we do not even know which Old World languages are most pertinent to the comparison. We list such similarities as have come to our attention and seem helpful, but we cannot be sure whether each comparison involves just a little more time depth than proto-Ancient American or goes back to the common period of all languages.

In judging the material presented in connection with any remote comparison, one should be forewarned against the assumption that distant relationship necessarily implies very different phonetic forms in all cases. It is true that a considerable amount of phonetic change can take place in a long time, but it does not always happen that way. Modern English has completely lost the syllable-final h which was preserved until fairly recent centuries (and is still found in the English of Scotland) but retains practically intact the old *n* of proto-Indo-European, which is therefore at least 5,000 years old. Modern Italian retains, relatively unchanged, probably more than half of the old Indo-European phonemes. In comparing Old and New World languages it would be possible to find forms that are considerably changed on both sides, if this were necessary to demonstrate the genuine character of the comparisons, but in practice it is much easier to operate in the main with the languages which have made relatively minor phonetic modifications.

The situation with regard to meanings is similar. One hundred and fifty centuries are sufficient to bring about enormous semantic changes, but in a large complex of related languages it is likely that at least a few will show values close to the original and to each other. In a study like the present one, it is convenient to cite comparisons with identical or closely similar meanings.

Phonetic Systems

A reconstruction of the consonants of proto-Ancient American gives us a fairly elaborate system of stops (including affricates), involving at least three types—simple, glottalized, and aspirate—in a number of contact positions: types *p ṗ ph* in positions *p t ȼ ƛ k q kᵂ qᵂ* (*ȼ* is *ts*-like sibilant affricate, *ƛ* the lateral or *tl*-affricate, *q* the velar *k*). Spirants include *s ʃ ł*. (*ʃ* represents the *sh*-sound and *ł* the lateral voiceless spirant, approximately *thl* in athlete). Glottal phonemes include the simple stop and spirant *ʔ h*. Sonorants are *m n l r w y*. Instead of the lateral affricate and spirant, there is equally good ground for reconstructing retroflex sounds, which may be represented by ᴛ and ʂ respectively; probably some dialects in the old days had the lateral and some the retroflex. The ancient system is fairly well preserved in some modern branches and much changed in others.

There is a general similarity between the American system and that reconstructed for Indo-European. Of the stop positions, the latter does not have the two affricates, but has five of the six others, lacking only the back labiovelar q^w. Since it has the two positions of non-labialized back palatals and one of the labiovelars, it seems possible that it may once have had the second one also, thereby completing the set; our theory (discussed below) is that the rounding "laryngeal," which gives k in syllable final in Tokarian but is otherwise reflected only in the rounding imparted to vowels, may go back to Gh^w (back velar rounded aspirate), while q^w and G^w simply fell together with k^w and g^w respectively. A retroflex series is found in the Indic branch of Indo-European, where it is generally assumed to have arisen under the influence of Dravidian languages. However, there is some basis for linking Dravidian with Indo-European on an earlier horizon. Semitic, which has also been compared with Indo-European, has a reflex stop and furthermore has a sibilant affricate like that reconstructed for proto-Ancient American and lacking in proto-Indo-European. The articulatory types usually reconstructed for Indo-European are three, p b bh. These seem to match p $\dot{p}$ ph respectively in America.

Similar consonant systems are also found in Caucassic and in Sino-Tibetan.

The vowels reconstructed for Amerindian are five or six—i u e o a and possibly i (high central unrounded). Something similar is to be found in Malayo-Polynesian and other Old World languages. Indo-European was formerly reconstructed with the same five vowels, but some scholars nowadays set up only two vowels, e o. In this new reconstruction, the vowel a is considered a secondary development under the influence of old h and x (represented in various ways, these being our preference), and the high vowels i u are merely the syllabic forms of the semi-consonants. However, it is not impossible that this two vowel system may be a simplification of an older one more like the American. Under the heading of morphology we present some evidence for an interchange of i with e and a, paralleled by interchange of u with o and a, which would bear out an original vocalic status for at least a part of the i- and u-phonemes, and a may not have had an h-influenced origin in all cases.

In proto-Ancient American we reconstruct two or more tonally differentiated accents, with a strong tendency for vowels to be lost in the syllables flanking the accented one. All this is highly reminiscent of Indo-European. The contrast between sustained or rising as against falling tone on the accented syllable is very similar between Takelma in America and Greek or Lithuanian in Indo-European. A slightly more complex tonal accent, which adds low level and rising as distinct from sustained high and which is found in some Zapotecan dialects, may be closer to the protosystem.

In establishing linguistic relationships, the phonemic system as such is usually not highly significant. Languages related at a moderate time depth may have rather different systems, and those closely parallel may be due to diffusional influences. The parallels we have noted in their totality seem great enough to indicate a historic connection, possibly that of common origin or possibly that of having once belonged to an interconnected culture area.

Morphologic Structure

A picture of proto-Ancient American morphology, derived from a consideration of recurring structural features in a large number of stocks, follows (Swadesh, 1958, p. 51):

It appears probable that use was made of the morphological techniques of root composition, the addition of prefixes and suffixes, reduplication and the alternation of vowels and consonants. The ancient language would have been considerably inflected, distinguishing categories like the following: singular, plural and perhaps dual number; at least masculine and feminine gender; the form of numbered objects, as round, long etc.; exclusive and inclusive in addition to the normal three persons; near or distant location; verbal aspects like aorist, durative and repetitive; such voices as passive and causative; augmentative and diminutive. Some of the categories may have been expressed by a variety of elements, in some cases slightly different, in other cases entirely so, in a manner similar to Latin inflexions.

Some American stocks have preserved large portions of this older structure, others have departed from it in many details. Indo-European coincides almost as well as the most conservative American stocks. A few features lacking in Indo-European are present in Malayo-Polynesian and other Old World languages. In many details the similarities are quite specific. For example, Tubatulabal prefixation of the stem vowel is reminiscent of the Greek "augment" used for the same function. Vowel mutation from front to back in the formation of nominal and verbal derivatives in Yokutsan parallels Indo-European ablaut.

American-style consonant and vowel interchange to indicate diminutive and augmentative has not previously been recognized in Indo-European reconstruction, but a reexamination of the data reveals many irregularities and variant roots with similar meanings, which appear to be traces of an old alternation of the same kind. The symbolism in America is still an active process in Chinookan and Sahaptian in northwestern North America, in Totonacan and Huave in Mexico, and perhaps in Quechua in South America. Remnants of it are found in any number of American stocks. As reconstructed for proto-Ancient American, the interchange among vowels shows mid-vowel e or o as the basic grade, high vowels i u for diminutive, and low vowel a for augmentative. Consonant interchange is both positional and articulatory. Under the former head we have three-way sets like S s $ł(ṣ)$, n l r, and t e $ƛ(\tau)$ for normal, diminutive and augmentative; and the two-consonant sets q k and q^w k^w for normal and diminutive. It is possible that in the k-series, too, there were three points of variation, k $ķ$ q and k^w $ķ^w$ q^w, but that the evidence is obscured by the falling together of the first and third or of all three in practically all of the component stocks. The application of the symbolism is subtly complex, with special turns like the play of diminutive and augmentative suffixes in Spanish, rather than like a strict inflection. One or both consonants of a stem may be modified in position or in articulation, or in both ways, and the vowel may or may not be changed. All the phonemes may be changed in the same direction, diminutive or augmentative, or one may be diminutive and the other augmentative, giving a blend; this gives different degrees and nuances, so that, for example, with the same basic stem one can express 'man,' 'little man,' 'large man,' 'old man,' 'little old man,' 'boy,' 'small boy,' 'large boy.' Certain stems relate to size in the abstract, and are used in specifically diminutive and augmentative forms to express small and large; the same stem with a blend of symbolism may express the idea of *long*, that is, large in one dimension and small in the other. The system may be used with verbal as well as nominal and adjectival stems.

Such a diminutive-augmentative symbolism does not occur as such in Indo-European, but there is evidence suggesting that it may have existed in an earlier pre-Indo-European stage. The interchange of r and l in familiar name forms in English and Spanish appears to be the same phenomenon as the Ancient American symbolism, for example in English Sal or Sally for Sara, Hal for Harold, Molly for Mary; in Spanish, Lico for Frederico, Lalo for Eduardo, Lola for Dolores. If this alternation can be shown to be archaic, it might be possible to relate it to Ancient American. Aside from this phenomenon, Indo-European vocabulary has many cases of unexplained alternation among precisely the phonemes that belong to diminutive-augmentative sets in America, except that types *b* and *bh* take the place of *ṗ* and *ph*. On the semantic side, there are any number of instances in Indo-European of the notions of large and small being expressed by similar roots, often with differences paralleling the American symbolism, sometimes without any difference in form, occasionally with what seems to be the contrary forms in the symbolic series. This state of affairs may reflect an old symbolic system which went out of service before proto-Indo-European times, leaving at first clear traces which were subsequently mutilated by the effect of sound changes and the use of old forms in different contexts without adjusting the phonemes to the implications of the context. Similar effects of obscuring the archaic symbolism are to be found in many American stocks, even though the old alternations still exist in sister stocks and even though there is a scattering of evidence in all the groups which confirms the reconstruction.

In many American stocks, the falling together of *r* and *l* confuses the picture of the old symbolism. This may also have happened in Indo-European in certain positions, possibly in the position before voiceless consonants. Vowel changes have also overlaid the old scheme both in certain American languages and in Sanskrit, with the falling together of *e o a*, or in Germanic, with the falling together of *e* with the vocalization of *y*. However, there is evidence that diminutive *i* may have been kept apart from the vocalization of *y* in Indo-European and only later developed to *e* in some of the branches, while eventually coinciding with *y* by receiving consonantal treatment in others. A structural circumstance must also have contributed to the confusion of diminutive and augmentative consonants, namely the possibility of adding suffixes of diminutive and augmentative meaning to the roots. When this took place after the quiescence of the alternation one could thereby obtain diminutive consonants in words implying large, and vice versa. With these explanations made, we now cite some of the examples of Indo-European forms which seem to bear out our hypothesis.

In giving forms from attested languages, we use normalized transcriptions for Sanskrit, Greek, Russian, and Latin, but traditional spellings in the other cases. Double letters represent long vowels; the two accents are differentiated by writing the acute sign over the first vowel for the falling and over the second for the rising. A rough separation is made into the diminutive and augmentative grades, blend forms being listed with the latter. Within each set semicolons set off series having more or less the same protoreconstruction.

*min/mil/ml/mel/mol 'little, small, soft'
Latin *minor*, German *minder* 'lesser'; Greek *minuthóo*, Latin *dee-minuti-re* 'diminish,' Latin *minutia* 'small thing,' French *mince* 'thin'; Russian *mᵞenᵞ-ſiy*, Tokarian B *men-ki* 'less'; Lithuanian *meñkas* 'insignificant'; Old Irish *menb*, Armenian *manr* 'small,' Sanskrit *manáak a* 'little,' Hittite *maninkuantes* 'short'; Latin *mollis* 'soft'; Russian *mᵞíliy* 'kindly,' English *mild*; Russian *málᵞenkiy* (from *ml*, with subsequent insertion of vowel), English *small* (*mol*); Latin *melior* 'better'; Sogdian *murzak* 'short' (normal change from *l* to *r*).

mn/men/man/mr/mar/maar 'much, large, strong,' often with augmentative suffix *-gho*
Russian *mnogo* 'much'; Gothic *manags*, English *many*; Old Irish *menicc* 'frequent, abundant'; Lithuanian *minià* 'multitude'; Irish *mor* 'many,' Latin *multus* 'much' (perhaps *mrtos*, with subsequent change of *r* to *l* before voiceless consonant), Greek *mála* 'very' (perhaps *mrha*), Tokarian *mírta·r* 'long.'

mik/mk/meeg 'small'
Greek *mikrós* 'small, short,' Latin *maker*, German *mager* 'thin'; English *meek*.

moq/maq/maaq/magh 'large, strong'
Old Irish *mochtae* 'large'; Greek *makros* 'long'; Hittite *makkes*, Latin *magnus* (perhaps voicing before *n*) 'big,' Russian *moc* 'power,' *moჳno* 'possible'; Lithuanian *mokë'ti* 'be able'; Sanskrit *maghá*, Gothic *magan*, *mahts*, English *might*, German *macht* 'power'; Tokarian A *ma·ka* 'much,' Lithuanian *magulas* 'numerous,' German *vermögen* 'power, capacity, possession.' *meG* perhaps originally 'biggish' (*G* augmentative by position, diminutive by type): Gothic *mikils*, Greek *mégas*, Armenian *mec* 'big.'

gl/gel/gol/gur 'cold, freeze, ice'
Latin *glakiees* 'ice'; English *chill*; German *kalt*, English *cold*, Tokarian *kuraſ* 'cold.'

qen/qan/qal/ghal/ghar 'hot'
Sanskrit *cándrah* 'brilliant'; Latin *kandee-re* 'be in flames,' *kandeela* 'candle'; Latin *kalidus* 'hot', German *lau* 'tepid' (*hlaw*), English *scald*; Irish *gealach* 'moon'; Irish *grian* 'sun,' Sanskrit *háras* 'heat.' English *kindle* perhaps from *Gen*. *xar/xal* with secondary meanings: Hittite

harkis, Tokarian *aarki,* Greek *alphos,* Latin *albus* 'white,' Greek *argos* 'brilliant,' Latin *argutus* 'clear,' *argentum* 'silver.'

The use of diminutive for 'cold' and augmentative for 'hot' is also found in America, likewise forms combining diminutive and augmentative grades (see pp. 918-19).

*gl/gil/kin 'small, young, child'

German *klein* 'small'; German *kind,* English *child.* Perhaps, based on the last meaning, compare **gen* 'be born.' **gen* 'knee' may be based on 'little hill' or 'little head,' cf. **xar* in Hittite *harsan* 'head.'

*Ger/qer/ghal/ghr/xal/xar/xan 'large, strong, old' and secondary meanings

Greek *géroon,* Sanskrit *járant-,* Armenian *cer* 'old'; Latin *kreskoo* 'grow,' *krassus* 'fat'; Cymbrian *gallu,* Breton *gal,* Lithuanian *galiu* 'power,' Russian *golᵛem* 'powerful'; German *grosz,* English *great,* German *greis* 'old man'; Latin *altus* 'high,' German *alt,* English *old,* Greek *ana* 'up,' Gothic *ana,* English *on,* Latin *antikᵂus* 'ancient,' *ante* 'before,' Latin *anus,* German *ahn-frau* 'old woman'; Hittite *halanta/harsan* 'head.' In still more variant meanings note **qordo* in Greek *kórdus* 'heap'; **ghordho* in Latin *hordus* 'horde,' Cymbrian *cordd* 'multitude'; **qerdho* in English 'herd'; Tokarian *kal-* 'stand.'

*tin/tun 'thin'

Latin *tenuis,* Russian *tonᵛkiy,* English *thin.* **dl* in Russian *dlᵛíniy* 'long'; **dol* in English *tall.*

*(s)tar/staar/str 'thick, strong'

Russian *tolstóy* 'thick,' *stáriy* 'old,' German *stark,* English strong.

Additional examples will be found in the material of the next section.

Sets of variants for back palatals in Indo-European turn out to include two "laryngeals." One is evidently the protophoneme that appears in Hittite as *h,* and which is reflected as *a*-vowel timbre in other languages. The other is recognizable by *o*-vowel timbre in most of the languages, but gives *k* in syllable final in Tokarian. We represent these as *x* and *xᵂ* respectively for proto-Indo-European, because their reflexes are so far removed from the *Gh* and *Ghᵂ* which one would expect from the parallel of the other series. In the material already cited, and in the lexical comparisons below, there is hardly a root beginning in the *k*-consonants which does not have a parallel with *x,* and the same holds true of *kᵂ* and *xᵂ.* Thus, the phonetic rhyme and semantic similarity of English *hear* and *ear* is found to correspond to the consonant grades, normal *k* and augmentative x, of one root, the first from *kaws and the second from *xaws (see pp. 919-20). Similarly, English wheel and Greek pólos ('axle') from *kʷel/kʷol may be related to Latin orbis ('orbit') from *xʷer. Additional examples, not otherwise listed in the material, include: German hasz and English hate from *kʷod, Latin odium from *xʷed; German gut and English good from *ghʷood, Frankish al-ood 'property' from *xal-xʷood ('all-goods'); Russian kostʸ 'bone' and Latin kosta 'rib' from *kʷost, Greek osteon, Sanskrit ásthi and Latin os (ossis) 'bone' from *xʷost; Latin kʷattwor, Greek tettares and Sanskrit catwaarah 'four' from *kʷektwoo-, Latin-Greek oktoo and Sanskrit aſtaa 'eight' from *xʷektoow; perhaps Sanskrit gaaúh, Greek bous, German kuh, English cow from *gʷoow, Latin owis, Sanskrit áwih, Greek ois 'sheep' from *xʷow.

Besides the question of phonologic consistency we have to consider, on the side of meaning, whether a diminutive-augmentative contrast is reflected in each case. This seems to be directly contradicted by diminutive consonants for 'cow' and augmentative for 'sheep.' The apparent contradiction might possibly be due to separate usages derived from the different areas in which each animal was first domesticated: those who named the sheep may have compared it with the dog, apparently called *kʷow with normal-grade consonant, as suggested by Greek kunos, kuoon, German hund, English hound, Vedic ſúnah (apparently kʷ was delabialized in Indic when closely followed by w, cf. also Sanskrit aſwah, Latin ekʷus 'horse' from *Pekʷwos, possibly Pe-kʷwos with the same root as 'sheep,' 'cow,' etc.; Greek híppos has unexplained h and vowel i and may represent a compound *sey-kʷwos); those who called the cow *gʷow, with diminutive consonant, may have been comparing it to the horse.

Evidence for an old diminutive-augmentative symbolism in pre-Indo-European may be one of the soundest structural parallels in support of genetic relationship with Ancient American. A possible rebuttal is that such associations of sound and meaning are a matter of common psychological tendencies in all human beings, but the fact that so many stocks in America and Indo-European itself have so far departed from the symbolic norms detracts from this argument. At last analysis the demonstration depends on the number and quality of specific resemblances in the application of the symbolism, and the joining of this evidence with the remaining structural and lexical parallels.

Along with its value as evidence of genetic unity, the phonologic interchanges bring complications to the comparative effort. For, they imply the propriety and the necessity of recognizing multiple equivalences among the phonemes; for example, the reflexes of *n* in one set of languages must be compared not only with those of *n* in the next group but also with those of *r* and *l*. This makes things easy for the careless comparativist, who is concerned only with piling up presumed cognates, but puts an additional burden on serious comparison. It is correct to accumulate as many similarities as possible, but eventually these have to be analyzed piece by piece and assessed as to the extent to which they contribute to proving relationship.

Lexical Comparisons

We present here a sampling of comparisons among specific meaningful elements. Each entry begins with a reconstruction in neutral form, that is non-diminutive and non-augmentative, but it is understood that every such form may imply one or more diminutive-augmentative variants and blends. A reconstructed meaning is given. Forms are cited from several American stocks, from Indo-European, and occasionally from other Old World groups. To simplify the presentation we give preference to forms that involve little phonologic, morphologic, and semantic complication. In some instances it is convenient to give a reconstructed protoform for a stock, with or without specific examples from component languages; if a form is found without change in a majority of the member languages, it is given without the asterisk conventionally used in citing reconstructions. In Malayo-Polynesian particularly we have used the device of giving a generalized or reconstructed form in order to avoid long listings of individual language citations, already conveniently assembled in Rivet's work. Only occasionally do we offer explanations of phonology and morphology, but of course we have always tried to bear in mind the pertinent guiding rules.

Pronoun elements, given first, need to be judged in the light of their morphology in the languages being compared. The basic elements are short affixes used with roots. Independent personal pronouns may consist of the affix attached to demonstrative roots, either all with the same one or possibly the first person with the near demonstrative, the second with the detached, and the third with the distant. As a result of this fact, along with later phonetic reduction, old demonstratives may take on the value of pronouns. There must have also been not one set of pronouns but two or more with different syntactic implications, such as subject or object or noun possessive, and there must have been gender distinctions at least in second and third persons, but, in the course of time, changes in usage caused eliminations and substitutions in different stocks. These considerations account for the existence of variant forms for expressing the pronouns and make it difficult to determine the exact function of each reconstructed element.

Near and far demonstratives at various times in the course of all the languages evidently were made by varying the vowels while keeping the consonants, e.g. Indo-European *ti 'this,' *to 'that.'

*(ʔe)ne 'I'. Often *(ʔi)ni, that is with vowel of near location.

AA Chinookan n- 'I, my'; Penan Sahaptian ʔini-, Klamath nu 'I'; Otian Miwok ka-ni 'I'; Mixean n- 'I, my'; Mayan -n, Huastec nanaa 'I'; Kanpanan Guambia na 'I'; Mapuche ni- 'I'; Algonkian ni- 'I'; Utaztecan ne/no/ni/na 'I, me, my.'

IE *ne 'we.'

MP Malayan *i-na(w) 'I'; Polynesian *na-ku 'my' (for the second syllable compare IE *ʔe-go 'I,' Germanic mi-k 'me,' Basque ni-k, and emphatic suffixes perhaps based on *ko and *kho in many American languages).

Basque ni(k) 'I'.

HS Hebrew ʔanii, Hausa ni, Somali-Galla ʔáni 'I.'

Note that demonstratives of the type ni/na are widespread in America and in other parts of the world. In Indo-European we find Hittite ana, Tokarian A an, Russian on 'that one, he,' and with l in Latin ille 'that.' A demonstrative ni with the n-stem and the vowel of near location could easily have become the expression for first person, without preventing other demonstrative formations, including IE *mi for first person singular and *wi, given below. On the other hand, the same roots could have been used with other vowels for the other persons. Once the pronoun becomes fixed, the vowel itself may be changed.

*ma/mu 'thou, thy.' Variants with i-vowel may be secondary.

AA Chinookan m(a)- 'thou, thy'; Penan Takelma-Kalapuya-Yokuts ma, Wintun-Maidu mi, Sahaptian ʔimi-, Molale ʔims, Klamath mi- 'thou, thy'; Otian mi 'thou'; Mixean mih 'thou'; Totonacan mi 'thou'; Misupan man 'thou'; Sonchonan Tsonekan ma, Moseten mi 'thou'; Utaztecan ma/mo/me 'thou, thy'; Hokan *ma/me/mi 'thou, thy.'

MP Melanesian *mu, Malay-Bugis mu, Dayak ma 'thou.'

*ta/tu 'thou, thy.' Variants with i-vowel may be secondary.

AA Yakonan Alsea -t 'thou'; Penan Takelma -ta-, Santiam ti- 'thou,' Santiam tup- 'ye'; Totonac -t(i) 'thou,' -tit 'ye'; Mayan *-te 'thou, thy,' Huastec tataa 'thou'; Tarasco thu 'thou,' -te 'thy' (with kinterms); Zuñi to 'thou'; Yamanan Alakaluf tawł 'thou.'

IE *te(w) 'thou'; Russian -tʸe, German -t, Sanskrit -dhwee 'ye' (verb ending).

HS Hebrew ʔataa 'thou.'

Uralic *-t 'thou, thy.'

Eskimo-Aleutian -t 'thou, thy.'

CC Avar dun, Dargua du, Kvarshi do 'thou.'

*(ʔe)wi 'me, I.' Perhaps originally suffix.

AA Tsimshian -u 'me'; Penan Takelma wi- 'my' (with kinterms), Santiam -w 'me'; Totonac -w(i) 'we'; Mayan Yucatec ʔu-, Quiche w- 'me'; Xilenca Lenca o-no, Chilanga u-na 'I'; Mataguayan Mataco o- 'I, me'; Jicaque hawm 'I'; Chitimacha ʔuʃ 'we'; Atakapa wi 'I'; Siouan *win 'I.'

IE Hittite wees, German wir, English we; Sanskrit -wa 'we two' (verb ending). Note that the stem *we/wo in other branches expresses second person, e.g. Latin wos, Russian vi 'ye.'

*te demonstrative.

AA Tsimsian t- 'he,' -t 'him'; Yakonan tey, Siuslaw ta 'this', Hanis tlte, Siuslaw tu, Alsea ʔantu 'that'; Penan Takelma ʔitaka, Yokutsan Tha 'that'; Mixean Copainalá teʔwi 'that'; Totonac taʔnu 'there'; Yuracare ati 'he, that'; Sonchonan Ona ta 'he'; Mataguayan Mataco tah 'this, that'; Mapuche twey 'that'; etc.

IE *ti/te/to demonstrative, *-tey third person of verb.

Basque d- 'he.'

*-ne nominalizing suffix, forming nouns of agent, instrument, adjectives, and infinitives.

AA *-ne/-le/-re. Yakonan Siuslaw -ni agent, Hanis -nu infinitive; Penan Takelma -n/-l nominalizer, Yokutsan -n action, substance, place, Molale -ni agent, Klamath -(ha)n participle, -li adjectival, Maidu -n infinitive; Otian Tuolumne -na instrument, -no season, Mutsun -n action, Totonac -n(iʔ) nominal and adjectival; Mayan -l nominal and verbal, -ba-l instrument, -ni-k present intransitive participle; Kanpanan Cholon -n infinitive; Quechumaran Quechua -*ni*, Aymara -*ñi* infinitive; Tarasco -*ni* infinitive, -*ri* agent, instrument; Misupan Misquito -*an* past participle; Mapuche -*n* infinitive.

IE *-*no*- infinitive, past participle, adjectival, with different functions in different divisions of the stock.

MP -*n*(*a*) adjectival.

*-*te* nominalizing suffix, similar in function to the preceding.

AA Penan Sahaptin -*ti* infinitive, nominalizer; Otian Mutsun -*ti* adjective and agent formative, Tuolumne -*to* place, -(*ma*)*ti* 'such a one' (forming nouns from adjectives), -*ti* diminutive nominalizer, -*Ti* augmentative nominalizer; Totonac -*t*(*iʔ*) nominalizer; Tarasco -(*pi*)*ti* adjectival, -*kata* past participle, -*ta* nominal; Sonchonan Moseten -*t* noun masculine; Utaztecan -*ta*/-*te* noun absolute.

IE *-*to*- past participle, *-*tey*-/-*tew*- infinitive.

*(*ʔe*)*ye* 'go, travel.'

AA Tsimsian *ye*- 'go'; Mixean *yoʔoy*- 'go'; Misupan Misquito *ya-man* 'foot,' *ya-bal* 'road'; Mapuche *yaw*- 'go'; Yamanan Yamana *koya* 'foot'; Coahuiltecan Comecrudo *kiye* 'go'; Wakashan Nootka *yaę*- 'go.'

IE Hittite *iya*, Latin *ii-re*, Sanskrit *yaa*-, Prussian *eeyt*, Tokarian *ya*(*a*)- 'go,' Lithuanian *yó*- 'ride,' Russian *yexa*- 'travel.'

Basque *yoan*, *ibilli* 'go.'

yew 'good, young.'

AA Misupan Esmeralda *yawa*, Misquito-Sumu-Ulua *yam* 'good,' Paya *yawiya*, Cacaopera *aydika*, Misquito *ayhki-ka* 'righthand'; Mataguayan Mataco *yuy* 'sharp'; Yuracare *yetta*, *emeheme* 'good'; Sonchonan Moseten *hem*, Tehuelche *hemso* 'good'; Wakashan Nootka *yuuł*- 'gentle, slow.' Paez *ew* 'good' may be from this root or from *(*ʔe*)*wen*, see below.

IE Latin *yuwenis*, Cymbrian *ieuanc*, Breton *youanc*, Lithuanian *yáunas*, Gothic *yungs* 'young'; Latin *yuus* 'right,' Sanskrit *yoof* 'benefit.'

wen 'desire, want to'; 2. 'satisfied, good.'

AA Penan Gashowu -*wali*, Santiam *hulyam*, Nezperce *wewelu*-, Maidu *wene* 'want,' Klamath *swanwi* 'in love'; Misupan Misquito *wlihka*- 'desire, want to.' 2. Yakonan Hanis *ʔan-wen* 'bad (not-good)'; Penan Molale-Sahaptin *wene* 'good'; Otian San José *welwel* 'good'; Mixean Popoluca *wił* 'good'; Mayan Huastec *winat* 'excellent,' Tzeltal-Tzotzil -*waʔel*,

Yucatec *winab* 'righthand'; Quechumaran Aymara *wali* 'good'; Tarasco *hulim* 'righthand'; Utaztecan Nahua *wel* 'good.'

IE **wel* 'want to, desire,' e.g. Latin *wole-re*, English *will*, Russian *vol^ye* 'desire' (noun), German *wahl* 'choice'; **wen* 'love, desire,' e.g. English *want*, Sanskrit *wanca-*, German *wünschen*, English *wish*, Latin *wenus* 'love, the Goddess of love,' *wenaa-re* 'hunt.' 2. English *well*; German *wonne* 'contentment'; perhaps Greek *eu-* 'good'; **wer* 'true, believe,' e.g. Latin *werus* 'true,' Russian *v^yer^yit^y* 'believe,' English *verily*.

Basque *ona* 'good.'

Uralic Finnish *onni* 'happiness,' Uiger *ona-* 'be happy.'

*wen 'round, ball, turn, return'; 2. 'go, travel, wander.'

AA Penan Santiam *wilwilo*, Atfalati *lulu*, Molale *Pitweliki* 'round,' Santiam *wiyat*, Molale *welimk* 'go around,' Patwin *were* 'year'; Otian Clearlake *po-wolo* 'round' (from **pol-wolo* 'full-round'), *wali* 'year'; Totonaco *ʃwiʔlaʔqa* 'rotate'; Mayan **wol* 'round,' Yucatec *walak̓*, Huastec *wilk̓inal* 'turn,' Yucatec *wowol* 'ball,' *-wol* 'round things'; Tarasco *wiriwirí-ṣi*, *wirí-piti* 'round'; Huave *pawal/piwil* 'round,' *wanean* 'turned'; Misupan Misquito *wilwa-* 'rotate,' *mlaka-* 'return, fold,' *walpa* 'stone,' Cacaopera *wara-* 'head'; Mataguayan Mataco *wela* 'moon.' 2. Yakonan Alsea *wil-* 'go,' Hanis *heʔwelc*, Miluk *hewel* 'road'; Penan Sahaptin *wina* 'go,' Klamath *swina* 'race,' Takelma *wiliw*, Nezperce *wlek*, Sahaptin *wayxt-* 'run,' Maidu *wileklék̓en* 'fast,' Nomlaki *wina*, Nisenan *hune* 'fly'; Otian Mariposa-Tuolumne-Amador *wiin-* 'go,' Santa Cruz *wina* 'fly'; Totonac *ƛaaʔwan-* 'go'; Mayan Chontal *wile*, Chol *wehlal*, Tzeltal *wil* 'fly'; Kanpanan Guambia *uni-* 'go'; Tarasco *wana-* 'go', *wiriá-* 'run'; Zuñi *wan* 'run to'; Mataguayan Mataco *welek* 'go.'

IE Latin *wolwe-re*, Greek *eluoo*, Old German *wellan* 'rotate,' Greek *heliks* 'spiral,' German *welle* 'wave'; English *wallow*; Sanskrit *wárta-*, Latin *werte-re* 'turn,' German *werden* 'become,' Latin *werge-re* 'incline,' English *wriggle*. 2. English *walk*, *wend*, *wander*.

MP **woli/huli* (from **hewli*) 'turn'; Java *vorivori* 'round'; MP **olu* 'head.' 2. Melanesian **wan* 'go.'

*wen 'person (human being), man, woman'; diminutive 'child,' sometimes 'woman.'

AA Penan Wintun *win-tuun*, Patwin *pat-win* 'person,' Sahaptin *ʔwinʃ*, Nisenan *win* 'man,' Klamath *wewens*, Nezperce *hac-wal*, Sahaptin *ʔas-wan* 'boy'; Mixean Copainalá *win* 'person, body'; Mayan **winaq* 'person, man'; Quechumaran *warmi* 'woman'; Tarasco *wali(ti)* 'woman,' *ei-were-ti* 'man,' *waei* 'child'; Yamanan Alakaluf *walk* 'woman,' Yamana *-wala* 'man,' *win* 'person'; Misupan Misquito *waynka* 'male'; Xilenca Lenca *wana* 'person'; Sonchonan Moseten *wenci* 'husband'; Mapuche *wenTi* 'man,' *mawon* 'woman,' *weñi* 'child'; Coahuiltecan Cotoname *wawnahe* 'man.'

IE Latin *wenetus* name of an ancient IE-speaking people, German *wende* name of a Slavic group within Germany; Tokarian *onk* 'man,' English *wench* 'girl'; Sanskrit *wrsan*, Greek *arséen* 'male,' Latin *wir*, Sanskrit *wiiráh*, Gothic *wer*, 'man,' German *wer(wolf)*, English *were(wolf)* 'man(wolf),' English *world*. Sanskrit *wrsan* and Greek *arséen* necessarily and Gothic-English-German *wer* probably come from a root **wer*. Latin *wir* and Sanskrit *wiiráh* seem to be based on **weyr*. However, this form may derive from the first as follows: the basic form of the root is **wen*, with the meaning 'person'; in the time of active diminutive-augmentative symbolism, **wer* augmentative meant 'man'; the blend form **wir*, with diminutive vocalism, meant 'little man' or 'old man,' and is the basis of the Latin; the long vowel of Sanskrit either goes back to a pre-Indo-European lengthening of the diminutive vowel to add to the diminutive effect, or is based on a later interpretation of **wir* as containing vocalized semiconsonant, or, in other words, **weyr* would be a reshaping of **wir*; the reduced grade of **weyr* can give either long or short vowel in Sanskrit according to rhythmic conditions.

MP **wina/wani* or compound formation **hina-wina/wani-hina* or re-duplication *waniwini* 'woman.' The specific variations in the various languages suggest a series of variant formations involving combinations of two roots, perhaps **wina* 'person' and *hina* 'female.' Also Iai *wana-kat* 'child,' North Melanesia *mwana* 'boy', *wene-liki* 'small.'

Basque *urricha* 'woman,' *arr* 'male,' *anre* 'lady.'

HS Somali *war*, Kafa *uro* 'man,' Somali *óori*, Kafa *ure* 'lady.'

*pew(n) 'burn, fire, red.'

Misupan Misquito *pawta*, Sumu *kuhpaw* 'fire,' Sumu *bawko* 'star,' Misquito-Taguasca *paw*, Ulua *puk-*, Matagalpa *pu* 'red', Misquito *pura* 'sky'; Penan Wintun-Patwin *poo* 'burn'; Mayan Pokomchi *poh*, Chorti *kapu* 'moon,' Chontal *pule* 'burn'; Quechumaran Quechua *pura* 'full moon,' *puncay* 'day'; Jicaque *pul* 'star'; Tucanoan Yupua *piiri* 'fire.' Some of these forms may belong with the next root.

IE *pewoor/pewoon 'fire': Armenian *hur*, Greek *puúr*, Umbrian *pir*, Prussian *panno* (*pwon-u* or with next root), Tokarian A *por*, Tokarian B *puwar*, German *feuer*, English *fire*; Gothic *foon*, German *funke*, Icelandic *funi* 'spark.' The word for 'fire' in Hittite is transcribed *pahhuwar*, but perhaps the reading should be *phuwar*, thus showing augmentative grade of the initial stop.

pen 'bright,' 'glow,' 'burn,' 'fire,' with many secondary meanings, including 'hot,' 'sun,' 'moon,' 'white,' 'red,' etc. Used in various diminutive and augmentative grades more than in the basic form, as *pel/p̓el/per/ phel/per/p̓er/pher*, which in IE give respectively *pel/bel/ber/bhel/per/ber/ bher*.

AA Tsimsian *pyelst*, Nisga *plist* 'star'; Penan Takelma *p̓ii* 'fire,' Yawelmani *pisi-* 'burn,' Molale *plak*, Nomlaki *pela* 'hot,' Santiam *pyan* 'sun,' Nisenan *poopila* 'summer'; Otian San José *pultwis*, *payan*, San Francisco etc. *paya* 'red'; Mayan Huastec *pil* 'firefly'; Kanpanan Guambia *pila* 'burn, year,' Guambia *pil*, Totero-Moguex 'pul,' Cholon *pel* 'moon'; Tarasco *cpíri* 'fire'; Misupan Paya *piri*, Misquito *pura* 'sky,' Paya *panwa*, *brana* 'red'; Xilencan Xinca *pari* 'sun, day'; Tucanoan Chunna *pero* 'fire'; Mataguayan *yapeł* 'burn,' *fala* 'sun, day'; Yamanan Alakaluf *apel* 'hot,' *aparaluk* 'star'; Coahuiltecan Chontal *epal* 'hot'; Chitimacha *pan* 'moon.' In various of the languages *y* is a secondary development from original *l* between vowels.

IE uses mainly augmentative *bh*, sometimes with *r* and sometimes with *l*: Sanskrit *bhraaja-* 'glow,' Lithuanian *brë'kšta* 'dawn,' Russian *brʸezg* 'the dawn,' Cymbrian *berth*, Swedish *brokig*, Gothic *berhts*, English *bright*, German *brennen*, English *burn*; Sanskrit *bhaalam*, Russian *blʸesk* 'brilliance,' Armenian *bal*, Gothic *bala* 'pallor,' Greek *phalós*, Russian *bʸéliy*, Lithuanian *bālas*, German *blank* 'white,' English *bald*, German *bleich*, *blasz*, Lettish *bāls* 'pale,' Old Irish *oíbell* 'heat, spark,' Greek *phlégoo*, Latin *flagraa-re* 'burn,' Greek *phlóks*, Icelandic *baal* 'flame,' Russian *blʸeknutʸ*, German *blitzen*, Latin *fulgee-re* 'to lighten,' Polish *blisk*, German *blitz* 'lightning,' English *blush*; German *farbe* 'color,' Lettish *pìrkstis* 'glowing ashes,' English *spark*; Latin *pulker* 'pretty.'

MP North Melanesia *pa(ra)para*, Tonga etc. *ma-fana*, Madagascar *ma-fana*, Indonesian *pana-s* 'hot'; East New Guinean *borabora*, *polapola*, *balabala*, Polynesian *falo*, *felo*, *fero* 'yellow'; North Melanesia *palapala* 'gray, whitish.'

Uralic Finnish *panu* 'fire.'
Basque *bero* 'hot, heat.'
CC Georgian *birbili* 'burning.'

*pen 'fly, wing, feather, hair, leaf.'

AA Tsimsian *plkʷa* 'feather'; Yakonan Alsea *pluplu* 'hair, fuzz,' *lpaʔan* 'wing,' Siuslaw *lpnat* 'bird'; Penan Yokutsan **khaa-phal* 'wing'; Kanpanan Guambia *palayi-* 'fly'; Quechumaran Quechua *pharpa* 'wing'; Misupan Misquito-Taguasca *lupul*, Paya *opra* 'fly,' *paya* 'leaf'; Xilencan Xinca *piya* 'leaf'; Sonchonan Moseten *pañ* 'feather,' *fin* 'hair'; Mataguayan Mataco *fiya* 'fly,' *afence* 'bird'; Comecrudan Chontal *i-pala* 'leaf (tree—).' This root occurs frequently in the meanings of 'tongue' and 'ear,' evidently derived from use in compositions meaning 'mouth-leaf' and 'head-leaf.'

IE Tokarian *plu*, English fly, German *fliege*, English (house)fly, Lithuanian *sparnas*, Lettish *spàrns*, German *flügel* 'wing,' Latin *pluuma*, Lithuanian *plùnksu*, Russian *pʸeró* 'feather,' Sanskrit *parṇá-* 'feather, leaf,' Latin *pilus* 'hair,' Tokarian *pilt* 'leaf.'

MP Polynesian **fulu*, Indonesian **bulu* 'feather, hair.'
Basque *biloa* 'hair.' Perhaps borrowing from Late Latin.
ST Tibetan *phir-* 'fly.'

*pet 'feather, fly.'

AA Yakonan Siuslaw *lput* 'feather,' Alsea *lpac* 'fly'; Penan Patwin *pute*, Nisenan *butuy* 'feather'; Otian Costanoan **te-pote* 'feather,' Clearlake *potul* 'fuzz,' Mariposa *tapa* 'fly'; Misupan Cacaopera *pit-* 'feather, wing,' Sumu-Ulua *butu-* 'feather'; Utaztecan Nahua *paλa-* 'fly.'

IE Greek *pterón*, Sanskrit *páttra-*, Latin *penna* (**pet-na*), Cymbrian *eterin*, English *feather*, Hittite *pattar* 'wing,' Sanskrit *páta-*, Greek *pétnumai* 'fly,' Latin *pete-re* 'attack,' Cymbrian *hedant* 'flying,' Russian *ptiɛe* 'bird.'

*pen 'flow, rain, river, water.'

AA Otian Rumsen *capur*, Santa Clara *tiprek*, Clearlake *poolpol* 'lake'; Mixean Oluta *piyik-* 'flow'; Kanpanan *pi* 'water'; Tarasco *hapónda* 'lake'; Misupan Misquito *plapa-* 'flow,' Paya *parmi, asu-pirwa* 'rain'; Yamanan Alakaluf *aperas* 'rain'; Coahuiltecan Chontal *pánaʔ* 'river.'

IE English *float, flow*, Latin *pluwius* 'rain,' Sanskrit *pláwa-*, Greek *pléoo*, Lithuanian *plaũkti* 'swim,' Armenian *heḷum*, Lithuanian *pìlti*, English *spill*; Old Dalmatian *balta*, Albanese *balt*, Lithuanian *balà*, Russian

bolóto 'marsh'; Old Irish *en* 'water,' Gothic *fani* 'slime,' Old Irish *enach*, Icelandic *fen*, Old English *fenn* 'marsh'; Greek *phlegma* 'slime.'
Basque *ubildu* 'flow,' *ubilla* 'liquid.'

*pen 'large,' 'heavy,' 'thick,' 'strong,' 'much,' 'full,' 'far'; diminutive with opposite meanings.

AA Chinookan Wasco *platax* 'heavy,' *palalay* 'many'; Penan Santiam *pala*, Patwin *ben* 'big,' Takelma *paáls*, Santiam *pows*, Yonkalla *puws* 'long,' Yonkala *pala?ya* 'far,' Atfalati *pala*, Wintun *buyaa*, Nomlaki *poya* 'many,' Patwin *buli* 'fat,' Wintun *paraa* 'full'; Otian Mariposa *tapal* wide, *?ipeelaka* 'grow,' Clearlake *pala* 'full'; Mayan Huastec *puulik*, Yucatec *polok* 'big,' Tzeltal *bayal*, Mam *banpun* 'many'; Huave *palan* 'complete, closed'; *cipiow* 'full'; Misupan Cacaopera *bulwika* 'full,' Misquito *poli* 'very,' Sumu *barak*, Cacaopera-Matagalpa *baybaka* 'old'; Jicaque *peluk* 'many,' *pone* 'broad,' *pune* 'thick,' *pones* 'big.' Diminutive Penan Chukchansi *payee?i* 'child,' *pay* 'baby,' *puunu* 'small,' *poytono* 'narrow'; Mayan Huastec *eipiil* 'small,' Yucatec *pal* 'child'; Paez *pil* 'thin'; Misupan Taguasca *-bine* 'child'; Yutaztecan Nahua *-pil-li* diminutive suffix.

IE **pel* 'full' (*l* perhaps by influence of **pel* 'flow,' thru verbs meaning 'spill,' 'pour,' 'fill'), e.g. Latin *pleenus*, English *full*; **bher* in Tokarian *pirkir* 'long,' Sanskrit *brhant-* 'big, powerful,' Armenian *barjr* 'high,' German *berg* 'mountain,' Latin *fortis* 'strong,' German *burg* 'fortress'; **per* in Armenian *heri*, Gothic *ferra*, English *far*, Icelandic *forn* 'old,' Sanskrit *párah* 'farther'; **pel(we)* 'multitude' in Sanskrit *púur*, Greek *pólis* 'city,' Latin *pleebs*, English *folk*, Greek *polús*, Gothic *filu*, German *viel* 'many'; **bal* Sanskrit *bálam* 'strength,' Latin *dee-bilis* 'weak,' Russian *bolᵘʃóy* 'big,' Dutch *pal* 'firm.' Derivatives with diminutive meaning have not yet been observed; possibly the augmentative carried the diminutive forms over to new meanings.

Basque *buru* 'head, upper part,' *burdin*, *burni* 'iron' (perhaps from 'strong').

HS Galla *boroo* 'top,' *borgi* 'mountain,' Somali *bur* 'mountain,' Somali *bir* 'iron.'

CC Udo *buul* 'head,' *burux* 'mountain.'

*men 'much,' 'large,' 'strong'; diminutive 'few,' 'small,' 'weak.'

AA Chinookan *mank* 'several'; Yakonan Hanis *mneni* 'thick'; Penan Yawelmani *mani* 'many,' Sahaptin *mla*, Nezperce *mi?lac* 'several'; Otian

Santa Clara *emen*, San José *hemen*, Rumsen *imey* 'many'; Mixean Aguacatec *mani* 'big'; Totonac *ɫmaaʔn* 'long'; Kanpanan Guambia *mancakin* 'many,' *mayele* 'all'; Quechumaran Quechua *mancay* 'plenty'; Huave *meawan* 'all'; Misupan Misquito *manas* 'many'; Xilencan Xinca *muʔla* 'broad.' Diminutive Otian *minwa* 'narrow'; Penan Sahaptin *manay* 'small, short'; Mapuche *muna* 'short'; Jicaque *mulway* 'short'; Comecrudan Chontal *miyú* 'thin.'

IE *mn etc., see p. 903.

MP Samoa *malu* 'soft.'

Basque *malba* 'weak,' *malso* 'slow,' *malfo, mardo* 'soft.'

HS Arabic *mals* 'smooth, soft,' *mald* 'soft.'

CC Chechen *meeliñ* 'weak,' *mellifi* 'little by little.'

Dravidian Tamil *mel* 'fine, tender.'

Mundan Santali *marang* 'big.'

*mek 'big,' 'old,' 'broad,' 'strong'; diminutive with opposite meanings.

AA Tsimsian *mik* 'mature'; Yakonan Alsea *makst* 'long in time'; Penan Takelma *maháy*, Yawelmani *mayaaha* (probably a type of internal reduplication), Nisenan *muk* 'big,' Nezperce *meχfem* 'mountain,' Yawelmani-Chukchansi *moxlo* 'old'; Mixean *miha 'big'; Totonac *maqat* 'far,' *maqaaʔs* 'of long duration'; Mayan Yucatec *muk* 'of long duration,' Tzeltal *muk̓* 'big'; Quechumaran Quechua *maqma* 'broad,' *maqhu* 'mountain'; Misupan Misquito *almuk* 'old'; Sonchonan Moseten *meke* 'mountain'; Comecrudo *maketyaw* 'far.' Diminutive Penan Klamath *muk̓ak̓* 'child'; Mixean Coatlán *muc* 'small,' Totontepec *muuckyin* 'narrow'; Mayan Lacandon *mehen* 'small'; Tucanoan Macuna *makaka* 'child'; Sonchonan Moseten *moci*, Ona *makka*, Tehuelche *mako* 'new.'

IE *moq etc., see p. 903.

MP Polynesian Maori *moko-rahi* 'big, extended,' *maha* 'plenty,' Pikiram *mokowa* 'far.'

Basque *mehe* 'thin,' *meharr* 'narrow.'

CC Karata *mika*, Andi *mici*, Georgian *mei-re* 'small.'

**men(te)* 'mind,' 'heart,' 'think,' 'understand,' 'hear.'

AA Chinookan Wasco *-mal* 'narrow'; Yakonan Hanis *mla*, Miluk *milam* 'liver'; Penan Takelma *muul-* 'liver, lungs,' *taa-míntha* 'teach,' Nezperce *tiʔmíne*, Sahaptin *tmna* 'heart'; Otian Mariposa-Santa Cruz-San José *mini* 'heart,' Clearlake *minic* 'hear'; Mayan Quiche *camanik* 'think,' Huastec *mamal* 'liver'; Kanpanan Guambia *manci* 'heart, liver,'

Cholon -*man* 'inside,' Guambia *meri* 'hear,' Cholon -*cman* 'know,' Xibito *manca* 'eye'; Tarasco *minzi-ta* 'mind, heart, stomach'; Huave -*meaɛ* 'heart'; Misupan Cacaopera *mil*, Taguasca *put-minik* 'heart,' *mantala* 'know'; Utaztecan Nahua *mati* 'think'; Sonchonan *hamni* 'liver'; Candoxi *mánk-ic* 'heart.'

IE Sanskrit *mánas-*, Latin *menti-*, English *mind*, Tokarian A *mnu*, Gothic *muns*, Lithuanian *mintìs* 'thought,' Sanskrit *mánya-* 'think,' Armenian *imanam* 'understand,' Greek *mémona*, Russian *po-mnᵘe-*, Lithuanian *miñti* 'remember,' Gothic *muna*, Old Irish *do-moiniur* 'believe,' Latin *mone-re*, German *mahnen* 'warn'; Greek *mnéesis* 'memory,' German *meinen* 'opine.'

MP **mana-wa* 'spirit,' 'heart,' 'stomach.'

Basque *mun* 'medulla,' *munak* (pl.) 'brains.'

*men 'dark,' 'black,' 'cloud.' Especially with *r* or *l*.

AA Penan Nomlaki-Wintun *molok*, Atfalati *muyem* 'black,' Patwin *sani-mel-be* 'night' ('day-dark-in'), Atfalati *mank* 'cloud'; Otian Clearlake *muluumulu*, Mutsun *humur*, Santa Cruz *murut*, *murcu*, Bodega *muluta* 'black,' Clearlake *molpa* 'dark,' Tuolumne *moli*, Mariposa *moolita*, Clearlake *mole* 'shadow,' Mutsun *muri*, Santa Cruz *mur* 'noche'; Mayan Huastec θ*amul* 'black,' Yucatec *muyal* 'cloud,' Cakchiquel *moyew* 'fog'; Misupan Cacaopera *mulka* 'dark'; Jicaque *mol* 'cloud'; Coahuiltecan Comecrudo -*mol* 'black'; Atakapa *mel* 'black'; Tunica *meli* 'black.'

IE Greek *mélaas*, Lettish *męlns* 'black,' Sanskrit *mlaana-* 'black, dark,' *mála-* 'dirtiness,' *maliná-* 'dirty, black,' Lithuanian *më'las* 'blue,' Prussian *melne* 'blue spot'; Armenian *mrayl* 'cloud, fog, darkness,' Czech *moratý* 'streaked with black,' Russian *marúʃka* 'spot,' English *murky*, Old German *merken* 'to mark.'

*men 'die,' 'sick,' 'bad,' 'not.'

AA Chinookan Kathlamet-Chinook -*mla* 'bad'; Penan Maidu *minel* 'die,' Wintun *milee*, Nomlaki *Pumaala* 'dull,' Wintun-Nomlaki -*mina*, Maidu-Nisenan *men* 'not'; Otian Santa Cruz *semon*, Mutsun *sun* (from **semn*, cf. also Kathlamet -*sim*) 'die'; Mayan Cakchiquel *mani*, Chol *maPanik*, Mam *mlay*, 'not,' Yucatec *manan* 'there isn't any'; Quechumaran Quechua *mana* 'not'; Zuñi -*Pamme* 'not'; Xilencan Xinca *marak* 'bad'; Comecrudan Chontal *mama-* 'die,' *maa* 'no'; Paez *ma* 'not'; Kanpanan Cholon *ma*, Itonama *maykana* 'not'; Yuman Diegueño *meley* 'die'; Coahuiltecan Karankawa *mal* 'dead.'

IE Sanskrit *mara-*, Lithuanian *mirti*, Latin *morii-re*, Russian *m^yer-* 'die,' Gothic *morθr*, English *murder*; Tokarian *ma·* 'not,' Avestan *maa*, Greek *meé*, Armenian *mi*, Albanese *mos* 'don't'; Latin *malus* 'bad'; Spanish *mancar* 'to lack.'

Basque *min* 'hurt,' *minkor* 'bitter,' *mindu* 'sour,' *malba* 'weak.'

HS Egyptian *mn*, Bari *min-* 'hurt, suffer.'

*new 'shiny,' 'new'; diminutive 'bright,' 'shiny,' 'white'; augmentative 'burn,' 'hot,' 'red.' With frequent interchange in the meanings of the grades.

AA Penan Nezperce *liw-*, Sahaptin *lu-*, Molale *new-*, Klamath *nu-*, Takelma *liwt-* 'burn'; Mixean Popoluca *-noʔ* 'burn'; Quechumaran Quechua *rupha-* 'burn'; Misupan Cacaopera *lawali* 'fire,' Misquito *anawa* 'ripe'; Huave *-liw* 'tender, new'; Xilencan Xinca *huroru* 'hot'; Mapuche *livliv-* 'burn'; Yamanan Yamana *lewn* 'sun'; Comecrudan Chontal *iñúʔ* 'hot'; Chitimacha *now-* 'cooked, ripe'; Atakapa *law* 'burn'; Yuman Diegueño *huraw* 'hot, summer.'

IE Sanskrit *náwa*, Armenian *nava-*, Latin *novus*, Greek *neos*, Old Lithuanian *navas*, Russian *nóviy*, Old Irish *nuuë*, Gothic *niuyis*, English *new*, German *nun*, English *now*; Sanskrit *rooká-*, *roocí-*, Armenian *lois*, Latin *luuks*, *luumen*, Slovene *lúc*, Gothic *liuhaθ*, English *light*, Armenian *lusin*, Latin *luuna*, Russian *lúna* 'moon,' Sanskrit *rukṣá-* 'bright,' Greek *leukós* 'bright, white,' Cymbrian *llug* 'sheen,' Icelandic *leygr* 'flame, fire,' Russian *luc* 'lightning,' Hittite *lukk-* 'give light, kindle,' Tokarian *luk-* 'give light'; Sanskrit *róohita-*, Greek *eruθrós*, Tokarian A *rtor*, Tokarian B *ritre*, Old Irish *ruuad*, Gothic *rauθs*, German *rot*, English *red*, Sanskrit *laahá-* 'reddish, copper,' Latin *ruubidus* 'dark red,' Russian *risiy* 'reddish'; Sanskrit *raaw-* 'sun'.

MP *arau 'sun'; San Cristobal *raurau* 'hot'; North Borneo *lau* 'day'; Anaiteum *lav* 'give light.'

Eskimo *nutaaRaq* 'new.'

*ʃew(ne) 'day,' 'sun,' 'fire.'

AA Tsimsian *sunt* 'coal'; Mixean Oluta *siwi*, Coatlan *ʂii* 'sun'; Misupan Misquito *aswa-* 'burn,' Paya *siwa* 'yellow'; Xilencan Lenca *sawa* 'day,' *sewla* 'red, ripe,' *ksowo* 'white,' Xinca *siriwi* 'red'; Comecrudo *-sowetyan* 'hot'; Mixtecan Mixtec *ti-siwi* 'burn'; Salina *suuneʔ* 'light'; Hokan Achomawi *ʓol* 'sun' (glottalization of *s*).

IE Vedic *súwar*, Sanskrit *suura-*, Avestan *hwari*, Greek *héelios*, Latin *sool*, Cymbrian *haul*, Gothic *sawil*, *sunnoo* (perhaps *suunnoo*), Icelandic *sool*, German *sonne*, English *sun*, Sanskrit *swara-* 'burn,' German *schwelen* 'heat up,' English *swarthy* (from 'sun-darkened'), German *schwarz* 'black.'

MP **sulu* 'torch.'

Basque *su* 'fire,' *suka-* 'scald.'

HS Egyptian *ſw* 'light,' Kredj *ʔoSo* 'fire,' Arabic *ſaway-* 'roast.'

*ſen(we) 'flow,' 'rain'; secondarily also 'water,' 'drink,' 'swim,' 'sea,' 'salt,' etc.

AA Yakonan Hanis *si* 'drink'; Penan Takelma *xiy* (*x* always from **s*, *y* sometimes from intervocalic *l*) 'water,' Chukchansi *seeʔal*, Yawelmani *şeʔel* 'rain'; Otian Mutsun-Rumsen-Santa Cruz *si* 'water,' Mutsun *solo* 'flow'; Totonac *siin* 'rain'; Mayan Chicomuceltec *siʔal* 'rain'; Kanpanan Guambia *se* 'rain'; Misupan Cacaopera *isola* 'sea'; Xilencan Xinca *suru* 'wet'; Coahuiltecan Chontal *snak-* 'drink.' Perhaps note also widespread **ſin/sin/łin* for 'mucus' and 'nose.'

IE Sanskrit *snaa-* 'bathe,' Greek *nekoo*, Latin *naa-re, nataa-re* 'swim,' English *snot, snout, snuff*; Greek *niphei*, 'to snow,' Latin *niks* (*niwis*), Russian *snʸeg*, Gothic *snaiws*, English *snow* (note regular loss of *s* before *n* or *l* at beginning of word in Greek and Latin); perhaps also Latin *sangʷis* 'blood'; Sanskrit *sreedha-*, Greek *o-listhanoo*, Gothic *sliwpah*, German *schleichen*, English *slip, slide*, German *schlucken* 'swallow in gulps,' German *schlamm* 'mud,' German *schleim*, English *slime*, Greek *leiboó*, Latin *libaz-re* 'make a libation,' Greek *louoó*, Latin *lawaa-re* 'wash,' Latin *solwe-re*, Greek *luoo* 'dissolve,' English *salve*, Latin *luubrikum* 'grease,' Greek *hélos* 'marsh,' Sanskrit *sáras-* 'sea,' *saráa* 'river,' Greek *hals* 'sea, salt' (with this secondary meaning, also Latin *sal*, Russian *solʸ*, Gothic *salt*, English *salt*); English *sleet*; Latin *sarpioo*, Russian *sʸerpʸ*, Lettish *sirpis* 'flow,' Sanskrit *siiráa* 'current,' Latin *serum* 'whey,' German *strom* (**sroom*), English *stream*. **naas* for 'nose' may be dissimilated from **snaas*, compare English *snot, snout* and AA coincidence of forms.

MP **tasi/hasi(na)* 'sea,' 'salt.' Perhaps an old compound **taha-sina* with much and varied reduction because of the great age of the formation. 'Nose' may be **isun*.

*ken especially diminutive 'cold,' 'ice,' 'snow,' 'white'; augmentative or blend formation 'hot,' 'burn,' 'red.'

AA Yakonan Hanis *kalu* 'winter,' *kayna* 'cold'; Penan Molale *keys* 'snow,' Wintun *ķilti i*, Patwin *ćil* 'sleet,' Wintun *kiki*, Maidu *koki* 'ice';

Otian Mariposa *kilime* 'ice,' Mariposa-Tuolumne *keela* 'snow,' Tuolumne-Amador *keleli-* 'white'; Mayan Lacandon *keʔel* 'cold,' Kekchi *ke* 'ice, snow, cold'; Quechumaran Aymara *khunu* 'snow'; Huave *-kind* 'cold'; Sonchonan Tehuelche *kel* 'snow,' *kekos* 'cold'; Yamanan Yamana *akila* 'ice.' Augmentative meanings (often with blend formations) Chinookan Wasco *-k̓la* 'hot,' *kalex* 'sun'; Yakonan Hanis *xalws*, Miluk *kalxawi* 'hot'; Penan Wintun-Nomlaki *qalaw*, Patwin *kul*, 'burn,' Klamath *kelp* 'hot,' Takelma *kuluk̓-* 'to flame'; Otian Mariposa *kula* 'coal'; Mayan *ʠin* 'sun, day'; Quechumaran Quechua *q̇uñi* 'hot,' *q̇unca* 'hearth'; Tarasco *kulí-* 'burn'; Zuñi *k̓al-* 'hot,' *ʔakli* 'fire'; Huave *-kanc* 'red'; Misupan Esmeralda *karo* 'red'; Sonchonan Tehuelche *kerenk*, Ona *kren* 'sun'; Mapuche *kel* 'red.'

IE see pp. 903 f.

MP Polynesian *kikila* 'lighten'; Melanesian *kar* 'day, sun.'

Basque *gelá* 'ice.' Possibly a borrowing from Latin.

ken 'perceive,' 'see,' 'hear,' 'know.'

AA Chinookan Kathlamet *-qlkl*, Chinook *-kl* 'see,' Kathlamet-Wasco *-kl* 'know'; Penan Sahaptin *kinu-t* 'see,' Klamath *kay* 'know'; Mixean Copainalá *ken* 'see'; Kanpanan Coconucan *kalu* 'ear'; Tarasco *kula-* 'hear'; Xilencan Chilanga *to-koro* 'ear'; Yuracare *kayle* 'know'; Jicaque *kuñuka* 'see'; Chitimacha *kani* 'eye.'

IE Russian *slífatʸ*, Greek *kluoo* 'hear,' Sanskrit *ſrnoo-*, Old German *hloosen*, English *listen*, Latin *klue-re* 'be famous,' Old German *hluut*, English *loud*; Irish *cluas*, Tokarian *kloſim* 'ear,' Russian *glaz* 'eye'; Sanskrit *janaa-*, Greek *gignooskoo*, Latin *noskoo*, Russian *znatʸ*, Old Irish *itar-gnini-*, Lithuanian *ʒina-*, Tokarian *kna·n*, Gothic *kunnan*, German *kennen*, English *know*; Latin *krede-re*, Vedic *ſrád-dadhaa-* ('heart-put') 'believe,' Greek *keer*, *kardia*, Latin *kor* (*kordis*), Russian *sʸerɕe*, German *herz*, English *heart*, Latin *kerebrum*, Sanskrit *ſirah*, German *hirn* 'brain' (but Greek *kara* 'head' and *kranion* 'skull' are perhaps better connected with *ken* 'large' in the secondary meaning of 'high' or 'upper').

Basque *ki-* 'know.'

HS Somali *qaan* 'know.'

kew 'ear, hear,' Possibly related to *kew* 'hollow,' well attested for AA and IE, though not cited in this paper.

AA Yakonan Siuslaw *kawyax* 'ear,' Miluk *kaʔw-* 'hear'; Penan

Takelma *taa-kaw-*, Santiam *kapt* 'hear'; Mixean Copainalá *kowi* 'ear'; Yamanan Alakaluf *telkawlu* 'ear.'

IE **qaus*: Greek *koeoo* 'observe,' Gothic *hausyan*, German *hören*, English *hear*; Greek *geuomai*, Latin *gustaa-re*, German *kosten* 'to taste'; **xaw(s)*: Latin *audii-re*, Greek *aioo* 'hear,' Latin *auris* (**ausis*), Russian *úxo*, Gothic *ausoo*, German *ohr*, English *ear*.

MP perhaps **tan-kaw* 'hear, ear,' e.g. Anaiteum *dongo* 'hear,' Tongo *toŋa*, Tagalog *tainga* 'ear.'

*kew 'high,' 'standing,' 'tree'; **kep* 'top,' 'peak,' 'head.' Originally two roots, which tend to become confused with each other, as well as with such others as **kew* 'hollow' (in the sense of 'vaulted') and **kew* 'ear' (because of location on top).

AA Tsimsian *-kaws* 'head,' *kakaws* 'horn'; Yakonan *kawax*, Miluk *kwna* 'up,' Siuslaw *kawix* 'summit,' *kawxn* 'sky,' *kawx* 'wood' (from 'tree'); Penan Maidu *kowkiŕu* 'standing'; Totonacan Totonac *kiʔwiʔ*, Tepehua *ḱiwi* 'tree'; Mixean *ko-* 'head'; Huave *kawiS* 'up.' Penan Molale *kpaw* 'tree,' Nezperce *qapqap* 'cottonwood,' Klamath *kapka* 'pine'; Nisenan *ḱepele* 'shoulder'; Mixean **kopk* 'mountain,' **kip* 'tree'; Mayan Cakchiquel *kapac* 'standing.'

IE Latin *kakuumen*, Sanskrit *kakúbh-* 'peak,' Lithuanian *kaukarà*, Old Icelandic *haugr*, German *hügel*, English *hill*, Old Persian *kaufa-* 'mountain,' Russian *kúca*, Albanese *kyipí*, Middle Irish *cuuan*, Lithuanian *kaũpas*, Gothic *hiuhma*, German *haufe*, English *heap*, Greek *kúmbee* 'head,' Gothic *hauhs*, German *hoch*, English *high*, German *haupt*, English *head*; **xaw(p)* Sanskrit *awa*, German *auf*, English *up*, Sanskrit *óojah* 'strength,' Greek *auksoo* 'increase,' Latin *auge-re* 'grow,' *awus* 'grandfather,' Gothic *awoo* 'grandmother.' Latin *kaput*, Greek *kephalós* Tokarian *fpa·l*, Sanskrit *kapaalah* 'head', Old German *gebal* 'top'; German *gipfel* 'peak'; **xap*: Greek *apo* 'far from,' Gothic *af* 'far,' German *ab*, English *off*; **xab*: Latin *ab* 'away from.'

MP **kau* 'tree,' Malay-Celebes-Sumatra *kapala* 'head.'

Basque *goya* 'high.'

*ken 'large' etc.; diminutive 'small' etc. Blend forms may give the meaning of 'long' and 'old,' which then become confused with those of **kʷen* in languages which coalesce *k* with *kʷ* either in all positions or before rounded vowels.

AA Chinookan *-qayχ* 'big,' *-khala* 'man,' Kathlamet-Wasco *-q̇iyukt* 'old'; Penan Takelma *kaay-* 'grow,' Yawelmani *kuyotum,* Maidu *keyi,* Nomlaki *k̓iyaas,* Patwin *ciyak* 'old,' Klamath *kélis* 'strong,' Chukchansi *kalcin* 'many'; Otian Clearlake *kilaa* 'old, many'; Mayan Lacandon *karem* 'big,' Kekchi *q̓eel* 'old'; Kanpanan Moquex *wakla* 'big,' Guambia *kali* 'old'; Paez *kula* 'big'; Tarasco *khéri* 'big,' *kani-k^wa* 'many,' *khé-* 'grow'; Quechumaran Quechua *qhari* 'man'; Coahuiltecan Comecrudo *-knah* 'old, man,' Cotoname *knah* 'good'; Jicaque *kokoy* 'old'; Xilencan Xinca *kara* 'heavy'; Yuracare *kalapeʃe* 'old'; Sonchonan Ona *kon* 'big,' *karcun* 'old,' Tehuelche *tekanek* 'long,' Ona *kar,* Tehuelche *khey* 'many'; Yamanan Alakaluf *hawkil* 'big.' Diminutive Tsimsian Nisga *łkul* 'narrow,' Tsimsian *t̓k̓iłk^w* 'child'; Yakonan Hanis *k̓ana* 'young,' Alsea *łk̓aylucant,* Siuslaw *-ma-k̓sk̓n* 'short,' Siuslaw *ya-k̓sk̓n,* Hanis *kays* 'small,' Hanis *k̓ilak* 'thin,' Miluk *k̓ilka* 'child,' Hanis *k̓ays* 'baby'; Penan Chukchansi *k̓olis* 'young,' Takelma *ta-skulí* 'short,' Santiam *cilek* 'near,' Klamath *k̓ick̓áni* 'small, young,' Molale *kuʔna,* Klamath *k̓ink̓ani,* Maidu *konoko* 'baby,' *kole* 'child'; Otian Mutsun *kuynu* 'narrow,' *koro* 'thin'; Mixean Copainalá *ciliy* 'baby'; Misupan Paya *akinatisi* 'few,' Matagalpa *kince* 'small.'

IE see p. 904.

*k^wen 'long,' 'far,' 'old.' In languages that lose the labialization, forms derived from this root may be indistinguishable from those belonging to the preceding.

AA Penan Sahaptin *k̓^walk,* Wintun *keleela* 'long,' Nomlaki *kelel,* Patwin *keleel* (necessarily from **k^w,* because original *k* becomes *c* in Patwin) 'far,' Sahaptin *k^wláwit,* Nezperce *kuléwit,* Wintun *kenwan,* Nomlaki *kenwani,* Nisenan *kulunti* 'late,' Nezperce *kunk̓u,* Sahaptin *k^walisim* 'always,' Takelma *k^walá* 'many,' Chukchansi *kalcin,* Maidu *kanite* 'all'; Mayan Cakchiquel *k̓ulahah* 'broad'; Quechumaran Quechua *kharu* 'far'; Misupan Paya *karhara* 'long,' *kara* 'far'; Xilencan Xinca *kerunu* 'long'; Tonkawa *k^walo* 'big'; Yuman **k^werak* 'old,' **kole* 'long, far'; Seri *ka-kol* 'long.'

IE Greek *téele* (*k^w* becomes *t* before front vowel), Cymbrian-Cornish-Breton *pell* 'far,' Sanskrit *cirás* 'of long duration,' *cara-má-* 'the last', Greek *télos,* Sanskrit *kúlam* 'multitude'; **g^wer* 'heavy'; Sanskrit *ghaná-* 'thick,' Greek *eu-θenées* 'abundant,' Lithuanian *ganà* 'sufficient,' Russian *do-gon^yat^y* 'suffice'; **x^wel*: Latin *ab-oleskere* 'grow old,' *ad-oleskere* grow up,' **x^wen* in Latin *onus* 'burden.'

MP Maori *kora-ha* 'big, extended,' Christmas Island *koroa, konui,* Magindano *kukula* 'far,' Polynesian **koro* 'weak with age,' Subanu *gulang* 'old.'

Basque *agurea* 'old man,' *gorratua* 'high.'

*kʷen 'woman,' 'wife.' Possibly **kʷen/kʷel,* diminutive forms of the preceding.

AA Otian Bodega *kuley,* Clearlake *kola* 'woman,' Clearlake *kule* 'wife'; Penan Maidu-Nisenan *kile* 'woman,' Maidu *kono* 'wife'; Kanpanan Itonama *kaneka-* 'woman,' Cholon *cala* 'wife'; Sonchonan Tehuelche *tarken* 'woman'; Mapuche *kure* 'wife'; Coahuiltecan Chontal *akáno* 'woman'; Zapotecan **kuna* 'woman.'

IE Greek *gunée,* Armenian *kin,* Avestan *graa,* Old Irish *ben,* Prussian *genna,* Russian *ʒená,* Tokarian A *ʃn-* (sing. *ʃim,* pl. *ʃnu*), Tokarian B *ʃana,* Gothic *kʷinoo,* Old German *kʷena,* Old Norse *kona,* Anglo-Saxon *kʷene* 'woman,' Cymbrian *ben-yw* 'feminine,' Cornish *ben-en* 'wife,' Albanese *zonjë* 'lady'; Tokarian *kuli* 'woman.'

*kʷen 'turn,' 'circle,' 'round,' 'bend.' 'knee,' 'elbow.'

AA Chinookan Wasco *kul* 'grind,' *-kuyikuyi* 'ring,' *-qulaʔwla* 'egg'; Yakonan Hanis *kʷl-* 'turn,' *kʷil-* 'bend,' Hanis *ma-kʷl,* Siuslaw *kʷlax,* Alsea *kʷlaws* 'egg'; Penan Klamath *kalkal,* Nisenan *kododoy* 'round,' Klamath *kulins* 'knee,' Maidu *kil-* 'turn,' *kol* 'drill,' Nisenan *kili* 'returning'; Otian Clearlake *to-kolo* 'knee,' Santa Cruz *kululis,* Monterrey *kulus,* Rumsen *kululse* 'elbow'; Totonacan Tepehua *-quluha* 'turn'; Mayan Mam *kololon,* Huastec *kʷecocol* 'round,' Cakchiquel *keen* 'grind,' Ixil-Aguacatec *kolol* 'egg'; Quechumaran Quechua *qurma* 'turn,' Aymara *qunquri* 'knee'; Tarasco *kulíʃata* 'ring'; Zuñi *ʔikʷalt* 'return'; Huave *-kʷireec* 'turn, run,' *-koon* 'fold'; Misupan Misquito *krukma* 'round,' Sumu-Ulua *kalas..mak* 'knee,' Misquito *karba-* 'turn'; Tucanoan Macuna *karariya,* Detoana *kalaria* 'egg'; Sonchonan Ona *kacer-kre* 'knee' (leg—); Mapuche *kura* 'stone'; Chimariko *koru-* 'bend.'

IE Greek *pólos* 'axis,' Sanskrit *kárṣa-,* Greek *telé-* (*t* from *kʷ* before front vowel), Albanese *syel* 'turn,' Sanskrit *cakrá-,* English *wheel,* Irish *cul,* Tokarian *kukil* 'vehicle,' Greek *kuklós* 'circle,' Latin *kolaa-re* 'plow,' Greek *klóothoo* 'spin,' *kloosteéros* 'spindle'; Greek *kurtos,* Latin *kurvus* 'curved,' Greek *krikos, kirkos* 'ring' (Latin *kirkus* perhaps borrowed from Greek); Greek *guros* 'circle,' German *kwer* 'crooked,' English *queer*; Latin *globus* 'sphere'; **xʷer*: Latin *orbis* 'circle'; **xʷel*: Greek *oolenee*, Latin *ulna*, Old German *elina*, Frankish *alina*, German *ellenbogen*, English *elbow*.

MP Maori *koru* 'folded,' *koro-hwana* 'curved,' Mangareva *ta-koro* 'curved,' Christmas Island *kori* 'to play.'

*kʷen 'neck,' 'throat,' 'swallow.' Perhaps related to the preceding in reference to the part of the body which turns.

'AA Yakonan Hanis *k̓ʷnc* 'neck,' *k̓ʷn* 'swallow'; Penan Takelma *kʷen*, Yawelmani-Yaudanchi *ʔookun*, Nisenan *k̓uyno*, Maidu *k̓uyi* 'neck,' Santiam-Atfalati *kʷinafu* 'swallow'; Mixean Copainalá *kini* 'neck'; Mayan Quiche-Cakchiquel-Aguacatec *qul*, Mam *qulh*, Yucatec *kal*, 'neck,' Cakchiquel *q̓ulih* 'swallow'; Quechumaran *kunqa* 'neck, throat'; Tarasco *kunah-* 'neck, swallow'; Misupan Misquito *karma* 'throat'; Yamanan Alakaluf *kyoltal-kʷar* 'neck.'

IE Latin *kollus*, Lettish *kokls*, Gothic-German *hals* (*kʷol, with labialization lost before rounded vowel) 'neck'; Sanskrit *gala-*, Persian *guluu*, Avestan *gariman-*, Armenian *kokorl* 'throat,' Old Irish *braagae* 'neck,' Sanskrit *girá-* 'swallow,' Latin *gurgulioo* 'windpipe,' German *kragen*, English *craw* (of bird), Sanskrit *griiwáa* 'nape,' Lettish *geris* 'drink'; English *swallow* (*s-ghʷol), *swill*, German *schwalch* 'throat'; Greek *bibrooskoo*, Latin *woraa-re* 'devour.'

REFERENCES

Bopp, F. 1840. "Über die Verwandschaft der malayisch-polynesischen Sprachen mit den indisch-europäischen," *Abhandlungen der königlischen Akademie der Wissenschaften zu Berlin*, 5th series, 27:171-332.

Hammerich, L. L. 1951. "Can Eskimo be related to Indo-European?" *International Journal of American Linguistics*, 17:217-23.

Mendoza, G. 1878. Estudio comparativo entre el sánskrito y el nagüatl, Mexico.

Radin, Paul. 1919. "The genetic relationship of the North American Indian languages," *University of California Publications in American Archaeology and Ethnology*, 14:489-552.

Rivet, Paul. 1925. "Les Australiens en Amérique," *Bulletin de la Société linguistique de Paris*, 26:23-63.

———, 1926 "Les Malayo-Polynésiaines en Amérique," *Journal de la Société des Americanistes de Paris*, 18:141-278.

Sauvageot, A. 1924. "Eskimo et Ouralian," *Journal de la Société des Americanistes de Paris*, 21:296-97.

Schott, Albert. 1936. "Indogermanisch-Semitisch-Sumerisch," *Germanen und Indogermanen*, 2:45-95.

Shafer, Robert. 1952. "Athapaskan and Sino-Tibetan," *International Journal of American Linguistics*, 18:12-19; discussion by Swadesh, *International Journal of American Linguistics*, 18:178-81.

Swadesh, Morris. 1954. "Perspectives and problems of Amerindian comparative linguistics," *Word*, 10:306-32.

——, 1956. "Problems of long-range comparison in Penutian," *Language*, 32:17-41.

——, 1958. "Materiales para un diccionario comparativo de las lenguas amerindias," *Cuadernos de Historia*, in press.

Thalbitzer, William. 1952. "Possible early contacts between Eskimo and Old World languages," in *Selected Papers of the XXIXth International Congress of Americanists*, pp. 50-54.

Trombetti, Alfredo. 1926. "Le origini della lingua basca," *Memorie della R. Accademmia delle Scienze dell'Istituto di Bologna*, Serie II, 8-9:1-164.

A SURVEY OF
AFRICAN PROSODIC SYSTEMS

By Joseph Greenberg

COLUMBIA UNIVERSITY

THIS IS THE FIRST attempt at a general survey of the prosodic verse forms of African poetry. It is therefore quite possible that certain phenomena have been overlooked—prosodic systems may exist of which the writer is ignorant. In addition to describing the facts, some historical analysis is likewise attempted. Here, too, the author is aware that certain of the results are merely tentative. Where such is the case, the appropriate qualifications and the existence of alternative hypotheses are indicated.

Only the basic facts concerning the prosodic systems are considered. Discussion of more subtle issues, comparable to such problems of classical metrics as the interrelation of stress and quantity in Latin verse, is not attempted here. It is believed that a general survey of the African terrain such as is attempted here must in most cases precede such detailed work. Moreover, in many instances our linguistic data are not sufficient for such problems at the present stage. Another omission concerns relations of literary dependence of specific poetic productions. Such data are obviously relevant to questions of historical relations among prosodic systems. Here again, except in a few instances, this field is as yet uncultivated. Therefore an attempt to evaluate evidence from this source would have extended greatly the already broad scope of the present paper. Considerations from this area have, therefore, been only infrequently utilized, although their importance is realized.

A mapping of prosodic verse forms in Africa shows a far from random distribution. Almost all examples occur in the northern half of the continent and in many of these, the borrowing and adaptation of Arabic models by peoples under Islamic influence is demonstrable. In certain other instances, notably in the Ethiopia-Somaliland area, one cannot always be certain of the direct or indirect Arabic origin of the existing verse forms. In addition to these and other instances in which Arabic influence, while possible—or even probable—is not certain, there are at least two authenticated instances of verse forms which are to all appearance indigenous, and not the result of Arabic influence.

Where Arabic origin is assured, it will be convenient to distinguish those instances in which the classical pre-Islamic forms, notably the standard *qaṣīdah* or "ode" have been adopted, from those in which post-classical medieval or modern Arabic forms are involved.

The descriptive sections of the present paper are accordingly divided into four parts: (1) indigenous African forms; (2) the influence of Pre-Islamic Arabic verse; (3) the influence of postclassical Arabic verse; (4) instances of possible though not certain Arabic influence. The main descriptive-historical treatment of African verse forms is preceded by a brief discussion of fundamental notions having to do with the nature and types of prosodic systems.

It is probable that there exists, in all human society, beyond the every-day use of language, a body of verbal tradition, written or unwritten which is distinguishable from ordinary languages by differences in vocabulary, grammar and other purely linguistic characteristics. Among the linguistic features which define such non-casual utterances, we find in certain instances adherence to rules which can be stated in terms of the sound structure alone within grammatically given stretches, such as the sentence. In such cases we talk of prosodic systems. Since the rules of prosodic systems can be stated in terms of the sound structure alone, it is feasible, in principle, to discover the existence of such systems without a knowledge of the grammar and semantics of the language. Thus, in the following text, certain regularities might be detected by an analyst entirely ignorant of the language, provided only that the transcription of sound units (phonemes) is accurate and that the boundaries of the relevant grammatical units are likewise given.

axi phani kwa upesi ilo ali karatasi na mwino mwema mweusi utilizao maozi na kalamu mahabubu ilo njema ya arabu nowe ina la wahabu mulu wethu muawazi.

If we divide the foregoing text into units (syllables), each consisting of a member of the class *a, e, i, o, u* (vowels), together with any non-vowels which precede up to but not including the preceding vowel, then the following phenomena may be noted. The syllables numbered 8, 16, 24 are the same (*si*); so are syllables 40, 48, and 56 (*bu*); syllables 32 and 64 are also identical (*zi*). All of these syllables have a number divisible by 8, and each is the final syllable of a grammatical unit, the word.

The language is Swahili and it would usually be stated that the poem is divided into lines of 8 syllables each and that the rhyme scheme is a a a b c c c b.

Such prosodic systems appear to be entirely absent among American Indians and to be confined to certain parts of Europe, Asia, and Africa.

The preceding was an example of the principle of syllable count, the occurrence of a certain number of syllables in each line. Relative to the line, which is the fundamental division in terms of which the pattern can be stated, one may classify the prosodic devices as follows: rhyme, alliteration, syllable count, quantity, stress, and tone.

Rhyme may be defined as similarity of sound sequence at some determinable place within the line, usually at the end. By *alliteration* is meant the recurrence of particular single sounds at certain fixed places, or merely a certain number of times within the line. A *quantitative* system is one in which syllables are classified as short or long and certain limitations of sequences are applied in terms of this division. A *stress* system involves a division of syllables into stressed and unstressed, again, with certain limitations on their sequence of occurrence. Similarly in *tonal* poetry, we classify syllables into types based on pitch characteristics and regulate the line in accordance with the permitted sequence of tonal types.

The application of any of these principles requires a numerical statement regarding the number of occurrences of the relevant characteristic in the line. This characteristic of prosodic systems may be called its metrical aspect. Thus, in the Swahili example cited, the occurrence of 8 syllables in a line is a metrical characteristic.

Metrical characteristics may be more or less rigid. On this basis they can be classified as fixed, alternative, bounded, maximal or minimal. These may be illustrated as follows. The requirement that every line have 6 syllables is a fixed metrical characteristic; that it may have either 6 or 8 an alternative; that it have no more than 8 or less than 5 bounded; that it have at most 6, a maximal, and that it have at least 6 syllables a minimal. An example of a minimal characteristic occurs below in the instance of Somali alliteration where the requirement is merely that every line have at least one occurrence of the basic consonant.

Quantity, stress, and tone can only be used as prosodic principles in those languages which have the required phonological characteristics. On the other hand, syllable count, alliteration, and rhyme can be applied in any language. This is an important factor in the consideration of the historical relationships of prosodic systems. Universally applicable principles like that of syllabic count can always be borrowed from one language to another, whereas quantitative patterns cannot be borrowed by a language which does not possess the linguistic distinction between short and long vowels.

It appears safe to conclude that except for possible recent influences of European rhymed poetry, the vast majority of African peoples south of the Sahara, including here the non-Moslem peoples of West Africa and all the Bantu peoples except the Islamicized Swahili, do not possess prosodic systems. The most conclusive evidence is the statement of a native speaker whose training would enable him to detect such a system did it exist. Several instances of such statements have been found. Babalola (1957, p. 7) says "Yoruba poetry has neither rhyme or regular metre. The 'line' of Ijala poetry is the sense group and its length varies." Nketia (1955, p. 77) a professionally trained musicologist and linguist arrives at the same conclusion regarding the Akan languages of Ghana.

There are two exceptions, it would appear, to this general rule. One of these is the occurrence of tone riddles among the Efik in Nigeria, and the other is a system of alliteration among the Somali. Particularly in the former instance, Arabic influence is entirely excluded by the nature of the system which involves significant pitch—a linguistic feature not found in Arabic.

The existence of tone-riddles among the Efik was discovered by Simmons (1955). The tone-riddle is here a specific subtype of riddle for which the indigenous name is *ukabade ikɔ* 'change of words.' The answer to the riddle has the same number of syllables and the same sequence of tones as the question. An example follows (Simmons, 1955, p. 423):

Query: àfák ɔkɔk kéták útɔ̀ŋ
     putting chew-stick under ear
Response: èsín ényìn kéŋkpɔ́ ówò
     putting eyes in thing of person

It is quite possible that tone-riddles, hitherto unreported, are found elsewhere among African peoples, particularly those in the same general area as the Efik.

The prosodic system of the Somali is about the minimum conceivable. The only requirement is that one particular consonant shall occur at least once in every line of the poem. All of the poetry seems to be sung. Kirk (1905) mentions three genres. Of these the *gerar*, sung on horseback, deals with warlike subjects; the *gabei*, usually sung around the fire, has a non-warlike, often amatory subject matter; and the *hes* is a dancing song with alternating men's and women's parts. In addition, there is the *hoyhoytan* or satire, mentioned by Cerulli (e.g. 1913, No. 16). The prosodic form described above occurs in all of these genres and in practically all published examples. It occurs likewise in the songs which occur in a narrative context in the folklore collection edited by Reinisch (1900).

The following is an example of a *gerar* in *g* (Kirk, 1905, p. 172).

> Ma sidi galoga
> o guluf mel ka daremei
> yan gamՑi wai haben
> sidi arka iyo gosha
> o gabnihi laga layei
> gurhan ma igu bote
> Like the bustard
> Who has seen an enemy somewhere
> I cannot sleep at night.
> Like the lion and the lioness
> Whose young have been slain
> I pace about distraught.

In some poems phonetically similar consonants are treated as equivalents for the purpose of alliteration. These are: *d* and *ḍ* (the latter a voiced apical stop); *s* and *sh*; *h* and *ḥ* (*ḥ* being an unvoiced pharyngeal); *γ* and *g*. In one extended example (Cerulli, 1913, No. 15) the liquids *l, r* and *n* are treated as equivalents and there is at least one probable example of *w* and *y* as rhymes.

We turn now to a consideration of classical Arabic prosody as a source of verse forms in a number of African languages. There exist extensive collections of Arabic poetry from the period immediately preceding and contemporary with Muhammad (570–632). These were all written down at a later period. Even if, as is probably the case, many examples are not authentic, the forms employed are certainly pre-Islamic.

The predominant type in these collections is the *qaṣīdah* or "ode," and it is the *qaṣīdah* which provides almost exclusively the basis for the descriptive science of prosody whose invention in the eighth century is attributed to Khalil b. Aḥmad. The *qaṣīdah* employs two prosodic principles simultaneously, quantity and rhyme. Each verse (*bayt* 'house, tent') consists of two hemistichs (*miṣraՑ* 'one of the two flaps of a tent door').

The rhyme which occurs at the end of each verse is identical throughout the poem. In addition, the first hemistich of the first verse (ʿarūd 'central tent-pole') usually but not always participates in the verse rhyme. If our unit is the hemistich, then the typical rhyme scheme is a a b a c a d a. If the ʿarūd does not rhyme we have a b c b d b e b. Every verse consists of a fixed sequence of long and short syllables which, with certain allowed substitutions, is constant throughout the poem. The last syllable of each hemistich is considered long regardless of its length in prose. A syllable is considered long if it consists either of a long vowel or of a vowel (normally short) followed by a consonant. There are 16 standard quantitative schemes, each of which has a name.

The quantitative and rhyme scheme of the qaṣīdah is illustrated here from the first two lines of the poem of Ṭarafah. Because of the length of the lines, each hemistich is written as a separate line. The end of each first hemistich is indicated by a comma and that of a verse by a period.

> lixawlata ʔaṭlālun biburqati thahmadi,
> talūhu kibāqi lwashmi fī ẓāhiri lyadi.
> wuqūfan bihā ṣaḥbī ʿalayya maṭayyahum,
> yaqūlūna lā tahlik ʔasan watajalladi.

There are traces yet of Khaula in the stony tract of Thahmad, apparent like the tattoo-mark seen on the back of a hand. There my companions halted their beasts awhile over me, saying "Don't perish of sorrow; bear it with fortitude."

The quantitative scheme of these two verses, which are in the meter Ṭawīl 'the long one' is as follows.

1. $\cup - \cup / \cup - - - / \cup - \cup / \cup - \cup -,$
   $\cup - \cup / \cup - - - / \cup - - / \cup - \cup -.$

2. $\cup - - / \cup - - - / \cup - \cup / \cup - \cup -,$
   $\cup - - / \cup - - - / \cup - \cup / \cup - \cup -.$

The rules of rhyme are rather complex. The following account omits certain refinements which are irrelevant for comparative study. Rhymes are of two types called "fettered" or "free." The "fettered" rhyme ends in a consonant. The vowel which precedes may, in practice, be any of the three short vowels of classical Arabic a, i, or u. The "free" rhyme ends in a vowel. This final vowel and the preceding consonant must always be the same. The preceding syllable must be one of the four following types and this type remains the same through the poem. These are: (1) ā only;

(2) *ī* or *ū*; (3) a short vowel followed by any consonant ("closed syllable"); (4) a short vowel *a*, *i*, or *u* not followed by a consonant in the same syllable. An example of the first type would be a rhyme -*ānū* which would have to be maintained unchanged through the entire poem. An example of the second type would be a poem in which every verse ended either in -*īlū* or -*ūlū*. In the third type -*ahmū*, -*ismū*, -*urmū*, etc. would rhyme. The fourth type is illustrated by the poem just cited in which the rhymed lines end in -*adī*. Lines ending in -*idī* and -*udī* might occur in such a poem.

A second pre-Islamic type is the *rajaz*. In his form the line is not divided into hemistichs. As in the *qaṣīdah* the same end rhyme occurs throughout the poem. The quantitative basis of each line, which is usually shorter than a hemistich of the *qaṣīdah* is the *rajaz* foot – – ᴗ –, which may be doubled or extended in other ways. Occasionally other feet are employed. Rajaz poets did not usually compose Qaṣīdahs and vice versa. Its subject matter was typically satire.

The following is an example of Rajaz (Ibn Hishām, p. 562):

> in tuqbilū nuʕāniq
> wanafrushu nnamāriq
> ʔin tudbirū nufāriq
> farāqa ghayri wāmiq

> If you advance we will embrace you
> And spread out the cushions.
> If you retreat we will separate from you
> A separation without love.

> – – ᴗ – ᴗ – –
> ᴗ – ᴗ – ᴗ – –
> – – ᴗ – ᴗ – –
> ᴗ – ᴗ – ᴗ – –

A still simpler form is *sajʕ* or rhymed prose. In *sajʕ*, each line is marked by end rhyme but there is no quantitative or other internal regulation. This form was characteristic of the *kāhins* or soothsayers. It was likewise employed by Muhammad in the Koran. In later times, it was cultivated as an art form as, for example, in the famous Assemblies (*maqāmāt*) of Al-Harīrī in the twelfth century.

Writers on Arabic prosody have often assumed that *sajʕ*, *rajaz*, and *qaṣīdah* constitute a historical progression with the *sajʕ* as the simplest coming first. This is quite possible, though it cannot be conclusively proven. In English, free verse, which is formally simpler, is more recent than rhymed form.[1]

Since the classical *qaṣīdah* employs the quantitative principle it can only be borrowed by languages in which there exists a linguistic distinction between short and long vowels. Such borrowings have occurred among two Mohammedan peoples of the Western Sudan—the Fulani and the Hausa.

The employment of the *qaṣīdah* form in Fulani is confined to learned poetry. There are apparently only two published instances, Reichardt (1859) and Gaden (1935). Both of these poems are written in Arabic script and are by known authors. The former is a poem of religious exhortation in the *mutadārik* meter, one of the standard sixteen but only known from postclassical examples. The latter is an account of the war of El Hadj Omar against the French, written in *Kāmīl*, a common classical meter. The Fulani language possesses a distinction of short and long vowels and contains the same syllable types as Arabic. It therefore lends itself without difficulty to the Arabic quantitative forms. Outside of the two examples cited, all published instances of Fulani songs or recited poetry are in the traditional African style, without prosodic rules. The occurrence of the *qaṣīdah* form in Fulani is then a learned exercise which has not been fully assimilated into Fulani culture.

Among the Hausa, there is likewise a distinction between learned and popular poetry. The former employs classical Arabic forms and is religious in subject matter. Unlike the Fulani instance, however, the quantitative principle in modified form has been thoroughly adopted and forms the basis of popular poetry. Even here, however, the indigenous African type without prosodic structure is retained in the songs of the spirit-possession cult and in the signal drumming which occurs in a variety of cultural contexts.

As in Fulani, the syllabic structure of the language is essentially like that of Arabic so that it lends itself without difficulty to quantitative schemes. Whereas the Arabic quantitative patterns are employed with great consistency in the learned poetry, the other chief device of the *qaṣīdah*, namely rhyme, tends to be used loosely. In some poems a considerable number of lines do not rhyme and in still others rhyme is not employed at all. In the popular poetry, rhyme does not occur except as an occasional device; it is not a constituent of the prosodic form.

Where rhyme is found in the learned poetry, the rules are simpler than those of classical Arabic. Since final syllables ending in a consonant are uncommon in the language, the rhyme is always equivalent to the "loose" rhyme of Arabic. No attention is paid to the phonetic structure of the syllable preceding the last or rhyme syllable. The rhyme, then, always consists of identity of the final syllable consisting of a consonant followed by a vowel.

Popular poetry makes use of quantitative sequences which are generally shorter than those of the classical Arabic meters. The lines are always paired, each corresponding functionally to a hemistich, or half-line of Arabic verse. In some poems, the first of each pair has a meter different from the second throughout. As in classical Arabic poetry, the last vowel is always treated as long. In any line, preliminary syllables up to four in number may be found which are not part of the quantitative pattern. A great variety of metrical forms occur in popular use.

The following is an example of Hausa popular verse in which the odd numbered lines have a different meter from that of the even numbered lines. Preliminary syllables which are not part of the metrical scheme are set off by commas in the scansion (Prietze, 1916, No. 6).

> dūniyā giširī čē
> da ḍanḍanā kan ḳārēta.
> dūniyā na dunānā
> karē ya ce yam māgārā.
> kō dūniyā tā ḳārē
> kāzā ba tā ḍaw tayki ba.
> kō dūniyā tā ḳārē
> kūsū ba zay haka rāmī ba.

The world is like salt; if you taste it, it is finished.
'The world is sinking away' says the dog to the dancers.
Even if the world were to end, the chicken could not lift a bag of grain.
Even if the world were to end, the rat could not dig a hole.

$$\_\ \cup\ \_\ \cup\ \cup\ \_\ \_,$$
$$\cup,\ \_\ \cup\ \_\ \_\ \_\ \_,$$
$$\_\ \cup\ \_\ \cup\ \cup\ \_\ \_,$$
$$\cup,\ \_\ \cup\ \_\ \_\ \_\ \_.$$
$$\_,\ \_\ \cup\ \_\ \_\ \_\ \_,$$
$$\_,\ \_\ \cup\ \_\ \_\ \_\ \_,$$
$$\_,\ \_\ \cup\ \_\ \_\ \_\ \_,$$
$$\_\ \cup\ \_\ \cup\ \cup\ \_\ \_\ \_.$$

This metrical scheme may be summarized as follows:

$$- \cup - \underset{\smile}{\overset{\frown}{}} - -,$$
$$- \cup - \underset{\smile}{\overset{\frown}{}} - - -.$$

We now turn to a consideration of postclassical Arabic verse forms. In the early Islamic period there arose the practice of improvisation by the insertion of new verses within some already well-known *qaṣīdah*. A fixed number of hemistichs, two or more, was added after the initial hemistich of each line of the original poem and rhymed with it. This process, known as *tasmīṭ* 'the stringing [of pearls],' produces a stanza form of rhyme. As noted earlier, if each hemistich of the *qaṣīdah* is considered a line, then the rhyme scheme of a poem which has the *ʿarūd* or first hemistich rhyme is a a / b a / c a / d a / .... If now we insert two new hemistichs in each line rhyming with the first hemistich we obtain the rhyme scheme a, a a, a / b, b b, a / c, c c, a / d, d d, a... where commas are used to set off the new inserted lines. Where the original *qaṣīdah* did not contain the initial hemistich rhyme the scheme became a a a b / c c c b / d d d b / .... The inserted lines were, of course, in the same quantitative meter as that of the original poem. Soon original poems were being composed in stanzas of this type. An example from the latter part of the eighth century is found in the *Dīwān* or collected poems of Abū Nuwas.

Later the basic *tasmīṭ* scheme was elaborated in Spain by the devising of new nonclassical meters, by varying the meters of different lines in the same stanza and by the development of more complex rhyme schemes. In this form it was called the *muwaššaḥ* ('girdled'). When written in the colloquial rather than classical meter it was called the *zajal*. From Spain, the *zajal* spread throughout the Moslem world. It was also imitated in Spanish, Provençal, and Italian. It was through the *zajal* that rhyme was introduced into Western Europe.[2]

The *tasmīṭ* and its later derivatives continue in use up to the present in both learned and popular poetry and examples are to be found in almost every collection of contemporary Arabic poetry.

One published example of the *tasmīṭ* in the Hausa language occurs alongside of the more common *qaṣīdah*. This is the "War Song of Abdallah dan Fodio" (Robinson, 1930, p. 133-44). Each line consists of two classical *ramal* feet ($- \cup - - / - \cup - -$) and the rhyme scheme is a a a a b, c c c c b, d d d d b....

The first two stanzas follow:

yan ʔuwā mun gōde ʔallā
mun yi ʔīmančī da sallā
har jihādi don ka jallā
mun ḳašē dangī na Dallā
sun sanī sū sun yi sarkī

mun ḳašē ʔalkāfirāwā
sū suwā nē Gōbirāwā
sun tafō don ḳādirāwā
sū da sāšin ʔAsbināwā
sun tafō sū duk da sarkī

Brethren we thank God;
We perform acts of faith and prayer
Even holy war for Thee the Exalted one:
We slew the breed of dogs,
They know (now) that their task was beyond their strength.

We have slain the unbelievers:
Who were they? The men of Gobir
They came against the followers of Abd-el-Kadr
They and half the men of Asben.
They came, all of them, together with their king.

Among the Kanuri, an important Moslem people immediately to the east of the Hausa, a single example of the *tasmīṭ* rhymed stanzas is forthcoming (Duisberg, 1913, pp. 169-85). It can hardly be accidental that, as in the Hausa example quoted above, we have the five-line stanza in place of the more common four-line scheme. Since the Kanuri language does not have significant distinctions of vowel length, the quantitative aspect of the *tasmīṭ* cannot be reproduced. The lines are of different length and it does not appear that any other prosodic principle is employed. The poem is an isolated example of rhyme in Kanuri. All the rest of the published poetry is in the traditional African style without prosodic organization.

It is among the Swahili that the *tasmīṭ* has scored its greatest success. It is by far the most common form in both learned and popular poetry, whether sung or recited. Swahili does not possess vowel quantitative distinctions. This principle has been replaced by that of syllabic count. By far the most popular variant is the four-line stanza in which each line contains eight syllables. Since all Swahili syllables end in a vowel, the rhymes would all be classified as "loose" in the Arabic terminology. As in Hausa, the rule of rhyme is identity of the last syllable. For Swahili, this simplification is practically inevitable on linguistic grounds. Since closed syllables and vowel length do not exist, the fourfold classification of Arabic penultimate syllables falls together in a single type. In the last syllable the phonetically similar vowels *e* and *i* are permitted to rhyme as well as the pair *o* and *u*.

The following is an example of the very common four-line stanza with eight syllables per line (Dammann, 1940, p. 214). The first three stanzas are as follows:

> axi phani kwa upesi
> ilo ali karatasi
> na wino mwema mweusi
> utilizao maozi
>
> na kalamu mahabubu
> ilo njema ya Arabu
> nowe ina la wahabu
> Mola wethu Muawazi
>
> nowe ina la wadudi
> 'bismilla' ni butadi
> ndiye pweke wa abadi
> mfalume mwenye ezi

My brother, give me good paper quickly and good black ink which comforts the eyes, and the beloved pen, the fine one of the Arabs, that I may write the name of the Munificent, our merciful Lord. I shall write the name of the Beloved; I shall begin "in the name of God." He is the unique one from eternity, the King, the Possessor of Power.

In addition to the more common four-line stanza, five-line stanzas are occasionally found. In one example, the "Song of Liongo" (Meinhof, 1924), the conscious following of Arabic models is evidenced by the author's mention of the technical term *taxmīs*, literally 'making five.' The predominance of the four-line stanza in Swahili is not surprising in view of other evidences of its popularity.[3] Occasional examples of more elaborate rhyme schemes reminiscent of the *zajal* of medieval Spain are found, for example, the following: a b c b d b e e e, f g h g i e e e, etc.

Besides the common eight-syllable line, longer types are sometimes found with internal caesuras, that is, obligatory word boundaries at certain fixed points. Among these are a ten-syllable line with caesura after the sixth syllable, an eleven-syllable line with caesura after the sixth syllable and, most elaborate of all, a fifteen-syllable line with two caesuras, one after the sixth and the other after the tenth syllable. An example of the latter follows: The caesuras have been marked by commas inserted in the text (Neuhaus, 1935, p. 145).

> baada humidi, na salati, ntawa hubiri
> kwanda kutukuza, maulidi, ni mzaffari
> alikaghirimu, laki tatu, za dananiri
> wakamuuliza, na fuuye, wakiiona.

After praise and prayer I will inform you. The celebrator of the Maulid (i.e. feast of Muhammad's birthday) is Jaʕfar. He spent 300,000 dinars. They asked him what use it was and they looked upon him.

There is also at least one published example of a Berber *tasmɪt* (De Calassanti-Motylinski, 1885).

Whereas in all of the examples previously considered, there can be no reasonable doubt of direct Arabic influence, there are a number of other prosodic systems in which the historical problem is more complex. Particularly in the Horn of Africa (Ethiopia and the Somalilands), a number of languages use rhyme as a principle of versification, sometimes in combination with other principles. The languages concerned are Geʕez (Classical Ethiopic), Amharic, Tigre, Tigrinya, Saho, and Galla. It will be convenient to refer to these as constituting an East African rhyming area.

The earliest examples of Geʕez verse, all apparently unpublished and dating from the fourteenth century when Geʕez was no longer a spoken language, appear from the descriptions to consist of lines of irregular length and without any principle of internal regulation. All the lines of the same poem have the same end rhyme consisting of identity of the last syllable. As a system this is equivalent to Arabic rhymed prose (*sajʕ*) and Cerulli at least has no doubt regarding its Arabic origin.[4] The writers of this verse all probably spoke Amharic as their first language. Alongside of external indications we have the fact that consonants are considered equivalents for rhyme when they have fallen together in the Amharic consonantal system and this in turn coincides with the Amharic tradition of pronouncing Geʕez.

The first recorded examples of Amharic poetry, the so-called Royal Songs—a collection of twelve poems celebrating the martial exploits of Ethiopian kings in their battles with the Moslems and dating from about the same period as the Geʕez poetry considered above—are likewise in rhymed prose, with the same rule of rhyme. As a further indication of the connection of the two traditions, we have a particular feature in regard to rhyme which characterizes both Ge'ez and Amharic poetry down to the present day. A final consonant of the line which in prose would be pronounced without a following vowel is followed by a central unsounded high vowel ə thus producing, in these cases, the identity of final syllable which is the rule of rhyme in both languages. In the Ethiopic syllabary a consonant which is not followed by a vowel and a consonant followed by ə are written with the same symbol. It is possible on the evidence of related languages that at the time when this syllabary was invented the final position consonant was actually followed by a vowel ə in the spoken language. It would then continue to be pronounced in poetic recitation, thus maintaining the identity of final syllable consisting of a consonant followed by a vowel as the principle of rhyme. This practice continues up to the present in Amharic poetry constructed on the more recent principle of rhyme combined with syllabic count. A final consonant which in spoken Amharic prose would not be followed by a vowel, is followed by ə in reading poetry and counts as a separate syllable.

The Amharic Royal Songs mentioned above differ from Ge'ez in rhyme only in that r and l freely rhyme, and while in some of the poems the same rhyme is maintained throughout, in others a new rhyme may be introduced at certain points. Thus, the seventh poem of this collection consists of 22 lines with the following rhymes q(ə), q(ə), q(ə), q(ə), q(ə), q(ə), ra, la, la, ra, la, ra, ra, la, ra, la, ra, la, la, la, ra, la.

In the fifteenth century strophic poems make their first appearance in Ge'ez liturgical poetry and they continue to be cultivated up to the present day. Three and five line strophes predominate with the same end rhyme according to the rules of the earlier rhymed prose in each strophe. The rhyme schemes are thus a a a b b b c c c... and a a a a a b b b b b c c c c c.... As in the earlier rhymed prose there is no metrical regulation of the line. The most famous early example of this form is the fifteenth-century *Weddase Maryam* or 'hymns in praise of Mary,' whose literary origin has been discussed in the literature. Ethiopian tradition refers the original to Ephrem Syrus, a well-known Syriac writer, but the theory of Arabic origin has been advanced. The latter is not an evidence of Moslem influence in this case, since by this time the various Christian churches of the Near East were using Arabic, the dominant spoken language, for literary purposes.

The relations of the Monophysite Ethiopian church to that of the

Syrian Monophysites is well documented. Regardless of the literary origins of the poem, the strophic rhyme scheme is similar to that of the later Syriac poetry. Since the Syriac use of rhyme is derived from Arabic this would, in the ultimate instance, be an example of the indirect influence of Arabic. Earlier Syriac poetry utilized the principle of syllabic count which existed before the Arabic principle of rhyme was superimposed. As has been noted, Geʿez poetry does not involve the principle of syllabic count. The most probable explanation of the Geʿez strophic forms is that the Syriac principle of rhymed stanzas was amalgamated in Ethiopic with the earlier practice of rhymed prose resulting in the typical strophic forms of Geʿez ecclesiastical poetry.

In Amharic, as in Geʿez, there is a contrast between earlier and later prosodic systems. The rhymed prose of the Royal Songs, the earliest surviving example of Amharic poetry, is succeeded by the principle of syllabic count combined with the rhyme of the earlier form. In the existing collections, short sung couplets consisting of two lines, almost always of twelve syllables each with a caesura after the sixth syllable are very common. Longer poems sometimes consist of sequences of such rhymed couplets and therefore have the rhyme scheme a a b b c c …. In other examples, a single rhyme is found throughout the poem, or there is occasional change of rhyme, just as earlier in some of the Royal Songs. Some published examples do not employ syllabic count and when monorhymed, coincide completely in form with the early rhymed prose.

The source of the principle of syllabic count in modern Amharic poetry is uncertain. It is possibly derived from the modern Arabic quatrain (ʿarobi) as described for Tunis by Stumme (1893). The ʿarobi is a four line stanza with rhyme pattern a b c b, or sometimes a b a b. In the Tunisian examples, syllabic count has replaced the classical quantitative meter as it has in much modern Arabic popular poetry, particularly from North Africa. Most of the ʿarobis in Stumme's collection have six syllables per line. In a collection of Berber poetry from the Riff, almost all the examples are twelve-syllable rhymed couplets with caesura after the sixth syllable (Renisio, 1932). These two instances suggest a wide extension for this form, particularly in North Africa. The difference between a rhymed couplet of twelve-syllable lines with caesura after the sixth, and a quatrain of six-syllable lines with the rhyme patterns a b c b is, of course, purely graphic, so that the most common Amharic verse form coincides completely in its prosodic rules with the ʿarobi. It is the absence of this form in published collections of popular verse of Arabic speaking areas nearer to Amharic than North Africa that suggests caution in accepting the ʕarobi as the model for modern Amharic verse. There is the further fact that languages other than Amharic in this area have syllabic count along with rhyme, and the historical connection of these verse forms to Amharic would have to be accounted for.

One example is Saho, a Cushitic language of Eritrea. The total published poetic material is apparently very small, being confined to a small collection of songs collected by Reinisch (1889–90, Vol. I). These are usually rhymed, though often only sporadically. However, numbers 4 and 7 of the collection show great regularity. Each is of six lines with rhyme scheme a b c b d b and with the same number of syllables in each line, five in the first instance, and four in the second. Again if we consider the lines as equivalent to Amharic hemistichs the resemblance is close, the main differences being in the number of syllables and the fact that the poems have six hemistichs rather than four. There are, however, occasional examples of six hemistichs or more in Amharic verse, the Tunisian ʕarobi and among the Beni Iznassen Berbers of the Riff. Besides, Amharic occasionally employs a ten-syllable line with caesura after the fifth syllable.

Number 7 of Reinisch (1889–90) will illustrate the form in Saho.

> sūm silēmān
> nō dēsamā
> lubāk belli
> dat haššamā
> ginni Falūm
> kä Gazāmā

Prince Sileman, our protector, like the lion is his black hair. He is like the Jinn of Falum and Gazama.

The extensive collections of Galla poetry display in their versification, a general resemblance to the Amharic couplet and the Saho examples just discussed. Galla poems are usually divided into four-line strophes with rhyme schemes a b a b or a b c b. The number of syllables in each line is fixed and is the same throughout the poem as a general rule. Poems with four-syllable lines are rare, with five frequent, with six or seven the most common of all, and with eight syllables likewise frequent. The examples with six syllables and rhyme scheme a b c b are, of course, formally identical with the usual Amharic couplet. There are cases of longer lines with a regular caesura. Thus there is one poem consisting of eleven-syllable lines with a caesura after the fourth syllable.

Rhyme is somewhat sporadic in Galla poetry but the number of syllables is fixed practically without exception. An occasional device of Galla poetry is vowel harmony between the first and third lines and between the second and fourth lines of the quatrain. In the following example this is carried out completely:

> lensan lon gusa
> bia garati
> densan lon busa
> iya nafati

> Lensa [a kind of grass] causes the cattle to dry up
> On the mountain;
> Flight exposes cattle,
> To screams of desperation.

Tigrinya is an Ethiopian Semitic language spoken to the north of Amharic and in the same general region as the extinct Geʿez, or classical Ethiopic. Unlike Amharic, Saho and Galla, there is no regular use of the rhymed couplet. Rhyme shifts at irregular intervals, as in some of the medieval Amharic Royal Songs, but these changes are more frequent, every four to seven lines on the average, with occasional unrhymed lines. In much of the poetry there seems to be no internal metrical regulation of the line but in other cases the principle of syllabic count is unmistakably present. In most of Conti Rossini's extensive collection (1903–5) we have a ten-syllable line with caesura after the fourth syllable. A single, quite long poem on the battle of Addi Cheleto (Conti Rossini, 1906) has five-syllable lines with the usual change of end rhyme at irregular intervals.

Tigrinya does not share the Geʿez-Amharic tradition of adding ə after a final consonant in recitation. The rhyme therefore, which consists in principle in identity of the last syllable, may be either CV or CVC. The equivalence of similar consonants for purposes of rhyme is carried very far, as in the neighboring Tigre. Not only are r and l treated as equivalents but also k, kʰ, and h, and likewise the pairs q and qʷ, g and gʷ, n and ñ, and the laryngeals ʕ and ʔ. In certain poems, much as in Tigre, all voiced stops b, d, j, g and gʷ are treated as equivalents. The rhymes of Conti Rossini (1903–5) No. 157 will illustrate this: gar, gar, gʷal, gʷal, gʷal, gʷal, jor, gar, bar, bar, gar.

The remaining language of the Ethiopian area for which extensive poetic collections exist is Tigre, another Semitic language, spoken north-east of Tigrinya. In Tigre poetry each line is divided into two hemistichs. There does not appear to be any principle of metrical organization within the line. As in Arabic and as in the earliest Geʿez poetry, the same rhyme is maintained throughout the entire poem.

The rule of rhyme is in principle close to that of Arabic classical poetry in that there is some regulation of the penultimate syllable in the line. Unlike Amharic and Geʿez no ǝ is added after final consonants. A marked feature of Tigre rhyme is the degree to which phonetically similar consonants are equated for purposes of rhyme; this has led previous observers to the conclusion that the consonants do not participate in the rhyme.[5] As a matter of fact, the rules are quite exact. Because an ǝ is not added to a final consonant in recitation, rhymes fall into two classes as in Arabic "fettered," ending in a consonant and "free," ending in a vowel. In "fettered" rhyme the final consonant which must always belong to the same class of phonetically similar consonants is always preceded by the same vowel. In "free" rhyme the final vowel must always be the same, the preceding consonant must belong to the same consonant class and the preceding syllable is likewise subject to some restrictions. If the syllable is open, i.e. ends in a vowel, it must be open through the whole poem and have the same vowel. If not, it must be closed through the whole poem with no restriction on the particular consonant which closes the penultimate syllable. Sometimes we have a rhyme in which the same final vowel is always preceded by two consonants, but there are no restrictions on the combinations allowed.

For purposes of rhyme the consonants fall into a number of almost mutually exclusive classes. These classes are the liquids (r, l, n, and occasionally m), the labials (b, m), the laryngeals (ḥ, ʿ, ʾ, and h), y, which forms a class by itself, and the obstruents consisting of the remaining consonants except w, for example t, d, ṭ, s, z, f, k, q, ǰ, š, etc. The con-sonant w never seems to be used in rhyme.

These rules of rhyme may be illustrated as follows. An example of fettered rhyme consisting of a final liquid always preceded by a is found in Littmann (1913–15), poem 71, which rhymes -an, -ar, -ar, -ar, -al, etc. The rule of loose rhyme in which the penultimate syllable is open and always has the same vowel is exemplified by poem 7 in the same collection. The rhyme here consists of final a, preceded by an obstruent, preceded by the vowel ä. The rhymes of this eight-line poem are -äka, -äta, -äsa,

-äta, -äta, -äsa, -äša, äta. An example of loose rhyme with penultimate closed syllable is poem 32 of Littmann, another eight-line poem in which the final vowel is *e* always preceded by an obstruent which is always preceded by a consonant without limitations as to class. The rhymes are *-mde, -rqe, -ǰǰe, -zze, -dde, -nte, -sse, -dde*.

Except for the hemistich division, the resemblance of Tigre verse prosody to Arabic rhymed prose is patent. Even the extensive substitution of similar consonants for each other in the rhyme has its parallel in the relative frequency of this practice, called *Pikfā* by the Arabs in rhymed prose and Rajaz.[6] The Tigre are Moslems and subject to strong Arabic cultural influence. As with the earliest Geʿez and Amharic rhymed prose we may hesitate between the alternative explanations of Arabic origin and continuation of a common South Semitic tradition.

In addition to the languages already mentioned, Beja should probably be included in the East African rhyming area. The small collection of Roper (1923) seems to be the only published material. These all are divided into four-line stanzas without any apparent metrical system. Rhyme is frequent but sporadic. Several poems, however, are rhymed throughout. The form, therefore, again approximates the rhymed prose of Tigre and the earlier Geʿez and Amharic poetry.

Two other peoples in Northern Africa have prosodic systems, the Nubians and the Berbers. The Nubians inhabit the Nile Valley of the northern part of the Sudan. There are also speakers of related dialects in the hills of Kordofan and still farther west. We are only concerned here with the Nile Nubians. But a small amount of poetic material has been published—much of it incidental to ethnologic texts in the form—for example, marriage songs. Except for some songs appended by Lepsius to his grammar (Lepsius, 1880), none of these show prosodic regulation. In Lepsius' material, the songs are all divided into stanzas of four lines each with rhymes a b a b or a a b b in each stanza and differing from stanza to stanza. The rhyme usually consists of repetition of the same word.

An example follows (Lepsius, 1880, p. 256):

> galaban šaǰan tōd wēki
> ekk aminsu dīkol wēki
> en anīsa mutta bōgsun
> sāla-būn olmisseg bōgsun

A son of worry and of sorrow we considered you. We considered you as one who died. Your friend cut her hair and threw it away. She is sick and has been weeping.

The eight-syllable line, of course, is reminiscent of Swahili although a direct influence from this quarter seems unlikely. The Nubians are Moslems and universally bilingual in Arabic. In one Nubian text, an Arabic poem of three lines occurs with end rhyme and eight syllables in each line (Junker and Schaefer, 1921–22, p. 90). Such eight-syllable lines, usually but not always quantitative, are common in Egyptian popular poetry. The knowledge of Egyptian Arabic poetry shown by this quotation in a Nubian text is very strong evidence for the Arabic origin of the principle of rhyme and the line of eight syllables in Nile Nubian poetry.

The Berber language is spoken widely in North Africa and the Sahara in many distinct dialectal variations, some of which deserve to be ranked as separate languages. We are dealing here with a number of largely independent local poetic traditions. The absence of any recorded poetic literature from many areas makes it difficult to draw valid conclusions of a historical nature at the present stage of our knowledge. Three main types of prosody can be distinguished in the existing material. These are: (1) absence of any prosodic principle; (2) rhyme unaccompanied by metrical regulation of the line; (3) rhyme combined with syllabic count.

The first of these types, the absence of any prosodic principle, seems particularly characteristic of the Shilḥ and Beraber group of southern and central Morocco. One poem recorded by Boulifa in the Demnat area of southern Morocco (Boulifa, 1908, p. 63) has end rhyme, shifting at intervals in the course of the poem. In the absence of rhyme, this form therefore approximates that of the medieval Amharic Royal Songs. There is some possibility that the poetry of this part of Morocco has a fixed number of stresses per line, but our linguistic knowledge is insufficient to verify the hypothesis.

The Riffian area of northern Morocco is one in which rhyme is normal. Biarnay's examples (1917) from the Ait Temseman are generally rhymed couplets, though a few are longer—the longest example running to eight lines. Renisio's Riffian material which shows two or sometimes three-line poems with rhyme, is drawn from three tribes, the Ait Ouriaghel, the Beni Tuzin, and the Beni Iznassen. Of these examples, a majority for all three tribes consists of 12-syllable lines with caesura after the sixth syllable. In the rest, the line does not appear to be metrically regulated. The typical form, as has been noted earlier, is therefore identical prosodically with the common modern Amharic couplet form.

The Zenaga of Mauretania, to judge from Nicolas's data, fall into the second category as defined above—that is rhyme without syllabic count. The typical form is here the single quatrain or a string of quatrains each with the rhyme scheme a b a b.

Tuareg poetry, of which Foucauld (1925–30) has made an extensive collection for the Ahaggar region, is characterized by poems of varying length, some quite long, with the same end rhyme throughout. Foucauld himself describes the poetry as quantitative. However, since there are so many inconsistencies in the application of the schemes as described, and since no linguistic basis in vowel quantitative distinctions has been reported in any other Berber dialect or indeed, by other students of the Tuareg languages, it appears that provisionally at least, we should deny a quantitative basis for this poetry. What does occur is syllabic count with regular caesura. Each type has an indigenous name, which is applied to the melody to which it is sung. The types found are a nine-syllable line with caesura after the fourth syllable, a ten-syllable line with caesura after the fifth syllable, and a ten-syllable line with caesura after the sixth syllable.

The remaining area for which extensive collections exist is that of the Kabyles in Algeria. The typical rhyme scheme here is a a b a a b a a b... or a a b a b a a b a b a a b a b.... In longer poems the rhyme may shift at irregular intervals. This poetry, unlike that of the Riffian Berbers and the Tuaregs is not sung. Much of it is by known individual poets. In some instances, syllabic count is not employed. In others (e.g. Luciani, 1899), the three lines of the stanza have seven, five, and seven syllables respectively. In the poetry of Sid Mojand (1914), each poem consists of three tercets, that is of nine lines, with the syllabic count seven, five, and seven for each tercet as in Luciani's collection.

There is also a single published example of the *tasmīṭ murabbaʿ* from the island of Djerba (De Calassanti-Motylinski, 1885). The apparent rarity of this form as compared to others with no direct Arabic parallel makes one hesitate to accept this as proof of the Arabic origin of Berber prosody. It is more likely a later case of local influence on an already established prosodic tradition, whether of ultimately Arabic provenience or not.

From the data just reviewed, the outstanding impression is that of the great prosodic variety of various Berber regional poetic traditions. In one matter, at least, there is agreement, suggesting a common basis for these local developments. This is the rule of rhyme. Unlike any other known African system, the rhyme involves phonetic similarity or identity from the last vowel until the end of the verse. If the final sound of the line is a vowel, this means that the only requirement is vocalic identity and there are no restrictions on the previous consonant. If the lines end in one or more consonant then both this consonant and the previous vowel are involved in the rhyme. Everywhere the pairs *n* and *m*, *r* and *l* are treated as equivalents for purposes of rhyme. Among the Tuareg these equivalences are carried much further. The unvoiced stops form one group, the voiced stops another. The unvoiced fricatives *f* and *s* rhyme with each other. A final cluster of two consonants may rhyme with a single consonant, if the final consonant of the cluster is a permitted rhyme in itself. As an example, we cite Foucauld (1925–30), No. 28, in which the rhyme consists of *a* followed by an unvoiced stop, most frequently *t*: *at, art, at, ayt, art, art, aq, ant, at, alt, at, ak, ak, at*.

A further evidence of the basic unity of Berber poetic tradition is the common term *izli* for a two- or three-line poem, regardless of the regional differences in prosodic form.

The possible origin of the Riffian couplet of twelve-syllable lines with caesura after the sixth syllable in the Arabic ʕarobi has already been mentioned. There is likewise a possible Arabic source for the common Kabyle rhyme scheme a a b a a b.... In Fuad Hasanein (1939), a manuscript collection from Egypt possibly dating from the 17th century, a single long stanzaic poem (No. 30) has the following elaborate variant of the basic fourfold *zajal*: a a b, a a b, a a b, c c d, e e f, e e f, e e f, c c d, etc. In each tercet, the first and third lines consist of two *rajaz* feet (– – ◡ – / – – ◡ –) and the second line of one (– – ◡ –). The syllabic count is thus 8, 4, 8. The common Kabyle type likewise has a different and smaller number of syllables for the second line as opposed to the first and third (7, 5, 7). Moreover, Sid Mojand always uses three of these tercets producing a nine-line poem whose rhyme scheme is identical with the portions of the above poem which have non-recurrent rhyme. In the actual singing of the *zajal* these recurrent and non-recurrent parts are separated by an instrumental interlude.

In general, since the Berbers are all Moslems, large numbers are bilingual in Arabic, and their language contains a very large number of Arabic loan words—there is a real basis for assuming Arabic influence in this, as in many other cultural features.

As was indicated in the opening section, this paper has been of a survey nature and many of the conclusions are merely of a tentative nature. The great variety of prosodic systems in Africa is apparent. It is hoped that the gaps in synchronic material and both synchronic and diachronic analyses that it reveals, will be a stimulus to further work in this area. The outstanding impression in the historic dimensions is the vast reach of certain and, in many cases highly probable, Arabic influence in the northern part of Africa—an influence well documented for many other aspects of the culture of the area.

Some further observations on the question of rhyme may be of interest. Unlike syllabic count which may arise independently through the mechanism of a varying text set to a constantly repeated melodic line, and quantitative verse which may originate in the same fashion when the language contains quantitative distinctions, it is not easy to discern any obvious way in which systematic rhyme can arise. Sporadic rhyme, particularly through the literary device of repetition of the same word occurs almost everywhere but its utilization as a prosodic principle is another matter. In Africa, the single ultimate origin of all rhyme either in a common South Semitic tradition, or, far more likely, through the direct or indirect intermediary of Arabic is highly probable. Outside of the area considered here, the eventual Arabic origin of rhyme in western European languages and in Hebrew, Syriac, and Coptic has been indicated. To this should be added Persian and certain languages influenced in turn by Persian literary forms. With the possible exception of Chinese, it is likely that all rhyme has a single origin.

We perhaps never think of rhyme as an invention. To speakers of English with its tradition of rhymed poetry, rhyme appears as something "natural." It seems likely rather that rhyme is one of those devices whose invention by no means lies on the surface, but whose inherent esthetic expressiveness and applicability to all languages leads to its facile adoption in almost all instances where a people become acquainted with the possibility of its employment.

NOTES

[1] Complexity which is in general an imprecise and difficult notion, can for prosodic forms be given objective, measurable meaning. One prosodic form is more complex

than another, if the probability of choosing a conforming example by random choice rom a set of utterances of the requisite length is less.

² The Arabic origin of rhyme in Europe has been disputed by some Romance scholars. The *prima facie* case for Arabic derivation appears very strong. Menendez Pidal (1943), the well-known Romance specialist, considers and rejects the arguments against Arabic origin.

³ Thus Hartmann (1897, p. 214) calls it the *tasmīṭ* par excellence. It was this form, moreover, which was introduced in Hebrew in the early tenth century (*ibid.*, p. 113). Likewise, the only rhymed poem in Coptic, the *Triadon* (Lemm, 1903), consists of quatrains with the *tasmīṭ* rhyme scheme.

⁴ Cerulli (1956, p. 85), states, "Certainly the introduction of rhymed prose in Ethiopic was an imitation of Arabic." Moreover, the use of rhymed prose in the introductory section of the prose biography of Lalibala (Perruchon, 1892) is quite in the Arabic style.

An alternative theory is that rhymed prose is an old South Semitic tradition brought into Ethiopia by the Semitic migrants from South Arabia and continued independently in both Arabic and Ethiopic.

In this case, South Arabic, a language distinct from Northern classical Arabic, known from a large inscriptional literature and still spoken in several forms on the South Arabian coast and on a few islands in the Indian Ocean, becomes of special importance inasmuch as it is more closely related to Ethiopic than North Arabic is. Mehri has rhyme but with a fixed number of stresses per line (Jahn, 1902). The South Arabic dialect spoken on the island of Soqotri shows, most surprisingly, syllabic count but no rhyme (Mueller, 1905). Of course, rhymed prose may have existed and been superseded. The case for Arabic origin, then, seems stronger than for a common South Semitic tradition.

⁵ Thus Noeldeke (1917–18, p. 14) remarks "This rhyme is more careful than appears at first glance. Still it pays little attention to the identity of consonants."

⁶ Goldziher (1896–99), part 1, p. 79.

REFERENCES

Babalola, Adeboye. 1957. Ijala: The Poetry of Yoruba Hunters, *Black Orpheus*, No. 1, pp. 5-7, Ibadan, Nigeria.

Basset, H. 1920. Essai sur la litterature des Berbères. Algiers.

Biarnay, S. 1917. Étude sur les dialectes Berbères au Rif. Paris.

Bloch, A. 1946. Vers und Sprache im Altarabischen. Basel.

Boulifa, Said. 1908. Textes Berbères en dialecte de l'Atlas. Paris.

—— 1934. Receuil de poesies Kabyles. Algiers.

Cerulli, E. 1913. "Conti e proverbi somali nel dialetto degli Habar Auwāl," *Rivista degl. Studi Orientali*, 7:797-836. Rome.

—— 1919-20. "Somali Songs and Little Texts," *Journal of the African Society*, 19:135-40.

—— 1956. Storia della letteratura etiopica. Milan.

Chaine, M. 1920-21. "La poesie chez les Ethiopiens: Poesie amharique," *Revue de l'Orient Chretien*, pp. 306-26; 401-25.

Conti Rossini, C. 1903-5. "Conti populari tigrai," *Zeitschrift für Assyriologie*, 17:23-52; 18:320-86.

—— 1906. "Poemetto lirico tigrai per la battaglia di Addi Cheleto," in *Orientalistische Studien Noeldeke gewidmet*, 2:925-39.

Dalman, G. A. 1901. Palästinischer Diwan. Leipzig.

Dammann, E. 1940. Dichtungen in der Lamu-Mundart des Swahili. Hamburg.

De Calassanti-Motylinski, A. 1885. "Chanson berbère de Djerba," *Bulletin de Correspondance Africaine*, pp. 461-64, Algiers.

Desparmet, J. 1905. "La poésie Arabe actuelle à Blida et sa métrique," *Actes du XIVe Congress Internationale des Orientalistes*, 3:437-602, Algiers.

Duisberg, A. von. 1913. Grundriss der Kanuri-Sprache in Bornu. Berlin.

Elder, E. E. 1926. Egyptian Colloquial Arabic Reader. Oxford.

Faitlovitch, J. 1910. "Versi abissini," *Giornale della Societa Asiatica Italiana*, 23:1-88.

Foucauld, C. E. 1925-30. Poésies touareges: dialecte de l'Ahaggar, 2 vols., Paris.

Freytag, G. W. 1880. Darstellung der Arabischen Verskunst. Bonn.

Fuad, Hasanein Ali. 1939. "Ägyptische Volkslieder," *Veröffentlichungen des Orientalischen Seminars der Universität Tübingen*. Heft 10.

Gaden, H. 1935. "La Vie d'el Hadj Omar, Qacida en Poular," *Travaux et Mémoires, Institut d'Ethnologie*, Vol. 21.

Gies, Hermann. 1879. *alfanūnu ssab*ʕ*atu:* Ein Beitrag zum Kenntnis sieben neuerer arabischen Versarten. Leipzig.

Goldziher, I. 1896-99. Abhandlungen zur Arabischen Philologie. Leiden.

Greenberg, J. H. 1947. "Swahili Prosody," *Journal of the American Oriental Society*, 67:24-30.

——— 1949. "Hausa Verse Prosody," *Journal of the American Oriental Society*, 69:125-35.

Grohmann, A. 1919. "Äthiopische Marienhymnen," *Sächsische Akademie der Wissenschaften, Abhandlungen, phil.-hist. Klasse*, Vol. 23.

Guidi, I. 1889. Le canzoni geez-amarina in onore di Re Abissini, Reale Academia dei Lincei, Rendiconti, pp. 52-66, Roma.

Hartmann, M. 1897. Das arabische Strophengedicht: I. Das Muwaššaḥ. Weimar.

Ibn Hishām. 1858. Das Leben Mahammeds nach Muhammed Ibn Ishak, ed. by F. Wustenfeld, Vol. I, Göttingen.

Jahn, A. 1902. Die Mehri-Sprache in Südarabien: Texte und Wörterbuch, Vienna.

Junker, H. and Schaefer, H. 1921-22. Nubische Texte im Kenzi-Dialekt, 2 vols., Vienna.

Justinard, L. 1925. "Poemes Chleuhs Receuillis au Sous," *Revue du Monde Musulman*, 60:63-107.

——— 1928. "Poesies en dialect du Sous Marocain d'apres un manuscrit arabico-berbere," *Journal asiatique*, 213:217-51.

Kirk, J. W. C. 1905. A Grammar of the Somali Language. Cambridge.

Kolmodin, J. 1912. "Traditions de Tsazzega et Hazzega, Textes tigrigna," *Archives d'Études Orientales*, 5:1.

Lemm, O. von. 1903. Das Triadon, ein Sahidisches Gedicht mit Arabischer Übersetzung. St. Petersburg.

Lepsius, K. R. 1880. Nubische Grammatik, mit einer Einleitung über die Völker und Sprachen Afrikas. Berlin.

Littmann, E. 1907. "Canzone tigre in onore del Governatore italiano," *Rivista degli Studi Orientali*, 1:211-15.

——— 1913-15. "Lieder der Tigre-Stamme," *Publications of the Princeton Expedition to Abyssinia*, Vol. 3, 4. Leyden.

——— 1914. Die altamharischen Kaiserlieder. Strassburg.

——— 1925. Galla Verskunst; ein Beitrag zur allgemeinen Verskunst nebst metrischen Übersetzungen. Tübingen.

Luciani, D. 1899. Chansons Kabyles de Smail Azikkiou. Algiers.

950 JOSEPH GREENBERG

Meinhof, C. 1924. "Das Lied des Liongo," *Zeitschrift für Eingeborenen-Sprachen*, 15:241-65.

Meissner, Bruno. 1902. "Neuarabische Gedichte aus dem Iraq," *Mitteilungen des Seminars für orientalische Sprachen*, 5:Abt. 2:77-131; 249-301.

Menendez Pidal, R. 1943. Poesia arabe y poesia europea. 2d ed., Buenos Aires.

Mueller, David H. 1905. Soqoṭri-Texte. Vienna.

Neuhaus, G. 1935. "Kitabu Maulidi," *Mitteilungen des Seminars für orientalische Sprachen*, 38:3:145-201.

Nicolas, F. 1953. La Langue Berbère de Mauretanie, Institut Français d'Afrique Noire, Memoires No. 33.

Nketia, J. H. 1955. Funeral Dirges of the Akan People. Achimota, Ghana.

Noeldeke, T. 1917-18. "Tigre-Lieder," *Zeitschrift für Assyriologie*, 31:1-25.

Perruchon, J. 1892. Vie de Lalibala, Roi d'Ethiopie. Paris.

Prietze, R. 1916. Haussa-Sänger mit Übersetzung und Erklärung, *Königliche Gesellschaft der Wissenschaften zu Göttingen, Nachrichten, Phil.-hist. Klasse*, pp. 163-230; 552-604.

Reichardt, C. J. 1859. Three Original Fulah Pieces. Berlin.

Reinhardt, C. 1894. Ein arabischer Dialekt gesprochen in 'Omàn und Zanzibar. Berlin.

Reinisch, L. 1889-90. Die Saho-Sprache. 2 vols., Vienna.

——— 1900. A. W. Schleichers Somali-Texte. Vienna.

Renisio. 1932. Étude sur les dialectes Berbères des Beni Iznassen, du Rif et des Senhaja de Srair. Paris.

Robinson, C. H. 1896. Specimens of Hausa Literature. Cambridge.

——— 1930. Hausa Grammar. 5th ed., London.

Roper, E. M. 1923. "Poetry of the Hadendiwa," *Sudan Notes and Records*, 10:147-58.

Serjeant, R. B. 1951. South Arabian Poetry. Vol. I, *Prose and Poetry from Ḥadramawt*. London.

Sid Mojand. 1914. El Jardin de los Deseos, poesias berberiscas de Sid Mojand, trans. and ed. by Isaac Munoz. Madrid and Buenos Aires.

Simmons, D. C. 1955. "Specimens of Efik Folklore," *Folklore* 66:417-24.

Socin, A. 1900. "Diwan aus Centralarabien," *Königliche Sächsische Gesellschaft der Wissenschaften, Abhandlungen, Phil.-hist. Klasse*, 19:Nos. 1-3.

Sonneck, C. 1902-6. Chants arabes du Maghreb. Étude sur le dialecte et la poesie populaire de l'Afrique du Nord. 3 vols., Paris.

Stumme, Hans. 1893. Tunisische Märchen und Gedichte. Leipzig.

——— 1895. Dichtkunst und Gedichte der Schluh. Leipzig.

——— 1896. Märchen und Gedichte aus der Stadt Tripolis in N.A., I. Teil. Leipzig.

Vito, L. de. 1893. Esercizi di lettera in lingua tigrigna. Rome.

A TENTATIVE CLASSIFICATION OF TAI DIALECTS

By Fang-Kuei Li

UNIVERSITY OF WASHINGTON

THE TAI DIALECTS are spoken in a vast territory which consists of Thailand, Laos, the northern part of Vietnam, West Burma (Shan states), and Southwest China. It is generally known that they are fairly similar to each other. No one has phrased this understanding better than the well-known French scholar H. Maspero, who said, "Malgré la multiplicité de ces dialectes et la vaste étendue des territoires qu'ils couvrent, leur parenté saute aux yeux immédiatement, ils sont, en effect, très proches les unes des autres aujourd'hui encore."[1] Maspero was, of course, aware of the problem of classifying these dialects, and proposed two schemes for their classification. One was based on the development of the Proto-Tai (PT) voiced stops *b-*, *d-*, and *g-*, and of the Proto-Tai preglottalized consonants (his mi-sourdes) *ᵓb* and *ᵓd-*. The other arrangement hinged on the development of the Proto-Tai clusters. The former seemed preferable, although neither was quite satisfactory to him. He modestly suggested that a more careful study of the vocabularies of the different Tai languages might offer a better classification.[2]

It is largely due to this important suggestion of Maspero that I offer the following tentative classification. In several earlier articles on comparative Tai phonology I tried to reconstruct several problematical initial consonant clusters in order to establish a phonological basis on which a reasonable classification might be made.[3] I made no attempt in these papers to classify the dialects, because I felt that some phonological problems had to be solved first. The relative order in which I listed forms from various dialects was not intended to imply any conclusions about the closeness of their relationships. I wish to make this clear, because of the statement by A. G. Haudricourt that I classified some dialects incorrectly.[4]

In order to provide material for discussion I have selected a number of words from a comparative dictionary of some twenty Tai dialects which

WORD LIST

	1	2	3	4	5	6	7
Meaning	sky	pungent hot	blind	below	classifier for animals	wing	beard
Tone class	C2	D1	D1	C1	A1, 2	D1, 2	B2
PT	v-	ph-	ʔb-	t-	t-, d-	p-, v-	m-
I							
Siamese	faa	phet	bɔɔt	tai	tua(A1)	piik(D1)	—
Lao	faa	phet	bɔɔt	të	tua(A1)	piik(D1)	—
Tai Noir	faa	—	bɔɔt	taë	too(A1)	piiʔ	—
Shan	pha	phet	mɔt	taï	to (A1)	pik (D1)	—
Lü	fa	phet	ʔbɔt	tai	to (A1)	pik (D1)	—
TB	fa	phet	bɔt	taë	to (A1)	piʔ (D1)	—
Ahom	phā	phit	båt	ka-teu	tu, tuw	pik	—
II							
Tay	faa	—	bɔt	tëï	tu (A1)	pik (D1)	mum
Tho	vaa	phët	bɔɔt	tɔ	tua (A1)	pik (D1)	muum
Nung	faa	phet	bɔt	tëï	tu (A1)	pik (D1)	mum
Lung-chow	faa	phit	boot	taï	tu (A1)	pik (D1)	mum
T'ien-pao	faa	—	ʔboot	—	—	pɔʔ (D1)	mum
Yung-ch'un	—	—	—	tai	—	viit (D2)	mum
III							
Wu-ming	—	—	—	—	tu (A2)	fïăt (D2)	mum
Ch'ien-chiang	—	—	—	—	tu (A2)	fuut (D2)	mum
T'se-heng	—	—	—	—	tuə (A2)	fïət (D2)	mum
Ling-yün	—	—	—	—	tuə (A2)	fïət (D2)	mum
Hsi-lin	—	—	—	—	tuə (A2)	fïət (D2)	mum
T'ien-chow	—	—	—	—	tuə (A2)	fiət (D2)	mum
Po-ai	—	—	—	—	tu (A2)	fït (D2)	mum

NOTE. For the tone classes A1, A2, B1, B2, etc., see my "Consonant Clusters in Tai,'' *Language*, 30:369-71. In the line designated by PT, only the Proto-Tai initials are reconstructed. TB refers to the Tai Blanc material of G. Minot.

I have compiled and which I hope to publish at a later date. The list here must necessarily be limited; only a small number of samples can be given for illustrative purposes. The sources of some of these dialects are well-known and have been used by Maspero and Wulff; the following later publications have not been generally used: G. Minot, "Dictionnaire tay blanc-français," *BEFEO* 40 (1940); Golap Chandra Borua, *Ahom-Assamese-English Dictionary* (Calcutta, 1920); F. K. Li, *The Tai Dialect of Lung-chow* (Shanghai, 1940); and F. K. Li, *The Tai Dialect of Wu-ming* (Taipei, 1956).

Examples from other dialects, such as Lü, T'ien-pao, Yung-ch'un,

WORD LIST *(Continued)*

	8	9	10	11	12	13	14
Meaning	to fear	mad	hunt	mother's (or wife's) mother	body	to be, become	young male animal
Tone class	A1	D2	B1	?	?	A1, 2	D1, 2
PT	xl-	b-	pr-	?	?	p-, b-	th-, d-
I							
Siamese	—	—	—	jaai(A2)	raaŋ(B2)	pen(A1)	thĭk(D1)
Lao	—	—	—	naai(A2)	haaŋ(B2)	pen(A1)	thĭk(D1)
Tai Noir	—	—	—	naai(A2)	—	peen(A1)	thĕk(D1)
Shan	—	—	—	nai(A2)	haŋ(B2)	pen(1)	thĭk(D1)
Lü	—	—	—	nai(A2)	—	pin(A1)	—
TB	—	—	—	nai(A2)	—	pin(A1)	thĕk(D1)
Ahom	—	—	—	—	rāng	pin	thek
II							
Tay	—	—	—	taai(A1)	daaŋ(A1)	pən(A2)	tĭk(D2)
Tho	laau	—	thau	taai(B1)	daaŋ(A1)	peen(A2)	tĕk(D2)
Nung	laau	paak	pheau, thau	taai(A1)	daaŋ(A1)	pen(A2)	tĭk(D2)
Lung-chow	laau	—	phjau	taai(A1)	daaŋ(A1)	pin(A2)	tək(D2)
T'ien-pao	laau	paaʔ	—	taai(A1)	'daaŋ(A1)	pan(A2)	taʔ(D2)
Yung-ch'un	—	baak	—	—	'daaŋ(A1)	ban(A2)	tok(D2)
III							
Wu-ming	lau	—	—	taai(A1)	ʔdaŋ(A1)	păn(A2)	tăk(D2)
Ch'ien-chiang	laau	paak	—	taai(A1)	ʔdaaŋ(A1)	pan(A2)	tak(D2)
T'se-heng	lao	pa	tau	tai(B1)	daŋ(A1)	pan(A2)	tak(D2)
Ling-yün	laau	paak	tau	taai(B1)	—	—	—
Hsi-lin	laau	paak	tau	taai(B1)	'daaŋ(A1)	pan(A2)	tak(D2)
T'ien-chow	laau	—	tau	taai(B1)	'daaŋ(A1)	pan(A2)	tak(D2)
Po-ai	laau	paak	tau	taai(B1)	naaŋ(A1)	pan(A2)	tak(D2)

Ch'ien-chiang, Ling-yun, Hsi-lin, T'ien-chow, and Po-ai,[5] are taken from my unpublished materials. Some of these have been briefly described and others referred to in my previous papers (see note 3).

The dialects are tentatively divided into three main groups:

I. The southwestern group

II. The central group

III. The northern (or northeastern) group

This classification is based on three types of evidence: the distribution of vocabulary, the distribution of certain special phonological features in the vocabulary, and specific phonological development characteristic of a certain group.

WORD LIST *(Continued)*

	15	16	17	18	19	20	21
Meaning	knife	to warn	we	road	to challenge	eye	to die
Tone class	D2	A1	A1	A1	C2	A1	A1
PT	m-	t-	t-	xr-?	d-	tr-	tr-
I							
Siamese	miit	tĭan	tuu	hon	thaa	taa	taai
Lao	miit	tĭan	tuu	hon	thaa	taa	taai
Tai Noir	miit	—	—	—	—	taa	taai
Shan	mit	—	tu	—	ta	ta	tai
Lü	mit	—	tu	hun	ta	ta	tai
TB	mit	—	—	—	—	ta	tai
Ahom	mit	tin	—	—	—	tā	tāi
II							
Tay	—	—	—	—	—	thaa, haa	thaai, haai, phaai
Tho	—	—	—	—	—	thaa	thaai
Nung	—	—	—	—	—	thaa, haa	thaai, haai
Lung-chow	—	—	—	—	—	haa	haai
T'ien-pao	mit	—	—	—	—	thaa	thaai
Yung-ch'un	—	—	—	—	—	thaa	thaai
III							
Wu-ming	mit	tĭăn	—	hon	—	ra	rai
Ch'ien-chiang	mit	—	—	—	—	taa	taai
T'se-heng	mit	tœn	tu	δon	ta	ta	tai
Ling-yün	mit	—	—	lon	—	taa	taai
Hsi-lin	mit	tĭən	—	lon	—	taa	taai
T'ien-chow	mit	—	tuu	hon	—	taa	taai
Po-ai	mit	tĭin	—	hɔn	taa	taa	taai

Distribution of Vocabulary

Forms which are found only in one group are not given here. Although they may be thought of as characteristic of one particular group, they are usually historically and phonologically difficult to evaluate, and can always be suspected of being loans from other languages. Nor is it necessary to list words that occur in all groups, except for special phonological developments which can be used as criteria of classification. The list presents three types of vocabulary: (1) vocabulary common to Groups I and II (Nos. 1-4); (2) vocabulary common to Groups II and III (Nos. 7-10); and (3) vocabulary common to Groups I and III (Nos. 15-19). In each column, the lack of a form in a given dialect is indicated by a

WORD LIST *(Continued)*

	22	23	24	25	26	27
Meaning	to ex-pose to the sun	to break	shower (rain, wind)	six	tail	head louse
Tone class	D1	D1	B1	D1	A1	A1
PT	pr-	pr-	xr-	xr-	thr-	thr-

I

Siamese	taak	tɛɛk	haa	hok	haaŋ	hau
Lao	taak	tɛɛk	haa	hok	haaŋ	hau
Tai Noir	taaʔ	tɛɛʔ	haa	hook	haaŋ	hau
Shan	tak	tɛk	ha	hok	haŋ	hǎu
Lü	tak	tɛk	ha	hok	haŋ	hǎu
TB	taʔ	tɛʔ	ha	hok	haŋ	hǎu
Ahom	tāk	tik (tek)	rā	ruk	rāng	rāo

II

Tay	thaak	thɛk	šaa	šok	thaaŋ, haaŋ	thəu, həu
Tho	thaak	thɛk	—	sok	thaaŋ	thau
Nung	pheaak	phɛk	šaa	hok	haaŋ	hau
Lung-chow	phjaak	pheek	haa	huk	haaŋ	hau
T'ien-pao	thaaʔ	theeʔ	khjaa	khjɔʔ	thaaŋ	thau
Yung-ch'un	thaak, phaak	—	—	lok	thɛɛŋ	thau

III

Wu-ming	rak	—	ra	rok	rĭǎŋ	rǎu
Ch'ien-chiang	taak	tɛɛk	—	ɣɔk	ɣĭĭŋ	ɣau
T'se-heng	ta	te	ða	ðok	ðəeŋ	ðau
Ling-yün	taak	teek	—	lok	lĭəŋ	lau
Hsi-lin	taak	teek	—	ðok	ðĭəŋ	lau
T'ien-chow	taak	teek	laa	lok	lĭəŋ	lau
Po-ai	taak	teek	laa	lɔk	lĭĭŋ	lau

dash. The dictionaries and glossaries vary in comprehensiveness, so that some missing forms may be accidental. But a form missing in all dialects of a group usually means that an altogether unrelated word is used, a fact significant for the study of the distribution of vocabulary.

Geographically, Group II lies more or less between Groups I and III. The sharing of vocabulary by Groups I and II or by Groups II and III is not surprising because their territories are contiguous. The vocabulary which is found common to Groups I and III, but not to Group II, is significant. It does not permit us to suppose that Group II is a merely transitional stage between I and III. It has to be considered as an independent unit, a deduction also evidenced by certain characteristic phonological developments (cf. *infra*). Only T'ien-pao and Yung-ch'un of Group II show some irregularities, i.e., T'ien-pao *mit*, 'knife,' is a word current in Groups I and III, and Yung-ch'un *viit*, 'wing,' is otherwise strictly a Group III word. Such irregularity in the occurrence of a dialect form is not unusual in border dialects. It is generally known in linguistic geography and indicates an iso-glossal line.

Distribution of Special Phonological Features in the Vocabulary

A number of irregular features show interesting distributions. These irregular features consist usually of an alternation of voiceless and voiced initials as indicated by the tone according to dialects. Such alternations of initials as well as certain other irregularities are phonologically difficult to explain, but their distribution may serve as a criterion for classifying the dialects. There are two types. 1. Features shared by Groups I and II. In Nos. 5 and 6, tones indicate Proto-Tai voiceless initials in Groups I and II but Proto-Tai voiced initials in Group III. 2. Features shared by Groups II and III. In Nos. 13 and 14, tones indicate Proto-Tai voiceless initials in Group I, but Proto-Tai voiced initials in Groups II and III. Similarly, Nos. 11 and 12 indicate that Groups II and III are in essential agreement, while Group I shows rather irregular features and must be marked off as distinct.

Characteristic Phonological Features of Group II

Here I include features which mark Group II as distinct from I and III. Nos. 20-23 show a secondarily developed aspirated initial (*th-*, *h-*, *ph-* from PT *tr̥-* and *pr-*) in Group II, while Groups I and III are in agreement (unaspirated *t-* from PT *tr-* and *pr-*).[6] Nos. 24-27 show that PT *xr-* and *thr-* have become **hr-* in Groups I and III. It is in turn simplified in Group I to *h-* in most instances (but *r-* in Ahom), and in Group III to **r-*, which appears as *r-*, *δ-*, *γ-*, or *l-*, according to dialects. In Group II, however, the initial consonant before the liquid was kept much longer, so that when the dialects later became separated a variety of forms (*th-*, *khj-*, *h-*, *š-*, etc.) developed to represent these Proto-Tai clusters. This again shows that Group II is not intermediate or transitional between I and III.

I shall not list the phonological features of Group III against Groups I and II, because I have published elsewhere a detailed description of the

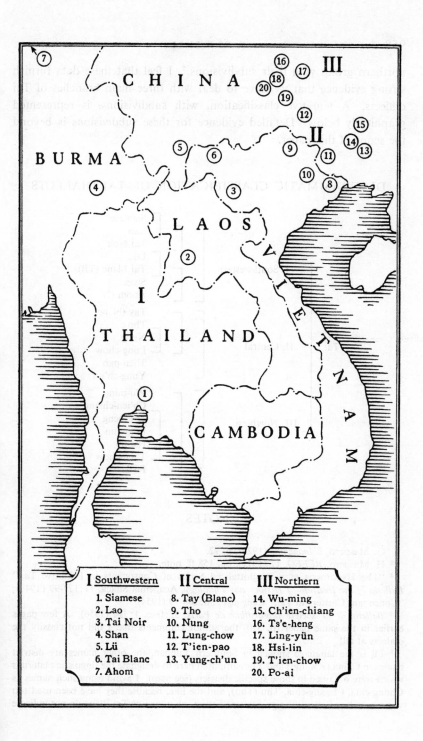

I Southwestern	II Central	III Northern
1. Siamese	8. Tay (Blanc)	14. Wu-ming
2. Lao	9. Tho	15. Ch'ien-chiang
3. Tai Noir	10. Nung	16. Ts'e-heng
4. Shan	11. Lung-chow	17. Ling-yün
5. Lü	12. T'ien-pao	18. Hsi-lin
6. Tai Blanc	13. Yung-ch'un	19. T'ien-chow
7. Ahom		20. Po-ai

northern group with their subdivisions.[7] I feel that these data furnish strong evidence that we have to deal with three main branches of Tai dialects. A tentative classification, with subdivisions, is represented graphically below. Detailed evidence for these subdivisions is beyond the scope of this paper.

DIAGRAMMATIC CLASSIFICATION OF TAI DIALECTS

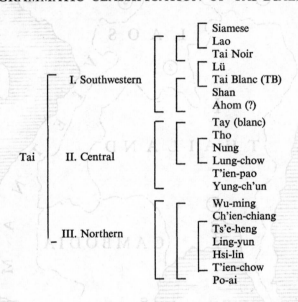

Tai

I. Southwestern
- Siamese
- Lao
- Tai Noir
- Lü
- Tai Blanc (TB)
- Shan
- Ahom (?)

II. Central
- Tay (blanc)
- Tho
- Nung
- Lung-chow
- T'ien-pao
- Yung-ch'un

III. Northern
- Wu-ming
- Ch'ien-chiang
- Ts'e-heng
- Ling-yun
- Hsi-lin
- T'ien-chow
- Po-ai

NOTES

[1] G. Maspero, *L'Indochine* (1929), p. 72.

[2] H. Maspero, *BEFEO*, 11 (1911), pp. 158 ff. note.

[3] "The Hypothesis of a Preglottalized Series of Consonants in Primitive Tai," *Bulletin of the Institute of History and Philology*, Academia Sinica, 11:177-99 (1947); "Consonant Clusters in Tai," *Language*, 30:368-79 (1954).

[4] *Bulletin de la Société linguistique de Paris*, 52:fasc. 1:314 (1956). A few pages earlier in the same paper (p. 310) the author comments that I did not classify the dialects at all!

[5] Lü is the language spoken in Southern Yunnan, the other names are district names in China (Kwangsi and Yunnan), used here to designate the linguistic materials which were obtained in those specific districts (see map). I avoid using such names as Chung-chia, Chuang-chia, Thu (Tho), and the like, because they have been used too vaguely to be of scientific significance. Even such names as Tai Blanc do not indicate

linguistic or ethnologic unity, i.e., the Tai Blanc of Minot (abbrev. here TB) and the Tai Blanc of Savina (abbrev. here Tay) are linguistically quite distinct. However in quoting other sources I have as a whole used without change the designations given by the respective authors, except that Dioi, which is too generalized, is here replaced by Ts'e-heng, the district where the Dio material was presumably obtained by Esquirol and Williatte.

[6] Wu-ming behaves differently and has *r-* for PT *tr-* and *pr-*, but it is essentially a Group III dialect.

[7] "The Jui Dialect of Po-ai and the Northern Tai," *Bulletin of the Institute of History and Philology*, Academia Sinica, Vol. 29 (1958).

ATHAPASKAN LANGUAGES OF THE PACIFIC COAST

By Harry Hoijer

UNIVERSITY OF CALIFORNIA, LOS ANGELES

THE ATHAPASKAN LANGUAGES are found in three major geographical groupings:

1. The northern group, spoken in a large and continuous region in Alaska and northwestern Canada. There are twenty-two or more languages in this division, but these languages probably divide into at least four sub-stocks and perhaps as many as nine (Osgood, 1936, pp. 21–22).

2. The Pacific Coast group, spoken along the Pacific coast in southwestern Oregon and the northern counties of California.

3. The southern group, spoken by the Navaho and Apache peoples of the American Southwest. These languages, seven in number, make up a single linguistic subdivision, now called Apachean (Hoijer, 1938).

It is the purpose of this paper to demonstrate that the Pacific Coast languages belong to a single sub-stock, which is distinct as a whole from Apachean and the several sub-stocks found in the north.

I

The Pacific Coast languages are found in two major geographical divisions: (1) southwestern Oregon and (2) northwestern California. Two languages formerly spoken near the mouth of the Columbia river (i.e.

Abbreviations used in this article are as follows: Beav=Beaver, one of the northern languages; Car=Carrier, a northern language; ChC=Chasta Costa; Chip=Chipewyan, a northern language; Coq=Coquille; EC=Euchre Creek; Gal=Galice; Matt=Mattole; Nav=Navaho; PA=Proto-Athapaskan; PCA=Pacific Coast Athapaskan; Sar=Sarci, a northern language; Tol=Tolowa; Ump=Umpqua; Wail=Wailaki.

Phonetic symbols used are those currently employed by Americanists. Note, however, the following: vowels are doubled to indicate length; acute accent marks high tone, grave accent low tone (these are indicated in the Apachean and northern languages; in Sarci, the absence of a tone marker means middle tone); α denotes *aa* central vowel, which is variously written by the authors cited; *L*, *Ł*, and *Ł'* are used for the lateral affricates *dl*, *tl*, and *t'l*. The orthography of forms cited from published sources is sometimes changed in the interests of uniformity.

Kwalhioqwa and Clatskanie) are sometimes included in this group, but the fragmentary data remaining on these two languages indicate that they do not belong linguistically with the Pacific Coast sub-stock.

The Oregon languages for which data are available are:

Umpqua (or Upper Umpqua), formerly spoken in the Umpqua river basin above the present site of Scottsburg, Oregon. My Umpqua material comes from Melville and Elizabeth Jacobs, who collected it in 1936. The language may now be extinct.

Coquille (or Upper Coquille), formerly spoken along the upper Coquille river down to the present site of Coquille, Oregon. Elizabeth Jacobs collected a considerable body of Coquille forms in 1933–34, which she has kindly put at my disposal. I gathered additional material in 1956 from Archie Johnson, an informant living in Siletz, Oregon. Coquille still has two or three speakers but all of them are sixty years of age or older.

Galice, formerly spoken on Galice Creek, a branch of the upper Rogue river. Galice was isolated from the main Oregon group by intervening Takelma bands. Melville Jacobs collected a large body of Galice text in 1933–34. I reviewed this material with Jacobs's informant (Hoxie Simmons, at Siletz, Oregon) in 1956 and added a considerable amount of lexical and grammatical data. Galice is now the best known language of the Oregon group. My informant, over eighty years of age, is apparently the only surviving speaker.

Chasta Costa (or Shasta Costa), formerly spoken on the lower Rogue river, about the mouth of one of its tributaries, the Illinois. My Chasta Costa data come from Sapir 1914; the language may now be extinct.

Euchre Creek, formerly spoken on the coast and the drainage about Euchre Creek. The scant data on this language were collected by Elizabeth Jacobs in 1933–34.

Tolowa, the southernmost member of the Oregon group, actually had most of its territory in northern California. It was spoken in the drainage of the Smith river and on the adjacent ocean front. I collected a small amount of Tolowa material in 1956 (from Mrs. Lopez, ninety-four years old, who lives in Crescent City, California). Three or four speakers remain, but all of them are sixty or more years of age.

Several other Oregon languages are mentioned in the literature:

Applegate, now extinct, was spoken on a branch of the upper Rogue river called Applegate Creek. I have seen no data on this language (except for a very small amount included in Sapir, 1914) but it is said to be essentially like Galice.

Chetco, formerly spoken on the lower Chetco river, north of the Tolowa. No Chetco data are available, although the language is said to be spoken by some three or more elderly people.

Tututni, a group of six or more dialects, said to be closely related, which were spoken on the coast from Chetco territory to that of the Euchre Creek people. No data are available on these dialects, some of which may still be spoken.

The California language group includes:

Hupa and the closely related and mutually intelligible *Chilula* and *Whilkut*. Hupa is still spoken in Hupa Valley on the Trinity river, a few miles above its confluence with the Klamath. Chilula and Whilkut were, and possibly still are, spoken on lower and upper Redwood Creek, respectively. My Hupa data come mainly from Sapir's field notes and those more recently collected by Mary Woodward. Additional material may be found in Goddard (1904, 1905). Goddard has also published (1914) the only available data on Chilula.

Mattole, formerly spoken on the lower Mattole and Bear rivers. Data on Mattole were published by Fang-Kuei Li (1930). He also obtained some words in the Bear river dialect, which appears to be "identical with Mattole in morphology, and probably in vocabulary, and differs only in a few phonetic respects...." (1930, p. 3).

Kato, the southernmost of the California languages, was spoken on the uppermost course of the South Fork of the Eel river. Data on Kato are taken from Goddard's two studies (1909, 1912). The language may still be spoken.

Wailaki, formerly spoken on the Eel river, north of the Kato. Li collected some Wailaki data in 1927; some of this is cited in Li (1930). Additional material may be found in Goddard (1923).

Between Wailaki and Hupa, and east of the Mattole, were three other languages: *Nongatl*, *Lassik*, and *Sinkyone*. There is too little information on these languages to include them in the present discussion.

II

Comparative studies of the Athapaskan languages have shown that the consonants develop differently depending upon their position in the morpheme and word. PA *x, for example, is retained as a stem initial in the Apachean languages, and is either retained or altered to *k* in PCA (see § 7). As a prefix initial, however, PA *x*, in some prefixes, is weakened to *h* in both Apachean and PCA, and, in other prefixes, undergoes even more radical changes (see Hoijer, 1938, pp. 75-76 and n. 3). PA *x* as a stem final shows still another development, too complex to summarize here (see Hoijer, 1938, p. 83 § 24). Vowels, in the Athapaskan languages, have been little studied comparatively, but it is evident that the development of these sounds is highly variable even between languages otherwise very much alike.

The major criterion for dividing the Athapaskan languages into sub-stocks is found in the development of initial stem consonants. Initials of prefixes, stem final consonants, and vowels, it appears, develop more diversely, and hence are useful mainly for determining differences within the several sub-stocks. In the present discussion we shall be concerned with stem initial consonants alone.

It might be noted, however, that none of the Pacific Coast languages so far studied possess tone phonemes. These have been found in all the Apachean languages and in Sarci, Chipewyan, Hare, and Kutchin of the

Table 1

	SURDS			FRICATIVES		NASALS
	Unaspirated	*Aspirated*	*Glottal*	*V. L.*	*Voiced*	*Voiced*
Bilabial						m
Apical	d	t	t'			n
Palatal	g^y	k^y	k'^y	x^y	y	
Velar	g	k	k'	x	γ	
Labio-velar	g^w	k^w	k'^w	x^w	$γ^w$	
Faucal	?					
s-consonants	j	c	c'	s	z	
š-consonants	ǰ	č	č'	š	ž	
Laterals	L	Ł	Ł'	ł	l	

north. Data on the remaining northern languages are uncertain on this point, but there is reason to believe that tone phonemes may be discovered in all of them. It follows, then, that this point has significance in setting the Pacific Coast languages apart from the rest.

III

PA consonants which functioned as stem initials are tabulated in Table 1. (Cf. Li's reconstructions in 1933, p. 431; both Li's reconstructions and mine are developed from an earlier unpublished one by Sapir.)

IV

Nine of the consonants listed in Table 1 are retained without change in PCA, and present no contrast between PCA, Apachean, and the northern languages. These consonants are $*d$, $*t$, $*t$', $*g$ (but see § 8), $*k$', $*ʔ$, $*y$, $*l$, and $*ł$. See examples 1-19, § 14.

V

PA $*m$ and $*n$. PA had only one bilabial consonant, which may be reconstructed either $*m$ or $*b$. The Apachean languages have both b and m (the former is usually the more frequent) and in one case, Chiricahua mbàʔ- 'coyote,' a b with strong nasal attack. In the north we find b alone (e.g. in Chip and Car), m alone (e.g. in Sar), or a bilabial spirant (e.g. in Anvik and Tena). The PCA development, shown below, is not distinctive.

PA $*m >$ Hupa, ChC, EC m, Wail, Matt, Kato b, Tol, Gal, Coq, Ump b or m (b is the more frequent except in Ump). See examples 20-23, § 14.

PA $*n >$ Gal n (when the stem has a nasalized vowel or a final nasal consonant), d (otherwise). PA $*n$ is retained unchanged in the rest of the PCA languages, in Apachean (but see Hoijer, 1938), and in most of the northern languages. See examples 24 and 25, § 14.

VI

PA $*x^y$ and the palatal stops $*g^y$, $*k^y$, and $*k'^y$ in Apachean regularly become s, j, c, and c', respectively. In most of the northern languages we find $š$ or $š^y$, $ǰ$, $č$, and $č$', respectively. The development in PCA is shown in Table 2 (an interrogation point indicates that cognates are lacking). Note that Kato and five of the Oregon languages resemble the northern languages. Hupa and Wail retain the original PA consonants (this retention is found also in one or two of the Alaskan languages), while

Matt and Ump each have an irregular and unique development. The correspondences clearly differentiate PCA as a whole from Apachean (but not from the northern languages), and suggest as well a line between the California languages (except Kato) and those of Oregon. See examples 26-34, § 14.

Table 2

PA	$*x^y$	$*g^y$	$*k^y$	$*k'^y$
Hupa	W	g^y	k^y	k'^y
Wail	(?)	g^y	k^y	k'^y
Matt	x (?)	j	$č^y$	c'^y
Kato	(?)	j	č	č'
EC	š	j	č	č'
Coq	š	j	č	č'
Tol	š	j	č	č'
Ump	(?)	j	š	(?)
Gal	š	j	č	č'

VII

PA $*k$, $*k^w$, $*x$, and $*x^w$ become k ($< *k$ and $*k^w$) and x ($< *x$ and $*x^w$) in Apachean and most of the northern languages. The development in PCA is shown in Table 3. See examples 35-40, § 14. Illustrations of PA $*x$, $*x^w$ are difficult to find in the material available to me, and my list of examples is therefore incomplete.

Table 3

PA	$*k$ and $*x$	$*k^w$ and $*x^w$
Hupa	x	x
Wail	k	k (?)
Matt	k	k
Kato	k	k
EC	x	x^w
Coq	x	x^w
Tol	x	x^w
ChC	x	x^w
Ump	x	x^w
Gal	k	k^w

In terms of the correspondences shown in Table 3, we may conclude that Proto-PCA had two consonants: *k or *x ($<$ PA *k and *x) and *k^w or *x^w ($<$ PA *k^w and *x^w), and that these first confusions clearly separate PCA from both Apachean and the northern languages. The California group then combined the two Proto-PCA consonants to one, while the Oregon group retained both.

VIII

PA *g, *g^w, *γ, and *γ^w go to g ($<$ *g and *g^w) and γ ($<$ *γ and *γ^w) in Apachean and many of the northern languages. The development of these consonants in PCA is in part parallel to the development of PA *k, *k^w, *x, and *x^w; it is shown in Table 4.

Table 4

PA	*g	*g^w	*γ	*γ^w
Hupa	g	g	w	w
Wail	g	g	g	g(?)
Matt	g	g	g, γ	g, γ
Kato	g	g	g	g, w(?)
EC	g	g^w	γ	γ^w
Coq	g	g^w	γ	γ, w(?)
Tol	g	g^w	γ	γ
ChC	g	g	γ	γ(?)
Ump	g	g	γ	γ
Gal	g	g^w	g, w	g, w

The shift from *γ to g, where it occurs, is not complete. In Matt, according to Li (1930, p. 9), γ remains in noun and postposition stems. Li adds: "It is probable that the retention of γ- is a conditioned phenomenon, that is, remaining after certain pronominal prefixes (possessive prefixes in the case of nouns and pronominal objects in the case of postpositions). The γ- never occurs as the initial of a verb-stem."

A similar phenomenon is found in Gal, where PA *γ becomes g in all verb stems but is shifted to w (not retained as γ) in some noun stems and postpositions. See examples 9, 10, and 41-47, § 14.

IX

PA $*k^{\prime w}$ seems to fall together with $*k^{\prime}$ in PCA, as it does in Apachean and many of the northern languages. However Gal has three stems beginning with $k^{\prime w}$: $-k^{\prime w}ad$ (a postposition) 'on top of,' $-k^{\prime w}as$ 'neck', and the verb stem $-k^{\prime w}al$ 'there is a lump or hump.' The first of these is also found in Kato $-k^{\prime w}at^{\prime}$ 'on' and EC $-k^{\prime w}ad$ 'on top of,' and the second in Coq $-k^{\prime w}as$ 'neck' and Ump $-k^{\prime w}as$ 'neck' (but note also Tol $-k^{\prime}as$ and Hupa, Matt $-k^{\prime}os$). The evidence of these comparisons only suggests that PA $*k^{\prime w}$ is preserved in some of the PCA languages.

X

The PA s-consonants (e.g. $*s$, $*z$, $*j$, $*c$, and $*c^{\prime}$) are retained in Apachean and in some of the northern languages, e.g. Sar, Beav, Kaska. In other northern languages, the whole set is shifted forward: see, for example, Chip and Slave θ, δ, $d\delta$, $t\theta$, $t^{\prime}\theta$. The PCA development is given in Table 5. See examples 48-59, § 14.

Table 5

PA	$*s$, $*z$	$*j$	$*c$	$*c^{\prime}$
Hupa	s	j	c	c'
Wail		s or c		c'
Matt		s or c		c'
Kato		s or c		c'
EC		s		c'
Coq		s		c'
Tol		s		c'
ChC	θ	θ or s		t'θ
Ump		s		c'
Gal		s		c'

Two points may be noted: (1) the confusion of PA $*s$ and $*z$, found in all PCA languages, and (2) the further confusion of PA *s, *z, *j, *c, which is complete in all the Oregon languages except ChC, partial in Wail, Matt, and Kato, and absent in Hupa. (Note also the unique development in ChC.) These correspondences, it is evident, clearly distinguish PCA from Apachean and the northern languages, and supply additional evidences for dividing PCA into two subdivisions, California and Oregon.

XI

The PA š-consonants (i.e. *š, *ž, *ǰ, *č, *č') are retained in Apachean, but go to s, z, j, c, and c', respectively, in most of the northern languages. For the PCA development, see Table 6 and examples 60-73, § 14.

Table 6

PA	*š, *ž	*ǰ	*č	*č'
Hupa	W	ǰ	čʷ	č'
Wail	š	ǰ	č	č'
Matt	x	ǰ	č	č'
Kato	š	ǰ	č	č'
EC	š	s	s, sʳ	c'
Coq	š	s	s, sʳ	c'
Tol	š	š, šʳ	š, šʳ	č'
ChC	š	(?)	s	c'
Ump	š	ǰ	š	č'
Gal	š	s	s, š	c'

Two conclusions may be drawn. First, the uniform confusion of PA *š, *ž in PCA clearly differentiates it from Apachean and the northern languages. Secondly, the line between the California and Oregon languages suggested earlier is here confirmed by the differential in the development of PA *ǰ, *č, and *č'.

XII

PA *L, *Ł, and *Ł' are retained in Apachean and in most of the northern languages. In PCA, however, PA *L goes to l or ł, PA *Ł to ł, and PA *Ł' is retained in all the languages except Wail and Tol, where it becomes t'. Here again the PCA languages are clearly set off from Apachean and the northern languages. See examples 74-83, § 14.

XIII

SUMMARY. The evidence presented in the preceding sections (1) clearly differentiates a PCA sub-stock of the greater Athapaskan family, and (2) strongly supports the hypothesis that this sub-stock has two main divisions, the Californian (Hupa, Wail, Matt, and Kato) and the Oregonian (Tol, ChC, Gal, Coq, EC, and Ump).

For point (1) we may cite: (a) the absence of pitch accent in PCA (§ 2), (b) the shift of PA *k, *x to x or k in PCA (§ 7), (c) the retention of the labio-velars x^w or k^w and g^w in some PCA languages, and the occasional occurrence of w from PA *γ^w (§§ 7, 8), (d) the shift from PA *γ to g in some PCA languages (§ 8), (e) the combining, in PCA, of PA *s and *z (§ 10), (f) the confusion, in most PCA languages, of PA *s, *z, *j, and *c (§ 10), (g) the combining in PCA of PA *$š$ and *$ž$ (§ 11), (h) the partial confusion in the Oregon languages of PA *j and *$č$ (§ 11), and (i) the shift of PA *L and *$Ł$ to PCA l or l and $ł$, respectively (§ 12).

Evidence for separating the PCA languages into a California and an Oregon division is found in: (a) the development of PA *m to b in most California languages and to m or b or m alone in those of Oregon (§ 5); (b) the irregular development of PA *g^y, *k^y, and *k'^y in the California languages (except Kato) as contrasted with the more regular shift to j, $č$, and $č'$ in all the languages of Oregon except Ump (although complete evidence is lacking, a similar division occurs in respect to PA *x^y; see § 6); (c) the shift of PA *k, *x to k in the California languages (except Hupa) and to x in those of Oregon (except Gal; see § 7); (d) the retention of the labio-velars or some trace of them in the languages of the Oregon group as compared to the complete loss of these consonants in the languages of California (§§ 7, 8, 9); (e) the complete confusion of PA *s, *z, *j, and *c in the Oregon languages as contrasted with their partial confusion in the California languages (§ 10); and (f) the confusion of PA *j, *$č$, and *$č'$ in the Oregon languages and their partial falling together with the PA s-consonants (in California this does not occur; see § 11).

The data presented do not permit a final statement of the relationships within the California and Oregon divisions, respectively. Hupa appears remote from the other three languages in the California group. Note, in particular, its distinctive treatment of PA *m, *x^y, *k and *x, *k^w and *x^w, *γ and *γ^w, *$š$ and *$ž$, and the retention in Hupa of PA *j and *c. Similarly, in the Oregon division, Gal, Ump, and ChC appear remote from each other and from the remaining three languages. See, for Gal, the treatment of PA *n, *k and *x, *k^w and *x^w, and *γ and *γ^w; for Ump, the development of PA *k^y, *k'^y, *j, and *$č$; and for ChC, the development of the PA s-consonants.

As a provisional hypothesis, subject to change after a more detailed comparison has been made, the following grouping of the PCA languages is proposed.

A. California Division
  1. Hupa
  2. Wailaki-Kato-Mattole
    a. Wailaki
    b. Kato
    c. Mattole

B. Oregon Division
  1. Southern group
    a. Euchre Creek-Coquille
      i. Euchre Creek
      ii. Coquille
    b. Tolowa
    c. Chasta Costa
  2. Galice (and Applegate?)
  3. Umpqua

XIV

The examples below illustrate briefly the phonetic correspondences described in the preceding sections. Data on the Apachean languages come from Sapir's and my own field notes (see also Hoijer, 1938). The northern languages cited are Beaver (from Goddard, 1917), Carrier (from Morice, 1932), Chipewyan (from Li, 1933), Hare (from field notes collected by Li), and Sarci (from Sapir's field notes).

1. Hupa -de, -$deʔ$ 'horn [of animal],' Matt, Kato -$deʔ$, Coq -daa, Tol, Ump, Gal -$deʔ$. Cf. Nav -$dèèʔ$, Chip -$dé$, Sar -$daʔ$, Car -de.

2. Hupa, Wail, Matt -$daʔ$ 'mouth,' EC -da, Coq, Tol, Ump, Gal -$daʔ$.

3. Hupa, Wail, Matt, Kato -$taʔ$ 'father,' Coq, Tol, Ump, Gal -$taʔ$. Cf. Nav -$tààʔ$, Chip -$tá$, Beav -$taʔ$.

4. Hupa $taak'$ 'three,' Matt $daak'eh$ (from an earlier *$taak'eh$?), Kato tak', Coq $taak'ai$, Tol $taak'i$, ChC $taayi$, Ump $taʔag$, Gal $taak'ad$. Cf. Nav $tááʔ$, Chip $tàyè$, Beav $tač'eh$.

5. Hupa tin 'road, path,' Matt $teeniŋ$, Kato $tanii$, EC $tane$, Coq $tanee$, Tol $teene$. Cf. Nav -$tìin$, Sar $tìna$, Chip -$tànè$.

6. Hupa *t'ehW* 'charcoal,' Wail *t'es*, Kato *t'eš*, Matt *t'eex.* Cf. Nav *t'èèš*, Sar *t'as.*

7. Hupa, Kato *t'eʔ* 'blanket,' EC *t'e*, Coq, Tol, Ump, Gal *t'eʔ.*

8. Hupa *-t'au* 'fly' (vb.), Matt *-t'ax*, *-t'aγ*, Kato *-t'ag*, *-t'ah*, EC *-t'a*, Coq, Tol, ChC, Gal *-t'ah.* Cf. Nav *-t'ááh*, *-t'àʔ*, Sar *-t'áh*, *-t'àài* (*-t'ag-*), Chip *-t'à.*

9. Hupa, Wail, Matt, Kato *-gai* 'white,' Coq, Tol, ChC *-gii*, Ump *-gei*, Gal *-gai.* Cf. Nav *-gàì*, Chip *-gàì*, Sar *-gáái.*

10. Matt *-gaaneʔ* 'arm,' EC, Coq *-gaane*, Tol, Ump, Gal *-gaaneʔ.* Cf. Nav *-gààn*, Chip *-gàné*, Sar *-gàn*, Car *-gan.*

11. Hupa, Wail, Matt, Kato *-k'ah* 'fat,' Coq *č'a-k'ah*, Tol *l-k'aa* 'be fat,' Gal *č'aa-k'ah* 'fat.' Cf. Nav *-k'àh* 'fat,' Chip *-k'à*, Sar *-k'ah*, Beav *k'a*, Car *-k'a.*

12. Matt, Kato *k'aʔ* 'arrow,' EC, Coq *k'aa-xas*, ChC *k'aa-xaθ*, Gal *k'aa-kas*, Ump *k'aa-xas.*

13. Hupa, Wail, Matt, Kato *ʔah* 'fog, cloud,' EC *ʔag*, Coq *ʔag*, Tol *ʔag-čo*, Gal *ʔag.* Cf. Nav *ʔááh* 'fog, mist,' Car *ʔa.*

14. Coq, EC *-ʔad* 'wife,' Ump *-ʔaag.* Cf. Nav *-ʔááá*, Car *-ʔad.*

15. Hupa *-ʔiŋ* 'look, see,' Matt *-ʔiŋ*, *-ʔiin*, *-ʔiŋʔ*, Kato *-ʔiŋʔ*, ChC *-ʔii.* Cf. Nav. *-ʔį́*, Chip *-ʔį́.*

16. Hupa, Wail *-yaŋ*, *-yaŋʔ* 'eat,' Matt *-yaŋ*, *-yaaʔn*, Kato *-yan*, *-yanʔ*, EC *-ya*, Coq *-yaa*, Tol *-yaŋ*, *-yą́ʔ*, ChC *-ya*, Ump *-ya*, Gal *-yą́ą*, *-yą́ʔ.* Cf. Nav *-yą́*, *-yą́ą́ʔ*, Chip *-yá.*

17. Hupa, Matt, Wail *łaan-* 'many,' Kato *łan*, *łaŋ-*, EC *łani*, Coq *łaa-de*, D Tol *łaan*, Gal *łą́ą.* Cf. Nav *łą́*, Car *łane*, Chip *łą́.*

18. Hupa *łaʔ* 'one,' Coq, Tol *łaʔ*, ChC *ła*, Ump *-łaʔ*, Gal *łaʔ.* Cf. Nav *łàʔ*, Chip *łą́*, *łá.*

19. Hupa, Matt, Kato *-łaʔ* 'hand,' EC, Coq, Tol *-łaʔ*, ChC *-la*, Ump, Gal *-łaʔ.* Cf. Nav *-làʔ*, Chip *-n-lá*, Car *-la.*

20. Hupa *-mit* 'stomach,' Wail *-bit'*, Matt *-baʔl*, Kato *-bat'*, EC *-mad*, Coq *-bad*, Tol *-met'*, Ump *-maʔ*, Gal *-baiʔ.* Cf. Nav *-bìd*, Chip *-bár*, Sar *-mìʔ*, Car *-bed*, Beav *-bad*, Tena *-vwad* (*vw* a bilabial spirant?).

21. Hupa *minʔ-ǰ* 'menstrual hut' (little house), Matt *biŋʔ* 'house,' EC *man*, Coq *banʔ*, Tol *manʔ*, ChC *man*, Ump *maʔ*, Gal *manʔ*, but *-badeʔ* in the possessive.

22. Hupa *maŋʔ* 'fly' (the insect), Matt *baʔ-ǰe*, Coq, Gal *banʔ*, Tol *banʔ*, Ump *baʔ-šŁ'e.*

23. Hupa *-miŋ* 'be full,' Matt *-biŋ*, *-biiʔn*, *-bil*, *-biŋʔ* 'become full,' Kato *-baŋʔ* 'be full,' Coq *-man*, EC *-man*, Tol *-man*, Gal *-man*, *-manʔ.*

24. Hupa, Wail -naaʔ 'eye,' Matt -naʔ, -naag-, Kato -naʔ, EC -naɣe, Coq -naɣeeʔ, Tol -naaɣeʔ, ChC -naɣe, Ump -naaɣe, Gal -daai. Cf. Nav -nááʔ, Chip -nà, -nà-, -nàɣá, Sar -ná-, -náɣ-, Car -na, Slav -na, Beav -daiʔ.

25. Hupa -naan 'drink' (vb.), Matt -naah, -naan, -naaʔn, -naal, -naŋʔ, Kato -nan, EC -na, Coq -naʔ, ChC -naa, Ump -na, Gal -naa, -naʔ. Cf. Nav -nééh, -nàʔ, -nàh 'liquid flows,' Chip -dá̜, -dà̜ 'drink,' Sar -dá(n-), -díč, -dànì. In Chip and Sar, the d initial results from coalescence of a prefix d- with a stem initial n.

26. Hupa Wiŋ 'song,' Matt xin-, EC, Coq šin, Tol šan, Gal šan. Cf. Nav sìn, Chip šan, Car šen.

27. Hupa, Wail -gᵛid 'be afraid,' Matt -ǰih, -ǰid, EC -ǰid, Coq -ǰad, Tol -ǰid, Gal -ǰad. Cf. Nav -ǰìd, Chip -ǰèr, Beav -ǰid, Sar -ǰiʔ(d-), Hare -ǰí, -ǰì.

28. Hupa di-gᵛaŋ 'here,' Kato ǰaŋ-haʔ, Coq ǰa-ǰi, Tol ǰaŋ, Ump yaa-ǰa 'it's here,' Gal ǰa̜a̜ 'here.' Cf. Nav ǰa̜a̜-di 'here,' Chip ǰa̜.

29. Hupa, Wail -kᵛid 'catch, grab,' Matt -čᵛoh, -čᵛod, Kato -čad, EC, Coq -čod, Gal -čoh, -čad. Cf. Nav -cóód, Chip -čù, Sar -čúʔ(d-), Beav -čuud.

30. Hupa -kᵛoh 'big,' Kato -čoo, ChC, Gal -čoh. Cf. Nav -cò, Chip -čòɣ.

31. Hupa -kᵛeʔ 'tail,' Matt -čᵛiiʔ, Kato -čiiʔ, Coq -čii-lah, Tol -čii-laʔ, Ump -šee-lah, Gal -čiʔ. Cf. Nav -cèèʔ, Beav -čeʔ, Sar -čaʔ.

32. Hupa xoh-k'ᵛid 'seven,' Matt ǰih-c'ᵛed 'eight,' ChC s-č'ade 'seven,' Tol s-č'eedeh. Cf. Nav còs-c'ìd.

33. Wail -k'ᵛit 'stretch, pull tight,' Matt -c'ᵛeʔl, -c'ᵛeʔd. Cf. Nav -c'ìd 'sinew,' Sar -č'ìd-, Hare -č'íréʔ.

34. Hupa -k'ᵛil, -k'ᵛil 'rip off, tear off,' Matt -c'ᵛeł, -c'ᵛel 'split with hand,' Kato -č'ał, -č'elʔ, 'split,' EC, Coq -č'ał 'crack, tear,' Gal -č'il. Cf. Nav -c'ìl, -c'ìl 'become cracked,' Sar -č'ùl, -č'úúl 'tear, rip,' Chip -č'ùl, -č'èl 'burst, split.'

35. Hupa -xeʔ 'foot,' Wail, Matt -keʔ, Kato -kʷeʔ, EC -xe, Coq -xee, Tol -xeʔ, ChC hwä (read xʷe?), Ump -xeʔ, Gal -keʔ. Cf. Nav -kèèʔ, Chip -ké, Sar -kaʔ, Beav -keʔ. The kʷ of Kato and hw (or xʷ) of ChC cannot be explained.

36. Hupa -xiW, -xiŋ 'float, travel by canoe,' Matt -kiix, -kiŋ, Kato -kas 'float' (?), EC -xeł 'move by boat, paddle,' Coq -xee, -xi, Tol -xeh, -xeʔ, -xeš, -xeł, ChC -xe, Gal -keš, -ki̜i̜, -kel. Cf. Nav -kééh, -kí̜, -kéél 'glide, slip,' Chip -káíh, -kí̜, -kèl, Sar -kàh, -kí(n-), -kál, Beav -ke, -ki̜, -kel.

37. Hupa xoŋʔ 'fire,' Matt -koŋʔ, Kato -kooŋʔ, EC xʷan, Coq xʷan,

Tol $x^w an\mathit{?}$, Ump $x^w an$, Gal $k^w an\mathit{?}$. Cf. Nav $k\grave{\varrho}\mathit{?}$, Chip $kún$, Sar $ko\mathit{?}$, Beav $kon\mathit{?}$.

38. Hupa xos 'mucous, cough,' Matt $-kos$ 'cough' (vb.), Kato $koos$ 'cough' (noun), EC $-x^w as$ 'cough' (vb.), Coq $-x^w as$, Tol $-x^w us$, ChC $-x^w a\theta$, Gal $-k^w as$. Cf. Nav $di\text{-}k\grave{o}s$ 'cough' (noun).

39. Hupa xai 'winter,' Matt $kaid$, Kato kai, Coq, Tol xai, Gal kai. Cf. Nav $x\grave{a}i$, Chip $x\grave{a}y\grave{e}$.

40. Kato kah 'goose,' ChC $xaa\mathit{?}\text{-}\check{c}us$. Cf. Chip $x\grave{a}$.

41. Hupa $-got'$ 'knee,' Matt $-go\mathit{?}\mathit{l}$, Kato $-goot'$, EC $-g^w ad$, Coq $-g^w ad$, Tol $-g^w eit'$, Ump $-go\mathit{?}$, Gal $-g^w ai\mathit{?}$. Cf. Nav $-g\grave{o}d$, Chip $-c\grave{a}\text{-}g\acute{o}r$, Sar $-gud$- 'knee, elbow.'

42. EC $-g^w a\check{s}$ 'fall, throw,' ChC $-ga\check{s}$, Gal $-g^w a\check{s}$. Cf. Nav $-g\grave{e}\grave{e}h$, $-g\grave{o}\mathit{?}$ 'fall,' Sar $-g\grave{u}h$, $-g\grave{u}\grave{u}l$.

43. Hupa $-wee$, $-wi\eta$ 'kill', Wail $-\gamma ee$, $-\gamma i\eta$, Matt $-gee$, $-giin$, Kato $-gii\eta$, EC $-\gamma e$, Coq $-\gamma e$, $-\gamma ii$, Ump $-\gamma e\mathit{l}$, Gal $-gee$, $gi\underset{.}{i}$. Cf. Nav $-\gamma é$, $-\gamma\underset{.}{i}$, Sar $-\gamma á$, $-\gamma\acute{i}(n\text{-})$.

44. Hupa $-wiW$, $-wi\eta$ 'carry a pack,' Wail $-\gamma i\check{s}$, $-\gamma i\eta$, Matt $-gix$, $-gi\eta$, $-giin$, Kato $-ga\check{s}$, $-gin$, EC $-\gamma e$, $-\gamma e\mathit{l}$, Coq $-\gamma e$, $-\gamma i$, Tol $-gee\mathit{l}$, Gal $-ge\check{s}$, $-gi\underset{.}{i}$. Cf. Nav $-\gamma\grave{e}\grave{e}h$, $-\gamma\underset{.}{i}$, Chip $-\gamma é$, $-\gamma\underset{.}{l}$.

45. Hupa $-wa\mathit{?}$ 'body hair,' Matt $-\gamma a\mathit{?}$ or $-ga\mathit{?}$ 'hair' (of animals), Kato $-ga\mathit{?}$ 'hair,' Coq $sa\text{-}\gamma aa$ 'head hair,' ChC $\theta a\text{-}ya$, Ump $\check{s}a\text{-}\gamma aal$, Gal $-wa\mathit{?}$ 'body hair,' $sa\text{-}gaa$ 'head hair.' Cf. Nav $-\gamma\grave{a}\grave{a}\mathit{?}$ 'hair, wool,' Chip $-\gamma\grave{a}$-, $-\gamma á$ 'hair.'

46. Hupa $-weeWe\mathit{?}$ 'eggs,' Matt $-\gamma eexe\mathit{?}$, Kato $-we\check{s}ii$, Coq $-\gamma aa\check{s}e\mathit{?}$, Tol $-\gamma eese\mathit{?}$, Ump $-\gamma eeye\mathit{?}$, Gal $-wee\check{s}e\mathit{?}$. Cf. Nav $-\gamma\grave{\underset{.}{e}}\grave{\underset{.}{e}}\check{z}i\grave{i}$, Chip $-\gamma ézé$, Sar $-\gamma as$-.

47. Matt $-gox^w$ 'snore, be sound asleep,' EC $-\gamma^w a\check{s}$, Coq $-\gamma^w o\check{s}$. Cf. Nav $-\gamma\grave{o}\check{s}$ 'sleep,' Chip $-\gamma\grave{u}s$ 'snore.'

48. Hupa, Wail $-sid$ 'become' (e.g. become awake, waken), Matt $-sih$, $-sid$ (in 'wake up someone'), $-cih$, $-cid$ (in 'become'), Kato $-sat'$, EC, Coq $-sad$. Cf. Nav $-z\acute{i}\acute{i}d$, $-z\grave{i}d$, Chip $-\delta ir$, $-\delta\grave{a}r$, Sar $-z\grave{i}\mathit{?}(d\text{-})$.

49. Hupa $-si\eta$, $-si\eta\mathit{?}$ 'think,' Matt $-siin$, $-sii\mathit{?}n$, Kato $-sa\eta$, EC, Coq $-san$, Tol $-sin$, Gal $-san$. Cf. Nav $-zin$, Chip $-\delta\grave{a}n$, Sar $-ziin$.

50. Hupa $-seel$ 'be warm, hot,' Matt $-sel$, Kato $-sal$, EC, Coq $-sal$, Gal $-sa\mathit{l}$, ChC $-\theta a\mathit{l}$ 'several wash.' Cf. Nav $-z\grave{i}l$ 'be warm,' Sar $-z\acute{i}l$, $-z\grave{i}\grave{i}l$, Chip $-\delta\grave{a}l$.

51. Kato sai 'sand,' EC, Ump see, Gal sai. Cf. Nav $s\acute{a}i$, Chip $\theta\grave{a}i$.

52. Hupa $-sit'$ 'liver,' Matt $-ci\mathit{?}\mathit{l}$, Tol $-set'$, Gal $-sa\mathit{?}\mathit{l}$. Cf. Nav $-z\grave{i}d$.

53. No clear examples of the development of PA $*j$ in PCA are available.

54. Hupa *ce* 'stone,' Matt *cee* or *see*, Kato *se*, EC, Coq, Tol *see*, ChC *se*, Ump, Gal *see*. Cf. Nav *cé*, Chip *tθè*, Sar *cá*.

55. Matt *-ciʔ* 'head,' Kato *-siiʔ*, Coq, Tol *-siʔ*, ChC *-θii*, Gal *-siʔ*. Cf. Nav *-cììʔ*, Chip *-tθí*.

56. Hupa, Matt *-cai*, *-caiʔ* 'be dry,' Wail *-jaiʔ*, Kato *-cai* or *-sai*. Cf. Nav *-càì*.

57. Hupa *-cow* 'yellow,' Wail *-sow*, Matt *-cow*, Kato *-coo*, ChC *-θo*. Cf. Nav *-cò*, Chip *-tθòγ*, Sar *-cúú*.

58. Hupa *-c'ooʔ* 'breast, milk,' Wail *-c'oʔ*, Matt, Kato *-C'ooʔ*, EC, Coq *-c'oowe*, Ump *-c'oweʔ*, Gal *-c'aweʔ*. Cf. Sar *-c'ow-*, Chip *t'θù*.

59. EC, Coq *-c'i* 'several sit,' ChC *-t'θi*, Gal *-c'eʔ*, *-c'ee*. Cf. Chip *-t'θí*, *-t'θì*, Sar *-c'í*, *-c'ìʔ*.

60. Hupa Wee '*I*', Matt, Kato *š'i* (Matt is exceptional here), EC *ši*, Coq, Tol, ChC, Ump, Gal *šii*. Cf. Nav *ší*, Chip *sì*.

61. Hupa *Waa* 'sun, moon,' Matt *xaa* 'light' (of sun, moon), Kato *ša* 'sun,' ChC, Ump, Gal *šaa*. Cf. Nav *šá*, Chip *sà*.

62. Hupa *-Win* 'be black,' Matt *-xin*, Kato *-šiinʔ*, *-šanʔ*, Coq, ChC *-šan*, Tol, Gal *-šan*. Cf. Nav *-žìn*, Chip *-zàn*.

63. Hupa *-oo-Weʔ* 'name,' EC *-oo-šii*, Coq *-oo-šaʔ*, Tol, Gal *-oo-šiʔ*. Cf. Nav *-í-žìʔ*, Chip *-ǹ-zí*.

64. Hupa *-We*, *-Weʔ* 'call by name,' Wail *-ši*, *-šiʔ*, Matt *-xaʔ*, EC *-ši*, *-šii*, Coq *-šii*, Gal *-šii*, *-šiʔ*. Cf. Sar *-zì*, *-zí*.

65. Hupa *jiŋ-* 'day,' Matt, Kato *jiŋ*, Coq *sas-*, Tol *šiiniiš*, Gal *sinis*, *sįs*. Cf. Nav *jį́*, Sar *jínis*.

66. Hupa *-jiwʔ* 'ear,' Matt *-jiiγeʔ*, EC *-saγe*, Coq *-saγeeʔ*, Tol *-š'eʔ*, Ump *-jaγeʔ*, Gal *-saai*. Cf. Nav *-jààʔ*, Sar *-jíγ-*.

67. Hupa *-c'iŋʔ* 'defecate,' Matt *-čiŋʔ*, *-čeʔn*, Kato *-čaŋ*, EC, Coq *-s'a*, Gal *-šąʔ*. Cf. Nav *-čįʔ*, *-čą̀ąʔ*, Chip *-cán*, *-cą́*.

68. Matt *-čiij* 'be red,' Kato *-čiiʔ*, *-čiig*, Coq *-sig*, Tol *-šiig*, ChC *-sag*, Gal *-sid*, Ump *šiiš* 'red paint.' Cf. Nav *-číʔ* 'be red,' Chip *cì* 'vermilion,' Sar *cíh* 'paint.'

69. Hupa *-c'ee*, *-c'iŋʔ* 'make [it] so,' Matt *-čii*, *-čiiʔn*, Wail *-čii*, *-čiŋʔ*, Kato *-čin*, *-čii*, ChC *-sii*. Cf. Nav *-čí*, *-čį́*, Chip *-cì*, *-cį̀*.

70. Matt *-čaŋʔ*, *-čeʔn* 'be bad,' EC, Coq *-san*, Tol *-š'an*. Cf. Nav *-čį̀h*, *-čįʔ* 'become bad,' Chip *-càné* 'bad point, weak point.'

71. Hupa *-č'ah*, *-č'aad* 'wear a hat,' Matt, Wail *č'ah* 'hat,' EC *-c'at'* 'wear a hat.' Cf. Nav *č'àh* 'hat,' Chip *c'à*.

72. Hupa *tes-č'e* 'wind,' Kato *-č'ii* 'wind blows,' EC *l-til-c'i* 'wind,'

Coq *ł-c'ii*, Tol *ł-č'ei*, Ump *č'iiš*, Gal *ł-c'ii*. Nav *-čĭ* 'wind,' Sar *-c'i* 'wind blows.'

73. Hupa *-č'aad* 'be sick, in pain,' Matt *-č'aah*, *-č'aad*, Kato *-č'a*, *-č'ad*, EC, Coq *-c'ad*, ChC *-c'ad*, Gal *-c'ah*. Cf. Chip *-c'ai*.

74. Hupa *łoʔ* 'laugh,' Matt *łoh*, Kato *-łaŋ* (cognate?), EC *-lo*, *-łak'*, Coq *-łoh*, Tol *-łoh*, ChC *-łoo*, Ump *-łoʔ*, Gal *-łoh*. Cf. Nav *Lò* 'laughter,' Chip *Lóy*, Sar *Lòòh*.

75. Hupa *łoʔn* 'mouse,' Matt *łoʔ-šgai*, Kato *łoon* 'rodent,' Coq *łamʔee* 'mouse,' Tol *łamʔe*, Ump *łoo-łgee*, Gal *łǫǫ-łgai*. Cf. Nav *Lǫ́ǫ́ʔ* 'prairie dog,' Sar *Lòòná* 'mouse,' Chip *-Lúnè*.

76. Hupa *lah* 'seaweed,' Matt *łoh-daiʔ*, Kato *lą̇d*, EC *laad*, Tol *lad*. Cf. Nav *Láád* 'moss, mould,' Chip *Làr*.

77. Matt *-laʔł*, *-łaʔd* 'throw mud,' EC, Coq *-le* 'dip up' (e.g. soup), Tol *-łee*, *-łek'* 'handle liquid,' Gal *-łeh*, *-łeʔ*. Cf. Nav *-Łèèh*, *-Łééʔ* 'wet object moves.'

78. Hupa *-laad* 'run,' Kato *-ład* 'jump.' Cf. Chip *-Łà*, *-Łá* 'move fast.'

79. EC, Coq *-ład* 'tremble,' Gal *-lad*. Cf. Nav *-Łìd* 'tremble.'

80. Hupa, Matt *Ł'oh* 'grass,' Wail *t'oh*, Kato *Ł'ooh*, Coq *Ł'oh*, ChC *Ł'ooh-de* 'tarweed,' Gal *Ł'oh* 'grass.' Cf. Nav *Ł'òh* 'grass,' Chip *Ł'òy*, Sar *-Ł'ò-*.

81. Hupa *xa-Ł'eʔ* 'night,' Kato *Ł'eʔ*, Coq, Gal *Ł'eʔ*, Tol *t'eeʔ*. Cf. Nav *Ł'ééʔ*, Chip *tà-Ł'èyè* 'darkness.'

82. Hupa *-Ł'ic'* 'hard,' Matt *-Ł'eʔc*, EC *-Ł'os*, Coq *-Ł'oʔs*, Tol *-t'eeʔs*, Gal *-Ł'aʔs*. Cf. Nav *-Ł'ìz*, Chip *-Ł'éδ* 'strong.'

83. Ump *xʷa-Ł'as* 'dirt, mud.' Cf. Nav *hàš-Ł'ìš*, Chip *-Ł'és*, Sar *Ł'is*.

REFERENCES

Goddard, P. E. 1904. Hupa Texts. University of California Publications in American Archeology and Ethnology, Vol. 1, No. 2.

—— 1905. The Morphology of the Hupa Language. University of California Publications in American Archeology and Ethnology, Vol. 3.

—— 1909. Kato Texts. University of California Publications in American Archeology and Ethnology, Vol. 5, No. 3.

—— 1912. Elements of the Kato Language. University of California Publications in American Archeology and Ethnology, Vol. 11, No. 1.

—— 1914. Chilula Texts. University of California Publications in American Archeology and Ethnology, Vol. 10, No. 7.

—— 1917. Beaver Dialect. Anthropological Papers, American Museum of Natural History, Vol. X, Part VI.

—— 1923. "Wailaka Texts," *International Journal of American Linguistics*, 2:Nos. 3-4:77-135.

Hoijer, Harry. 1938. "The Southern Athapaskan Languages," *American Anthropologist,* 40:75-87.

Li, Fang-Kuei. 1930. Mattole, an Athabaskan Language. Chicago: University of Chicago Press.

———— 1933. "Chipewyan Consonants," *Bulletin of the Institute of History and Philology of the Academia Sinica,* Vol. I (Peiping).

Morice, A. G. 1932. The Carrier Language. Vienna: Anthropos. 2 vols.

Osgood, Cornelius. 1936. The Distribution of the Northern Athapaskan Indians. Yale University Publications in Anthropology, No. 7.

Petitot, E. 1876. Dictionnaire de la Langue Dènè-Dindjié. Paris.

Sapir, Edward. 1914. Notes on Chasta Costa Phonology and Morphology. University of Pennsylvania, University Museum, Anthropological Publications, Vol. II, No. 2.

SOME GENETIC AFFILIATIONS OF ALGONKIAN

By Mary R. Haas

UNIVERSITY OF CALIFORNIA, BERKELEY

THE GEOGRAPHICAL SPREAD of the Algonkian languages is greater than the spread of any other linguistic family of North America. Tribes speaking these languages occupied almost the whole of the north central and northeastern part of the continent (including the Atlantic seaboard at least as far south as North Carolina) with additional enclaves in the west central plains and in the Southeast. Notwithstanding this great areal sweep these languages bear a close relationship to one another, the degree of closeness being roughly comparable to that which the Romance languages, or the Germanic languages, bear to one another. On the face of it, then, it seems logical to suppose that the Algonkian family is probably related to some other languages or language families in North America, just as we now know that Romance and Germanic are related not only to each other but also to several other languages and language families in Europe and Asia.

The present paper assesses the most important theories ofAlgonkian affiliations made in the past and proceeds thence to the proposal of new theories.[1]

Algonkian and Ritwan

The first breakthrough in the search for congeners for the Algonkian languages came in 1913 when Sapir suggested an affiliation with Ritwan, i.e. Wiyot and Yurok, isolated languages of northern California. Unfortunately, Sapir's suggestion was roundly denied by the brilliant Algonkianist Truman Michelson (1914), giving rise to the famous Sapir-Michelson controversy over the issue in the pages of the *American Anthropologist* in 1913–15. Though some scholars went on record in support of Sapir's hypothesis (Dixon and Kroeber, 1919; Radin, 1919), the general consensus of opinion seemed to be that the matter was controversial. As a result, the whole issue remained enshrouded in a cloud of doubt for very nearly half a century.

The second half of the twentieth century, however, at last finds us adequately equipped to take a new look at the problem. On the Algonkian side of the picture our information, especially about the nature of Proto–Central Algonkian, is much better and much fuller than it was in 1913. In 1925 Leonard Bloomfield placed Algonkian comparative studies on a firm basis by the publication of "On the Sound System of Central Algonquian." Michelson made important progress in bringing the Plains languages into the picture by the publication of an article entitled "Phonetic Shifts in Algonquian Languages" (1935). Several important articles on problems of Proto–Central Algonkian consonant clusters appeared in 1941 (Voegelin, Siebert, Geary). And finally, the most important single work, Bloomfield's masterly sketch of "Algonquian," appeared in 1946. This work contains all of the sound correspondences for Proto–Central Algonkian (together with reconstructions) and at the same time presents the total grammatical structure in all its complexity (again with reconstructions). This important work has also served as the point of departure for C. F. Hockett's proposed Central Algonkian comparative dictionary, the first installment of which appeared in print late in 1957.

In the meantime considerable progress has also been made on the Ritwan side of the picture. When Sapir first proposed the Algonkian-Ritwan connection, he not only had none of the Algonkian material discussed in the preceding paragraph, he was also handicapped by the sketchiness of the available Wiyot and Yurok material. At that time this consisted almost entirely of what is to be found in Kroeber's "Languages of the Coast of California North of San Francisco" (1911: Wiyot, pp. 384-413; Yurok, pp. 414-26). In 1925 extensive materials on Wiyot became available with the publication of Reichard's *Wiyot Grammar and Texts*. Extensive materials on Yurok are still unavailable in print but are due to make their appearance shortly (Robins, 1958). Furthermore, new, recently recorded materials on Wiyot (Teeter, unpublished field notes) have served to clarify a number of points, both phonological and grammatical, left vague in the Reichard work.

With so much new material at hand a reexamination of the whole problem of the possibility of an Algonkian-Ritwan connection became imperative. The results of this reexamination are such that it is possible to state unequivocally that Algonkian and Ritwan are related. The evidence for this assertion is presented in a separate paper entitled "Algonkian-Ritwan: the End of a Controversy" (Haas, 1958a).[2] A synopsis of that evidence is shown in Table 1.

The Algonkian forms quoted are usually reconstructed PCA (Proto–Central Algonkian) taken largely from Bloomfield (1946), Hockett (1957), and Michelson (1935), but a few forms are taken from Geary (1941) and Voegelin (1941). Occasional forms taken from Siebert (1941) are, properly speaking, PCEA (Proto–Central-Eastern Algonkian) since the revised reconstructions he proposed are based on evidence found in the Eastern languages only. In rare instances, when the desired reconstruction was unavailable in the literature, I have provided a reconstruction of my own based on whatever evidence I could find in the daughter languages.[3]

The Wiyot forms are taken from Teeter (unpublished notes),[4] or, when unavailable in his notes, from Reichard (1925). Robins (1958) is the source for most of the Yurok forms, though a few have been taken from my own field notes on the language.

Table 1

ALGONKIAN-RITWAN RELATIONS

Gloss	PCA or PCEA	Wiyot	Yurok
One	*kot-, *kwet-	kuʔc	koht-
Two	*niˑš-	ɹiʔt-	niʔiy-
Three	*neʔθ-	ɹiʔg-	nahks-
Four	*nyeˑw-	ɹiyoˑʔw-	—
Arm (finger)	*-θen(cyeˑ)-	šoˑn-	-sen
Bone	*waθkan-	watkaɹ-	wəlkəˑʔ
my Eye	*neški·n(šekw)-	ɹali·ɹ	neslin
his Leg (foot)	*wexka·c-	wačko·č	wacka
his Liver	*weθkwan-	watwaɹ	wəlkun
his Mouth	*wetoˑn-	walul-	weluł
his Tongue	*wi·θan-	wi·t-	weypł
his Tooth	*wi·pit-	wapt-	warpeł
his Tail	*waθany-	wadi·ʔl	wələy
Bear	*maθkw-	βokw	—
Deer	*atehkw-	hołakw	—
Grease	*pemi	puʔm	pemey
Louse	*ehkw-	hikw	mohkoh
Tree	*-a·htekw-	-o·tiʔ	tepo·
Woman	*eθkwe·w-	—	-ahpew
Drink	*mene	βaɹo-	meno(kʷolum)
Suckle	*no·n-	-ɹun(oč)-	newon
Steal	*kemot-	komar-	kemol-
Long	*kenw-	łoʔw	knew-
You	*ki·l-	gi·l	ke·ʔl
Obviative	*-ali	-aʔl	—

Linguistic forms in the text are preceded by an asterisk when they are reconstructions, and enclosed in diagonals when they are actual speech forms. The phonetic symbols used have the usual values assigned to them in American Indian linguistic work. However, Teeter uses the symbol /r/ for a voiced flap and /r/ for a voiced retroflex in Wiyot words. The Wiyot /r/ is very much like the only consonantal /r/ of Yurok. But Yurok also has a strongly retroflexed vocalic *r* written /ə/ in this paper in place of the symbol /ɹ/ used by Robins.

This synopsis (Table 1) is sufficient to demonstrate the genetic affinity of these languages for all practical purposes. All items listed are of the type generally considered to be "basic." No less than three consecutive phonemes are being compared in every instance, and in several instances as many as six consecutive phonemes are compared. Over and above the phonological evidence, we find that in several items two consecutive cognate morphemes are combined in the same order, e.g. MY EYE (MY+EYE), HIS LEG (HIS+LEG), and so forth. It has become traditional in comparative Algonkian studies to quote fully inflected forms wherever possible (Bloomfield, 1946; Hockett, 1957). It is not without significance that it is often possible to adhere to this tradition when Wiyot and Yurok are brought into the picture. The chances that resemblances of the types mentioned here could be accidental are so infinitesimal that the possibility need not be considered.

Algonkian and Mosan

Nothing daunted by the Michelson attack on his Algonkian-Ritwan hypothesis, Sapir suggested even broader possible affiliations for Algonkian a few years later. In his famous 1929 encyclopaedia article on "Central and North American Indian Languages" he placed Algonkian-Ritwan, Kutenai, and Mosan (Wakashan, Chemakuan, Salishan) together as one of his proposed six superstocks.[5] No evidence of any kind has ever been presented for this broader series of connections. Mosan itself is actually a superstock, and a great deal more work remains to be done before the intricacies of the relationship between Chemakuan, Wakashan, and Salishan are fully understood. Recent work by Swadesh (1953a, b), however, appears to be sufficient to establish the validity of their relationship to one another.

The question which next arises, then, is how we are to go about discovering whether or not Algonkian is related to Mosan. Swadesh assumes that the relationship of the three branches of Mosan to one another, though valid, is remote. If this is true, and if we assume that even so there may be some validity to the Algonkian-Mosan hypothesis, then it appears that it ought to be much more profitable to attempt to compare Algonkian with the separate branches of Mosan rather than to Proto-Mosan. A cursory examination of some of the material pertinent to this question (Swadesh, 1953a, b, 1955; Andrade, 1953) has revealed a few suggestive details. One of these is discussed below.

ONE. Bloomfield (1946) reconstructs PCA *nekotwi 'one,' Hockett (1957) reconstructs PCA *kotak- 'other.' Haas (1958b) makes a revised reconstruction *kwet- 'one, other' with a variant *nekwet- 'one' (but not 'other').

Table 1 shows Wiyot /kuʔc/ 'one,' Yurok /koht-/ 'one' (with certain classifiers). Haas (1958a) reconstructs PAR *kwet- 'one.'

Swadesh (1955) cites Chemakum /kʷi·l, kʷa·l/ (etc.) 'one,' Quileute /wi·l, wa·l/ 'one' and reconstructs Proto-Chemakuan *wi·l, *wa·l 'one.' It would seem that *kʷi·l, *kʷa·l might be equally plausible as a reconstruction. But either way the protoform appears to be comparable to PAR *kwet-.

Swadesh (1953a) reconstructs Proto-Salishan *nk-, *nkʷ- 'one,' which compares nicely with PCA *nekwet-. Swadesh further cites Nootka /n'up-/, classifier base for 'one,' which may also be comparable to the same PCA form. But observe that his Proto-Wakashan reconstruction *n'am- appears less likely as a comparison and that his Proto-Mosan reconstruction *na(m)- (or possibly *nama-) appears less likely still.

Assuming—pending the accumulation of further evidence—that the forms from the various languages and proto languages quoted above are actually cognate, it is clear that it is no more difficult (in this one example, at least) to fit in the Algonkian and Ritwan forms than it is to fit together the Chemakuan, Salishan, and Wakashan forms. Indeed the comparison of Proto-Salishan *nk-, *nkʷ- with Proto-Chemakuan *kʷi·l, *kʷa·l (or Swadesh's *wi·l, *wa·l) is rendered considerably more plausible by the introduction of PCA evidence in the form of *kwet-, *nekwet-. This, then, bears out my contention that it may turn out to be more profitable to begin work on the problem of Algonkian-Mosan affiliation by comparing Proto-Algonkian to Proto-Chemakuan, Proto-Salishan, and Proto-Wakashan rather than to Proto-Mosan. In part this appears to be due to the fact that Swadesh is attempting to explain too much by means of his

Proto-Mosan reconstructions, including as he does under 'one,' for example, words from various languages glossed 'all, alone, only, very much' as well as 'one.' There is, however, another and even greater difficulty which is inherent in all remote comparisons, namely that the further back in time one goes, the fewer the number of reconstructions that can be arrived at with evidence contributed from all the branches of the stock being subsumed in the reconstruction system.

Table 2

ALGONKIAN-MOSAN RELATIONS

Gloss	PCA or PCEA	Chemakum	Quileute
Bad	*maci	—	basi[?]
Big	*me[?]θ-, *me[?]ši	ma·t'ča-	—
Cover	*pet-	(ha)p'ili-	—
Crane	*mo·sk(aho·siw)-	mu·q'ʷa	—
Cry	*se·kw-	—	-c'aq(s)
Ear	*-hta·(waka·y)-	-t'a	—
Eye	*-(ški·)nšekw-	łaq'u·	daq'u·
Fish	*name·-	t'imi(qł)	—
Foot (1)	*-ka·t-	(la·?a)kʷut	(la?la)wit
Foot (2)	*-sit-	—	-č'iłi
Foot (3)	*-ešk-	—	-(d)ask
Head	*-štikw(a·n)-	-t'i·qʷ	-t'i·qʷ
Hip	*-θo·(kan)-	—	-t'u(s)
Mouth	*weto·n-, *oto·n- 'his mouth'	—	?u·lit
Neck	*-hkwe·-	-q'u(s)	-q'u(s)
Not	*kat-	kʷa·?al(χa)	wal
One	*kwet-, *kot-	kʷi·ł	wi·ł
See (look)	*wa·p-, *-a·p-	hu·pa?a-	—
Sharp(en)	*ki·n-t-	—	kidi·(qit) 'whetstone'
Steal	*kemot-	kʷut-	-k'o·t-
Swallow (v.)	*kwan-, *kon-	—	-k'a?d(as) 'throat'
Tail	*-aθany-	—	t'a·d(ax)
Through	*ša·pw-	ła·?ap(a·ti)-	-la?ap(a?a) 'sew'
Try	*kwat-, *kot-	—	kwat-

Still further proof of the profit which may be expected to ensue if Algonkian is compared to the branches rather than to the superstock as a whole is shown in Table 2. This table contains a set of possible comparisons between PCA and Chemakuan (Chemakum plus Quileute).

Chemakum forms are taken from Swadesh (1955), Quileute from Andrade (1933–38). In assessing these comparisons it must be borne in mind that Quileute /b, d/ normally correspond to Chemakum /m, n/ and the phonemes of both languages come from Proto-Chemakuan *m, *n. I retain Swadesh's transcription for these languages except that (1) long vowels are written by a single vowel letter followed by a raised dot instead of doubled vowel letters, and (2) /č/ is used for the sibilant affricate in place of the cyrillic symbol used by Swadesh.

Sound correspondences deserving special comment are the following:

PCA *t, Ch /t, t́/, Q /t, t́/: ear, foot (1), head, steal, try.

PCA *t, Ch /l, ĺ/, Q/ l, ĺ/:cover, foot (2), mouth, not, one.

PCA *n, Ch (n), Q /d/: sharp, swallow, tail.

PCA *n, Ch /t, t́/, Q /t, t́/: fish, mouth.

PCA *s, Ch (?), Q /č, č́/: cry, foot (2).

PCA *š, Ch /ĺ/, Q /ll/: through. In 'eye' Ch /ĺ/ may correspond to PCA *(n)š, Q /d/ to PCA *n(š).

PCA *θ, Ch (?), Q /t, t́/: hip, tail.

PCA *k, *kw, Ch /kʷ/, Q /w/: foot (1), not, one.

PCA *kʷ, Ch /q', q'ʷ/, Q /q', q'ʷ/: cry, eye, head.

This list of sound correspondences is far from exhaustive; it is intended only to be suggestive and is based on an admittedly sketchy preliminary attempt at comparison. But thirty years have elapsed since Sapir postulated his Algonkian-Mosan hypothesis, and in all that time no other evidence for the assumption, or any part of the assumption, has ever been published.

The comparisons presented in Table 2, then—preliminary though they may be—greatly strengthen the case for a probable genetic affiliation between Algonkian and Chemakuan, and hence probably also to Wakashan and Salishan. But at the present stage of the investigation, it would appear that this relationship will not turn out to be as close as that between Algonkian and Ritwan (Table 1).

Algonkian and the Gulf Languages

In a symposium held during the winter meetings of the American Anthropological Association in 1957, I presented evidence for a new and hitherto unsuspected genetic affiliation for Algonkian. This is a relationship with the Gulf languages which comprise the Muskogean family of languages plus Natchez, Tunica, Chitimacha, and Atakapa. Detailed evidence for this relationship is given in an article entitled "A New Linguistic Relationship in North America: Algonkian and the Gulf Languages" (Haas, 1958c).

Table 3 has been prepared to give a synopsis of the evidence for the Algonkian-Gulf relationship. The PCA (or PCEA) material is taken from the sources mentioned previously. The PM (Proto-Muskogean) forms are reconstructions taken from my own files. The principal sound correspondences for PM and a number of reconstructions are already available in print (Haas 1941, 1946b, 1947, 1949, 1950, 1956). Since the PCA and PM forms are reconstructions they are preceded by asterisks in the table. The rest of the Gulf languages are all single-language families and therefore actual speech forms are quoted for these in lieu of reconstructed forms.[6] Natchez is quoted from Haas (unpublished), Tunica from Haas (1953), Chitimacha from Swadesh (unpublished), and Atakapa from Gatschet and Swanton (1932).

Table 3

ALGONKIAN-GULF RELATIONS

Gloss	PCA or PCEA	PM	Natchez	Tunica	Chitimacha	Atakapa
Beat	*pak-	—	pa·k-	péka	—	pak
Cold	*tahk-	—	takap-	láka	č'aki	—
Cut (break)	*ki·šk-	*kač-	kec-	káhču	—	kec
Die	*nepe-	*ili-	—	lúpi	nu·p-	(pix)
Fish	*name·-	*NaNi/u	ʔeN	níni	(ni-)	nti
Hand	*-neθk-i	*-mkʷi	—	'-hkeni	—	nok
Name	*-i·n-	—	ʔinu	—	nuy-t-	eŋ
Neck	*-hkwe·-	*nukkʷi	kʷaht	—	k'eʔ	koy
Night	*tepeθk-	—	tewe	láwu	tapk'i	iti
One	*kwet-, *nekwet-	—	wi·t(a·N)	—	ʔunk'u	(ta)nuk
Scrape	*ka·šk-	*ka·s-	ko·c-	kósa	k'atka-	kau-š
See	*ne·w-	—	ʔeL-	héra	heč-t-	ini
Sharp(en)	*ki·n-t-	*xʷulut-	pilit-	kíri	kihci	kini
Shoot	*pemw-, *-el-	—	-epenel-	—	pa·hma-	pem
Split	*pa·θ-k-	*pał-	pa·L-	pása	šap-t-	pał
Swallow (v.)	*kwan-, *kon-	*kʷalak-	-akun-	kóra	ka·č-t-	kul
Tail	*-aθany-	*haci	ʔisi	-ása	(m)ahči	—
Three	*neʔθ-	—	ne·-	ʔéni-	—	lat
Through	*ša·pw-	*łuput-	—	šíhpu	—	łop
Tree	*meʔtekw-	*itti/u	cu·	ríhku	šuš	—
Turn	*kwetekw-	—	kitip-	kúra	kut'ih-t-	—

The synopsis in Table 3 should be sufficient to demonstrate the genetic affinity between Algonkian and Gulf for all practical purposes. The items shown have been selected from a list of over 125 comparisons between Algonkian and/or Ritwan and one or more of the Gulf languages. Only one principle of selection was used, namely, that a form cognate to the PCA form be present in at least three of the five Gulf languages. The items which make up the resulting list are all of the type generally considered to be "basic," that is, of a type unlikely to be borrowed. And in spite of the fact that it is often considered easier to find cognates among noun-like words than among verb-like words, a surprising number of the latter turned up as a result of this method of selection.

A word of caution needs to be inserted at this point. The postulation of a relationship between Algonkian and the Gulf languages does not necessarily mean that we must assume a greater time depth for Algonkian-Gulf than we would have to assume for the Gulf languages without Algonkian. After many years devoted to a study of the problem, I have been unable to come to any other conclusion than that the relationship of the various Gulf languages to one another is already quite remote. Algonkian, then, simply forms another link in this chain of relationships. And there may very well be additional links in the chain which will have to be fitted in before the whole story can be told. Indeed the next section of the present paper postulates the addition of one more link, namely Tonkawa.

Algonkian and Tonkawa

In connection with my work on the Gulf languages I have made note, from time to time, of probable comparisons between these languages and Tonkawa. Once I had worked out the evidence for the affiliation of Algonkian and Gulf, it was logical to look at the Tonkawa material in the light of this new hypothesis. In some instances it was necessary only to add Algonkian to the Gulf-Tonkawa comparisons already at hand. In a few instances, however, plausible comparisons between Algonkian and Tonkawa were found for which Gulf comparisons were lacking. A synopsis of the Algonkian-Gulf-Tonkawa comparisons is presented in Table 4. The Tonkawa forms are taken from Hoijer (1949). The Gulf column shows a comparison from only one of the Gulf languages, usually Natchez (Nt), but occasionally Tunica (Tn), Chitimacha (Cht), At (Atakapa), or Creek (Cr), the latter a Muskogean language. Important comparisons between Algonkian and Tonkawa for which Gulf comparisons appear to be lacking are the words for JEALOUS, LAND, NEW, and TONGUE.

Table 4

ALGONKIAN-GULF-TONKAWA COMPARISONS

Gloss	PCA or PCEA	Gulf	Tonkawa
Beat	*pak-	Nt: pa·k-	-paxa-
Black (blue)	*kaθk-	Cht: kat'i-	xʔat(on)
Close (cover)	*kep-	Nt: kap-	-kapa-
Cold	*tahk-	Nt: takap-	-tike-
Cut (break)	*ki·šk-	Nt: kec-	kes(ʔace)-
Dig	*wa·l-	Tn: wéra	kʷan(ʔase)-
Hand (arm)	*-neθk-	At: nok	-noto(·n)
Hot	*kešy-	Nt: ke·s-	ka·le-; xal(al)
Jealous	*kya··	—	cʔeyʔe-
Land	*axky-	—	ha·c
Look	*-a·p-	Tn: pó	hapa(xa)-
New (young)	*wešk-, *ošk-	—	hos(as)
One	*kwet-, *kot-	Nt: wi·t(a·N)	we·(ʔis)
Plural	*-aki	Cr: -aki	-ka
Scrape (scratch)	*ka·šk-	Tn: kósa	xʔas(ʔake)-
See	*ne·w-	Nt: ʔeL-	helʔe(ya)-
Sharp(en)	*ki·n-t-	At: kini	xʔelʔe-
Skin (hide)	*lo·k- (or *θ-)	Nt: toloks	ʔok
Sky	*ki·šek-	Nt: ʔisak	cʔel
Spotted	*ketak-	Tn: kéra	kelʔis
Stink (break wind)	*pec-	Nt: pic-	(xʔo)poco-
Stink (defecate)	*mi·s-	Nt: mis-	mos(koy)
Swallow (throat)	*kwan-, *kon-	Nt: -akun-	(wa)wana-
Tail	*-aθany-	Tn: -ása	tan
Tongue (lick)	*-i·θan-	—	(ne)tale-

Sound correspondences deserving special notice are the following:

PCA *k, Tnk /k/: close, cut, hot, plural, spotted

PCA *k, Tnk /x, xʔ/: beat, black, hot (2), scrape, sharp

PCA *kw, Tnk /w/: one, swallow

PCA *ky (or in one instance *k/i), Tnk /c, cʔ/: jealous, land, sky

PCA *n, Tnk /n/: hand, swallow, tail

PCA *n, Tnk /l/: see, sharp, tongue

PCA *š, Tnk /l/: hot, sky

PCA *θ, Tnk /t/: tail, tongue

PCA *šk, Tnk /s/: cut, new, scrape

PCA *θk, Tnk /t/: black, hand

The last two sets of sound correspondences are remarkable for a special reason connected with PCA phonology. The exact phonetic nature of the first component of any PCA consonant cluster is unknown. Therefore the actual symbol used (e.g. š, θ) need not be interpreted as having the same phonemic value as that same symbol used alone. But the regularity of the sound correspondences within Central Algonkian are such that any given PCA consonant cluster always has the same reflex in any given Central Algonkian language. It is therefore not without considerable significance that Tonkawa shows this same regularity in its reflexes.

As is well known, Tonkawa has long been assumed to be related to the Coahuiltecan languages, and both in turn are assumed to be related to the Hokan languages (Sapir, 1917). The postulation of an Algonkian-Tonkawa connection is not intended to deny the possibility of other affiliations for Tonkawa. Up to the present, however, attempts to compare Tonkawa with Hokan have been sporadic and haphazard and, so far as I am aware, nothing has yet been presented which has the kind of internal consistency and regularity to be found in Table 4. What future researches will bring remains to be seen.

Summary

The sequence of affiliations suggested for Algonkian in the preceding sections of this paper leads up to the conclusion that all of these language groups are related in some way. A summary of the evidence is presented in Table 5. Salishan and most Wakashan forms are quoted from Swadesh (1953b), but some Kwakiutl is from Boas (1947) and some Nootka is from Sapir and Swadesh (1939). Numbers are used to distinguish the branches of Salishan and Wakashan. In the Salishan row, (1) is Bella Coola, (2) is Interior Salish, and (3) is Pacific Coast Salish. In the Wakashan row, (1) is Kwakiutl, (2a) is Nootka, and (2b) is Nitinat.

Conclusion

The purpose of this paper has been fourfold: (1) to validate the Algonkian-Ritwan connection, (2) to show that the possibility of an Algonkian-Mosan affiliation merits further investigation, (3) to show that the Gulf languages and Tonkawa are also related to Algonkian, and (4) to suggest

Table 5

RELATION OF ALGONKIAN TO OTHER LANGUAGE GROUPS

	One	Fish	Hand	Neck	Sharp(en)	Spit(tle)	Swallow[a]	Tail
PCAlgonkian	*kwet-	*name-	*-neθk-	*-hkwe-	*kin-t-	*sekw-	*kwan-	*-aθany-
Wiyot	ku?c ↓	nepuy	—	peh(tun)	k'were-	(pa)luk-	—	-adi·?l-
Yurok	koht- ↓	—	—	—	—	lohpǝ(yeł)	—	-łey
Chemakum	kʷi·ł ↓	t'imi(qł)	-kʷanut	-q'us	—	tuxʷ-	—	—
Quileute	wi·ł ↓	—	—	-q'us	kidi-	tuxʷ-	-k'a?d(as)	-t'a·?d(ax)
Salishan	nk'ʷ- (2) ↑	—	—	-?χu (1)	kʷi- (2a)	łχʷt (1)	—	—
Wakashan	n'up- (2a) ↑	me (1)	-n'uk (2a)	—	—	tuxʷ- (2b)	wan(i·q) (2a)	—
PMuskogean	—	*NaNi/u	*-mkʷi	*(nu)kkʷi	*xʷulut-	*tuxʷ-	*kʷalak-	*haci
Natchez	wi·t-	?eN	—	kʷaht	pilit-	cuh-	-akun-	?isi
Tunica	—	níni	'-hkeni	k'e?	kiri	čúhu	kóra	-ása
Chitimacha	↑	(ni-)	—	koy	kihci	—	ka·č-t-	(m)ahči
Atakapa	(ta)nuk	nti-	nok	—	kini	(ki)tuš	kul	—
Tonkawa	we-	—	-noto(-n)	—	x?e?e-	-toxo-	-wana-	tan

[a] Also often 'throat.'

that all these languages are probably related to one another. The first two points were already suggested by Sapir; the last two points are new.

It would be unwise at this stage to make conjectures beyond what the evidence presented so far indicates. But we cannot close our eyes to the fact that other affiliations have been suggested for the Gulf languages and Tonkawa, namely that they belong together with a number of other families and stocks (including, among others, Siouan, Iroquoian, and Hokan) in a superstock named "Hokan-Siouan" by Sapir (1929). Hints of a possible relationship between Hokan and Penutian (in the broad sense of that term) have also been alluded to from time to time in the literature. Clearly we do not yet have all the answers.

Forty years ago Paul Radin published a short paper entitled "The Genetic Relationship of the North American Indian Languages" (1919) in which he set forth the theory that all the languages of North America except Eskimoan are related. At the time the paper appeared his theory was considered extremely unlikely and his arguments a tour de force. Present thinking has modified this earlier judgment, and recent investigations (while they still fall short of complete agreement) are nevertheless propelling us nearer and nearer to his point of view. In a volume of papers prepared in his honor, it is particularly fitting that Dr. Radin be given due credit for having envisaged, so many years ago, some of the directions in which future investigations were sure to proceed.

NOTES

[1] Grateful acknowledgment is made to the Research Committee of the University of California, Berkeley, for funds to employ part-time research assistants who have aided (1) in the preparation of an alphabetized file of Proto-Central Algonkian reconstructions, (2) in making other needed indexes, and (3) in the processing of some of my Natchez and Muskogean field notes. My thanks are due to Mr. Harvey Pitkin and Mr. Wick R. Miller, advanced graduate students in linguistics, who have, at different times, assisted me in this capacity.

[2] Karl V. Teeter has also written a paper entitled "Wiyot and Algonquian: a Preliminary Study" (unpublished).

[3] Strictly speaking, the type of broader comparative work that I am undertaking in connection with Algonkian would be greatly facilitated if it were possible to quote true PA (Proto-Algonkian) reconstructions rather than PCA reconstructions. Comparative Algonkian studies, however, have not yet progressed to the point where this is possible. Until such time as this possibility becomes a reality, then, we shall have to make do with PCA. Even with this restriction, however, the results are surprisingly rewarding.

[4] The field work of Karl V. Teeter on Wiyot (1956 and 1957) and of R. H. Robins on Yurok (1951) was carried out under the sponsorship of the Survey of California

Indian Languages, Department of Linguistics, University of California, Berkeley.

[5] To the best of my knowledge, the first published statement concerning this particular series of affiliations appears in Radin's "The Genetic Relationship of North American Indian Languages" (1919). In this paper, Radin suggests three subgroups, the first of which comprises "Salish, Kwakiutl, Kutenai, Algonkin" (p. 492). Perhaps this grouping resulted from discussions between Radin and Sapir, since Sapir had the greater firsthand familiarity with these particular languages.

[6] Several attempts at comparing two or more Gulf languages have been made from time to time, viz. Tunica, Chitimacha, and Atakapa (Swanton, 1919), Atakapa and Chitimacha (Swadesh, 1946b, 1947), Natchez and Muskogean (Swanton, 1924; Haas, 1956), and finally, Muskogean, Natchez, Tunica, Chitimacha, and Atakapa (two etymologies; Haas, 1951, 1952).

REFERENCES

Andrade, Manuel J. 1933–38. "Quileute," in *Handbook of American Indian Languages*, ed. by Franz Boas, Vol. 3, pp. 149-292).

—— 1953. "Notes on the Relations between Chemakum and Quileute," *International Journal of American Linguistics*, 19:212-15.

Bloomfield, Leonard. 1925. "On the Sound System of Central Algonquian," *Language*, 1:130-56.

—— 1946. "Algonquian," in Harry Hoijer and others, *Linguistic Structures of Native America* (Viking Fund Publications in Anthropology, No. 6), pp. 85-129.

Boas, Franz. 1947. "Kwakiutl Grammar with a Glossary of the Suffixes," *Transactions of the American Philosophical Society*, n.s., 37:201-377.

Dixon, Roland B., and Alfred L. Kroeber. 1919. "Linguistic Families of California," *University of California Publications in American Archaeology and Ethnology*, 16:47-118.

Gatschet, Albert S., and John R. Swanton. 1932. A Dictionary of the Atakapa Language. Bureau of American Ethnology, Bulletin 108, Washington, D.C.

Geary, James A. 1941. "Proto-Algonquian *çk: Further Examples," *Language*, 17:304-10.

Haas, Mary R. 1936-37. Field Notes on Natchez (unpublished).

—— 1941. "The Classification of the Muskogean Languages," in *Language, Culture, and Personality*, ed. by L. Spier, Menasha, Wisconsin, pp. 41-56.

—— 1946a. "A Grammatical Sketch of Tunica," in Harry Hoijer and others, *Linguistic Structures of Native America* (Viking Fund Publications in Anthropology, No. 6), pp. 337-66.

—— 1946b. "A Proto-Muskogean Paradigm," *Language*, 22:326-32.

—— 1947. "Development of Proto-Muskogean *kʷ," *International Journal of American Linguistics*, 13:135-37.

—— 1949. "The Position of Apalachee in the Muskogean Family," *International Journal of American Linguistics*, 15:121-27.

—— 1950. "On the Historical Development of Certain Long Vowels in Creek," *International Journal of American Linguistics*, 16:122-25.

—— 1951. "The Proto-Gulf Word for *Water* (with Notes on Siouan-Yuchi)," *International Journal of American Linguistics*, 17:71-79.

—— 1952. "The Proto-Gulf Word for *Land* (with a Note on Proto-Siouan)," *International Journal of American Linguistics*, 18:238-40.

—— 1953. "Tunica Dictionary," *University of California Publications in Linguistics*, 6:175-332.

———— 1956. "Natchez and the Muskogean Languages," *Language*, 32:61-72.

———— 1958a. "Algonkian-Ritwan: the End of a Controversy," *International Journal of American Linguistics*, 24:159-73.

———— 1958b. "Some Notes on PCA Stems in /k-/," *International Journal of American Linguistics*, 24:241-45.

———— 1958c. "A New Linguistic Relationship in North America; Algonkian and the Gulf Languages" *Southwestern Journal of Anthropology*, 14:231-64.

Hockett, Charles F. 1957. "Central Algonquian Vocabulary: Stems in /k-/," *International Journal of American Linguistics*, 23:247-68.

Hoijer, Harry. 1933–38. "Tonkawa, an Indian Language of Texas," in *Handbook of American Indian Languages*, ed. by Franz Boas, Vol. 3, pp. 1-148.

———— 1946. "Tonkawa," in Harry Hoijer and others, *Linguistic Structures of Native America* (Viking Fund Publications in Anthropology, No. 6), pp. 289-311.

———— 1949. "An Analytical Dictionary of the Tonkawa Language," *University of California Publications in Linguistics*, 5:1-74.

Kroeber, Alfred L. 1911. "The Languages of the Coast of California North of San Francisco," *University of California Publications in American Archaeology and Ethnology*, 9:273-435 (Wiyot, pp. 384-413; Yurok, pp. 414-426).

Michelson, Truman. 1914. "Two Alleged Algonquian Languages of California," *American Anthropologist*, 16:361-67.

———— 1915. "Rejoinder [to Sapir, 1915]" *American Anthropologist*, 17:194-98.

———— 1935. "Phonetic Shifts in Algonquian Languages," *International Journal of American Linguistics*, 8:131-71.

Radin, Paul. 1919. "The Genetic Relationship of the North American Indian Languages," *University of California Publications in Archaeology and Ethnology*, 14:489-502.

Reichard, Gladys A. 1925. "Wiyot Grammar and Texts," *University of California Publications in American Archaeology and Ethnology*, 22:1-215.

Robins, R. H. 1958. "The Yurok Language," *University of California Publications in Linguistics*, 15:1-300.

Sapir, Edward. 1913. "Wiyot and Yurok, Algonkin Languages of California," *American Anthropologist*, 15:617-46.

———— 1915a. "Algonkin Languages of California: a Reply [to Michelson, 1914]," *American Anthropologist*, 17:188-94.

———— 1915b. "Epilogue [to the Sapir-Michelson exchange]," *American Anthropologist*, 17:198.

———— 1917. "The Hokan and Coahuiltecan Languages," *International Journal of American Linguistics*, 1:280-90.

———— 1923. "The Algonkin Affinity of Yurok and Wiyot Kinship Terms," *Journal de la Société des Americanistes de Paris*, 15:37-74.

———— 1929. "Central and North American Languages," in *Encyclopaedia Britannica*, 14th ed., Vol. 5, pp. 138-41. Reprinted in *Selected Writings of Edward Sapir*, ed. by David G. Mandelbaum, pp. 169-78. University of California Press, 1949.

Sapir, Edward, and Morris Swadesh. 1939. Nootka Texts: Tales and Ethnological Narratives with Grammatical Notes and Lexical Materials. University of Pennsylvania, Philadelphia.

Siebert, Frank T., Jr. 1941. "Certain Proto-Algonquian Consonant Clusters," *Language*, 17:298-303.

Swadesh, Morris. 1946a. "Chitimacha," in Harry Hoijer and others, *Linguistic Structures of Native America* (Viking Fund Publications in Anthropology, No. 6), pp. 312-36.

—— 1946b. "Phonologic Formulas for Atakapa-Chitimacha," *International Journal of American Linguistics*, 12:113-32.

—— 1947. "Atakapa-Chitimacha *kᵂ," *International Journal of American Linguistics*, 13:120-21.

—— 1953a. "Mosan I: A Problem of Remote Common Origin," *International Journal of American Linguistics*, 19:26-44.

—— 1953b. "Mosan II: Comparative Vocabulary," *International Journal of American Linguistics*, 19:223-36.

—— 1955. "Chemakum Lexicon Compared with Quileute," *International Journal of American Linguistics*, 21:60-72.

—— Unpub. Chitimacha Vocabulary (typescript).

Swanton, John R. 1919. A Structural and Lexical Comparison of the Tunica, Chitimacha and Atakapa Languages. Bureau of American Ethnology, Bulletin 68, Washington, D.C.

—— 1924. "The Muskhogean Connection of the Natchez Language," *International Journal of American Linguistics*, 3:46-75.

Teeter, Karl V. 1956–57. Field notes on Wiyot recorded for the Survey of California Indian Languages, Department of Linguistics, University of California, Berkeley.

—— Unpub. "Wiyot and Algonquian: A Preliminary Study" (typescript).

Voegelin, Charles F. 1941. "Proto-Algonquian Consonant Clusters in Delaware," *Language*, 17:143-47.

YUROK SPEECH USAGES

By A. L. Kroeber

UNIVERSITY OF CALIFORNIA

PAUL RADIN has always been sensitive to the relations of particular cultures to particular languages, and has consistently stressed a textual foundation for ethnological documents.

The following are some reactions—all obtained from Robert Spott, co-author of *Yurok Narratives*—to special forms of Yurok speech, ranging from baby talk to ritualistic phrases, and including samples of metaphors, generalizing terms, circumlocutions, and technical terms reflecting institutions.

The Indians of northwest California seem to have been strongly aware of proper speech. The Hupa distinguished in pronominal gender between adult Hupa on the one hand and foreigners and Hupa children on the other, according to Goddard (1905, p. 30).

Spott said that the Karok in their World Renewal or "New Years" at Panamnik, Orleans, made Yurok, Hupa, and other foreign visitors camp below "Tui" (Ullathorn?) Creek until the smoke of the sacred fire lit by the ritualist had gone down—unless the foreigners spoke Karok well, in which case they were treated like natives. Thus, the children of a Yurok who was part Karok himself but had raised them in Weitchpec, could speak some Karok, but not well enough, and so were also kept below "Tui." In all Karok world renewals the formulist made one fire which (or the smoke of which) it was forbidden and dangerous to view. It is not known whether the purpose of the discrimination according to speaking ability was to protect visitors or to set the home nationality apart from foreigners.

From here on the data are Spott's, with comment by myself enclosed in square brackets.

Children's Talk

In adult Yurok, *kútskuts* means angleworm, and *lekwo* is used for an aged person dragging himself along on his rump.

[It will be seen that small children duplicate monosyllabic kinship terms; that they turn voiced fricative into unvoiced stop; that they pronounce *l* for *r*; that their duplicated words are mostly accented (stress plus pitch in adult speech) finally, but unduplicated disyllables, initially even when adults stress them finally; that grammatical elements are mostly omitted. All these features recur or have resemblances in young children's versions of other languages.]

Children say: Adults say:

p p p	eat	[nep]
kikí	urinate	ahki; ki·hk, defecates indoors
p'ū'	defecate	pú'ne [break wind]; kwonoł
kokók	mother	ko·k [vocative]
totót, dodót	father	to·t [vocative]
kútskuts	grandmother	ku·ts
pah	water	pa'
lékwo	drink	negwó'
kíko	acorns	kegó'
népa	salmon	nepúi
po·o	stand	kó·'o-pes
nà·ma	walk	nä'·ä·pes; [n-eg-a·ma, (dog) walks (on fours)]
na·	no	pa·

Adults do not reciprocate with baby talk, in order that the children may sooner learn to talk correctly.

Sense and Control

mä'-tp'ol, 'without sense or discretion'; i.e., small children who cannot be trusted to understand or take care of themselves; *hu·ksa*, 'children in general'; *kits-tup'ôl*, 'has [reached] sense'; *kits-nimi-tup'ol*, 'no longer has sense, second childhood'; *mos-tup'ol*, 'insane from a curse,' as for instance uttered by a man finding his house robbed and wishing evil to the thief. A man from house *leki·ł* at *Tsa·hpekw* became that way: he tore off his clothes, went into the woods for days "to stay with beings there"; between times, he was sober.

kits-ni-kerhpéyu, 'crazy sexually'; *kerhpéyu mel wéntsauks*, 'crazy after (with) women.'

witunú·menok, 'crazy from crying too much,' or from the earth where a *sa'äl* spirit is in brush of creek.

upä'·'äl, 'quarrelsome'; *u-wegó·*, 'fights all the time' (-*eg*-, iterative infix).

wá'asoi, 'poor'; *mel wegá'asoi*, 'because always poor,' means they are greedy for food [infix -*eg*-, iterative].

Imperfections of Speech

tswegí·n, 'talk, language.'

ki-tswí·gin, 'he talks articulately,' when a child has outgrown baby talk.

m·ä-tswí·gin, (adult) 'talks inarticulately'—perhaps intelligible to his family, but others have difficulty understanding him.

ninó·hsun we-só·n, 'he just grew up that way'—naturally, not through sickness.

u'-melú·l, 'speaks gasping or brokenly.'

mä'-skui u'-melú·l, 'not-good his speaking brokenly.'

kwetlóni·p, 'stutter, stammer.'

Near-Homonyms

winó'σs, 'its cradle, baby-basket'; *winó's,* 'will you please' [give it], [*wenó's,* 'hand it here']; *wenó·s,* [her] 'husband'; *wénos,* 'come here!'

perérkr, 'starvation formula, famine witchcraft' (Spott and Kroeber, 1942, No. 18, p. 202); *per'érkr,* 'dried mussels.'

umá', 'bewitcher', also his "devil"; *umá',* 'a small diving duck'; *umä'ⁱ,* 'girl who has not yet borne a child.'

"Woge Language"

This is ritual language, as used in formulas and prayers, which were instituted by the woge, the first race, the immortals, who withdrew as human beings came into the world. [Most of the terms are metaphors.]

olo·lékw-is-o'l, 'person, human beings' ["who live in settlements"?—cf. *oló·lekw,* 'village, town']. Ordinary word: *ôl.*

no'óhpu·k [cf. *nohpu·k,* 'born from "half" (matrilocal) marriage'], 'children'. Ordinary word: *hú·ksa.*

megá·wil, 'woman', term used in boat on ocean. Ordinary word: *wéntsauks.*

no·hpétuks, 'dog', ("salmon beetle," "maggots in food,"), used in boat on ocean, on ritual trail, etc. Ordinary word: *tsis,* or *megó·kw* ('barks').

ôl eká, 'earth' ("what people grasp, hold on to"). Ordinary word: *lkel,* 'ground', *we-lkél'oná,* 'world'.

mel-kétso', 'sun' ("with light"). Ordinary word: *wonä'ᵘsläi.*

mel-hégwomi wés-kwel or *ne-wés,* 'fire' ("what they warm their bodies with"). Ordinary word: *mets.*

lá·yo, 'Klamath river' (cf. *láyeks,* 'road'). Ordinary word: *werói,* 'stream', *u-megwó,* 'river, large stream.'

kits-ségeyóil ("growth is burned dry"), [*-eg*, iterative infix]. Ordinary word: *kisén*.

mégworets, 'boat' (cf. *u-megwó*, 'river'). Ordinary word: *yots*.

kits-ká·hselumiso·n, 'the dead' ("unknowing ones"). Ordinary word: *késamui*.

kyéhkwin kiwinó'omun o·l eká, 'as long as people endure' [hold on to from generation to generation].

hí"i'i'i'i'i, *k'eléu koní·'i*, 'hi-i-i-i-i-i, to you I blow' [this offering of grains of tobacco from my palm].

Metaphorical Phrases or Sayings

kits-ká·hsilumisó·n wi-la'a o'tep, 'those-who-have-been-left-behind [the dead] their-trail [tree-] it stands.'

ki'mole'ṇ ho'ohkoł u-tegeräu, 'evil at-night bewitch-by-praying' [*-eg-*, iterative infix. The first word means also bad, ugly, worn-out, tattered].

nä'äptsus e'gó·r, 'steps over the home hearth' [marries a house mate].

tsisä'osó·n, 'grow up like dogs' [marry kin].

pekwón opyú·weg o'wé·n po'ntét-mel pí·gäl; Pekwon, 'living-house-in-which-they-dance its-women ashes-with they-fight-with-one-another' (and before breakfast at that!). Such has been the way in that house, and men are advised not to take a wife from it.

If trading of sisters in marriage was contemplated, a reference to the negotiator or marriage broker (*hegi'm*) that one wished to drink (women being water fetchers), was a suggestion that one was ready to trade sisters

Collective Terms

Probably in formal ritual speeches ("woge talk"):

neryérmert ("moving about inland"), 'game, of all species.'

skewégoneł, 'fish of all kinds.'

nunépeu, same (cf. *nepúi*, 'salmon of any species').

pegáwuks kolsónkeł, 'dressed skins, tanned furs.'

Probably secular:

herérhkerł, 'fresh-caught' (fish or game).

wó·weł, 'acorns, hazelnuts, pine nuts, pepper nuts.'

slo·weł, 'pinole, fine-ground seeds,' of whatever herb.

Wealth

S'er'is is treasure of feathers or fur. Does not include dentalia or obsidian blades. Also used specifically for woodpecker-crest head-bands (*regä"i, plegóhk*). *S'eris kits-k'ewé'yono*, 'paid feather-treasure,' was said when *regä"i* were included in bride-payment.

tsi·k, dentalia.

ní·gem, obsidian or flint blades.

hiwónison tsi·k, 'top money,' highest grade dentalia (won, "up, above").

keits'i wesega"aigek, 'completely rich'; he does not have to try to acquire more.

mi·kisó·tak upyúr, 'able to outfit two dances at once, upriver and downriver.'

kegéi-mel wesega"aigek, 'doctoring-from wealthy.' This is better to have than weregild wealth, but not so clean as wish wealth. Is kept separate.

tspok-sínmił (by "willing, thinking"), *meihkwílel-mel* ("by tears") *wino·'hkwomis* ("acquired"), is the purest wealth.

Feuds

ekór, 'to murder,' kill a person.

kits-ekóri'm, '(watch your step, someone in your family) has done a killing.'

ekór o'tép, 'murder it stands,' a plank erected by a murderer to draw to itself the curses wished on him by the relatives of his victim. It might be very slightly shaped in silhouette to suggest a human being. The spot would be remembered long after the plank had fallen, and would retain the name *ekór o'tép*. [Powers, 1877, p. 57, gives the first description.]

Wohpukítslo·, 'thrown into the middle of the river,' said of a person shot and killed. An actual throwing into water was called *pa'ä'ł-iklo·*.

(ki-)mu·łkoik', 'to settle for a killing'; the modern word is *ki-mä·hpäu*, or *kits-mäuhpe-lik*, 'it has been paid for and settled.'

Cursing

"Cursing" was by words (*we-negó·no'm*), or by gesture of extended hand with spread fingers (*o-kwegétsip, u-kmegó·wei* by children and adults respectively); obscene talk was counted the same. Sample expressions were: *tsórrikik 'o'ló; híwos tsor 'o'ló·, híwos tsor so·tos*, referring to place after death; or asking "where is your father, etc.?" if the kinsman was dead.

Fine for spoken curse was: 2 necklaces *terk^utem* (bead dentalia);

among poorer people, 1 or 2 digger-pine or yew seed necklaces, or an elk-horn spoon, or a steatite dish; or, between women, a cooking basket (*mu'rip*); or, lately, $2.50 to $5.00; double that among the rich. The gesture curse was more serious: the wealthy paid or exacted up to $30.00 or $40.00.

If there were provocation—work spoiled or one's property left disordered by others—the one at fault was not likely to claim a fine; but a bystander might claim it, pretending to feel included in the abuse because no names were mentioned. Then the *hohpkusin* (judge, arbiter) would rule that the fault justified anger, though warning against its repetition. If pay tendered for cursing was refused as insufficient, the *hohpkusin* might warn the aggrieved not to retaliate, under liability of a doubled fine because settlement had been offered.

Children, sometimes up to ca. 14, were not fined for cursing because *nimoka-tép'ol*, 'without discretion.'

Threat by aiming an arrow, *ha'érekwets*, was serious; the fine was "nearly half" that for shooting.

The Ocean

Substitute words for woman and dog used while in a boat on the ocean have been mentioned under "Woge Language."

Women were allowed on the ocean in boats unless menstruant; they were asked if they were so. Dogs were never taken on the ocean in boats.

Some women were bad sea voyagers, so walked part way between the mouth of the Klamath and Crescent City (Kohpei). Some chiefly feared passing the Klamath mouth bar, so embarked or disembarked at Hostsegep, a short mile north of mouth (Waterman, 1920, map 5:36, cites Otsegep erroneously as a seastack off shore, but the situation is about right). Yet this was not a really safe landing. Better, 5 miles north at a promontory 1 mile north of Omen-hipur, was an always safe landing behind the seastack called *wéntsauks hélku olégem*, 'women inland-of-it disembark.' This rock was toward shore from a larger one near a point called *erwergérl*. (Waterman, 1920, map 5:12, gives *owergerl* as nearly 1 mile offshore from Omen-hipur; but this outside rock is called *tertús*, 'knobby, lumpy.')

Ocean: *pískäl*, from *píska*, 'salt.' [The Yurok in English frequently say "saltwater" for "ocean."] Another word, *sepolá*, 'prairie', was also used, especially [?] upriver.

tegwoli-két'o, 'both oceans together'; *tegwoli,* 'across sky, behind sky'; *oket'o, oket'uł,* 'lake, body of water.'

piskäł nike'm, 'sea food'; *hełkä'u nike'm,* 'inland food.'

tsegyéł, (Porphyra), 'edible seaweed.'

wahtéi, po'yół, 'inedible sea-mosses'; *piskäł ni-ha'ä'i umép'o,* 'ocean rock whiskers,' another kind; *werłkił,* 'kelp.'

Orthography of Yurok Words

I have written *ts* for a sound between *ch* and *ts,* while *s* is a sibilant neither quite *s* nor *sh*; *g* as a sonant fricative could well have been expressed by gamma; crossed *l, (ł)* is surd *l*; an apostrophe following a stop makes this glottalized; the raised period indicates a long vowel; all initial vowels are perhaps preceded by a glottal stop. Consonantal *r* is much as in American English; and (against linguistic rule) I denote vocalic *r* by the two letters *er,* which are also spoken as Americans would speak them.

REFERENCES

Goddard, P. E. 1905. Morphology of the Hupa Language. University of California Publications in American Archaeology and Ethnology, Vol. 3.

Kroeber, A.L. 1925. Handbook of Indians of California. Bureau of American Ethnology Bulletin 78.

Powers, Stephen. 1877. Tribes of California. Contributions to North American Ethnology, Vol. 3.

Spott, Robert, and A. L. Kroeber. 1942. Yurok Narratives. University of California Publications in American Archaeology and Ethnology, Vol. 35.

Waterman, T. T. 1920. Yurok Geography. University of California Publications in American Archaeology and Ethnology, Vol. 16.

A BIBLIOGRAPHY OF
WRITINGS BY PAUL RADIN

Compiled by Richard Werbner

BRANDEIS UNIVERSITY

1906

"Zur Netztechnik der Sudamerikanischer Indianer," *Zeitschrift für Ethnologie,* 388:926-38.

With V. Frič, "Contributions to the Study of the Bororo Indians," *Journal of the Royal Anthropological Institute of Great Britain and Ireland,* Vol. 36.

Editor, "Notes on the Grave-Posts of the Kadiueo," by V. Frič, *Man,* 6:71-72.

———— "Note on the Mask-Dances of the Čamacoco," by V. Frič, *Man,* 6:116-19.

1909

"Winnebago Tales," *Journal of American Folklore,* 22:288-313.

1910

"The Clan Organization of the Winnebago," *American Anthropologist,* N.S., 12: No. 2:209-19. Reprinted 1910 by New Era Printing Co., Lancaster, Pa.

With J. O. Dorsey, "The Winnebago Tribe," in *Handbook of American Indians North of Mexico,* 2:958-61. Bureau of American Ethnology Bulletin 30. Washington, D.C.

1911

"Some Aspects of Winnebago Archaeology," *American Anthropologist,* N.S., 13: No. 4:517-38.

"The Ritual and Significance of the Winnebago Medicine Dance," *Journal of American Folklore,* 24:No. 92:148-208.

"Winnebago Text," in *Handbook of American Indian Languages,* 1:959-65. Ed. by Franz Boas. Bureau of American Ethnology Bulletin 40. Washington, D.C.

With Oliver Lamere, "Descriptions of a Winnebago Funeral," *American Anthropologist,* N.S., 13:No. 3:437-44.

Translator, Legends of the Jews, by Louis Ginzburg. Vol. III. Philadelphia, Jewish Publication Society.

1912

"On Ojibwa Work in Southeastern Ontario," in *Summary Report of the Canada Geological Survey,* pp. 482-83. Ottawa.

Appendix to *The Indian Tribes of the Upper Mississippi Valley,* by Emma H. Blair. Vol. II. Cleveland, Arthur H. Clark Co.

With Louis H. Gray, "The Eskimos," in *Encyclopaedia of Religion and Ethics,* ed. by James Hastings, pp. 391-95.

1913

"On Ojibwa Work, 1913," in *Reports from the Anthropological Division of the Canada Geological Survey,* p. 374. Ottawa.

"Personal Reminiscences of a Winnebago Indian," *Journal of American Folklore*, 26:No. 102:293-318.

1914

Some Myths and Tales of the Ojibwa of South-Eastern Ontario. Ottawa. Anthropology Series of the Canada Geological Survey, Memoir 48, No. 2.

"The Influence of the Whites on Winnebago Culture," in *Proceedings of the Wisconsin State Historical Society*, 1913, pp. 137-45. Madison, Wisconsin.

"Introductive Enquiry in the Study of Ojibwa Religion," in *Papers and Records of the Ontario Historical Society*, Vol. XII. Reprinted by The Griffin and Richmond Co., Ltd, Hamilton, Ont.

"Religion of the North American Indians," *Journal of American Folklore*, 27:No. 106:335-73.

"A Sketch of the Peyote Cult of the Winnebago: A Study in Borrowing," *Journal of Religious Psychology*, Vol. 7 (January). Reprinted Worcester, Mass.

"Some Aspects of Puberty Fasting among the Ojibwa," *Museum Bulletin of the Canada Geological Survey*, No. 2, pp. 517-38.

1915

Literary Aspects of North American Mythology. Ottawa. Anthropology Series of the Canada Geological Survey, No. 6. Museum Bulletin No. 16.

The Social Organization of the Winnebago Indians, an Interpretation. Ottawa. Anthropology Series of the Canada Geological Survey, No. 5. Museum Bulletin No. 10.

"The Hare Cycle of the Winnebago Indians," in *Studies in North American Mythology*, Vol. 1, Part 1. Santa Fe, New Mexico.

"Religion of the North American Indians," in *Anthropology in North America*, by Franz Boas and others, pp. 259-305. New York, G. E. Stechert.

"A Semi-Historical Account of the War of the Winnebago and the Foxes," in *Proceedings of the Wisconsin Historical Society*, 1914, pp. 191-207. Madison, Wisconsin.

"The Winnebago Myth of the Twins," in *Papers of the Southwestern Authropological Society*, 1:1-56.

Editor, with Aurelio M. Espinosa, "Folk-Tales from Oaxaca," *Journal of American Folklore*, 28:No. 110:370-408.

1916

"The Native Problem in Mexico," *New Republic*, 9:90-91.

"On the Relationship of Huave and Mixe," *American Anthropologist*, N.S., 18:No. 3:411-21.

1917

Editor, with Aurelio M. Espinosa. El Folk-Lore de Oaxaca. New York, G. E. Stechert.

1918

"Ethnology and History," *University of California Chronicle*, 20:No. 2:16-21.

1919

"The Genetic Relationship of Huave and Mixe," *Journal de Société des Américanistes de Paris*, N.S., 11:489-99.

"The Genetic Relationship of the North American Indian Languages," *University of California Publications in American Archaeology and Ethnology,* 14:489-502.

1920

"The Autobiography of a Winnebago Indian," *University of California Publications in American Archaeology and Ethnology,* 16:381-473.

"The Sources and Authenticity of the History of the Ancient Mexicans," *University of California Publications in American Archaeology and Ethnology,* 17:1-150.

1922

"Thunder-Cloud, a Winnebago Shaman, Relates and Prays," in *American Indian Life,* by Elsie Clewes Parson, pp. 75-80. New York, B. W. Huebsch.

1923

"The Winnebago Tribe," in *Thirty-seventh Annual Report of the United States Bureau of American Ethnology,* pp. 35-550. Washington, D.C.

1924

Monotheism among Primitive Peoples. London, G. Allen and Unwin. The Arthur Davis Memorial Lecture before the Jewish Historical Society. Foreword by Israel Zangwill.

Reissued 1954. Basel, Ethnographical Museum. Special Publication of Bollingen Foundation, No. 4.

"The Adoption of an Alphabet by an Aboriginal People," *Cambridge University Reporter* (Proceedings of Cambridge Philological Society), November 25, pp. 24-31.

"Ojibwa Ethnological Chit-chat," *American Anthropologist,* N.S., 26:491-530.

"The Relationship of Maya to Zoque-Huave," *Journal de Société des Américanistes de Paris,* N.S., 16:317-24.

"Wappo Texts, First Series," *University of California Publications in American Archaeology and Ethnology,* 19:1-147.

1925

"The Distribution and Phonetics of the Zapotec Dialects, A Preliminary Sketch," *Journal de Société des Américanistes de Paris,* 17:27-76.

"Maya, Nahuatl, and Tarascan Kinship Terms," *American Anthropologist,* N.S., 27:100-2.

Translator, The Practice and Theory of Individual Psychology, by Alfred Adler. New York, Harcourt Brace and Co.; London, Kegan Paul, Trench, Trubner and Co., Ltd.

———— Language, A Linguistic Introduction to History, by Joseph Vendryes. London, Kegan Paul, Trench, Trubner and Co., Ltd.; New York, Knopf. History of Civilization Series. Introduction by Henri Berr.

Translator, with V. C. C. Collum, The Earth before History: Man's Origin and the Origin of Life, by Edmond Perrier. New York, Knopf. History of Civilization Series.

Review of Erwin Rohde, *Psyche,* in New York *Herald Tribune,* December 13, p. 17.

1926

"Literary Aspects of Winnebago Mythology," *Journal of American Folklore,* 39:18-52.

"Winnebago Myth Cycles," *Primitive Culture,* 1:8-86.

Editor, Crashing Thunder: The Autobiography of an American Indian. New York and London, Appleton and Company.

Reviews

Gustave Glotz, *The Aegean Civilization,* in New York *Herald Tribune,* February 28, p. 11.

L. H. Dudley Buxton, *The Peoples of Asia,* V. G. Childe, *The Dawn of Civilization,* and C. L. Delaporte, *Mesopotamia,* in New York *Herald Tribune,* April 4, p. 16.

Karl Kautsky, *Are the Jews a Race,* in New York *Herald Tribune,* April 25, p. 11.

H. E. Barnes, *History and Social Intelligence,* in New York *Herald Tribune,* June 27, p. 4.

L. I. Newman, *Jewish Influences on Christian Reform Movements,* in New York *Herald Tribune,* July 4, p. 6.

Durant Drake, *The Mind and Its Place in Nature,* New York *Herald Tribune,* July 18, p. 10.

H. E. Barnes, *The History and Prospects of the Social Sciences,* in New York *Herald Tribune,* August 15, p. 8.

J. Y. Simpson, *Landmarks in the Struggle between Science and Religion,* in New York *Herald Tribune,* October 17, p. 12.

James H. Breasted, *The Conquest of Civilization,* and James H. Robinson, *The Ordeal of Civilization,* in New York *Herald Tribune,* November 7, p. 4.

Géza Roheim, *Social Anthropology,* in New York *Herald Tribune,* November 28, p. 20.

Lynn Thorndike, *A Short History of Civilization,* in New York *Herald Tribune,* December 5, p. 16.

Georg Brandes, *Jesus: A Myth,* and Maurice Goguel, *Jesus the Nazarene,* in New York *Herald Tribune,* December 26, p. 11.

1927

Primitive Man as Philosopher. New York, Appleton & Co. Foreword by John Dewey. Enlarged ed. 1957. New York, Dover Publications.

The Story of the American Indian. New York, Boni and Liveright.

Revised ed. 1934. New York, Liveright.

Translated 1936 as *Histoire de la civilisation Indienne* by Eva Métraux. Paris, Payot.

Reviews

R. M. Eaton, *Symbolism and Truth,* C. Morgan Lloyd, *Life, Mind and Spirit,* R. M. Ogden, *Psychology and Education,* and Paul Masson-Oursel, *Comparative Philosophy,* in New York *Herald Tribune,* February 18, p. 14.

Mary Stuart, *The Psychology of Time,* and C. Nordmann, *The Tyranny of Time,* in New York *Herald Tribune,* February 20, p. 13.

Louis Ginzberg, *The Legends of the Jews,* W. Landsell, *Israel and Babylon,* Reuben Levy, *Deutero-Isaiah,* and Edmond Flag, *The Jewish Anthology,* in New York *Herald Tribune,* February 27, p. 25.

N. K. McKnechie, *The Heir of All the Ages: The Family Tree of Mr. Smith,* in New York *Herald Tribune,* March 17, p. 16.

Ettie A. Rout, *Maori Symbolism,* in New York *Herald Tribune,* May 22, p. 11.

Max Schmidt, *The Primitive Races of Mankind,* in New York *Herald Tribune,* June 12, p. 18.

Lewis Spence, *The History of Atlantis,* in New York *Herald Tribune,* June 26, p. 9.

Sir Bertram C. A. Windle, *The Catholic Church and Its Reactions with Science,* in New York *Herald Tribune,* July 24, p. 8.

G. A. Grinnel, *By Cheyenne Campfires,* in New York *Herald Tribune,* August 21, p. 15.

1928

"Ethnological Notes on the Ojibwa of Southeastern Ontario," *American Anthropologist,* N.S., 30:659-68.

With A. B. Reagan, "Ojibwa Myths and Tales," *Journal of American Folklore,* 41:61-146.

Reviews

Sir Bertram C. A. Windle, *Religions Past and Present,* in New York *Herald Tribune,* March 4, p. 22.

E. R. Bevan and C. Singer, *The Legacy of Israel,* in New York *Herald Tribune,* March 25, p. 21.

Thomas Gann, *Maya Cities,* in New York *Herald Tribune,* May 27, p. 20.

Long Lance, Chief Buffalo Child, *Long Lance,* in New York *Herald Tribune,* October 14, p. 7.

1929

A Grammar of the Wappo Language. University of California Publications in American Archaeology and Ethnology, Vol. 27. Berkeley, Calif.

"A History of Ethnological Theories," *American Anthropologist,* N.S., 31:9-33.

"Huave Texts," *International Journal of American Linguistics,* 5:1-56.

1930

"A Preliminary Sketch of the Zapotec Language," *Language,* 6:64-85.

1931

"Concept of Right and Wrong," in *The Making of Man,* by Vernon F. Calverton, pp. 818-27. New York. Modern Library.

"Mexican Kinship Terms," *University of California Publications in American Archaeology and Ethnology,* 31:1-14.

"The Thunderbird Warclub: A Winnebago Tale," *Journal of American Folklore,* 44:143-65.

1932

Social Anthropology. New York and London, McGraw-Hill.

"Ancestor Worship," in *Encyclopaedia of the Social Sciences,* 2:53-58. New York.

1933

The Method and Theory of Ethnology: An Essay in Criticism. New York and London, McGraw-Hill.

"Mixe Texts," *Journal de Société des Américanistes de Paris*, N.S., 25:41-64.
"Notes on the Tlappanecan Language of Guerrero," *International Journal of American Linguistics*, 8:45-72.
Review of Edward Moffat Weyer, Jr., *The Eskimo: Their Environment and Folkways*, in *American Anthropologist*, 35:60-61.

1934

The Racial Myth. New York, Whittlesey House.
"The Method and Theory of Ethnology: A Reply to R. R. Marett's Review," *American Anthropologist*, N.S., 36:315-16.

1935

An Historical Legend of the Zapotecs. Berkeley, Calif. Ibero-Americana Series.
The Italians of San Francisco: Their Adjustment and Acculturation. San Francisco.
SERA Projects 2-f2-98 and 3-f2-145.
The Survey of San Francisco's Minorities: Its Purposes and Results. San Francisco.
SERA Projects 2-f2-98 and 3-f2-145.

1936

"Ojibwa and Ottawa Puberty Dreams," in *Essays in Anthropology Presented to A. L. Kroeber,* ed. by Robert H. Lowie, pp. 233-64. Berkeley, Calif.

1937

Primitive Religion: Its Nature and Origin. New York, Viking Press.
Enlarged ed. 1957. New York, Dover Publications.
Translated 1941 as *La Religion Primitive: sa Nature et son Origine* by Alfred Métraux. Paris, Gallimard.
"Economic Factors in Primitive Religion," *Science and Society*, Vol. 1, No. 3.

1938

Review of Evelyn Lend, *The Underground Struggle in Germany,* in *Emanu-el* and *The Jewish Journal,* San Francisco, December 16.

1939

An Annotated Bibliography of the Opponents and Friends of J. J. Fernandez de Lizardi. San Francisco, Sutro Library. Occasional Papers, Mexican History Series, No. 2, Part 2.
An Annotated Bibliography of the Poems and Pamphlets of J. J. Fernandez de Lizardi. San Francisco, Sutro Library. Occasional Papers, Mexican History Series, No. 2, Part 1.
An Annotated Bibliography of Some Newly Discovered Poems and Pamphlets of J. J. Fernandez de Lizardi (El Pensador Mexicano). San Francisco, Sutro Library. Occasional Papers, Mexican History Series, No. 1, Part 1.
An Annotated Bibliography and Summary of F. Coles' "A Perfect Diurnal of Some Passages in Parliament (1643-1649)." San Francisco, Sutro Library. Occasional Papers, English Series, No. 2.
Catalogue of the Mexican Pamphlets in the Sutro Collection (1623-1888). San Francisco, Sutro Library. Works Progress Administration 665-08-3-236, ten parts.
Introduction to *Two Pamphlets on the History of the Jews in England* by William

Arnall and Francis Goldsmid. San Francisco, Sutro Library. Occasional Papers, English Series, No. 4.

"Bibliographical Notes from the Sutro Library," *Bulletin of the Sutro Library,* 2:5-8; 4:6-8.

"Brief Sketch of the Sutro Library," *Bulletin of the Sutro Library,* 1:2-3.

Editor, The First Mexican Constitution: The Constitution of Apatzingan. San Francisco, Sutro Library. Reprint Series, No. 7.

Translator, "Dr. Martin Luther's Christian Farewell and Death," *Bulletin of the Sutro Library,* 1:5-7.

Review of Franz Boas, *The Mind of Primitive Man,* in New Republic, 98:300-3. Reprinted 1939 in *Books That Changed Our Minds,* ed. by Malcolm Cowley and Bernard Smith, pp. 127-42. New York, Doubleday.

1940

An Annotated Bibliography of the Poems and Pamphlets of J. J. Fernandez de Lizardi: The First Period (1808-1819). San Francisco, Sutro Library. Occasional Papers, Mexican History Series, No. 2, Part 1 (January).

An Annotated Bibliography of the Poems and Pamphlets of J. J. Fernandez de Lizardi: The Second Period (1820-1823). San Francisco, Sutro Library. Occasional Papers, Mexican History Series, No. 2, Part 1 (February).

Summary of Work (1939-1940). San Francisco. Works Projects Administration, 665-08-3-236.

Introduction to *The Early Pamphlets of Rafael Davila (1820-1822).* San Francisco, Sutro Library. Occasional Papers, Reprint Series, No. 17.

Introduction to *Pamphlets on Religion and Democracy—16th to 19th Centuries.* San Francisco, Sutro Library. Also introductions to specific documents in the volume *Pamphlets on Religion and Civil Power:* pp. i-iv, *The Trial of Peter Zenger;* p. 180, *The Origin and End of Evil Power;* p. 220, *A Perswasive to Moderation . . . ;* p. 351, *The Civil and Municipal Disabilities of the Jews.*

"The Sutro Library," *Women's City Club Magazine,* San Francisco, July.

Editor, The Golden Mountain: Chinese Tales Told in California by Jon Lee. San Francisco, Sutro Library. Occasional Papers, Manuscript Series, No. 1.

Reviews

A. L. Kroeber, *Cultural and Natural Areas of Native North America,* in Oakland *Tribune,* February 4.

Edwin R. Embree, *Indians of the Americas,* in Oakland *Tribune,* February 11.

Clark Wissler, *Indians of the United States: Four Centuries of Their History and Culture,* in Oakland *Tribune,* March 3.

Sir Charles Oman, *On the Writing of History,* in Oakland *Tribune,* March 24.

1942

Indians of South America. Garden City, N. Y., Doubleday. American Museum of Natural History Science Series, Vol. 8.

Translated 1948 as *Los Indios de la América del Sur* by Luis Echávarri. Buenos Aires, Pleamar.

Introduction to *How Man Became a Giant,* by M. Il'in (pseud. of I. Y. Marshak), trans. by A. Komarov and E. A. Furman. Philadelphia and New York, J. B. Lippincott.

Introduction to *The Unpublished Letters of Adolphe F. Bandelier concerning the Writing and Publishing of the Delight-Makers.* New York, Charles P. Everitt.

Editor, "The Tragedy of the Seventh Day, by Jon Lee," *California Folklore Quarterly*, 1:No. 4:337-67.

1943

"Cuentos y Leyendas de los Zapotecos," *Tlalocan*, 1:3-30, 134-54.

Editor, "Some Chinese Customs and Beliefs in California, by Jon Lee," *California Folklore Quarterly*, 2:No. 3:191-204.

Review of Leslie A. White, ed., *The Bandelier-Morgan Letters (1873-1883)*, in *American Anthropologist*, N.S., 45:457.

1944

"The Classification of the Languages of Mexico," *Tlalocan*, 1:259-65.

"Cuentos y Leyendas de los Zapotecos," *Tlalocan*, 1:194-226.

"The Nature and Problems of Mexican Indian Mythology," *Journal of American Folklore*, 57:26-36.

1945

Cuentos de Mitla. Sacramento, Calif., The House of Tlaloc.
　Reprinted, with corrections and additions, from *Tlalocan*, Vol. I, Nos. 1, 2, and 3.

The Road of Life and Death: A Ritual Drama of the American Indians. New York, Pantheon Books. Bollingen Series, No. 5. Foreword by Mark Van Doren.

"The Journey of the Soul to Spiritland," *Circle*, 5:70-73.

Review of E. A. Burbank, *Burbank among the Indians*, as told to Ernest Royce, ed. by Frank J. Taylor, in New York *Herald Tribune*, August 5.

Review of Victor Wolfgang Von Hagen, *The Aztec and Maya Paper Makers*, in *Hispanic American Historical Review*, 25:364-65.

1946

"Annotated Bibliography of the Poems and Pamphlets of Fernandez de Lizardi (1824-1827)," *Hispanic American Historical Review*, 26:289-91.

"Three Conversions," *Circle*, 7-8:90-96.

"Zapotec Texts: Dialect of Juchitan-Tehuano," *International Journal of American Linguistics*, 12:152-72.

Editor, "Folktales of Japan as Told in California," *Journal of American Folklore*, 59:289-308.

———— "Japanese Ceremonies and Festivals in California," *Southwestern Journal of Anthropology*, 2:152-79.

Reviews

　Gordon Macgregor, *Warriors without Weapons: A Study of the Society and Personality Development of the Pine Ridge Sioux*, in New York *Herald Tribune*, October 13.

　Vito Alessio Robles, ed., *El pensàmiento del padre Mier*, in *Hispanic American Historical Review*, 26:105-6.

　Ralph Beals, *Ethnology of the Western Mixe*, in *Hispanic American Historical Review*, 26:114.

　Miguel Covarrubias and Daniel F. Rubin de la Borbolla, eds., *El arte indígena de Norteamérica: Exposición celebrada en el museo del xx de Marzo al xx de Abril de 1945*, in *Hispanic American Historical Review*, 26:237.

　El Norte de México y el sur de Estados Unidos: Tercera reunión de mesa redonda

sobre problemas antropológicas de México y leutro America, 25 de Agosto a 2 de Septiembre de 1943, in *Hispanic American Historical Review,* 26:237-38.
Elsie Clews Parsons, *Peguche, Canton of Otavalo, Province of Imbabura, Ecuador: A Study of Andean Indians,* in *Hispanic American Historical Review,* 26:245-46.

1947

Review of A. J. Toynbee, *A Study of History,* in *Kenyon Review,* 9:622-28.

1948

Winnebago Hero Cycles: A Study in Aboriginal Literature. Bloomington, Ind. Indiana University Publications in Anthropology and Linguistics, Memoir 1. Also *International Journal of American Linguistics* Memoir 1; Supplement to *International Journal of American Linguistics,* Vol. 14, No. 3.
"Music and Medicine among Primitive Peoples," in *Music and Medicine,* ed. by Dorothy Schullian and Max Schoen, pp. 3-24. New York, Schuman.
Reviews
  Miguel Covarrubias, *Mexico South, the Isthmus of Tehuantepec,* in *Hispanic American Historical Review,* 28:126-27.
  J. H. Steward, ed., *Handbook of South American Indians,* in *Hispanic American Historical Review,* 28:537-40.

1949

Winnebago Culture as Described by Themselves. Supplement to *International Journal of American Linguistics,* Vol. 15, No. 1. Special Publication of the Bollingen Foundation, No. 1.
"The Basic Myth of the American Indians," *Eranos Jahrbuch,* 17:359-419.
Review of Clyde Kluckhohn and Henry A. Murray, *Personality in Nature, Society, and Culture,* and Clyde Kluckhohn, *Mirror for Man,* in *Kenyon Review,* 11:523-26.

1950

The Origin Myth of the Medicine Rite: Three Versions—The Historical Origins of the Medicine Rite. Supplement to *International Journal of American Linguistics,* Vol. 16, No. 1. Special Publication of the Bollingen Foundation, No. 2.
"The Religious Experiences of an American Indian," *Eranos Jahrbuch,* 18:250-90.

1951

Die Religiöse Erfahrung der Naturvölker. Zurich, Rhein-Verlag.
"The Esoteric Rituals of the North American Indians," *Eranos Jahrbuch,* 19:282-349.
"Primitive Literature," in *The World through Literature,* ed. by C. G. E. Laird, pp. 3-43. New York, Appleton.
Introduction to *The Two Crosses of Todos Santos, Survivals of Mayan Religious Ritual,* by Maud Oakes. New York, Pantheon Books. Bollingen Series, No. 27.

1952

Editor, African Folktales and Sculpture. New York, Pantheon Books. Bollingen Series, No. 32.

1010 RICHARD WERBNER

Translated 1955 as *Fiabe africane* by Adriana Motti. Turin, Einaudi. Preface by Italo Calvino.
Review of Ramon Menendez Pidal, *The Spaniards and Their History,* in *Kenyon Review,* 14:340-44.

1953

The World of Primitive Man. New York, Schuman. Life of Science Library.
Translated 1953 as *Gott und Mensch in der Primitiven Welt* by Margherita von Wyss. Zurich, Rhein-Verlag. Revised and enlarged ed.

1954

The Evolution of an American Indian Prose Epic: A Study in Comparative Literature, Part I. Basel, Ethnographical Museum. Special Publication of the Bollingen Foundation, No. 3.
"Eine Erweckung, nacherzählt und eingeleitet von Paul Radin," *Du,* December, 1954, pp. 31-32. Translated by Harry Kahn.

1955

"The Dreams of an American Indian: Their Meaning and Function," in *Studien zur Analytischen Psychologie C. G. Jungs,* Band II, pp. 146-70. Zurich, Rascher Verlag.
"The Literature of Primitive Peoples," *Diogenes,* 12:1-28.

1956

The Evolution of an American Indian Prose Epic: A Study in Comparative Literature, Part II. Basel, Ethnographical Museum. Special Publication of the Bollingen Foundation, No. 5.
The Trickster: A Study in American Indian Mythology. London, L. Routledge; New York, Philosophical Library. Commentaries by C. G. Jung and Karl Kerenyi.
Translated 1954 as *Der Göttliche Schelm: ein Indianischer Mythenzyklus* by Ilse Kramer. Zurich, Rhein-Verlag.
Translated 1958 as *Le Fripon Divin: Un Mythe Indien* by Arthur Reiss. Geneva, Georg.

1958

"Robert H. Lowie, 1883–1957," *American Anthropologist,* 60:358-61.
Introductions to Volumes I and II of *Primitive Culture,* by Edward B. Tylor. New York, Harper Torchbook Series. Vol. I, *The Origins of Culture,* pp. ix-xv; Vol. II, *Religion in Primitive Culture,* pp. ix-xvii.

1959

The Sacral Chief among the American Indians. Leiden, E. J. Brill. Studies in the History of Religions. *Numen,* Supplement IV.
"Parent and Child in Primitive Mythology," in *The Family: Its Function and Destiny,* ed. by Ruth Nanda Anshen. New York, Harper & Brothers. Rev. ed. Science of Culture Series, Vol. V.

INDEX